UNIVERSITY CASEBOOK SERIES

CASES AND MATERIALS

CIVIL PROCEDURE

SECOND EDITION

by

A. LEO LEVIN
Leon Meltzer Professor of Law Emeritus
University of Pennsylvania Law School

PHILIP SHUCHMAN
Justice Joseph Weintraub Professor of Law
Rutgers University Law School

CHARLES M. YABLON
Professor of Law
Benjamin N. Cardozo School of Law
Yeshiva University

NEW YORK, NEW YORK
FOUNDATION PRESS
2000

COPYRIGHT © 1961, 1974, 1992 FOUNDATION PRESS
COPYRIGHT © 2000 By FOUNDATION PRESS
                        11 Penn Plaza, Tenth Floor
                        New York, NY 10001
                        Phone Toll Free 1–877–888–1330
                        Fax (212) 760–8705
                        fdpress.com
All rights reserved
Printed in the United States of America

ISBN 1–56662–755–9

 TEXT IS PRINTED ON 10% POST CONSUMER RECYCLED PAPER

ACKNOWLEDGMENTS

We gratefully acknowledge the permission given by the following publishers and authors to reprint excerpts from the works indicated:

Brazil, Civil Discovery: Lawyers' Views of its Effectiveness, Its Principal Problems and Abuses, 1980 American Bar Foundation Research Journal 789. Reprinted by permission of Wayne D. Brazil.

Brickman, Contingent Fees Without Contingencies: Hamlet Without the Prince of Denmark? 37 UCLA L. Rev. 29 (1989).
Originally published in 37 UCLA L. Rev. 29, Copyright © 1989, The Regents of the University of California. All rights reserved.

Sherman L. Cohn, New Developments in Federal Litigation: Discovery Defenses, American Inns of Court Federal Practice Digest, 209-210 (Jan. 1994).

David, Book Review (California Pleadings by James Chadbourn), 8 UCLA L. Rev. 994 (1961)
Originally published in 8 UCLA L. Rev. 994, Copyright © 1961, The Regents of the University of California. All rights reserved.

Fox, Upstate-Downstate Gap in Injury Awards, New York Law Journal, (January 4, 1988). Reprinted with permission of the New York Law Journal, Copyright © 1988, The New York Law Publishing Company.

Graham, Discovery of Experts Under Rule 26(b)(4) of the Federal Rules of Civil Procedure, 1977 University of Illinois Law Forum 169. Reprinted by permission of Michael H. Graham and the Board of Trustees of the University of Illinois.

Deborah R. Hensler and Mark A. Peterson, Reinventing Civil Litigation: Evaluating Proposals for Change: Understanding Mass Personal Injury Litigation: a Socio-Legal Analysis, 59 Brooklyn Law Review 961 (1993). Copyright © 1993, Deborah R. Hensler and Mark A. Peterson.

Kakalik, King, Traynor, Ebener & Picus, Costs and Compensation Paid in Aviation Accident Litigation, Rand Institute for Civil Justice, 1988. Reprinted with permission of the Rand Institute for Civil Justice.

Keeton, The Function of the Local Rules and the Tension with Uniformity, 50 University of Pittsburgh Law Review 853 (1989). Reprinted with permission of Robert E. Keeton and the University of Pittsburgh Law Review.

Levin and Colliers, Containing the Cost of Litigation, 37 Rutgers Law Review 219 (1985). Reprinted by permission of the authors and Rutgers Law Review.

Levin and Golash, Alternate Dispute Resolution in Federal District Courts, 37 Florida Law Review 29 (1985). Reprinted with the permission the University of Florida Law Review. Copyright © 1985.

Levin and Wooley, Dispatch and Delay: A Field Study of Judicial Administration in Pennsylvania (1961). Reprinted by permission of the University of Pennsylvania.

Levine, Northern District of California Adopts Early Neutral Evolution to Expedite Dispute Resolution, 72 Judicature 235 (1989). Reprinted by permission of the author and the American Judicature Society.

McCaskill, The Modern Philosophy of Pleading: A Dialogue Outside the Shades, 38 ABA Journal, 123 (1952).
Reprinted with permission from volume 38 of the ABA Journal, The Lawyer's Magazine, published by the American Bar Association.

McMunigal, The Costs of Settlements: The Impact of Scarcity of Adjudication on Litigating Lawyers, 37 UCLA L. Rev. 833 (1990).
Originally published in 37 UCLA L. Rev. 833, Copyright © 1990, The Regents of the University of California. All rights reserved.

Mengler, Burbank & Rowe, Congress Accepts Supreme Court's Invitation to Codify Supplemental Jurisdiction, 74 Judicature 213 (1990-91). Reprinted with permission of the American Judicature Society.

Merryman, How Others Do It: The French and German Judiciaries, 61 Southern California Law Review 1865 (1988). Reprinted with permission of John Henry Merryman and the Southern California Law Review.

Morgan, Variance Problem, 32 Nebraska Law Review 357 (1953). Reprinted with permission of the Nebraska Law Review.

Peckham, The Federal Judge As Case Manager: The New Role in Guiding a Case From Filing to Disposition, 60 California Law Review 770 (1981). Reprinted with permission of the California Law Review, Inc. Copyright © 1981.

Plucknett, A Concise History of the Common Law (5th Ed. 1956) 383-85. Reprinted with permission of Little, Brown & Company.

Resnik, Managerial Judges, 96 Harvard Law Review 374 (1982). Copyright © 1982 by the Harvard Law Review Association.

Restatement of the Law, 2d, Judgments. Copyright © 1982 by the American Law Institute. Reprinted with permission of the American Law Institute.

Richey, Rule 16: A Survey of Some Considerations for the Bench and Bar, 126 F.R.D. 599, 615-16 (1989). Reprinted with permission of the author.

Schuck, The Role of Judges in Settling Complex Cases: The Agent Orange Example, 53 University of Chicago Law Review 337 (1986). Reprinted with permission of the author and the University of Chicago Law Review.

Schwarzer, Slaying the Monsters of Cost and Delay: Would Disclosure Be More Effective Than Discovery?, 74 Judicature 178 (1991). Reprinted with permission of William Schwarzer and the American Judicature Society.

Shuchman, Travel Costs for Service of Civil Process, 5 Connecticut Law Review 458 (1973). Reprinted by permission of the Connecticut Law Review.

Shuchman, Discovering the Law of Discovery Through Low Level Investigations, 38 George Washington Law Review 32 (1969). Reprinted by permission of the George Washington Law Review © 1969.

Siegel, Changes in Federal Jurisdiction and Practice Under the New Judicial Improvements and Access to Justice Act, 123 F.R.D. 399, 405-07 (1989).

Allan Stein, Forward to Symposium on the Entire Controversy Doctrine, 28 Rutgers Law Journal 1 (1996). Reprinted with permission of the Rutgers Law Journal.

Traynor, The Riddle of Harmless Error (1970). Reprinted by permission of Madeline (Mrs. Roger J.) Traynor.

Tuerkheimer, Service of Process in New York City: A Proposed End to Unregulated Criminality. 72 Columbia Law Review 847 (1972).
> Copyright © 1972 by the Directors of the Columbia Law Review Association, Inc. All rights reserved. This article originally appeared at 72 Colum. L. Rev. 847 (1972). Reprinted by permission.

Waggoner, Section 1404(a), "Where it Might Have Been Brought": Brought By Whom? 1988 Brigham Young University Law Review 67 (1988). Reprinted by permission of the Brigham Young University Law Review.

Yablon, Stupid Lawyer Tricks: An Essay on Discovery Abuse, 96 Columbia Law Review 1618 (1996).

Zeisel, Social Research and the Law: The Ideal and the Practical, printed in Law and Sociology 130-32 (William M. Evan, Ed. 1962). Reprinted with permission of The Free Press, A Division of MacMillan Inc., Copyright © 1962 by the Free Press.

Note, Abuse of Process: Sewer Service, 3 Columbia Journal of Law and Social Problems 17 (1967). Reprinted by permission of the Columbia Journal of Law and Social Problems.

*

PREFACE

Civil procedure does not lack for technicalities, fine points of doctrine which able lawyers feel compelled to master because they are important to understanding what the subject is all about—and because they are crucial in the practice. Neither does it lack for larger, more difficult questions that today command the interest of Congress as well as of the judges and justices who formulate, promulgate and apply procedural rules. Is the cost of litigation denying access to justice to large segments of our society? Does award of attorney fees to a prevailing party solve the problem? Is discovery abuse both prevalent and serious and, if so, what can be done about it?

We know that expense and delay in federal civil litigation appeared important enough to Congress for it to require, as it did in the Civil Justice Improvements Act of 1990, that each United States district court formulate a plan designed to contribute to their reduction.

This book is based on the premise that both types of questions are important. It does not ignore the larger issues; neither does it ignore or short-change the specifics of rule and statute.

Our hope, and our experience in using these materials, is that this combination makes for an especially valuable and interesting educational experience. We might say that we aspire to studying law, together with our students, in what Holmes called "the grand manner," and, in addition, we like to think that there can be joy in the enterprise.

A number of conventions have guided us in the editing of these materials. We have felt free to omit citations, particularly string citations, without noting the omission. We have followed a similar practice with respect to footnotes while at the same time retaining the original numbering, so that gaps in the sequence are to be expected. All footnotes by the editors are indicated by letters rather than numbers, and are thus identified as editorial insertions.

This is a successor edition to the casebook which bore the name of the late, beloved Professor James H. Chadbourn. He challenged, inspired, stimulated and, above all, taught generations of students at the University of Pennsylvania, U.C.L.A. and Harvard University. And always there was for him and for them joy in the enterprise. We can do no less than acknowledge our debt to him.

We are also indebted to Professor Peter Lushing for helpful comments, to Malia Brink, Katherine Lipton Chabinsky, Maria Chinzi, Adoni Economou, Bryan D. Glass, Michelle Hangley, Judith Nason, Michael J. Richter, Eric Roberson, Paul Scott, Steven Spielvogel, Roberta Stonehill and

Helen S. Unangst for able and dedicated research assistance. Above all, we are indebted to our students who, as we used these materials together, have helped shape us as well as this book.

A.L.L.
P.S.
C.Y.

SUMMARY OF CONTENTS

*

TABLE OF CONTENTS

*

TABLE OF CASES

Principal cases are in bold type. Non-principal cases are in roman type. References are to Pages.

*

CASES AND MATERIALS

CIVIL PROCEDURE

*

INTRODUCTION

LITIGATING A DISPUTE: AN OVERVIEW

From grievance to lawsuit: To understand civil litigation it is helpful to realize how very few claims result in lawsuits. It is a long road from a grievance to a lawyer's office. It is an even longer road from the lawyer's office to the courthouse and relatively few potential plaintiffs complete the journey. Far from representing an unhappy situation, in most cases this represents a very fortunate state of affairs. A satisfactory settlement may have been obtained without judicial action, occasionally even without the intervention of a lawyer. In a pioneering study published in 1959, Kalven, Zeisel and Buchholz found that "On the average, in the United States only about one fifth of all personal injury claims are ever filed in court, only about 5 per cent ever reach the trial stage, and only 2 or 3 per cent ever reach the stage where they are decided by the verdict of a jury or the judgment of a court."[1] A more recent study, ranging over a far wider spectrum of types of disputes, found a similarly low proportion of grievances to lawsuits.[2]

There are many reasons for disputants to avoid a lawsuit, and certainly to avoid trial. Litigation is hardly conducive to a continuing relationship between two business people. Besides, litigation is expensive and the outcome is rarely assured.[3] For one thing, facts tend to be slippery, witnesses less than completely reliable and juries not altogether predictable. Finally, extra-judicial alternatives, such as commercial arbitration, may be both available and attractive.

In all of this the role of the lawyer can be exceedingly important. Negotiation without adequate background knowledge can be a hazardous game. The law does not always conform to a layman's sense of equity, particularly where that layman is the individual who considers himself aggrieved. In addition, as has already been suggested, the facts may turn out to be quite different than they appeared to be at the first telling. Moreover, it may require a lawyer's training and skill to sift through a mass of detail as presented by a party and to determine what is and what is not acceptable as evidence in a court of law. Obviously, such judgments affect the settlement value of a case and may even determine whether or not the dispute can be resolved without filing suit.

1. Zeisel, Kalven & Buchholz, Delay in the Court (1959) 105. For an analysis of the dramatic attrition, primarily by settlement, in cases which were already listed for trial see Levin and Woolley, Dispatch and Delay: A Field Study of Judicial Administration in Pennsylvania (1961) 66. See also Shuchman, Problems of Knowledge in Legal Scholarship (1979) 61–64.

2. For detailed discussion of "The Dispute Pyramid" see Galanter, Reading the Landscape of Disputes: What We Know and Don't Know (and Think We Know) about our Allegedly Contentious and Litigious Society, 31 U.C.L.A. L.Rev. 4, 6–36 (1983).

3. Mr. Justice Brennan, while still a state court judge, observed that "a case settled is a case best disposed of, because then one of the parties certainly avoids the heartache of losing at the trial." Proceedings of the Attorney General's Conference on Court Congestion and Delay in Litigation 87 (1956), quoted in Levin and Woolley, Dispatch and Delay: A Field Study of Judicial Administration in Pennsylvania (1961) 232 n. 23.

Cases do get filed, of course, and many are tried to verdict. Why? Sometimes a trial is necessary so that disputes of fact may be resolved in court: did the defendant's car run the red light at an excessive rate of speed? Were the goods shipped by plaintiff to the defendant defective? Sometimes the parties find they need an authoritative resolution of an issue of law: in a medical malpractice situation does the statute of limitations begin to run from the time of the doctor's negligence, from the time the plaintiff realized something was wrong, or, perhaps, from some other point in the history of plaintiff's troubles? Finally, there are times when resort to the coercive power of the state is necessary if one aggrieved is to obtain redress. Nothing short of a judgment, and sometimes execution by a sheriff, will suffice.

Choosing an appropriate court: Suppose two residents of New York, each doing business exclusively in New York, enter into a contract that is to be performed in New York. If a dispute arises out of that contract, it would be quite unreasonable to permit the plaintiff to sue the defendant in a California court. California, you will readily conclude, has no authority to order a New York resident, the defendant in our hypothetical, to defend the action in California under pain of a default judgment. Nor does Idaho, Montana, Alaska or even Connecticut or New Jersey. These courts, we say, lack jurisdiction over the defendant in this type of case. In our federal system the United States Supreme Court will police a violation of that rule.

The problem changes radically, however, if the defendant is a resident of California, or if the contract was to be performed in California, or if the parties had agreed in advance to litigate any dispute over the contract in California. Determining when a court has *personal jurisdiction* over a defendant, as we term it, is an increasingly important aspect of international trade.

To say that a given lawsuit will be brought in New York or Texas, for example, does not yet specify the court in which the action will be filed. Within each state of the United States there co-exist two separate judicial systems, state and federal. With respect to some cases, patent litigation or bankruptcy, for example, the federal courts have *exclusive jurisdiction* and with respect to still other claims, e.g. divorce, they have, for all intents and purposes, no jurisdiction at all. However, state and federal courts have *concurrent jurisdiction* with respect to some lawsuits. Thus, for example, if the parties are citizens of different states and the case meets the other requirements of *diversity jurisdiction,* it may be heard in federal court. But the state courts, too, are competent to hear the case and, in the first instance, a choice must be made by plaintiff. More generally, before filing an action the lawyer must choose a particular judicial system, one which has jurisdiction over the subject matter of the claim or, more succinctly, the court must have *subject matter jurisdiction.*

It is helpful to think for a moment of the structure of a judicial system. This can help us visualize relationships between different courts within the same system and also understand similarities between courts of different systems which have identical functions but very different names.

The federal judicial system is relatively simple, consisting of three tiers: 95 district courts, which are *courts of general jurisdiction,* 12 regional courts of appeals[4], which are intermediate appellate courts and the *United States Supreme Court.* These are the basic components of the system, and you will be concerned primarily with them.[5]

The prototypical state court structure includes an additional tier, *courts of limited jurisdiction.*[6] With respect to civil cases the limitation usually concerns the amount in controversy, $10,000 in many states.[7] In Georgia, the Municipal Courts and the City Court of Atlanta, some 390 courts in all, may not hear cases in which over $7,500 is in controversy, although even with respect to these courts jurisdictional amount is not uniform.

In many states there are *family courts.* In Indiana there are 52 city courts and 25 town courts. In California there is a huge judicial system, with well over 1300 judicial officers. In New York there is a complex structure with an even greater number of judicial officers. Some unusual courts reflect local conditions. For example, in Colorado one can find a water court, and in some urban areas, a housing court.

Your primary concern, however, will be with the *courts of general jurisdiction,* those with no upper limit on the amount in controversy in civil cases. In many states these are known as district courts, but the nomenclature is far from uniform. In Pennsylvania and Ohio they are known as Courts of Common Pleas; the term superior court is not uncommon and in New York the trial court of general jurisdiction is known as the Supreme Court. With the trial court identified as Supreme, there is an obvious need for different names for the courts which review the Supreme Court's judgments. The intermediate appellate court is called the Appellate Division of the Supreme Court, or more commonly simply the Appellate Division, and the highest court in New York is the Court of Appeals.

Assume for the moment that we are dealing with a claim that must be brought in the court of general jurisdiction of the state in question. There still remain the options and limitations of the law of *venue,* those rules that determine where within a given judicial system an action may be brought. Philadelphia is sufficiently distant from Pitts-

---

4. A thirteenth federal court, the United States Court of Appeals for the Federal Circuit, hears appeals primarily from certain federal courts and tribunals dealing with specialized matters such as patents, tariffs and monetary claims against the federal government.

5. Courts with specially defined jurisdiction, such as bankruptcy courts or the Tax Court, will not be of concern at this early stage of your legal education.

6. See State Court Caseload Statistics: Annual Report 1988 (1990) 183. The material

relevant to state courts that follows in this section is taken from that publication, a joint effort of the Conference of State Court Administrators, State Justice Institute and National Center for State Courts' Court Statistics Project. See *id.* 179 et seq.

7. In the federal system, the district court has jurisdiction of diversity cases only if the amount in controversy exceeds $75,000. If it does not, the case must be brought in state court.

burgh, Los Angeles from San Francisco, not to mention Chicago and Carbondale, that litigating in one rather than another may impose substantial burdens. Of even greater potential significance, there is evidence that the size of a verdict may vary with the venue. An able lawyer will not ignore these factors in deciding where to bring suit.

Service of process: The most elementary view of fundamental fairness would require that a defendant be notified of any lawsuit instituted against her, particularly when the failure to respond to the allegations may subject the defendant to an enforceable default judgment. What kind of notice should suffice is a far more difficult question. Is a news story in the local newspaper adequate? A legal notice in the classified ad section of the same paper? Word of mouth in a neighborhood with a well developed grapevine? A piece of paper affixed to the door of defendant's usual place of abode?

These questions may not be subject to categorical response, at least not all of them. However, they invite us to consider under what circumstances a particular form of service will pass constitutional muster, that is, will be held to meet the requirements of *due process.* As one moves to more familiar forms of communication such as ordinary first-class mail, a rather different type of question commands our attention. Procedural rules may demand adherence to stricter standards than are required to meet the bare minimum necessary to satisfy due process. It thus becomes appropriate to inquire whether rules of procedure should specify registered mail, for example, rather than ordinary mail in order to increase the probability of defendant's receiving notice. Even this apparently simple question forces us to think carefully about two types of issues. First, does a rule requiring the use of registered mail, or in-hand service—manual delivery of a complaint to a defendant in person—actually increase the probability of the defendant's receiving notice? Second, if it does, is the benefit worth the extra cost and effort?

The document that informs an individual that a lawsuit has been filed against him is called a *summons* and, typically, it is signed by the clerk of court or a deputy clerk. It makes for efficiency to have an acceptable form for documents of this type and such forms are to be found in appendices to Rules of Procedure. In the federal system Form 1 of the Appendix of Forms sets forth a summons. Names will vary. In Iowa, Form 1 in the Appendix of Forms is entitled Form of Original Notice for Personal Service, with other forms, suitable for use in specialized situations, following. In Pennsylvania, what is termed a Form of Writ of Summons may be found in Rule 1351, the first rule in the chapter on Forms.

The pleadings: It is hard to conceive of a case coming to trial without the plaintiff having informed the defendant of what relief she is seeking and why it is that she believes herself entitled to that relief. Does plaintiff seek money damages or an order of the court prohibiting the defendant from engaging in specified activity—an injunction? If plaintiff seeks money damages, what is the basis of her claim? Injuries sustained in an automobile accident, or is it defendant's alleged failure to fulfill a contractual obligation? Without some indication of what plaintiff seeks, and the factual basis for that claim, defendant could be hard pressed to prepare for trial. The statements of the contentions of the parties we call pleadings.

Today pleadings are in the form of written documents. Plaintiff's statement is called a *complaint*. There was a time when the parties set forth their respective contentions orally in open court and some forms of dispute resolution provide for such a procedure today. Whatever the method, some statement of what the dispute is about is a necessary component of a rational system.

Federal Rule of Civil Procedure 4 provides that the complaint be served together with the summons. As you can readily imagine, there is no reason inherent in the nature of things that would preclude its being served after service of process has been completed. Understandably, state practice may differ with respect to detail, and it is helpful to recognize that it is possible to achieve both fairness and efficiency, the fundamental purposes of rules governing civil procedure, with substantial variation in the technical details.

Defendant must be allowed to respond to plaintiff's contentions. This defendant does by way of an *answer*. The answer, too, is filed with the court and also served on the other parties to the litigation, although the form of service on opposing parties who are already in the lawsuit is far simpler, involving far fewer requirements, than is true of the papers that are used to initiate the litigation.

Basically, defendant has three options. She may deny the allegations of the complaint: I did not sell you defective goods, I was not driving negligently, I am not the manufacturer of the power tool that disintegrated in your hands. Defendant may, however, admit all the allegations of the complaint, but add allegations of fact which, if proved, will change the legal result: Yes, I admit you were injured while I was driving at a speed in excess of 100 miles per hour, but before you got in my stock car racer I warned you of the dangers, you said you understood them and were willing to accept the risks and, what's more, you signed a duly notarized document to that effect.

There is a third possibility. Defendant may simply say "So what?" The technical term, when the "so-what" is addressed to the complaint, is a *motion to dismiss*. Some cases you will read, however, use the term *demurrer*, a device formerly utilized for a challenge to the legal sufficiency of any pleading. If, for example, plaintiff alleges that at a very important social occasion defendant intentionally failed to greet the plaintiff, as a result of which plaintiff fell ill, developed ulcers, required psychiatric treatment and suffered other grievous injuries too sad to recount, no matter how elegant the pleading, how exquisite and persuasive the proof, plaintiff cannot recover simply because the law does not redress an injury resulting from such conduct by the defendant. Phrased differently, defendant has no legal obligation to greet the plaintiff and is not subject to answering in damages for failure to do so.

The pleading stage may, but need not be concluded with the filing of an answer. There are situations in which it is desirable to allow the plaintiff to respond to new matter contained in the answer; that pleading is called a *reply*. In some situations plaintiff is required to reply. For example, defendant may counterclaim, i.e., include in his answer a claim that he has against the plaintiff. Defendant may deny negligence and assert that it was plaintiff's negligence that caused the accident. In this situation a reply is required, but the pleading process ends here. The time and effort required for further development of the respective positions of the parties by exchange of written assertions is simply not worthwhile. We will deem the allegations of the last pleading filed to have been denied or avoided and get on with the business of litigating the case.

The scope of an action; multiple parties and multiple claims: The paradigmatic lawsuit has a single plaintiff suing one defendant on a single claim. Plaintiff may, however, have more than one claim against defendant, related or unrelated, and in many situations it may be efficient to allow these claims to be brought together and even to be tried together. Sometimes plaintiff's claim runs against two people, e.g. where each has signed a contract that plaintiff claims to have been breached. Clearly, it makes sense to have both defendants joined in the one action if service can be had on both.

A lawsuit may begin as a two-party action with the need to include additional parties soon becoming apparent. Plaintiff is a passenger injured in a two-car accident, who sues only one of the drivers. The defendant may *implead* the other driver, serving him and making him a party to the litigation. With multiple parties there may be *claims, counterclaims* and *cross-claims* as each of the litigants seeks to adjudicate her rights against one or more of the others. What constraints on the proliferation of claims and parties the law should recognize to insure optimal efficiency, avoiding both repetitive litigation and unmanageable law suits, is a question that requires careful study.

Preparation for trial; discovery: Once issue is joined, i.e. the pleadings have been completed, one might think the case ready for trial. That, indeed, once was the situation. Today we allow the parties the opportunity to seek evidence from their opponents and, generally, to learn more of the adversaries' contentions. We also make it possible for the parties to place non-litigants under oath and to examine and cross-examine them in advance of the trial. This process we call *discovery*.

Three of the mechanisms utilized in discovery have assumed particular importance. First, there are *interrogatories*, questions propounded in written form to another party, which questions must be answered under oath. There is also a procedure by which a litigant can ask for, and receive, relevant documents in the possession of another party. Finally, there are *depositions*. Any person, including but not limited to parties, may be called for interrogation under oath, with examination by the party seeking the deposition and cross-examination by any other party. Typically, such depositions are taken in a lawyer's office or other convenient place. A transcript is prepared and, the deposition having been given under oath, it may have tremendous impact at trial, in some cases even determining the outcome of the litigation.

We have noted the three most significant methods of obtaining discovery, but we have hardly begun to exhaust the possibilities. What is important for present purposes is the fact that discovery can be both expensive and time-consuming. It is not at all unusual for depositions to be taken on the east coast, the west coast and in the southwest region of the country, all in the same case. The more complex the litigation, the greater the number of depositions that can be expected and the longer each is likely to be. Of course, where huge sums are at stake it is understandable that the cost of litigation should increase. However, in many cases discovery has been converted into a tactical weapon designed to inflict economic hardship on an opponent, perhaps for the purpose of forcing a more advantageous settlement.

Our present system of pretrial discovery invites controversy concerning the propriety of a particular deposition, or a particular line of questioning. The trial judge, or in some situations a magistrate whose function it is to assume some of the burdens of the judge, is asked to resolve that controversy. The motion practice ancillary to discovery is quite extensive. As you can readily imagine, even the time spent appearing in court to argue such motions adds significantly to the cost of litigation and some judges have taken to deciding discovery motions on the papers alone, which no doubt is a less costly process, but which hardly eliminates the cost of preparing the papers, including those opposing the motion, nor the time between objection and decision. As a result, some judges make provision for such motions to be made by telephone conference call, sometimes from the site of the deposition itself, with a ruling usually forthcoming immediately.

Discovery remains one of the most controversial aspects of contemporary civil procedure, and the rules governing the procedures for gathering information prior to trial continue to be debated and frequently changed. Some would like to see more limits on the scope and amount of discovery that may be taken. Others would like the disclosure of certain basic information about the case to be automatic and therefore less subject to legal wrangling and tactics. Recent changes in the Federal Rules of Civil Procedure have moved in both these directions, instituting new limitations on discovery as well as a new rules requiring immediate disclosure which are applicable in many federal district courts. Additional changes along these lines may be forthcoming.

Summary Judgment: There are situations in which, quite early in the litigation, it becomes clear that there is no genuine controversy with respect to any material issue in the case. Plaintiff, for example, takes out a $30,000,000 insurance policy on what he claims were very valuable statues, which were lost at sea. Under the applicable substantive law he had the obligation of disclosing to the insurance carrier that a prior policy on the same statues had been cancelled, and he had failed to do so, precluding recovery. There would be little point to litigating the actual value of the statues; the substantive law precludes recovery in any event. In this situation the law provides for what is termed "summary judgment," a prompt disposition terminating the case early on.

Too much "efficiency" can be a dangerous thing. Summary judgment forever denies the losing party the opportunity to present his case in court. How can we assure that it will in fact be used to terminate litigation where it will spare the parties pointless expenditure of time and resources, and yet assure that it will not be used unfairly? This precise question has been the subject of a number of recent Supreme Court cases.

Settlements; alternative dispute resolution: In only about 5% of all civil cases terminated in federal court during the past statistical year did a trial even begin. State courts exhibit a similar phenomenon. What happens to the other 95%? Some are decided on motion, no doubt some are simply dropped by plaintiffs who thought better of suing, but the common assumption, supported by such facts as we have, is that the vast preponderance of those cases are settled.

Often settlement occurs without the intervention of any third parties. The lawyers involved consider the strength and weaknesses of their respective positions, the risks of adjudication, not excluding the vagaries of juries, the cost of proceeding to trial, and determine that it would be beneficial to settle. Often the judges, on their own initiative or as a result of a request by one or both of the parties, will attempt to see whether settlement is possible. It is useful to remember that a case that has settled does not have to be tried, and crowded dockets are the rule, the universal rule in large urban centers.

Some courts have instituted formal programs intended to bring about settlement: *mediation* supervised by third parties and court-annexed *arbitration* that is mandatory but non-binding are two common devices. Whether this type of arbitration is viewed by the participants as a form of adjudication or simply as a settlement device is a question that can be postponed. What is important to emphasize at this juncture is that there is a very long road between the pleadings and the trial and the vast majority of litigants never complete the journey.

Managing the case: Many cases are quite simple. They present no discovery problems and they move through the system from summons to judgment in a straightforward manner. These need hardly any judicial management. At the other end of the spectrum are the complex cases. Typically, they involve huge sums, large numbers of parties, and seemingly incessant wrangling over discovery. They require a firm judicial hand from the very beginning of the litigation until it is concluded. The Federal Rules of Civil Procedure provide for appropriate tools with which a judge can effectively manage litigation that requires it. Some are permissive, some are mandatory. They range from *scheduling orders* to *pretrial conferences.* Such devices, too, develop rules governing their operation and their effect. Thus, you will be obliged to consider whether a *pretrial order* developed at a pretrial conference supersedes the pleading and whether, and under what circumstances, it may be amended.

The trial: The heart of the trial is the presentation of evidence. A witness is called and will be questioned by the side calling her. This is known as *direct examination. Cross examination* follows after which *redirect* and further cross examination may follow. The taking of testimony may or may not proceed smoothly; objections may be interposed in which event the judge will rule on them. Documents may be offered into evidence and, if appropriate, will be admitted.

The evidence introduced at a trial may be likened to pieces of a jig-saw puzzle; the relevance and significance of each piece is often not clear to the trier of fact, particularly in a jury trial. To make the process more intelligible the actual taking of testimony is preceded by opening statements offered by the lawyers for each party. Typically, counsel will describe what she intends to prove, providing something of a big picture of the case. At the close of the testimony each side will offer closing arguments.

Ordinarily, the plaintiff has the *burden of proof* and will present her evidence first. When plaintiff has "closed", i.e. completed her case, defendant will present his evidence. Finally, there will be the opportunity, analogous to redirect and re-cross, for the parties to present further evidence, subject to some potentially rigid requirements designed to assure that such further proceedings have been necessitated by the flow of events.

The case may be tried to a jury or tried to the court. In the latter event, the judge, as the trier of fact, will be obliged to issue both findings of fact and conclusions of law. Until this point in the case, the non-jury case has the virtue of simplicity and an added measure of flexibility with respect to the law of evidence, much of which is designed to protect—some say insulate—the jury. At this point, however, the non-jury case may be subjected to far greater delay as the judge makes up her mind and prepares the requisite documents explaining and supporting her decision.

In the case of the jury trial, the trier of fact brings in a verdict. It may be a *general verdict,* defendant is or is not liable to plaintiff and, where liability is found, the amount of the damages assessed. At the option of the judge, however, it is possible to have a *special verdict:* the jury may be required to answer a series of questions concerning issues in the case, with the ultimate judgment molded by the judge based upon these responses. At first blush, the procedure appears attractive, conducive to a more rational process of decision. However, it can involve a variety of costs, and problems, including inconsistent responses by the jury, and is therefore used infrequently.

Where trial is to a jury several additional procedures are required. The jury must be selected; those who are thought to be biased, e.g., are not permitted to sit. To determine bias, it is appropriate that the *venire,* those called for jury service, be questioned either by the attorneys, the judge, or both. This we refer to as the *voir dire.* Where the questioning reveals a reason in law for not seating a particular person, there will be a *challenge for cause.* In addition, each side is permitted a certain number of *peremptory challenges,* authority to prevent a prospective juror from sitting without assigning a reason. Obviously, selection of the venire itself must be free from bias based on race, sex or religion.

When the testimony has been concluded, the jury must be instructed on the applicable law. This is the judge's function, but the judge is assisted by counsel's requests, technically termed points for charge.

Ultimately, there will be a *judgment* terminating the case. It may state that defendant has prevailed, it may adjudge that defendant shall pay plaintiff a specified sum or return certain property or refrain from engaging in certain activity. It is the judgment that concludes the case at the trial level, although even this simple statement is subject to exceptions and qualifications, something you have already come to expect of the law.

Post-trial motions: A verdict may have been outrageously high, the result of what the law likes to term "passion and prejudice." A new trial may be required even on the question of liability. Yet, it may appear perfectly clear to the judge that the right party won, that is the evidence clearly supported the finding of liability. Rather than force a new trial, a *remittitur* may be appropriate. Defendant will not be granted a new trial if plaintiff consents to accepting a lesser amount fixed by the judge. Sometimes the judge recognizes that he has committed error, serious error, and there would be little point in allowing the verdict to stand, only to have the judgment reversed on appeal. A new trial is appropriate. In certain very limited situations a new trial may be granted simply because the judge feels that, although there was no technical error, something went wrong in the trial process and the result "offends the conscience of the court." It is even possible for the judge to overturn the jury's decision and grant a *judgment as a matter of law* (formerly known as a judgment notwithstanding the verdict (j.n.o.v.)). This can be done if the judge finds that the evidence is not legally sufficient to support the jury's verdict.

Appeals: In this country we operate on the premise that every aggrieved litigant is entitled to one appeal as of right. It will normally be limited to an appeal from the *final judgment.* This limitation makes perfect sense when you realize that in the course of a typical case a trial judge will make many rulings, in some cases hundreds. To halt the proceedings so that each and every one of them might be promptly reviewed by a higher court would be intolerable. Yet, there are situations in which it would be highly desirable to gain the benefit of an appellate decision without awaiting final judgment.

Suppose that in a case requiring a long and complex trial there is a challenge to the jurisdiction of the trial court, a challenge which turns on a point of law. Suppose further that the trial judge and the litigants all agree that a determination of this point of law in advance of trial would be highly desirable. Should there not be a mechanism for prompt review, i.e. an *interlocutory appeal?*

Interlocutory appeals are available in very limited situations almost everywhere, and rather freely in some jurisdictions. In the federal system there exist both judicially-created doctrines and statutory procedures for avoiding the final judgment rule, each with its own requirements, each applicable in narrowly defined circumstances.

Appeals may be to an intermediate appellate court, as is the case in the federal system and in most states, or directly to the highest court of a state, depending on the jurisdiction. On appeal, the judgment may be affirmed, or it may be reversed. If a new trial is ordered, the trial process starts all over again.

CHAPTER I

SERVICE OF PROCESS

A. PERSONAL AND ABODE SERVICE

Terlizzi v. Brodie

Supreme Court of New York, Appellate Division, Second Dept., 1972.
38 A.D.2d 762, 329 N.Y.S.2d 589.

■ Before LATHAM, ACTING P.J., and SHAPIRO, GULOTTA, BRENNAN and BENJAMIN, JJ.

■ MEMORANDUM BY THE COURT.

In a negligence action to recover damages for personal injuries, defendants appeal, as limited by their brief, from so much of an order of the Supreme Court, Kings County, dated July 23, 1971, as, after granting reargument of their motion to vacate service of the summons, adhered to the original decision denying the motion.

Order reversed insofar as appealed from, on the law and on the facts, and motion granted with $10 costs and disbursements.

In May or June, 1968 defendants, New Jersey residents, were in an automobile collision in New Jersey which caused plaintiffs, New York residents, to sustain injuries. In February, 1971 defendants were called at home and told that they had been chosen to receive two tickets to a Broadway show as a promotional venture to get their opinion on a questionnaire of the new 7:30 P.M. curtain time. After the performance and while still in the theatre, defendants were served with a summons in this action by a man who had been sitting behind them. No questionnaire had been given them. Plaintiffs have presented no facts concerning the service to refute defendants' claim and have not submitted an affidavit of the investigator retained to effect service.

It has long been held that where a defendant has been lured into this jurisdiction by fraud or deceit in order that he may be served, the service so effected is invalid (Neotex Mfg. Co. v. Eidinger, 250 App.Div. 504, 294 N.Y.S. 767; Shillman v. Toulson, 211 App.Div. 336, 207 N.Y.S. 296; Garabettian v. Garabettian, 206 App.Div. 502, 201 N.Y.S. 548).

In our opinion, the service was invalid and the motion should have been granted.

NOTES

A. Writing on New York Trial Practice in the N.Y.L.J. of September 8, 1972, Dean (now Judge) McLaughlin refers to the principal case and asks, "Query: Would the result have been the same if the plaintiff had in fact prepared a questionnaire and had given it to the defendants?''

B. In Gumperz v. Hofman, 245 App.Div. 622, 283 N.Y.S. 823 (1st Dept.1935) plaintiff appealed from an order granting defendant's motion to vacate service of summons. The opinion reads as follows:

UNTERMYER, JUSTICE. The defendant, a physician who resides in Buenos Aires, was sojourning at a hotel in the city of New York when served with a summons in this action. According to the defendant's affidavit, the process server called several times at the defendant's rooms while the defendant was absent and on each occasion left a message that Dr. Goldman had called. Eventually the process server, still representing himself to be Dr. Goldman with a letter from the president of the New York County Medical Society to be personally delivered to the defendant, arranged with the defendant to meet him in the lobby of the hotel. When the defendant arrived, he was served with the summons in this action. The process server, in fact, was not a doctor, though his name was Goldman; he was not sent by the president of the New York County Medical Society, and he had no letter for delivery to the defendant. The Special Term vacated the service upon the ground that "the alleged service of the summons was effected through fraud and deceit." Even though we agree with the Special Term in its determination of the facts, we are of opinion that service of the summons ought not to have been set aside.

Order reversed, and motion denied.

C. Are these cases distinguishable?

D. *Gumperz* assumes, and *Terlizzi* appears to assume, that in-hand service within a state on an individual who happens to be in that state, albeit as a transient, creates jurisdiction over that person so long as no force or fraud is involved. This is not a self-evident proposition and it will be examined in Chapter II.

Daks Auto Leasing Corp. v. Connell

District Court of New York, 1989.
142 Misc.2d 354, 537 N.Y.S.2d 469.

■ CHARLES G. HEINE, JUDGE.

Defendant's motion for an order pursuant to CPLR Section 3211(a), par. (8) dismissing the complaint on the basis that the Court has no personal jurisdiction over the defendant is granted.

The summons and complaint in this action were served upon the manager of the trailer park where the defendant's trailer is located, but at a trailer other than the one where the defendant resided. Plaintiff contends that personal service was sufficiently made upon the defendant pursuant to CPLR Section 308 subd. (2). This Court disagrees. Section 308 subd. (2) of the Civil Practice Law and Rules provides that personal service upon a natural person is made when the summons is delivered to a person of suitable age and discretion at the actual place of business, dwelling place or usual place of abode of the person to be served, and by mailing the summons to the last known residence or place of business. In the instant case, the manager of the trailer park qualifies as a person of "suitable age and discretion" within the contemplation of CPLR Section 308 subd. (2). The person served must objectively be of sufficient maturity, understanding and responsibility under the circumstances so as to be reasonably likely to convey the summons to the defendant. The Courts have sustained delivery to adult relatives, landlords, employers, co-workers and apartment house doormen as persons of suitable age and discretion. *See, Roldan v. Thorpe*, 117 A.D.2d 790, 499 N.Y.S.2d 114 (Second Dept. 1986). However, the critical issue in the instant case is whether the trailer manager was served at the "actual dwelling place" or "usual place of abode" of the defendant.

While there are no cases involving personal service upon an individual at a trailer park, analogous situations have been encountered by other Courts. The "actual dwelling place" or "usual place of abode" of a tenant in a multiple dwelling has been held to be the apartment of the tenant. Family Fin. Corp. v. Canuelas, 94 Misc.2d 241, 404 N.Y.S.2d 248 (1978). This general rule was recognized in F.I. duPont, Glore Forgan v. S. Chen, 41 N.Y.2d 794, 396 N.Y.S.2d 343, 364 N.E.2d 1115 (1977) where the Court of Appeals established an exception to the rule. The Court held that there was personal jurisdiction over the tenant in a large apartment building by service of process in the lobby upon the doorman, who denied the process server access to defendant's apartment. The Court reached this conclusion on the basis that since the process server is not permitted to proceed to the actual apartment by the doorman or some other employee, the outer bounds of the actual dwelling place must be deemed to extend to the location at which the process server's progress is arrested. In this case, the location was the lobby of the apartment house. *Id.*, 396 N.Y.S.2d 343, at 346, 364 N.E.2d 1115 at 1117.

In Roldan v. Thorpe, 117 A.D.2d 790, 499 N.Y.S.2d 114 (Second Dept.1986), the Appellate Division of the Second Department used the analysis of the Court of Appeals in *F.I. duPont, supra,* to find that personal service upon a landlord of a single family house, where the defendant resided in the basement apartment, was service upon a "person of suitable age and discretion," and service was made at the "actual dwelling place" or "usual place of abode." F.I. duPont, Glore Forgan & Co. v. S. Chen, 41 N.Y.2d 794, 396 N.Y.S.2d 343, 364 N.E.2d 1115 (1977). The Court found that the "outer bounds" of the defendant's "actual dwelling place" extended to the front of the house (the third mode of access to the defendant's basement apartment) where the process server was met by the landlord. *Roldan,* 499 N.Y.S.2d 114, at 117. The Court reached this conclusion because the defendant's apartment was not identifiable in any way, the house was small and private, the locked gate barred access to defendant's apartment through rear or side door, and defendant possessed keys to the gate.

In the instant case, the Court finds that the service of the summons and complaint upon the manager of the trailer park was not at the "actual dwelling place" or "usual place of abode" of the defendant. There is no indication that the process server made the attempt to serve the defendant at his trailer. Furthermore, there is no evidence that shows the process server was prevented from entering the trailer park and serving defendant at his trailer, unlike the situations in *F.I. duPont* and *Roldan* where the process server was hindered from service because of the actions of defendant.

The Court of Appeals in *F.I. duPont, supra,* recognizes the rule that the "actual dwelling place" or "usual place of abode" of a tenant in a multiple dwelling is the apartment of the tenant. Accordingly, this Court finds that the defendant's trailer in a trailer park is the "actual dwelling place" or "usual place of abode," and not the trailer park itself. The plaintiff has not shown extenuating circumstances for the Court to carve an exception to the general rule, as the Courts did in *F.I. duPont* and *Roldan.*

Accordingly, the complaint is dismissed since the Court lacks personal jurisdiction over the defendant.

Churchill v. Barach

United States District Court, District of Nevada, 1994.
863 F. Supp. 1266.

■ Pro, District Judge.

I. FACTUAL BACKGROUND AND PROCEDURAL HISTORY

JoAnn Churchill, a former ticket agent for Continental Airlines, sought to recover for personal injuries which she alleges were sustained as a result of a letter Barach wrote to Continental complaining about Churchill's inappropriate behavior towards him during an incident that occurred at McCarran International Airport in Las Vegas, Nevada.

[The Court dismissed Churchill's first complaint without prejudice due to improper service.]

On March 7, 1994, Churchill refiled her Complaint against Barach alleging the same causes of action contained in her first Complaint. Churchill again attempted to serve Barach on July 1, 1994. At that time, a deputy sheriff or marshall left a Summons and Complaint with the doorman at Barach's apartment building located at 349 East 49th Street, New York, New York. Churchill also mailed a copy of the Summons and Complaint to Barach at his New York address, and filed an Affidavit of Service with this Court on July 20, 1994. Barach has acknowledged that he received the copies left with the doorman and the copies sent by mail.

Defendant Barach now moves to dismiss the entire action on the grounds that Churchill failed to properly serve process on him in accordance with the requirements of Rule 4 of the Federal Rules of Civil Procedure. Alternatively, Barach seeks dismissal of Churchill's claims for failure to state a claim upon which relief can be granted. Fed. R. Civ. P. 12(b)(6).

A. Motion to Dismiss for Insufficient Service of Process

Rule 4 of the Federal Rules of Civil Procedure governs service of process in federal court. Rule 4(e) provides for service upon individuals within a judicial district of the United States and authorizes nationwide long-arm jurisdiction over defendants. Subsections (1) and (2) of Rule 4(e) set forth that service may properly be effected (1) by a method approved by the law of the state in which the federal court sits, in this case, Nevada, Fed. R. Civ. P. 4(e)(1); (2) by a method approved by the law of the state in which service is effected, in this case, New York, Fed. R. Civ. P. 4(e)(1); (3) by delivering a copy of the summons and of the complaint to the individual personally, Fed. R. Civ. P. 4(e)(2); (4) by leaving copies thereof at the individual's dwelling house or usual place of abode with some person of suitable age and discretion then residing therein, id.; or (5) by delivering a copy of the summons and of the complaint to an agent authorized by appointment or by law to receive service of process. Barach contends that Churchill has failed to comply with any of the approved methods of service under Rule 4 and, therefore, this case must be dismissed because the 120–day period provided by Fed. R. Civ. P. 4(m) has expired.

[T]he Court concludes that Churchill attempted to effect service pursuant to a method approved by New York law, specifically N.Y. Civ. Prac. L. & R. ("NYCPLR") § 308(2). According to NYCPLR § 308(2) personal service may be effected by:

> (1) delivering the summons within the state to a person of suitable age and discretion at the dwelling place of the person to be served; and (2) by mailing the summons to the person to be served at his last known residence in an envelop bearing the legend "personal and confidential" and not indicating on the outside thereof that the communication is from an attorney or concerns an action against the person to be served; and (3) such delivery and mailing must be effected within twenty days of each other; and (4) proof of such service shall be filed with the clerk of the court designated in the summons within twenty days of either such delivery or mailing, whichever is effected later. Service shall be complete ten days after such filing.

The Court finds that Churchill's efforts to effect service pursuant to § 308(2) were untimely under Fed. R. Civ. P. 4(m). Even assuming for the moment that Churchill complied with all the elements of service required by § 308(2), it is clear from the record that service was not complete until after the 120–day limit had expired. Churchill filed her Complaint on March 7, 1994. Counting forward 120 days reveals that Churchill was required to effectively complete service by July 5, 1994, to be in compliance with Rule 4(m). Churchill, however, did not file a proof of service with this Court until July 20, 1994, fifteen days after expiration of the period. Furthermore, according to § 308(2), service was not "complete" until ten days thereafter on July 30, 1994. The result is that Churchill did not properly effect service under New York law until 25 days after the 120–day period provided for by Rule 4(m) had expired.

In her Opposition however, Churchill does not argue that she properly effected service under New York law. Instead, she argues that

Barach was properly served under Rule 4(e)(2), and that said service was effected in a timely manner.

Churchill relies upon the subsection of Rule 4(e)(2) which provides that service may be effected "by leaving copies [of the summons and of the complaint] at the individual's dwelling house or usual place of abode with some person of suitable age and discretion then residing therein." Barach responds that service upon the doorman of his apartment building was invalid because the doorman was not "residing" at Barach's "dwelling house or usual place of abode."

It is undisputed that Barach resides within one of the apartments in the apartment building located at 349 East 49th Street. Thus, that apartment is properly considered Barach's "dwelling house or usual place of abode." Further, the Court finds that the doorman, Mr. Kolja Curanovic, is a "person of suitable age and discretion." Accordingly, whether service was properly effected under Rule 4(e) will turn upon this Court's construction of the phrase "residing therein," and whether that phrase, under the facts of this case, encompasses Barach's doorman. For the reasons that follow, the Court finds that it does.

The phrase "residing therein" is not defined by the Federal Rules. The Court finds that Plaintiff is entitled to a liberal construction of Rule 4(e) and the terms contained therein because Barach has had actual notice that a suit has been filed against him. As the Fifth Circuit explained in *Nowell v. Nowell*, 384 F.2d 951, 953 (5th Cir. 1967), during its analysis of former Rule 4(d)(1):

> The appropriate construction of Rule 4(d)(1) [now Rule 4(e)(2)] varies according to whether the defendant received notice of the suit. 4(d)(1) should be broadly construed where the defendant, as in this case, received notice of the suit. This rule of construction is, of course, subject to the limitation that the construction of the statute's language must be natural rather than an artificial one . . . the practicalities of the particular fact situation determines whether service meets the requirements of 4(d)(1).

In cases arising under similar facts, the courts have been inclined to construe the "residing therein" requirement liberally in order to find valid service of process. See *Hartford Fire Ins. Co. v. Perinovic* (holding that doorman at defendant's condominium building was "residing therein" for purposes of service of process); *Three Crown Limited Partnership v. Caxton Corp* (holding, without discussion, that service upon 20-year-old doorman was sufficient to satisfy requirements of Rule 4(d)(1)); *Nowell* (finding service upon apartment manager sufficient); *Smith v. Kincaid* (finding service upon landlady sufficient).

Furthermore, the doorman of Barach's apartment building has acknowledged that his "regular duties include screening callers, announcing visitors, and accepting messages and packages for delivery to the tenants of the building." It has been recognized that:

> Arguably, since hotel managers and landladies normally are under an obligation to transmit all incoming messages and mail to guests

and tenants, there appears to be no valid objection to permitting delivery to such persons, at least in terms of questioning the likelihood of notice or fairness to defendant. This obligation to relay information to guests and occupants should be a sufficient basis for distinguishing those cases in which service has been disallowed when left with a resident of a multiple unit dwelling who is not living in defendant's place of abode.

4A Charles A. Wright & Arthur R. Miller, Federal Practice and Procedure § 1096, at 82–83 (1987).

The Court finds the aforementioned authority persuasive and thus concludes that under the facts of this case, in leaving copies of the summons and complaint with Barach's doorman, Churchill left them at Barach's "usual place of abode with some person of suitable age and discretion then residing therein." Barach therefore received valid service under Rule 4(e). Furthermore, said service was timely as it occurred on July 1, 1994—four days prior to the expiration of the service period provided for by Rule 4(m).

[The Court went on to find that Churchill had failed to state a claim upon which relief could be granted, and dismissed the claim pursuant to Rule 12(b)(6).]

IT IS THEREFORE ORDERED THAT Defendant's Motion to Dismiss is Granted.

QUESTIONS

If defendant concedes having received notice of the lawsuit, should non-compliance with the specific requirements of the rules be considered significant? Why?

Is the *Churchill* court suggesting that if defendant has in fact received notice, compliance with the requirements of the rule is irrelevant? If not, what then is the rationale of *Churchill*?

B. ABUSE OF PROCESS

Tuerkheimer, Service of Process in New York City: A Proposed End to Unregulated Criminality

72 Columbia L.Rev. 847 (1972).

In June of 1971, the United States Court of Appeals for the Second Circuit, in United States v. Wiseman,[2] affirmed the convictions of two process servers for violations of the 1866 Civil Rights Act[3] and the general aiding and abetting section of title 18.

2. 445 F.2d 792 (2d Cir.), cert. denied, 404 U.S. 967 (1971).

3. 18 U.S.C.A. § 242 (Supp.1973). In pertinent part the statute provides:

Whoever, under color of any law, statute, ordinance, regulation, or custom willfully subjects any inhabitant of any State * * * to the deprivation of any rights, privileges, or

The basis for these convictions was the defendants' systematic practice of signing affidavits affirming that they had delivered summonses to named defendants when, in fact, they had never made, nor even attempted to make, such service. The result was a large number of default judgments entered against parties who had no way of knowing that proceedings had been instituted against them.

* * *

A contribution by attorneys to the elimination of sewer service would be most welcome. However, on the basis of what we know, it is illusory to expect or to rely on such a prospect.

V. Recommendations

B. *Causes of Sewer Service*

Before discussing recommendations for changes in the law, it may be helpful to attempt to illuminate the main causes for the persistence of the practice of sewer service. There appear to be four reasons why it has existed on such a broad scale for so long a time.

Despite the critical function of service of process, the area has remained largely unregulated. With the increase in consumer spending,[38] process servers and process serving agencies have acquired the power to affect the property, peace of mind, and fortunes of thousands of individuals. One New York court has stated that "[t]he service of process is an act of public power * * *."[39] Yet New York law establishes no requirements for process servers other than that they be eighteen years old and not a party to the suit. Apart from general penal statutes, process servers are not regulated in any way even though their work involves substantial temptation to improper conduct. The temptation has two sources. First, the victims are remote, disorganized, and usually lack the know-how and resources to complain. Second, it is not easy for process servers, almost all of whom are white, to venture alone into black neighborhoods, find a specific person, inform him that he is being sued, and then hand him a piece of paper setting in operation machinery that may end with property attachment and income execution. Such work carries obvious risks and these risks in turn invite shortcuts. The easiest shortcut is the one leading to the nearest sewer.

A second reason for the prevalence of sewer service is that, as already noted, the collection bar has been allowed to insulate itself from responsibility for the sewer service practices on which it relies for its profitable operation. Because of their reliance on the mails, collection attorneys are invariably presented with substantial data pointing

---

immunities secured or protected by the Constitution or the laws of the United States * * * shall be fined not more than $1000 or imprisoned not more than one year, or both * * *.

The Second Circuit found process service to be a "public function" and therefore found Wiseman to have acted under color of law within the meaning of the Act. United States v. Wiseman, 445 F.2d at 796.

38. From 1945 to 1969, the outstanding consumer installment debt went from $2.5 billion to $97 billion.

39. In re Bonesteel Will, 16 A.D.2d 324, 326, 228 N.Y.S.2d 301, 304 (3d Dep't 1962).

to the unreliability of affidavits of service.[40] Yet, they can with impunity close their eyes to such evidence and continue to operate as in the past.

A third cause of sewer service, although somewhat less significant today, is that its victims have been too poor and disorganized to do anything about it. Since a pioneer study conducted by the Congress of Racial Equality in 1965, some organizational resources have been directed to this problem. But while legislative reform designed to eliminate the traditional powerlessness of sewer service victims is certainly a possibility, it is likely to be difficult to achieve. Hence, it might be well to exhaust other alternatives first.

The fourth reason why sewer service has flourished is that local law enforcement agencies have done little to curb it. The crimes involved are both large in number and pernicious in effect, yet investigative and prosecutorial discretion has not been inclined towards this area. The results have been twofold. First, sewer service has continued largely unchecked. Second, federal law enforcement authorities have had to pick up the slack through the initiation of both criminal and civil actions by the Justice Department. Such expansion of federal authority into areas of primary state responsibility, although constitutional, runs contrary to notions of federalism and risks potential abuses, which could be avoided if local officials acted.

* * *

Joint Investigative Report Into the Practice of Sewer Service in N.Y. City
April 1986.

Fraudulent service of process by licensed process servers, commonly known as "sewer service," has been a perennial matter of public concern. Despite enforcement and legislative efforts in the past decade to combat this pernicious practice, sewer service continues to plague our courts and deny due process to our citizens.

This report * * * describes the investigations and enforcement actions taken over a two-year period, and proposes additional remedies to the problem.

THE THREE–PRONGED INVESTIGATION

To identify, expose and prosecute process servers engaging in sewer service, the Attorney General, DCA[a], and DOI[b] employed three

---

40. An interesting insight into what returned mail can reveal was provided by the seizure of certain of returned correspondence from Attorneys Service Company. Apparently a number of process servers working for the company purported to make substituted service, which required leaving the summons and complaint at the residence or business of the defendant and mailing them to his home. In one case the mailing was returned with the notation "moved, left no address." Never-theless, *thereafter,* in a non-military affidavit, a process server swore to having a conversation with the defendant at the same address. In another case where the returned correspondence was stamped "no such number" the proprietor of the process service agency filled in the non-military affidavit alleging a conversation with the defendant at the same address *after* the envelope had been returned.

    a. Department of Consumer Affairs.

    b. Department of Investigations.

separate investigative techniques. These included 1) actual surveillance of a number of major process servers; 2) use of an undercover agent to demonstrate the physical impossibility of serving the volume of process claimed by most process servers, and, at the same time, to demonstrate the difficulty of making a living by serving process legally; and 3) cross-referencing records of different process server agencies for a specified time period. The results of each of these techniques is summarized below.

Criminal Investigation—Method I

In November and December 1985, DOI conducted a criminal investigation of certain major process servers identified by DCA, and thereafter turned over evidence resulting from that investigation and prosecution. Indictments of five process servers have been handed up by a grand jury. The Attorney General's investigation is continuing.

"Operation Double–Fault"—Method II

An undercover investigation was undertaken in October, 1985 by DOI, known as "Operation Double Fault". It demonstrated that it is physically impossible to serve legally the volume generally claimed by most full-time process servers, and that process servers could not make a living wage if service was performed legally, given the current economics of the industry.

From October 2, 1985 until November 4, 1985, an undercover detective furnished with a license by DCA, worked as a process server for four licensed agencies in Manhattan. During the course of the investigation, the detective attempted to serve 401 pieces of process.[1] A team of investigators assisted the detective in sorting the process by zip codes and in planning routes to ensure maximum speed and efficiency. In addition, the detective was accompanied on a daily basis by a driver so that parking problems would be eliminated. The detective personally made every attempted service and completed the required mailings and affidavits himself, in accordance with law.

Despite working six days a week and an average of fifteen hours per day, the detective was able to serve only 214 pieces of process. The remaining process was unservable because the party to be served was unknown at the address indicated, or because the address did not exist. The percentage of unservable process—46%—was much higher than can be reasonably presumed for the industry.

The detective made 537 visits to the various premises in his attempts to make proper service. The 214 instances of completed

---

1. The detective actually received a total of 526 pieces of process during the investigation. However, due to the enormous amount of time and energy expended on the initial 401 pieces, it became physically impossible to attempt to serve the remaining 125 within the month's time. Consequently, these 125 pieces were returned to their source agency at the conclusion of the investigation.

service were distributed as follows among the various categories of service.

	Number	Percentage
Personal Service	83	39%
Substituted Service [2]	117	55%
Nail and Mail Service	14	7%
Totals	214	101% [3]

The percentage of service accomplished by nail and mail was much smaller than process servers ordinarily report according to DCA.

The detective's income for the month, based on payment of $3.00 per service, totalled only about $600.00 before his expenses and taxes were taken into consideration. This represents a wage of less than one half the current $3.35 per hour federal minimum wage.

In sum, the results of "Operation Double Fault" clearly demonstrate the impossibility of lawfully serving the large amount of process regularly claimed to be served by many process servers in the time they claim such services are made.

Cross–Referencing of Records—Method III

Most individual process servers obtain their process from process service agencies. While aware that such process servers obtain process simultaneously from other agencies, each agency wears blinders to the consequences of this fact. Each agency is content to rely on the information furnished by the individual process servers for the process distributed by that agency only without inquiring as to what services were made for other agencies.

Few conflicts (defined as two or more services usually within five minutes or less with a significant distance separating the locations) or duplications (defined as two or more services at the exact same time) are found in an agency's records because individual process servers are adept at calling in a full day's service to *each* agency which superficially appears in perfect order.

In March 1984, DCA dispatched teams of inspectors simultaneously to visit seventeen process service agencies. DCA inspectors reviewed the agencies' business records of actual and attempted services for the month of February 1984.

Since each agency's records reflected the services for process distributed by that agency only, it was impossible to obtain a complete picture of each individual process server's daily activities from those records alone.

It was necessary to first divide the records of each agency according to individual process servers to obtain a more accurate picture of 37 individual process servers identified as having worked for more than one agency. A master list was prepared to each of the 37 process

---

2. Includes cases where process was left with an individual on behalf of a business.

3. Due to rounding off of percentages.

servers. From such list, a chronological log for a seven-to ten-day period[4] was created. The chronological daily log included the date and time of each service, and the address where the service allegedly occurred.

It soon became apparent that many of the claimed services occurred simultaneously or within such close proximity in time as to be physically impossible, evidencing the "Superman Syndrome." Numerous duplications and conflicts were uncovered. Thereafter, affidavits of service were reviewed in the cases where either conflicts or duplications were identified.

Findings

A total of 4,661 services were recorded for 37 process servers for the period examined; an average of 126 services per process server. Examination of the integrated logs revealed that for 95%, or 35 of the 37 process servers, there was some evidence of conflicts or duplications in the services they claimed to have performed. For those 35 process servers, who claimed to perform a total of 4,661 services, there were 1,721 services (or 39%) which were either conflicts or duplications.[5] Of those, 640, or 37%, represented services with duplicated times; 1,081, or 63% represented services with conflicting times.

* * *

Conclusion

This report reflects the findings and actions resulting from an intensive two-year investigation conducted by state and city officials into the problem of sewer service in New York City. Every investigative technique confirms beyond doubt the pervasive, wanton disregard for the law by the private process server industry.

As we have shown, the documentation of individual instances of sewer service is an extremely difficult and painstaking process requiring the allocation of a large amount of resources. The case-by-case approach is wholly inadequate to provide essential consumer protection in the face of the enormous number of instances of sewer service.

NOTE ON PROFESSIONAL CONSTRAINTS

Rule 5.3 of the A.B.A. Model Rules of Professional Conduct provides:

With respect to a nonlawyer employed or retained by or associated with a lawyer:

(a) a partner in a law firm shall make reasonable efforts to ensure that the firm has in effect measures giving reasonable assurance that the

---

4. Although in most instances February 1st through 10th was used, the actual days varies in that some individual process servers did not serve any papers for a few of these days. In these instances, a later 7–10 day period in February was selected.

5. In some instances, a service was both a duplication of another service and in conflict with a third service, in which case it was counted as both a duplication and a conflict.

person's conduct is compatible with the professional obligations of the lawyer;

(b) a lawyer having direct supervisory authority over the nonlawyer shall make reasonable efforts to ensure that the person's conduct is compatible with the professional obligations of the lawyer; and

(c) a lawyer shall be responsible for conduct of such a person that would be a violation of the Rules of Professional Conduct if engaged in by a lawyer if:

(1) the lawyer orders or, with the knowledge of the specific conduct, ratifies the conduct involved; or

(2) the lawyer is a partner in the law firm in which the person is employed, or has direct supervisory authority over the person, and knows of the conduct at a time when its consequences can be avoided or mitigated but fails to take reasonable remedial action.

NOTE

Does Rule 5.3 now impose responsibility on the lawyers for sewer service? What if the lawyer had reason to know that something was probably amiss?

COST OF SERVICE

A. SHUCHMAN, TRAVEL COSTS FOR SERVICE OF CIVIL PROCESS, 5 Conn.L.Rev. 458 (1973):

The import of this investigation is simply stated: Deputy sheriffs and constables in Connecticut overcharge an average of 230 percent or about $2.70 for travel in civil cases in which they make service of process. These overcharges are evident in over four-fifths of the sample cases we examined. Given that nearly 70,000 civil suits are now started annually, the total of this petty theft will be nearly $200,000. Then, too, there is legal vigorish: An average of about $1.50 is permitted for "copies" never made and for "endorsements" that are meaningless. These legal but unnecessary charges will total about $100,000 a year. Thus about $300,000 of unlawful costs and unnecessary costs is paid by the litigants in civil suits, but mostly by the defendants in those lawsuits. The systems of compensation for service of process from the courts in several other states are similar and we expect that replication of this study in those states would show similar results.

B. A recent article directed to California practitioners surveys various alternative professional process services. "The fees vary, but you can generally figure on paying between $15 and $40 for most serves * * *. [R]ush jobs run higher, often including an inflated hourly rate coupled to mileage and expenses. For urgent, difficult and dangerous serves, an attorney might hire a private investigator and run up a bill as high as $500." Setterberg, Service with a Smile, 5 Cal.Lawyer 55 (July, 1985).

C. In July, 1990, a Philadelphia firm's fee schedule for service of process gave charges of $40 for service on one defendant in Philadelphia; an additional $10 for each additional defendant at the same address and $20 for each additional defendant at another address in Philadelphia.

N.Y. CIVIL PRACTICE LAW AND RULES

§ 308.   Personal Service Upon a Natural Person

Personal service upon a natural person shall be made by any of the following methods:

1.   by delivering the summons within the state to the person to be served; or

2.   by delivering the summons within the state to a person of suitable age and discretion at the actual place of business, dwelling place or usual place of abode of the person to be served and by either mailing the summons to the person to be served at his or her last known residence or by mailing the summons by first class mail to the person to be served at his or her actual place of business in an envelope bearing the legend "personal and confidential" and not indicating on the outside thereof, by return address or otherwise, that the communication is from an attorney or concerns an action against the person to be served, such delivery and mailing to be effected within twenty days of each other; proof of such service shall be filed with the clerk of the court designated in the summons within twenty days of either such delivery or mailing, whichever is effected later; service shall be complete ten days after such filing; proof of service shall identify such person of suitable age and discretion and state the date, time and place of service, except in matrimonial actions where service hereunder may be made pursuant to an order made in accordance with the provisions of subdivision a of section two hundred thirty-two of the domestic relations law; or

3.   by delivering the summons within the state to the agent for service of the person to be served as designated under rule 318, except in matrimonial actions where service hereunder may be made pursuant to an order made in accordance with the provisions of subdivision a of section two hundred thirty-two of the domestic relations law;

4.   where service under paragraphs one and two cannot be made with due diligence, by affixing the summons to the door of either the actual place of business, dwelling place or usual place of abode within the state of the person to be served and by either mailing the summons to such person at his or her last known residence or by mailing the summons by first class mail to the person to be served at his or her actual place of business in an envelope bearing the legend "personal and confidential" and not indicating on the outside thereof, by return address or otherwise, that the communication is from an attorney or concerns an action against the person to be served, such affixing and mailing to be effected within twenty days of each other; proof of such service shall be filed with the clerk of the court designated in the

summons within twenty days of either such affixing or mailing, whichever is effected later; service shall be complete ten days after such filing, except in matrimonial actions where service hereunder may be made pursuant to an order made in accordance with the provisions of subdivision a of section two hundred thirty-two of the domestic relations law;

5. in such manner as the court, upon motion without notice, directs, if service is impracticable under paragraphs one, two and four of this section.

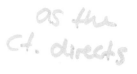

as the Ct. directs

QUESTIONS ON SEWER SERVICE AND DEFAULT JUDGMENTS

What factors appear to be related to the question of the reliability of the return of service? Consider the following: economic incentives (are the process servers civil service employees on a salary or are they paid on a "piece work" basis?); type of action (contract, rent claims and personal injury); kind of neighborhood; whether the plaintiff or the lawyer may choose the process server.

A small sampling in Connecticut revealed almost no default judgments in personal injury actions. The economic motives for avoiding defaults result from the fact that defendant's insurance carrier is the party who will pay any judgment. About nine-tenths of all personal injury actions are settled before trial.

Would you be inclined to have different rules for service of process for different types of claims, larger and smaller claims, and different defendants?

Some states permit service of process at the last known abode of the defendant. Sometimes abode service is permitted only after attempts at personal service have proved fruitless.

Given the transient conditions of the near-poor, is abode service likely to be the best means of giving notice to such persons? What alternatives might be preferable?

The usual execution process in the consumer credit cases is by wage garnishment. Many defendants claim that their first notice of a lawsuit is when their wages are garnished. Would it help to enact a rule of civil procedure providing for answer on the merits—notwithstanding the default judgment—within, say, 30 days of the first wage garnishment? (Would you prescribe that the money be held by the employer until the later of appearance and defense or the expiration of the 30 day period?)

In some states, court clerks stamp the name, address and telephone number of the nearest legal aid office on the summons or complaint in collection and rent cases. In other jurisdictions, before a default judgment can be finally entered, the clerk of the court writes a letter to the defendant advising him that request for a default judgment has been made and that he has two weeks within which to appear and state that he wishes to defend on the merits. Since many default judgments are followed by wage garnishment, would it be better from the standpoint of notice to commence the action by notice of wage garnishment served on the defendant's employer? What other problems would this create?

Kleeman v. Rheingold

Court of Appeals of New York, 1993.
81 N.Y.2d 270, 598 N.Y.S.2d 149, 614 N.E.2d 712.

■ TITONE, JUDGE.

In a prior action brought to recover damages for alleged medical malpractice, plaintiff was nonsuited for failure properly to serve the defendant doctor before the Statute of Limitations on her claim expired. The threshold issue in this second malpractice action, which was brought by plaintiff against the lawyers she retained to prosecute the first, is whether an attorney may be held vicariously liable to his or her client for the negligence of a process server whom the attorney has hired on behalf of that client.

According to the allegations in the present complaint, plaintiff, a victim of alleged medical malpractice, had originally retained defendant and his law firm to pursue her claim against Dr. Neils Lauersen. With only five days remaining before the Statute of Limitations on the claim would expire, defendant promptly prepared a summons and complaint. On November 5, 1978, two days before the Statute of Limitations was to run, defendant delivered the prepared documents to Fischer's Service Bureau, a process service agency regularly used by defendant's law firm, with the instruction that process was to be served "immediately." It is undisputed that Fischer's, not defendant, selected the licensed process server who would actually deliver the papers and that Fischer's and the process server, rather than defendant, determined the precise manner of effecting service.

Although the process server used by Fischer's apparently delivered the papers on time, plaintiff's medical malpractice claim was ultimately dismissed when a traverse hearing revealed that the process server had given the papers to Dr. Lauersen's secretary rather than Dr. Lauersen himself. By the time the traverse hearing was held, the Statute of Limitations had expired and plaintiff had no further legal recourse against the allegedly negligent doctor. Defendants then attempted to recover on plaintiff's behalf by "alleging various and different theories of liability against certain other parties." These claims, however, were all resolved against plaintiff in January of 1987.

Plaintiff subsequently commenced the present legal malpractice action against defendant and his law firm, claiming that they should be held liable for the negligence of the process server who had been retained to serve Dr. Lauersen on plaintiff's behalf. Defendants moved for summary judgment and plaintiff cross-moved. Plaintiff argued that defendants' liability could be predicated on a nondelegable duty of attorneys to exercise care in assuring proper service of their clients' legal process. Alternatively, plaintiff argued that the process server was defendants' agent and that, under settled agency law principles, they could therefore be held accountable for the process server's wrongful acts. Finally, plaintiff contended that defendants should be held liable because of their own negligence in selecting a process serving agency that was "not a particularly respected or reliable entity," in failing to supervise or monitor the work of that agency and, finally, in neglecting to file the summons and complaint with the appropriate County Clerk so as to obtain a 60–day toll of the Statute of Limitations on plaintiff's claim pursuant to CPLR 203(b)(5).

The trial court rejected all of plaintiff's arguments, concluding that a process server is an "independent contractor" rather than an agent of the employing attorney, since "[t]he attorney does not have control over the manner in which the task is performed." Accordingly, the court held, the relationship between the process server and the attorney here did not provide a cognizable basis for holding the latter vicariously liable for the acts of the former. On reargument, the court also rejected plaintiff's claims regarding defendants' failure to supervise the process server, holding that defendants' duty was satisfied when they took the necessary steps to commence the action by retaining the services of a licensed process server.

On plaintiff's appeal, a divided Appellate Division affirmed for essentially the same reasons. We now modify by denying defendants' motion for summary judgment. As plaintiff's attorneys, defendants had a nondelegable duty to her and, accordingly, they cannot evade legal responsibility for the negligent performance of that duty by assigning the task of serving process to an "independent contractor."

The general rule is that a party who retains an independent contractor, as distinguished from a mere employee or servant, is not liable for the independent contractor's negligent acts. Although several justifications have been offered in support of this rule, the most commonly accepted rationale is based on the premise that one who employs an independent contractor has no right to control the manner in which the work is to be done and, thus, the risk of loss is more sensibly placed on the contractor.

Despite the courts' frequent recitation of the general rule against vicarious liability, the common law has produced a wide variety of so-called "exceptions." Indeed, it has been observed that the general rule "is now primarily important as a preamble to the catalog of its exceptions." These exceptions, most of which are derived from various public policy concerns, fall roughly into three basic categories: negligence of the employer in selecting, instructing or supervising the contractor; employment for work that is especially or "inherently" dangerous; and, finally, instances in which the employer is under a specific nondelegable duty.

The exception that concerns us here—the exception for nondelegable duties—has been defined as one that "requires the person upon whom it is imposed to answer for it that care is exercised by anyone, even though he be an independent contractor, to whom the performance of the duty is entrusted." The exception is often invoked where the particular duty in question is one that is imposed by regulation or statute. However, the class of duties considered "nondelegable" is not limited to statutorily imposed duties. To the contrary, examples of nondelegable common-law duties abound.

There are no clearly defined criteria for identifying duties that are nondelegable. Indeed, whether a particular duty is properly catego-rized as "nondelegable" necessarily entails a sui generis inquiry, since the conclusion ultimately rests on policy considerations.

The most often cited formulation is that a duty will be deemed nondelegable when " 'the responsibility is so important to the commu-nity that the employer should not be permitted to transfer it to another.' " This flexible formula recognizes that the "privilege to farm out [work] has its limits" and that those limits are best defined by reference to the gravity of the public policies that are implicated.

Viewed in the light of these principles, the duty at issue here—that owed by an attorney to his or her client to exercise care in the service of process—fits squarely and neatly within the category of obligations that the law regards as "nondelegable." Manifestly, when an individual retains an attorney to commence an action, timely and accurate service of process is an integral part of the task that the attorney undertakes. Furthermore, proper service of process is a particularly critical component of a lawyer's over-all responsibility for commencing a client's lawsuit, since a mistake or oversight in this area can deprive the client of his or her day in court regardless of how meritorious the client's claim may be. Given the central importance of this duty, our State's attorneys cannot be allowed to evade responsibil-ity for its careful performance by the simple expedient of "farming out" the task to independent contractors.

The existence of an extensive and comprehensive Code of Profes-sional Responsibility that governs the obligations of attorneys to their clients reinforces our conclusion. Under the Code, a lawyer may not "seek, by contract or other means, to limit prospectively the lawyer's individual liability to a client for malpractice." Moreover, the Code forbids lawyers from "[n]eglect[ing] legal matter[s] entrusted to [them]," enjoins them to assist in "secur[ing] and protect[ing] avail-able legal rights" and requires them to represent their clients as zealously as the "bounds of the law" permit. All of the latter ethical and disciplinary considerations are implicated when a client's lawsuit is undermined—or even defeated—as a consequence of carelessness in the service of process.

Our conclusion is also supported by the perceptions of the lay public and the average client, who may reasonably assume that all of the tasks associated with the commencement of an action, including its formal initiation through service of process, will be performed either by the attorney or someone acting under the attorney's di-rection. While it may be a common practice among attorneys to retain outside agencies like Fischer's to assist them in effecting service, that custom is not necessarily one of which the general public is aware. Even where a client is expressly made aware that a process serving agency will be retained, it is unlikely that the client will understand or appreciate that the process serving agency's legal status as an "independent contractor" could render the retained attorney immune from liability for the agency's negligence. Under established principles, the client's reasonable expectations and beliefs about who will render a particular service are a significant factor in identifying duties that should be deemed to be "nondelegable."

Finally, we conclude that permitting lawyers to transfer their duty of care to process servers would be contrary to sound public policy. In this State, licensed attorneys have been granted an exclusive franchise to practice law, with the understanding that they have both the specialized knowledge and the character required to represent clients in a competent, diligent and careful manner. Under this system, lawyers are authorized to hold themselves out as being uniquely qualified to manage their clients' legal affairs, a task that unquestionably includes the commencement of lawsuits. While it is true that the State also licenses nonlawyers to perform certain discrete, law-related tasks such as service of process, the existence of that licensing system certainly does not evince a governmental intent to relieve attorneys of the responsibilities implicit in their franchise. To the contrary, the purpose of the licensing system for process servers is to "combat a continuing and pervasive problem of unscrupulous service practices" in order to protect defendants who might otherwise be deprived of their day in court or be victimized by "fraudulent default judgments." That purpose is obviously unrelated to the entirely separate goal of assuring clients who are would-be plaintiffs that their process will be timely served in a manner that complies with the complex requirements of CPLR articles 2 and 3, as well as with the numerous other statutory provisions relating to commencement of actions and the formidable body of case law illuminating those statutes. The responsibility for achieving that goal—and the liability for negligent failures to achieve it—must remain squarely on the shoulders of trained and licensed attorneys who, as members of a "learned profession," alone have the necessary knowledge and experience to protect their clients' rights.

[T]he nondelegable duty of care that we have recognized in this case is limited to the discrete and unique function of commencing an action through service of process. Furthermore, the duty extends only to clients who have retained an attorney for the purpose of commencing a lawsuit. We do not decide here the entirely separate question of an attorney's liability for the wrongs that a retained process server may commit against a potential defendant or another third party. Nor do we consider the right of an attorney who has been held liable for the negligence of a retained process server to pursue whatever contractual or tort remedies that the attorney may have against that process server. We hold only that an attorney has a nondelegable duty to his or her clients to exercise due care in the service of process and that, accordingly, an attorney may be held liable to the client for negligent service of process, even though the task may have been "farmed out" to an independent contractor.

In view of this conclusion, it is evident that the courts below erred in granting defendants' motion for summary judgment dismissing the complaint. If there was negligence in the effort to effect service of process in plaintiff's failed action against Dr. Lauersen, plaintiff is entitled to hold defendant vicariously liable, and she may recover in damages if she can demonstrate that this negligence was the proximate cause of any pecuniary injury she sustained. We note, however, that plaintiff is not herself entitled to summary judgment on the liability question at this point in the litigation, since she still must demonstrate both that the retained process server acted negligently and that she would have prevailed in the underlying action against Lauersen if the negligence had not occurred. Thus, the denial of plaintiff's cross motion for partial summary judgment was proper. Finally, since we are holding that neither party is entitled to summary judgment on plaintiff's single cause of action for legal malpractice, we need not now consider the viability of the other theories that plaintiff has advanced to support defendants' liability. At this point in the litigation, it suffices to hold that defendants' nondelegable duty to plaintiff provides a legally viable basis for imposing liability on them.

Accordingly, the order of the Appellate Division should be modified, with costs to plaintiff, by denying defendants' motion for summary judgment dismissing the complaint and, as modified, affirmed.

C.   SERVICE AND WAIVER OF SERVICE BY MAIL

Bernard v. Husky Truck Stop d/b/a Goodland Car and Truck Plaza a/k/a Fastway, Inc.

United States District Court, District of Kansas, 1994.
1994 WL 171732.

■ LUNGSTRUM, DISTRICT JUDGE

I.   Introduction

This case involves a personal injury action brought by plaintiff Jay Bernard for injuries he allegedly suffered when he slipped and fell at a restaurant/truck stop owned by defendant Fastway, Inc. The matter is currently before the court on defendant's motion to dismiss pursuant to Fed. R. Civ. P. 12(b)(5). For the reasons set forth below, the motion to dismiss is granted.

II.   Legal Standards

The defendant challenges the sufficiency of the plaintiff's service of process. In opposing a motion to dismiss filed before trial, plaintiff has the burden of making a prima facie showing that statutory and due process requirements are satisfied so as to permit the court to exercise personal jurisdiction over the defendant. *Carrothers Const. Co., Inc. v. Quality Service & Supply, Inc.*, 586 F.Supp. 134, 135–36 (D.Kan. 1984). The parties may submit affidavits and other documentary evidence for the court's consideration. *Slawson v. Hair*, 716 F.Supp. 1373, 1374 (D.Kan. 1989). Plaintiff is entitled to the benefit of any factual doubt. *Ammon v. Kaplow*, 468 F.Supp. 1304, 1309 (D.Kan. 1979).

III. Factual Background

Applying these principles, the court considers the following facts to be relevant and controlling of defendant's motion. This case involves a personal injury action brought by plaintiff for a slip and fall accident at a restaurant/truck stop owned by defendant. Plaintiff originally filed an action in this court on July 24, 1991 that was styled as Case No. 91–2274–GTV. Subsequently, that case was dismissed without prejudice in December, 1992. Plaintiff filed the current action on June 14, 1993. Plaintiff attempted to serve defendant by mail on August 28, 1993. However, instead of issuing a summons and mailing a copy of the summons and complaint to the proper defendant, Fastway, Inc., plaintiff issued a summons and mailed a copy of the summons and complaint to "Husky Truck Stop," which was neither the proper defendant in the case nor a proper person to receive service on behalf of Fastway, Inc. under either the Federal or State rules of procedure. In an order dated December 28, 1993, this court ruled that plaintiff had failed to execute proper service on defendant. As a result of this ruling, pursuant to K.S.A. § 60–203(b), plaintiff had 90 days from the date of the ruling within which to effectuate proper service in order for the action to be deemed to have commenced at the time of the filing of the complaint.

Following the court's December 28, 1993 ruling, plaintiff attempted to serve defendant by mail. Plaintiff's first attempt, which was mailed on January 18, 1994, was returned from the post office indicating defendant was no longer at that address. On March 4, 1994 plaintiff mailed a Notice of Lawsuit and Request for Waiver of Summons; a Waiver of Summons; and a copy of the Complaint filed herein to defendant's correct address by certified mail. On March 9, 1994, plaintiff's counsel received a domestic return receipt indicating that the above-named documents were received by the president of defendant corporation, Don Baldwin, on March 7, 1994. Plaintiff did not include a summons in the materials sent to defendant. Indeed, plaintiff never obtained a summons from the clerk of this court.

IV. Discussion

Federal Rule of Civil Procedure 4 provides several methods by which a plaintiff may effectuate service of process. Rule 4(h)(1) provides that service upon a domestic corporation, from which a waiver of service has not been obtained and filed, shall be effected either (i) pursuant to the law of the state in which the district court is located; or (ii) by delivering a copy of the summons and complaint to an officer, a managing or general agent, or any other agent authorized by appointment or law to receive service of process. Additionally, Rule 4(d) provides an alternate method whereby a plaintiff may notify a defendant of the commencement of an action and request that the defendant waive service.

It is apparent that plaintiff did not comply with any of the methods for obtaining service of process provided in Rule 4. Plaintiff did not deliver a copy of the summons and complaint to an officer, a managing or general agent, or any other agent authorized by appointment or law to receive service on process. As noted, no summons was ever issued by the clerk of this court. Similarly, plaintiff did not obtain a waiver of service as provided in Rule 4(d). Rule 4(d) provides a specific mechanism by which a plaintiff can obtain a waiver of service from a defendant. A plaintiff must mail a notice and request for waiver of service to the defendant which includes all the requirements contained in 4(d)(2)(A)-(G). However, the mere mailing of the notice and request by a plaintiff does not effectuate service. The defendant must return the waiver of service to the plaintiff, who must then file the waiver with the court. If the defendant fails to return the waiver, then the plaintiff must effectuate service in a manner provided in subdivision (e), (f) or (h) of Rule 4. See Fed. R. Civ. P. 4(d)(5). In the present case, plaintiff did not receive the waiver from the defendant and no such waiver was ever filed with the court. Consequently, plaintiff did not effectuate proper service on defendant merely by mailing the notice and request for waiver to the defendant.

Having determined that plaintiff failed to comply with the methods for obtaining service specifically provided in Rule 4, the court now examines whether plaintiff complied with the law of Kansas for obtaining service of process. K.S.A. § 60–303 sets forth the proper methods to obtain service under Kansas law, including service by mail. The statute provides, in pertinent part, that:

> The ... attorney for the party ... shall cause a copy of the process and petition ... to be placed in an envelope addressed to the person to be served in accordance with K.S.A. 60–304 ... adequate postage to be affixed and the sealed envelope to be placed in the United States mail as certified mail return receipt requested with instructions to the delivering postal employee to show to whom delivered, date of delivery, and address where delivered.

> The ... party's attorney ... shall execute a return on service stating the nature of the process, the date on which the process was mailed, and the name and address on the envelope containing the process mailed as certified mail return receipt requested. The ... party's attorney shall file the return on service and the return receipt or return envelope in the records of the action.

K.S.A. § 60–303(b).

In order to effectuate service by mail in Kansas, a plaintiff must deliver a copy of the summons and petition to the defendant. In the present case, plaintiff not only did not mail a copy of a summons to defendant, in fact, no summons was ever issued by the clerk of this court. Plaintiff contends that under K.S.A. § 60–302, the notice and waiver sent to defendant should qualify as an adequate summons under state law. K.S.A. § 60–302 provides that "the summons shall be signed by the clerk, dated the day it is issued, be under the seal of the court and shall be in substantial conformity with the forms for summons contained in the appendix of forms following K.S.A. 60–269." Plaintiff contends that the notice and waiver of service he sent "was in substantial conformity" with the forms for summons contained in the appendix of forms following K.S.A. § 60–269.

The court does not believe that plaintiff's failure to have a summons issued and delivered to defendant can be saved by the "substantial conformity" language contained in K.S.A. § 60–302. The statute specifically provides that the summons shall be "signed by the clerk." The court finds that this language clearly contemplates that a summons must be issued by the clerk of the court, and plaintiff's self-generated notice and waiver of service does not comply with the form of summons requirement contained in K.S.A. § 60–203.

[The Court went on to find that the plaintiff had not demonstrated excusable neglect that would prevent dismissal of the case under Fed. R. Civ. P. 4(m).]

IT IS, THEREFORE, BY THE COURT ORDERED THAT defendant's motion to dismiss is granted.

John Magnuson v. Video Yesteryear

United States Court of Appeals for the Ninth Circuit, 1996.
85 F.3d 1424.

■ D.W. NELSON, CIRCUIT JUDGE:

FACTUAL AND PROCEDURAL BACKGROUND

This appeal involves the rights to "Lenny Bruce," a black-and-white film created by John Magnuson and the American satirist Lenny Bruce. In the film, which was shot in a New York night club in 1965, Magnuson and Bruce sought to convey Bruce's version of the events that gave rise to his arrest and conviction for obscenity. The film was produced by the California corporation, Imagination, Inc. ("Imagination"), of which Magnuson was the chief executive officer. Imagination paid the production and post-production expenses and employed the camera and sound crews for the film, while Bruce was the sole author of the material used in the film. There is no existing written agreement between Bruce, Magnuson or Imagination concerning rights to the film.

In 1979, VY purchased a copy of the Lenny Bruce film which did not include a copyright notice. VY conducted a search with the U.S. Copyright Office to determine whether any film entitled "Lenny Bruce in Concert" had been registered, although the film in question has never gone by that title. The search produced no results, and VY, concluding that the Lenny Bruce film was in the public domain, began marketing the film on video tape in 1979. The video was not authorized by Magnuson and contains a copyright notice claiming a 1983 copyright belonging to VY.

Magnuson filed an action for copyright infringement against VY and trial was scheduled to begin on March 7, 1994, with a pretrial conference set for March 2, 1994. On February 22, 1994, VY sent by Federal Express and by facsimile ("fax") an offer of judgment pursuant to Fed. R. Civ. P. 68 for $3,000. Magnuson's attorney rejected the offer because it was untimely, having been served less than ten court days before the scheduled trial date. The district court held in favor of Magnuson on the copyright claim and awarded $375 in damages. It rejected Magnuson's request for attorney's fees pursuant to *17 U.S.C. § 505*. It also rejected VY's request for attorney's fees pursuant to Fed. R. Civ. P. 68, but awarded costs under that rule, finding that the offer had been timely. VY appeals the district court's holding with respect to copyright infringement and its denial of VY's request for attorney's fees. On cross-appeal, Magnuson challenges the district court's award of costs to VY and the denial of its request for attorney's fees.

II.   Service of VY's Rule 68 Offer

Magnuson contends that VY's Rule 68 offer was defectively served, and therefore, that neither costs nor attorney's fees should be awarded to VY. We agree.

The district court held that while service by fax was inadequate, service of the offer by Federal Express was acceptable because of "the reality that the offer was received more than ten days prior to the [actual] commencement of the trial." However, the district court declined to take a position as to whether service by Federal Express is permitted by federal or local rules of civil procedure and how such service might affect the computation of the date by which the offer should have been served. It also failed to cite any case law in support of the proposition that actual notice suffices where service of process is defective.

In cases involving Rule 68 offers, service of process must comply with Fed. R. Civ. P. 5(b), *Grosvenor v. Brienen*, 801 F.2d 944, 948 (7th Cir.1986) (holding that an oral offer does not satisfy service requirements of Rule 5(b) in the context of Rule 68); *Stewart v. County of Sonoma*, 634 F. Supp. 773, 775 (N.D.Cal.1986). Service by fax does not satisfy Fed. R. Civ. P. 5(b). *Mushroom Assocs. v. Monterey Mushrooms, Inc.*, 1992 WL 442898, 25 U.S.P.Q.2d (BNA) 1304 (N.D. Cal. 1992), 1992 WL 442898 * 4; *Salley v. Board of Governors, Univ. of N.C.*, 136 F.R.D. 417, 419 (M.D.N.C.1991). Thus, the district court correctly held that service of process by fax of the Rule 68 offer was inadequate, even though Magnuson apparently did receive a faxed copy of the offer. The district court erred, however, in holding that service of the offer by Federal Express was adequate. The handful of cases that have addressed the issue of service by Federal Express come almost entirely from district courts outside of this circuit, and they are not consistent. Therefore, we will provide a brief overview of the scant law that exists in this area.

The Seventh Circuit has held that delivery by Federal Express is not "mail" for the purposes of Rule 4. *Audio Enterprises, Inc. v. B & W Loudspeakers*, 957 F.2d 406, 409 (7th Cir.1992). In Audio Enterprises, the court reasoned that "Rule 4(c)(2)(C)(ii) specifies first class mail, postage prepaid. Federal Express is not first class mail." [a]*Id.* Similarly, the Fifth Circuit has held that Federal Express is not mail for purposes of Fed. R. App. P. 25(a). *Prince v. Poulos*, 876 F.2d 30, 32 n. 1 (5th Cir.1989). The Prince court rejected the appellant's argument that the appellee's brief should have been delivered by Federal Express to satisfy the requirement of Rule 25(a) that the most "expeditious form of delivery by mail" be utilized. The court relied upon the definition of "mail" in Webster's New Collegiate Dictionary (1973), which defines mail as "letters ... conveyed under public authority." *Id.* at 32 n.1. Because Federal Express delivery service is not public authority, the court reasoned, it is not mail.

In fact, two district court cases have held that Rule 5 allows service by Federal Express. In *Edmond v. U.S. Postal Service*, 727 F. Supp. 7, 11 (D.D.C.1989), the court held that a plaintiff had been validly served by Federal Express under Rule 5(b). The court cited no authority and provided no explanation of its reasoning. In another case, *United States v. Certain Real Properties and Premises Known as 63–29 Trimble Road*, 812 F. Supp. 332, 334 (E.D.N.Y.1992), the court followed Edmond, finding that service by Federal Express satisfied Fed. R. Civ. P. 5(b). The court in Trimble Road explained that Rule 5, in contrast to Rule 4, does not prohibit service by Federal Express because it does not specify that service must be made by first class mail, postage prepaid, as does Rule 4. Id. It also distinguishes Prince v. Poulos by noting that that case involved Fed. R. App. P. 25 and whether service by Federal Express was required, rather than permitted. Id.

If there is any question of whether the term "mail" encompasses private delivery services today, there is little doubt that "mail" meant "U.S. mail" in 1937, when Rule 5 was adopted. The suggestion that in failing to specify that mail must be "first class, postage prepaid" Rule 5 was intended to authorize service by private delivery service in an era that predates modern overnight delivery services makes little sense. Thus, the distinction drawn by the Trimble Road court does not withstand scrutiny, and this panel declines to adopt the rule of Trimble Road and Edmond.

Nor, on a practical level, does it make sense to adopt an approach that interprets the term "mail" differently for the purposes of different rules within the Federal Rules of Civil Procedure. If we were to hold that Federal Express is "mail" for the purposes of Rule 5 (even though it is not for Rule 4), we would then have to address whether Federal Express is "mail" under Rule 6(e), which adds three days to computations of time where service is by mail. Given that Federal Express is generally used for overnight delivery, one could argue that Congress did not intend that Rule 6(e) apply to service by Federal Express, i.e., that Federal Express is not mail under Rule 6. It seems clear that in interpreting the term "mail" differently for the purposes of different rules within the Federal Rules of Civil Procedure, courts are likely to

---

a. Note that this section of rule 4 has since been changed. See Rule 4(d)(2)(B).

cause great confusion. Thus, we hold that Federal Express does not satisfy the requirements of Rule 5(b).

Furthermore, the local rules for district courts in the Northern District of California that were applicable at the time of service in this case also did not permit service by Federal Express. Prior to their amendment in 1995, these rules allowed service by mail but did not explicitly define "mail." However, they did specify that "all papers required to be served shall, when served by mail, be served by first class or priority mail...." Local Rules of Practice for the United States District Court for the Northern District of California, Rule 210–2 (1994). As the court stated in Audio Enterprises, "Federal Express is not first class mail." 957 F.2d at 409. Neither is it priority mail. (In 1995, the local rules for the Northern District of California added a provision allowing service by private delivery service or fax with the written consent of the receiving party. See Local Rule 5–3.)

Thus, the next question we must address is whether actual notice in this case suffices. We hold that it does not. In *Salley*, the court stated that

> actual notice by a means other than that authorized by Rule 5(b) does not constitute valid service and is not an exception to the rule. Therefore, a party must advance some other compelling circumstance, in addition to actual notice in order to have the Court excuse noncompliance with Rule 5(b).

136 F.R.D. at 420. In that case, the plaintiff alleged that service of a discovery request by fax was invalid. *Id.* at 420. The court found "exceptional good cause" because the receiving party had explicitly consented to service of discovery requests by fax on several previous occasions. Id. We adopt the rule of Salley and require that a party demonstrate exceptional good cause for failing to comply with Rule 5(b).

Here, there is no indication of good cause. VY declined to address Magnuson's argument that the offer was not validly served, or alternatively, untimely, in either its opening or reply briefs. It has not explained why it could not have served Magnuson personally and has not presented evidence that Magnuson consented to service by fax or by Federal Express. Because VY did not serve its Rule 68 offer in compliance with Fed. R. Civ. P. 5(b) and did not offer good cause for its failure to validly serve the offer, we reverse the district court's award of costs to VY pursuant to Rule 68.

SERVICE BY ELECTRONIC MAIL AND FAX

Even though service of process cannot generally be accomplished by electronic mail or facsimile transmissions, local practice may provide that once a lawsuit has been commenced in the traditional fashion, further documents may be filed with the court and served on opponents electronically.

The United States District Court for the Eastern District of Pennsylvania for example, has a detailed protocol for such filings including the admonition that documents filed electronically *"must not* [emphasis in original] be followed by paper submissions of the same documents."

NOTE ON PROVING SERVICE BY MAIL

In *Green v. WCI Holdings*, 136 F.3d 313 (2d Cir.1998) the United States Court of Appeals for the Second Circuit considered plaintiff's arguments that defendant's motion to dismiss had not been served in a timely manner. In that case, the partes had agreed to extend defendant's time to answer the complaint to April 2, 1992. The stipulation containing that agreement was "so ordered" by the district court. On April 3, 1992, defendants filed with the court a motion to dismiss the complaint pursuant to Federal Rule of Civil Procedure 12(b)(1) and 12(b)(6). The motion was dated April 2, 1992, and an affidavit of service was attached declaring that it had been served on the plaintiff by placing it in a mailbox on April 2, 1992 at 5:30 p.m. Greene received a copy of the motion to dismiss in the mail on April 4, 1992. The envelope was postmarked April 3, 1992. Plaintiff argued, among other things, that the district court erred in holding that the motion had been served when the defendants' claim was placed in the mailbox on April 2 rather than when it was postmarked on April 3. The Second Circuit stated:

"Federal Rule of Civil Procedure 5(b) plainly provides that 'service by mail is complete upon mailing.' The question is what constitutes a 'mailing'—is it the placing of an envelope in a mail box or the postmarking of it by postal service employees? Although the Second Circuit has not addressed this precise issue, there is nothing in Rule 5(b) or our case law to indicate that the date of postmark, or the date of receipt, rather than the date of placing it in the mail controls. See, e.g., *United States v. White*, 980 F.2d 836, 840 n. 8 (2d Cir.1992) (service effected when papers were mailed regardless of when they were received).

"The First Circuit addressed the issue of what constitutes service by mail in *Rivera v. M/T Fossarina*, 840 F.2d 152 (1st Cir.1988), and held that 'for service by mail to be valid under Rule 5(b) the pleading or document has to be "placed in an envelope addressed to . . . the opposing attorney . . . and deposited in a United States post office or post office box." ' *Id.* at 155 (quoting 4A Charles Allan Wright & Arthur R. Miller, Federal Practice and Procedure § 1148, at 432–33 (2d ed. 1987)). Similarly, the D.C. Circuit has held that, under Rule 5(b), ' "service is deemed complete at the instant the documents are placed into the hands of the United States Post Office or a Post Office Box.' " *United States v. Kennedy*, 133 F.3d 53, 328 U.S.App.D.C. 190, 1998 WL 11780, at *6 (D.C.Cir.1998) (quoting 1 James Wm. Moore, et al., Moore's Federal Practice § 5.04[2][a][ii], at 5–28 (3d ed. 1997)). We think this is the sensible rule, and, hence, hold that service under Rule 5(b) is accomplished when the envelope is deposited at a post office or in a mail box.

"Greene further argues that, apart from the legal issue of when 'mailing' is complete, the defendants' factual allegation that they placed the envelope in the mailbox on April 2, 1992, is false. The magistrate judge and district court considered and rejected this argument, and their decision to believe the defendants' affidavit (which stated that the envelope had been placed in the mailbox on April 2) was not clearly erroneous. Accordingly, Greene's motion for default judgment was properly denied.

SERVICE AND WAIVER UNDER THE 1993 AMENDMENTS

Complying with the technical requirements of effective service can be both expensive and time consuming. Technical compliance often requires hiring a process server to make one or more trips to defendant's residence, substantially increasing the cost to plaintiffs of litigating cases with small monetary claims. Where defendant is a foreign national, expense can be multiplied and delay increased exponentially. There are likely to be complex procedures mandated by international treaty, not to mention the cost of translation even where the defendant is fluent in English. Is it possible to cut through this maze of technicalities without increasing the risk that some hapless defendant will in fact go without notice that he or she is being sued?

Federal Rule of Civil Procedure 4(d), as amended in 1993, provides for waiver of service on request. Once defendant has executed such a waiver and plaintiff has filed same with the court, there is no longer any need for formal service. What could be simpler? However, to make it advantageous for defendants to consent to the waiver, and to avoid undesirable side effects, the Rule contains a complex scheme of carrots, sticks and other technical provisions. The text of the Rule and the Advisory Committee Notes, from which this brief description is drawn, run on for pages.

First, failure to waive service subjects a defendant resident in the United States to payment of the costs incurred by plaintiff in effecting service and, in addition, reasonable attorney fees incurred in bringing a motion to collect those costs. To avoid possible conflict with foreign law and to retain the status of the request for waiver as a private non-judicial act, no such penalty will follow with respect to a defendant resident abroad.

A defendant who wishes to object to venue, or even to jurisdiction over the person, may still waive service of process while preserving the right to raise those objections. FRCP 4(d)(1). The time for filing an answer is extended to 60 days from the date on which plaintiff sent the waiver, longer if the request was addressed outside the country. FRCP 4(d)(3).

A request for a waiver, even if received in timely fashion, does not constitute service and will not stop the running of the statute of limitations. The fact that the defendant "signed a certified mail receipt for the Notice and Waiver" is of no significance. *Sentry Ins. v. Apolinario*, 1995 WL 91421 (E.D. Pa. 1995). Litigants are warned against the risk of losing a claim in an effort to achieve a bit of incremental efficiency. If there is no waiver, either because it was not requested or because defendants refuse to waive, service must still be made as provided in Rule 4.

If the defendant is a corporation, Rule 4(d)(2)(A) requires that the request for waiver be addressed to an individual qualified to receive service. The "general mail rooms of large organizations cannot" be expected to identify the proper recipient if this is not done. When considering cases where the U.S. government is the defendant, the Advisory Committee simply gave up and made the waiver provisions inapplicable. It noted that the federal government's "mail receiving facilities are inadequate to assure that the notice is actually received by the correct person in the Department of Justice.''

As *Husky Truck Stop* makes abundantly clear, Rule 4(d)'s attempt to avoid unnecessary technicalities is not an invitation to sloppiness. The penalty for sloppiness may still be dismissal.

If costs are awarded, the amount must be reasonable. After denying costs because the requirements of Rule 4(d)(2) had not been met, one court took occasion to add:

> The Court would be remiss, however, not to take notice of the amount claimed for attorney's fees that were incurred in bringing this Motion for costs. The Court is concerned by the claim of four hundred eighty-seven and 50/100 dollars ($487.50) to bring what amounts to a seven paragraph motion that covers little more than one page and cites no case law.

> By way of comparison, the United States District Court for the Eastern District of Pennsylvania recently granted just such a motion for costs pursuant to rule 4(d)(2). In that case the court found it reasonable to award seventy-five dollars ($75.00) per defendant that failed to waive service according to the rule. *Thompson v. Kramer*, 1994 WL 725953 (E.D. Pa. 1994).

Spivey v. Board of Church Extension and Home Mission, 160 F.R.D. 660, 663 (M.D.Fla.1995) (Kovachevich, District Judge).

Two other amendments to Rule 4 deserve mention. All references to ''service by mail'' under Rule 4 have been deleted. Since Rules 4(e)(1) and 4(h)(1) authorize service to be made in federal court pursuant to the law of the state in which the district court is located, however, and since many state statutes permit service by mail, the procedure is still available to many federal litigants. The old federal provision covering service by mail had given rise to confusion and uncertainties, which the drafters of the new Rule 4 hoped to eliminate by deleting the term.

A second major change relates to service on individuals in a foreign country. Rules 4(f) and 4(h)(2). Litigation brought in courts in the United States against foreign defendants is becoming increasingly important. These rules, and the Advisory Committee notes thereto, expressly set out the sources of authority for U.S. courts to acquire personal jurisdiction over foreign defendants and the procedures for effectuating service in such cases.

Petrucelli v. Bohringer and Ratzinger

United States Court of Appeals for the Third Circuit, 1995.
46 F.3d 1298.

■ COWEN, CIRCUIT JUDGE.

This appeal arises from an order dismissing a personal injury suit without prejudice after the plaintiff failed to serve a summons upon the defendant within 120 days of filing the complaint as required by

Rule 4 of the Federal Rules of Civil Procedure. The issue of whether, subsequent to a recent rule change, Rule 4(m) permits a district court to extend time for service even absent a showing of good cause is one of first impression at the federal appellate level. We conclude that, under the former rule, the district court did not abuse its discretion in refusing to extend time beyond the 120 days within which service was to be effected after finding no good cause present. Nevertheless, because we conclude that the new rule affords a district judge greater discretion, we remand to the district court for reconsideration on this issue only.

* * *

B.   Denial of Motion to Extend Time for Service

Petrucelli next argues that the district court should have granted his alternative motion for an extension of the 120–day limit to serve Jake Diel, pursuant to Rule 4(j). When Petrucelli argued his motion to extend time for service before the district court in May of 1992 and when the district court entered its memorandum order in August of 1992 denying Petrucelli's motion, former Rule 4(j) had not yet been amended. In 1992, Rule 4(j) read in pertinent part:

> Summons: Time Limit for Service. If a service of the summons and complaint is not made upon a defendant within 120 days after the filing of the complaint and the party on whose behalf such service was required cannot show good cause why such service was not made within that period, the action *shall* be dismissed as to that defendant without prejudice upon the court's own initiative with notice to such party or upon motion.

Fed. R. Civ. P. 4(j) (1991) (emphasis added). Under this rule, a district court was required to dismiss a case if service of process was not effected within the 120 day period, unless the plaintiff showed good cause for the delinquency.

As of December 1, 1993, Rule 4(j) was amended and redesignated as Rule 4(m). While the change in designation from (j) to (m) is of no import, the language in this subdivision was substantially modified. Although counsel for Petrucelli failed to bring this substantive change to our attention, our own research has revealed this critical change in the rule.

Initially, we question whether Rule 4(m) applies to these proceedings in light of the fact that service of process was attempted in 1991, two years prior to the rule change. If former Rule 4(j) still applies to this case and we conclude that the district court did not abuse its discretion in finding that there was no good cause shown for failing to timely serve Jake Diel, we would have no choice but to affirm the order of the district court dismissing this case. However, we are guided by the order of the Supreme Court which stated, "the foregoing amendments to the Federal Rules of Civil Procedure shall take effect on December 1, 1993, and shall govern ... insofar as just and practicable, all proceedings in civil cases then pending." See The Order of the United States Supreme Court Adopting and Amending the Federal Rules of Civil Procedure (April 22, 1993). Because we believe it to be "just and practicable," we conclude that Rule 4(m) applies retroactively to these proceedings.

Determining that Rule 4(m) applies to the case before us does not, however, end our inquiry. In this case of first impression before a federal Court of Appeals, we must decide the manner in which a district court should now proceed when employing a Rule 4(m) analysis. Rule 4(m) states in relevant part:

> Time Limit for Service. If service of the summons and complaint is not made upon a defendant within 120 days after the filing of the complaint, the court, upon motion or on its own initiative after notice to the plaintiff, *shall dismiss the action without prejudice as to that defendant or direct that service be effected within a specified time; provided that if the plaintiff shows good cause for the failure, the court shall* extend the time for service for an appropriate period.

Fed. R. Civ. P. 4(m) (1993) (emphasis added). As mentioned previously, the former rule required the court to dismiss the case absent a showing of good cause. We read the new rule to require a court to extend time if good cause is shown and to allow a court discretion to dismiss or extend time absent a showing of good cause. We reach this conclusion for several reasons.

Initially, we find that the plain language of the rule itself explains that in all cases, the court has the option of dismissing the action or extending time for service. The fact that the word "shall" is used along with the disjunctive "or" in the first clause indicates that the court has discretion to choose one of these options. As an exception to this general provision, the second clause notes that if good cause exists, the district court has no choice but to extend time for service. Thus, the logical inference that can be drawn from these two clauses is that the district court may, in its discretion, extend time even absent a finding of good cause.

Next, we find the Advisory Committee note on the Rule 4(m) amendment to be instructive. The Committee explained:

> The new subdivision explicitly provides that the court *shall allow additional time if there is good cause* for the plaintiff's failure to effect service in the prescribed 120 days, and *authorizes the court to relieve a plaintiff* of the consequences of an application of this subdivision *even if there is no good cause shown.*

Fed. R. Civ. P. 4(m) advisory committee's note (1993) (emphasis added). Thus, the "even if" language of the note indicates that the district court may extend time for service where there is no good cause shown.

We hold that as a result of the rule change which led to Rule 4(m), when entertaining a motion to extend time for service, the district court must proceed in the following manner. First, the district court should determine whether good cause exists for an extension of time. If good cause is present, the district court must extend time for service and the inquiry is ended. If, however, good cause does not exist, the court may in its discretion decide whether to dismiss the case without prejudice or extend time for service.

The Advisory Committee note provides some guidance as to what factors the district court should consider when deciding to exercise its discretion to extend time for service in the absence of a finding of good cause. Although the list is not exhaustive, the Committee explained that, "[r]elief may be justified, *for example*, if the applicable statute of limitations would bar the refiled action, or if the defendant is evading service or conceals a defect in attempted service." Id. (citation omitted) (emphasis added).

We hold that a district court may not consider the fact that the statute of limitations has run until after it has conducted an examination of good cause. If the district court determines that good cause does not exist, only then may it consider whether the running of the statute of limitations would warrant granting an extension of time. We emphasize that the running of the statute of limitations does not require the district court to extend time for service of process. Rather, absent a finding of good cause, a district court may in its discretion still dismiss the case, even after considering that the statute of limitations has run and the refiling of an action is barred.

T & S Rentals v. United States

United States District Court for the Northern District of West Virginia, 1996.
164 F.R.D. 422.

■ KEELEY, DISTRICT JUDGE.

[Plaintiffs, claiming that the Federal Aviation Administration's negligence caused a plane crash that destroyed an airplane belonging to one plaintiff and killed the plane's occupants, filed their complaint on the day before the statute of limitations expired.]

Federal Rule of Civil Procedure 4(m) allows a plaintiff 120 days from the filing of the complaint in which to effect such service on a defendant. While the copies of the complaint and summons were placed in the mail on the 119th day after the complaint was filed, they did not reach the defendants and, therefore, were not effectively served, until August 4, 1995, the 121st day.

* * *

The plaintiffs argue that the amended language of Rule 4(m) gives the Court discretion to extend the period for service of process in the absence of "good cause." In support of their argument, plaintiffs cite *Petrucelli v. Bohringer and Ratzinger*, 46 F.3d 1298 (3d Cir.1995), in which the Third Circuit discussed the practical differences between Rule 4(m) and its predecessor. According to the Third Circuit,

the former rule required the court to dismiss the case absent a showing of good cause. We read the new rule to require a Court to extend time if good cause is shown and to allow a court discretion to dismiss or extend time absent a showing of good cause.

Id. at 1305. The court based its interpretation of Rule 4(m) on "the plain language of the rule itself," and on an Advisory Committee Note to rule 4(m) which states:

> The new subdivision explicitly provides that the court shall allow additional time if there is good cause for the plaintiff's failure to effect service in the prescribed 120 days, *and authorizes the court to relieve a plaintiff of the consequences of an application of this subdivision even if there is no good cause shown.*

Fed. R. Civ. P. 4(m), Advisory Committee's Note (1993) (emphasis added).

While the reasoning of the Third Circuit in *Petrucelli* might be persuasive if this Court were writing on a blank slate, the Fourth Circuit Court of Appeals has already interpreted Rule 4(m) and this Court is constrained to follow that interpretation. In *Mendez v. Elliot*, 45 F.3d 75 (4th Cir.1995), the court stated:

> Rule 4(j) was edited without a change in substance and renumbered as Rule 4(m), effective Dec. 1, 1993. Rule 4(m) requires that if the complaint is not served within 120 days after it is filed, the complaint must be dismissed absent a showing of good cause.

Id. at 78.

The plaintiffs urge this Court not to follow *Mendez* because its analysis is not as thorough as that in *Petrucelli*. *Mendez*, they argue, does not take into account differences in the plain language of Rules 4(j) and 4(m), or the advisory committee note mentioned earlier. Although it is true that *Mendez* does not discuss the advisory committee note, it is binding Fourth Circuit precedent that this Court may not ignore simply because another circuit's interpretation is urged to be more logical. Indeed, other district courts in this circuit have applied *Mendez* in circumstances similar to those found here.

Accordingly, under *Mendez*, in order to withstand the defendant's motion to dismiss, the plaintiffs must demonstrate that they had "good cause" for not serving the defendants with a copy of their complaint and summons within the 120 day window provided by rule 4(m). *Mendez*, 45 F.3d at 78.

III. "GOOD CAUSE" UNDER RULE 4(m)

Although the concept of "good cause" remains unchanged despite the renumbering of Rule 4(j) as Rule 4(m), its exact definition cannot be gleaned by reference to the language of the rules themselves. In *Quann v. Whitegate–Edgewater*, 112 F.R.D. 649 (D.Md. 1986), the district court sought to define the parameters of "good cause" within the meaning of Fed. R. Civ. P. 4(j). After examining the legislative history of 4(j), the court concluded that "good cause" existed in situations in which a plaintiff, who was not in technical compliance with the 120 day time limit for service, had nonetheless made "reasonable, diligent" efforts to effect service on the defendant.

In assessing the reasonableness and diligence of the plaintiff's efforts to serve process, the *Quann* court looked to past instances in which other courts had found "good cause" for nonconforming service. In doing so, it found that Fed. R. Civ. P. 4(j)'s legislative history and supporting case law indicated that a defendant's active evasion of service in the face of plaintiffs' attempts to effect such service would constitute "good cause." The *Quann* court also referenced several cases in which courts had found "good cause" where a plaintiff had immediately corrected a technically flawed service that had been effected within the 120 day period.

The court, however, recognized that "inadvertent or heedless non-service is what amended Rule 4(j) is aimed [to eliminate]," and held that "good cause" did not exist in the case before it because the delay in service was attributable to attorney inadvertence and not to external factors that would reasonably stifle a plaintiff's due diligence. As a basis for this conclusion, the court cited the fact that the plaintiff had been unable, up to that point, to offer any meaningful explanation for the delay, as well as the fact that there were no obstructions to service such as the lack of an address or an evasive defendant.

The delay in service in the present case apparently resulted from attorney inadvertence. The only explanation for the delay in service offered by the plaintiffs is the supposed complexities of complying with Fed. R. Civ. P. 4(i), which governs service of process on government agencies and requires that a plaintiff who is suing an agency, officer, or corporation of the United States effect service upon the United States Attorney for the judicial district in which the proceedings are commenced, the Attorney General of the United States, and the agency or officer whose ruling or order is being challenged. Subsection (3) of Rule 4(i) reads:

> The court shall allow a reasonable time for service of process under this subdivision for the purpose of curing the failure to serve multiple officers, agencies, or corporations of the United States if the plaintiff has effected service on either the United States Attorney or the Attorney General of the United States.

Fed. R. Civ. P. 4(i)(3) (1993). The Advisory Committee's Notes to Rule 4(m) specifically state that 4(i)(3) constitutes a "specific instance of good cause."

Section 4(i)(3) is inapplicable to the present case, however. Neither the United States Attorney for the Northern District of West Virginia nor the Attorney General was served within the 120 day period. Both were served on the 121st day. The complexities of compliance with Rule 4(i), therefore, did not cause the failure of the plaintiffs to effect service in the present case.

Plaintiffs also argue that service on the 121st day constitutes good cause when, as here, the applicable statute of limitations bars the refiling of the action. In support of this contention, they cite *Tyson v. Sunnyvale*, 159 F.R.D. 528 (N.D.Cal.1995), in which the district court found "good cause" under Rule 4(m) as a result of the fact that the applicable statute of limitations barred refiling of the claims in issue.

The holding in *Tyson* flies in the face of *Quann*'s notion that "good cause" is a product of a plaintiff's reasonable, diligent efforts to effect service within the statutory period. Indeed, if the Court were to adopt the rule in *Tyson*, plaintiffs would never be obliged to effect service within the statutory window for, as long as the refiling of the claim eventually became time-barred, they would always have "good cause" for an extension. This result is detrimental to the principal aim of Fed. R. Civ. P. 4(m), which is to encourage more efficient, speedy and inexpensive litigation by transferring the burden of effecting service to the litigants. Under *Tyson*, this burden would remain with the court because plaintiffs would need do no more than simply wait for the court to instruct them to effect service, after the applicable statute of limitations had run on their claims. Realization of the goals of Rule 4(m), therefore, requires a rule that has stiff consequences for non-compliance.

Moreover, the Fourth Circuit has indicated that the fact that a claim may be time barred should not have an impact on the "good cause" analysis under Rule 4(m). In *Mendez, supra*, the court stated:

> Under Rule 4(j), if a plaintiff is not diligent and fails to serve the complaint within 120 days or such further time period as ordered by the court for good cause, the case shall be dismissed without prejudice. The 'without prejudice' condition permits a plaintiff to refile the complaint as if it had never been filed. Rule 4(j) does not, however, give the appellant a right to refile without the consequences of time defenses, such as the statute of limitations.

Id. at 78. The mere fact that a claim would be time-barred if refiled, therefore, does not constitute "good cause" within the meaning of Fed. R. Civ. P. 4(m).

In this case, it is critical that the plaintiffs had almost four months (from April 5 to August 1) after this suit was filed in which to effect proper service. Although all that was required was the timely placing of two copies of the complaint and summons in the mail, they did not do this and have offered no explanation for their failure. Having waited one day too long to effect service of process on the defendants, the plaintiffs must now live with the consequences of that inadvertence.

Accordingly, the plaintiffs have not shown "good cause" within the meaning of Fed. R. Civ. P. 4(m) because they have not demonstrated their "reasonable, diligent efforts to effect service on the defendant." Since service was effected outside the 120 day window provided by Rule 4(m), the complaint must be dismissed, without prejudice, pursuant to Fed. R. Civ. P. 12(b)(3).

IV. DISCRETIONARY EXTENSION UNDER PETRUCELLI

Even if the Court heeded the plaintiffs' urging and followed the interpretation of Fed. R. Civ. P. 4(m) adopted by the Third Circuit Court of Appeals in *Petrucelli v. Bohringer & Ratzinger*, the plaintiffs would not be entitled to a discretionary extension of the 120–day service limit. Although they argue that there are several factors that militate in favor of such an extension, the Court does not agree.

The first factor the plaintiffs rely on is that dismissal at this stage would be final since the applicable statute of limitations now bars refiling of their suit. As discussed in *Mendez*, this argument is unpersuasive. If there are no consequences for failure to meet the service deadline, the stated policies underlying the transfer of the burden of service to the litigants will be undermined.

As their second factor, the plaintiffs cite their good faith effort to comply with the complexities of Rule 4(i)'s multiple service requirement as proper grounds for a discretionary extension. Arguing that the difficult and burdensome nature of these service requirements warrants a one-day extension of the service period, the plaintiffs rely on *Espinoza v. United States*, 52 F.3d 838 (10th Cir.1995), in which the Tenth Circuit, after adopting the *Petrucelli* interpretation, recognized the complexities of Rule 4(i):

> The complex nature of the requirements of Fed. R. Civ. P. 4(i), particularly when the plaintiff is proceeding pro se, should be a factor for the district court's consideration when it determines whether a permissive [discretionary] extension of time should be granted under Rule 4(m).

Id. at 842. The court then granted the plaintiff a discretionary extension of the service period, even though he had not made a showing of "good cause."

Espinoza, where the plaintiff was pro se, is clearly distinguishable from the present case. Here, the plaintiffs have been represented by counsel throughout the course of these proceedings, from the administrative action before the FAA to the filing of the claim in this Court.

Furthermore, if, as the plaintiffs argue, the root of this problem lay in determining who was supposed to be served under Rule 4(i), one would have expected that at least some defendants would have been served before the deadline. Instead, all the defendants were served at the same time . . . one day after the statutory window ended. This congruence suggests that attorney inattention, and not an excusable inability to grasp the requirements of Rule 4(i), was at the center of this failure to effect timely service.

As their third factor, the plaintiffs cite the lack of prejudice that would result to the defendant were this suit allowed to proceed. This consideration does not constitute "good cause" under Fed. R. Civ. P. 4(m), however. Nor would this Court find that a mere absence of prejudice to the defendant warrants a discretionary extension in a case such as this one.

Finally, as their fourth factor, the plaintiffs argue that the defendant's conduct during the course of this proceeding estops it from filing a motion to dismiss. Specifically, they assert that the defendant evinced a willingness to litigate this matter fully by insisting on compliance with a scheduling order and noticing depositions, and it cannot now seek to dismiss the complaint.

That argument is without merit. There is nothing duplicitous about preparing for trial on the one hand, while asserting a meritorious defense pursuant to Rule 12 on the other. As to the depositions, if plaintiffs found the dates to be onerous or impractical, they should have objected instead of raising the issue at this stage. Estoppel is not available to the plaintiffs in this situation.

V.   CONCLUSION

Under the Fourth Circuit's holding in *Mendez v. Elliot*, the plaintiffs must show "good cause" for their failure to effect service within Fed. R. Civ. P. 4(m)'s 120 day period in order to defeat the defendant's motion to dismiss. The Court concludes that the plaintiffs have failed to do so as a consequence of which their claim must be DISMISSED.

Even if the Fourth Circuit were to distinguish *Mendez* and to adopt the Third Circuit's interpretation of Rule 4(m) in *Petrucelli v. Bohringer and Ratzinger*, there are no factors that would warrant a discretionary extension in the absence of "good cause."

ORDER

For the reasons stated in the accompanying memorandum, the plaintiffs' complaint is DISMISSED without prejudice.

NOTE ON "GOOD CAUSE" UNDER RULE 4(m)

Courts frequently show no sympathy with the plight of a plaintiff who, because the statute of limitations has run, will not be able to pursue her claim at all if her complaint is dismissed for failure to serve process. In *Tuke v. United States*, 76 F.3d 155, 156 (7th Cir.1996), Judge Easterbrook wrote:

> An attorney who files suit when the statute of limitations is about to expire must take special care to achieve timely service of process, because a slip-up is fatal. [The plaintiff's attorney] filed this suit under the Federal Tort Claims Act at the end of the limitations period yet treated service casually. He did not bother to read Fed. R. Civ. P. 4, which governs service in federal litigation, and relied on his adversary to tell him what he must do. When he got that advice, he tarried in following it. The delay has cost his client the litigation and exposes [the attorney] to a suit for malpractice.... Where is the "good cause" that Rule 4(m) requires for belated service? Failure to read a rule is the antithesis of good cause. Ignorance may be an explanation but is not an excuse.

QUESTIONS

1.   Does a plaintiff have "good cause" to delay service under Rule 4(m) because of emotional distress resulting from her daughter's murder? See *Braithwaite v. Johns Hopkins Hospital*, 160 F.R.D. 75 (D.Md.1995).

2.   Suppose service can readily be effected long before 120 days after the commencement of the action. Is plaintiff under any obligation to do so?

In *Henderson v. United States*, 517 U.S. 654 , 116 S. Ct. 1638 (1996) the United States Supreme Court rejected the Government's view that Rule 4 establishes "only an outer boundary for timely service," but held instead that it grants "an irreducible allowance."

D. Service by "Posting"

Greene v. Lindsey

Supreme Court of the United States, 1982.
456 U.S. 444, 102 S.Ct. 1874, 72 L.Ed.2d 249.

■ Justice Brennan delivered the opinion of the Court.

A Kentucky statute provides that in forcible entry or detainer actions, service of process may be made under certain circumstances by posting a summons on the door of a tenant's apartment. The question presented is whether this statute, as applied to tenants in a public housing project, fails to afford those tenants the notice of proceedings initiated against them required by the Due Process Clause of the Fourteenth Amendment.

* * *

In each instance, notice took the form of posting a copy of the writ of forcible entry and detainer on the door of the tenant's apartment.[1] Appellees claim never to have seen these posted summonses; they state that they did not learn of the eviction proceedings until they were served with writs of possession, executed after default judgments had been entered against them, and after their opportunity for appeal had lapsed.

* * *

"The fundamental requisite of due process of law is the opportunity to be heard." Grannis v. Ordean, 234 U.S. 385, 394, 34 S.Ct. 779, 783, 58 L.Ed. 1363 (1914). And the "right to be heard has little reality or worth unless one is informed that the matter is pending and can choose for himself whether to appear or default, acquiesce or contest," *Mullane, supra,* at 314, 70 S.Ct., at 657. Personal service guarantees actual notice of the pendency of a legal action; it thus presents the ideal circumstance under which to commence legal proceedings against a person, and has traditionally been deemed necessary in actions styled *in personam.* McDonald v. Mabee, 243 U.S.

---

1. "Posting" refers to the practice of placing the writ on the property by use of a thumbtack, adhesive tape, or other means. App. 74, 77 (deposition of process servers). Appellants describe the usual method of effecting service pursuant to § 454.030 in the following terms:

"The officer of the court who is charged with serving notice in a forcible entry and detainer action, usually a Jefferson County Deputy Sheriff, takes the following steps in notifying a tenant. First, the officer goes to the apartment in an effort to effectuate personal in-hand service. Second, if the named tenant is absent or will not appear at the door, personal in-hand service is made on any member of the tenant's family over sixteen years of age. Finally, if no one answers the door, a copy of the notice is posted on the premises, usually the door." Brief for Appellants 3.

90, 92, 37 S.Ct. 343, 344, 61 L.Ed. 608 (1917). Nevertheless, certain less rigorous notice procedures have enjoyed substantial acceptance throughout our legal history; in light of this history and the practical obstacles to providing personal service in every instance, we have allowed judicial proceedings to be prosecuted in some situations on the basis of procedures that do not carry with them the same certainty of actual notice that inheres in personal service. But we have also clearly recognized that the Due Process Clause does prescribe a constitutional minimum: "An elementary and fundamental requirement of due process in any proceeding which is to be accorded finality is *notice reasonably calculated, under all the circumstances, to apprise interested parties of the pendency of the action* and afford them an opportunity to present their objections." *Mullane,* 339 U.S., at 314, 70 S.Ct. at 657 (emphasis added). It is against this standard that we evaluate the procedures employed in this case.

Appellants argue that because a forcible entry and detainer action is an action *in rem,* notice by posting is *ipso facto* constitutionally adequate. Appellees concede that posting has traditionally been deemed appropriate for *in rem* proceedings, but argue that detainer actions can now encompass more than the simple issue of the tenant's continued right to possession, and that they therefore require the more exacting forms of notice customarily provided for proceedings *in personam.* Appellants counter by conceding that if the particular detainer proceeding was one in which the landlord sought to recover past due rent, personal service would be required by Kentucky law, but argue that such claims are unusual in such proceedings, and that in the case before us the landlord claimed only a right to recover possession.

As in *Mullane,* we decline to resolve the constitutional question based upon the determination whether the particular action is more properly characterized as one *in rem* or *in personam.* 339 U.S., at 312, 70 S.Ct., at 656. That is not to say that the nature of the action has no bearing on a constitutional assessment of the reasonableness of the procedures employed. The character of the action reflects the extent to which the court purports to extend its power, and thus may roughly describe the scope of potential adverse consequences to the person claiming a right to more effective notice. But " '[a]ll proceedings, like all rights, are really against persons.' "[3] In this case, appellees have been deprived of a significant interest in property: indeed, of the right to continued residence in their homes. In light of this deprivation, it will not suffice to recite that because the action is *in rem,* it is only necessary to serve notice "upon the thing itself."[5] The sufficiency of notice must be tested with reference to its ability to inform people of the pendency of proceedings that affect their interests. In arriving at the constitutional assessment, we look to the realities of the case before us: In determining the constitutionality of a procedure estab-

---

3. Shaffer v. Heitner, 433 U.S. 186, 207, n. 22, 97 S.Ct., at 2581, n. 22 (1977), quoting *Tyler v. Court of Registration,* 175 Mass. 71, 76, 55 N.E. 812, 814 (Holmes, C.J.), writ of error dism'd 179 U.S. 405 (1900).

5. *The Mary,* 9 Cranch 126, 144 (1815).

lished by the State to provide notice in a particular class of cases, "its effect must be judged in the light of its practical application to the affairs of men as they are ordinarily conducted." North Laramie Land Co. v. Hoffman, 268 U.S. 276, 283, 45 S.Ct. 491, 494, 69 L.Ed. 953 (1925).

It is, of course, reasonable to assume that a property owner will maintain superintendence of his property, and to presume that actions physically disturbing his holdings will come to his attention. See *Mullane, supra.*[6] The frequent restatement of this rule impresses upon the property owner the fact that a failure to maintain watch over his property may have significant legal consequences for him, providing a spur to his attentiveness, and a consequent reinforcement to the empirical foundation of the principle. Upon this understanding, a State may in turn conclude that in most cases, the secure posting of a notice on the property of a person is likely to offer that property owner sufficient warning of the pendency of proceedings possibly affecting his interests.

The empirical basis of the presumption that notice posted upon property is adequate to alert the owner or occupant of property of the pendency of legal proceedings would appear to make the presumption particularly well founded where notice is posted at a residence. With respect to claims affecting the continued possession of that residence, the application of this presumption seems particularly apt: If the tenant has a continuing interest in maintaining possession of the property for his use and occupancy, he might reasonably be expected to frequent the premises; if he no longer occupies the premises, then the injury that might result from his not having received actual notice as a consequence of the posted notice is reduced. Short of providing personal service, then, posting notice on the door of a person's home would, in many or perhaps most instances, constitute not only a constitutionally acceptable means of service, but indeed a singularly appropriate and effective way of ensuring that a person who cannot conveniently be served personally is actually apprised of proceedings against him.

But whatever the efficacy of posting in many cases, it is clear that, in the circumstances of this case, merely posting notice on an apartment door does not satisfy minimum standards of due process. In a

6. As we noted in *Mullane:*

"The ways of an owner with tangible property are such that he usually arranges means to learn of any direct attack upon his possessory or proprietary rights. Hence, * * * entry upon real estate in the name of law may reasonably be expected to come promptly to the owner's attention. * * * A state may indulge the assumption that one who has left tangible property in the state either has abandoned it, in which case proceedings against it deprive him of nothing, * * * or that he has left some caretaker under a duty to let him know that it is

being jeopardized." 339 U.S., at 316, 70 S.Ct., at 658.

Of course, the *Mullane* discussion of the special notice rules with respect to proceedings affecting property ownership focused on the forms of notice that might be appropriate as a supplement to the direct disturbance of the property itself. But where the State has reason to believe the premises to be occupied or under the charge of a caretaker, notice posted on the premises, if sufficiently apparent, is itself a form of disturbance, likely to come to the attention of the occupants or the caretaker.

significant number of instances, reliance on posting pursuant to the provisions of § 454.030 results in a failure to provide actual notice to the tenant concerned. Indeed, appellees claim to have suffered precisely such a failure of actual notice. As the process servers were well aware, notices posted on apartment doors in the area where these tenants lived were "not infrequently" removed by children or other tenants before they could have their intended effect. Under these conditions, notice by posting on the apartment door cannot be considered a "reliable means of acquainting interested parties of the fact that their rights are before the courts." *Mullane,* 339 U.S., at 315, 70 S.Ct., at 657.

Of course, the reasonableness of the notice provided must be tested with reference to the existence of "feasible and customary" alternatives and supplements to the form of notice chosen. *Ibid.* In this connection, we reject appellants' characterization of the procedure contemplated by § 454.030 as one in which " 'posting' is used as a method of service only as a last resort." Brief for Appellants 7. To be sure, the statute requires the officer serving notice to make a visit to the tenant's home and to attempt to serve the writ personally on the tenant or some member of his family. But if no one is at home at the time of that visit, as is apparently true in a "good percentage" of cases, posting follows forthwith. Neither the statute, nor the practice of the process servers, makes provision for even a second attempt at personal service, perhaps at some time of day when the tenant is more likely to be at home. The failure to effect personal service on the first visit hardly suggests that the tenant has abandoned his interest in the apartment such that mere *pro forma* notice might be held constitutionally adequate. Cf. *Mullane,* 339 U.S., at 317–318, 70 S.Ct., at 658.

As noted by the Court of Appeals, and as we noted in *Mullane,* the mails provide an "efficient and inexpensive means of communication," *id.,* at 319, 70 S.Ct., at 659, upon which prudent men will ordinarily rely in the conduct of important affairs, *id.,* at 319–320, 70 S.Ct., at 659. Notice by mail in the circumstances of this case would surely go a long way toward providing the constitutionally required assurance that the State has not allowed its power to be invoked against a person who has had no opportunity to present a defense despite a continuing interest in the resolution of the controversy.[9] Particularly where the subject matter of the action also happens to be the mailing address of the defendant, and where personal service is ineffectual, notice by mail may reasonably be relied upon to provide

---

9. The dissent apparently wishes to dispute the District Court's finding that "notices posted on apartment doors are often removed," and further questions our reliance on the observation in *Mullane* that the mails are a reliable means of communication—in light of its own observation that "unattended mailboxes are subject to plunder." *Post,* at 460. The dissent misconstrues the constitutional standard. In light of the findings of the courts below, we hold only that posted notice pursuant to § 454.030 is constitutionally inadequate. It is not our responsibility to prescribe the form of service that the Commonwealth should adopt. But even conceding that process served by mail is far from the ideal means of providing the notice the Due Process Clause of the Fourteenth Amendment requires, we have no hesitation in concluding that posted service *accompanied by* mail service, is constitutionally preferable to posted service alone.

interested persons with actual notice of judicial proceedings. We need not go so far as to insist that in order to "dispense with personal service the substitute that is most likely to reach the defendant is the least that ought to be required," McDonald v. Mabee, 243 U.S., at 92, 37 S.Ct., at 344, in order to recognize that where an inexpensive and efficient mechanism such as mail service is available to enhance the reliability of an otherwise unreliable notice procedure, the State's continued exclusive reliance on an ineffective means of service is not notice "reasonably calculated to reach those who could easily be informed by other means at hand." *Mullane, supra,* at 319.[10]

■ JUSTICE O'CONNOR, with whom THE CHIEF JUSTICE and JUSTICE REHNQUIST join, dissenting.

* * *

At a minimum, the Fourteenth Amendment requires "notice reasonably calculated, under all the circumstances, to apprise interested parties of the pendency of the action." Mullane v. Central Hanover Bank & Trust Co., 339 U.S. 306, 314 (1950). The question before the Court is whether the notice provided by Kentucky's statute meets this standard. In answering that question, the first "circumstances" to be considered are the nature and purpose of the action for which notice is required.

Kentucky's forcible entry and detainer action is a summary proceeding for quickly determining whether or not a landlord has the right to immediate possession of leased premises and, if so, for enabling the landlord speedily to obtain the property from the person in wrongful possession * * * The means chosen for making service of process, therefore, must be prompt and certain, for otherwise the principal purpose of a forcible entry and detainer action could be thwarted before the judicial proceedings even began.

The Kentucky statute meets this need. It directs the process server to attempt personal service on the tenant at his residence. Ky.Rev.Stat. § 454.030 (1975). If the process server cannot find the tenant on the premises, the statute directs the server to explain and leave a copy of the notice with a family member over the age of 16. *Ibid.* If both of these attempts fail, Kentucky authorizes the server, as a last resort, to post a copy of the notice in a conspicuous place on the premises.

* * *

The Court nonetheless rejects these established procedures as unconstitutional, though it does not cite a single case, other than the decision below, supporting its position that notice by posting is constitutionally inadequate in summary eviction proceedings. Instead,

---

10. "Where the names and post-office addresses of those affected by a proceeding are at hand, the reasons disappear for resort to means less likely than the mails to apprise them of its pendency." 339 U.S., at 318, 70 S.Ct., at 659. *See* Schroeder v. City of New York, 371 U.S. 208, 213, 83 S.Ct. 279, 282, 9 L.Ed.2d 255 (1962).

the Court relies solely on the deposition testimony of a few Kentucky process servers.

* * *

Plainly, such conflicting testimony falls well short of what this Court should require before rushing to scrap Kentucky's considered legislative judgment that, as a last resort, posted notice is an appropriate form of service of process for forcible entry and detainer actions.

The Court, however, holds that notice via the mails is so far superior to posted notice that the difference is of constitutional dimension.[2] How the Court reaches this judgment remains a mystery, especially since the Court is unable, on the present record, to evaluate the risks that notice mailed to public housing projects might fail due to loss, misdelivery, lengthy delay, or theft. Furthermore, the advantages of the mails over posting, if any, are far from obvious. It is no secret, after all, that unattended mailboxes are subject to plunder by thieves. Moreover, unlike the use of the mails, posting notice at least gives assurance that the notice has gotten as far as the tenant's door.

* * *

NOTE

In Mennonite Board of Missions v. Adams, 462 U.S. 791, 103 S.Ct. 2706, 77 L.Ed.2d 180 (1983), the United States Supreme Court held that notice to a mortgagee by local newspaper publication and by posting at the courthouse (both for three consecutive weeks by statute) was not adequate notice of a foreclosure proceeding to sell the mortgaged property for nonpayment of taxes. The recorded mortgage identified the mortgagee as a corporation of Wayne County, Ohio. The foreclosure took place in Indiana. The Court's opinion includes the following:

> Since a mortgagee clearly has a legally protected property interest, he is entitled to notice reasonably calculated to apprise him of a pending tax sale. Cf. Wiswall v. Sampson, 14 How. 52, 67, 14 L.Ed. 322 (1852). When the mortgagee is identified in a mortgage that is publicly recorded, constructive notice by publication must be supplemented by notice mailed to the mortgagee's last known available address, or by personal service. But unless the mortgagee is not reasonably identifiable, constructive notice alone does not satisfy the mandate of *Mullane*.

> * * *

> Notice by mail or other means as certain to ensure actual notice is a minimum constitutional precondition to a proceeding which will adversely affect the liberty or property interests of *any* party, whether unlettered or well versed in commercial practice, if its name and address are reasonably ascertainable. Furthermore, a mortgagee's knowledge of delinquency in the payment of

2. The Court gives lip service to the principle that "[i]t is not our responsibility to prescribe the form of service that [Kentucky] should adopt," *ante,* at 455, n. 9, but then goes on to do just that, first by explaining to the state legislature that, unlike notice by posting, notice by mail "would surely go a long way toward" satisfying the Court, *ante,* at 455, and then by remarking that, in the Court's view, the combination of posted service and mail service would be "constitutionally preferable" to posted service alone, *ante,* at 455, n. 9.

taxes is not equivalent to notice that a tax sale is pending. The latter "was the information which the [county] was constitutionally obliged * * * to give personally to the appellant—an obligation which the mailing of a single letter would have discharged." Schroeder v. New York City, 371 U.S., at 214.

462 U.S. at 798, 103 S.Ct. at 2711.

Seiler v. Ricci's Towing Services

Supreme Court of New York, Appellate Division, Fourth Department, 1996.
227 A.D.2d 920, 643 N.Y.S.2d 789.

■ JUDGES: GREEN, J. P., FALLON, WESLEY, DAVIS and BOEHM, JJ.

Plaintiff and Timothy Guilford (defendant) were involved in a motor vehicle accident on October 4, 1990. Although defendant was then living at 4940 Lake Road in the Town of Avon, his license indicated that he lived at 8085 West Henrietta Road in the Town of Rush and that was the address used by the police on the accident report. Defendant had lived at the West Henrietta Road address before the accident, but had moved to Lake Road without informing the Commissioner of Motor Vehicles. About two years after the accident, defendant moved from Lake Road to 65 Picture Book Trailer Park in the Town of West Bloomfield. On May 3, 1993, 31 months after the accident, plaintiff's process server attempted to serve a summons and complaint upon defendant at the West Henrietta Road address by affixing a copy of the summons and complaint to the door of the house and mailing copies to the same address, pursuant to CPLR 308(4). Supreme Court denied the motion of defendant to dismiss the complaint based upon his affirmative defenses of lack of personal jurisdiction and expiration of the Statute of Limitations and granted the cross motion of plaintiff to strike those affirmative defenses. We reverse.

We have held that a defendant is not estopped from raising defective service as a defense where he did not engage in conduct calculated to prevent plaintiff from learning his new address, even where he "neglected to contact authorities to inform them of his change of address. 'Since potential defendants ordinarily have no affirmative duty to keep those who might sue them abreast of their whereabouts' (*Feinstein v. Bergner*, 48 N.Y.2d 234, 241–242), there is no basis upon which to invoke an estoppel" (*Marsh v. Phillips*, 167 A.D.2d 905, 906). The Second Department cases relied upon by defendant (see, *Sherrill v. Pettiford*, 172 A.D.2d 512; *Anello v. Barry*, 149 A.D.2d 640; *Lavery v. Lopez*, 131 A.D.2d 820; *Hill v. Jones*, 113 A.D.2d 874; *Kramer v. Ryder Truck Rental*, 112 A.D.2d 194) are not controlling and, in any event, are inapposite. Here, there is nothing in the record to indicate that defendant had not advised the Commissioner of Motor Vehicles of his new address at 65 Picture Book Trailer Park prior to the date of attempted service. Further, at the time that service was attempted, defendant was no longer at the Lake Road address where he was living at the time of the accident. Therefore, even if the correct address had been listed on defendant's license, that address would not have been current when service was attempted.

Gardner v. Tully

Supreme Court of New York, Appellate Division, Second Department, 1996.
227 A.D.2d 587; 643 N.Y.S.2d 204.

■ JUDGES: BRACKEN, J. P., THOMPSON, KRAUSMAN and GOLDSTEIN, JJ., concur.

The plaintiff was involved in an accident on February 25, 1991, with an automobile operated by the defendant Philip R. Tully and owned by his wife Patricia Tully. The police officer at the accident scene used the driver's license and registration presented by the defendant Philip R. Tully to prepare an accident report which set forth a Bethpage address for the defendants, even though they had moved to Huntington Station some 10 months before the accident. Finding herself unable to serve the defendants in Bethpage, the plaintiff requested information from the Department of Motor Vehicles, whose documentation showed the defendants' residence to be in Bellmore. In fact, however, only the defendant's father, named Philip Tully, lived at the Bellmore address. After verifying the defendants' residence with a Bellmore neighbor, the plaintiff's process server served process by means of the affix and mail method set forth in CPLR 308 (4). The plaintiff's subsequent motion for leave to enter a default judgment was served upon the defendants by certified mail at that location, and a signed receipt was given to the postal delivery person. When the defendants failed to answer or oppose the plaintiff's motion, an inquest was held and the plaintiff entered a default judgment. Thereafter, the defendants moved to vacate the default, and their application was granted by the Supreme Court.

It is well settled that where, as here, a defendant has knowingly displayed an incorrect address to a plaintiff and the police at the scene of a motor vehicle accident, he is thereafter estopped from contesting jurisdiction and from challenging the diligence of the plaintiff's process server in ascertaining the defendant's correct address (see, e.g., *Anello v. Barry*, 149 A.D.2d 640, 540 N.Y.S.2d 460; *Lavery v. Lopez*, 131 A.D.2d 820, 517 N.Y.S.2d 182; *Treutlein v. Gutierrez*, 129 A.D.2d 791, 514 N.Y.S.2d 781; *Hill v. Jones*, 113 A.D.2d 874, 493 N.Y.S.2d 603). This is particularly so where a defendant has failed to keep the Department of Motor Vehicles apprised of any change of address, as required by Vehicle and Traffic Law § 505 (5), with the result that the plaintiff's process server is misdirected in his or her efforts to locate and serve the defendant (*McNeil v. Tomlin*, 82 A.D.2d 825, 439 N.Y.S.2d 430; *see also, Harrington v. Dickinson*, 159 A.D.2d 876, 553 N.Y.S.2d 219; *Kramer v. Ryder Truck Rental*, 112 A.D.2d 194, 490 N.Y.S.2d 863). Accordingly, the order appealed from is reversed and the motion to vacate the default judgment is denied.

QUESTION

Seiler v. Ricci's Towing and *Gardner v. Tully* were decided within a few days of each other. Can the holdings of the two cases be reconciled?

E. Substituted Service

FASHIONING A PROCEDURE FOR THE INDIVIDUAL CASE

I

Krueger v. Williams, and its companion case *Rodgers v. Davis,* 410 Mich. 144, 300 N.W.2d 910 (1981), *appeal denied,* 452 U.S. 956, 101 S.Ct. 3102, 69 L.Ed.2d 967 (1981) discussed the adequacy of various means of substituted service of process pursuant to Michigan's GCR 1963, 105.8 [now redesignated MCR 2.105]:

> Discretion of the Court. The Court in which an action has been commenced may, in its discretion, allow service of process to be made upon a defendant in any other manner which is reasonably calculated to give him actual notice of the proceedings and an opportunity to be heard, if an order permitting such service is entered before service of process is made upon showing to the court that service of process cannot reasonably be made in the manner provided for under other rules.

In *Krueger,* plaintiff had an automobile accident with a Michigan resident who subsequently moved out of state. When service could not be made on the named defendant, plaintiff requested permission to serve process on defendant's insurance carrier. In reversing the trial court's denial of this request, the Michigan Supreme Court explained:

> Plaintiff attempted service of process by compliance with the non-resident motorist statute * * *. Because the letter was returned unopened, this type of service was unavailable.

> Plaintiff made diligent efforts to locate the defendant. An investigator was hired and various locations checked. Affidavits of two investigators as well as plaintiff's attorney were filed reflecting these efforts. Plaintiff has demonstrated that there were no other means available to her to effect service of process except by appealing to the court, in its discretion, to allow her to serve the defendant's liability insurer. * * * Plaintiff has made diligent attempts to serve defendant. Plaintiff's need to utilize constructive service in this case is obvious. Our mobile society affords elusive defendants the potential to escape liability by avoiding service of process. The insurance company, while undertaking negotiations to settle this controversy, was aware of the possibility that a suit would be filed. We would allow constructive service under these circumstances.

In *Rodgers,* plaintiffs were passengers on a city street car that was struck by a Detroit police vehicle chasing a Ford Mustang. Among others, suit was brought against the owners and alleged driver of the Mustang. The trial court granted plaintiffs' motion for substituted service by mail (to defendant's last known address) and publication but this was reversed by the Michigan Supreme Court:

> A truly diligent search for an absentee defendant is absolutely necessary to supply a fair foundation for and legitimacy to the ordering of substituted service. "[W]hen notice is a person's due, process which is a mere gesture is not due process." *Mullane,* 339 U.S. 306, 315.

> The verified motion for substituted service presented on behalf of plaintiffs in Rodgers is insufficient. It fails to show with particularity either that service of process could not reasonably have been made according to prescribed methods or that no better alternative means of giving notice were available than publication.

> The only evidence in the record of plaintiffs' efforts to personally serve defendants appears in a conclusory statement contained in plaintiffs' motion for substituted service supported by a general affidavit by one of their attorneys that the motion's allegations are "true to the best of his knowledge, except those matters therein stated to be on information and belief, and as to those matters he believes the same to be true". In short, there is no direct sworn testimony.

> The motion first asserts that personal service on defendants "is not possible". It then states the last known address of one defendant and that the whereabouts of the other defendants are "unknown". The motion further alleges that despite "diligent attempts" by office staff and investigative agencies, plaintiffs have been unable to locate defendants. In short, the pleadings contain insufficient factual assertions as to what diligent attempts were undertaken to find and serve defendants under other rules. Further, the pleadings offer no explanation as to why other means better calculated to impart actual notice than publication were not reasonably available.

II

In *Omni Capital International v. Rudolf Wolff & Co., Ltd.*, 484 U.S. 97, 108 S.Ct. 404, 98 L.Ed.2d 415 (1987) plaintiffs (petitioners in the Supreme Court) sued defendant, a British corporation, and Gourlay, a resident and citizen of the United Kingdom, in a federal court in Louisiana seeking damages under the Commodities and Exchange Act (CEA). The Court held that service of a summons on these foreign defendants was not authorized under Rule 4 of the Federal Rules. Justice Blackmun, speaking for a unanimous Court, held that service was not authorized by federal statute, since the CEA contained no express provision for such service, and the parties had conceded that Louisiana's long-arm statute also did not authorize such service. Finally, he declined to "fill the 'interstices in the law inadvertently left by legislative enactment' by creating [a judicial] rule authorizing service of process in this litigation." Justice Blackmun stated that:

"We would consider it unwise for a court to make its own rule authorizing service of summons. It seems likely that Congress has been acting on the assumption that federal courts cannot add to the scope of service of summons Congress has authorized. This Court in the past repeatedly has stated that a legislative grant of authority is necessary. * * *

"The strength of this long-standing assumption, and the network of statutory enactments and judicial decisions tied to it, argue strongly against devising common-law service of process provisions at this late date for at least two reasons. First, since Congress concededly has the power to limit service of process, circumspection is called for in going beyond what Congress has authorized. Second, as statutes and rules have always provided the measures for service, courts are inappropriate forums for deciding whether to extend them. Legislative rulemaking better ensures proper consideration of a service rule's ramifications within the pre-existing structure and is more likely to lead to consistent application.

"Nothing about this case impels us to a different conclusion. If we do not create a rule here, the only harm to federal interests is the inability of a private litigant to bring a CEA action in the United States against an alien defendant who is not within the reach of the state long-arm statute. Since the CEA authorizes broader service of process in other enforcement actions, aliens cannot consider themselves immune from the Act's provisions. Also, a British court may be willing to enforce the CEA itself, if Omni brings suit against Wolff and Gourlay there.

"We are not blind to the consequences of the inability to serve process on Wolff and Gourlay. A narrowly tailored service of process provision, authorizing service on an alien in a federal-question case when the alien is not amenable to service under the applicable state long-arm statute, might well serve the ends of the CEA and other federal statutes. It is not for the federal courts, however, to create such a rule as a matter of common law. That responsibility, in our view, better rests with those who propose the Federal Rules of Civil Procedure and with Congress. * * *

The 1993 amendments to the Federal Rules of Civil Procedure addressed the problem raised in *Omni* and resolved it in favor of jurisdiction. Specifically, Rule 4(k)(2) allows a federal court to exercise personal jurisdiction over a defendant on a federal claim as long as such jurisdiction is consistent with the Due Process Clause of the Fifth Amendment. Even if the defendant would not be subject to the personal jurisdiction of any state court, a defendant may be subject to the jurisdiction of a federal court if the "significant affiliating contacts with the United States" are present, and the choice of forum is not so inconvenient as to deny "fair play and substantial justice." See Advisory Committee Note to FRCP Rule 4(k).

NOTE

The problems of fashioning a procedure for procuring the defendant's appearance suitable to the individual case have a long history as is shown in the following extract:

Plucknett, a Concise History of the Common Law

(5th ed. 1956), 383–385.

SECURING THE DEFENDANT'S APPEARANCE

If private endeavors failed, the next step was to get the defendant into court. The coercive power of the State generally has no difficulty in doing this under modern conditions, but early law found it immensely difficult. It first resorted to long and patient persuasion, in the hope that the adversary would promise to come into court. Appearance, in fact, was contractual—one of the earliest contracts which the law undertook to enforce. Slowly, however, the State assumed coercive powers and undertook to compel appearance, but even when this was accomplished the forms were still relics of the earlier method. Instead of the party voluntarily giving gages and finding friends who would be his pledges, the sheriff is sent to take them, and if they are not forthcoming he will in the end seize the recalcitrant one's property as a security for his appearance.

In the King's Court we find a compromise between the old oral procedure and the newer machinery of written documents. The plaintiff began the proceedings by purchasing an original writ suited to his case. We find little more trace of the actual requirement of previous demands for right, although formal words long survived in the declaration on writs of debt saying that "the defendant though often requested has not paid the said sum to the plaintiff, but has so far refused, and still refuses". If the older writs require the sheriff to urge the defendant to do right, the more modern type, represented by novel disseisin and trespass, begins at once with an order to summon.

Most original writs were not "served"; they went to the sheriff, and he carried out the order through machinery which looks very old. He appointed two "good summoners" (and at first they were certainly not officials) who went to the party and summoned him. In Glanvill's day they had to come to court in order to testify whether they had properly summoned the defendant. Thrice was the party summoned, and if he had not yet appeared, process issued to take his land. This oral summons was a weak point, and disputes whether summons had been duly made were frequent. The early stringent proof of summons by the testimony of the summoners was soon relaxed, and it became general to allow wager of law—an easy "proof" of non-summons—as a means of "curing a default".

Instead of merely failing to appear, the defendant might send certain excuses called "essoins". A number of "essoiners" were sent to explain that the party was sick, abroad, on the King's service, cut off by a flood, a broken bridge, and so forth. These secured delays of varying length, and in early times were verified. The court would send four knights to see whether the party was actually in bed. As one was entitled to an essoin if one had previously appeared, it was possible to spin out a long series of appearances and essoins. Worse still, in certain actions, especially debt, it was necessary to have all the co-defendants in court together. This might never happen if they arranged to cast essoins in turn. This practice of "fourcher" was particularly favoured by executors, until it was stopped by statute.

F.   PROBLEMS OF FEDERALISM

NOTE ON A PROBLEM IN FEDERALISM

If Jones of New York sues Smith of New Jersey in a federal court sitting in the latter state, what law shall the federal Judge apply to the case? In 1938 the U.S. Supreme Court, reversing a decision of almost 100 years' standing, held that in diversity cases the federal courts are constitutionally obliged to apply the laws of the respective states in which they sit. Erie Railroad Co. v. Tompkins, 304 U.S. 64, 58 S.Ct. 817 (1938). This famous case promptly spawned a spate of law review comment which continues unabated to the present. In the words of one learned gentleman, Erie "received quite a play in the magazines."

Nineteen thirty-eight was also the year the Federal Rules of Civil Procedure took effect. Erie applied only to substantive law, the rules to procedure. It will not surprise you, sophisticated in the law as you have already become, to note the publication one year later of an article entitled "Categorization and Federalism: 'Substance' and 'Procedure' after Erie Railroad v. Tompkins"[47] devoted to the question of how you tell which is which. Consider the following excerpt as a guide to the case materials which follow:

"If Mr. Justice Brandeis' opinion in the Tompkins case can be said to have a theme, that theme, constantly recurring, is this necessity of preventing a dual system of courts from spawning dual systems of justice. Built into that theme were phrases from the larger problems of adjusting a concurrent jurisdiction to function properly in cases not involving a federal question—one spearhead of national encroachment upon domestic polity.

"Out of this emphasis certainly comes the most important check on any proposed 'procedural' classification: will an independent federal rule be productive of diverse results in the two systems of tribunals where state courts utilize a varying rule? Certain unfairnesses still remain—the character of federal juries and judges as contrasted with that of state juries and judges will continue to offer advantages to certain litigants which may vitally bear on the result of cases. But, in spite of these vestiges, the softening of the incompatibilities inherent in concurrent jurisdiction, accomplished by the abolition of 'general law', should be further effected by refusal to sanction 'procedural' deviations which would bring about the same sort of invidious discrimination."

As *Hanna v. Plumer* shows, no simple answers served to resolve these problems. They continue to arise, albeit in new forms. They may appear to concern details of court procedure, seemingly of little moment to anyone other than the litigants. Yet, they continue to command the serious concern of courts and commentators, for in a larger sense they relate to the nature of "our federalism."

Hanna v. Plumer

Supreme Court of the United States, 1965.
380 U.S. 460, 85 S.Ct. 1136, 14 L.Ed.2d 8.

■ MR. CHIEF JUSTICE WARREN delivered the opinion of the Court.

The question to be decided is whether, in a civil action where the jurisdiction of the United States district court is based upon diversity

---

47.   By Tunks, 34 Ill.L.Rev. 271 (1939).

of citizenship between the parties, service of process shall be made in the manner prescribed by state law or that set forth in Rule 4(d)(1) of the Federal Rules of Civil Procedure.

On February 6, 1963, petitioner, a citizen of Ohio, filed her complaint in the District Court for the District of Massachusetts, claiming damages in excess of $10,000 for personal injuries resulting from an automobile accident in South Carolina, allegedly caused by the negligence of one Louise Plumer Osgood, a Massachusetts citizen deceased at the time of the filing of the complaint. Respondent, Mrs. Osgood's executor and also a Massachusetts citizen, was named as defendant. On February 8, service was made by leaving copies of the summons and the complaint with respondent's wife at his residence, concededly in compliance with Rule 4(d)(1), which provides:

"The summons and complaint shall be served together. The plaintiff shall furnish the person making service with such copies as are necessary. Service shall be made as follows:

"(1) Upon an individual other than an infant or an incompetent person, by delivering a copy of the summons and of the complaint to him personally or by leaving copies thereof at his dwelling house or usual place of abode with some person of suitable age and discretion then residing therein * * *."

Respondent filed his answer on February 26, alleging, *inter alia* that the action could not be maintained because it had been brought "contrary to and in violation of the provisions of Massachusetts General Laws (Ter.Ed.) Chapter 197, Section 9." That section provides:

"Except as provided in this chapter, an executor or administrator shall not be held to answer to an action by a creditor of the deceased which is not commenced within one year from the time of his giving bond for the performance of his trust, or to such an action which is commenced within said year unless before the expiration thereof the writ in such action has been served by delivery in hand upon such executor or administrator or service thereof accepted by him or a notice stating the name of the estate, the name and address of the creditor, the amount of the claim and the court in which the action has been brought has been filed in the proper registry of probate. * * * "Mass.Gen.Laws Ann., c. 197, § 9 (1958).

On October 17, 1963, the District Court granted respondent's motion for summary judgment, citing Ragan v. Merchants Transfer Co., 337 U.S. 530, 69 S.Ct. 1233, 93 L.Ed. 1520, and Guaranty Trust Co. v. York, 326 U.S. 99, 65 S.Ct. 1464, 89 L.Ed. 2079, in support of its conclusion that the adequacy of the service was to be measured by § 9, with which, the court held, petitioner had not complied. On appeal, petitioner admitted noncompliance with § 9, but argued that Rule

4(d)(1) defines the method by which service of process is to be effected in diversity actions. The Court of Appeals for the First Circuit, finding that "[r]elatively recent amendments [to § 9] evince a clear legislative purpose to require personal notification within the year,"[1] concluded that the conflict of state and federal rules was over "a substantive rather than a procedural matter," and unanimously affirmed. 331 F.2d 157. Because of the threat to the goal of uniformity of federal procedure posed by the decision below, we granted certiorari, 379 U.S. 813.

We conclude that the adoption of Rule 4(d)(1), designed to control service of process in diversity actions, neither exceeded the congressional mandate embodied in the Rules Enabling Act nor transgressed constitutional bounds, and that the Rule is therefore the standard against which the District Court should have measured the adequacy of the service. Accordingly, we reverse the decision of the Court of Appeals.

The Rules Enabling Act, 28 U.S.C.A. § 2072 (1958 ed.), provides in pertinent part:

> "The Supreme Court shall have the power to prescribe, by general rules, the forms of process, writs, pleadings, and motions, and the practice and procedure of the district courts of the United States in civil actions.

> "Such rules shall not abridge, enlarge or modify any substantive right and shall preserve the right of trial by jury * * *."

Under the cases construing the scope of the Enabling Act, Rule 4(d)(1) clearly passes muster. Prescribing the manner in which a defendant is to be notified that a suit has been instituted against him, it relates to the "practice and procedure of the district courts." Cf. Insurance Co. v. Bangs, 103 U.S. 435, 439, 26 L.Ed. 580.

> "The test must be whether a rule really regulates procedure—the judicial process for enforcing rights and duties recognized by substantive law and for justly administering remedy and redress for disregard or infraction of them." Sibbach v. Wilson & Co., 312 U.S. 1, 14, 61 S.Ct. 422, 426, 85 L.Ed. 479.

In Mississippi Pub. Corp. v. Murphree, 326 U.S. 438, 66 S.Ct. 242, 90 L.Ed. 185, this Court upheld Rule 4(f), which permits service of a summons anywhere within the State (and not merely the district) in which a district court sits:

> "We think that Rule 4(f) is in harmony with the Enabling Act * * *. Undoubtedly most alterations of the rules of practice and procedure may and often do affect the rights of litigants. Congress' prohibition of any alteration of substantive rights of litigants was obviously not addressed to such incidental effects as necessar-

---

1. Section 9 is in part a statute of limitations, providing that an executor need not "answer to an action * * * which is not commenced within one year from the time of his giving bond * * *." This part of the stat-ute, the purpose of which is to speed the settlement of estates, * * * is not involved in this case, since the action clearly was timely commenced.

ily attend the adoption of the prescribed new rules of procedure upon the rights of litigants who, agreeably to rules of practice and procedure, have been brought before a court authorized to determine their rights. Sibbach v. Wilson & Co., 312 U.S. 1, 11–14, 61 S.Ct. 422, 425–427, 85 L.Ed. 479. The fact that the application of Rule 4(f) will operate to subject petitioner's rights to adjudication by the district court for northern Mississippi will undoubtedly affect those rights. But it does not operate to abridge, enlarge or modify the rules of decision by which that court will adjudicate its rights." Id., at 445–446, 66 S.Ct. at 246.

Thus were there no conflicting state procedure, Rule 4(d)(1) would clearly control. National Rental v. Szukhent, 375 U.S. 311, 316, 84 S.Ct. 411, 414, 11 L.Ed.2d 354. However, respondent, focusing on the contrary Massachusetts rule, calls to the Court's attention another line of cases, a line which—like the Federal Rules—had its birth in 1938. Erie R. Co. v. Tompkins, 304 U.S. 64, 58 S.Ct. 817, 82 L.Ed. 1188, overruling Swift v. Tyson, 16 Pet. 1, 10 L.Ed. 865, held that federal courts sitting in diversity cases, when deciding questions of "substantive" law, are bound by state court decisions as well as state statutes. The broad command of *Erie* was therefore identical to that of the Enabling Act: federal courts are to apply state substantive law and federal procedural law. However, as subsequent cases sharpened the distinction between substance and procedure, the line of cases following *Erie* diverged markedly from the line construing the Enabling Act. Guaranty Trust Co. v. York, 326 U.S. 99, 65 S.Ct. 1464, 89 L.Ed. 2079, made it clear that *Erie*-type problems were not to be solved by reference to any traditional or common-sense substance-procedure distinction:

> "And so the question is not whether a statute of limitations is deemed a matter of 'procedure' in some sense. The question is * * * does it significantly affect the result of a litigation for a federal court to disregard a law of a State that would be controlling in an action upon the same claim by the same parties in a State court?"

326 U.S., at 109.

Respondent, by placing primary reliance on *York* and *Ragan,* suggests that the *Erie* doctrine acts as a check on the Federal Rules of Civil Procedure, that despite the clear command of Rule 4(d)(1), *Erie* and its progeny demand the application of the Massachusetts rule. Reduced to essentials, the argument is: (1) *Erie,* as refined in *York,* demands that federal courts apply state law whenever application of federal law in its stead will alter the outcome of the case. (2) In this case, a determination that the Massachusetts service requirements obtain will result in immediate victory for respondent. If, on the other hand, it should be held that Rule 4(d)(1) is applicable, the litigation will continue, with possible victory for petitioner. (3) Therefore, *Erie* demands application of the Massachusetts rule. The syllogism possesses an appealing simplicity, but is for several reasons invalid.

In the first place, it is doubtful that, even if there were no Federal Rule making it clear that in-hand service is not required in diversity actions, the *Erie* rule would have obligated the District Court to follow the Massachusetts procedure. "Outcome-determination" analysis was never intended to serve as a talisman. Byrd v. Blue Ridge Cooperative, 356 U.S. 525, 537, 78 S.Ct. 893, 900, 2 L.Ed.2d 953. Indeed, the message of *York* itself is that choices between state and federal law are to be made not by application of any automatic, "litmus paper" criterion, but rather by reference to the policies underlying the *Erie* rule. Guaranty Trust Co. v. York, supra, at 108–112, 65 S.Ct. at 1469–1471.

The *Erie* rule is rooted in part in a realization that it would be unfair for the character or result of a litigation materially to differ because the suit had been brought in a federal court.

> "Diversity of citizenship jurisdiction was conferred in order to prevent apprehended discrimination in state courts against those not citizens of the State. Swift v. Tyson introduced grave discrimination by non-citizens against citizens. It made rights enjoyed under the unwritten 'general law' vary according to whether enforcement was sought in the state or in the federal court; and the privilege of selecting the court in which the right should be determined was conferred upon the non-citizen. Thus, the doctrine rendered impossible equal protection of the law." Erie R. Co. v. Tompkins, supra, at 74–75, 58 S.Ct. at 820–821.

The decision was also in part a reaction to the practice of "forum-shopping" which had grown up in response to the rule of Swift v. Tyson, 304 U.S., at 73–74, 58 S.Ct. at 819–820. That the *York* test was an attempt to effectuate these policies is demonstrated by the fact that the opinion framed the inquiry in terms of "substantial" variations between state and federal litigation. 326 U.S., at 109, 65 S.Ct. at 1469. Not only are nonsubstantial, or trivial, variations not likely to raise the sort of equal protection problems which troubled the Court in *Erie;* they are also unlikely to influence the choice of a forum. The "outcome-determination" test therefore cannot be read without reference to the twin aims of the *Erie* rule: discouragement of forum-shopping and avoidance of inequitable administration of the laws.

The difference between the conclusion that the Massachusetts rule is applicable, and the conclusion that it is not, is of course at this point "outcome-determinative" in the sense that if we hold the state rule to apply, respondent prevails, whereas if we hold that Rule 4(d)(1) governs, the litigation will continue. But in this sense *every* procedural variation is "outcome-determinative." For example, having brought suit in a federal court, a plaintiff cannot then insist on the right to file subsequent pleadings in accord with the time limits applicable in the state courts, even though enforcement of the federal timetable will, if he continues to insist that he must meet only the state time limit, result in determination of the controversy against him. So it is here. Though choice of the federal or state rule will at this point have a marked effect upon the outcome of the litigation, the difference between the two rules would be of scant, if any, relevance to the choice of a forum. Petitioner, in choosing her forum, was not presented with a situation where application of the state rule would wholly bar recovery; rather, adherence to the state rule would have resulted only in altering the way in which process was served. Moreover, it is difficult to argue that permitting service of defendant's wife to take the place of in-hand service of defendant himself alters the mode of enforcement of state-created rights in a fashion sufficiently "substantial" to raise the sort of equal protection problems to which the *Erie* opinion alluded.

There is, however, a more fundamental flaw in respondent's syllogism: the incorrect assumption that the rule of Erie R. Co. v. Tompkins constitutes the appropriate test of the validity and therefore the applicability of a Federal Rule of Civil Procedure. The *Erie* rule has never been invoked to void a Federal Rule. It is true that there have been cases where this Court has held applicable a state rule in the face of an argument that the situation was governed by one of the Federal Rules. But the holding of each such case was not that *Erie* commanded displacement of a Federal Rule by an inconsistent state rule, but rather that the scope of the Federal Rule was not as broad as the losing party urged, and therefore, there being no Federal Rule which covered the point in dispute, *Erie* commanded the enforcement of state law.

> "Respondent contends, in the first place, that the charge was correct because of the fact that Rule 8(c) of the Rules of Civil Procedure makes contributory negligence an affirmative defense. We do not agree. Rule 8(c) covers only the manner of pleading. The question of the burden of establishing contributory negligence is a question of local law which federal courts in diversity of citizenship cases (Erie R. Co. v. Tompkins, 304 U.S. 64, 58 S.Ct. 817, 82 L.Ed. 1188) must apply." Palmer v. Hoffman, 318 U.S. 109, 117, 63 S.Ct. 477, 482, 87 L.Ed. 645.

(Here, of course, the clash is unavoidable: Rule 4(d)(1) says—implicitly, but with unmistakable clarity—that in-hand service is not required in federal courts.) At the same time, in cases adjudicating the validity of Federal Rules, we have not applied the *York* rule or other refinements of *Erie,* but have to this day continued to decide questions concerning the scope of the Enabling Act and the constitutionality of specific Federal Rules in light of the distinction set forth in *Sibbach.* E.g., Schlagenhauf v. Holder, 379 U.S. 104, 85 S.Ct. 234, 13 L.Ed.2d 152.

Nor has the development of two separate lines of cases been inadvertent. The line between "substance" and "procedure" shifts as the legal context changes. "Each implies different variables depending upon the particular problem for which it is used." Guaranty Trust Co. v. York, supra, at 108; Cook, The Logical and Legal Bases of the Conflict of Laws, pp. 154–183 (1942). It is true that both the Enabling Act and the *Erie* rule say, roughly, that federal courts are to apply state "substantive" law and federal "procedural" law, but from that it need not follow that the tests are identical. For they were designed to control very different sorts of decisions. When a situation is covered by one of the Federal Rules, the question facing the court is a far cry from the typical, relatively unguided *Erie* choice: the court has been instructed to apply the Federal Rule, and can refuse to do so only if the Advisory Committee, this Court, and Congress erred in their prima facie judgment that the Rule in question transgresses neither the terms of the Enabling Act nor constitutional restrictions.

We are reminded by the *Erie* opinion that neither Congress nor the federal courts can, under the guise of formulating rules of decision for federal courts, fashion rules which are not supported by a grant of federal authority contained in Article I or some other section of the Constitution; in such areas state law must govern because there can be no other law. But the opinion in *Erie,* which involved no Federal Rule and dealt with a question which was "substantive" in every traditional sense (whether the railroad owed a duty of care to Tompkins as a trespasser or a licensee), surely neither said nor implied that measures like Rule 4(d)(1) are unconstitutional. For the constitutional provision for a federal court system (augmented by the Necessary and Proper Clause) carries with it congressional power to make rules governing the practice and pleading in those courts, which in turn includes a power to regulate matters which, though falling within the uncertain area between substance and procedure, are rationally capable of classification as either. Cf. M'Culloch v. Maryland, 4 Wheat. 316, 421, 4 L.Ed. 579. Neither *York* nor the cases following it ever suggested that the rule there laid down for coping with situations where no Federal Rule applies is coextensive with the limitation on Congress to which *Erie* had adverted. Although this Court has never before been confronted with a case where the applicable Federal Rule is in direct collision with the law of the relevant State, courts of appeals faced with such clashes have rightly discerned the implications of our decisions.

"One of the shaping purposes of the Federal Rules is to bring about uniformity in the federal courts by getting away from local rules. This is especially true of matters which relate to the administration of legal proceedings, an area in which federal courts have traditionally exerted strong inherent power, completely aside from the powers Congress expressly conferred in the Rules. The purpose of the Erie doctrine, even as extended in York and Ragan, was never to bottle up federal courts with 'outcome-determinative' and 'integral-relations' stoppers—when there are 'affirmative countervailing [federal] considerations' and when there is a Congressional mandate (the Rules) supported by constitutional authority." Lumbermen's Mutual Casualty Co. v. Wright, 322 F.2d 759, 764 (C.A. 5th Cir.1963).

Erie and its offspring cast no doubt on the long-recognized power of Congress to prescribe housekeeping rules for federal courts even though some of those rules will inevitably differ from comparable state rules. Cf. Herron v. Southern Pacific Co., 283 U.S. 91, 51 S.Ct. 383, 75 L.Ed. 857. "When, because the plaintiff happens to be a non-resident, such a right is enforceable in a federal as well as in a State court, the forms and mode of enforcing the right may at times, naturally enough, vary because the two judicial systems are not identic." Guaranty Trust Co. v. York, supra, 326 U.S. at 108, 65 S.Ct. at 1469; Cohen v. Beneficial Loan Corp., 337 U.S. 541, 555, 69 S.Ct. 1221, 1229. Thus, though a court, in measuring a Federal Rule against the standards contained in the Enabling Act and the Constitution, need not wholly blind itself to the degree to which the Rule makes the character and result of the federal litigation stray from the course it would follow in state courts, Sibbach v. Wilson & Co., supra, at 13–14, it cannot be forgotten that the *Erie* rule, and the guidelines suggested in *York,* were created to serve another purpose altogether. To hold that a Federal Rule of Civil Procedure must cease to function whenever it alters the mode of enforcing state-created rights would be to disembowel either the Constitution's grant of power over federal procedure or Congress' attempt to exercise that power in the Enabling Act. Rule 4(d)(1) is valid and controls the instant case.

Reversed.[1]

G. THE CONDITIONS OF EFFECTIVE CONSENT

National Equipment Rental v. Szukhent

Supreme Court of the United States, 1964.
375 U.S. 311, 84 S.Ct. 411, 11 L.Ed.2d 354.

■ MR. JUSTICE STEWART delivered the opinion of the Court.

The Federal Rules of Civil Procedure provide that service of process upon an individual may be made "by delivering a copy of the summons and of the complaint to an agent authorized by appointment * * * to receive service of process." The petitioner is a corporation with its principal place of business in New York. It sued the respondents, residents of Michigan, in a New York federal court, claiming that the respondents had defaulted under a farm equipment lease. The only question now before us is whether the person upon whom the summons and complaint were served was "an agent authorized by appointment" to receive the same, so as to subject the respondents to the jurisdiction of the federal court in New York.

The respondents obtained certain farm equipment from the petitioner under a lease executed in 1961. The lease was on a printed form less than a page and a half in length, and consisted of 18 numbered paragraphs. The last numbered paragraph, appearing just above the respondents' signatures and printed in the same type used in the remainder of the instrument, provided that "the Lessee hereby designates Florence Weinberg, 47–21 Forty-first Street, Long Island City, N.Y., as agent for the purpose of accepting service of any process

---

1. Justice Harlan's concurring opinion is omitted.

within the State of New York." The respondents were not acquainted with Florence Weinberg.

In 1962 the petitioner commenced the present action by filing in the federal court in New York a complaint which alleged that the respondents had failed to make any of the periodic payments specified by the lease. The Marshal delivered two copies of the summons and complaint to Florence Weinberg. That same day she mailed the summons and complaint to the respondents, together with a letter stating that the documents had been served upon her as the respondents' agent for the purpose of accepting service of process in New York, in accordance with the agreement contained in the lease.[54] The petitioner itself also notified the respondents by certified mail of the service of process upon Florence Weinberg.

Upon motion of the respondents, the District Court quashed service of the summons and complaint, holding that, although Florence Weinberg had promptly notified the respondents of the service of process and mailed copies of the summons and complaint to them, the lease agreement itself had not explicitly required her to do so, and there was therefore a "failure of the agency arrangement to achieve intrinsic and continuing reality." 30 F.R.D. 3, 5. The Court of Appeals affirmed, 311 F.2d 79, and we granted certiorari, 372 U.S. 974, 83 S.Ct. 1110, 10 L.Ed.2d 141. For the reasons stated in this opinion, we have concluded that Florence Weinberg was "an agent authorized by appointment * * * to receive service of process," and accordingly we reverse the judgment before us.

We need not and do not in this case reach the situation where no personal notice has been given to the defendant. Since the respondents did in fact receive complete and timely notice of the lawsuit pending against them, no due process claim has been made. The case before us is therefore quite different from cases where there was no actual notice, such as Schroeder v. City of New York, 371 U.S. 208, 83 S.Ct. 279, 9 L.Ed.2d 255; Walker v. Hutchinson City, 352 U.S. 112, 77 S.Ct. 200, 1 L.Ed.2d 178; and Mullane v. Central Hanover Tr. Co., 339 U.S. 306, 70 S.Ct. 652, 94 L.Ed. 865. Similarly, as the Court of Appeals recognized, this Court's decision in Wuchter v. Pizzutti, 276 U.S. 13, 48 S.Ct. 259, 72 L.Ed. 466, is inapposite here. In that case a state nonresident motorist statute which failed to provide explicitly for communication of notice was held unconstitutional, despite the fact that notice had been given to the defendant in that particular case. *Wuchter* dealt with the limitations imposed by the Fourteenth Amendment upon a statutory scheme by which a State attempts to subject nonresident individuals to the jurisdiction of its courts. The question presented here, on the other hand, is whether a party to a private

54. The complaint, summons, and covering letter were sent by certified mail, and the letter read as follows:

"Gentlemen:

"Please take notice that the enclosed Summons and Complaint was duly served upon me this day by the United States Marshal, as your agent for the purpose of accepting service of process within the State of New York, in accordance with your contract with National Equipment Rental, Ltd.

"Very truly yours,

"Florence Weinberg"

contract may appoint an agent to receive service of process within the meaning of Federal Rule of Civil Procedure 4(d)(1), where the agent is not personally known to the party, and where the agent has not expressly undertaken to transmit notice to the party.

The purpose underlying the contractual provision here at issue seems clear. The clause was inserted by the petitioner and agreed to by the respondents in order to assure that any litigation under the lease should be conducted in the State of New York. The contract specifically provided that "This agreement shall be deemed to have been made in Nassau County, New York, regardless of the order in which the signatures of the parties shall be affixed hereto, and shall be interpreted, and the rights and liabilities of the parties here determined, in accordance with the laws of the State of New York." And it is settled, as the courts below recognized, that parties to a contract may agree in advance to submit to the jurisdiction of a given court, to permit notice to be served by the opposing party, or even to waive notice altogether.

* * *

Under well-settled general principles of the law of agency, Florence Weinberg's prompt acceptance and transmittal to the respondents of the summons and complaint pursuant to the authorization was itself sufficient to validate the agency, even though there was no explicit previous promise on her part to do so. "The principal's authorization may neither expressly nor impliedly request any expression of assent by the agent as a condition of the authority, and in such a case any exercise of power by the agent within the scope of the authorization, during the term for which it was given, or within a reasonable time if no fixed term was mentioned, will bind the principal." 2 Williston on Contracts (3d ed. 1959), § 274.

We deal here with a Federal Rule, applicable to federal courts in all 50 States. But even if we were to assume that this uniform federal standard should give way to contrary local policies, there is no relevant concept of state law which would invalidate the agency here at issue. In Michigan, where the respondents reside, the statute which validates service of process under the circumstances present in this case contains no provision requiring that the appointed agent expressly undertake to notify the principal of the service of process. Similarly, New York law, which it was agreed should be applicable to the lease provisions, does not require any such express promise by the agent in order to create a valid agency for receipt of process. The New York statutory short form of general power of attorney, which specifically includes the power to accept service of process, is entirely silent as to any such requirement. Indeed, the identical contractual provision at issue here has been held by a New York court to create a valid agency for service of process under the law of that State. National Equipment Rental v. Graphic Art Designers, 36 Misc.2d 442, 234 N.Y.S.2d 61.

It is argued, finally, that the agency sought to be created in this case was invalid because Florence Weinberg may have had a conflict of interest. This argument is based upon the fact that she was not personally known to the respondents at the time of her appointment and upon a suggestion in the record that she may be related to an officer of the petitioner corporation. But such a contention ignores the narrowly limited nature of the agency here involved. Florence Weinberg was appointed the respondents' agent for the single purpose of receiving service of process. An agent with authority so limited can in no meaningful sense be deemed to have had an interest antagonistic to the respondents, since both the petitioner and the respondents had an equal interest in assuring that, in the event of litigation, the latter be given that adequate and timely notice which is a prerequisite to a valid judgment.[56]

A different case would be presented if Florence Weinberg had not given prompt notice to the respondents, for then the claim might well be made that her failure to do so had operated to invalidate the agency. We hold only that, prompt notice to the respondents having been given, Florence Weinberg was their "agent authorized by appointment" to receive process within the meaning of Federal Rule of Civil Procedure 4(d)(1).

The judgment of the Court of Appeals is reversed and the case is remanded for further proceedings consistent with this opinion.

It is so ordered.

■ Mr. Justice Black, dissenting.

The petitioner, National Equipment Rental, Ltd., is a Delaware corporation with its principal place of business in greater New York City. From that location it does a nationwide equipment rental business. The respondents, Steve and Robert Szukhent, father and son farming in Michigan, leased from National two incubators for their farm, signing in Michigan a lease contract which was a standard printed form obviously prepared by the New York company's lawyers. Included in the 18 paragraphs of fine print was the following provision:

> " * * * the Lessee hereby designates Florence Weinberg, 47–21 Forty-first Street, Long Island City, N.Y., as agent for the purpose of accepting service of any process within the State of New York."

---

56. There is no allegation that Weinberg had any pecuniary interest in the subject matter of the litigation. Nor is the issue here the applicability of a statute which permits service on a foreign corporation by service on persons who are generally authorized to act as agents of the corporation, when the agent upon whom service is made has a personal interest in suppressing notice of service: see, e.g., John W. Masury & Son v. Lowther, 299 Mich. 516, 300 N.W. 866 (1941) (involving a garnishment proceeding in which service under such a statute was attempted upon that employee of the foreign corporation who had incurred the debt on which the suit was based, who therefore had a personal interest in concealing from his employer the fact of service, and who did not notify the employer that service had been made). See Hartsock v. Commodity Credit Corp., 10 F.R.D. 181, also involving a situation where the agent "sustains such a relation to plaintiff or the claim in suit as to make it to his interest to suppress the fact of service * * *." 10 F.R.D., at 184.

The New York company later brought this suit for breach of the lease in the United States District Court for the Eastern District of New York.

* * *

The record on the motion to quash shows that the Szukhents had never had any dealings with Mrs. Weinberg their supposed agent. They had never met, seen, or heard of her. She did not sign the lease, was not a party to it, received no compensation from the Szukhents, and undertook no obligation to them. In fact, she was handpicked by the New York company to accept service of process in any suits that might thereafter be filed by the company. Only after this suit was brought was it reluctantly revealed that Mrs. Weinberg was in truth the wife of one of the company's officers. The district judge, applying New York law to these facts, held that there had been no effective appointment of Mrs. Weinberg as agent of the Szukhents, that the service on her as their "agent" was therefore invalid, and that the service should be quashed. 30 F.R.D. 3 (D.C.E.D.N.Y.). The Court of Appeals, one judge dissenting, affirmed, agreeing that no valid agency had been created. 311 F.2d 79 (C.A.2d Cir. 1962) . This Court now reverses both courts below and holds that the contractual provision purporting to appoint Mrs. Weinberg as agent is valid and that service of process on her as agent was therefore valid and effective under Rule 4(d)(1) as on an "agent authorized by appointment * * * to receive service of process." I disagree with that holding, believing that (1) whether Mrs. Weinberg was a valid agent upon whom service could validly be effected under Rule 4(d)(1) should be determined under New York law and that we should accept the holdings of the federal district judge and the Court of Appeals sitting in New York that under that State's law the purported appointment of Mrs. Weinberg was invalid and ineffective; (2) if, however, Rule 4(d)(1) is to be read as calling upon us to formulate a new federal definition of agency for purposes of service of process, I think our formulation should exclude Mrs. Weinberg from the category of an "agent authorized by appointment * * * to receive service of process"; and (3) upholding service of process in this case raises serious questions as to whether these Michigan farmers have been denied due process of law in violation of the Fifth and Fourteenth Amendments.

I

No federal statute has undertaken to regulate the sort of agency transaction here involved. There is only Rule 4(d)(1), which says nothing more than that in federal courts personal jurisdiction may be obtained by service on an "agent." The Rule does not attempt to define who is an "agent." To me it is evident that the draftsmen of the Rules did not, by using the word "agent," show any intention of throwing out the traditional body of state law and creating a new and different federal doctrine in this branch of the law of agency. Therefore, it is to the law of New York—the State where this action was brought in federal court, the place where the contract was deemed by the parties to have been made, and the State the law of which was specified as determining rights and liabilities under the contract—that we should turn to test the validity of the appointment.

I agree with the district judge that this agency is invalid under the laws of New York. * * *

II

If Rule 4(d)(1) is to be read as requiring this Court to formulate new federal standards of agency to be resolved in each case as a federal question, rather than as leaving the question to state law, I think the standards we formulate should clearly and unequivocally denounce as invalid any alleged service of process on nonresidents based on purported agency contracts having no more substance than that naming Mrs. Weinberg.

In the first place, we should interpret the federal rule as contemplating a genuine agent, not a sham. Here the "agent," Mrs. Weinberg, was unknown to respondents. She was chosen by the New York company, was under its supervision, and, indeed, was the wife of one of its officers—facts no one ever told these farmers.[a]

* * *

QUESTIONS

Is there anything in the opinions to show that the Szukhents were not represented by counsel? Would it have made any difference to Justice Black?

Notice Justice Black's repeated references to "these Michigan farmers." Would Justice Black have been less aroused if the defendant were a corporation conducting a commercial farm operation? Note that the jurisdiction of the federal courts in diversity cases was then predicated upon the amount in controversy exceeding $10,000. Today, the amount in controversy would have to exceed $50,000.

NOTE: CONFESSION OF JUDGMENT

In *D.H. Overmyer Co. v. Frick Co.*, 405 U.S. 174, 92 S.Ct. 775, 31 L.Ed.2d 124 (1972) the Supreme Court upheld the constitutionality of a confession of judgment, specifically a cognovit note described by the Court in the following terms:

> This case presents the issue of the constitutionality, under the Due Process Clause of the Fourteenth Amendment, of the cognovit note authorized by Ohio Rev.Code § 2323.13.
>
> The cognovit is the ancient legal device by which the debtor consents in advance to the holder's obtaining a judgment without notice or hearing, and possibly even with the appearance, on the debtor's behalf, of an attorney designated by the holder.
>
> Statutory treatment varies widely. Some States specifically authorize the cognovit. Others disallow it. Some go so far as to make its employment a misdemeanor. The majority, however, regulate its use and many prohibit the device in small loans and consumer sales.

a. The dissenting opinion of Justice Brennan is omitted.

The concurring opinion of Justice Douglas, joined by Justice Marshall, emphasizes that whatever hardship resulted from "the Ohio confession of judgment scheme * * * was voluntarily and understandingly self-inflicted through the arm's length bargaining of these corporate parties." Justice Blackmun, speaking for the Court, emphasized the availability of a post-judgment procedure by means of which an aggrieved party could seek to have the judgment vacated. Both parties were business firms, negotiating at arm's length and represented by counsel.

In a companion case, *Swarb v. Lennox*, 405 U.S. 191, 92 S.Ct. 767, 31 L.Ed.2d 138 (1972) the Court decided that the cognovit could not be used against low-income consumer debtors who were not represented by counsel.

Peralta v. Heights Medical Center, Inc.

Supreme Court of the United States, 1988.
485 U.S. 80, 108 S.Ct. 896, 99 L.Ed.2d 75.

■ JUSTICE WHITE delivered the opinion of the Court.

Heights Medical Center, Inc. (hereafter appellee), sued appellant Peralta in February 1982 to recover some $5,600 allegedly due under appellant's guarantee of a hospital debt incurred by one of his employees. Citation issued, the return showing personal, but untimely, service. Appellant did not appear or answer, and on July 20, 1982, default judgment was entered for the amount claimed, plus attorney's fees and costs.

In June 1984, appellant began a bill of review proceeding in the Texas courts to set aside the default judgment and obtain other relief. * * * [I]t was alleged that the return of service itself showed a defective service and that appellant in fact had not been personally served at all. The judgment was therefore void under Texas law. It was also alleged that the judgment was abstracted and recorded in the county real property records, thereby creating a cloud on appellant's title, that a writ of attachment was issued, and that, unbeknownst to him, his real property was sold to satisfy the judgment and for much less than its true value. Appellant prayed that the default judgment be vacated, the abstract of judgment be expunged from the county real property records, the constable's sale be voided, and that judgment for damages be entered against the Medical Center and * * * the purchasers at the constable's sale.

* * *

Appellee filed a motion for summary judgment asserting that in a bill of review proceeding such as appellant filed, it must be shown that the petitioner had a meritorious defense to the action in which judgment had been entered, that petitioner was prevented from proving his defense by the fraud, accident, or wrongful act of the opposing party, and that there had been no fault or negligence on petitioner's part. Although it was assumed for the purposes of summary judgment that there had been defective service and that this lapse excused proof of the second and third requirement for obtaining a bill of review, it was assertedly necessary, nevertheless, to show a

meritorious defense, which appellant had conceded he did not have.
* * *

In opposition to summary judgment, appellant denied that he had been personally served and that he had notice of the judgment. The case proceeded through the Texas courts on that basis, and it is not denied by appellee that under our cases, a judgment entered without notice or service is constitutionally infirm. "An elementary and fundamental requirement of due process in any proceeding which is to be accorded finality is notice reasonably calculated, under the circumstances, to apprise interested parties of the pendency of the action and afford them the opportunity to present their objections." Mullane v. Central Hanover Bank & Trust Co., 339 U.S. 306, 314, 70 S.Ct. 652, 657, 94 L.Ed. 865 (1950). Failure to give notice violates "the most rudimentary demands of due process of law." Armstrong v. Manzo, 380 U.S. 545, 550, 85 S.Ct. 1187, 1190, 14 L.Ed.2d 62 (1965). * * *

The Texas courts nevertheless held, as appellee urged them to do, that to have the judgment set aside, appellant was required to show that he had a meritorious defense, apparently on the ground that without a defense, the same judgment would again be entered on retrial and hence appellant had suffered no harm from the judgment entered without notice. But this reasoning is untenable. As appellant asserts, had he had notice of the suit, he might have impleaded the employee whose debt had been guaranteed, worked out a settlement, or paid the debt. He would also have preferred to sell his property himself in order to raise funds rather than to suffer it sold at a constable's auction.

Nor is there any doubt that the entry of the judgment itself had serious consequences. It is not denied that the judgment was entered on the county records, became a lien on appellant's property, and was the basis for issuance of a writ of execution under which appellant's property was promptly sold without notice. Even if no execution sale had yet occurred, the lien encumbered the property and impaired appellant's ability to mortgage or alienate it; and state procedures for creating and enforcing such liens are subject to the strictures of due process. Here, we assume that the judgment against him and the ensuing consequences occurred without notice to appellant, notice at a meaningful time and in a meaningful manner that would have given him an opportunity to be heard. * * *

The Texas court held that the default judgment must stand absent a showing of a meritorious defense to the action in which judgment was entered without proper notice to appellant, a judgment that had substantial adverse consequences to appellant. By reason of the Due Process Clause of the Fourteenth Amendment, that holding is plainly infirm.

Where a person has been deprived of property in a manner contrary to the most basic tenets of due process, "it is no answer to say that in his particular case due process of law would have led to the same result because he had no adequate defense upon the merits." Coe v. Armour Fertilizer Works, 237 U.S. 413, 424, 35 S.Ct. 625, 629,

59 L.Ed. 1027 (1915). As we observed in Armstrong v. Manzo, supra, at 552, only "wip[ing] the slate clean * * * would have restored the petitioner to the position he would have occupied had due process of law been accorded to him in the first place." The Due Process Clause demands no less in this case.

The judgment below is

Reversed.

H. IMMUNITY FROM SERVICE

Fun–Damental Too v. Hwung, Gemmy Industries (Hong Kong), High Quality, Ltd., and Gem Office Products, Inc.

United States District Court for the Southern District of New York, 1997.
111 F.3d 993.

■ MICHAEL B. MUKASEY, U.S.D.J.

Fun–Damental Too, Ltd. sues Hwung–Hsiang Hwung, Gemmy Industries (Hong Kong), Ltd. ("Gemmy Hong Kong"), High Quality, Ltd., and Gem Office Products, Inc., for false designation of origin and trade dress infringement in violation of § 43(a) of the Lanham Act, *15 U.S.C. § 1125*(a), injury to business reputation and dilution under New York General Business Law § 368–d, and unfair competition and tortious interference with prospective contractual relations under New York State law. Defendants move to dismiss pursuant to Fed. R. Civ. P. 12(b)(2) for lack of personal jurisdiction, and Fed. R. Civ. P. 12(b)(5) for insufficiency of service of process. For the reasons outlined below, defendants' motion to dismiss pursuant to Fed. R. Civ. P. 12(b)(5) is granted.

This action is related to another action, Fun–Damental Too, Ltd. v. Gemmy Industries Corp. and Kay–Bee Toy & Hobby Shops, Inc., 96 Civ. 1103 (S.D.N.Y. filed Feb. 14, 1996) ("Fun–Damental I"). I have previously issued two opinions in that case which describe the facts underlying this controversy. * * *

Plaintiff, a Pennsylvania limited partnership, developed, manufactures and markets a toy called the Toilet Bank. (Compl. PP 1, 28) Plaintiff made substantial sales of the Toilet Bank in 1994 and 1995. In Fun–Damental I, plaintiff alleged that Gemmy Industries distributed, and Kay–Bee sold, a "knock-off" of the Toilet Bank under the name "Currency Can" (the "Can"), thereby infringing on its trade dress. In March, 1996, I enjoined Gemmy Industries and Kay–Bee from selling the Can during the pendency of that action. See 1996 WL 125641 (S.D.N.Y. March 20, 1996)

Plaintiff alleges here that these defendants also infringed on the Toilet Bank's trade dress through their role in the development and sale of the Can. Gemmy Hong Kong and High Quality are Hong Kong corporations and Gem Office Products is a Taiwanese corporation. Hwung, an officer, director and principal shareholder of defendants, and president of Gemmy Industries, a defendant in Fun–Damental I, is a citizen of Taiwan. Plaintiff alleges that defendants conspired with Gemmy Industries to manufacture, market, and distribute the Can in the United States. * * *

Plaintiff commenced this action on February 7, 1997. On February 11, 1997, plaintiff served Hwung with a summons and complaint while Hwung was testifying at a deposition in New York in Fun–Damental I. Defendants now move to dismiss for lack of personal jurisdiction and for insufficiency of service of process.

II.

Plaintiff claims that it properly served Hwung personally in New York on February 11, 1997. Defendants argue that Hwung was immune from service while he was in New York because he was here solely to testify at a deposition in Fun–Damental I and therefore, that service was invalid.

"It is well established that witnesses, parties and attorneys coming from another jurisdiction are exempt from service of civil process while in attendance upon court, and during a reasonable time in coming and going." *Cabiri v. Assasie–Gyimah*, 921 F. Supp. 1189, 1193 (S.D.N.Y.1996).[1] "The immunity has been liberally construed to cover all stages of the case, including motion, deposition practice and appeals." 2 Jack B. Weinstein, Harold L. Korn & Arthur R. Miller, New York Civil Practice CPLR, P 308.05, at 3–254.46 (1997). If a witness or party could be served while attending such a proceeding, it "might tend to discourage[] the voluntary attendance of those whose presence is necessary or convenient to the judicial administration of pending litigation." *Lamb v. Schmitt*, 285 U.S. 222, 225, 76 L. Ed. 720, 52 S. Ct. 317 (1932). Here, Hwung was served while he was in New York for a deposition in a pending matter.

However, plaintiff claims first that Hwung waived his immunity by visiting Gemmy Industries' showroom the night before testifying at the deposition and thereby conducting business unrelated to the deposition. "If, while in the jurisdiction, the person claiming immunity engages in activities of a business nature totally unrelated to the litigation which he is attending, the rule is that immunity from process is in effect waived." *Uniroyal, Inc. v. Sperberg*, 63 F.R.D. 55, 58 (S.D.N.Y.1973) (quoting *Dillingham v. Anderson*, 126 F. Supp. 221, 224 (D.Haw.1954)). "The criterion seems to be, however, not the fact of engaging in other than litigious matters, but rather, the degree and proportion of the activity." *Dillingham*, 126 F. Supp. at 224. The immunity is not considered waived if the unrelated business dealings

---

1. "The question of immunity from service of process ... is viewed as a procedural question controlled by federal precedents rather than by state law." 4 Charles Alan Wright & Arthur R. Miller, Federal Practice and Procedure: Civil 2d § 1076, at 500 (1987).

are of "a mere casual and unforeseen nature" or are "trivial and insubstantial." *Uniroyal*, 63 F.R.D. at 58.

Here, Hwung arrived in New York at 6 p.m. on February 10, 1997, the evening before the deposition. (Hwung dep. at 46) He then visited Gemmy Industries' showroom for about an hour with Dan Flaherty, the vice-president of Gemmy Industries, and Jim Vandyssel, one of its salespeople. Hwung testified that Flaherty and Vandyssel showed him Gemmy Industries' products and told him that a Toy Fair, then occurring in New York, was going well. Hwung stated also that he did not discuss customers with Flaherty and Vandyssel. Hwung then had dinner with Flaherty, and he testified that they did not discuss business during dinner.

Hwung's activities the night before his deposition were not sufficient to waive immunity from service of process. It is undisputed that Hwung would not have been in New York were it not for the deposition. Hwung's visit to the Gemmy Industries' showroom, absent transaction of business, is trivial and insubstantial. Hwung merely viewed the company's products in a casual manner, and since, as he states, he is not involved in the sale of those products (id. at 53–54), this viewing was more informational than integral to his job. Certainly, visiting the showroom was much more trivial than the types of business transactions which previously have been found to waive immunity from service. See, e.g., *Uniroyal*, 63 F.R.D. at 58 (immunity waived when witness met with bank to discuss personal affairs, had meeting with magazine publisher, and visited with family for three days); *Dillingham*, 126 F. Supp. at 222–24 (immunity waived when witness, an insurance agent, secured release of obligation under lease, sublet leased offices for one month, contacted insurers with regard to insurance coverage for insureds, paid premiums for an insured, and made arrangements with Hawaiian resident for referral of insurance prospects). Moreover, Hwung's dinner with Flaherty does not waive his immunity. It is not reasonably to be expected or required that a foreign businessman entering New York for a deposition eat dinner alone, rather than with a business associate, and such a meal, without allegation or evidence that specific business was conducted, cannot by itself waive immunity from service.

Plaintiff argues second that the general immunity rule is inapplicable here because this action is closely related to Fun–Damental I and therefore Hwung was not immune from service of process in this action while he was attending a deposition in Fun–Damental I. In Lamb, the Supreme Court carved out an exception to the general immunity rule, and held that a witness is not immune if the immunity would undermine the purpose of the action in which the witness is participating when served. 285 U.S. at 226–27. The Court reasoned that in such cases, the negative effects of the immunity outweigh its benefits. *Id*. at 226. The Court stated, "The test is whether the immunity itself, if allowed, would so obstruct judicial administration in the very cause for the protection of which it is invoked as to justify withholding it." *Id*. at 228.

The Second Circuit has interpreted this exception narrowly, holding that even if there is a close relationship between two actions, the immunity is waived only if the Supreme Court's specific test is met. See, e.g., *Shapiro & Son Curtain Corp. v. Glass*, 348 F.2d 460, 461 (2d Cir.), cert. denied, 382 U.S. 942, 15 L. Ed. 2d 351, 86 S. Ct. 397 (1965); *In re Equitable Plan Co.*, 277 F.2d 319, 320–21 (2d Cir.1960); see also *American Centennial Ins. Co. v. Handal*, 901 F. Supp. 892, 895–96 (D.N.J.1995) (citing Second Circuit cases for the proposition that the "theory evolving from Lamb is that immunity should be granted to non-residents, even when the second action is factually similar to the first, unless the grant of immunity would obstruct justice in the first suit.").

For example, in Shapiro & Son, Shapiro was sued by Everwear Candlewick for allegedly breaching an agreement. Shapiro counterclaimed, alleging that Everwear had conspired to interfere with its business. 348 F.2d at 461. Shapiro then filed a second action against Basil Glass, a director of Everwear, alleging that Glass dominated and controlled Everwear, and that Glass conspired with Everwear and others to interfere with Shapiro's business. The Glass complaint noted that the claim was cognizable only after the first action against Everwear was concluded. Id. Glass was served while he was attending a deposition in the Everwear case. The Court found that Glass was immune from service and that the Lamb exception did not apply because, although the two actions were related, there was no showing that immunity from service would so obstruct administration of the Everwear action as to justify withholding immunity. Id.

Likewise, in *NASL Marketing, Inc. v. De Vries*, 94 F.R.D. 309, 310–11 (S.D.N.Y.1982), Judge Weinfeld held that the defendant was immune from process served upon him while attending an arbitration in New York. He reasoned that even though the legal action and arbitration were closely related in that the second action sought to hold defendant personally liable for the arbitration award, the defendant was immune because the plaintiff "failed to show that any of the acts charged in the [second] complaint have so interfered with its rights as determined in the arbitration to justify the withholding of immunity." *Id. at 311.*

On the other hand, in *McDonnell v. American Leduc Petroleums, Ltd.*, 456 F.2d 1170 (2d Cir.1972), one of the defendants, who allegedly engaged in fraudulent dealings with a debtor, was served while attending a Section 167 bankruptcy proceeding relating to this same debtor. The Court found that "the very purpose of a section 167 investigation is to uncover for the trustee conducting it possible causes of action, including actions against those called to testify," and therefore that "the present action against [the defendant] carried out the purpose of the earlier section 167 proceeding." *Id.* Thus, the Court applied the Lamb exception because the application of immunity would have undermined the purpose of the action which the immunity was intended to benefit.

In Cabiri, the Court stated that "McDonnell stands for the proposition that where there is a close relationship between the two actions, and both involve vindication of the same cluster of rights and interests, then immunity from service of process should be withheld." 921 F. Supp. at 1194. However, this interpretation of McDonnell is too broad; as noted above, the Second Circuit has applied the Lamb exception only where the Supreme Court's test is met—i.e., where immunity would obstruct judicial administration in the action which the immunity is designed to benefit—and that test was met in McDonnell. See *Viking Penguin, Inc. v. Janklow*, 98 F.R.D. 763, 766 (S.D.N.Y. 1983) (refusing to apply Lamb exception, even though claims closely related, because immunity would not obstruct prosecution of first action); *NASL Marketing, Inc.*, 94 F.R.D. at 310–11 (same); *United Nations v. Adler*, 90 F. Supp. 440, 442 (S.D.N.Y.1950) (same).

Here, granting Hwung immunity from service of process while in New York to attend the deposition will not obstruct the administration or purpose of Fun–Damental I. In Fun–Damental I, plaintiff alleges that Gemmy Industries and Kay–Bee infringed on its trade dress and seeks injunctive relief and damages. Plaintiff's attempt to obtain relief from those defendants will not be assisted by the prosecution of this action. Although plaintiff in this action seeks relief similar to that sought in Fun–Damental I, it seeks that relief from different defendants and its ability to obtain relief against the Fun–Damental I defendants will not be helped or hindered by this action. Therefore, the Lamb exception is inapplicable.

Accordingly, plaintiff's service of process on Hwung while he was attending the deposition in New York was invalid. Because plaintiff has alleged no other service on defendants, the action must be dismissed. Because I dismiss for insufficiency of service of process, I need not address defendants' motion to dismiss for lack of personal jurisdiction.

* * *

For the above reasons, defendants' motion to dismiss pursuant to Fed. R. Civ. P. 12(b)(5) is granted.

CHAPTER II

JURISDICTION AND VENUE

INTRODUCTION TO PERSONAL JURISDICTION

Notice alone is not enough to subject a defendant to the adjudicatory power of any court in which the plaintiff chooses to sue. Most of us would assume, for example, that a resident of France would not be obligated to come to New York to defend a lawsuit arising out of an automobile accident which occurred in France, even if a summons from a New York court were personally served on the French defendant in Paris, defendant received actual notice and the service met all the requirements of New York law. To have valid authority to adjudicate with respect to a potential defendant, there must be both legally adequate notice to that defendant, and a legally adequate relationship, or nexus, between the actions of the defendant and the forum state. This latter requirement is often described as the need for a court to have *personal jurisdiction* over the defendant.

What legal rules determine when a sufficient relationship exists between defendant and the forum state to subject the defendant to personal jurisdiction in the courts of that state? The regulatory structure is similar to the one we have already studied in Chapter I in connection with notice. The states, through statute and case law, set forth the legal standards which determine when their courts can exercise personal jurisdiction over various types of defendants with various types of relationships to the forum state. The states' power to exercise such personal jurisdiction is limited, however, by constitutional standards articulated by the United States Supreme Court pursuant to the Due Process Clause of the Fourteenth Amendment. While states do not have to confer on their courts the power to exercise personal jurisdiction to the fullest extent of the United States Constitution, many states do precisely that. Under our constitutional system, however, no state can validly exercise personal jurisdiction when doing so would exceed that state's power under the Due Process Clause.

The Supreme Court's view of the limits the Constitution places on states' power to exercise personal jurisdiction has changed over time. In the landmark case of *Pennoyer v. Neff*, 95 U.S. 714 (1877), the territorial limits of the state itself were seen as also limiting the state's power to exercise personal jurisdiction. If a defendant was geographically situated within the state, and could be served there, the state could validly exercise personal jurisdiction over that defendant. But if a potential defendant was a non-resident of the forum state, not subject to service in the state and owned no property there, under *Pennoyer* there could be no constitutionally valid exercise of personal jurisdiction over such a defendant. (Non-residents who did own property within the forum state were a different story, one we will consider a little later in this chapter.)

The expansion of interstate travel and interstate business activities in the late nineteenth and twentieth centuries created many more occasions for lawsuits against out-of-state defendants. In the cases that follow we see the Supreme Court redefining the constitutional limits on the exercise of personal jurisdiction by state courts, and lower courts seeking to understand and apply those limits. Which cases expand state power relative to the prior standards and which contract it? Who benefits and who is hurt by these changes?

A.　Contacts With the Forum State Based on the Stream of Commerce

International Shoe v. State of Washington

Supreme Court of the United States, 1945.
326 U.S. 310, 66 S. Ct. 154, 90 L. Ed. 95.

■ Mr. Chief Justice Stone delivered the opinion of the Court.

The questions for decision are (1) whether, within the limitations of the due process clause of the Fourteenth Amendment, appellant, a Delaware corporation, has by its activities in the State of Washington rendered itself amenable to proceedings in the courts of that state to recover unpaid contributions to the state unemployment compensation fund exacted by state statutes, and (2) whether the state can exact those contributions consistently with the due process clause of the Fourteenth Amendment.

The statutes in question set up a comprehensive scheme of unemployment compensation, the costs of which are defrayed by contributions required to be made by employers to a state unemployment compensation fund. The assessment and collection of the contributions and the fund are administered by appellees.

In this case notice of assessment for the years in question was personally served upon a sales solicitor employed by appellant in the State of Washington, and a copy of the notice was mailed by registered mail to appellant at its address in St. Louis, Missouri. Appellant appeared specially before the office of unemployment and moved to set aside the order and notice of assessment on the ground that the service upon appellant's salesman was not proper service upon appellant; that appellant was not a corporation of the State of Washington and was not doing business within the state; that it had no agent within the state upon whom service could be made; and that appellant is not an employer and does not furnish employment within the meaning of the statute.

The motion was heard on evidence and a stipulation of facts by the appeal tribunal which denied the motion and ruled that appellee

Commissioner was entitled to recover the unpaid contributions. That action was affirmed by the Commissioner; both the Superior Court and the Supreme Court affirmed. 22 Wash. 2d 146, 154 P. 2d 801. Appellant in each of these courts assailed the statute as applied, as a violation of the due process clause of the Fourteenth Amendment, and as imposing a constitutionally prohibited burden on interstate commerce. The cause comes here on appeal under § 237 (a) of the Judicial Code, 28 U. S. C. § 344 (a), appellant assigning as error that the challenged statutes as applied infringe the due process clause of the Fourteenth Amendment and the commerce clause.

Appellant has no office in Washington and makes no contracts either for sale or purchase of merchandise there. It maintains no stock of merchandise in that state and makes there no deliveries of goods in intrastate commerce. During the years from 1937 to 1940, now in question, appellant employed eleven to thirteen salesmen under direct supervision and control of sales managers located in St. Louis. These salesmen resided in Washington; their principal activities were confined to that state; and they were compensated by commissions based upon the amount of their sales. The commissions for each year totaled more than $31,000. Appellant supplies its salesmen with a line of samples, each consisting of one shoe of a pair, which they display to prospective purchasers. On occasion they rent permanent sample rooms, for exhibiting samples, in business buildings, or rent rooms in hotels or business buildings temporarily for that purpose. The cost of such rentals is reimbursed by appellant.

The authority of the salesmen is limited to exhibiting their samples and soliciting orders from prospective buyers, at prices and on terms fixed by appellant. The salesmen transmit the orders to appellant's office in St. Louis for acceptance or rejection, and when accepted the merchandise for filling the orders is shipped f. o. b. from points outside Washington to the purchasers within the state. All the merchandise shipped into Washington is invoiced at the place of shipment from which collections are made. No salesman has authority to enter into contracts or to make collections.

The Supreme Court of Washington was of opinion that the regular and systematic solicitation of orders in the state by appellant's salesmen, resulting in a continuous flow of appellant's product into the state, was sufficient to constitute doing business in the state so as to make appellant amenable to suit in its courts. But it was also of opinion that there were sufficient additional activities shown to bring the case within the rule frequently stated, that solicitation within a state by the agents of a foreign corporation plus some additional activities there are sufficient to render the corporation amenable to suit brought in the courts of the state to enforce an obligation arising out of its activities there. The court found such additional activities in the salesmen's display of samples sometimes in permanent display rooms, and the salesmen's residence within the state, continued over a period of years, all resulting in a substantial volume of merchandise regularly shipped by appellant to purchasers within the state.

Appellant also insists that its activities within the state were not sufficient to manifest its "presence" there and that in its absence the state courts were without jurisdiction, that consequently it was a denial of due process for the state to subject appellant to suit. And appellant further argues that since it was not present within the state, it is a denial of due process to subject it to taxation or other money exaction.

Historically the jurisdiction of courts to render judgment in personam is grounded on their de facto power over the defendant's person. Hence his presence within the territorial jurisdiction of a court was prerequisite to its rendition of a judgment personally binding him. Pennoyer v. Neff, 95 U.S. 714, 733. But now that the *capias ad respondendum* has given way to personal service of summons or other form of notice, due process requires only that in order to subject a defendant to a judgment in personam, if he be not present within the territory of the forum, he have certain minimum contacts with it such that the maintenance of the suit does not offend "traditional notions of fair play and substantial justice." Milliken v. Meyer, 311 U.S. 457, 463. See Holmes, J., in McDonald v. Mabee, 243 U.S. 90, 91. Compare Hoopeston Canning Co. v. Cullen, 318 U.S. 313, 316, 319. See Blackmer v. United States, 284 U.S. 421; Hess v. Pawloski, 274 U.S. 352; Young v. Masci, 289 U.S. 253.

Since the corporate personality is a fiction, although a fiction intended to be acted upon as though it were a fact, it is clear that unlike an individual its "presence" without, as well as within, the state of its origin can be manifested only by activities carried on in its behalf by those who are authorized to act for it. To say that the corporation is so far "present" there as to satisfy due process requirements, for purposes of taxation or the maintenance of suits against it in the courts of the state, is to beg the question to be decided. For the terms "present" or "presence" are used merely to symbolize those activities of the corporation's agent within the state which courts will deem to be sufficient to satisfy the demands of due process. Those demands may be met by such contacts of the corporation with the state of the forum as make it reasonable, in the context of our federal system of government, to require the corporation to defend the particular suit which is brought there. An "estimate of the inconveniences" which would result to the corporation from a trial away from its "home" or principal place of business is relevant in this connection.

"Presence" in the state in this sense has never been doubted when the activities of the corporation there have not only been continuous and systematic, but also give rise to the liabilities sued on, even though no consent to be sued or authorization to an agent to accept service of process has been given. Conversely it has been generally recognized that the casual presence of the corporate agent or even his conduct of single or isolated items of activities in a state in the corporation's behalf are not enough to subject it to suit on causes of action unconnected with the activities there. To require the corporation in such circumstances to defend the suit away from its home or other jurisdiction where it carries on more substantial activities has been thought to lay too great and unreasonable a burden on the corporation to comport with due process.

While it has been held, in cases on which appellant relies, that continuous activity of some sorts within a state is not enough to support the demand that the corporation be amenable to suits unrelated to that activity, there have been instances in which the continuous corporate operations within a state were thought so substantial and of such a nature as to justify suit against it on causes of action arising from dealings entirely distinct from those activities.

Finally, although the commission of some single or occasional acts of the corporate agent in a state sufficient to impose an obligation or liability on the corporation has not been thought to confer upon the state authority to enforce it, other such acts, because of their nature and quality and the circumstances of their commission, may be deemed sufficient to render the corporation liable to suit. True, some of the decisions holding the corporation amenable to suit have been supported by resort to the legal fiction that it has given its consent to service and suit, consent being implied from its presence in the state through the acts of its authorized agents. But more realistically it may be said that those authorized acts were of such a nature as to justify the fiction.

It is evident that the criteria by which we mark the boundary line between those activities which justify the subjection of a corporation to suit, and those which do not, cannot be simply mechanical or quantitative. Whether due process is satisfied must depend rather upon the quality and nature of the activity in relation to the fair and orderly administration of the laws which it was the purpose of the due process clause to insure. That clause does not contemplate that a state may make binding a judgment in personam against an individual or corporate defendant with which the state has no contacts, ties, or relations.

But to the extent that a corporation exercises the privilege of conducting activities within a state, it enjoys the benefits and protection of the laws of that state. The exercise of that privilege may give rise to obligations, and, so far as those obligations arise out of or are connected with the activities within the state, a procedure which requires the corporation to respond to a suit brought to enforce them can, in most instances, hardly be said to be undue.

Applying these standards, the activities carried on in behalf of appellant in the State of Washington were neither irregular nor casual. They were systematic and continuous throughout the years in question. They resulted in a large volume of interstate business, in the course of which appellant received the benefits and protection of the laws of the state, including the right to resort to the courts for the enforcement of its rights. The obligation which is here sued upon arose out of those very activities. It is evident that these operations establish sufficient contacts or ties with the state of the forum to make it reasonable and just, according to our traditional conception of fair play and substantial justice, to permit the state to enforce the obligations which appellant has incurred there.

Affirmed.

■ Mr. Justice Jackson took no part in the consideration or decision of this case.

■ Mr. Justice Black delivered the following opinion.

I believe that the Federal Constitution leaves to each State, without any "ifs" or "buts," a power to tax and to open the doors of its courts for its citizens to sue corporations whose agents do business in those States. Believing that the Constitution gave the States that power, I think it a judicial deprivation to condition its exercise upon this Court's notion of "fair play," however appealing that term may be. Nor can I stretch the meaning of due process so far as to authorize this Court to deprive a State of the right to afford judicial protection to its citizens on the ground that it would be more "convenient" for the corporation to be sued somewhere else.

There is a strong emotional appeal in the words "fair play," "justice," and "reasonableness." But they were not chosen by those who wrote the original Constitution or the Fourteenth Amendment as a measuring rod for this Court to use in invalidating State or Federal laws passed by elected legislative representatives. No one, not even those who most feared a democratic government, ever formally proposed that courts should be given power to invalidate legislation under any such elastic standards. Express prohibitions against certain types of legislation are found in the Constitution, and under the long-settled practice, courts invalidate laws found to conflict with them. This requires interpretation, and interpretation, it is true, may result in extension of the Constitution's purpose. But that is no reason for reading the due process clause so as to restrict a State's power to tax and sue those whose activities affect persons and businesses within the State, provided proper service can be had. Superimposing the natural justice conception the Constitution's specific prohibitions could operate as a drastic abridgment of democratic safeguards they embody, such as freedom of speech, press and religion, and the right to counsel.

World–Wide Volkswagen Corp. v. Woodson

Supreme Court of the United States, 1980.
444 U.S. 286, 100 S.Ct. 559, 62 L.Ed.2d 490.

■ Mr. Justice White delivered the opinion of the Court.

The issue before us is whether, consistently with the Due Process Clause of the Fourteenth Amendment, an Oklahoma court may exercise *in personam* jurisdiction over a nonresident automobile retailer and its wholesale distributor in a products-liability action, when the defendants' only connection with Oklahoma is the fact that an automobile sold in New York to New York residents became involved in an accident in Oklahoma.

I

Respondents Harry and Kay Robinson purchased a new Audi automobile from petitioner Seaway Volkswagen, Inc. (Seaway), in Massena, N.Y., in 1976. The following year the Robinson family, who resided in New York, left that State for a new home in Arizona. As they passed through the State of Oklahoma, another car struck their Audi in the rear, causing a fire which severely burned Kay Robinson and her two children.[1]

The Robinsons subsequently brought a products-liability action in the District Court for Creek County, Okla., claiming that their injuries resulted from defective design and placement of the Audi's gas tank and fuel system. They joined as defendants the automobile's manufacturer, Audi NSU Auto Union Aktiengesellschaft (Audi); its importer, Volkswagen of America, Inc. (Volkswagen); its regional distributor, petitioner World–Wide Volkswagen Corp. (World–Wide); and its retail dealer, petitioner Seaway. Seaway and World–Wide entered special appearances,[3] claiming that Oklahoma's exercise of jurisdiction over them would offend the limitations on the State's jurisdiction imposed by the Due Process Clause of the Fourteenth Amendment.

The facts presented to the District Court showed that World–Wide is incorporated and has its business office in New York. It distributes vehicles, parts, and accessories, under contract with Volkswagen, to retail dealers in New York, New Jersey, and Connecticut. Seaway, one of those retail dealers, is incorporated and has its place of business in New York. Insofar as the record reveals, Seaway and World–Wide are fully independent corporations whose relations with each other and with Volkswagen and Audi are contractual only. Respondents adduced no evidence that either World–Wide or Seaway does any business in Oklahoma, ships or sells any products to or in that State, has an agent to receive process there, or purchases advertisements in any media calculated to reach Oklahoma. In fact, as respondents' counsel conceded at oral argument, Tr. of Oral Arg. 32, there was no showing that any automobile sold by World–Wide or Seaway has ever entered Oklahoma with the single exception of the vehicle involved in the present case.

Despite the apparent paucity of contacts between petitioners and Oklahoma, the District Court rejected their constitutional claim and reaffirmed that ruling in denying petitioners' motion for reconsideration. Petitioners then sought a writ of prohibition in the Supreme Court of Oklahoma to restrain the District Judge, respondent Charles S. Woodson, from exercising *in personam* jurisdiction over them. They renewed their contention that, because they had no "minimal contacts," App. 32, with the State of Oklahoma, the actions of the District Judge were in violation of their rights under the Due Process Clause.

1. The driver of the other automobile does not figure in the present litigation.

3. Volkswagen also entered a special appearance in the District Court, but unlike World–Wide and Seaway did not seek review in the Supreme Court of Oklahoma and is not a petitioner here. Both Volkswagen and Audi remain as defendants in the litigation pending before the District Court in Oklahoma.

The Supreme Court of Oklahoma denied the writ, 585 P.2d 351 (1978), holding that personal jurisdiction over petitioners was authorized by Oklahoma's "long-arm" statute. Okla.Stat., Tit. 12, § 1701.03(a)(4) (1971).[7] Although the court noted that the proper approach was to test jurisdiction against both statutory and constitutional standards, its analysis did not distinguish these questions, probably because § 1701.03(a)(4) has been interpreted as conferring jurisdiction to the limits permitted by the United States Constitution. * * *

We granted certiorari, 440 U.S. 907 (1979), to consider an important constitutional question with respect to state-court jurisdiction and to resolve a conflict between the Supreme Court of Oklahoma and the highest courts of at least four other States. We reverse.

II

The Due Process Clause of the Fourteenth Amendment limits the power of a state court to render a valid personal judgment against a nonresident defendant. Kulko v. California Superior Court, 436 U.S. 84, 91, 98 S.Ct. 1690, 1696, 56 L.Ed.2d 132 (1978). A judgment rendered in violation of due process is void in the rendering State and is not entitled to full faith and credit elsewhere. Pennoyer v. Neff, 95 U.S. 714, 732–733, 24 L.Ed. 565 (1877). Due process requires that the defendant be given adequate notice of the suit, Mullane v. Central Hanover Trust Co., 339 U.S. 306, 313–314, 70 S.Ct. 652, 657, 94 L.Ed. 865 (1950), and be subject to the personal jurisdiction of the court, International Shoe Co. v. Washington, 326 U.S. 310, 66 S.Ct. 154, 90 L.Ed. 95 (1945). In the present case, it is not contended that notice was inadequate; the only question is whether these particular petitioners were subject to the jurisdiction of the Oklahoma courts.

As has long been settled, and as we reaffirm today, a state court may exercise personal jurisdiction over a nonresident defendant only so long as there exist "minimum contacts" between the defendant and the forum State. *International Shoe Co. v. Washington, supra,* at 316, 66 S.Ct., at 158. The concept of minimum contacts, in turn, can be seen to perform two related, but distinguishable, functions. It protects the defendant against the burdens of litigating in a distant or inconvenient forum. And it acts to ensure that the States, through their courts, do not reach out beyond the limits imposed on them by their status as coequal sovereigns in a federal system.

---

7. This subsection provides:
"A court may exercise personal jurisdiction over a person, who acts directly or by an agent, as to a cause of action or claim for relief arising from the person's * * * causing tortious injury in this state by an act or omission outside this state if he regularly does or solicits business or engages in any other persistent course of conduct, or derives substantial revenue from goods used or consumed or services rendered, in this state. * * * "

The State Supreme Court rejected jurisdiction based on § 1701.03(a)(3), which authorizes jurisdiction over any person "causing tortious injury in this state by an act or omission in this state." Something in addition to the infliction of tortious injury was required.

The protection against inconvenient litigation is typically described in terms of "reasonableness" or "fairness." We have said that the defendant's contacts with the forum State must be such that maintenance of the suit "does not offend 'traditional notions of fair play and substantial justice.' " *International Shoe Co. v. Washington, supra,* at 316, 66 S.Ct., at 158, quoting Milliken v. Meyer, 311 U.S. 457, 463, 61 S.Ct. 339, 342, 85 L.Ed. 278 (1940). The relationship between the defendant and the forum must be such that it is "reasonable * * * to require the corporation to defend the particular suit which is brought there." 326 U.S., at 317, 66 S.Ct., at 158. Implicit in this emphasis on reasonableness is the understanding that the burden on the defendant, while always a primary concern, will in an appropriate case be considered in light of other relevant factors, including the forum State's interest in adjudicating the dispute, see McGee v. International Life Ins. Co., 355 U.S. 220, 223, 78 S.Ct. 199, 201, 2 L.Ed.2d 223 (1957); the plaintiff's interest in obtaining convenient and effective relief, see *Kulko v. California Superior Court, supra,* at 92, at least when that interest is not adequately protected by the plaintiff's power to choose the forum, cf. Shaffer v. Heitner, 433 U.S. 186, 211, n. 37, 97 S.Ct. 2569, 2583, n. 37, 53 L.Ed.2d 683 (1977); the interstate judicial system's interest in obtaining the most efficient resolution of controversies; and the shared interest of the several States in furthering fundamental substantive social policies, see *Kulko v. California Superior Court, supra,* at 93, 98, 98 S.Ct., at 1697, 1700.

The limits imposed on state jurisdiction by the Due Process Clause, in its role as a guarantor against inconvenient litigation, have been substantially relaxed over the years. As we noted in *McGee v. International Life Ins. Co., supra,* at 222–223, 78 S.Ct., at 201, this trend is largely attributable to a fundamental transformation in the American economy:

> "Today many commercial transactions touch two or more States and may involve parties separated by the full continent. With this increasing nationalization of commerce has come a great increase in the amount of business conducted by mail across state lines. At the same time modern transportation and communication have made it much less burdensome for a party sued to defend himself in a State where he engages in economic activity."

The historical developments noted in *McGee,* of course, have only accelerated in the generation since that case was decided.

Nevertheless, we have never accepted the proposition that state lines are irrelevant for jurisdictional purposes, nor could we, and remain faithful to the principles of interstate federalism embodied in the Constitution. The economic interdependence of the States was foreseen and desired by the Framers. In the Commerce Clause, they provided that the Nation was to be a common market, a "free trade unit" in which the States are debarred from acting as separable economic entities. H.P. Hood & Sons, Inc. v. Du Mond, 336 U.S. 525, 538, 69 S.Ct. 657, 665, 93 L.Ed. 865 (1949). But the Framers also intended that the States retain many essential attributes of sovereignty, including, in particular, the sovereign power to try causes in their courts. The sovereignty of each State, in turn, implied a limitation on the sovereignty of all of its sister States—a limitation express or implicit in both the original scheme of the Constitution and the Fourteenth Amendment.

Hence, even while abandoning the shibboleth that "[t]he authority of every tribunal is necessarily restricted by the territorial limits of the State in which it is established," *Pennoyer v. Neff, supra,* at 720, we emphasized that the reasonableness of asserting jurisdiction over the defendant must be assessed "in the context of our federal system of government," International Shoe Co. v. Washington, 326 U.S., at 317, 66 S.Ct., at 158, and stressed that the Due Process Clause ensures not only fairness, but also the "orderly administration of the laws," *id.,* at 319. As we noted in Hanson v. Denckla, 357 U.S. 235, 250–251, 78 S.Ct. 1228, 2 L.Ed.2d 1283 (1958):

> "As technological progress has increased the flow of commerce between the States, the need for jurisdiction over nonresidents has undergone a similar increase. At the same time, progress in communications and transportation has made the defense of a suit in a foreign tribunal less burdensome. In response to these changes, the requirements for personal jurisdiction over nonresidents have evolved from the rigid rule of Pennoyer v. Neff, 95 U.S. 714, 24 L.Ed. 565, to the flexible standard of International Shoe Co. v. Washington, 326 U.S. 310, 66 S.Ct. 154, 90 L.Ed. 95. But it is a mistake to assume that this trend heralds the eventual demise of all restrictions on the personal jurisdiction of state courts. [Citation omitted.] Those restrictions are more than a guarantee of immunity from inconvenient or distant litigation. They are a consequence of territorial limitations on the power of the respective States."

Thus, the Due Process Clause "does not contemplate that a state may make binding a judgment *in personam* against an individual or corporate defendant with which the state has no contacts, ties, or relations." *International Shoe Co. v. Washington, supra,* at 319. Even if the defendant would suffer minimal or no inconvenience from being forced to litigate before the tribunals of another State; even if the forum State has a strong interest in applying its law to the controversy; even if the forum State is the most convenient location for litigation, the Due Process Clause, acting as an instrument of interstate federalism, may sometimes act to divest the State of its power to render a valid judgment. *Hanson v. Denckla, supra,* at 251, 254, 78 S.Ct., at 1238, 1240.

III

Applying these principles to the case at hand,[10] we find in the record before us a total absence of those affiliating circumstances that

---

10. Respondents argue, as a threshold matter, that petitioners waived any objections to personal jurisdiction by (1) joining with their special appearances a challenge to

are a necessary predicate to any exercise of state-court jurisdiction. Petitioners carry on no activity whatsoever in Oklahoma. They close no sales and perform no services there. They avail themselves of none of the privileges and benefits of Oklahoma law. They solicit no business there either through salespersons or through advertising reasonably calculated to reach the State. Nor does the record show that they regularly sell cars at wholesale or retail to Oklahoma customers or residents or that they indirectly, through others, serve or seek to serve the Oklahoma market. In short, respondents seek to base jurisdiction on one, isolated occurrence and whatever inferences can be drawn therefrom: the fortuitous circumstance that a single Audi automobile, sold in New York to New York residents, happened to suffer an accident while passing through Oklahoma.

It is argued, however, that because an automobile is mobile by its very design and purpose it was "foreseeable" that the Robinsons' Audi would cause injury in Oklahoma. Yet "foreseeability" alone has never been a sufficient benchmark for personal jurisdiction under the Due Process Clause. In *Hanson v. Denckla, supra,* it was no doubt foreseeable that the settlor of a Delaware trust would subsequently move to Florida and seek to exercise a power of appointment there; yet we held that Florida courts could not constitutionally exercise jurisdiction over a Delaware trustee that had no other contacts with the forum State. In Kulko v. California Superior Court, 436 U.S. 84, 98 S.Ct. 1690, 56 L.Ed.2d 132 (1978), it was surely "foreseeable" that a divorced wife would move to California from New York, the domicile of the marriage, and that a minor daughter would live with the mother. Yet we held that California could not exercise jurisdiction in a child-support action over the former husband who had remained in New York.

If foreseeability were the criterion, a local California tire retailer could be forced to defend in Pennsylvania when a blowout occurs there, see Erlanger Mills, Inc. v. Cohoes Fibre Mills, Inc., 239 F.2d 502, 507 (C.A.4 1956); a Wisconsin seller of a defective automobile jack could be haled before a distant court for damage caused in New Jersey, Reilly v. Phil Tolkan Pontiac, Inc., 372 F.Supp. 1205 (D.N.J. 1974); or a Florida soft-drink concessionaire could be summoned to Alaska to account for injuries happening there, see Uppgren v. Executive Aviation Services, Inc., 304 F.Supp. 165, 170–171 (D.Minn.1969). Every seller of chattels would in effect appoint the chattel his agent for service of process. His amenability to suit would travel with the chattel. We recently abandoned the outworn rule of Harris v. Balk, 198 U.S. 215, 25 S.Ct. 625, 49 L.Ed. 1023 (1905), that the interest of a creditor in a debt could be extinguished or otherwise affected by any State having transitory jurisdiction over the debtor. Shaffer v. Heitner,

the District Court's subject-matter jurisdiction, see n. 4, *supra,* and (2) taking depositions on the merits of the case in Oklahoma. The trial court, however, characterized the appearances as "special," and the Oklahoma Supreme Court, rather than finding jurisdiction waived, reached and decided the statutory and constitutional questions. Cf. Kulko v. California Superior Court, 436 U.S. 84, 91, n. 5, 98 S.Ct. 1690, 1696, n. 5, 56 L.Ed.2d 132 (1978).

433 U.S. 186, 97 S.Ct. 2569, 53 L.Ed.2d 683 (1977). Having interred the mechanical rule that a creditor's amenability to a *quasi in rem* action travels with his debtor, we are unwilling to endorse an analogous principle in the present case.[11]

This is not to say, of course, that foreseeability is wholly irrelevant. But the foreseeability that is critical to due process analysis is not the mere likelihood that a product will find its way into the forum State. Rather, it is that the defendant's conduct and connection with the forum State are such that he should reasonably anticipate being haled into court there. See *Kulko v. California Superior Court, supra,* at 97–98, 98 S.Ct., at 1699–1700; Shaffer v. Heitner, 433 U.S., at 216, 97 S.Ct., at 2586; and see *id.,* at 217–219, 97 S.Ct., at 2586–2587 (STEVENS, J., concurring in judgment). The Due Process Clause, by ensuring the "orderly administration of the laws," International Shoe Co. v. Washington, 326 U.S., at 319, 66 S.Ct., at 159, gives a degree of predictability to the legal system that allows potential defendants to structure their primary conduct with some minimum assurance as to where that conduct will and will not render them liable to suit.

When a corporation "purposefully avails itself of the privilege of conducting activities within the forum State." Hanson v. Denckla, 357 U.S., at 253, 78 S.Ct., at 1240, it has clear notice that it is subject to suit there, and can act to alleviate the risk of burdensome litigation by procuring insurance, passing the expected costs on to customers, or, if the risks are too great, severing its connection with the State. Hence if the sale of a product of a manufacturer or distributor such as Audi or Volkswagen is not simply an isolated occurrence, but arises from the efforts of the manufacturer or distributor to serve, directly or indirectly, the market for its product in other States, it is not unreasonable to subject it to suit in one of those States if its allegedly defective merchandise has there been the source of injury to its owner or to others. The forum State does not exceed its powers under the Due Process Clause if it asserts personal jurisdiction over a corporation that delivers its products into the stream of commerce with the expectation that they will be purchased by consumers in the forum State. Cf. Gray v. American Radiator & Standard Sanitary Corp., 22 Ill.2d 432, 176 N.E.2d 761 (1961).

But there is no such or similar basis for Oklahoma jurisdiction over World–Wide or Seaway in this case. Seaway's sales are made in Massena, N.Y. World–Wide's market, although substantially larger, is

---

11. Respondents' counsel, at oral argument, see Tr. of Oral Arg. 19–22, 29, sought to limit the reach of the foreseeability standard by suggesting that there is something unique about automobiles. It is true that automobiles are uniquely mobile, see Tyson v. Whitaker & Son, Inc., 407 A.2d 1, 6, and n. 11 (Me.1979) (McKusick, C.J.), that they did play a crucial role in the expansion of personal jurisdiction through the fiction of implied consent, *e.g.*, Hess v. Pawloski, 274 U.S. 352, 47 S.Ct. 632, 71 L.Ed. 1091 (1927), and that some of the cases have treated the automobile as a "dangerous instrumentality." But today, under the regime of *International Shoe*, we see no difference for jurisdictional purposes between an automobile and any other chattel. The "dangerous instrumentality" concept apparently was never used to support personal jurisdiction; and to the extent it has relevance today it bears not on jurisdiction but on the possible desirability of imposing substantive principles of tort law such as strict liability.

limited to dealers in New York, New Jersey, and Connecticut. There is no evidence of record that any automobiles distributed by World–Wide are sold to retail customers outside this tristate area. It is foreseeable that the purchasers of automobiles sold by World–Wide and Seaway may take them to Oklahoma. But the mere "unilateral activity of those who claim some relationship with a nonresident defendant cannot satisfy the requirement of contact with the forum State." Hanson v. Denckla, supra, at 253, 78 S.Ct., at 1239–1240.

In a variant on the previous argument, it is contended that jurisdiction can be supported by the fact that petitioners earn substantial revenue from goods used in Oklahoma. The Oklahoma Supreme Court so found, 585 P.2d, at 354–355, drawing the inference that because one automobile sold by petitioners had been used in Oklahoma, others might have been used there also. While this inference seems less than compelling on the facts of the instant case, we need not question the court's factual findings in order to reject its reasoning.

This argument seems to make the point that the purchase of automobiles in New York, from which the petitioners earn substantial revenue, would not occur *but for* the fact that the automobiles are capable of use in distant States like Oklahoma. Respondents observe that the very purpose of an automobile is to travel, and that travel of automobiles sold by petitioners is facilitated by an extensive chain of Volkswagen service centers throughout the country, including some in Oklahoma. However, financial benefits accruing to the defendant from a collateral relation to the forum State will not support jurisdiction if they do not stem from a constitutionally cognizable contact with that State. See Kulko v. California Superior Court, 436 U.S., at 94–95, 98 S.Ct., at 1698–1699. In our view, whatever marginal revenues petitioners may receive by virtue of the fact that their products are capable of use in Oklahoma is far too attenuated a contact to justify that State's exercise of *in personam* jurisdiction over them.

Because we find that petitioners have no "contacts, ties, or relations" with the State of Oklahoma, *International Shoe Co. v. Washington, supra,* at 319, 66 S.Ct., at 159, the judgment of the Supreme Court of Oklahoma is

Reversed.

■ Mr. Justice Brennan, dissenting.[a]

The Court holds that the Due Process Clause of the Fourteenth Amendment bars the States from asserting jurisdiction over the defendants in these two cases. In each case the Court so decides because it fails to find the "minimum contacts" that have been required since International Shoe Co. v. Washington, 326 U.S. 310, 316, 66 S.Ct. 154, 158, 90 L.Ed. 95 (1945). Because I believe that the Court reads *International Shoe* and its progeny too narrowly, and because I

----

a. Justice Brennan's dissent, in the instant case and in a companion case, appears   at 444 U.S. 286, 100 S.Ct. 580, 62 L.Ed.2d 490 (1980).

believe that the standards enunciated by those cases may already be obsolete as constitutional boundaries, I dissent.

I

The Court's opinions focus tightly on the existence of contacts between the forum and the defendant. In so doing, they accord too little weight to the strength of the forum State's interest in the case and fail to explore whether there would be any actual inconvenience to the defendant. The essential inquiry in locating the constitutional limits on state-court jurisdiction over absent defendants is whether the particular exercise of jurisdiction offends " 'traditional notions of fair play and substantial justice.' " *International Shoe, supra,* at 316, quoting Milliken v. Meyer, 311 U.S. 457, 463 (1940). The clear focus in *International Shoe* was on fairness and reasonableness. Kulko v. California Superior Court, 436 U.S. 84, 92 (1978). The Court specifically declined to establish a mechanical test based on the quantum of contacts between a State and the defendant * * * The existence of contacts, so long as there were some, was merely one way of giving content to the determination of fairness and reasonableness.

Surely *International Shoe* contemplated that the significance of the contacts necessary to support jurisdiction would diminish if some other consideration helped establish that jurisdiction would be fair and reasonable. The interests of the State and other parties in proceeding with the case in a particular forum are such considerations.

* * *

Another consideration is the actual burden a defendant must bear in defending the suit in the forum. *McGee, supra.* Because lesser burdens reduce the unfairness to the defendant, jurisdiction may be justified despite less significant contacts. The burden, of course, must be of constitutional dimension. Due process limits on jurisdiction do not protect a defendant from all inconvenience of travel, *McGee, supra,* at 224, and it would not be sensible to make the constitutional rule turn solely on the number of miles the defendant must travel to the courtroom.[1] Instead, the constitutionally significant "burden" to be analyzed relates to the mobility of the defendant's defense. For instance, if having to travel to a foreign forum would hamper the defense because witnesses or evidence or the defendant himself were immobile, or if there were a disproportionately large number of witnesses or amount of evidence that would have to be transported at the defendant's expense, or if being away from home for the duration of the trial would work some special hardship on the defendant, then the Constitution would require special consideration for the defendant's interests.

That considerations other than contacts between the forum and the defendant are relevant necessarily means that the Constitution

---

1. In fact, a courtroom just across the state line from a defendant may often be far more convenient for the defendant than a courtroom in a distant corner of his own State.

does not require that trial be held in the State which has the "best contacts" with the defendant. * * * The defendant has no constitutional entitlement to the best forum or, for that matter, to any particular forum. Under even the most restrictive view of *International Shoe,* several States could have jurisdiction over a particular cause of action. We need only determine whether the forum States in these cases satisfy the constitutional minimum.

II

In each of these cases, I would find that the forum State has an interest in permitting the litigation to go forward, the litigation is connected to the forum, the defendant is linked to the forum, and the burden of defending is not unreasonable. Accordingly, I would hold that it is neither unfair nor unreasonable to require these defendants to defend in the forum State. * * *

[T]he interest of the forum State and its connection to the litigation is strong. The automobile accident underlying the litigation occurred in Oklahoma. The plaintiffs were hospitalized in Oklahoma when they brought suit. Essential witnesses and evidence were in Oklahoma. See Shaffer v. Heitner, 433 U.S., at 208. The State has a legitimate interest in enforcing its laws designed to keep its highway system safe, and the trial can proceed at least as efficiently in Oklahoma as anywhere else.

The petitioners are not unconnected with the forum. Although both sell automobiles within limited sales territories, each sold the automobile which in fact was driven to Oklahoma where it was involved in an accident. It may be true, as the Court suggests, that each sincerely intended to limit its commercial impact to the limited territory, and that each intended to accept the benefits and protection of the laws only of those States within the territory. But obviously these were unrealistic hopes that cannot be treated as an automatic constitutional shield.[9]

An automobile simply is not a stationary item or one designed to be used in one place. An automobile is *intended* to be moved around. Someone in the business of selling large numbers of automobiles can hardly plead ignorance of their mobility or pretend that the automobiles stay put after they are sold. It is not merely that a dealer in automobiles foresees that they will move. * * * The dealer actually intends that the purchasers will use the automobiles to travel to distant States where the dealer does not directly "do business." The sale of an automobile does *purposefully* inject the vehicle into the stream of interstate commerce so that it can travel to distant States.

---

9. Moreover, imposing liability in this case would not so undermine certainty as to destroy an automobile dealer's ability to do business. According jurisdiction does not expand liability except in the marginal case where a plaintiff cannot afford to bring an action except in the plaintiff's own State. In addition, these petitioners are represented by insurance companies. They not only could, but did, purchase insurance to protect them should they stand trial and lose the case. The costs of the insurance no doubt are passed on to customers.

See *Kulko,* 436 U.S., at 94; Hanson v. Denckla, 357 U.S. 235, 253 (1958).

* * *

The Court accepts that a State may exercise jurisdiction over a distributor which "serves" that State "indirectly" by "deliver[ing] its products into the stream of commerce with the expectation that they will be purchased by consumers in the forum State." * * * It is difficult to see why the Constitution should distinguish between a case involving goods which reach a distant State through a chain of distribution and a case involving goods which reach the same State because a consumer, using them as the dealer knew the customer would, took them there.[11] In each case the seller purposefully injects the goods into the stream of commerce and those goods predictably are used in the forum State.

Furthermore, an automobile seller derives substantial benefits from States other than its own. A large part of the value of automobiles is the extensive, nationwide network of highways. Significant portions of that network have been constructed by and are maintained by the individual States, including Oklahoma. The States, through their highway programs, contribute in a very direct and important way to the value of petitioners' businesses. Additionally, a network of other related dealerships with their service departments operates throughout the country under the protection of the laws of the various States, including Oklahoma, and enhances the value of petitioners' businesses by facilitating their customers' traveling.

Thus, the Court errs in its conclusion, * * * (emphasis added), that "petitioners have *no* 'contacts, ties, or relations' " with Oklahoma. There obviously are contacts, and, given Oklahoma's connection to the litigation, the contacts are sufficiently significant to make it fair and reasonable for the petitioners to submit to Oklahoma's jurisdiction.

III

It may be that affirmance of the judgments in these cases would approach the outer limits of *International Shoe*'s jurisdictional principle. But that principle, with its almost exclusive focus on the rights of defendants, may be outdated.

* * *

In answering the question whether or not it is fair and reasonable to allow a particular forum to hold a trial binding on a particular defendant, the interests of the forum State and other parties loom large in today's world and surely are entitled to as much weight as are the interests of the defendant. The "orderly administration of the laws" provides a firm basis for according some protection to the

---

11. For example, I cannot understand the constitutional distinction between selling an item in New Jersey and selling an item in New York expecting it to be used in New Jersey.

interests of plaintiffs and States as well as of defendants.[14] Certainly, I cannot see how a defendant's right to due process is violated if the defendant suffers no inconvenience. * * *

The conclusion I draw is that constitutional concepts of fairness no longer require the extreme concern for defendants that was once necessary. * * * When an action in fact causes injury in another State, the actor should be prepared to answer for it there unless defending in that State would be unfair for some reason other than that a state boundary must be crossed.

In effect the Court is allowing defendants to assert the sovereign rights of their home States. The expressed fear is that otherwise all limits on personal jurisdiction would disappear. But the argument's premise is wrong. I would not abolish limits on jurisdiction or strip state boundaries of all significance; I would still require the plaintiff to demonstrate sufficient contacts among the parties, the forum, and the litigation to make the forum a reasonable State in which to hold the trial. * * *

The plaintiffs * * * brought suit in a forum with which they had significant contacts and which had significant contacts with the litigation. I am not convinced that the defendants would suffer any "heavy and disproportionate burden" in defending the suits. Accordingly, I would hold that the Constitution should not shield the defendants from appearing and defending in the plaintiffs' chosen fora.[b]

NOTES

A. The Oklahoma statute is set forth in note 7 of the Supreme Court opinion. Could that statute have been interpreted so that under Oklahoma law there was no personal jurisdiction over these defendants? Is such a reading less plausible than the one adopted by the Oklahoma Supreme Court?

B. Note 1 of the United States Supreme Court opinion refers to the driver of the other car who "does not figure in the present litigation." If this suit included the Oklahoma driver as a party plaintiff would that fact weigh in favor of Oklahoma having jurisdiction over the defendants?

Asahi Metal Ind. v. Superior Court of California

Supreme Court of the United States, 1987.
480 U.S. 102, 107 S.Ct. 1026, 94 L.Ed.2d 92.

■ Justice O'Connor announced the judgment of the Court and delivered the unanimous opinion of the Court with respect to Part I, the

---

14. The Court has recognized that there are cases where the interests of justice can turn the focus of the jurisdictional inquiry away from the contacts between a defendant and the forum State. For instance, the Court indicated that the requirement of contacts may be greatly relaxed (if indeed any personal contacts would be required) where a plaintiff is suing a nonresident defendant to enforce a judgment procured in another State. Shaffer v. Heitner, 433 U.S., at 210–211, nn. 36, 37.

b. The dissenting opinions of Justices Marshall and Blackmun, which argue that Seaway (the retailer) and WorldWide (the regional distributor) had enough contacts with Oklahoma to satisfy due process requirements are omitted.

opinion of the Court with respect to Part II–B, in which THE CHIEF JUSTICE, JUSTICE BRENNAN, JUSTICE WHITE, JUSTICE MARSHALL, JUSTICE BLACKMUN, JUSTICE POWELL, and JUSTICE STEVENS join, and an opinion with respect to Parts II–A and III, in which THE CHIEF JUSTICE, JUSTICE POWELL, and JUSTICE SCALIA join.

This case presents the question whether the mere awareness on the part of a foreign defendant that the components it manufactured, sold, and delivered outside the United States would reach the forum state in the stream of commerce constitutes "minimum contacts" between the defendant and the forum state such that the exercise of jurisdiction "does not offend 'traditional notions of fair play and substantial justice.'" International Shoe Co. v. Washington, 326 U.S. 310, 316, 66 S.Ct. 154, 158, 90 L.Ed. 95 (1945), quoting Milliken v. Meyer, 311 U.S. 457, 463, 61 S.Ct. 339, 342, 85 L.Ed. 278 (1940).

I

On September 23, 1978, on Interstate Highway 80 in Solano County, California, Gary Zurcher lost control of his Honda motorcycle and collided with a tractor. Zurcher was severely injured, and his passenger and wife, Ruth Ann Moreno, was killed. In September 1979, Zurcher filed a product liability action in the Superior Court of the State of California in and for the County of Solano. Zurcher alleged that the 1978 accident was caused by a sudden loss of air and an explosion in the rear tire of the motorcycle, and alleged that the motorcycle tire, tube, and sealant were defective. Zurcher's complaint named, *inter alia,* Cheng Shin Rubber Industrial Co., Ltd. (Cheng Shin), the Taiwanese manufacturer of the tube. Cheng Shin in turn filed a cross-complaint[a] seeking indemnification from its codefendants and from petitioner, Asahi Metal Industry Co., Ltd. (Asahi), the manufacturer of the tube's valve assembly. Zurcher's claims against Cheng Shin and the other defendants were eventually settled and dismissed, leaving only Cheng Shin's indemnity action against Asahi.

California's long-arm statute authorizes the exercise of jurisdiction "on any basis not inconsistent with the Constitution of this state or of the United States." Cal.Code Civ.Proc.Ann. § 410.10 (West 1973). Asahi moved to quash Cheng Shin's service of summons arguing the State could not exert jurisdiction over it consistent with the Due Process Clause of the Fourteenth Amendment.

In relation to the motion, the following information was submitted by Asahi and Cheng Shin. Asahi is a Japanese corporation. It manufactures tire valve assemblies in Japan and sells the assemblies to Cheng Shin, and to several other tire manufacturers, for use as components in finished tire tubes. Asahi's sales to Cheng Shin took place in Taiwan. The shipments from Asahi to Cheng Shin were sent from Japan to Taiwan. Cheng Shin bought and incorporated into its tire tubes 150,000 Asahi valve assemblies in 1978; 500,000 in 1979;

a. Although termed a cross-complaint under California practice, this is equivalent to a third party complaint under F.R.C.P. 14.

500,000 in 1980; 100,000 in 1981; and 100,000 in 1982. Sales to Cheng Shin accounted for 1.24 percent of Asahi's income in 1981 and 0.44 percent in 1982. Cheng Shin alleged that approximately 20 percent of its sales in the United States are in California. Cheng Shin purchases valve assemblies from other suppliers as well, and sells finished tubes throughout the world.

In 1983 an attorney for Cheng Shin conducted an informal examination of the valve stems of the tire tubes sold in one cyclery in Solano County. The attorney declared that of the approximately 115 tire tubes in the store, 97 were purportedly manufactured in Japan or Taiwan, and of those 97, 21 valve stems were marked with the circled letter "A", apparently Asahi's trademark. Of the 21 Asahi valve stems, 12 were incorporated into Cheng Shin tire tubes. The store contained 41 other Cheng Shin tubes that incorporated the valve assemblies of other manufacturers. Declaration of Kenneth B. Shepard in Opposition to Motion to Quash Subpoena, App. to Brief for Respondent 5–6. An affidavit of a manager of Cheng Shin whose duties included the purchasing of component parts stated: " 'In discussions with Asahi regarding the purchase of valve stem assemblies the fact that my Company sells tubes throughout the world and specifically the United States has been discussed. I am informed and believe that Asahi was fully aware that valve stem assemblies sold to my Company and to others would end up throughout the United States and in California.' " 39 Cal.3d 35, 48, n. 4, 216 Cal.Rptr. 385, 392, n. 4, 702 P.2d 543, 549–550, n. 4 (1985). An affidavit of the president of Asahi, on the other hand, declared that Asahi " 'has never contemplated that its limited sales of tire valves to Cheng Shin in Taiwan would subject it to lawsuits in California.' " *Ibid.* The record does not include any contract between Cheng Shin and Asahi. Tr. of Oral Arg. 24.

Primarily on the basis of the above information, the Superior Court denied the motion to quash summons, stating that "Asahi obviously does business on an international scale. It is not unreasonable that they defend claims of defect in their product on an international scale." Order Denying Motion to Quash Summons, Zurcher v. Dunlop Tire & Rubber Co., No. 76180 (Super.Ct., Solano County, Cal., Apr. 20, 1983).

The Court of Appeal of the State of California issued a peremptory writ of mandate commanding the Superior Court to quash service of summons. The court concluded that "it would be unreasonable to require Asahi to respond in California solely on the basis of ultimately realized foreseeability that the product into which its component was embodied would be sold all over the world including California." App. to Pet. for cert. B5–B6.

The Supreme Court of the State of California reversed and discharged the writ issued by the Court of Appeal. 39 Cal.3d 35, 216 Cal.Rptr. 385, 702 P.2d 543 (1985). The court observed that "Asahi has no offices, property or agents in California. It solicits no business in California and has made no direct sales [in California]." *Id.*, at 48, 216 Cal.Rptr., at 392, n. 4, 702 P.2d, at 549–550, n. 4. Moreover, "Asahi did not design or control the system of distribution that carried its valve assemblies into California." *Id.,* 49, 216 Cal.Rptr., at 392, 702 P.2d, at 549. Nevertheless, the court found the exercise of jurisdiction over Asahi to be consistent with the Due Process Clause. It concluded that Asahi knew that some of the valve assemblies sold to Cheng Shin would be incorporated into tire tubes sold in California, and that Asahi benefited indirectly from the sale in California of products incorporating its components. The court considered Asahi's intentional act of placing its components into the stream of commerce—that is, by delivering the components to Cheng Shin in Taiwan—coupled with Asahi's awareness that some of the components would eventually find their way into California, sufficient to form the basis for state court jurisdiction under the Due Process Clause.

We granted certiorari, 475 U.S.1044, 106 S.Ct. 1258, 89 L.Ed.2d 569 (1986), and now reverse.

II facts

A

The Due Process Clause of the Fourteenth Amendment limits the power of a state court to exert personal jurisdiction over a nonresident defendant. "[T]he constitutional touchstone" of the determination whether an exercise of personal jurisdiction comports with due process "remains whether the defendant purposefully established 'minimum contacts' in the forum State." Burger King Corp. v. Rudzewicz, 471 U.S. 462, 474, 105 S.Ct. 2174, 2183, 85 L.Ed.2d 528 (1985), quoting International Shoe Co. v. Washington, 326 U.S. 310, 316, 66 S.Ct. 154, 158, 90 L.Ed. 95 (1945). Most recently we have reaffirmed the oft-quoted reasoning of Hanson v. Denckla, 357 U.S. 235, 253, 78 S.Ct. 1228, 1239, 2 L.Ed.2d 1283 (1958), that minimum contacts must have a basis in "some act by which the defendant purposefully avails itself of the privilege of conducting activities within the forum State, thus invoking the benefits and protections of its laws." *Burger King,* 471 U.S., at 475, 105 S.Ct., at 2183. "Jurisdiction is proper * * * where the contacts proximately result from actions by the defendant *himself* that create a 'substantial connection' with the forum State." *Ibid.,* quoting McGee v. International Life Insurance Co., 355 U.S. 220, 223, 78 S.Ct. 199, 201, 2 L.Ed.2d 223 (1957) (emphasis in original).

Applying the principle that minimum contacts must be based on an act of the defendant, the Court in World–Wide Volkswagen Corp. v. Woodson, 444 U.S, 286, 100 S.Ct. 559, 62 L.Ed.2d 490 (1980), rejected the assertion that a *consumer's* unilateral act of bringing the defendant's product into the forum State was a sufficient constitutional basis for personal jurisdiction over the defendant. It had been argued in *World–Wide Volkswagen* that because an automobile retailer and its wholesale distributor sold a product mobile by design and purpose, they could foresee being haled into court in the distant States into which their customers might drive. The Court rejected this concept of foreseeability as an insufficient basis for jurisdiction under the Due Process Clause. * * * The Court disclaimed, however, the idea that "foreseeability is wholly irrelevant" to personal jurisdiction, concluding that "[t]he forum State does not exceed its powers under the Due Process Clause if it asserts personal jurisdiction over a corporation that delivers its products into the stream of commerce with the expectation that they will be purchased by consumers in the forum State." *Id.,* 297–298, 100 S.Ct., at 567 (citation omitted).

* * *

In *World–Wide Volkswagen* itself, the state court sought to base jurisdiction not on any act of the defendant, but on the foreseeable unilateral actions of the consumer. Since *World–Wide Volkswagen,* lower courts have been confronted with cases in which the defendant acted by placing a product in the stream of commerce, and the stream eventually swept defendant's product into the forum State, but the defendant did nothing else to purposefully avail itself of the market in the forum state. Some courts have understood the Due Process Clause, as interpreted in *World–Wide Volkswagen,* to allow an exercise of personal jurisdiction to be based on no more than the defendant's act of placing the product in the stream of commerce. Other courts have understood the Due Process Clause and the above-quoted language in *World–Wide Volkswagen* to require the action of the defendant to be more purposefully directed at the forum State than the mere act of placing a product in the stream of commerce.

The reasoning of the Supreme Court of California in the present case illustrates the former interpretation of *World–Wide Volkswagen.* The Supreme Court of California held that, because the stream of commerce eventually brought some valves Asahi sold Cheng Shin into California, Asahi's awareness that its valves would be sold in California was sufficient to permit California to exercise jurisdiction over Asahi consistent with the requirements of the Due Process Clause. The Supreme Court of California's position was consistent with those courts that have held that mere foreseeability or awareness was a constitutionally sufficient basis for personal jurisdiction if the defendant's product made its way into the forum State while still in the stream of commerce. See Bean Dredging Corp. v. Dredge Technology Corp., 744 F.2d 1081 (5th Cir.1984); Hendrick v. Daiko Shoji Co., 715 F.2d 1355 (9th Cir.1983).

Other courts, however, have understood the Due Process Clause to require something more than that the defendant was aware of its product's entry into the forum State through the stream of commerce in order for the state to exert jurisdiction over the defendant. In the present case, for example, the State Court of Appeal did not read the Due Process Clause, as interpreted by *World–Wide Volkswagen,* to allow "mere foreseeability that the product will enter the forum state [to] be enough by itself to establish jurisdiction over the distributor and retailer." App. to Pet. for cert. B5. In Humble v. Toyota Motor Co., Ltd., 727 F.2d 709 (8th Cir.1984), an injured car passenger brought suit against Arakawa Auto Body Company, a Japanese corporation that manufactured car seats for Toyota. Arakawa did no business in the United States; it had no office, affiliate, subsidiary, or agent in the

United States; it manufactured its component parts outside the United States and delivered them to Toyota Motor Company in Japan. The Court of Appeals, adopting the reasoning of the District Court in that case, noted that although it "does not doubt that Arakawa could have foreseen that its product would find its way into the United States," it would be "manifestly unjust" to require Arakawa to defend itself in the United States. * * * See generally Max Daetwyler Corp. v. R. Meyer, 762 F.2d 290, 299 (3d Cir.1985) (collecting "stream of commerce" cases in which the "manufacturers involved had made deliberate decisions to market their products in the forum state").

We now find this latter position to be consonant with the requirements of due process. The "substantial connection," *Burger King,* 471 U.S., at 475, 105 S.Ct., at 2184; *McGee,* 355 U.S., at 223, 78 S.Ct., at 201, between the defendant and the forum State necessary for a finding of minimum contacts must come about by *an action of the defendant purposefully directed toward the forum State. Burger King, supra,* 471 U.S., at 476, 105 S.Ct., at 2184; Keeton v. Hustler Magazine, Inc., 465 U.S. 770, 774, 104 S.Ct. 1473, 1478, 79 L.Ed.2d 790 (1984). The placement of a product into the stream of commerce, without more, is not an act of the defendant purposefully directed toward the forum State. Additional conduct of the defendant may indicate an intent or purpose to serve the market in the forum State, for example, designing the product for the market in the forum State, advertising in the forum State, establishing channels for providing regular advice to customers in the forum State, or marketing the product through a distributor who has agreed to serve as the sales agent in the forum State. But a defendant's awareness that the stream of commerce may or will sweep the product into the forum State does not convert the mere act of placing the product into the stream into an act purposefully directed toward the forum State.

Assuming, *arguendo,* that respondents have established Asahi's awareness that some of the valves sold to Cheng Shin would be incorporated into tire tubes sold in California, respondents have not demonstrated any action by Asahi to purposefully avail itself of the California market. Asahi does not do business in California. It has no office, agents, employees, or property in California. It does not advertise or otherwise solicit business in California. It did not create, control, or employ the distribution system that brought its valves to California. Cf. Hicks v. Kawasaki Heavy Industries, 452 F.Supp. 130 (1978). There is no evidence that Asahi designed its product in anticipation of sales in California. Cf. Rockwell International Corp. v. Costruzioni Aeronautiche Giovanni Agusta, 553 F.Supp. 328 (E.D.Pa. 1982). On the basis of these facts, the exertion of personal jurisdiction over Asahi by the Superior Court of California* exceeds the limits of Due Process.

---

* We have no occasion here to determine whether Congress could, consistent with the Due Process Clause of the Fifth Amendment, authorize federal court personal jurisdiction over alien defendants based on the aggregate of *national* contacts, rather than on the contacts between the defendant and the State in which the federal court sits. * * *

Wheat

B

The strictures of the Due Process Clause forbid a state court from exercising personal jurisdiction over Asahi under circumstances that would offend "traditional notions of fair play and substantial justice." International Shoe Co. v. Washington, 326 U.S., at 316, 66 S.Ct., at 158; quoting Milliken v. Meyer, 311 U.S., at 463, 61 S.Ct., at 342.

We have previously explained that the determination of the reasonableness of the exercise of jurisdiction in each case will depend on an evaluation of several factors. A court must consider the burden on the defendant, the interests of the forum state, and the plaintiff's interest in obtaining relief. It must also weigh in its determination "the interstate judicial system's interest in obtaining the most efficient resolution of controversies; and the shared interest of the several States in furthering fundamental substantive social policies." *World-Wide Volkswagen*, 444 U.S., at 292, 100 S.Ct., at 564 (citations omitted).

A consideration of these factors in the present case clearly reveals the unreasonableness of the assertion of jurisdiction over Asahi, even apart from the question of the placement of goods in the stream of commerce.

Certainly the burden on the defendant in this case is severe. Asahi has been commanded by the Supreme Court of California not only to traverse the distance between Asahi's headquarters in Japan and the Superior Court of California in and for the County of Solano, but also to submit its dispute with Cheng Shin to a foreign nation's judicial system. The unique burdens placed upon one who must defend oneself in a foreign legal system should have significant weight in assessing the reasonableness of stretching the long arm of personal jurisdiction over national borders.

When minimum contacts have been established, often the interests of the plaintiff and the forum in the exercise of jurisdiction will justify even the serious burdens placed on the alien defendant. In the present case, however, the interests of the plaintiff and the forum in California's assertion of jurisdiction over Asahi are slight. All that remains is a claim for indemnification asserted by Cheng Shin, a Taiwanese corporation, against Asahi. The transaction on which the indemnification claim is based took place in Taiwan; Asahi's components were shipped from Japan to Taiwan. Cheng Shin has not demonstrated that it is more convenient for it to litigate its indemnification claim against Asahi in California rather than in Taiwan or Japan.

Because the plaintiff is not a California resident, California's legitimate interests in the dispute have considerably diminished. The Supreme Court of California argued that the State had an interest in "protecting its consumers by ensuring that foreign manufacturers comply with the state's safety standards." 39 Cal.3d, at 49, 216 Cal.Rptr., at 392, 702 P.2d, at 550. The State Supreme Court's definition of California's interest, however, was overly broad. The dispute between Cheng Shin and Asahi is primarily about indemnification rather than safety standards. Moreover, it is not at all clear at this point that California law should govern the question whether a Japanese corporation should indemnify a Taiwanese corporation on the basis of a sale made in Taiwan and a shipment of goods from Japan to Taiwan. Phillips Petroleum v. Shutts, 472 U.S. 797, 105 S.Ct. 2965, 86 L.Ed.2d 628 (1985); Allstate Insurance Co. v. Hague, 449 U.S. 302, 312–313, 101 S.Ct. 633, 639–640, 66 L.Ed.2d 521 (1981). The possibility of being haled into a California court as a result of an accident involving Asahi's components undoubtedly creates an additional deterrent to the manufacture of unsafe components; however, similar pressures will be placed on Asahi by the purchasers of its components as long as those who use Asahi components in their final products, and sell those products in California, are subject to the application of California tort law.

World–Wide Volkswagen also admonished courts to take into consideration the interests of the "several States," in addition to the forum state, in the efficient judicial resolution of the dispute and the advancement of substantive policies. In the present case, this advice calls for a court to consider the procedural and substantive policies of other *nations* whose interests are affected by the assertion of jurisdiction by the California court. The procedural and substantive interests of other nations in a state court's assertion of jurisdiction over an alien defendant will differ from case to case. In every case, however, those interests, as well as the Federal interest in its foreign relations policies, will be best served by a careful inquiry into the reasonableness of the assertion of jurisdiction in the particular case, and an unwillingness to find the serious burdens on an alien defendant outweighed by minimal interests on the part of the plaintiff or the forum State. "Great care and reserve should be exercised when extending our notions of personal jurisdiction into the international field." United States v. First National City Bank, 379 U.S. 378, 404, 85 S.Ct. 528, 542, 13 L.Ed.2d 365 (1965) (Harlan, J., dissenting). See Born, Reflections on Judicial Jurisdiction in International Cases, to be published in 17 Ga.J. Int'l & Comp. L. 1 (1987).

Considering the international context, the heavy burden on the alien defendant, and the slight interests of the plaintiff and the forum State, the exercise of personal jurisdiction by a California court over Asahi in this instance would be unreasonable and unfair.

III

Because the facts of this case do not establish minimum contacts such that the exercise of personal jurisdiction is consistent with fair play and substantial justice, the judgment of Supreme Court of California is reversed, and the case is remanded for further proceedings not inconsistent with this opinion.

It is so ordered.

■ JUSTICE BRENNAN, with whom JUSTICE WHITE, JUSTICE MARSHALL, and JUSTICE BLACKMUN join, concurring in part and in the judgment.

I do not agree with the plurality's interpretation of the stream-of-commerce theory, nor with its conclusion that Asahi did not "purposely avail itself of the California market." *Ante,* at 1034. I do agree, however, with the Court's conclusion in Part II–B that the exercise of personal jurisdiction over Asahi in this case would not comport with "fair play and substantial justice," International Shoe Co. v. Washington, 326 U.S. 310, 320, 66 S.Ct. 154, 160, 90 L.Ed. 95 (1945). This is one of those rare cases in which "minimum requirements inherent in the concept of 'fair play and substantial justice' * * * defeat the reasonableness of jurisdiction even [though] the defendant has purposefully engaged in forum activities." Burger King Corp. v. Rudzewicz, 471 U.S. 462, 477–478, 105 S.Ct. 2174, 2184–2185, 85 L.Ed.2d 528 (1985). I therefore join Parts I and II–B of the Court's opinion, and write separately to explain my disagreement with Part II–A.

The plurality states that "a defendant's awareness that the stream of commerce may or will sweep the product into the forum State does not convert the mere act of placing the product into the stream into an act purposefully directed toward the forum State." *Ante,* at 1033. The plurality would therefore require a plaintiff to show "[a]dditional conduct" directed toward the forum before finding the exercise of jurisdiction over the defendant to be consistent with the Due Process Clause. * * * I see no need for such a showing, however. The stream of commerce refers not to unpredictable currents or eddies, but to the regular and anticipated flow of products from manufacture to distribution to retail sale. As long as a participant in this process is aware that the final product is being marketed in the forum State, the possibility of a lawsuit there cannot come as a surprise. Nor will the litigation present a burden for which there is no corresponding benefit. A defendant who has placed goods in the stream of commerce benefits economically from the retail sale of the final product in the forum State, and indirectly benefits from the State's laws that regulate and facilitate commercial activity. These benefits accrue regardless of whether that participant directly conducts business in the forum State, or engages in additional conduct directed toward that State. Accordingly, most courts and commentators have found that jurisdiction premised on the placement of a product into the stream of commerce is consistent with the Due Process Clause, and have not required a showing of additional conduct.

The plurality's endorsement of what appears to be the minority view among Federal Courts of Appeals[2] represents a marked retreat

---

2. The Court of Appeals for the Eighth Circuit appears to be the only Circuit Court to have expressly adopted a narrow construction of the stream-of-commerce theory analogous to the one the plurality articulates today, although the Court of Appeals for the Eleventh Circuit has implicitly adopted it. See Humble v. Toyota Motor Co., Ltd., 727 F.2d 709 (8th Cir.1984); Banton Industries, Inc. v. Dimatic Die & Tool Co., 801 F.2d 1283 (11th Cir.1986). Two other Courts of Appeals have found the theory inapplicable when only a single sale occurred in the forum State, but do not appear committed to the interpretation of the theory that the Court adopts today. *E.g.* Chung v. NANA Development Corp., 783 F.2d 1124 4th Cir. cert. denied, 749 U.S. 948, 107 S.Ct. 431, 93 L.Ed.2d 381 (1986); Dalmau Rodriguez v. Hughes Aircraft Co., 781 F.2d 9 (1st Cir.1986). Similarly, the Court of Appeals for the Third Circuit has not interpreted the theory as the plurality

from its analysis in World–Wide Volkswagen v. Woodson, 444 U.S. 286, 100 S.Ct. 559, 62 L.Ed.2d 490 (1980). * * *

■ JUSTICE STEVENS, with whom JUSTICE WHITE and JUSTICE BLACKMUN join, concurring in part and concurring in the judgment.

The judgment of the Supreme Court of California should be reversed for the reasons stated in Part II–B of the Court's opinion. While I join Parts I and II–B, I do not join Part II–A for two reasons. First, it is not necessary to the Court's decision. An examination of minimum contacts is not always necessary to determine whether a state court's assertion of personal jurisdiction is constitutional. See Burger King Corp. v. Rudzewicz, 471 U.S. 462, 476–478 (1985). Part II–B establishes, after considering the factors set forth in World–Wide Volkswagen Corp. v. Woodson, 444 U.S. 286, 292 (1980), that California's exercise of jurisdiction over Asahi in this case would be "unreasonable and unfair." * * * This finding alone requires reversal; this case fits within the rule that "minimum requirements inherent in the concept of 'fair play and substantial justice' may defeat the reasonableness of jurisdiction even if the defendant has purposefully engaged in forum activities." *Burger King,* 471 U.S., at 477–478 (quoting International Shoe Co. v. Washington, 326 U.S. 310, 320 (1945)). Accordingly, I see no reason in this case for the plurality to articulate "purposeful direction" or any other test as the nexus between an act of a defendant and the forum State that is necessary to establish minimum contacts.

Second, even assuming that the test ought to be formulated here, Part II–A misapplies it to the facts of this case. The plurality seems to assume that an unwavering line can be drawn between "mere awareness" that a component will find its way into the forum State and "purposeful availment" of the forum's market. * * * Over the course of its dealings with Cheng Shin, Asahi has arguably engaged in a higher quantum of conduct than "[t]he placement of a product into the stream of commerce, without more * * *." * * * Whether or not this conduct rises to the level of purposeful availment requires a constitutional determination that is affected by the volume, the value, and the hazardous character of the components. In most circumstances I would be inclined to conclude that a regular course of dealing that results in deliveries of over 100,000 units annually over a period of several years would constitute "purposeful availment" even though the item delivered to the forum State was a standard product marketed throughout the world.

has today, but has rejected stream-of-commerce arguments for jurisdiction when the relationship between the distributor and the defendant "remains in dispute" and "evidence indicating that [defendant] could anticipate either use of its product or litigation in [the forum State] is totally lacking," Max Daetwyler Corp. v. R. Meyer, 762 F.2d 290, 298, 300, n. 13, cert. denied, 474 U.S. 980, 106 S.Ct. 383, 88 L.Ed.2d 336 (1985), and when the defendant's product was not sold in the forum State and defendant "did not take advantage of an indirect marketing scheme," DeJames v. Magnificence Carriers, Inc., 654 F.2d 280, 285, cert. denied, 454 U.S. 1085, 102 S.Ct. 642, 70 L.Ed.2d 620 (1981).

NOTES

A. Justice O'Connor describes the results of an "informal" survey of valve stems taken in one cyclery. Is a survey limited to one store at one point in time of a quality that should be considered by the court? Should the attorney in question have felt obligated to do more? Were the results of the survey relevant to whether Asahi should be compelled to litigate in California? On what theory?

B. Part II–A of the opinion deals with the limits of the stream of commerce rationale for asserting jurisdiction. Does Justice O'Connor speak for the Court on this point?

C. In assessing the precedential value of *Asahi* it is necessary to identify the crucial variables and to ask what differences in the facts would cause a different result. Suppose Asahi had sold all its valves to Cheng Shin. Would that have made a difference? Suppose that Asahi knew that thousands of its valves were going to be on United States highways? On California highways? Suppose the original plaintiffs had not settled with Cheng Shin?

NOTE ON STREAM OF COMMERCE AFTER ASAHI

In *Barone v. Rich Brothers Interstate Display Fireworks*, 25 F.3d 610 (8th Cir.) cert. denied, 115 S. Ct. 359 (1994), plaintiff was injured in Nebraska when a fireworks display he was helping to set up went awry. Among the defendants was a fireworks manufacturer, Hosoya Fireworks Co. of Tokyo, Japan who had sold to the distributor, Rich Bros. Interstate Display Fireworks Co. of Sioux Falls, South Dakota. Hosoya moved to dismiss for lack of personal jurisdiction. The district court granted that motion and the United States Court of Appeals for the Eighth Circuit, in holding that there was personal jurisdiction in Nebraska over Hosoya the Court stated:

"The Supreme Court most recently examined the 'stream of commerce' theory of personal jurisdiction in *Asahi Metal Industry Co. v. Superior Court of California*, 480 U.S. 102, 94 L. Ed. 2d 92, 107 S. Ct. 1026 (1987).

"The plaintiff in Asahi eventually settled his suit, but the action for indemnity between the Taiwanese company that sold the final product into California and the Japanese company that manufactured the allegedly defective component part remained to be litigated. The Supreme Court eventually held that the exercise of personal jurisdiction over the component manufacturer in a California state court did not comport with due process because it was unreasonable to subject the Japanese company to suit in California when neither the plaintiff nor the forum state had any significant interest in the outcome and when it would place a severe burden on the Japanese company. The Court split badly on the question of whether the Japanese company had sufficient contacts with the forum state, with four justices indicating that it did not, four justices indicating that it did, and three justices indicating that, although it was unnecessary to reach the question, they believed that 'a regular course of dealing that results in deliveries of over 100,000 units annually over a period of several years would constitute "purposeful availment" even though the item delivered to the forum State was a standard product marketed throughout the world.' " Id. at 122.

"In short, Asahi stands for no more than that it is unreasonable to adjudicate third-party litigation between two foreign companies in this country absent consent by the nonresident defendant. Should one engage in vote counting, which we are loath to do, it appears that five justices agreed that continuous placement of a significant number of products into the stream of commerce with knowledge that the product would be distributed into the forum state represents sufficient minimum contacts to satisfy due process. In doing so, those justices simply followed the Court's earlier statement in World–Wide Volkswagen that when a manufacturer or distributor attempts to serve a market "directly or indirectly ... , it is not unreasonable to subject it to suit in [that market] if its allegedly defective merchandise has there been the source of injury to its owner or to others."

"Hosoya has reaped the benefits of its network of distributors, and it is only reasonable and just that it should now be held accountable in the forum of the plaintiff's choice (as long as that choice of forum comports with due process, which we believe it does). More than reasonable foreseeability is at stake here, as it must be under existing case law, for Hosoya has purposefully reaped the benefits not only of South Dakota's laws, but of Nebraska's as well."

The issue raised in *Barone* remains unsettled. Some courts have held, following Justice White's statement in *World-Wide Volkswagen*, that placing goods in the stream of commerce with knowledge that they will ultimately be sold in the forum state is sufficient to satisfy Due Process requirements. Other courts have adopted Justice O'Connor's view, stated in the plurality opinion in *Asahi*, that the Due Process clause requires more to establish personal jurisdiction than merely placing goods in the stream of commerce with knowledge that "may or will" make their way into the forum state. *See e.g. Lesnick v. Hollingsworth & Vose Co.*, 35 F.3d 939 (4th Cir.1994). Which of these courts are correctly following Supreme Court precedent?

NOTE ON RULE 4(k)(2) AND NATIONAL CONTACTS

Plaintiff, a Danish manufacturer, sues an English subsidiary of a major American corporation in the United States District Court for the Southern District of New York alleging violations of federal antitrust law. Plaintiff and defendant both produce a certain type of printing system, and plaintiff alleges that defendant engaged in activities overseas which had an anticompetitive effect and excluded plaintiff from selling in certain foreign and United States markets.

Defendant has no offices, employees, or bank accounts in the United States, files no U.S. tax returns, and is not licensed to conduct business in any state. However, it exports millions of dollars worth of products to the United States, sometimes through its U.S. parent company. It also sends representatives to trade shows in various states in the U.S.

Defendant contends it does not have sufficient contacts with New York to subject it to personal jurisdiction under New York law. Indeed, under the facts defendant is not subject to personal jurisdiction in any state in the United States. Can the district court assert personal jurisdiction under Rule 4(k)(2)? See *Eskofot A/S v. E.I. Du Pont De Nemours & Co.*, 872 F. Supp. 81 (S.D.N.Y.1995).

Personal Jurisdiction and the Internet

The growth of commercial and other activities over the Internet has raised new issues of personal jurisdiction. To what extent does a company (or individual) that conducts activities over the Internet subject itself to personal jurisdiction? Courts are just beginning to grapple with these issues. One influential application of general personal jurisdiction principles to Internet activities was provided by the Court in *Zippo Manufacturing v. Zippo Dot Com*, 952 F. Supp. 1119 (W.D.Pa.1997). It stated:

"The Internet makes it possible to conduct business throughout the world entirely from a desktop. With this global revolution looming on the horizon, the development of the law concerning the permissible scope of personal jurisdiction based on Internet use is in its infant stages. The cases are scant. Nevertheless, our review of the available cases and materials reveals that the likelihood that personal jurisdiction can be constitutionally exercised is directly proportionate to the nature and quality of commercial activity that an entity conducts over the Internet. This sliding scale is consistent with well developed personal jurisdiction principles. At one end of the spectrum are situations where a defendant clearly does business over the Internet. If the defendant enters into contracts with residents of a foreign jurisdiction that involve the knowing and repeated transmission of computer files over the Internet, personal jurisdiction is proper. At the opposite end are situations where a defendant has simply posted information on an Internet Web site which is accessible to users in foreign jurisdictions. A passive Web site that does little more than make information available to those who are interested in it is not grounds for the exercise of personal jurisdiction. The middle ground is occupied by interactive Web sites where a user can exchange information with the host computer. In these cases, the exercise of jurisdiction is determined by examining the level of interactivity and commercial nature of the exchange of information that occurs on the Web site."

B. DOING HARM WITHIN THE FORUM STATE

Keeton v. Hustler Magazine, Inc.

Supreme Court of the United States, 1984.
465 U.S. 770, 104 S.Ct. 1473, 79 L.Ed.2d 790.

■ JUSTICE REHNQUIST delivered the opinion of the Court.

Petitioner Keeton is a resident of New York. Her only connection with New Hampshire is the circulation there of copies of a magazine that she assists in producing. The magazine bears petitioner's name in several places crediting her with editorial and other work. Respondent Hustler Magazine, Inc., is an Ohio corporation, with its principal place of business in California. Respondent's contacts with New Hampshire consist of the sale of some 10,000 to 15,000 copies of Hustler Magazine in that State each month. * * * Petitioner claims to have been libeled in five separate issues of respondent's magazine published between September 1975 and May 1976.[1]

The Court of Appeals, in its opinion affirming the District Court's dismissal of petitioner's complaint, held that petitioner's lack of contacts with New Hampshire rendered the State's interest in redressing the tort of libel to petitioner too attenuated for an assertion of personal jurisdiction over respondent. The Court of Appeals observed that the "single publication rule" ordinarily applicable in multistate libel cases would require it to award petitioner "damages caused in *all* states" should she prevail in her suit, even though the bulk of petitioner's alleged injuries had been sustained outside New Hamp-

---

1. Initially, petitioner brought suit for libel and invasion of privacy in Ohio, where the magazine was published. Her libel claim, however, was dismissed as barred by the Ohio statute of limitations, and her invasion-of-privacy claim was dismissed as barred by the New York statute of limitations, which the Ohio court considered to be "migratory." Petitioner then filed the present action in October 1980.

shire. 682 F.2d, at 35.[2] The court also stressed New Hampshire's unusually long (6–year) limitations period for libel actions. New Hampshire was the only State where petitioner's suit would not have been time-barred when it was filed. Under these circumstances, the Court of Appeals concluded that it would be "unfair" to assert jurisdiction over respondent. New Hampshire has a minimal interest in applying its unusual statute of limitations to, and awarding damages for, injuries to a nonresident occurring outside the State, particularly since petitioner suffered such a small proportion of her total claimed injury within the State. *Id.,* at 35–36.

We conclude that the Court of Appeals erred when it affirmed the dismissal of petitioner's suit for lack of personal jurisdiction. Respondent's regular circulation of magazines in the forum State is sufficient to support an assertion of jurisdiction in a libel action based on the contents of the magazine.

* * *

The District Court found that "[t]he general course of conduct in circulating magazines throughout the state was purposefully directed at New Hampshire, and inevitably affected persons in the state." App. to Pet. for Cert. 5a. Such regular monthly sales of thousands of magazines cannot by any stretch of the imagination be characterized as random, isolated, or fortuitous. It is, therefore, unquestionable that New Hampshire jurisdiction over a complaint based on those contacts would ordinarily satisfy the requirement of the Due Process Clause that a State's assertion of personal jurisdiction over a nonresident defendant be predicated on "minimum contacts" between the defendant and the State. * * * And, as the Court of Appeals acknowledged, New Hampshire has adopted a "long-arm" statute authorizing service of process on nonresident corporations whenever permitted by the Due Process Clause. 682 F.2d, at 33.[4] Thus, all the requisites for personal jurisdiction over Hustler Magazine, Inc., in New Hampshire are present.

We think that the three concerns advanced by the Court of Appeals, whether considered singly or together, are not sufficiently

---

2. The "single publication rule" has been summarized as follows:

"As to any single publication, (a) only one action for damages can be maintained; (b) all damages suffered in all jurisdictions can be recovered in the one action; and (c) a judgment for or against the plaintiff upon the merits of any action for damages bars any other action for damages between the same parties in all jurisdictions." Restatement (Second) of Torts § 577A(4) (1977).

4. New Hampshire Rev.Stat.Ann. § 300:14 (1977) provides in relevant part:

"If a foreign corporation * * * commits a tort in whole or in part in New Hampshire, such ac[t] shall be deemed to be doing business in New Hampshire by such foreign corporation and shall be deemed equivalent to the appointment by such foreign corporation of the secretary of the state of New Hampshire and his successors to be its true and lawful attorney upon whom may be served all lawful process in any actions or proceedings against such foreign corporation arising from or growing out of such * * * tort."

This statute has been construed in the New Hampshire courts to extend jurisdiction over nonresident corporations to the fullest extent permitted under the Federal Constitution. See, *e.g.,* Roy v. North American Newspaper Alliance, Inc., 106 N.H. 92, 95, 205 A.2d 844, 846 (1964).

weighty to merit a different result. The "single publication rule," New Hampshire's unusually long statute of limitations, and plaintiff's lack of contacts with the forum State do not defeat jurisdiction otherwise proper under both New Hampshire law and the Due Process Clause.

In judging minimum contacts, a court properly focuses on "the relationship among the defendant, the forum, and the litigation." Shaffer v. Heitner, 433 U.S. 186, 204, 97 S.Ct. 2569, 2579, 53 L.Ed.2d 683 (1977). * * * Thus, it is certainly relevant to the jurisdictional inquiry that petitioner is *seeking* to recover damages suffered in all States in this one suit. The contacts between respondent and the forum must be judged in the light of that claim, rather than a claim only for damages sustained in New Hampshire. That is, the contacts between respondent and New Hampshire must be such that it is "fair" to compel respondent to defend a multistate lawsuit in New Hampshire seeking nationwide damages for all copies of the five issues in question, even though only a small portion of those copies were distributed in New Hampshire.

The Court of Appeals expressed the view that New Hampshire's "interest" in asserting jurisdiction over plaintiff's multistate claim was minimal. We agree that the "fairness" of haling respondent into a New Hampshire court depends to some extent on whether respondent's activities relating to New Hampshire are such as to give that State a legitimate interest in holding respondent answerable on a claim related to those activities. * * *

The Court of Appeals acknowledged that petitioner was suing, at least in part, for damages suffered in New Hampshire. 682 F.2d, at 34. And it is beyond dispute that New Hampshire has a significant interest in redressing injuries that actually occur within the State. * * * This interest extends to libel actions brought by nonresidents. False statements of fact harm both the subject of the falsehood *and* the readers of the statement. New Hampshire may rightly employ its libel laws to discourage the deception of its citizens. * * *

New Hampshire may also extend its concern to the injury that in-state libel causes within New Hampshire to a nonresident. The tort of libel is generally held to occur wherever the offending material is circulated. Restatement (Second) of Torts § 577A, Comment a (1977). The reputation of the libel victim may suffer harm even in a State in which he has hitherto been anonymous. The communication of the libel may create a negative reputation among the residents of a jurisdiction where the plaintiff's previous reputation was, however small, at least unblemished.

New Hampshire has clearly expressed its interest in protecting such persons from libel, as well as in safeguarding its populace from falsehoods. * * * Moreover, in 1971 New Hampshire specifically deleted from its long-arm statute the requirement that a tort be committed "against a resident of New Hampshire."

* * * In sum, the combination of New Hampshire's interest in redressing injuries that occur within the State and its interest in

cooperating with other States in the application of the "single publication rule" demonstrates the propriety of requiring respondent to answer to a multistate libel action in New Hampshire.

The Court of Appeals also thought that there was an element of due process "unfairness" arising from the fact that the statutes of limitations in every jurisdiction except New Hampshire had run on the plaintiff's claim in this case. * * * The question of the applicability of New Hampshire's statute of limitations to claims for out-of-state damages presents itself in the course of litigation only after jurisdiction over respondent is established, and we do not think that such choice-of-law concerns should complicate or distort the jurisdictional inquiry.

* * *

Finally, implicit in the Court of Appeals' analysis of New Hampshire's interest is an emphasis on the extremely limited contacts of the *plaintiff* with New Hampshire. But we have not to date required a plaintiff to have "minimum contacts" with the forum State before permitting that State to assert personal jurisdiction over a nonresident defendant. On the contrary, we have upheld the assertion of jurisdiction where such contacts were entirely lacking. * * * In the instant case, respondent's activities in the forum may not be so substantial as to support jurisdiction over a cause of action unrelated to those activities. But respondent is carrying on a "part of its general business" in New Hampshire, and that is sufficient to support jurisdiction when the cause of action arises out of the very activity being conducted, in part, in New Hampshire.

The plaintiff's residence is not, of course, completely irrelevant to the jurisdictional inquiry. As noted, that inquiry focuses on the relations among the defendant, the forum, and the litigation. Plaintiff's residence may well play an important role in determining the propriety of entertaining a suit against the defendant in the forum. That is, plaintiff's residence in the forum may, because of defendant's relationship with the plaintiff, enhance defendant's contacts with the forum. Plaintiff's residence may be the focus of the activities of the defendant out of which the suit arises. But plaintiff's residence in the forum State is not a separate requirement, and lack of residence will not defeat jurisdiction established on the basis of defendant's contacts.

It is undoubtedly true that the bulk of the harm done to petitioner occurred outside New Hampshire. But that will be true in almost every libel action brought somewhere other than the plaintiff's domicile. There is no justification for restricting libel actions to the plaintiff's home forum. The victim of a libel, like the victim of any other tort, may choose to bring suit in any forum with which the defendant has "certain minimum contacts * * * such that the maintenance of the suit does not offend 'traditional notions of fair play and substantial justice.'"

Where, as in this case, respondent Hustler Magazine, Inc., has continuously and deliberately exploited the New Hampshire market, it must reasonably anticipate being haled into court there in a libel action based on the contents of its magazine. * * * And, since respondent can be charged with knowledge of the "single publication rule," it must anticipate that such a suit will seek nationwide damages. Respondent produces a national publication aimed at a nationwide audience. There is no unfairness in calling it to answer for the contents of that publication wherever a substantial number of copies are regularly sold and distributed.

The judgment of the Court of Appeals is reversed, and the cause is remanded for proceedings consistent with this opinion.[a]

* * *

NOTES

A jury awarded Keeton $2 million. That verdict was appealed to the Court of Appeals for the First Circuit which certified two questions to the New Hampshire Supreme Court:

> 1. Does New Hampshire follow an interstate single publication rule in libel cases?

> 2. If so, does New Hampshire permit a plaintiff to recover for distribution of a libel in jurisdictions whose own statutes of limitations would bar recovery, where neither party is a New Hampshire resident, where the only factual connection with New Hampshire is the distribution there of one percent or less of the total circulation of the material, and where the relevant statute of limitations has expired in every jurisdiction but New Hampshire?

828 F.2d 64, 67 (1st Cir.1987).

The New Hampshire Supreme Court, in a 3 to 2 opinion, responded "that New Hampshire follows the single publication rule * * * and that, in the circumstances described, we would apply our own statute of limitations to the plaintiff's entire libel action under that rule." Keeton v. Hustler Magazine, Inc., 131 N.H. 6, 549 A.2d 1187, 1188 (1988).

Calder v. Jones

Supreme Court of the United States, 1984.
465 U.S. 783, 104 S.Ct. 1482, 79 L.Ed.2d 804.

■ Justice Rehnquist delivered the opinion of the Court.

Respondent Shirley Jones brought suit in California Superior Court claiming that she had been libeled in an article written and edited by petitioners in Florida. The article was published in a national magazine with a large circulation in California. Petitioners were served with process by mail in Florida and caused special appearances to be entered on their behalf, moving to quash the service of process for lack of personal jurisdiction. The Superior Court granted the motion on the ground that First Amendment concerns weighed against an assertion of jurisdiction otherwise proper under the Due Process Clause. The California Court of Appeal reversed, rejecting the sugges-

---

a. Justice Brennan's concurring opinion is omitted.

tion that First Amendment considerations enter into the jurisdictional analysis. We now affirm.

Respondent lives and works in California. She and her husband brought this suit against the National Enquirer, Inc., its local distributing company, and petitioners for libel, invasion of privacy, and intentional infliction of emotional harm. The Enquirer is a Florida corporation with its principal place of business in Florida. It publishes a national weekly newspaper with a total circulation of over 5 million. About 600,000 of those copies, almost twice the level of the next highest State, are sold in California. Respondent's and her husband's claims were based on an article that appeared in the Enquirer's October 9, 1979, issue. Both the Enquirer and the distributing company answered the complaint and made no objection to the jurisdiction of the California court.

Petitioner South is a reporter employed by the Enquirer. He is a resident of Florida, though he frequently travels to California on business. South wrote the first draft of the challenged article, and his byline appeared on it. He did most of his research in Florida, relying on phone calls to sources in California for the information contained in the article. Shortly before publication, South called respondent's home and read to her husband a draft of the article so as to elicit his comments upon it. Aside from his frequent trips and phone calls, South has no other relevant contacts with California.

Petitioner Calder is also a Florida resident. He has been to California only twice—once, on a pleasure trip, prior to the publication of the article and once after to testify in an unrelated trial. Calder is president and editor of the Enquirer. He "oversee[s] just about every function of the Enquirer." App. 24. He reviewed and approved the initial evaluation of the subject of the article and edited it in its final form. He also declined to print a retraction requested by respondent. Calder has no other relevant contacts with California.

* * *

The allegedly libelous story concerned the California activities of a California resident. It impugned the professionalism of an entertainer whose television career was centered in California. The article was drawn from California sources, and the brunt of the harm, in terms both of respondent's emotional distress and the injury to her professional reputation, was suffered in California. In sum, California is the focal point both of the story and of the harm suffered. Jurisdiction over petitioners is therefore proper in California based on the "effects" of their Florida conduct in California.

* * *

Petitioners argue that they are not responsible for the circulation of the article in California. A reporter and an editor, they claim, have no direct economic stake in their employer's sales in a distant State. Nor are ordinary employees able to control their employer's marketing activity. The mere fact that they can "foresee" that the article will be circulated and have an effect in California is not sufficient for an assertion of jurisdiction. * * * They do not "in effect appoint the [article their] agent for service of process." * * * Petitioners liken themselves to a welder employed in Florida who works on a boiler which subsequently explodes in California. Cases which hold that jurisdiction will be proper over the manufacturer, Buckeye Boiler Co. v. Superior Court, 71 Cal.2d 893, 458 P.2d 57 (1969); Gray v. American Radiator & Standard Sanitary Corp., 22 Ill.2d 432, 176 N.E.2d 761 (1961), should not be applied to the welder who has no control over and derives no direct benefit from his employer's sales in that distant State.

Petitioners' analogy does not wash. Whatever the status of their hypothetical welder, petitioners are not charged with mere untargeted negligence. Rather, their intentional, and allegedly tortious, actions were expressly aimed at California. Petitioner South wrote and petitioner Calder edited an article that they knew would have a potentially devastating impact upon respondent. And they knew that the brunt of that injury would be felt by respondent in the State in which she lives and works and in which the National Enquirer has its largest circulation. Under the circumstances, petitioners must "reasonably anticipate being haled into court there" to answer for the truth of the statements made in their article. An individual injured in California need not go to Florida to seek redress from persons who, though remaining in Florida, knowingly cause the injury in California.

Petitioners are correct that their contacts with California are not to be judged according to their employer's activities there. On the other hand, their status as employees does not somehow insulate them from jurisdiction. Each defendant's contacts with the forum State must be assessed individually. * * * In this case, petitioners are primary participants in an alleged wrongdoing intentionally directed at a California resident, and jurisdiction over them is proper on that basis.

We also reject the suggestion that First Amendment concerns enter into the jurisdictional analysis. The infusion of such considerations would needlessly complicate an already imprecise inquiry. * * *

We hold that jurisdiction over petitioners in California is proper because of their intentional conduct in Florida calculated to cause injury to respondent in California. The judgment of the California Court of Appeal is

Affirmed.[a]

NOTE ON LONG ARM STATUTES

State statutes which expressly give the courts of a state power to adjudicate claims against non-residents are commonly referred to as "long-arm statutes"

---

a. *Calder,* a companion case to *Keeton,* was decided the same day.

(presumably because of their extensive reach). Pertinent portions of some representative long-arm statutes are provided below:

NEW YORK CIVIL PRACTICE LAW AND RULES (1998)

§ 302.   Personal jurisdiction by acts of non-domiciliaries

(a) Acts which are the basis of jurisdiction. As to a cause of action arising from any of the acts enumerated in this section, a court may exercise personal jurisdiction over any non-domiciliary, or his executor or administrator, who in person or through an agent:

1.   transacts any business within the state or contracts anywhere to supply goods or services in the state; or

2.   commits a tortious act within the state, except as to a cause of action for defamation of character arising from the act; or

3.   commits a tortious act without the state causing injury to person or property within the state, except as to a cause of action for defamation of character arising from the act, if he

(i) regularly does or solicits business, or engages in any other persistent course of conduct, or derives substantial revenue from goods used or consumed or services rendered, in the state, or

(ii) expects or should reasonably expect the act to have consequences in the state and derives substantial revenue from interstate or international commerce; or

4.   owns, uses or possesses any real property situated within the state.

COLORADO REVISED STATUTES (1997)

§ 13–1–124.   Jurisdiction of Courts

(1) Engaging in any act enumerated in this section by any person, whether or not a resident of the state of Colorado, either in person or by an agent, submits such person and, if a natural person, such person's personal representative to the jurisdiction of the courts of this state concerning any cause of action arising from:

(a) The transaction of any business within this state;

(b) The commission of a tortious act within this state;

(c) The ownership, use, or possession of any real property situated in this state;

(d) Contracting to insure any person, property, or risk residing or located within this state at the time of contracting;

(e) The maintenance of a matrimonial domicile within this state with respect to all issues relating to obligations for support to children and spouse in any action for dissolution of marriage, legal separation, declaration of invalidity of marriage, or support of children if one of the parties of the marriage continues without interruption to be domiciled within the state;

CALIFORNIA CODE OF CIVIL PROCEDURE (1997)

§ 410.10.   Jurisdiction exercisable

A court of this state may exercise jurisdiction on any basis not inconsistent with the Constitution of this state or of the United States.

QUESTION

Which of these statutes do you think would be interpreted to extend the state's power to hear cases involving out-of-state defendants to the full limits of the United States Constitution? (Two of the three have been so interpreted.)

Talbot v. Johnson Newspaper Corp.

Court of Appeals of New York, 1988.
71 N.Y.2d 827, 527 N.Y.S.2d 729, 522 N.E.2d 1027.

■ Memorandum.

The order of the Appellate Division, 123 A.D.2d 147, 511 N.Y.S.2d 152, should be affirmed, with costs.

Leon Talbot and Jane Talbot commenced defamation action against Stuart MacLaren, his daughter Patricia MacLaren, and Johnson Newspaper Corp. (as well as several individual media defendants), seeking damages for injury to his reputation as a coach at St. Lawrence University, caused by two letters written by Stuart MacLaren. The letters dealt with two incidents recounted by Patricia MacLaren to her father, which occurred in May 1982, allegedly involving Leon Talbot. In the first, a St. Lawrence student was struck and killed by a vehicle driven by a second student shortly after he left a party at the Talbots' home; he was charged with operating a vehicle while his condition was impaired by alcohol, a charge that was eventually dismissed. Patricia MacLaren, then a St. Lawrence senior, assisted in identifying the body and notifying the deceased's roommates. The second incident occurred approximately two weeks later at a fraternity party where MacLaren observed an individual she believed to be Leon Talbot in a severely intoxicated state.

More than two years after his daughter's graduation, Stuart Mac-Laren, a California resident, wrote from there to the university president and board of trustees criticizing the handling of the student's death, describing his daughter's account of the coach's behavior at the campus party, and questioning the propriety of university requests for contributions from alumni in light of these events. In October 1984, defendant newspaper featured the letter (which had been sent to it by a trustee) in an article. The article quoted from the letter as well as a telephone interview with Patricia MacLaren, also in California, in which she said, "I have no doubt in my mind that I saw the coach guzzling beer at the party." Talbot insisted that the individual she saw must have been a look-alike. Four days later, the newspaper published a second article entitled "Coach's Double Fell Asleep on Frat Sofa," which reported that a man bearing an uncanny resemblance to Talbot was the person described in the MacLaren letter. A subsequent letter written by Stuart MacLaren reiterated that his daughter still maintained that the man on the sofa was Leon Talbot.

The MacLarens—both California residents who conducted no business in New York—moved to dismiss the action against them for want of personal jurisdiction. Special Term denied the motion, concluding that the requirements of CPLR 302(a)(1) were satisfied by Patricia MacLaren's pursuit of a college degree here and by both MacLarens' interest in maintaining the value of that degree, and that there was a substantial relationship between the business transaction and the cause of action: "[a]bsent the four-year educational contract, the MacLarens would not even have been in New York at the time of the basketball coach's alleged intoxication". The Appellate Division reversed and dismissed the complaint against the MacLarens.

We agree with the Appellate Division that CPLR 302(a)(1)—the section that governs the issue in this defamation action—does not support the exercise of personal jurisdiction over the MacLarens. Essential to the maintenance of this action against the MacLarens are some "purposeful activities" within the State and a "substantial relationship" between those activities and the transaction out of which the cause of action arose (McGowan v. Smith, 52 N.Y.2d 268, 272, 437 N.Y.S.2d 643, 419 N.E.2d 321). Even if Patricia MacLaren's previous enrollment and attendance at a New York university satisfied the requirement of purposeful activities in New York, there was no showing that—years after termination of that relationship—there was the required nexus between the MacLarens' New York "business" and the present cause of action. While appellants urge that jurisdiction may constitutionally be premised on broader standards articulated by the United States Supreme Court (*see, e.g.,* Asahi Metal Indus. v. Superior Ct., 480 U.S. 102, 107 S.Ct. 1026, 1033, 94 L.Ed.2d 92), the New York long-arm statute (CPLR 302) does not provide for in personam jurisdiction in every case in which due process would permit it (Banco Ambrosiano v. Artoc Bank & Trust, 62 N.Y.2d 65, 71, 476 N.Y.S.2d 64, 464 N.E.2d 432).

Burt v. Board of Regents

United States Court of Appeals, Tenth Circuit, 1985.
757 F.2d 242.
Cert. granted, *Connolly v. Burt*, 474 U.S. 1004, 88 L. Ed. 2d 454, 106 S. Ct. 521 (1985); and vacated, remanded with instructions to dismiss as moot, *Connolly v. Burt*, 475 U.S. 1063, 89 L. Ed. 2d 599, 106 S. Ct. 1372 (1986)

■ SEYMOUR, CIRCUIT JUDGE.

Andrew K. Burt, a Colorado resident at the time this action was filed, brought suit against the Board of Regents of the University of Nebraska and John F. Connolly, Chairman of the Department of Orthopedic Surgery at the University. Dr. Burt, a medical doctor, had completed a residency program in orthopedic surgery under Dr. Connolly at the University. Dr. Burt subsequently applied for staff privileges at several Colorado hospitals, which directed inquiries to Dr. Connolly about Dr. Burt's orthopedic residency and general medical competence. Dr. Connolly responded with a very unfavorable letter and Dr. Burt was denied staff privileges. Dr. Burt filed this suit seeking damages for defamation, breach of contract, interference with prospective advantage, outrageous conduct, and the deprivation of property and liberty interests protected by the United States Constitution. The district court granted defendants' motions to dismiss, ruling that the Board of Regents was immune under the Eleventh Amendment, and that the court did not have personal jurisdiction over Dr. Connolly. Dr. Burt appeals the jurisdictional issue, and we reverse.

Dr. Burt alleges in his complaint that the statements by Dr. Connolly were false, willful and wanton, made with malice, and published in Colorado. He further alleges that as a result of these statements he was unable to practice medicine in Colorado. Dr. Burt asserts that the court has personal jurisdiction over Dr. Connolly pursuant to Colorado's long-arm statute, which provides in pertinent part:

> "Engaging in any act enumerated in this section by any person, whether or not a resident of the state of Colorado, either in person or by an agent, submits such person, and if a natural person his personal representative to the jurisdiction of the courts of this state concerning any cause of action arising from:

* * *

> The commission of a tortious act within this state * * *."

Colo.Rev.Stat. § 13–1–124(1)(b) (1973).

In response, Dr. Connolly filed an affidavit asserting that he is a resident of Nebraska and that he has never done business of any kind in Colorado. Dr. Connolly further states that he owns no property in Colorado and was never physically present in Colorado in connection with the claim asserted by Dr. Burt.

The Colorado long-arm statute was intended to extend the jurisdiction of the Colorado courts to the fullest extent permitted by the due process clause of the United States Constitution. Behagen v. Amateur Basketball Association of America, 744 F.2d 731, 733 (10th Cir.1984). In this case the district court concluded that the action was technically within the reach of the long-arm statute because the alleged tort of defamation occurred in Colorado. The court held, however, that personal jurisdiction over Dr. Connolly was precluded by the requirements of federal due process because he lacked sufficient minimum contacts with the forum state.

* * *

Nor are we persuaded by Dr. Connolly's claim that it violates due process to hale him into court in Colorado because the letter was, in effect, solicited by Dr. Burt, who gave Dr. Connolly's name to the hospitals. Dr. Burt solicited a letter of reference; he did not solicit a malicious falsehood. Taking Dr. Burt's allegations as true, as we must on a motion to dismiss, we hold that no due process notions of fairness are violated by requiring one who intentionally libels another to answer for the truth of his statements in any state where the libel causes harm to the victim. To the extent that Dr. Connolly's statements damaged Dr. Burt's reputation and his ability to practice his profession, the damage occurred in Colorado.

Accordingly, we conclude that the district court erred in its determination that it lacked personal jurisdiction over Dr. Connolly. The judgment is reversed on that ground and remanded for further proceedings.[a]

Covenant Bank for Savings v. Cohen

United States District Court District of New Jersey, 1992.
806 F. Supp. 52.

■ BROTMAN, DISTRICT JUDGE.

Presently before the court are motions brought by defendants Bank Hapoalim and David Barr to dismiss the complaint for lack of personal jurisdiction and to grant partial summary judgment. For the reasons set forth below, the court holds that an assertion of jurisdiction over these two defendants would be inconsistent with constitutional due process. Because of this holding, the court does not consider the motion for partial summary judgment.

The present dispute arises out of a series of loan transactions between plaintiff Covenant Bank for Savings ("Covenant") and defendant Brad Cohen in July 1989. Covenant alleges that it made loans to Brad Cohen in the amount of $690,000. These loans were allegedly evidenced by promissory notes dated October 26, 1990. Covenant claims that Brad Cohen has defaulted on all of these loans and asks the court to award damages. By its opinion and order dated September 25, 1992, this court instructed the clerk of the court to enter a default against Brad Cohen, pursuant to Federal Rule of Civil Procedure 55(a), for failure to defend the present action.

Covenant has also stated claims against defendants Bank Hapoalim ("Hapoalim") and David Barr, a former employee of Hapoalim. In count four of the complaint, Covenant alleges fraud in that Hapoalim and Barr defendants drafted and provided Covenant with a false credit report concerning Brad Cohen. Count five sounds in negligence, alleging that defendants violated their duty of care in giving false credit information. Both claims arise from an alleged conversation in July 1989 between the plaintiff bank and Mr. Barr.

Defendants ask this court to dismiss the claims against them for lack of personal jurisdiction, pursuant to Federal Rule of Civil Procedure 12(b)(2). Plaintiff bears the burden of proving the existence of "sufficient contacts between the defendant[s] and the forum state to support jurisdiction." *Provident National Bank v. California Federal Savings & Loan Association*, 819 F.2d 434, 437 (3d Cir.1987). This court may exercise personal jurisdiction over a party pursuant to New Jersey law and the Due Process clause. Because New Jersey extends its jurisdictional reach to the fullest limits permitted by the federal

---

a. The dissenting opinion of Circuit Judge Seth is omitted.

Constitution, the sole inquiry before this court is whether an assertion of personal jurisdiction over defendants Hapoalim and David Barr comports with constitutional due process.

The court considers first whether there is specific jurisdiction over Hapoalim and Mr. Barr. The underlying transaction which gives rise to plaintiff's claims against these defendants consists of a single inquiry, initiated by Covenant, directed to Mr. Barr at his office at Hapoalim in Philadelphia. There is no allegation that defendants solicited or initiated the contact with Covenant. Nor are there allegations of other contacts between defendants and the forum state that are connected to plaintiff's claims.

This single, unsolicited contact with a plaintiff located in New Jersey is not sufficient to justify an assertion of personal jurisdiction. The case law clearly establishes that a resident plaintiff's unilateral acts, directed to a nonresident defendant, do not create sufficient minimum contacts between the nonresident defendant and the forum, even where the plaintiff's claim arises out of these acts. See *Time Share Vacation Club v. Atlantic Resorts, Ltd.*, 735 F.2d 61, 65 (3d Cir.1984); *Reliance Steel Products Co. v. Watson, Ess, Marshall & Enggas*, 675 F.2d 587, 589 (3d Cir.1982); *Baron & Co., Inc. v. Bank of New Jersey*, 497 F. Supp. 534, 537 (E.D.Pa.1980).[4] Rather, "it is essential in each case that there be some act by which the defendant purposefully avails itself of the privilege of conducting activities within the forum State, thus invoking the benefits and protection of its laws." *Hanson v. Denckla*, 357 U.S. 235, 253, 2 L. Ed. 2d 1283, 78 S. Ct. 1228 (1958). Hapoalim and Mr. Barr responded to an unsolicited inquiry, initiated by Covenant, for information on the credit worthiness of Larry Cohen and Brad Cohen. Although the communication might have been tortious, it did not in any way represent a deliberate and purposeful contact with New Jersey.

Covenant attempts to establish minimum contacts based not on the telephone call itself but on the telephone call's impact in New Jersey. Covenant argues that the court may exercise personal jurisdiction "over non-residents in tort cases based upon a single deliberate contact with New Jersey where a contact resulted in the alleged injury." Pl.'s Brief at 9 (quoting *United States Golf Association v. U.S. Amateur Golf Association*, 690 F. Supp. 317 (D.N.J.1988)).

It is true that due process is satisfied when a forum asserts jurisdiction over a defendant who undertakes affirmative acts which the defendant should reasonably foresee would lead to economic damages within the forum. See *Calder v. Jones*, 465 U.S. 783, 79 L. Ed. 2d 804, 104 S. Ct. 1482 (1984) (permitting personal jurisdiction over two nonresidents who wrote and edited allegedly libelous article in

---

4. Covenant cites Southeast Guaranty Trust Co., Ltd. v. Rodman & Renshaw, 358 F. Supp. 1001, 1009 (N.D.Ill.1973), for the proposition that a misrepresentation, communicated by a nonresident defendant during a single telephone call initiated by a resident plaintiff, is a sufficient contact to confer jurisdiction. Pl.'s Brief at 10. The court finds Southeast Guaranty Trust on point, but refuses to follow its holding because it is incompatible with more recent Third Circuit law.

their capacity as employees of publication which was distributed in forum state); see also Carteret Savings Bank, 954 F.2d at 147–48. But the Calder "effects" test requires as a predicate for its application that the nonresident defendant purposefully and deliberately direct his act toward the forum state. Viewing the facts most favorably for the plaintiff, the court assumes that defendants' alleged act of misrepresentation was intentional. It is, however, necessary to distinguish between a defendant's acts which: (1) are aimed at a plaintiff who is located in the forum and (2) are aimed at the forum itself. In the first instance, defendant's actions, directed at the plaintiff, have only an unintended effect in the forum, such as economic damage. In the second instance, the defendant performs an act with "the very purpose of having an effect" in the forum. *Narco Avionics, Inc. v. Sportsman's Market, Inc.*, 792 F. Supp. 398, 408 (E.D.Pa.1992). Only the latter kind of intentional act constitutes a purposeful and deliberate contact with the forum which makes it fair and reasonable for the forum to exercise personal jurisdiction. Defendants' sole act was to respond to Covenant's unsolicited request for information. While defendants' response may have caused plaintiff damages in New Jersey, defendants did not perform this act with the "very purpose" of having such an impact in New Jersey. Accordingly, the Calder "effects" test does not apply.

QUESTION

Has the district court successfully distinguished *Calder*? Do you think the court's proposed distinction between different kinds of intentional acts is a practicable one?

C. DOING BUSINESS IN THE FORUM STATE: THE CONCEPT OF GENERAL JURISDICTION

Helicopteros Nacionales de Colombia v. Hall

Supreme Court of the United States, 1984.
466 U.S. 408, 104 S.Ct.1868, 80 L.Ed.2d 404.

■ JUSTICE BLACKMUN delivered the opinion of the Court.

We granted certiorari in this case, 460 U.S. 1021, 103 S.Ct. 1270, 75 L.Ed.2d 493 (1983), to decide whether the Supreme Court of Texas correctly ruled that the contacts of a foreign corporation with the State of Texas were sufficient to allow a Texas state court to assert jurisdiction over the corporation in a cause of action not arising out of or related to the corporation's activities within the State.

I

Petitioner Helicopteros Nacionales de Colombia, S.A. (Helicol), is a Colombian corporation with its principal place of business in the city of Bogota in that country. It is engaged in the business of providing helicopter transportation for oil and construction companies in South America. On January 26, 1976, a helicopter owned by Helicol crashed in Peru. Four United States citizens were among those who lost their lives in the accident. Respondents are the survivors and representatives of the four decedents.

At the time of the crash, respondents' decedents were employed by Consorcio, a Peruvian consortium, and were working on a pipeline in Peru. Consorcio is the alter ego of a joint venture named Williams–Sedco–Horn (WSH). The venture had its headquarters in Houston, Tex. Consorcio had been formed to enable the venturers to enter into a contract with Petro Peru, the Peruvian state-owned oil company. Consorcio was to construct a pipeline for Petro Peru running from the interior of Peru westward to the Pacific Ocean. Peruvian law forbade construction of the pipeline by any non-Peruvian entity.

Consorcio/WSH needed helicopters to move personnel, materials, and equipment into and out of the construction area. In 1974, upon request of Consorcio/WSH, the chief executive officer of Helicol, Francisco Restrepo, flew to the United States and conferred in Houston with representatives of the three joint venturers. At that meeting, there was a discussion of prices, availability, working conditions, fuel, supplies, and housing. Restrepo represented that Helicol could have the first helicopter on the job in 15 days. The Consorcio/WSH representatives decided to accept the contract proposed by Restrepo. Helicol began performing before the agreement was formally signed in Peru on November 11, 1974. The contract was written in Spanish on official government stationery and provided that the residence of all the parties would be Lima, Peru. It further stated that controversies arising out of the contract would be submitted to the jurisdiction of Peruvian courts. In addition, it provided that Consorcio/WSH would make payments to Helicol's account with the Bank of America in New York City.

Aside from the negotiation session in Houston between Restrepo and the representatives of Consorcio/WSH, Helicol had other contacts with Texas. During the years 1970–1977, it purchased helicopters (approximately 80% of its fleet), spare parts, and accessories for more than $4 million from Bell Helicopter Company in Fort Worth. In that period, Helicol sent prospective pilots to Fort Worth for training and to ferry the aircraft to South America. It also sent management and maintenance personnel to visit Bell Helicopter in Fort Worth during the same period in order to receive "plant familiarization" and for technical consultation. Helicol received into its New York City and Panama City, Fla., bank accounts over $5 million in payments from Consorcio/WSH drawn upon First City National Bank of Houston.

Beyond the foregoing, there have been no other business contacts between Helicol and the State of Texas. Helicol never has been authorized to do business in Texas and never has had an agent for the service of process within the State. It never has performed helicopter operations in Texas or sold any product that reached Texas, never solicited business in Texas, never signed any contract in Texas, never had any employee based there, and never recruited an employee in Texas. In addition, Helicol never has owned real or personal property in Texas and never has maintained an office or establishment there. Helicol has maintained no records in Texas and has no shareholders in that State. None of the respondents or their decedents were domiciled in Texas, Tr. of Oral Arg. 17, 18,[5] but all of the decedents were hired in Houston by Consorcio/WSH to work on the Petro Peru pipeline project.

Respondents instituted wrongful-death actions in the District Court of Harris County, Tex., against Consorcio/WSH, Bell Helicopter Company, and Helicol. Helicol filed special appearances and moved to dismiss the actions for lack of *in personam* jurisdiction over it. The motion was denied. After a consolidated jury trial, judgment was entered against Helicol on a jury verdict of $1,141,200 in favor of respondents.[6]

The Texas Court of Civil Appeals, Houston, First District, reversed the judgment of the District Court, holding that *in personam* jurisdiction over Helicol was lacking. 616 S.W.2d 247 (1981). The Supreme Court of Texas, with three justices dissenting, initially affirmed the judgment of the Court of Civil Appeals. App. to Pet. for Cert. 46a–62a. Seven months later, however, on motion for rehearing, the court withdrew its prior opinions and, again with three justices dissenting, reversed the judgment of the intermediate court. 638 S.W.2d 870 (1982). In ruling that the Texas courts had *in personam* jurisdiction, the Texas Supreme Court first held that the State's long-arm statute reaches as far as the Due Process Clause of the Fourteenth Amendment permits. Id. at 872.[7] Thus, the only question remaining for the

---

5. Respondents' lack of residential or other contacts with Texas of itself does not defeat otherwise proper jurisdiction. Keeton v. Hustler Magazine, Inc., 465 U.S. 770, 780, 104 S.Ct. 1473, 1481, 79 L.Ed.2d 790 (1984); Calder v. Jones, 465 U.S. 783, 788, 104 S.Ct. 1482, 1486, 79 L.Ed.2d 804 (1984). We mention respondents' lack of contacts merely to show that nothing in the nature of the relationship between respondents and Helicol could possibly enhance Helicol's contacts with Texas. The harm suffered by respondents did not occur in Texas. Nor is it alleged that any negligence on the part of Helicol took place in Texas.

6. Defendants Consorcio/WSH and Bell Helicopter Company were granted directed verdicts with respect to respondents' claims against them. Bell Helicopter was granted a directed verdict on Helicol's cross-claim against it. App. 167a. Consorcio/WSH, as cross-plaintiff in a claim against Helicol, obtained a judgment in the amount of $70,000.

7. The State's long-arm statute is Tex. Rev.Civ.Stat.Ann., Art. 2031b (Vernon 1964 and Supp. 1982–1983). It reads in relevant part:

"Sec. 3. Any foreign corporation * * * that engages in business in this State, irrespective of any Statute or law respecting designation or maintenance of resident agents, and does not maintain a place of regular business in this State or a designated agent upon whom service may be made upon causes of action arising out of such business done in this State, the act or acts of engaging in such business within this State shall be deemed equivalent to an appointment by such foreign corporation * * * of the Secretary of State of Texas as agent upon whom service of process may be made in any action, suit or proceedings arising out of such business done in this State, wherein such corporation * * * is a party or is to be made a party.

"Sec. 4. For the purpose of this Act, and without including other acts that may constitute doing business, any foreign corporation * * * shall be deemed doing business in this State by entering into contract by mail or otherwise with a resident of Texas to be performed in whole or in part by either party in this State, or the committing of any tort in

court to decide was whether it was consistent with the Due Process Clause for Texas courts to assert *in personam* jurisdiction over Helicol.

II

The Due Process Clause of the Fourteenth Amendment operates to limit the power of a State to assert *in personam* jurisdiction over a nonresident defendant. Pennoyer v. Neff, 95 U.S. 714, 24 L.Ed. 565 (1877). Due process requirements are satisfied when *in personam* jurisdiction is asserted over a nonresident corporate defendant that has "certain minimum contacts with [the forum] such that the maintenance of the suit does not offend 'traditional notions of fair play and substantial justice.' " International Shoe Co. v. Washington, 326 U.S. 310, 316, 66 S.Ct. 154, 158, 90 L.Ed. 95 (1945), quoting Milliken v. Meyer, 311 U.S. 457, 463, 61 S.Ct. 339, 342, 85 L.Ed.2d 278 (1940). When a controversy is related to or "arises out of' a defendant's contacts with the forum, the Court has said that a "relationship among the defendant, the forum, and the litigation" is the essential foundation of *in personam* jurisdiction. Shaffer v. Heitner, 433 U.S. 186, 204, 97 S.Ct. 2569, 2579, 53 L.Ed.2d 683 (1977).[8]

Even when the cause of action does not arise out of or relate to the foreign corporation's activities in the forum State,[9] due process is not offended by a State's subjecting the corporation to its *in personam* jurisdiction when there are sufficient contacts between the State and the foreign corporation. Perkins v. Benguet Consolidated Mining Co., 342 U.S. 437, 72 S.Ct. 413, 96 L.Ed. 485 (1952); see Keeton v. Hustler Magazine, Inc., 465 U.S. 770, 779–780, 104 S.Ct. 1473, 1480–1481, 79 L.Ed.2d 790 (1984). In *Perkins,* the Court addressed a situation in which state courts had asserted general jurisdiction over a defendant foreign corporation. During the Japanese occupation of the Philippine Islands, the president and general manager of a Philippine mining corporation maintained an office in Ohio from which he conducted activities on behalf of the company. He kept company files and held directors' meetings in the office, carried on correspondence relating to the business, distributed salary checks drawn on two active Ohio bank accounts, engaged an Ohio bank to act as transfer agent, and supervised policies dealing with the rehabilitation of the corporation's

whole or in part in this State. The act of recruiting Texas residents, directly or through an intermediary located in Texas, for employment inside or outside of Texas shall be deemed doing business in this State."

The last sentence of § 4 was added by 1979 Tex.Gen.Laws, ch. 245, § 1, and became effective August 27, 1979. * * *

8. It has been said that when a State exercises personal jurisdiction over a defendant in a suit arising out of or related to the defendant's contacts with the forum, the State is exercising "specific jurisdiction" over the defendant. *See* Von Mehren & Trautman,

Jurisdiction to Adjudicate: A Suggested Analysis, 79 Harv.L.Rev. 1121, 1144–1164 (1966).

9. When a State exercises personal jurisdiction over a defendant in a suit not arising out of or related to the defendant's contacts with the forum, the State has been said to be exercising "general jurisdiction" over the defendant. See Brilmayer, How Contacts Count: Due Process Limitations on State Court Jurisdiction. 1980 S.Ct.Rev. 77, 80–81; Von Mehren & Trautman, 79 Harv.L.Rev., at 1136–1144; Calder v. Jones, 465 U.S., at 786, 104 S.Ct., at 1485.

properties in the Philippines. In short, the foreign corporation, through its president, "ha[d] been carrying on in Ohio a continuous and systematic, but limited, part of its general business," and the exercise of general jurisdiction over the Philippine corporation by an Ohio court was "reasonable and just." 342 U.S., at 438, 445, 72 S.Ct., at 414, 418.

All parties to the present case concede that respondents' claims against Helicol did not "arise out of," and are not related to, Helicol's activities within Texas. We thus must explore the nature of Helicol's contacts with the State of Texas to determine whether they constitute the kind of continuous and systematic general business contacts the Court found to exist in *Perkins.* We hold that they do not.

It is undisputed that Helicol does not have a place of business in Texas and never has been licensed to do business in the State. Basically, Helicol's contacts with Texas consisted of sending its chief executive officer to Houston for a contract-negotiation session; accepting into its New York bank account checks drawn on a Houston bank; purchasing helicopters, equipment, and training services from Bell Helicopter for substantial sums; and sending personnel to Bell's facilities in Fort Worth for training.

The one trip to Houston by Helicol's chief executive officer for the purpose of negotiating the transportation-services contract with Consorcio/WSH cannot be described or regarded as a contact of a "continuous and systematic" nature, as *Perkins* described it, see also International Shoe Co. v. Washington, 326 U.S., at 320, 66 S.Ct., at 160, and thus cannot support an assertion of *in personam* jurisdiction over Helicol by a Texas court. Similarly, Helicol's acceptance from Consorcio/WSH of checks drawn on a Texas bank is of negligible significance for purposes of determining whether Helicol had sufficient contacts in Texas. There is no indication that Helicol ever requested that the checks be drawn on a Texas bank or that there was any negotiation between Helicol and Consorcio/WSH with respect to the location or identity of the bank on which checks would be drawn. Common sense and everyday experience suggest that, absent unusual circumstances, the bank on which a check is drawn is generally of little consequence to the payee and is a matter left to the discretion of the drawer. Such unilateral activity of another party or a third person is not an appropriate consideration when determining whether a defendant has sufficient contacts with a forum State to justify an assertion of jurisdiction. * * *

The Texas Supreme Court focused on the purchases and the related training trips in finding contacts sufficient to support an assertion of jurisdiction. We do not agree with that assessment, for the Court's opinion in Rosenberg Bros. & Co. v. Curtis Brown Co., 260 U.S. 516, 43 S.Ct. 170, 67 L.Ed. 372 (1923) (Brandeis, J., for a unanimous tribunal), makes clear that purchases and related trips, standing alone, are not a sufficient basis for a State's assertion of jurisdiction.

The defendant in *Rosenberg* was a small retailer in Tulsa, Okla., who dealt in men's clothing and furnishings. It never had applied for a license to do business in New York, nor had it at any time authorized suit to be brought against it there. It never had an established place of business in New York and never regularly carried on business in that State. Its only connection with New York was that it purchased from New York wholesalers a large portion of the merchandise sold in its Tulsa store. The purchases sometimes were made by correspondence and sometimes through visits to New York by an officer of the defendant. The Court concluded: "Visits on such business, even if occurring at regular intervals, would not warrant the inference that the corporation was present within the jurisdiction of [New York]." *Id.*, at 518.

This Court in *International Shoe* acknowledged and did not repudiate its holding in *Rosenberg.* See 326 U.S., at 318, 66 S.Ct., at 159. In accordance with *Rosenberg,* we hold that mere purchases, even if occurring at regular intervals, are not enough to warrant a State's assertion of *in personam* jurisdiction over a nonresident corporation in a cause of action not related to those purchase transactions.[12] Nor can we conclude that the fact that Helicol sent personnel into Texas for training in connection with the purchase of helicopters and equipment in that State in any way enhanced the nature of Helicol's contacts with Texas. The training was a part of the package of goods and services purchased by Helicol from Bell Helicopter. The brief presence of Helicol employees in Texas for the purpose of attending the training sessions is no more a significant contact than were the trips to New York made by the buyer for the retail store in *Rosenberg.*
* * *

III

We hold that Helicol's contacts with the State of Texas were insufficient to satisfy the requirements of the Due Process Clause of the Fourteenth Amendment.[13] Accordingly, we reverse the judgment of the Supreme Court of Texas.

12. This Court in *International Shoe* cited *Rosenberg* for the proposition that "the commission of some single or occasional acts of the corporate agent in a state sufficient to impose an obligation or liability on the corporation has not been thought to confer upon the state authority to enforce it." 326 U.S., at 318, 66 S.Ct., at 159. Arguably, therefore, *Rosenberg* also stands for the proposition that mere purchases are not a sufficient basis for either general or specific jurisdiction. Because the case before us is one in which there has been an assertion of general jurisdiction over a foreign defendant, we need not decide the continuing validity of *Rosenberg* with respect to an assertion of specific jurisdiction, *i.e.*, where the cause of action arises out of or relates to the purchases by the defendant in the forum State.

13. As an alternative to traditional minimum-contacts analysis, respondents suggest that the Court hold that the State of Texas had personal jurisdiction over Helicol under a doctrine of "jurisdiction by necessity." See Shaffer v. Heitner, 433 U.S. 186, 211, n. 37, 97 S.Ct. 2569, 2583, n. 37, 53 L.Ed.2d 683 (1977). We conclude, however, that respondents failed to carry their burden of showing that all three defendants could not be sued together in a single forum. It is not clear from the record, for example, whether suit could have been brought against all three defendants in either Colombia or Peru. We decline to consider adoption of a doctrine of jurisdiction by necessity—a potentially far-reaching modification of existing law—in the absence of a more complete record.

It is so ordered.

■ JUSTICE BRENNAN, dissenting.

Decisions applying the Due Process Clause of the Fourteenth Amendment to determine whether a State may constitutionally assert *in personam* jurisdiction over a particular defendant for a particular cause of action most often turn on a weighing of facts. * * *

To a large extent, today's decision follows the usual pattern. Based on essentially undisputed facts, the Court concludes that petitioner Helicol's contacts with the State of Texas were insufficient to allow the Texas state courts constitutionally to assert "general jurisdiction" over all claims filed against this foreign corporation. Although my independent weighing of the facts leads me to a different conclusion, * * * the Court's holding on this issue is neither implausible nor unexpected.

What is troubling about the Court's opinion, however, are the implications that might be drawn from the way in which the Court approaches the constitutional issue it addresses. First, the Court limits its discussion to an assertion of general jurisdiction of the Texas courts because, in its view, the underlying cause of action does "not aris[e] out of or relat[e] to the corporation's activities within the State." *Ante,* at 409. Then, the Court relies on a 1923 decision in Rosenberg Bros. & Co. v. Curtis Brown Co., 260 U.S. 516, 43 S.Ct. 170, 67 L.Ed. 372, without considering whether that case retains any validity after our more recent pronouncements concerning the permissible reach of a State's jurisdiction. By posing and deciding the question presented in this manner, I fear that the Court is saying more than it realizes about constitutional limitations on the potential reach of *in personam* jurisdiction. In particular, by relying on a precedent whose premises have long been discarded, and by refusing to consider any distinction between controversies that "relate to" a defendant's contacts with the forum and causes of action that "arise out of" such contacts, the Court may be placing severe limitations on the type and amount of contacts that will satisfy the constitutional minimum.

NOTES

A. The Texas Supreme Court in its substituted opinion of October 6, 1982, Hall v. Helicopteros Nacionales De Colombia, 638 S.W.2d 870, 871–872 (Tex.1982) referred to Helicol's committing the following acts in Texas:

a. Purchased substantially all of its helicopter fleet in Fort Worth, Texas;

b. Did approximately $4,000,000 worth of business in Fort Worth, Texas, from 1970 through 1976 as purchaser of equipment, parts and services. This consisted of spending an average of $50,000 per month with Bell Helicopter Company, a Texas corporation;

c. Negotiated in Houston, Harris County, Texas, with a Texas resident, which negotiation resulted in the contract to provide the helicopter service involving the crash leading to this cause of action (previously mentioned), and wherein Helicol agreed to obtain liability insurance payable in American dollars to cover a claim such as this;

d.   Sent pilots to Fort Worth, Texas to pick up helicopters as they were purchased from Bell Helicopter and fly them from Fort Worth to Colombia;

e.   Sent maintenance personnel and pilots to Texas to be trained;

f.   Had employees in Texas on a year-round rotation basis;

g.   Received roughly $5,000,000 under the terms and provisions of the contract in question here which payments were made from First City National Bank in Houston, Texas; and

h.   Directed the First City National Bank of Houston, Texas to make payments to Rocky Mountain Helicopters pursuant to the contract in question. (Involved leasing of a large helicopter capable of moving heavier loads for Williams–Sedco–Horn.)

B.   Entering into a contract or, more generally doing business, within the forum state may be urged as sufficient contact to support a finding of jurisdiction either with respect to a dispute arising out of the contract in question or one that is not related to that particular contract or business. Should there be any difference in the standard applied in these two situations? If so, in which should a court more readily find jurisdiction?

For a fact situation in which the dispute arose out of the contract see Burger King Corp. v. Rudzewicz, 471 U.S. 462, 105 S.Ct. 2174, 85 L.Ed.2d 528 (1985).

D.   Location of Person or Property Within the Forum State: In Rem and Quasi-In-Rem Jurisdiction

NOTE ON QUASI-IN-REM JURISDICTION

Suppose a dispute has arisen over the ownership of a two acre parcel of land in downtown Metrocenter, located in State X. Surely State X has jurisdiction to resolve that dispute, by litigation in its courts, even though none of the disputants resides within the state. There are various ways of articulating why that is so, but there is no doubt that it is so.

If the property in question is not real property, but personal property, gold bars in a vault located in State X, for example, the result is the same. The policies that support this conclusion are not identical with those in the first case, but they are similar. If the property in question is intangible personal property, a bank account, for example, the result will be identical.

Where litigation purported to determine the rights of the parties before it in a given piece of property against the whole world, for example the rights of all to Metroacre located in State X, or the rights of the whole world to a late model Cadillac being confiscated for drug running, the litigation was said to be in rem, distinguishing it from jurisdiction over the person (in personam) with which we have been dealing. Note that if a lawsuit properly in rem results in a judgment, it ends the matter even against individuals who never were in that suit.

Legal doctrine developed a hybrid basis of jurisdiction, termed quasi-in-rem. If plaintiff had a claim against defendant who was not subjected to the in personam jurisdiction of the court but who had money in a State X bank account, plaintiff might subject that bank account to the power of the court in State X, following procedures dictated by statute and the court would then assert jurisdiction over the defendant to determine, as between P and D and based solely on the claim being asserted in that lawsuit, who had the superior right to the money in the bank account. This did not preclude assertion of a superior right to the bank account on the part of some third party; it could not result in D being obliged to pay more than the amount of money actually in the bank account, at least not if D defaulted.

How far should we carry that interesting theory? If L (lender) lends money to B (borrower) the debt is really property owned by L, intangible property to be sure, but still property. In theory that "property" is located wherever B goes, or at least wherever B can be served in a lawsuit. Now suppose P (plaintiff) wishes to sue L on an unrelated claim and decides to commence the law suit by subjecting that debt owed by B to L to the jurisdiction of the court in some third state, Z, doing so by serving papers on B which say: don't pay your debt to L, that property of L's is subject to our jurisdiction; wait until we adjudicate the case of P vs. L. Does Z have quasi-in-rem jurisdiction over P's claim against L? Any limit on where L might find herself litigating?

In Harris v. Balk, 198 U.S. 215, 25 S.Ct. 625, 49 L.Ed. 1023 (1905), Epstein in Baltimore claimed that Balk, a resident of North Carolina, owed him $344. Harris, a North Carolina resident, but present on business in Baltimore to buy goods, owed Balk $180. Epstein garnished the $180. debt owed by Harris to Balk (quasi in rem jurisdiction). Epstein had to file a bond for the defendant Balk's protection. Default judgment was entered on the Maryland action which Harris later paid to the $180. limit of his debt to Balk. When Harris returned to North Carolina Balk sued Harris for the same $180. Harris asserted his satisfaction of the Maryland judgment as a defense.

The Supreme Court held that the judgment against the garnishee was valid in Maryland because jurisdiction over the garnishee had been obtained by personal service in Maryland. That valid judgment barred defendant Balk's later action against the garnishee in North Carolina for the same property, the $180. debt.

Balk got prompt notice of the attachment. Under Maryland law, Balk had a year and a day to appear in the Maryland proceeding and raise any defense he might have had and, if successful, open the default judgment. Epstein's bond had to last that long under Maryland law. Thus, Balk had notice, ample opportunity to appear and defend, and the protection of Epstein's bond.

The garnishee will want to give the defendant, whose property he has, notice of the attachment proceedings which may affect defendant's property. This will protect the garnishee from double liability. State statutes vary with some requiring that the plaintiff be responsible for giving notice to the defendant by service of a copy of the complaint and writ of garnishment (as often called attachment).

Shaffer v. Heitner

Supreme Court of the United States, 1977.
433 U.S. 186, 97 S.Ct. 2569, 53 L.Ed.2d 683.

■ MR. JUSTICE MARSHALL delivered the opinion of the Court.

The controversy in this case concerns the constitutionality of a Delaware statute that allows a court of that State to take jurisdiction of a lawsuit by sequestering any property of the defendant that happens to be located in Delaware. Appellants contend that the sequestration statute as applied in this case violates the Due Process Clause of the Fourteenth Amendment both because it permits the state courts to exercise jurisdiction despite the absence of sufficient contacts among the defendants, the litigation, and the State of Delaware and because it authorizes the deprivation of defendants' property without providing adequate procedural safeguards. We find it necessary to consider only the first of these contentions.

I

Appellee Heitner, a nonresident of Delaware, is the owner of one share of stock in the Greyhound Corp., a business incorporated under the laws of Delaware with its principal place of business in Phoenix, Ariz. On May 22, 1974, he filed a shareholder's derivative suit in the Court of Chancery for New Castle County, Del., in which he named as defendants Greyhound, its wholly owned subsidiary Greyhound Lines, Inc.,[1] and 28 present or former officers or directors of one or both of the corporations. In essence, Heitner alleged that the individual defendants had violated their duties to Greyhound by causing it and its subsidiary to engage in actions that resulted in the corporations being held liable for substantial damages in a private antitrust suit[2] and a large fine in a criminal contempt action.[3] The activities which led to these penalties took place in Oregon.

Simultaneously with his complaint, Heitner filed a motion for an order of sequestration of the Delaware property of the individual defendants pursuant to Del.Code Ann., Tit. 10, § 366 (1975).[4] This motion was accompanied by a supporting affidavit of counsel which stated that the individual defendants were nonresidents of Delaware. The affidavit identified the property to be sequestered as

> "common stock, 3% Second Cumulative Preferred Stock and stock unit credits of the Defendant Greyhound Corporation. * * *.

---

1. Greyhound Lines, Inc., is incorporated in California and has its principal place of business in Phoenix, Ariz.

2. A judgment of $13,146,090 plus attorneys' fees was entered against Greyhound in Mt. Hood Stages, Inc. v. Greyhound Corp., 1972–3 Trade Cas. ¶ 74,824, aff'd, 555 F.2d 687 (9th Cir.1977); App. 10.

3. See United States v. Greyhound Corp., 363 F.Supp. 525 (N.D.Ill.1973) and 370 F.Supp. 881 (N.D.Ill.), aff'd, 508 F.2d 529 (7th Cir.1974). Greyhound was fined $100,-000 and Greyhound Lines $500,000.

4. Section 366 provides:

"(a) If it appears in any complaint filed in the Court of Chancery that the defendant or any one or more of the defendants is a nonresident of the State, the Court may make an order directing such nonresident defendant or defendants to appear by a day certain to be designated. Such order shall be served on such nonresident defendant or defendants by mail or otherwise, if practicable, and shall be published in such manner as the Court directs, not less than once a week for 3 consecutive weeks. The Court may compel the appearance of the defendant by the seizure of all or any part of his property, which property may be sold under the order of the Court to pay the demand of the plaintiff, if the defendant does not appear, or otherwise defaults. Any defendant whose property shall have been so seized and who shall have entered a general appearance in the cause may, upon notice to the plaintiff, petition the Court for an order releasing such property or any part thereof from the seizure. The Court shall release such property unless the plaintiff shall satisfy the Court that because of other circumstances there is a reasonable possibility that such release may render it substantially less likely that plaintiff will obtain satisfaction of any judgment secured. If such petition shall not be granted, or if no such petition shall be filed, such property shall remain subject to seizure and may be sold to satisfy any judgment entered in the cause. The Court may at any time release such property or any part thereof upon the giving of sufficient security.

The requested sequestration order was signed the day the motion was filed. Pursuant to that order, the sequestrator "seized" approximately 82,000 shares of Greyhound common stock belonging to 19 of the defendants,[7] and options belonging to another 2 defendants. These seizures were accomplished by placing "stop transfer" orders or their equivalents on the books of the Greyhound Corp. So far as the record shows, none of the certificates representing the seized property was physically present in Delaware. The stock was considered to be in Delaware, and so subject to seizure, by virtue of Del.Code Ann., Tit. 8, § 169 (1975), which makes Delaware the situs of ownership of all stock in Delaware corporations.

All 28 defendants were notified of the initiation of the suit by certified mail directed to their last known addresses and by publication in a New Castle County newspaper. The 21 defendants whose property was seized (hereafter referred to as appellants) responded by entering a special appearance for the purpose of moving to quash service of process and to vacate the sequestration order. They contended that the *ex parte* sequestration procedure did not accord them due process of law and that the property seized was not capable of attachment in Delaware. In addition, appellants asserted that under the rule of International Shoe Co. v. Washington, 326 U.S. 310, 66 S.Ct. 154, 90 L.Ed. 95 (1945), they did not have sufficient contacts with Delaware to sustain the jurisdiction of that State's courts.

II

The Delaware courts rejected appellants' jurisdictional challenge by noting that this suit was brought as a *quasi in rem* proceeding. Since *quasi in rem* jurisdiction is traditionally based on attachment or seizure of property present in the jurisdiction, not on contacts between the defendant and the State, the courts considered appellants' claimed lack of contacts with Delaware to be unimportant. This categorical analysis assumes the continued soundness of the conceptual structure founded on the century-old case of Pennoyer v. Neff, 95 U.S. 714, 24 L.Ed. 565 (1877).

Pennoyer was an ejectment action brought in federal court under the diversity jurisdiction. Pennoyer, the defendant in that action, held the land under a deed purchased in a sheriff's sale conducted to realize on a judgment for attorney's fees obtained against Neff in a previous action by one Mitchell. At the time of Mitchell's suit in an Oregon State court, Neff was a nonresident of Oregon. An Oregon statute allowed service by publication on nonresidents who had property in the State, and Mitchell had used that procedure to bring Neff before the court. The United States Circuit Court for the District of Oregon, in which Neff brought his ejectment action, refused to

---

7. The closing price of Greyhound stock on the day the sequestration order was issued was $14⅜, New York Times, May 23, 1974, p.   62. Thus, the value of the sequestered stock was approximately $1.2 million.

recognize the validity of the judgment against Neff in Mitchell's suit, and accordingly awarded the land to Neff. This Court affirmed.

* * *

From our perspective, the importance of *Pennoyer* is not its result, but the fact that its principles and corollaries derived from them became the basic elements of the constitutional doctrine governing state-court jurisdiction. See, *e.g.,* Hazard, A General Theory of State–Court Jurisdiction, 1965 Sup.Ct.Rev. 241 (hereafter Hazard). As we have noted, under *Pennoyer* state authority to adjudicate was based on the jurisdiction's power over either persons or property. This fundamental concept is embodied in the very vocabulary which we use to describe judgments. If a court's jurisdiction is based on its authority over the defendant's person, the action and judgment are denominated *"in personam"* and can impose a personal obligation on the defendant in favor of the plaintiff. If jurisdiction is based on the court's power over property within its territory, the action is called *"in rem"* or *"quasi in rem."* The effect of a judgment in such a case is limited to the property that supports jurisdiction and does not impose a personal liability on the property owner, since he is not before the court.[17]

* * *

The *Pennoyer* rules generally favored nonresident defendants by making them harder to sue. This advantage was reduced, however, by the ability of a resident plaintiff to satisfy a claim against a nonresident defendant by bringing into court any property of the defendant located in the plaintiff's State. See, *e.g.,* Zammit, Quasi–In–Rem Jurisdiction: Outmoded and Unconstitutional?, 49 St. John's L.Rev. 668, 670 (1975). For example, in the well-known case of Harris v. Balk, 198 U.S. 215, 25 S.Ct. 625, 49 L.Ed. 1023 (1905), Epstein, a resident of Maryland, had a claim against Balk, a resident of North Carolina. Harris, another North Carolina resident, owed money to Balk. When Harris happened to visit Maryland, Epstein garnished his debt to Balk. Harris did not contest the debt to Balk and paid it to Epstein's North Carolina attorney. When Balk later sued Harris in North Carolina, this Court held that the Full Faith and Credit Clause, U.S. Const., Art. IV, § 1, required that Harris' payment to Epstein be treated as a discharge of his debt to Balk. This Court reasoned that the debt Harris owed Balk was an intangible form of property belonging to Balk, and that the location of that property traveled with the debtor. By obtaining personal jurisdiction over Harris, Epstein had "arrested" his debt to

---

17. "A judgment *in rem* affects the interests of all persons in designated property. A judgment *quasi in rem* affects the interests of particular persons in designated property. The latter is of two types. In one the plaintiff is seeking to secure a pre-existing claim in the subject property and to extinguish or establish the nonexistence of similar interests of particular persons. In the other the plain- tiff seeks to apply what he concedes to be the property of the defendant to the satisfaction of a claim against him. Restatement, Judgments, 5–9." Hanson v. Denckla, 357 U.S. 235, 246 n. 12, 78 S.Ct. 1228, 1235, 2 L.Ed.2d 1283 (1958).

As did the Court in *Hanson,* we will for convenience generally use the term *"in rem"* in place of *"in rem* and *quasi in rem."*

Balk, 198 U.S., at 223, and brought it into the Maryland court. Under the structure established by *Pennoyer,* Epstein was then entitled to proceed against that debt to vindicate his claim against Balk, even though Balk himself was not subject to the jurisdiction of a Maryland tribunal.

* * *

The advent of automobiles, with the concomitant increase in the incidence of individuals causing injury in States where they were not subject to *in personam* actions under *Pennoyer,* required further moderation of the territorial limits on jurisdictional power. This modification, like the accommodation to the realities of interstate corporate activities, was accomplished by use of a legal fiction that left the conceptual structure established in *Pennoyer* theoretically unaltered. Cf. Olberding v. Illinois Central R. Co., 346 U.S. 338, 340–341, 74 S.Ct. 83, 85–86, 98 L.Ed. 39 (1953). The fiction used was that the out-of-state motorist, who it was assumed could be excluded altogether from the State's highways, had by using those highways appointed a designated state official as his agent to accept process. See Hess v. Pawloski, 274 U.S. 352, 47 S.Ct. 632, 71 L.Ed. 1091 (1927). Since the motorist's "agent" could be personally served within the State, the state courts could obtain *in personam* jurisdiction over the nonresident driver.

The motorists' consent theory was easy to administer since it required only a finding that the out-of-state driver had used the State's roads. By contrast, both the fictions of implied consent to service on the part of a foreign corporation and of corporate presence required a finding that the corporation was "doing business" in the forum State. Defining the criteria for making that finding and deciding whether they were met absorbed much judicial energy. See, *e.g.,* International Shoe Co. v. Washington, 326 U.S., at 317–319, 66 S.Ct., at 158–160. While the essentially quantitative tests which emerged from these cases purported simply to identify circumstances under which presence or consent could be attributed to the corporation, it became clear that they were in fact attempting to ascertain "what dealings make it just to subject a foreign corporation to local suit." Hutchinson v. Chase & Gilbert, 45 F.2d 139, 141 (2d Cir.1930) (L. Hand, J.). In *International Shoe,* we acknowledged that fact.

The question in *International Shoe* was whether the corporation was subject to the judicial and taxing jurisdiction of Washington. Mr. Chief Justice Stone's opinion for the Court began its analysis of that question by noting that the historical basis of *in personam* jurisdiction was a court's power over the defendant's person. That power, however, was no longer the central concern:

> "But now that the *capias ad respondendum* has given way to personal service of summons or other form of notice, due process requires only that in order to subject a defendant to a judgment *in personam,* if he be not present within the territory of the forum, he have certain minimum contacts with it such that the

maintenance of the suit does not offend 'traditional notions of fair play and substantial justice.' Milliken v. Meyer, 311 U.S. 457, 463, 61 S.Ct. 339, 343, 85 L.Ed. 278." 326 U.S., at 316, 66 S.Ct., at 158.

Thus, the inquiry into the State's jurisdiction over a foreign corporation appropriately focused not on whether the corporation was "present" but on whether there have been

"such contacts of the corporation with the state of the forum as make it reasonable, in the context of our federal system of government, to require the corporation to defend the particular suit which is brought there." *Id.*, at 317, 66 S.Ct., at 158.

Mechanical or quantitative evaluations of the defendant's activities in the forum could not resolve the question of reasonableness:

"Whether due process is satisfied must depend rather upon the quality and nature of the activity in relation to the fair and orderly administration of the laws which it was the purpose of the due process clause to insure. That clause does not contemplate that a state may make binding a judgment *in personam* against an individual or corporate defendant with which the state has no contacts, ties, or relations." *Id.*, at 319, 66 S.Ct., at 160.

Thus, the relationship among the defendant, the forum, and the litigation, rather than the mutually exclusive sovereignty of the States on which the rules of *Pennoyer* rest, became the central concern of the inquiry into personal jurisdiction. The immediate effect of this departure from *Pennoyer*'s conceptual apparatus was to increase the ability of the state courts to obtain personal jurisdiction over nonresident defendants.

No equally dramatic change has occurred in the law governing jurisdiction *in rem.* There have, however, been intimations that the collapse of the *in personam* wing of *Pennoyer* has not left that decision unweakened as a foundation for *in rem* jurisdiction. Well-reasoned lower court opinions have questioned the proposition that the presence of property in a State gives that State jurisdiction to adjudicate rights to the property regardless of the relationship of the underlying dispute and the property owner to the forum. The overwhelming majority of commentators have also rejected *Pennoyer*'s premise that a proceeding "against" property is not a proceeding against the owners of that property. Accordingly, they urge that the "traditional notions of fair play and substantial justice" that govern a State's power to adjudicate *in personam* should also govern its power to adjudicate personal rights to property located in the State. * * *

Although this Court has not addressed this argument directly, we have held that property cannot be subjected to a court's judgment unless reasonable and appropriate efforts have been made to give the property owners actual notice of the action. This conclusion recognizes, contrary to *Pennoyer,* that an adverse judgment *in rem* directly affects the property owner by divesting him of his rights in the property before the court. Schroeder v. City of New York, *supra,* at 213, 83 S.Ct., at 282; cf. Continental Grain Co. v. Barge FBL–585, 364

U.S. 19, 80 S.Ct. 1470, 4 L.Ed.2d 1540 (1960) (separate actions against barge and barge owner are one "civil action" for purpose of transfer under 28 U.S.C. § 1404(a)). Moreover, in *Mullane* we held that Fourteenth Amendment rights cannot depend on the classification of an action as *in rem* or *in personam,* since that is

> "a classification for which the standards are so elusive and confused generally and which, being primarily for state courts to define, may and do vary from state to state." 339 U.S., at 312, 70 S.Ct., at 656.

It is clear, therefore, that the law of state-court jurisdiction no longer stands securely on the foundation established in *Pennoyer.* We think that the time is ripe to consider whether the standard of fairness and substantial justice set forth in *International Shoe* should be held to govern actions *in rem* as well as *in personam.*

III

The case for applying to jurisdiction *in rem* the same test of "fair play and substantial justice" as governs assertions of jurisdiction *in personam* is simple and straightforward. It is premised on recognition that "[t]he phrase, 'judicial jurisdiction over a thing,' is a customary elliptical way of referring to jurisdiction over the interests of persons in a thing." Restatement (Second) of Conflict of Laws § 56, Introductory Note (1971) (hereafter Restatement). This recognition leads to the conclusion that in order to justify an exercise of jurisdiction *in rem,* the basis for jurisdiction must be sufficient to justify exercising "jurisdiction over the interests of persons in a thing." The standard for determining whether an exercise of jurisdiction over the interests of persons is consistent with the Due Process Clause is the minimum-contacts standard elucidated in *International Shoe.*

This argument, of course, does not ignore the fact that the presence of property in a State may bear on the existence of jurisdiction by providing contacts among the forum State, the defendant, and the litigation. For example, when claims to the property itself are the source of the underlying controversy between the plaintiff and the defendant, it would be unusual for the State where the property is located not to have jurisdiction. In such cases, the defendant's claim to property located in the State would normally indicate that he expected to benefit from the State's protection of his interest. The State's strong interests in assuring the marketability of property within its borders and in providing a procedure for peaceful resolution of disputes about the possession of that property would also support jurisdiction, as would the likelihood that important records and witnesses will be found in the State. The presence of property may also favor jurisdiction in cases, such as suits for injury suffered on the land of an absentee owner, where the defendant's ownership of the property is conceded but the cause of action is otherwise related to rights and duties growing out of that ownership.

It appears, therefore, that jurisdiction over many types of actions which now are or might be brought *in rem* would not be affected by a holding that any assertion of state-court jurisdiction must satisfy the *International Shoe* standard. For the type of *quasi in rem* action typified by *Harris v. Balk* and the present case, however, accepting the proposed analysis would result in significant change. These are cases where the property which now serves as the basis for state-court jurisdiction is completely unrelated to the plaintiff's cause of action. Thus, although the presence of the defendant's property in a State might suggest the existence of other ties among the defendant, the State, and the litigation, the presence of the property alone would not support the State's jurisdiction. If those other ties did not exist, cases over which the State is now thought to have jurisdiction could not be brought in that forum.

* * *

Moreover, we know of nothing to justify the assumption that a debtor can avoid paying his obligations by removing his property to a State in which his creditor cannot obtain personal jurisdiction over him. The Full Faith and Credit Clause, after all, makes the valid *in personam* judgment of one State enforceable in all other States.[36]

* * *

IV

The Delaware courts based their assertion of jurisdiction in this case solely on the statutory presence of appellants' property in Delaware. Yet that property is not the subject matter of this litigation, nor is the underlying cause of action related to the property. Appellants' holdings in Greyhound do not, therefore, provide contacts with Delaware sufficient to support the jurisdiction of that State's courts over appellants. If it exists, that jurisdiction must have some other foundation.

Appellee Heitner did not allege and does not now claim that appellants have ever set foot in Delaware. Nor does he identify any act related to his cause of action as having taken place in Delaware. Nevertheless, he contends that appellants' positions as directors and officers of a corporation chartered in Delaware provide sufficient "contacts, ties, or relations," International Shoe Co. v. Washington, 326 U.S., at 319, 66 S.Ct., at 160, with that State to give its courts jurisdiction over appellants in this stockholder's derivative action. This argument is based primarily on what Heitner asserts to be the strong interest of Delaware in supervising the management of a Delaware corporation. That interest is said to derive from the role of Delaware law in establishing the corporation and defining the obligations owed to it by its officers and directors. In order to protect this interest,

---

36. Once it has been determined by a court of competent jurisdiction that the defendant is a debtor of the plaintiff, there would seem to be no unfairness in allowing an action to realize on that debt in a State where the defendant has property, whether or not that State would have jurisdiction to determine the existence of the debt as an original matter.

appellee concludes, Delaware's courts must have jurisdiction over corporate fiduciaries such as appellants.

This argument is undercut by the failure of the Delaware Legislature to assert the state interest appellee finds so compelling. Delaware law bases jurisdiction, not on appellants' status as corporate fiduciaries, but rather on the presence of their property in the State. Although the sequestration procedure used here may be most frequently used in derivative suits against officers and directors, Hughes Tool Co. v. Fawcett Publications, Inc., 290 A.2d 693, 695 (Del.Ch. 1972), the authorizing statute evinces no specific concern with such actions. Sequestration can be used in any suit against a nonresident, see, *e.g.,* U.S. Industries, Inc. v. Gregg, 540 F.2d 142 (3d Cir.1976), cert. pending, No. 76–359 (breach of contract); *Hughes Tool Co. v. Fawcett Publications, Inc., supra* (same), and reaches corporate fiduciaries only if they happen to own interests in a Delaware corporation, or other property in the State. But as Heitner's failure to secure jurisdiction over seven of the defendants named in his complaint demonstrates, there is no necessary relationship between holding a position as a corporate fiduciary and owning stock or other interests in the corporation. If Delaware perceived its interest in securing jurisdiction over corporate fiduciaries to be as great as Heitner suggests, we would expect it to have enacted a statute more clearly designed to protect that interest.

* * *

Appellee suggests that by accepting positions as officers or directors of a Delaware corporation, appellants performed the acts required by *Hanson v. Denckla.* He notes that Delaware law provides substantial benefits to corporate officers and directors, and that these benefits were at least in part the incentive for appellants to assume their positions. It is, he says, "only fair and just" to require appellants, in return for these benefits, to respond in the State of Delaware when they are accused of misusing their power. Brief for Appellee 15.

But like Heitner's first argument, this line of reasoning establishes only that it is appropriate for Delaware law to govern the obligations of appellants to Greyhound and its stockholders. It does not demonstrate that appellants have "purposefully avail[ed themselves] of the privilege of conducting activities within the forum State," *Hanson v. Denckla, supra,* at 253, in a way that would justify bringing them before a Delaware tribunal. Appellants have simply had nothing to do with the State of Delaware. Moreover, appellants had no reason to expect to be haled before a Delaware court. Delaware, unlike some States, has not enacted a statute that treats acceptance of a directorship as consent to jurisdiction in the State. And "[i]t strains reason * * * to suggest that anyone buying securities in a corporation formed in Delaware 'impliedly consents' to subject himself to Delaware's * * * jurisdiction on any cause of action." Folk & Moyer, *supra,* n. 10, at 785. Appellants, who were not required to acquire interests in Greyhound in order to hold their positions, did not by acquiring those interests surrender their right to be brought to judgment only in States with which they had had "minimum contacts."

The Due Process Clause

> "does not contemplate that a state may make binding a judgment * * * against an individual or corporate defendant with which the state has no contacts, ties, or relations." International Shoe Co. v. Washington, 326 U.S., at 319.

Delaware's assertion of jurisdiction over appellants in this case is inconsistent with that constitutional limitation on state power. The judgment of the Delaware Supreme Court must, therefore, be reversed.

It is so ordered.[a]

NOTE

After the Supreme Court's decision in *Shaffer v. Heitner,* many courts and commentators viewed the decision as the "death knell" of quasi in rem jurisdiction. However, New York, among other states, has reinvigorated the doctrine and applied it in a number of multi-million dollar commercial and tort cases. According to Chief Judge Wachtler, writing for a unanimous Court of Appeals in Banco Ambrosiano, S.P.A. v. Artoc Bank & Trust Limited, 62 N.Y.2d 65, 476 N.Y.S.2d 64, 464 N.E.2d 432 (1984):

> Although it may appear, at first blush, that the usefulness of quasi-in-rem jurisdiction has been eliminated by *Shaffer,* inasmuch as the minimum contacts necessary to support it will also generally provide in personam jurisdiction, that is not the case, at least in New York. As noted above CPLR 302 does not provide for in personam jurisdiction in every case in which due process would permit it. Thus a "gap" exists in which the necessary minimum contacts, including the presence of defendant's property within the State, are present, but personal jurisdiction is not authorized by CPLR 302. It is appropriate, in such a case, to fill that gap utilizing quasi-in-rem principles.

An assertion of quasi in rem jurisdiction is constitutionally impermissible, the opinion continues, only when the "property has no relation to the cause of action, and there are no other ties, among the defendant, the forum and the litigation." In *Ambrosiano,* the requisite minimum contacts were found to exist where an Italian bank, suing to recover a fifteen million dollar loan it had made to a Bahamian banking corporation, sought to attach eight million dollars in the defendant's New York bank account. The Court of Appeals held that the facts that the defendant had maintained an account in a correspondent bank in New York, that it was through this bank that the loan at issue was effectuated, that the defendant had used this bank on a regular basis to accomplish its international banking business, and furthermore, that the loan at issue was to be repaid to the plaintiff's own New York bank account created sufficient minimum contacts with the state of New York for the court to exercise quasi in rem jurisdiction.

According to Professor Mushlin, "The New Quasi In Rem Jurisdiction: New York's Revival of a Doctrine Whose Time Has Passed," 55 Brooklyn L.Rev. 1059 (1990), about ten other states have indicated that they too, are willing to invoke quasi in rem jurisdiction in the post-*Shaffer* era.

---

a. The concurring opinions of Justice Powell and Justice Stevens and the opinion of Justice Brennan, concurring in part and dissenting in part, are omitted.

E. TRANSIENT JURISDICTION

Humphrey v. Langford

Supreme Court of Georgia, 1980.
246 Ga. 732, 273 S.E.2d 22.

■ BOWLES, JUSTICE.

The Humphreys are the former owners of a South Carolina heating and air conditioning business. Langford purchased the business at a time when all parties were residents of South Carolina. The contract of sale was executed in South Carolina. Subsequently the Humphreys moved to Bryan County, Georgia, and instituted this lawsuit in Chatham County, Georgia concerning the sales agreement. Langford, still a resident of South Carolina, was in Chatham County one day to bowl. While there, he was served with the complaint and summons in this case.

* * * Corporate presence can only be manifested by corporate activity and therefore a minimum contacts analysis seems appropriate. However, when an individual is personally served within the state, we are talking about actual presence. Minimum contacts analysis is not necessary. It could be forcefully argued, however, that personal presence in a state fulfills the minimum contacts requirement.

* * * We believe that it is not practical to have classifications of sojourners in the state. Where does a court draw the line between sojourners here for an evening of bowling and sojourners who commute to the state on a daily basis? Some individuals are constant or perennial sojourners. Some have no identifiable place of residence. Still others are able to avoid personal service by remaining away from an otherwise identifiable place of abode. Others to avoid a responsibility can terminate on a moments notice a legal residence and otherwise disrupt the judicial process. Others can terminate residence in a forum favorable to the plaintiff and establish residence in a forum considered favorable to the defendant. One of two joint obligors may never be reached with process where they are residents of different states, and there is no basis for federal court jurisdiction, if it were not for a sojourner jurisdiction rule. If they cannot be sued where they are found, they may not be sued at all. Due process is not solely for the protection of the judicial defendant. Plaintiffs have rights that must also be protected. A balancing of rights appears constitutionally fair. When a sojourner is sued in this state, the plaintiff does not select the venue. The venue is where the defendant is of his own volition and is served. This sovereign state has an adequate court system and is capable of rendering justice between litigants as well as any court system. A party who is obligated on a transitory cause of action and who is a sojourner to this state, is required to abide by the laws of this state and could expect to be protected by those laws as well. To accept

the state's benefits and to avoid its responsibilities creates an imbalance which we cannot recognize. For these reasons we do not believe Langford's due process rights are being violated by requiring him to defend this lawsuit in this state.

Judgment reversed.

yes you can serve
① "balance of rights"

Burnham v. Superior Court of California

Supreme Court of the United States, 1990.
495 U.S. 604, 110 S.Ct. 2105, 109 L.Ed.2d 631.

■ JUSTICE SCALIA announced the judgment of the Court and delivered an opinion in which THE CHIEF JUSTICE and JUSTICE KENNEDY join, and in which JUSTICE WHITE joins with respect to Parts I, II–A, II–B, and II–C.

The question presented is whether the Due Process Clause of the Fourteenth Amendment denies California courts jurisdiction over a nonresident, who was personally served with process while temporarily in that State, in a suit unrelated to his activities in the State.

I

Petitioner Dennis Burnham married Francie Burnham in 1976, in West Virginia. In 1977 the couple moved to New Jersey, where their two children were born. In July 1987 the Burnhams decided to separate. They agreed that Mrs. Burnham, who intended to move to California, would take custody of the children. Shortly before Mrs. Burnham departed for California that same month, she and petitioner agreed that she would file for divorce on grounds of "irreconcilable differences."

In October 1987, petitioner filed for divorce in New Jersey state court on grounds of "desertion." Petitioner did not, however, obtain an issuance of summons against his wife, and did not attempt to serve her with process. Mrs. Burnham, after unsuccessfully demanding that petitioner adhere to their prior agreement to submit to an "irreconcilable differences" divorce, brought suit for divorce in California state court in early January 1988.

In late January, petitioner visited southern California on business, after which he went north to visit his children in the San Francisco Bay area, where his wife resided. He took the older child to San Francisco for the weekend. Upon returning the child to Mrs. Burnham's home on January 24, 1988, petitioner was served with a California court summons and a copy of Mrs. Burnham's divorce petition. He then returned to New Jersey.

Later that year, petitioner made a special appearance in the California Superior Court, moving to quash the service of process on the ground that the court lacked personal jurisdiction over him because his only contacts with California were a few short visits to the State for the purposes of conducting business and visiting his children. The Superior Court denied the motion, and the California Court of Appeal denied mandamus relief, rejecting petitioner's contention that the Due Process Clause prohibited California courts from asserting jurisdiction over him because he lacked "minimum contacts" with the State. The court held it to be "a valid jurisdictional predicate for *in personam* jurisdiction" that the "defendant [was] present in the forum state and personally served with process."

II

A

* * *

To determine whether the assertion of personal jurisdiction is consistent with due process, we have long relied on the principles traditionally followed by American courts in marking out the territorial limits of each State's authority. That criterion was first announced in *Pennoyer v. Neff,* in which we stated that due process "mean[s] a course of legal proceedings according to those rules and principles which have been established in our systems of jurisprudence for the protection and enforcement of private rights," including the "well-established principles of public law respecting the jurisdiction of an independent State over persons and property." In what has become the classic expression of the criterion, we said in International Shoe Co. v. Washington, 326 U.S. 310, 66 S.Ct. 154, 90 L.Ed. 95 (1945), that a State court's assertion of personal jurisdiction satisfies the Due Process Clause if it does not violate " 'traditional notions of fair play and substantial justice.' " *Id.,* at 316, 66 S.Ct., at 158, quoting Milliken v. Meyer, 311 U.S. 457, 463, 61 S.Ct. 339, 343, 85 L.Ed. 278 (1940). See also Insurance Corp. of Ireland v. Compagnie des Bauxites de Guinee, 456 U.S. 694, 703, 102 S.Ct. 2099, 2105, 72 L.Ed.2d 492 (1982). Since *International Shoe,* we have only been called upon to decide whether these "traditional notions" permit States to exercise jurisdiction over absent defendants in a manner that deviates from the rules of jurisdiction applied in the 19th century. We have held such deviations permissible, but only with respect to suits arising out of the absent defendant's contacts with the State.[1] See, *e.g.,* Helicopteros Nacionales de Colombia v. Hall, 466 U.S. 408, 414, 104 S.Ct. 1868, 1872, 80 L.Ed.2d 404 (1984). The question we must decide today is whether due process requires a similar connection between the litigation and the defendant's contacts with the State in cases where the

---

1. We have said that "[e]ven when the cause of action does not arise out of or relate to the foreign corporation's activities in the forum State, due process is not offended by a State's subjecting the corporation to its *in personam* jurisdiction when there are sufficient contacts between the State and the foreign corporation." Helicopteros Nacionales de Colombia v. Hall, 466 U.S., at 414, 104 S.Ct., at 1872. Our only holding supporting that statement, however, involved "regular service of summons upon [the corporation's] president while he was in [the forum State] acting in that capacity." See Perkins v. Benguet Consolidated Mining Co., 342 U.S. 437, 440, 72 S.Ct. 413, 415, 96 L.Ed. 485 (1952). It may be that whatever special rule exists permitting "continuous and systematic" contacts, *id.,* at 438, 72 S.Ct., at 414, to support jurisdiction with respect to matters unrelated to activity in the forum, applies *only* to corporations, which have never fitted comfortably in a jurisdictional regime based primarily upon "de facto power over the defendant's person." International Shoe Co. v. Washington, 326 U.S. 310, 316, 66 S.Ct. 154, 158, 90 L.Ed. 95 (1945). We express no views on these matters—and, for simplicity's sake, omit reference to this aspect of "contacts"-based jurisdiction in our discussion.

defendant is physically present in the State at the time process is served upon him.

B

Among the most firmly established principles of personal jurisdiction in American tradition is that the courts of a State have jurisdiction over nonresidents who are physically present in the State. The view developed early that each State had the power to hale before its courts any individual who could be found within its borders, and that once having acquired jurisdiction over such a person by properly serving him with process, the State could retain jurisdiction to enter judgment against him, no matter how fleeting his visit.

* * *

Decisions in the courts of many States in the 19th and early 20th centuries held that personal service upon a physically present defendant sufficed to confer jurisdiction, without regard to whether the defendant was only briefly in the State or whether the cause of action was related to his activities there. * * * Most States, moreover, had statutes or common-law rules that exempted from service of process individuals who were brought into the forum by force or fraud, see, *e.g.,* Wanzer v. Bright, 52 Ill. 35 (1869), or who were there as a party or witness in unrelated judicial proceedings. These exceptions obviously rested upon the premise that service of process conferred jurisdiction.

* * *

This American jurisdictional practice is, moreover, not merely old; it is continuing. It remains the practice of, not only a substantial number of the States, but as far as we are aware *all* the States and the federal government—if one disregards (as one must for this purpose) the few opinions since 1978 that have erroneously said, on grounds similar to those that petitioner presses here, that this Court's due-process decisions render the practice unconstitutional. We do not know of a single State or federal statute, or a single judicial decision resting upon State law, that has abandoned in–State service as a basis of jurisdiction. Many recent cases reaffirm it.

C

Despite this formidable body of precedent, petitioner contends, in reliance on our decisions applying the *International Shoe* standard, that in the absence of "continuous and systematic" contacts with the forum, see note 1, *supra,* a nonresident defendant can be subjected to judgment only as to matters that arise out of or relate to his contacts with the forum. This argument rests on a thorough misunderstanding of our cases.

The view of most courts in the 19th century was that a court simply could not exercise *in personam* jurisdiction over a nonresident who had not been personally served with process in the forum. * * * *Pennoyer v. Neff,* while renowned for its statement of the principle that the Fourteenth Amendment prohibits such an exercise of jurisdiction, in fact set that forth only as dictum, and decided the case (which involved a judgment rendered more than two years before the Fourteenth Amendment's ratification) under "well-established principles of public law." 95 U.S., at 722. Those principles, embodied in the Due Process Clause, required (we said) that when proceedings "involv[e] merely a determination of the personal liability of the defendant, he must be brought within [the court's] jurisdiction by service of process within the State, or his voluntary appearance." *Id.*, at 733. We invoked that rule in a series of subsequent cases, as either a matter of due process or a "fundamental principl[e] of jurisprudence."

Later years, however, saw the weakening of the *Pennoyer* rule. In the late 19th and early 20th centuries, changes in the technology of transportation and communication, and the tremendous growth of interstate business activity, led to an "inevitable relaxation of the strict limits on state jurisdiction" over nonresident individuals and corporations. Hanson v. Denckla, 357 U.S. 235, 260, 78 S.Ct. 1228, 1243, 2 L.Ed.2d 1283 (1958) (Black, J., dissenting). States required, for example, that nonresident corporations appoint an in-state agent upon whom process could be served as a condition of transacting business within their borders, see, *e.g.,* St. Clair v. Cox, 106 U.S. 350, 1 S.Ct. 354, 27 L.Ed. 222 (1882), and provided in-state "substituted service" for nonresident motorists who caused injury in the State and left before personal service could be accomplished, see, *e.g.,* Kane v. New Jersey, 242 U.S. 160, 37 S.Ct. 30, 61 L.Ed. 222 (1916); Hess v. Pawloski, 274 U.S. 352, 47 S.Ct. 632, 71 L.Ed. 1091 (1927). We initially upheld these laws under the Due Process Clause on grounds that they complied with *Pennoyer's* rigid requirement of either "consent," see, *e.g.,* Hess v. Pawloski, *supra,* at 356, 47 S.Ct., at 633, or "presence," *see, e.g.,* Philadelphia & Reading R. Co. v. McKibbin, 243 U.S. 264, 265, 37 S.Ct. 280, 280, 61 L.Ed. 710 (1917). As many observed, however, the consent and presence were purely fictional. Our opinion in *International Shoe* cast those fictions aside, and made explicit the underlying basis of these decisions: due process does not necessarily *require* the States to adhere to the unbending territorial limits on jurisdiction set forth in *Pennoyer.* The validity of assertion of jurisdiction over a nonconsenting defendant who is not present in the forum depends upon whether "the quality and nature of [his] activity" in relation to the forum, 326 U.S., at 319, 66 S.Ct., at 160, renders such jurisdiction consistent with " 'traditional notions of fair play and substantial justice.' " *Id.,* at 316, 66 S.Ct., at 158 (citation omitted). Subsequent cases have derived from the *International Shoe* standard the general rule that a State may dispense with in-forum personal service on nonresident defendants in suits arising out of their activities in the State. See generally Helicopteros Nacionales de Colombia v. Hall, 466 U.S., at 414–415, 104 S.Ct., at 1872.

* * *

Nothing in *International Shoe* or the cases that have followed it, however, offers support for the very different proposition petitioner seeks to establish today: that a defendant's presence in the forum is not only unnecessary to validate novel nontraditional assertions of jurisdiction, but is itself no longer sufficient to establish jurisdiction. That proposition is unfaithful to both elementary logic and the foundations of our due process jurisprudence. The distinction between what is needed to support novel procedures and what is needed to sustain traditional ones is fundamental[.] * * * The short of the matter is that jurisdiction based on physical presence alone constitutes due process because it is one of the continuing traditions of our legal system that define the due process standard of "traditional notions of fair play and substantial justice." That standard was developed by *analogy* to "physical presence," and it would be perverse to say it could now be turned against that touchstone of jurisdiction.

D

Petitioner's strongest argument, though we ultimately reject it, relies upon our decision in Shaffer v. Heitner, 433 U.S. 186, 97 S.Ct. 2569, 53 L.Ed.2d 683 (1977). In that case, a Delaware court hearing a shareholder's derivative suit against a corporation's directors secured jurisdiction *quasi in rem* by sequestering the out-of-State defendants' stock in the company, the situs of which was Delaware under Delaware law. Reasoning that Delaware's sequestration procedure was simply a mechanism to compel the absent defendants to appear in a suit to determine their personal rights and obligations, we concluded that the normal rules we had developed under *International Shoe* for jurisdiction over suits against absent defendants should apply—viz., Delaware could not hear the suit because the defendants' sole contact with the State (ownership of property there) was unrelated to the lawsuit. 433 U.S., at 213–215, 97 S.Ct., at 2584–2585.

It goes too far to say, as petitioner contends, that *Shaffer* compels the conclusion that a State lacks jurisdiction over an individual unless the litigation arises out of his activities in the State. *Shaffer*, like *International Shoe*, involved jurisdiction over an *absent defendant*, and it stands for nothing more than the proposition that when the "minimum contact" that is a substitute for physical presence consists of property ownership it must, like other minimum contacts, be related to the litigation. Petitioner wrenches out of its context our statement in *Shaffer* that "all assertions of state-court jurisdiction must be evaluated according to the standards set forth in *International Shoe* and its progeny," 433 U.S., at 212, 97 S.Ct., at 2584. When read together with the two sentences that preceded it, the meaning of this statement becomes clear:

> "The fiction that an assertion of jurisdiction over property is anything but an assertion of jurisdiction over the owner of the property supports an ancient form without substantial modern justification. Its continued acceptance would serve only to allow state-court jurisdiction that is fundamentally unfair to the defendant.

"We *therefore conclude* that all assertions of state-court jurisdiction must be evaluated according to the standards set forth in *International Shoe* and its progeny." *Ibid.* (emphasis added).

Shaffer was saying, in other words, not that all bases for the assertion of *in personam* jurisdiction (including, presumably, in-state service) must be treated alike and subjected to the "minimum contacts" analysis of *International Shoe;* but rather that *quasi in rem* jurisdiction, that fictional "ancient form," and *in personam* jurisdiction, are really one and the same and must be treated alike—leading to the conclusion that *quasi in rem* jurisdiction, *i.e.,* that form of *in personam* jurisdiction based upon a "property ownership" contact and by definition unaccompanied by personal, in-state service, must satisfy the litigation-relatedness requirement of *International Shoe.* The logic of *Shaffer*'s holding—which places all suits against absent nonresidents on the same constitutional footing, regardless of whether a separate Latin label is attached to one particular basis of contact—does not compel the conclusion that physically present defendants must be treated identically to absent ones. As we have demonstrated at length, our tradition has treated the two classes of defendants quite differently, and it is unreasonable to read *Shaffer* as casually obliterating that distinction. *International Shoe* confined its "minimum contacts" requirement to situations in which the defendant "be not present within the territory of the forum," 326 U.S., at 316, 66 S.Ct., at 158, and nothing in *Shaffer* expands that requirement beyond that.

It is fair to say, however, that while our holding today does not contradict *Shaffer,* our basic approach to the due process question is different. We have conducted no independent inquiry into the desirability or fairness of the prevailing in-state service rule, leaving that judgment to the legislatures that are free to amend it; for our purposes, its validation is its pedigree, as the phrase *"traditional notions* of fair play and substantial justice" makes clear. *Shaffer* did conduct such an independent inquiry, asserting that " 'traditional notions of fair play and substantial justice' can be as readily offended by the perpetuation of ancient forms that are no longer justified as by the adoption of new procedures that are inconsistent with the basic values of our constitutional heritage." 433 U.S., at 212, 97 S.Ct., at 2584. Perhaps that assertion can be sustained when the "perpetuation of ancient forms" is engaged in by only a very small minority of the States.[4] Where, however, as in the present case, a jurisdictional principle is both firmly approved by tradition and still favored, it is impossible to imagine what standard we could appeal to for the judgment that it is "no longer justified." While in no way receding from or casting doubt upon the holding of *Shaffer* or any other case, we reaffirm today our time-honored approach. For new procedures, hitherto unknown, the Due Process Clause requires analysis to determine whether "traditional notions of fair play and substantial justice" have been offended.

---

4. *Shaffer* may have involved a unique state procedure in one respect: Justice Stevens noted that Delaware was the only State that treated the place of incorporation as the situs of corporate stock when both owner and custodian were elsewhere. See 433 U.S., at 218, 97 S.Ct., at 2587 (opinion concurring in judgment).

International Shoe, 326 U.S., at 316, 66 S.Ct., at 158. But a doctrine of personal jurisdiction that dates back to the adoption of the Fourteenth Amendment and is still generally observed unquestionably meets that standard.

III

*   *   *

But the concurrence's proposed standard of "contemporary notions of due process" requires more: it measures state-court jurisdiction not only against traditional doctrines in this country, including current state-court practice, but against each Justice's subjective assessment of what is fair and just. Authority for that seductive standard is not to be found in any of our personal jurisdiction cases. It is, indeed, an outright break with the test of "traditional notions of fair play and substantial justice," which would have to be reformulated "*our* notions of fair play and substantial justice."

The subjectivity, and hence inadequacy, of this approach becomes apparent when the concurrence tries to explain *why* the assertion of jurisdiction in the present case meets its standard of continuing-American-tradition-*plus*-innate-fairness. Justice Brennan lists the "benefits" Mr. Burnham derived from the State of California—the fact that, during the few days he was there, "his health and safety [were] guaranteed by the State's police, fire, and emergency medical services; he [was] free to travel on the State's roads and waterways; he likely enjoy[ed] the fruits of the State's economy." Three days' worth of these benefits strike us as powerfully inadequate to establish, as an abstract matter, that it is "fair" for California to decree the ownership of all Mr. Burnham's worldly goods acquired during the ten years of his marriage, and the custody over his children. We daresay a contractual exchange swapping those benefits for that power would not survive the "unconscionability" provision of the Uniform Commercial Code. Even less persuasive are the other "fairness" factors alluded to by Justice Brennan. It would create "an asymmetry," we are told, if Burnham were *permitted* (as he is) to appear in California courts as a plaintiff, but were not *compelled* to appear in California courts as defendant; and travel being as easy as it is nowadays, and modern procedural devices being so convenient, it is no great hardship to appear in California courts. The problem with these assertions is that they justify the exercise of jurisdiction over *everyone, whether or not* he ever comes to California. The only "fairness" elements setting Mr. Burnham apart from the rest of the world are the three-days' "benefits" referred to above—and even those, do not set him apart from many other people who have enjoyed three days in the Golden State (savoring the fruits of its economy, the availability of its roads and police services) but who were fortunate enough not to be served with process while they were there and thus are not (simply by reason of that savoring) subject to the general jurisdiction of California's courts. See, *e.g.,* Helicopteros Nacionales de Colombia v. Hall, 466 U.S., at 414–416, 104 S.Ct., at 1872–1873. In other words, even if one agreed with Justice Brennan's conception of an equitable bargain, the "benefits" we have been discussing would explain why it is "fair" to assert general jurisdiction over Burnham-returned-to-New–Jersey-after-service only at the expense of proving that it is also "fair" to assert general jurisdiction over Burnham-returned-to-New–Jersey-*without*-service— which we *know* does not conform with "contemporary notions of due process."

There is, we must acknowledge, one factor mentioned by Justice Brennan that *both* relates distinctively to the assertion of jurisdiction on the basis of personal in-state service *and* is fully persuasive— namely, the fact that a defendant voluntarily present in a particular State has a "reasonable expectatio[n]" that he is subject to suit there. By formulating it as a "reasonable expectation" Justice Brennan makes that seem like a "fairness" factor; but in reality, of course, it is just tradition masquerading as "fairness." The only reason for charging Mr. Burnham with the reasonable expectation of being subject to suit is that the States of the Union assert adjudicatory jurisdiction over the person, and have always asserted adjudicatory jurisdiction over the person, by serving him with process during his temporary physical presence in their territory. That continuing tradition, which anyone entering California should have known about, renders it "fair" for Mr. Burnham, who voluntarily entered California, to be sued there for divorce—at least "fair" in the limited sense that he has no one but himself to blame.

* * *

Since Justice Brennan's only criterion of constitutionality is "fairness," the phrase "as a rule" represents nothing more than his estimation that, *usually,* all the elements of "fairness" he discusses in the present case will exist. But what if they do not? Suppose, for example, that a defendant in Mr. Burnham's situation enjoys not three days' worth of California's "benefits," but fifteen minutes' worth. Or suppose we remove one of those "benefits"—"enjoy[ment of] the fruits of the State's economy"—by positing that Mr. Burnham had not come to California on business, but only to visit his children. Or suppose that Mr. Burnham were demonstrably so impecunious as to be unable to take advantage of the modern means of transportation and communication that Justice Brennan finds so relevant. Or suppose, finally, that the California courts lacked the "variety of procedural devices," *post,* at 2125, that Justice Brennan says can reduce the burden upon out-of-state litigants. One may also make additional suppositions, relating not to the absence of the factors that Justice Brennan discusses, but to the presence of additional factors bearing upon the ultimate criterion of "fairness." What if, for example, Mr. Burnham were visiting a sick child? Or a dying child? *Cf.* Kulko v. California Superior Court, 436 U.S. 84, 93, 98 S.Ct. 1690, 1697, 56 L.Ed.2d 132 (1978) (finding the exercise of long-arm jurisdiction over an absent parent unreasonable because it would "discourage parents from entering into reasonable visitation agreements"). Since, so far as one can tell, Justice Brennan's approval of applying the in-state service rule in the present case rests on the presence of *all* the factors he lists, and on the absence of any others, every different case will present a different litigable issue. Thus, despite the fact that he manages to work the word "rule" into his formulation, Justice Brennan's approach does not establish a rule of law at all, but only a "totality of the circumstances" test, guaranteeing what traditional territorial rules of jurisdiction were designed precisely to avoid: uncertainty and litigation over the preliminary issue of the forum's competence. It may be that those evils, necessarily accompanying a free-standing "reasonableness" inquiry, must be accepted at the margins, when we evaluate *non*-traditional forms of jurisdiction newly adopted by the states, see, *e.g.,* Asahi Metal Industry Co., Ltd. v. Superior Court of California, 480 U.S. 102, 115, 107 S.Ct. 1026, 1035, 94 L.Ed.2d 92 (1987). But that is no reason for injecting them into the core of our American practice, exposing to such a "reasonableness" inquiry the ground of jurisdiction that has hitherto been considered the very *baseline* of reasonableness, physical presence.

* * *

Because the Due Process Clause does not prohibit the California courts from exercising jurisdiction over petitioner based on the fact of in-state service of process, the judgment is

Affirmed.

■ JUSTICE WHITE, concurring in part and concurring in the judgment.

I join Part I and Parts II–A, II–B, and II–C of Justice Scalia's opinion and concur in the judgment of affirmance. The rule allowing jurisdiction to be obtained over a non-resident by personal service in the forum state, without more, has been and is so widely accepted throughout this country that I could not possibly strike it down, either on its face or as applied in this case, on the ground that it denies due process of law guaranteed by the Fourteenth Amendment. Although the Court has the authority under the Amendment to examine even traditionally accepted procedures and declare them invalid, *e.g.,* Shaffer v. Heitner, 433 U.S. 186, 97 S.Ct. 2569, 53 L.Ed.2d 683 (1977), there has been no showing here or elsewhere that as a general proposition the rule is so arbitrary and lacking in common sense in so many instances that it should be held violative of Due Process in every case. Furthermore, until such a showing is made, which would be difficult indeed, claims in individual cases that the rule would operate unfairly as applied to the particular non-resident involved need not be entertained. At least this would be the case where presence in the forum state is intentional, which would almost always be the fact. Otherwise, there would be endless, fact-specific litigation in the trial and appellate courts, including this one. Here, personal service in California, without more, is enough, and I agree that the judgment should be affirmed.

■ JUSTICE BRENNAN, with whom JUSTICE MARSHALL, JUSTICE BLACKMUN, and JUSTICE O'CONNOR join, concurring in the judgment.

I agree with Justice Scalia that the Due Process Clause of the Fourteenth Amendment generally permits a state court to exercise jurisdiction over a defendant if he is served with process while voluntarily present in the forum State.[1] I do not perceive the need, however, to decide that a jurisdictional rule that " 'has been immemorially the actual law of the land,' " automatically comports with due process simply by virtue of its "pedigree." Although I agree that history is an important factor in establishing whether a jurisdictional rule satisfies due process requirements, I cannot agree that it is the *only* factor such that all traditional rules of jurisdiction are, *ipso facto,* forever constitutional. Unlike Justice Scalia, I would undertake an "independent inquiry into the * * * fairness of the prevailing in-state service rule." *Ante,* at 2116. I therefore concur only in the judgment.

I

I believe that the approach adopted by Justice Scalia's opinion today—reliance solely on historical pedigree—is foreclosed by our decisions in International Shoe Co. v. Washington, 326 U.S. 310, 66 S.Ct. 154, 90 L.Ed. 95 (1945), and Shaffer v. Heitner, 433 U.S. 186, 97 S.Ct. 2569, 53 L.Ed.2d 683 (1977). In *International Shoe,* we held that a state court's assertion of personal jurisdiction does not violate the Due Process Clause if it is consistent with " 'traditional notions of fair play and substantial justice.' " 326 U.S., at 316, 66 S.Ct., at 158, quoting Milliken v. Meyer, 311 U.S. 457, 463, 61 S.Ct. 339, 342–343, 85 L.Ed. 278 (1940). In *Shaffer,* we stated that "*all* assertions of state-court jurisdiction must be evaluated according to the standards set forth in *International Shoe* and its progeny." 433 U.S., at 212, 97 S.Ct., at 2584 (emphasis added). The critical insight of *Shaffer* is that all rules of jurisdiction, even ancient ones, must satisfy contemporary notions of due process. No longer were we content to limit our jurisdictional analysis to pronouncements that "[t]he foundation of jurisdiction is physical power," McDonald v. Mabee, 243 U.S. 90, 91, 37 S.Ct. 343, 343, 61 L.Ed. 608 (1917), and that "every State possesses exclusive jurisdiction and sovereignty over persons and property within its territory." Pennoyer v. Neff, 95 U.S. 714, 722, 24 L.Ed. 565 (1877). While acknowledging that "history must be considered as supporting the proposition that jurisdiction based solely on the presence of property satisfie[d] the demands of due process," we found that this factor could not be "decisive." 433 U.S., at 211–212, 97 S.Ct., at 2583. We recognized that " '[t]raditional notions of fair play and substantial justice' can be as readily offended by the perpetuation of ancient forms that are no longer justified as by the adoption of new procedures that are inconsistent with the basic values of our constitutional heritage." *Id.,* at 212, 97 S.Ct., at 2584 (citations omitted). I agree with this approach and continue to believe that "the minimum-contacts analysis developed in *International Shoe* * * * represents a far more sensible construct for the exercise of state-court jurisdiction

---

1. I use the term "transient jurisdiction" to refer to jurisdiction premised solely on the fact that a person is served with process while physically present in the forum State.

than the patchwork of legal and factual fictions that has been generated from the decision in *Pennoyer v. Neff."* *Id.,* at 219, 97 S.Ct., at 2588 (citation omitted) (Brennan, J., concurring in part and dissenting in part).

While our *holding* in *Shaffer* may have been limited to *quasi in rem* jurisdiction, our mode of analysis was not. Indeed, that we were willing in *Shaffer* to examine anew the appropriateness of the *quasi in rem* rule—until that time dutifully accepted by American courts for at least a century—demonstrates that we did not believe that the "pedigree" of a jurisdictional practice was dispositive in deciding whether it was consistent with due process. We later characterized *Shaffer* as "abandon[ing] the outworn rule of Harris v. Balk, 198 U.S. 215 [25 S.Ct. 625, 49 L.Ed. 1023] (1905), that the interest of a creditor in a debt could be extinguished or otherwise affected by any State having transitory jurisdiction over the debtor." World–Wide Volkswagen Corp. v. Woodson, 444 U.S. 286, 296, 100 S.Ct. 559, 565, 62 L.Ed.2d 490 (1980); see also Rush v. Savchuk, 444 U.S. 320, 325–326, 100 S.Ct. 571, 575–576, 62 L.Ed.2d 516 (1980). If we could discard an "ancient form without substantial modern justification" in *Shaffer, supra,* 433 U.S., at 212, 97 S.Ct., at 2584, we can do so again. Lower courts,[4] commentators,[5] and the American Law Institute[6] all have interpreted *International Shoe* and *Shaffer* to mean that *every* assertion of state-court jurisdiction, even one pursuant to a "traditional" rule such as transient jurisdiction, must comport with contemporary notions of due process. Notwithstanding the nimble gymnastics of Justice Scalia's opinion today, it is not faithful to our decision in *Shaffer.*

4. Some lower courts have concluded that transient jurisdiction did not survive *Shaffer.* See Nehemiah v. Athletics Congress of U.S.A., 765 F.2d 42, 46–47 (3d Cir.1985); Schreiber v. Allis–Chalmers Corp., 448 F.Supp. 1079, 1088–1091 (Kan.1978), rev'd on other grounds, 611 F.2d 790 (10th Cir. 1979); Harold M. Pitman Co. v. Typecraft Software Ltd., 626 F.Supp. 305, 310–314 (N.D.Ill.1986); Bershaw v. Sarbacher, 40 Wash.App. 653, 657, 700 P.2d 347, 349 (1985). Others have held that transient jurisdiction is alive and well. But even cases falling into the latter category have engaged in the type of due process analysis that Justice Scalia's opinion claims is unnecessary today.

* * *

5. Although commentators have disagreed over whether the rule of transient jurisdiction is consistent with modern conceptions of due process, that they have engaged in such a debate at all shows that they have rejected the methodology employed by Justice Scalia's opinion today.

* * *

6. See Restatement (Second) of Conflict of Laws § 24, Comment *b,* p. 29 (Proposed Revisions 1986) ("One basic principle underlies all rules of jurisdiction. This principle is that a state does not have jurisdiction in the absence of some reasonable basis for exercising it. With respect to judicial jurisdiction, this principle was laid down by the Supreme Court of the United States in *International Shoe* * * *."); *id.,* at 30 ("Three factors are primarily responsible for existing rules of judicial jurisdiction. Present-day notions of fair play and substantial justice constitute the first factor"); *id.,* at 41, § 28, Comment *b,* ("The Supreme Court held in *Shaffer v. Heitner* that the presence of a thing in a state gives that state jurisdiction to determine interests in the thing only in situations where the exercise of such jurisdiction would be reasonable * * *. It must likewise follow that considerations of reasonableness qualify the power of a state to exercise personal jurisdiction over an individual on the basis of his physical presence within its territory"); Restatement (Second) of Judgments § 8, Comment *a,* p. 64 (Tent. Draft No. 5, Mar. 10, 1978) (*Shaffer* establishes " 'minimum contacts' in place of presence as the principal basis for territorial jurisdiction").

II

Tradition, though alone not dispositive, is of course *relevant* to the question whether the rule of transient jurisdiction is consistent with due process.[7] Tradition is salient not in the sense that practices of the past are automatically reasonable today; indeed, under such a standard, the legitimacy of transient jurisdiction would be called into question because the rule's historical "pedigree" is a matter of intense debate. The rule was a stranger to the common law and was rather weakly implanted in American jurisprudence "at the crucial time for present purposes: 1868, when the Fourteenth Amendment was adopted." *Ante,* at 2111. For much of the 19th century, American courts did not uniformly recognize the concept of transient jurisdiction, and it appears that the transient rule did not receive wide currency until well after our decision in Pennoyer v. Neff, 95 U.S. 714, 24 L.Ed. 565 (1877).

Rather, I find the historical background relevant because, however murky the jurisprudential origins of transient jurisdiction, the fact that American courts have announced the rule for perhaps a century (first in dicta, more recently in holdings) provides a defendant voluntarily present in a particular State *today* "clear notice that [he] is subject to suit" in the forum. World–Wide Volkswagen Corp. v. Woodson, 444 U.S. 286, 297, 100 S.Ct. 559, 567, 62 L.Ed.2d 490 (1980). Regardless of whether Justice Story's account of the rule's genesis is mythical, our common understanding *now,* fortified by a century of judicial practice, is that jurisdiction is often a function of geography. The transient rule is consistent with reasonable expectations and is entitled to a strong presumption that it comports with due process. "If I visit another State, * * * I knowingly assume some risk that the State will exercise its power over my property or my person while there. My contact with the State, though minimal, gives rise to predictable risks." *Shaffer,* 433 U.S., at 218, 97 S.Ct., at 2587 (Stevens, J., concurring in judgment); see also Burger King Corp. v. Rudzewicz, 471 U.S. 462, 476, 105 S.Ct. 2174, 2184, 85 L.Ed.2d 528 (1985) ("[t]erritorial presence frequently will enhance a potential defendant's affiliation with a State and reinforce the reasonable foreseeability of suit there"); Glen, An Analysis of "Mere Presence" and Other Traditional Bases of Jurisdiction, 45 Brooklyn L.Rev. 607, 611–612 (1979). Thus, proposed revisions to the Restatement (Second) of Conflict of Laws § 28, p. 39 (1986), provide that "[a] state has power to exercise judicial jurisdiction over an individual who is present within its territory unless the individual's

7. I do not propose that the "contemporary notions of due process" to be applied are no more than "each Justice's subjective assessment of what is fair and just." Rather, the inquiry is guided by our decisions beginning with International Shoe Co. v. Washington, 326 U.S. 310, 66 S.Ct. 154, 90 L.Ed. 95 (1945), and the specific factors that we have developed to ascertain whether a jurisdictional rule comports with "traditional notions of fair play and substantial justice." See, *e.g.,* Asahi Metal Industry Co. v. Superior Court of California, Solano County, 480 U.S. 102, 113, 107 S.Ct. 1026, 1033, 94 L.Ed.2d 92 (1987) (noting "several factors," including "the burden on the defendant, the interests of the forum State, and the plaintiff's interest in obtaining relief"). This analysis may not be "mechanical or quantitative," *International Shoe,* 326 U.S., at 319, 66 S.Ct. at 159, but neither is it "freestanding," *ante,* at 2119, or dependent on personal whim. Our experience with this approach demonstrates that it is well within our competence to employ.

relationship to the state is so attenuated as to make the exercise of such jurisdiction unreasonable."[11]

By visiting the forum State, a transient defendant actually "avail[s]" himself, *Burger King, supra,* at 476, 105 S.Ct., at 2184, of significant benefits provided by the State. His health and safety are guaranteed by the State's police, fire, and emergency medical services; he is free to travel on the State's roads and waterways; he likely enjoys the fruits of the State's economy as well. Moreover, the Privileges and Immunities Clause of Article IV prevents a state government from discriminating against a transient defendant by denying him the protections of its law or the right of access to its courts. Subject only to the doctrine of *forum non conveniens,* an out-of-state plaintiff may use state courts in all circumstances in which those courts would be available to state citizens. Without transient jurisdiction, an asymmetry would arise: a transient would have the full benefit of the power of the forum State's courts as a plaintiff while retaining immunity from their authority as a defendant. See Maltz, Sovereign Authority, Fairness, and Personal Jurisdiction: The Case for the Doctrine of Transient Jurisdiction, 66 Wash.U.L.Q. 671, 698–699 (1988).

The potential burdens on a transient defendant are slight. " '[M]odern transportation and communications have made it much less burdensome for a party sued to defend himself' " in a State outside his place of residence. *Burger King,* 471 U.S., at 474, 105 S.Ct., at 2183, quoting McGee v. International Life Insurance Co., 355 U.S. 220, 223, 78 S.Ct. 199, 201, 2 L.Ed.2d 223 (1957). That the defendant has already journeyed at least once before to the forum—as evidenced by the fact that he was served with process there—is an indication that suit in the forum likely would not be prohibitively inconvenient. Finally, any burdens that do arise can be ameliorated by a variety of procedural devices.[13] For these reasons, as a rule the exercise of personal jurisdiction over a defendant based on his voluntary presence in the forum will satisfy the requirements of due process.

In this case, it is undisputed that petitioner was served with process while voluntarily and knowingly in the State of California. I therefore concur in the judgment.

■ Justice Stevens, concurring in the judgment.

---

11. As the Restatement suggests, there may be cases in which a defendant's involuntary or unknowing presence in a State does not support the exercise of personal jurisdiction over him. The facts of the instant case do not require us to determine the outer limits of the transient jurisdiction rule.

13. For example, in the federal system, a transient defendant can avoid protracted litigation of a spurious suit through a motion to dismiss for failure to state a claim or through a motion for summary judgment. Fed.Rules Civ.Proc. 12(b)(6) and 56. He can use relatively inexpensive methods of discovery, such as oral deposition by telephone (Rule 30(b)(7)), deposition upon written questions (Rule 31), interrogatories (Rule 33), and requests for admission (Rule 36), while enjoying protection from harassment (Rule 26(c)), and possibly obtaining costs and attorney's fees for some of the work involved (Rule 37(a)(4), (b)–(d)). Moreover, a change of venue may be possible. 28 U.S.C. § 1404. In state court, many of the same procedural protections are available, as is the doctrine of *forum non conveniens,* under which the suit may be dismissed.

As I explained in my separate writing, I did not join the Court's opinion in Shaffer v. Heitner, 433 U.S. 186, 97 S.Ct. 2569, 53 L.Ed.2d 683 (1977), because I was concerned by its unnecessarily broad reach. *Id.*, at 217–219, 97 S.Ct., at 2586–2588 (opinion concurring in judgment). The same concern prevents me from joining either Justice Scalia's or Justice Brennan's opinion in this case. For me, it is sufficient to note that the historical evidence and consensus identified by Justice Scalia, the considerations of fairness identified by Justice Brennan, and the common sense displayed by Justice White, all combine to demonstrate that this is, indeed, a very easy case. Accordingly, I agree that the judgment should be affirmed.

QUESTIONS

1. How persuasive is Justice Scalia's argument that "jurisdiction based on physical presence alone constitutes due process because it is one of the continuing traditions of the legal system which define the due process standard of 'traditional notions of fair play and substantial justice' "? In light of this, consider Justice Holmes' remarks in his article "The Path of the Law," 10 Harv.L.Rev. 457, 469 (1897):

> It is revolting to have no better reason for a rule of law than that so it was laid down in the time of Henry IV. It is still more revolting if the grounds upon which it was laid down have vanished long since, and the rule simply persists from blind imitation of the past.

Is this applicable to the *Burnham* decision?

> Consider Justice Scalia's criticism of a possible alternative which:

> [M]easures state-court jurisdiction not only against traditional doctrines in this country, including current state-court practice, but against each Justice's subjective assessment of what is fair and just. Authority for that seductive standard is not to be found in any of our personal jurisdiction cases. It is, indeed, an outright break with the test of "traditional notions of fair play and substantial justice," which would have to be reformulated "*our* notions of fair play and substantial justice."

2. Under *Burnham* is service made on a passenger in an airplane flying over the forum state sufficient to confer personal jurisdiction over the passenger in that state?

F. OBJECTING TO JURISDICTION

NOTE: THE RATIONALE OF A SPECIAL APPEARANCE

I

One can hardly object to a rule that denies a defendant the opportunity to defend on the merits and, if unsuccessful, avoiding an adverse judgment by demonstrating that the court was altogether lacking in jurisdiction over defendant's person because there never had been proper service of process. Any other rule would be grossly inefficient and, one might add, rather unfair to plaintiff. In conceptual terms, we say that defendant, by litigating has entered a general appearance in the action, thereby consenting to the jurisdiction of the court.

Having conceptualized the issue in these terms, the question arises as to what, short of a trial on the merits, will be considered a general appearance, precluding a subsequent objection to the jurisdiction of the court. Suppose defendant unsuccessfully presses a motion to dismiss for failure of the plaintiff to state a claim? It is, of course, conceivable that the mere appearance before the court to notify the court that it has no jurisdiction over the defendant and that defendant objects to the continuation of the case could be held to be a general appearance. Indeed, this was the law in Texas and Mississippi well into the modern period and the United States Supreme Court held that the procedure did not violate due process so long as the defendant could raise the objection at the point that plaintiff sought to execute on the resulting default judgment, a judgment that would clearly be void as violative of due process. This is, however, hardly efficient, and it certainly puts defendant to some tough choices, especially in close cases.

At the present time there is no judicial system in this country that does not provide for a procedure by which a litigant can object to the jurisdiction of the court without thereby risking an adverse judgment. However, for a variety of reasons, some historical and some grounded in policy considerations, technical rules apply and failure to follow them can result in a litigant's having been held to have made a general appearance. Even the nomenclature—special appearance—reflects judicial malaise at allowing a party to come into court to advise the court that she really does not have to be there.

Consider the following extract from California Dental Association v. American Dental Association, 23 Cal.3d 346, 152 Cal.Rptr. 546, 590 P.2d 401, 405 (1979), decided by the California Supreme Court sitting en banc:

The ADA contends that California courts do not have personal jurisdiction over it in the case before us. We disagree. Code of Civil Procedure section 410.50, subdivision (a), declares: "Except as otherwise provided by statute, the court in which an action is pending has jurisdiction over a party from the time summons is served on him as provided by Chapter 4 * * *. *A general appearance by a party is equivalent to personal service of summons on such party.*" (Italics added.) Thus, although a defendant may make a special appearance to challenge the jurisdiction of the court over his person (Judson v. Superior Court (1942) 21 Cal.2d 11, 13, 129 P.2d 361, overruled on other grounds in Goodwine v. Superior Court (1965) 63 Cal.2d 481, 484, 47 Cal.Rptr. 201, 407 P.2d 1; Jardine v. Superior Court (1931) 213 Cal. 301, 2 P.2d 756; Lander v. Fleming (1874) 47 Cal. 614), when he simultaneously answers to the merits he is no longer entitled to make this challenge. (Cason v. Glass Bottle Blowers Assn. (1951) 37 Cal.2d 134, 140, 231 P.2d 6; Childs v. Lanterman (1894) 103 Cal. 387, 37

P. 382; Ghiradelli v. Greene (1880) 56 Cal. 629.) It is well settled that "if a defendant wishes to insist upon the objection that he is not in court for want of jurisdiction over his person, he must specially appear for that purpose only, and must keep out for all purposes except to make that objection" (Olcese v. Justice's Court (1909) 156 Cal. 82, 87, 103 P. 317, 319); otherwise, he waives "any right [he] may have to insist that jurisdiction of [his] person had not been obtained." (Remsberg v. Hackney Manufacturing Co. (1917) 174 Cal. 799, 801, 164 P. 792, 793.)

In the case before us, the ADA has not only raised jurisdictional challenges but has also defended against all of the CDA's claims on the merits. We therefore conclude that under these circumstances the exercise of jurisdiction over the ADA by California courts is appropriate.

Special rules may also apply to appeal from an adverse decision on jurisdiction. An interlocutory appeal may or may not be allowed; it may even be required if the jurisdictional point is not to be waived.

II

The Federal Rules take a radically different approach. Under these rules, there is no special appearance. The objection to jurisdiction over the person is not lost by virtue of being presented together with a defense on the merits. See F.R.C.P. 12(b). However, there are situations in which improper procedure will result in loss of the opportunity to object to jurisdiction over the person even under the Federal Rules. See F.R.C.P. 12(g) and 12(h)(1).

It should not be assumed that states which follow the Federal Rules generally have abolished the special appearance, and because of the importance that the question can assume in litigation, local law should be checked with particular care.

III

A special appearance may raise issues of fact as well as issues of law. When must these be resolved? Must there be an evidentiary hearing? Who has the burden of proof, or are the various burdens shared? Note that in some cases, for example a special appearance turning on the identity of the person to whom the summons was handed, may have no relationship to the underlying dispute. In others, for example the place a contract was to be performed, may control the right of recovery as well as the jurisdictional question.

Compare the approach taken in the following two cases.

Bruce Ball v. Metallurgie Hoboken–Overpelt

United States Court of Appeals for the Second Circuit, 1990.
902 F.2d 194.

* * * Prior to discovery, a plaintiff challenged by a jurisdiction testing motion may defeat the motion by pleading in good faith, see

Fed.R.Civ.P. 11, legally sufficient allegations of jurisdiction. At that preliminary stage, the plaintiff's prima facie showing may be established solely by allegations. After discovery, the plaintiff's prima facie showing, necessary to defeat a jurisdiction testing motion, must include an averment of facts that, if credited by the trier, would suffice to establish jurisdiction over the defendant. At that point, the prima facie showing must be factually supported.

Where the jurisdictional issue is in dispute, the plaintiff's averment of jurisdictional facts will normally be met in one of three ways: (1) by a Rule 12(b)(2) motion, which assumes the truth of the plaintiff's factual allegations for purposes of the motion and challenges their sufficiency, (2) by a Rule 56 motion, which asserts that there are undisputed facts demonstrating the absence of jurisdiction, or (3) by a request for an adjudication of disputed jurisdictional facts, either at a hearing on the issue of jurisdiction or in the course of trial on the merits. If the defendant is content to challenge only the sufficiency of the plaintiff's factual allegation, in effect demurring by filing a Rule 12(b)(2) motion, the plaintiff need persuade the court only that its factual allegations constitute a prima facie showing of jurisdiction. If the defendant asserts in a Rule 56 motion that undisputed facts show the absence of jurisdiction, the court proceeds, as with any summary judgment motion, to determine if undisputed facts exist that warrant the relief sought. If the defendant contests the plaintiff's factual allegations, then a hearing is required, at which the plaintiff must prove the existence of jurisdiction by a preponderance of the evidence.

C.W. Brown Mach. Shop v. Stanley Machinery

Court of Appeals of Texas, 2d Dist., 1984.
670 S.W.2d 791, 792.

* * *

The sole question on appeal is whether the trial court erred in dismissing appellant's cause of action for want of jurisdiction. In the instant case, a review of the record reveals that no findings of fact or conclusions of law were requested or filed with this court. Case law dictates that where no findings of fact or conclusions of law are filed, the judgment of the trial court must be affirmed if it can be upheld on any legal theory that finds support in the evidence. * * *

Process was served on the Texas Secretary of State as the presumed agent of appellee pursuant to the Texas long-arm statute, TEX.REV.CIV.STAT.ANN. art. 2031b (Vernon 1964 & Supp.1984). Citation was received by appellee by certified mail in Massachusetts. Appellee entered a special appearance pursuant to TEX.R.CIV.P. 120a objecting to the jurisdiction of the court over appellee on the ground that appellee is not amenable to process issued by the courts of this state. After holding a hearing, the court dismissed the cause of action for want of jurisdiction. TEX.R.CIV.P. 120a governs special appearances. The purpose of the rule is to allow a defendant to make a special appearance in a cause in order to attack the court's jurisdiction over his person without subjecting himself to the jurisdiction of the court generally. * * * The Texas long-arm statute requires that in the interest of notions of fair play and substantial justice, consideration must be given to the quality, nature, and extent of the activity in Texas and the benefits and protection of the laws of Texas afforded to the defendant. The burden of proof is upon the defendant filing a special appearance to show that it is not subject to the long-arm process. * * *

Insurance Corporation of Ireland v. Compagnie des Bauxites de Guinee

Supreme Court of the United States, 1982.
456 U.S. 694, 102 S.Ct. 2099, 72 L.Ed.2d 492.

■ Justice White delivered the opinion of the Court.

* * *

The question presented by this case is whether this Rule [37(b)] is applicable to facts that form the basis for personal jurisdiction over a defendant. May a district court, as a sanction for failure to comply with a discovery order directed at establishing jurisdictional facts, proceed on the basis that personal jurisdiction over the recalcitrant party has been established? Petitioners urge that such an application of the Rule would violate due process: If a court does not have jurisdiction over a party, then it may not create that jurisdiction by judicial fiat. They contend also that until a court has jurisdiction over a party, that party need not comply with orders of the court; failure to comply, therefore, cannot provide the ground for a sanction. In our view, petitioners are attempting to create a logical conundrum out of a fairly straightforward matter.

* * *

In December 1975, CBG filed a two-count suit in the Western District of Pennsylvania, asserting jurisdiction based on diversity of citizenship. The first count was against INA; the second against the excess insurers. INA did not challenge personal or subject-matter jurisdiction of the District Court. The answer of the excess insurers, however, raised a number of defenses, including lack of *in personam* jurisdiction. Subsequently, this alleged lack of personal jurisdiction became the basis of a motion for summary judgment filed by the excess insurers.[5] The issue in this case requires an account of respondent's attempt to use discovery in order to demonstrate the court's personal jurisdiction over the excess insurers.[a]

5. The motion for summary judgment was filed on May 20, 1977. In it, 17 of the excess insurers alleged a lack of *in personam* jurisdiction and all 21 excess insurers sought dismissal on the ground of *forum non conve-* *niens*. The District Court denied the motion on April 19, 1979.

a. At an earlier stage in this litigation Judge Aldisert, writing for the Court of Ap-

Respondent's first discovery request—asking for "[c]opies of all business interruption insurance policies issued by Defendant during the period from January 1, 1972 to December 31, 1975"—was served on each defendant in August 1976. In January 1977, the excess insurers objected, on grounds of burdensomeness, to producing such policies. Several months later, respondent filed a motion to compel petitioners to produce the requested documents. In June 1978, the court orally overruled petitioners' objections. This was followed by a second discovery request in which respondent narrowed the files it was seeking to policies which "were delivered in * * * Pennsylvania * * * or covered a risk located in * * * Pennsylvania." Petitioners now objected that these documents were not in their custody or control; rather, they were kept by the brokers in London. The court ordered petitioners to request the information from the brokers, limiting the request to policies covering the period from 1971 to date. That was in July 1978; petitioners were given 90 days to produce the information. On November 8, petitioners were given an additional 30 days to complete discovery. On November 24, petitioners filed an affidavit offering to make their records, allegedly some 4 million files, available at their offices in London for inspection by respondent. Respondent countered with a motion to compel production of the previously requested documents. On December 21, 1978, the court, noting that no conscientious effort had yet been made to produce the requested information and that no objection had been entered to the discovery order in July, gave petitioners 60 more days to produce the requested information. The District Judge also issued the following warning:

> "[I]f you don't get it to him in 60 days, I am going to enter an order saying that because you failed to give the information as requested, that I am going to assume, under Rule of Civil Procedure 37(b), subsection 2(A), that there is jurisdiction." 1 App. 115a.

A few moments later he restated the warning as follows: "I will assume that jurisdiction is here with this court unless you produce statistics and other information in that regard that would indicate otherwise." *Id.,* at 116a.

On April 19, 1979, the court, after concluding that the requested material had not been produced, imposed the threatened sanction, finding that "for the purpose of this litigation the Excess Insurers are subject to the in personam jurisdiction of this Court due to their business contacts with Pennsylvania." *Id.,* at 201a. Independently of the sanction, the District Court found two other grounds for holding that it had personal jurisdiction over petitioners. First, on the record

peals, commented on the protracted pretrial proceedings:

This is an unfortunate case filed in the district court in 1975 which still admits of no resolution on the merits but bears the scars of over five years of pre-trial skirmishing.

Compagnie des Bauxites de Guinea v. Ins. Co. of N. Am., 651 F.2d 877, 879 (3d Cir.1981).

established, it found that petitioners had sufficient business contacts with Pennsylvania to fall within the Pennsylvania long-arm statute. Second, in adopting the terms of the INA contract with CBG—a Pennsylvania insurance contract—the excess insurers implicitly agreed to submit to the jurisdiction of the court.[6]

Except with respect to three excess insurers, the Court of Appeals for the Third Circuit affirmed the jurisdictional holding, relying entirely upon the validity of the sanction.[7] Compagnie des Bauxites de Guinea v. Insurance Co. of North America, 651 F.2d 877 (1981). That court specifically found that the discovery orders of the District Court did not constitute an abuse of discretion and that imposition of the sanction fell within the limits of trial court discretion. * * * Furthermore, it held that the sanction did not violate petitioners' due process rights, because it was no broader than "reasonably necessary" under the circumstances.

Because the decision below directly conflicts with the decision of the Court of Appeals for the Fifth Circuit in Familia De Boom v. Arosa Mercantil, S.A., 629 F.2d 1134 (1980), we granted certiorari. 454 U.S. 963, 102 S.Ct. 502, 70 L.Ed.2d 377 (1981).

* * *

Because the requirement of personal jurisdiction represents first of all an individual right, it can, like other such rights, be waived. In *McDonald v. Mabee, supra,* the Court indicated that regardless of the power of the State to serve process, an individual may submit to the jurisdiction of the court by appearance. A variety of legal arrangements have been taken to represent express or implied consent to the personal jurisdiction of the court. In National Equipment Rental, Ltd. v. Szukhent, 375 U.S. 311, 316, 84 S.Ct. 411, 414, 11 L.Ed.2d 354 (1964), we stated that "parties to a contract may agree in advance to submit to the jurisdiction of a given court," and in Petrowski v. Hawkeye–Security Co., 350 U.S. 495, 76 S.Ct. 490, 100 L.Ed. 639 (1956), the Court upheld the personal jurisdiction of a District Court on the basis of a stipulation entered into by the defendant. In addition, lower federal courts have found such consent implicit in agreements to arbitrate. * * *

6. On March 22, 1979, the excess insurers instituted a suit against CBG in England, attacking the validity of the insurance contract. In its April 19 decision, the District Court found that "the commencement of the separate action in England [was] oppressive, unfair, and an act of bad faith under all of the circumstances." 1 App. 203a. It, therefore, enjoined the continuation of that suit. This aspect of the District Court decision was reversed by the Court of Appeals. Respondent seeks certiorari review of that decision (see n. 1, *supra*).

7. It reversed as to three of the excess insurers on the grounds that they had complied with the discovery orders and that their contacts with Pennsylvania were not sufficient to justify exercise of the Pennsylvania long-arm statute. It also held that the District Court had abused its discretion in enjoining the action in England. Judge Gibbons dissented on the propriety of the sanction, arguing that the District Court had abused its discretion. He also expressed some doubt that a Rule 37 sanction could ever be used as the source of personal jurisdiction. 651 F.2d, at 892, n. 4.

In sum, the requirement of personal jurisdiction may be intentionally waived, or for various reasons a defendant may be estopped from raising the issue. These characteristics portray it for what it is—a legal right protecting the individual. The plaintiff's demonstration of certain historical facts may make clear to the court that it has personal jurisdiction over the defendant as a matter of law—*i.e.,* certain factual showings will have legal consequences—but this is not the only way in which the personal jurisdiction of the court may arise. The actions of the defendant may amount to a legal submission to the jurisdiction of the court, whether voluntary or not.

The expression of legal rights is often subject to certain procedural rules: The failure to follow those rules may well result in a curtailment of the rights. Thus, the failure to enter a timely objection to personal jurisdiction constitutes, under Rule 12(h)(1), a waiver of the objection. A sanction under Rule 37(b)(2)(A) consisting of a finding of personal jurisdiction has precisely the same effect. As a general proposition, the Rule 37 sanction applied to a finding of personal jurisdiction creates no more of a due process problem than the Rule 12 waiver. Although "a court cannot conclude all persons interested by its mere assertion of its own power," Chicago Life Ins. Co. v. Cherry*, at 29, 37 S.Ct. at 493, not all rules that establish legal consequences to a party's own behavior are "mere assertions" of power.

* * *

Petitioners argue that a sanction consisting of a finding of personal jurisdiction differs from all other instances in which a sanction is imposed * * * because a party need not obey the orders of a court until it is established that the court has personal jurisdiction over that party. If there is no obligation to obey a judicial order, a sanction cannot be applied for the failure to comply. Until the court has established personal jurisdiction, moreover, any assertion of judicial power over the party violates due process.

This argument again assumes that there is something unique about the requirement of personal jurisdiction, which prevents it from being established or waived like other rights. A defendant is always free to ignore the judicial proceedings, risk a default judgment, and then challenge that judgment on jurisdictional grounds in a collateral proceeding. * * * By submitting to the jurisdiction of the court for the limited purpose of challenging jurisdiction, the defendant agrees to abide by that court's determination on the issue of jurisdiction: That decision will be res judicata on that issue in any further proceedings. * * *

Because the application of a legal presumption to the issue of personal jurisdiction does not in itself violate the Due Process Clause and because there was no abuse of the discretion granted a district

* 244 U.S. 25 (1917).

court under Rule 37(b)(2), we affirm the judgment of the Court of Appeals.

So ordered.[b]

Lauro Lines v. Chasser

Supreme Court of the United States, 1989.
490 U.S. 495, 109 S.Ct. 1976, 104 L.Ed.2d 548.

■ BRENNAN, J., delivered the opinion for a unanimous Court.

We granted certiorari to consider whether an interlocutory order of a United States District Court denying a defendant's motion to dismiss a damages action on the basis of a contractual forum-selection clause is immediately appealable under 28 U.S.C. § 1291 as a collateral final order. We hold that it is not.

I

The individual respondents were, or represent the estates of persons who were, passengers aboard the cruise ship Achille Lauro when it was hijacked by terrorists in the Mediterranean in October 1985. Petitioner Lauro Lines s.r.l., an Italian company, owns the Achille Lauro. Respondents filed suits against Lauro Lines in the District Court for the Southern District of New York to recover damages for injuries sustained as a result of the hijacking, and for the wrongful death of passenger Leon Klinghoffer. Lauro Lines moved before trial to dismiss the actions, citing the forum-selection clause printed on each passenger ticket. This clause purported to obligate the passenger to institute any suit arising in connection with the contract in Naples, Italy, and to renounce the right to sue elsewhere.

The District Court denied petitioner's motions to dismiss, holding that the ticket as a whole did not give reasonable notice to passengers that they were waiving the opportunity to sue in a domestic forum. Without moving for certification for immediate appeal pursuant to 28 U.S.C. § 1292(b), Lauro Lines sought to appeal the District Court's orders. The Court of Appeals for the Second Circuit dismissed petitioner's appeal on the ground that the District Court's orders denying petitioner's motions to dismiss were interlocutory and not appealable under § 1291. The court held that the orders did not fall within the exception to the rule of nonappealability carved out for collateral final orders in *Cohen v. Beneficial Industrial Loan Corp.,* 337 U.S. 541, 69 S.Ct. 1221, 93 L.Ed. 1528 (1949). 844 F.2d 50 (1988). We granted certiorari to resolve a disagreement among the Courts of Appeals. * * *

II

Title 28 U.S.C. § 1291 provides for appeal to the courts of appeals only from "final decisions of the district courts of the United States." For purposes of § 1291, a final judgment is generally regarded as "a

---

b.   Justice Powell's concurrence is omitted.

decision by the District Court that 'ends the litigation on the merits and leaves nothing for the court to do but execute the judgment.' " Van Cauwenberghe v. Biard, 486 U.S. 517, 521, 108 S.Ct. 1945, 1949, 100 L.Ed.2d 517 (1988), quoting *Catlin v. United States,* 324 U.S. 229, 233, 65 S.Ct. 631, 633, 89 L.Ed. 911 (1945). An order denying a motion to dismiss a civil action on the ground that a contractual forum-selection clause requires that such suit be brought in another jurisdiction is not a decision on the merits that ends the litigation. On the contrary, such an order "ensures that litigation will continue in the District Court." Gulfstream Aerospace Corp. v. Mayacamas Corp., 485 U.S. 271, 275, 106 S.Ct. 1133, 1136, 99 L.Ed.2d 296 (1988). Section 1291 thus permits an appeal only if an order denying a motion to dismiss based upon a forum-selection clause falls within the "narrow exception to the normal application of the final judgment rule [that] has come to be known as the collateral order doctrine." Midland Asphalt Corp. v. United States, 489 U.S. 794, 798, 109 S.Ct. 1494, 1497, 103 L.Ed.2d 879 (1989). That exception is for a "small class" of pre-judgment orders that "finally determine claims of right separable from, and collateral to, rights asserted in the action, [and that are] too important to be denied review and too independent of the cause itself to require that appellate consideration be deferred until the whole case is adjudicated." *Cohen, supra,* 337 U.S., at 546, 69 S.Ct., at 1226. We have held that to fall within the *Cohen* exception, an order must satisfy at least three conditions: "It must 'conclusively determine the disputed question,' 'resolve an important issue completely separate from the merits of the action,' and 'be effectively unreviewable on appeal from a final judgment.' " Richardson–Merrell Inc. v. Koller, 472 U.S. 424, 431, 105 S.Ct. 2757, 2761, 86 L.Ed.2d 340 (1985), quoting Coopers & Lybrand v. Livesay, 437 U.S. 463, 468, 98 S.Ct. 2454, 2458, 57 L.Ed.2d 351 (1978). For present purposes, we need not decide whether an order denying a dismissal motion based upon a contractual forum-selection clause conclusively determines a disputed issue, or whether it resolves an important issue that is independent of the merits of the action, for the District Court's orders fail to satisfy the third requirement of the collateral order test.

We recently reiterated the "general rule" that an order is "effectively unreviewable" only "where the order at issue involves 'an asserted right the legal and practical value of which would be destroyed if it were not vindicated before trial.' " Midland Asphalt Corp., *supra,* 489 U.S., at 799, 109 S.Ct., at 1498, quoting *United States v. MacDonald,* 435 U.S. 850, 860, 98 S.Ct. 1547, 1552, 56 L.Ed.2d 18 (1978). If it is eventually decided that the District Court erred in allowing trial in this case to take place in New York, petitioner will have been put to unnecessary trouble and expense, and the value of its contractual right to an Italian forum will have been diminished. It is always true, however, that "there is value * * * in triumphing before trial, rather than after it," *MacDonald, supra,* at 860, n. 7, 98 S.Ct., at 1553, n. 7, and this Court has declined to find the costs associated with unnecessary litigation to be enough to warrant allowing the immediate appeal of a pretrial order. See *Richardson–Merrell Inc.,* *supra,* 472 U.S., at 436, 105 S.Ct., at 2764 ("[T]he possibility that a ruling may be erroneous and may impose additional litigation expense is not sufficient to set aside the finality requirement imposed by Congress" in § 1291). Instead, we have insisted that the right asserted be one that is essentially destroyed if its vindication must be postponed until trial is completed. * * *

On the other hand, we have declined to hold the collateral order doctrine applicable where a district court has denied a claim, not that the defendant has a right not to be sued at all, but that the suit against the defendant is not properly before the particular court because it lacks jurisdiction. In Van Cauwenberghe v. Biard, 486 U.S. 517, 108 S.Ct. 1945, 100 L.Ed.2d 517 (1988), a civil defendant moved for dismissal on the ground that he had been immune from service of process because his presence in the United States had been compelled by extradition to face criminal charges. We noted that, after *Mitchell,* "[t]he critical question . . . is whether 'the essence' of the claimed right is a right not to stand trial," 486 U.S., at 524, 108 S.Ct., at 1950, and held that the immunity from service of process defendant asserted did not amount to an immunity from suit—even though service was essential to the trial court's jurisdiction over the defendant. See also Catlin v. United States, 324 U.S., at 236, 65 S.Ct., at 635 (order denying motion to dismiss petition for condemnation of land not immediately appealable, "even when the motion is based upon jurisdictional grounds").

Lauro Lines argues here that its contractual forum-selection clause provided it with a right to trial before a tribunal in Italy, and with a concomitant right not to be sued anywhere else. This "right not to be haled for trial before tribunals outside the agreed forum," petitioner claims, cannot effectively be vindicated by appeal after trial in an improper forum. Brief for Petitioner 38–39. There is no obviously correct way to characterize the right embodied in petitioner's forum-selection provision: "all litigants who have a meritorious pretrial claim for dismissal can reasonably claim a right not to stand trial." *Van Cauwenberghe, supra,* 486 U.S., at 524, 108 S.Ct., at 1950. The right appears most like that to be free from trial if it is characterized—as by petitioner—as a right not to be sued at all except in a Neapolitan forum. It appears less like a right not to be subjected to suit if characterized—as by the Court of Appeals—as "a right to have the binding adjudication of claims occur in a certain forum." 844 F.2d, at 55. Cf. *Van Cauwenberghe, supra,* 486 U.S., at 526–527. Even assuming that the former characterization is proper, however, petitioner is obviously not entitled under the forum-selection clause of its contract to avoid suit altogether, and an entitlement to avoid suit is different in kind from an entitlement to be sued only in a particular forum. Petitioner's claim that it may be sued only in Naples, while not perfectly secured by appeal after final judgment, is adequately vindicable at that stage—surely as effectively vindicable as a claim that the trial court lacked personal jurisdiction over the defendant—and hence does not fall within the third prong of the collateral order doctrine.

Petitioner argues that there is a strong federal policy favoring the enforcement of foreign forum-selection clauses, citing The Bremen v. Zapata Off–Shore Co., 407 U.S. 1, 92 S.Ct. 1907, 32 L.Ed.2d 513 (1972), and that "the essential concomitant of this strong federal policy * * * is the right of immediate appellate review of district court orders denying their enforcement." Brief for Petitioner 40–41. A policy favoring enforcement of forum-selection clauses, however, would go to the merits of petitioner's claim that its ticket-agreement requires that any suit be filed in Italy and that the agreement should be enforced by the federal courts. Immediate appealability of a prejudgment order denying enforcement, insofar as it depends upon satisfaction of the third prong of the collateral order test, turns on the precise contours of the right asserted, and not upon the likelihood of eventual success on the merits. The Court of Appeals properly dismissed petitioner's appeal, and its judgment is

Affirmed.

■ Justice Scalia, concurring.

I join the opinion of the Court, and write separately only to make express what seems to me implicit in its analysis.

* * *

While it is true, therefore, that the "right not to be sued elsewhere than in Naples" is not fully vindicated—indeed, to be utterly frank, is positively destroyed—by permitting the trial to occur and reversing its outcome, that is vindication enough because the right is not sufficiently important to overcome the policies militating against interlocutory appeals. We have made that judgment when the right not to be tried in a particular court has been created through jurisdictional limitations established by Congress or by international treaty, see *Van Cauwenberghe, supra.* The same judgment applies—if anything, *a fortiori*—when the right has been created by private agreement.

NOTE: INTERLOCUTORY APPEAL

The Court notes that defendant did not move "for certification" for immediate appeal pursuant to 28 U.S.C. § 1292(b). That section provides as follows:

§ 1292.   Interlocutory decisions

(b) When a district judge, in making in a civil action an order not otherwise appealable under this section, shall be of the opinion that such order involves a controlling question of law as to which there is substantial ground for difference of opinion and that an immediate appeal from the order may materially advance the ultimate termination of the litigation, he shall so state in writing in such order. The Court of Appeals which would have jurisdiction of an appeal of such action may thereupon, in its discretion, permit an appeal to be taken from such order, if application is made to it within ten days after the entry of the order: *Provided, however,* That application for an appeal hereunder shall not stay proceedings in the district court unless the district judge or the Court of Appeals or a judge thereof shall so order.

Was this an appropriate case for certification? Was there a reason for defendant to have proceeded under § 1291, which provides for appeal as of right?

G.   SUPPLEMENTAL JURISDICTION

INTRODUCTORY NOTE: SUBJECT MATTER JURISDICTION

Not every court is competent to hear every type of case. There may be limitations imposed legislatively in terms of the amount in controversy. There may be limitations in terms of the subject matter of the action; not every court is competent to grant a divorce or to probate a will. In the federal system there are both constitutional and statutory limitations on the competence of courts; some of the more important limitations will be discussed below. What bears particular emphasis at this juncture is the fact that not even the consent of all the litigants can confer the power to adjudicate where subject-matter jurisdiction is lacking.

In this regard subject-matter jurisdiction stands in sharp contrast to personal jurisdiction. F.R.C.P. 12(h)(3) makes this abundantly clear by providing that "Whenever it appears by suggestion of the parties or otherwise that the court lacks jurisdiction over the subject matter, the court shall dismiss the action." Should the court find that it has no jurisdiction over the subject matter it is obligated to dismiss, even if it must act on its own motion.

Two major sources of jurisdiction account for the vast majority of civil litigation in the federal courts. The first is federal question jurisdiction; the second is jurisdiction based on diversity of citizenship. Section 1331 of title 28 of the U.S. Code governs the former, except that there are special statutes governing what are termed the federal specialties: e.g., patent and copyright law, bankruptcy, admiralty. And a huge volume of cases involve the United States as plaintiff: see section 1345.

Section 1332 governs suits in which jurisdiction is based on diversity of citizenship. A complex body of law governs the definition of diversity for jurisdictional purposes. Some provisions have their basis in explicit provisions of a statute: see section 1332(c) defining the citizenship of a corporation for present purposes. Some rules have been developed judicially, the most important of which requires what is termed "complete diversity," i.e. that the citizenship of each defendant be diverse from that of each plaintiff. Thus, if P of Pennsylvania sues D–1 of Delaware and D–2 of Pennsylvania, complete diversity is lacking and a federal court will not entertain the suit. The requirement, it bears emphasis, is not a constitutional limitation, but is based rather on the Court's reading of the diversity statute. Thus, in cases where the Congress has made a contrary intention unambiguous, e.g., in certain cases of interpleader, jurisdiction will be upheld.

Congress has also provided for removal to federal court of cases brought in state court, thus giving the defendant rather than the plaintiff the choice of judicial system. As the governing statute (28 U.S.C. § 1441) makes clear, however, there are limitations. Thus, if a non-resident plaintiff sues a defendant in the latter's home state, removal is not an option.

The cases that follow explore some of the problems presented by joinder of claims and of parties where some of the claims would, and some would not be independently cognizable in federal court. When may a federal court retain the entire case, when may it remand? When must a federal court dismiss certain counts and retain others? In considering these questions it is useful to distinguish between what is mandated constitutionally and what follows as a result of the Court's interpretation of what the Congress has enacted.

Carnegie–Mellon University v. Cohill

Supreme Court of the United States, 1988.
484 U.S. 343, 108 S.Ct. 614, 98 L.Ed.2d 720.

■ JUSTICE MARSHALL delivered the opinion of the Court.

The question before us is whether a federal district court has discretion under the doctrine of pendent jurisdiction to remand a properly removed case to state court when all federal-law claims in the action have been eliminated and only pendent state-law claims remain.

I

Respondents, William and Carrie Boyle, commenced this action by filing a complaint against petitioners, Carnegie–Mellon University (CMU) and John Kordesich, in the Court of Common Pleas of Allegheny County, Pennsylvania. CMU is William Boyle's former employer; Kordesich is William Boyle's former supervisor. In the complaint, William Boyle charged CMU with violation of federal and state age-discrimination laws, wrongful discharge, breach of contract, intentional infliction of emotional distress, defamation, and misrepresentation. He stated many of the same claims, as well as tortious interference with a contractual relationship, against Kordesich. Carrie Boyle claimed that these alleged wrongs had caused her to suffer a loss of consortium, loss of companionship, and loss of her husband's household services. All of respondents' claims arose from CMU's discharge of William Boyle.

Petitioners removed the case from state court to the United States District Court for the Western District of Pennsylvania under 28 U.S.C. § 1441(a), which allows a defendant to remove an action that falls within the original jurisdiction of the federal district courts. Petitioners stated that the entire lawsuit fell within the original jurisdiction, and hence within the removal jurisdiction, of the District Court because the complaint stated a claim arising under the Age Discrimination in Employment Act of 1967, 81 Stat. 602, as amended, 29 U.S.C. §§ 621–

634, and the state-law claims in the complaint were pendent to this federal-law claim. Respondents did not contest the removal.

Six months later, respondents moved to amend their complaint to delete the allegations of age discrimination and defamation and the request for damages for loss of consortium. In this motion, respondents stated that they now believed these claims were not tenable. At the same time, respondents filed a motion, conditional upon amendment of the complaint, to remand the suit to state court. Respondents noted that the amendment would eliminate their sole federal-law claim, which had provided the basis for removal of the case, and argued that a remand to state court was appropriate in these circumstances.

After granting the motion to amend, the District Court remanded the remaining claims to the state court in which respondents initially had filed the action. Boyle v. Carnegie–Mellon University, 648 F.Supp. 1318 (W.D.Pa. 1985). In its opinion, the District Court first examined whether any provision of the federal removal statute, 28 U.S.C. §§ 1441–1451, supported a remand. The court noted that two sections of the statute authorize district courts to remand after removal. Under 28 U.S.C. § 1447(c), a court shall remand any case that "was removed improvidently and without jurisdiction"; under 28 U.S.C. § 1441(c), a court may remand any claim that is both independently nonremovable and "separate and independent" of the claim providing the basis for removal of the case. The court held that § 1447(c) did not apply because the removal was jurisdictionally proper and that § 1441(c) did not apply because the remaining state-law claims in the case, although independently nonremovable, were pendent to, rather than separate and independent of, the federal-law claim that had provided the basis for removal. The District Court then stated that in Thermtron Products, Inc. v. Hermansdorfer, 423 U.S. 336, 96 S.Ct. 584, 46 L.Ed.2d 542 (1976), this Court had suggested that a district court could not remand a removed case or claim without specific statutory authorization. The District Court noted, however, that a number of appellate decisions since *Thermtron* had approved the remand of removed pendent state-law claims when the federal-law claim providing the basis for removal had been eliminated from the suit. The court found these later decisions persuasive and consequently opted to remand respondents' remaining state-law claims.

Petitioners filed a petition for writ of mandamus with the United States Court of Appeals for the Third Circuit, and a divided panel granted the petition.[4] Both the majority and the dissent agreed with the District Court's conclusion that neither § 1447(c) nor § 1441(c) authorized a remand in this case. The majority, after noting a division among the Circuits on the question, held that under *Thermtron* this absence of statutory authorization precluded the District Court from

---

4. Petitioners also appealed the District Court's decision. The Court of Appeals, however, dismissed the appeal on the ground that 28 U.S.C. § 1447(d) of the removal statute bars appeals from remands to state courts with a single exception not applicable to this case.

ordering a remand. The dissent countered that *Thermtron*'s admonition against remanding removed cases to state court without specific statutory authorization did not extend to cases involving pendent jurisdiction. The dissent noted that under the pendent jurisdiction doctrine, a district court has discretion to dismiss without prejudice cases involving pendent claims, and argued that fairness, efficiency, comity, and common sense supported the authority of removal courts to remand such cases as well.

The Court of Appeals granted respondents' petition for rehearing *en banc* and vacated the panel opinions and writ of mandamus. 41 FEP Cases 1888 (3d Cir.1986) (en banc). After the rehearing, the en banc court divided evenly on the question whether the District Court had authority to remand respondents' case to state court. Civ. Action No. 85–3619 (3d Cir., Nov. 24, 1986). Accordingly, the court issued an order denying petitioners' application for a writ of mandamus. This order effectively left undisturbed the remand of respondents' case.

We granted certiorari, 479 U.S. 1083, 107 S.Ct. 1283, 94 L.Ed.2d 141 (1987), to resolve the split among the Circuits as to whether a district court has discretion to remand a removed case to state court when all federal-law claims have dropped out of the action and only pendent state-law claims remain.[5] We now affirm.

II

The modern doctrine of pendent jurisdiction stems from this Court's decision in Mine Workers v. Gibbs, 383 U.S. 715, 86 S.Ct. 1130, 16 L.Ed.2d 218 (1966). Prior to *Gibbs,* this Court had recognized that considerations of judicial economy and procedural convenience justified the recognition of power in the federal courts to decide certain state-law claims involved in cases raising federal questions. See Hurn v. Oursler, 289 U.S. 238, 243–247, 53 S.Ct. 586, 588–90, 77 L.Ed. 1148 (1933). The test for determining when a federal court had jurisdiction over such state-law claims was murky, however, and the lower courts experienced considerable difficulty in applying it.[6] In *Gibbs,* the Court responded to this confusion, and the resulting hesitancy of federal courts to recognize jurisdiction over state-law claims, by establishing a new yardstick for deciding whether a federal court has jurisdiction over a state-law claim brought in a case that also involves a federal question. The Court stated that a federal court has

---

5. Compare *In re Romulus Community Schools,* 729 F.2d 431 (6th Cir.1984), Fox v. Custis, 712 F.2d 84 (4th Cir.1983), and Hofbauer v. Northwestern National Bank of Rochester, 700 F.2d 1197 (8th Cir.1983) (approving remand of remaining pendent state-law claims when all federal claims were eliminated from case), with Cook v. Weber, 698 F.2d 907 (7th Cir.1983), and *In re Greyhound Lines, Inc.,* 598 F.2d 883 (5th Cir.1979) (disapproving such remands).

6. The test established in *Hurn v. Oursler* provided that if a plaintiff presented "two distinct grounds," one state and one federal, "in support of a single cause of action," the federal court had jurisdiction over the entire action, but that if the plaintiff's assertions amounted to "two separate and distinct causes of action," the federal court had jurisdiction only over the federal "cause of action." 289 U.S., at 246, 53 S.Ct., at 590. The difficulty with this test, as many commentators noted, was that it centered on the inherently elusive concept of a "cause of action." See, *e.g.,* Shulman & Jaegerman, Some Jurisdictional Limitations on Federal Procedure, 45 Yale L.J. 393, 397–410 (1936).

jurisdiction over an entire action, including state-law claims, whenever the federal-law claims and state-law claims in the case "derive from a common nucleus of operative fact" and are "such that [a plaintiff] would ordinarily be expected to try them all in one judicial proceeding." Mine Workers v. Gibbs, 383 U.S., at 725, 86 S.Ct., at 1138. The Court intended this standard not only to clarify, but also to broaden, the scope of federal pendent jurisdiction. See *ibid.* (stating that the prior approach, at least as applied by lower courts, was "unnecessarily grudging"). According to *Gibbs,* "considerations of judicial economy, convenience and fairness to litigants" support a wide-ranging power in the federal courts to decide state-law claims in cases that also present federal questions. *Id.,* at 726, 86 S.Ct., at 1139.

At the same time, however, *Gibbs* drew a distinction between the power of a federal court to hear state-law claims and the discretionary exercise of that power. The *Gibbs* Court recognized that a federal court's determination of state-law claims could conflict with the principle of comity to the States and with the promotion of justice between the litigating parties. For this reason, *Gibbs* emphasized that "pendent jurisdiction is a doctrine of discretion, not of plaintiff's right." *Ibid.* Under *Gibbs,* a federal court should consider and weigh in each case, and at every stage of the litigation, the values of judicial economy, convenience, fairness, and comity in order to decide whether to exercise jurisdiction over a case brought in that court involving pendent state-law claims. When the balance of these factors indicates that a case properly belongs in state court, as when the federal-law claims have dropped out of the lawsuit in its early stages and only state-law claims remain,[7] the federal court should decline the exercise of jurisdiction by dismissing the case without prejudice. *Id.,* at 726–727, 86 S.Ct., at 1139. As articulated by *Gibbs,* the doctrine of pendent jurisdiction thus is a doctrine of flexibility, designed to allow courts to deal with cases involving pendent claims in the manner that most sensibly accommodates a range of concerns and values.

In the case before us, respondents' complaint stated a single federal-law claim and a number of state-law claims. The state-law claims fell within the jurisdiction of the District Court to which the action was removed because they derived from the same nucleus of operative fact as the federal-law claim: CMU's dismissal of William Boyle. Under the pendent jurisdiction doctrine set forth in *Gibbs,* however, the District Court had to consider throughout the litigation

7. In *Gibbs,* the Court stated that "if the federal claims are dismissed before trial the state claims should be dismissed as well." *Mine Workers v. Gibbs,* 383 U.S., at 726, 86 S.Ct., at 1139. More recently, we have made clear that this statement does not establish a mandatory rule to be applied inflexibly in all cases. See Rosado v. Wyman, 397 U.S. 397, 403–405, 90 S.Ct. 1207, 1213–14, 25 L.Ed.2d 442 (1970). The statement simply recognizes that in the usual case in which all federal-law claims are eliminated before trial, the balance of factors to be considered under the pendent jurisdiction doctrine—judicial economy, convenience, fairness, and comity—will point toward declining to exercise jurisdiction over the remaining state-law claims.

The Court in *Gibbs* also indicated that these factors usually will favor a decision to relinquish jurisdiction when "state issues substantially predominate, whether in terms of proof of the scope of the issues raised or of the comprehensiveness of the remedy sought." Mine Workers v. Gibbs, *supra,* at 726, 86 S.Ct., at 1139.

whether to exercise its jurisdiction over the case. When the single federal-law claim in the action was eliminated at an early stage of the litigation, the District Court had a powerful reason to choose not to continue to exercise jurisdiction. The question that this case presents is whether the District Court could relinquish jurisdiction over the case only by dismissing it without prejudice or whether the District Court could relinquish jurisdiction over the case by remanding it to state court as well.

This Court's crafting of the pendent jurisdiction doctrine in *Gibbs* strongly supports the conclusion that when a district court may relinquish jurisdiction over a removed case involving pendent claims, the court has discretion to remand the case to state court. *Gibbs* itself does not directly address this issue; because the plaintiff in *Gibbs* filed his suit in federal court, remand was not an option in the case, and the Court spoke only of dismissal. But *Gibbs* establishes that the pendent jurisdiction doctrine is designed to enable courts to handle cases involving state-law claims in the way that will best accommodate the values of economy, convenience, fairness, and comity, and *Gibbs* further establishes that the judicial branch is to shape and apply the doctrine in that light. Because in some circumstances a remand of a removed case involving pendent claims will better accommodate these values than will dismissal of the case, the animating principle behind the pendent jurisdiction doctrine supports giving a district court discretion to remand when the exercise of pendent jurisdiction is inappropriate.

As many lower courts have noted,[8] a remand generally will be preferable to a dismissal when the statute of limitations on the plaintiff's state-law claims has expired before the federal court has determined that it should relinquish jurisdiction over the case. In such a case, a dismissal will foreclose the plaintiff from litigating his claims. This consequence may work injustice to the plaintiff: although he has brought his suit in timely manner, he is time-barred from pressing his case.[9] Equally important, and more easily overlooked, the foreclosure of the state-law claims may conflict with the principle of comity to States. The preclusion of valid state-law claims initially brought in timely manner in state court undermines the State's interest in enforc-

---

8. *See, e.g., In re Romulus Community Schools,* 729 F.2d, at 439; Kaib v. Pennzoil Co., 545 F.Supp. 1267, 1271 (W.D.Pa.1982).

9. Moreover, if a plaintiff bringing suit in state court knows that, notwithstanding the expiration of a statute of limitations, a federal court to which a case is removed must dismiss the case upon deciding that the exercise of pendent jurisdiction would be inappropriate, the plaintiff may well decline to allege any federal-law claims. By forgoing all federal-law claims, the plaintiff can insulate himself from the risk that the combination of removal, dismissal under the pendent jurisdiction doctrine, and the expiration of a statute of limitations will foreclose him from litigating his state-law claims. Such protec-

tion will appear especially attractive to a plaintiff who has any doubt about the validity of his federal-law claims, because he will know that if the district court dismisses these claims on the merits prior to trial, the court may well decide that the rest of the case is unsuitable for resolution in a federal court and therefore dismiss the remaining claims. Thus, a rule that would require federal courts to dismiss a removed case that is not suitable for resolution in a federal court would operate not only to foreclose some plaintiffs from litigating their state-law claims, but also to chill other plaintiffs from bringing their federal-law claims.

ing its law. The operation of state statutes of limitations thus provides a potent reason for giving federal district courts discretion to remand, as well as to dismiss, removed pendent claims.[10]

Even when the applicable statute of limitations has not expired, a remand may best promote the values of economy, convenience, fairness, and comity. Both litigants and States have an interest in the prompt and efficient resolution of controversies based on state law. Any time a district court dismisses, rather than remands, a removed case involving pendent claims, the parties will have to refile their papers in state court, at some expense of time and money. Moreover, the state court will have to reprocess the case, and this procedure will involve similar costs. Dismissal of the claim therefore will increase both the expense and the time involved in enforcing state law. Under the analysis set forth in *Gibbs,* this consequence, even taken alone, provides good reason to grant federal courts wide discretion to remand cases involving pendent claims when the exercise of pendent jurisdiction over such cases would be inappropriate.

Petitioners argue that the federal removal statute prohibits a district court from remanding properly removed cases involving pendent claims. This argument is based not on the language of Congress, but on its silence. Petitioners note that the removal statute explicitly authorizes remands in two situations. By failing similarly to provide for remands of removed cases involving pendent claims, petitioners assert, Congress intended to preclude district courts from remanding such cases.

We cannot accept petitioners' reasoning. We do not dispute that Congress could set a limitation of this kind on the federal courts' administration of the doctrine of pendent jurisdiction. But Congress has not done so, expressly or otherwise, in the removal statute. The principal flaw in petitioners' argument is that it fails to recognize that the removal statute does not address specifically *any* aspect of a district court's power to dispose of pendent state-law claims after removal: just as the statute makes no reference to a district court's power to remand pendent claims, so too the statute makes no reference to a district court's power to dismiss them. Yet petitioners

---

10. Petitioners argue that the federal courts do not need discretion to remand because they can retain jurisdiction over any case in which the statute of limitations has expired. See Brief for Petitioners 20. At least one Court of Appeals has made the identical argument. See Cook v. Weber, 698 F.2d, at 909. This solution to the problem of an expired statute of limitations, however, is far from satisfying. Under petitioners' suggested approach, district courts would retain jurisdiction over cases that apart from the statute-of-limitations concern properly belong in state courts. There is no reason to compel or encourage district courts to retain jurisdiction over such cases when the alternative of a remand is readily available.

In similar vein, the dissent argues that federal courts do not need discretion to remand because some States have savings clauses that alleviate the statute-of-limitations problem arising from the dismissal of cases. But the existence of such clauses in some States, while diminishing the reason for remand in particular cases, hardly reverses our general conclusion that the balance of factors to be weighed under *Gibbs,* considered in light of the range of state statutes of limitations, supports giving federal district courts the authority to remand cases involving pendent claims.

concede, as they must, that a federal court has discretion to dismiss a removed case involving pendent claims. Given that Congress's silence in the removal statute does not negate the power to dismiss such cases, that silence cannot sensibly be read to negate the power to remand them.

* * *

As petitioners point out, this Court's opinion in Thermtron Products, Inc. v. Hermansdorfer, 423 U.S. 336, 96 S.Ct. 584, 46 L.Ed.2d 542 (1976), contains some language that could be read to support the opposite conclusion. In *Thermtron,* a District Court remanded a properly removed case to state court on the ground that the federal docket was overcrowded. This Court held that the remand was improper. In so doing, the Court stated several times that a district court may not remand a case to a state court on a ground not specified in the removal statute. * * * Petitioners, again noting that the removal statute does not explicitly authorize the remand of cases involving pendent state-law claims, argue that *Thermtron* thus compels a holding that such remands are impermissible.

* * *

The *Thermtron* decision was a response to a clearly impermissible remand, of a kind very different from that at issue here. In *Thermtron,* the District Court had no authority to decline to hear the removed case. The court had diversity jurisdiction over the case, which is not discretionary. Thus, the District Court could not properly have eliminated the case from its docket, whether by a remand or by a dismissal. In contrast, when a removed case involves pendent state-law claims, a district court has undoubted discretion to decline to hear the case. The only remaining issue is whether the district court may decline jurisdiction through a remand as well as through a dismissal. The *Thermtron* opinion itself recognized this distinction by stating that federal courts have no greater power to remand cases because of an overcrowded docket than they have to dismiss cases on that ground. The implication of this statement, which is confirmed by common sense, is that an entirely different situation is presented when the district court has clear power to decline to exercise jurisdiction. *Thermtron* therefore does not control the decision in this case.

Petitioners also argue that giving district courts discretion to remand cases involving pendent state-law claims will allow plaintiffs to secure a state forum through the use of manipulative tactics. Petitioners' concern appears to be that a plaintiff whose suit has been removed to federal court will be able to regain a state forum simply by deleting all federal-law claims from the complaint and requesting that the district court remand the case. This concern, however, hardly justifies a categorical prohibition on the remand of cases involving state-law claims regardless of whether the plaintiff has attempted to manipulate the forum and regardless of the other circumstances in the case. A district court can consider whether the plaintiff has engaged in any manipulative tactics when it decides whether to remand a case. If the plaintiff has attempted to manipulate the forum, the court should take this behavior into account in determining whether the balance of factors to be considered under the pendent jurisdiction doctrine support a remand in the case. The district courts thus can guard against forum manipulation without a blanket rule that would prohibit the remand of all cases involving pendent state-law claims.

We conclude that a district court has discretion to remand to state court a removed case involving pendent claims upon a proper determination that retaining jurisdiction over the case would be inappropriate. The discretion to remand enables district courts to deal with cases involving pendent claims in the manner that best serves the principles of economy, convenience, fairness, and comity which underlie the pendent jurisdiction doctrine. Such discretion is precluded neither by the removal statute nor by our decision in *Thermtron*. We therefore affirm the decision below denying the petition for a writ of mandamus.

It is so ordered.[a]

Owen Equipment & Erection Co. v. Kroger, Administratrix

Supreme Court of the United States, 1978.
437 U.S. 365, 98 S.Ct. 2396, 57 L.Ed.2d 274.

■ MR. JUSTICE STEWART delivered the opinion of the Court.

In an action in which federal jurisdiction is based on diversity of citizenship, may the plaintiff assert a claim against a third-party defendant when there is no independent basis for federal jurisdiction over that claim? The Court of Appeals for the Eighth Circuit held in this case that such a claim is within the ancillary jurisdiction of the federal courts. We granted certiorari, 434 U.S. 1008, 98 S.Ct. 715, 54 L.Ed.2d 749, because this decision conflicts with several recent decisions of other Courts of Appeals.

I

On January 18, 1972, James Kroger was electrocuted when the boom of a steel crane next to which he was walking came too close to a high-tension electric power line. The respondent (his widow, who is the administratrix of his estate) filed a wrongful-death action in the United States District Court for the District of Nebraska against the Omaha Public Power District (OPPD). Her complaint alleged that OPPD's negligent construction, maintenance, and operation of the power line had caused Kroger's death. Federal jurisdiction was based on diversity of citizenship, since the respondent was a citizen of Iowa and OPPD was a Nebraska corporation.

OPPD then filed a third-party complaint pursuant to Fed. Rule Civ.Proc. 14(a) against the petitioner, Owen Equipment and Erection

---

a. The dissent of Justice White joined   is omitted.
by Justice Scalia and Chief Justice Rehnquist

Co. (Owen), alleging that the crane was owned and operated by Owen, and that Owen's negligence had been the proximate cause of Kroger's death.[3] OPPD later moved for summary judgment on the respondent's complaint against it. While this motion was pending, the respondent was granted leave to file an amended complaint naming Owen as an additional defendant. Thereafter, the District Court granted OPPD's motion for summary judgment in an unreported opinion.[4] The case thus went to trial between the respondent and the petitioner alone.

The respondent's amended complaint alleged that Owen was "a Nebraska corporation with its principal place of business in Nebraska." Owen's answer admitted that it was "a corporation organized and existing under the laws of the State of Nebraska," and denied every other allegation of the complaint. On the third day of trial, however, it was disclosed that the petitioner's principal place of business was in Iowa, not Nebraska,[5] and that the petitioner and the respondent were thus both citizens of Iowa. The petitioner then moved to dismiss the complaint for lack of jurisdiction. The District Court reserved decision on the motion, and the jury thereafter returned a verdict in favor of the respondent. In an unreported opinion issued after the trial, the District Court denied the petitioner's motion to dismiss the complaint.

The judgment was affirmed on appeal. 558 F.2d 417. The Court of Appeals held that under this Court's decision in Mine Workers v. Gibbs, 383 U.S. 715, 86 S.Ct. 1130, 16 L.Ed.2d 218, the District Court had jurisdictional power, in its discretion, to adjudicate the respondent's claim against the petitioner because that claim arose from the "core of 'operative facts' giving rise to both [respondent's] claim against OPPD and OPPD's claim against Owen." 558 F.2d, at 424. It further held that the District Court had properly exercised its discretion in proceeding to decide the case even after summary judgment had been granted to OPPD, because the petitioner had concealed its Iowa citizenship from the respondent. Rehearing en banc was denied by an equally divided court. * * *

III

The relevant statute in this case, 28 U.S.C. § 1332(a)(1), confers upon federal courts jurisdiction over "civil actions where the matter in controversy exceeds the sum or value of $10,000 * * * and is between

3. Under Rule 14(a), a third-party defendant may not be impleaded merely because he may be liable to the plaintiff. * * * While the third-party complaint in this case alleged merely that Owen's negligence caused Kroger's death, and the basis of Owen's alleged liability to OPPD is nowhere spelled out, OPPD evidently relied upon the state common-law right of contribution among joint tortfeasors. * * * The petitioner has never challenged the propriety of the third-party complaint as such.

4. Judgment was entered pursuant to Fed. Rule Civ.Proc. 54(b), and the Court of Appeals affirmed. Kroger v. Omaha Public Power Dist., 523 F.2d 161 8th Cir.

5. The problem apparently was one of geography. Although the Missouri River generally marks the boundary between Iowa and Nebraska, Carter Lake, Iowa, where the accident occurred and where Owen had its main office, lies west of the river, adjacent to Omaha, Neb. Apparently the river once avulsed at one of its bends, cutting Carter Lake off from the rest of Iowa.

* * * citizens of different States." This statute and its predecessors have consistently been held to require complete diversity of citizenship. That is, diversity jurisdiction does not exist unless *each defendant is a citizen of a different State from* each plaintiff. Over the years Congress has repeatedly re-enacted or amended the statute conferring diversity jurisdiction, leaving intact this rule of complete diversity. Whatever may have been the original purposes of diversity-of-citizenship jurisdiction, this subsequent history clearly demonstrates a congressional mandate that diversity jurisdiction is not to be available when any plaintiff is a citizen of the same State as any defendant.

Thus it is clear that the respondent could not originally have brought suit in federal court naming Owen and OPPD as codefendants, since citizens of Iowa would have been on both sides of the litigation. Yet the identical lawsuit resulted when she amended her complaint. Complete diversity was destroyed just as surely as if she had sued Owen initially. In either situation, in the plain language of the statute, the "matter in controversy" could not be "between * * * citizens of different States."

It is a fundamental precept that federal courts are courts of limited jurisdiction. The limits upon federal jurisdiction, whether imposed by the Constitution or by Congress, must be neither disregarded nor evaded. Yet under the reasoning of the Court of Appeals in this case, a plaintiff could defeat the statutory requirement of complete diversity by the simple expedient of suing only those defendants who were of diverse citizenship and waiting for them to implead nondiverse defendants.[17] If, as the Court of Appeals thought, a "common nucleus of operative fact" were the only requirement for ancillary jurisdiction in a diversity case, there would be no principled reason why the respondent in this case could not have joined her cause of action against Owen in her original complaint as ancillary to her claim against OPPD. Congress' requirement of complete diversity would thus have been evaded completely.

It is true, as the Court of Appeals noted, that the exercise of ancillary jurisdiction over nonfederal claims has often been upheld in situations involving impleader, cross-claims or counterclaims. But in determining whether jurisdiction over a nonfederal claim exists, the context in which the nonfederal claim is asserted is crucial. * * * And the claim here arises in a setting quite different from the kinds of nonfederal claims that have been viewed in other cases as falling within the ancillary jurisdiction of the federal courts.

---

17. This is not an unlikely hypothesis, since a defendant in a tort suit such as this one would surely try to limit his liability by impleading any joint tortfeasors for indemnity or contribution. Some commentators have suggested that the possible abuse of third-party practice could be dealt with under 28 U.S.C. § 1359, which forbids collusive attempts to create federal jurisdiction. * * *

The dissenting opinion today also expresses this view. * * * But there is nothing necessarily collusive about a plaintiff's selectively suing only those tortfeasors of diverse citizenship, or about the named defendants' desire to implead joint tortfeasors. Nonetheless, the requirement of complete diversity would be eviscerated by such a course of events.

First, the nonfederal claim in this case was simply not ancillary to the federal one in the same sense that, for example, the impleader by a defendant of a third-party defendant always is. A third-party complaint depends at least in part upon the resolution of the primary lawsuit. See n. 3, *supra.* Its relation to the original complaint is thus not mere factual similarity but logical dependence. The respondent's claim against the petitioner, however, was entirely separate from her original claim against OPPD, since the petitioner's liability to her depended not at all upon whether or not OPPD was also liable. Far from being an ancillary and dependent claim, it was a new and independent one.

Second, the nonfederal claim here was asserted by the plaintiff, who voluntarily chose to bring suit upon a state-law claim in a federal court. By contrast, ancillary jurisdiction typically involves claims by a defending party haled into court against his will, or by another person whose rights might be irretrievably lost unless he could assert them in an ongoing action in a federal court. A plaintiff cannot complain if ancillary jurisdiction does not encompass all of his possible claims in a case such as this one, since it is he who has chosen the federal rather than the state forum and must thus accept its limitations. "[T]he efficiency plaintiff seeks so avidly is available without question in the state courts." Kenrose Mfg. Co. v. Fred Whitaker Co., 512 F.2d 890, 894 (4th Cir. 1972).

It is not unreasonable to assume that, in generally requiring complete diversity, Congress did not intend to confine the jurisdiction of federal courts so inflexibly that they are unable to protect legal rights or effectively to resolve an entire logically entwined lawsuit. Those practical needs are the basis of the doctrine of ancillary jurisdiction. But neither the convenience of litigants nor considerations of judicial economy can suffice to justify extension of the doctrine of ancillary jurisdiction to a plaintiff's cause of action against a citizen of the same State in a diversity case. Congress has established the basic rule that diversity jurisdiction exists under 28 U.S.C. § 1332 only when there is complete diversity of citizenship. * * * To allow the requirement of complete diversity to be circumvented as it was in this case would simply flout the congressional command.[21]

Accordingly, the judgment of the Court of Appeals is reversed.

It is so ordered.[a]

Mengler, Burbank & Rowe, Congress Accepts Supreme Court's Invitation to Codify Supplemental Jurisdiction

74 Judicature 213 (Dec.–Jan., 1991).

* * *

The 5–4 decision in Finley v. United States, 490 U.S. 545, 109 S.Ct. 2003, 104 L.Ed.2d 593 (1989) resolved the uncertainty over

---

21. Our holding is that the District Court lacked power to entertain the respondent's lawsuit against the petitioner. Thus, the asserted inequity in the respondent's alleged concealment of its citizenship is irrelevant. Federal judicial power does not depend upon "prior action or consent of the parties." American Fire & Cas. Co. v. Finn, 341 U.S., at 17–18, 71 S.Ct., at 542.

a. The dissent of Justice White, with whom Justice Brennan joined, is omitted.

pendent party jurisdiction, by rejecting Barbara Finley's invocation of pendent party jurisdiction in the context of a Federal Tort Claims Act suit. Finley's husband and children were killed when a plane in which they were flying struck electric transmission wires during its approach to a San Diego airfield. Finley sued the utility company in state court, but when she learned that the Federal Aviation Administration might have been responsible, she brought an action under the FTCA in federal district court, which has exclusive jurisdiction over FTCA suits. Later, Finley tried to append a state law tort claim against a nondiverse defendant, the utility company.

Finley thus presented the Court with a compelling case for recognizing pendent party jurisdiction: the plaintiff's federal question claim could not be heard in state court, the federal and state law claims were closely linked, and requiring Finley to pursue her claims in two different forums would be sheer waste of judicial resources (or would force her to abandon one if she chose to bring only a single action).

* * *

Section 1367

With a few exceptions discussed below, section 1367 codifies supplemental jurisdiction as it existed before the *Finley* decision. Theoretical arguments can be made for broadening supplemental jurisdiction even as it existed prior to *Finley*. But expanding supplemental jurisdiction would require relaxing the requirements for diversity jurisdiction and would cut against the dominant perception, shared by the Federal Courts Study Committee, that federal courts should focus more of their resources on federal question cases and fewer (or none at all) on diversity cases. In order to repair *Finley's* damage in a noncontroversial manner without expanding the scope of diversity jurisdiction, the statutory measure was therefore framed to restore and regularize supplemental jurisdiction, not to revamp it.

Section 1367(a), for example, generally authorizes the district courts to exercise jurisdiction over a supplemental claim whenever it forms part of the same constitutional case or controversy as the claim that provides the basis of the district court's original jurisdiction. In reaching to the limits of Article III, subsection (a) codifies supplemental jurisdiction at the outer constitutional boundary that existed before *Finley's* statutory revisionism. Typically, courts have understood the same constitutional case or controversy to include all claims arising out of a single transaction or occurrence or related series of transactions or occurrences.

The second sentence of subsection (a), making explicit the federal courts' authority to hear supplemental claims "that involve the joinder or intervention of additional parties," in part simply reinstates the prior settled law. Thus, for example, as under pre-*Finley* practice, impleader claims against nondiverse third-party defendants are authorized, as are compulsory counterclaims and cross-claims involving additional parties. The second sentence, however, modifies current law by overruling *Finley*. Congress thus has resolved the controversy over pendent party jurisdiction by providing the explicit statutory authorization found lacking and regarded as necessary by the *Finley* majority.

Subsection (b) restricts the federal courts' exercise of supplemental jurisdiction in diversity cases by, in effect, codifying the principal rationale of *Owen Equipment & Erection Co. v. Kroger.* * * *

Thearo Snider and Phillip Steele v. Stimson Lumber Company

United States District Court for the Eastern District of California, 1996.
914 F. Supp. 388.

■ Lawrence K. Karlton, Chief Judge Emeritus,

On August 10, 1995, plaintiffs Thearo Snider and Phillip Steele filed this action on behalf of themselves and all others similarly situated. The named defendants are Stimson Lumber Company and Stimson Trading Company, a fictitious business name of Stimson Lumber.

The complaint alleges that defendants manufactured and sold defective hardboard siding. Plaintiffs claim that they purchased the defective siding from defendants, or their agents, and installed it on their dwellings. According to plaintiffs, the siding warped, buckled, cracked, and slipped as a result of weather, exposure and other factors. They allege injury in excess of $50,000.

The complaint contains counts in strict liability, negligence, negligent infliction of emotional distress, and violation of RICO. Plaintiffs also seek to represent a class of over a thousand people who have allegedly installed defendants' siding.

Defendants' motion seeks, inter alia, to dismiss the class claims because of a failure to allege that each member of the class has sustained damages in excess of the jurisdiction amount.

Aggregation of Class Claims

Defendants contend that plaintiffs fail to satisfy the amount in controversy requirement for a class action because they do not allege that each member's claim exceeds the jurisdictional minimum. The Supreme Court has previously held that in a diversity based class action, where the class members assert separate and distinct claims, each class member must independently meet the amount-in-controversy requirement to establish diversity jurisdiction over his or her claim. Zahn v. International Paper Co., 414 U.S. 291, 301, 38 L. Ed. 2d 511, 94 S. Ct. 505 (1973); Snyder v. Harris, 394 U.S. 332, 338, 22 L. Ed. 2d 319, 89 S. Ct. 1053 (1969). On the other hand, where the plaintiffs have joined together to "enforce a single title or right, in which they have a common and undivided interest, it is enough if their interests collectively equal the jurisdictional amount." Troy Bank v. G. A. Whitehead & Co., 222 U.S. 39, 40–41, 56 L. Ed. 81, 32 S. Ct. 9 (1911), cited in Zahn,, 414 U.S. at 294.

Plaintiffs do not attempt to argue that all class members have a common and undivided interest such that they can evade the non-aggregation rule of Zahn. Rather, plaintiffs contend that in 28 U.S.C. § 1367 Congress overruled Zahn.

28 U.S.C. § 1367 contains two subsections which raise the question of whether Zahn is still good law. First, subsection 1367(a) provides district courts with supplemental jurisdiction over related claims. Second, subsection 1367(b) carves out exceptions to this grant of jurisdiction for diversity cases. Class actions are not among the exceptions listed in § 1367(b). Thus, the court is presented with a question of statutory construction as to whether the absence of class actions in the list of exceptions constitutes an overruling of the non-aggregation doctrine.

As with any issue of statutory interpretation, the first question which a district court must address is whether there is a binding construction of the statute. Neither the Supreme Court nor the Ninth Circuit has determined whether supplemental jurisdiction under § 1367 extends to claims of class members in diversity who do not meet the amount in controversy jurisdictional requirement. Accordingly, the court must undertake its own explication employing the traditional methods of statutory construction.

Analysis of § 1367 commences with application of the plain meaning rule. Connecticut Nat. Bank v. Germain, 503 U.S. 249, 253–54, 117 L. Ed. 2d 391, 112 S. Ct. 1146 (1992). Under the rule, the inquiry ends with the words of § 1367 if they are clear and unambiguous. Id. If the language of the statute is ambiguous, however, the court may resort to textual and extrinsic aids to construction. See Dodd v. John Hancock Mut. Life Ins. Co., 688 F. Supp. 564, 569 (E.D.Cal. 1988).

Recently, the Fifth Circuit has held that the plain language of § 1367—i.e. the absence of an exception for class actions in subsection (b)—clearly and unambiguously vested federal courts with the power to hear supplemental claims in class actions based in diversity without regard to the amount in controversy of each individual claim. In re Abbott Laboratories, 51 F.3d 524, 527–28 (5th Cir.1995). As that court conceded, its conclusion is inconsistent with that of a number of district courts that have examined the issue. Id. at 528 n.8 (citing twelve district court decisions holding that § 1367 did not overrule Zahn, and three non-class action cases holding that § 1367 supersedes Zahn). With due respect to the Fifth Circuit, this court cannot agree with it, since I do not find the language of § 1367 clear and unambiguous.

Under § 1367(a) supplemental jurisdiction depends upon all claims forming part of the same case or controversy. It does not follow, however, as the Fifth Circuit assumes, that the claims of class members asserting a similar wrong but distinct injury and damages form part of the same case or controversy. Indeed, class action doctrine teaches otherwise.

Class actions are a procedural device permitting a single suit where there are common questions, and thereby sometimes providing for vindication of rights when economic reality would not otherwise permit suit. See 7 Charles A. Wright and Arthur R. Miller, Federal Practice and Procedure § 1751, at 509, § 1754, at 543 (1972). Nonetheless, a class action involving separate and distinct claims by definition involves "several or distinct rights." 7 Id. § 1756, at 554. Class members can litigate these claims together, not because they are one "case or controversy," but "simply because the different claims [involve] common questions of law or fact." Snyder v. Harris, 394 U.S. at 335. Accordingly, when class members assert separate and distinct claims, there are as many "cases or controversies" in a class action as there are class members. Simply put, claims related to those asserted by other class members may suffice to support recognition of a class, but that does not mean they "form part of the same case or controversy under Article III of the United States Constitution" within the meaning of 28 U.S.C. § 1367.

The reading of the supplemental jurisdiction statute in light of class action doctrine reflects the distinction Snyder and Zahn recognized between class actions involving the enforcement of a single title or right, and those where all plaintiffs assert separate and distinct claims. The former permits aggregation, while the latter requires each class member to allege the jurisdictional amount of damages. See Snyder, 394 U.S. at 334–35 and Zahn, 414 U.S. at 293–94. While the non-aggregation doctrine for separate and distinct claims is based upon the Supreme Court's interpretation of the statutory phrase "matter in controversy," Snyder, 394 U.S. at 336, the logical inference is that a class action asserting a common and undivided interest involves a single "case or controversy," but that a class action containing separate and distinct claims comprises a different "case or controversy" for each class member's claim. Read in this light, the text of § 1367 does not clearly and unambiguously create supplemental jurisdiction over separate and distinct claims in a class action based in diversity. Indeed, given the assumption that Congress knows the law, Cannon v. University of Chicago, 441 U.S. 677, 696–97, 60 L. Ed. 2d 560, 99 S. Ct. 1946 (1979), it appears to this court that a reading of the statute in light of the law in existence during the passage of § 1367 is a more natural and appropriate one.

Even if § 1367 is susceptible to the Fifth Circuit's reading, the fact that it is not unreasonable to interpret the statute consistent with the non-aggregation rule demonstrates that the text is not conclusive. Since ambiguity exists, resort may be had to the legislative history to resolve the question of construction. See Catholic Social Services Inc. v. Meese, 685 F. Supp. 1149, 1152 (E.D.Cal.1988); see also Leroy Cattle Co., Inc. v. Fina Oil & Chemical Co., 1994 WL 151105, at *15 n.

10 (D. Kan. 1994), ("It is unlikely that so much scholarly effort would have been expended on the meaning and purpose of § 1367 if its meaning and purpose were clear.").

As the Fifth Circuit itself acknowledged, the legislative history of § 1367 strongly indicates that Congress did not intend to overrule Zahn. Abbott Laboratories, 51 F.3d at 527–28. The history demonstrates that Congress passed § 1367 essentially to "restore the pre-Finley understandings of the authorization for and limits on other forms of supplemental jurisdiction." H.R. Rep. No. 734, 101st Cong., 2d Sess. 28 (1990), reprinted in 1990 U.S.C.C.A.N. 6860, 6874. Indeed, the legislative history explains that "the section is not intended to affect the jurisdictional requirements of 28 U.S.C. § 1332 in diversity-only class actions, as those requirements were interpreted prior to Finley," 1990 U.S.C.C.A.N. at 6875, and cites, inter alia, to Zahn as a pre-Finley case untouched by the Act. Id. at 6875 n.17. In the words of the Fifth Circuit, "the House Committee on the Judiciary considered the bill that became § 1367 to be a 'noncontroversial' collection of 'relatively modest proposals,' not the sort of legislative action that would upset any long-established precedent like Zahn." Abbott Laboratories, 51 F.3d at 528, quoting 1990 U.S.C.C.A.N. at 6861.

Given the ambiguity of the statute and the longstanding precedent against the aggregation of separate and distinct claims, resort to the legislative history is appropriate. That history demonstrates that Congress did not intend § 1367 to overrule Zahn. Accordingly, this court, joining the vast majority of district courts around the country, concludes that where plaintiffs base jurisdiction of a class action upon diversity and allege separate and distinct claims, they must allege that each class member has a $50,000 claim to maintain the case.

Stromberg Metal Works and Comfort Control, Inc. v. Press Mechanical, Inc.

United States Court of Appeals for the Seventh Circuit, 1996.
77 F.3d 928.

■ Before Easterbrook, Rovner, and Evans, Circuit Judges.

■ Easterbrook, Circuit Judge.

Bechtel Power Corporation is the owner's contracting agent for the Calvert Cliffs nuclear power station under construction in Lusby, Maryland. Bechtel hired Press Mechanical to work on the heating, ventilation, and air conditioning system of the power station's diesel generator building. The contract between Bechtel and Press calls for the application of Maryland law and requires Press to "bind every subcontractor to . . . the terms of the construction documents as far as applicable to the work performed by the subcontractor". Press engaged Stromberg Metal Works and Comfort Control to do some of the HVAC work required by the Bechtel–Press contract. Press issued purchase orders, which provide on the front that the work is to be done "in strict accordance with the plans, specifications and other contract documents listed below"—which include the master contract that selects Maryland law. Preprinted on the back of each purchase order is this sentence: "This order shall be governed by the laws of the State of Illinois."

The contract between Press and Bechtel provides that Bechtel will pay Press for work done by a subcontractor only if Press certifies that the subcontractor has been paid, or that a bond secures payment. The project's owner needs clean title, which means that Bechtel or the owner may have to pay the subcontractor directly if necessary to clear a mechanic's or materialman's lien. No one wants to pay twice for the same work. Hence the requirement that Press pay the subcontractor before Bechtel will pay Press. According to the complaint, whose allegations we must accept, Press represented to Bechtel that it had paid more than $425,000 to Stromberg, and more than $27,000 to Comfort Control, for their work under the subcontracts. Bechtel then reimbursed Press. But the representation was false; Press had paid only $18,000 to Stromberg and nothing to Comfort Control. Press is insolvent and has made an assignment for the benefit of its creditors. Apparently Stromberg and Comfort Control do not have liens on their work (the reason for this is not clear, but we need not pursue the question). Having paid Press, Bechtel is unwilling to pay the subcontractors directly, and Press cannot. Stromberg and Comfort Control filed this action under the diversity jurisdiction seeking to collect from Lester H. Goldwyn, John P. Goldwyn, and George E. Zielinski, who it believes controlled Press and were responsible for the false certification to Bechtel and the nonpayment of the debts on the subcontracts. They invoke the Maryland Construction Trust Fund Statute. One clause of this law, Md. Real Property Code § 9–201(b)(1), provides that funds received by a contractor "for work done or materials furnished ... for or about a building by any subcontractor" are held in trust for the subcontractor, and § 9–202 adds:

Any officer, director, or managing agent of any contractor or subcontractor, who knowingly retains or uses the moneys held in trust under § 9–201 of this subtitle, or any part thereof, for any purpose other than to pay those subcontractors for whom the moneys are held in trust, shall be personally liable to any person damaged by the action.

Illinois law lacks any comparable provision, so plaintiffs' case depends on the application of Maryland law. Zielinski and the Goldwyns believe that they have defenses even if Maryland law applies, but we need not decide whether that is so. Similarly, we sidestep the question whether the current version of the Maryland law (which we have quoted) differs materially from the version in force when Press failed to pay Stromberg and Comfort Control.

I

Stromberg's claim exceeds $50,000, but Comfort Control's claim does not, so the immediate question is: does the supplemental jurisdiction permit a court to hear a claim by a party whose loss does not meet the jurisdictional minimum? In Clark v. Paul Gray, Inc., 306 U.S. 583, 83 L. Ed. 1001, 59 S. Ct. 744 (1939), the Supreme Court held not, but 28 U.S.C. § 1367, enacted in 1990, may have altered that result. One court of appeals has held that § 1367 supersedes Clark and allows pendent-party jurisdiction when the additional parties have claims worth less than $50,000. In re Abbott Laboratories, 51 F.3d 524, 527–29 (5th Cir.1995). (Actually, the fifth circuit held that § 1367 alters the result of Zahn v. International Paper Co., 414 U.S. 291, 38 L. Ed. 2d 511, 94 S. Ct. 505 (1973); we discuss below whether there is a material difference between Clark and Zahn.) No other court of appeals has addressed this question; we recently remarked on its unsettled nature. Anthony v. Security Pacific Financial Services, Inc., 75 F.3d 311 (7th Cir. 1996), slip op. 6–7 & n.2. Most district judges, within and without this circuit, have held that the old rule retains vitality. The district court in this case followed the majority view and dismissed Comfort Control's claim for want of jurisdiction. But we are reluctant to create a conflict among the circuits on a jurisdictional issue. We follow Abbott Laboratories, which has strong support from the statutory text.

Section 1367(a) provides that "district courts shall have supplemental jurisdiction over all other claims that are so related to claims in the action within such original jurisdiction that they form part of the same case or controversy under Article III of the United States Constitution." To emphasize the inclusiveness of "all", the section continues: "Such supplemental jurisdiction shall include claims that involve the joinder or intervention of additional parties." Abbott Laboratories observed that this language is direct and unambiguous. We held in Brazinski v. Amoco Petroleum Additives Co., 6 F.3d 1176 (7th Cir. 1993), that § 1367(a) permits the adjudication of a claim by a pendent party that neither arises under federal law nor is supported by diversity of citizenship. If § 1367(a) allows suit by a pendent plaintiff who meets the jurisdictional amount but not the diversity requirement, it also allows suit by a pendent plaintiff who satisfies the diversity requirement but not the jurisdictional amount.

Although the final sentence of § 1367(a) might have been designed to do nothing more than reverse the outcome of Finley v. United States, 490 U.S. 545, 104 L. Ed. 2d 593, 109 S. Ct. 2003 (1989), which held that pendent-party jurisdiction is unavailable when the principal claim arises under federal law, the text is not limited to federal-question cases, and § 1367(b) shows that the statute governs diversity litigation as well. Section 1367(b) begins: "In any civil action of which the district courts have original jurisdiction founded solely on section 1332 of this title, the district courts shall not have supplemental jurisdiction" in defined circumstances. So although, as Abbott Laboratories discussed, some legislative history suggests that the responsible committees did not expect § 1367 to upset Zahn, the text is not limited in this way. When text and legislative history disagree, the text controls. In re Sinclair, 870 F.2d 1340 (7th Cir.1989).

The Goldwyns ask us to distinguish Abbott Laboratories on the ground that it, like Zahn, involved a class action. Zahn held that every member of a class must satisfy the jurisdictional minimum, and Abbott Laboratories concluded that under § 1367 only the named class representatives need do so. Our case, by contrast, has just two plaintiffs. But § 1367 does not distinguish class actions from other cases; neither did Zahn. Indeed, the point of Zahn was that the class device made no difference. Snyder v. Harris, 394 U.S. 332, 22 L. Ed. 2d 319, 89 S. Ct. 1053 (1969), held that Fed. R. Civ. P. 23 does not alter the rule that multiple persons' claims cannot be combined to reach the minimum amount in controversy. Then Zahn added that each unnamed class member must satisfy the jurisdictional amount even if the class representatives do so without aggregation. The Court started from the proposition, established in Clark, that § 1332 applies to each party independently. See also Scott v. Frazier, 253 U.S. 243, 64 L. Ed. 883, 40 S. Ct. 503 (1920). Zahn holds that the unnamed class members remain ''parties'' for this purpose. In modern terms, this means that Rule 23 does not authorize pendent-party jurisdiction. See also Fed. R. Civ. P. 82 (''these rules shall not be construed to extend or limit the jurisdiction of the United States district courts''). Zahn added only that the status of the pendent parties as class members (rather than as named representatives) does not make a difference. Section 1367(a) has changed the basic rule by authorizing pendent-party jurisdiction, and that change affects Clark and Zahn equally. To the extent practical considerations enter in, it is hard to avoid remarking that allowing thousands of small claims into federal court via the class device is a substantially greater expansion of jurisdiction than is allowing a single pendent party. It is therefore easy to imagine wanting to overturn Clark but not Zahn; it is much harder to imagine wanting to overturn Zahn but not Clark, and we have no reason to believe that Congress harbored such a secret desire.

Section 1367(b) specifies exceptions to § 1367(a) for diversity cases. It forbids the exercise of supplemental jurisdiction in diversity litigation over claims by plaintiffs against persons made parties under Rule 14, 19, 20, or 24 of the Federal Rules of Civil Procedure, or over claims by persons proposed to be joined as plaintiffs under Rule 19 of such rules, or seeking to intervene as plaintiffs under Rule 24 of such rules, when exercising supplemental jurisdiction over such claims would be inconsistent with the jurisdictional requirements of section 1332.

Thus plaintiffs joined under Fed. R. Civ. P. 19, or intervening under Fed. R. Civ. P. 24, must satisfy the requirements of § 1332. Comfort Control is not an intervenor, and it does not come under Rule 19 either. That rule calls for the joinder of necessary parties. Comfort Control is not an indispensable party to litigation by Stromberg, or the reverse; joinder is strictly for convenience, and is authorized by Fed. R. Civ. P. 20. Now this does point up an apparent incongruity in § 1367(b). Claims against persons made parties under Rule 20 are forbidden, but claims by parties who join under Rule 20 are allowed. Similarly, claims by parties joined under Rule 19 because they are essential to adjudication are forbidden (if that spoils diversity), but claims by parties joined under Rule 20 for convenience are allowed. What sense can this make? Some scholars have suggested that it makes none, and they call on courts to fix the statute by inventive construction. E.g., Thomas D. Rowe, Jr., Stephen B. Burbank & Thomas M. Mengler, Compounding or Creating Confusion About Supplemental Jurisdiction? A Reply to Professor Freer, 40 Emory L.J. 943, 961 n.91 (1991). Whether § 1367(b) is a model drafting exercise may be doubted, but the language draws an important line. The complete diversity rule of Strawbridge v. Curtiss, 7 U.S. (3 Cranch) 267, 2 L. Ed. 435 (1806), excludes from federal court cases in which citizens of the same state are on each side. Supplemental jurisdiction has the potential to move from complete to minimal diversity. Suppose a citizen of Illinois sues a citizen of Indiana under § 1332 and adds a citizen of Illinois as a supplemental defendant. If this strategy works, then Strawbridge is no longer controlling. Similarly, suppose two parties (one from Illinois, one from Indiana) who claim an interest in the same property want to adjudicate their rights against a third party, a citizen of Illinois. Without a provision like § 1367(b), it would be easy for the Indiana claimant to start the suit, leading the defendant to add the Illinois claimant under Rule 19. As written, § 1367(b) keeps cases of this kind out of federal court entirely, just as Strawbridge does. See also Owen Equipment & Erection Co. v. Kroger, 437 U.S. 365, 57 L. Ed. 2d 274, 98 S. Ct. 2396 (1978). But if it is possible for the principal action to be in federal court without any jurisdictional qualms then § 1367(b) does not block adding an additional plaintiff with a closely related claim against the defendants who are already in the federal forum.

"Closely related" is a vital qualification. Section 1367(c)(2) provides that the district court may dismiss a supplemental claim that "substantially predominates over the claim or claims over which the district court has original jurisdiction". And § 1367(a) itself applies only if the supplemental claims are "so related to claims in the action within [the] original jurisdiction that they form part of the same case or controversy under Article III of the United States Constitution." The claims of Stromberg and Comfort Control satisfy these requirements, however. The two plaintiffs are affiliated corporations under common control. The claims arose out of the same construction project. According to the complaint, the defendants pursued a single course of action—fraudulently representing to Bechtel that the subcontractors had been paid, and thus obtaining money intended for the subcontractors without remitting it—that injured both plaintiffs. The same form of purchase order was used for both subcontracts, so factual and legal issues are identical. This strikes us as exactly the sort of case in which pendent-party jurisdiction is appropriate. It is two for the price of one: to decide either plaintiff's claim is to decide both, and neither private interests nor judicial economy would be promoted by resolving Stromberg's claim in federal court while trundling Comfort Control off to state court to get a second opinion. These plaintiffs' claims are more closely related than the claims in Brazinski, where the pendent plaintiff ultimately lost on legal and factual grounds that were specific to the pendent claim. If Brazinski was within the supplemental jurisdiction, this case is too. See also, e.g., Baer v. First Options of Chicago, Inc., 72 F.3d 1294 (7th Cir.1995), slip op. 6–14; Myers v. County of Lake, 30 F.3d 847 (7th Cir.1994).

II

Stromberg lost on the merits in the district court because the judge thought that Stromberg had assented to the application of Illinois law. Press is an Illinois corporation with its principal place of business in Illinois; Stromberg and Comfort Control are Maryland corporations; Stromberg's place of business is Washington, D.C., and Comfort Control's is in Maryland. The subcontracts had enough of a link to Illinois that an Illinois court would permit the parties to select Illinois law. See Hofeld v. Nationwide Life Insurance Co., 59 Ill. 2d 522, 322 N.E.2d 454 (1975). (Because the district court is in Illinois, that state's choice-of-law rules apply. Klaxon Co. v. Stentor Electric Manufacturing Co., 313 U.S. 487, 85 L. Ed. 1477, 61 S. Ct. 1020 (1941).) "The law of the state chosen by the parties to govern their contractual rights and duties will be applied if the particular issue is one which the parties could have resolved by an explicit provision in their agreement directed to that issue." Restatement (2d) of Conflict of Laws § 187(1) (1971). Maryland does not insist that its Construction Trust Fund Statute be applied to all work performed in that state; the statute does not include a rule forbidding waivers. Because plaintiffs could have agreed by contract to surrender their rights under that law, they were free to accomplish the same thing by choosing Illinois law in gross. The parties dispute whether and how Illinois would apply § 187(2) of the Restatement, which deals with what happens "if the particular issue is one which the parties could not have resolved by an explicit provision in their agreement directed to that issue". Because individual liability could be created or avoided by contract, Illinois would stop with the approach of § 187(1).

All questions of contract to one side, Illinois law is presumptively applicable because plaintiffs want to hold corporate officers liable for corporate acts. Efforts to "pierce the corporate veil" are governed by the law of the state of incorporation, see Kern v. Chicago & Eastern Illinois R.R., 6 Ill. App. 3d 247, 250–51, 285 N.E.2d 501, 503–04 (1st Dist. 1972), which for Press is Illinois. So unless the parties agreed to the application of Maryland law, it is not necessary to turn over the purchase order and read the choice-of-law clause on the reverse. By "the parties" we mean the persons sought to be held liable. Even the strongest language choosing Maryland law for purposes of interpreting the subcontracts would not necessarily bind Zielinski and the Goldwyns for purposes of personal liability—they did not sign the contracts. Corporate officers' decisions may be imputed to the corporation; things do not work the other way 'round. Citizens Electric Corp. v. Bituminous Fire & Marine Insurance Co., 68 F.3d 1016, 1021–22 (7th Cir.1995); Mark I, Inc. v. Gruber, 38 F.3d 369 (7th Cir.1994); In re Kubly, 818 F.2d 643 (7th Cir.1987). Plaintiffs therefore need to prevail on two sequential questions: first, they must establish that the subcontracts bind Press to Maryland law; second, they must show that Press's officers have made the same choice for their personal liability. The first hurdle is insuperable, so we need not discuss the second.

One way to establish that Maryland law applies would be to show that subcontractors are third-party beneficiaries of the rules Bechtel established for the project—rules that appear in the Bechtel–Press contract. See E. Allan Farnsworth, 3 Farnsworth on Contracts § 10.4 (1990). Owners and their agents have powerful reasons to want all work on a project done according to one set of laws. For example, the owner must decide whether to require contractors to post bonds securing payment of subcontractors. The decision whether to require such a bond could be influenced by the existence of a law such as Maryland's Construction Trust Fund Statute. When corporate managers have more incentive to pay their subcontractors (as they do under Maryland law, to avoid personal liability), there is less need for bonds. Then, too, the price of the Bechtel–Press contract may well have depended on assumptions about liability for defects (which depends on state law), on the likelihood that the contractor could excuse noncompliance with the contract (state law, again), and so on. The last thing Bechtel wanted to hear from Press was a claim that it could not complete the work on time because some peculiarity of Illinois law entitled one of the subcontractors to delay performance. Press promised Bechtel that it would bind all of its subcontractors to the requirements of the main contract, and one function of such a clause may be to give subcontractors the right to enforce the terms of the main contract against Press when the contract and subcontract differ. Curiously, however, Stromberg and Comfort Control do not contend that they are third-party beneficiaries of the Bechtel–Press contract. Nor do they contend that the Bechtel–Press contract estops Press to claim the benefits of Illinois law, to the extent it differs from the rules of Maryland law. In civil litigation courts confine themselves to the arguments advanced by the parties—here, that the subcontract itself selects Maryland law, and that when preprinted and individually negotiated terms conflict the negotiated terms prevail. The latter proposition is sound, 2 Farnsworth on Contracts § 7.11 at 264, but the former is not.

Negotiated language on the front of each purchase order reads:

Seller shall furnish and install all duct work, hangers, HVAC, equipment and appurtenances and install all owner-furnished equipment in strict accordance with the plans, specifications and other contract documents listed below, as well as Bechtel procurement specification DG–80491, Bechtel design specification SP–782 and all shop drawings prepared by buyer. All work to be performed under the direct supervision and control of buyer's project manager, project superintendent (or their designee) and shall adhere to all project requirements, including, but not limited to, Buyer's Quality Assurance Safety and Fitness for Duty programs.

Plaintiffs emphasize the words "other contract documents" and "all project requirements", but the context in which these words appear establishes that they refer to the technical requirements of the work. Stromberg and Comfort Control agreed to do exactly what Press had promised Bechtel it would do. A more backhanded way of selecting Maryland law would be difficult to imagine. True, the Bechtel documents include that provision, but they are crammed with other requirements that are not plausible candidates for imputing to the subcontract. Reading the language typed on the purchase orders as limited to the nature of the work the subcontractors agreed to do makes so much more sense than reading it as incorporating the whole Bechtel–Press contract that the judge was entitled to dismiss the complaint under Fed. R. Civ. P. 12(b)(6). Plaintiffs do not want to offer any additional facts (the subcontracts include integration clauses) and do not argue that this issue is one for a jury to decide. All they have is the bald language, and it is not enough.

The judgment with respect to Stromberg is affirmed. The judgment dismissing Comfort Control as a plaintiff is vacated, and the case is remanded with instructions to enter judgment on the merits.

H. VENUE

1. Basic Considerations

VENUE IN STATE AND FEDERAL COURTS: AN OVERVIEW

The fact that an action may be brought in California, or Texas or New York does not mean that it may be brought anywhere within those states that plaintiff chooses to file. The law of venue, largely statutory in both state and federal systems, limits plaintiff's options.

These limitations are of great significance to the parties. Hundreds of miles and vast cultural differences often separate one section of a state from another. In the federal system, the option to bring an action in the District of Alaska, the Southern District of Texas, or the Northern District of New York may have far-reaching consequences.

In all these situations we assume that the court in question has both subject matter and personal jurisdiction, but that is not enough. Venue requirements must also be satisfied.

In the states certain patterns have developed. Actions regarding interests in land must ordinarily be brought in the county or other judicial subdivision where the property is located.

In transitory actions the plaintiff often has choices: where the defendant resides or does business, or where the cause of action or claim for relief arose. Venue is often properly laid where the plaintiff resides and sometimes where the plaintiff does business. Some states permit the parties to a contract to use forum selection clauses which fix venue.

In the federal system, the basic patterns are described in 28 U.S.C. § 1391, although special venue provisions applicable to specific areas of the law, *e.g.,* patent infringement litigation, are to be found in connection with these specialties. Section 1391 has been amended a number of times in recent years. The changes were designed to reduce difference in venue requirements for cases based on diversity of citizenship and those arising under federal question jurisdiction. They also sought to create fallback venue provisions that could be used when no other proper venue for the action was available.

Parsing the words of the statute, one can recognize any number of policy questions as well as technical problems. Is it better, in matters of venue, to serve the convenience of plaintiffs or of defendants? If two motorists, one from Florida and one from Maine, are involved in an auto accident in Wyoming, what venue options should the law provide? Does it help or hinder to substitute for "the judicial district in which the claim arose" the present provision: "a judicial district in which a substantial part of the events or omissions giving rise to the claim occurred?"

Examine the current text of § 1391(a) and (b) to see how and to what extent it answers these questions. What kinds of cases will provide many venue choices? When will venue choices be limited?

Siegel, Changes in Federal Jurisdiction and Practice Under the New Judicial Improvements and Access to Justice Act
123 F.R.D. 399, 405–407 (1989).

The main venue provision altered by the amendment* is § 1391(c) of Title 28. It affects the venue of an action against a corporate defendant. (No change is made in respect of actions by a corporate plaintiff, * * *) The old subdivision (c) read as follows:

> A corporation may be sued in any judicial district in which it is incorporated or licensed to do business or is doing business, and such judicial district shall be regarded as the residence of such corporation for venue purposes.

The new subdivision (c) is even more generous in permitting venue choices in actions against corporations, but in at least one respect, as will be shown, the choice is curtailed. The new subdivision reads:

> For purposes of venue under this chapter, a defendant that is a corporation shall be deemed to reside in any judicial district in which it is subject to personal jurisdiction at the time the action is commenced. In a State which has more than one judicial district and in which a defendant that is a corporation is subject to personal jurisdiction at the time an action is commenced, such corporation shall be deemed to reside in any district in that State within which its contacts would be sufficient to subject it to

---

* Pub.L. 100–702 (1988).

personal jurisdiction if that district were a separate State, and, if there is no such district, the corporation shall be deemed to reside in the district within which it has the most significant contacts.

The old subdivision allowed venue in any of several districts, including any in which the corporation was merely "doing business". The new one makes the corporation's amenability to jurisdiction the venue standard: as long as the corporation is subject to personal jurisdiction in the district—even if it has to be served with process through (e.g.) a state official or outside the state the court sits in—that district qualifies as proper venue in an action against the corporation.

Probably the most important instance in which this will expand the venue option is the case in which jurisdiction rests on something like a state "longarm" statute, adopted for application in the federal court by Rule 4(e) of the Federal Rules of Civil Procedure. Whatever contacts the corporation may have had with the state in respect of the claim, if they suffice for jurisdiction they suffice for venue. Many a reader may assume that this was always so, but some courts held the other way, refusing to find a corporation to be "doing business" in the state under the old statute (so as to satisfy venue) merely because it was doing just enough to meet the demands of a state longarm statute (and thus satisfy jurisdiction). The new statute works just such an assimilation.

* * *

While a superficial reading of the statute tends to suggest only an expansion of corporate venue, it was in fact a curtailment of corporate venue that may have been the amendment's prime intent. (See House Report 100–889, p. 70, U.S.Code Cong. & Admin.News 1988, pp. 5982, 6031.) Under case law, a corporation "licensed" to do business in a state used to be deemed, for a venue measure, to be doing that business in all parts of the state. In multi-district states, it sometimes meant that a corporation with all of its contacts in district A might end up being sued in district B, farther away from its base and likely a less appropriate district for the action.

Under the second sentence of the amended subdivision (c), that should not happen. It requires that the corporation be sued only in that district with which it had the jurisdictional contacts. And should those contacts be so divided between the two districts that while they suffice in the aggregate for jurisdiction, the contacts with either district, measured alone, would not, the court is directed to set venue in the district with the "most significant" of the contacts.

* * *

Under the first sentence of subdivision (c), the measure of whether the defendant is subject to personal jurisdiction is based on "the time the action is commenced". That may not be very important when longarm jurisdiction is being used, because longarm jurisdiction ordinarily depends on some act or acts the defendant performed in the past (and, of course, that the claim arises out of those acts). But it may be quite important when the claim itself did not arise in the state and when jurisdiction is based only on the corporation's current physical presence in the state. That's the "doing business" test, and it ordinarily requires a showing that the defendant was doing business in the state when the action was commenced. (The "doing business" test explicitly listed as a venue basis under the old subdivision (c) remains a venue basis under the new one for the obvious reason that doing business in a state also makes the corporation amenable to jurisdiction there.)

Zeisel, Social Research on the Law: The Ideal and the Practical
Law and Sociology 130–132 (W.M. Evan, Ed. 1962).

The question is one of theoretical and practical concern to lawyers. Do juries in some regions or cities give higher damage awards in comparable tort cases than in other regions or cities? Since there are some 60,000 civil jury trials held each year in the United States, it seemed tempting simply to compare the average awards made in different states or cities. The first obstacle that arose was that only few courts have ever recorded this type of information. On closer inspection, it turned out that this was not a key deficiency. Even if the data were available they would mean little, because the cases that came to trial varied so immensely that "average awards" had little meaning. We thought, then, that certain of the more frequent standard injuries, such as a lost leg, might supply a sufficient number of comparable cases. But it soon became clear that these legs were lost by young people, old people, rich ones, poor ones, men, and women. Hence, the value of a leg varied almost as widely as the value of all injuries. Since it is not feasible to try the same case fifty times in fifty different courts, what was one to do?

In place of the unobtainable comparable verdicts, the research device eventually resorted to was a plan to use estimates of these verdicts by informed experts. Experts can be useful provided that the particular request is within the expert's routine experience, and that individual idiosyncrasies do not endanger the result. All of these safeguards were incorporated in the design. Five personal injury cases were described in such detail as is customarily requested by the insurance adjustor who evaluates claims. Through the cooperation of three nationwide insurance companies these five cases were then submitted to their local adjustors with this question: "How much, judging from your experience, would you expect a jury in your court to award from this case?" The question was asked for a selected number of courts that together constituted a representative sample of various regions and community sizes.

The logical chain that supports this research approach runs as follows. The adjustors make their living by being right on the types of guesses that were asked. These guesses are informed by continuous comparison with the subsequent court verdicts, if the claim should reach that stage. If one conceives of the ongoing jury trials as a series of "experiments," our experts extract the essence of the experience and apply it to five standard cases. We attempted to eliminate personal idiosyncrasies by submitting several cases, with the intention of using an average, and by having in each case *three* experts, representing the three cooperative insurance companies. We could, therefore, expect that if these verdict-guesses showed systematic variations, they would truly reflect geographic variations in jury behavior. In fact, as Table 2 shows, such variations did emerge.

Table 2

Regional Variation of Estimated Jury Awards for Identical Claims

(In percent deviation from the national average = 100)

City Size	West	Midwest	South	East
Large	+ 20	+ 2	0	+ 19
Medium	+ 8	− 11	− 9	+ 10
Small	0	− 21	− 15	− 6

Awards for identical claims vary roughly between 80 percent of the national average in the rural South and Midwest, and 120 percent in the metropolitan cities on the East and West coasts. If one were to translate this table into a formula, one would say: add 10 percent to the average if the trial takes place on the East or West coast; add another 10 percent if it is conducted in a large metropolitan city; subtract 10 percent if it is conducted in the South or Midwest; and another 10 percent if it takes place in the rural area.

M. Fox, Upstate–Downstate Gap in Injury Awards, N.Y.Law Journal

January 4, 1988, at 1, col. 3.

Plaintiffs' attorneys in personal injury cases enjoy telling about a colleague who was sued for legal malpractice after shunning jurisdiction in the Bronx and moving his case to Broome County.

That apocryphal tale illustrates the difference between upstate and downstate in terms of jury awards.

Median Awards Lower

The difference is re-enforced by statistics showing that the median awards in four upstate counties were substantially lower than in the metropolitan New York area over a corresponding period.

Attorneys for both plaintiffs and defendants, however, agree that in "catastrophe" cases where there are clear showings of negligence, the difference in jury awards may not be significant.

* * *

Different Lifestyles

But aside from "catastrophic" suits, verdicts away from the metropolitan New York area reflect differences in lifestyles, cost-of-living factors, economic values and philosophies. According to unofficial statistics compiled for the Law Journal by the New York Jury Verdict Reporter covering verdicts in Albany, Erie, Monroe and Onondaga Counties between 1983 and 1986, the median award in personal injury actions in those jurisdictions was a fraction of those returned in urban and most suburban communities downstate. In Albany, Erie, Monroe and Onondaga Counties, respectively, the median awards were $25,000, $50,000, $34,000 and $27,559.

* * * the results were based upon representative statistics and not all verdicts in those four counties were included. (There were no figures on verdicts available from smaller counties.)

In contrast, in 1984, the last year for which complete records are available for metropolitan New York, the median award in the Bronx for personal injury cases was $147,000 followed, respectively, by New York County ($113,750), Kings ($101,000) and Queens ($94,000).

* * *

Attorneys who prosecute and defend personal injury cases said juries in New York City often have their own set of values in determining what is proper compensation, particularly when the City of New York or large corporate entities are involved. Increasingly, as demographics change, juries consist of poor persons described by one attorney as "embittered toward an impersonal city, who are not part of the system but with an opportunity to express their frustration."

* * *

Interestingly, while Bronx juries are infamous for "giving away the courthouse," * * * just across the county line in Westchester there is a complete turnaround. The Jury Verdict Reporter found the median award there in 1984 was $42,000, the lowest in the metropolitan area.

* * *

Westchester juries, not surprisingly, also rank as a leader in returning verdicts in favor of defendants. In 1984, 55 percent of all cases sustained defendants, second only to 61 percent in Nassau County.

* * *

NOTE

Do these data cast doubt on the conclusions reached by Zeisel, supra? Are median awards a satisfactory measure of geographic differences in the size of jury verdicts?

Walter Koschak v. Gates Construction Corporation

Supreme Court of New York, Appellate Division, First Department, 1996.
225 A.D.2d 315, 639 N.Y.S.2d 10.

■ Before ROSENBERGER, J. P., WALLACH, RUBIN and TOM, JJ.

■ MEMORANDUM OPINION

This litigation was instituted in December 1990 by plaintiffs Walter and Carol Koschak. Plaintiffs seek recovery for personal injuries allegedly sustained by Walter Koschak on March 8, 1989 while working on a barge in Liberty State Park, New Jersey. At the time of the accident, plaintiffs resided on Staten Island, and defendant maintained its principal place of business in Little Ferry, New Jersey.

In an affidavit dated August 2, 1993, Walter Koschak stated that, on December 3, 1990, some eighteen months after the subject occurrence and just seven days before the complaint was verified, plaintiffs moved to 117 Pilot Street in the City Island section of the Bronx. In the course of subsequent hearings, it was disclosed that the house to which plaintiffs relocated had been purchased on October 26, 1990 by Paul C. Matthews, the attorney who then represented them. Matthews conceded that the contract of sale had been assigned to him by plaintiffs after they had been refused financing to acquire the home. Carol Koschak admitted that plaintiffs could not have moved to City Island without Matthews' help and that plaintiffs paid no rent for the first fourteen months of their occupancy.

By their own admission, plaintiffs owed Matthews a sum in excess of $23,000. However, in view of the failure to produce either receipts demonstrating payment of rent or Matthews' tax returns declaring rental income, plaintiffs offered no proof that their alleged payment of some $29,400 (comprising both rent and the cost of improvements to the dwelling) was actually made. Indeed, Matthews subsequently conceded that he had not declared any rental income for the premises. It is further evident that affidavits submitted by plaintiffs to this Court, in connection with a motion to disqualify counsel, falsely represented the circumstances under which they came to reside in their current abode.

Defendant originally brought its motion to change venue to Richmond County in July 1993. A subsequent affidavit by defense counsel in support of the motion states that he first learned from another attorney during June 1993 that Matthews might "own real property in the Bronx and that he might be harboring clients in said property." Supreme Court denied the motion to change venue based upon a finding that, at the time suit was instituted, plaintiffs actually resided in Bronx County.

The paramount concern of this Court is the preservation of the integrity of the judicial process. It does not advance that end to permit a party to obtain what is perceived to be an advantageous forum by rank manipulation of the rules for setting venue. While Supreme Court's decision is in accordance with the letter of the law, our courts have eschewed literal application of venue rules to preclude forum shopping (e.g., *Philogene v. Fuller Auto Leasing*, 167 A.D.2d 178, 179 ["misleading tactics of plaintiff's attorney"]; *Turner v. Turner*, 84 Misc.2d 229 [transitory residence]; *Saphir v. Kruse*, 5 Misc. 2d 415 [assignment of claim]). Where, as here, venue is designated as a result of duplicity, in which plaintiffs have participated, it amounts to a fraud upon the court and will not be permitted to stand.

2.   Forum Non Conveniens; Transfer of Venue

Gulf Oil Corp. v. Gilbert

Supreme Court of the United States, 1947.
330 U.S. 501, 67 S.Ct. 839, 91 L.Ed. 1055.

■ JUSTICE JACKSON delivered the opinion of the Court.

The questions are whether the United States District Court has inherent power to dismiss a suit pursuant to the doctrine of *forum non conveniens* and, if so, whether that power was abused in this case.

The respondent-plaintiff brought this action in the Southern District of New York, but resides at Lynchburg, Virginia, where he operated a public warehouse. He alleges that the petitioner-defendant, in violation of the ordinances of Lynchburg, so carelessly handled a delivery of gasoline to his warehouse tanks and pumps as to cause an explosion and fire which consumed the warehouse building to his damage of $41,889.10, destroyed merchandise and fixtures to his damage of $3,602.40, caused injury to his business and profits of $20,038.27, and burned the property of customers in his custody under warehousing agreements to the extent of $300,000. He asks judgment of $365,529.77 with costs and disbursements, and interest from the date of the fire. The action clearly is one in tort.

The petitioner-defendant is a corporation organized under the laws of Pennsylvania, qualified to do business in both Virginia and New York, and it has designated officials of each state as agents to receive service of process. When sued in New York, the defendant, invoking the doctrine of *forum non conveniens,* claimed that the appropriate place for trial is Virginia, where the plaintiff lives and defendant does business, where all events in litigation took place, where most of the witnesses reside, and where both state and federal courts are available to plaintiff and are able to obtain jurisdiction of the defendant.

The case, on its merits, involves no federal question and was brought in the United States District Court solely because of diversity in citizenship of the parties. Because of the character of its jurisdiction and the holdings of and under Erie Railroad Co. v. Tompkins, 304 U.S. 64, 58 S.Ct. 817, 82 L.Ed. 1188, the District Court considered that the law of New York as to *forum non conveniens* applied and that it required the case to be left to Virginia courts. It therefore dismissed.

The Circuit Court of Appeals disagreed as to the applicability of New York law, took a restrictive view of the application of the entire doctrine in federal courts and, one judge dissenting, reversed. The case is here on certiorari. 328 U.S. 830.

I.

It is conceded that the venue statutes of the United States permitted the plaintiff to commence his action in the Southern District of New York and empower that court to entertain it. But that does not settle the question whether it must do so. Indeed, the doctrine of *forum non conveniens* can never apply if there is absence of jurisdiction or mistake of venue.

* * *

II.

The principle of *forum non conveniens* is simply that a court may resist imposition upon its jurisdiction even when jurisdiction is authorized by the letter of a general venue statute. These statutes are drawn with a necessary generality and usually give a plaintiff a choice of courts, so that he may be quite sure of some place in which to pursue his remedy. But the open door may admit those who seek not simply justice but perhaps justice blended with some harassment. A plaintiff sometimes is under temptation to resort to a strategy of forcing the trial at a most inconvenient place for an adversary, even at some inconvenience to himself.

Many of the states have met misuse of venue by investing courts with a discretion to change the place of trial on various grounds, such as the convenience of witnesses and the ends of justice. The federal law contains no such express criteria to guide the district court in exercising its power. But the problem is a very old one affecting the administration of the courts as well as the rights of litigants, and both in England and in this country the common law worked out techniques and criteria for dealing with it.

Wisely, it has not been attempted to catalogue the circumstances which will justify or require either grant or denial of remedy. The doctrine leaves much to the discretion of the court to which plaintiff resorts, and experience has not shown a judicial tendency to renounce one's own jurisdiction so strong as to result in many abuses.

If the combination and weight of factors requisite to given results are difficult to forecast or state, those to be considered are not difficult to name. An interest to be considered, and the one likely to be most pressed, is the private interest of the litigant. Important considerations are the relative ease of access to sources of proof; availability of compulsory process for attendance of unwilling, and the cost of obtaining attendance of willing, witnesses; possibility of view of premises, if view would be appropriate to the action; and all other practical problems that make trial of a case easy, expeditious and inexpensive. There may also be questions as to the enforcibility of a judgment if one is obtained. The court will weigh relative advantages and obstacles to fair trial. It is often said that the plaintiff may not, by choice of an inconvenient forum, "vex," "harass," or "oppress" the defendant by inflicting upon him expense or trouble not necessary to his own right to pursue his remedy. But unless the balance is strongly in favor of the defendant, the plaintiff's choice of forum should rarely be disturbed.

Factors of public interest also have place in applying the doctrine. Administrative difficulties follow for courts when litigation is piled up in congested centers instead of being handled at its origin. Jury duty is a burden that ought not to be imposed upon the people of a community which has no relation to the litigation. In cases which touch the affairs of many persons, there is reason for holding the trial in their view and reach rather than in remote parts of the country where they can learn of it by report only. There is a local interest in having localized controversies decided at home. There is an appropriateness, too, in having the trial of a diversity case in a forum that is at home with the state law that must govern the case, rather than having a court in some other forum untangle problems in conflict of laws, and in law foreign to itself.

* * *

III.

Turning to the question whether this is one of those rather rare cases where the doctrine should be applied, we look first to the interests of the litigants.

The plaintiff himself is not a resident of New York, nor did any event connected with the case take place there, nor does any witness, with the possible exception of experts, live there. No one connected with that side of the case save counsel for the plaintiff resides there, and he has candidly told us that he was retained by insurance companies interested presumably because of subrogation. His affidavits and argument are devoted to controverting claims as to defendant's inconvenience rather than to showing that the present forum serves any convenience of his own, with one exception. The only justification for trial in New York advanced here is one rejected by the district court and is set forth in the brief as follows:

> "This Court can readily realize that an action of this type, involving as it does a claim for damages in an amount close to $400,000, is one which may stagger the imagination of a local jury which is surely unaccustomed to dealing with amounts of such a nature. Furthermore, removed from Lynchburg, the respondent will have an opportunity to try this case free from local influences and preconceived notions which may make it difficult to procure a jury which has no previous knowledge of any of the facts herein."

This unproven premise that jurors of New York live on terms of intimacy with $400,000 transactions is not an assumption we easily make. Nor can we assume that a jury from Lynchburg and vicinity would be "staggered" by contemplating the value of a warehouse building that stood in their region, or of merchandise and fixtures such as were used there, nor are they likely to be staggered by the value of chattels which the people of that neighborhood put in storage. It is a strange argument on behalf of a Virginia plaintiff that the community which gave him patronage to make his business valuable is not capable of furnishing jurors who know the value of the goods they store, the building they are stored in, or the business their patronage creates. And there is no specification of any local influence, other than accurate knowledge of local conditions, that would make a fair trial improbable. The net of this is that we cannot say the District Court was bound to entertain a provincial fear of the provincialism of a Virginia jury. That leaves the Virginia plaintiff without even a suggested reason for transporting this suit to New York.

Defendant points out that not only the plaintiff, but every person who participated in the acts charged to be negligent, resides in or near Lynchburg. It also claims a need to interplead an alleged independent contractor which made the delivery of the gasoline and which is a Virginia corporation domiciled in Lynchburg, that it cannot interplead in New York. There also are approximately 350 persons residing in and around Lynchburg who stored with plaintiff the goods for the damage to which he seeks to recover. The extent to which they have left the community since the fire and the number of them who will actually be needed is in dispute. The complaint alleges that defendant's conduct violated Lynchburg ordinances. Conditions are said to require proof by firemen and by many others. The learned and experienced trial judge was not unaware that litigants generally manage to try their cases with fewer witnesses than they predict in such motions as this. But he was justified in concluding that this trial is likely to be long and to involve calling many witnesses, and that Lynchburg, some 400 miles from New York, is the source of all proofs for either side, with possible exception of experts. Certainly to fix the place of trial at a point where litigants cannot compel personal attendance and may be forced to try their cases on deposition, is to create a condition not satisfactory to court, jury or most litigants. Nor is it necessarily cured by the statement of plaintiff's counsel that he will see to getting many of the witnesses to the trial and that some of them "would be delighted to come to New York to testify." There may be circumstances where such a proposal should be given weight. In others, the offer may not turn out to be as generous as defendant or court might suppose it to be. Such matters are for the District Court to decide in exercise of a sound discretion.

The court likewise could well have concluded that the task of the trial court would be simplified by trial in Virginia. If trial was in a state court, it could apply its own law to events occurring there. If in federal court by reason of diversity of citizenship, the court would apply the law of its own state in which it is likely to be experienced. The course of adjudication in New York federal court might be beset with conflict of laws problems all avoided if the case is litigated in Virginia where it arose.

We are convinced that the District Court did not exceed its powers or the bounds of its discretion in dismissing plaintiff's complaint and remitting him to the courts of his own community. The Circuit Court of Appeals took too restrictive a view of the doctrine as approved by this Court. Its judgment is

Reversed.[a]

■ Justice Black, dissenting.

* * *

It may be that a statute should be passed authorizing the federal district courts to decline to try so-called common law cases according to the convenience of the parties. But whether there should be such a statute and determination of its scope and the safeguards which should surround it, are, in my judgment, questions of policy which Congress should decide. There are strong arguments presented by the Court in its opinion why federal courts exercising their common law jurisdiction should have the discretionary powers which equity courts have always possessed in dispensing equitable relief. I think equally strong arguments could be advanced to show that they should not. For any individual or corporate defendant who does part of his business in states other than the one in which he is sued will almost invariably be put to some inconvenience to defend himself. It will be a poorly represented multistate defendant who cannot produce substantial evidence and good reasons fitting the rule now adopted by this Court tending to establish that the forum of the action against him is most inconvenient. The Court's new rule will thus clutter the very threshold of the federal courts with a preliminary trial of fact concerning the relative convenience of forums. The preliminary disposition of this factual question will, I believe, produce the very kind of uncertainty, confusion, and hardship which stalled and handicapped persons seeking compensation for maritime injuries following this Court's decision in Southern Pacific Co. v. Jensen, 244 U.S. 205, 37 S.Ct. 524, 61 L.Ed. 1086. The broad and indefinite discretion left to federal courts to decide the question of convenience from the welter of factors which are relevant to such a judgment, will inevitably produce a complex of close and indistinguishable decisions from which accurate prediction of the proper forum will become difficult, if not impossible. Yet plaintiffs will be asked "to determine with certainty before bringing their actions that factual question over which courts regularly divide among themselves and within their own membership. As penalty for error, the injured individual may not only suffer serious financial loss through the delay and expense of litigation, but discover that his claim has been barred by the statute of limitations in the proper forum while he was erroneously pursuing it elsewhere." Davis v. Dept. of Labor & Industries, 317 U.S. 249, 254, 63 S.Ct. 225, 228, 87 L.Ed. 246.

This very case illustrates the hazards of delay. It must be begun anew in another forum after the District Court, the Circuit Court of Appeals, and now this Court, have had their time-consuming say as to the relative convenience of the forum in which the plaintiff chose to seek redress. Whether the statute of limitations has run against the plaintiff, we do not know. The convenience which the individual defendant will enjoy from the Court's new rule of *forum non conveniens* in law actions may be thought to justify its inherent delays,

---

a. Justice Reed and Justice Burton dissented without opinion.

uncertainties, administrative complications and hardships. But in any event, Congress has not yet said so; and I do not think that this Court should, 150 years after the passage of the Judiciary Act, fill in what it thinks is a deficiency in the deliberate policy which Congress adopted. Whether the doctrine of forum non conveniens is good or bad, I should wait for Congress to adopt it.

■ Justice Rutledge joins in this opinion.

Ferens v. John Deere Co.

Supreme Court of the United States, 1990.
494 U.S. 516, 110 S.Ct. 1274, 108 L.Ed.2d 443.

■ Kennedy, J., delivered the opinion of the Court, in which Rehnquist, C.J., and White, Stevens, and O'Connor, JJ., joined. Scalia, J., filed a dissenting opinion, in which Brennan, Marshall, and Blackmun, JJ., joined.

[Section 1404(a) of Title 28 states:] "For the convenience of parties and witnesses, in the interest of justice, a district court may transfer any civil action to any other district or division where it might have been brought." 28 U.S.C. § 1404(a) (1982 ed.). In Van Dusen v. Barrack, 376 U.S. 612, 84 S.Ct. 805, 11 L.Ed.2d 945 (1964), we held that, following a transfer under § 1404(a) initiated by a defendant, the transferee court must follow the choice of law rules that prevailed in the transferor court. We now decide that, when a plaintiff moves for the transfer, the same rule applies.

I

Albert Ferens lost his right hand when, the allegation is, it became caught in his combine harvester, manufactured by Deere & Company. The accident occurred while Ferens was working with the combine on his farm in Pennsylvania. For reasons not explained in the record, Ferens delayed filing a tort suit and Pennsylvania's 2–year limitations period expired. In the third year, he and his wife sued Deere in the United States District Court for the Western District of Pennsylvania, raising contract and warranty claims as to which the Pennsylvania limitations period had not yet run. The District Court had diversity jurisdiction, as Ferens and his wife are Pennsylvania residents, and Deere is incorporated in Delaware with its principal place of business in Illinois.

Not to be deprived of a tort action, the Ferenses in the same year filed a second diversity suit against Deere in the United States District Court for the Southern District of Mississippi, alleging negligence and products liability. Diversity jurisdiction and venue were proper. The Ferenses sued Deere in the District Court in Mississippi because they knew that, under Klaxon Co. v. Stentor Electric Mfg. Co., 313 U.S. 487, 496, 61 S.Ct. 1020, 1021, 85 L.Ed. 1477 (1941), the federal court in the exercise of diversity jurisdiction must apply the same choice of law rules that Mississippi state courts would apply if they were deciding the case. A Mississippi court would rule that Pennsylvania substantive law controls the personal injury claim but that Mississippi's own law governs the limitation period.

* * *

The Mississippi courts, as a result, would apply Mississippi's 6–year statute of limitations to the tort claim arising under Pennsylvania law and the tort action would not be time-barred under the Mississippi statute. See Miss.Code Ann. § 15–1–49 (1972).

The issue now before us arose when the Ferenses took their forum shopping a step further: having chosen the federal court in Mississippi to take advantage of the State's limitations period, they next moved, under § 1404(a), to transfer the action to the federal court in Pennsylvania on the ground that Pennsylvania was a more convenient forum. The Ferenses acted on the assumption that, after the transfer, the choice of law rules in the Mississippi forum, including a rule requiring application of the Mississippi statute of limitations, would continue to govern the suit.

Deere put up no opposition, and the District Court in Mississippi granted the § 1404(a) motion. The Court accepted the Ferenses' arguments that they resided in Pennsylvania; that the accident occurred there; that the claim had no connection to Mississippi; that a substantial number of witnesses resided in the Western District of Pennsylvania but none resided in Mississippi; that most of documentary evidence was located in the Western District of Pennsylvania but none was located in Mississippi; and that the warranty action pending in the Western District of Pennsylvania presented common questions of law and fact.

The District Court in Pennsylvania consolidated the transferred tort action with the Ferenses' pending warranty action but declined to honor the Mississippi statute of limitations as the District Court in Mississippi would have done. It ruled instead that, because the Ferenses had moved for transfer as plaintiffs, the rule in *Van Dusen* did not apply. Invoking the 2–year limitations period set by Pennsylvania law, the District Court dismissed their tort action. Ferens v. Deere & Co., 639 F.Supp. 1484 (W.D.Pa.1986).

The Court of Appeals for the Third Circuit affirmed, but not, at first, on grounds that the Ferenses had lost their entitlement to Mississippi choice of law rules by their invoking § 1404(a). The Court of Appeals relied at the outset on the separate theory that applying Mississippi's statute of limitations would violate due process because Mississippi had no legitimate interest in the case. Ferens v. Deere & Co., 819 F.2d 423 (1987). We vacated this decision and remanded in light of Sun Oil Co. v. Wortman, 486 U.S. 717, 108 S.Ct. 2117, 100 L.Ed.2d 743 (1988), in which we held that a State may choose to apply its own statute of limitations to claims governed by the substantive laws of another State without violating either the Full Faith and Credit Clause or the Due Process Clause. Ferens v. Deere & Co., 487 U.S. 1212, 108 S.Ct. 2862, 101 L.Ed.2d 898 (1988). On remand, the Court of Appeals again affirmed, this time confronting the Van Dusen question and ruling that a transferor court's choice of law rules do not apply after a transfer under § 1404(a) on a motion by a plaintiff 862 F.2d 31 (3d Cir.1988).

II

Section 1404(a) states only that a district court may transfer venue for the convenience of the parties and witnesses when in the interest of justice. It says nothing about choice of law, and nothing about affording plaintiffs different treatment from defendants. We touched upon these issues in Van Dusen, but left open the question presented in this case. See 376 U.S., at 640, 84 S.Ct., at 821. In Van Dusen, an airplane flying from Boston to Philadelphia crashed into Boston Harbor soon after take-off. The personal representatives of the accident victims brought more than 100 actions in the District Court for the District of Massachusetts and more than 40 actions in the District Court for the Eastern District of Pennsylvania. When the defendants moved to transfer the actions brought in Pennsylvania to the federal court in Massachusetts, a number of the Pennsylvania plaintiffs objected because they lacked capacity under Massachusetts law to sue as representatives of the decedents. The plaintiffs also averred that the transfer would deprive them of the benefits of Pennsylvania's choice of law rules because the transferee forum would apply to their wrongful death claims a different substantive rule. The plaintiffs obtained from the Court of Appeals a writ of mandamus ordering the District Court to vacate the transfer. See id., at 613–615, 84 S.Ct. at 807–08.

We reversed. After considering issues not related to the present dispute, we held that the Court of Appeals erred in its assumption that Massachusetts law would govern the action following transfer. The legislative history of § 1404(a) showed that Congress had enacted the statute because broad venue provisions in federal acts often resulted in inconvenient forums and that Congress had decided to respond to this problem by permitting transfer to a convenient federal court under § 1404(a). 376 U.S., at 634–636, 84 S.Ct. at 818–19. We said:

"This legislative background supports the view that § 1404(a) was not designed to narrow the plaintiff's venue privilege or to defeat the state-law advantages that might accrue from the exercise of this venue privilege but rather the provision was simply to counteract the inconveniences that flowed from the venue statutes by permitting transfer to a convenient federal court. The legislative history of § 1404(a) certainly does not justify the rather startling conclusion that one might 'get a change of a law as a bonus for a change of venue.' Indeed, an interpretation accepting such a rule would go far to frustrate the remedial purposes of § 1404(a). If a change in the law were in the offing, the parties might well regard the section primarily as a forum-shopping instrument. And, more importantly, courts would at least be reluctant to grant transfers, despite considerations of convenience, if to do so might conceivably prejudice the claim of a plaintiff who initially selected a permissible forum. We believe, therefore, that both the history and purposes of § 1404(a) indicate that it should be regarded as a federal judicial housekeeping measure, dealing with the placement of litigation in the federal courts and generally intended, on the basis of convenience and fairness, simply to authorize a change of courtrooms." *Id.,* at 635–637, 84 S.Ct., at 818–19 (footnotes omitted).

We thus held that the law applicable to a diversity case does not change upon a transfer initiated by a defendant.

III

The quoted part of *Van Dusen* reveals three independent reasons for our decision. First, § 1404(a) should not deprive parties of state law advantages that exist absent diversity jurisdiction. Second, § 1404(a) should not create or multiply opportunities for forum shopping. Third, the decision to transfer venue under § 1404(a) should turn on considerations of convenience and the interest of justice rather than on the possible prejudice resulting from a change of law. * * * We decide that, in addition to other considerations, these policies require a transferee forum to apply the law of the transferor court, regardless of who initiates the transfer. A transfer under § 1404(a), in other words, does not change the law applicable to a diversity case.

A

The policy that § 1404(a) should not deprive parties of state law advantages, although perhaps discernible in the legislative history, has its real foundation in Erie R. Co. v. Tompkins, 304 U.S. 64, 58 S.Ct. 817, 82 L.Ed. 1188 (1938). See *Van Dusen,* 376 U.S., at 637, 84 S.Ct., at 819. The *Erie* rule remains a vital expression of the federal system and the concomitant integrity of the separate States. We explained *Erie* in Guaranty Trust Co. v. York, 326 U.S. 99, 109, 65 S.Ct. 1464, 1470, 89 L.Ed. 2079 (1945), as follows:

"In essence, the intent of [the *Erie*] decision was to insure that, in all cases where a federal court is exercising jurisdiction solely because of the diversity of citizenship of the parties, the outcome of the litigation in the federal court should be substantially the same, so far as legal rules determine the outcome of a litigation, as it would be if tried in a State court. The nub of the policy that underlies Erie R. Co. v. Tompkins is that for the same transaction the accident of a suit by a non-resident litigant in a federal court instead of in a State court a block away should not lead to a substantially different result."

In Hanna v. Plumer, 380 U.S. 460, 473, 85 S.Ct. 1136, 1145, 14 L.Ed.2d 8 (1965), we held that Congress has the power to prescribe procedural rules that differ from state law rules even at the expense of altering the outcome of litigation. This case does not involve a conflict. As in Van Dusen, our interpretation of § 1404(a) is in full accord with the Erie rule.

The Erie policy had a clear implication for Van Dusen. The existence of diversity jurisdiction gave the defendants the opportunity to make a motion to transfer venue under § 1404(a), and if the applicable law were to change after transfer, the plaintiff's venue privilege and resulting state-law advantages could be defeated at the defendant's option. 376 U.S., at 638, 84 S.Ct., at 820. To allow the transfer and at the same time preserve the plaintiff's state-law advantages, we held that the choice of law rules should not change following a transfer initiated by a defendant. *Id.,* at 639, 84 S.Ct., at 821.

Transfers initiated by a plaintiff involve some different considerations, but lead to the same result. Applying the transferor law, of course, will not deprive the plaintiff of any state law advantages. A defendant, in one sense, also will lose no legal advantage if the transferor law controls after a transfer initiated by the plaintiff; the same law, after all, would have applied if the plaintiff had not made the motion. In another sense, however, a defendant may lose a nonlegal advantage. Deere, for example, would lose whatever advantage inheres in not having to litigate in Pennsylvania, or, put another way, in forcing the Ferenses to litigate in Mississippi or not at all.

We, nonetheless, find the advantage that the defendant loses slight. A plaintiff always can sue in the favorable state court or sue in diversity and not seek a transfer. By asking for application of the Mississippi statute of limitations following a transfer to Pennsylvania on grounds of convenience, the Ferenses are seeking to deprive Deere only of the advantage of using against them the inconvenience of litigating in Mississippi. The text of § 1404(a) may not say anything about choice of law, but we think it not the purpose of the section to protect a party's ability to use inconvenience as a shield to discourage or hinder litigation otherwise proper. The section exists to eliminate inconvenience without altering permissible choices under the venue statutes. See Van Dusen, supra, at 634–635, 84 S.Ct. at 818–19. This interpretation should come as little surprise. As in our previous cases, we think that "[t]o construe § 1404(a) this way merely carries out its design to protect litigants, witnesses and the public against unnecessary inconvenience and expense, not to provide a shelter for * * * proceedings in costly and inconvenient forums." Continental Grain Co. v. Barge FBL–585, 364 U.S. 19, 27, 80 S.Ct. 1470, 1475, 4 L.Ed.2d 1540 (1960). By creating an opportunity to have venue transferred between courts in different States on the basis of convenience, an option that does not exist absent federal jurisdiction, Congress, with respect to diversity, retained the Erie policy while diminishing the incidents of inconvenience.

* * *

C

Van Dusen also made clear that the decision to transfer venue under § 1404(a) should turn on considerations of convenience rather than on the possibility of prejudice resulting from a change in the applicable law. See 376 U.S., at 636, 84 S.Ct., at 819; Piper Aircraft Co. v. Reyno, 454 U.S. 235, 253–254, and n. 20, 102 S.Ct. 252, 264–65, and n. 20, 70 L.Ed.2d 419 (1981). We reasoned in Van Dusen that, if the law changed following a transfer initiated by the defendant, a district court "would at least be reluctant to grant transfers, despite considerations of convenience, if to do so might conceivably prejudice the claim of a plaintiff." 376 U.S., at 636, 84 S.Ct., at 819. The court, to determine the prejudice, might have to make an elaborate survey of the law, including statutes of limitations, burdens of proof, presumptions, and the like. This would turn what is supposed to be a statute for convenience of the courts into one expending extensive judicial time and resources. Because this difficult task is contrary to the purpose of the statute, in Van Dusen we made it unnecessary by ruling that a transfer of venue by the defendant does not result in a change of law. This same policy requires application of the transferor law when a plaintiff initiates a transfer.

If the law were to change following a transfer initiated by a plaintiff, a district court in a similar fashion would be at least reluctant to grant a transfer that would prejudice the defendant. Hardship might occur because plaintiffs may find as many opportunities to exploit application of the transferee law as they would find opportunities for exploiting application of the transferor law. See Note, 63 Cornell L.Rev., at 156. If the transferee law were to apply, moreover, the plaintiff simply would not move to transfer unless the benefits of convenience outweighed the loss of favorable law.

Some might think that a plaintiff should pay the price for choosing an inconvenient forum by being put to a choice of law versus forum. But this assumes that § 1404(a) is for the benefit only of the moving party. By the statute's own terms, it is not. Section 1404(a) also exists for the benefit of the witnesses and the interest of justice, which must include the convenience of the court. Litigation in an inconvenient forum does not harm the plaintiff alone.

* * *

The desire to take a punitive view of the plaintiff's actions should not obscure the systemic costs of litigating in an inconvenient place.

D

This case involves some considerations to which we perhaps did not give sufficient attention in *Van Dusen*. Foresight and judicial economy now seem to favor the simple rule that the law does not change following a transfer of venue under § 1404(a). Affording transfers initiated by plaintiffs different treatment from transfers initiated by defendants may seem quite workable in this case, but the simplicity is an illusion. If we were to hold that the transferee law applies following a § 1404(a) motion by a plaintiff, cases such as this would not arise in the future. Although applying the transferee law, no doubt, would catch the Ferenses by surprise, in the future no plaintiffs in their position would move for a change of venue.

Other cases, however, would produce undesirable complications. The rule would leave unclear which law should apply when both a defendant and a plaintiff move for a transfer of venue or when the court transfers venue on its own motion. See Note, 63 Cornell L.Rev., at 158. The rule also might require variation in certain situations, such as when the plaintiff moves for a transfer following a removal from state court by the defendant, or when only one of several plaintiffs requests the transfer, or when circumstances change through no fault of the plaintiff making a once convenient forum inconvenient. True, we could reserve any consideration of these questions for a later day. But we have a duty, in deciding this case, to consider whether our decision will create litigation and uncertainty. On the basis of these considerations, we again conclude that the transferor law should apply regardless who makes the § 1404(a) motion.

IV

Some may object that a district court in Pennsylvania should not have to apply a Mississippi statute of limitations to a Pennsylvania cause of action. This point, although understandable, should have little to do with the outcome of this case. Congress gave the Ferenses the power to seek a transfer in § 1404(a) and our decision in *Van Dusen* already could require a district court in Pennsylvania to apply the Mississippi statute of limitations to Pennsylvania claims. Our rule may seem too generous because it allows the Ferenses to have both their choice of law and their choice of forum, or even to reward the Ferenses for conduct that seems manipulative. We nonetheless see no alternative rule that would produce a more acceptable result. Deciding that the transferee law should apply, in effect, would tell the Ferenses that they should have continued to litigate their warranty action in Pennsylvania and their tort action in Mississippi. Some might find this preferable, but we do not. We have made quite clear that "[t]o permit a situation in which two cases involving precisely the same issues are simultaneously pending in different District Courts leads to the wastefulness of time, energy and money that § 1404(a) was designed to prevent." *Continental Grain,* 364 U.S., at 26, 80 S.Ct. at 1474.

From a substantive standpoint, two further objections give us pause but do not persuade us to change our rule. First, one might ask why we require the Ferenses to file in the District Court in Mississippi at all. Efficiency might seem to dictate a rule allowing plaintiffs in the Ferenses' position not to file in an inconvenient forum and then to return to a convenient forum though a transfer of venue, but instead simply to file in the convenient forum and ask for the law of the inconvenient forum to apply. Although our rule may invoke certain formality, one must remember that § 1404(a) does not provide for an automatic transfer of venue. The section, instead, permits a transfer only when convenient and "in the interest of justice." Plaintiffs in the position of the Ferenses must go to the distant forum because they have no guarantee, until the court there examines the facts, that they may obtain a transfer. No one has contested the justice of transferring this particular case, but the option remains open to defendants in future cases. Although a court cannot ignore the systemic costs of inconvenience, it may consider the course that the litigation already has taken in determining the interest of justice.

Second, one might contend that, because no *per se* rule requiring a court to apply either the transferor law or the transferee law will seem appropriate in all circumstances, we should develop more sophisticated federal choice of law rules for diversity actions involving transfers. See Note, 75 Yale L.J., at 130–135. To a large extent, however, state conflicts of law rules already ensure that appropriate laws will apply to diversity cases. Federal law, as a general matter, does not interfere with these rules. See *Sun Oil,* 486 U.S., at 727–729. In addition, even if more elaborate federal choice of law rules would not run afoul of *Klaxon* and *Erie,* we believe that applying the law of the transferor forum effects the appropriate balance between fairness and simplicity. Cf. R. Leflar, American Conflicts Law § 143, p. 293 (3d ed. 1977) (arguing against a federal common law of conflicts).

For the foregoing reasons, we conclude that Mississippi's statute of limitations should govern the Ferenses' action. We reverse and remand for proceedings consistent with this opinion.

It is so ordered.

■ JUSTICE SCALIA, with whom JUSTICE BRENNAN, JUSTICE MARSHALL, and JUSTICE BLACKMUN join, dissenting.

Plaintiffs, having filed this diversity action in Federal District Court in Mississippi, successfully moved for a transfer of venue to the District Court in Pennsylvania where their warranty action was then pending. The question we must decide is which State's choice-of-law principles will govern the case now that it is to be litigated in that court.

The Rules of Decision Act, first placed in the Judicial Code by the Judiciary Act of 1789, currently provides:

> "The laws of the several states, except where the Constitution or treaties of the United States or Acts of Congress otherwise require or provide, shall be regarded as rules of decision in civil actions in the courts of the United States, in cases where they apply." 28 U.S.C. § 1652 (1982 ed.).

In Erie R. Co. v. Tompkins, 304 U.S. 64, 58 S.Ct. 817, 82 L.Ed. 1188 (1938), we held that the Act requires a federal court to apply, in diversity cases, the law of the State in which it sits, both statutory law and common law established by the courts. Three years later, in Klaxon Co. v. Stentor Electric Mfg. Co., 313 U.S. 487, 494, 61 S.Ct. 1020, 1020, 85 L.Ed. 1477 (1941), we considered "whether in diversity cases the federal courts must follow conflict of laws rules prevailing in the states in which they sit." We answered the question in the affirmative, reasoning that, were the rule otherwise, "the accident of diversity of citizenship would constantly disturb equal administration of justice in coordinate state and federal courts sitting side by side," a state of affairs that "would do violence to the principle of uniformity within a state, upon which the *Tompkins* decision is based." *Id.,* at

496, 61 S.Ct. at 1021. See also Griffin v. McCoach, 313 U.S. 498, 503, 61 S.Ct. 1023, 1025, 85 L.Ed. 1481 (1941).

Although the venue provision of § 1404(a) was enacted after *Klaxon,* see 62 Stat. 937, we have repeatedly reaffirmed *Klaxon* since then. See Nolan v. Transocean Air Lines, 365 U.S. 293, 81 S.Ct. 555, 5 L.Ed.2d 571 (1961); Day & Zimmerman, Inc. v. Challoner, 423 U.S. 3, 96 S.Ct. 167, 46 L.Ed.2d 3 (1975).

The question we must answer today is whether 28 U.S.C. § 1404(a) (1982 ed.) and the policies underlying *Klaxon*—namely, uniformity within a State and the avoidance of forum shopping—produce a result different from *Klaxon* when the suit in question was not filed in the federal court initially, but was transferred there under § 1404(a) on plaintiff's motion. In Van Dusen v. Barrack, 376 U.S. 612, 84 S.Ct. 805, 11 L.Ed.2d 945 (1964), we held that a result different from *Klaxon* is produced when a suit has been transferred under § 1404(a) on defendant's motion. Our reasons were two. First, we thought it highly unlikely that Congress, in enacting § 1404(a), meant to provide defendants with a device by which to manipulate the substantive rules that would be applied. *Id.,* at 633–636, 84 S.Ct., at 817–19. That conclusion rested upon the fact that the law grants the plaintiff the advantage of choosing the venue in which his action will be tried, with whatever state-law advantages accompany that choice. A defensive use of § 1404(a) in order to deprive the plaintiff of this "venue privilege," *id.,* at 634, 84 S.Ct., at 818, would allow the defendant to " 'get a change of law as a bonus for a change of venue,' " *id.,* at 636, 84 S.Ct., at 819 (citation omitted), and would permit the defendant to engage in forum shopping among States, a privilege that the *Klaxon* regime reserved for plaintiffs. Second, we concluded that the policies of *Erie* and *Klaxon* would be undermined by application of the transferee court's choice-of-law principles in the case of a defendant-initiated transfer, *id.,* at 637–640, 84 S.Ct., at 819–21, because then "the 'accident' of federal diversity jurisdiction" would enable the defendant "to utilize a transfer to achieve a result in federal court which could not have been achieved in the courts of the State where the action was filed," *id.,* at 638, 84 S.Ct., at 820. The goal of *Erie* and *Klaxon,* we reasoned, was to prevent "forum shopping" as between state and federal systems; the plaintiff makes a choice of forum-law by filing the complaint, and that choice must be honored in federal court, just as it would have been honored in state court, where the defendant would not have been able to transfer the case to another State.

We left open in *Van Dusen* the question presented today, viz., whether "the same considerations would govern" if a plaintiff sought a § 1404(a) transfer. 376 U.S., at 640, 84 S.Ct., at 821. In my view, neither of those considerations is served—and indeed both are positively defeated—by a departure from *Klaxon* in that context. First, just as it is unlikely that Congress, in enacting § 1404(a), meant to provide the defendant with a vehicle by which to manipulate in his favor the substantive law to be applied in a diversity case, so too is it unlikely that Congress meant to provide the *plaintiff* with a vehicle by which to appropriate the law of a distant and inconvenient forum in which he does not intend to litigate, and to carry that prize back to the State in which he wishes to try the case. Second, application of the transferor court's law in this context would encourage forum-shopping between federal and state courts in the same jurisdiction on the basis of differential substantive law. It is true, of course, that the plaintiffs here did not select the *Mississippi* federal court in preference to the Mississippi state courts because of any differential substantive law; the former, like the latter, would have applied Mississippi choice-of-law rules, and thus the Mississippi statute of limitations. But one must be blind to reality to say that it is the *Mississippi* federal court in which these plaintiffs have chosen to sue. That was merely a way station en route to suit in the *Pennsylvania* federal court. The plaintiffs were seeking to achieve exactly what *Klaxon* was designed to prevent: the use of a Pennsylvania federal court instead of a Pennsylvania state court in order to obtain application of a different substantive law. Our decision in *Van Dusen* compromised "the principle of uniformity within a state," *Klaxon,* 313 U.S., at 496, 61 S.Ct., at 1021, only in the abstract, but today's decision compromises it precisely in the respect that matters—*i.e.,* insofar as it bears upon the plaintiff's choice between a state and a federal forum. The significant federal judicial policy expressed in *Erie* and *Klaxon* is reduced to a laughingstock if it can so readily be evaded through filing-and-transfer.

The Court is undoubtedly correct that applying the *Klaxon* rule after a plaintiff-initiated transfer would deter a plaintiff in a situation such as exists here from seeking a transfer, since that would deprive him of the favorable substantive law. But that proves only that this disposition achieves what *Erie* and *Klaxon* are designed to achieve: preventing the plaintiff from using "the accident of diversity of citizenship," *Klaxon,* 313 U.S., at 496, 61 S.Ct., at 1021, to obtain the application of a different law within the State where he wishes to litigate. In the context of the present case, he must either litigate in the State of Mississippi under Mississippi law, or in the Commonwealth of Pennsylvania under Pennsylvania law.

The Court expresses concern, * * * that if normal *Erie–Klaxon* principles were applied a district judge might be reluctant to order a transfer, even when faced with the prospect of a trial that would be manifestly inconvenient to the parties, for fear that in doing so he would be ordering what is tantamount to a dismissal on the merits. But where the plaintiff himself has moved for a transfer, surely the principle of *volenti non fit injuria* suffices to allay that concern. The Court asserts that in some cases it is the defendant who will be prejudiced by a transfer-induced change in the applicable law. That seems likely to be quite rare, since it assumes that the plaintiff has gone to the trouble of bringing the suit in a *less* convenient forum, where the law is *less* favorable to him. But where the defendant is disadvantaged by a plaintiff-initiated transfer, I do not see how it can reasonably be said that he has been "prejudiced," since the plaintiff could have brought the suit in the "plaintiff's-law forum" with the law more favorable to him (and the more convenient forum) in the first place. Prejudice to the defendant, it seems to me, occurs only when the plaintiff is enabled to have his cake and eat it too—to litigate in the more convenient forum that he desires, but with the law of the distant forum that he desires.

The Court suggests that applying the choice-of-law rules of the forum court to a transferred case ignores the interest of the federal courts themselves in avoiding the "systemic costs of litigating in an inconvenient place," Gulf Oil Corp. v. Gilbert, 330 U.S. 501, 509, 67 S.Ct. 839, 843, 91 L.Ed. 1055 (1947). The point, apparently, is that these systemic costs will increase because the change in law attendant to transfer will not only deter the plaintiff from moving to transfer but will also deter the court from ordering *sua sponte* a transfer that will harm the plaintiff's case. Justice Jackson's remarks were addressed, however, not to the operation of § 1404(a), but to "those rather rare cases where the doctrine [of *forum non conveniens*] should be applied." 330 U.S., at 509, 67 S.Ct., at 843. Where the systemic costs are that severe, transfer ordinarily will occur whether the plaintiff moves for it or not; the district judge can be expected to order it *sua sponte*. I do not think that the prospect of depriving the plaintiff of favorable law will any more deter a district judge from transferring[1] than it would have deterred a district judge, under the prior regime, from ordering a dismissal *sua sponte* pursuant to the doctrine of *forum non conveniens*. In fact the deterrence to *sua sponte* transfer will be considerably less, since transfer involves no risk of statute-of-limitations bars to refiling.

Thus, it seems to me that a proper calculation of systemic costs would go as follows: Saved by the Court's rule will be the incremental cost of trying in forums that are inconvenient (but not so inconvenient as to prompt the court's *sua sponte* transfer) those suits that are now filed in such forums for choice-of-law purposes. But incurred by the Court's rule will be the costs of considering and effecting transfer, not only in those suits but in the indeterminate number of additional suits that will be filed in inconvenient forums now that filing-and-transfer is an approved form of shopping for law; plus the costs attending the necessity for transferee courts to figure out the choice-of-law rules (and probably the substantive law) of distant States much more often than our *Van Dusen* decision would require. It should be noted that the file-and-transfer ploy sanctioned by the Court today will be available not merely to achieve the relatively rare (and generally unneeded) benefit of a longer statute of limitations, but also to bring home to the desired state of litigation all sorts of favorable choice-of-law rules

---

1. The prospective transferor court would not be deterred at all, of course, if we simply extended the *Van Dusen* rule to court-initiated transfers. In my view that would be inappropriate, however, since court-initiated transfer, like plaintiff-initiated transfer, does not confer upon the defendant the advantage of forum-shopping for law, Van Dusen v. Barrack, 376 U.S. 612, 636, 84 S.Ct. 805, 819, 11 L.Ed.2d 945 (1964), and does not enable the defendant "to utilize a transfer to achieve a result in federal court which could not have been achieved in the courts of the State where the action was filed," *id.,* at 638, 84 S.Ct., at 820.

regarding substantive liability—in an era when the diversity among the States in choice-of-law principles has become kaleidoscopic.[2]

The Court points out, apparently to deprecate the prospect that filing-and-transfer will become a regular litigation strategy, that there is "no guarantee" that a plaintiff will be accorded a transfer; that while "[n]o one has contested the justice of transferring this particular case," that option "remains open to defendants in future cases"; and that "[a]lthough a court cannot ignore the systemic costs of inconvenience, it may consider the course that the litigation already has taken in determining the interest of justice." I am not sure what this means—except that it plainly does not mean what it must mean to foreclose the filing-and-transfer option, namely, that transfer can be denied because the plaintiff was law-shopping. The whole theory of the Court's opinion is that it is not in accord with the policy of § 1404(a) to deprive the plaintiff of the "state-law advantages" to which his "venue privilege" entitles him. The Court explicitly repudiates "[t]he desire to take a punitive view of the plaintiff's actions," *ante,* at 1283, and to make him "pay the price for choosing an inconvenient forum by being put to a choice of law versus forum." Thus, all the Court is saying by its "no guarantee" language is that the plaintiff must be careful to choose a *really inconvenient* forum if he wants to be sure about getting a transfer. That will often not be difficult. In sum, it seems to me quite likely that today's decision will cost the federal courts more time than it will save them.

Thus, even as an exercise in giving the most extensive possible scope to the policies of § 1404(a), the Court's opinion seems to me unsuccessful. But as I indicated by beginning this opinion with the Rules of Decision Act, that should not be the object of the exercise at all. The Court and I reach different results largely because we approach the question from different directions. For the Court, this case involves an "interpretation of § 1404(a)," and the central issue is whether *Klaxon* stands in the way of the policies of that statute. For me, the case involves an interpretation of the Rules of Decision Act, and the central issue is whether § 1404(a) alters the "principle of uniformity within a state" which *Klaxon* says that Act embodies. I think my approach preferable, not only because the Rules of Decision Act does, and § 1404(a) does not, address the specific subject of which law to apply, but also because, as the Court acknowledges, our jurisprudence under that statute is "a vital expression of the federal system and the concomitant integrity of the separate States," *ante,* at 1280. To ask, as in effect the Court does, whether *Erie* gets in the way of § 1404(a), rather than whether § 1404(a) requires adjustment of *Erie,* seems to me the expression of a mistaken sense of priorities.

For the foregoing reasons, I respectfully dissent.

---

2. The current edition of Professor Leflar's treatise on American Conflicts Law lists 10 separate theories of choice of law that are applied, individually or in various combinations, by the 50 States. See R. Leflar, L. McDougall III, & R. Felix, American Conflicts Law §§ 86–91, 93–96 (4th ed.1986). See also Kay, Theory into Practice: Choice of Law in the Courts, 34 Mercer L.Rev. 521, 525–584, 591–592 (1983).

Waggoner, Section 1404(a), "Where it Might Have Been Brought": Brought by Whom?

1988 B.Y.U. L.Rev. 67, 69–73 (1988).

* * *

Section 1404(a) authorizes transfer of civil actions from one federal district court to another, even though venue and personal jurisdiction were proper where the action was filed. Such transfers are to be made, much as under the common law doctrine of forum non conveniens, "for the convenience of parties and witnesses, in the interest of justice." Under forum non conveniens a court dismisses or stays an action; under section 1404(a) the court transfers the action.

The decision to transfer is more complicated than the decision to dismiss or stay. To dismiss or stay an action, a court need only determine that the action should not proceed in that court. To transfer requires a further inquiry: "If not here, where?" Section 1404(a) provides that an action may be transferred only to a court "where it might have been brought." That last requirement * * * "has engendered much controversy in the courts."

III.   Interpreting "Where It Might Have Been Brought"

The United States Supreme Court in *Blaski** divided over the two interpretations adopted by various lower courts of "where [the action] might have been brought." The majority held that that phrase refers to the time the action was commenced, not later when the motion to transfer was made. Transfer would be allowed only to districts in which, at the time the action was commenced, plaintiff could have satisfied personal jurisdiction and venue over the defendant. The dissent would have extended the phrase to the time when the motion to transfer was made. Because a defendant may create personal jurisdiction and venue by consent,[11] the dissent would allow the defendant, via a consent in his motion to transfer, to make a particular district one "where [the action] might have been brought."

Let us examine these two interpretations, taking first the common ground and then the areas of disagreement. The common ground concerns transfers sought by plaintiff. In this situation restricting transfer of an action to courts "where it might have been brought" would seem to be intended to preserve normal concepts of personal jurisdiction and venue. There would be little point in having those concepts if plaintiff could, after filing in a court satisfying them, transfer to any other court without regard to them.[13] Thus, transfers sought by plaintiffs should be allowed only to courts where venue and personal jurisdiction would be satisfied for this plaintiff's assertion of

---

* 363 U.S. 335 (1960).

11. *See, e.g.,* The Bremen v. Zapata Off–Shore Co., 407 U.S. 1 (1972); National Equip. Rental v. Szukhent, 375 U.S. 311 (1964).

13. It would still be necessary to satisfy the "convenience" and "justice" require-ments, but more than that would be required for venue and personal jurisdiction. *See* 28 U.S.C. § 1391 (1982); *see also* World–Wide Volkswagen Corp. v. Woodson, 444 U.S. 286 (1980).

this claim against this defendant. This is the interpretation adopted in the circuit courts of appeal even before *Blaski,* and it would seem to be acceptable to both majority and dissent. The disagreement concerns transfers sought by the defendant.

A.   *The Blaski Majority*

The majority would allow transfers at defendant's request only to courts where plaintiff might have brought the action, i.e., where plaintiff could have satisfied personal jurisdiction and venue. This approach does not always produce a sensible result.

In order to illustrate, let us consider a hypothetical dispute between two corporations, Interstate and Local. A claim between the two corporations satisfies federal subject matter jurisdiction. Interstate, let us suppose, is engaged in continuous and substantial business in every state of the Union; in each state it has factories, offices, stores, and employees. Local is a retail store (not franchised[15]) which sells over the counter to the ultimate consumer and which buys from local wholesalers. Assume further that the claim arose at Local's place of business.

If Local is the plaintiff, the case would have satisfied personal jurisdiction[16] and venue in every district, so "where it might have been brought" would include all federal district courts. Interstate can have the case transferred anywhere. This is true even though plaintiff Local has no contacts with any other district and might be seriously inconvenienced by the transfer. Thus the majority's interpretation provides no protection to a local plaintiff suing an interstate defendant.

If Interstate is the plaintiff, personal jurisdiction will be satisfied only in Local's state,[18] so Local cannot have the case transferred. This is true, even though plaintiff Interstate has substantial contacts in all other districts and would not likely be seriously inconvenienced by any transfer. Thus the majority's interpretation allows an interstate plaintiff, even with no apparent interest in resisting a transfer, to prevent transfer sought by a local defendant. This result—an interstate defendant sued by a local plaintiff has many potential transferee districts to which it may force the plaintiff to go, but a local defendant sued by an interstate plaintiff has few or none—seems anomalous.

"These hypotheticals may be interesting," the reader may be thinking, "but are they realistic? Why would a local defendant want a transfer? Would a court transfer a local plaintiff suing an interstate defendant?" Yes, the hypotheticals are realistic, they are based (within

15. *Cf.* Burger King Corp. v. Rudzewicz, 471 U.S. 462 (1985) (court at franchisor's headquarters may obtain personal jurisdiction over out-of-state franchisee).

16. If defendant's contacts with the forum are sufficiently continuous and substantial, defendant may be subject to personal jurisdiction even for claims unrelated to those contacts. *See* Helicopteros Nacionales de Columbia, S.A. v. Hall, 466 U.S. 408 (1984); Perkins v. Benguet Consol. Mining Co., 342 U.S. 437 (1952); International Shoe Co. v. Washington, 326 U.S. 310 (1945).

18. Venue, but not personal jurisdiction, would be satisfied in plaintiff Interstate's residence if subject matter jurisdiction is based on diversity. *See* 28 U.S.C. § 1391(a) (1982).

normal limits of poetic license) on two leading Supreme Court decisions interpreting section 1404(a), Blaski[19] and Van Dusen v. Barrack.[20] A local defendant might want to transfer a case to consolidate it with others to spread the costs of defense. A court might similarly transfer a local plaintiff to ease consolidation.

The preceding analysis considered only the "where it might have been brought" restriction. Might the problem of anomalous transfer opportunities, created by the *Blaski* majority's interpretation of that restriction, be solved by the "convenience" and "justice" requirement?

In the "local plaintiff v. interstate defendant" hypothetical, "convenience" and "justice" might have been adequate safeguards, as any transfer of such a plaintiff is likely to cause the plaintiff substantial inconvenience, since by hypothesis that plaintiff has contacts only in the forum. Congress was not content to rely solely on a court's estimate of "convenience" and "justice," however, because it added the "where it might have been brought" restriction. Yet that restriction is given no purposeful content under the prevailing interpretation. The proposed interpretation, if it replaced that now prevailing, would provide such purposive content.

A different situation is presented when a local defendant seeks transfer of an action brought by an interstate plaintiff. Here some transfers might well satisfy the "convenience" and "justice" requirement, yet no transfer is allowed under the prevailing interpretation of "where it might have been brought," even though no policy is served by such an interpretation.

* * *

Thus far we have considered only a two-party action. Might the advantages of consolidating multi-party litigation justify the conventional *Blaski* interpretation over the proposed interpretation? Consider the facts of *Van Dusen v. Barrack.* An airliner bound from Boston to Philadelphia crashed on takeoff. Over 100 wrongful death actions were filed in the federal court for Massachusetts; over 45 were filed in the federal court for the Eastern District of Pennsylvania. Defendants in the Pennsylvania cases sought a transfer to Massachusetts. Because it is clear that the Pennsylvania plaintiffs could have satisfied personal jurisdiction and venue in the Massachusetts court, the transfer would satisfy the "where it might have been brought" requirement as conventionally interpreted. However, it is uncertain whether an accused tort-feasor can assert personal jurisdiction at the accident site over non-resident victims and their estates.[24]

* * *

19. A patent holder sued a small business for infringement. A patent holder may be viewed as interstate because of the nationwide rights the patent creates.

20. 376 U.S. 612 (1964). A personal injury action was held transferable from plaintiff's residence to the accident site, without inquiry as to the extent of plaintiff's interstate activities or contacts with the accident site.

24. Limits on service of process from federal courts generally follow those of the state in which the federal court sits. *See* Fed.R.Civ.P. 4(e), (f); *see also* Arrowsmith v.

Piper Aircraft Co. v. Reyno

Supreme Court of the United States, 1981.
454 U.S. 235, 102 S.Ct. 252, 70 L.Ed.2d 419.

■ JUSTICE MARSHALL delivered the opinion of the Court.

These cases arise out of an air crash that took place in Scotland. Respondent, acting as representative of the estates of several Scottish citizens killed in the accident, brought wrongful-death actions against petitioners that were ultimately transferred to the United States District Court for the Middle District of Pennsylvania. Petitioners moved to dismiss on the ground of *forum non conveniens.* After noting that an alternative forum existed in Scotland, the District Court granted their motions. 479 F.Supp. 727 (1979). The United States Court of Appeals for the Third Circuit reversed. 630 F.2d 149 (1980). The Court of Appeals based its decision, at least in part, on the ground that dismissal is automatically barred where the law of the alternative forum is less favorable to the plaintiff than the law of the forum chosen by the plaintiff. Because we conclude that the possibility of an unfavorable change in law should not, by itself, bar dismissal, and because we conclude that the District Court did not otherwise abuse its discretion, we reverse.

I

A

In July 1976, a small commercial aircraft crashed in the Scottish highlands during the course of a charter flight from Blackpool to Perth. The pilot and five passengers were killed instantly. The decedents were all Scottish subjects and residents, as are their heirs and next of kin. There were no eyewitnesses to the accident. At the time of the crash the plane was subject to Scottish air traffic control.

The aircraft, a twin-engine Piper Aztec, was manufactured in Pennsylvania by petitioner Piper Aircraft Co. (Piper). The propellers were manufactured in Ohio by petitioner Hartzell Propeller, Inc. (Hartzell). At the time of the crash the aircraft was registered in Great Britain and was owned and maintained by Air Navigation and Trading Co., Ltd. (Air Navigation). It was operated by McDonald Aviation, Ltd. (McDonald), a Scottish air taxi service. Both Air Navigation and McDonald were organized in the United Kingdom. The wreckage of the plane is now in a hangar in Farnsborough, England.

The British Department of Trade investigated the accident shortly after it occurred. A preliminary report found that the plane crashed after developing a spin, and suggested that mechanical failure in the plane or the propeller was responsible. At Hartzell's request, this report was reviewed by a three-member Review Board, which held a

United Press Int'l, 320 F.2d 219 (2d Cir. 1963) (en banc). *But see* National Equip. Rental v. Szukhent, 375 U.S. 311 (1964) (federal law determines who is "an agent authorized by appointment or by law to receive service of process" under Fed.R.Civ. P. 4(d)(1)). Thus determination of federal personal jurisdiction requires reference to the personal jurisdiction of state courts.

9–day adversary hearing attended by all interested parties. The Review Board found no evidence of defective equipment and indicated that pilot error may have contributed to the accident. The pilot, who had obtained his commercial pilot's license only three months earlier, was flying over high ground at an altitude considerably lower than the minimum height required by his company's operations manual.

In July 1977, a California probate court appointed respondent Gaynell Reyno administratrix of the estates of the five passengers. Reyno is not related to and does not know any of the decedents or their survivors; she was a legal secretary to the attorney who filed this lawsuit.[a] Several days after her appointment, Reyno commenced separate wrongful-death actions against Piper and Hartzell in the Superior Court of California, claiming negligence and strict liability. Air Navigation, McDonald, and the estate of the pilot are not parties to this litigation. The survivors of the five passengers whose estates are represented by Reyno filed a separate action in the United Kingdom against Air Navigation, McDonald, and the pilot's estate.[2] Reyno candidly admits that the action against Piper and Hartzell was filed in the United States because its laws regarding liability, capacity to sue, and damages are more favorable to her position than are those of Scotland. Scottish law does not recognize strict liability in tort. Moreover, it permits wrongful-death actions only when brought by a decedent's relatives. The relatives may sue only for "loss of support and society."

On petitioners' motion, the suit was removed to the United States District Court for the Central District of California. Piper then moved for transfer to the United States District Court for the Middle District of Pennsylvania, pursuant to 28 U.S.C. § 1404(a). Hartzell moved to dismiss for lack of personal jurisdiction, or in the alternative, to transfer.[3] In December 1977, the District Court quashed service on Hartzell and transferred the case to the Middle District of Pennsylvania. Respondent then properly served process on Hartzell.

B

In May 1978, after the suit had been transferred, both Hartzell and Piper moved to dismiss the action on the ground of *forum non conveniens.* The District Court granted these motions in October 1979. It relied on the balancing test set forth by this Court in Gulf Oil Corp. v. Gilbert, 330 U.S. 501, 67 S.Ct. 839, 91 L.Ed. 1055 (1947), and its companion case, Koster v. Lumbermens Mut. Cas. Co., 330 U.S.

a. Until the late sixties federal courts had allowed jurisdiction to be "manufactured" by the appointment of an out of state representative by an otherwise non-diverse party. Since that time, federal courts have rejected subject matter jurisdiction in cases where the appointment is found, as a factual matter, to have been made for the purpose of creating jurisdiction. Note that this was no problem in *Piper* because plaintiffs were aliens. Note also that under a 1988 amendment to the federal diversity statute, 28 U.S.C. § 1332(c)(2), the citizenship of important categories of legal representatives is always disregarded for diversity purposes.

2. The pilot's estate has also filed suit in the United Kingdom against Air Navigation, McDonald, Piper, and Hartzell.

3. The District Court concluded that it could not assert personal jurisdiction over Hartzell consistent with due process. However, it decided not to dismiss Hartzell because the corporation would be amenable to process in Pennsylvania.

518, 67 S.Ct. 828, 91 L.Ed. 1067 (1947). In those decisions, the Court stated that a plaintiff's choice of forum should rarely be disturbed. However, when an alternative forum has jurisdiction to hear the case, and when trial in the chosen forum would "establish * * * oppressiveness and vexation to a defendant * * * out of all proportion to plaintiff's convenience," or when the "chosen forum [is] inappropriate because of considerations affecting the court's own administrative and legal problems," the court may, in the exercise of its sound discretion, dismiss the case. *Koster, supra,* at 524, 67 S.Ct., at 831–832. To guide trial court discretion, the Court provided a list of "private interest factors" affecting the convenience of the litigants, and a list of "public interest factors" affecting the convenience of the forum. *Gilbert, supra,* at 508–509, 67 S.Ct., at 843.[6]

After describing our decisions in *Gilbert* and *Koster,* the District Court analyzed the facts of these cases. It began by observing that an alternative forum existed in Scotland; Piper and Hartzell had agreed to submit to the jurisdiction of the Scottish courts and to waive any statute of limitations defense that might be available. It then stated that plaintiff's choice of forum was entitled to little weight. The court recognized that a plaintiff's choice ordinarily deserves substantial deference. It noted, however, that Reyno "is a representative of foreign citizens and residents seeking a forum in the United States because of the more liberal rules concerning products liability law," and that "the courts have been less solicitous when the plaintiff is not an American citizen or resident, and particularly when the foreign citizens seek to benefit from the more liberal tort rules provided for the protection of citizens and residents of the United States." 479 F.Supp., at 731.

The District Court next examined several factors relating to the private interests of the litigants, and determined that these factors strongly pointed towards Scotland as the appropriate forum. Although evidence concerning the design, manufacture, and testing of the plane and propeller is located in the United States, the connections with Scotland are otherwise "overwhelming." *Id.,* at 732. The real parties in interest are citizens of Scotland, as were all the decedents. Witnesses who could testify regarding the maintenance of the aircraft, the training of the pilot, and the investigation of the accident—all essential to the defense—are in Great Britain. Moreover, all witnesses to damages are located in Scotland. Trial would be aided by familiarity with Scottish topography, and by easy access to the wreckage.

6. The factors pertaining to the private interests of the litigants included the "relative ease of access to sources of proof; availability of compulsory process for attendance of unwilling, and the cost of obtaining attendance of willing, witnesses; possibility of view of premises, if view would be appropriate to the action; and all other practical problems that make trial of a case easy, expeditious and inexpensive." *Gilbert,* 330 U.S., at 508, 67 S.Ct., at 843. The public factors bearing on the question included the administrative difficulties flowing from court congestion; the "local interest in having localized controversies decided at home"; the interest in having the trial of a diversity case in a forum that is at home with the law that must govern the action; the avoidance of unnecessary problems in conflict of laws, or in the application of foreign law; and the unfairness of burdening citizens in an unrelated forum with jury duty. *Id.,* at 509, 67 S.Ct., at 843.

The District Court reasoned that because crucial witnesses and evidence were beyond the reach of compulsory process, and because the defendants would not be able to implead potential Scottish third-party defendants, it would be "unfair to make Piper and Hartzell proceed to trial in this forum." *Id.,* at 733. The survivors had brought separate actions in Scotland against the pilot, McDonald, and Air Navigation. "[I]t would be fairer to all parties and less costly if the entire case was presented to one jury with available testimony from all relevant witnesses." *Ibid.* Although the court recognized that if trial were held in the United States, Piper and Hartzell could file indemnity or contribution actions against the Scottish defendants, it believed that there was a significant risk of inconsistent verdicts.[7]

The District Court concluded that the relevant public interests also pointed strongly towards dismissal. The court determined that Pennsylvania law would apply to Piper and Scottish law to Hartzell if the case were tried in the Middle District of Pennsylvania.[8] As a result, "trial in this forum would be hopelessly complex and confusing for a jury." *Id.,* at 734. In addition, the court noted that it was unfamiliar with Scottish law and thus would have to rely upon experts from that country. The court also found that the trial would be enormously costly and time-consuming; that it would be unfair to burden citizens with jury duty when the Middle District of Pennsylvania has little connection with the controversy; and that Scotland has a substantial interest in the outcome of the litigation.

In opposing the motions to dismiss, respondent contended that dismissal would be unfair because Scottish law was less favorable. The District Court explicitly rejected this claim. It reasoned that the possibility that dismissal might lead to an unfavorable change in the law did not deserve significant weight; any deficiency in the foreign law was a "matter to be dealt with in the foreign forum." *Id.,* at 738.

C

On appeal, the United States Court of Appeals for the Third Circuit reversed and remanded for trial. The decision to reverse appears to be based on two alternative grounds. First, the Court held that the District Court abused its discretion in conducting the *Gilbert*

---

7. The District Court explained that inconsistent verdicts might result if petitioners were held liable on the basis of strict liability here, and then required to prove negligence in an indemnity action in Scotland. Moreover, even if the same standard of liability applied, there was a danger that different juries would find different facts and produce inconsistent results.

8. Under Klaxon v. Stentor Electric Mfg. Co., 313 U.S. 487, 61 S.Ct. 1020, 85 L.Ed. 1477 (1941), a court ordinarily must apply the choice-of-law rules of the State in which it sits. However, where a case is transferred pursuant to 28 U.S.C. § 1404(a), it must apply the choice-of-law rules of the State from which the case was transferred.

Van Dusen v. Barrack, 376 U.S. 612, 84 S.Ct. 805, 11 L.Ed.2d 945 (1964). Relying on these two cases, the District Court concluded that California choice-of-law rules would apply to Piper, and Pennsylvania choice-of-law rules would apply to Hartzell. It further concluded that California applied a "governmental interests" analysis in resolving choice-of-law problems, and that Pennsylvania employed a "significant contacts" analysis. The court used the "governmental interests" analysis to determine that Pennsylvania liability rules would apply to Piper, and the "significant contacts" analysis to determine that Scottish liability rules would apply to Hartzell.

analysis. Second, the Court held that dismissal is never appropriate where the law of the alternative forum is less favorable to the plaintiff.

The Court of Appeals began its review of the District Court's *Gilbert* analysis by noting that the plaintiff's choice of forum deserved substantial weight, even though the real parties in interest are nonresidents. * * *

In other words, the court decided that dismissal is automatically barred if it would lead to a change in the applicable law unfavorable to the plaintiff.

We granted certiorari in these cases to consider the questions they raise concerning the proper application of the doctrine of *forum non conveniens.* 450 U.S. 909, 101 S.Ct. 1346, 67 L.Ed.2d 333 (1981).

II

The Court of Appeals erred in holding that plaintiffs may defeat a motion to dismiss on the ground of *forum non conveniens* merely by showing that the substantive law that would be applied in the alternative forum is less favorable to the plaintiffs than that of the present forum. The possibility of a change in substantive law should ordinarily not be given conclusive or even substantial weight in the *forum non conveniens* inquiry.

We expressly rejected the position adopted by the Court of Appeals in our decision in Canada Malting Co. v. Paterson Steamships, Ltd., 285 U.S. 413, 52 S.Ct. 413, 76 L.Ed. 837 (1932). That case arose out of a collision between two vessels in American waters. The Canadian owners of cargo lost in the accident sued the Canadian owners of one of the vessels in Federal District Court. The cargo owners chose an American court in large part because the relevant American liability rules were more favorable than the Canadian rules. The District Court dismissed on grounds of *forum non conveniens.* The plaintiffs argued that dismissal was inappropriate because Canadian laws were less favorable to them. This Court nonetheless affirmed:

> "We have no occasion to enquire by what law the rights of the parties are governed, as we are of the opinion that, under any view of that question, it lay within the discretion of the District Court to decline to assume jurisdiction over the controversy * * *. '[T]he court will not take cognizance of the case if justice would be as well done by remitting the parties to their home forum.' " *Id.,* at 419–420 (quoting Charter Shipping Co. v. Bowring, Jones & Tidy, Ltd., 281 U.S. 515, 517, 50 S.Ct. 400, 414, 74 L.Ed. 1008 (1930)).

The Court further stated that "[t]here was no basis for the contention that the District Court abused its discretion." 285 U.S., at 423.

It is true that *Canada Malting* was decided before *Gilbert,* and that the doctrine of *forum non conveniens* was not fully crystallized until our decision in that case.[13] However, *Gilbert* in no way affects the

---

13. In other words, *Gilbert* held that dismissal may be warranted where a plaintiff

validity of *Canada Malting*. Indeed, by holding that the central focus of the *forum non conveniens* inquiry is convenience, *Gilbert* implicitly recognized that dismissal may not be barred solely because of the possibility of an unfavorable change in law. Under *Gilbert*, dismissal will ordinarily be appropriate where trial in the plaintiff's chosen forum imposes a heavy burden on the defendant or the court, and where the plaintiff is unable to offer any specific reasons of convenience supporting his choice. If substantial weight were given to the possibility of an unfavorable change in law, however, dismissal might be barred even where trial in the chosen forum was plainly inconvenient.

The Court of Appeals' decision is inconsistent with this Court's earlier *forum non conveniens* decisions in another respect. Those decisions have repeatedly emphasized the need to retain flexibility. In *Gilbert*, the Court refused to identify specific circumstances "which will justify or require either grant or denial of remedy." 330 U.S., at 508, 67 S.Ct., at 843. Similarly, in *Koster*, the Court rejected the contention that where a trial would involve inquiry into the internal affairs of a foreign corporation, dismissal was always appropriate. "That is one, but only one, factor which may show convenience." 330 U.S., at 527, 67 S.Ct., at 833. And in Williams v. Green Bay & Western R. Co., 326 U.S. 549, 557, 66 S.Ct. 284, 288, 90 L.Ed. 311 (1946), we stated that we would not lay down a rigid rule to govern discretion, and that "[e]ach case turns on its facts." If central emphasis were placed on any one factor, the *forum non conveniens* doctrine would lose much of the very flexibility that makes it so valuable.

In fact, if conclusive or substantial weight were given to the possibility of a change in law, the *forum non conveniens* doctrine would become virtually useless. Jurisdiction and venue requirements are often easily satisfied. As a result, many plaintiffs are able to choose from among several forums. Ordinarily, these plaintiffs will select that forum whose choice-of-law rules are most advantageous. Thus, if the possibility of an unfavorable change in substantive law is given substantial weight in the *forum non conveniens* inquiry, dismissal would rarely be proper.

Except for the court below, every Federal Court of Appeals that has considered this question after *Gilbert* has held that dismissal on grounds of *forum non conveniens* may be granted even though the law applicable in the alternative forum is less favorable to the plaintiff's chance of recovery.

* * *

The Court of Appeals' approach is not only inconsistent with the purpose of the *forum non conveniens* doctrine, but also poses substantial practical problems. If the possibility of a change in law were given substantial weight, deciding motions to dismiss on the ground of

chooses a particular forum, not because it is convenient, but solely in order to harass the defendant or take advantage of favorable law. This is precisely the situation in which the Court of Appeals' rule would bar dismissal.

forum non conveniens would become quite difficult. Choice-of-law analysis would become extremely important, and the courts would frequently be required to interpret the law of foreign jurisdictions. First, the trial court would have to determine what law would apply if the case were tried in the chosen forum, and what law would apply if the case were tried in the alternative forum. It would then have to compare the rights, remedies, and procedures available under the law that would be applied in each forum. Dismissal would be appropriate only if the court concluded that the law applied by the alternative forum is as favorable to the plaintiff as that of the chosen forum. The doctrine of *forum non conveniens*, however, is designed in part to help courts avoid conducting complex exercises in comparative law. As we stated in *Gilbert*, the public interest factors point towards dismissal where the court would be required to "untangle problems in conflict of laws, and in law foreign to itself." 330 U.S., at 509, 67 S.Ct., at 843.

Upholding the decision of the Court of Appeals would result in other practical problems. At least where the foreign plaintiff named an American manufacturer as defendant,[17] a court could not dismiss the case on grounds of *forum non conveniens* where dismissal might lead to an unfavorable change in law. The American courts, which are already extremely attractive to foreign plaintiffs,[18] would become even more attractive. The flow of litigation into the United States would increase and further congest already crowded courts.[19]

---

17. In fact, the defendant might not even have to be American. A foreign plaintiff seeking damages for an accident that occurred abroad might be able to obtain service of process on a foreign defendant who does business in the United States. Under the Court of Appeals' holding, dismissal would be barred if the law in the alternative forum were less favorable to the plaintiff—even though none of the parties are American, and even though there is absolutely no nexus between the subject matter of the litigation and the United States.

18. First, all but 6 of the 50 American States—Delaware, Massachusetts, Michigan, North Carolina, Virginia, and Wyoming—offer strict liability. 1 CCH Prod. Liability Rep. § 4016 (1981). Rules roughly equivalent to American strict liability are effective in France, Belgium, and Luxembourg. West Germany and Japan have a strict liability statute for pharmaceuticals. However, strict liability remains primarily an American innovation. Second, the tort plaintiff may choose, at least potentially, from among 50 jurisdictions if he decides to file suit in the United States. Each of these jurisdictions applies its own set of malleable choice-of-law rules. Third, jury trials are almost always available in the United States, while they are never provided in civil law jurisdictions. G. Gloss, Comparative Law 12 (1979); J. Merryman, The Civil Law Tradition 121 (1969). Even in the United Kingdom, most civil actions are not tried before a jury. 1 G. Keeton, The

United Kingdom: The Development of its Laws and Constitutions 309 (1955). Fourth, unlike most foreign jurisdictions, American courts allow contingent attorney's fees, and do not tax losing parties with their opponents' attorney's fees. R. Schlesinger, Comparative Law: Cases, Text, Materials 275–277 (3d ed. 1970); Orban, Product Liability: A Comparative Legal Restatement—Foreign National Law and the EEC Directive, 8 Ga.J. Int'l & Comp.L. 342, 393 (1978). Fifth, discovery is more extensive in American than in foreign courts. R. Schlesinger, *supra*, at 307, 310, and n. 33.

19. In holding that the possibility of a change in law unfavorable to the plaintiff should not be given substantial weight, we also necessarily hold that the possibility of a change in law favorable to defendant should not be considered. Respondent suggests that Piper and Hartzell filed the motion to dismiss, not simply because trial in the United States would be inconvenient, but also because they believe the laws of Scotland are more favorable. She argues that this should be taken into account in the analysis of the private interests. We recognize, of course, that Piper and Hartzell may be engaged in reverse forum-shopping. However, this possibility ordinarily should not enter into a trial court's analysis of the private interests. If the defendant is able to overcome the presumption in favor of plaintiff by showing that trial in the chosen forum would be unnecessarily

The Court of Appeals based its decision, at least in part, on an analogy between dismissals on grounds of *forum non conveniens* and transfers between federal courts pursuant to § 1404(a). In Van Dusen v. Barrack, 376 U.S. 612, 84 S.Ct. 805, 11 L.Ed.2d 945 (1964), this Court ruled that a § 1404(a) transfer should not result in a change in the applicable law. Relying on dictum in an earlier Third Circuit opinion interpreting *Van Dusen,* the court below held that that principle is also applicable to a dismissal on *forum non conveniens* grounds. * * * However, § 1404(a) transfers are different than dismissals on the ground of *forum non conveniens.*

Congress enacted § 1404(a) to permit change of venue between federal courts. Although the statute was drafted in accordance with the doctrine of *forum non conveniens,* * * * it was intended to be a revision rather than a codification of the common law. * * * District courts were given more discretion to transfer under § 1404(a) than they had to dismiss on grounds of *forum non conveniens.* * * *

The reasoning employed in *Van Dusen v. Barrack* is simply inapplicable to dismissals on grounds of *forum non conveniens.* That case did not discuss the common-law doctrine. Rather, it focused on "the construction and application" of § 1404(a). 376 U.S., at 613, 84 S.Ct., at 807–08. Emphasizing the remedial purpose of the statute, *Barrack* concluded that Congress could not have intended a transfer to be accompanied by a change in law. * * * The statute was designed as a "federal housekeeping measure," allowing easy change of venue within a unified federal system. * * * The Court feared that if a change in venue were accompanied by a change in law, forum-shopping parties would take unfair advantage of the relaxed standards for transfer. The rule was necessary to ensure the just and efficient operation of the statute.

We do not hold that the possibility of an unfavorable change in law should *never* be a relevant consideration in a *forum non conveniens* inquiry. Of course, if the remedy provided by the alternative forum is so clearly inadequate or unsatisfactory that it is no remedy at all, the unfavorable change in law may be given substantial weight; the district court may conclude that dismissal would not be in the interests of justice.[22] In these cases, however, the remedies that would be provided by the Scottish courts do not fall within this category. Although the relatives of the decedents may not be able to rely on a strict liability theory, and although their potential damages award may be smaller, there is no danger that they will be deprived of any remedy or treated unfairly.

burdensome, dismissal is appropriate—regardless of the fact that defendant may also be motivated by a desire to obtain a more favorable forum.

22. At the outset of any *forum non conveniens* inquiry, the court must determine whether there exists an alternative forum. Ordinarily, this requirement will be satisfied when the defendant is "amenable to process" in the other jurisdiction. *Gilbert,* 330 U.S., at 506–507, 67 S.Ct., at 842. In rare circumstances, however, where the remedy offered by the other forum is clearly unsatisfactory, the other forum may not be an adequate alternative, and the initial requirement may not be satisfied. Thus, for example, dismissal would not be appropriate where the alternative forum does not permit litigation of the subject matter of the dispute.

III

The Court of Appeals also erred in rejecting the District Court's *Gilbert* analysis. The Court of Appeals stated that more weight should have been given to the plaintiff's choice of forum, and criticized the District Court's analysis of the private and public interests. However, the District Court's decision regarding the deference due plaintiff's choice of forum was appropriate. Furthermore, we do not believe that the District Court abused its discretion in weighing the private and public interests.

A

The District Court acknowledged that there is ordinarily a strong presumption in favor of the plaintiff's choice of forum, which may be overcome only when the private and public interest factors clearly point towards trial in the alternative forum. It held, however, that the presumption applies with less force when the plaintiff or real parties in interest are foreign.

The District Court's distinction between resident or citizen plaintiffs and foreign plaintiffs is fully justified. In *Koster*, the Court indicated that a plaintiff's choice of forum is entitled to greater deference when the plaintiff has chosen the home forum. 330 U.S., at 524, 67 S.Ct., at 831–832.[23] When the home forum has been chosen, it is reasonable to assume that this choice is convenient. When the plaintiff is foreign, however, this assumption is much less reasonable. Because the central purpose of any *forum non conveniens* inquiry is to ensure that the trial is convenient, a foreign plaintiff's choice deserves less deference.[24]

B

The *forum non conveniens* determination is committed to the sound discretion of the trial court. It may be reversed only when there has been a clear abuse of discretion; where the court has considered all relevant public and private interest factors, and where its balancing of these factors is reasonable, its decision deserves substantial deference. *Gilbert*, 330 U.S., at 511–512, 67 S.Ct., at 844–845; *Koster*, 330 U.S., at 531, 67 S.Ct., at 835. Here, the Court of Appeals expressly acknowledged that the standard of review was one of abuse of discretion. In examining the District Court's analysis of the public and

---

23. In *Koster,* we stated that "[i]n any balancing of conveniences, a real showing of convenience by a plaintiff who has sued in his home forum will normally outweigh the inconvenience the defendant may have shown." 330 U.S., at 524, 67 S.Ct., at 831–832. * * * Citizens or residents deserve somewhat more deference than foreign plaintiffs, but dismissal should not be automatically barred when a plaintiff has filed suit in his home forum. As always, if the balance of conveniences suggests that trial in the chosen forum would be unnecessarily burdensome for the defendant or the court, dismissal is proper. * * *

24. Respondent argues that since plaintiffs will ordinarily file suit in the jurisdiction that offers the most favorable law, establishing a strong presumption in favor of both home and foreign plaintiffs will ensure that defendants will always be held to the highest possible standard of accountability for their purported wrongdoing. However, the deference accorded a plaintiff's choice of forum has never been intended to guarantee that the plaintiff will be able to select the law that will govern the case.

private interests, however, the Court of Appeals seems to have lost sight of this rule, and substituted its own judgment for that of the District Court.

(1)

In analyzing the private interest factors, the District Court stated that the connections with Scotland are "overwhelming." 479 F.Supp., at 732. This characterization may be somewhat exaggerated. Particularly with respect to the question of relative ease of access to sources of proof, the private interests point in both directions. As respondent emphasizes, records concerning the design, manufacture, and testing of the propeller and plane are located in the United States. She would have greater access to sources of proof relevant to her strict liability and negligence theories if trial were held here.[25] However, the District Court did not act unreasonably in concluding that fewer evidentiary problems would be posed if the trial were held in Scotland. A large proportion of the relevant evidence is located in Great Britain.

The Court of Appeals found that the problems of proof could not be given any weight because Piper and Hartzell failed to describe with specificity the evidence they would not be able to obtain if trial were held in the United States. It suggested that defendants seeking *forum non conveniens* dismissal must submit affidavits identifying the witnesses they would call and the testimony these witnesses would provide if the trial were held in the alternative forum. Such detail is not necessary. Piper and Hartzell have moved for dismissal precisely because many crucial witnesses are located beyond the reach of compulsory process, and thus are difficult to identify or interview. Requiring extensive investigation would defeat the purpose of their motion. Of course, defendants must provide enough information to enable the District Court to balance the parties' interests. Our examination of the record convinces us that sufficient information was provided here. Both Piper and Hartzell submitted affidavits describing the evidentiary problems they would face if the trial were held in the United States.[27]

The District Court correctly concluded that the problems posed by the inability to implead potential third-party defendants clearly supported holding the trial in Scotland. Joinder of the pilot's estate, Air Navigation, and McDonald is crucial to the presentation of petitioners' defense. If Piper and Hartzell can show that the accident was caused not by a design defect, but rather by the negligence of the pilot, the plane's owners, or the charter company, they will be relieved of all liability. It is true, of course, that if Hartzell and Piper were

---

25. In the future, where similar problems are presented, district courts might dismiss subject to the condition that defendant corporations agree to provide the records relevant to the plaintiff's claims.

27. * * * The affidavit provided to the District Court by Piper states that it would call the following witnesses: the relatives of the decedents; the owners and employees of McDonald; the persons responsible for the training and licensing of the pilot; the persons responsible for servicing and maintaining the aircraft; and two or three of its own employees involved in the design and manufacture of the aircraft.

found liable after a trial in the United States, they could institute an action for indemnity or contribution against these parties in Scotland. It would be far more convenient, however, to resolve all claims in one trial. The Court of Appeals rejected this argument. Forcing petitioners to rely on actions for indemnity or contributions would be "burdensome" but not "unfair." 630 F.2d, at 162. Finding that trial in the plaintiff's chosen forum would be burdensome, however, is sufficient to support dismissal on grounds of *forum non conveniens.*

(2)

The District Court's review of the factors relating to the public interest was also reasonable. On the basis of its choice-of-law analysis, it concluded that if the case were tried in the Middle District of Pennsylvania, Pennsylvania law would apply to Piper and Scottish law to Hartzell. It stated that a trial involving two sets of laws would be confusing to the jury. It also noted its own lack of familiarity with Scottish law. Consideration of these problems was clearly appropriate under *Gilbert;* in that case we explicitly held that the need to apply foreign law pointed towards dismissal.[29] The Court of Appeals found that the District Court's choice-of-law analysis was incorrect, and that American law would apply to both Hartzell and Piper. Thus, lack of familiarity with foreign law would not be a problem. Even if the Court of Appeals' conclusion is correct, however, all other public interest factors favored trial in Scotland.

Scotland has a very strong interest in this litigation. The accident occurred in its airspace. All of the decedents were Scottish. Apart from Piper and Hartzell, all potential plaintiffs and defendants are either Scottish or English. As we stated in *Gilbert,* there is "a local interest in having localized controversies decided at home." 330 U.S., at 509, 67 S.Ct., at 843. Respondent argues that American citizens have an interest in ensuring that American manufacturers are deterred from producing defective products, and that additional deterrence might be obtained if Piper and Hartzell were tried in the United States, where they could be sued on the basis of both negligence and strict liability. However, the incremental deterrence that would be gained if this trial were held in an American court is likely to be insignificant. The American interest in this accident is simply not sufficient to justify the enormous commitment of judicial time and resources that would inevitably be required if the case were to be tried here.

IV

The Court of Appeals erred in holding that the possibility of an unfavorable change in law bars dismissal on the ground of *forum non conveniens.* It also erred in rejecting the District Court's *Gilbert* analysis. The District Court properly decided that the presumption in favor of the respondent's forum choice applied with less than maxi-

---

29. Many *forum non conveniens* decisions have held that the need to apply foreign law favors dismissal. * * * Of course, this factor alone is not sufficient to warrant dis-

missal when a balancing of all relevant factors shows that the plaintiff's chosen forum is appropriate. * * *

mum force because the real parties in interest are foreign. It did n
act unreasonably in deciding that the private interests pointed towa
trial in Scotland. Nor did it act unreasonably in deciding that
public interests favored trial in Scotland. Thus, the judgment of
Court of Appeals is

Reversed.

■ JUSTICE POWELL took no part in the decision of these cases.

■ JUSTICE O'CONNOR took no part in the consideration or decision of
these cases.

■ JUSTICE WHITE, concurring in part and dissenting in part.

I join Parts I and II of the Court's opinion. However, like JUSTICE
BRENNAN and JUSTICE STEVENS, I would not proceed to deal with the issues
addressed in Part III. To that extent, I am in dissent.

■ JUSTICE STEVENS, with whom JUSTICE BRENNAN joins, dissenting.

[O]nly one question is presented for review to this Court:

"Whether, in an action in federal district court brought by
foreign plaintiffs against American defendants, the plaintiffs may
defeat a motion to dismiss on the ground of *forum non conveniens* merely by showing that the substantive law that would be
applied if the case were litigated in the district court is more
favorable to them than the law that would be applied by the
courts of their own nation."

[T]he Court limited its grant of certiorari, see 450 U.S. 909, 101
S.Ct. 1346, 67 L.Ed.2d 332, to the same question. * * * I agree that
this question should be answered in the negative. Having decided that
question, I would simply remand the case to the Court of Appeals for
further consideration of the question whether the District Court
correctly decided that Pennsylvania was not a convenient forum in
which to litigate a claim against a Pennsylvania company that a plane
was defectively designed and manufactured in Pennsylvania.

NOTE

Most of the Courts of Appeals have held that the denial of a forum non
conveniens motion is not appealable. Carlenstolpe v. Merck & Co., Inc., 819 F.2d 33
(2d Cir.1987) is an example which provides a brief survey.

In virtually all international tort cases the plaintiff is seeking to obtain a forum
in the U.S. One conspicuous exception is defamation. If the offending language is
English, the preferred forum often is London.

While in the United States defamation plaintiffs must prove that the statements are incorrect, in England the burden is on the defendants to prove the truth
of their statements. Under the standard "English Rule" of litigation, the losing
party must pay the costs and counsel fees of the winner. Also, far less discovery is
permitted and there is less delay.

Several well-known U.S. and U.K. figures have successfully sued U.S. publications for defamation in England. The judgments (and settlements) are much smaller
than in the U.S. See, *New York Observer*, September 23, 1991, p. 1.

MacLeod v. MacLeod

Supreme Court of Maine, 1978.
383 A.2d 39.

■ McKusick, Chief Justice.

The plaintiff, Maggie S. MacLeod, appeals an order of the Superior Court, Lincoln County, dismissing this action brought against her former husband, Walter E. MacLeod.

We sustain the appeal. We hold that the Superior Court erred in granting defendant's motion to dismiss on the ground of *forum non conveniens.* We do grant the defendant, however, relief from having to defend Mrs. MacLeod's suit in Maine. We direct the Superior Court to stay this Maine action conditioned upon Mr. MacLeod's submitting to suit in Virginia, which is, he argues and we agree, a more appropriate forum than Maine.

The plaintiff and the defendant were married in New York City on October 15, 1955. Their one child, Scott Michael MacLeod, was born the following year. Encountering marital difficulties, they on June 15, 1971 entered into a separation agreement whereby Mrs. MacLeod was given custody of their son, and Mr. MacLeod agreed to pay his wife child support and alimony, as well as certain storage and travel expenses. The separation agreement does not recite where it was entered into, but the record otherwise shows that the MacLeods were living in France at the time, Mr. MacLeod being an employee of the Central Intelligence Agency.

The couple was divorced on June 12, 1973, by decree of the Tribunal de Grande Instance de Paris (in this record translated as the "County Court") in Paris, France, where Mrs. MacLeod was then living. The French divorce decree gave a San Francisco APO address as Mr. MacLeod's "domicile"; the record before the court shows that he was working for the CIA in Bangkok, Thailand, at the time. The French court awarded custody of their son to Mrs. MacLeod and ordered Mr. MacLeod to pay the plaintiff child "upkeep" and alimony in a total amount of 3150 francs a month.

Mrs. MacLeod instituted the present action in Superior Court, Lincoln County, in July 1977. In her complaint, she alleged that she resided in the Commonwealth of Virginia and that the defendant was a resident of Newcastle in Lincoln County, Maine.[1] In one count of her complaint Mrs. MacLeod attempts to collect an amount of $19,490 alleged to be due to her from the defendant under the French divorce judgment as child "upkeep" and alimony; and by another she seeks damages of an unstated amount for the defendant's alleged default on the separation agreement.

On July 30, 1977, Mrs. MacLeod succeeded in obtaining personal service upon the defendant at his parents' home in Newcastle, Maine.

---

1. Despite plaintiff's allegation in her complaint that defendant resided in Newcastle, Maine, the defendant's affidavit that he now resides in Thailand is not contradicted and must for present purposes be taken as fact.

At the time, Mr. MacLeod was in Maine to attend his parents' golden wedding anniversary.

On August 15, 1977, the defendant filed a motion to dismiss, supported by his affidavit stating that (i) he now resides in Bangkok, Thailand, and during the past ten years, as a CIA employee, has lived in four different foreign countries; (ii) although he is an American citizen, his sole contact with the United States is his Virginia driver's license; and (iii) he has never resided, held property, or paid taxes in the State of Maine.

Following a hearing on the defendant's motion to dismiss, the Superior Court justice dismissed the action "with prejudice"[2] on the grounds that "neither party is a resident of the State of Maine, and that the Court, in its discretion, declines to exercise jurisdiction over this matter." Both parties interpret this cryptic statement to be an invocation of the doctrine of *forum non conveniens.*

The present action concerns a nonresident plaintiff suing a nonresident defendant upon transitory causes of action which did not arise in the State of Maine. Given those facts, the trial court could rightly consider exercising its discretionary power, notwithstanding the existence of both subject matter and personal jurisdiction, to decline jurisdiction over the action. Foss v. Richards, 126 Me. 419, 139 A. 313 (1927). Dismissal for *forum non conveniens,* although discretionary, must be predicated upon the trial court's initial determination that dismissal will further the ends of justice and promote convenience of the suit for all parties. * * *

For reasons of both justice and comity, a nonresident plaintiff in a transitory action is usually entitled to have his complaint heard and resolved by the forum of his choice. Dismissal of his action by a court with legal power to grant relief places the plaintiff in the position of having expended time and money in a wasted action, and during the period of his reliance he risks running afoul of the statutes of limitations in other jurisdictions. In recognition of the harshness of dismissal, a court will not dismiss for *forum non conveniens* unless the ends of justice strongly militate in favor of relegating the plaintiff to an alternative forum. * * *

The many factors to be weighed in applying the doctrine of *forum non conveniens* have been identified by the Supreme Court of the United States [in *Gulf Oil v. Gilbert*]. * * *

Whatever relative weight is given those factors bearing upon justice and convenience in a particular action, however, courts unanimously agree that the availability of an *alternative* forum is essential to exercise of the power to dismiss for *forum non conveniens.* * * *

---

2. Since we sustain Mrs. MacLeod's appeal, the dismissal of her action "with prejudice" as well as the clerk's docket entry of "Judgment for the Defendant" are vacated. For future guidance of the Superior Court, however, we note that a dismissal because of *forum non conveniens* is not an adjudication on the merits. See Rule 41(b)(3). M.R.Civ.P. (exception for dismissals "for improper venue"): 46 *Am.Jur.2d* "Judgments" § 505.

The present record is barren of any facts whatsoever indicating that this plaintiff, a Virginia resident, has available *any* "alternative" forum, at least within American territory, let alone one that is in addition "more appropriate." The defendant, according to his own uncontradicted affidavit, is now a resident of Thailand. The defendant's sole "contacts" with any state are those he has with Virginia by virtue of his possession of a driver's license from that state and the fact that the CIA, his former employer, maintains its headquarters there. Virginia is also, of course, the present residence of his former wife. Those limited contacts are not such, however, as to render him personally subject to the jurisdiction of any court located in the Commonwealth of Virginia. Nor does the record display any other facts so much as hinting that the defendant is subject to personal jurisdiction anywhere else in American territory. We would ill serve the interests of justice and comity should we shut the doors of the Maine Courts to this plaintiff who has in reality no "alternative" forum.[6]

Therefore, the presiding justice erred in dismissing the plaintiff's action. Our holding does not, however, lead us to reverse and remand for trial. The relative considerations of convenience to the parties and the respective interests of Virginia and Maine, the two states principally concerned with resolving this dispute, warrant our attention. Upon examination of those factors, we agree with the implicit conclusion of the Superior Court that Maine is not the best place for this action to be tried. Virginia, the state of the plaintiff's residence, would obviously be the forum preferred by the plaintiff, who also will undoubtedly be her own principal witness at any trial. From the point of view of her former husband, the defendant, no state is going to be particularly convenient for trial, but Virginia will not be obviously more inconvenient than Maine. In fact, the defendant does possess minimal ties with Virginia which perhaps balance the practical fact that his parents happen to live in Maine. From the standpoint of the State of Maine, it is generally undesirable to expend our judicial resources in resolving a dispute between nonresident parties *if* such is avoidable without depriving the plaintiff of a forum. On the other hand, the Commonwealth of Virginia owes its domiciliary, Mrs. MacLeod, an obligation to provide her with a forum. The public interests involved are also uniquely concerns of Virginia. That state has an immediate, pecuniary interest in enforcing the plaintiff's right to alimony and support payments. Maine shares those concerns only secondarily, as a feature of comity.

In sum, the particular circumstances of this action dictate that the ends of justice would be best served if this action were heard in Virginia, the state of plaintiff's residence. This transfer of the action

6. Thailand, the country of the defendant's residence, is of course technically one other forum suggested by these facts as a place where plaintiff might be able to prosecute her suit against the defendant. We do not believe, however, that the foreign forum is an "alternative" within the meaning of that requirement, at least in the factual circumstances of this case. * * * In any event, the defendant does not urge that Thailand is an appropriate forum.

can in practical effect be accomplished by the Superior Court's staying the Maine action conditioned upon acceptance by the defendant, Mr. MacLeod, of service in a Virginia suit to be newly commenced by Mrs. MacLeod on the same causes of action. In other words, the court below would grant Mr. MacLeod part of the relief he sought by his motion to dismiss, *i.e.,* avoidance of defending his former wife's suit in Maine, but only on condition that he, by submitting to the jurisdiction of a Virginia court, assure the existence of a true alternative forum.

Before granting the defendant this conditional relief, we appropriately should examine whether the plaintiff would thereby lose any substantial rights which she gained by successfully serving Mr. MacLeod in Maine on July 30, 1977. There is nothing before us to suggest that Mrs. MacLeod picked Maine as the forum for her suit because of any advantages of Maine substantive law or conflicts rules; it would appear that Maine was her choice only because it was the sole place within American territory where she could catch Mr. MacLeod for service of process. In this Maine action, however, Mrs. MacLeod does have the existing advantage of having commenced suit on July 30, 1977, perhaps a fact of some significance in determining whether recovery of any of the monthly payments under either the separation agreement of June 15, 1971, or the divorce decree of June 12, 1973, are now barred by the passage of time. The benefit of that date of commencement of suit can be preserved to Mrs. MacLeod by imposing as another condition for granting the stay a stipulation that the defendant in the prospective Virginia action will not assert any statute-of-limitations defense inconsistent with treating the Virginia action as having been commenced on July 30, 1977.

Until the Virginia action is commenced and thereafter until it goes to final judgment, the Superior Court will keep jurisdiction over this action; and if an appropriate Virginia court for any reason fails to get or maintain personal jurisdiction over the defendant or the statute of limitations applicable in the Virginia action is not applied as if the Virginia action was commenced on July 30, 1977, the Superior Court may lift the stay of this action.

* * *

NOTE: FORUM NON CONVENIENS IN A STATE COURT

Piper Aircraft and *Union Carbide* involve foreign plaintiffs asserting personal injury and products liability claims against United States corporations where the injuries and occurred abroad. Often in such cases, the federal courts dismiss based on forum non conveniens and the criteria for the application of that doctrine set forth in *Piper*.

The states have their own forum non conveniens doctrines. Most states apply standards that more or less follow federal law. See e.g. *Stangvik v. Shiley, Inc.*, 54 Cal. 3d 744, 819 P.2d 14, 1 Cal Rptr. 2d 556 (Cal. 1991) (discussing the propriety of adopting federal forum non conveniens criteria).

In 1993, Texas added a provision for cases involving personal injury or wrongful death. It stated that if the claimant in such cases is not a legal resident of the United States the court may decline to exercise jurisdiction under the doctrine of forum non conveniens if it finds that "in the interest of justice" the action "would more properly be heard in a forum outside this state." Tex. Civ. Prac. & Rem. Code Ann. § 71.051 (Supp. 1993).

The Illinois Supreme Court "has consistently appeared willing to review lower court decisions" (on forum non conveniens). "Since 1981" (to the middle of 1984) "the Illinois Supreme Court has decided at least nine cases involving the doctrine." Furlang & Bedell, Recent Developments in Forum Non Conveniens, Chicago Bar Record, Sept.–Oct. 1984 (p. 114).

NOTE

In re Union Carbide Corp. (BHOPAL)

United States Court of Appeals, Second Circuit, 1987.
809 F.2d 195, *cert. denied*, 484 U.S. 871, 108 S.Ct. 198, 98 L.Ed.2d 150 (1987).

■ MANSFIELD, CIRCUIT JUDGE:

* * *

The conditions imposed by the district court upon its forum non conveniens dismissal stand on a different footing. Plaintiffs and the UOI,[a] however, contend that UCC,[b] having been granted the *forum non conveniens* dismissal that it sought and having consented to the district court's order, has waived its right to appellate review of these conditions. We disagree. UCC expressly reserved its right to appeal Judge Keenan's order. Moreover, it has made a sufficient showing of prejudice from the second and third conditions of the court's order to entitle it to seek appellate review. UCC's position is comparable to that of a prevailing party which, upon being granted injunctive relief, is permitted to challenge by appeal conditions attaching to the injunction that are found to be objectionable.

* * *

The first condition, that UCC consent to the Indian court's personal jurisdiction over it and waive the statute of limitations as a defense, are not unusual and have been imposed in numerous cases where the foreign court would not provide an adequate alternative in the absence of such a condition. See, e.g., Schertenleib, supra, 589 F.2d at 1166; Bailey v. Dolphin Int'l, Inc., 697 F.2d 1268, 1280 (5th Cir.1983). The remaining two conditions, however, pose problems.

In requiring that UCC consent to enforceability of an Indian judgment against it, the district court proceeded at least in part on the erroneous assumption that, absent such a requirement, the plaintiffs, if they should succeed in obtaining an Indian judgment against UCC, might not be able to enforce it against UCC in the United States. The law, however, is to the contrary. Under New York law, which governs actions brought in New York to enforce foreign judgments, *see* Island Territory of Curacao v. Solitron Devices, Inc., 489 F.2d 1313, 1318 (2d Cir.1973), *cert. denied*, 416 U.S. 986, 94 S.Ct. 2389, 40 L.Ed.2d 763 (1974), a foreign-country judgment that is final, conclusive and enforceable where rendered must be recognized and will be enforced as "conclusive between the parties to the extent that it grants or denies recovery of a sum of money" except that it is not deemed to be conclusive if:

a. Union of India which also represents the Indian plaintiffs.

b. Union Carbide Corp.

1.   the judgment was rendered under a system which does not provide impartial tribunals or procedures compatible with the requirements of due process of law;

2.   the foreign court did not have personal jurisdiction over the defendant.

Art. 53, Recognition of Foreign Country Money Judgments, 7B N.Y.Civ.Prac.L. & R. §§ 5301–09 (McKinney 1978). Although § 5304 further provides that under certain specified conditions a foreign country judgment need not be recognized, none of these conditions would apply to the present cases except for the possibility of failure to provide UCC with sufficient notice of proceedings or the existence of fraud in obtaining the judgment, which do not presently exist but conceivably could occur in the future.[c] * * *

---

c.   The Court of Appeals also refused to permit enforcement of the District Court order that required UCC to consent to the broader discovery under the Federal Rules of Civil Procedure in the Indian forum.

CHAPTER III

Pleadings

A. The Purpose of the Pleadings

Messick v. Turnage

Supreme Court of North Carolina, 1954.
240 N.C. 625, 83 S.E.2d 654.

In this action the plaintiff seeks to recover damages on account of injuries she received while a patron in defendant's moving picture theatre. The allegations in her complaint are in substance that she purchased a ticket and entered the theatre during a hard rain; that falling plaster and water behind her so frightened her that she involuntarily jumped from her seat, striking the metal part of the seat in front, causing her injury. The particular breach of duty on the part of the defendant which she alleges is actionable negligence is set out in the following words: "That the defendant failed to maintain a safe theatre and auditorium for plaintiff's enjoyment, in that the defendant knew or should have known by reasonable observation which was his duty, that said roof was leaking and in bad repair."

She further alleges somewhat indefinitely that this condition caused the plaster to give way. The other allegations of negligence are too general, too indefinite, and too vague to be availing.

The defendant answered, denying negligence, and denying that the roof was leaking or in bad repair.

The evidence, in the light most favorable to the plaintiff, tended to show the theatre consisted of a main floor and a balcony which extended over the rear part of the main floor on either side and to the rear. A restroom on the level with the balcony floor was maintained for the patrons of the theatre. A valve in one of the fixtures in the restroom failed to close, causing water to spill out to the floor. This floor was of tile, sloping toward the center, and fitted with a drainpipe sufficient in size to carry all overflow. This pipe was covered with a grill. Cigarette butts and other debris had clogged the pipe. Water covered the floor to a depth sufficient to overflow a three-quarter-inch strip at the door. The balcony was covered with a carpet which soaked up the overflowing water. Seepage from the carpet through the floor of the balcony softened the plaster under the balcony. Suddenly this plaster gave way, and, to use plaintiff's own words, "I thought the whole balcony was coming down behind me, it made so much fuss. I did not know what was going on at the second when it happened, and it startled me so I hit my leg on the back of the seat." The plaintiff's evidence further tended to show the door to the restroom was closed. The sound of running water could not be heard from the outside. Water could not be discovered from the outside, except by examination or stepping on the carpet. At the close of plaintiff's evidence, motion for judgment of nonsuit was made and sustained. The plaintiff appealed. * * *

HIGGINS, JUSTICE. The negligence sufficiently pleaded in the complaint is to the effect that the defendant "knew or should have known * * * that said roof was leaking and in bad repair * * *." There is not a suggestion in the evidence that the roof was leaking and in bad repair. It was incumbent upon the plaintiff not only to prove negligence proximately causing her injury, but it was her duty to prove negligence substantially as alleged in her complaint. This she failed to do. Proof without allegation is as unavailing as allegation without proof.

Affirmed.

NOTE

For a more recent example, in a commercial context, see New Style Homes, Inc. v. Fletcher, 606 S.W.2d 510 (Mo.App.1980), in which Dixon J. observed:

> Defendant Atlas Surety Corporation appeals from a money judgment entered in a court-tried case. The basic and dispositive issue is the contradiction between the pleading, the proof, and the judgment entered. The proof does not follow the pleading; and the findings of fact, conclusions of law, and the judgment do not follow either the proof or the pleadings.

* * *

> The failure of proof in this case does not require outright reversal since it appears that there may be proof available but not offered on the issues.

The Variance Problem

Morgan, The Variance Problem

32 Neb.L.Rev. 357 (1953).

Since the introduction of the system of written pleadings, lawyers have been plagued with the problem of a discrepancy—or variance—between pleading and proof. Under the early common law method of oral pleadings, there was no such problem because the practice of summoning witnesses to testify to the facts was unknown. Issue was reached by a debate between counsel in court and each attorney was responsible for the truth of the facts pleaded. At any time during this proceeding, counsel could examine their clients on fresh facts and adjust the form of the pleadings to these new issues.

Under the system of written pleadings which was later introduced at common law, this was impossible. The pleadings were closed and issue reached before the parties got into court. Witnesses were summoned to testify to the truth or untruth of the facts alleged in the pleadings. Consequently it might easily happen that the proved facts did not support the facts pleaded, i.e., there might be a variance between proof and pleadings. And at common law the slightest discrepancy might prove fatal to the success of a party, regardless of the merits of his claim. For example, in an early decision concerning an action for a false charge of felony, the declaration stated that the defendant went before Richard Cavendish, Baron Waterpark of *Water-fork*, a justice of the peace, and falsely charged the plaintiff with the felony. The evidence showed that the charge was made before Richard Cavendish, Baron Waterpark of *Waterpark*. This variance was considered fatal and the plaintiff nonsuited.

Such a highly formalistic concept may obviously work injustice. From this extreme case, however, we cannot conclude that the variance problem is merely an example of common law technicality and formalism and that all variances should be disregarded under a modern system of pleading. There still remains the fact that either party should be able to rely on his opponent's statement of his position to give notice of what the issues will be at trial, so that he may, if he wishes, prepare to meet that position at trial by argument and evidence. Under the common law and the codes, this notice was designed to be given in the written pleadings.

Conflicting with this desirable goal, is the interest of the other party in having his claim or defense decided according to the merits of the actual facts as they appear at the trial. After all, it is expected that controversies will be decided in accordance with the facts and that rules of procedure will effectuate this goal and not stand in its way. It is not only a goal which is desirable from the point of view of the actual parties to the litigation, but also one which the public expects will be effectuated, and when it is not, causes a great undercurrent of dissatisfaction with the judicial process.

The Managerial Problem

David, Book Review
[Of Chadbourn, California Pleading (1961)].
8 U.C.L.A.L.Rev. 994 (1961).

* * *

The California courts now proceed by the most direct line to develop the issues for trial, and he who attempts to revert to the sporting theory of justice, by semantic demurrers and bold motions to strike, will have the judge to deal with in our metropolitan courts. Except for developing accurate issues and the truth as soon as possible, judges have no disposition to add to, or prolong, the pleading stage of the lawsuit; at least not when over 6,000 demurrers and half that number of motions to strike are presented annually in the law and motion departments of the Los Angeles Superior Court. Motions for summary judgment, and the pretrial conference take the sword out of the pleader's hands, and attempt to substitute Diogenes' lantern.

In *California Pleading* one notes emphasis upon testing complaints by their adequacy to notify the opponent of the nature of the controversy. Perhaps there should be more emphasis upon the necessity that complaints be in such form that positive and unequivocal admissions or denials can be made of their averments. This basic necessity underlies rules against inclusion of evidentiary matter, conclusions of law, and for the exclusion of conclusionary adjectives and adverbs characterizing action. One can deny a collision happened, or can admit it happened, but how can one adequately deny or affirm an indefinite collective, such as "wrongful," "wilful," "negligent?" These give no notice of the premises to be denied or admitted. Or, how can one deal with a rambling narrative? It may give notice of the controversy, but may not present identifiable ultimates which should be put in issue.

* * *

The pleading of ultimate facts requires the pleader to determine which facts are ultimate. Until there have been thorough discovery procedures, he may not know, or suspect, the full nature of the evidentiary material.

* * *

In a footnote, Judge David adds that "[T]here is little or no published data showing the actual impact of law and motion matters, principally pleading, in any court. In eleven months of 1956, in one of the two law and motion departments of the Superior Court of Los Angeles County in which I presided, there were 2,343 demurrers and 906 motions to strike, out of a total of 5,965 law and motion matters. In the first six months of 1957 there were 4,546 law and motion matters, excluding continuances. Of these, 1,677 were demurrers and 496 were motions to strike. In 1956 (eleven months) there were 244 motions for summary judgment. In the first six months of 1957 there were 149 such motions."

"In the 1956 figures, there were 1866 demurrers to the original complaint or answer filed; 353 to the first amended pleading; 85 to the second amended pleading; 23 to the third amended pleading; 7 to the fourth amended pleading; 6 to the fifth amended pleading; 1 to the 7th amended pleading; and 2 to the 8th amended pleading."

B. SPECIFICITY: THE DETAIL REQUIRED

1. Federal Rules and State Adaptations

Dioguardi v. Durning

United States Court of Appeals, Second Circuit, 1944.
139 F.2d 774.

■ CLARK, CIRCUIT JUDGE.

In his complaint, obviously home drawn, plaintiff attempts to assert a series of grievances against the Collector of Customs at the

Port of New York growing out of his endeavors to import merchandise from Italy "of great value," consisting of bottles of "tonics." We may pass certain of his claims as either inadequate or inadequately stated and consider only these two: (1) that on the auction day, October 9, 1940, when defendant sold the merchandise at "public custom," "he sold my merchandise to another bidder with my price of $110, and not of his price of $120," and (2) "that three weeks before the sale, two cases, of 19 bottles each case, disappeared." Plaintiff does not make wholly clear how these goods came into the collector's hand, since he alleges compliance with the revenue laws; but he does say he made a claim for "refund of merchandise which was two-thirds paid in Milano, Italy," and that the collector denied the claim. These and other circumstances alleged indicate (what, indeed, plaintiff's brief asserts) that his original dispute was with his consignor as to whether anything more was due upon the merchandise, and that the collector, having held it for a year (presumably as unclaimed merchandise under 19 U.S.C.A. § 1491), then sold it, or such part of it as was left, at public auction. For his asserted injuries plaintiff claimed $5,000 damages, together with interest and costs, against the defendant individually and as collector. This complaint was dismissed by the District Court, with leave, however, to plaintiff to amend, on motion of the United States Attorney, appearing for the defendant, on the ground that it "fails to state facts sufficient to constitute a cause of action."

Thereupon plaintiff filed an amended complaint, wherein, with an obviously heightened conviction that he was being unjustly treated, he vigorously reiterates his claims, including those quoted above and now stated as that his "medicinal extracts" were given to the Springdale Distilling Company "with my betting [bidding?] price of $110: and not their price of $120," and "It isnt so easy to do away with two cases with 37 bottles of one quart. Being protected, they can take this chance." An earlier paragraph suggests that defendant had explained the loss of the two cases by "saying that they had leaked, which could never be true in the manner they were bottled." On defendant's motion for dismissal on the same ground as before, the court made a final judgment dismissing the complaint, and plaintiff now comes to us with increased volubility, if not clarity.

It would seem, however, that he has stated enough to withstand a mere formal motion, directed only to the face of the complaint, and that here is another instance of judicial haste which in the long run makes waste. Under the new rules of civil procedure, there is no pleading requirement of stating "facts sufficient to constitute a cause of action," but only that there be "a short and plain statement of the claim showing that the pleader is entitled to relief," Federal Rules of Civil Procedure, rule 8(a), 28 U.S.C.A. following section 723c; and the motion for dismissal under Rule 12(b) is for failure to state "a claim upon which relief can be granted." The District Court does not state why it concluded that the complaints showed no claim upon which relief could be granted; and the United States Attorney's brief before us does not help us, for it is limited to the prognostication—unfortunately ill founded so far as we are concerned—that "the most cursory examination" of them will show the correctness of the District Court's action.

We think that, however inartistically they may be stated, the plaintiff has disclosed his claims that the collector has converted or otherwise done away with two of his cases of medicinal tonics and has sold the rest in a manner incompatible with the public auction he had announced—and, indeed, required. * * * [As to] this latter claim, it may be that the collector's only error is a failure to collect an additional ten dollars from the Springdale Distilling Company; but giving the plaintiff the benefit of reasonable intendments in his allegations (as we must on this motion), the claim appears to be in effect that he was actually the first bidder at the price for which they were sold, and hence was entitled to the merchandise. Of course, defendant did not need to move on the complaint alone; he could have disclosed the facts from his point of view, in advance of a trial if he chose, by asking for a pre-trial hearing or by moving for a summary judgment with supporting affidavits. But, as it stands, we do not see how the plaintiff may properly be deprived of his day in court to show what he obviously so firmly believes and what for present purposes defendant must be taken as admitting. It appears to be well settled that the collector may be held personally for a default or for negligence in the performance of his duties. * * *

On remand, the District Court may find substance in other claims asserted by plaintiff, which include a failure properly to catalogue the items (as the cited Regulations provide), or to allow plaintiff to buy at a discount from the catalogue price just before the auction sale (a claim whose basis is not apparent), and a violation of an agreement to deliver the merchandise to the plaintiff as soon as he paid for it, by stopping the payments. In view of plaintiff's limited ability to write and speak English, it will be difficult for the District Court to arrive at justice unless he consents to receive legal assistance in the presentation of his case. The record indicates that he refused further help from a lawyer suggested by the court, and his brief (which was a recital of facts, rather than an argument of law) shows distrust of a lawyer of standing at this bar. It is the plaintiff's privilege to decline all legal help, * * * but we fear that he will be indeed ill advised to attempt to meet a motion for summary judgment or other similar presentation of the merits without competent advice and assistance.

Judgment is reversed and the action is remanded for further proceedings not inconsistent with this opinion.

NOTE

The Dioguardi case was treated at some length in McCaskill, The Modern Philosophy of Pleading: A Dialogue Outside the Shades, 38 A.B.A.J. 123, 126 (1952):

FATHER: Common law pleading was not concerned with fair notice, but only with forming issues, and rested upon the untenable ground that the parties knew nothing about a case except what was stated in the pleadings. This we know is nonsense, because the parties were participants in the events out of which the litigation arose. To get away from this foolishness, we discarded common law pleading and adopted a procedure so simple a 16–year-old boy may draft pleadings.[1] Read Moore's Federal Practice and Clark on Code Pleading. They are the leading modern texts.

SON: Is this a Hadacol for pleading aches and fevers, cancers and corns? If pleadings now are so simple, why such long texts by these authors?

FATHER: To explain simplicity, that is, to show the kind of simplicity; that it is the simplicity of the common man and not the simplicity which comes from knowledge and technical expertness.

SON: Tell me more about that Dioguardi case before Judge Clark. It sounds interesting. * * *

SON: What happened on the remandment?

FATHER: If you insist, there was a trial on the amended home drawn complaint. Dioguardi failed to prove a right to relief, and judgment went for defendant. Dioguardi again appealed to the Court of Appeals, where that judgment was affirmed.

SON: Who, then, wasted time, the District Court or Judge Clark?

FATHER: You are forgetting the satisfaction given Dioguardi and the public by the full hearing on the evidence. Such a procedure gives the public greater confidence in the courts than decisions on pleadings alone. The courts should take time to do that and it is not wasted time. You see, the District Court there got reversed by not following the postponement procedure. Do you think it will sustain any more motions on pleadings?

Moore v. Agency for International Development

United States Court of Appeals, District of Columbia Circuit, 1993.
994 F.2d 874

■ Henderson, Circuit Judge

Brian P. Moore filed a pro se complaint against the Agency for International Development (AID) and against Ronald W. Roskens, its Director, and George Wachtenheim, the Former Acting Director of AID/Bolivia, in their official and individual capacities. Moore alleged various violations of his civil rights, libel and slander, personal injury and loss of property resulting from the defendants' actions. Roskens resides in Virginia and Wachtenheim resides in Honduras. The district court dismissed all of the claims with prejudice. It dismissed the constitutional claims against Roskens and Wachtenheim because of improper service of process, lack of venue and failure to meet this circuit's heightened pleading standard. Moore appeals the dismissal of his constitutional claims against the defendants in their individual

---

1. The reference is to Clark, Institute on Federal Rules 220 (Proceedings at Cleveland, 1938): "I was interested to hear recently from one of the lawyers who was really criticizing this section of the rules. * * * He said, 'Why, a sixteen-year-old boy could plead under these rules!'

"Well, I would say, in answer, Why not, if he tells the court what his case is about? And that is what we are trying to ask the lawyers to do, and to do quite simply."—Note by Eds.

capacities only. Because Moore is a pro se plaintiff, we remand to allow him to amend his complaint and to correct his service of process. In addition, because Congress amended 28 U.S.C. § 1391, the general venue statute, while this case was pending in district court, we remand to allow the district court to reconsider whether venue lies in this jurisdiction.

I

Because the appeal arises in part from a rule 12(b)(6) motion to dismiss, we accept Moore's allegations of facts in the complaint as true. Moore is a former employee of Management Sciences for Health (MSH), a Massachusetts corporation that had a contract with AID to provide medical services in Bolivia. Beginning in February 1987, he served as "chief of party," MSH's technical advisor for the project. According to Moore, in April 1987, Wachtenheim libeled and slandered him, both personally and professionally, to other AID officials.[2] Peter Rozzelle of MSH verbally informed Moore that AID had conditioned renewal of its contract with MSH on Moore's termination from the project. In early May 1987, MSH terminated Moore effective May 15, 1987.

Since his termination, Moore has been unable to find similar work with private international health care consultants who contract with AID. He asserts that these organizations have not hired him because of their fear that they would not obtain contracts with AID.

Moore argues that AID's directive to terminate him denied him due process and that it interfered with his "right to employment and equal treatment under the law." Moore's complaint does not explain how Roskens was involved in his termination but his brief asserts that "this directive was communicated to MSH through AID agents Ronald W. Roskens and George Wachtenheim."

Moore filed suit on April 13, 1990, in the United States District Court for the District of Columbia. He served the United States Attorney General on April 26, 1990. He then served the United States Attorney on May 3, 1990. On July 2, 1990, an Assistant United States Attorney (AUSA) made an appearance for the defendants.

The defendants moved to dismiss or in the alternative for summary judgment. They argued that the defendants were not properly served, that venue did not lie in the District of Columbia and that Moore's constitutional claims failed to satisfy this circuit's heightened pleading standard. Moore conceded that he did not properly serve the defendants and asked the district court for an opportunity to correct his service of process. He opposed the defendants' other two arguments. The district court agreed with the defendants and dismissed the claims with prejudice. Moore, now represented by counsel, appeals.

---

2. Wachtenheim had been Moore's Peace Corps Director in Peru during 1971–72. Moore had opposed certain political appointees and certain projects conducted by the Peace Corps in Peru. Moore's activities had apparently adversely affected Wachtenheim's employment status there.

II.

As noted, Moore brought this suit pro se. Pro se litigants are allowed more latitude than litigants represented by counsel to correct defects in service of process and pleadings. See *Haines v. Kerner*, 404 U.S. 519, 520, 30 L. Ed. 2d 652, 92 S. Ct. 594 (1972) (pro se complaints held to "less stringent standards than formal pleadings drafted by lawyers"); *Redwood v. Council of the Dist. of Columbia*, 679 F.2d 931, 933 (D.C.Cir.1982). In *Neal v. Kelly*, 963 F.2d 453 (D.C.Cir.1992), we discussed the importance of providing pro se litigants with the necessary knowledge to participate effectively in the trial process. District courts do not need to provide detailed guidance to pro se litigants but should supply minimal notice of the consequences of not complying with procedural rules. See *Eldridge v. Block*, 832 F.2d 1132, 1136 (9th Cir.1987).The assistance provided by the district courts, however, "does not constitute a license for a plaintiff filing pro se to ignore the Federal Rules of Civil Procedure." *Jarrell v. Tisch*, 656 F. Supp. 237, 239 (D.D.C.1987).

III.

Although Moore's allegations in his complaint are sketchy, he appears to assert that Roskens and Wachtenheim, acting in bad faith and with malice, caused his termination and interfered with future job prospects. Assuming, without deciding, that their actions violated his constitutional rights, Moore must nonetheless satisfy this circuit's heightened pleading standard applicable to *Bivens* actions in order to overcome their defense of qualified immunity.[5] To meet the heightened pleading standard, Moore must produce " 'some direct evidence that the officials' actions were improperly motivated . . . if the case is to proceed to trial.' " *Whitacre v. Davey*, 890 F.2d 1168, 1171 (quoting *Martin v. District of Columbia Metro. Police Dep't*, 812 F.2d 1425, 1435 (D.C.Cir.1987)). Moore concedes that his complaint does not meet this standard. He contends, however, that the district court should have alerted him to the defects and allowed him to amend his complaint.

We have long recognized that leave to amend a complaint "shall be freely given when justice so requires." *Wyant v. Crittenden*, 113 F.2d 170, 175 (D.C.Cir.1940); Fed. R. Civ. P. 15(a). As we noted in *Wyant*, this principle "would appear to be particularly appropriate when the party seeking to amend is permitted to proceed in forma pauperis and, because of his circumstances, does so without benefit of counsel."

Moreover, the district court should give the pro se litigant at least minimal notice of our pleading requirements. In *Hudson v. Hardy*, 412 F.2d 1091, 1094 (D.C.Cir.1968), we held that "before entering summary judgment against [a pro se prisoner] appellant, the District Court, as a bare minimum, should have provided him with fair notice

---

5. In *Bivens v. Six Unknown Named Agents of Fed. Bureau of Narcotics*, 403 U.S. 388, 29 L. Ed. 2d 619, 91 S. Ct. 1999 (1971), the Supreme Court held that a plaintiff may recover money damages from federal officers who violate his constitutional rights.

of the requirements of the summary judgment rule." The form of notice must be "sufficiently understandable to one in appellant's circumstances fairly to apprise him of what is required." Id. The same principle applies here. Because there is no indication that any of the defendants would have been prejudiced by allowing Moore leave to amend or that amendment would have been futile, the district court should have permitted Moore to amend his complaint.

To sum up, we remand so that the district court, applying section 1391(b) as amended, can reconsider whether venue lies in this jurisdiction. If the district court concludes that venue does lie, it should then allow Moore to correct his service of process and to amend his complaint in order to comply with this circuit's heightened pleading standard.[8]

Sutton v. Duke

Supreme Court of North Carolina, 1970.
277 N.C. 94, 176 S.E.2d 161.

At the October 1969 Session of Greene, defendants demurred to plaintiff's complaint (filed 27 June 1969) upon the ground that it failed to state a cause of action. Hubbard, J., sustained the demurrers and dismissed the action. In an opinion filed 31 December 1969 the Court of Appeals reversed; upon defendants' petition we allowed certiorari.

In summary the complaint alleges: About 9:20 p.m. on 22 April 1967 plaintiff's automobile, which he was operating at 50 MPH on Rural Paved Road 1743 in Greene County, collided with a mule which belonged to W.I. Herring. The mule was at large in consequence of the following series of events. Defendant Marvin Duke, the president of defendant Kinston Fertilizer Company, owned a white pony. On 22 April 1967, and for sometime prior thereto, the pony was kept about 100 feet from Road No. 1743 within a one-acre enclosure on the premises of defendant Fertilizer Company. Inside the fenced area were storage and other facilities used by Fertilizer Company for business purposes. The tracks of defendant Seaboard Coast Line Railroad ran beside the enclosure and a spur track extended into the stockade through a gate. From time to time defendant Railroad delivered fertilizer and other supplies over the spur track to Fertilizer Company's storehouse in the enclosure.

All defendants and their agents knew that the pony was kept within the fenced area and that it would likely run at large if the gate was left open. On 22 April 1967 defendant Railroad delivered a carload of materials and supplies to Fertilizer Company, and "the defendants jointly and severally through their respective servants and agents and the said Marvin Duke, individually, said agents and servants then and

8. We note that the Supreme Court recently rejected a heightened pleading requirement as applied to an entity, not an individual, defendant. See *Leatherman v. Tarrant* *County Narcotics Intelligence & Coordination Unit,* 507 U.S. 163, 122 L. Ed. 2d 517, 113 S. Ct. 1160, 1162 (1993).

there acting within the scope of and pursuant to their employment, did negligently and carelessly and unlawfully leave the gate to the enclosure wherein said pony was customarily retained, open, enabling said pony to escape and run at large.''

On the opposite side of Road No. 1745, about 500 yards from the enclosure where the white pony was kept, Mr. Herring maintained an enclosure in which he kept four mules. Just before 8:00 p.m. on 22 April 1967, the pony, which was "being negligently permitted to run at large," came to the vicinity of the mule lot. There the pony "did agitate, excite, and attract said mules * * * in such a way that the said mules were caused to break down and break out of the Herring enclosure." Thereafter three of the mules ran at large, and plaintiff struck one of them at a point about three-fourths of a mile from the place where the animals were customarily retained and about 300 feet south of the intersection of N.C. Highway No. 91 with Rural Paved Road No. 1745. Plaintiff, traveling north, met and passed an automobile with its headlights burning. As the two cars came abreast, plaintiff saw a mule standing in his lane of traffic. Despite his efforts to avoid striking the mule, he collided with it. The collision wrecked his car and caused him serious and permanent personal injuries. He was damaged in the sum of $130,000.00.

Defendants demurred to the complaint upon the ground that their alleged acts and omissions, if they constituted negligence, were not a proximate cause of plaintiff's injuries.

Sharp, Justice. The demurrer in this case was interposed under G.S. § 1–127(6). This section was repealed by N.C.Sess.L. ch. 934, § 4(1967), which enacted the new North Carolina Rules of Civil Procedure (NCRCP). These rules became effective 1 January 1970 and were made applicable "to actions and proceedings pending on that date as well as to actions and proceedings commenced on and after that date." N.C.Sess.L. ch. 803 (1969). The decision of the Court of Appeals, which reversed the trial court's judgment sustaining the demurrer and dismissing the action, was filed 31 December 1969. Thus, this appeal was caught *in limine* by Rule 7(c) which says, "Demurrers, pleas and exceptions for insufficiency shall not be used."

When, however, a pleader has failed "to state a claim upon which relief can be granted," his adversary is now permitted by Rule 12(b)(6) to assert that defense either in a responsive pleading or by motion to dismiss.

Accordingly we treat the demurrer in this case as a motion to dismiss under our Rule 12(b)(6) and consider whether plaintiff has stated in his complaint "a claim upon which relief can be granted." Our general directive is Rule 8(a)(1) which requires that any "pleading which sets forth a claim for relief * * * shall contain (1) A short and plain statement of the claim *sufficiently particular to give the court and the parties notice of the transactions, occurrences, or series of transactions or occurrences, intended to be proved* showing that the pleader is entitled to relief, and (2) A demand for judgment for the relief to which he deems himself entitled. * * * "(Emphasis added.) This rule replaces G.S. § 1–122 (repealed 1 January 1970), which provided that "the complaint must contain * * * a plain and concise statement of the facts constituting a cause of action. * * * "

* * *

By repealing G.S. § 1–122, which required a complaint to state "the facts constituting a cause of action," and substituting in lieu thereof the requirement that a "claim for relief" shall be stated with sufficient particularity to give *notice* of the events intended to be proved showing that the pleader is entitled to relief, the legislature obviously intended to change our prior law. We do not assume its choice of "new semantics" was either accidental or casual. Considering the inspiration, origin, and legislative history of the NCRCP and the absence from it of the words "facts" and the phrase "facts constituting a cause of action" we conclude that the legislature intended to relax somewhat the strict requirements of detailed *fact* pleading and to adopt the concept of "notice pleading." However, the additional requirements in our Rule 8(a)(1) manifest the legislative intent to require a more specific statement, or notice in more detail, than Federal Rule 8(a)(2) requires.

* * *

The attempts of the federal court to state the scope and philosophy of their rules was summarized by Mister Justice Black in Conley v. Gibson, 355 U.S. 41, 78 S.Ct. 99, 2 L.Ed.2d 80, the case most frequently cited and quoted on the point we consider here. Speaking for a unanimous Court, he said: " * * * [T]he Federal Rules of Civil Procedure do not require a claimant to set out in detail the facts upon which he bases his claim. To the contrary, all the Rules require is 'a short and plain statement of the claim' that will give the defendant fair notice of what the plaintiff's claim is and the grounds upon which it rests. The illustrative forms appended to the Rules plainly demonstrate this. Such simplified 'notice pleading' is made possible by the liberal opportunity for discovery and the other pretrial procedures established by the Rules to disclose more precisely the basis of both claim and defense and to define more narrowly the disputed facts and issues." Id. at 17–18, 78 S.Ct. at 103. Thus, under the federal rules "a case consists not in the pleadings, but in the evidence, for which the pleadings furnish the basis." De Loach v. Crowleys, Inc., 128 F.2d 378 (5th Cir.1942).

Under the "notice theory of pleading" a statement of claim is adequate if it gives sufficient notice of the claim asserted "to enable the adverse party to answer and prepare for trial, to allow for the application of the doctrine of res judicata, and to show the type of case brought. * * * " Moore § 8.13. "Mere vagueness or lack of detail is not ground for a motion to dismiss." Such a deficiency "should be attacked by a motion for a more definite statement." Moore § 12.08 and cases cited therein.

In further appraising the sufficiency of a complaint Mister Justice Black said, in Conley v. Gibson, *supra,* 355 U.S. at 45–46, 78 S.Ct. at 102, "[W]e follow, of course, the accepted rule that a complaint should not be dismissed for failure to state a claim unless it appears beyond doubt that the plaintiff can prove no set of facts in support of his claim which would entitle him to relief." "This rule," said the Court in American Dairy Queen Corporation v. Augustyn, D.C., 278 F.Supp. 717, "generally precludes dismissal except in those instances where the face of the complaint discloses some insurmountable bar to recovery." If the complaint discloses an unconditional affirmative defense which defeats the claim asserted or pleads facts which deny the right to any relief on the alleged claim it will be dismissed. Moore § 12.08 summarizes the federal decisions as follows: " 'A [complaint] may be dismissed on motion if clearly without any merit; and this want of merit may consist in an absence of law to support a claim of the sort made, or of facts sufficient to make a good claim, or in the disclosure of some fact which will necessarily defeat the claim.' But a complaint should not be dismissed for insufficiency *unless it appears to a certainty that plaintiff is entitled to no relief under any state of facts which could be proved in support of the claim."*

Since the sufficiency of a statement will vary with the circumstances of each case, generalizations by the court are of little more help to a pleader than the rules themselves.

* * *

The difference in the degree of specificity required by the NCRCP, CPLR, and the Federal Rules cannot be formularized. It is best realized by a comparison of the various forms of complaint illustrating the respective rules. * * * Under the "notice theory" of pleading contemplated by Rule 8(a)(1), detailed fact-pleading is no longer required. A pleading complies with the rule if it gives sufficient notice of the events or transactions which produced the claim to enable the adverse party to understand the nature of it and the basis for it, to file a responsive pleading, and—by using the rules provided for obtaining pretrial discovery—to get any additional information he may need to prepare for trial.

At the beginning of this opinion we noted that the motion to dismiss, which tested "the legal sufficiency of the complaint," performed a function of the demurrer under the former practice. The motion to dismiss, however, will *only* be allowed when, under the former practice, a demurrer would have been sustained because the complaint affirmatively disclosed that the plaintiff had no cause of action against the defendant.

If the complaint disclosed "a defective cause of action" no amendment could supply the deficiency, and the action was dismissed.

If, on the contrary, the complaint contained "a defective statement of a good cause of action," that is, if it was deficient in factual allegations which presumably could be supplied, the demurrer was sustained but plaintiff was allowed to amend.

When Rule 7(c) abolished demurrers and decreed that pleas "for insufficiency shall not be used" it also abolished the concept of "a defective statement of a good cause of action." Thus, generally speaking, the motion to dismiss under Rule 12(b)(6) may be successfully interposed to a complaint which states a defective claim or cause of action but not to one which was formerly labeled a "defective statement of a good cause of action." For such complaint, as we have already noted, other provisions of Rule 12, the rules governing discovery, and the motion for summary judgment provide procedures adequate to supply information not furnished by the complaint.

We come now to the specific question in the instant case, do the facts alleged absolutely absolve defendants of legal responsibility for plaintiff's collision with the Herring mule? Had the pony suddenly appeared on the highway in front of plaintiff's automobile it is clear that all those whose negligence was responsible for permitting it to escape would be liable to plaintiff for the injuries resulting from his collision with it. One who fails to close the gate which provides ingress and egress to an enclosure in which he knows a pony is kept, can reasonably anticipate that it will escape and run at large. He can also reasonably foresee the probability that the animal will go upon a nearby highway and cause injury to travelers and vehicles thereon. However, it was not the pony with which plaintiff collided; it was a mule which—along with three others—became so excited by the presence of the pony at large outside the mule enclosure that it broke out, wandered onto the highway three-fourths of a mile away, and caused the collision in which plaintiff was injured.

On the facts alleged, we can assume that "but for" defendants' negligence in permitting the pony to escape the mules would not have broken out and that plaintiff would not have collided with one of them. The question remains, however, whether defendants' negligence was a proximate, or legal, cause of the collision, that is, whether the law extends their responsibility to such a consequence.

In this jurisdiction, to warrant a finding that negligence, not amounting to a wilful or wanton wrong, was a proximate cause of an injury, it must appear that the tortfeasor should have reasonably foreseen that injurious consequences were likely to follow from his negligent conduct. It is not necessary that a defendant anticipate the particular consequences which ultimately result from his negligence. It is only required "that a person of ordinary prudence could have reasonably foreseen that such a result, *or some similar injurious result,* was probable under the facts as they existed." (Italics ours) Adams v. State Board of Education, 248 N.C. 506, 103 S.E.2d 854; 3 Strong. N.C. Index Negligence § 7 (1960). However, we have also said that a defendant is liable for the consequences of his negligence if he "might have foreseen that some injury would result from his act or omission, or that *consequences of a generally injurious nature* might have been expected." (Emphasis added) Williams v. Boulerice, 268 N.C. 62, 149 S.E.2d 590. * * *

Definitions and general statements made with reference to specific situations are of little help in those cases in which the defendant's negligence is followed, not by reasonably foreseeable consequences but by events which, prima facie, he could not have anticipated. * * *

On the basis of the facts which plaintiff has alleged it would seem that the "mule delivery" was a consequence of the pony's escape which could not reasonably have been foreseen. However, we cannot say on the basis of the "bare bones pleadings" that plaintiff cannot prove otherwise, or that he can prove no facts which would entitle him to recover from defendants (or some of them) for the damages resulting from the collision. To dismiss the action now would be "to go too fast too soon." Barber v. Motor Vessel "Blue Cat," 372 F.2d 626, 629 (5th Cir.1967). This case is not yet ripe for a determination that there can be no liability as a matter of law. *Inter alia,* these questions arise: Had the pony ever escaped and agitated the Herring mules prior to 22 April 1967? If so, did defendants, or any of them, know of the incident? Did defendants have any reason to believe that the Herring fence was inadequate to confine the mules? Had the mules, to the knowledge of defendants, ever escaped before?

We hold that the face of the complaint shows no insurmountable bar to recovery on the claim alleged and that it gives defendants sufficient notice of the nature and basis of plaintiff's claim to enable them to answer and to prepare for trial. Indeed, defendants Duke and Fertilizer Company have not only filed answers; each has filed a third-party complaint against W.I. Herring. By utilizing the discovery rules defendants may ascertain more precisely the details of plaintiff's claim and whether he can prove facts which will entitle him to have a jury decide the merits of his claim.

Affirmed.

2.   Special Matters

Leatherman v. Tarrant County Narcotics Intelligence and Coordination Unit

Supreme Court of the United States, 1993.
507 U.S. 163, 113 S. Ct. 1160, 122 L.Ed. 2d 517.

■ CHIEF JUSTICE REHNQUIST delivered the opinion of the Court.

We granted certiorari to decide whether a federal court may apply a "heightened pleading standard"—more stringent than the usual pleading requirements of Rule 8(a) of the Federal Rules of Civil Procedure—in civil rights cases alleging municipal liability under 42 U.S.C. § 1983. We hold it may not.

We review here a decision granting a motion to dismiss, and therefore must accept as true all the factual allegations in the complaint. See *United States v. Gaubert*, 499 U.S. 315, 113 L. Ed. 2d 335, 111 S. Ct. 1267 (1991). This action arose out of two separate incidents involving the execution of search warrants by local law enforcement officers.

Each involved the forcible entry into a home based on the detection of odors associated with the manufacture of narcotics. One homeowner claimed that he was assaulted by the officers after they had entered; another claimed that the police had entered her home in her absence and killed her two dogs. Plaintiffs sued several local officials in their official capacity and the county and two municipal corporations that employed the police officers involved in the incidents, asserting that the police conduct had violated the Fourth Amendment to the United States Constitution. The stated basis for municipal liability under *Monell v. New York City Dept. of Social Services*, 436 U.S. 658, 56 L. Ed. 2d 611, 98 S. Ct. 2018 (1978), was the failure of these bodies adequately to train the police officers involved.

The United States District Court for the Northern District of Texas ordered the complaints dismissed, because they failed to meet the "heightened pleading standard" required by the decisional law of the Court of Appeals for the Fifth Circuit. The Fifth Circuit, in turn, affirmed the judgment of dismissal, and we granted certiorari to resolve a conflict among the Courts of Appeals concerning the applicability of a heightened pleading standard to § 1983 actions alleging municipal liability. Compare, e. g., *Karim-Panahi v. Los Angeles Police Dept.*, 839 F.2d 621, 624 (9th Cir.1988) ("a claim of municipal liability under section 1983 is sufficient to withstand a motion to dismiss even if the claim is based on nothing more than a bare allegation that the individual officers' conduct conformed to official policy, custom, or practice"). We now reverse.

Respondents seek to defend the Fifth Circuit's application of a more rigorous pleading standard on two grounds. First, respondents claim that municipalities' freedom from respondeat superior liability, see *Monell*, supra, necessarily includes immunity from suit. In this sense, respondents assert, municipalities are no different from state or local officials sued in their individual capacity. Respondents reason that a more relaxed pleading requirement would subject municipalities to expensive and time consuming discovery in every § 1983 case, eviscerating their immunity from suit and disrupting municipal functions.

This argument wrongly equates freedom from liability with immunity from suit. To be sure, we reaffirmed in *Monell* that "a municipality cannot be held liable under § 1983 on a respondeat superior theory." 436 U.S. at 691. But, contrary to respondents' assertions, this protection against liability does not encompass immunity from suit. Indeed, this argument is flatly contradicted by Monell and our later decisions involving municipal liability under § 1983. These decisions make it quite clear that, unlike various government officials, municipalities do not enjoy immunity from suit—either absolute or qualified—under § 1983. In short, a municipality can be sued under § 1983, but it cannot be held liable unless a municipal policy or custom caused the constitutional injury. We thus have no occasion to consider whether our qualified immunity jurisprudence would require a heightened pleading in cases involving individual government officials.

Second, respondents contend that the Fifth Circuit's heightened pleading standard is not really that at all. According to respondents, the degree of factual specificity required of a complaint by the Federal Rules of Civil Procedure varies according to the complexity of the underlying substantive law. To establish municipal liability under § 1983, respondents argue, a plaintiff must do more than plead a single instance of misconduct. This requirement, respondents insist, is consistent with a plaintiff's Rule 11 obligation to make a reasonable pre-filing inquiry into the facts.

But examination of the Fifth Circuit's decision in this case makes it quite evident that the "heightened pleading standard" is just what it purports to be: a more demanding rule for pleading a complaint under § 1983 than for pleading other kinds of claims for relief. This rule was adopted by the Fifth Circuit in *Elliott v. Perez*, 751 F.2d 1472 (1985), and described in this language:

> "In cases against government officials involving the likely defense of immunity we require of trial judges that they demand that the plaintiff's complaints state with factual detail and particularity the basis for the claim which necessarily includes why the defendant-official cannot successfully maintain the defense of immunity." Id., at 1473.

In later cases, the Fifth Circuit extended this rule to complaints against municipal corporations asserting liability under § 1983. See, e.g., *Palmer v. San Antonio*, 810 F.2d 514 (1987).

We think that it is impossible to square the "heightened pleading standard" applied by the Fifth Circuit in this case with the liberal system of "notice pleading" set up by the Federal Rules. Rule 8(a)(2) requires that a complaint include only "a short and plain statement of the claim showing that the pleader is entitled to relief." In *Conley v. Gibson*, 355 U.S. 41, 2 L.Ed.2d 80, 78 S.Ct. 99 (1957), we said in effect that the Rule meant what it said:

> "The Federal Rules of Civil Procedure do not require a claimant to set out in detail the facts upon which he bases his claim. To the contrary, all the Rules require is 'a short and plain statement of the claim' that will give the defendant fair notice of what the plaintiff's claim is and the grounds upon which it rests." Id. at 47 (footnote omitted).

Rule 9(b) does impose a particularity requirement in two specific instances. It provides that "in all averments of fraud or mistake, the circumstances constituting fraud or mistake shall be stated with particularity." Thus, the Federal Rules do address in Rule 9(b) the question of the need for greater particularity in pleading certain actions, but do not include among the enumerated actions any reference to complaints alleging municipal liability under § 1983. *Expressio unius est exclusio alterius.*

The phenomenon of litigation against municipal corporations based on claimed constitutional violations by their employees dates from our decision in *Monell*, supra, where we for the first time construed § 1983 to allow such municipal liability. Perhaps if Rules 8 and 9 were re-written today, claims against municipalities under § 1983 might be subjected to the added specificity requirement of Rule 9(b). But that is a result which must be obtained by the process of amending the Federal Rules, and not by judicial interpretation. In the absence of such an amendment, federal courts and litigants must rely on summary judgment and control of discovery to weed out unmeritorious claims sooner rather than later.

QUESTIONS

1. Articulate the distinction Justice Rehnquist makes between "freedom from liability" and "immunity from suit". How do these substantive law concepts relate to a heightened pleading standard? If government officials, unlike municipal governments, do have a qualified immunity from suit, how would *Leatherman* affect the application of a heightened pleading requirement to suits against such officials?

2. Look up the phrase *"expressio unius est exclusio alterius"*. State in English the statutory construction argument being made by the Court.

NOTE ON *LEATHERMAN* AND HEIGHTENED PLEADING

Noting that *Leatherman* expressly left the question open, a number of circuits have continued to require a heightened pleading standard for claims against government officials who have qualified immunity. See, *Moore v. Agency for International Development*, 994 F. 2d 874 (D.C.Cir.1993), *Branch v. Tunnell*, 14 F.3d 449 (9th Cir.1994). In *Castro v. United States*, 34 F. 3d 106 (2d Cir.1994), the Second Circuit refused to apply a heightened pleading requirement in a § 1983 action where the claims against individual defendants were subject to qualified immunity. The court stated that "qualified immunity is an affirmative defense that a defendant has the burden of pleading in his answer" and that, plaintiff "need not plead facts showing the absence of such a defense." Id. at 111. The opinion did not mention *Leatherman*.

In other contexts, however, *Leatherman* has been cited to reject heightened pleading requirements for matter not expressly subjected to the specificity requirements of Rule 9. *Mendocino Environmental Ctr. v. Mendocino Cty.*, 14 F.3d 457 (9th Cir.1994), *Adams v. Watson*, 10 F.3d 915 (1st Cir.1993), *Mid America Title Co. v. Kirk*, 991 F.2d 417, 422 (7th Cir.1993).

NOTE: IS FACT PLEADING BEING REVIVED?

I. Testing the Complaint

F.R.C.P. 8(a)(2) describes what plaintiff should include in the complaint. The illustrative forms appended to the Rules make clear the simplicity and the brevity that is intended. The elaborate provisions for discovery are intended to provide the litigants with detailed information relevant to the lawsuit.

Suppose plaintiff does not comply with the mandate of Rule 8(a). In the rare case that a complaint is "so vague or ambiguous" that the defendant cannot frame a responsive pleading, Rule 8(e) provides for a motion for a more definite statement.

This is a little used device. The standard for granting the motion is quite rigorous and it is doubtful that granting the motion accomplishes very much.

Of greater significance is the motion to dismiss for failure to state a claim upon which relief can be granted, Rule 12(b)(6). The standard for grant of the motion is not explicit in the text of the rule. Long ago the Supreme Court articulated a test intended to discourage fruitless skirmishing about the language of the pleading, jousting that serves primarily to delay rather than to expedite disposition of the case. In Conley v. Gibson, 355 U.S. 41, 78 S.Ct. 99, 2 L.Ed.2d 80 (1957), the Court said that a complaint should be dismissed under 12(b)(6) only if it appears "beyond doubt that the plaintiff can prove no set of facts in support of his claim which would entitle him to relief."

In Car Carriers, Inc. v. Ford Motor Co., 745 F.2d 1101, 1106 (7th Cir.1984), an anti-trust case, the court acknowledged the statement of the Supreme Court, indeed quoted it, but added: "Nevertheless, as this court has recognized, *Conley* has never been interpreted literally." Instead, the opinion goes on, the complaint "must contain either direct or inferential allegations respecting all the material elements necessary to sustain a recovery under *some* viable legal theory."

What accounts for this remarkable, but by no means atypical statement of the court of appeals? Is the answer to be found in the subject matter of the litigation? The Federal rules are said to be trans-substantive, that is applicable without regard to the subject matter of the litigation. Is that an oversimplification? Or do attitudes toward the desirable level of specificity in pleading swing, pendulum-like, from time to time?

We turn to an analysis of the underlying dynamics, the concerns which make for changing judicial attitudes on the contemporary scene.

II.   Pleading Requirements as a Function of Time and Money

We need not rehearse why it was that the Federal Rules chose to deemphasize pleading and to rely instead on discovery to provide for adequate preparation for trial. But discovery proved expensive and the more unfocused the pleadings the wider the permissible range of discovery. The cost of litigation was escalating, particularly in complex cases. Moreover, managing such cases, including the resolution of discovery disputes, was burdensome for the judges, a situation aggravated by mounting caseloads. Were there cases in which it would be useful to demand greater specificity in plaintiff's pleading?

In an important article, The Revival of Fact Pleading under the Federal Rules of Civil Procedure, 86 Colum.L.Rev. 433, 436 (1986), Professor Richard Marcus identifies two broad categories of such cases: "those in which more specificity is likely to disclose a fatal defect in a plaintiff's case, and those in which sufficient detail will enable the court to make a reliable determination that defendant did not violate plaintiff's rights."

In terms of the subject matter of the litigation, Professor Marcus found that the decisions generally fell into one of three categories: securities fraud, civil rights, and conspiracy cases.

Will the effort prove successful? Are there alternative devices such as summary judgment or sanctions for frivolous complaints that are preferable? Writing of the 1983 amendments to the Federal Rules of Civil Procedure, the reporter to the Advisory Committee on Civil Rules, Professor Arthur Miller, had this to say about 12(b)(6) motions: "a wonderful tool on paper, but have you ever looked at the batting average of rule 12(b)(6) motions? I think it was last effectively used during the McKinley administration." (Quoted in Marcus, supra at 444–445.) This hardly ends the inquiry, but it does help define it.

One is reminded of the observation of Professor Judith Resnik that "The history of procedure is a series of attempts to solve the problems created by the preceding generation's procedural reforms." (Tiers, 57 S.Cal.L.Rev. 837, 1030 (1984)) This is hardly an argument for the status quo, whatever it may be. Perhaps it is appropriate to inquire whether the end result of change, or a series of changes, is to facilitate access to justice and to enhance the quality of justice once access is gained.

Finally, one should consider the impact on pleading of the disclosure provisions of F.R.C.P. 26(a), which are discussed extensively in Chapter IV. That Rule mandates the initial disclosure, by each party, of specified information "relevant to disputed facts alleged with particularity in the pleadings." Does this provide litigants with a new and powerful incentive to go beyond notice pleading and allege with particularity as many facts as possible?

Varley v. Motyl

Supreme Court of Connecticut, 1952.
139 Conn. 128, 90 A.2d 869.

■ JENNINGS, ASSOCIATE JUSTICE. This is an action for personal injuries, allegedly sustained by the plaintiffs on December 25, 1945, when their automobile, which had stopped in a line of traffic, was negligently bumped from the rear by the defendants' car. * * *

The other exception concerns a single ruling upon evidence relating to John's heart condition. His attorney in the course of his examination of John asked: "And your heart condition since this accident, will you tell us up to the present time has it been better or worse than it was prior to the accident?" Counsel for the defendants objected, stating: "There is no claim in the complaint of an aggravation of a pre-existing heart condition * * *. At no time in this complaint did Mr. Cole ever disclose that his client had a pre-existing heart condition which he claimed was aggravated by the accident." To this John's counsel replied that he did not so claim, "because the man had no trouble with his heart with the exception of a mild attack three years before and the attack in 1940. Other than that he had no heart condition." The court allowed the question and John answered: "Worse than it was before." The only material allegation in the complaint is that the injuries sustained in the accident "affected and injured his heart." The importance of determining whether or not, in the absence of any allegation thereof in the complaint, John was entitled to prove that the pre-existing diseased condition of his heart was aggravated by the accident is clear.

Whether the court erred in admitting this evidence depends upon the answer to the question whether the allegation in the complaint that the accident affected and injured John's heart lays a proper foundation for evidence of the aggravation of a pre-existing heart condition. The admissibility of this evidence has been argued as though the only question was whether the damage claimed was special, requiring a specific allegation, or general. Ordinarily, such things as loss of earnings, doctors' and hospital bills are referred to as special damages. Since they do not necessarily follow an injury, the defendant is entitled to notice of them by a special allegation. Tomlinson v. Derby, 43 Conn. 562, 567. An injury to the heart, for example, does not necessarily follow an accident either. John therefore properly alleged injury to his heart as special damage. The question is not between special and general damages. It is whether the complaint containing this allegation gave sufficient notice of the type of injury which would be claimed. * * *

There is authority for the defendants' position that the aggravation of a pre-existing condition must be specially alleged. Littman v. Bell Telephone Co., 315 Pa. 370, 380, 172 A. 687; Samuels v. New York Rys. Corporation, 226 App.Div. 94, 96, 234 N.Y.S. 377. In most of the states, evidence offered under circumstances similar to those in the case at bar is admitted. St. Louis Trust Co. v. Murmann, 90 Mo.App. 555, 559; Leingang v. Geller, Ward & Hasner Hardware Co., 335 Mo. 549, 556, 73 S.W.2d 256; Conrad v. Shuford, 174 N.C. 719, 720, 94 S.E. 424; Wadell v. Public Service Coordinated Transport, 3 N.J.Super. 132, 135, 65 A.2d 766; Virginia Ry. & Power Co. v. Hubbard, 120 Va. 664, 669, 91 S.E. 618; Frick v. Washington Water Power Co., 76 Wash. 12, 13, 135 P. 470. As is well pointed out in the dissent in this case, the complaint does not conform to good pleading. We hold, however, that the allegation that the defendants' negligence "affected and injured" John's heart was sufficient notice of a claim of aggravation of a pre-existing heart ailment. On the practical side it may be noted that few if any hearts are perfect after beating sixty-one years. It may be true that the defendants did not appreciate the fact that the injury to the heart alleged in the complaint might appear in evidence to be an injury in the nature of an aggravation of a pre-existing condition. They at least were fairly apprised that such might be the evidence and if they felt that the allegation was at all ambiguous they were privileged to move for a more specific statement.

There is error on the appeal of John Varley and the case is remanded with direction to enter judgment on the verdict. * * *

■ BROWN, CHIEF JUSTICE (dissenting). * * * It is my conclusion that the court committed reversible error in that case, as claimed by the defendants' bill of exceptions, in allowing John, hereinafter called the plaintiff, to testify to aggravation of a pre-existing heart condition as an element of damage and that, in consequence, by setting aside the verdict it reached the correct result. * * *

The controlling rule of law in this jurisdiction as to the necessity and manner of pleading special damage and the reasons for it are succinctly stated in Tomlinson v. Derby, 43 Conn. 562. As we there say 43 Conn. at page 566, in this state "we still adhere closely to the technical rule of the common law, that where the damages are special the matter must be distinctly averred in the declaration in order to apprise the defendant of the nature of the claim." As we further say 43 Conn. at page 567, with reference to the need and the nature of the averments so required, "[i]t is difficult to lay down any general rule by which to determine when the law implies the damage and when it does not. It would seem however that *when the consequences of an* *injury are peculiar to the circumstances and condition of the injured party,* the law could not imply the damage simply from the act causing the injury" (italics supplied). By the same token, the law cannot imply "aggravation of a pre-existing heart condition" simply from the fact that the plaintiff's heart was "affected and injured." That this is so is emphasized by our further statement in the Tomlinson case 43 Conn. p. 567, that "the sole object of the rule that requires special damage to be averred is to advise the defendant of the claim." The factual situation which existed in the instant case cogently illustrates how well founded is this reason for the rule. It is hard to conceive of a more apt and accurate description of the situation of this plaintiff than that stated in the words which I have italicized. * * *

* * * The allegations of injury sustained by both plaintiffs are identical, except that in John's complaint injury to "heart and lungs" is substituted for injury to "shoulder" and "abdomen" in Hilma's. With this qualification, the injuries alleged as to each would seem to include about all of the ills to which flesh could be heir in consequence of such an accident. The anatomical afflictions are enumerated ad nauseam and, as the record discloses, with but slight regard to what the evidence actually tended to prove. These ills of the plaintiffs are set forth in such detail that, as counsel well observed in argument, a motion for a "less" rather than a "more" specific statement would have to be utilized to ascertain what the plaintiffs' injuries really were.

This type of pleading, which might well be termed a common counts for negligence actions, is not designed to give the defendant the information to which he is entitled in order to prepare his defense properly. It is violative of the purpose and spirit of our rules of practice. It tends to needless trouble not only for opposing counsel but for the court as well. Allegations of personal injuries in a tort case should be confined to an honest and fair statement of what the attorney has reason to believe he can offer evidence to prove and ought not to omit the allegation of material factors as to damage upon which he expects to rely. * * *

While there is a conflict of authority upon the question whether aggravation of a pre-existing condition must be alleged to permit recovery for it, very substantial authority supports the conclusion which I have reached. Littman v. Bell Telephone Co., 315 Pa. 370, 380, 172 A. 687; * * *

NOTE

In suing on a written contract the plaintiff normally has the option of pleading the contract verbatim, or by exhibit or according to legal effect. See Form 3 of the Federal Rules of Civil Procedure and Advisory Committee Note 1 accompanying it.

Stern v. Leucadia Nat. Corp.

United States Court of Appeals, Second Circuit, 1988.
844 F.2d 997.

■ MAHONEY, CIRCUIT JUDGE:

Jonathan Stern brought this action on behalf of himself and a class of investors who purchased common stock of the GATX Corporation

("GATX") between January 9, 1986 and March 26, 1986, inclusive. Stern complained that defendants violated Section 10(b) of the Securities Exchange Act of 1934, 15 U.S.C. § 78j(b) (1982) ("Section 10(b)"), and Rule 10b–5 promulgated thereunder, 17 C.F.R. § 240.10b–5 (1987) ("Rule 10b–5"), by leading the investing public to believe that defendant Leucadia National Corporation ("Leucadia National") would merge with GATX, when in fact defendants sought only to inflate artificially the market price of GATX common stock, and thereafter to sell off their shares at a substantial profit.

Defendants moved to dismiss the complaint pursuant to Fed. R.Civ.P. 9(b) and 12(b)(6). The United States District Court for the Southern District of New York, Gerard L. Goettel, *Judge,* granted the motion, according plaintiff leave to replead within twenty days. Stern v. Leucadia Nat'l Corp., 644 F.Supp. 1108 (S.D.N.Y.1986). Upon the filing of the amended complaint, defendants moved to dismiss on the same grounds as before; in addition, defendants requested that sanctions be awarded under Fed.R.Civ.P. 11. By endorsement, the district court granted defendants' second motion to dismiss and awarded Rule 11 sanctions with respect to that motion.

Stern appeals. We affirm as to the dismissal, and reverse as to the sanctions.

I. BACKGROUND

Except for the allegations pertaining to Jonathan Stern and his counsel, plaintiff's amended complaint is pleaded entirely upon information and belief. In view of our disposition of this appeal, we assume the truth of his allegations.[1] * * *

A. *The Defendants*

Stern alleges that defendants Ian N. Cumming and Joseph S. Steinberg control an interlocking network consisting of the corporate defendants. * * *

Stern alleges that defendants conspired with, and aided and abetted, one another in violating Section 10(b) and Rule 10b–5, and that Leucadia National, Cumming and Steinberg were each a controlling person of each of the other defendants (except possibly Carl Marks) within the meaning of Section 20(a) of the Securities Exchange Act of 1934, 15 U.S.C. § 78t(a) (1982).

---

1. We note in this regard that the district court's dismissal of the amended complaint placed no reliance on the fact that virtually all of plaintiff's allegations were stated upon information and belief, nor do appellees urge the point here. The general rule (with certain exceptions), however, which we discuss in more detail hereinafter, is that fraud allegations premised upon information and belief do not satisfy Rule 9(b). Our consideration of appellant's claims on the merits under the circumstances of this appeal should not be construed to undermine that general rule, or to condone the practice of pleading virtually an entire fraud complaint upon information and belief.

B. *The Allegations of the Amended Complaint*

In light of our view of the noncompliance of plaintiff's amended complaint with Fed.R.Civ.P. 9(b), it is appropriate to outline the allegations of that complaint in some detail. That outline follows.

The Events

On January 9, 1986, Leucadia National, LNC, AIC, Charter, LI, Uintah and TLC (collectively the "Leucadia group") filed a Schedule 13D statement with the Securities and Exchange Commission reporting that they had purchased, or had acquired options to purchase, 5.26% of GATX's outstanding shares. The statement indicated that the Leucadia group deemed GATX's common stock undervalued, and might seek control of GATX. Preliminary to any such determination, the group stated it might explore the feasibility of various strategies for gaining control, including: (1) merger; (2) acquisition of additional GATX common or preferred stock (subject to its availability at favorable prices and the availability of any requisite financing) in open market or privately negotiated purchases, by tender offer, or otherwise; (3) solicitation of proxies to elect its nominees as directors of GATX; or (4) joining forces with interested third parties to obtain control of GATX. The group noted that, depending upon the course it chose, it might dispose of shares of GATX common stock in the open market, in privately negotiated transactions, or otherwise. The statement cautioned, however, "that the possible activities of [the Leucadia group] are subject to change at any time and there is no assurance that [it] will actually purchase any additional shares of the Common Stock or any shares of preferred stock or seek to influence or obtain control of [GATX]." The same day, the Dow Jones News Service ("DJNS") reported the Leucadia group's stake in GATX and its plans with respect thereto as described above. On January 10, GATX common closed at $38½ on the New York Stock Exchange ("NYSE"), up $3⅝ from its closing price the day before.

On January 30, 1986, the Leucadia group filed the first of seven amendments to the Schedule 13D statement[.]

* * *

On March 24, DJNS and the *Wall Street Journal* reported GATX's acceptance of Leucadia's cash merger proposal. The reports repeated that the merger was contingent on GATX shareholder approval and Leucadia's ability to obtain financing, and that Merrill Lynch was "highly confident" that the necessary financing could be obtained. According to the reports, the deadline for completing the definitive merger agreement was midnight on March 25, 1986.

On March 31, 1986, the Leucadia group filed the seventh and last amendment to its Schedule 13D statement, disclosing information which had already been reported by DJNS and the *Wall Street Journal* on March 26 and 27. The amendment stated that on March 25, Leucadia National had advised GATX that Leucadia National would require additional time to determine whether to proceed with the transaction because it had become evident that day that certain additional financing would be required; that Leucadia National had requested a seven day extension for consummation of a definite merger agreement; that GATX had refused that request on March 27; and that the Leucadia group would continue to evaluate the situation, and would specifically consider making another merger proposal to GATX, acquiring additional GATX common stock, or disposing of its holdings of GATX common stock.

Leucadia National stated that its need for additional financing and time arose from its sudden discovery, on March 25, that a merger with GATX would trigger a requirement that some of the latter's debt be paid on an accelerated basis.

The Allegations of Fraud

Plaintiff claims, however, that Leucadia never intended to merge with or otherwise acquire GATX, and never intended to seek additional financing during the requested extension. Plaintiff maintains that Leucadia's eleventh-hour discovery that additional financing would be necessary was "merely a pretext because Leucadia had long been in possession of all of GATX's debt documents and the alleged information suddenly discovered by Leucadia was not new or unusual * * *." * * *

Stern alleges that the defendants conspired, and aided and abetted one another, to create the impression, via their filings, that GATX was genuinely "in play," when in fact defendants intended only to inflate the market price of GATX's stock, and thereafter to extract greenmail from GATX or sell their holdings to another bidder for GATX at a premium. Thus, according to plaintiffs, defendants violated Section 10(b) and Rule 10b–5 because their filings, replete with material misstatements and omissions, led "the reasonable investor to believe that, subject to certain essentially mechanical conditions, defendants would seek to merge with GATX when in truth defendants had no genuine intention of carrying out the merger even were the announced conditions were [sic] met."

Plaintiff purchased his shares of GATX on March 3, 1986 at $41.50 per share. He sold his shares for $35.25 on April 8, 1986.

C. *Action by the District Court*

The district court dismissed Stern's original complaint, finding that it failed adequately to allege "the element of material representation or omission, and the element of reliance and causation," 644 F.Supp. at 1111, with respect to the Leucadia group; that the claim against the other defendants (with the exception of Carl Marks) rested "solely upon the vague allegation that they either control or are part of an interlocking network of corporations affecting the management of the signing defendants," 644 F.Supp. at 1112; and, as to Carl Marks, that plaintiff failed to allege facts indicating that Carl Marks' Schedule 14B filings "contained false or misleading material facts," or that Carl Marks conspired with, or aided or abetted, the other defendants, 644 F.Supp. at 1112.

The district court granted leave to amend within twenty days, "if such repleading can allege sufficient facts" in support of Stern's allegations. 644 F.Supp. at 1112. Plaintiff filed his amended complaint, which was very similar to the first, but contained some new matter, consisting essentially of (1) further elaboration concerning the alleged purpose of defendants' statements and omissions; (2) summaries and quotations of news reports and commentaries concerning defendants' bid for GATX, some of which referred to other occasions on which Leucadia National had assertedly received greenmail from corporate targets; (3) allegations that the Leucadia group had long known, because of its possession of the relevant GATX documents, that the accelerated payment of certain GATX debt would be required as a result of the merger, and its request for additional time to arrange financing was accordingly a pretext; and (4) an allegation concerning the increase in the price of GATX's common stock as a result of the initial filing of the Leucadia group's Schedule 13D statement.

Defendants renewed their motions to dismiss and requested sanctions. At the hearing on this motion, Judge Goettel announced that he would grant the motion to dismiss "entirely on the original opinion" and, deeming the amended complaint "repetitious", would "grant Rule 11 sanctions as to the costs for making the second motion to dismiss, but only the second motion." A corresponding endorsement was then entered. Upon application, Rule 11 sanctions were awarded in the amount of $7,500.00 for legal fees.

This appeal followed.

II. DISCUSSION

On appeal, Stern contends that the district court's Rule 12(b)(6) ruling improperly implicated factual issues more appropriately resolved on the merits by the trier of fact; that the complaint complied with Rule 9(b); and that sanctions were improperly imposed. We need address only the latter two contentions.

A. *The Sufficiency of the Complaint under Rule 9(b)*

As this court has recently observed, Fed.R.Civ.P. 9(b) is designed to further three goals: (1) providing a defendant fair notice of plaintiff's claim, to enable preparation of a defense; (2) protecting a defendant from harm to his reputation or goodwill; and (3) reducing the number of strike suits.

The Rule 9(b) balance has been struck in a number of ways. Thus, fraud pleadings generally cannot be based on information and belief. On the other hand, fraud allegations may be so pleaded as to facts peculiarly within the opposing party's knowledge; even then, however, the allegations must be accompanied by a statement of facts upon which the belief is founded. Further, Rule 9(b) permits "[m]alice, intent, knowledge, and other condition of mind" to be "averred generally." In this regard, we have noted that it would be unworkable and unfair to require great specificity in pleading scienter, since "a plaintiff realistically cannot be expected to plead a defendant's actual state of mind." Nonetheless, circumstances must be pleaded that provide a factual foundation for otherwise conclusory allegations of scienter.

Judged by these standards, we have no difficulty agreeing with the court below that Stern's amended complaint does not pass muster under Rule 9(b). It contains little by way of embellishment of the bald allegation that "Leucadia never had any intention of merging or otherwise acquiring GATX, never had any intention of merging or otherwise acquiring GATX at a price equivalent to $40 per share, [and] never had any intention of utilizing the requested extension to seek additional financing." It is not enough to quote press speculation about defendants' motives and press reports of other occasions on which Leucadia National assertedly obtained greenmail from other corporate targets. Nor does it suffice to assert conclusory suspicions as to defendants' motives based solely upon the fact that they had GATX's loan agreements for a considerable period of time before concluding that certain of their provisions would require additional financing for the proposed merger. Such allegations simply do not provide the "specific, well-pleaded facts" upon which Judge Goettel correctly insisted in offering plaintiff an opportunity to replead its complaint.

As the district court pointed out, furthermore, many of Stern's allegations undercut his claim of fraud. For example, (1) the Leucadia group's Schedule 13D statements were all conditional; (2) the earlier filings indicated that Leucadia might dispose of its stock instead of attempting to gain control of GATX; (3) later filings noted that Leucadia National cash merger proposal depended upon, *inter alia,* arrangement of financing and acquisition of shareholder approval; and (4) Leucadia National agreed to pay Merrill Lynch a substantial fee if it sold more than 51% of its holdings in GATX. *See generally* 644 F.Supp. at 1111. Finally, Leucadia National never called off the merger; it asked GATX for a brief extension of time to obtain additional financing, which GATX declined to provide.

We conclude that the district court correctly dismissed plaintiff's amended complaint for failure to comply with Fed.R.Civ.P. 9(b).

NOTE ON PLEADING SECURITIES FRAUD

Rule 9(b) clearly requires some form of heightened pleading in connection with fraud actions, including securities fraud claims such as those brought pursuant to Section 10(b) of the Securities Exchange Act of 1934 and Rule 10b–5 promulgated thereunder. There has been substantial disagreement, however, over how much specificity is required in such cases. Some courts have held that a statement of the "bare bones of the fraudulent scheme" is sufficient. *Morgan v. Kobrin Securities Inc.*, 649 F. Supp. 1023, 1028 (N.D.Ill.1986); *In Re Midlantic Corp. Shareholder Litigation*, 758 F. Supp. 226 (D.N.J.1990). Other courts have required that facts be pleaded which give rise to a strong inference of fraudulent intent. *In Re Gupta Corp. Securities Litig.*, 900 F. Supp. 1217, 1229 (N.D.Cal.1994).

The Private Securities Litigation Reform Act of 1995, passed by Congress over the veto of President Clinton, appears to resolve this issue. That statute adds a new section to the Securities Exchange Act of 1934, § 21D(b)(2), which requires that in any private action under the Securities Exchange Act for damages in which plaintiff must prove that defendant acted with a particular state of mind (i.e. scienter), the plaintiff must "state with particularity facts giving rise to a strong inference that defendant acted with the required state of mind." The statute goes on to state that "a court shall, on the motion of any defendant, dismiss the complaint if the requirements of [§ 21D(b)(2)] are not met." For a thorough discussion of the issues raised by this statute in light of prior case law, see Elliot J. Weiss, The New Securities Fraud Pleading Requirement: Speed Bump or Road Block?, 38 Ariz. L. Rev. 675 (1996).

In April 1997 the Securities and Exchange Commission filed a "Report to the President and the Congress on the First Year of Practice under the Private Securities Litigation Reform Act of 1995," as required by law. The report was quite tentative in tone, but it did make clear that the total number of companies sued in securities class actions in federal court was down for the twelve months following passage of the Act.

It was also pointed out that the number of such class actions filed in state court had apparently increased during the same period. In 1998, Congress sought to close this perceived "loophole" for avoiding the stricter federal pleading requirements by enacting the Securities Litigation Uniform Standards Act, which effectively prevented securities class action plaintiffs from filing their suits in state court. Since that time, there has been another marked increase in securities class actions filed in federal court, but there also appear to be an increased number of such cases being dismissed by federal courts at the pleading stage. See, Robert L. Sharpe Jr., Four Years After Securities Reform, Shareholder Suits Still Big Business, THE LEGAL INTELLIGENCER, (August 12, 1999) p.1.

* * *

NOTE: CONDITIONS PRECEDENT AND SUBSEQUENT

Liability under a contract, particularly an insurance policy, is frequently subject to the performance or occurrence of a large number of conditions: that the premiums have been paid in advance, that no gasoline or kerosene be stored on the premises insured against fire, that accounts of bonded employes be audited at specified intervals, that notice of loss be forwarded in writing to the company within a specified period. The law of contracts has categorized conditions as either conditions precedent as to which plaintiff had the burden of pleading and proving or conditions subsequent as to which defendant had those burdens.

A great deal of ink has been spilled over the years in the effort to describe how one tells which is which. Often it gets down to whether the contract utilized the words "provided that" rather than "except" in introducing the condition. Moreover, except for the burdens described above, it really made no difference; failure to perform or non-occurrence of a condition would have the same effect in law no matter how denominated.

F.R.C.P. 9(c) provides for a conclusory allegation by the plaintiff and specific allegations by the defendant if the performance or occurrence of any condition is to be put in issue. The respective burdens of proof remain unchanged. The rule applies equally to statutory conditions on the right to sue, as is true in litigation brought by the Equal Employment Opportunity Commission.

Howard v. Barr

United States District Court, Western District of Kentucky, 1953.
114 F.Supp. 48.

■ SHELBOURNE, CHIEF JUDGE. These actions were filed August 10, 1951, under the authority of Title 28 U.S.C.A. § 1332, to recover for personal injury and property damage alleged to have been sustained by the plaintiffs, husband and wife, in an accident which occurred on August 6, 1951, at the intersection of Clay Street and Fehr Avenue, in the City of Louisville, Kentucky. They have been consolidated for the purpose of hearing.[a]

* * *

The plaintiff Ozia C. Howard is entitled to recover damages from the defendant Orlin Barr in the amount of $500 for personal injuries and pain and suffering. He is not entitled to recover his medical expenses, since such are special damages and were not pleaded in his complaint. Rule 54(c), Rules of Civil Procedure * * *.[b]

C.　SANCTIONS FOR IMPROPER PLEADING: RULE 11

INTRODUCTORY NOTE TO RULE 11

Rule 11 of the Federal Rules of Civil Procedure was designed to deter frivolous, dishonest and otherwise improper pleading. It was totally ineffective. Indeed, for decades it was virtually ignored. In 1983, Rule 11 was amended. As amended, it specified that the signature on a pleading constituted a certificate by the signer, made after reasonable inquiry into both the law and the facts, that the pleading was well grounded and not filed for any improper purpose.

The amendment went further. It charged the trial judge with the obligation to act on her own motion if opposing parties chose to ignore the offense and, in addition, made the imposition of sanctions mandatory once a violation of the Rule had been found.

While the sanction imposed could be as mild as a reprimand, the 1983 Rule also included specific reference to assessing reasonable attorneys fees. In more than a few instances, sanctions of over $100,000 were imposed. Indeed, one study found an average sanction of over $44,000 and a median sanction of $5,000.

The profession was quite divided in its reaction to Rule 11. Books and articles poured forth—almost two dozen of the former and close to 125 of the latter between 1985 and 1990. Uniformity and predictability were hardly the hallmarks of implementation of the new rule. Some circuits were known as vigorously in favor of substantial sanctions, others as rather lenient. In addition, the attitudes of individual trial judges varied substantially.

In 1993 Rule 11 was amended again, and it is the 1993 version on which we will focus. To understand the 1993 changes, however, it is necessary to look back. The *George* case, with which the chapter opens, was decided under the 1983 version of the Rule. It is the operation of the 1983 Rule which is the subject of the Burbank

---

a. A default judgment was entered under F.R.C.P. 55(b)(2).

b. Some states now treat medical expenses for serious injuries as damages to be expected and therefore general.

study which follows *George*. *Cooter & Gell* is the Supreme Court's most extensive consideration of Rule 11 issues although, a we shall see, it too has been superseded to some extent by the 1993 revisions.

George v. Bethlehem Steel Corp.

United States District Court, Northern District of Indiana, 1987.
116 F.R.D. 628.

■ MOODY, DISTRICT JUDGE.

This matter comes before the court on defendant Bethlehem Steel Corporation's ("Bethlehem") petition for attorney fees and expenses filed April 30, 1987. Plaintiff George filed a "Motion to Strike, or in the Alternative, for More Particular Statement" on May 12, 1987. Subsequently, on June 29, 1987, Bethlehem filed a Supplemental Memorandum in Support of its original motion to which the plaintiff responded on July 14, 1987. The defendant replied to the plaintiff's response on July 21, 1987. For reasons discussed below, Bethlehem's motion for attorney's fees and expenses is GRANTED.

I.

Plaintiff George, a black male, filed his complaint in this action on July 23, 1985 alleging that Bethlehem, as his employer, violated Title VII, 42 U.S.C. §§ 2000e–5 *et seq.*, by failing to recall him on the basis of his race and sex. At the beginning of the trial, the court, as is its custom with *pro se* litigants, instructed plaintiff George on the relevant burdens of proof and his obligations as a plaintiff in a Title VII case. At trial, however, George offered only four documents and his own testimony in support of his case. Therefore, in an order dated June 16, 1987, the court found for defendant and concluded that plaintiff George lacked any factual basis to raise an inference of discrimination, let alone to file a federal lawsuit, against Bethlehem.

At the end of the trial, the court granted Bethlehem leave to file a petition for fees by May 1, 1987 and George was given until May 8, 1987 to respond. Bethlehem filed its petition for fees on April 30 and George moved to strike the petition for failure to provide the particularized grounds for the relief sought. Because neither party presented substantive arguments on whether the facts in this case warranted an award or sanction of fees, the court directed the parties attention to recent Seventh Circuit opinions. Both parties have now supplemented their previous motions with substantive arguments concerning the award of attorney's fees in this case.

II.

The defendant supports its request for fees and expenses pursuant to Rule 11 of the Federal Rules of Civil Procedure. In relevant part, Rule 11 provides:

[a] party who is not represented by an attorney shall sign his pleading, motion, or other paper and state his address ... [t]he signature of an attorney or party constitutes a certificate by him

that he has read the pleading, motion, or other paper; that to the best of his knowledge, information, and *belief formed after reasonable inquiry it is well grounded in fact and is warranted by existing law* or a good faith argument for the extension, modification, or reversal of existing law, and that it is not interposed for any improper purpose, such as to harass or to cause unnecessary delay or needless increase in the cost of litigation * * * [i]f a pleading, motion, or other paper is *signed in violation of this rule, the court, upon motion or upon its own initiative, shall impose upon the person who signed it, a represented party, or both, an appropriate sanction,* which may include an order to pay to the other party or parties the amount of the reasonable expenses incurred because of the filing of the pleading, motion, or other paper, including a reasonable attorney's fee. (emphasis added).

Rule 11 applies to *pro se* plaintiffs like Mr. George. Shrock v. Altru Nurses Registry, 810 F.2d 658 (7th Cir.1987). In *Shrock,* the court held that "Rule 11, as recently amended, by its terms requires—it does not merely permit—the district court to impose sanctions on a plaintiff who files a complaint without some minimum of previous investigation". *Id.* at 661.

Defendant Bethlehem alleges that plaintiff George failed to investigate the factual basis of the suit. In particular, Bethlehem argues that George knew all along that his Union, and not Bethlehem, decided who was to be recalled to work on the United Way campaign. Thus, if Bethlehem was to be held liable for discrimination, George was required to investigate the reasons for the Union's decision, determine that the Union acted unlawfully, and finally, show that Bethlehem should not have followed the Union's recommendation. George produced no evidence concerning the Union's conduct in this case.

Furthermore, as stated in this court's order dated June 16, 1987, the plaintiff failed to investigate the law required to prove discrimination in Title VII cases. A plaintiff bringing a Title VII case alleging unlawful discrimination must present evidence demonstrating actual discriminatory intent, or at least raising the inference of bad intent, on the part of the defendant. George presented no such evidence at trial. In fact, he offered no witnesses, apart from himself, and his documentary evidence was, at best, neutral. George presented no evidence showing that other union members, with recall rights identical to his own, were recalled while he was not.

Because the plaintiff did not make the minimum factual and legal investigation as required in Rule 11, he is subject to sanctions. In deciding whether to award defendants attorney's fees in civil rights cases, a district court must "strike a careful balance between the desire to encourage private litigants with valid claims to bring suit to indicate civil rights and the need to deter frivolous actions brought primarily to harass the defendant without hope of success." Coates v. Betchel, 811 F.2d 1045, 1049–50 (7th Cir.1987) (assessing fees under § 1988). The court is not insensitive to the possible chilling effect an imposition of sanctions might have in this case; quite to the contrary, the court holds that a "chilling" effect is most appropriate here.

"Mounting federal caseloads and growing public dissatisfaction with the costs and delays of litigation have made it imperative that the federal courts impose sanctions on persons and firms that abuse their right of access to these courts. The rules whether statutory or judge-made, designed to discourage groundless litigation are being and will continue to be enforced in this circuit to the hilt." Dries & Krump Mfg. v. International Ass'n. of Machinists, 802 F.2d 247, 255 (7th Cir.1986). Based on the foregoing, the court concludes that sanctions are warranted in this case.

III.

In its motion for sanctions, Bethlehem submitted a detailed summary of attorney's fees totall[ing] $8,938.50 and actual expenses of $667.08. Sanctions under Rule 11 serve several purposes including punishment, deterrence and compensation. A. Levin & S. Sobel, Achieving Balance in the Developing Law of Sanctions, 36 Cath. U.L.Rev. 587, 599 (1987). Generally, when assessing attorneys' fees under Rule 11, courts are concerned more with reasonableness and fairness in determining how large a sanction to impose, rather than with the actual fees incurred. Id. at 598–99 (citing United Food & Commercial Workers Union Local No. 115 v. Armour & Co., 106 F.R.D. 345, 349 (N.D.Cal.1985) ("rule 11 only authorizes 'reasonable' fees, not necessarily actual fees")).

In the present case, George has challenged neither the amount nor the accuracy of Bethlehem's fees and expenses; likewise, the court has no reason to doubt the defendant's assessment of its costs. Nevertheless, the court finds that a sanction of over $9,000.00 would be excessive in this case.

Two factors lead the court to this conclusion. First, although it is true that the court has found that this action was frivolous and that George was under a duty to cease the pursuit [of] his claim much sooner, there is a correlative duty on defendants of a frivolous lawsuit to use reasonable means to terminate litigation and to prevent the costs of a frivolous suit from becoming excessive. United Foods, 106 F.R.D. at 348.

> The duty is one of mitigation * * * [i]f a party eventually wins rule 11 sanctions, but has failed to use the least expensive route to early resolution, the court may rule that not all the expenses the successful party incurred in making formal motions were reasonable attorney's fees that should be awarded under rule 11.

Id., see also Michigan National Bank v. Kroger, Co., 619 F.Supp. 1149, 1159 (D.C.Mich.1985). Here, Bethlehem did file a motion to dismiss before trial, however, its motion did not address the merits (or the obvious lack of merits) of George's claim; instead, Bethlehem's dismissal motion was based on the technical filing requirements with the

Equal Employment Opportunity Commission ("EEOC").[2] Bethlehem never filed a summary judgment motion which would have alerted the court to the frivolous nature of George's case.

Second, although as previously stated, subjective state of mind is not a factor to be considered in determining whether a violation of Rule 11 has occurred, it has been held that the "egregiousness of the conduct involved" is a proper consideration "in determining an appropriate sanction." Continental Air Lines v. Group Systems Intern., 109 F.R.D. 594, 600 (C.D.Cal.1986) (citing Kendrick v. Zanides, 609 F.Supp. 1162, 1173 (N.D.Cal.1985)). Here, Bethlehem has not argued and the court has not found that George proceeded in bad faith or with vexatious intent.

Therefore, based on these considerations, the court finds that the sum of $5,000.00 is an appropriate sanction under Rule 11.

CONCLUSION

The court ORDERS that plaintiff Jerry D. George shall PAY defendant Bethlehem Steel Corporation $5,000.00 as a Fed.R.Civ.P. 11 sanction.

Burbank (Reporter), Rule 11 in Transition—The Report of
the Third Circuit Task Force on FRCP 11 (1989)

CIVIL RIGHTS PLAINTIFFS

Probably no group of lawyers has been more concerned about the impact of amended Rule 11 on their clients and their practice than lawyers who specialize in plaintiffs' civil rights (including employment discrimination) law. Their concerns have been fueled by published statistics suggesting that requests for sanctions in civil rights cases constitute a disproportionate slice of the Rule 11 pie and that civil rights plaintiffs (and/or their lawyers) are both more likely to be "targets" of Rule 11 motions and more likely to be sanctioned than the general population of plaintiffs (and plaintiffs' lawyers) in federal court. * * *

Again, the data from our sanction survey furnish less reason for concern, simply as a matter of raw statistics, than do previously published data. See supra at 57. Requests for sanctions in civil rights cases constituted only a slightly larger slice of our pie (24/132 or 18.2%) than one would expect on the basis of civil filings in this circuit (16% of civil filings in the period ending June 30, 1988) (1988 Annual Report of the Director, Table C3). The same is true of civil rights cases as a proportion of all cases in the survey. See supra at 61. Yet, plaintiffs (and/or their counsel) were sanctioned on motion in civil rights (including employment discrimination) cases in our survey at a rate (8/17 or 47.1%) that is considerably higher than the rate (6/71 or 8.45%) for plaintiffs in non-civil rights cases.

---

2. The court denied Bethlehem's motion because, even though George's filing with the state agency was untimely, his federal claim was not barred because he filed with the EEOC within the 300–day deadline. Martinez v. United Automobile Aerospace & Agricultural Implement Workers, 772 F.2d 348 (7th Cir.1985).

In this context above all, it is important to reaffirm the limited utility of our statistics for inferences about Rule 11 experience in other circuits. Apart from differences in doctrine under and judicial attitudes about Rule 11 in general, and apart from differences in local legal culture, we are aware that civil rights cases constitute a far higher share of the civil litigation pie in some circuits than they do here (e.g., 23.2% of cases filed in the Eleventh Circuit in the same period). Because, as we discuss below, frivolous civil rights cases are deemed to be a problem in many parts of the country, we expect that the size of that perceived problem may affect experience under Rule 11.

In pondering the differential impact on civil rights plaintiffs that emerges from our data, we have deemed it useful to consider other aspects of such cases that may set them apart, both factual and legal. We have also deemed it useful to advert to the characteristics of civil rights cases in our sanction survey in which sanctions were imposed (briefly summarized in Appendix A).

We start with the observations that seven of nine civil rights cases within our survey in which plaintiffs (or their counsel) were sanctioned, on motion and *sua sponte,* involved claims under 42 U.S.C. § 1983, that five of the nine involved *pro se* plaintiffs (including one attorney), and that "civil rights" is an elusive, or at least capacious, category, potentially embracing everything from a Title VII action alleging sex discrimination in a law firm to a § 1983 action alleging improper medical care in a state prison. * * *

If the question is the adequacy of the factual inquiry grounding a complaint (or factual frivolousness), amended Rule 11 should not impose a disproportionate burden on civil rights plaintiffs relying on § 1983 in those circuits, including this one, that impose special pleading requirements on § 1983 claimants. Indeed, it should have less impact than in other types of cases, which may explain why our Court of Appeals recently observed:

> In reviewing the sufficiency of civil rights complaints, we cannot avoid noting the difficulty plaintiffs and their counsel may have in attempting to accommodate this court's requirement of factual specificity with amended Fed.R.Civ.P. 11 * * * [T]he Advisory Committee has explained that, "[t]he standard is one of reasonableness under the circumstances." * * * One of the circumstances to be considered is whether the plaintiff is in a position to know or acquire the relevant factual details * * *

Colburn v. Upper Darby Township, 838 F.2d 663, 667 (3d Cir.1988).

Although courts of appeals imposing special pleading requirements in civil rights cases have employed the device of factual specificity, the concern in many such cases would appear to be that they are *legally* frivolous and that the incremental gains that might result from full-dress treatment, including in particular discovery, are not worth the costs of such treatment.

Whatever the place of law in general on a spectrum of "underdeterminacy," *see supra,* chapter 2, at 18–19, the law governing § 1983 actions must be relatively far out on that spectrum. Recent years have witnessed reversals, false starts, hesitations and agonizing reappraisals by the Supreme Court, and the lower federal courts and litigants have been left if not at sea, then certainly in no safe harbor. Much of the § 1983 landscape is characterized by, in the words of the Court, "contours * * * 'in a state of evolving definition and uncertainty.' " City of St. Louis v. Praprotnik, 108 S.Ct. 915, 922 (1988). Constitutional litigation is by nature dynamic, if for no other reason than the relative impotence of stare decisis. The changing jurisprudence of § 1983, a primary vehicle of constitutional litigation, has given a new meaning to dynamism. See *Szabo Food Service, Inc. v. Canteen Corp.*, 823 F.2d 1073, 1085–86 (7th Cir.1987) (Cudahy, J., dissenting), *cert. dismissed*, 108 S.Ct. 1101 (1988). The concern of the plaintiffs' civil rights bar is that Rule 11 has added a stick of dynamite to what is already a minefield. * * *

APPENDIX A

* * *

B.   There were 10 "Civil Rights" cases in which sanctions were imposed (*2 sua sponte*):

1.   In July, the case was one in which a disappointed husband sought collaterally to attack a state court property settlement under § 1983.

2.   In the September case, a probationary county employee who had resigned sued the county and certain individuals under § 1983 for wrongful termination, alleging violation of her First Amendment and due process rights.

3.   In October, sanctions were imposed for a remand petition after plaintiff had voluntarily dismissed the only federal count in a complaint alleging wrongful discharge/job discrimination (the count asserted failure "to provide plaintiff with equal conditions of employment in violation of federal and/or state civil rights law").

4.   The November case involved a collateral attack on state proceedings claiming religious discrimination in employment in which defendants had prevailed. In the federal action, brought under § 1983 and Title VII, the pro se plaintiff (an attorney) alleged that an attorney for the township had suborned perjury.

5.   In January, a court imposed sanctions on plaintiff's attorney for bringing an action seeking a declaration that state courts have concurrent jurisdiction over Title VII claims after the contrary was established as the law of the circuit and for adding a time-barred count under Title VII itself.

6.   In the February case, a § 1983 action by a terminated federal employee who had brought three other lawsuits, the court denied Rule 11 sanctions in the form of attorney's fees but required that all future complaints filed by the pro se plaintiff against the defendants be

filed in strict compliance with Rules 8 and 11 and be accompanied by a memorandum of law and affidavit under penalty of perjury.

7–9.   In one April case, the court sanctioned a pro se tax protestor whose § 1983 action had been dismissed but who continued to file motions and papers even in the face of an injunction. In another April case, a court sanctioned defendant in a Title VII case sua sponte under Rules 11 and 37 for interrupting a deposition and seeking a protective order. In the third April case, the court adopted the magistrate's recommendation that a pro se § 1983 plaintiff be sanctioned for bringing a federal lawsuit that apparently sought to attack a state judgment collaterally.

10.   In May, a court sua sponte fined a pro se § 1983 plaintiff (prisoner) $40 for "continuous filing of frivolous lawsuits."

NOTE

42 U.S.C. § 1983. Civil action for deprivation of rights.

Every person who, under color of any statute, ordinance, regulation, custom, or usage, of any State or Territory or the District of Columbia, subjects, or causes to be subjected, any citizen of the United States or other person within the jurisdiction thereof to the deprivation of any rights, privileges, or immunities secured by the Constitution and laws, shall be liable to the party injured in an action at law, suit in equity, or other proper proceeding for redress. For the purposes of this section, any Act of Congress applicable exclusively to the District of Columbia shall be considered to be a statute of the District of Columbia.

Cooter & Gell v. Hartmarx Corp.

Supreme Court of the United States, 1990.
496 U.S. 384, 110 S.Ct. 2447, 110 L.Ed.2d 359.

■ JUSTICE O'CONNOR delivered the opinion of the Court.

This case presents three issues related to the application of Rule 11 of the Federal Rules of Civil Procedure: whether a district court may impose Rule 11 sanctions on a plaintiff who has voluntarily dismissed his complaint pursuant to Rule 41(a)(1)(i) of the Federal Rules of Civil Procedure; what constitutes the appropriate standard of appellate review of a district court's imposition of Rule 11 sanctions; and whether Rule 11 authorizes awards of attorney's fees incurred on appeal of a Rule 11 sanction.

I

In 1983, Danik, Inc., owned and operated a number of discount men's clothing stores in the Washington, D.C., area. In June 1983, Intercontinental Apparel, a subsidiary of respondent Hartmarx Corp., brought a breach-of-contract action against Danik in the United States District Court for the District of Columbia. Danik, represented by the law firm of Cooter & Gell (petitioner), responded to the suit by filing a counterclaim against Intercontinental, alleging violations of the Robinson–Patman Act, 49 Stat. 1526, 15 U.S.C. § 13 et seq. In March 1984, the District Court granted summary judgment for Intercontinental in its suit against Danik, and, in February 1985, a jury returned a verdict for Intercontinental on Danik's counterclaim. Both judgments were affirmed on appeal.

While this litigation was proceeding, petitioner prepared two additional antitrust complaints against Hartmarx and its two subsidiaries, respondents Hart, Schaffner & Marx and Hickey–Freeman Co. One of the complaints, the one giving rise to the Rule 11 sanction at issue in this case, alleged a nationwide conspiracy to fix prices and to eliminate competition through an exclusive retail agent policy and uniform pricing scheme, as well as other unfair competition practices such as resale price maintenance and territorial restrictions. App. 3–14.

Petitioner filed the two complaints in November 1983. Respondents moved to dismiss the antitrust complaint at issue, alleging, among other things, that Danik's allegations had no basis in fact. Respondents also moved for sanctions under Rule 11. In opposition to the Rule 11 motion, petitioner filed three affidavits setting forth the prefiling research that supported the allegations in the complaint. Id., at 16–17, 22–23, 24–27. In essence, petitioner's research consisted of telephone calls to salespersons in a number of men's clothing stores in New York City, Philadelphia, Baltimore, and Washington, D.C. Petitioner inferred from this research that only one store in each major metropolitan area nationwide sold Hart, Schaffner & Marx suits.

In April 1984, petitioner filed a notice of voluntary dismissal of the complaint, pursuant to Rule 41(a)(1)(i). The dismissal became effective in July 1984, when the District Court granted petitioner's motion to dispense with notice of dismissal to putative class members. In June 1984, before the dismissal became effective, the District Court heard oral argument on the Rule 11 motion. The District Court took the Rule 11 motion under advisement.

In December 1987, 3½ years after its hearing on the motion and after dismissal of the complaint, the District Court ordered respondents to submit a statement of costs and attorney's fees. Respondents filed a statement requesting $61,917.99 in attorney's fees. Two months later, the District Court granted respondent's motion for Rule 11 sanctions, holding that petitioner's prefiling inquiry was grossly inadequate. Specifically, the District Court found that the allegations in the complaint regarding exclusive retail agency arrangements for Hickey–Freeman clothing were completely baseless because petitioner researched only the availability of Hart, Schaffner & Marx menswear. In addition, the District Court found that petitioner's limited survey of only four Eastern cities did not support the allegation that respondents had exclusive retailer agreements in every major city in the United States. Accordingly, the District Court determined that petitioner violated Rule 11 and imposed a sanction of $21,452.52 against petitioner and $10,701.26 against Danik.

The Court of Appeals for the District of Columbia Circuit affirmed the imposition of Rule 11 sanctions. Danik, Inc. v. Hartmarx Corp.,

277 U.S.App.D.C. 333, 875 F.2d 890 (1989). Three aspects of its decision are at issue here. First, the Court of Appeals rejected petitioner's argument that Danik's voluntary dismissal of the antitrust complaint divested the District Court of jurisdiction to rule upon the Rule 11 motion. After reviewing the decisions of other circuits considering the issue, the Court of Appeals concluded that "the policies behind Rule 11 do not permit a party to escape its sanction by merely dismissing an unfounded case." Id., at 337, 875 F.2d, at 894. The court reasoned that because Rule 11 sanctions served to punish and deter, they secured the proper functioning of the legal system "independent of the burdened party's interest in recovering its expenses." Id., at 338, 875 F.2d, at 895. Accordingly, the court held that such sanctions must "be available in appropriate circumstances notwithstanding a private party's effort to cut its losses and run out of court, using Rule 41 as an emergency exit." Ibid.

Second, the Court of Appeals affirmed the District Court's determination that petitioner had violated Rule 11. Petitioner's arguments failed to "cal[l] into doubt" the two fatal deficiencies identified by the District Court. Rather, petitioner's "account of their efforts d[id] no more than confirm these shortcomings." Ibid.

Third, the Court of Appeals considered respondent's claim that petitioner should also pay the expenses respondent incurred in defending its Rule 11 award on appeal. Relying on Westmoreland v. CBS, Inc., 248 U.S.App.D.C. 255, 770 F.2d 1168 (1985), the Court of Appeals held that an appellant who successfully defends a Rule 11 award was entitled to recover its attorney's fees on appeal and remanded the case to the district court to determine the amount of reasonable attorney's fees and to enter an appropriate award.

II

The Rules Enabling Act, 28 U.S.C. § 2072, authorizes the Court to "prescribe general rules of practice and procedure and rules of evidence for cases in the United States district courts (including proceedings before Magistrates thereof) and courts of appeals." The Court has no authority to enact rules that "abridge, enlarge or modify any substantive right." Ibid. Pursuant to this authority, the Court promulgated the Federal Rules of Civil Procedure to "govern the procedure in the United States district courts in all suits of a civil nature." Fed.Rule Civ.Proc. 1. We therefore interpret Rule 11 according to its plain meaning, see Pavelic & LeFlore v. Marvel Entertainment Group, 493 U.S. 120, 110 S.Ct. 456, 458, 107 L.Ed.2d 438 (1989),[a] in light of the scope of the congressional authorization.

* * *

a. In Pavelic & LeFlore v. Marvel Entertainment Group, the district court imposed sanctions which included a $200,000 Rule 11 sanction to be paid half by the party and half by the law firm representing the party. The individual lawyer had signed on behalf of the law firm. The district court held that Rule 11 sanctions could be and should be imposed on the law firm of the signing lawyer. The Second Circuit Court of Appeals affirmed. The federal Supreme Court reversed holding that Rule 11 sanctions can

An interpretation of the current Rule 11 must be guided, in part, by an understanding of the deficiencies in the original version of Rule 11 that led to its revision. The 1938 version of Rule 11 required an attorney to certify by signing the pleading "that to the best of his knowledge, information, and belief there is good ground to support [the pleading]; and that it is not interposed for delay * * * or is signed with intent to defeat the purpose of this rule." 28 U.S.C., pp. 2616–2617 (1940 ed.) An attorney who willfully violated the rule could be "subjected to appropriate disciplinary action." Ibid. Moreover, the pleading could "be stricken as sham and false and the action [could] proceed as though the pleading had not been served." Ibid. In operation, the rule did not have the deterrent effect expected by its drafters. See Advisory Committee Note on Rule 11, 28 U.S.C.App., pp. 575–576. The Advisory Committee identified two problems with the old Rule. First, the Rule engendered confusion regarding when a pleading should be struck, what standard of conduct would make an attorney liable to sanctions, and what sanctions were available. Second, courts were reluctant to impose disciplinary measures on attorneys, see ibid., and attorneys were slow to invoke the rule. Vairo, Rule 11: A Critical Analysis, 118 F.R.D. 189, 191 (1988).

To ameliorate these problems, and in response to concerns that abusive litigation practices abounded in the federal courts, the rule was amended in 1983. See Schwarzer, Sanctions Under the New Federal Rule 11—A Closer Look, 104 F.R.D. 181 (1985). It is now clear that the central purpose of Rule 11 is to deter baseless filings in District Court and thus, consistent with the Rule Enabling Act's grant of authority, streamline the administration and procedure of the federal courts. See Advisory Committee Note on Rule 11, 28 U.S.C.App., p. 576. Rule 11 imposes a duty on attorneys to certify that they have conducted a reasonable inquiry and have determined that any papers filed with the court are well-grounded in fact, legally tenable, and "not interposed for any improper purpose." An attorney who signs the paper without such a substantiated belief "shall" be penalized by "an appropriate sanction." Such a sanction may, but need not, include payment of the other parties' expenses. See ibid. Although the rule must be read in light of concerns that it will spawn satellite litigation and chill vigorous advocacy, ibid., any interpretation must give effect to the rule's central goal of deterrence.

III

We first address the question whether petitioner's dismissal of its antitrust complaint pursuant to Rule 41(a)(1)(i) deprived the District Court of the jurisdiction to award attorney's fees.

* * *

Rule 41(a) permits a plaintiff to dismiss an action without prejudice only when he files a notice of dismissal before the defendant files

only be imposed on the individual lawyer-signer and not on the signer's law firm even where the individual lawyer explicitly signs on behalf of the law firm. Eds.

an answer or motion for summary judgment and only if the plaintiff has never previously dismissed an action "based on or including the same claim." Once the defendant has filed a summary judgment motion or answer, the plaintiff may dismiss the action only by stipulation, Rule 41(a)(1)(ii), or by order of the court, "upon such terms and conditions as the court deems proper." Rule 41(a)(2). If the plaintiff invokes Rule 41(a)(1) a second time for an "action based on or including the same claim," the action must be dismissed with prejudice.

Petitioner contends that filing a notice of voluntary dismissal pursuant to this rule automatically deprives a court of jurisdiction over the action, rendering the court powerless to impose sanctions thereafter. Of the Circuit Courts to consider this issue, only the Court of Appeals for the Second Circuit has held that a voluntary dismissal acts as a jurisdictional bar to further Rule 11 proceedings.

* * *

In our view, nothing in the language of Rule 41(a)(1)(i), Rule 11, or other statute or Federal Rule terminates a district court's authority to impose sanctions after such a dismissal.

* * *

IV

Petitioner further contends that the Court of Appeals did not apply a sufficiently rigorous standard in reviewing the District Court's imposition of Rule 11 sanctions. Determining whether an attorney has violated Rule 11 involves a consideration of three types of issues. The court must consider factual questions regarding the nature of the attorney's prefiling inquiry and the factual basis of the pleading or other paper. Legal issues are raised in considering whether a pleading is "warranted by existing law or a good faith argument" for changing the law and whether the attorney's conduct violated Rule 11. Finally, the district court must exercise its discretion to tailor an "appropriate sanction."

The Court of Appeals in this case did not specify the applicable standard of review. There is, however, precedent in the District of Columbia Circuit for applying an abuse of discretion standard to the determination whether a filing had an insufficient factual basis or was interposed for an improper purpose, but reviewing *de novo* the question whether a pleading or motion is legally sufficient. See, *e.g.*, International Brotherhood of Teamsters, Chauffeurs, Warehousemen & Helpers of America (Airline Div.) v. Association of Flight Attendants, 274 U.S.App.D.C. 370, 373, 864 F.2d 173, 176 (1988); Westmoreland v. CBS, Inc., 248 U.S.App.D.C., at 261, 770 F.2d, at 1174–1175. Petitioner contends that the Court of Appeals for the Ninth Circuit has adopted the appropriate approach. That Circuit reviews findings of historical fact under the clearly erroneous standard, the determination that counsel violated Rule 11 under a *de novo* standard, and the choice of sanction under an abuse-of-discretion standard.

* * *

Although the Courts of Appeal use different verbal formulas to characterize their standards of review, the scope of actual disagreement is narrow. No dispute exists that the appellate courts should review the district court's selection of a sanction under a deferential standard. In directing the district court to impose an "appropriate" sanction, Rule 11 itself indicates that the district court is empowered to exercise its discretion. See also Advisory Committee Note on Rule 11, 28 U.S.C.App., p. 576 (suggesting a district court "has discretion to tailor sanctions to the particular facts of the case, with which it should be well acquainted").

The Circuits also agree that, in the absence of any language to the contrary in Rule 11, courts should adhere to their usual practice of reviewing the district court's finding of facts under a deferential standard. See Fed.Rule Civ.Proc. 52(a) ("Findings of fact * * * shall not be set aside unless clearly erroneous, and due regard shall be given to the opportunity of the trial court to judge of the credibility of the witnesses"). In practice, the "clearly erroneous" standard requires the appellate court to uphold any district court determination that falls within a broad range of permissible conclusions. See, *e.g.,* Anderson v. Bessemer City, 470 U.S. 564, 573–574, 105 S.Ct. 1504, 1511–1512, 84 L.Ed.2d 518 (1985) ("If the district court's account of the evidence is plausible in light of the record viewed in its entirety, the court of appeals may not reverse it even though convinced that had it been sitting as the trier of fact, it would have weighed the evidence differently. Where there are two permissible views of the evidence, the factfinder's choice between them cannot be clearly erroneous"); Inwood Laboratories, Inc. v. Ives Laboratories, Inc., 456 U.S. 844, 857–858, 102 S.Ct. 2182, 2190–2191, 72 L.Ed.2d 606 (1982). When an appellate court reviews a district court's factual findings, the abuse of discretion and clearly erroneous standards are indistinguishable: A court of appeals would be justified in concluding that a district court had abused its discretion in making a factual finding only if the finding were clearly erroneous.

The scope of disagreement over the appropriate standard of review can thus be confined to a narrow issue: whether the court of appeals must defer to the district court's legal conclusions in Rule 11 proceedings. A number of factors have led the majority of Circuits, as well as a number of commentators, see, *e.g.,* C. Shaffer & P. Sandler, Sanctions: Rule 11 and Other Powers 14–15 (2d ed. 1988) (hereinafter Shaffer & Sandler); American Judicature Society, Rule 11 in Transition, The Report of the Third Circuit Task Force on Federal Rule of Civil Procedure 11, 45–49 (Burbank, reporter 1989), to conclude that appellate courts should review all aspects of a district court's imposition of Rule 11 sanctions under a deferential standard.

The Court has long noted the difficulty of distinguishing between legal and factual issues. See Pullman–Standard v. Swint, 456 U.S. 273, 288, 102 S.Ct. 1781, 1789, 72 L.Ed.2d 66 (1982) ("Rule 52(a) does not furnish particular guidance with respect to distinguishing law from fact. Nor do we yet know of any other rule or principle that will unerringly distinguish a factual finding from a legal conclusion"). Making such distinctions is particularly difficult in the Rule 11 context. Rather than mandating an inquiry into purely legal questions, such as whether the attorney's legal argument was correct, the rule requires a court to consider issues rooted in factual determinations. For example, to determine whether an attorney's prefiling inquiry was reasonable, a court must consider all the circumstances of a case. An inquiry that is unreasonable when an attorney has months to prepare a complaint may be reasonable when he has only a few days before the statute of limitations runs. In considering whether a complaint was supported by fact and law "to the best of the signer's knowledge, information, and belief," a court must make some assessment of the signer's credibility. Issues involving credibility are normally considered factual matters. See Fed.Rule Civ.Proc. 52; see also United States v. Oregon Medical Society, 343 U.S. 326, 332, 72 S.Ct. 690, 695, 96 L.Ed. 978 (1952). The considerations involved in the Rule 11 context are similar to those involved in determining negligence, which is generally reviewed deferentially. See Mars Steel Corp. v. Continental Bank, N.A., supra, at 932; see also 9 C. Wright & A. Miller, Federal Practice and Procedure § 2590 (1971); McAllister v. United States, 348 U.S. 19, 20–22, 75 S.Ct. 6, 7–9, 99 L.Ed. 20 (1954) (holding that the District Court's findings of negligence were not clearly erroneous). Familiar with the issues and litigants, the district court is better situated than the court of appeals to marshall the pertinent facts and apply the fact-dependent legal standard mandated by Rule 11. Of course, this standard would not preclude the appellate court's correction of a district court's legal errors, e.g., determining that Rule 11 sanctions could be imposed upon the signing attorney's law firm, see Pavelic & LeFlore v. Marvel Entertainment Group, 493 U.S. 120, 110 S.Ct. 456, 107 L.Ed.2d 438 (1989), or relying on a materially incorrect view of the relevant law in determining that a pleading was not "warranted by existing law or a good faith argument" for changing the law. An appellate court would be justified in concluding that, in making such errors, the district court abused its discretion. "[I]f a district court's findings rest on an erroneous view of the law, they may be set aside on that basis." Pullman–Standard v. Swint, 456 U.S., *supra,* at 287, 102 S.Ct., at 1789. See also Icicle Seafoods, Inc. v. Worthington, 475 U.S. 709, 714, 106 S.Ct. 1527, 1530, 89 L.Ed.2d 739 (1986) ("If [the Court of Appeals] believed that the District Court's factual findings were unassailable, but that the proper rule of law was misapplied to those findings, it could have reversed the District Court's judgment").

Pierce v. Underwood, 487 U.S. 552, 108 S.Ct. 2541, 101 L.Ed.2d 490 (1988), strongly supports applying a unitary abuse of discretion standard to all aspects of a Rule 11 proceeding. In *Pierce,* the Court held a District Court's determination under the Equal Access to Justice

Act (EAJA), 28 U.S.C. § 2412(d) (1982 ed.), that "the position of the United States was substantially justified" should be reviewed for an abuse of discretion. As a position is "substantially justified" if it "has a reasonable basis in law and fact," 487 U.S., at 566, n. 2, 108 S.Ct., at 2550, n. 2, EAJA requires an inquiry similar to the Rule 11 inquiry as to whether a pleading is "well grounded in fact" and legally tenable. Although the EAJA and Rule 11 are not completely analogous, the reasoning in *Pierce* is relevant for determining the Rule 11 standard of review.

Two factors the Court found significant in *Pierce* are equally pertinent here. First, the Court indicated that " 'as a matter of the sound administration of justice,' " deference was owed to the " 'judicial actor * * * better positioned than another to decide the issue in question.' " 487 U.S., at 559–560, 108 S.Ct., at 2547, quoting Miller v. Fenton, 474 U.S. 104, 114, 106 S.Ct. 445, 451, 88 L.Ed.2d 405 (1985). Because a determination whether a legal position is "substantially justified" depends greatly on factual determinations, the Court reasoned that the district court was "better positioned" to make such factual determinations. See 487 U.S., at 560, 108 S.Ct., at 2547. A district court's ruling that a litigant's position is factually well grounded and legally tenable for Rule 11 purposes is similarly fact-specific. *Pierce* also concluded that district court's rulings on legal issues should be reviewed deferentially. See *id.,* at 560–561, 108 S.Ct., at 2547–2548. According to the Court, review of legal issues under a *de novo* standard would require the courts of appeals to invest time and energy in the unproductive task of determining "not what the law now is, but what the Government was substantially justified in believing it to have been." *Ibid.* Likewise, an appellate court reviewing legal issues in the Rule 11 context would be required to determine whether, at the time the attorney filed the pleading or other paper, his legal argument would have appeared plausible. Such determinations "will either fail to produce the normal law-clarifying benefits that come from an appellate decision on a question of law, or else will strangely distort the appellate process" by establishing circuit law in "a most peculiar, second-handed fashion." *Id.,* at 561, 108 S.Ct., at 2548.

Second, *Pierce* noted that only deferential review gave the district court the necessary flexibility to resolve questions involving " 'multifarious, fleeting, special, narrow facts that utterly resist generalization.' " *Id.,* at 561–562, 108 S.Ct., at 2548. The question whether the government has taken a "substantially justified" position under all the circumstances involves the consideration of unique factors that are "little susceptible * * * of useful generalization." *Ibid.* The issues involved in determining whether an attorney has violated Rule 11 likewise involve "fact-intensive, close calls." Shaffer & Sandler 15. Contrary to petitioner's contentions, *Pierce v. Underwood* is not distinguishable on the ground that sanctions under Rule 11 are mandatory: that sanctions "shall" be imposed when a violation is found does not have any bearing on how to review the question whether the attorney's conduct violated Rule 11.

Rule 11's policy goals also support adopting an abuse-of-discretion standard. The district court is best acquainted with the local bar's litigation practices and thus best situated to determine when a sanction is warranted to serve Rule 11's goal of specific and general deterrence. Deference to the determination of courts on the front lines of litigation will enhance these courts' ability to control the litigants before them. Such deference will streamline the litigation process by freeing appellate courts from the duty of reweighing evidence and reconsidering facts already weighed and considered by the district court; it will also discourage litigants from pursuing marginal appeals, thus reducing the amount of satellite litigation.

Although district courts' identification of what conduct violates Rule 11 may vary, see Schwarzer, Rule 11 Revisited, 101 Harv.L.Rev. 1013, 1015–1017 (1988); Note, A Uniform Approach to Rule 11 Sanctions, 97 Yale L.J. 901 (1988), some variation in the application of a standard based on reasonableness is inevitable. "Fact-bound resolutions cannot be made uniform through appellate review, de novo or otherwise." Mars Steel Corp. v. Continental Bank N.A., 880 F.2d, at 936; see also Shaffer & Sandler 14–15. An appellate court's review of whether a legal position was reasonable or plausible enough under the circumstances is unlikely to establish clear guidelines for lower courts; nor will it clarify the underlying principles of law. See *Pierce, supra,* 487 U.S., at 560–561, 108 S.Ct., at 2547–2548.

In light of our consideration of the purposes and policies of Rule 11 and in accordance with our analysis of analogous EAJA provisions, we reject petitioner's contention that the Court of Appeals should have applied a three-tiered standard of review. Rather, an appellate court should apply an abuse-of-discretion standard in reviewing all aspects of a district court's Rule 11 determination. A district court would necessarily abuse its discretion if it based its ruling on an erroneous view of the law or on a clearly erroneous assessment of the evidence. Here, the Court of Appeals determined that the District Court "applied the correct legal standard and offered substantial justification for its finding of a Rule 11 violation." 277 U.S.App.D.C., at 339, 875 F.2d, at 896. Its affirmance of the District Court's liability determination is consistent with the deferential standard we adopt today.

V

Finally, the Court of Appeals held that respondents were entitled to be reimbursed for attorney's fees they had incurred in defending their award on appeal. Accordingly, it remanded to the District Court "to determine such expenses and, ultimately, to enter an appropriate award." * * *

On its face, Rule 11 does not apply to appellate proceedings. Its provision allowing the court to include "an order to pay to the other party or parties the amount of the reasonable expense, incurred because of the filing of the pleading, motion, or other paper, including a reasonable attorney's fee" must be interpreted in light of Federal

Rule of Civil Procedure 1, which indicates that the rules only "govern the procedure in the United States district courts." Neither the language of Rule 11 nor the Advisory Committee Note suggests that the Rule could require payment for any activities outside the context of district court proceedings.

* * *

To avoid this somewhat anomalous result, Rules 11 and 38 are better read together as allowing expenses incurred on appeal to be shifted onto appellants only when those expenses are caused by a frivolous appeal, and not merely because a Rule 11 sanction upheld on appeal can ultimately be traced to a baseless filing in district court.

Limiting Rule 11's scope in this manner accords with the policy of not discouraging meritorious appeals. If appellants were routinely compelled to shoulder the appellees' attorney's fees, valid challenges to district court decisions would be discouraged. The knowledge that, after an unsuccessful appeal of a Rule 11 sanction, the district court that originally imposed the sanction would also decide whether the appellant should pay his opponent's attorney's fee would be likely to chill all but the bravest litigants from taking an appeal. See Webster v. Sowders, 846 F.2d 1032, 1040 (6th Cir.1988) ("Appeals of district court orders should not be deterred by threats [of Rule 11 sanctions] from district judges"). Moreover, including appellate attorney's fees in a Rule 11 sanction might have the undesirable effect of encouraging additional satellite litigation. For example, if a district court included appellate attorney's fees in the Rule 11 sanction on remand, the losing party might again appeal the amount of the award.

It is possible that disallowing an award of appellate attorney's fees under Rule 11 would discourage litigants from defending the award on appeal when appellate expenses are likely to exceed the amount of the sanction. There is some doubt whether this proposition is empirically correct. See American Judicature Society, Rule 11 in Transition, The Report of the Third Circuit Task Force on Federal Rule of Civil Procedure 11, p. 15 (Burbank, reporter 1989). The courts of appeals have ample authority to protect the beneficiaries of Rule 11 sanctions by awarding damages and single or double costs under Rule 38—which they may do, as we have noted, when the appellant had no reasonable prospect of meeting the difficult standard of abuse of discretion. Beyond that protection, however, the risk of expending the value of one's award in the course of defending it is a natural concomitant of the American Rule, i.e., that "the prevailing litigant is ordinarily not entitled to collect a reasonable attorneys' fee from the loser." Alyeska Pipeline Service Co. v. Wilderness Society, 421 U.S. 240, 247, 95 S.Ct. 1612, 1616, 44 L.Ed.2d 141 (1975). Whenever damages awards at the trial level are small, a successful plaintiff will have less incentive to defend the award on appeal. As Rule 11 is not a fee-shifting statute, the policies for allowing district courts to require the losing party to pay appellate, as well as district court attorneys' fees, are not applicable. "A movant under Rule 11 has no entitlement to fees or any other sanction, and the contrary view can only breed appellate litigation." American Judicature Society, supra, at 49.

We affirm the Court of Appeals' conclusion that a voluntary dismissal does not deprive a district court of jurisdiction over a Rule 11 motion and hold that an appellate court should review the district court's decision in a Rule 11 proceeding for an abuse of discretion. As Rule 11 does not authorize a district court to award attorneys' fees incurred on appeal, we reverse that portion of the Court of Appeals' judgment remanding the case to the district court for a determination of reasonable appellate expenses. For the foregoing reasons, the judgment of the court below is affirmed in part and reversed in part.

It is so ordered.

■ JUSTICE STEVENS, concurring in part and dissenting in part.

* * *

I agree that dismissal of an action pursuant to Rule 41(a)(1) does not deprive the district court of jurisdiction to resolve collateral issues.[3] A court thus may impose sanctions for contempt on a party who has voluntarily dismissed his complaint or impose sanctions under 28 U.S.C. § 1927 against lawyers who have multiplied court proceedings vexatiously. A court may also impose sanctions under Rule 11 for a complaint that is not withdrawn before a responsive pleading is filed or for other pleadings that are not well grounded and find no warrant in the law or arguments for its extension, modification or reversal. If a plaintiff files a false or frivolous affidavit in response to a motion to dismiss for lack of jurisdiction, I have no doubt that he can be sanctioned for that filing. In those cases, the action of the party constitutes an abuse of judicial resources. But when a plaintiff has voluntarily dismissed a complaint pursuant to Rule 41(a)(1), a collateral proceeding to examine whether the complaint is well grounded will stretch out the matter long beyond the time in which either the plaintiff or the defendant would otherwise want to litigate the merits of the claim. An interpretation that can only have the unfortunate consequences of encouraging the filing of sanction motions and discouraging voluntary dismissals cannot be a sensible interpretation of Rules that are designed "to secure the just, speedy, and inexpensive determination of every action." Fed.Rule Civil Proc. 1.

Despite the changes that have taken place at the bar since I left the active practice 20 years ago, I still believe that most lawyers are wise enough to know that their most precious asset is their professional reputation. Filing unmeritorious pleadings inevitably tarnishes that asset. Those who do not understand this simple truth can be dealt with in appropriate disciplinary proceedings, state law actions for malicious prosecution or abuse of process, or, in extreme cases, contempt proceedings. It is an unnecessary waste of judicial resources and an unwarranted perversion of the Federal Rules to hold such lawyers liable for Rule 11 sanctions in actions in federal court.

---

3. I also join Parts IV and V of the Court's opinion.

I respectfully dissent.

* * *

QUESTIONS ON THE 1993 REVISIONS TO RULE 11

Students should analyze the current version of Rule 11 with some care. You should also review the Advisory Committee Note that accompanied those changes. The following questions are designed to guide your analysis of the more substantial changes in the Rule.

1. Do the standards of Rule 11 apply separately to each factual allegation and legal contention in a pleading, or do they apply to the pleading as a whole?

2. When may a pleader allege facts for which he has no evidentiary support and still satisfy Rule 11?

3. Old Rule 11 required that the pleading be warranted by existing law or a "good faith" argument for the extension, modification, or reversal of existing law. Current Rule 11 substitutes the word "nonfrivolous" for "good faith". In what situations will this change potentially make a difference?

4. Suppose plaintiff's attorney files a case based on a novel theory of liability which she believes is warranted by a nonfrivolous argument for the establishment of new law. Suppose that two weeks later the highest court in the state comes down with a controlling precedent rejecting that theory of liability. If plaintiff's attorney continues to litigate the case, even to defend against a motion to dismiss, is she in violation of Rule 11?

5. Under current Rule 11, is the holding of *Cooter & Gell* that an action voluntarily dismissed pursuant to Rule 41(a) is subject to Rule 11 sanctions still correct? How can an attorney presented with a Rule 11 motion insulate herself from any potential sanction?

6. An overworked associate at a large law firm signs a motion asserting a legal theory later found to be frivolous under Rule 11. Absent other facts, on whom should the court impose sanctions? Suppose the client had insisted on that legal argument being made?

7. If a judge finds that a pleading has been signed by an attorney in violation of Rule 11(b), must she impose sanctions under the current version of Rule 11?

8. If the *George* case were being decided today, what arguments could you make as to why no monetary sanctions should be imposed?

Moore v. Keegan Management Company

United States Court of Appeals for the Ninth Circuit, 1996.
78 F.3D 431.

■ POOLE, CIRCUIT JUDGE:

The merits of this case, a securities class-action, are not at issue. The sole question on appeal is whether plaintiffs' counsel may be sanctioned for initiating this lawsuit.

Defendant Keegan Management was a franchisee of nutri/system weight loss centers ("nutri/system"). It sold weight loss programs. In December 1989, Keegan made an initial public offering ("IPO") of stock at $7 per share. Stock rose to $10 per share within a few months.

In early 1990, controversy over the nutri/system program broke out. A series of personal injury lawsuits alleging gall bladder problems resulting from weight-loss programs were filed against nutri/system. In March, Congressional hearings on the diet industry aired testimony discussing the health risks associated with such programs, including the risk of gallstones from rapid weight loss. The Wall Street Journal published an article discussing health problems associated with the nutri/system program. Amidst these events and other reports, Keegan's stock fell to 10% of its peak value.

Appellant law firms Lieff, Cabraser & Heimann and Feldman, Waldman & Kline were approached in late 1990 by potential clients interested in filing securities fraud suits against Keegan based on the possibility that Keegan had knowingly or recklessly failed to disclose health risks associated with its program in the 1989 IPO. Attorneys Elizabeth Cabraser of Lieff, Cabraser and Richard Jaeger of Feldman, Waldman & Kline ultimately filed separate class action suits on February 19 and March 4, 1991. The two suits, *Moore v. Keegan* and *Crespo v. Keegan*, were consolidated. These suits alleged that Keegan misrepresented the nutri/system program as safe at a time when it knew, or was reckless in not knowing, that the program might lead to gall bladder problems.

Keegan moved for summary judgment, and the district court granted the motion in May 1992. The district court found plaintiffs' evidence of scienter, and any known link between weight loss and gall bladder problems prior to December 1989, entirely lacking. That summer, Keegan moved for rule 11 sanctions, but withdrew its motion as part of settlement negotiations. The parties reached a settlement in November 1992. However, prior to approval of that settlement, the district court sua sponte issued an order to show cause why rule 11 sanctions should not be entered. The court conducted a hearing on April 27, 1993. On March 31, 1994, the district court entered sanctions against Cabraser and Jaeger in the amount of $25,000 each pursuant to Rule 11 and 28 U.S.C. § 1927. It also sanctioned the attorneys' firms $25,000 each pursuant to § 1927 and its inherent power. The district court concluded that the attorneys had been reckless in filing a complaint when they could at best only guess that Keegan recklessly failed to disclose health risks when issuing the IPO. The attorneys and firms have timely appealed.

II

At the time the complaint in this case was filed, Rule 11 provided in relevant part that by signing a filing, an attorney certified that [1] to the best of the signer's knowledge, information, and belief formed after reasonable inquiry it is well grounded in fact and is warranted by existing law or a good faith argument for the extension, modification, or reversal of existing law, and that [2] it is not interposed for any improper purpose, such as to harass or to cause unnecessary delay or needless increase in the cost of litigation. Fed. R. Civ. P. 11. The district court sanctioned cabraser and jaeger pursuant to the first prong, the "frivolousness prong." We review the district court's entry of rule 11 sanctions for an abuse of discretion. *Cooter & Gell v. Hartmarx Corp.*, 496 U.S. 384, 405, 110 L.Ed. 2d 359, 110 S.Ct. 2447 (1990); *Newton v. Thomason*, 22 F.3D 1455, 1463 (9th Cir.1994).

Cabraser and Jaeger raise several challenges to these sanctions. We need address only one. Cabraser and Jaeger argue that the district court erred by failing to consider after-acquired factual evidence that would have adequately supported the complaint. We agree.

Under the district court's understanding of the law, the key question was, "what did plaintiffs know when they filed their lawsuit?" Applying this understanding, the district court excluded from consideration any evidence supporting the suit which was unknown to counsel at the time of filing. This included a scientific study published in August 1989—several months before the IPO—suggesting a weight loss/gallstone link, as well as a declaration from plaintiffs' expert Dr. J.W. Marks reviewing the scientific literature and asserting that such a link was well-established prior to the IPO. These exclusions were dispositive; the district court acknowledged that "if, prior to filing the complaint, plaintiffs had in their possession the same information that they offered in opposition to summary judgment, it would have been sufficient to justify filing this lawsuit."

In effect, the district court applied a subjective-objective test. Objectively, would a reasonable attorney have believed plaintiffs' complaint to be well-founded in fact based on what plaintiffs' attorneys subjectively knew at the time? Appellants argue that an objective-objective test should apply: would a reasonable attorney have believed plaintiffs' complaint to be well-founded in fact based on what a reasonable attorney would have known at the time? Alternatively, the issue may be framed as whether the "reasonable inquiry" and "well-founded" requirements are conjunctive or disjunctive. An attorney may not be sanctioned for a complaint that is not well-founded, so long as she conducted a reasonable inquiry. May she be sanctioned for a complaint which is well-founded, solely because she failed to conduct a reasonable inquiry?

We conclude that the answer is no. In *Townsend v. Holman Consulting Corp.*, 929 F.2d 1358 (9th Cir.1990) (en banc), an en banc panel of this court canvassed the circuit's Rule 11 law. It explained the requirements for sanctioning an attorney under the frivolousness prong:

> our cases have established that sanctions must be imposed on the signer of a paper if ... The paper is "frivolous." The word "frivolous" does not appear anywhere in the text of the rule; rather, it is a shorthand that this court has used to denote a filing that is both baseless and made without a reasonable and competent inquiry.

Id. at 1362.

Townsend thus approves of the conjunctive requirement and the objective-objective rule. *Townsend* goes on to expressly embrace an objective-objective analysis in dismissing an attorney's lack of awareness of favorable precedent: "the fact that [counsel] did not cite that case . . . Does not render his argument sanctionable, since, objectively, his request was warranted by existing law." Id. at 1367.

Some language in our prior cases suggests the opposite result. We have held that "an attorney violates rule 11 whenever he signs a pleading, motion, or other paper without having conducted a reasonable inquiry into whether his paper is frivolous, legally unreasonable, or without factual foundation." *Unioil, Inc. v. E.F. Hutton & Co.,* 809 F.2d 548, 557 (9th Cir.1986) cert. denied, 484 U.S. 822 (1987). Under *Unioil,* it appears not to matter whether a filing is frivolous, so long as the signing attorney has failed to conduct a reasonable inquiry. This language accords with the district court's subjective-objective approach, but is inconsistent with *Townsend.* To the extent *Unioil* endorses a subjective-objective test and authorizes sanctions solely for an unreasonable inquiry, we believe it has been implicitly overruled by the en banc decision in *Townsend.*[4]

Townsend compels our result. Its conclusion, we believe, is firmly rooted in the text and policies underlying Rule 11. Rule 11 must be read not only to give effect to the rule's central deterrent goals, but also "in light of concerns that it will spawn satellite litigation and chill vigorous advocacy[.]" *Cooter & Gell,* 496 U.S. at 393. We do little to undermine the deterrent goals of the rule by not sanctioning complaints which have merit on their face. The potential for such sanctions, however, may do much to increase the frequency of the collateral litigation that is rule 11's unfortunate side effect.

■ O' SCANNLAIN, CIRCUIT JUDGE, concurring in part and dissenting in part:

I respectfully dissent from part II.

The court concludes that the district court's imposition of rule 11 sanctions should be reversed, insisting that it is appropriate for a complaint to be filed on the basis of a hunch if it is ultimately well-grounded in fact and law.

In support of its ruling, the court cites our decision in *Townsend v. Holman Consulting Corp.,* 929 F.2d 1358 (9th Cir.1990) (en banc), which noted that a filing is frivolous if it is "both baseless and made without a reasonable and competent inquiry." Id. at 1362. The court appears to hold that this language implicitly overrules *Unioil, Inc. v.*

---

4. We note in passing that while there is a split among the circuits on this question, our approach accords with that taken by the majority of the circuits to have considered the question. Compare *Jones v. International Riding Helmets, Ltd.,* 49 F.3d 692, 695 (11th Cir.1995) (requiring lack of reasonable inquiry and frivolousness); *Kale v. Combined Insurance Company,* 861 F.2d 746, 759 (1st Cir.1988) (same); *Calloway v. Marvel Entertainment Group,* 854 F.2d 1452, 1470 (2d Cir.1988) (same), rev'd in part on other grounds sub nom. *Pavelic & LeFlore v. Marvel Entertainment Group,* 493 U.S. 120, 107 L. Ed. 2d 438, 110 S. Ct. 456 (1989) with *Garr v. U.S. Healthcare, Inc.,* 22 F.3d 1274 (3d Cir. 1994) (sanctioning based solely on failure to conduct reasonable inquiry); *Matter of Excello Press, Inc.,* 967 F.2d 1109, 1112 (7th Cir.1992) (holding that proper focus is reasonableness of inquiry, not frivolousness).

E.F. Hutton & Co., 809 F.2d 548 (9th Cir.1986), Which held that "an attorney violates rule 11 whenever he signs a pleading, motion or other paper without having conducted a reasonable inquiry into whether his paper is frivolous, legally unreasonable, or without factual foundation." Id. at 557. Since the *Townsend* language which the court cites is mere dicta, I must strongly disagree with the assertion that *Unioil* has been overruled.

The opinion also fails to evaluate what, in fact, happened in this case. The record is devoid of any showing of pre-filing investigation by the attorneys; rather the complaint appears to have been filed solely on the basis of several news reports and interviews with personal injury attorneys who had an interest in pending litigation involving the company. Although the case eventually stumbled upon some merit, Rule 11, properly construed, as it provided prior to 1993 (which would be appropriate under the circumstances), requires independent judgment and does not allow post-complaint information to serve as adequate justification.

While I agree that we must avoid the spawning of satellite litigation and the chilling of vigorous advocacy, we must also recall that the supreme court case instructing such behavior, *Cooter & Gell v. Hartmarx Corp. et al.*, 496 U.S. 384, 110 L. Ed. 2d 359, 110 S. Ct. 2447 (1990), Reminds us that Rule 11's primary function is to deter frivolous litigation. The rule's central goal is what compelled the third circuit, in *Garr v. U.S. Healthcare*, 22 F. 3d 1274 (3d Cir.1994), To find that "a shot in the dark is a sanctionable event, even if it somehow hits the mark." (citing *Vista Mfg., Inc. v. Trac–4 Inc.*, 131 F.R.D. 134, 138 (N.D.Ind.1990)). After all, if a "lucky shot could save the signer from sanctions, the purpose of rule 11 'to deter baseless filings' would be frustrated." *Garr*, 22 F.3D at 1279.

QUESTIONS

1. Do the 1993 revisions to Rule 11 shed any light on the issue raised in *Moore v. Keegan Management*?

2. Is a claim sanctionable under Rule 11 if it is not objectively frivolous but is brought, in whole or in part, for an improper purpose? See *Sussman v. Bank of Israel*, 56 F.3d 450 (2d Cir.1995), holding that it is not.

3. Is a claim sanctionable under Rule 11 if the attorney had a reasonable evidentiary basis for making the factual allegations in the complaint, but did not believe those allegations to be true? See *Jones v. International Riding Helmets*, 49 F.3d 692 (11th Cir.1995), holding that it is.

Union Planters Bank v. L & J Development Company, Inc.

United States Court of Appeals for the Sixth Circuit, 1997.
115 F.3d 378.

■ MOORE, CIRCUIT JUDGE.

Sunburst Bank brought an action against L & J Development Company and John and Lynn Jemison seeking to recover on a promissory note. The case was tried by United States District Judge Jerome Turner, who found for Sunburst. Soon thereafter, Sunburst was acquired by Union Planters Bank, a banking institution with whom the judge had economic relations. Subsequent to the merger, Judge Turner awarded $50,000 in sanctions under Rule 11 of the Federal Rules of Civil Procedure against the Jemisons and their attorneys, payable to Sunburst, and the next day recused himself from one claim that remained to be tried. The Jemisons and one of their attorneys now appeal the sanctions order and assert that Judge Turner should have recused himself from hearing the sanctions motion. For the reasons that follow, we affirm.

I.   BACKGROUND

In 1987, Sunburst Bank, a Mississippi corporation, extended a commercial loan in the amount of $1,225,000 to L & J Development Co., Inc. ("L & J"), a Tennessee corporation. John W. Jemison of Houston, Texas, acting as the president of L & J, executed a promissory note in the same amount, secured by a deed of trust encumbering certain rental property owned by L & J, assignments of rents and a life insurance policy, and a personal guaranty from Jemison and his wife, Lynn. L & J defaulted.

In 1993, Sunburst filed suit against L & J and the Jemisons in the Chancery Court of Shelby County, Tennessee, seeking to recover on the note and the guaranty. The suit was removed to the U.S. District Court for the Western District of Tennessee where it was assigned to Judge Jerome Turner. L & J and the Jemisons answered and counterclaimed, claiming, inter alia, that the trust deed had been materially altered by Sunburst. J.A. at 24–28. Their attorney, Larry K. Scroggs, signed the pleading. In addition to their counterclaim, L & J and the Jemisons filed suit in Texas against Sunburst for material alteration of a trust deed. The Texas case was later transferred to the Western District of Tennessee, assigned case number 93–3075, and consolidated with the pending Sunburst suit, case number 93–2371.

L & J thereafter petitioned for Chapter 11 bankruptcy relief in the U.S. Bankruptcy Court for the Southern District of Texas. The bankruptcy case was transferred to the U.S. Bankruptcy Court for the Western District of Tennessee. L & J retained William M. Gotten, its bankruptcy counsel, to represent the company's interests in the consolidated Tennessee litigation. Scroggs continued representing the Jemisons.

In July 1994, Union Planters Bank publicly announced that it was planning to acquire Sunburst. Following the announcement, L & J and the Jemisons filed a "Suggestion of Possible Conflict," noting that Judge Turner's former law firm had represented Union Planters for many years. Judge Turner convened the parties in his chambers on August 18, 1994, after which he entered an order reciting that his contacts with his former law firm presented no conflict. Regarding the judge's personal business ties with Union Planters, the order stated that "the parties have suggested to the court that they do not view the court's business relationships with Union Planters National Bank as a conflict and do not wish the court to recuse itself." For this reason, and because the merger was not imminent, Judge Turner concluded that recusal was neither required nor appropriate at that time.

Sunburst moved for summary judgment, claiming that L & J's own loan closing attorney, Alison Wetter, admitted in a deposition that she had probably altered the trust deed by changing $1,225,520 to $1,225,000 to reflect the actual loan amount. Wetter also testified that Mr. Jemison signed the deed in her office at the closing. Mr. Jemison, however, testified that he signed only one trust deed in the amount of $1,225,520 at Sunburst Bank sometime before the closing. Finding disputed issues of fact concerning who altered the deed and whether the Jemisons executed a superseding guaranty, Judge Turner denied Sunburst's motion for summary judgment.

Judge Turner conducted a bench trial on the consolidated claims in November 1994. Mr. Jemison testified at trial consistent with his prior deposition testimony. On December 2, 1994, Judge Turner found for Sunburst on all claims and defenses. In the court's opinion, the "overwhelming weight of the evidence" established that the Jemisons' closing attorney Wetter corrected the trust deed before Mr. Jemison signed it at her office.

On August 16, 1994, several months before trial, Sunburst served on the Jemisons a motion for sanctions which it then filed with the court on November 17, 1994. A hearing was held on December 21, 1994, where, although the sanctions motion was mentioned, the discussion primarily focused on Sunburst's renewed motion for summary judgment and the question of recusal from the remaining untried claim. Earlier that day Sunburst had submitted six affidavits detailing legal expenses incurred by the bank in defending the Jemisons' claims. Union Planters's acquisition of Sunburst took effect on December 31, 1994.

On March 28, 1995, Judge Turner imposed sanctions in the amount of $45,000 against the Jemisons, and $2,500 each against attorneys Scroggs and Gotten, all payable to Sunburst.

The next day, March 29, 1995, Judge Turner transferred the garnishment claim remaining in case number 93–3075 to another judge "[b]ecause Sunburst Bank has been acquired by Union Planters National Bank, a banking institution with whom the presiding judge currently has substantial economic relations and because the plaintiffs in this case have requested the court to recuse itself on the remaining untried issue."Judge Turner noted that "the parties specifically declined to request recusal on [the sanctions] issue." The Jemisons and Gotten, L & J's attorney, now appeal the sanctions order.

B. Rule 11 Sanctions

Turning to the merits of the sanctions order, the Jemisons and Gotten, L & J's attorney, challenge several aspects of the district court's application of Rule 11. In this circuit, the test for the imposition of Rule 11 sanctions remains, after the 1993 amendments, "whether the individual's conduct was reasonable under the circumstances." Lemaster v. United States, 891 F.2d 115, 118 (6th Cir.1989) (quotation omitted); see Ridder v. Springfield, 109 F.3d 288, 293 (6th Cir.1997); Fed. R. Civ. P. 11(b) (requiring "inquiry reasonable under the circumstances"). On appeal, "[w]e review all aspects of a court's Rule 11 determination for abuse of discretion."

Applying Rule 11, as amended in 1993, the district court found six specific violations of the rule: (1) asserting and, in Mr. Jemison's case, testifying that Sunburst altered the deed, knowing that such assertions lacked evidentiary support; (2) pursuing the alteration defense in order to delay and gain settlement leverage; (3) asserting and, in Mr. Jemison's case, testifying that Sunburst committed wrongful conduct in connection with the Jemisons' personal guaranty, knowing that such assertions lacked evidentiary support; (4) pursuing the superseding guaranty defense in order to delay and gain settlement leverage; (5) asserting affirmative damage claims without first conducting reasonable inquiry into their evidentiary support; and (6) pursuing the damage claims after discovery and trial revealed them to be without evidentiary support.

The district court specifically found that the Jemisons were actively at fault and "the root cause of the violations in this case"; accordingly, they received the bulk of the sanction. The court noted that the litigation revolved primarily "around a $520 clerical error in a $1.2 million loan ... [that] was quickly corrected by Mr. Jemison's own closing attorney, in his favor, and with his knowledge and consent," and that "the alleged 'superseding guaranty' exists only in Mr. Jemison's imagination." The record adequately supports these findings, and the Jemisons have not shown them to be erroneous in any way.

Rule 11 explicitly allows for the imposition of sanctions upon a party responsible for the rule's violation, provided that a represented party is not sanctioned for a violation of subsection (b)(2) involving unwarranted legal contentions. See Fed. R. Civ. P. 11(c), (c)(2)(A). Here, the sanctions order speaks to the Jemisons' "improper purpose" in " 'string[ing] along' Sunburst with delaying tactics," and their advancement of claims lacking legitimate evidentiary support that unnecessarily multiplied the proceedings. A cursory review of the order thus shows that the Jemisons were sanctioned for improper motivations and unfounded factual, not legal, contentions. Because the Jemisons were sanctioned for misrepresenting key facts during both deposition and trial testimony, and knowingly bringing and pursuing claims devoid of evidentiary support, we refuse to hold that the district court abused its discretion by sanctioning the represented parties.

Furthermore, the district court's imposition of sanctions without a full evidentiary hearing did not violate due process. The Jemisons were notified well in advance that Sunburst would be seeking sanctions against them individually and against their attorneys,[3] and they filed a written response to Sunburst's request for sanctions. Significantly, Judge Turner presided over the pretrial and trial proceedings and thus was intimately familiar with the basic facts of the litigation, including the Jemisons' financial position and the relative behavior of the Jemisons and their attorneys. See Silverman v. Mutual Trust Life Ins. Co. (In re Big Rapids Mall Assoc.), 98 F.3d 926, 929 (6th Cir. 1996) (recognizing that an evidentiary hearing is "not necessarily required where the court has full knowledge of the facts and is familiar with the conduct of the attorneys."); INVST Fin. Group, Inc. v. Chem–Nuclear Sys., Inc., 815 F.2d 391, 405 (6th Cir.1986) (explaining that "no hearing is required where an attorney is sanctioned for filing frivolous motions ungrounded in law or fact, and where the judge imposing sanctions has participated in the proceedings."), cert. denied sub nom. Garratt v. INVST Fin. Group, Inc., 484 U.S. 927, 98 L. Ed. 2d 251, 108 S. Ct. 291 (1987). Having been afforded ample notice and a meaningful opportunity to be heard on the sanctions issue, the Jemisons and their attorneys received appropriate due process.

When it is the client who acts improperly by providing false testimony, a question arises whether sanctions should properly be assessed against the attorney. See In re Big Rapids, 98 F.3d at 932 (holding that without specific findings of wrongdoing, sanctioning the attorneys in that case amounted to vicarious liability for the perceived unreliability of their clients' testimony). However, attorneys are obligated under Rule 11 "to conduct an appropriate investigation into the facts that is reasonable under the circumstances." Fed. R. Civ. P. 11, Advisory Committee Notes (1993 Amendments). Here, Judge Turner concluded that, as to the alteration issue, Mr. Jemison's "direct statements and Wetter's lack of memory, although borderline, provide an objectively reasonable basis for Jemison's attorneys to have proceeded as they did." Yet, as to the Jemisons' claims of a superseding guaranty and their entitlement to affirmative damages from Sunburst, the attorneys had not conducted an appropriate inquiry reasonably necessary to assure that such claims were supported by the evidence and not interposed for improper purposes. A simple inquiry into whether the Jemisons had executed a superseding guaranty, or a demand that the Jemisons produce the purported document, would have revealed to the attorneys involved that the existence of this superseding guaranty was, if not entirely illusory, at the very least, questionable. Cf. Mann v. G & G Mfg., Inc., 900 F.2d 953, 959–60 (6th Cir.) (holding that counsel should have known that client's claim was not well-grounded in fact when reasonable pre-filing inquiry would have revealed deficiencies in the client's theory of causation), cert.

3. By serving the sanctions motion on the Jemisons in August and then waiting until November to file it with the court, Sunburst fully complied with Rule 11's "safe harbor" procedural prerequisite. See Fed. R. Civ. P. 11(c)(1)(A); Ridder v. Springfield, 109 F.3d 288, 294–95 (6th Cir.1997).

denied sub nom. Sloan v. G & G Mfg., Inc., 498 U.S. 959, 112 L. Ed. 2d 398, 111 S. Ct. 387 (1990). Accordingly, we agree that sanctions were appropriately awarded against Gotten, L & J's attorney, for failing to investigate and verify, within reason, a major factual premise behind the asserted legal claims of his client.

The Jemisons also claim that the denial of Sunburst's motion for summary judgment serves to insulate them from all Rule 11 reproach. Before Rule 11 was amended in 1993, it was clear in this circuit that "mere survival of a summary judgment motion . . . does not insulate the party from sanctions if it is later determined that all factual claims were groundless." Lemaster, 891 F.2d at 121. While it is true that the drafters of the 1993 amendments contemplated that a party having evidence sufficient to defeat a motion for summary judgment "would have sufficient 'evidentiary support' for purposes of [Rule 11(b)(3)]," FED. R. CIV. P. 11, Advisory Committee Notes (1993 Amendments), we are not persuaded that the drafters intended the anomaly of insulating from the rule's reach a dishonest litigant who presented false testimony sufficient to overcome summary judgment. Rather, the presentation of false testimony strongly suggests that sanctions are needed to deter the litigant from displaying similarly abusive tactics in the future. Consistent with the purposes behind Rule 11, we hold that litigants cannot avoid sanction under the rule simply by defeating summary judgment on the basis of false evidence. In this case the Jemisons were not rendered sanction-proof because their false testimony sufficed to defeat summary judgment. The district court found that Mr. Jemison's deposition testimony regarding the superseding guaranty was "quite simply, false," a finding that has not been shown to be erroneous. Had Mr. Jemison testified truthfully, in all likelihood, Sunburst would have been granted summary judgment, and both Sunburst and the court would have been spared the need to undergo a full trial.

Even though Rule 11 now "de-emphasizes monetary sanctions and discourages direct payouts to the opposing party," Ridder, 109 F.3d at 294, the rule explicitly allows for expenses "incurred as a direct result of the violation" to be paid directly to the other party "if imposed on motion and warranted for effective deterrence." Fed. R. Civ. P. 11 (c)(2). The drafters note that a direct payout to the injured party is particularly appropriate for Rule 11(b)(1) violations involving improper motivations of the type found here. See Fed. R. Civ. P. 11, Advisory Committee Notes (1993 Amendments). Judge Turner also recognized that the Jemisons' wealth was "largely protected from any efforts by Sunburst to execute or garnish," and that this supported the order to pay the sanctions directly to the injured party. Moreover, the Jemisons never challenged their ability to pay nor opposed Sunburst's affidavits detailing the bank's expenses incurred in contesting the Jemisons' claims. Thus, we agree that the present case called for a direct payout to the injured party in an amount that we believe was based upon the evidentiary showing, necessary for deterrence, and well within the court's discretion.

III.   CONCLUSION

Having reviewed the circumstances of this case, we are convinced that the district court did not abuse its discretion in sanctioning the persons directly responsible for, and those attorneys who could have easily unmasked, the blatant litigation abuses occurring below. The order of the district court imposing sanctions is AFFIRMED.

NOTE ON RULE 11 IN PRIVATE SECURITIES ACTIONS

The Private Securities Litigation Reform Act of 1995 provides for substantially more stringent standards and sanctions to be applied in private securities litigation than current Rule 11 requires for other litigation. The Act requires that upon final adjudication of any private securities litigation, the court must make specific findings as to whether all parties and lawyers involved had complied with the requirements of Rule 11. If any lawyer or party is found to have violated Rule 11, sanctions are mandatory and there is a rebuttable presumption in favor of "an award to the opposing party of the reasonable attorneys' fees and other expenses incurred as a direct result of the violation."

NOTE ON WILLY v. COASTAL

In Willy v. Coastal Corp., 112 S. Ct. 1076 (1992), a unanimous Supreme Court held that Rule 11 sanctions may be imposed even where it is subsequently determined that the federal court never had subject matter jurisdiction. Plaintiff had commenced suit in state court. Defendant removed to federal court over plaintiff's objection, and ultimately, the U.S. Court of Appeals ordered the case remanded for lack of subject matter jurisdiction.

The offenses catalogued "included a 1,200–page unindexed, unnumbered pile of materials that the District Court determined to be a 'to be a conscious and wanton affront to the judicial process, this court, and opposing counsel'." The Court also noted "careless pleading, such as reliance on a nonexistent Federal Rule of Evidence."

The Court concluded, "The interest in having the rules of procedure obeyed ...does not disappear upon a subsequent determination that the court was without subject matter jurisdiction."

DO LAWYERS REALLY BRING FRIVOLOUS SUITS?

Professor Yablon argues that lawyers bring suits with a low probability of success if the potential recovery is high enough, as well as suits with a high probability of success, but that they rarely bring suits that the perceive as truly frivolous, that is, suits they know or ought to know have no chance of success. From this premise he argues that any rule designed to deter the "frivolous" suit will inevitably also deter the filing of a certain number of meritorious suits. See Yablon, The Good, The Bad and the Frivolous Case: An Essay on Probability and Rule 11, 44 U.C.L.A. L. Rev. 65 (1996).

This, of course, changes the terms of the debate and raises serious policy questions.

D. ALTERNATIVE PLEADING

McCormick v. Kopmann

Court of Appeals, Third District, 1959.
23 Ill.App.2d 189, 161 N.E.2d 720.

■ REYNOLDS, PRESIDING JUSTICE.

On the evening of November 21, 1956, Lewis McCormick was killed on Main Street in Gifford, Illinois, when a truck being operated by defendant Lorence Kopmann collided with the automobile which McCormick was driving.

This action was brought by McCormick's widow in the Circuit Court of Champaign County against Kopmann and Anna, John and Mary Huls. The complaint contains four counts; the issues raised on this appeal concern only the first and fourth counts.

Count I is brought by plaintiff as Administratrix of McCormick's Estate, against Kopmann, under the Illinois Wrongful Death Act. Plaintiff sues for the benefit of herself and her eight children, to recover for the pecuniary injury suffered by them as a result of McCormick's death. It is charged that Kopmann negligently drove his truck across the center line of Main Street and collided with McCormick's automobile. In paragraph 3 of Count I, plaintiff alleges:

> "That at the time of the occurrence herein described, and for a reasonable period of time preceding it, the said decedent was in the exercise of ordinary care for his own safety and that of his property."

Count IV is brought by plaintiff as Administratrix of McCormick's Estate, against the Huls, under the Illinois Dram Shop Act. Plaintiff avers that Count IV is brought "in the alternative to Count I." She sues for the benefit of herself and her four minor children, to recover for the injury to their means of support suffered as a result of McCormick's death. It is alleged that Anna Huls operated a dramshop in Penfield, Illinois; that John and Mary Huls operated a dramshop in Gifford; that on November 21, 1956 the Huls sold alcoholic beverages to McCormick which he consumed and which rendered him intoxicated; and that "as a result of such intoxication" McCormick drove his automobile "in such a manner as to cause a collision with a truck" being driven by Kopmann on Main Street in Gifford.

Kopmann, defendant under Count I, moved to dismiss the complaint on the theory that the allegations of that Count I and Count IV were fatally repugnant and could not stand together, because McCormick could not be free from contributory negligence as alleged in Count I, if his intoxication caused the accident as alleged in Count IV. Kopmann also urged that the allegation in Count IV that McCormick's intoxication was the proximate cause of his death, is a binding judicial admission which precludes an action under the Wrongful Death Act. Kopmann's motion was denied. He raised the same defenses in his answer.

The Huls, defendants under Count IV, answered. They did not file a motion directed against Count IV.

Neither defendant sought a severance (see Civil Practice Act, Sections 44(2) and 51), and both counts came on for trial at the same time.

Plaintiff introduced proof that at the time of the collision, McCormick was proceeding North in the northbound traffic lane, and that Kopmann's truck, travelling South, crossed the center line and struck McCormick's car. Plaintiff also introduced testimony that prior to the accident McCormick drank a bottle of beer in Anna Huls' tavern in Penfield and one or two bottles of beer in John and Mary Huls' tavern in Gifford. Plaintiff's witness Roy Lowe, who was with McCormick during the afternoon and evening of November 21, and who was seated in the front seat of McCormick's car when the collision occurred, testified on cross examination that in his opinion McCormick was sober at the time of the accident.

At the close of plaintiff's evidence, all defendants moved for directed verdicts. The motions were denied.

Kopmann, the defendant under the Wrongful Death count, introduced testimony that at the time of the collision, his truck was in the proper lane; that McCormick's automobile was backed across the center line of Main Street, thus encroaching on the southbound lane, and blocking it; that the parking lights on McCormick's automobile were turned on, but not the headlights; that Kopmann tried to swerve to avoid hitting McCormick's car; and that there was an odor of alcohol on McCormick's breath immediately after the accident. Over plaintiff's objection, the trial court permitted Kopmann's counsel to read to the jury the allegations of Count IV relating to McCormick's intoxication, as an admission.

The Huls, defendants under the Dram Shop count, introduced opinion testimony of a number of witnesses that McCormick was not intoxicated at the time of the accident. Anna Huls testified that McCormick drank one bottle of beer in her tavern. Several witnesses testified that McCormick had no alcoholic beverages in John and Mary Huls' tavern.

All defendants moved for directed verdicts at the close of all the proof. The motions were denied. The jury was instructed that Count IV was an alternative to Count I; that Illinois law permits a party who is uncertain as to which state of facts is true to plead in the alternative, and that it is for the jury to determine the facts. At Kopmann's request, the court instructed the jury on the law of contributory negligence, and further:

> " * * * if you find from all of the evidence in the case that (McCormick) was operating his automobile while intoxicated and that such intoxication, if any, contributed proximately to cause the

collision in question, then in that case * * * you should find the defendant, Lorence Kopmann, not guilty.''

The jury returned a verdict against Kopmann for $15,500 under Count I. The jury found the Huls not guilty under Count IV. Kopmann's motions for judgment notwithstanding the verdict, and in the alternative for a new trial, were denied.

Kopmann has appealed. His first contention is that the trial court erred in denying his pre-trial motion to dismiss the complaint. Kopmann is correct in asserting that the complaint contains inconsistent allegations. The allegation of Count I that McCormick was free from contributory negligence, cannot be reconciled with the allegation of Count IV that McCormick's intoxication was the proximate cause of his death. Freedom from contributory negligence is a prerequisite to recovery under the Wrongful Death Act. Russell v. Richardson, 308 Ill.App. 11, at page 27, 31 N.E.2d 427, at page 434. If the jury had found that McCormick was intoxicated and that his intoxication caused the accident, it could not at the same time have found that McCormick was not contributorily negligent. The Illinois Supreme Court has held that ''voluntary intoxication will not excuse a person from exercising such care as may reasonably be expected from one who is sober.''

In addition to this factual inconsistency, it has been held that compensation awarded under the Wrongful Death Act includes reparation for the loss of support compensable under the Dram Shop Act.

Counts I and IV, therefore, are mutually exclusive; plaintiff may not recover upon both counts. It does not follow, however, that these counts may not be pleaded together. Section 24(1) of the Illinois Civil Practice Act (Ill.Rev.Stat.Ch. 110, Sec. 24) authorizes joinder of defendants against whom a liability is asserted in the alternative arising out of the same transaction. Section 24(3) of the Act provides:

> ''If the plaintiff is in doubt as to the person from whom he is entitled to redress, he may join two or more defendants, and state his claim against them in the alternative in the same count or plead separate counts in the alternative against different defendants, to the intent that the question which, if any, of the defendants is liable, and to what extent, may be determined as between the parties.''

Section 34 of the Act states in part that ''Relief, whether based on one or more counts, may be asked in the alternative.''

Section 43(2) of the Act provides:

> ''When a party is in doubt as to which of two or more statements of fact is true, he may, regardless of consistency, state them in the alternative or hypothetically in the same or different counts or defenses, whether legal or equitable. A bad alternative does not affect a good one.''

Thus, the Civil Practice Act expressly permits a plaintiff to plead inconsistent counts in the alternative, where he is genuinely in doubt as to what the facts are and what the evidence will show. The legal sufficiency of each count presents a separate question. It is not ground for dismissal that allegations in one count contradict those in an alternative count. * * *

A recent decision concerning alternative pleading is Urnest v. Sabre Metal Products, Inc. and Edward Yucis, 22 Ill.App.2d 172, 159 N.E.2d 512. In Count I, brought against the defendant corporation, plaintiff alleged that the corporation's agent Yucis contracted to employ plaintiff as general manager of the corporation; that Yucis was authorized to enter into this agreement; that the corporation ratified the contract, and that the corporation breached the contract. Plaintiff sought damages for breach of contract. In Count II, brought against Yucis, plaintiff averred that Yucis fraudulently represented that he was authorized to contract on the corporation's behalf and that the corporation had ratified his acts, whereas Yucis had no such authority and no ratification had taken place. Plaintiff sought damages for fraud and deceit. The motions of both defendants to strike the complaint were allowed, whereupon plaintiff appealed. The court held that the inconsistency between the counts was not ground for dismissal:

> " * * * The allegations in count two are inconsistent with and contradictory of the allegations of count one; however, such pleading is permitted under section 43(2) of the Civil Practice Act (Ill.Rev.Stat.1957, chap. 110, par. 43(2)). Freeman & Co. v. [Robert G.] Regan Co., 332 Ill.App. 637 [76 N.E.2d 514]. The theory is that on the trial the proof will determine on which set of facts, if any, the plaintiff is entitled to recover. Where the pleading is in the alternative in different counts, each count stands alone and the inconsistent statements contained in a count cannot be used to contradict statements in another count. The intent of the cited section of the Practice Act is that counts can be pleaded in the alternative regardless of consistency."

* * *

The 1955 revision of Section 43(2) of the Civil Practice Act was designed to make it clear that inconsistent facts or theories could be pleaded alternatively, whether in the same or different counts. In their note respecting the revised section, the drafters of the 1955 Act, having explained why clarifying language was needed, concluded: "Under the revision the inconsistency may exist either in the statement of the facts, or in the legal theories adopted." S.H.A. ch. 110, sec. 43, p. 514. This provision was modelled after Rule 8(e)(2) of the Federal Rules of Civil Procedure, 28 U.S.C.A. Federal courts have held that where the plaintiff in personal injury cases is uncertain as to who is liable, he may assert his claims against the several defendants alternatively.

Sound policy weighs in favor of alternative pleading, so that controversies may be settled and complete justice accomplished in a single action. If the right is abused, as where the pleader has knowledge of the true facts (viz., he knows that the facts belie the alternative) pleading in the alternative is not justified. Thus in Church v.

Adler, 350 Ill.App. 471 at page 483, 113 N.E.2d 327 at page 332, we
said:

> " * * * alternative pleading is not permitted when in the nature
> of things the pleader must know which of the inconsistent aver-
> ments is true and which is false. Plaintiff must know whether she
> will be sick, sore, lame and disordered for the rest of her life or
> whether on the contrary she has regained her health, as alleged in
> Count II. She must make up her mind which is the fact, and strike
> the inconsistent allegation from her pleading on remand."

There is nothing in the record before us to indicate that plaintiff
knew in advance of the trial, that the averments of Count I, and not
Count IV, were true. In fact, at the trial, Kopmann attempted to
establish the truth of the allegations of Count IV that McCormick was
intoxicated at the time of the collision and that his intoxication caused
his death. He can hardly be heard now to say that before the trial,
plaintiff should have known that these were not the facts. Where, as in
the Church case, the injured party is still living and able to recollect
the events surrounding the accident, pleading in the alternative may
not be justified, but where, as in the case at bar, the key witness is
deceased, pleading alternative sets of facts is often the only feasible
way to proceed.

We hold that, in the absence of a severance, plaintiff had the right
to go to trial on both Counts I and IV, and to adduce all the proof she
had under both Count I and Count IV.

* * *

* * * Plaintiff pleaded alternative counts because she was uncertain as to what the true facts were. Even assuming she introduced
proof to support all essential allegations of both Count I and Count
IV, she was entitled to have all the evidence submitted to the trier of
fact, and to have the jury decide where the truth lay. She was not
foreclosed *ipso facto* from going to the jury under Count I, merely
because she submitted proof, under Count IV, tending to prove that
McCormick's intoxication proximately caused his death. If this were
the rule, one who in good faith tried his case on alternative theories,
pursuant to the authorization, if not the encouragement of Section 43,
would run the risk of having his entire case dismissed. The provisions
of the Civil Practice Act authorizing alternative pleading, necessarily
contemplate that the pleader adduce proof in support of both sets of
allegations or legal theories, leaving to the jury the determination of
the facts.

Furthermore, in testing the sufficiency of the proof as against a
motion for directed verdict, the sufficiency of the proof to support
each count is to be judged separately as to each count, just as the legal
sufficiency of each count is separately judged at the pleading stage. As
to each count, the court will look only to the proof and inferences
therefrom favorable to the plaintiff; the court cannot weigh conflicting
evidence. Proof unfavorable to the plaintiff, even though the plaintiff
herself introduced that proof, cannot be considered. The determina-

tion to be made is whether there is any evidence (all unfavorable evidence excluded) upon which the jury could base a verdict for the plaintiff under the count in question, and if there is, the motion as to that count must be denied and the issues submitted to the jury. Lindroth v. Walgreen Co., 407 Ill. 121, 130, 94 N.E.2d 847; Kiriluk v. Cohn, 16 Ill.App.2d 385, 388–389, 148 N.E.2d 607. Judged by these well-settled tests, it is clear that plaintiff's proof under Count I was sufficient to require the case to be submitted to the jury.

What we have said is not to say that a plaintiff assumes no risks in adducing proof to support inconsistent counts. The proof in support of one inconsistent count necessarily tends to negate the proof under the other count and to have its effect upon the jury. While the fact alone of inconsistent evidence will not bar submission of the case to the jury, it may very well affect the matter of the weight of the evidence and warrant the granting of a new trial, even though, as we have held, it does not warrant *ipso facto* a directed verdict or judgment notwithstanding the verdict.

Kopmann argues that plaintiff should have been required to elect between her alternative counts before going to the jury. The doctrine known as "election of remedies" has no application to the case at bar. Here, either of two defendants may be liable to plaintiff, depending upon what the jury finds the facts to be. It has been aptly said that "truth cannot be stated until known, and, for purposes of judicial administration, cannot be known until the trier of facts decides the fact issues." McCaskill, Illinois Civil Practice Act Annotated (1933), p. 103. Plaintiff need not choose between the alternative counts. Such a requirement would, to a large extent, nullify the salutary purposes of alternative pleading. Since she could bring actions against the defendants seriatim, or at the same time in separate suits, she is entitled to join them in a single action, introduce all her proof, and submit the entire case to the jury under appropriate instructions.

Kopmann contends he was prejudiced because Counts I and IV were submitted together to the jury, in that the jury was confused by plaintiff's inconsistent positions as to liability. We believe this argument is no longer open to Kopmann, since he failed to seek a separate trial pursuant to Section 51 of the Illinois Civil Practice Act. We also note that Kopmann's counsel repeatedly sought to establish McCormick's intoxication, indicating that this issue would have been injected into the case whether or not Count IV was presented concurrently with Count I. And, in any event, the jury was carefully instructed as to the law and the position of each party. The verdict itself shows that the instructions were understood and followed.

Kopmann argues that the practical effect of the trial court's instructions was to direct the jury to determine whether he or the Huls were liable to plaintiff, depending upon whether or not McCormick was intoxicated. The instructions given, belie this contention. At Kopmann's request, the jury was repeatedly admonished that Kopmann was not liable to plaintiff if the jury found McCormick was guilty of contributory negligence, as well as if the jury found McCormick was intoxicated and his intoxication contributed proximately to cause the accident. No error was committed in this regard.

* * *

Plaintiff has perfected a cross appeal, contending that the verdict is inadequate as a matter of law. We believe the jury could reasonably fix plaintiff's damages under Count I at $15,500. The Supreme Court has but recently reminded us that courts of review must examine verdicts in cases such as this "with humble deference to the discretion of the jury in making its determination and to the ruling of the trial judge on the post-trial motions." Lau v. West Towns Bus Co., 16 Ill.2d 442, 453, 158 N.E.2d 63, 69.

We conclude that the verdict and judgment below are correct and the judgment is affirmed.

Judgment affirmed.

E.   ALLOCATION OF THE BURDENS: PLEADING AND PROVING

Ingraham v. United States

United States Court of Appeals, Fifth Circuit, 1987.
808 F.2d 1075.

■ POLITZ, CIRCUIT JUDGE:

The appellees in these consolidated cases sued the United States, under the Federal Tort Claims Act, for severe injuries caused by the negligence of government physicians. In each case, after entry of adverse judgment the government moved for relief from the judgment to the extent that the damages exceeded the limit imposed on medical malpractice awards by the Medical Liability and Insurance Improvement Act of Texas, Tex.Rev.Civ.Stat.Ann. art. 4590i. The respective district courts denied these posttrial motions. Concluding that the government did not raise the issue timely before the trial courts, that the issues were not preserved for appeal, and, in the Bonds case, that the challenged awards were not otherwise excessive, we affirm both judgments.

Background

In 1977, in response to what was perceived to be a medical malpractice crisis, the Legislature of Texas, like several other state legislatures, adopted certain limitations on damages to be awarded in actions against health care providers, for injuries caused by negligence in the rendering of medical care and treatment. Of particular significance to these appeals is the $500,000 cap placed on the ex delicto recovery,[1] not applicable to past and future medical expenses.[2]

---

1. Tex. Rev. Civ. Stat. Ann. art. 4590i, § 11.02(a), provides:

In an action on a health care liability claim where final judgment is rendered

On February 12, 1979, Dwight L. Ingraham was operated on by an Air Force surgeon. During the back surgery a drill was negligently used and Ingraham's spinal cord was damaged, causing severe and permanent injuries. The court awarded Ingraham judgment for $1,264,000. This total included $364,000 for lost wages and $900,000 for pain, suffering, and disability. There is no reference to the Medical Liability and Insurance Improvement Act of Texas in the pleadings, nor was any reference made to the Act during the trial. After entry of judgment the United States filed a notice of appeal. Thereafter, urging the Act's limitations, the government sought relief from judgment under Fed. R.Civ.P. 60(b). The district court denied that motion. No appeal was taken from that ruling.

Similarly, in March of 1979, Jocelyn and David Bonds, and their infant daughter Stephanie, were victims of the negligent performance by an Air Force physician. Because of the mismanagement of the 43rd week of Jocelyn Bonds's first pregnancy, and the negligent failure to perform timely a caesarean section delivery, Stephanie suffered asphyxiation *in utero*. The loss of oxygen caused extensive brain damage, resulting in spastic quadriparesis, cortical blindness, seizures, and mental retardation. In their FTCA action the court awarded Stephanie $1,814,959.70 for medical expenses and $1,675,596.90 for the other losses. Jocelyn Bonds was awarded $750,000 for her losses, including loss of the society of her daughter. As in the Ingraham case, the government did not invoke the Texas malpractice limitation in pleading or at trial. Postjudgment the government filed a motion to amend the judgment under Fed.R.Civ.P. 59, but, again, there was no mention of the limitations Act. Subsequently, three months after entry of the judgment, the government filed a pleading entitled "Motion for Reconsideration," in which it advanced the malpractice Act. That motion was denied. The government appealed the judgment and motion to amend, but did not appeal the denial of the "motion for reconsideration."

These appeals do not challenge the courts' findings of liability, but object only to quantum, contending that damages are limited by the Medical Liability and Insurance Improvement Act and, in the case of Stephanie and Jocelyn Bonds, are otherwise excessive.

Analysis

Appellees maintain that we should not consider the statutory limitation of liability invoked on appeal because it is an affirmative defense under Rule 8(c) of the Federal Rules of Civil Procedure, and the failure to raise it timely constitutes a waiver. We find this argument persuasive.

against a physician or health care provider, the limit of civil liability for damages of the physician or health care provider shall be limited to an amount not to exceed $500,000.

2. Tex. Rev. Civ. Stat. Ann. art. 4590i, § 11.02(b), provides:

Subsection (a) of this section does not apply to the amount of damages awarded on a health care liability claim for the expenses of necessary medical, hospital, and custodial care received before judgment or required in the future for treatment of the injury.

Rule 8(c) first lists 19 specific affirmative defenses, and concludes with the residuary clause "any other matter constituting an avoidance or affirmative defense." In the years since adoption of the rule, the residuary clause has provided the authority for a substantial number of additional defenses which must be timely and affirmatively pleaded. These include: exclusions from a policy of liability insurance; breach of warranty; concealment of an alleged prior undissolved marriage; voidable preference in bankruptcy; noncooperation of an insured; statutory limitation on liability; the claim that a written contract was incomplete; judgment against a defendant's joint tortfeasor; circuity of action; discharge of a contract obligation through novation or extension; recission or mutual abandonment of a contract; failure to mitigate damages; adhesion contract; statutory exemption; failure to exhaust state remedies; immunity from suit; good faith belief in lawfulness of action; the claim that a lender's sale of collateral was not commercially reasonable; a settlement agreement or release barring an action; and custom of trade or business. * * *

Determining whether a given defense is "affirmative" within the ambit of Rule 8(c) is not without some difficulty. We find the salient comments of Judge Charles E. Clark, Dean of the Yale Law School, later Chief Judge of the United States Second Circuit Court of Appeals, and the principal author of the Federal Rules, to be instructive:

> [J]ust as certain disfavored allegations made by the plaintiff * * * must be set forth with the greatest particularity, so like disfavored defenses must be particularly alleged by the defendant. These may include such matters as fraud, statute of frauds * * *, statute of limitations, truth in slander and libel * * * and so on. In other cases the mere question of convenience may seem prominent, as in the case of payment, where the defendant can more easily show the affirmative payment at a certain time than the plaintiff can the negative of nonpayment over a period of time. Again it may be an issue which may be generally used for dilatory tactics, such as the question of the plaintiff's right to sue * * * a vital question, but one usually raised by the defendant on technical grounds. These have been thought of as issues "likely to take the opposite party by surprise," which perhaps conveys the general idea of fairness or the lack thereof, though there is little real surprise where the case is well prepared in advance.

Clark, *Code Pleading,* 2d ed. 1947, § 96 at 609–10, *quoted in* 5 C. Wright & A. Miller, *Federal Practice and Procedure: Civil,* § 1271, p. 313 (1969).

Also pertinent to the analysis is the logical relationship between the defense and the cause of action asserted by the plaintiff. This inquiry requires a determination (1) whether the matter at issue fairly may be said to constitute a necessary or extrinsic element in the plaintiff's cause of action; (2) which party, if either, has better access to relevant evidence; and (3) policy considerations: should the matter be indulged or disfavored?

Central to requiring the pleading of affirmative defenses is the prevention of unfair surprise. A defendant should not be permitted to "lie behind a log" and ambush a plaintiff with an unexpected defense. The instant cases illustrate this consideration. Plaintiffs submit that, had they known the statute would be applied, they would have made greater efforts to prove medical damages which were not subject to the statutory limit. In addition, plaintiffs maintain that they would have had an opportunity and the incentive to introduce evidence to support their constitutional attacks on the statute.

This distinction separates the present cases from our recent decision in Lucas v. United States, 807 F.2d 414 (5th Cir.1986). In *Lucas,* although the limitation of recovery issue was not pleaded, it was raised at trial. We held that the trial court was within its discretion to permit the defendant to effectively amend its pleadings and advance the defense. The treatment we accorded this issue in *Lucas* is consistent with long-standing precedent of this and other circuits that " 'where [an affirmative defense] is raised in the trial court in a manner that does not result in unfair surprise, * * * technical failure to comply with Rule 8(c) is not fatal.' " Bull's Corner Restaurant v. Director, Federal Emergency Management Agency, 759 F.2d 500, 502 (5th Cir.1985), *quoting* Allied Chemical Corp. v. Mackay, 695 F.2d 854, 855 (5th Cir.1983); *see also* Dickinson v. Auto Center Mfg. Co., 733 F.2d 1092 (5th Cir.1983).

We view the limitation on damages as an "avoidance" within the intendment of the residuary clause of 8(c). Black's Law Dictionary, 5th ed. 1979, defines an avoidance in pleadings as "the allegation or statement of new matter, in opposition to a former pleading, which, admitting the facts alleged in such former pleading, shows cause why they should not have their ordinary legal effect." Applied to the present discussion, a plaintiff pleads the traditional tort theory of malpractice and seeks full damages. The defendant responds that assuming recovery is in order under the ordinary tort principles, because of the new statutory limitation, the traditional precedents "should not have their ordinary legal effect."

Considering these factors, against the backdrop and with the illumination provided by other applications of Rule 8(c), we conclude that the Texas statutory limit on medical malpractice damages is an affirmative defense which must be pleaded timely and that in the cases at bar the defense has been waived.

* * *

NOTES

1. Justice White wrote the following opinion dissenting from the Supreme Court's denial of certiorari in Ida J. Taylor v. United States, 485 U.S. 992, 108 S.Ct. 1300, 99 L.Ed.2d 510:

"Petitioner's husband was left comatose when he was disconnected from his ventilator while in a military hospital. She brought suit against the Government under the Federal Tort Claims Act for personal injury as a result of negligence, and won a judgment of $500,000 for emotional distress and loss of consortium. In a postjudgment motion, the Government argued for the first time that Cal.Civ.Code Ann. § 3333.2 (West Supp.1988) limits noneconomic damages to $250,000 in this case. The District Court rejected this claim, which it noted had not been raised before or during the trial. The Ninth Circuit reversed, holding that the Government had not waived the application of the state statute by failing to plead it, and therefore the damages recovered by petitioner must be limited to $250,000.

"Under the accepted interpretation of Rule 8(c) of the Federal Rules of Civil Procedure, any matter 'constituting an avoidance or affirmative defense' to the matters raised in the plaintiff's complaint must be pleaded in a timely manner or it is deemed to be waived. As a matter of California law, the state statute at issue in this case is understood to be an affirmative defense. The Ninth Circuit held, however, that this determination is not binding on a federal court because the proper characterization of the statute in this case, which was brought in federal court, is a matter of federal procedural law. The court ruled that this statute is a mere limitation of liability, rather than an avoidance or an affirmative defense. This conclusion conflicts with the decisions of two other Courts of Appeals. In Ingraham v. United States, 808 F.2d 1075, 1078–1079 (1987), the Fifth Circuit held that an identical statutory limitation on damages recoverable in the State of Texas is an affirmative defense that is waived under the Federal Rules by failure to plead it in a timely manner. And in Jakobsen v. Massachusetts Port Authority, 520 F.2d 810, 813 (1975), the First Circuit held that a statutory limitation on liability is an affirmative defense under Rule 8(c). Both courts also ruled that any such statute is deemed to be waived when the application of the statute is not raised during the trial but instead is raised for the first time after the trial, on appeal. I would grant certiorari to resolve this conflict among the Courts of Appeals.

2. In Jakobsen v. Massachusetts Port Authority, 520 F.2d 810, 813 (1st Cir.1975), cited in Taylor, the defendant state agency raised the defense of its liability being limited to $5000 by statute for the first time in a motion for a directed verdict after the presentation of evidence, and in its requested instructions.

"The district court, without opinion, rejected the defense then and again upon consideration of a motion for judgment notwithstanding the verdict. We affirm—not because of any position that we take on the purported statutory limitation, but because the Port Authority's failure to plead and its belated raising of the defense amounted, in our view, to a waiver thereof. The Port Authority raised in its answer, besides a general denial, only the defenses of lack of statutory notice, contributory negligence, and assumption of risk. The defense in question was not identified until the close of evidence, and was fully articulated only in the motion for judgment notwithstanding the verdict. Under Rule 8(c), Fed.R.Civ.P., certain specified defenses and 'any other matter constituting an avoidance or affirmative defense' must be pleaded affirmatively. While a statutory limitation on liability is not enumerated among the listed defenses, we think it falls within the Rule's residuary clause. The Port Authority's defense shares the common characteristic of a bar to the right of recovery even if the general complaint were more or less admitted to. *See* C. Wright & A. Miller, Federal Procedure and Practice, § 1270, at 292 (1969). *Compare* Rule 9(a), Fed.R.Civ.P. (lack of capacity to be sued may be raised only by 'specific negative averment').

"The ordinary consequence of failing to plead an affirmative defense is its forced waiver and its exclusion from the case. *See* Wright & Miller, *supra,* § 1278, at 339 & n. 29, and cases cited therein.

"Doubtless, when there is no prejudice and when fairness dictates, the strictures of this rule may be relaxed. Under Rule 15 the district court may and should liberally allow an amendment to the pleadings if prejudice does not result. And if an affirmative defense is actually tried by implied consent, the pleadings may be later made to conform. Fed.R.Civ.P. 15(b). But the defense in question was not tried by implied consent. * * * "

F. RELATION BACK AND OTHER PROBLEMS OF STATUTES OF LIMITATIONS

1. Amending After the Statute Has Run

Duffy v. Horton Memorial Hospital

Court of Appeals of New York, 1985.
66 N.Y.2d 473, 497 N.Y.S.2d 890, 488 N.E.2d 820.

■ TITONE, JUSTICE.

The question presented is whether a plaintiff's direct claim against a third-party defendant, which is asserted in an amended complaint, relates back to the date of service of the third-party complaint for purposes of the Statute of Limitations, pursuant to CPLR 203(e), where the third-party complaint and the amended complaint are based on the same transaction or occurrence. We hold that it does. * * *

Plaintiff and her husband commenced this medical malpractice action in August 1979, alleging that defendants had failed to recognize and diagnose an early stage of the husband's lung cancer. The husband's condition deteriorated and he died in May 1981. Special Term subsequently granted plaintiff's motion for substitution and for an amendment of the complaint to add a wrongful death claim.

In June 1981, defendants brought a timely third-party action against Dr. Isidore Greenberg, the family physician who had treated the husband before and after a 1978 hospital examination. A deposition of Dr. Greenberg was conducted in October 1982, after which plaintiff sought to amend her complaint to name him as a defendant.[2] Plaintiff urged that the claim was not barred by the Statute of Limitations because of the provisions of CPLR 203(e): "A claim asserted in an amended pleading is deemed to have been interposed, at the time the claims in the original pleading were interposed, unless the original pleading does not give notice of the transactions, occurrences, or series of transactions or occurrences, to be proved pursuant to the amended pleading."

2. CPLR 1009 permits a plaintiff to amend the complaint as of right within 20 days after service of the third-party complaint (*see,* Johnson v. Equitable Life Assur. Socy., 22 A.D.2d 141, 254 N.Y.S.2d 261, *aff'd.* 18 N.Y.2d 933, 277 N.Y.S.2d 136, 223 N.E.2d 562). After that time period expires, plaintiff must obtain leave of court (Siegel, N.Y.Prac. § 164).

Special Term initially granted the motion, but reversed itself on reargument * * *. The Appellate Division, Third Department, affirmed, adhering to its position that a plaintiff's direct claim against a third-party defendant cannot be asserted after the Statute of Limitations has run. The appeal to this court has been taken by permission of the Appellate Division, which has certified the question of whether its order was correctly made.

* * *

The language of the governing statute, CPLR 203(e), is not particularly helpful, since it does not state whether or not it is applicable to an amended complaint served upon someone not named in the original complaint. Analysis should, therefore, turn on the policy considerations underlying Statutes of Limitations. * * *

We have emphasized that the primary purpose of a limitations period is fairness to a defendant (Flanagan v. Mount Eden Gen. Hosp., 24 N.Y.2d 427, 429, 301 N.Y.S.2d 23, 248 N.E.2d 871). A defendant should " 'be secure in his reasonable expectation that the slate has been wiped clean of ancient obligations, and he ought not to be called on to resist a claim where the "evidence has been lost, memories have faded, and witnesses have disappeared" ' " (*id.*, quoting Developments in the Law: Statutes of Limitations, 63 Harv.L.Rev. 1177, 1185). There is also the need to protect the judicial system from the burden of adjudicating stale and groundless claims. * * *

An amendment which merely adds a new theory of recovery or defense arising out of a transaction or occurrence already in litigation clearly does not conflict with these policies. * * * A party is likely to have collected and preserved available evidence relating to the entire transaction or occurrence and the defendant's sense of security has already been disturbed by the pending action. * * *

The situation is far more difficult, however, when an amendment is sought to add a new party defendant. It is one thing to permit an amendment to relate back as applied to parties before the court. It is quite another thing to permit an amendment to relate back when a new party is sought to be added by the amendment against whom the Statute of Limitations has run. * * *

Thus, if the new defendant has been a complete stranger to the suit up to the point of the requested amendment, the bar of the Statute of Limitations must be applied (*see*, Arnold v. Mayal Realty Co., 299 N.Y. 57, 85 N.E.2d 616; *Bringing in Party—Limitations*, Ann., 8 A.L.R.2d 6, §§ 53, 58). But where, within the statutory period, a potential defendant is fully aware that a claim is being made against him with respect to the transaction or occurrence involved in the suit, and is, in fact, a participant in the litigation, permitting an amendment to relate back would not necessarily be at odds with the policies underlying the Statute of Limitations. * * * In such cases, there is room for the exercise of a sound judicial discretion to determine whether, on the facts, there is any operative prejudice precluding a retroactive amendment. * * *

It is evident that when a third party has been served with the third-party complaint, and all prior pleadings in the action as required by CPLR 1007, the third-party defendant has actual notice of the plaintiff's potential claim at that time. The third-party defendant must gather evidence and vigorously prepare a defense. There is no temporal repose. Consequently, an amendment of the complaint may be permitted, in the court's discretion, and a direct claim asserted against the third-party defendant, which, for the purposes of computing the Statute of Limitations period, relates back to the date of service of the third-party complaint (*see,* McLaughlin, Practice Commentaries, McKinney's Cons. Laws of N.Y., Book 7B, C203:11, p. 124; Siegel, N.Y.Prac. § 49, at 17–18 [1985 Supp.]; 6 Wright and Miller, Federal Practice & Procedure § 1498).

In this case, both Special Term and the Appellate Division erred in denying the motion to amend solely upon the ground that the claim would be barred by the Statute of Limitations. Accordingly, we must remit the matter to the Appellate Division to give that court the opportunity to exercise its discretion in determining whether an amendment is warranted. * * *

NOTE

Following remand, the Appellate Division had to rule on another appeal reported at 119 A.D.2d 847, 500 N.Y.S.2d 420 (1986):

HARVEY, JUSTICE.

Appeal from an order of the Supreme Court at Special Term (Williams, J.), entered January 3, 1984 in Sullivan County, which granted third-party defendants' motion for reargument and denied plaintiff leave to serve an amended complaint.

When this case was previously before this court (109 A.D.2d 927, 486 N.Y.S.2d 402), we affirmed Special Term's holding that plaintiff's direct claim against third-party defendant, asserted in an amended complaint, did not relate back to the date of service of the third-party complaint for purposes of the Statute of Limitations (*see,* CPLR 203[e]). The Court of Appeals reversed (66 N.Y.2d 473, 497 N.Y.S.2d 890, 488 N.E.2d 820). Since this court had denied plaintiff's motion to amend solely on the ground that the claim would be barred by the Statute of Limitations, the Court of Appeals remitted the matter for the exercise of our discretion in determining whether amendment of plaintiff's complaint would be warranted (CPLR 5613).

Leave to amend pleadings "shall be freely given" absent prejudice or surprise resulting from the delay (CPLR 3025[b]: * * * Here, third-party defendant was apprised of the underlying lawsuit. Plaintiff's amended complaint asserting a direct claim against third-party defendant involves the same transactions and facts as the underlying suit. No prejudice or surprise has been shown. We find plaintiff's supporting papers adequate to allow her to amend her complaint to assert a direct cause of action against third-party defendant. * * *

Meredith v. United Air Lines

United States District Court, Southern District of California, 1966.
41 F.R.D. 34.

◼ IRVING HILL, DISTRICT JUDGE.

This case enables the Court to use the 1966 amendment of Federal Civil Rule 15(c) for the beneficial purposes for which the amendment was intended.

The instant case is a personal injury action based on negligence. On January 22, 1963, Plaintiff, Mrs. Meredith, was a paying passenger on a United Air Lines flight from Seattle to Los Angeles. She is a resident of Washington. Near the end of the flight, while the plane was over the vicinity of Bakersfield, California, she was standing in the restroom when she alleges that she was thrown to the floor by an abrupt and sharp movement of the aircraft, with resultant serious injury and permanent disability.

Plaintiff's husband employed California counsel shortly after the accident. Counsel apparently engaged in quite a lengthy series of settlement negotiations with the insurers for United Air Lines. At some time in those negotiations, Plaintiff's counsel learned that there had been a near-collision between the United plane and a military-type jet fighter plane. Mrs. Meredith and her husband were also told of the near-collision by one of Mrs. Meredith's fellow passengers who was an eye witness. He stated that the abrupt veering off of the passenger plane had been caused by a military-type plane bearing U.S. Government insignia, coming right at it. Mr. and Mrs. Meredith informed counsel of this information in September, 1963. It is not clear which of these two disclosures of the near-collision came to counsel's attention first; they probably occurred at about the same time.[2] In any event that was all the information counsel had when the complaint was prepared and they made the natural assumption that the unidentified military-type plane was government-owned and government-operated.

The instant complaint was filed on January 9, 1964. It is in two counts. Count 1 names United Air Lines alone and is based on diversity. Count 2 names both United Air Lines and the United States, charging the concurrent negligence of both. It alleges that a government plane of "description unknown" was a contributing cause of the injury. The United States is sued under the Federal Tort Claims Act.

Thus far I have discussed the facts which were known to Plaintiff and her counsel up to the filing of the complaint. Important events, unknown to them, had occurred in the meantime. Very shortly after the accident, the Civil Aeronautics Board conducted an investigation of the near-collision. Therein the Government took the position that it had no jet aircraft of a military-type operating anywhere near the scene of the near-collision. The Government also contended therein that if a military-type airplane was involved, it must have been one of two military aircraft being operated in the general area by Lockheed Aircraft Corporation, a supplier of military aircraft to the Government. It appeared that Lockheed, on the date in question, was conducting a

---

2. As will be discussed in Footnote 3, infra, Plaintiff's attorney had earlier received hearsay information about there having been a Civil Aeronautics Board investigation of the incident. But that hearsay information was extremely indefinite and did not put him on notice that a near-collision with a military-type airplane had been a cause of the accident.

pre-delivery test of a new military-type jet aircraft manufactured for the Government. The test also involved the use of another military-type jet plane as a target. Both were being flown by Lockheed's pilots. The Civil Aeronautics Board apprised Lockheed of these facts and made Lockheed a party to the investigation. Statements were taken therein from Lockheed's pilots and other of its employees. Generally Lockheed denied that the tests were conducted in the vicinity of Bakersfield, but one of its pilots stated to the Civil Aeronautics Board that he was "in the vicinity of Bakersfield" after having been released from the tests. The tests were being directed from Palmdale which is about 75 air miles from Bakersfield.

Unfortunately, neither Plaintiff nor her attorney was made aware of the facts which the Civil Aeronautics Board investigation developed.[3]

After extensions of time to plead, the Government filed an answer on June 26, 1964, which, for the first time, advised Plaintiff and her attorney of the Government's position that it was not operating the military-type aircraft. At the same time, the Government noticed a motion to bring Lockheed into the case as a Third–Party Defendant. The Motion was granted on July 13, 1964. On July 21, 1964, the Government filed a Third–Party Complaint against Lockheed. In the Third–Party Complaint, after describing both of the planes which were being operated by Lockheed in the general area as aforesaid, the Government asserted that the unknown military-type plane referred to in Plaintiff's Complaint was one of those two. The Third–Party Complaint sought indemnification from Lockheed in the event the Government was held liable.

After thus learning of Lockheed's possible involvement, Plaintiff's attorney acted promptly. On September 2, 1964, he moved to sue Lockheed under Civil Rule 14(a) and filed a proposed Amended Complaint. After some lapse of time, that Motion was heard and granted, and on November 20, 1964, an Amended Complaint was filed naming Lockheed as an additional Defendant in Count 2.

Since the first effort to bring Lockheed into the case as a party defendant occurred more than one year after the accident, and since the California statute of limitations for negligence is one year (Code of Civil Procedure § 340(3)), Lockheed has moved to dismiss the Amended Complaint as to it. All parties agreed in oral argument that the California one-year statute of limitations applies.

Plaintiff resists the Motion to Dismiss on two alternative grounds. First, she asks the Court to hold that the statute of limitations has been tolled because of Lockheed's "fraudulent concealment" of its possible implication. Second, she urges that the Amended Complaint should be

3. Plaintiff's attorney, Mr. Downing, in an affidavit filed September 2, 1964, states that he was informed "soon after the accident" of the Civil Aeronautics Board investigation and that "after four weeks' investigation, [the Civil Aeronautics Board] issued a statement that [it] had not been able to determine the presence or existence of any military airplanes in or about the area of the accident at the time of the accident." Under all of the facts, I believe that the attorney had no duty to follow the matter further.

deemed to relate back to the date on which the original Complaint was filed.

At the hearing on the Motion to Dismiss I gave the parties a substantial additional period of time in which to conduct further discovery. I asked them to file such affidavits as they might wish to file on several factual matters:

(1) What notice Lockheed had had of the pendency of the claim.

(2) Whether Lockheed would be prejudiced by being brought into the action at this time, particularly as to whether Lockheed had made a factual investigation while the facts were fresh in memory.

(3) When Plaintiff first knew or should have known of Lockheed's possible involvement.

Only Plaintiff filed an affidavit as requested.

As will be seen infra, I hold that under Civil Rule 15(c) as amended in 1966, the Amended Complaint should be deemed to relate back to the date of filing the original Complaint. Thus, it is unnecessary to consider whether there has been any "fraudulent" or other concealment which would toll the statute of limitations under California law.

In reaching my conclusion I have considered the following questions:

I. Does this case meet the requirements of present Civil Rule 15(c)?

II. Can Rule 15(c) as amended in 1966 be validly applied to the instant case?

I

DOES THIS CASE MEET THE REQUIREMENTS OF PRESENT CIVIL RULE 15(c)?

Civil Rule 15(c) as amended by the recent amendments which became effective July 1, 1966, reads as follows:

"Whenever the claim or defense asserted in the amended pleading arose out of the conduct, transaction, or occurrence set forth or attempted to be set forth in the original pleading, the amendment relates back to the date of the original pleading. *An amendment changing the party against whom a claim is asserted relates back if the foregoing provision is satisfied and, within the period provided by law for commencing the action against him, the party to be brought in by amendment (1) has received such notice of the institution of the action that he will not be prejudiced in maintaining his defense on the merits, and (2) knew or should have known that, but for a mistake concerning the identity of the proper party, the action would have been brought against him.*"

The italicized portion was added by the 1966 amendments.

In determining whether the instant case meets the requirements of Section 15(c) as amended, several inquiries must be made. First, does the claim asserted against Lockheed in the amended pleading arise "out of the conduct, transaction, or occurrence set forth * * * in the original pleading * * * "? Obviously it does.

Second, has Lockheed, the party brought in by the amendment, "received such notice of the institution of the action that [it] will not be prejudiced in maintaining [its] defense on the merits"?

And third, did Lockheed know or should it have known "that, but for a mistake concerning the identity of the proper party, the action would have been brought against [it]"? Both of these requirements also seem amply satisfied by the facts of the instant case.

Lockheed was brought into the Civil Aeronautics Board inquiry and fully investigated the occurrence within a few weeks after it happened. So Lockheed clearly will not be prejudiced in maintaining its defense. Lockheed learned that a passenger on the United plane had been injured not more than a month after the incident and probably within two days afterward. As a result of hearing of the injuries, one of the Lockheed pilots made a written report of the facts to company counsel. This, in my view, is sufficient to have put Lockheed on notice of the instant litigation. Moreover, though Lockheed was specifically afforded the opportunity to file an affidavit clarifying when it in fact gained knowledge of the pendency and institution of Plaintiff's claim, it has filed no such affidavit. I must therefore assume that Lockheed knew of the pendency of the claim before Plaintiff filed the action, and knew of the filing of the action when, or shortly after, it was commenced.

Such knowledge leads to the inescapable conclusion that Lockheed also knew or should have known "that, but for a mistake concerning the identity of the proper party, the action would have been brought against [it]." Lockheed should have known at an early moment that there was a strong possibility of a mistake of identity on the part of Plaintiff and her counsel. It seems obvious that if Plaintiff had known that the Government had no planes operating in the vicinity and that Lockheed had a plane or planes so operating with Government insignia thereon, Plaintiff would have originally named Lockheed at least as a co-defendant with the Government.

One further question remains. Is the instant amendment to the Complaint "[a]n amendment *changing* the party against whom a claim is asserted * * * "? [Italics supplied.] I believe that it is. The instant amendment does add Lockheed as a Defendant while also retaining the Government as a Defendant. Under the circumstances, Plaintiff's counsel could not safely substitute Lockheed for the Government, since Lockheed continues to deny that any of its planes caused the near-collision. Ownership of the aircraft being tested is an unresolved factual and legal question and it is conceivable that Lockheed's pilot, if he caused the near-collision, might be held to be an agent of the

Government. The word "changing" must be given a sensible and practical construction. It would be unfair indeed to deny Plaintiff the benefits of Rule 15(c) as amended, merely because her counsel, in the necessary protection of her interests, have not substituted Lockheed in place of the Government.

I conclude that the present case meets all of the requirements of Rule 15(c) as amended.

* * *

Lockheed's Motion to Dismiss is denied.

NOTES

A.   In Craig v. United States, 413 F.2d 854 (9th Cir.1969), a plane crashed while trying to land on an aircraft carrier on the high seas. The pilot was killed and a seaman injured. Suit for wrongful death of the pilot was brought within the statute of limitations, but amendment to add Litton Systems as a defendant was sought after the statute had already run. Litton admittedly knew of the incident prior to the running of the statute as a result of an action by the injured seaman. Leave to amend was denied, the court emphasizing that Rule 15(c) required notice of the institution of the action within the prescribed period; notice of the incident did not suffice.

Does *Meredith* meet this test? Did the court in *Meredith* recognize that the rule requires more than knowledge of the incident? Did it find that Lockheed had knowledge of the institution of the action before the statute had run? What in the record could support such a finding?

B.   Under Rule 15(c) for a party to be brought in by amendment after the statute of limitations has run, certain conditions must be satisfied "within the period provided by law for commencing the action" against that party. Precisely what this means divided the Supreme Court in Schiavone v. Fortune, 477 U.S. 21, 106 S.Ct. 2379, 91 L.Ed.2d 18 (1986). In that case, an action for defamation based on an article that appeared in Fortune magazine, was commenced with Fortune named as defendant. Fortune, however, is the name of an internal division of Time, Incorporated, rather than an independent legal entity. After the statute of limitations had run plaintiff sought to amend to name "Fortune, also known as Time, Incorporated" as defendant.

The action had been filed some ten days before the one year statute of limitations had expired and service of process was attempted by mail on a duly qualified agent of Time for receipt of service of process in New Jersey. Service was refused because Time had not been named. If Time had been properly named as defendant, service would have been good because the action is commenced when the complaint is filed (Rule 3) and under Rule 4(j) plaintiff has an additional 120 days in which to complete service. But Time had not been named in the original complaint and the Supreme Court was faced with deciding precisely what Rule 15(c) permits. The majority refused to allow the amendment to relate back, arguing that the language of the Rule was clear: notice had to reach the party sought to be added by amendment within the statutory period. The dissent argued that there were two components to the period described in the Rule: the first was the one year provided for in the relevant statute of limitations; the second was the added period provided by Rule 4(j).

Under the amendments to the Federal Rules of Civil Procedure transmitted by the Supreme Court to Congress on April 30, 1991 (effective December 1, 1991) the period during which notice must be received by the party to be added is stated to include the period provided by Rule 4(j).

The majority opinion in *Schiavone* includes the following passage:

> We cannot understand why, in litigation of this asserted magnitude, Time was not named specifically as the defendant in the caption and in the body of each complaint. This was not a situation where the ascertainment of the defendant's identity was difficult for the plaintiffs. An examination of the magazine's masthead clearly would have revealed the corporate entity responsible for the publication.

In a footnote the opinion sets forth verbatim the precise language of the masthead as it appeared in the issue of Fortune in which the alleged defamation was published and also quotes the same portion of the masthead as it appeared in several later issues, each of which includes not only the correct corporate name, but also appropriate addresses. Is any of this relevant to the proper application of Rule 15(c)? Is it irrelevant to a practicing lawyer?

C. In some state courts the legal relationship between the party originally named and the party sought to be added by amendment after the statute of limitations has run is of particular importance. Capital Dimensions v. Samuel Oberman, Inc., 104 A.D.2d 432, 478 N.Y.S.2d 950 (2d Dept.1984) is illustrative:

> In order to determine whether parties are "united in interest" for the purpose of determining whether the claims asserted in an amended complaint relate back to the date of service of the original summons and complaint, the "jural relationship of the parties whose interests are said to be united" and "the nature of the claim asserted against them by the plaintiff" must be examined (Connell v. Hayden, 83 A.D.2d 30, 42–43, 443 N.Y.S.2d 383). Thus, partners are united in interest because by statute (Partnership Law, §§ 24, 26) they are "fully, personally, and vicariously liable for the torts of their co-partners committed within the scope of the partnership business" (Connell v. Hayden, *supra,* p. 46, 443 N.Y.S.2d 383). Similarly, business corporations and their employees are united in interest because corporations are vicariously liable for the torts of their employees committed within the scope of the corporate business, as are any other parties who have a master and servant relationship (Connell v. Hayden, *supra,* p. 46, 443 N.Y.S.2d 383).

> However, if the only relationship between the original parties and the parties sought to be added is that of joint tort-feasors, the parties are not united in interest because each tort-feasor, acting independently, is liable to the plaintiff only because of his own fault; the fault of his codefendant is not imputed to him. In such circumstances, neither codefendant is responsible for the acts or omissions of the other (Connell v. Hayden, supra, pp. 44–45, 443 N.Y.S.2d 383).

In the present case, although the corporations sought to be added by plaintiff in its amended complaint may be controlled by the same principal and operate as a single unit, the corporations are, nevertheless, separate and distinct business entities which have no jural relationship other than that of alleged joint tort-feasors. It is entirely possible that one or more of the corporations may be responsible for the alleged harm to plaintiff. Since the fault of one corporation cannot be imputed to a codefendant corporation (Connell v. Hayden, supra, pp. 44–45, 443 N.Y.S.2d 383), the corporate defendants sought to be added by plaintiff are not united in interest with the original defendant Samuel Oberman Company, Inc. Similarly, there is no proof that the individually named defendant, Sidney Slotnick, is a servant of any of the proposed new corporate defendants. Accordingly, the motion for leave to serve a supplemental summons and an amended complaint against the additional corporate defendants, the date of claim interposition upon them to relate back to the date of service of the original summons and complaint, should have been denied.

D. "Doe" Practice: Another Form of Relation Back: Several states have what has been termed the "Doe Defendant" practice. The general requirements are that plaintiff must start suit in a timely manner and describe by their functions or activities the unknown potential defendants. These may be identified in the complaint as Does numbers 1 through 10, for example.

If plaintiff then discovers the identities of the Doe Defendants after the statute of limitations would have expired, plaintiff has from the date of discovery an additional period of time within which to serve complaints on these defendants. The general requirements are discussed in Hogan, California's Unique Doe Defendant Practice: A Fiction Stranger than Truth, 30 Stan.L.Rev. 51 (1977).

Britt v. Arvanitis

United States Court of Appeals, Third Circuit, 1978.
590 F.2d 57.

■ HANNUM, DISTRICT JUDGE. * * *

On March 20, 1970, appellant underwent a gastrectomy for correction of a chronic duodenal ulcer. Initial recovery appeared to be normal, but in 1972 he began to experience sharp pain in the upper abdomen near the locus of the gastrectomy. These episodes became more frequent and intense and on October 17, 1974, appellant had exploratory surgery in an attempt to determine the source of his continuing discomfort. As a result of this second operation, it was discovered, in January 1975, that some of the sutures used in the 1970 operation were defective. The complaint was filed in the District Court on October 1, 1975, naming as defendants the doctor who performed the gastrectomy, the hospital in which it occurred, the administrator of the hospital, and, because Ethicon, Inc.'s identity was at that time unknown, "John Doe" as manufacturer of the wire sutures. Discovery elicited the name of Ethicon, Inc. as the manufacturer of the sutures, which information was given to plaintiff November 9, 1976. Thereafter, by notice of motion dated November 18, 1976, plaintiff sought leave to amend the complaint and name Ethicon, Inc. in place of the "John Doe" originally denominated. A consent order allowing the amendment was filed January 24, 1977 and the amended complaint was filed February 28, 1977 with service on Ethicon, Inc. effected on March 2, 1977. Ethicon, Inc. raised the Statute of Limitations defense by moving to vacate the District Court's Order allowing the amendment and the Court below granted summary judgment for appellee.

In so ruling, the District Court held first, that appellants' cause of action accrued, for Statute of Limitations purposes, in January, 1975 when it was first ascertained that the sutures were defective; and second, since the amended complaint was filed more than two years after the accrual date, the action was barred by the two year Statute of Limitations. Finally, the District Court held that the amendment did not relate back to the date the original complaint was filed (concededly within the two year period) because the amendment replacing John

Doe with Ethicon, Inc. effectively introduced a new party to the action and the notice provisions of Fed.R.Civ.P. 15(c) which allow relation back of an amendment in such circumstances were not met.

* * *

In the present case, it is not disputed that at the time the original complaint was filed, appellants were unaware of the precise identity of the potential defendant. They were, however, able to describe the defendant in terms of what it did or failed to do, indeed, they did so by describing "John Doe" as "a manufacturer of wire surgical sutures." * * *

[W]e * * * hold that appellants' cause of action accrued, and the limitations period began to run, in January, 1975 when it was first established that the wire sutures used in the 1970 operation were causative factors in appellants' damages. * * * [A]s to whether Fed.R.Civ.P. 15(c) allows the complaint to relate back, we conclude that it does not. Since the replacement of a "John Doe" defendant with a named party introduces a new litigant, * * * all conditions of Rule 15(c) must be met for the amendment to relate back. It is undisputed that the claim asserted in the amended complaint arose out of the same conduct, transaction, or occurrence set forth in the original complaint. It is equally clear, however, that Ethicon, Inc. had no notice of the action, informal or otherwise, prior to the running of the Statute of Limitations. Thus, the notice provisions of Rule 15(c) have not been satisfied. Accordingly, the amended complaint does not relate back to the filling date of the original complaint. The Statute of Limitations having run in January, 1977 and the amended complaint having been filed on February 28, 1977, the action is barred * * *.

NOTE ON DOE PRACTICE IN FEDERAL COURTS

In 1991, the Federal Rules were amended to add a new Rule 15(c)(1), which was designed, according to the note of the Advisory Committee, "to make it clear that the rule does not apply to preclude any relation back that may be permitted under the applicable limitations law." Since then, federal courts in New Jersey and elsewhere have permitted relation back based on Doe practice in federal court in cases arising under New Jersey law or that of other states that utilize the practice. See, e.g. *Cruz v. City of Camden*, 898 F. Supp. 1100 (D.N.J.1995); *Wilson v. City of Atlantic City*, 142 F.R.D. 603 (D.N.J.1992); *Jordan v. Tapper*, 143 F.R.D. 575 (D.N.J.1992).

However, when the amendment is one changing the party "or the naming of the party" against whom the claim is asserted, these cases generally require that plaintiff must also satisfy the specific notice requirements of Rule 15(c)(3).

2. The Governing Limitations Period

Baratta v. Kozlowski

Supreme Court, Appellate Division, Second Department, 1983.
94 A.D.2d 454, 464 N.Y.S.2d 803.

■ LAZER, JUSTICE.

The primary focus of these appeals is application of the Statute of Limitations when the same conduct or transaction produces separate causes of action sounding in tort and in contract. Asserting that the "essence" of the instant action is tort, defendants have unsuccessfully sought its dismissal, on the basis of untimeliness and other alleged defects and they now seek corrective relief from us. Resolution of the issues implicates the recent and portentous holding of the Court of Appeals in Video Corp. of America v. Flatto Assoc., 58 N.Y.2d 1026, 462 N.Y.S.2d 439, 448 N.E.2d 1350.

I

From 1968 through 1975, the Bank of Babylon (the Bank) purchased and retained $120,000 worth of bonds at the direction and for the account of plaintiff. When return of the bonds was requested by plaintiff in November, 1976, Edward Kozlowski, the president of the Bank, admitted that he had utilized the bonds for his own purposes and that they would not be returned. When plaintiff, who was a director of the Bank, reported this state of facts to the Bank's counsel, he was advised not to press any claim because to do so would damage the Bank and ruin Kozlowski's career. Kozlowski subsequently requested time to make restitution, furnished plaintiff with a written admission of liability, and provided some small cash payments for a few months. At a later point—between July and October 1977—Kozlowski informed plaintiff that he would be unable to return the bonds or their proceeds.

In October of 1977, upon notifying the Bank counsel of his intention to report the embezzlement, plaintiff was told that Kozlowski had threatened to kill him if suit was brought. These threats to plaintiff's life were repeated to him by the lawyer in September, 1978 and December, 1980. Despite his earlier declaration of inability to pay, in January of 1980 Kozlowski renewed his promise of full restitution, paid the plaintiff $300 at that time, and returned $10,000 worth of bonds the following month. In the absence of further payments, however, plaintiff finally reported the embezzlement directly to the Bank in February of 1981, but his demand for restitution was rejected. By May of 1981, when plaintiff sued Kozlowski, the Bank and its parent company, Irving Bank Corporation, four and one-half years had elapsed since return of the bonds had first been requested. After commencement of the action, Kozlowski returned an additional $30,000 worth of bonds and pleaded guilty to grand larceny in the third degree. Still unaccounted for are $80,000 worth of bonds.

II

Plaintiff's 10 causes of action include claims for conversion, money had and received, breach of fiduciary duty, breach of contract, negligence and fraud. At the outset, we conclude that the complaint against the Irving Bank should be dismissed. The Irving Bank was not a party to any contract with plaintiff and it may not be held liable for the torts of its subsidiary because the complaint fails to allege that it exercised complete domination and control over the subsidiary. Subsequent references to the defendants in this opinion do not include the Irving Bank.

The crux of defendants' challenge to timeliness is that the essence of the action is tort and since more than three years elapsed between accrual of the tort claims and the institution of suit, the complaint must be dismissed. We reject the Bank's assertion that the action accrued when the bonds were converted because where there is a delivery of personal property "not to be returned specifically or in kind at a fixed time or upon a fixed contingency" an action for conversion does not accrue until there is a demand for return of the property (see CPLR 206, subd. [a], par. 2; see, also, 1 Weinstein–Korn–Miller, N.Y.Civ.Prac., par. 206.02). Here, the bonds were not to be returned at a set time and accrual must therefore be computed from the time of demand in November, 1976, shortly after plaintiff learned of the wrong. Since the action was commenced four and one-half years after its causes of action accrued, we must decide whether it is the three-year Statute of Limitations governing conversion, negligence and breach of fiduciary duty * * * or the six-year statute governing contractual and quasi-contractual claims (see CPLR 213, subd. 2) that applies. Plaintiff argues, nonetheless, that this question need not be reached because Kozlowski's requests for delay, promises of restitution, threats of death, together with his admission of liability, estop defendants from raising time-bar as a defense. Only one of these contentions gives us pause.

While it is quite questionable whether mere oral promises can form the basis of estoppel in this State (see Scheuer v. Scheuer, 308 N.Y. 447, 126 N.E.2d 555; Shapley v. Abbott, 42 N.Y. 443), plaintiff relies on cases where estoppel was invoked against insurers who promised settlement and implied that the commencement of an action was unnecessary. There is no need to resolve that aspect of the estoppel question, however, because the instant promises were repudiated prior to the expiration of the Statute of Limitations while the plaintiff still had ample time to commence a tort action * * * When Kozlowski repudiated his earlier promises by telling plaintiff in the latter half of 1977 that he would neither return the bonds nor pay for them, not even one year had elapsed since the cause of action for conversion had accrued. Plaintiff's failure to bring suit within the two years remaining under the tort Statute of Limitations constituted a failure to exercise due diligence as a matter of law and estoppel based on the promises of payment is unavailable to defeat the defense of the Statute of Limitations (see 509 Sixth Ave. Corp. v. New York City Transit Authority, 24 A.D.2d 975, 265 N.Y.S.2d 429 [6 months remaining], supra; Ball v. Utica Mut. Ins. Co. of Utica, 60 Misc.2d 459, 303 N.Y.S.2d 233 [10 months]; Di Biase v. A & D, Inc., 351 A.2d 865 [Del] [2 years]; Sabath v. Mansfield, 60 Ill.App.3d 1008, 18 Ill.Dec. 8, 377 N.E.2d 161 [8 months]; Ford v. Rogovin, 289 Mass. 549, 199 N.E. 719 [Mass] [10 months]; Huhtala v. Travelers Ins. Co., 65 Mich.App. 581, 237 N.W.2d 567 [2 years]; Troutman v. Southern Railway Co., 296 F.Supp. 963 [1 year]; but see Arbutina v. Bahuleyan, 75 A.D.2d 84, 428 N.Y.S.2d 99 [2 months]; Redington v. Hartford Acc. & Indem. Co., 463

F.Supp. 83 [7 months]). Nor does Kozlowski's alleged renewal of his promise of full restitution in January, 1980 resuscitate the claim of estoppel, for by then the tort statute had run and renewal of the promises could not create a new estoppel or revive one that derived from earlier conduct (see 1 Williston, Contracts, § 186; 1A Corbin, Contracts, § 221).

We turn, then, to the more difficult aspect of the estoppel question—the effect of the death threats that were never repudiated and which continued for the two years following Kozlowski's repudiation of his promises of restitution. It is well settled that duress and undue influence are grounds for rescission of a contract where the complaining party is compelled to agree to the contract by means of a wrongful threat which precludes the exercise of free will. Furthermore, when duress is part of the cause of action alleged, the limitations period is tolled until the termination of the duress. Although such duress does not prevent the accrual of the cause of action, it tolls the running of the limitations statute because the offensive conduct is regarded as a continuous wrong.

Where the underlying action is unrelated to duress, however, the Statute of Limitations is not tolled by duress. The Court of Appeals so held in Piper v. Hoard, 107 N.Y. 67, 71 [1887], declaring that "the statute begins to run irrespective of * * * whether [the injured party] has enough of courage and independence to resist a hostile influence, and assert his rights or not". Not only has *Piper* never been overturned, but more recently the First Department has decided that a defendant's alleged threats of physical violence and loss of employment against the plaintiff "are insufficient to estop defendant * * * from arguing the defense of Statute of Limitations" (Stadtman v. Cambere, 73 A.D.2d 501, 422 N.Y.S.2d 102). Neither case provides any reasoning.

While other jurisdictions have suggested or assumed the possibility for the purpose of argument that duress might toll the limitations period for causes of action not based on duress, the ultimate resolution in each case was to reject duress as a toll on the facts presented. * * * Whether reluctance to recognize duress as a toll lies in the undesirability of a rule that turns on the reasonableness of reliance upon threats of physical or economic harm, the ease of fabrication of such threats * * * or simply in the judicial reluctance to create an entirely new defense to the Statute of Limitations * * * we do not assay to answer, for we are not inclined in this case to attempt overthrow of the old rule. Although *stare decisis* is not intended to effect a "petrifying rigidity" (Bing v. Thunig, 2 N.Y.2d 656, 667, 163 N.Y.S.2d 3, 143 N.E.2d 3), the substantive result we otherwise arrive at militates against use of this litigation to expand existing rules of estoppel. Thus, we decline the proffered opportunity to seek to relegate *Piper* to the ages or to announce that in this Department, duress independent of the grounds stated in a cause of action, will toll the Statute of Limitations.

III

We arrive, then, at the substance of the timeliness issues. The Bank contends that the essence of the action is conversion and that under the three-year tort limitation period (see CPLR 214, subd. 3) the action must be dismissed as untimely. Plaintiff responds that the essence of the action rule does not apply where the claim is for damages to pecuniary interest rather than personal injury, and therefore his action was timely under the six-year contract statute.

Fundamental to the difference between tort and contract actions is the nature of the interests protected. Tort actions were created to protect the interest in freedom from various kinds of harm and are based primarily on social policy. Contract actions derive, of course, from agreements entered into between parties. Tort and contract concepts are not wholly discrete, however, and the same facts may give rise to liability under both (Victorson v. Bock Laundry, 37 N.Y.2d 395, 373 N.Y.S.2d 39, 335 N.E.2d 275). "Between actions plainly *ex contractu* and those as clearly *ex delicto* there exists what has been termed a border-land, where the lines of distinction are shadowy and obscure, and the tort and the contract so approach each other, and become so nearly coincident as to make their practical separation somewhat difficult" (Rich v. New York Cent. and Hudson Riv. R.R. Co., 87 N.Y. 382, 390). Where tort and contract theories are both available to a plaintiff, the critical question often has been whether the plaintiff is entitled to the more favorable limitation period or whether the court must itself decide on the particular facts pleaded that the "gravamen" of the action is one or the other.

In resolving conflicts between the tort and contract limitations periods, the judiciary historically has looked toward the "essence of the action", a rule primarily applied to personal injury lawsuits * * * but sometimes applied to pecuniary interest cases as well * * * 25 Misc.2d 122, 204 N.Y.S.2d 410). In recent times, however, the Court of Appeals has disavowed blanket application of the essence of the action rule beyond personal injury actions and recognized that different policy considerations are involved in actions for damages to property or pecuniary interests (Sears, Roebuck & Co. v. Enco Assoc., 43 N.Y.2d 389, 401 N.Y.S.2d 767, 372 N.E.2d 555; Matter of Paver & Wildfoerster [Catholic High School Assn.], 38 N.Y.2d 669, 382 N.Y.S.2d 22, 345 N.E.2d 565). In the most notable case, a firm of architects contracted with Sears Roebuck to design plans and supervise the construction of parking ramps at one of its stores. Sears Roebuck ultimately sued the architects for negligence and breach of contract based on the failure to use professional care. With timeliness the issue, the Court of Appeals applied the six-year statute and reinstated the tort and contract causes of action while limiting proof on the issues of damages to the contract measure * * * The court held * * * that when damage to property or pecuniary interests is involved, the six-year statute governs regardless of how the theory of liability is described, as long as the asserted liability "had its genesis in the contractual relationship of the parties".

The significance and meaning of *Sears* were recently illuminated in a case that has not yet attracted the attention it merits, for the Court of Appeals now has explicitly declared that an action for failure to exercise due care in the performance of a contract, where the plaintiff seeks damages for injury to property or pecuniary interests, is governed by the six-year Statute of Limitations (see Video Corp. of Amer. v. Flatto Assoc., 58 N.Y.2d 1026, 462 N.Y.S.2d 439, 448 N.E.2d 1350, *supra*). Since *Video Corp.* involved no written contract and dealt with the failure of an insurance broker to obtain adequate insurance coverage, the holding was an apparent response to the restrictive manner in which three departments of the Appellate Division interpreted *Sears* when confronted with malpractice claims against accountants, lawyers and insurance brokers. All three departments had viewed *Sears* as solely applicable to cases involving detailed written agreements. * * * In rejecting this restriction, the Court of Appeals in *Video Corp.* reached out to specifically overrule Gilbert Props. v. Millstein, 33 N.Y.2d 857, 352 N.Y.S.2d 198, 307 N.E.2d 257, a malpractice action against an attorney, and Adler & Topal v. Exclusive Envelope Corp. [, 84 A.D.2d 365, 446 N.Y.S.2d 337], a case that was not even before the court, involving an informal contract for accounting services.

Although the Court of Appeals cited Prosser in concluding that different policy considerations pertain where damages to property or pecuniary interests are involved as opposed to personal injuries * * *, the considerations were not particularized and further elucidation was not provided by the Prosser citation (see Prosser, Torts [4th ed.], § 92, p. 621). We perceive one of the considerations as the recognition that determination of the essence of an action where pecuniary interests are involved is difficult almost to the point of requiring arbitrary resolution. *Video Corp.* seems to draw a bright line which will ease selection of limitations periods for property or pecuniary interest cases, a process previously described as a "snarl of utter confusion" (see Prosser, The Borderline of Tort and Contracts, p. 434). The *Video Corp.* result is also consonant with Siegel's observation that "it does seem wrong to restrict a plaintiff, injured in effect by two wrongs, to the shorter of their time periods" (Siegel, N.Y. Practice, p. 40), for a wrongdoer should not be permitted to allege his own wrong for the purpose of defeating an action on the basis of the Statute of Limitations (see Ganley v. Troy City Nat. Bank, 98 N.Y. 487, 494; Angell, Limitations [5th ed.], § 72; 1 Wood, Limitations of Actions [3rd ed.], § 57b). Those who seek recompense for injury to property or pecuniary interests can now select a remedy less likely to be frustrated by time restrictions, provided they are willing to limit themselves to contractual damages.

With this jurisprudential backdrop, we proceed to the selection of the limitations period that governs the current claims. The complaint sufficiently alleges the creation of a bailment contract with the Bank since the plaintiff was entitled to the return of the identical bonds deposited with the Bank for safekeeping * * *. As bailee, the Bank was required, of course, to exercise reasonable care so as to prevent loss of or damage to the property * * *. Since the claimed damage is to property or pecuniary interests and the asserted liability not only relates in part to an alleged failure to use due care, but also "had its genesis in the contractual relationship of the parties" (Sears, Roebuck & Co. v. Enco Assoc., 43 N.Y.2d 389, 396, 401 N.Y.S.2d 767, 372 N.E.2d 555, *supra*), application of the six-year Statute of Limitations to the claims against the Bank is mandated by *Sears* and *Video Corp.* Thus, the complaint against the Bank is not barred by the Statute of Limitations. While plaintiff is limited to the contract measure of damages, the difference between tort and contract damages in this case is hardly discernible since both standards would permit recovery of the value of the bonds plus accrued interest. There may be a real distinction as far as punitive damages are concerned since they are rarely available for mere breach of contract, but that is an issue we need not decide at this juncture.

While Kozlowski was not a party to the bailment contract, the six-year Statute of Limitations applies to the causes against him based on plaintiff's claim of unjust enrichment. It is well-settled that a plaintiff may elect to waive a conversion claim and sue in assumpsit or quasi-contract * * *. This election proceeds upon the theory that the plaintiff is deemed to ratify the conversion and proceed upon an implied contract of sale of the converted property to the wrongdoer. * * * There is no election as of yet, since inconsistent theories may be advanced in pleadings (see CPLR 3002, 3014; Cohn v. Lionel Corp., 21 N.Y.2d 559, 289 N.Y.S.2d 404, 236 N.E.2d 634), with the choice usually not required to be made until the trial at a time within the discretion of the Trial Judge * * *.

IV

Finally, we must dispose of two other challenges to the complaint based on the asserted insufficiency of certain causes of action. We agree with the Bank that no action for unjust enrichment lies against it because it was not enriched by Kozlowski's embezzlement. A quasi-contractual obligation is one imposed by law when the acts of the parties or others have placed in the possession of the defendant money or its equivalent "under such circumstances that in equity and good conscience he ought not to retain it" (Miller v. Schloss, 218 N.Y. 400, 407, 113 N.E. 337; see, also, Bradkin v. Leverton, 26 N.Y.2d 192, 197, 309 N.Y.S.2d 192, 257 N.E.2d 643). Although performance of any wrongful act by the defendant is not required * * * there must be unjust enrichment as between the parties to the transaction (McGrath v. Hilding, 41 N.Y.2d 625, 394 N.Y.S.2d 603, 363 N.E.2d 328; Restatement, Restitution, § 1). The enrichment may either be the receipt of money or its equivalent * * * or by being saved from expenses or loss. Since the complaint alleges that Kozlowski converted the bonds "to his own use and benefit", the Bank was not enriched by the conversion. * * * While a principal may be liable in tort for the actions of its embezzling agent, it cannot be held for unjust enrichment for the simple reason that it has not been enriched. Accordingly, the second cause of action for money had and received should be dismissed as to the Bank.

In addition, the seventh cause of action for fraud should be dismissed. It alleges that Kozlowski and the Bank falsely misrepresented to the plaintiff that the bonds would be returned, thereby causing him loss when the Statute of Limitations expired. If the failure to commence an action before the expiration of the Statute of Limitations is due to fraud practiced upon the plaintiff, a cause of action will lie for the loss sustained. * * * Here, however, the misrepresentations caused plaintiff no loss since he had two years to sue in tort after Kozlowski repudiated the fraud.

* * *

Order of the Supreme Court, Suffolk County, dated March 29, 1982 modified, on the law, and defendants' motions granted to the extent that the complaint is dismissed against defendant Irving Bank, the second and seventh causes of action are dismissed as against defendant Bank of Babylon, and the seventh cause of action is dismissed as against defendant Kozlowski, and the motions are otherwise denied. As so modified, order affirmed, without costs or disbursements.

NOTE: PRIVATE CONTRACTUAL LIMITATIONS

The most common form of *private* limitation on a suit is the statutory and contractual standard form of casualty insurance which bars suit on the policy "unless commenced within twelve months after the fire" or "within twelve months next after discovery by the insured of the occurrence which gives rise to the claim."

In Fratto v. New Amsterdam Casualty Co., 434 Pa. 136, 252 A.2d 606 (1969) the insured brought an action in federal district court against an insurance company in April 1963, for a 1962 fire loss. In June 1963, insured brought a second action in federal district court against nine other insurance companies. Both actions were consolidated for trial.

In June 1965, the second action against the several insurance companies was dismissed on the court's motion for failure to meet the jurisdictional amount.

Later that month the insured started suit in state court on the same facts and cause of action as in the federal suit that had been dismissed.

Defendant insurance companies moved for summary judgment which was granted. Since the fire loss was in 1962 and suit in state court was not until 1965, the state action was barred because the standard fire insurance contract provided that the suit must be brought within twelve months after the event (fire). Motion granted, and the Pennsylvania Supreme Court affirmed on the narrow issue of whether insurance company defendants' admission of jurisdiction in the federal district court lulled the plaintiff into a false sense of security thus enabling the defendants to take advantage of the plaintiff. If so, defendant insurance companies are estopped from raising the policy limitation (action within 12 months) as a bar to an action in the state court. Here plaintiff was thought not to have been misled regarding the insurers' intentions. Since the matter was being litigated, the parties were dealing at arms length and hence no lulling.

Should this kind of contractual statute of limitations be tolled during the time when the insured could have started suit but did not because of ongoing negotiations in which the insurer had not denied its liability? Ford Motor Co. v. Lumbermens Mutual Cas. Co., 413 Mich. 22, 319 N.W.2d 320 (1982) held that the period of limitations is tolled from the time the insured gives notice of the loss until the insurer explicitly or formally denies liability. This seems a minority view.

The standard policy provisions give 60 days for the insured to supply proofs of loss and another 60 days after that for the insurer to pay the claim. Of course there can be waiver if both parties take the full 60 days and protracted negotiations follow during the next several months. Most of the reported cases seem to be decided on whether negotiations were terminated with a reasonable amount of time remaining in which the insured could file suit. Vestevich v. Liberty Mutual Ins. Co., 47 Mich.App. 490, 209 N.W.2d 486 (1973) held that 50 days remaining is a reasonable time and if suit is not started within the 50 days, the claim is barred.

SAVINGS STATUTES

Markoff v. South Nassau Community Hosp.

Court of Appeals of New York, 1984.
61 N.Y.2d 283, 473 N.Y.S.2d 766, 461 N.E.2d 1253.

■ COOKE, CHIEF JUDGE.

When an action that has been timely commenced is later dismissed, CPLR 205 (subd. [a]) provides that, even if the Statute of Limitations has or will run, a new action may be commenced within six months of the termination, except if the dismissal was on the merits, for failure to prosecute, or by voluntary discontinuance. An action will not be deemed "commenced," however, until there has been proper service of a summons upon a defendant in compliance with the appropriate method prescribed by the CPLR. Therefore, when an action is dismissed for lack of personal jurisdiction because service of the summons was defective, or because service never occurred, CPLR 205 (subd. [a]) will not apply notwithstanding a defendant's actual notice, because the action was never "commenced," within the meaning of that statute.

Milton Markoff was treated by defendant doctors at defendant South Nassau Community Hospital in October, 1978. Eight months after his discharge, Mr. Markoff died, allegedly as a result of defendants' malpractice. Plaintiff Ruth Markoff, individually and as executrix of the estate of her husband, sought to commence an action for medical malpractice and wrongful death.

On March 19, 1981, following an initial unsuccessful attempt to effect service on July 14, 1980, plaintiff obtained an ex parte order authorizing expedient service upon defendants pursuant to CPLR 308 (subd. 5). Pursuant to this, summonses were left for defendants at the hospital on March 30, 1981. Defendants' answer asserted the defense of lack of personal jurisdiction, and they moved to vacate the ex parte order. Vacatur was granted in May, 1981. The action was terminated for lack of personal jurisdiction, due to the absence of any valid service, by an order dated September 23, 1981.

Meanwhile, in late August and early September, 1981, plaintiff had personally served defendants in compliance with CPLR 308 (subd. 1). On October 22, 1981, defendants served an answer that raised the Statute of Limitations as a defense. Plaintiff, in turn, notified defendants that they were in default because the answer was untimely. Defendants successfully moved to vacate the default. Defendants also succeeded in having the action dismissed as barred by the Statute of Limitations, notwithstanding plaintiff's invocation of CPLR 205.

The Appellate Division, 91 A.D.2d 1064, 458 N.Y.S.2d 672, affirmed the order vacating the ex parte order authorizing expedient service and the order dismissing the complaint as barred by the Statute of Limitations. This court now affirms.

In the present case, the Statutes of Limitations expired in June, 1981, for the wrongful death action and in April, 1981, for the medical malpractice action. Proper service did not occur until the following August and September. Thus, plaintiff's action is time barred unless she may take advantage of CPLR 205.[2]

CPLR 205 (subd. [a]) provides that when "an action is timely commenced" but it is later terminated, the plaintiff may commence a new action within six months after the termination. The new action must arise from the same transaction or occurrence, and the new action must have been timely if it had been commenced when the prior action was instituted. The statute by its express terms provides that it is not applicable when the action is terminated by voluntary discontinuance, a dismissal for neglect to prosecute, or a final judgment on the merits.

The requisite predicate for the application of CPLR 205 (subd. [a]) is that the terminated action must have been "timely commenced" (see Carrick v. Central Gen. Hosp., 51 N.Y.2d 242, 250, 434 N.Y.S.2d 130, 414 N.E.2d 632). An action is "commenced," within the meaning of any statute governing limitation, including CPLR 205 (subd. [a]) when there has been service of a summons (see CPLR 203, subd. [b]). Service is only effective, however, when it is made pursuant to the appropriate method authorized by the CPLR. Actual notice alone will not sustain the service or subject a person to the court's jurisdiction when there has not been compliance with prescribed conditions of service.

Therefore, when an action is dismissed for lack of personal jurisdiction due to a lack of or improper service, it has not been "commenced" for purposes of CPLR 205 (subd. [a]). This failure precludes the application of the statute.[3]

---

2. Plaintiff also challenges both the vacatur of service and the vacatur of defendants' default in answering. Both orders are matters to be determined within the discretion of the Appellate Division. As such, this court may only reverse if the Appellate Division abused its discretion as a matter of law. It was not such an abuse of discretion to affirm the vacatur of the ex parte order authorizing expedient service. The plaintiff's conclusory affidavit stating that service was impracticable under the other provisions of CPLR 308, without specifying why or that prior attempts were made, was insufficient to justify the order of expedient service under CPLR 308 (subd. 5). * * *

3. To the extent that Amato v. Svedi, 35 A.D.2d 672, 315 N.Y.S.2d 63, supports the

In so holding, the court does not create a new exception outside those expressly provided in the statute. Rather, it merely recognizes that timely commencement of the prior action is a condition precedent to the invocation of CPLR 205 (subd. [a]), and that an action dismissed for lack of personal jurisdiction based upon improper service has not satisfied that condition.

When the ex parte order authorizing the alternative method of service was vacated here, the service made in March, 1981 was nullified. Plaintiff never made a proper service until after the pertinent Statutes of Limitations had run. Consequently, the prior action was never timely commenced and she is barred from taking advantage of CPLR 205 (subd. [a]).

Accordingly, the order of the Appellate Division should be affirmed, with costs.

NOTE ON MARKOFF

In 1992, the New York legislature amended the Civil Practice Law and Rules to provide that, in the major trial courts of New York (supreme and county courts), actions would be commenced for statute of limitations purposes from the filing of the summons and complaint. Similar to the system under the Federal Rules, plaintiff then has 120 days to serve the defendant and file proof of service with the court.

Under CPLR 306–b(a) any action in which proof of service is not filed within 120 days from filing is "deemed dismissed" with respect to an unserved defendant. However, CPLR-b(b) contains a savings clause. It provides that plaintiff can commence "a new action" within 120 days of the 306–b(a) dismissal, even if the statute of limitations has run. Does this mean *Markoff* has been legislatively overruled?

The answer, like many aspects of New York procedure, is unclear and rather complicated. Far from being legislatively repealed, CPLR 205(a), the savings statute involved in *Markoff*, was amended in 1992 to expressly incorporate the *Markoff* holding. CPLR 205(a) now provides that the six month period provided in that section for commencing a new action is available:

> If an action is timely commenced and is terminated in any other manner than by a voluntary discontinuance, *a failure to obtain personal jurisdiction over the defendant*, a dismissal of the complaint for neglect to prosecute the action, or a final judgment upon the merits. . . .

(emphasis added)

However, under CPLR 306–b(a), an action is now commenced by filing, so an action may be timely commenced even though no service has been made. If the action is then deemed dismissed for failure to effect proper service of file proof of service within 120 days, under CPLR 306–b(b), plaintiff has another 120 days to commence a new action and make effective service. Could the plaintiff in *Markoff* have made use of this provision if it had existed in 1981?

view that CPLR 205 (subd. [a]) does apply if a defendant receives actual notice but there is a technical flaw in the method of service resulting in a dismissal for lack of personal jurisdiction, that decision is in error. A careful reading of *Amato* reveals that the dismissal there was based upon the absence of subject matter jurisdiction, and the references to a lack of "personal jurisdiction" are inadvertent.

NOTE ON THE ACCRUAL AND "DISCOVERY" RULES

Justice Stevens, dissenting in United States v. Kubrick, 444 U.S. 111, 125 (1979) justifies the "discovery" rule, the application of which can toll the statute of limitations:

"Normally a tort claim accrues at the time of the plaintiff's injury. In most cases that event provides adequate notice to the plaintiff of the possibility that his legal rights have been invaded. It is well settled, however, that the normal rule does not apply to medical malpractice claims under the Federal Tort Claims Act. The reason for this exception is essentially the same as the reason for the general rule itself. The victim of medical malpractice frequently has no reason to believe that his legal rights have been invaded simply because some misfortune has followed medical treatment. Sometimes he may not even be aware of the actual injury until years have passed; at other times, he may recognize the harm but not know its cause; or, as in this case, he may have knowledge of the injury and its cause, but have no reason to suspect that a physician has been guilty of any malpractice. In such cases—until today—the rule that has been applied in the federal courts is that the statute of limitations does not begin to run until after fair notice of the invasion of the plaintiff's legal rights.

"Essentially, there are two possible approaches to construction of the word 'accrues' in statutes of limitations: (1) a claim might be deemed to 'accrue' at the moment of injury without regard to the potentially harsh consequence of barring a meritorious claim before the plaintiff has a reasonable chance to assert his legal rights, or (2) it might 'accrue' when a diligent plaintiff has knowledge of facts sufficient to put him on notice of an invasion of his legal rights. The benefits that flow from certainty in the administration of our affairs favor the former approach in most commercial situations. But in medical malpractice cases the harsh consequences of that approach have generally been considered unacceptable."

G. Denial and Reply

David v. Crompton & Knowles Corp.

United States District Court, Eastern District of Pennsylvania, 1973.
58 F.R.D. 444.

■ Huyett, District Judge.

The present case is a products liability action involving a serious personal injury. Defendant, Crompton & Knowles Corporation (Crompton), seeks to amend its answer to Paragraph 5 of the complaint which alleges that Crompton designed, manufactured and sold a shredding machine, 600 AAZ Series 11, to Crown Products Corporation (Crown). In its answer to the complaint Crompton averred that it was without sufficient knowledge or information to admit or deny the allegation and demanded proof. It now seeks to deny that it designed, manufactured and sold the machine in question.

Crompton bases its proffered denial upon information which it claims it discovered during 1972. It alleges that the machine was designed, manufactured and sold by James Hunter Corporation (Hunter) prior to its purchase of Hunter, and that it did not assume liabilities for the negligent design, manufacture or sale of machines by Hunter prior to its purchase of Hunter's assets in 1961.

An answer to an averment in a complaint which states that the party lacks sufficient information or knowledge to admit or deny the averments is permitted by Fed.R.Civ.P. 8(b) and it has the effect of a denial. A party, however, may not deny sufficient information or knowledge with impunity, but is subject to the requirements of honesty in pleading. *See,* 2A J. Moore, Federal Practice ¶ 8.22 (1968). An averment will be deemed admitted when the matter is obviously one as to which defendant has knowledge or information. Mesirow v. Duggan, 240 F.2d 751 (8 Cir.), cert. denied sub nom. Duggan v. Green, 355 U.S. 864, 78 S.Ct. 93, 2 L.Ed.2d 70 (1957). Crompton claims that it only recently discovered the information which it now uses as a basis to deny the allegations of Paragraph 5. Plaintiff contends that Crompton's denial of knowledge or information was patently false and should be treated as an admission.

The request for leave to amend assumes significance if Crompton's original answer to Paragraph 5 is deemed an admission. If it is considered an admission, then it is necessary to decide whether an amendment which might greatly affect plaintiff's right to recovery should be allowed, but if it is not deemed admitted and is considered denied in the original answer, then the amendment will only serve as a clarification.

The machine which was involved in the accident was designed, manufactured and sold by Hunter to Crown in 1961. Crompton admits that it was aware that the machine was a Hunter product at the time it answered the complaint or very shortly thereafter.[3] Nevertheless, in answers to interrogatories and in a third-party complaint Crompton indicated that it was responsible for the design, manufacture and sale of the machine which was made prior to its purchase of Hunter. Crompton relies entirely on its claim that it has only recently discovered that the contract by which it purchased Hunter did not make it responsible for liabilities of this kind.

In Mesirow v. Duggan, *supra,* the court held that if the matter alleged in the averment was a matter of record peculiarly within the control and knowledge of the defendant, an answer that defendant was without knowledge or information sufficient to form a belief did not constitute a denial under Fed.R.Civ.P. 8(b). *See also,* American Photocopy Equipment Co. v. Rovico, Inc., 359 F.2d 745 (7 Cir.1966); Harvey Aluminum, Inc. v. N.L.R.B., 335 F.2d 749 (9 Cir.1964); Squire v. Levan, 32 F.Supp. 437 (E.D.Pa.1940); 2A J. Moore, Federal Practice ¶ 8.22 (1968). In the present case Crompton admits knowledge of Hunter's role in the design, manufacture and sale of the machine. Its assertion of lack of knowledge or information, therefore, must have been in relation to responsibility which it assumed for such a claim. Any responsibility, of course, arises from the agreement of sale be-

3. In answers to interrogatories Crompton asserted that it learned of the action from Hunter, which is now a division of Crompton.

tween Crompton and Hunter. The terms of this agreement are certainly peculiarly within the control and knowledge of Crompton, one of the parties to the agreement. It does not seem too burdensome to hold Crompton to knowledge of the terms of its purchase agreement and their effect on its rights and liabilities more than nine years after the sale of Hunter was completed. The averment of lack of knowledge or information sufficient to admit or deny the allegations of Paragraph 5 is not proper under these circumstances and plaintiff's allegation should be deemed admitted.

The next question is whether Crompton should now be permitted to amend its answer to deny the allegation in Paragraph 5. Crompton relies upon Fed.R.Civ.P. 15(a) which provides that leave to amend an answer should be freely given when justice requires. The Federal Rules clearly favor a liberal attitude towards amendments. The purpose of a permissive attitude is to encourage decision of the case on the merits by allowing parties to present the real issues of the case. *See,* United States v. E.B. Hougham, 364 U.S. 310, 317, 81 S.Ct. 13, 5 L.Ed.2d 8 (1960).

A court may deny a request to amend if it bases such denial upon a valid ground. Among the reasons commonly cited for denying permission to amend are that the amendment will result in undue prejudice to the other party, Zenith Radio Corp. v. Hazeltine Research, Inc., 401 U.S. 321, 330, 91 S.Ct. 795, 28 L.Ed.2d 77 (1971), or that it has been unduly delayed, Albee Homes, Inc. v. Lutman, 406 F.2d 11, 14 (3d Cir.1969). See, 3 J. Moore, Federal Practice ¶ 15.08[4] at 897–898 (1968). Plaintiff claims that Crompton should be denied leave to amend because of undue delay by defendant and prejudice to plaintiff if Crompton's motion is granted.

Crompton, as indicated above, knew the basic facts surrounding the manufacture and delivery of the machine no later than October 1, 1971 when it filed answers to interrogatories. It almost certainly knew the essential facts much earlier. Crompton had examined the machinery in question by June, 1971. It had received information concerning the machine from plaintiff's counsel in March, 1971. The proffered reason for this delay, Crompton's recent discovery that it was not liable for such liabilities of Hunter, cannot be considered good cause for the reasons discussed above.

The effect of this delay could be highly prejudicial to the plaintiff. The action arose on November 27, 1969. The two-year statute of limitation expired on November 27, 1971. Plaintiff is now barred from instituting this action against another party.

* * *

Under the circumstances of this case defendant's motion to amend will be denied. This may be burdensome to defendant and may deny to it an otherwise valid defense, but that is a situation of its own making. To allow the amendment would be to penalize the plaintiff who is without fault and leave him without a possible remedy for very severe injuries.

NOTES

A. Is any particular form required for a specific denial? Suppose defendant denies "that plaintiff did sell and deliver 50 bales of hay to said defendant on January 2, 1974." Is any part of this an admission? See discussion of the negative pregnant in Wright and Miller, Federal Practice and Procedure: Civil § 1267 (1969).

In Freedom National Bank v. Northern Ill. Corp., 202 F.2d 601, 605 (7th Cir.1953) the court said:

> " * * * An examination of the pleadings reveals the fact that in its answer to the complaint the defendant expressly admitted the allegation of the complaint that on August 2, 1948, several months after the conversion, the Trailmobile trailer was valued at $4,000. And to the allegation of the complaint that at the time of the conversion, in January 1948, the value of the trailer exceeded $4,718.25, the defendant in its answer denied only that the value at that time *exceeded* that sum. By denying that the value of the trailer at that time exceeded that sum, the defendant impliedly admitted that the value then equalled the sum of $4,718.25.

> "That which a defendant admits in his answer is binding upon him until he withdraws the admission by a proper amended or supplemental pleading. No such amended or supplemental pleading was filed by the defendant in this case. The plaintiff, therefore, had the right to rely on the defendant's admission of value and was under no duty to adduce evidence to prove the $4,000 valuation found by the court."

B. The distinction between a "reply" to a counterclaim and an "answer" to a complaint, crossclaim, or third-party complaint is of little importance because procedurally and functionally they are the same. However, a reply is necessary and mandatory only when an answer contains what has been denominated as a counterclaim. Failure to reply to an answer with a denominated counterclaim (or to respond to a court ordered reply) constitutes an admission.

Beeck v. Aquaslide 'N' Dive Corp.

United States Court of Appeals for the Eighth Circuit, 1977.
562 F.2d 537.

■ BENSON, DISTRICT JUDGE.

This case is an appeal from the trial court's exercise of discretion on procedural matters in a diversity personal injury action.

Jerry A. Beeck was severely injured on July 15, 1972, while using a water slide. He and his wife, Judy A. Beeck, sued Aquaslide 'N' Dive Corporation (Aquaslide), a Texas corporation, alleging it manufactured the slide involved in the accident, and sought to recover substantial damages on theories of negligence, strict liability and breach of implied warranty.

Aquaslide initially admitted manufacture of the slide, but later moved to amend its answer to deny manufacture; the motion was resisted. The district court granted leave to amend.[2] On motion of the defendant, a separate trial was held on the issue of "whether the defendant designed, manufactured or sold the slide in question." This

2. Beeck v. Aquaslide 'N' Dive Corporation, 67 F.R.D. 411 (S.D.Iowa 1975).

motion was also resisted by the plaintiffs. The issue was tried to a jury, which returned a verdict for the defendant, after which the trial court entered summary judgment of dismissal of the case. Plaintiffs took this appeal, and stated the issues presented for review to be:

1. Where the manufacturer of the product, a water slide, admitted in its Answer and later in its Answer to Interrogatories both filed prior to the running of the statute of limitations that it designed, manufactured and sold the water slide in question, was it an abuse of the trial court's discretion to grant leave to amend to the manufacturer in order to deny these admissions after the running of the statute of limitations?

2. After granting the manufacturer's Motion for Leave to Amend in order to deny the prior admissions of design, manufacture and sale of the water slide in question, was it an abuse of the trial court's discretion to further grant the manufacturer's Motion for a Separate Trial on the issue of manufacture?

I. Facts

A brief review of the facts found by the trial court in its order granting leave to amend, and which do not appear to have been in dispute, is essential to a full understanding of appellants' claims.

In 1971 Kimberly Village Home Association of Davenport, Iowa, ordered an Aquaslide product from one George Boldt, who was a local distributor handling defendant's products. The order was forwarded by Boldt to Sentry Pool and Chemical Supply Co. in Rock Island, Illinois, and Sentry forwarded the order to Purity Swimming Pool Supply in Hammond, Indiana. A slide was delivered from a Purity warehouse to Kimberly Village, and was installed by Kimberly employees. On July 15, 1972, Jerry A. Beeck was injured while using the slide at a social gathering sponsored at Kimberly Village by his employer, Harker Wholesale Meats, Inc. Soon after the accident investigations were undertaken by representatives of the separate insurers of Harker and Kimberly Village. On October 31, 1972, Aquaslide first learned of the accident through a letter sent by a representative of Kimberly's insurer to Aquaslide, advising that "one of your Queen Model #Q–3D slides" was involved in the accident. Aquaslide forwarded this notification to its insurer. Aquaslide's insurance adjuster made an on-site investigation of the slide in May, 1973, and also interviewed persons connected with the ordering and assembly of the slide. An inter-office letter dated September 23, 1973, indicates that Aquaslide's insurer was of the opinion the "Aquaslide in question was definitely manufactured by our insured." The complaint was filed October 15, 1973.[3] Investigators for three different insurance companies, representing Harker, Kimberly and the defendant, had concluded that the slide had been manufactured by Aquaslide, and the defendant, with no information to the contrary, answered the complaint on December 12, 1973, and

3. Aquaslide 'N' Dive Corporation was the sole defendant named in the complaint.

admitted that it "designed, manufactured, assembled and sold" the slide in question.[4]

The statute of limitations on plaintiff's personal injury claim expired on July 15, 1974. About six and one-half months later Carl Meyer, president and owner of Aquaslide, visited the site of the accident prior to the taking of his deposition by the plaintiff.[5] From his on-site inspection of the slide, he determined it was not a product of the defendant. Thereafter, Aquaslide moved the court for leave to amend its answer to deny manufacture of the slide.

II. Leave to Amend

Amendment of pleadings in civil actions is governed by Rule 15(a), F.R.Civ.P., which provides in part that once issue is joined in a lawsuit, a party may amend his pleading "only by leave of court or by written consent of the adverse party; and leave shall be freely given when justice so requires."

In Foman v. Davis, 371 U.S. 178, 83 S.Ct. 227, 9 L.Ed.2d 222 (1962), the Supreme Court had occasion to construe that portion of Rule 15(a) set out above:

> Rule 15(a) declares that leave to amend "shall be freely given when justice so requires," this mandate is to be heeded. * * * If the underlying facts or circumstances relied upon by a plaintiff may be a proper subject of relief, he ought to be afforded an opportunity to test his claim on the merits. In the absence of any apparent or declared reason—such as undue delay, bad faith or dilatory motive on the part of the movant, repeated failure to cure deficiencies by amendments previously allowed, undue prejudice to the opposing party by virtue of allowance of the amendment, futility of amendment, etc.—the leave sought should, as the rules require, be "freely given." Of course, the grant or denial of an opportunity to amend is within the discretion of the District Court, * * *.

371 U.S. at 182, 83 S.Ct. at 230. *See also* McIndoo v. Burnett, 494 F.2d 1311 (8th Cir.1974); Standard Title Ins. Co. v. Roberts, 349 F.2d 613 (8th Cir.1965).

This Court in Hanson v. Hunt Oil Co., 398 F.2d 578, 582 (8th Cir.1968), held that "[p]rejudice *must be shown.*" (Emphasis added). The burden is on the party opposing the amendment to show such prejudice. In ruling on a motion for leave to amend, the trial court must inquire into the issue of prejudice to the opposing party, in light of the particular facts of the case. Standard Title Ins. Co. v. Roberts, 349 F.2d at 622.

Certain principles apply to appellate review of a trial court's grant or denial of a motion to amend pleadings. First, as noted in *Foman v.*

---

4. In answers to interrogatories filed on June 3, 1974, Aquaslide again admitted manufacture of the slide in question.

5. Plaintiffs apparently requested Meyer to inspect the slide prior to the taking of his deposition to determine whether it was defectively installed or assembled.

Davis, allowance or denial of leave to amend lies within the sound discretion of the trial court, and is reviewable only for an abuse of discretion. The appellate court must view the case in the posture in which the trial court acted in ruling on the motion to amend.

It is evident from the order of the district court that in the exercise of its discretion in ruling on defendant's motion for leave to amend, it searched the record for evidence of bad faith, prejudice and undue delay which might be sufficient to overbalance the mandate of Rule 15(a), F.R.Civ.P., and *Foman v. Davis*, that leave to amend should be "freely given." Plaintiffs had not at any time conceded that the slide in question had not been manufactured by the defendant, and at the time the motion for leave to amend was at issue, the court had to decide whether the defendant should be permitted to litigate a material factual issue on its merits.

In inquiring into the issue of bad faith, the court noted the fact that the defendant, in initially concluding that it had manufactured the slide, relied upon the conclusions of three different insurance companies,[6] each of which had conducted an investigation into the circumstances surrounding the accident. This reliance upon investigations of three insurance companies, and the fact that "no contention has been made by anyone that the defendant influenced this possibly erroneous conclusion," persuaded the court that "defendant has not acted in such bad faith as to be precluded from contesting the issue of manufacture at trial." The court further found "[t]o the extent that 'blame' is to be spread regarding the original identification, the record indicates that it should be shared equally."

In considering the issue of prejudice that might result to the plaintiffs from the granting of the motion for leave to amend, the trial court held that the facts presented to it did not support plaintiffs' assertion that, because of the running of the two year Iowa statute of limitations on personal injury claims, the allowance of the amendment would sound the "death knell" of the litigation. In order to accept plaintiffs' argument, the court would have had to assume that the defendant would prevail at trial on the factual issue of manufacture of the slide, and further that plaintiffs would be foreclosed, should the amendment be allowed, from proceeding against other parties if they were unsuccessful in pressing their claim against Aquaslide. On the state of the record before it, the trial court was unwilling to make such assumptions,[7] and concluded "[u]nder these circumstances, the Court

---

6. The insurer of Beeck's employer, the insurer of Kimberly Village, as well as the defendant's insurer had each concluded the slide in question was an Aquaslide.

7. The district court noted in its order granting leave to amend that plaintiffs may be able to sue other parties as a result of the substituting of a "counterfeit" slide for the Aquaslide, if indeed this occurred. The court added:

[a]gain, the Court is handicapped by an unclear record on this issue. If, in fact, the slide in question is not an Aquaslide, the replacement entered the picture somewhere along the Boldt to Sentry, Sentry to Purity, Purity to Kimberly Village chain of distribution. Depending upon the circumstances of its entry, a cause of action sounding in fraud or contract might lie. If so, the applicable statute of limitations period would not have run. Further, as defendant points out,

deems that the possible prejudice to the plaintiffs is an insufficient basis on which to deny the proposed amendment." The court reasoned that the amendment would merely allow the defendant to contest a disputed factual issue at trial, and further that it would be prejudicial to the defendant to deny the amendment.

The court also held that defendant and its insurance carrier, in investigating the circumstances surrounding the accident, had not been so lacking in diligence as to dictate a denial of the right to litigate the factual issue of manufacture of the slide.

On this record we hold that the trial court did not abuse its discretion in allowing the defendant to amend its answer.

III.   Separate Trials

After Aquaslide was granted leave to amend its answer, it moved pursuant to Rule 42(b), F.R.Civ.P., for a separate trial on the issue of manufacture of the slide involved in the accident. The grounds upon which the motion was based were:

> (1) a separate trial solely on the issue of whether the slide was manufactured by Aquaslide would save considerable trial time and unnecessary expense and preparation for all parties and the court, and (2) a separate trial solely on the issue of manufacture would protect Aquaslide from substantial prejudice.

The court granted the motion for a separate trial on the issue of manufacture, and this grant of a separate trial is challenged by appellants as being an abuse of discretion.

A trial court's severance of trial will not be disturbed on appeal except for an abuse of discretion. * * *

The record indicates that Carl Meyer, president and owner of Aquaslide, designs the slides sold by Aquaslide. The slide which plaintiff Jerry A. Beeck was using at the time of his accident was very similar in appearance to an Aquaslide product, and was without identifying marks. Kimberly Village had in fact ordered an Aquaslide for its swimming pool, and thought it had received one. After Meyer's inspection and Aquaslide's subsequent assertion that it was not an Aquaslide product, plaintiffs elected to stand on their contention that it was in fact an Aquaslide. This raised a substantial issue of material fact which, if resolved in defendant's favor, would exonerate defendant from liability.

Plaintiff Jerry A. Beeck had been severely injured, and he and his wife together were seeking damages arising out of those injuries in the sum of $2,225,000.00. Evidence of plaintiffs' injuries and damages would clearly have taken up several days of trial time, and because of the severity of the injuries, may have been prejudicial to the defendant's claim of non-manufacture. The jury, by special interrogatory,

the doctrine of equitable estoppel might possibly preclude another defendant from asserting the two-year statute as a defense.   67 F.R.D. at 415.

found that the slide had not been manufactured by Aquaslide. That finding has not been questioned on appeal. Judicial economy, beneficial to all the parties, was obviously served by the trial court's grant of a separate trial. We hold the Rule 42(b) separation was not an abuse of discretion.

The judgment of the district court is affirmed.

CHAPTER IV

DISCOVERY

A. THE ROLE OF DISCOVERY IN THE LITIGATION PROCESS

The 1993 amendments to the Federal Rules of Civil Procedure constituted the most sweeping changes in the Federal Rules dealing with discovery in over twenty years. In many federal district courts, however, there has been virtually no modification at all in the way discovery is conducted. The explanation for this apparent anomaly is that those rules which contained the most extensive changes also included provisions which allow a particular district court, an individual judge, and sometimes the parties to the action to opt out of using the new rules.

As of March 1996, the 1993 discovery rules had become fully effective in only half of the federal district courts. Other courts promulgated local rules or district-wide standing orders which had the effect of suspending or limiting application of the national rules, or leaving the decision whether to follow the national rules up to the individual judge. New amendments to the Federal Rules, which are scheduled to take effect in December 2000, would prevent district courts from opting out of these changes through local rules, but preserve the power of judges to modify the rules by order in individual cases. The new amendments also change the scope of discovery in significant ways.

To better understand the current state of discovery, a student must appreciate the tremendous dissatisfaction with federal discovery that developed over the last twenty years. There was a strong consensus among lawyers, judges and academics (with a few prominent dissenters) that discovery, as it was being conducted in many federal cases, was overly expensive and time consuming, and encouraged abusive tactics by lawyers.

It is important to remember that throughout the ongoing debate over discovery, no one has proposed eliminating it entirely. Discovery is designed to have some important benefits that without which the court system could not function fairly and effectively. Having looked at the problems of the old system and the goals that discovery is intended to achieve, a student will be in a better position to evaluate the new system of disclosure and the seemingly inevitable proposals for further change.

1. Discovery: The Major Premises

Blank v. Ronson Corp.

United States District Court, Southern District of New York, 1983.
97 F.R.D. 744.

■ Whitman Knapp, District Judge.

Plaintiff has brought this proposed class action for securities fraud charging Ronson Corporation and several individual defendants with a "common scheme" artificially to inflate the market price of Ronson stock by failing to disclose (or misstating) adverse material information. Interrogatories were served by defendants in connection with a pending motion for class certification. Not satisfied with plaintiff's answers, defendants noticed the deposition of the named plaintiff to elicit further information, ostensibly required to oppose the motion for class certification. The case is now before us on plaintiff's motion for a protective order to quash the notice of deposition.

There has been much criticism of late regarding the abuses of discovery. *See, e.g.,* Sherman & Kinnard, Federal Court Discovery in 80's—Making the Rules Work, 94 F.R.D. 245 (1983); Second Report of the Special Committee for the Study of Discovery Abuse, 92 F.R.D. 137 (1982). The motion before us aptly illustrates the cause of such criticism.

Defendants' lawyers have served a set of 94 interrogatories concerning the motion for class certification. Plaintiff's counsel, in response, vouchsafes 74 pages of purported answers. Although we have before us two highly competent law firms, there is, in this vast expanse of paper, no indication that any lawyer (or even moderately competent paralegal) ever looked at the interrogatories or at the answers. It is, on the contrary, obvious that they have all been produced by some word-processing machine's memory of prior litigation. For an example we need go no further than defendant's interrogatory #1. It asks for the basis of plaintiff's claim that the class members are sufficiently numerous to justify a class action, and for an estimate of the class size. This information, aside from being obvious, has (a) already been made public by Ronson Corporation itself, and is (b) specifically set forth in the plaintiff's previously filed motion for class certification as follows:

> Ronson's public reports indicate that * * * there were 4,412,575 shares of common stock outstanding and more than 7,622 stockholders who are members of the class.

Plaintiff, with appropriate display of outrage, objects to this interrogatory on the ground, among others, that it seeks "privileged information."[1] By not citing other examples we by no means wish to suggest that the foregoing is the most absurd one.

---

1. The complete "response" to interrogatory #1 reads:

Plaintiff objects to this Interrogatory on the ground that it is incomprehensible. Plaintiff also objects to this Interrogato-

Accordingly, the Court, on its own motion, strikes both the interrogatories and the purported answers. To the extent that they may already have been filed, we direct the Clerk to return them to the respective parties. The parties are, furthermore, ordered never to refer to them again in this litigation.

The following schedule, announced at oral argument on the motion for a protective order on May 13, 1983, is hereby confirmed:

1. Defendants, on or before May 20, 1983, may propound new interrogatories tailored specifically to the motion for class certification.

2. Thereafter, on or before May 27, 1983, plaintiff shall respond in simple, short, declarative sentences. Plaintiff may then also supplement the already-filed motion for class certification.

3. Thereafter, on or before June 10, 1983, defendants shall answer the motion for class certification on the basis of the information at hand. Should defendants be of the view that the Court lacks specific information necessary to decide the motion, they may also submit a document captioned "REQUEST FOR ADDITIONAL FACTS" setting forth in numbered paragraphs specific items of additional information they believe should be before the Court, with a citation to authority supporting the need for such additional information.

4. Should defendants submit a Request, plaintiff shall provide, on or before June 17, 1983, the additional information and/or submit a document captioned "PLAINTIFF'S OBJECTIONS TO DEFENDANTS' REQUEST FOR ADDITIONAL FACTS" detailing, as to each numbered item, where in plaintiff's answers to interrogatories we may find the supposedly omitted fact, or stating why any specific requested information is not needed.

5. On June 24, 1983 at 2:00 P.M. the parties will come to court prepared to argue the motion for class certification. However, based on the parties' submissions, the Court may then adjourn oral argument pending further discovery by such method as the Court may direct.

At oral argument defendants will be prepared to explain, if required to do so, the reason for each interrogatory posed—*i.e.,* precisely what information was expected and why it was necessary. Should the defendants be unable to justify any interrogatory it will again be struck and appropriate sanctions will be imposed. By the same token, the plaintiff will be prepared to justify every answer, objection, or late submission. If any such justification is found to be wanting, similar sanctions will be imposed.

ry on the grounds that, to the extent it is comprehensible, it is vexatious, calls for information outside plaintiff's knowledge, calls for legal conclusions, is not reasonably calculated to lead to the discovery of admissible evidence, calls for privileged information and/or information protected by the attorney work product doctrine, is premature, and calls for speculation.

NOTES

    A.   Who won the motion before the Court in *Blank v. Ronson?*

    B.   Do you think Judge Knapp's order will improve the subsequent stages of the litigation?

Schwarzer, Slaying the Monsters of Cost and Delay: Would Disclosure Be More Effective Than Discovery?

74 *Judicature* 178 (1991).

    A 6–year–old descendant of the photographer Edward Steichen won a long battle for a Matisse painting on Friday when her family settled a law suit over it with the Museum of Modern Art.

    But the child, Ariana Rodina Calderone Stahmer of Pennington, N.J., will probably never see the painting on her bedroom wall.

    The family said it would have to sell "Vue de Collioure a l'Eglise," which Henri Matisse painted in 1905 and gave three years later to Mr. Steichen, to pay more than $100,000 in legal fees that they incurred fighting for it.[1]

    When the framers of the Federal Rules of Civil Procedure drafted the discovery rules more than 50 years ago, their purpose was to bring about the just, speedy and inexpensive determination of every action. Discovery was intended to provide each side with all relevant information about the case to help bring about settlement or, if not, avoid trial by ambush. Discovery was designed to be conducted by the lawyers, with little involvement of the judge.

    Discovery seemed to work well for about 35 years, but then things began to go awry and discovery started to become a problem. Discovery, rather than trial, became the main event in litigation. Depositions came to be seen as often pivotal to the resolution of cases, leading to long and arduous deposition campaigns. The ingenuity and aggressiveness of lawyers made discovery, and with it civil litigation, increasingly expensive, burdensome and time-consuming. Cases began to turn on the capacity of a party to endure the discovery process. And to an extent, discovery was driven by its profit potential for lawyers.

    Widespread dissatisfaction and concern over discovery led to amendment of the federal rules, first in 1980 and again in 1983. The 1980 amendment created the discovery conference in Rule 26(f). In 1983, Rule 26(b)(1) was amended to give trial judges extensive discretionary power to manage discovery, to prevent duplication and unreasonable burdens, and to apply the principle of proportionality to limit discovery. Rule 26(g), which paralleled Rule 11, authorized judges to impose sanctions for discovery demands and responses that were unreasonably burdensome and expensive in light of the amount and issues at stake or duplicated prior discovery. These amendments, by specifying judicial authority to address the sources of trouble,

---

    1.   New York Times, Aug. 12, 1990, at p. 26.

appeared to be a sensible approach to the problem. Although they gave judges all the tools they needed to deal with it, and obligated parties to avoid burdensome and harassing practices, they have largely failed to accomplish their purpose and the discovery problem persists.

Much time and effort has been devoted to analyzing that problem. Not everyone agrees either on the existence of a problem or on its dimensions. Nor does every case necessarily present a problem. There is widespread agreement, however, that discovery, as it is now conducted, spawns some abuse and, more importantly, is prone to overuse leading to expense and delay. * * * Discovery is abused when it is used as a weapon to burden, discourage or exhaust the opponent, rather than to obtain needed information. The adversary process presents an invitation, and a convenient justification, for lawyers to conduct aggressive discovery campaigns. Discovery being inherently costly and burdensome, lawyers cannot be expected to ignore that calculus in planning their litigation strategy, particularly when urged on by clients who favor hardball tactics. At what point aggressive discovery becomes abusive is not readily defined; standards of professionalism provide little guidance. Lawyers generally find it easier to detect abuse in the conduct of their opponents than in their own. For all of these reasons, abuse is extremely difficult for courts to identify, prevent and control, even with the powers at hand.

More significant than abuse as a cause of the discovery problem is excess. Under the existing discovery system, the adversary process drives lawyers to overdiscover. Fearing surprise at trial and the risk of malpractice liability, and hoping that more discovery may produce that priceless gem of evidence that will ensure victory, lawyers leave no stone unturned. They take depositions that are unnecessary or last too long, make document requests and productions that are too voluminous, and inflict interrogatories, often generated by word processors with little regard to the issues in the case, the answers to which are burdensome to prepare but will probably never be used in the litigation. All of this activity tends to lead to numerous discovery disputes, the cost of which may be disproportionate to what is at stake in the litigation.

As a result, discovery has become a major source of profit for litigating firms; some have estimated that they may derive half or more of their gross income from discovery. Lawyers are making careers of discovery without ever trying a case. Discovery offers opportunities for associates and paralegals to run up chargeable hours to meet firm requirements. Overall the discovery system creates the wrong incentives and breeds a conflict of interest between lawyer and client.

To some extent, overdiscovery also results from lack of competence and professionalism. When lawyers do not know how to conduct effective discovery, have failed to learn enough about their case to know what is and is not needed, or lack the judgment or confidence to limit their discovery, activity mushrooms. The same result follows when the tactical premise of discovery is that the opponent will conceal, evade and obstruct and that those tactics must be anticipated or countered.

Overdiscovery, though prevalent in larger cases, is not limited to them. It can occur in the $50,000 case as much as in the $50,000,000 case. It is lack of proportionality as much as the absolute volume of activity that marks overdiscovery. Repeatedly lawyers engage in discovery campaigns with little or no thought of how the cost will relate to the likely recovery or exposure in the case. And though Rule 26 permits the judge to limit discovery by "taking into account the . . . amount in controversy, limitations on the parties' resources, and the importance of the issues at stake in the litigation", it is difficult to do and rarely done.

With all of these factors operating, discovery generates cost and delay that are pricing civil litigation in the federal courts out of the market. Litigating a case in a metropolitan federal court involving less than $100,000, or perhaps even $200,000, is rarely economically feasible, and, whatever the amount involved, the costs incurred will likely end up being disproportionate to what is at stake. Even in large cases, in which each side's attorneys fees during the discovery stage have been known to run at a rate of $1,000,000 per month, decisions about strategy often turn more on the cost of the litigation than on its merits. In short, the transaction costs of dispute resolution have reached unaffordable levels, and must be brought down.

NOTE: BRAZIL'S STUDY OF CIVIL DISCOVERY

In the summer of 1979, Wayne Brazil and an associate conducted interviews with 180 Chicago litigators to assess their attitudes toward and experiences with the system of civil discovery. The author selected a diverse group of attorneys who were classified into sets of contrasting subgroups: (1) case size, those whose median size case was $1,000,000 or more contrasted with those whose median size case was $25,000 or less, (2) area of practice, securities/antitrust contrasted with tort actions arising from motor vehicle accidents, (3) the attorney's principal clients, corporations contrasted with individuals, and (4) where they litigated, federal court in contrast to state court. Below is an excerpt from an article which discusses the results of this study.

The primary conclusion of the study is that discovery is abused far more in larger cases in which the issues are more complex, more money is at stake, more money is available for use in litigation, and in which lawyers are more likely to engage in evasive tactical machinations. "These factors conspire to create strong incentives, numerous opportunities, and ample resources to obstruct or burden the discovery process and to misuse its tools in pursuit of adversarial advantages. * * * [O]ne generalization is clearly safe: the discovery process is much less likely to distribute information evenly among the parties and much more likely to be heavily encumbered by various forms of resistance, abuse, and tactical jockeying in large, complex cases than it is in smaller, more routine lawsuits."

Brazil, Civil Discovery: Lawyers' Views of Its Effectiveness, Its Principal Problems and Abuses

1980 A.B.F. Research J. 789.

II.   The Health of the System as a Whole

"The rules are excellent. The enforcement of the rules stinks. The system moves poorly."

—a Chicago litigator

* * *

The existence of this tension or inconsistency between many of the lawyers' relatively positive general impressions of discovery and their specific descriptions of its shortcomings illustrates another communication problem that may have affected responses to many of the questions posed during the interviews. That problem was caused by "professional acculturation," a phrase I use to describe how lawyers who have been educated for our adversarial system and who have practiced in it and become accommodated to it tend to make certain assumptions about it and to accept uncritically many of its principal features. After such acculturation lawyers sometimes lose their consciousness of the system as a system and embrace its premises with an unarticulated sense of their inevitability.

* * *

Some examples are in order. One litigator responded to the initial, open-end question about how well discovery is working by declaring that the "system is excellent." He proceeded to report, however, that during the preceding five years opponents had impaired his discovery efforts in 95 percent of his cases by failing for protracted periods (a year or more) to respond to his discovery requests and in 50 percent of his cases by providing evasive or incomplete answers to his probes. Later in the interview he said he was having difficulty discovering the information he needed in "virtually all" of his currently active civil cases (of which he said there were about 200). In conjunction with this response he made an observation that may help explain how an attorney who has difficulty with discovery in almost all of his cases can characterize the system as "excellent." After conceding that he was having difficulty in virtually all of his active cases he added "that's the nature of the beast—but it's more irritating than substantially troublesome." Thus, to this litigator, difficulty inhered in "the nature of the beast" discovery. "Answers" that were evasive or incomplete or that were not even offered for a year or more had become mere irritants because they were perceived as inevitable. Since such irritants were inevitable, "realistic" lawyers accepted them. And since realistic lawyers assumed that such inevitable defects would accompany any system, these lawyers evaluated the current system of civil discovery as if such defects did not exist. Hence a system which would appear seriously flawed when judged by detached standards can be considered "excellent" by an acculturated lawyer.

* * *

[Some specifics are helpful.] When asked if they would "favor or oppose more frequent use of sanctions for discovery abuse" 90 percent of the lawyers whose median size case was $1,000,000 or more favored more frequent use of sanctions. As figure 26 shows, the percentage of favorable responses to this proposal was almost as high in the other subgroups of attorneys who tended to handle larger and more complex matters. Moreover, such positive reactions to the possibility of more vigorous enforcement of the discovery rules were not confined to the big case lawyers. Just under 80 percent of all the lawyers asked (136 of 174) said they would welcome more aggressive use of the sanctioning power. The sharp division of feelings among predominantly smaller case attorneys about a general expansion of judicial involvement in discovery was replaced by a clear vote of approval for "more frequent use of sanctions for discovery abuse." Approximately three of every four lawyers whose typical cases were small and filed in state court said they would like to see the courts impose sanctions more often. Figure 26 shows the percentages of attorneys in eight subgroups who shared this view.

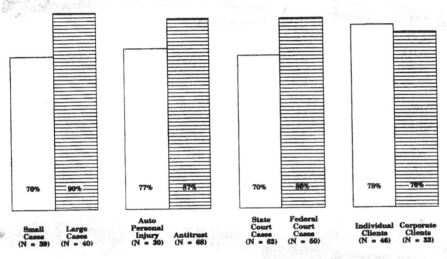

| 76% | 90% | 77% | 87% | 70% | 86% | 78% | 76% |

| Small Cases (N = 39) | Large Cases (N = 40) | Auto Personal Injury (N = 30) | Antitrust (N = 68) | State Court Cases (N = 63) | Federal Court Cases (N = 50) | Individual Clients (N = 46) | Corporate Clients (N = 33) |

Fig. 26. Percentages of attorneys who favor more frequent use of sanctions by subgroup set   [25A]

The 31 lawyers who opposed more frequent imposition of sanctions tended to be involved in modest sized cases (their median size case was $175,000, compared to $150,000 for the sample as a whole), to practice in small law firms (the median size firm in which these attorneys worked was 7, while for the entire sample it was 20), and to spend most of their time on matters filed in state court (the median percent of time consumed by state court matters for the 31 opponents of increased use of the sanctioning power was 85 percent, while for all lawyers it was 50 percent).

Several of the attorneys who opposed more frequent use of sanctions volunteered reasons for their positions. Some thought that the process for imposing sanctions too often is arbitrary and unpredictable, sometimes imposing penalties where none are deserved and, on a regular basis, punishing only the unlucky few who are caught committing practices in which large numbers of attorneys routinely engage. Increasing the frequency of sanctions would extend the reach of a process these lawyers do not respect. Some litigators also contended that it would be unfair to invigorate enforcement of the discovery rules because for a long time some forms of abuse have been widespread and tolerated, by court and counsel alike, under the "unwritten rules" of the system. Finally, a few lawyers said they objected because they perceived sanctions as ineffectual devices for curbing abuse; these lawyers simply did not believe that more vigorous enforcement would substantially deter violators of the rules. The vast majority of their fellow litigators, however, were not prepared to give up without a fight; most lawyers want the courts to get tougher with abusers of the system. * * *

Connolly, Holleman & Kuhlman, Judicial Controls and the Civil Litigative Process: Discovery

Federal Judicial Center (1978).
Levin, Foreword (p. xi).

This report should be viewed as a beginning. It explores from one perspective the operation of the federal rules governing discovery as revealed in more than 7,000 docketed requests appearing in more than 3,000 terminated cases in six United States district courts. (A survey of practitioners in the six districts suggests that the docketed requests cover the great bulk of discovery activity.) The report is a continuation of the Center's District Court Studies Project, the first report of which (*Case Management and Court Management in United States District Courts*) appeared several months ago.

The instant report does not study "discovery abuse" as such, or even attempt a rigorous definition. Its data, however, are relevant to wide-spread concerns that the discovery process consumes too much time, too much energy, and too much money. As the report itself indicates:

> It is possible for a single discovery request to be abusive, as it is possible for sixty-two requests to be appropriate, relevant, and facilitative in the just disposition of a particular case. The data do suggest, however, that discovery abuse, to the extent it exists, does not permeate the vast majority of federal filings. In half the filings, there is no discovery—abusive or otherwise. In the remaining half of the filings, abuse—to the extent it exists—must be found in the *quality* of the discovery requests, not in the *quantity*, since fewer than 5 percent of the filings involved more than ten requests.

One of the most cogent findings in this report is that the imposition of what the report defines as "strong judicial controls" will shorten the time consumed by discovery without impairing discovery rights. Shortened discovery time is in turn associated with shortened case disposition time.

* * *

Chapter III: Quantifying the Use of Discovery (p. 28)

The Extent of Discovery Use

Table 9 shows that approximately 52 percent of the cases in the study sample had no recorded discovery requests. Cases having discovery (discovered cases) ranged from those with only one discovery request (10.5 percent of the total) to a case with sixty-two requests. It is interesting to note that 95.1 percent of the cases had ten or fewer discovery requests.

In order to simplify these data, cases having discovery are grouped into three volume categories as follows:

Low Volume	Those discovered cases having one to three discovery requests
Moderate Volume	Those discovered cases having three to ten requests
High Volume	Those discovered cases having eleven or more requests

Table 9

Number of Cases by Number of Discovery Requests

No. of Requests	No. of Cases	Percent of Cases	Cumulated Percent
0	1,610	51.7	51.7
1	326	10.5	62.2
2	316	10.1	72.3
3	213	6.8	79.2
4	159	5.1	84.3
5	119	3.8	88.1
6	72	2.3	90.4
7	50	1.6	92.0
8	42	1.3	93.4
9	28	0.9	94.3
10	27	0.9	95.1
11	31	1.0	96.1
12	18	0.6	96.7
13	22	0.7	97.4
14	15	0.5	97.9
15	7	0.2	98.1
16	6	0.2	98.3
17	3	0.1	98.4
18	8	0.3	98.7
19	2	0.1	98.7
20	5	0.2	98.9
21	1	0.0	98.9
22	4	0.1	99.1
23	3	0.1	99.2
24	2	0.1	99.2
25	3	0.1	99.3
26	1	0.0	99.4
27	2	0.1	99.4

No. of Requests	No. of Cases	Percent of Cases	Cumulated Percent
28	1	0.0	99.5
29	3	0.1	99.6
30	1	0.0	99.6
31	2	0.1	99.6
32	1	0.0	99.7
33	2	0.1	99.7
34	1	0.0	99.8
35	1	0.0	99.8
42	1	0.0	99.8
43	1	0.0	99.9
46	1	0.0	99.9
52	1	0.0	99.9
53	1	0.0	100.0 [a]
62	1	0.0	100.0
	3,114	100.0	

[a]This percentage was rounded up to 100.0%.

TABLE 10

ANALYSIS OF DISCOVERY IN DISCOVERED CASES

Volume Categories	No. Cases	% Cases	Average Requests per Case
Low	642	42.7	1.49
Moderate	710	47.2	4.94
High	152	10.1	17.47

FIGURE 1

PROPORTIONS OF REQUEST TYPES FOR DISCOVERED CASES

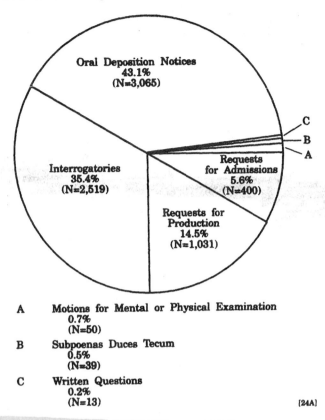

Oral Deposition Notices
43.1%
(N=3,065)

C

B

A

Interrogatories
35.4%
(N=2,519)

Requests
for Admissions
5.6%
(N=400)

Requests for
Production
14.5%
(N=1,031)

A Motions for Mental or Physical Examination
0.7%
(N=50)

B Subpoenas Duces Tecum
0.5%
(N=39)

C Written Questions
0.2%
(N=13)   [24A]

NOTE: DIFFERING PERSPECTIVES ON "THE PROBLEM"

During the last quarter of 1987 Louis Harris and Associates conducted a study of *Judges' Opinions on Procedural Issues.* One thousand judges, state and federal, were surveyed. Abuse of the discovery process headed the list of "Causes of Delays in Litigation" among both federal and state judges. Forty-seven per cent of the federal judges ranked such abuse as a major cause of delay with 46% ranking it as a minor cause in their jurisdictions. Only 8% did not consider it a cause of delay or were not sure. Among the state judges 89% considered it either as a major or minor cause, with 11% of the view that it was not a cause.

One year later the same organization surveyed over one thousand federal judges and litigators and in 1989 published the results in *Procedural Reform of the Civil Justice System.* Among the major findings: "Transaction costs are perceived to be a problem;" "Judges and lawyers agree that transaction costs lead to unequal justice" (giving an unfair advantage to litigants with greater resources); and "Discovery abuse is considered the most important cause of the problem."

To cite one example, The Civil Justice Reform Act of 1990, signed into law on December 1, 1990, reflects a continuing concern over the costs and delays in civil litigation and the view, expressed by Senator Biden in his statement introducing the bill, that "Discovery abuse is a principal cause of high litigation transaction costs".

The Act calls for continued research and experimentation by the federal courts in methods of reducing costs and moving cases more quickly to trial. The statute also requires that each federal district court undertake a "civil justice delay and expense reduction plan" whose provisions would include:

> (2) early and ongoing control of the pretrial process through involvement of a judicial officer in—(C) controlling the extent of discovery and the time for completion of discovery, and ensuring compliance with appropriate requested discovery in a timely fashion;

Notwithstanding the loud, sustained and often strident chorus of complaints about abuse and overuse of discovery, virtually no one has suggested that discovery be abolished. There have been many suggestions for curtailing and controlling discovery, but the major premise that discovery is a useful, perhaps an indispensable tool, in civil litigation remains unchallenged.

To advance the inquiry it is useful to make explicit what it is that discovery is intended to accomplish and how it was envisioned that the pretrial phase of litigation would operate, to make the whole enterprise feasible. And as we set about the task, we should not forget that those responsible for the federal rules viewed the provisions governing discovery as central to the scheme of the new rules and an accomplishment of which they were very proud.

2.   The Scope of Discovery

What Discovery Was Intended to Accomplish: An Overview of Goals and Mechanisms

Stated simply, the discovery rules sought full and equal mutual disclosure of the facts between parties to civil litigation. Relevant documents would be exchanged during the pretrial phase, facilitating access to proof by both sides and reducing the risk of surprise at the trial. Witnesses were expected to tell their stories on the record, under oath, subject to cross-examination, and to do so almost immediately after a law suit was filed, often long before trial. The risk of perjury was to be reduced, and the probability of settlement enhanced.

Without provisions for liberal discovery a plaintiff suing a large corporation to recover for alleged employment discrimination might find proof impossible; that's the easy case. Discovery was, however, designed to accomplish more. It was designed to replace the pleadings as the primary source of information concerning the opposing parties' contentions. It was designed to reveal to each of the litigants tactical strengths and weaknesses of the opposing parties.

Perhaps most important of all, discovery was intended to accomplish all this with minimal intervention by the court. Those responsible for the original rules, promulgated in 1938, intended to design a system in which incentives and disincentives would assure smooth functioning of the pretrial phase of litigation without the need for judicial policing of the parties or their counsel.

To learn precisely how all this was to come about it is necessary to read the rules themselves. Close reading of Rules 26 to 37 will prove rewarding in presenting the basic pattern and, in addition, will aid in developing the skill of using "statutory" materials to help determine specific, detailed procedures useful in meeting various needs of counsel.

A few questions may prove of help in focusing study of the text of the rules themselves. What is subject to discovery? If requested information seems rather irrelevant to Litigant A, but Litigant B insists the information sought can be useful to her, what standard governs? Suppose defendant sends a list of 100 questions to plaintiff asking about the litigation in question. No officer before whom they shall be answered is named. What should plaintiff do? What are the relevant rules? Will it make any difference in which district court the litigation has been filed? (See local rules reprinted infra.)

Suppose the defendant sends the same list to Ms. Witness. Is the problem different? Should it be?

Who is present at a deposition? What rules indicate the answer? May you ask a witness "What did John Smith tell Uncle Bill Aunt Clara had told him about the accident?" Suppose a party thinks that a particular question is irrelevant. What should he do? Suppose a witness thinks a question calls for privileged matter? Suppose a party whose deposition is being taken simply declines to answer. What may his opponent do? What provisions in the rules are intended to limit the frequency with which depositions are interrupted for judicial rulings?

The range of factual and legal situations and the ingenuity of lawyers are such that these rules have occasioned a vast amount of litigation, much of which is determined finally by trial courts. The remainder of the chapter treats a number of illustrative and recurring contemporary problems. The materials may illumine an overall set of values implicit in these conflicts. They may also help focus on prosaic details of procedure and of judicial case management that in the ultimate may, for many litigants, grant or deny access to justice. In a particular case the issue is rarely phrased in terms so majestic; the question may be whether to accept or reject an "unfair" settlement. But if, as Professor Maurice Rosenberg has pointed out, "Costs of discovery can be so high that they force settlements that would not occur, or, more likely, force settlements on different terms than would otherwise have been reached," may that not be the same thing?

Josephs v. Harris Corp.

United States Court of Appeals, Third Circuit, 1982.
677 F.2d 985.

■ SLOVITER, CIRCUIT JUDGE.

I.

In this products liability action filed in federal court on the basis of diversity jurisdiction, plaintiff Howard Jay Josephs appeals following a jury verdict in favor of the defendant, Harris Corporation. Josephs was injured while cleaning a printing press which was manufactured by Harris Corporation in 1963, and sold in a used condition by Harris to Josephs' employer, Pocono Press, Inc., in 1973. Josephs alleged that his injuries were caused by a defective design and by Harris' failure to adequately warn and instruct on the safe operation of the press. After a three-day trial, the jury found by special interrogatory that "the Harris Press [was not] defective at the time of its sale to Pocono Press." Accordingly, judgment was entered for the defendant and plaintiff appeals.

Plaintiff claims (1) that the court erred in granting defendant's in limine motion which precluded plaintiff from introducing any testimony relating to standards and publications promulgated and published subsequent to 1963, the year that defendant manufactured the press in issue, when in fact defendant resold the press to plaintiff's employer in 1973; (2) that the court erred in refusing to allow plaintiff redirect examination of his expert witness and cross-examination of defendant's witnesses with regard to standards, publications or textual material adopted or published subsequent to 1963; (3) that the court erred in excluding evidence of or reference to remedial measures undertaken and warnings issued by defendant subsequent to plaintiff's injury; and (4) that the court erred in denying plaintiff's motion to compel answers to interrogatories requesting information as to prior accidents involving the press which injured Josephs and as to similar Harris presses.

II.

FACTS

On the date of the accident, June 18, 1979, Josephs was employed for the summer by Pocono Press, Inc.[2] as a pressman's helper. He was nineteen years of age and had begun working at Pocono Press a few weeks earlier. As a pressman's helper, Josephs' duties included cleaning the printing press at the end of the day.

The press in question, Harris Model LUM, stood over seven feet tall and had five different control stations. At each control station there was a series of three buttons, positioned vertically. The top button was labeled "safe", and when pushed in the machine would not run. This

---

2. Pocono Press, Inc. is a small family run corporation. Its president, Jay Josephs, is   the father of the plaintiff.

button also had a lock out feature, *i.e.,* it was surrounded by a ring which when rotated clockwise prevented the press from being operated from any control station. The middle button was labeled "jog" and when depressed the press ran forward; when released the press stopped by inertia. The third button was labeled "reverse" and operated in the same manner as the "jog" button except that the press ran in the opposite direction.

In order to clean the LUM press, it was necessary for someone to crawl under the press and wipe the cylinders. On June 18, 1979, Josephs was lying underneath the press wiping the second, or bottom cylinder, with a cleaning cloth and solvent. Only a small portion of the cylinder is exposed beneath the press. After cleaning the exposed portion, Josephs had to use the "jog" button to inch the cylinder around, thus exposing more of the cylinder's surface. The process of jogging and wiping would normally continue until the entire surface of the cylinder was cleaned.

The control box that is used while cleaning the cylinder is located underneath the press. Because of the way Josephs was positioned, he could not see the control buttons and the cylinder at the same time. He was using his left hand to push the "jog" button and his right hand to wipe the cylinder. Although Josephs cannot recall the actual accident, and there was no one watching him clean the cylinder, it appears that he was pushing the jog button to advance the cylinder when the cleaning rag in his right hand got caught in the cylinder. His hand was dragged in with the cleanup rag, causing the injury for which suit was brought, a crush amputation of the thumb and portions of the first three fingers.

In face of the jury's adverse verdict, Josephs must demonstrate that the court's evidentiary rulings and discovery rulings which he challenges were not only erroneous but were so prejudicial as to amount to reversible error. Fed.R.Civ.P. 61; Fed.R.Evid. 103(a).

* * *

IV.

DISCOVERY RULING

As part of his discovery, Josephs served interrogatories on the defendant Harris requesting, *inter alia,* the name of any person known to Harris to have been injured by the LUM and nine other models of Harris presses.[4] Harris objected to the interrogatories as being irrelevant, oppressive, and unduly burdensome, and failed to reply. Josephs filed a motion for an order compelling discovery; the district court denied Josephs' motion, as well as his subsequent motion for reconsideration. The basis for the district court's ruling denying this discovery does not appear on the record. Under the

---

4. Plaintiff's interrogatories to defendant, numbered 51 and 52, were:

51. (a) State the name, address and dates of injury of any or all persons known to Harris and/or its insurance carrier to have been injured through the use of a Harris two-color offset printing press, Model LUM during the period

Federal Rules of Civil Procedure, discovery is not limited to information which is admissible at trial but instead is allowed "if the information sought appears reasonably calculated to lead to the discovery of admissible evidence." Fed.R.Civ.P. 26(b)(1). In this case, the information requested was patently relevant to the issue of duty to warn and may have led to relevant evidence regarding the existence of a defect. *See* Bowman v. General Motors Corp., 64 F.R.D. 62 (E.D.Pa.1974) (Becker, J.) (permitting discovery of information about the design and testing of models allegedly similar to the one at issue in that case). The district court's discovery ruling in this case precluded plaintiff from discovery of data relating to the issue of the safety record of the press in question although the district court apparently instructed the jury that the safety record of that press was relevant in connection with its consideration of the design of that press.

Harris claims that the information sought was burdensome and oppressive. However, the mere statement by a party that the interrogatory was "overly broad, burdensome, oppressive and irrelevant" is not adequate to voice a successful objection to an interrogatory. On the contrary, the party resisting discovery "must show specifically how * * * each interrogatory is not relevant or how each question is overly broad, burdensome or oppressive." Roesberg v. Johns–Manville Corp., 85 F.R.D. 292, 296–97 (E.D.Pa.1980) (citations omitted). In this case Harris failed to make the requisite showing. In light of our remand because of the court's erroneous exclusionary ruling, we need not decide whether the court's failure to require defendant to supply the requested discovery information would in itself have warranted a reversal. On remand, however, the court should give plaintiff the opportunity to elicit the appropriate information.

For the reasons set forth above, we will vacate the judgment for defendant and remand this matter to the district court for a new trial.

QUESTIONS

A. What must a party show in order successfully to oppose a discovery demand as being outside the permissible scope of discovery under Rule 26(b)?

from the date the model was first manufactured to the present, and

(b) Identify those persons injured while allegedly engaged in cleaning the second cylinder and, if any of those persons had an attorney, set forth the name and address of said attorney.

(c) As to each and every person identified in 51(b), indicate whether legal action was instituted and, if so, indicate the court term and number of said legal action.

52. (a) State the names, addresses and dates of injury of any and all persons known to Harris and/or its insurance carriers to have been injured through the use of the following Harris Presses.

MODEL	NUMBER OF COLORS	NORMAL SIZE
LXE	2	22 × 29
LTP	2	24 × 36
LWQ, L238A	2	25 × 38
LWQ, LWR, LWR–M, L438A	4	25 × 38
L638A	6	25 × 38

(b) Identify those persons injured while allegedly engaged in cleaning the second cylinder and, if any of those persons had an attorney, set forth the name and address of said attorney.

(c) As to each and every person identified in 52(b), indicate whether legal action was instituted and, if so, indicate the court term and number of said legal action.

App. at 29a–31a.

B. Was it proper for plaintiff to request information about prior lawsuits against defendants?

C. Under the *Josephs* case, what must a party show to establish the "burdensomeness" of a discovery demand?

Gheesling v. Chater, Commissioner of Social Security

United States District Court for the District of Kansas, 1995.
162 F.R.D. 649.

■ REID, UNITED STATES MAGISTRATE JUDGE

Plaintiff's motion seeks further responses to request for production number 5, and interrogatories 4, 5, 6, 7, and 11. In plaintiff's reply, he indicates that he will submit a revised request for production number 5 that will be clear as to certain matters. Therefore, the court will not rule on that matter at this time.

Before discussing the specifics of the remaining disputes, the court will set forth its general rules regarding discovery. This court has always taken a very liberal position in regards to discovery. That position has been as follows. Relevancy has been defined as encompassing any matter that bears on, or that reasonably could lead to other matter that could bear on, any issue that is or may be in the case. Discovery is not limited to issues raised by the pleadings, for discovery itself is designed to help define and clarify the issues. *Oppenheimer Fund, Inc. v. Sanders,* 437 U.S. 340, 351, 98 S. Ct. 2380, 2389, 57 L. Ed. 2d 253 (1978). A request for discovery should be considered relevant if there is any possibility that the information sought may be relevant to the subject matter of this action. Discovery should ordinarily be allowed under the concept of relevancy unless it is clear that the information sought can have no possible bearing upon the subject matter of this action.

However, though the scope of discovery is broad, it is not unlimited. If the plaintiff has failed to specify how the information is relevant, and the court cannot determine how the information sought is relevant, a court will not require the defendant to produce the information.

In employment discrimination cases, discovery is usually limited to information about employees in the same department or office absent a showing of a more particularized need for, and the likely relevance of, broader information. See *Earley v. Champion International Corp.,* 907 F.2d 1077, 1084–85 (11th Cir.1990); *James v. Newspaper Agency Corp.,* 591 F.2d 579, 582 (10th Cir.1979); *Serina v. Albertson's, Inc.,* 128 F.R.D. 290, 291–92 (M.D.Fla.1989); *Prouty v. National Railroad Passenger Corp.,* 99 F.R.D. 545, 547 (D.D.C.1983). When the employment decisions were made locally, discovery may properly be limited to the employing unit. *Scales v. J.C. Bradford and Co.,* 925 F.2d 901, 907 (6th Cir.1991); Earley, 907 F.2d at 1084. In the absence of any evidence that there were hiring or firing practices and procedures applicable to all the employing units, discovery may be limited to plaintiff's employing unit. See *Joslin Dry Goods Co. v. Equal Employment Opportunity Commission*, 483 F.2d 178, 184 (10th Cir. 1973).

A party opposing a discovery request cannot make conclusory allegations that a request is irrelevant, immaterial, unduly burdensome, or overly broad. Instead, the party resisting discovery must show specifically how each discovery request is irrelevant, immaterial, unduly burdensome or overly broad. *McLeod, Alexander, Powel & Apffel, P.C. v. Quarles*, 894 F.2d 1482, 1484–85 (5th Cir.1990); *Panola Land Buyers Ass'n v. Shuman*, 762 F.2d 1550, 1559 (11th Cir.1985); *Josephs v. Harris Corp.*, 677 F.2d 985, 992 (3d Cir.1982).

Interrogatories 4–6 seek information regarding the number of attorney-advisors who were promoted to supervisory attorney-advisor, how many supervisory attorney-advisor positions were filled over a six year period, and how many persons over the age of 50 applied for these positions. While discovery is not limited to issues raised by the pleadings, and is very broad in scope, there are limits to the scope of discovery. As noted above, discovery is generally limited to the employing unit. However, in their reply brief, plaintiff states that "discovery has established the fact that 126 such positions exist and that only one filled in a six-year time span between 1988 and 1994 went to an applicant who was over 50" (Doc. 38 at 2). This information, if it is nationwide, could possibly indicate a hiring practice applicable to all employing units. On the other hand, the court is concerned due to the cost and burden of obtaining this information from the different units nationwide. Therefore, the court will order plaintiff to provide to the court the discovered material that shows that only 1 out of 126 positions were filled by a person over the age of 50, along with any other relevant material, i.e., the source of the information, etc. Plaintiff will provide this information to the court by May 12, 1995. Defendant will have until May 23, 1995 to file a brief setting forth their objections to having the answers to these interrogatories provided in light of this discovered material.

Interrogatory number seven seeks the identification of any EEO complaint concerning administrator Melvin Werner, who was the hiring person for the position in question. The court finds the request to be clear; plaintiff seeks any EEO complaints made against Mr. Werner. The only possible relevant inquiry in this case would be an inquiry into complaints of age discrimination; any other EEO complaints have no conceivable relevance to an age discrimination case. Defendant need only respond as to any allegations of age discrimination.

Interrogatory number eleven seeks the performance ratings of plaintiff and Gene Michael Kelly from 1991–1993. Apparently, Mr. Kelly obtained the job in question. The court finds that the material sought is relevant, or could lead to relevant evidence, and orders defendants to provide the material.

IT IS THEREFORE ORDERED that the motion to compel is granted in part, and denied in part, as set forth above.

Read up to here for 2/8

QUESTIONS

A. The court stated that information on patterns of racial or sexual discrimination by the same employer would be undiscoverable as irrelevant in this age discrimination case. Why would patterns of other types of discrimination be irrelevant?

B. Does the decision of the court appear well-tailored to avoiding unnecessary costs?

NOTE ON PROPOSED CHANGES TO THE SCOPE OF DISCOVERY

Proposed amendments to Rule 26(b)(1) of the Federal Rules of Civil Procedure have been approved by the Judicial Conference of the United States and appear likely to become effective in December 2000. The new Rule would change the basic scope of federal discovery from "any matter, not privileged, which is relevant to the subject matter in the pending action" to "any matter, not privileged, that is relevant to the claim or defense of any party." Discovery relevant to the "subject matter involved in the action" may still be ordered by the court "for good cause."

The Note of the Advisory Committee states, in part:

> "The Committee intends that the parties and the court focus on the actual claims and defenses involved in the action. The dividing line between information relevant to the claims and defenses and that relevant only to the subject matter of the action cannot be defined with precision. A variety of types of information not directly pertinent to the incident in suit could be relevant to the claims or defenses raised in a given action. For example, other incidents of the same type, or involving the same product, could be properly discoverable under the revised standard. Information about organizational arrangements or filing systems of a party could be discoverable if likely to yield or lead to the discovery of admissible information.

> "The rule change signals to the court that it has authority to confine discovery to the claims and defenses asserted in the pleadings, and signals to the parties that they have no entitlement to discovery to develop new claims or defenses that are not already identified in the pleadings."

Do you think the *Josephs* and *Gheesling* cases would have been decided differently if new Rule 26(b)(1) had been in effect?

3. The New System of Disclosure

Dixon v. The CertainTeed Corporation

United States District Court for the District of Kansas, 1996.
164 F.R.D. 685.

■ Rushfelt, Magistrate Judge

CertainTeed removed this action from state court to the District of Kansas. At that time the action came under the control of the Federal Rules of Civil Procedure. Attached as Exhibit A to the Notice of Removal was the latest petition of plaintiff. Upon removal to this district that petition became the controlling pleading in this case. It thus set the initial framework for required disclosures under Fed. R.

Civ. P. 26(a). In the context of Rule 26(a), amendments to pleadings became important later.

Plaintiff alleged that "he leaned on a railing, which was not securely attached and which gave way, causing [him] to fall several feet to the floor, and suffer bodily injury." He further alleged that "defendant was negligent . . . [and] failed to exercise reasonable care to keep its premises in a reasonably safe and suitable condition." He claimed damages for "defendant's negligence and/or the aforesaid conduct and/or omissions of defendant." CertainTeed admitted that plaintiff fell and was injured at its plant. It otherwise denied the allegations in PP 4–8 of the petition of plaintiff.

Plaintiff pleads the following facts with sufficient particularity to require responsive disclosures: (1) that he leaned on the railing; (2) the railing was not securely attached; and (3) the railing gave way, causing him to fall several feet to the floor. The denial of CertainTeed places these facts in dispute. Thus it should have identified all individuals likely to have discoverable information relevant to the stability and safety of the railing. It likewise should have identified all documents or tangible items in its possession, custody, or control, relevant to the disputed facts.

CertainTeed initially identified 31 individuals likely to have discoverable information. It has subsequently identified other such individuals. It has not disclosed, however, the addresses or telephone numbers of current employees. It contends that Rule 26(a) does not require such disclosure. In a novel approach it cites correspondence between counsel for the parties as support for such proposition. The cited "authority" consists only of a collection of letters between counsel. They contain no legal citation for the proposition plaintiff asserts. Identification of individuals pursuant to Fed. R. Civ. P. 26(a)(1) includes providing their addresses and telephone numbers, if known. The rule expressly states as much. Pursuant to Rule 26(a)(1), therefore, CertainTeed shall disclose the addresses and telephone numbers of all the identified employees. It may not satisfy this obligation by disclosing its business address and phone number, unless it knows of no other address and number.

CertainTeed expresses concern that counsel for plaintiff will contact its employees outside its presence. It may not pose its concern as cause to unilaterally disregard its duties of disclosure under Rule 26(a). Nor will the court indulge in speculation that counsel will unethically use the disclosed information. The court expects counsel to abide by the canons of legal ethics. It assumes attorneys will be ethical, absent some evidence to show otherwise.

The court notes that an ethical rule

> prohibits communications by a lawyer for one party concerning the matter in representation with persons having managerial responsibility on behalf of the organization, *and with any other person whose act or omission in connection with that matter*

may be imputed to the organization for purposes of civil or criminal liability.

See *Aiken v. Business & Indus. Health Group, Inc*, 885 F. Supp. 1474, 1477 (D.Kan.1995) (quoting Model Rule of Professional Conduct 4.2 cmt. (1983)) (emphasis added). Counsel should also note *Chancellor v. Boeing Co.*, 678 F. Supp. 250 (D.Kan.1988). The latter case specifically relates to current employees.

In this instance the parties dispute the cause of the allegedly unsafe railing. Many employees of defendant CertainTeed may have knowledge of facts relevant to the alleged negligence. Their acts or omissions could conceivably be imputed to CertainTeed, as employer. Counsel for plaintiff must assess these possibilities, in deciding to what extent he may or may not contact employees or issue subpoenas for their testimony. The court notes that plaintiff, apparently to avoid an ethical problem, has suggested that his attorney interview current employees in the presence of counsel for CertainTeed.

The court next addresses the request for leave to take additional depositions. Fed. R. Civ. P. 30(a)(2) provides:

> A party must obtain leave of the court, which shall be granted to the extent consistent with the principles stated in Rule 26(b)(2) . . . if, without the written stipulation of the parties.
>
> (A) a proposed deposition would result in more than ten depositions being taken or Rule 31 by the plaintiffs, or the defendants, or by third-party defendants; [or]
>
> (B) the person to be examined already has been deposed in the case. . . .

The motion for additional depositions invites consideration of both subdivisions (A) and (B). Fed. R. Civ. P. 26(b)(2) directs the court to limit discovery

> if it determines that: (i) the discovery sought is unreasonably cumulative or duplicative, or is obtainable from some other source that is more convenient, less burdensome, or less expensive; (ii) the party seeking discovery has had ample opportunity by discovery in the action to obtain the information sought; or (iii) the burden or expense of the proposed discovery outweighs its likely benefit, taking into account the needs of the case, the amount in controversy, the parties' resources, the importance of the issues at stake in the litigation, and the importance of the proposed discovery in resolving the issues.

Plaintiff has already taken more than 40 depositions. He seeks leave to take 17 more and to redepose two witnesses.

"The propriety of deposing someone a second time addresses the discretion of the court." *In re Starcom, Inc. v. US Telecom, Inc.*, No. 87–2540–O, unpublished op. at 1 (D. Kan. June 20, 1990). Absent some showing of a need or good reason for doing so, "the court will generally not require a deponent to appear for a second deposition." *Lone Star Indus., Inc. v. River's Bend* Red–E–Mix, Inc., No. 90–2349–V, unpublished op. at 4 (D. Kan. Oct. 6, 1992). "Courts generally disfavor repeat depositions." *In re Starcom, Inc.*, at 1–2.

In this instance the adequacy of the initial disclosures by defendant affects the question of redeposing the two witnesses. The Advisory Committee Notes to the 1993 amendments to Rule 26, therefore, provide helpful guidance:

A major purpose of [Rule 26(a)] is to accelerate the exchange of basic information about the case and to eliminate the paper work involved in requesting such information, and the rule should be applied in a manner to achieve those objectives. . . .

* * *

. . . The [1993] revision puts in place a series of disclosure obligations that . . . are designed to eliminate certain discovery, help focus the discovery that is needed, and facilitate preparation for trial or settlement.

Subparagraph [(a)(1)](A) requires identification of all persons who, based on the investigation conducted thus far, are likely to have discoverable information relevant to the factual disputes between the parties. All persons with such information should be disclosed, whether or not their testimony will be supportive of the position of the disclosing party. As officers of the court, counsel are expected to disclose the identity of those persons who may be used by them as witnesses or who, if their potential testimony were known, might reasonably be expected to be deposed or called as a witness by any of the other parties. Indicating briefly the general topics on which such persons have information should not be burdensome, and will assist other parties in deciding which depositions will actually be needed.

Subparagraph [(a)(1)](B) is included as a substitute for the inquiries routinely made about the existence and location of documents and other tangible things in the possession, custody, or control of the disclosing party. Although unlike subdivision (a)(3)(C), an itemized listing of each exhibit is not required, the disclosure should describe and categorize, to the extent identified during the initial investigation . . . sufficiently to enable opposing parties (1) to make an informed decision concerning which documents might need to be examined, at least initially, and (2) to frame their document requests in a manner likely to avoid squabbles resulting from the wording of the requests. As with potential witnesses, the requirement for disclosure of documents applies to all potentially relevant items then known to the party, whether or not supportive of its contentions in the case.

* * *

The initial disclosure requirements of subparagraphs (A) and (B) are limited to identification of potential evidence "relevant to disputed facts alleged with particularity in the pleadings." There is no need for a party to identify potential evidence with respect to allegations that are admitted.... The greater the specificity and clarity of the allegations in the pleadings, the more complete should be the listing of potential witnesses and types of documentary evidence. Although paragraphs (1)(A) and (1)(B) by their terms refer to the factual disputes defined in the pleadings, the rule contemplates that these issues would be informally refined and clarified during the meeting of the parties under subdivision (f) and that the disclosure obligations would be adjusted in light of these discussions. The disclosure requirements should, in short, be applied with common sense in light of the principles of Rule 1, keeping in mind the salutary purposes that the rule is intended to accomplish. The litigants should not indulge in gamesmanship with respect to the disclosure obligations.

* * *

Before making its disclosures, a party has the obligation under subdivision (g)(1) to make a reasonable inquiry into the facts of the case. The rule does not demand an exhaustive investigation at this stage of the case, but one that is reasonable under the circumstances, focusing on the facts that are alleged with particularity in the pleadings. The type of investigation that can be expected at this point will vary based upon such factors as the number and complexity of the issues; the location, nature, number, and availability of potentially relevant witnesses and documents; the extent of past working relationships between the attorney and the client, particularly in handling related or similar litigation; and of course how long the party has to conduct an investigation, either before or after filing of the case.... The party should make its initial disclosures based on the pleadings and the information then reasonably available to it. As its investigation continues and as the issues in the pleadings are clarified, it should supplement its disclosures as required by subdivision (e)(1)....

A reasonable investigation by CertainTeed should have uncovered the fact that a safety team had inspected its premises, including the location of the accident of plaintiff, just two weeks prior to such accident. CertainTeed removed this action from state court on August 5, 1994. On September 27, 1994 the parties agreed to exchange information required by Fed. R. Civ. P. 26(a) by November 7, 1994. (See Report of Parties' Planning Meeting, doc. 11, P 2, hereinafter Report.) CertainTeed thus had three months from the date of removal to the date their disclosures were due to conduct its own investigation. A reasonable investigation during that period should have uncovered the fact that a safety team had inspected its premises only two weeks before the accident. Defendant has provided nothing of record to suggest otherwise.

The Report, moreover, indicates that discovery would be needed on "Safety rules, regulations, and procedures in [CertainTeed's] plant." If before the planning meeting CertainTeed was unaware of the pertinence of information concerning reports of safety teams about the specific area of the accident, it could no longer make such claim.

Rule 26(a) contemplates that the factual disputes defined in the pleadings "would be informally refined and clarified during the meeting of the parties under subdivision (f) and that the disclosure obligations would be adjusted in light of these discussions." Fed. R. Civ. P. 26(a) advisory committee notes (1993 Amend.).

CertainTeed should have identified at the initial disclosure stage the report of its safety team about its inspection of the plant two weeks prior to the accident. The safety report in turn would have identified the members of such safety teams. Plaintiff has shown good reason to redepose Ms. Lovell. He may redepose her for the limited purpose of inquiring about her participation on the safety team and related matters. Redeposing her does not appear to violate Fed. R. Civ. P. 26(b)(2).

From the information the parties have provided, the court cannot determine if CertainTeed should have identified in its initial disclosures the construction log herein discussed. The court cannot find that such a log by its nature would necessarily contain information relevant to this action. The court does not know whether the log relates either to construction of the railing or to its immediate vicinity. The court cannot find, therefore, that CertainTeed had a duty to disclose its identity. Once it became aware of the log with its statements by Mr. Hall, however, it had a duty to supplement its initial disclosures to identify it. Nothing indicates that CertainTeed failed to timely supplement its disclosures with such information. As far as the court knows, CertainTeed disclosed the log as soon as it discovered its relevance. The court will not attribute to defendant intentional delay and violation of the Federal Rules of Civil Procedure without adequate evidence of such conduct.

Plaintiff has shown good reason, nevertheless, to redepose Mr. Hall. While conducting the first deposition, all parties were apparently unaware of his statements to Precision Constructors, Inc. regarding the railing in question. Had plaintiff known of such statements, he probably would have inquired about them at the first deposition. Redeposing him for the limited purpose of inquiring about these statements does not violate Fed. R. Civ. P. 26(b)(2) in this instance. Plaintiff may redepose him for that limited purpose.

Plaintiff also seeks leave to take 17 additional depositions. He has already taken more than 40 with the agreement of defendant. Fed. R. Civ. P. 30(a)(2)(A)

> provides a limit on the number of depositions the parties may take, absent leave of court or stipulation with the other parties. One aim of this [Rule] is to assure judicial review under the standards stated in Rule 26(b)(2) before any side will be allowed to take more than ten depositions in a case without agreement of the other parties. A second objective is to emphasize that counsel have a professional obligation to develop a mutual cost-effective plan for discovery in the case.

Id. Advisory Committee Notes (1993 Amend.).

Plaintiff has suggested that he can obtain the information sought by the requested depositions instead through informal interviews with the 17 proposed deponents. He also appears to concede that informal interviews would be more convenient, less burdensome, and less expensive. The court, therefore, denies the request for leave to take additional depositions. Plaintiff may pursue his suggested method of obtaining the information sought, i.e. informal interviews; provided he does so within the ethical constraints described by *Aiken* and *Chancellor*, supra. The mere fact that many individuals may have discoverable information does not necessarily entitle a party to depose each such individual. Advisory Committee's Notes to the 1993 amendments to Rule 26 highlight that a brief synopsis of "the general topics on which [persons identified] have information . . . will assist other parties in deciding which depositions will actually be needed."

The rulings of the court necessitate consideration of sanctions. Fed. R. Civ. P. 37(c)(1) provides:

A party that without substantial justification fails to disclose information required by Rule 26(a) or 26(e)(1) shall not, unless such failure is harmless, be permitted to use as evidence at a trial, at a hearing, or on a motion any witness or information not so disclosed. In addition to or in lieu of this sanction, the court, on motion and after affording an opportunity to be heard, may impose other appropriate sanctions. In addition to requiring payment of reasonable expenses, including attorney's fees, caused by the failure, these sanctions may include any of the actions authorized under subparagraphs (A), (B), and (C) of subdivision (b)(2) of this rule and may include informing the jury of the failure to make the disclosure.

CertainTeed had no substantial justification for excluding identification of its safety reports from its initial disclosures. In accordance with Rule 37(c)(1), therefore, CertainTeed shall within twenty days of the date of this order show cause why the next deposition of Ms. Lovell should not be at its expense.

The sustaining of a motion to compel, furthermore, invites consideration of Fed. R. Civ. P. 37(a)(4)(A). It provides:

If the motion is granted or if the disclosure or requested discovery is provided after the motion was filed, the court shall, after affording an opportunity to be heard, require the party or deponent whose conduct necessitated the motion or the party or attorney advising such conduct or both of them to pay to the moving party the reasonable expenses incurred in making the motion, including attorney's fees, unless the court finds that the motion was filed without the movant's first making a good faith effort to obtain the disclosure or discovery without court action, or that the opposing party's nondisclosure, response, or objection was substantially justified or that other circumstances make an award of expenses unjust.

The concerns of CertainTeed about the ethics of opposing counsel does not eliminate the requirement of Rule 26(a)(1)(A) that it disclose the known addresses and telephone numbers of those current employees identified pursuant to Rule 26. Although such concerns may be understandable, they do not excuse the unilateral decision of CertainTeed to not make the required disclosures. It appears that the failure to disclose was a deliberate choice to violate the clear mandate of Rule 26. Thus in accordance with Fed. R. Civ. P. 37(a)(4)(A) CertainTeed and its counsel shall have twenty days from the date of this order to show cause why the court should not order either or both of them to pay the reasonable costs and expenses incurred by plaintiff upon the motion to compel. Within ten days of the date of this order, plaintiff shall submit an affidavit of time and expenses incurred upon the motion.

The court overrules all other requests for sanctions made in conjunction with these two motions. It finds no justification for additional sanctions under the circumstances.

In summary, the court sustains in part and defers ruling in part the Motion To Compel CertainTeed Corporation to Disclose The Addresses And Telephone Numbers Of Individuals Identified Pursuant To Rule 26 and For Sanctions. Within twenty days of the date of this order, CertainTeed shall disclose the addresses and telephone numbers of its current employees identified pursuant to Fed. R. Civ. P. 26(a)(1). The court defers ruling on the issue of sanctions, until CertainTeed and its counsel have had an opportunity to be heard in accordance with Fed. R. Civ. P. 37(a)(4)(A). It, furthermore, sustains in part, overrules in part, and defers ruling in part the Motion For Leave To Take Additional Depositions of CertainTeed Employees and For Sanctions. Plaintiff may redepose Ms. Lovell and Mr. Hall. In accordance with Fed. R. Civ. P. 37(c)(1), the court defers ruling on sanctions for the failure of CertainTeed to identify safety reports of members of safety teams at the initial disclosure stage of this action. The court otherwise overrules the motion.

QUESTIONS

A. The court in *CertainTeed* limits the obligation to disclose to information relevant to "disputed facts alleged with particularity in the pleadings," which, indeed, is the formulation of the national rule. Does this invite a return to fact pleading, involving an implied amendment of Rule 8(a)?

B. Is it desirable to invite greater detail in the pleadings?

C. Can you suggest a preferable formulation?

NOTE ON MANDATORY DISCLOSURE

In its Report setting forth the proposed changes to the Federal Rules of Civil Procedure in 1993, the Advisory Committee on Civil Rules to the United States Judicial Conference Committee on Rules of Practice and Procedure noted that its proposed changes to Rule 26 of the Federal Rules of Civil Procedure "have provoked the most intense division within the bench and bar of any of the proposed amendments." Indeed, three Justices of the United States Supreme Court dissented from the Supreme Court's order transmitting the proposed rule to Congress, stating that the "proposed radical reforms to the discovery process are potentially disastrous and certainly premature."

Although the Rules were transmitted to Congress, it was widely expected that during the six month period before they became effective under 28 U.S.C. § 2074, Congress would act to delete or at least delay imposition of the new mandatory disclosure system. Such a bill was passed by the House of Representatives, but the Senate recessed for Thanksgiving without taking any action, and all the proposed Rules, including the mandatory disclosure provisions, became effective on December 1, 1993. The controversy surrounding them, however, continues today.

Mandatory Disclosure Under Rule 26(a)

The heart of the new system is amended Rule 26(a), which provides for mandatory disclosure by each party of a substantial amount of relevant information shortly after the commencement of the litigation and without the need for a discovery request by the opposing party. Commentators have begun to refer to this mandated provision of information to the other side as "disclosure" to contrast it with the traditional system of depositions, interrogatories and document requests initiated by the opposing parties, which continues to be available and is referred to as "discovery". Because nomenclature in this area remains far from uniform, students should be sensitive to context in determining what is meant by the terms "disclosure" and "discovery". For purposes of this text, however, we will limit the term "disclosure" to the 26(a) procedure and its analogues in local court rules. We will use the term "discovery" for the other methods of obtaining information under Rules 26 through 37.

The new proposed amendments to Rule 26(a), which have been approved by the United States Judicial Conference, and will become effective in December 2000 unless Congress acts to the contrary, will significantly narrow the scope of the disclosure obligation while creating greater uniformity among district courts with respect to disclosure procedures.

Under current Rule 26(a)(1), each party is required to provide to the others, without awaiting a discovery request, identifying disclosures regarding witnesses likely to have information and documents "relevant to disputed facts alleged with particularity in the pleadings". Under the proposed new Rule 26(a)(1) each party would only be required to disclose identifying facts concerning witnesses likely to have information or documents "that the disclosing party may use to support its claims or defenses, unless solely for impeachment."

The other disclosures required under Rule 26(a)(1), computations of damages by the party claiming those damages, and any insurance policies that may be available to satisfy a judgment in the case, (Rule 26(a)(1)(C) and (D)) remain unchanged.

Current Rule 26(f) provides that the parties will meet "as soon as practicable" to arrange for these required disclosures and to agree on a discovery plan. The Rules contemplate that this meeting will generally be held within 75 days after defendant first appears in the action. (Defendant's appearance is usually made by filing an answer or a motion pursuant to Rule 12.) Disclosure under 26(a) is required to be made at or within 10 days after the discovery meeting. The proposed amendments extend these deadlines slightly and make it clear that the discovery "conference" need not involve a face to face meeting (unless the court so orders), but may be conducted over the telephone or by other electronic means.

Rule 26(a)(2) requires substantial disclosure of information relating to expert testimony. These provisions are discussed more fully later in this chapter. Rule 26(a)(3) requires substantial pretrial disclosure of evidence that will be presented at trial. These Rules would remain essentially unchanged by the 2000 amendments.

A major purpose of the disclosure requirements, as the Advisory Committee Notes to the 1993 rules state, is to "accelerate the exchange of basic information about the case and to eliminate the paper work involved in requesting such information."

The rules continue to permit discovery to be conducted through depositions, interrogatories, document demands and the other discovery devices set forth in Rule 26 through 37. Rule 30(a) restricts the number of depositions that may be taken without leave of the court to 10, and Rule 33 limits the number of interrogatories that may be taken without court order to 25. Rule 26(b)(2) currently authorizes the district court, by local rule or order, to alter these limits and to impose other limitations on discovery, but the proposed 2000 amendments would eliminate the power of district courts to alter these limits by local rule and would presumptively limit the duration of each deposition to seven hours.

The question remains, has the disclosure system, either in its current or revised form, effectively addressed the problems of cost, delay and abuse which first led to calls for reform of the system. As you read, consider whether these problems exist where the system of disclosure has been implemented or whether the system has improved.

Scheetz v. Bridgestone/Firestone, Inc.

United States District Court, District of Montana, 1993.
152 F.R.D. 628.

■ HATFIELD, CHIEF JUDGE

The subject motion seeks to compel the defendant, Bridgestone/Firestone, Inc. to file a pre-discovery disclosure statement sufficient to satisfy the prescriptions of [Local] Rule 200–5(a).[9] The plaintiffs contend the disclosure statement served and filed by Bridgestone/Firestone fails to comply with the requirements of Rule 200–5 because it is deficient in the following respects:

First, the statement does not contain the factual basis of every defense advanced by the defendants;

---

9. Rule 200–5(a) provides:

(a) Pre–Discovery Disclosure

(1) Except with leave of court, a party may not seek discovery from any source before making an appropriate pre-discovery disclosure and may not seek discovery from another party before serving that party with an appropriate disclosure.

The disclosure shall contain the following information:

(i) the factual basis of every claim or defense advanced by the disclosing party;

(ii) the legal theory upon which each claim or defense is based;

(iii) the identity of all persons known or believed to have discoverable information about the claims or defenses, and a summary of that information;

(iv) a description, including the location and custodian of any tangible evidence or relevant documents that are reasonably likely to bear on the claims or defenses;

(v) a computation of any damages claimed; and

(vi) the substance of any insurance agreement that may cover any resulting judgment.

Second, the statement does not identify all persons known or believed to have discoverable information about the claims or defenses, together with a summary of that information; and

Third, the statement fails to give a description including the location and custodian of tangible evidence and relevant documents that bear upon claims or defenses.

Bridgestone/Firestone retorts that its disclosure statement satisfies the "spirit" of Rule 200–5 and that plaintiffs' reliance upon the rule is simple "gamesmanship".

Magistrate Judge Holter, having reviewed the initial pre-discovery disclosure statement of Bridgestone/Firestone, together with the supplement to that statement, concluded, without discussion, the statement complied with Rule 200–5. The order is reviewed for clear error. Fed.R.Civ.P. 72(a).

The plaintiffs' objection calls upon the court to construe the mandate of Rule 200–5(a) in the context of litigation properly characterized as "complex". In view of the somewhat novel nature of mandatory pre-discovery disclosure, the task would, at first blush, appear formidable. However, when one reviews the language of Rule 200–5, in conjunction with the Civil Justice Expense and Delay Reduction Plan of the District of Montana, not only does the task prove significantly less onerous, but the error of the defendants' position becomes evident.

On April 1, 1992, the District of Montana adopted a comprehensive Civil Justice Expense and Delay Reduction Plan (the "Plan"). Following the express recommendation of the Advisory Group that the Plan require the prompt disclosure of information in the form of a "pre-discovery disclosure" statement ... Rule 200–5 provides, in essence, that a party may not seek discovery from another party before serving that party with an appropriate pre-discovery disclosure statement. "The intent of the provision is to ensure that the specifically delineated items of information are promptly disclosed early in the course of litigation, avoiding unnecessary and protracted discovery and to enhance the prospect of early resolution through settlement." The obligation created by Rule 200–5(a) must be defined and, accordingly, the language of the various provisions of the rule construed in a manner which will effect the Rule's intended purpose, i.e., the avoidance of unnecessary and protracted discovery through the mandatory exchange of essential information.

The present dispute places subsections (i), (iii) and (iv) of Rule 200–5(a)(1) under scrutiny, and calls upon the court to construe the terms of those subsections, both generally and with specific reference to the facts and circumstances of this case. In order that the dispute is placed in its proper perspective, analysis begins with a review of the circumstances underlying the case.[10]

---

10. Fed.R.Civ.P. 26 (amended December 1, 1993), likewise contemplates this broad disclosure, as the Committee Notes to the Rule reflect in the following terms:

The product at issue in this action is the now notorious RH5 degrees rim, a multi-piece wheel assembly designed, manufactured and marketed by the predecessor in interest of Bridgestone/Firestone. Litigation involving the RH5 degrees assembly has spanned a period of time in excess of a decade, and included multi-district litigation that occurred in the 1970's. Plaintiffs' counsel in the present case, Mr. John Risjord, was, in fact, lead plaintiffs' counsel in the multi-district litigation and has prosecuted numerous cases involving the RH5 degrees assembly. The controversy which exists between the parties regarding the proper interpretation to be afforded Rule 200–5 may be said to have its genesis in the fact that Mr. Risjord has represented numerous plaintiffs in the prosecution of actions against Firestone, and its successor, for damages allegedly sustained as a result of the defective design of the RH5 degrees assembly. This conclusion is borne out by the fact that Bridgestone/Firestone frames the determinative issue as follows: "Whether Firestone should be compelled under the circumstances of this case . . . to identify in any greater detail historical witnesses or categories and locations of historical documents about which plaintiffs' counsel not only possesses full knowledge, but has also previously deposed the witnesses themselves (or at least had the opportunity to depose them) and reviewed and selected copies of the documents."

Contrary to the suggestion of Bridgestone/Firestone, however, the fact the plaintiffs in this case are represented by counsel who has participated in innumerable cases involving the RH5 degrees assembly is irrelevant to a determination as to the sufficiency of the defendants' disclosure statement. Simply stated, Mr. Risjord's involvement in the present case does not operate to relieve Bridgestone/Firestone from complying with the mandate of Rule 200–5.

The COMMENT to Part IV,(B)(1) of the Plan notes that the mandatory pre-discovery disclosure requirement was patterned after the proposed amendment to Fed.R.Civ.P. 26 as set forth in the Preliminary Draft of the Proposed Amendments of the Federal Rules of Civil Procedure and Federal Rules of Evidence, August 1991. The Rule requires litigants to disclose specified core information about the case; namely, potential witnesses, documentary evidence, damage claims, and insurance. The objectives of subpart B(1), and accordingly of Rule 200–5(a), are the same as those which underly the amendments to the Federal Rules of Civil Procedure approved by both the Advisory Committee on Civil Rules on April 15, 1992, and the Committee on Rules of Practice and Procedure of the Judicial Conference of the United States in September of 1992, i.e., the elimination of the time and expense of preparing formal discovery requests with respect to

Rule 26(a)(1)(A) requires identification of all persons who, based on the investigation conducted thus far, are likely to have discoverable information relevant to the factual disputes between the parties. All persons with such information should be disclosed, whether or not their testimony will be supportive of the position of the disclosing party. As officers of the court, counsel are expected to disclose the identity of those persons who may be used by them as witnesses or who, if their potential testimony were known, might reasonably be expected to be deposed or called as a witness by any of the other parties.

that information and to enable the parties to plan more effectively for the discovery that would be needed.[11]

The language utilized in Rule 200–5, in essence, is akin to the language of Fed.R.Civ.P. 26(a)(1)(A) (amended December 1, 1993).

A reading of Rule 200–5, in its entirety, evinces that the initial disclosure of a party must, at the very least, identify those potential witnesses and documents which would support each claim for relief asserted by the disclosing party, or every defense asserted by the disclosing party to any claim for relief advanced against that party in any pleading. However, contrary to the suggestion of Bridgestone/Firestone, the initial disclosure required by Rule 200–5 is not limited to identifying those potential witnesses and documents supporting the disclosing party's contentions. Rather, the obligation imposed by the rule requires the disclosure of the identity of all potential witnesses, documents and tangible evidence that are relevant to the disputed facts as framed by the pleadings.[12]

Rule 200–5(a) imposes upon the defendant in this case, Bridgestone/Firestone, inter alia, the following obligations: First, to identify all persons known or believed to have discoverable information that would bear upon the claim asserted by the plaintiff in this action, i.e., that the RH5 degrees assembly, at the time it left the hands of Firestone, was in a defective condition, unreasonably dangerous to the ultimate user or consumer of the RH5 degrees assembly, or any defense to that claim. Together with identifying those persons, Bridgestone/Firestone must provide a summary of the information each person possesses. Second, to provide a description of all tangible evidence and documents that are reasonably likely to bear on the claim advanced by the plaintiff and the defenses asserted to that claim. With regard to each item of tangible evidence and document Bridgestone/Firestone shall set forth the location of the tangible item or document and the individual who has custody of that item or document.

---

11. The August 1991 published draft of proposed Rule 26(a)(1)(A) called for parties to identify "each individual likely to have information that bears significantly on any claims or defense." The language subsequently approved on April 15, 1992, by the Advisory Committee on Civil Rules and approved by the Committee on Rules of Practice and Procedure of the Judicial Conference of the United States calls for the parties to identify "each individual likely to have discoverable information relevant to disputed facts alleged with particularity in the pleadings." The change "was made primarily at the insistence of many commentators who objected to the lack of use of familiar terms such as 'relevancy' or 'discoverable information' to the problems created by the vague allegations tolerated under notice pleading, and to the imposition of a duty to exercise judgment, arguably conflicting with an attorney's responsibility to a client, in identifying which potential witnesses would be most beneficial to an adversary."

12. This construction of Rule 200–5 is consistent with the view adopted by the Advisory Committee on Civil Rules regarding the obligation of mandatory disclosure created by the proposed amendments to Fed.R.Civ.P. 26. In relation to its April 15, 1992, approval of the proposed amendments to Fed.R.Civ.P. 26, the Advisory Committee offered the following observation: "One committee member preferred, as suggested by many critics, that initial disclosures be limited to potential witnesses and documents supporting the parties' contentions; the other members, however, remained of the view that the obligation should relate to all such witnesses and documents." *Id.*

Bridgestone/Firestone shall not be allowed to effectively defeat the goal of the Plan, and necessarily the CJRA, through the mere expediency of declaring that counsel for the adverse party is aware of the information falling within the purview of Rule 200–5(a)(1)(iii) and (iv).[13]

Therefore, for the reasons set forth herein,

IT IS HEREBY ORDERED that the defendant Bridgestone/Firestone, Inc., shall, within twenty (20) days of the date hereof, file a supplemental pre-discovery disclosure statement that satisfies the prescriptions of Rule 200–5, RULES OF PROCEDURE OF THE UNITED STATES DISTRICT COURT FOR THE DISTRICT OF MONTANA, as those prescriptions are more specifically delineated herein.

QUESTIONS

A. Do you think the disclosure shortened the discovery process in this case? Is this the right question to ask?

B. Is disclosure likely to have made the discovery process less costly in this case?

C. Is this case idiosyncratic because the lawyer was already aware of the background facts? Would a different lawyer have been able to tell that disclosure was incomplete?

NOTE ON LOCAL COURT RULES REGULATING DISCOVERY

The 1993 Amendments to the Federal Rules made two important changes in the discovery process. (1) Federal Rule 26(a) established a new system of mandatory disclosure that requires each party to provide a opposing parties with substantial information *without a request*, at the earliest possible date. (2) Federal Rule 30(a)(2)(A) and Federal Rule 33(a) set up presumptive limits on discovery by confirming the number of depositions (10) and interrogatories (25) a party can use without obtaining permission from the court.

Currently, by their terms, these Federal Rules may be modified or limited by local rule. Federal Rule 26(a)(1) expressly provides that the disclosure system may be altered or suspended by an order of an individual judge, the stipulation of the parties, or a local rule of a court, and Federal Rule 26(b)(2) permits a court to alter the presumptive limits by local rule. In recent years, a number of federal courts have experimented with different approaches to the discovery process, promulgating local rules that have the effect of changing or rejecting the new Federal Rules. The *Bridgestone* case provides an illustration of one local approach to changing the

---

13. The proposed amendment to Fed. R.Civ.P. 26 requiring mandatory early pre-discovery disclosure has "provoked the most intense division within the bench and bar of any of the proposed amendments [to the Federal Rules of Civil Procedure]." See, Issues and Changes, Attachment B to letter from Advisory Committee on Civil Rules to Robert E. Keeton, Chairman, Standing Committee on Rules of Practice and Procedure of the Judicial Conference of the United States (May 1, 1992). Perhaps, the critics of mandatory pre-discovery disclosure may ultimately be vindicated in their assertion that the notion of cooperative discovery will prove counter-productive to the goals of efficiency and expediency envisioned by the CJRA. However, an informed decision as to whether or not this cooperative discovery technique will operate to reduce cost and delay can only be made with the assistance of empirical data.

disclosure requirements. The new amendments to the Federal Rules scheduled to become effective in December 2000 would eliminate the power of district courts to modify the disclosure requirements or the presumptive limits on discovery by local rule, although they could still be altered by stipulation or judicial order in an individual case.

Consider the following reports, which provide some of the basis for the Advisory Committee's decision to impose greater uniformity among the district courts through the 2000 amendments.

Stienstra, Implementation of Disclosure in United States District Courts

164 F.R.D. LXXXIII (1996).

Rule 26(a), which requires initial disclosure, has been more frequently rejected than have the other sections of Rule 26. Altogether, exactly half the districts have implemented 26(a)(1), and half have not. Compared to March 1994, this is an increase of two courts. The overall change across courts is, however, slightly greater, as one or two courts decided this past year to reverse earlier decisions to implement the rule and several who hadn't implemented the rule decided to do so.

Of the forty-seven districts that have not implemented the rule, three require initial disclosure through local rules, orders, or the CJRA plan, one requires disclosure in a specified set of case types, and seventeen—two more than were reported last year—specifically give individual judges authority to require initial disclosure. Six courts have implemented Rule 26(a)(1) with a significant revision. Typically the revision excludes either the requirement to disclose adverse material or the requirement to submit a computation of damages.

Although Rule 26 does not include provisions for opting out of expert disclosure, 26(a)(2), and pretrial disclosure, 26(a)(3), about a fifth of the districts have interpreted the federal rule that way. Still, the great majority require expert and pretrial disclosure—78 and 76 courts, respectively, an increase of four courts in both categories since March 1994. Of the courts adopting expert disclosure, seven have made a significant revision in their implementation of the rule; the most common revision is to exempt parties from submitting the experts' signed report.

FJC Report: Disclosure and Discovery

Federal Judicial Center Report, Discovery and Disclosure: Practice, Problems, and Proposals for Change (1997)

With what frequency in initial disclosure used? What are its effects? What or problems arise in initial disclosure?

The most controversy of the 1993 amendments is the revision of Fed. R. Civ. P. (hereafter Rule) 26(a)(1), which permits each district to delete whether to require attorneys to disclose specified types of information early in the litigation without requests from opposing counsel. The rule drafters intended to achieve a number of outcomes, including less formal discovery, lower litigation costs, and earlier settlements. Because Rule 26(a)(1) permits districts, as well as attorneys by stipulation, to opt out of the rule, it has been unclear how many cases have actually been subject to the rule, much less what its impact has been.

Frequency of initial disclosure

We found that over half of the attorneys (58%) who engaged in some discovery or disclosure either provided or received initial disclosure in their case (Table 2). The vast majority of attorneys (89%) who reported that initial disclosure in their case also reported other types of discovery, indicating that initial disclosure seldom replaces discovery entirely.

Given the unexpectedly high incidence of initial disclosure, we examined whether the cases in our sample might over represent the amount of disclosure. We concluded that they do not, but also found surprisingly, that more than a third of the attorneys in our sample who had engaged in initial disclosure had litigated their case in a district classified as having opted out of Rule 26(a)(1)'s requirements (Table 15). These data, together with the finding that 58% of cases with some discovery also involved disclosure suggest that initial disclosure requirements may be more prevalent than some believe.

Table 2

**Percentage of attorneys reporting that specific forms
of discovery and disclosure occurred, in cases
involving some discovery or disclosure**

Discovery activity	
Document Production	84%
Interrogatories	81%
Depositions	67%
Initial disclosure (Rule 26 (a)(1) or local provision	58%
Requests for admission	31%
Expert disclosure	20%
Physical or mental exam	13%
Other formal discovery (subpoenas, inspections)	9%

Table 15

Percentage of attorneys who did not use initial disclosure in their case, by type of disclosure requirement in district in which case was filed

judge discretion	National rule in effect	Less stringent local variation	No disclosure required	Individual
Disclosure	73%	73%	35%	37%
No disclosure	27%	27%	65%	63%

Effects of initial disclosure

In general, initial disclosure appears to be having its intended effects. Among those who believed there was an effect, the effects were most often of the type intended by the drafters of the1993 amendments. Far more attorneys reported that initial disclosure decreased litigation expense, time from filing to disposition, the amount of discovery, and the number of discovery disputes than said it increased them. At the same time, may more attorneys said initial disclosure increased overall procedural fairness, the fairness of the case outcome, and the prospects of settlement than said it decreased them (Table 17)
* * *

Nonetheless, more than a third of the attorneys (37%) who participated in initial disclosure identified one or more problems wlth the process (and generally with other aspects of discovery in their cases). The most frequently identified problem was incomplete disclosure (19% of attorneys who participated in disclosure). Relatively few attorneys reported that disclosure requirements led to motions to compel, motions for sanctions, or other satellite litigation (Table 18). Problems in initial disclosure arose more frequently in cases involving large stakes and expenses or that were characterized [by the attorneys] as complex or contentious.

Table 17

Percentage of attorneys reporting specific effects of initial disclosure in their case

Effect of initial disclosure on	Increased	Had no effect	Decreased
Your client's litigation expenses	16%	45%	39%
Time from filing to disposition	7%	62%	32%
Overall procedural fairness	37%	54%	9%
Fairness of case outcome	25%	70%	5%
Prospects of settlement	36%	59%	6%
Amount of discovery	10%	47%	43%
Number of discovery disputes	5%	62%	33%

Table 18

Percentage of attorneys reporting specific problems with initial disclosure, in cases where initial disclosure was reported

Type of Problem	All Respondents
Disclosure was too brief or incomplete	19%
A party failed to supplement or update the disclosures	12%
Some disclosed materials were also requested in discovery	11%
A party disclosed required information and another party did not disclose required information	11%
Disclosure occurred only after a motion to compel or an order from the court	6%
Other	3%
Disclosure was excessive	2%
Sanctions were imposed for failure to disclose	1%

Is nonuniformity in the disclosure rules a problem?

Although for some time them has been growing concern about nonuniformity in the Federal Rules of Civil Procedure, those concerns became far greater after 1993 when the revisions to Rule 26 explicitly permitted districts to opt out of the rule's initial disclosure requirements. Since that time, an increasing number of voices among both the bench and bar have asserted that nonuniformity in the discovery rules-and in the disclosure rules in particular-is a serious problem and should be resolved.

That opinion is shared by the attorneys in our sample, at least with regard to nonuniformity of disclosure *across* districts. A clear majority—60%—of the attorneys with opinions on this subject said nonuniformity in the disclosure rules creates problems (Table 34). Most said the problems are moderate, but attorneys who practice in four or more districts (10% of the respondents) are more likely than other attorneys to see such problems as serious. Even these national practitioners, however, are more likely to label the problems moderate than serious.

When asked about uniformity of disclosure requirements *within* districts about 25% of the attorneys said that there are problems with nonuniformity of disclosure rules within the districts in which the sample case was files. Almost half said that there is no significant lack of uniformity within the district in which the case was filed (Table 34).

Table 34

Percentage of attorneys holding certain opinions regarding the effect of nonuniformity concerning disclosure within a district and across districts

Attorney Opinion	Within a district	Across districts
There is no significant lack of uniformity	47%	13%
Lack of uniformity creates serious problems	6%	16%
Lack of uniformity creates moderate problems	21%	44%
Lack of uniformity creates minor or no problems	27%	28%

NOTE ON STANDING ORDERS AND CONTROL OF THE DISCOVERY PROCESS BY INDIVIDUAL JUDGES

In addition to and consistent with the requirements of the Federal Rules of Civil Procedure and any applicable local court rules, individual judges may also promulgate rules to regulate the discovery process in cases that come before them. These rules may take the form of "standing orders" applicable to all cases or all cases of a certain type which are assigned to the judge, or they may be contained in a pretrial order applicable only to an individual case. Such rules, like local court rules, may limit the number or scope of certain discovery devices, provide procedures for making discovery motions, refer discovery disputes to magistrate judges, and seek to regulate the discovery process in other ways.

For example, Rule 2.1: Procedures for Individual Judges for the District Court for the Southern District of Alabama states as follows:

Attorneys practicing before this Court are advised that the judges of this Court have adopted different pretrial orders, copies of which are available from the clerk's office * * * Some of the rules have been reduced to writing. Attorneys shall check with the clerk of the Court in order to ascertain whether a particular judge has any such printed rules.

In Keeton, The Function of the Local Rules and the Tension With Uniformity, 50 U. of Pitt.L.Rev. 853, 900–01 (1989), Judge Robert Keeton of the United States Court for the District of Massachusetts provided an example of an order regarding discovery he has issued in some cases. It states in part:

Discovery disputes have arisen in this case. On the basis of an examination of matters on file, the court is concerned that this may be an instance in which counsel on both sides are taking positions that do not comply with either the letter or the spirit of the Federal Rules of Civil Procedure. An excessive discovery demand, knowingly made, violates Rule 11 and Rule 26(g). An inadequate response, knowingly made, violates Rule 11, Rules 26(g), and other rules as well. . . .

The court will not serve, or acquiesce in a magistrate's serving, as a mediator for settlement of disputes over discovery in which each party takes unreasonable positions with the purpose of conceding what is plainly due under the rules only when before the court or magistrate. If counsel makes excessive demands or insufficient responses after this cautionary order by the court, an order may be entered providing for more stringent controls over discovery, including the following:

(1) Having determined that both sides have been unreasonable, the court may impose an appropriate sanction, pursuant to FED.R.CIV.P. 26(g) and 37. An appropriate sanction in this case may include an order in which the court declines to undertake the burdensome task of working out some compromise position that is a reasonable accommodation within the range counsel should have agreed upon; the court may instead determine only which side has been more unreasonable and, as a sanction for misconduct, enter an order that discovery proceed in accordance with the other side's position.

QUESTIONS

A. What do you think of the approach to resolving discovery disputes implied by Judge Keeton's order? Is it an effective way of reducing unreasonable discovery positions? Will it provide equitable results?

B. Should a court enforce a discovery request that may be improper or beyond the authorized scope of discovery?

Grass v. E. I. Dupont De Nemours and Company

United States Court of Appeals for the Fourth Circuit, 1997.
114 F.3d 1176 (Unpublished Opinion).

■ PER CURIAM:

In this personal injury action removed to the district court from the Circuit Court of Kanawha County, West Virginia, John T. Grass, Jr., appeals the summary judgment granted to E.I. duPont de Nemours & Co., Inc. We affirm.

I.

Grass worked at duPont's chemical plant in Belle, West Virginia, for approximately ten years, until November 18, 1983. Grass's health has deteriorated since his termination, and he is currently afflicted with a host of cardiovascular and respiratory ailments; Grass's difficulties are compounded as the result of a debilitating stroke he suffered in early 1995.

Grass believes that duPont, by insisting that he work in extreme heat and in proximity to certain hazardous materials, is responsible for his infirmities. He seeks recovery under W. Va. Code § 23–4–2(c)(2), which excepts from workers' compensation immunity those employers that act with "deliberate intention" to harm an employee.

II.

As an initial matter, Grass maintains that an action brought pursuant to § 23–4–2(c)(2) arises "under the workmen's compensation laws" of West Virginia and is, therefore, not susceptible to removal to the district court. See *28 U.S.C. § 1445*(c). He asks that we reconsider our decision to the contrary in *Arthur v. E.I. Dupont de Nemours & Co., 58 F.3d 121, 128 (4th Cir.1995)*. We must decline Grass's request, for we are bound to faithfully apply circuit precedent until it is either overruled en banc or superseded by a decision of the Supreme Court.

III.

Grass next asserts that the district court abused its discretion by not enforcing against duPont Fed. R. Civ. P. 26(a)(1), which dictates that all parties to a civil action disclose, more or less concurrently, certain information at the initial stages of discovery. The plain language of the rule, however, permits its default requirements to be amended by stipulation of the parties, and that is precisely what occurred here. On September 25, 1995, the parties filed with the district court a report of their discovery planning meeting, held pursuant to Fed. R. Civ. P. 26(f), wherein it was agreed that

> the plaintiff will make initial disclosures as required by Rule 26(a)(1) ... on or before October 9, 1995. Such disclosures ... will include ... (1) a list of the specific chemical(s) to which the plaintiff was exposed, (2) the location of each such chemical exposure, (3) the time and duration of each such chemical exposure, (4) the resulting disease process, and (5) proof of causation of each disease process.... The Defendant will make initial disclosures thirty days after plaintiff has provided initial disclosures.

Grass did provide some information to duPont, but, as the district court found, these disclosures fell short of what the agreement required. Consequently, duPont was not compelled to make any disclosures at all.

Moreover, Grass, through counsel, represented to the district court that further discovery would bear neither on duPont's motion for summary judgment nor on his own cross-motion. In so doing, Grass essentially gambled that the materials already before the court were sufficient to permit his claims to proceed to trial. Having lost that gamble, Grass cannot now be heard to complain that he should have been prevented from placing the bet.

QUESTIONS

    A. Was the result in *Grass v. E.I. Dupont* equitable?

    B. What are the dangers and advantages of allowing parties to waive the disclosure rules by agreement?

Arche, Inc. v. Azaleia, U.S.A.

United States District Court, Southern District of New York, 1995.
882 F.Supp. 334.

■ KAPLAN, DISTRICT JUDGE.

Plaintiff, a French manufacturer of ladies' footwear, claims that defendants, a Brazilian footwear manufacturer and its U.S. distributor, have violated their rights under the Lanham Act, among other legal doctrines, by imitating the trade dress of plaintiff's so-called P-sole shoes. The matter is before the Court on defendants' motions in limine. Defendants seek to exclude plaintiff's consumer survey, including the testimony of the interviewer and eight interview respondents, on the ground that plaintiff failed to comply with discovery requirements.

. . .

The Consumer and Affiliated Witnesses

Defendants move to exclude any testimony concerning actual consumer confusion by three consumer witnesses (Geri Bondanza,

Michele Breier and Sara Horowitz) and by a number of other witnesses who are employees or customers of Arche or have had, directly or indirectly, some affiliation or connection with it in the past (the "Affiliated Witnesses"). They assert that such evidence should be precluded as a sanction for plaintiff's alleged violation of FED. R. CIV. P. 26(e).

In April 1993, defendants served an interrogatory calling upon plaintiff to identify anyone alleged to have been confused between plaintiff's and defendants' shoes and to provide certain other information. Arche shortly thereafter responded that instances of actual confusion at the retail level had been reported to it, that it did not yet have the information requested, and that it would provide the information when it became available. The interrogatory answer never was supplemented. In consequence, defendants never were told in discovery whether they had to meet evidence of instances of actual confusion, apart from what they learned of Ms. Goldberg's sojourn in Washington Square Park, if indeed that is properly so characterized.

It is not clear from the pretrial order whether plaintiff proposes to adduce testimony from any of these witnesses that should have been provided in response to the interrogatory. Plaintiff, however, resists any order of preclusion, thus suggesting that Arche does so intend.

Plaintiff does not directly dispute the contention that any information regarding witnesses to instances of actual consumer confusion should have been disclosed in response to the interrogatory or in a supplement thereto. It simply argues that defendants had an opportunity to depose all of these witnesses. It may not so easily avoid its responsibilities.

Having served the interrogatory, defendants were entitled to know whether plaintiff intended to call witnesses to instances of actual consumer confusion and, if so, the requested information concerning each. That information was important to permit defendants to decide which depositions to take in order to prepare the case for trial on an economical basis. To suggest, as plaintiff in substance does, that defendants should have deposed a broad range of people to find out whether they had knowledge of any actual consumer confusion mocks the discovery rules.

The factors relevant to determining sanctions for failure to supplement the interrogatory answer are the explanation for the failure, the importance of the testimony, the need for time to meet the testimony, and the possibility of a continuance. Outley v. City of New York, 837 F.2d 587, 590 (2d Cir.1988). Here, any testimony concerning instances of actual consumer confusion would be quite significant for the reasons outlined above. No excuse has been offered by plaintiff for the failure to supplement the interrogatory answer. The deposition testimony of Ms. Verbrugghen, supra n.4, was evasive and disregarded Arche's obligations under Rule 30(b)(6). A continuance is inappropriate, as this is at least the third trial setting (dated back to 1993) in this case already and plaintiff failed either to specify which of, and to what extent, these witnesses would testify to instances of actual confusion or to tender them for examination in the two months since defendants made this motion. Balancing these factors, I grant defendants' motion to the extent of precluding any testimony by these witnesses with respect to instances of actual confusion unless plaintiff can demonstrate that the information neither was known nor should have been known to plaintiff or its counsel prior to the date of this order.

Conclusion

In sum, defendants' motions are granted to the extent that plaintiff is precluded from adducing (a) the cumulative survey results and any opinion testimony based thereon and (b) testimony from the consumer and Affiliated Witnesses concerning any instances of actual consumer confusion to the extent described above. The motions otherwise are denied on the basis previously outlined.

NOTE: SANCTIONS FOR FAILURE TO DISCLOSE

Disclosure imposes the obligation to furnish an adversary with information that the adversary has not requested. In that sense it is self-executing. As a result, failure to disclose relevant information that has never been requested may result in the imposition of sanctions on the culpable party, raising the question of what sanctions are appropriate.

Thus, in *Asia Strategic Investment Alliances, Ltd. v. General Electric Capital Services*, 1997 WL 122568 (D.Kan.), plaintiff failed to make disclosure but the court found "no indication that plaintiff acted in bad faith or with callous disregard of the rules of discovery." As a result the court refused to exclude the evidence at trial, but did make an award of "reasonable attorneys' fees and expenses incurred due to the failure to disclose."

B.   LIMITATIONS ON OBTAINING DISCOVERY

1.   The Work Product Protection

(a) MATERIALS PREPARED IN ANTICIPATION OF LITIGATION

Hickman v. Taylor

Supreme Court of the United States, 1947.
329 U.S. 495, 67 S.Ct. 385, 91 L.Ed. 451.

■ Mr. Justice Murphy delivered the opinion of the Court.

This case presents an important problem under the Federal Rules of Civil Procedure, 28 U.S.C.A. following section 723c, as to the extent to which a party may inquire into oral and written statements of witnesses, or other information, secured by an adverse party's counsel in the course of preparation for possible litigation after a claim has arisen. Examination into a person's files and records, including those resulting from the professional activities of an attorney, must be judged with care. It is not without reason that various safeguards have been established to preclude unwarranted excursions into the privacy of a man's work. At the same time, public policy supports reasonable and necessary inquiries. Properly to balance these competing interests is a delicate and difficult task.

On February 7, 1943, the tug "J.M. Taylor" sank while engaged in helping to tow a car float of the Baltimore & Ohio Railroad across the Delaware River at Philadelphia. The accident was apparently unusual in nature, the cause of it still being unknown. Five of the nine crew members were drowned. Three days later the tug owners and the underwriters employed a law firm, of which respondent Fortenbaugh is a member, to defend them against potential suits by representatives of the deceased crew members and to sue the railroad for damages to the tug.

A public hearing was held on March 4, 1943, before the United States Steamboat Inspectors, at which the four survivors were examined. This testimony was recorded and made available to all interested parties. Shortly thereafter, Fortenbaugh privately interviewed the survivors and took statements from them with an eye toward the anticipated litigation; the survivors signed these statements on March 29. Fortenbaugh also interviewed other persons believed to have some information relating to the accident and in some cases he made memoranda of what they told him. At the time when Fortenbaugh secured the statements of the survivors, representatives of two of the deceased crew members had been in communication with him. Ultimately claims were presented by representatives of all five of the deceased; four of the claims, however, were settled without litigation. The fifth claimant, petitioner herein, brought suit in a federal court under the Jones Act on November 26, 1943, naming as defendants the two tug owners, individually and as partners, and the railroad.

One year later, petitioner filed 39 interrogatories directed to the tug owners. The 38th interrogatory read: "State whether any statements of the members of the crews of the Tugs 'J.M. Taylor' and 'Philadelphia' or of any other vessel were taken in connection with the towing of the car float and the sinking of the Tug 'John M. Taylor'.

"Attach hereto exact copies of all such statements if in writing, and if oral, set forth in detail the exact provisions of any such oral statements or reports."

Supplemental interrogatories asked whether any oral or written statements, records, reports or other memoranda had been made concerning any matter relative to the towing operation, the sinking of the tug, the salvaging and repair of the tug, and the death of the deceased. If the answer was in the affirmative, the tug owners were then requested to set forth the nature of all such records, reports, statements or other memoranda.

The tug owners, through Fortenbaugh, answered all of the interrogatories except No. 38 and the supplemental ones just described. While admitting that statements of the survivors had been taken, they declined to summarize or set forth the contents. They did so on the ground that such requests called "for privileged matter obtained in preparation for litigation" and constituted "an attempt to obtain indirectly counsel's private files." It was claimed that answering these requests "would involve practically turning over not only the complete files, but also the telephone records and, almost, the thoughts of counsel."

In connection with the hearing on these objections, Fortenbaugh made a written statement and gave an informal oral deposition explaining the circumstances under which he had taken the statements. But he was not expressly asked in the deposition to produce the statements. The District Court for the Eastern District of Pennsylvania, sitting en banc, held that the requested matters were not privileged. 4 F.R.D. 479. The court then decreed that the tug owners and Fortenbaugh, as counsel and agent for the tug owners forthwith "Answer Plaintiff's 38th interrogatory and supplemental interrogatories; produce all written statements of witnesses obtained by Mr. Fortenbaugh, as counsel and agent for Defendants; state in substance any fact concerning this case which Defendants learned through oral statements made by witnesses to Mr. Fortenbaugh whether or not included in his private memoranda and produce Mr. Fortenbaugh's memoranda containing statements of fact by witnesses or to submit these memoranda to the Court for determination of those portions which should be revealed to Plaintiff." Upon their refusal, the court adjudged them in contempt and ordered them imprisoned until they complied.

The Third Circuit Court of Appeals, also sitting en banc, reversed the judgment of the District Court. 153 F.2d 212. It held that the information here sought was part of the "work product of the lawyer" and hence privileged from discovery under the Federal Rules of Civil Procedure. The importance of the problem, which has engendered a great divergence of views among district courts, led us to grant certiorari. 328 U.S. 876, 66 S.Ct. 1337.

The pre-trial deposition-discovery mechanism established by Rules 26 to 37 is one of the most significant innovations of the Federal Rules of Civil Procedure. Under the prior federal practice, the pre-trial functions of notice-giving issue-formulation and fact-revelation were performed primarily and inadequately by the pleadings. Inquiry into the issues and the facts before trial was narrowly confined and was often cumbersome in method. The new rules, however, restrict the pleadings to the task of general notice-giving and invest the deposition-discovery process with a vital role in the preparation for trial. The various instruments of discovery now serve (1) as a device, along with the pre-trial hearing under Rule 16, to narrow and clarify the basic issues between the parties, and (2) as a device for ascertaining the facts, or information as to the existence or whereabouts of facts, relative to those issues. Thus civil trials in the federal courts no longer need be carried on in the dark. The way is now clear, consistent with recognized privileges, for the parties to obtain the fullest possible knowledge of the issues and facts before trial.

There is an initial question as to which of the deposition-discovery rules is involved in this case. Petitioner, in filing his interrogatories, thought that he was proceeding under Rule 33. That rule provides that a party may serve upon any adverse party written interrogatories to be answered by the party served. The District Court proceeded on the same assumption in its opinion, although its order to produce and its contempt order stated that both Rules 33 and 34 were involved. Rule 34 establishes a procedure whereby, upon motion of any party showing good cause therefor and upon notice to all other parties, the court may order any party to produce and permit the inspection and copying or photographing of any designated documents, etc., not privileged, which constitute or contain evidence material to any matter involved in the action and which are in his possession, custody or control.

The Circuit Court of Appeals, however, felt that Rule 26 was the crucial one. Petitioner, it said, was proceeding by interrogatories and, in connection with those interrogatories, wanted copies of memoranda and statements secured from witnesses. While the court believed that Rule 33 was involved, at least as to the defending tug owners, it stated that this rule could not be used as the basis for condemning Fortenbaugh's failure to disclose or produce the memoranda and statements, since the rule applies only to interrogatories addressed to adverse parties, not to their agents or counsel. And Rule 34 was said to be inapplicable since petitioner was not trying to see an original document and to copy or photograph it, within the scope of that rule. The court then concluded that Rule 26 must be the one really involved. That provides that the testimony of any person, whether a party or not, may be taken by any party by deposition upon oral examination or written interrogatories for the purpose of discovery or for use as evidence; and that the deponent may be examined regarding any matter, not privileged, which is relevant to the subject matter involved in the pending action, whether relating to the claim or defense of the examining party or of any other party, including the existence, description, nature, custody, condition and location of any books, documents or other tangible things.[a]

The matter is not without difficulty in light of the events that transpired below. We believe, however, that petitioner was proceeding primarily under Rule 33. He addressed simple interrogatories solely to the individual tug owners, the adverse parties, as contemplated by that rule. He did not, and could not under Rule 33, address such interrogatories to their counsel, Fortenbaugh. Nor did he direct these interrogatories either to the tug owners or to Fortenbaugh by way of deposition; Rule 26 thus could not come into operation. And it does not appear from the record that petitioner filed a motion under Rule 34 for a court order directing the production of the documents in question. Indeed, such an order could not have been entered as to

---

a. The Federal Rules relating to discovery have been substantially amended and renumbered since the time of *Hickman v. Taylor*. At that time, Rule 26(a) provided that "the testimony of any person, whether a party or not, may be taken at the instance of any party by deposition upon oral examination or written interrogatories." The successor to that Rule is to be found today as Rules 30(a) and 31(a). Moreover, Rule 26(b)(3), which codifies the work product protection, was not added to the Federal Rules until 1970.

Fortenbaugh since Rule 34, like Rule 33, is limited to parties to the proceeding, thereby excluding their counsel or agents.

Thus to the extent that petitioner was seeking the production of the memoranda and statements gathered by Fortenbaugh in the course of his activities as counsel, petitioner misconceived his remedy. Rule 33 did not permit him to obtain such memoranda and statements as adjuncts to the interrogatories addressed to the individual tug owners. A party clearly cannot refuse to answer interrogatories on the ground that the information sought is solely within the knowledge of his attorney. But that is not this case. Here production was sought of documents prepared by a party's attorney after the claim has arisen. Rule 33 does not make provision for such production, even when sought in connection with permissible interrogatories. Moreover, since petitioner was also foreclosed from securing them through an order under Rule 34, his only recourse was to take Fortenbaugh's deposition under Rule 26 and to attempt to force Fortenbaugh to produce the materials by use of a subpoena *duces tecum* in accordance with Rule 45. Holtzoff, "Instruments of Discovery under the Federal Rules of Civil Procedure," 41 Mich.L.Rev. 205, 220. But despite petitioner's faulty choice of action, the District Court entered an order, apparently under Rule 34, commanding the tug owners and Fortenbaugh, as their agent and counsel, to produce the materials in question. Their refusal led to the anomalous result of holding the tug owners in contempt for failure to produce that which was in the possession of their counsel and of holding Fortenbaugh in contempt for failure to produce that which he could not be compelled to produce under either Rule 33 or Rule 34.

But under the circumstances we deem it unnecessary and unwise to rest our decision upon this procedural irregularity, an irregularity which is not strongly urged upon us and which was disregarded in the two courts below. It matters little at this late stage whether Fortenbaugh fails to answer interrogatories filed under Rule 26 or under Rule 33 or whether he refuses to produce the memoranda and statements pursuant to a subpoena under Rule 45 or a court order under Rule 34. The deposition-discovery rules create integrated procedural devices. And the basic question at stake is whether any of those devices may be used to inquire into materials collected by an adverse party's counsel in the course of preparation for possible litigation. The fact that the petitioner may have used the wrong method does not destroy the main thrust of his attempt. Nor does it relieve us of the responsibility of dealing with the problem raised by that attempt. It would be inconsistent with the liberal atmosphere surrounding these rules to insist that petitioner now go through the empty formality of pursuing the right procedural device only to reestablish precisely the same basic problem now confronting us. We do not mean to say, however, that there may not be situations in which the failure to proceed in accordance with a specific rule would be important or decisive. But in the present circumstances, for the purposes of this decision, the procedural irregularity is not material. Having noted the proper procedure, we may accordingly turn our attention to the substance of the underlying problem.

In urging that he has a right to inquire into the materials secured and prepared by Fortenbaugh, petitioner emphasizes that the deposition-discovery portions of the Federal Rules of Civil Procedure are designed to enable the parties to discover the true facts and to compel their disclosure wherever they may be found. It is said that inquiry may be made under these rules, epitomized by Rule 26, as to any relevant matter which is not privileged; and since the discovery provisions are to be applied as broadly and liberally as possible, the privilege limitation must be restricted to its narrowest bounds. On the premise that the attorney-client privilege is the one involved in this case, petitioner argues that it must be strictly confined to confidential communications made by a client to his attorney. And since the materials here in issue were secured by Fortenbaugh from third persons rather than from his clients, the tug owners, the conclusion is reached that these materials are proper subjects for discovery under Rule 26.

As additional support for this result, petitioner claims that to prohibit discovery under these circumstances would give a corporate defendant a tremendous advantage in a suit by an individual plaintiff. Thus in a suit by an injured employee against a railroad or in a suit by an insured person against an insurance company the corporate defendant could pull a dark veil of secrecy over all the pertinent facts it can collect after the claim arises merely on the assertion that such facts were gathered by its large staff of attorneys and claim agents. At the same time, the individual plaintiff, who often has direct knowledge of the matter in issue and has no counsel until some time after his claim arises could be compelled to disclose all the intimate details of his case. By endowing with immunity from disclosure all that a lawyer discovers in the course of his duties, it is said, the rights of individual litigants in such cases are drained of vitality and the lawsuit becomes more of a battle of deception than a search for truth.

But framing the problem in terms of assisting individual plaintiffs in their suits against corporate defendants is unsatisfactory. Discovery concededly may work to the disadvantage as well as to the advantage of individual plaintiffs. Discovery, in other words, is not a one-way proposition. It is available in all types of cases at the behest of any party, individual or corporate, plaintiff or defendant. The problem thus far transcends the situation confronting this petitioner. And we must view that problem in light of the limitless situations where the particular kind of discovery sought by petitioner might be used.

We agree, of course, that the deposition-discovery rules are to be accorded a broad and liberal treatment. No longer can the time-honored cry of "fishing expedition" serve to preclude a party from inquiring into the facts underlying his opponent's case. Mutual knowledge of all the relevant facts gathered by both parties is essential to proper litigation. To that end, either party may compel the other to disgorge whatever facts he has in his possession. The deposition-discovery procedure simply advances the stage at which the disclosure can be compelled from the time of trial to the period preceding it, thus reducing the possibility of surprise. But discovery, like all matters of procedure, has ultimate and necessary boundaries. As indicated by Rules 30(b) and (d) and 31(d), limitations inevitably arise when it can be shown that the examination is being conducted in bad faith or in such a manner as to annoy, embarrass or oppress the person subject to the inquiry. And as Rule 26(b) provides, further limitations come into existence when the inquiry touches upon the irrelevant or encroaches upon the recognized domains of privilege.

We also agree that the memoranda, statements and mental impressions in issue in this case fall outside the scope of the attorney-client privilege and hence are not protected from discovery on that basis. It is unnecessary here to delineate the content and scope of that privilege as recognized in the federal courts. For present purposes, it suffices to note that the protective cloak of this privilege does not extend to information which an attorney secures from a witness while acting for his client in anticipation of litigation. Nor does this privilege concern the memoranda, briefs, communications and other writings prepared by counsel for his own use in prosecuting his client's case; and it is equally unrelated to writings which reflect an attorney's mental impressions, conclusions, opinions or legal theories.

But the impropriety of invoking that privilege does not provide an answer to the problem before us. Petitioner has made more than an ordinary request for relevant, non-privileged facts in the possession of his adversaries or their counsel. He has sought discovery as of right of oral and written statements of witnesses whose identity is well known and whose availability to petitioner appears unimpaired. He has sought production of these matters after making the most searching inquiries of his opponents as to the circumstances surrounding the fatal accident, which inquiries were sworn to have been answered to the best of their information and belief. Interrogatories were directed toward all the events prior to, during and subsequent to the sinking of the tug. Full and honest answers to such broad inquiries would necessarily have included all pertinent information gleaned by Fortenbaugh through his interviews with the witnesses. Petitioner makes no suggestion, and we cannot assume, that the tug owners or Fortenbaugh were incomplete or dishonest in the framing of their answers. In addition, petitioner was free to examine the public testimony of the witnesses taken before the United States Steamboat Inspectors. We are thus dealing with an attempt to secure the production of written statements and mental impressions contained in the files and the mind of the attorney Fortenbaugh without any showing of necessity or any indication or claim that denial of such production would unduly prejudice the preparation of petitioner's case or cause him any hardship or injustice. For aught that appears, the essence of what petitioner seeks either has been revealed to him already through the interrogatories or is readily available to him direct from the witnesses for the asking.

The District Court, after hearing objections to petitioner's request, commanded Fortenbaugh to produce all written statements of witnesses and to state in substance any facts learned through oral statements of witnesses to him. Fortenbaugh was to submit any memoranda he had made of the oral statements so that the court might determine what portions should be revealed to petitioner. All of this was ordered without any showing by petitioner, or any requirement that he make a proper showing, of the necessity for the production of any of this material or any demonstration that denial of production would cause hardship or injustice. The court simply ordered production on the theory that the facts sought were material and were not privileged as constituting attorney-client communications.

In our opinion, neither Rule 26 nor any other rule dealing with discovery contemplates production under such circumstances. That is not because the subject matter is privileged or irrelevant, as those concepts are used in these rules. Here is simply an attempt, without purported necessity or justification, to secure written statements, private memoranda and personal recollections prepared or formed by an adverse party's counsel in the course of his legal duties. As such, it falls outside the arena of discovery and contravenes the public policy underlying the orderly prosecution and defense of legal claims. Not even the most liberal of discovery theories can justify unwarranted inquiries into the files and the mental impressions of an attorney.

Historically, a lawyer is an officer of the court and is bound to work for the advancement of justice while faithfully protecting the rightful interests of his clients. In performing his various duties, however, it is essential that a lawyer work with a certain degree of privacy, free from unnecessary intrusion by opposing parties and their counsel. Proper preparation of a client's case demands that he assemble information, sift what he considers to be the relevant from the irrelevant facts, prepare his legal theories and plan his strategy without undue and needless interference. That is the historical and the necessary way in which lawyers act within the framework of our system of jurisprudence to promote justice and to protect their clients' interests. This work is reflected, of course, in interviews, statements, memoranda, correspondence, briefs, mental impressions, personal beliefs, and countless other tangible and intangible ways—aptly though roughly termed by the Circuit Court of Appeals in this case * * * as the "Work product of the lawyer." Were such materials open to opposing counsel on mere demand, much of what is now put down in writing would remain unwritten. An attorney's thoughts, heretofore inviolate, would not be his own. Inefficiency, unfairness and sharp practices would inevitably develop in the giving of legal advice and in the preparation of cases for trial. The effect on the legal profession would be demoralizing. And the interests of the clients and the cause of justice would be poorly served.

We do not mean to say that all written materials obtained or prepared by an adversary's counsel with an eye toward litigation are necessarily free from discovery in all cases. Where relevant and non-privileged facts remain hidden in an attorney's file and where production of those facts is essential to the preparation of one's case, discovery may properly be had. Such written statements and documents might, under certain circumstances, be admissible in evidence or give clues as to the existence or location of relevant facts. Or they might be useful for purposes of impeachment or corroboration. And production might be justified where the witnesses are no longer available or can be reached only with difficulty. Were production of written statements and documents to be precluded under such circumstances, the liberal ideals of the deposition-discovery portions of the Federal Rules of Civil Procedure would be stripped of much of their meaning. But the general policy against invading the privacy of an attorney's course of preparation is so well recognized and so essential to an orderly working of our system of legal procedure that a burden rests on the one who would invade that privacy to establish adequate reasons to justify production through a subpoena or court order. That burden, we believe, is necessarily implicit in the rules as now constituted.

Rule 30(b), as presently written, gives the trial judge the requisite discretion to make a judgment as to whether discovery should be allowed as to written statements secured from witnesses. But in the instant case there was no room for that discretion to operate in favor of the petitioner. No attempt was made to establish any reason why Fortenbaugh should be forced to produce the written statements. There was only a naked, general demand for these materials as of right and a finding by the District Court that no recognizable privilege was involved. That was insufficient to justify discovery under these circumstances and the court should have sustained the refusal of the tug owners and Fortenbaugh to produce.

* * *

* * * Petitioner's counsel frankly admits that he wants the oral statements only to help prepare himself to examine witnesses and to make sure that he has overlooked nothing. That is insufficient under the circumstances to permit him an exception to the policy underlying the privacy of Fortenbaugh's professional activities. If there should be a rare situation justifying production of these matters, petitioner's case is not of that type.

We fully appreciate the wide-spread controversy among the members of the legal profession over the problem raised by this case. It is a problem that rests on what has been one of the most hazy frontiers of the discovery process. But until some rule or statute definitely prescribes otherwise, we are not justified in permitting discovery in a situation of this nature as a matter of unqualified right. When Rule 26 and the other discovery rules were adopted, this Court and the members of the bar in general certainly did not believe or contemplate that all the files and mental processes of lawyers were thereby opened to the free scrutiny of their adversaries. And we refuse to interpret the rules at this time so as to reach so harsh and unwarranted a result.

We therefore affirm the judgment of the Circuit Court of Appeals.

■ MR. JUSTICE JACKSON, concurring.

* * *

The primary effect of the practice advocated here would be on the legal profession itself. But it too often is overlooked that the lawyer and the law office are indispensable parts of our administration of justice. Law-abiding people can go nowhere else to learn the ever changing and constantly multiplying rules by which they must behave and to obtain redress for their wrongs. The welfare and tone of the legal profession is therefore of prime consequence to society, which would feel the consequences of such a practice as petitioner urges secondarily but certainly.

* * *

Counsel for the petitioner candidly said on argument that he wanted this information to help prepare himself to examine witnesses, to make sure he overlooked nothing. He bases his claim to it in his brief on the view that the Rules were to do away with the old situation where a law suit developed into "a battle of wits between counsel." But a common law trial is and always should be an adversary proceeding. Discovery was hardly intended to enable a learned profession to perform its functions either without wits or on wits borrowed from the adversary.

The real purpose and the probable effect of the practice ordered by the district court would be to put trials on a level even lower than a "battle of wits." I can conceive of no practice more demoralizing to the Bar than to require a lawyer to write out and deliver to his adversary an account of what witnesses have told him. Even if his recollection were perfect, the statement would be his language permeated with his inferences. Every one who has tried it knows that it is almost impossible so fairly to record the expressions and emphasis of a witness that when he testifies in the environment of the court and under the influence of the leading question there will not be departures in some respects. Whenever the testimony of the witness would differ from the "exact" statement the lawyer had delivered, the lawyer's statement would be whipped out to impeach the witness. Counsel producing his adversary's "inexact" statement could lose nothing by saying, "Here is a contradiction, gentlemen of the jury. I do not know whether it is my adversary or his witness who is not telling the truth, but one is not." Of course, if this practice were adopted, that scene would be repeated over and over again. The lawyer who delivers such statements often would find himself branded a deceiver afraid to take the stand to support his own version of the witness's conversation with him, or else he will have to go on the stand to defend his own credibility—perhaps against that of his chief witness, or possibly even his client.

* * *

And what is the lawyer to do who has interviewed one whom he believes to be a biased, lying or hostile witness to get his unfavorable statements and know what to meet? He must record and deliver such statements even though he would not vouch for the credibility of the witness by calling him. Perhaps the other side would not want to call him either, but the attorney is open to the charge of suppressing evidence at the trial if he fails to call such a hostile witness even though he never regarded him as reliable or truthful.

Having been supplied the names of the witnesses, petitioner's lawyer gives no reason why he cannot interview them himself. If an employee-witness refuses to tell his story, he, too, may be examined under the Rules. He may be compelled on discovery as fully as on the trial to disclose his version of the facts. But that is his own disclosure—it can be used to impeach him if he contradicts it and such a deposition is not useful to promote an unseemly disagreement between the witness and the counsel in the case.

* * *

QUESTIONS

A. Why was the discovery ruling in *Hickman* appealable prior to the final determination of the litigation? Are most such discovery rulings immediately appealable?

B. Do you think the Court's ruling would have been different if the crewmen who had been interviewed by opposing counsel were no longer available for questioning?

C. If the crewmen were unavailable for questioning, would prior evaluations of their credibility by opposing counsel be discoverable?

Brannan v. Great Lakes Dredge & Dock Company

United States District Court For the Southern District of New York, 1998.
1998 WL 229521.

■ CHIN, D.J.

Defendant Great Lakes Dredge & Dock Company moves this Court to compel a further deposition of plaintiff Thomas W. Brannan, Jr. prior to disclosing surveillance videotapes of him. Plaintiff submits that defendant should not be permitted to obtain a second deposition of him and that defendant should either be required to produce the surveillance videotapes forthwith, or be precluded from using such tapes at trial. Defendant's motion is granted for the reasons, and subject to the limitations, set forth below.

BACKGROUND

Plaintiff was seriously injured on May 20, 1995 while working as an employee of defendant and a member of the crew of its dredge. The instant action relating to plaintiff's injury was filed on June 4, 1996.

On January 14, 1997, plaintiff appeared for deposition. At that time, there was no dispute that plaintiff was still disabled from the May 20, 1995 accident. Defendant, therefore, chose not to ask plaintiff questions concerning his disability and/or limitations as of that time. Later, however, defendant became suspicious that plaintiff was exaggerating his disability and decided to place him under surveillance. Eventually, videotapes were made. Defendant did not inform plaintiff or the Court of these facts until the parties appeared on February 5, 1998 for a settlement conference.

After disclosing the existence of the videotapes, defendant offered to produce the tapes to plaintiff but on the condition that plaintiff first submit to further deposition on the question of the extent of his disability. Plaintiff refused, arguing that the videotapes should either be disclosed to him forthwith or be precluded from use at trial.

This motion followed.

DISCUSSION

A.   Discovery of Impeachment Videotape

The impeachment value of videotape surveillance is well recognized by courts in this district. See, e.g., *Ramos v. Falacara*, 1994 WL 132298, *1 (S.D.N.Y. Apr.14, 1994); *Weinhold v. Witte Heavy Lift, Inc.*, No. 90 Civ. 2096, 1994 WL 132392, *1 (S.D.N.Y. Apr. 11, 1994); *Daniels v. National R.R. Passenger Corp.*, 110 F.R.D. 160, 161 (S.D.N.Y.1986). Moreover, despite the general rule of liberal pre-trial disclosure, surveillance videotapes may be protected from disclosure provided their use at trial is limited to impeachment. Disclosure of impeachment videotapes is warranted only if the party who has the tapes is afforded the opportunity to take the deposition of the surveilled party so that the position of that party to be impeached is committed. *Martin v. Long Island Railroad*, 63 F.R.D. 53, 55 (E.D.N.Y. 1974). Where surveillance materials are used for purposes beyond impeachment as "substantive evidence," however, the materials must be produced before trial without limitation.

B.   Application

Despite the recognized impeachment value of surveillance videotapes, plaintiff maintains that defendant must immediately produce the videotapes or be precluded from using them at trial. Plaintiff claims that defendant deliberately waited until after discovery was closed before notifying him and the Court of the existence of the videotapes, and that defendant did so in an effort to "intimidate plaintiff into agreeing to settle his case for an amount more to the liking of defendant." (Pl. Opp. at 9). Because discovery is closed and plaintiff requested production of any surveillance videotapes on September 30, 1996, he argues that defendant is not entitled to redepose plaintiff prior to producing the videotapes.

Although I appreciate plaintiff's concerns about the sequence of events and timing, his objections to an additional deposition are overruled. On March 31, 1997, defendant responded to plaintiff's

September 1996 discovery request for, inter alia, surveillance materials, by stating that "none have been taken of plaintiff, but if any . . .
[videotapes] are taken by defendant, production of such documents
will be refused on the grounds that they will be materials prepared in
anticipation of litigation and trial for which plaintiff has not shown
substantial need." (Pl. Opp. at 3–4). Defendant did not decide to put
plaintiff under surveillance, therefore, until sometime after March 31,
1997. That decision was made to "determine the extent of plaintiff's
recovery from his injuries, and to confirm whether or not he was, in
fact, exaggerating his complaints of disability." (Def. Mem. at 2).

This is a classic case of making surveillance videotapes for impeachment. Indeed, nowhere does plaintiff allege that the videotapes
are anything other than impeachment evidence. Even though discovery
is closed in this case, defendant is entitled to lock-in plaintiff's position
on his condition as of the time of the videotapes prior to giving
plaintiff access to the videotapes. Therefore, plaintiff is entitled to
production of the videotapes provided he first make himself available
for further deposition on the question of the extent of his injuries
and/or recovery as of the time the videotapes were made. Defendant is
not permitted to examine plaintiff on other matters. Furthermore, the
videotapes will be admissible at trial only for impeachment and only
on the question of the extent of plaintiff's disability as of the time the
videotapes were made.

CONCLUSION

Accordingly, defendant is not required to produce copies of its
surveillance videotapes to plaintiff unless plaintiff submits to further
deposition limited to the extent of his disability and/or recovery as of
the time the videotapes were made. Any further deposition of plaintiff
must take place within 30 days from the date of this order, and the
videotapes are to be produced immediately following any such deposition. In view of defendant's delay in making the videotapes, plaintiff's
reasonable expenses incurred in connection with any such deposition
shall be borne by defendant. If plaintiff decides not to submit to
further deposition, defendant may still use the videotapes at trial for
impeachment purposes only, but defendant is not required to produce
the tapes before trial.

The parties shall appear for a pre-trial conference on June 19,
1998 at 11:00 a.m.

QUESTIONS

A.   Why should the defendant have to produce the videotape at all if it is
investigative material prepared in anticipation of trial?

B.   Is making the plaintiff available for another deposition prior to allowing
discovery of the videotape sufficient protection for the party who ordered the
videotape?

C.   What rule governing discovery of surveillance materials best promotes
accuracy in fact finding?

NOTE: WORK PRODUCT AND THE 1993 AMENDMENTS TO THE FEDERAL RULES

The December 1, 1993 amendments to the federal discovery rules left Rule 26(b)(3), which sets forth the scope of the work product protection, unchanged. It did add new Rule 26(b)(5), which provides that whenever otherwise discoverable information is withheld on the basis of privilege or work product protection, the claim of privilege or protection must be made expressly, and a description of the withheld information must be provided that "will enable other parties to assess the applicability of the privilege or protection." This description is commonly known as a privilege log.

Thus, in *Sheehan v. Mellon Bank v. Four Diamonds, Inc.*, 1996 WL 243470 (E.D.Pa.), a third-party plaintiff claiming attorney-client and work product privilege provided a list of the type of documents with respect to which he was asserting privilege. The court found the list to be insufficient under the Rule. Its instructions to the third-party plaintiff illustrate what the court would consider adequate. The court instructed the party to provide a revised privilege log containing a "factual briefing to clarify the issues presented.... [In addition, the] briefs should, as applicable, answer the following questions:

* * *

2. Whom did Mr. Bloom represent? If he represented Plaintiffs, did he represent them as officers of Four Diamonds or in their individual capacity?

3. Generally, what is the nature and time period of Mr. Bloom's representation?

* * *

5. For whom is Mr. Bloom asserting privilege?

* * *

7. In what way, if any, was Mr. Bloom's representation provided in anticipation of litigation?"

Upjohn Co. v. United States

Supreme Court of the United States, 1981.
449 U.S. 383, 101 S.Ct. 677, 66 L.Ed.2d 584.

■ JUSTICE REHNQUIST delivered the opinion of the Court.

We granted certiorari in this case to address important questions concerning the scope of the attorney-client privilege in the corporate context and the applicability of the work-product doctrine in proceedings to enforce tax summonses. 445 U.S. 925, 100 S.Ct. 1310, 63 L.Ed.2d 758. With respect to the privilege question the parties and various *amici* have described our task as one of choosing between two "tests" which have gained adherents in the courts of appeals. We are acutely aware, however, that we sit to decide concrete cases and not abstract propositions of law. We decline to lay down a broad rule or series of rules to govern all conceivable future questions in this area, even were we able to do so. We can and do, however, conclude that the attorney-client privilege protects the communications involved in this case from compelled disclosure and that the work-product doctrine does apply in tax summons enforcement proceedings.

I

Petitioner Upjohn Co. manufactures and sells pharmaceuticals here and abroad. In January 1976 independent accountants conducting an audit of one of Upjohn's foreign subsidiaries discovered that the subsidiary made payments to or for the benefit of foreign government officials in order to secure government business. The accountants so informed petitioner, Mr. Gerard Thomas, Upjohn's Vice President, Secretary, and General Counsel. Thomas is a member of the Michigan and New York Bars, and has been Upjohn's General Counsel for 20 years. He consulted with outside counsel and R.T. Parfet, Jr., Upjohn's Chairman of the Board. It was decided that the company would conduct an internal investigation of what were termed "questionable payments." As part of this investigation the attorneys prepared a letter containing a questionnaire which was sent to "All Foreign General and Area Managers" over the Chairman's signature. The letter began by noting recent disclosures that several American companies made "possibly illegal" payments to foreign government officials and emphasized that the management needed full information concerning any such payments made by Upjohn. The letter indicated that the Chairman had asked Thomas, identified as "the company's General Counsel," "to conduct an investigation for the purpose of determining the nature and magnitude of any payments made by the Upjohn Company or any of its subsidiaries to any employee or official of a foreign government." The questionnaire sought detailed information concerning such payments. Managers were instructed to treat the investigation as "highly confidential" and not to discuss it with anyone other than Upjohn employees who might be helpful in providing the requested information. Responses were to be sent directly to Thomas. Thomas and outside counsel also interviewed the recipients of the questionnaire and some 33 other Upjohn officers or employees as part of the investigation.

On March 26, 1976, the company voluntarily submitted a preliminary report to the Securities and Exchange Commission on Form 8–K disclosing certain questionable payments.[1] A copy of the report was simultaneously submitted to the Internal Revenue Service, which immediately began an investigation to determine the tax consequences of the payments. Special agents conducting the investigation were given lists by Upjohn of all those interviewed and all who had responded to the questionnaire. On November 23, 1976, the Service issued a summons pursuant to 26 U.S.C. § 7602 demanding production of:

> "All files relative to the investigation conducted under the supervision of Gerard Thomas to identify payments to employees of foreign governments and any political contributions made by the Upjohn Company or any of its affiliates since January 1, 1971 and to determine whether any funds of the Upjohn Company had

---

1. On July 28, 1976, the company filed an amendment to this report disclosing fur-   ther payments.

been improperly accounted for on the corporate books during the same period.

"The records should include but not be limited to written questionnaires sent to managers of the Upjohn Company's foreign affiliates, and memorandums or notes of the interviews conducted in the United States and abroad with officers and employees of the Upjohn Company and its subsidiaries."

The company declined to produce the documents specified in the second paragraph on the grounds that they were protected from disclosure by the attorney-client privilege and constituted the work product of attorneys prepared in anticipation of litigation. On August 31, 1977, the United States filed a petition seeking enforcement of the summons under 26 U.S.C. §§ 7402(b) and 7604(a) in the United States District Court for the Western District of Michigan. That court adopted the recommendation of a Magistrate who concluded that the summons should be enforced. Petitioners appealed to the Court of Appeals for the Sixth Circuit which rejected the Magistrate's finding of a waiver of the attorney-client privilege, 600 F.2d 1223, 1227, n. 12, but agreed that the privilege did not apply "[t]o the extent that the communications were made by officers and agents not responsible for directing Upjohn's actions in response to legal advice * * * for the simple reason that the communications were not the 'client's.' "*Id.,* at 1225. The court reasoned that accepting petitioners' claim for a broader application of the privilege would encourage upper-echelon management to ignore unpleasant facts and create too broad a "zone of silence." Noting that Upjohn's counsel had interviewed officials such as the Chairman and President, the Court of Appeals remanded to the District Court so that a determination of who was within the "control group" could be made. In a concluding footnote the court stated that the work-product doctrine "is not applicable to administrative summonses issued under 26 U.S.C. § 7602." *Id.,* at 1228, n. 13.

* * *

[The Court then went on to consider whether the communications between Upjohn employees and Upjohn's in-house corporate counsel would be privileged as "attorney-client communications" and therefore exempt from discovery. The Court rejected the court of appeals' position that only communications between corporate counsel and senior management of Upjohn (the so-called "control group") were privileged. It noted that such a rule would "frustrate the very purpose of the privilege by discouraging the communication of relevant information by employees of the client to attorneys seeking to render legal advice to the client corporation." 449 U.S. at 392, 101 S.Ct. at 684.

Rather, it noted that the communications at issue, even those involving Upjohn employees who were not senior management, "were made by Upjohn employees to counsel for Upjohn acting as such, at the direction of corporate superiors in order to secure legal advice from counsel", *Id.* at 394, 101 S.Ct. at 685, and that such communications "must be protected against compelled disclosure" *Id.* at 395, 101 S.Ct. at 685. The Court noted, however, that the attorney-client privilege only protected the *communications* between Upjohn employees and counsel, not the underlying facts which were the subject of those communications. Such facts could be discovered, if, for example, the Government lawyers chose to depose the same Upjohn employees who filled out the questionnaires involved in *Upjohn.*]

III

Our decision that the communications by Upjohn employees to counsel are covered by the attorney-client privilege disposes of the case so far as the responses to the questionnaires and any notes reflecting responses to interview questions are concerned. The summons reaches further, however, and Thomas has testified that his notes and memoranda of interviews go beyond recording responses to his questions. To the extent that the material subject to the summons is not protected by the attorney-client privilege as disclosing communications between an employee and counsel, we must reach the ruling by the Court of Appeals that the work-product doctrine does not apply to summonses issued under 26 U.S.C. § 7602.[6]

The Government concedes, wisely, that the Court of Appeals erred and that the work-product doctrine does apply to IRS summonses. Brief for Respondents 16, 48. This doctrine was announced by the Court over 30 years ago in Hickman v. Taylor, 329 U.S. 495, 67 S.Ct. 385, 91 L.Ed. 451 (1947). In that case the Court rejected "an attempt, without purported necessity or justification, to secure written statements, private memoranda and personal recollections prepared or formed by an adverse party's counsel in the course of his legal duties." *Id.,* at 510, 67 S.Ct., at 393. The Court noted that "it is essential that a lawyer work with a certain degree of privacy" and reasoned that if discovery of the material sought were permitted

> "much of what is now put down in writing would remain unwritten. An attorney's thoughts, heretofore inviolate, would not be his own. Inefficiency, unfairness and sharp practices would inevitably develop in the giving of legal advice and in the preparation of cases for trial. The effect on the legal profession would be demoralizing. And the interests of the clients and the cause of justice would be poorly served." *Id.,* at 511, 67 S.Ct., at 393–394.

The "strong public policy" underlying the work-product doctrine was reaffirmed recently in United States v. Nobles, 422 U.S. 225, 236–240, 95 S.Ct. 2160, 2169–2171, 45 L.Ed.2d 141 (1975), and has been substantially incorporated in Federal Rule of Civil Procedure 26(b)(3).[7]

---

6. The following discussion will also be relevant to counsel's notes and memoranda of interviews with the seven former employees should it be determined that the attorney-client privilege does not apply to them. See n. 3, *supra.*

7. This provides, in pertinent part:

"[A] party may obtain discovery of documents and tangible things otherwise discoverable under subdivision (b)(1) of this rule and prepared in anticipation of litigation or for trial by or for another party or by or for that other party's representative (including his attorney, consultant, surety, indemnitor, insurer, or

As we stated last Term, the obligation imposed by a tax summons remains "subject to the traditional privileges and limitations." United States v. Euge, 444 U.S. 707, 714, 100 S.Ct. 874, 879–880, 63 L.Ed.2d 141 (1980). Nothing in the language of the IRS summons provisions or their legislative history suggests an intent on the part of Congress to preclude application of the work-product doctrine. Rule 26(b)(3) codifies the work-product doctrine, and the Federal Rules of Civil Procedure are made applicable to summons enforcement proceedings by Rule 81(a)(3). See Donaldson v. United States, 400 U.S. 517, 528, 91 S.Ct. 534, 541, 27 L.Ed.2d 580 (1971). While conceding the applicability of the work-product doctrine, the Government asserts that it has made a sufficient showing of necessity to overcome its protections. The Magistrate apparently so found, 78–1 USTC ¶ 9277, p. 83,605. The Government relies on the following language in *Hickman:*

> "We do not mean to say that all written materials obtained or prepared by an adversary's counsel with an eye toward litigation are necessarily free from discovery in all cases. Where relevant and nonprivileged facts remain hidden in an attorney's file and where production of those facts is essential to the preparation of one's case, discovery may properly be had * * *. And production might be justified where the witnesses are no longer available or can be reached only with difficulty." 329 U.S., at 511, 67 S.Ct., at 394.

The Government stresses that interviewees are scattered across the globe and that Upjohn has forbidden its employees to answer questions it considers irrelevant. The above-quoted language from *Hickman,* however, did not apply to "oral statements made by witnesses * * * whether presently in the form of [the attorney's] mental impressions or memoranda." *Id.,* at 512, 67 S.Ct., at 394. As to such material the Court did "not believe that any showing of necessity can be made under the circumstances of this case so as to justify production * * *. If there should be a rare situation justifying production of these matters petitioner's case is not of that type." *Id.* at 512–513, 67 S.Ct., at 394–395. See also *Nobles, supra,* 422 U.S., at 252–253, 95 S.Ct., at 2177 (White, J., concurring). Forcing an attorney to disclose notes and memoranda of witnesses' oral statements is particularly disfavored because it tends to reveal the attorney's mental processes, 329 U.S., at 513, 67 S.Ct., at 394–395 ("what he saw fit to write down regarding witnesses' remarks"); *id,* at 516–517, 67 S.Ct., at 396 ("the statement would be his [the attorney's] language, permeated with his inferences") (JACKSON, J., concurring).[8]

agent) only upon a showing that the party seeking discovery has substantial need of the materials in the preparation of his case and that he is unable without undue hardship to obtain the substantial equivalent of the materials by other means. In ordering discovery of such materials when the required showing has been made, the court shall protect against disclosure of the mental impressions, conclusions, opinions, or legal theories of an attorney or other representative of a party concerning the litigation."

8. Thomas described his notes of the interviews as containing "what I considered to be the important questions, the substance of the responses to them, my beliefs as to the importance of these, my beliefs as to how they related to the inquiry, my thoughts as to how they related to other questions. In some instances they might even suggest other questions that I would have to ask or things

Rule 26 accords special protection to work product revealing the attorney's mental processes. The Rule permits disclosure of documents and tangible things constituting attorney work product upon a showing of substantial need and inability to obtain the equivalent without undue hardship. This was the standard applied by the Magistrate, 78–1 USTC ¶ 9277, p. 83,604. Rule 26 goes on, however, to state that "[i]n ordering discovery of such materials when the required showing has been made, the court shall protect against disclosure of the mental impressions, conclusions, opinions or legal theories of an attorney or other representative of a party concerning the litigation." Although this language does not specifically refer to memoranda based on oral statements of witnesses, the *Hickman* court stressed the danger that compelled disclosure of such memoranda would reveal the attorney's mental processes. It is clear that this is the sort of material the draftsmen of the Rule had in mind as deserving special protection. See Notes of Advisory Committee on 1970 Amendment to Rules, 28 U.S.C.App., p. 442 ("The subdivision * * * goes on to protect against disclosure the mental impressions, conclusions, opinions, or legal theories * * * of an attorney or other representative of a party. The *Hickman* opinion drew special attention to the need for protecting an attorney against discovery of memoranda prepared from recollection of oral interviews. The courts have steadfastly safeguarded against disclosure of lawyers' mental impressions and legal theories * * * ").

Based on the foregoing, some courts have concluded that *no* showing of necessity can overcome protection of work product which is based on oral statements from witnesses. See, *e.g., In re Grand Jury Proceedings,* 473 F.2d 840, 848 (C.A.8 1973) (personal recollections, notes, and memoranda pertaining to conversation with witnesses); *In re Grand Jury Investigation,* 412 F.Supp. 943, 949 (E.D.Pa.1976) (notes of conversation with witnesses "are so much a product of the lawyer's thinking and so little probative of the witness's actual words that they are absolutely protected from disclosure"). Those courts declining to adopt an absolute rule have nonetheless recognized that such material is entitled to special protection. See, *e.g., In re Grand Jury Investigation,* 599 F.2d 1224, 1231 (C.A.3 1979) ("special considerations * * * must shape any ruling on the discoverability of interview memoranda * * *; such documents will be discoverable only in a 'rare situation' "); Cf. *In re Grand Jury Subpoena,* 599 F.2d 504, 511– 512 (C.A.2 1979).

We do not decide the issue at this time. It is clear that the Magistrate applied the wrong standard when he concluded that the Government had made a sufficient showing of necessity to overcome the protections of the work-product doctrine. The Magistrate applied the "substantial need" and "without undue hardship" standard articulated in the first part of Rule 26(b)(3). The notes and memoranda sought by the Government here, however, are work product based on oral statements. If they reveal communications, they are, in this case,

that I needed to find elsewhere." 78–1 USTC ¶ 9277, p. 83,599.

protected by the attorney-client privilege. To the extent they do not reveal communications, they reveal the attorneys' mental processes in evaluating the communications. As Rule 26 and *Hickman* make clear, such work product cannot be disclosed simply on a showing of substantial need and inability to obtain the equivalent without undue hardship.

While we are not prepared at this juncture to say that such material is always protected by the work-product rule, we think a far stronger showing of necessity and unavailability by other means than was made by the Government or applied by the Magistrate in this case would be necessary to compel disclosure. Since the Court of Appeals thought that the work-product protection was never applicable in an enforcement proceeding such as this, and since the Magistrate whose recommendations the District Court adopted applied too lenient a standard of protection, we think the best procedure with respect to this aspect of the case would be to reverse the judgment of the Court of Appeals for the Sixth Circuit and remand the case to it for such further proceedings in connection with the work-product claim as are consistent with this opinion.

Accordingly, the judgment of the Court of Appeals is reversed, and the case remanded for further proceedings.[a]

QUESTION

Why do the federal courts provide such powerful protection against discovery of the mental impressions and opinions of attorneys?

United States v. Adlman

United States Court of Appeals for the Second Circuit, 1998.
134 F.3d 1194.

■ Leval, Circuit Judge:

This appeal concerns the proper interpretation of Federal Rule of Civil Procedure 26(b)(3) ("the Rule"), which grants limited protection against discovery to documents and materials prepared "in anticipation of litigation." Specifically, we must address whether a study prepared for an attorney assessing the likely result of an expected litigation is ineligible for protection under the Rule if the primary or ultimate purpose of making the study was to assess the desirability of a business transaction, which, if undertaken, would give rise to the litigation. We hold that a document created because of anticipated litigation, which tends to reveal mental impressions, conclusions, opinions or theories concerning the litigation, does not lose work-product protection merely because it is intended to assist in the making of a business decision influenced by the likely outcome of the anticipated litigation. Where a document was created because of anticipated litigation, and would not have been prepared in substan-

---

a. Concurring opinion of Justice Burger omitted.

tially similar form but for the prospect of that litigation, it falls within Rule 26(b)(3).

The district court ruled that the document sought by the IRS in this case did not fall within the scope of Rule 26(b)(3) and ordered its production. Because we cannot determine whether the district court used the correct standard in reaching its decision, we vacate the judgment and remand for reconsideration.

Background

Sequa Corporation is an aerospace manufacturer with annual revenues of nearly $2 billion. Prior to 1989, Atlantic Research Corporation ("ARC") and Chromalloy Gas Turbine Corporation ("Chromalloy") were wholly-owned Sequa subsidiaries. Appellant Monroe Adlman is an attorney and Vice President for Taxes at Sequa.

In the spring of 1989, Sequa contemplated merging Chromalloy and ARC. The contemplated merger was expected to produce an enormous loss and tax refund, which Adlman expected would be challenged by the IRS and would result in litigation. Adlman asked Paul Sheahen, an accountant and lawyer at Arthur Andersen & Co. ("Arthur Andersen"), to evaluate the tax implications of the proposed restructuring. Sheahen did so and set forth his study in a memorandum (the "Memorandum"). He submitted the Memorandum in draft form to Adlman in August 1989. After further consultation, on September 5, 1989, Sheahen sent Adlman the final version. The Memorandum was a 58–page detailed legal analysis of likely IRS challenges to the reorganization and the resulting tax refund claim; it contained discussion of statutory provisions, IRS regulations, legislative history, and prior judicial and IRS rulings relevant to the claim. It proposed possible legal theories or strategies for Sequa to adopt in response, recommended preferred methods of structuring the transaction, and made predictions about the likely outcome of litigation.

Sequa decided to go ahead with the restructuring, which was completed in December 1989 in essentially the form recommended by Arthur Andersen.

In an ensuing audit of Sequa's 1986–1989 tax returns, the IRS requested a number of documents concerning the restructuring transaction. Sequa acknowledged the existence of the Memorandum, but cited work-product privilege as grounds for declining to produce it. On September 23, 1993, the IRS served a summons on Adlman for production of the Memorandum.

When Adlman declined to comply, the IRS instituted an action in the United States District Court for the Southern District of New York to enforce the subpoena. Adlman defended on the grounds that the Memorandum was protected by both the attorney-client and work-product privileges. The district court (Knapp, J.) in its first decision rejected Adlman's claim that the Memorandum was protected by attorney-client privilege, finding that Adlman had not consulted Arthur Andersen in order to obtain assistance in furnishing legal advice to

Sequa. It rejected Adlman's claim of work-product privilege because the Memorandum was prepared for litigation based on actions or events that had not yet occurred at the time of its creation. The court granted the IRS's petition to enforce the summons.

On appeal, we affirmed denial of Adlman's claim of attorney-client privilege. We vacated the district court's enforcement order, however, because the district court had evaluated Adlman's claim of work-product privilege under the wrong standard. Although the non-occurrence of events giving rise to litigation prior to preparation of the documents is a factor to be considered, we explained, it does not necessarily preclude application of work-product privilege. For example, where a party faces the choice of whether to engage in a particular course of conduct virtually certain to result in litigation and prepares documents analyzing whether to engage in the conduct based on its assessment of the likely result of the anticipated litigation, we concluded that the preparatory documents should receive protection under Rule 26(b)(3). We therefore remanded for reconsideration whether the Memorandum was protected work product.

On remand, Adlman argued that the Memorandum was protected by Rule 26(b)(3) because it included legal opinions prepared in reasonable anticipation of litigation. Litigation was virtually certain to result from the reorganization and Sequa's consequent claim of tax losses.

The district court again rejected the claim of work-product privilege, concluding that the Memorandum was not prepared in anticipation of litigation. *1996 WL 84502,* at *1 (S.D.N.Y. Feb. 27, 1996). Adlman appeals.

Discussion

This case involves a question of first impression in this circuit: whether Rule 26(b)(3) is inapplicable to a litigation analysis prepared by a party or its representative in order to inform a business decision which turns on the party's assessment of the likely outcome of litigation expected to result from the transaction. Answering that question requires that we determine the proper interpretation of Rule 26(b)(3)'s requirement that documents be prepared "in anticipation of litigation" in order to qualify for work-product protection.

In *Hickman v. Taylor,* the Supreme Court held that notes taken by the defendant's attorney during interviews with witnesses to the event that eventually gave rise to the lawsuit in the case were not discoverable by the plaintiff.

Were the attorney's work accessible to an adversary, the Hickman court cautioned, "much of what is now put down in writing would remain unwritten" for fear that the attorney's work would redound to the benefit of the opposing party. Legal advice might be marred by "inefficiency, unfairness and sharp practices," and the "effect on the legal profession would be demoralizing." Neither the interests of clients nor the cause of justice would be served, the court observed, if work product were freely discoverable.

The Supreme Court has reaffirmed the "strong public policy" underlying the work-product privilege in the decades since Hickman. See *United States v. Nobles*, 422 U.S. 225, 236, 95 S. Ct. 2160, 2169, 45 L. Ed. 2d 141 (1975); *Upjohn Co. v. United States*, 449 U.S. 383, 398, 101 S. Ct. 677, 687, 66 L. Ed. 2d 584 (1981). It has also made clear that documents that "tend[] to reveal the attorney's mental process"—described by commentators as "opinion work product," see Special Project, The Work Product Doctrine, 68 Cornell L. Rev. 760, 817 (1983)—receive special protection not accorded to factual material. *Upjohn*, 449 U.S. at 399, 101 S. Ct. at 687. Special treatment for opinion work product is justified because, "at its core, the work-product doctrine shelters the mental processes of the attorney, providing a privileged area within which he can analyze and prepare his client's case." *Nobles*, 422 U.S. at 238, 95 S. Ct. at 2170.

II.

The first problem we face is to determine the meaning of the phrase prepared "in anticipation of litigation." The phrase has never been interpreted by our circuit; furthermore, courts and commentators have expressed a range of views as to its meaning. It is universally agreed that a document whose purpose is to assist in preparation for litigation is within the scope of the Rule and thus eligible to receive protection if the other conditions of protection prescribed by the Rule are met. The issue is less clear, however, as to documents which, although prepared because of expected litigation, are intended to inform a business decision influenced by the prospects of the litigation. The formulation applied by some courts in determining whether documents are protected by work-product privilege is whether they are prepared "primarily or exclusively to assist in litigation"—a formulation that would potentially exclude documents containing analysis of expected litigation, if their primary, ultimate, or exclusive purpose is to assist in making the business decision. Others ask whether the documents were prepared "because of" existing or expected litigation—a formulation that would include such documents, despite the fact that their purpose is not to "assist in" litigation. Because we believe that protection of documents of this type is more consistent with both the literal terms and the purposes of the Rule, we adopt the latter formulation.

1.   "Primarily to assist in" litigation.

The "primarily to assist in litigation" formulation is exemplified by a line of cases from the United States Court of Appeals for the Fifth Circuit. In *United States v. Davis*, 636 F.2d 1028 (5th Cir.), cert. denied, 454 U.S. 862, 102 S. Ct. 320, 70 L. Ed. 2d 162 (1981), the Fifth Circuit denied protection to documents made in the course of preparation of a tax return. This result was well justified as there was no showing whatsoever of anticipation of litigation. In what might be characterized as a dictum, or in any event a statement going far beyond the issues raised in the case, the court asserted that the Rule applies only if the "primary motivating purpose behind the creation of the document was to aid in possible future litigation." 636 F.2d at 1040.

Then, in *United States v. El Paso Co.*, 682 F.2d 530 (5th Cir. 1982), cert. denied, 466 U.S. 944, 104 S. Ct. 1927, 80 L. Ed. 2d 473 (1984), a large public corporation sought to shield documents that analyzed prospective liabilities that might result from litigation with the IRS over its tax returns. The documents were prepared not to assist in litigation but to establish and justify appropriate reserves in El Paso's financial statements. Treating the Davis dictum as law, the Fifth Circuit held that because the "primary motivating force [behind the preparation of the documents was] not to ready El Paso for litigation" but rather "to bring its financial books into conformity with generally accepted auditing principles," 682 F.2d at 543, and because the documents' liability analysis was "only a means to a business end," id., the documents were not prepared "in anticipation of litigation" within the meaning of the Rule and enjoyed no work-product protection.

We believe that a requirement that documents be produced primarily or exclusively to assist in litigation in order to be protected is at odds with the text and the policies of the Rule. Nowhere does Rule 26(b)(3) state that a document must have been prepared to aid in the conduct of litigation in order to constitute work product, much less primarily or exclusively to aid in litigation. Preparing a document "in anticipation of litigation" is sufficient.

The text of Rule 26(b)(3) does not limit its protection to materials prepared to assist at trial. To the contrary, the text of the Rule clearly sweeps more broadly. It expressly states that work-product privilege applies not only to documents "prepared . . . for trial" but also to those prepared "in anticipation of litigation." If the drafters of the Rule intended to limit its protection to documents made to assist in preparation for litigation, this would have been adequately conveyed by the phrase "prepared . . . for trial." The fact that documents prepared "in anticipation of litigation" were also included confirms that the drafters considered this to be a different, and broader category. Nothing in the Rule states or suggests that documents prepared "in anticipation of litigation" with the purpose of assisting in the making of a business decision do not fall within its scope.

In addition, the Rule takes pains to grant special protection to the type of materials at issue in this case—documents setting forth legal analysis. Where the Rule has explicitly established a special level of protection against disclosure for documents revealing an attorney's (or other representative's) opinions and legal theories concerning litigation, it would oddly undermine its purposes if such documents were excluded from protection merely because they were prepared to assist in the making of a business decision expected to result in the litigation.

Admittedly, there are fragmentary references in the caption to the Rule and in its commentary that can be read to lend support to a contrary interpretation. The caption, for example, refers to "Trial Preparation," and the Advisory Committee Notes make occasional reference to "trial preparation materials." We attach small importance to those references. Given that the text of the Rule (and of the commentary) expressly goes beyond documents "prepared . . . for trial" to encompass also those documents "prepared in anticipation of litigation," we cannot read the references in the caption and commentary as overriding the text of the Rule.

In addition to the plain language of the Rule, the policies underlying the work-product doctrine suggest strongly that work-product protection should not be denied to a document that analyzes expected litigation merely because it is prepared to assist in a business decision. Framing the inquiry as whether the primary or exclusive purpose of the document was to assist in litigation threatens to deny protection to documents that implicate key concerns underlying the work-product doctrine.

The problem is aptly illustrated by several hypothetical fact situations likely to recur:

(i) A company contemplating a transaction recognizes that the transaction will result in litigation; whether to undertake the transaction and, if so, how to proceed with the transaction, may well be influenced by the company's evaluation of the likelihood of success in litigation. Thus, a memorandum may be prepared in expectation of litigation with the primary purpose of helping the company decide whether to undertake the contemplated transaction. An example would be a publisher contemplating publication of a book where the publisher has received a threat of suit from a competitor purporting to hold exclusive publication rights. The publisher commissions its attorneys to prepare an evaluation of the likelihood of success in the litigation, which includes the attorneys' evaluation of various legal strategies that might be pursued. If the publisher decides to go ahead with publication and is sued, under the "primarily to assist in litigation" formulation the study will likely be disclosed to the opposing lawyers because its principal purpose was not to assist in litigation but to inform the business decision whether to publish. We can see no reason under the words or policies of the Rule why such a document should not be protected. See *United States v. Adlman*, 68 F.3d at 1501.

(ii) A company is engaged in, or contemplates, some kind of partnership, merger, joint undertaking, or business association with another company; the other company reasonably requests that the company furnish a candid assessment by the company's attorneys of its likelihood of success in existing litigations. For instance, the company's bank may request such a report from the company's attorneys concerning its likelihood of success in an important litigation to inform its lending policy toward the company. Or a securities underwriter contemplating a public offering of the company's securities may wish to see such a study to decide whether to go ahead with the offering without waiting for the termination of the litigation. Such a study would be created to inform the judgment of the business associate concerning its business decisions. No part of its purpose would be to aid in the conduct of the litigation. Nonetheless it would reveal the attorneys' most intimate strategies and assessments concerning the litigation. We can see no reason why, under the Rule, the litigation adversary should have access to it. But under the Fifth Circuit's "to assist" test, it would likely be discoverable by the litigation adversary.

(iii) A business entity prepares financial statements to assist its executives, stockholders, prospective investors, business partners, and others in evaluating future courses of action. Financial statements include reserves for projected litigation. The company's independent auditor requests a memorandum prepared by the company's attorneys estimating the likelihood of success in litigation and an accompanying analysis of the company's legal strategies and options to assist it in estimating what should be reserved for litigation losses.

In each scenario, the company involved would require legal analysis that falls squarely within Hickman's area of primary concern—analysis that candidly discusses the attorney's litigation strategies, appraisal of likelihood of success, and perhaps the feasibility of reasonable settlement. The interpretation of Rule 26(b)(3) advocated by the IRS imposes an untenable choice upon a company in these circumstances. If the company declines to make such analysis or scrimps on candor and completeness to avoid prejudicing its litigation prospects, it subjects itself and its co-venturers to ill-informed decisionmaking. On the other hand, a study reflecting the company's litigation strategy and its assessment of its strengths and weaknesses cannot be turned over to litigation adversaries without serious prejudice to the company's prospects in the litigation.

We see no basis for adopting a test under which an attorney's assessment of the likely outcome of litigation is freely available to his litigation adversary merely because the document was created for a business purpose rather than for litigation assistance. The fact that a document's purpose is business-related appears irrelevant to the question whether it should be protected under Rule 26(b)(3).

2. Prepared "because of" litigation.

The formulation of the work-product rule used by the Wright & Miller treatise, and cited by the Third, Fourth, Seventh, Eighth and D.C. Circuits, is that documents should be deemed prepared "in anticipation of litigation," and thus within the scope of the Rule, if "in light of the nature of the document and the factual situation in the particular case, the document can fairly be said to have been prepared or obtained because of the prospect of litigation." Charles Alan Wright, Arthur R. Miller, and Richard L. Marcus, 8 Federal Practice & Procedure § 2024, at 343 (1994) (emphasis added). See *In re Grand Jury Proceedings*, 604 F.2d 798, 803 (3d Cir.1979); *National Union Fire Ins. Co. v. Murray Sheet Metal Co., Inc.*, 967 F.2d 980, 984 (4th Cir.1992); *Binks Mfg. Co. v. National Presto Indus., Inc.*, 709 F.2d 1109, 1118–19 (7th Cir.1983); *Simon v. G.D. Searle & Co.*, 816 F.2d

397, 401 (8th Cir.), cert. denied, 484 U.S. 917, 108 S. Ct. 268, 98 L. Ed. 2d 225 (1987); *Senate of Puerto Rico v. United States Dep't of Justice,* 262 U.S. App. D.C. 166, 823 F.2d 574, 586 n. 42 (D.C.Cir. 1987).

The Wright & Miller "because of" formulation accords with the plain language of Rule 26(b)(3) and the purposes underlying the work-product doctrine. Where a document is created because of the prospect of litigation, analyzing the likely outcome of that litigation, it does not lose protection under this formulation merely because it is created in order to assist with a business decision.

Conversely, it should be emphasized that the "because of" formulation that we adopt here withholds protection from documents that are prepared in the ordinary course of business or that would have been created in essentially similar form irrespective of the litigation. It is well established that work-product privilege does not apply to such documents. See Fed. R. Civ. P. 26(b)(3), Advisory Committee's note ("Materials assembled in the ordinary course of business . . . are not under the qualified immunity provided by this subdivision.") Even if such documents might also help in preparation for litigation, they do not qualify for protection because it could not fairly be said that they were created "because of" actual or impending litigation. See Wright & Miller § 2024, at 346 ("even though litigation is already in prospect, there is no work-product immunity for documents prepared in the regular course of business rather than for purposes of the litigation").

In short, we find that the Wright & Miller "because of" test appropriately focuses on both what should be eligible for the Rule's protection and what should not. We believe this is the proper test to determine whether a document was prepared "in anticipation of litigation" and is thus eligible for protection depending on the further findings required by the Rule.

We remand with instructions to the district court to reconsider the issue under the Wright & Miller test of whether "the document can fairly be said to have been prepared . . . because of the prospect of litigation." Wright & Miller, § 2024 at 343. There is little doubt under the evidence that Sequa had the prospect of litigation in mind when it directed the preparation of the Memorandum by Arthur Andersen. Whether it can fairly be said that the Memorandum was prepared because of that expected litigation really turns on whether it would have been prepared irrespective of the expected litigation with the IRS.

If the district court concludes that substantially the same Memorandum would have been prepared in any event—as part of the ordinary course of business of undertaking the restructuring—then the court should conclude the Memorandum was not prepared because of the expected litigation and should adhere to its prior ruling denying the protection of the Rule.

On the other hand, if the court finds the Memorandum would not have been prepared but for Sequa's anticipation of litigation with the

IRS over the losses generated by the restructuring, then judgment should be entered in favor of Sequa.

■ KEARSE, CIRCUIT JUDGE, dissenting:

I respectfully dissent. It does not appear to me that the district court applied an erroneous standard in this case. Accordingly, I would affirm.

The attorney work product privilege accords limited protection for materials that were "prepared in anticipation of litigation or for trial." See Fed. R. Civ. P. 26(b)(3). Where the only prospect of litigation is what would be anticipated if the party undertakes a contemplated transaction but not otherwise, and the materials in question were prepared in connection with providing legal advice to the party as to whether or not to undertake that transaction, I do not regard the materials as having been prepared "in anticipation of litigation." I regard the majority as having extended the work product privilege to a stage that precedes any possible "anticipation" of litigation.

This does not mean, as suggested by the majority opinion, that such materials will normally be discoverable. Documents in which a party's attorney assesses the legal advisability of contemplated business transactions, including the possibility and efficacy of litigation if the client elects to proceed with the transaction, will normally be protected from discovery, by the attorney-client privilege, so long as the client meets the usual requirements of, inter alia, maintaining confidentiality and showing that it was seeking legal advice. The assertion of attorney-client privilege in the present case was rejected only because the client had failed to make any record that distinguished the present consultation of its accounting firm from its normal business consultations. See *United States v. Adlman*, 68 F.3d 1495, 1499–1500 (2d Cir.1995).

I disagree with the majority's expansion of the work-product privilege to afford protection to documents not prepared in anticipation of litigation but instead prepared in order to permit the client to determine whether to undertake a business transaction, where there will be no anticipation of litigation unless the transaction is undertaken.

QUESTIONS

A. What kinds of information will be protected as work product under the "because of" litigation test that would not be protected under the "primarily to assist in litigation" standard?

B. How do you think the district court will go about deciding whether, in the absence of a litigation concern, a document "substantially similar" to the Arthur Andersen report would have been prepared?

C. What concerns about the expansion of work product protection do you think underlie Judge Kearse's dissent?

NOTE: ACCOUNTANTS' WORK PRODUCT

The federal courts do not recognize an accountant-client privilege. In *United States v. Arthur Young & Company*, 465 U.S. 805, 104 S.Ct. 1495, 79 L.Ed.2d 826 (1984) defendants sought to assert a work product immunity for tax accrual work papers prepared by accountants which were sought by the Internal Revenue Service in connection with a tax investigation. In rejecting the claim of accountants' work product immunity, the Court (Burger Ch. J.) stated:

> Nor do we find persuasive the argument that a work-product immunity for accountants' tax accrual workpapers is a fitting analogue to the attorney work-product doctrine established in Hickman v. Taylor, 329 U.S. 495, 67 S.Ct. 385, 91 L.Ed. 451 (1947). The Hickman work-product doctrine was founded upon the private attorney's role as the client's confidential adviser and advocate, a loyal representative whose duty it is to present the client's case in the most favorable possible light. An independent certified public accountant performs a different role. By certifying the public reports that collectively depict a corporation's financial status, the independent auditor assumes a *public* responsibility transcending any employment relationship with the client. The independent public accountant performing this special function owes ultimate allegiance to the corporation's creditors and stockholders, as well as to the investing public. This "public watchdog" function demands that the accountant maintain total independence from the client at all times and requires complete fidelity to the public trust. To insulate from disclosure a certified public accountant's interpretations of the client's financial statements would be to ignore the significance of the accountant's role as a disinterested analyst charged with public obligations.

The Supreme Court's refusal to create a common law analogue to the work product protection for accountants in *Arthur Young* does not mean that accountants' work papers can never be protected from discovery. As the *Adlman* case indicates, material prepared by an accountant in connection with an anticipated or pending litigation might well fall within the protection of Rule 26(b)(3).

In *United States v. Rockwell International*, 897 F.2d 1255 (3d Cir.1990), the Internal Revenue Service sought disclosure of Rockwell's "free reserve file", a file containing "the summary of deferred tax items in which potential tax liabilities are set aside for possible subsequent adjustments". That file was maintained in the office of Rockwell's in-house tax counsel, and maintained with the assistance of in-house attorneys and accountants. It was said to contain calculations of Rockwell's contingent future tax liability as well as the attorney's "mental impressions as to settlement positions, litigation strategy and interpretations of trends in the tax law". The contents of the file were discussed but never surrendered to outside auditors.

The Third Circuit held that such documents were potentially protected as work product, if they were in fact prepared to aid Rockwell in future litigation with the IRS and not to comply with generally accepted accounting principles and federal SEC reporting requirements. The case was remanded to the district court to "determine with specificity Rockwell's motivation in creating and maintaining the free reserve file". *Id.* at 1266.

Although federal courts have been hesitant to form any type of special privilege for accountants and their clients, a number of states, such as New York, provide such a privilege by statute. The rationale for adopting accountant-client privilege is that accountants are under an ethical obligation to preserve the confidences of their clients, but accountant-client privilege statutes rarely if ever apply to criminal proceedings.

QUESTIONS

A. Do you agree with those states that have an accountant-client privilege or with the federal policy for disallowing it?

B. If a state law claim is tried in a federal court under diversity jurisdiction, would the accountant-client privilege statute of the state be applicable in that case?

C. A is injured in an automobile accident with a car driven by B. While in the hospital, A is visited by a claims adjuster for B's insurance company, who asks A for a statement describing the accident. A provides the statement, which is recorded by the claims adjuster on a small tape recorder. Subsequently, A becomes concerned that the statement contains an error in the description of the accident, and that it might be used to impeach A's testimony at trial. Can A obtain a copy of A's own statement from B? Must A show "substantial need"? See Rule 26(b)(3).

D. Is information about a defendant's wealth and insurance coverage discoverable in a personal injury lawsuit? See Rule 26(b)(2). What possible relevance might such information have to the pending action?

(b) EXPERTS AND THEIR REPORTS

Zarecki v. National Railroad Passenger Corporation, d/b/a Amtrak

United States District Court for the Northern District of Illinois, 1996.
914 F. Supp. 1566.

■ CASTILLO, DISTRICT JUDGE

Plaintiff Judy Zarecki ("Zarecki"), a reservation sales agent for National Railroad Passenger Corp. d/b/a ("Amtrak"), was diagnosed with carpal tunnel syndrome while employed at Amtrak. Zarecki alleges that her condition developed because Amtrak required her to perform her job in an unsafe manner and failed to provide her with safe equipment. She seeks relief under the Federal Employers Liability Act ("FELA"), 45 U.S.C. §§ 51–60 (1988), alleging that Amtrak was negligent. Amtrak now moves for summary judgment. For the reasons stated herein, Amtrak's motion is granted.

RELEVANT FACTS

The following undisputed facts are gleaned from the parties' respective Local Rule 12(M) statements of material facts and accompanying exhibits.

Zarecki began working for Amtrak as a reservation sales agent on November 1, 1983. Her duties included answering phones, checking schedules and routes, and making reservations. Like most modern day ticketing agents, Zarecki used a personal computer, an accompanying computer keyboard, and a phone headset with a microphone so that her hands were free to operate the keyboard. Zarecki performed these tasks while seated in an adjustable chair.

Zarecki has worked full time during her approximate twelve years at Amtrak. During each eight-hour work day, Zarecki had two scheduled breaks, one eighteen minute break and another forty-eight minute break for lunch. In addition, she was free to take a break and use the washroom, water fountain or coffee machine.

Although Zarecki did complain to fellow employees about her working conditions at Amtrak, she did not complain to any supervisor before she was first diagnosed with carpal tunnel syndrome. Zarecki specifically testified that she never complained to anyone at Amtrak about her working conditions before 1994 except for fellow workers. She did, however, complain to her supervisor in 1994.

Zarecki was diagnosed with carpal tunnel syndrome in 1992.[3] Zarecki first tried to alleviate her pain by taking medication, but eventually decided to undergo surgery in 1994 upon the suggestion of her physician. (Id. at 100). She returned to work without restrictions in August of 1994.

Zarecki contends that Amtrak caused her condition in one or more of the following ways: (1) failing to provide safe equipment and work space; (2) failing to provide proper work methods to avoid the repetitive nature of the work; (3) failing to provide proper training; (4) failing to properly supervise; and (5) failing to warn of the possibility of acquiring carpal tunnel syndrome.

Amtrak has submitted the report of an ergonomist, David T. Ridyard, President of Applied Ergonomics Technology, who investigated the work conditions at Amtrak and formed an opinion as to the risk of developing carpal tunnel syndrome from performing Zarecki's job. Ridyard's report notes that three potential carpal tunnel "risk factors" are generally associated with computer keying activities: (1) a very high number of repetitions; (2) non-neutral wrist postures; and (3) forceful exertions. Although these risk factors are generally associated with keying activities, Ridyard found that all of these factors were essentially absent at the Chicago Amtrak facility and he concluded that "there are no potential carpal tunnel syndrome and other upper extremity cumulative trauma disorder risk factors at the Chicago Amtrak facility" where Zarecki worked.

Ridyard found that the number of keystrokes (per hand) per minute of a reservation sales agent at Amtrak was approximately 7 to 8, which is equivalent to approximately two words per minute. To assess this factor, Ridyard recorded the number of keystrokes during one-minute observations of twelve different sales representatives who were randomly selected. Ridyard also found that the sales agents could maintain their wrists in a neutral position, meaning that they were not bent significantly in any direction. None of the conditions that adversely affect a computer operator's ability to maintain neutral wrist positions, such as desks and chairs that are at an improper height, existed

---

3. Carpal tunnel syndrome. A condition resulting from pressure on the median nerve as it traverses the carpal tunnel (a deep space in the palmar or palm surface of the wrist); usually by fibers of the transverse carpal ligament. The condition is characterized by pain, tingling, burning, numbness, etc. in the areas supplied by the nerve, i.e., in the skin of the palm, fingers, wrist, etc. There may also bone swelling of the fingers and atrophy of some of the muscles of the hand, especially those at the based of the thumb. 1 Schmidt's Attorney's Dictionary of Medicine, (MB) No. 28, at C–76 (Feb. 1995).

at the Chicago Amtrak facility. Indeed, Zarecki admits that she was able to keep her hands in a neutral position. Finally, Ridyard found that the keyboards could be operated with low finger forces.

Ridyard's expert report, which is uncontroverted, presents an evidentiary hurdle that Zarecki must overcome in order to survive Amtrak's motion for summary judgment. However, instead of presenting her own expert testimony regarding risk factors for carpal tunnel syndrome present at Amtrak's workstations, Zarecki relies almost exclusively on an affidavit by her treating physician, Dr. Farrell, to defeat Amtrak's motion for summary judgment.

* * *

Zarecki's Negligence Claim

Under FELA, railroad companies are liable in damages to any employee who suffers injury due to the railroad's negligence. 45 U.S.C § 51. To recover under FELA, Zarecki must prove the common-law elements of negligence including duty, breach, foreseeability, and causation. Fulk v. Illinois Cent. R.R. Co., 22 F.3d 120, 124 (7th Cir.), cert. denied, 130 L. Ed. 2d 125, 115 S. Ct. 193 (1994). The evidence required to establish liability in a FELA action however is less than that required in an ordinary negligence action. Harbin v. Burlington N. Ry. Co., 921 F.2d at 129, 131–132 (7th Cir. 1990). The common law standard of proximate cause is not applicable to FELA. Crane v. Cedar Rapids & Iowa City R.R. Co., 395 U.S. 164, 166, 23 L. Ed. 2d 176, 89 S. Ct. 1706 (1969). The Supreme Court has described the test for causation as "whether the proofs justify with reason the conclusion that employer negligence played any part, even the slightest, in producing the injury." Rogers v. Missouri Pac. R.R. Co., 352 U.S. 500, 506, 1 L. Ed. 2d 493, 77 S. Ct. 443 (1957).

Under FELA, a railroad has a duty to provide employees: (1) a reasonably safe workplace; (2) safe equipment; (3) proper training; and (4) suitable methods to perform the assigned work. Aparicio v. Norfolk & W. Ry. Co., 874 F. Supp. 154, 158 (N.D.Ohio 1994). Whether the duty has been breached is viewed from an objective standard of reasonableness. The standard is the degree of care a person of ordinary, reasonable prudence would observe under similar circumstances. The scope of the railroad's duty, however, is limited to hazards it could have foreseen. Gallose v. Long Island R. Co., 878 F.2d 80, 85 (2d Cir.1989).

In order for Zarecki to prove that Amtrak breached its duty, she must offer evidence that shows (or, for purposes of the present motion, raises a genuine issue of material fact as to) either that the equipment she was provided, or the manner in which she was required to use it, was unsafe. Zarecki maintains that the keyboard and the chair she used while working were unsafe, but she provides no evidentiary support for this contention. The only evidence she provides is her own testimony that Amtrak did not provide her with an adjustable keyboard or a chair without armrests at all times; however, she offers no evidence that using a non-adjustable keyboard or a chair with armrests was unsafe or otherwise causally related to her carpal tunnel syndrome.

Zarecki also maintains that the manner in which Amtrak required her to perform her job was unsafe; again however, she fails to provide any probative evidence to support this contention. Her evidence consists only of her testimony that her job requires her to handle approximately 95–150 calls per day and to enter data continuously using a computer keyboard. Additionally, she testified that she is allowed to take two scheduled breaks along with other breaks to use the washroom, coffee machine, and water fountain. Amtrak is correct in asserting that this testimony is only a description of her job and not evidence that she is required to perform her job in an unsafe manner. Absent any additional evidence suggesting that these work conditions exceed some minimal safety threshold, Zarecki's testimony, even when viewed in the light most favorable to her, fails to raise a genuine issue of material fact as to the safety (or lack thereof) of her working conditions.

Essentially, this Court has concluded that Zarecki's claims survive or fall on the basis of the Court's evaluation of Dr. Farrell's affidavit. Zarecki attempts to use Dr. Farrell's affidavit to prove that the keyboard, chair, and manner in which she was required to use them were unsafe and that they caused her injury.

The first issue that this Court must address is whether Dr. Farrell's affidavit is admissible.

* * *

On April 28, 1995, the Court ordered both parties to comply with Rule 26(a) by July 28, 1995. Rule 26(a) (2) requires parties to disclose the identity of any person who may be used at trial as an expert witness. FED. R. CIV. P. 26(A)(2)(A). The disclosure must be accompanied by a written report prepared and signed by the witness that contains: (1) a complete statement of all opinions to be expressed and the basis for the opinions; (2) the data or other information considered by the witness in forming the opinions; (3) any exhibits to be used as a summary of or in support for the opinions; (4) the witness qualifications and compensation; and (5) any other cases in which the witness has testified as an expert within the preceding four years. FED. R. CIV. P. 26(a) (2) (B). The Rule also requires that "These disclosures be made at the times and in the sequence directed by the court." FED. R. CIV. P. 26(a)(2)(C). The requirement of a written report in Fed. R. Civ. P. 26(a) (2) (B) applies only to those experts who are retained or specially employed to provide expert testimony. See FED. R. CIV. P. 26 advisory committee notes (1993). Zarecki did not disclose Dr. Farrell as an expert witness pursuant to Rule 26(a). She contends, however, that she need not have disclosed Dr. Farrell as an expert because he is her treating physician and his testimony pertains to information obtained during the course of his treatment of her and not obtained in preparation for trial. The Court cannot agree.

Zarecki is correct, of course, in asserting that under certain circumstances a treating physician need not be disclosed as an expert. See generally Richardson v. Consolidated Rail Corp., 17 F.3d 213, 218 (7th Cir.1994). In particular, as the Seventh Circuit observed in Patel v. Gayes, 984 F.2d 214 (7th Cir.1993), where a witness will testify as to information acquired not "in preparation for trial but rather because he was an actor or viewer with respect to transactions or occurrences that are part of the subject matter of the lawsuit," that witness need not be disclosed as an expert. Id. at 217. Thus, "rule 26 focuses not on the status of the witness but rather on the substance of the testimony." Id. at 218. In a related vein, in O'Conner v. Commonwealth Edison Co., 13 F.3d 1090 (7th Cir.1994), the Seventh Circuit rejected a plaintiff's argument that his treating physician was exempt from the Federal Rules of Evidence governing expert testimony, stating "we do not distinguish the treating physician from other experts when the treating physician is offering expert testimony regarding causation." Id. at 1105 n.14. In the instant case, the Court has little difficulty concluding that Dr. Farrell is being offered as an expert who should have been disclosed pursuant to Rule 26 (a) (2) and this Court's expert-disclosure order. In the first place it is instructive to note that Dr. Farrell's affidavit states, "I have been retained as an expert witness." (Farrell Aff. P 1.). Of course, we are not slaves to labels and so we look to the substance of Dr. Farrell's testimony. Dr. Farrell's testimony goes far beyond any personal observations that he might have made during the course of treating Zarecki; instead, he purports to offer conclusions as to the ultimate cause of Zarecki's carpal tunnel syndrome (see id. P 7) and the foreseeability of Zarecki's injuries based on the work conditions at Amtrack (id. P 8). Dr. Farrell also states that he makes his affidavit "on personal and professional knowledge and upon my personal examination of Judy Zarecki, and the medical records of Judy Zarecki." (Id. P 9) (emphasis added). Plainly, Dr. Farrell's opinions as to ultimate causation and foreseeability are not derived solely from his treatment of Zarecki or his personal observations-there is, for instance no suggestion in the record that he ever actually investigated the specific nature of Zarecki's work conditions; instead, he is purporting to speak as an expert on these issues based on some unspecified body of professional knowledge. Accordingly, he should have been disclosed pursuant to Rule 26(a)(2). In view of Zarecki's failure to comply with the disclosure requirements of Rule 26(a)(2), it is within this Court's sound discretion to strike Dr. Farrell's affidavit. Patel v. Gayes, 984 F.2d at 217; see also Sylla–Sawdon v. Uniroyal Goodrich Tire Co., 47 F.3d 277, 284 (8th Cir. 1995) (finding no abuse of discretion in excluding expert testimony that was not properly disclosed). However, our decision to strike Dr. Farrell's testimony is not based on this ground alone.

* * *

Ms. Zarecki's present medical conditions are unfortunate. However, the law does not provide a remedy for every medical malady. Under the circumstances of this case, Ms. Zarecki has simply not presented enough evidence to proceed to trial. In essence, a trial will only delay the inevitable conclusion of this case—a judgment in favor of Amtrak. For all of the foregoing reasons, defendant Amtrak's motion for summary judgment is granted. This case is dismissed with prejudice. Both sides are to bear their own costs.

QUESTIONS

A. The case was dismissed with prejudice. What does that mean?

B. Do you think that the grant of summary judgment was appropriate? Is it relevant that the only evidence available for the court's consideration, after the exclusion of Dr. Farrell's opinion, was the opinion of a defense witness?

NOTE: DISCOVERY OF EXPERTS

The 1993 amendments substantially changed the provisions for the discovery of experts. Rule 26(a)(2) requires the disclosure of the identity and written report of any expert witness who may testify at trial. The report must state fully the testimony the expert will present, and it must be accompanied by materials considered by the expert in forming her opinion as well as any exhibits that will be introduced at trial. Rule 26(b)(4)(A) then provides that an opposing party, at their own expense, may depose the expert witness after receipt of the written report but before trial.

Additionally, Rule 26(b)(4)(C) stipulates that the party seeking discovery of research or investigations used by another party's expert in forming an opinion must pay "a fair portion of the fees and expenses reasonably incurred by the latter party in obtaining facts and opinions from the expert." In other words, in order to use research results obtained at the expense of an opposing party, a party must contribute to the cost of obtaining those results.

The provisions for the discovery of experts were designed to achieve an open exchange of the substance of expert testimony. According to the Advisory Committee Note, "[g]iven this obligation of disclosure, litigants should no longer be able to argue that materials furnished to their experts should be used in forming their opinions ... are privileged or other wise protected from disclosure when such persons are testifying or being deposed." Now, both the cost and content of expert testimony must be shared. The proposed 2000 amendments leave these provisions unchanged.

David Wakabayashi v. The Hertz Corporation v. General Motors Corporation

Supreme Court of Hawaii, 1983.
66 Hawaii 265, 660 P.2d 1309.

■ NAKAMURA, JUSTICE.

The Hertz Corporation (Hertz) appeals from a judgment awarding David Wakabayashi (Wakabayashi) $150,000 for injuries sustained in a single-car accident involving an automobile he rented from Hertz and the vehicle's manufacturer, General Motors Corporation (General Motors), appeals from a judgment indemnifying the rental agency for its liability. Finding no reversible error affecting the verdict in favor of

Wakabayashi, we affirm the judgment against Hertz. But we conclude General Motors should not have been denied permission to depose the plaintiff's expert; and as the denial prejudiced its defense of Hertz' third-party suit, we reverse the judgment against General Motors and remand the case for further proceedings consistent with this opinion.

I

On February 17, 1977 Wakabayashi, a Los Angeles optometrist attending a convention in Honolulu, rented a 1975 Chevrolet Chevelle from Hertz. The vehicle had been purchased new by Hertz from Aloha Motors, Inc. on July 23, 1975 and had been driven 22,577 miles prior to its rental to Wakabayashi. Three days later Wakabayashi, after having driven the Chevelle slightly more than 120 miles in the interim, drove to the entrance of the basement garage of the Ala Moana Hotel and stopped to obtain a parking stub from the attendant. He claims he placed the car's gear in the "park" position, keeping his right foot on the brake pedal, and, upon receiving a stub from the attendant, he shifted into "drive" and released his foot from the brake pedal. While it is unclear exactly what occurred next, the evidence indicates Wakabayashi either touched the accelerator pedal or was about to touch it when the Chevelle shot forward with a roar down the entrance ramp and into the garage. Wakabayashi testified he put his foot on the brake pedal, and though there was resistance, the vehicle did not come to a stop. To avoid striking a pedestrian in its path, Wakabayashi swerved and rammed the Chevelle into a concrete pillar.

Wakabayashi brought an action seeking damages from Hertz on the theory of strict products liability. Hertz answered with a twofold defense, claiming the Chevelle was not defective but asserting that if it were, the vehicle's manufacturer was responsible for the defect. Consistent with the latter position, Hertz filed a third-party action against General Motors.

At trial, Wakabayashi conceded he could not offer direct evidence of a specific defect that caused the Chevelle to accelerate out of control. He nevertheless convinced the trial judge that the evidence consisting of his own testimony and the statements of his passengers and the parking attendant, who observed the rear brake lights on the Chevelle as it sped down the ramp, was sufficient to enable the jury to determine the vehicle was defective when rented and to hold Hertz liable for the injuries he sustained.

Hertz' principal defense consisted of testimony that an examination of the Chevelle following the accident uncovered no defects in the vehicle. General Motors relied primarily on the apparent absence of any broken part or other identifiable defect and on expert testimony that the Chevelle consequently could not have accelerated in the manner described by Wakabayashi unless he had depressed the accelerator pedal rather than the brake pedal.

Answering special interrogatories propounded by the trial court, the jury found the Chevelle was defective, the defect was a proximate cause of the accident, Wakabayashi suffered damages amounting to

$150,000 as a result of the accident, and the defect was present when the vehicle was initially sold. Judgments in the sum of $150,000 for Wakabayashi and against Hertz and in a like sum against General Motors on Hertz' third-party claim were entered on the basis of the jury verdict. Hertz and General Motors perfected timely appeals, which by stipulation were consolidated for argument and disposition.

* * *

B.

Hertz next avers reversible error was committed when the trial court, at Wakabayashi's instance, prevented the defendants from apprising the jury of the fact that the plaintiff's expert had examined the damaged vehicle. It claims the ruling was prejudicial because the jury was then unable to infer from the plaintiff's failure to call him as a witness that the Chevelle harbored no defect that would cause an accident. While the court later permitted evidence that the expert in question examined the vehicle as the plaintiff's representative to be presented to the jury, Hertz maintains it was nevertheless denied the opportunity of presenting this proof in an effective manner since it had rested its case before the earlier ruling was rescinded.

Our review of the record, however, leads us to conclude the claim of reversible error lacks merit, as we do not believe Hertz was actually prejudiced by the trial court's initial reaction that the evidence in question should not be considered by the jury.

* * *

III

Although General Motors raises several issues, we confine our discussion to the assertion that its pre-trial efforts to discover facts known or opinions held by the expert who had inspected the damaged Chevelle on Wakabayashi's behalf should not have been foreclosed. And as we agree the trial court's error in this regard was prejudicial to General Motors, we find it unnecessary to reach the remainder of the questions posed.[1]

A.

General Motors made two attempts to depose Wakabayashi's expert pursuant to Rule 26(b)(4)(B) of the Hawaii Rules of Civil Procedure, which under some circumstances sanctions discovery of

---

1. These questions are:

(1) Whether the trial court erred in denying General Motors' motion for a directed verdict, on the ground that Hertz failed to produce substantial evidence of a defect in the 1975 Chevrolet Chevelle at the time of its sale by General Motors;

(2) Whether the trial court improperly permitted Wakabayashi to introduce evidence of other accidents involving General Motors automobiles; and

(3) Whether the trial court erred in allowing Wakabayashi to cross-examine a General Motors witness about other accidents not entered into evidence.

facts known or opinions held by an expert who has been retained by another party but is not expected to testify at trial.[2]

In the first, it argued the precondition of "exceptional circumstances" demanded by Rule 26(b)(4)(B) had been satisfied since Wakabayashi's expert had inspected the ill-starred Chevelle prior to its destruction by Hertz and the first-hand information he had secured was unavailable to General Motors due to its being brought into the controversy after the vehicle's demolition. While the motion seeking leave to depose the expert was denied, the trial court suggested the possibility of its renewal if the deposition of Hertz' expert showed the facts known or opinions held by the plaintiff's expert differed from that of the rental agency's expert.

The second attempt to discover relevant information within the knowledge of Wakabayashi's expert was mounted after General Motors learned when it deposed Hertz' expert that the plaintiff's expert had independently examined the damaged vehicle and its parts rather than in conjunction with the other expert as it had theretofore supposed. And as the deposition further revealed that neither had discussed his findings or opinions with the other after his inspection, General Motors argued the circumstances were indeed exceptional and that it should be allowed to depose Wakabayashi's expert even though he was not expected to be called as a witness at trial. The renewed motion was nevertheless denied.

B.

"The Hawaii Rules of Civil Procedure, like the federal procedural rules, reflect a basic philosophy that a party to a civil action should be entitled to the disclosure of all relevant information in the possession of another person prior to trial, unless the information is privileged." Mehau v. Gannett Pacific Corporation, 66 Haw. 133, 155, 658 P.2d 312, 326 (1983). Still, "[t]he extent to which discovery is permitted under Rule 26 (as well as under Rules 33 and 34) is subject to considerable latitude and [the] discretion [of the trial court]." In re Goodfader, 45 Haw. 317, 335, 367 P.2d 472, 483 (1961). Thus the exercise of such discretion will not be disturbed in the absence of a clear abuse of discretion that results in substantial prejudice to a party.

---

2. Rule 26, HRCP reads in relevant part:

GENERAL PROVISIONS GOVERNING DISCOVERY.

* * *

(b) Scope of Discovery. Unless otherwise limited by order of the court in accordance with these rules, the scope of discovery is as follows:

* * *

(4) *Trial Preparation: Experts.* Discovery of facts known and opinions held by experts, otherwise discoverable under the provisions of subdivision (b)(1) of this rule and acquired or developed in anticipation of litigation or for trial, may be obtained only as follows:

* * *

(B) A party may discover facts known or opinions held by an expert who has been retained or specially employed by another party in anticipation of litigation or preparation for trial and who is not expected to be called as a witness at trial, only as provided in Rule 35(b) or upon a showing of exceptional circumstances under which it is impracticable for the party seeking discovery to obtain facts or opinions on the same subject by other means.

However, we cannot but agree with General Motors that the "circumstances" in which it found itself in preparing for trial were "exceptional" and fairness impelled that it be allowed to discover facts known or opinions held by plaintiff's expert. For it had been placed in the difficult position of defending the integrity of the mechanism of an automobile five years after its manufacture and after its demolition as well, and the only other expert opinion available on the condition of the Chevelle after the crash was that of the expert retained by Hertz, the primary adversary.

The trial court, in our opinion, committed reversible error as the "exceptional circumstances" prescribed as a prerequisite for the allowance of the discovery sought by General Motors were definitely present and the denial of its Motion to Compel Production of Expert Witness for Deposition resulted in substantial prejudice.

The judgment in favor of David Wakabayashi is affirmed and the judgment in favor of Hertz is reversed. The case is remanded for the retrial of Hertz' claim against General Motors.

NOTES

A. Was Hertz' position as to the existence of a defect really adverse to that of GM in the *Wakabayashi* case?

B. Doesn't 26(b)(4)(B) create a situation in which only expert testimony helpful to the party retaining the expert is likely to be disclosed? Can such a result be justified?

Johnson v. H.K. Webster, Inc.

United States Court of Appeals, First Circuit, 1985.
775 F.2d 1.

■ Davis, Circuit Judge.

In this diversity tort case, defendant H.K. Webster, Inc. (Webster) appeals from a judgment entered on a jury verdict in favor of plaintiff Raymond Johnson (Johnson). The jury also found, in response to a special interrogatory, that the cause of the accident in which Johnson's foot was crushed in a grain conveyor designed by Webster was 51% Webster's negligent design of the machinery and 49% Johnson's negligent conduct in working near the device's exposed hazardous parts. The jury awarded Johnson $400,000 in damages under the applicable Maine comparative negligence statute.

* * *

I. *Background*

In 1973, Webster designed an "undertrack grain conveyor" for Cohen Milling Company (Cohen) in Saco, Maine. The conveyor serves to transport grains and meals from railroad hopper cars through an underground pipeline to storage silos located at the side of the track. Under Webster's design, a hopper car full of grain is positioned over a

14 inch by 48 inch trench underneath the track. Ideally, when the trap on the underside of the hopper car is released, the grain flows down into the trench. In the trench is an auger, a screwlike device which pushes the grain through a pipeline into the storage bins.[4]

Webster's design of the conveyor included a removable metal grate which fits over the undertrack trench. The spaces in the grate were about five inches square, sufficiently small to keep an adult's feet out of the trench, but large enough to allow most grains to pass through smoothly. But in the early 1970's (and to a certain extent, still today), the grain mills faced a problem of lumping. Certain products such as soybean meal would coagulate into large balls, often a foot in diameter. The spaces in a grate over the undertrack trench designed to keep feet out were too small to allow lumped materials to pass through. Webster's design therefore specifically called for a removable grate to allow lumped materials to pass to the auger unimpeded.

Appellee Johnson worked for Cohen in its milling operation. On September 16, 1980, Johnson emptied a hopper car of corn (a non-lumping grain) into the conveyor. He then moved the car down the track and began to sweep the corn lying at the sides of the trench. As was the habit at Cohen, the grate was not covering the trench into the conveyor. Believing he was to the side of the trench, but actually standing in front of it, Johnson stepped back into the conveyor. The auger gripped and crushed his right foot. After a series of surgical efforts to save the foot, doctors were forced to amputate Johnson's right leg below the knee.

Johnson filed suit against Webster in 1982 alleging negligent design of the conveyor, breach of warranty and strict liability in tort. After extensive discovery, the case came up for trial in 1984. At the start of the trial, Johnson dropped the breach of warranty counts.

A major procedural issue at trial, now raised before us, was the admissibility of testimony offered by two of Johnson's witnesses, Robert Flynn and Igor Paul. In each instance, Webster contended that the opinions advanced by the witnesses were not properly disclosed to defendant in response to pretrial interrogatories. The trial court limited Flynn's testimony to matters raised at his deposition and admitted all of Paul's testimony.

At trial, Johnson proved approximately $422,000 in monetary losses from the accident, including $53,000 in medical expenses, $69,000 in lost earnings up to trial, and $300,000 in lost future earnings. After receiving unchallenged instructions from the trial judge, the jury returned a verdict in Webster's favor on the product liability count and in Johnson's favor on the negligence count. As already noted, the jury awarded damages in the amount of $400,000 and found fault of 51% on Webster's part, 49% on Johnson's.

---

4. In the record, the auger in the Webster grain conveyor is likened to the inner mechanism of a meat grinder, which grips meat inserted in the top of the grinder and presses it against the grinding blades.

[After determining that any errors regarding Flynn's testimony were at most harmless error, the court went on to consider the testimony of Igor Paul]

III.   *Testimony of Igor Paul*

At the time of the trial, Professor Igor Paul was on the faculty of the Massachusetts Institute of Technology in the Department of Mechanical Engineering. Soon after the accident, Johnson engaged Paul to examine the conveyor and its safety features. In May 1983, Paul issued an opinion regarding the safety features, which reads in pertinent part:

> In my professional opinion the design of the underground auger conveyor designed and installed by [Webster] * * * was improper, inadequate and defective in failing to provide effective permanent or safety-interlocked removable grate guarding for the intake area of the conveyor trough * * *. The large opening above the auger screw in this design should have been provided with a grate guard safety interlocked to two hermetically sealed power interrupt switches in a self-testing interlock circuit which would stop auger motion whenever the guard was removed for any reason * * * and would not allow powered auger motion until the guard was replaced.

As Paul would later testify, the system he described would render the conveyor nonfunctional when the grate was removed. The self-testing interlock circuit would insure that, if the system failed, it would fail on the side of safety and the system would shut down completely.

Soon after he received the opinion, Johnson notified Webster that Paul would testify that the conveyor was unsafe "because it could be operated while the safety grate was not in place * * * [and] regarding various safety devices which should have been included as part of the grain auger." Webster took Paul's deposition in September 1983 and questioned him extensively about his inspection of the conveyor site and his opinion regarding its safety. During his deposition, Paul indicated that his inspection of the conveyor was not complete. Just before trial, Johnson confirmed in a submission to the trial court that "there is no need to anticipate any testimony different [from] that given at his [Paul's] deposition."

Subsequent to his deposition, Paul became aware of the lumping problem associated with certain grains. This made his grate interlock system impossible to use since Cohen would have to remove the grate to feed the lumped material into the conveyor. Under Paul's theory, the power would then shut off and the conveyor would be useless. For operation with lumping grains, the conveyor would have to operate without the grate in place.

At trial, Paul testified as to other specific methods of guarding the conveyor trench. He pointed out that "if you just cannot feed material through a safety grate, then you have to provide alternate ways of guarding." He listed several possible devices which could be used on

Cohen's conveyor, including: a split grate which could open but which would still provide a type of fence around the trench; a plain fence around the trench; and, "if you had to go to that extreme . . . an interlock side grating so that you could only operate the auger if the grate were removed, if there was a railroad car in place." This last device would have prevented the conveyor from operating when the grate was not in place unless a railroad car was stationed over the trench.

Webster asserts that this testimony should have been excluded because Johnson never disclosed prior to trial that Paul had formulated possible safety procedures (besides the type of grate interlock he specifically mentioned at his deposition) for use at the Cohen conveyor. Webster relies on Fed.R.Civ.P. 26(e) which states:

> *Supplementation of Responses:* A party who has responded to a request for discovery with a response that was complete when made is under no duty to supplement his response to include information thereafter acquired, except as follows:
>
> (1) A party is under a duty reasonably to supplement his response with respect to any request addressed to * * * (B) the identity of each person expected to be called as an expert witness at trial, the subject matter on which he is expected to testify, and the substance of his testimony.

In appellant's view, Johnson had a duty to inform it of Paul's alternate ideas regarding possible safety devices for the Cohen conveyor.

The 1970 Amendments to the Federal Rules of Civil Procedure added several new provisions on pretrial discovery of expert witnesses, including Rules 26(b)(4) and 26(e), *supra.* The court in Smith v. Ford Motor Co., 626 F.2d 784, 791–93 (10th Cir.1980), *cert. denied,* 450 U.S. 918, 101 S.Ct. 1363, 67 L.Ed.2d 344 (1981), has provided a detailed description of the origins and purposes of the new treatment of expert discovery in the Federal Rules. Briefly, the ill which the amendments sought to cure was the heavy burden placed on a cross-examiner confronted by an opponent's expert whose testimony had just been revealed for the first time in open court. As the Advisory Committee Note to Rule 26(b)(4) states, this situation "produces in acute form the very evils that discovery has been created to prevent. Effective cross-examination of an expert witness requires advance preparation." The Advisory Committee thus proposed Amendments to Rule 26 on the ground that, under the old prohibition against discovery of expert witnesses, "the narrowing of issues and elimination of surprise which discovery normally produces are frustrated." In order to enforce the Rule, the Advisory Committee Note to Rule 26(e) calls for "sanctions imposed by the trial court, including exclusion of evidence, continuance, or other actions as the court may deem appropriate."

Rule 26(e)'s supplementation requirement is not absolute. As the rule itself makes clear, the instances in which a party must supplement discovery are limited; if the rule called for supplementation in all instances, the actual trial would be merely a recital of earlier responses to written interrogatories and deposition questions. For instance, nothing in the rule or the Advisory Committee Note forecloses an expert from revising or further clarifying opinions during redirect examination or surrebuttal in response to points raised by the opposing party during its cross-examination or the presentation of its case. We must therefore not read Rule 26 mechanically, but rather in light of its dual purposes, "narrowing of issues and elimination of surprise."[7]

The cases which have considered objections to proffered testimony because it was not earlier disclosed have reflected this need to balance fairness to the opposing party with the realities of adversarial litigation. For example, in *Smith v. Ford Motor Co., supra,* the court reversed a judgment because the trial judge improperly admitted testimony from a medical expert relating to the connection between plaintiff's injuries and an alleged defect in plaintiff's automobile. Plaintiff had stated that the expert would testify only as to plaintiff's injuries. The appellate court noted that plaintiff had "misled Ford into believing that his testimony would relate solely to plaintiff's injuries and not to their relationship to a defective seat belt." 626 F.2d at 797. Similarly in Holiday Inns, Inc. v. Robertshaw Controls Co., 560 F.2d 856 (7th Cir.1977), the court held that testimony regarding plaintiff's alternate theory as to the origins of a fire in a hotel kitchen should be excluded. Plaintiff alleged during pretrial discovery that a control thermostat in a deep fat frier malfunctioned. Defendant in an interrogatory asked specifically if plaintiff alleged any other causes. Plaintiff responded in the negative. The court ruled that plaintiff could not then present evidence at trial that the frier lacked an oil level sensing device because "that resulted in defendant's being surprised at trial by plaintiff's alternative theory." 560 F.2d at 858.

On the other hand, in Stich v. United States, 730 F.2d 115 (3d Cir.1984), *cert. denied,* 469 U.S. 917, 105 S.Ct. 294, 83 L.Ed.2d 229 (1984), the Third Circuit approved a district court's ruling allowing medical testimony based on research published only a few weeks before trial. The appellate court noted that "plaintiffs could adequately prepare to cross-examine [the witness] from already available data." *Id.* at 118. In Murphy v. Magnolia Elec. Power Ass'n., 639 F.2d 232, 234, 235 (5th Cir.1981), the court held that plaintiff's expert should have been allowed to testify as a rebuttal witness "despite the fact that appellants breached their duty under Fed.R.Civ.P. 26(e)," given "the absence of prejudice and the essential nature of the evidence involved."

---

7. The parties have called to our attention the four-part test enunciated by the Third Circuit in Meyers v. Pennypack Woods Home Ownership Ass'n., 559 F.2d 894, 904–05 (3d Cir.1977). That case differs because it concerned a witness who had never been put on a witness list. That type of case does not involve the precise problems which arise when, as here, a witness is expected but the particular testimony may not be. We agree with the Third Circuit that the two most important factors to be considered are the prejudice and surprise suffered by the opposing party, and that party's ability to cure the prejudice.

As these cases demonstrate, the emphasis in evaluating the decision to admit testimony over a Rule 26(e) objection entails careful balancing. Trial and appellate courts should look to the conduct of the trial, the importance of the evidence to its proponent, and the ability of the defendant to formulate a response. DeMarines v. KLM Royal Dutch Airlines, 580 F.2d 1193, 1201–02 (3d Cir.1978). It is noteworthy that, in those cases in which testimony was held properly excluded, the courts have found some evasion or concealment, intentional or not, on the part of the litigant offering the evidence.

Closely linked to the issue of surprise and prejudice—its converse side—is the question of whether the party objecting to the evidence might have been able to confront the evidence with a minimum of disruption to the trial. Courts have often found it significant whether the objecting party sought a continuance to prepare to rebut the testimony. The Advisory Committee Note to Rule 26(e) expressly states that one possible sanction for a party's failure to provide supplemental responses is the granting of a continuance; here, Webster asked the trial judge for the far more drastic remedy of excluding the testimony in issue. Courts have looked with disfavor upon parties who claim surprise and prejudice but who do not ask for a recess so they may attempt to counter the opponent's testimony. * * *

Although the issue of the exclusion of Paul's testimony because of Johnson's presumed duty to supplement his original response regarding that presumed testimony does present a close question, we do not conclude that Webster has demonstrated an abuse of the trial judge's discretion to control discovery and the admission of evidence. *See* Part II, *supra.* Johnson had clearly indicated that Paul would discuss safety devices using interlock circuitry (though a different type of such circuitry), and Paul never departed from that general scheme. Webster says that this case is identical to *Holiday Inns, supra,* because Paul's testimony at trial related to an apparatus different from the device discussed in detail at his deposition, but it is clear that, unlike the plaintiff in *Holiday Inns,* Johnson responded correctly to the interrogatory and adequately informed Webster of the general technology on which it would, and in fact did, rely.[8] *See* DeMarines v. KLM Royal Dutch Airlines, 580 F.2d at 1201–02 (in which the court ruled that defendant's expert's testimony regarding the particulars of plaintiff's exact physical condition prior to an accident should be admitted when defendant had stated generally that it would raise plaintiff's pre-existing illness as an element of the case).

Moreover, Webster presented the judge solely with a motion to exclude the testimony, the most drastic remedy. Webster never asked for a trial continuance so it could prepare to respond.[9] One excuse

---

8. Five days before Paul testified, Johnson had expressly asked Mr. Ralph Webster (a leading officer of appellant) about interlocks keyed "to the presence of the train or the placement of the grate," and Mr. Webster had replied, "I think it's a concept that is worth consideration" and that he would "have to know more about that." It seems fair to say that the concept was not entirely strange or bizarre to Mr. Webster.

9. As indicated in footnote 8, *supra,* that matter had been mentioned at the trial some five days before Paul brought it up.

given us is that the trial judge never recognized any prejudice to Webster, so he would not have granted a continuance. However, the trial judge did not say that he saw no prejudice to Webster. He ruled merely that in this situation he saw no reason to grant a motion to strike.

Nor is it a proper excuse that Webster could not retain an expert knowledgeable in the proposed circuitry (*i.e.,* an interlock circuit between the grate and the railroad cars) in time to counter Paul's testimony. As shown in footnote 8, *supra,* Webster already knew (at least five days before) that the subject was on plaintiff's mind. But Webster never retained an expert on interlock circuitry at all. Its experts were familiar with the designs of grain mills and conveyors. The intention was simply to rebut Paul's original opinion regarding the interlocked grate with testimony on how that solution would be impossible given the lumping problem. In his testimony, Paul surmounted that difficulty by applying the same technology in a different way. Webster was then prepared only to rebut a particularly narrow point as to interlock circuitry, but that point never materialized. We cannot say, because Webster's original trial strategy approached the interlock issue so narrowly and it did not properly seek to cure its limited preparation when the new techniques surfaced, that the trial judge was in error. *See Phil Crowley Steel Corp., supra,* 601 F.2d at 344 (in which the court ruled that undisclosed expert testimony correctly stating plaintiff's damages should not be struck merely because the other party was prepared at trial only to rebut the previously disclosed incorrect testimony).

* * *

Graham, Discovery of Experts Under Rule 26(b)(4) of the Federal Rules of Civil Procedure

1977 U of Illinois Law Forum, 169.

I.   The Questionnaire

To ascertain actual practice of the discovery of expert witnesses expected to be called at trial in federal district courts throughout the United States a survey questionnaire was prepared. The questionnaire sought to determine whether discovery actually proceeded beyond the answer to interrogatories either voluntarily or on order of the court. In addition, the questionnaire attempted to reveal not only the manner of any such further discovery, and whether it was limited in scope, but also whether the discovery was subject to restrictions relating to timing and mutuality.

The questionnaire was mailed to each federal district judge, United States magistrate, United States Attorneys' office, the regional offices of the Securities and Exchange Commission and Department of Justice, Antitrust Division, and to ten practicing attorneys in each state selected on the basis of their participation in federal court litigation.

II.   Results of the Survey

The results of the survey indicate that the actual practice of discovery of expert witnesses expected to be called at trial varies widely from the two-step procedure of Rule 26(b)(4)(A). The interrogatory overwhelmingly is recognized as a totally unsatisfactory method of providing adequate preparation for cross-examination and rebuttal. In practice, full discovery is the rule, and practitioners use all available means of disclosure including both the discovery of expert's reports and depositions.

To gain a full perspective on the actual practice of the discovery of experts expected to testify the survey posed a series of questions. One question attempted to reveal the attitude of the respondents to the interrogatory. Another group of questions attempted to discover the actual manner of discovery, the voluntariness of the discovery, the scope of the discovery of experts expected to be called at trial, and the timing and mutuality of the discovery used.

* * *

B.   Manner of Disclosure

The following three questions were designed to ascertain the usual pattern of discovery of experts expected to be called at trial:

1) The normal pattern of discovery of an adverse party's expert expected to be called at trial can best be described as follows:

2) In my experience in the federal district court in which I now practice or preside, in the course of discovery of an adverse party's expert, Rule 34 demands are made, interrogatories are propounded and answered, reports are furnished and/or the expert is deposed in the following percentage of cases.

		% of Cases Occurring
a.	Rule 34 Demand Made	_____%
b.	Interrogatories Propounded	_____%
c.	Interrogatories Actually Answered	_____%
d.	Expert's Report Furnished	_____%
e.	Deposition Taken	_____%

3) In what percentage of cases involving experts expected to testify are both the expert's report furnished and the expert deposed? _____%

Manner of Discovery—Average Percentage of State Responses

		% of Cases Occurring
a.	Rule 34 Demand Made	36.07%
b.	Interrogatories Propounded	67.76%
c.	Interrogatories Answered	60.73%
d.	Expert Report Furnished	71.74%
e.	Deposition Taken	60.07%

Moreover, the survey revealed from the responses to question 3 that in 48.46% of all cases both the expert's report is furnished and the expert is deposed.

C.   Voluntary Disclosure

The survey responses indicate that the extensive discovery of experts expected to testify occurs voluntarily without resort to judicial compulsion. * * *

V.   DISCOVERY OF AN ADVERSE PARTY'S EXPERT NOT EXPECTED TO BE CALLED

One of the most surprising responses to the questionnaire was to a question designed to ascertain the pattern of discovery of an expert witness that an adverse party retained or specially employed but did not expect to call at trial. As stated in Rule 26(b)(4)(B) discovery of such an expert should occur only in "exceptional circumstances." The survey responses, however, indicate that discovery of even these experts does occur to some extent:

> III.   With respect to an expert who has been retained or specially employed by your adversary but is *not* expected to be called to testify, is it fair to say that no discovery of that expert would *normally* take place?

Total Responses	Yes	No	% Yes	% No	Confidence Interval % Yes
197	142	55	72.08	27.92	63.5–79.9

The replies to the survey thus reveal that disclosure beyond acquisition of the name of the expert occurs without any showing of exceptional circumstances. Whether this is a result of a failure to understand the provisions of Rule 26(b)(4)(B) or of a developed practice favoring full disclosure despite Rule 26(b)(4)(B) is not clear. Nevertheless, reports of such experts are furnished and depositions conducted voluntarily in many instances.

QUESTION

Do the 1993 changes in the Federal Rules adequately address the problems noted in Graham's study?

Minnesota Mining and Manufacturing Company v. Signtech USA, Ltd.

United States District Court for the District of Minnesota, 1998.
177 F.R.D. 459.

■ LEBEDOFF, UNITED STATES MAGISTRATE JUDGE.

The above-entitled matter came on for hearing before the undersigned Magistrate Judge of District Court on November 18, 1997, on a motion by Defendant Signtech USA, Ltd. (Signtech) to compel discovery and extend the periods for expert rebuttal reports and discovery. The discovery Signtech seeks is Plaintiff Minnesota Mining and Manufacturing Company's (3M) expert reports under Fed. R. Civ. P. 26(a)(2)(B), for the expert witnesses identified in 3M's Rule 26(a)(2)(A) Expert Witness Disclosures.

3M has refused to impose the written report requirement on its six employee experts, asserting that these employee experts—all of whom will testify based on their experience and knowledge gained through their regular employment at 3M—are outside the mandates of Rule 26 and should not be treated as experts who are specially hired for litigation. 3M believes that Signtech should take the depositions of 3M's expert witnesses in lieu of the written reports.

Signtech acknowledges that Fed. R. Civ. P. 26(a)(2)(B) requires a party to produce a written report prepare and signed by each witness

> who is retained or specially employed to provide expert testimony in the case or whose duties as an employee of the party regularly involve giving expert testimony.

Signtech argues however that to literally construe this Rule, as 3M is doing, is at odds with the purpose of discovery under the Federal Rules, the 1993 Amendments to the Federal Rules, and the specific case law. Signtech points to the Advisory Committee Notes on the 1993 Amendments to the Federal Rules, submitting that they clearly set out a policy of broadened disclosure for expert witnesses. For example, the Advisory Committee Notes on the 1993 Amendments with regard to Rule 26(a) reads:

> A major purpose of the revision is to accelerate the exchange of basic information about the case and to eliminate the paper work involved in requesting such information, and the rule should be applied in a manner to achieve these objectives.

And, the Advisory Committee Notes on the 1993 Amendments state the following with regard to Rule 26(a)(2)(B):

> The information disclosed under the former rule in answering interrogatories about the "substance" of expert testimony was frequently so sketchy and vague that it rarely dispensed with the need to depose the expert and often was even of little help in preparing for a deposition of the witness.

In addition, Signtech submits that the Advisory Committee Notes on the 1993 Amendments state the following with regard to Rule 26(b)(4)(A):

> Revised subdivision (b)(4)(A) authorizes the deposition of expert witnesses. Since deposition of experts required to prepare a written report may be taken only after the report has been served, the length of the deposition of such experts should be reduced, and in many cases the report may eliminate the need for a deposition. (emphasis added)

Signtech avers that its construction of Rule 26(a)(2)(B) is supported by the rulings in several cases, including: *Sylla–Sawdon v.*

Uniroyal Goodrich Tire Co., 47 F.3d 277, 284 (8th Cir.1995) (affirming the purpose of the 1993 amendments to Rule 26 as "the elimination of unfair surprise to the opposing party and the conservation of resources", and commenting on problems with the earlier Rule being of little help in preparing for the deposition of a witness); *Sullivan v. Glock*, 175 F.R.D. 497, 1997 WL 621558 (D.Md.) and *Day v. Consolidated Rail Corp.*, 1996 WL 257654 (S.D.N.Y.1996) (although Rule 26(a)(2)(B) reports are not required from "hybrid" fact/expert witnesses, true expert witnesses must provide such reports). In particular, Signtech directs this Court's attention to Day v. Consolidated Rail Corp., asserting that it contains identical circumstances to the present case.

Indeed, this Court finds the *Day* court's rationale to be instructive and compelling. Wrote the court in *Day*:

> The argument about Mr. Heide [that an expert witness report is not required from him] is premised on the undisputed fact that he is an employee of defendant Con Rail ... According to defendant, Mr. Heide's job duties at Con Rail do not regularly involve giving expert testimony and he was not "retained or specially employed to provide expert testimony in this case." Accordingly, defendant argues that it need not provide the information otherwise required for expert witnesses.

> [T]he reading proposed by defendant would create a distinction seemingly at odds with the evident purpose of promoting full pretrial disclosure of expert information. The logic of defendant's position would be to create a category of expert trial witness for whom no written disclosure is required—a result plainly not contemplated by the drafters of the current version of the rules and not justified by any articulated policy. The implausibility of defendant's position on this point is underscored by the language of the relevant Advisory Committee notes both for the current version of the rules and for its predecessor. [quotations omitted].

> Although Rule 26(b)(4)(A), governing depositions of experts, appears to imply that some category of experts may be exempt from the report requirements, that exemption is apparently addressed to experts who are testifying as fact witnesses, although they may also express some expert opinions ... In such an instance, we may infer that the reasons for requiring an expert's report are far less compelling and may unfairly burden a non-party who is appearing principally because he or she witnessed certain events relevant to the lawsuit.

> In a case such as this, in which it appears that the witness in question ... although employed by the defendant, is being called solely or principally to offer expert testimony, there is little justification for construing the rules as excusing the report requirement. Since his duties do not normally involve giving expert testimony, he may fairly be viewed as having been "retained" or "specially employed" for that purpose.

Id.

As Signtech points out, 3M's disclosed witnesses will be testifying as experts, not as factor hybrid fact/expert witnesses. See Plaintiff's Rule 26(a)(2)(A) Expert Disclosures, attached as Exhibit E to Defendant's Memorandum in Support of Motion to Compel Discovery). In addition, 3M has insisted that these witnesses do not have duties which regularly involve giving expert testimony. See Letter of October 23, 1997, letter attached as Exhibit D to Defendant's Memorandum. Therefore, argues Signtech, under Day these experts must be view as "retained" or "specially employed" to give expert testimony, and 3M must provide expert reports.

3M asserts that the Day case was wrongly decided and urges this Court not to follow its lead in re-writing the rule.

While there are merits to both arguments, the Court finds the rationale of the Day case out of the esteemed Southern District of New York to be highly applicable here. This Court joins in finding that requiring testifying experts to submit written reports is entirely consistent with the spirit of Rule 26(a)(2)(B). It is not only likely that such reports will serve to streamline or even eliminate the necessity for deposition testimony, but they will undoubtedly serve to minimize the element of surprise. Defendant Signtech's motion to compel 3M to provide expert reports under Fed. R. Civ. P. 26(a)(2)(B) for the expert witnesses identified in 3M's Rule 26(a)(2)(A) Expert Witness Disclosures is granted. 3M shall produce and deliver to counsel for Signtech these expert witness reports no later than December 22, 1997.

Defendant Signtech has also moved for an extension of the period for providing its rebuttal reports and for an extension of the discovery schedule. Signtech believes a reasonable extension for it to produce rebuttal reports would be 30 days from the date that 3M provides its Rule 26(a)(2)(B) reports to Signtech. The Court agrees. The date by which Defendant Signtech shall produce rebuttal reports is extended to January 21, 1998.

Finally, Signtech submits that because it cannot take depositions of 3M's experts until the Rule 26(a)(2)(B) reports are provided, the period during which the parties may conduct discovery should be extended. Again, the Court agrees. The period during which the parties may conduct discovery is extended to February 27, 1998; and the date by which all non-dispositive motions must be filed and heard is extended to February 27, 1998. Commensurately, and to avoid an additional motion to extend the pretrial schedule, until further notice all dispositive motions must be noticed, served and filed, in accordance with the local rules adopted by the Court on 11/1/96, prior to March 27, 1998; and this case will considered ready for trial as of July 1, 1998.

* * *

QUESTION

A.   The issue in the case is whether employee experts should have to submit written reports or simply be deposed. Either method is a means of discovery. Would one be more likely to eliminate unfair surprise to the opposing party? Would one be more likely to conserve resources such as time, cost or man-power?

   B.   Do you agree with the court's decision?

Kennedy v. Baptist Memorial Hospital–Booneville

United States District Court for the Northern District of Mississippi, Eastern Division, 1998. 179 F.R.D. 520.

■ SENTER, CHIEF JUDGE.

   This cause presents the court with an intriguing question regarding the interplay of two discovery rules relating to an expert witness and his report and the competing interests underlying each rule. Presently before the court is plaintiffs' objection to the January 23, 1998, order of the magistrate judge denying plaintiffs' motion to compel.

   The pertinent facts are as follows: By letter dated October 13, 1997, Dr. Frank W. Ling, an expert retained by defendant Dr. D. J. Williams, advised Williams' counsel, Honorable Robert Upchurch, of his opinion regarding the alleged negligence of Dr. Williams in the treatment and care of plaintiffs' decedent. Of particular relevance to Ling's opinion are the following statements: (1) "As an obstetrician/gynecologist, I do not feel qualified to make a specific statement as to cause of death," and (2) "It appears that Dr. Williams was a victim of miscommunication from Dr. Stallworth. Dr. Stallworth appears to have misrepresented the severity of the injuries suffered by the patient." That report was forwarded to the court and counsel for plaintiffs, Honorable Shane Langston.

   The next day, Dr. Ling forwarded a second letter to Mr. Upchurch. This version of Ling's opinion reflects some editorial changes and several substantive changes of opinion and deletions from the October 13 letter. Of critical importance, Dr. Ling opined that "the information contained in the autopsy reports does not support blood loss as a probable cause of Ms. Kennedy's death. There are other probable causes . . . including closed head trauma or amniotic fluid embolism" and made no mention of Dr. Stallworth whatsoever. This letter was likewise forwarded to the court and Mr. Langston.

   With both reports in hand, Mr. Langston requested that Mr. Upchurch provide him with "the data and other information considered by the witness in forming the opinions," Fed. R. Civ. P. 26(a)(2)(B), so as to explain the changes in Ling's opinion. Upchurch refused, and plaintiffs moved to compel the production of this information. After conducting an in camera review of the requested documents, the magistrate judge concluded:

   The documents in question are communications between counsel and his retained expert over what is required in a Rule 26 expert report. Contrary to plaintiffs' beliefs, the records do not contain factual matters for the expert to consider; they contain the areas to be covered by the report and then proposed changes to [the] report which appear to the court to be editorial in nature. In any event, the plaintiff[s] [have] copies of both the original report and subsequent report of Dr. Ling and may cross-examine him about the differences. No further production is warranted as the court finds the documents protected by the work-product privilege.

The instant Rule 72 objection followed.

Having carefully considered the matter, the court is of the opinion that the magistrate judge's ruling is, in part, clearly erroneous and contrary to law. Without so stating, the magistrate judge chose to follow the line of cases which holds that "the data or other information" which must be divulged by the expert under 26(a)(2)(B) includes only factual materials, not core attorney work product considered by the expert which remains protected under Fed. R. Civ. P. 26(b)(3). See *Magee v. Paul Revere Life Insurance Co.*, 172 F.R.D. 627 (E.D.N.Y.1997); *Haworth, Inc. v. Herman Miller, Inc.*, 162 F.R.D. 289 (W.D.Mich.1995); *All West Pet Supply Co. v. Hill's Pet Products Division*, 152 F.R.D. 634 (D.Kan.1993).

Plaintiffs advance the opposite position. See *Musselman v. Phillips*, 176 F.R.D. 194 (D.Md.1997) (when attorney communicates otherwise protected work product—whether factual in nature or containing attorney's opinions or impressions—that information is discoverable if considered by expert retained to render opinion at trial); *B.C.F. Oil Refining, Inc. v. Consolidated Edison Co. of New York, Inc.*, 171 F.R.D. 57 (S.D.N.Y.1997) (all materials, not just factual information, furnished to expert must be disclosed in expert report); *Karn v. Rand*, 168 F.R.D. 633 (N.D. Ill. 1996) (when attorney furnishes work product—either factual or containing attorney's impressions—to expert retained to provide opinion testimony at trial, opposing party is entitled to discover that communication if considered by expert in developing opinion).

In this instance, the court chooses to take a more moderate position than either of these. While as a general rule, the court has no hesitation in finding that communications between an attorney and his retained expert are not discoverable—an attorney should be able to communicate freely with his retained expert without fear that his "mental impressions, conclusions, opinions, or legal theories," Fed. R. Civ. P. 26(b)(3), will be disclosed—the factual setting of this case causes it to fall outside that general rule. Here, counsel for Williams opened the door to additional discovery of "the data and other information considered by [Dr. Ling] in forming [his] opinions," Fed. R. Civ. P. 26(a)(2)(B), including any communications or documents normally protected by the work product privilege, when he inadvertently sent out the October 13 letter and followed it shortly thereafter with a revised version of that letter which, in this court's view, incorporated more than editorial changes. Obviously, some additional information was presented to Dr. Ling in the twenty-four-hour period between the two letters which, among other things, caused him to change his opinion regarding his expertise to opine on the cause of death and the alleged culpability of Dr. Stallworth, and as Dr. Ling could not otherwise explain those changes (indeed, he denied that his opinion had changed in any manner), plaintiffs are entitled "to ascertain whether the opinion which is to be offered at trial is that of the expert, as opposed to the attorney." *Musselman v. Phillips*, 176 F.R.D. 194, 201 (D.Md.1997). Otherwise, under the facts of this case, plaintiffs will not be able to cross-examine Dr. Ling effectively or to impeach his credibility. Therefore, while the court finds that communications between Upchurch or members of his firm and staff and Ling occurring before October 13, 1997, are protected by the attorney work product privilege, it is of the opinion that any communications between those persons occurring between the issuance of the two letters is discoverable.

In reaching this decision, the court wants to make clear that this holding is peculiar to the facts at hand and cannot in any way be taken as an open invitation to others to begin requesting production of documents and communications which they know to be protected by the attorney work product privilege. Only when an event occurs which puts the opponent on notice that counsel may have "interjected him or herself into the process by which a testifying expert forms the opinions to be testified to at trial," *Musselman*, 176 F.R.D. at 200, will be this holding be of any precedential value in this court.

An appropriate order shall issue.

NOTE

In Musselman v. Phillips, 176 F.R.D. 194 (D.Md.1997), the court held that when an attorney furnishes work product to an expert witness before his opinion report has been submitted, that work product is discoverable. The court gave two rationales for its holding: (1) giving the work product to the expert waived the protection and (2) the need for opposing parties to have a complete view of material on which an expert has formed his opinion will always prevail over work product protection. The foundation for this holding is the Advisory Committee Note to Rule 26(a)(2)(disclosure of expert's report) which states in part:

> The report is to disclose the data and other information considered by the expert and any exhibits or charts that summarize or support the expert's opinions. Given this obligation of disclosure, litigants should no longer be able to argue that materials furnished to their experts to be used in forming their opinions—whether or not ultimately relied upon by the expert—are privileged or otherwise protected from disclosure when such persons are testifying or being deposed.

The court in *Musselman* interpreted this commentary to say that all information furnished to an expert before he submits his report is discoverable, including anything provided by the attorney. A growing number of cases are in accord with the holding in *Musselman* and claim this rule is clear, necessary for effective cross examination and not harmful to the core doctrine of work product because an attorney may avoid any problems by not furnishing any of his theories to the expert.

The courts which maintain work product protection,[1] even when the work product has been furnished to an expert, maintain a distinction between factual

---

1. See e.g. Magee v. Paul Revere Life Insurance Co., 172 F.R.D. 627 (E.D.N.Y. 1997).

materials given to an expert and communication of theories and impressions. These courts conclude that the commentary of the Advisory Committee was not meant completely to override the strict protection traditionally given to attorney mental impressions.

A. Which of these tenets does the court in *Kennedy* agree with generally? Is the decision in this case an exception to their general rule? If so, why?

B. Does the attorney's error impact on Dr. Ling's credibility at trial?

4. Protective Orders

(a) LIMITATIONS BASED ON CONTENT OF THE DISCLOSURE

Seattle Times Co. v. Rhinehart

Supreme Court of the United States, 1984.
467 U.S. 20, 104 S.Ct. 2199, 81 L.Ed.2d 17.

■ JUSTICE POWELL delivered the opinion of the Court.

This case presents the issue whether parties to civil litigation have a First Amendment right to disseminate, in advance of trial, information gained through the pretrial discovery process.

I

Respondent Rhinehart is the spiritual leader of a religious group, the Aquarian Foundation. The Foundation has fewer than 1,000 members, most of whom live in the State of Washington. Aquarian beliefs include life after death and the ability to communicate with the dead through a medium. Rhinehart is the primary Aquarian medium.

In recent years, the Seattle Times and the Walla Walla Union–Bulletin have published stories about Rhinehart and the Foundation. Altogether 11 articles appeared in the newspapers during the years 1973, 1978, and 1979. The five articles that appeared in 1973 focused on Rhinehart and the manner in which he operated the Foundation. They described seances conducted by Rhinehart in which people paid him to put them in touch with deceased relatives and friends. The articles also stated that Rhinehart had sold magical "stones" that had been "expelled" from his body. One article referred to Rhinehart's conviction, later vacated, for sodomy. The four articles that appeared in 1978 concentrated on an "extravaganza" sponsored by Rhinehart at the Walla Walla State Penitentiary. The articles stated that he had treated 1,100 inmates to a 6–hourlong show, during which he gave away between $35,000 and $50,000 in cash and prizes. One article described a "chorus line of girls [who] shed their gowns and bikinis and sang * * *." App. 25a. The two articles that appeared in 1979 referred to a purported connection between Rhinehart and Lou Ferrigno, star of the popular television program, "The Incredible Hulk."

II

Rhinehart brought this action in the Washington Superior Court on behalf of himself and the Foundation against the Seattle Times, the Walla Walla Union–Bulletin, the authors of the articles, and the spouses of the authors. Five female members of the Foundation who had participated in the presentation at the penitentiary joined the suit as plaintiffs.[1] The complaint alleges that the articles contained statements that were "fictional and untrue," and that the defendants—petitioners here—knew, or should have known, they were false. According to the complaint, the articles "did and were calculated to hold [Rhinehart] up to public scorn, hatred and ridicule, and to impeach his honesty, integrity, virtue, religious philosophy, reputation as a person and in his profession as a spiritual leader." *Id.,* at 8a. With respect to the Foundation, the complaint also states: "[T]he articles have, or may have had, the effect of discouraging contributions by the membership and public and thereby diminished the financial ability of the Foundation to pursue its corporate purposes." *Id.,* at 9a. The complaint alleges that the articles misrepresented the role of the Foundation's "choir" and falsely implied that female members of the Foundation had "stripped off all their clothes and wantonly danced naked * * *." *Id.,* at 6a. The complaint requests $14,100,000 in damages for the alleged defamation and invasions of privacy.[2]

Petitioners filed an answer, denying many of the allegations of the complaint and asserting affirmative defenses.[3] Petitioners promptly initiated extensive discovery. They deposed Rhinehart, requested production of documents pertaining to the financial affairs of Rhinehart and the Foundation, and served extensive interrogatories on Rhinehart and the other respondents. Respondents turned over a number of financial documents, including several of Rhinehart's income tax returns. Respondents refused, however, to disclose certain financial information,[4] the identity of the Foundation's donors during the preceding 10 years, and a list of its members during that period.

---

1. The record is unclear as to whether all five of the female plaintiffs participated in the "chorus line" described in the 1978 articles. The record also does not disclose whether any of the female plaintiffs were mentioned by name in the articles.

2. Although the complaint does not allege specifically that the articles caused a decline in membership of the Foundation, respondents' answers to petitioners' interrogatories raised this issue. In response to petitioners' request that respondents explain the damages they are seeking, respondents claimed that the Foundation had experienced a drop in membership in Hawaii and Washington "from about 300 people to about 150 people, and [a] concurrent drop in contributions." Record 503.

3. Affirmative defenses included contentions that the articles were substantially true and accurate, that they were privileged under the First and Fourteenth Amendments, that the statute of limitations had run as to the 1973 articles, that the individual respondents had consented to any invasions of privacy, and that respondents had no reasonable expectation of privacy when performing before 1,100 prisoners.

4. Rhinehart also refused to reveal the current address of his residence. He submitted an affidavit stating that he had relocated out of fear for his safety and that disclosure of his current address would subject him to risks of bodily harm. Petitioners promptly moved for an order compelling Rhinehart to give his address and the trial court granted the motion.

Petitioners filed a motion under the State's Civil Rule 37 requesting an order compelling discovery.[5] In their supporting memorandum, petitioners recognized that the principal issue as to discovery was respondents' "refusa[l] to permit any effective inquiry into their financial affairs, such as the source of their donations, their financial transactions, uses of their wealth and assets, and their financial condition in general." Respondents opposed the motion, arguing in particular that compelled production of the identities of the Foundation's donors and members would violate the First Amendment rights of members and donors to privacy, freedom of religion, and freedom of association. Respondents also moved for a protective order preventing petitioners from disseminating any information gained through discovery. Respondents noted that petitioners had stated their intention to continue publishing articles about respondents and this litigation, and their intent to use information gained through discovery in future articles.

In a lengthy ruling, the trial court initially granted the motion to compel and ordered respondents to identify all donors who made contributions during the five years preceding the date of the complaint, along with the amounts donated. The court also required respondents to divulge enough membership information to substantiate any claims of diminished membership. Relying on *In re Halkin*, 194 U.S. App.D.C. 257, 598 F.2d 176 (1979),[6] the court refused to issue a protective order. It stated that the facts alleged by respondents in support of their motion for such an order were too conclusory to warrant a finding of "good cause" as required by Washington Superior Court Civil Rule 26(c). The court stated, however, that the denial of respondents' motion was "without prejudice to [respondents'] right to move for a protective order in respect to specifically described discovery materials and a factual showing of good cause for restraining defendants in their use of those materials."

Respondents filed a motion for reconsideration in which they renewed their motion for a protective order. They submitted affidavits of several Foundation members to support their request. The affidavits detailed a series of letters and telephone calls defaming the Foundation, its members, and Rhinehart—including several that threatened

---

5. Washington Superior Court Civil Rule 37 provides in relevant part: "A party, upon reasonable notice to other parties and all persons affected thereby, may apply to the court in the county where the deposition was taken, or in the county where the action is pending, for an order compelling discovery * * *."

6. The *Halkin* decision was debated by the courts below. Prior to *Halkin*, the only Federal Court of Appeals to consider the question directly had understood that the First Amendment did not affect a trial court's authority to restrict dissemination of information produced during pretrial discovery. See International Products Corp. v. Koons, 325 F.2d 403, 407–08 (C.A.2 1963). *Halkin* considered the issue at length. Characterizing a protective order as a "paradigmatic prior restraint," *Halkin* held that such orders require close scrutiny. The court also held that before a court should issue a protective order that restricts expression, it must be satisfied that "the harm posed by dissemination must be substantial and serious; the restraining order must be narrowly drawn and precise; and there must be no alternative means of protecting the public interest which intrudes less directly on expression." 194 U.S.App.D.C. at 272, 598 F.2d, at 191 (footnotes omitted).

physical harm to those associated with the Foundation. The affiants also described incidents at the Foundation's headquarters involving attacks, threats, and assaults directed at Foundation members by anonymous individuals and groups. In general, the affidavits averred that public release of the donor lists would adversely affect Foundation membership and income and would subject its members to additional harassment and reprisals.

Persuaded by these affidavits, the trial court issued a protective order covering all information obtained through the discovery process that pertained to "the financial affairs of the various plaintiffs, the names and addresses of Aquarian Foundation members, contributors, or clients, and the names and addresses of those who have been contributors, clients, or donors to any of the various plaintiffs." The order prohibited petitioners from publishing, disseminating, or using the information in any way except where necessary to prepare for and try the case. By its terms, the order did not apply to information gained by means other than the discovery process.[8] In an accompanying opinion, the trial court recognized that the protective order would restrict petitioners' right to publish information obtained by discovery, but the court reasoned that the restriction was necessary to avoid the "chilling effect" that dissemination would have on "a party's willingness to bring his case to court."

Respondents appealed from the trial court's production order, and petitioners appealed from the protective order. The Supreme Court of Washington affirmed both. 98 Wash.2d 226, 654 P.2d 673 (1982). With respect to the protective order, the court reasoned:

"Assuming then that a protective order may fall, ostensibly, at least, within the definition of a 'prior restraint of free expression', we are convinced that the interest of the judiciary in the integrity of its discovery processes is sufficient to meet the 'heavy burden' of justification. The need to preserve that integrity is adequate to sustain a rule like CR 26(c) which authorizes a trial court to protect the confidentiality of information given for purposes of litigation." *Id.,* at 256, 654 P.2d at 690.[9]

---

8. The relevant portions of the protective order state:

"2. Plaintiffs' motion for a protective order is granted with respect to information gained by the defendants through the use of all of the discovery processes regarding the financial affairs of the various plaintiffs, the names and addresses of Aquarian Foundation members, contributors, or clients, and the names and addresses of those who have been contributors, clients, or donors to any of the various plaintiffs.

"3. The defendants and each of them shall make no use of and shall not disseminate the information defined in paragraph 2 which is gained through discovery, other than such use as is neces-

sary in order for the discovering party to prepare and try the case. As a result, information gained by a defendant through the discovery process may not be published by any of the defendants or made available to any news media for publication or dissemination. This protective order has no application except to information gained by the defendants through the use of the discovery processes." App. 65a.

9. Although the Washington Supreme Court assumed, *arguendo,* that a protective order could be viewed as an infringement on First Amendment rights, the court also stated:

"A persuasive argument can be made that when persons are required to give

The court noted that "[t]he information to be discovered concerned the financial affairs of the plaintiff Rhinehart and his organization, in which he and his associates had a recognizable privacy interest; and the giving of publicity to these matters would allegedly and understandably result in annoyance, embarrassment and even oppression." *Id.,* at 256–257, 654 P.2d, at 690. Therefore, the court concluded, the trial court had not abused its discretion in issuing the protective order.[10]

The Supreme Court of Washington recognized that its holding conflicts with the holdings of the United States Court of Appeals for the District of Columbia Circuit in *In re Halkin,* 194 U.S.App.D.C. 257, 598 F.2d 176 (1979),[11] and applies a different standard from that of the Court of Appeals for the First Circuit in *In re San Juan Star Co.,* 662 F.2d 108 (1981).[12] We granted certiorari to resolve the conflict.[13] 464 U.S. 812, 104 S.Ct. 64, 78 L.Ed.2d 80 (1983). We affirm.

III

Most States, including Washington, have adopted discovery provisions modeled on Rules 26 through 37 of the Federal Rules of Civil Procedure. F. James & G. Hazard, Civil Procedure 179 (1977).[14] Rule 26(b)(1) provides that a party "may obtain discovery regarding any matter, not privileged, which is relevant to the subject matter involved in the pending action." It further provides that discovery is not limited to matters that will be admissible at trial so long as the information sought "appears—reasonably calculated to lead to the discovery of admissible evidence." Wash.Super.Ct.Civil Rule 26(b)(1).

The Rules do not differentiate between information that is private or intimate and that to which no privacy interests attach. Under the

information which they would otherwise be entitled to keep to themselves, in order to secure a government benefit or perform an obligation to that government, those receiving that information waive the right to use it for any purpose except those which are authorized by the agency of government which exacted the information." 98 Wash.2d, at 239, 654 P.2d, at 681.

10. The Washington Supreme Court also held that, because the protective order shields respondents from "abuse of the discovery privilege," respondents could not object to the order compelling production. We do not consider here that aspect of the Washington Supreme Court's decision.

11. See n. 6, *supra.*

12. In *San Juan Star,* the Court of Appeals for the First Circuit considered and rejected *Halkin's* approach to the constitutionality of protective orders. Although the *San Juan* court held that protective orders may implicate First Amendment interests, the court reasoned that such interests are somewhat lessened in the civil discovery context. The court stated: "In general, then, we find the appropriate measure of such limitations in a standard of 'good cause' that incorporates a 'heightened sensitivity' to the First Amendment concerns at stake * * *." 662 F.2d at 116.

13. The holding of the Supreme Court of Washington is consistent with the decision of the Court of Appeals for the Second Circuit in International Products Corp. v. Koons, 325 F.2d at 407–408.

14. See Bushman v. New Holland Division, 83 Wash.2d 429, 433, 518 P.2d 1078, 1080 (1974). The Washington Supreme Court has stated that when the language of a Washington Rule and its federal counterpart are the same, courts should look to decisions interpreting the Federal Rule for guidance. American Discount Corp. v. Saratoga West, Inc., 81 Wash.2d 34, 37–38, 499 P.2d 869, 871 (1972). The Washington Rule that provides for the scope of civil discovery and the issuance of protective orders is virtually identical to its counterpart in the Federal Rules of Civil Procedure. Compare Wash.Super.Ct.Civ.Rules 26(b) and (c) with Fed.Rules Civ.Proc. 26(b) and (c).

Rules, the only express limitations are that the information sought is not privileged, and is relevant to the subject matter of the pending action. Thus, the Rules often allow extensive intrusion into the affairs of both litigants and third parties.[16] If a litigant fails to comply with a request for discovery, the court may issue an order directing compliance that is enforceable by the court's contempt powers. Wash.Super.Ct.Civil Rule 37(b).[17]

Petitioners argue that the First Amendment imposes strict limits on the availability of any judicial order that has the effect of restricting expression. They contend that civil discovery is not different from other sources of information, and that therefore the information is "protected speech" for First Amendment purposes. Petitioners assert the right in this case to disseminate any information gained through discovery. They do recognize that in limited circumstances, not thought to be present here, some information may be restrained. They submit, however:

> "When a protective order seeks to limit expression, it may do so only if the proponent shows a compelling governmental interest. Mere speculation and conjecture are insufficient. Any restraining order, moreover, must be narrowly drawn and precise. Finally, before issuing such an order a court must determine that there are no alternatives which intrude less directly on expression." Brief for Petitioners 10.

We think the rule urged by petitioners would impose an unwarranted restriction on the duty and discretion of a trial court to oversee the discovery process.

IV

It is, of course, clear that information obtained through civil discovery authorized by modern rules of civil procedure would rarely, if ever, fall within the classes of unprotected speech identified by decisions of this Court. In this case, as petitioners argue, there certainly is a public interest in knowing more about respondents. This interest may well include most—and possibly all—of what has been discovered as a result of the court's order under Rule 26(b)(1). It does not necessarily follow, however, that a litigant has an unrestrained right to disseminate information that has been obtained through pretrial discovery. For even though the broad sweep of the First Amendment seems to prohibit all restraints on free expression, this Court has observed that "[f]reedom of speech * * * does not compre-

---

16. Under Rules 30 and 31, a litigant may depose a third party by oral or written examination. The litigant can compel the third party to be deposed and to produce tangible evidence at the deposition by serving the third party with a subpoena pursuant to Rule 45. Rule 45(b)(1) authorizes a trial court to quash or modify a subpoena of tangible evidence "if it is unreasonable and oppressive." Rule 45(f) provides: "Failure by any person without adequate excuse to obey a subpoena served upon him may be deemed a contempt of the court from which the subpoena issued."

17. In addition to its contempt power, Rule 37(b)(2), authorizes a trial court to enforce an order compelling discovery by other means including, for example, regarding designated facts as established for purposes of the action. Cf. Fed.Rule Civ.Proc. 37(b)(2)(A).

hend the right to speak on any subject at any time." American Communications Assn. v. Douds, 339 U.S. 382, 394–395, 70 S.Ct. 674, 681–682, 94 L.Ed. 925 (1950).

The critical question that this case presents is whether a litigant's freedom comprehends the right to disseminate information that he has obtained pursuant to a court order that both granted him access to that information and placed restraints on the way in which the information might be used. In addressing that question it is necessary to consider whether the "practice in question [furthers] an important or substantial governmental interest unrelated to the suppression of expression" and whether "the limitation of First Amendment freedoms [is] no greater than is necessary or essential to the protection of the particular governmental interest involved."

A

At the outset, it is important to recognize the extent of the impairment of First Amendment rights that a protective order, such as the one at issue here, may cause. As in all civil litigation, petitioners gained the information they wish to disseminate only by virtue of the trial court's discovery processes. As the Rules authorizing discovery were adopted by the state legislature, the processes thereunder are a matter of legislative grace. A litigant has no First Amendment right of access to information made available only for purposes of trying his suit. Zemel v. Rusk, 381 U.S. 1, 16–17, 85 S.Ct. 1271, 1280–1281, 14 L.Ed.2d 179 (1965) ("The right to speak and publish does not carry with it the unrestrained right to gather information"). Thus, continued court control over the discovered information does not raise the same specter of government censorship that such control might suggest in other situations. See In re Halkin, 194 U.S.App.D.C., at 287, 598 F.2d, at 206–207 (WILKEY, J., dissenting).[18]

Moreover, pretrial depositions and interrogatories are not public components of a civil trial.[19] Such proceedings were not open to the

---

18. Although litigants do not "surrender their First Amendment rights at the courthouse door," *In re Halkin*, 194 U.S.App. D.C., at 268, 598 F.2d, at 186, those rights may be subordinated to other interests that arise in this setting. For instance, on several occasions this Court has approved restriction on the communications of trial participants where necessary to ensure a fair trial for a criminal defendant. See Nebraska Press Assn. v. Stuart, 427 U.S. 539, 563, 96 S.Ct. 2791, 2804–2805, 49 L.Ed.2d 683 (1976); *id.*, at 601, and n. 27, 96 S.Ct., at 2823 and n. 27 (BRENNAN, J., concurring in judgment); Oklahoma Publishing Co. v. District Court, 430 U.S. 308, 310–311, 97 S.Ct. 1045, 1046–1047, 51 L.Ed.2d 355 (1977); Sheppard v. Maxwell, 384 U.S. 333, 361, 86 S.Ct. 1507, 1521–1522, 16 L.Ed.2d 600 (1966). "In the conduct of a case, a court often finds it necessary to restrict the free expression of participants, including counsel, witnesses, and jurors." Gulf

Oil Co. v. Bernard, 452 U.S. 89, 104, n. 21, 101 S.Ct. 2193, 2201–2202 n. 21, 68 L.Ed.2d 693 (1981).

19. Discovery rarely takes place in public. Depositions are scheduled at times and places most convenient to those involved. Interrogatories are answered in private. Rules of Civil Procedure may require parties to file with the clerk of the court interrogatory answers, responses to requests for admissions, and deposition transcripts. See Fed.Rule Civ. Proc. 5(d). Jurisdictions that require filing of discovery materials customarily provide that trial courts may order that the materials not be filed or that they be filed under seal. See *ibid.*; Wash.Super.Ct.Civil Rule 26(c). Federal district courts may adopt local rules providing that the fruits of discovery are not to be filed except on order of the court. See, *e.g.,* C.D.Cal.Rule 8.3; S.D.N.Y.Civ.Rule 19. Thus, to the extent that courthouse records could

public at common law, Gannett Co. v. DePasquale, 443 U.S. 368, 389, 99 S.Ct. 2898, 2910, 61 L.Ed.2d 608 (1979), and, in general, they are conducted in private as a matter of modern practice. See *id.,* at 396, 99 S.Ct. at 2913–2914 (BURGER, C.J., concurring); Marcus, Myth and Reality in Protective Order Litigation, 69 Cornell L.Rev. 1 (1983). Much of the information that surfaces during pretrial discovery may be unrelated, or only tangentially related, to the underlying cause of action. Therefore, restraints placed on discovered, but not yet admitted, information are not a restriction on a traditionally public source of information.

Finally, it is significant to note that an order prohibiting dissemination of discovered information before trial is not the kind of classic prior restraint that requires exacting First Amendment scrutiny. See *Gannett Co. v. DePasquale, supra,* at 399, 99 S.Ct., at 2915 (POWELL, J., concurring). As in this case, such a protective order prevents a party from disseminating only that information obtained through use of the discovery process. Thus, the party may disseminate the identical information covered by the protective order as long as the information is gained through means independent of the court's processes. In sum, judicial limitations on a party's ability to disseminate information discovered in advance of trial implicates the First Amendment rights of the restricted party to a far lesser extent than would restraints on dissemination of information in a different context. Therefore, our consideration of the provision for protective orders contained in the Washington Civil Rules takes into account the unique position that such orders occupy in relation to the First Amendment.

B

Rule 26(c) furthers a substantial governmental interest unrelated to the suppression of expression. *Procunier, supra,* at 413, 94 S.Ct., at 1811.[a] The Washington Civil Rules enable parties to litigation to obtain information "relevant to the subject matter involved" that they believe will be helpful in the preparation and trial of the case. Rule 26, however, must be viewed in its entirety. Liberal discovery is provided for the sole purpose of assisting in the preparation and trial, or the settlement, of litigated disputes. Because of the liberality of pretrial discovery permitted by Rule 26(b)(1), it is necessary for the trial court to have the authority to issue protective orders conferred by Rule 26(c). It is clear from experience that pretrial discovery by depositions and interrogatories has a significant potential for abuse.[20] This abuse is

serve as a source of public information, access to that source customarily is subject to the control of the trial court.

a. Procunier v. Martinez, 416 U.S. 396, 413, 94 S.Ct. 1800, 1811, 40 L.Ed.2d 224 (1974).

20. See Comments of the Advisory Committee on the 1983 Amendments to Fed. Rule Civ.Proc. 26, 28 U.S.C.App., pp. 729–730 (1982 ed., Supp. I). In Herbert v. Lando, 441 U.S. 153, 99 S.Ct. 1635, 60 L.Ed.2d 115

(1979), the Court observed: "There have been repeated expressions of concern about undue and uncontrolled discovery, and voices from this Court have joined the chorus. But until and unless there are major changes in the present Rules of Civil Procedure, reliance must be had on what in fact and in law are ample powers of the district judge to prevent abuse." *Id.,* at 176–177, 99 S.Ct. at 1648– 1649 (footnote omitted); see also *id.,* at 179, 99 S.Ct., at 1650 (POWELL, J., concurring). But

not limited to matters of delay and expense; discovery also may seriously implicate privacy interests of litigants and third parties.[21] The Rules do not distinguish between public and private information. Nor do they apply only to parties to the litigation, as relevant information in the hands of third parties may be subject to discovery.

There is an opportunity, therefore, for litigants to obtain—incidentally or purposefully—information that not only is irrelevant but if publicly released could be damaging to reputation and privacy. The government clearly has a substantial interest in preventing this sort of abuse of its processes.

* * *

C

We also find that the provision for protective orders in the Washington Rules requires, in itself, no heightened First Amendment scrutiny. To be sure, Rule 26(c) confers broad discretion on the trial court to decide when a protective order is appropriate and what degree of protection is required. The Legislature of the State of Washington, following the example of the Congress in its approval of the Federal Rules of Civil Procedure, has determined that such discretion is necessary, and we find no reason to disagree. The trial court is in the best position to weigh fairly the competing needs and interests of parties affected by discovery.[23] The unique character of the discovery process requires that the trial court have substantial latitude to fashion protective orders.

V

The facts in this case illustrate the concerns that justifiably may prompt a court to issue a protective order. As we have noted, the trial court's order allowing discovery was extremely broad. It compelled respondents—among other things—to identify all persons who had made donations over a 5–year period to Rhinehart and the Aquarian Foundation, together with the amounts donated. In effect the order would compel disclosure of membership as well as sources of financial support. The Supreme Court of Washington found that dissemination of this information would "result in annoyance, embarrassment and even oppression." 98 Wash.2d at 257, 654 P.2d, at 690. It is sufficient for purposes of our decision that the highest court in the State found

abuses of the Rules by litigants, and sometimes the inadequate oversight of discovery by trial courts, do not in any respect lessen the importance of discovery in civil litigation and the government's substantial interest in protecting the integrity of the discovery process.

21. Cf. Whalen v. Roe, 429 U.S. 589, 599, 97 S.Ct. 869, 876, 51 L.Ed.2d 64 (1977); Cox Broadcasting Corp. v. Cohn, 420 U.S. 469, 488–491, 95 S.Ct. 1029, 1042–1044, 43 L.Ed.2d 328 (1975). Rule 26(c) includes among its express purposes the protection of a "party or person from annoyance, embarrassment, oppression or undue burden or ex-

pense." Although the Rule contains no specific reference to privacy or to other rights or interests that may be implicated, such matters are implicit in the broad purpose and language of the Rule.

23. In addition, heightened First Amendment scrutiny of each request for a protective order would necessitate burdensome evidentiary findings and could lead to time-consuming interlocutory appeals, as this case illustrates. *See, e.g.* Zenith Radio Corp. v. Matsushita Electric Industrial Co., 529 F.Supp. 866 (E.D.Pa.1981).

no abuse of discretion in the trial court's decision to issue a protective order pursuant to a constitutional state law. We therefore hold that where, as in this case, a protective order is entered on a showing of good cause as required by Rule 26(c), is limited to the context of pretrial civil discovery, and does not restrict the dissemination of the information if gained from other sources, it does not offend the First Amendment.[24]

The judgment accordingly is *Affirmed.*

■ JUSTICE BRENNAN, with whom JUSTICE MARSHALL joins, concurring.

The Court today recognizes that pretrial protective orders, designed to limit the dissemination of information gained through the civil discovery process, are subject to scrutiny under the First Amendment. As the Court acknowledges, before approving such protective orders, "it is necessary to consider whether the 'practice in question [furthers] an important or substantial governmental interest unrelated to the suppression of expression' and whether 'the limitation of First Amendment freedoms [is] no greater than is necessary or essential to the protection of the particular governmental interest involved.'" (quoting Procunier v. Martinez, 416 U.S. 396, 413, 94 S.Ct. 1800, 1811, 40 L.Ed.2d 224 (1974)).

In this case, the respondents opposed discovery, and in the alternative sought a protective order for discovered materials, because the "compelled production of the identities of the Foundation's donors and members would violate the First Amendment rights of members and donors to privacy, freedom of religion, and freedom of association." The Supreme Court of Washington found that these interests constituted the requisite "good cause" under the State's Rule 26(c) (upon "good cause shown," the court may make "any order which justice requires to protect a party or person from annoyance, embarrassment, oppression, or undue burden or expense"). 98 Wash.2d 226, 256, 654 P.2d 673, 690 (1982). Given this finding, the court approved a protective order limited to "information * * * regarding the financial affairs of the various [respondents], the names and addresses of Aquarian Foundation members, contributors, or clients, and the names and addresses of those who have been contributors, clients, or donors to any of the various [respondents]." I agree that the respondents' interests in privacy and religious freedom are sufficient to justify this protective order and to overcome the protections afforded free expression by the First Amendment. I therefore join the Court's opinion.

NOTES

A. Note the Court's discussion of the disparate approaches to this issue taken by lower courts in *In re Halkin* (note 6 of the Court's opinion), *In re San Juan Star*

24. It is apparent that substantial government interests were implicated. Respondents, in requesting the protective order, relied upon the rights of privacy and religious association. Both the trial court and the Supreme Court of Washington also emphasized that the right of persons to resort to the courts for redress of grievances would have been "chilled." See n. 22, supra.

Co. (note 12 of the Court's opinion), and the Supreme Court of Washington in *Rhinehart.* Which approach is closest to Justice Powell's?

B.   In *Richmond Newspapers v. Virginia*, 448 U.S. 555, 100 S.Ct. 2814, 65 L.Ed.2d 973 (1980), the Supreme Court held that there was a First Amendment right of access to criminal trials for the press and the public which could not be abrogated without an overriding showing of need for such exclusion. Is *Seattle Times* inconsistent with *Richmond*?

Procter & Gamble Co. v. Bankers Trust Co.

U.S. Court of Appeals for the Sixth Circuit, 1996.
78 F.3d 219.

■ Merritt, Chief Judge.

In a case of widespread interest to the press, the District Court issued an injunction prohibiting Business Week magazine from publishing an article disclosing the contents of documents placed under the seal of secrecy by the parties to a lawsuit. This appeal raises the issue of whether the bedrock First Amendment principle that the press shall not be subjected to prior restraints can be set aside when a federal court perceives a threat to the secrecy of material placed under seal by stipulation of the parties. We are guided by the holding of the First Circuit in *In the Matter of Providence Journal Company*, 820 F.2d 1342, 1351, *modified on reh'g by* 820 F.2d 1354 (1st Cir.1987), *cert. granted and dismissed on other grounds*, that even a temporary restraint on pure speech is improper "absent the most compelling circumstances." Such circumstances are not present in the case at bar, and we therefore hold that the District Court erred in granting the orders challenged here.

I.   Facts

On October 27, 1994, Procter & Gamble ("P & G") filed a complaint against Bankers Trust ("Bankers") claiming a loss of over $100 million due to alleged fraud by Bankers in the sale of derivatives to P & G. The case has received widespread coverage, especially in the business press.

The suit was filed against both Bankers Trust and an affiliate, BT Securities. This opinion will refer to them collectively as "Bankers."

In January of 1995, Bankers and P & G agreed to a broad stipulated protective order as part of the discovery process. The order provided that parties and non-parties to the litigation—without court approval for "good cause" as required by Rule 26(e) of the Civil Rules—could, in their discretion, designate discovery material as "confidential" and could have such material filed under seal if the parties agreed that it reflected "trade secrets or other confidential research, development or commercial information...." The parties and not the court would determine whether particular documents met the requirements of Rule 26. The protective order further provided that the parties could modify its terms without approval of the court.

Business Week, a magazine owned by McGraw–Hill, had obtained documents from the Bankers/P & G litigation that the parties wanted to remain secret. The documents in question were materials supporting a motion by P & G for leave to amend its complaint. Although the motion itself was not sealed, the accompanying documents, which contained a supporting memorandum of law, a proposed Second Amended Complaint containing RICO allegations, and a RICO case statement, were filed in secret pursuant to the protective order. Neither Bankers nor P & G could say at that time how Business Week had obtained the documents.

The hearings revealed that the documents had found their way to Business Week through an unusual chain of people and events. Business Week's editor on the story, Zachary Schiller, testified on the basis of his reporter's notes to a tantalizing, off-the-record phone call from an employee in the public relations department of P & G who suggested that some documents that would be of interest to Business Week were about to be filed at the courthouse. (It seems that the tactics of P & G's public relations office were a little different from those of its lawyers.) Schiller notified several Business Week journalists that he was seeking information about the mysterious filing.

While Schiller was away from his office, a New York-based journalist for Business Week contacted an acquaintance who was a partner at the New York law firm representing Bankers Trust. Neither the partner (who was not working on the P & G case) nor the journalist (who had not previously been covering the story), appeared to know that the material was under seal. The journalist simply asked for the documents, and the partner obtained copies and gave them to her. The circle of irony became complete. Banker's New York lawyers unwittingly also followed tactics different from those of its litigators. It appears that Business Week found out about the sealed material because of a P & G leak and got the documents through a leak from Banker's Trust.

With this information before it, the District Court entered two orders on October 3rd, three weeks after its initial order restraining publication. In one order, the District Court concluded that Business Week "knowingly violated the protective order" by obtaining the documents and was therefore prohibited and permanently enjoined from using "the confidential materials that it obtained unlawfully." J.A. at 49. ("I conclude as a matter of law that Business Week cannot be permitted to use the confidential materials it obtained to publish its story." J.A. at 47.) This injunction remains in effect. In the other order, the District Court determined that, because the parties could not provide a "substantial government interest" in keeping the documents confidential, "the sealed documents should no longer be protected" and should be released into the public domain.

II. Analysis

B. Prior restraint

(1) The permanent injunction

It has long been established that a prior restraint comes to a court "with a heavy presumption against its constitutional validity." Bantam

Books v. Sullivan, 372 U.S. 58, 70, 9 L. Ed. 2d 584, 83 S. Ct. 631 (1963). In this case, the news magazine Business Week obtained information from a confidential source and prepared a story on a matter of public concern. Following standard journalistic protocol, Business Week sought comment from the parties and proceeded to take the story to print. Instead, the magazine received a facsimile transmission from a Federal District Court prohibiting publication of the information and citing "irreparable harm" as the reason. J.A. at 23.

The critical starting point for our analysis, therefore, is that we face the classic case of a prior restraint. Indeed, "prohibiting the publication of a news story . . . is the essence of censorship," and is allowed only under exceptional circumstances. Providence Journal, 820 F.2d at 1345. Justice Blackmun recently summarized the state of prior restraint doctrine as follows:

> Although the prohibition against prior restraints is by no means absolute, the gagging of publication has been considered acceptable only in "exceptional cases." Even where questions of allegedly urgent national security, or competing constitutional interests, are concerned, we have imposed this "most extraordinary remedy" only where the evil that would result from the reportage is both great and certain and cannot be militated by less intrusive measures. CBS v. Davis, 127 L. Ed. 2d 358, 114 S. Ct. 912, 914 (1994) (Blackmun, J., in chambers) (citations omitted).

Thus, we ask whether Business Week's planned publication of these particular documents posed such a grave threat to a critical government interest or to a constitutional right as to justify the District Court's three injunctive orders.

Before proceeding to this constitutional inquiry, however, we must clear up the considerable confusion generated by the proceedings below. Not only did the District Court fail to conduct any First Amendment inquiry before granting the two TROs, but it compounded the harm by holding hearings on issues that bore no relation to the right of Business Week to disseminate the information in its possession. Weeks passed with the "gag order" in effect, while the court inquired painstakingly into how Business Week obtained the documents and whether or not its personnel had been aware that they were sealed. While these might be appropriate lines of inquiry for a contempt proceeding or a criminal prosecution, they are not appropriate bases for issuing a prior restraint.

Furthermore, when the District Court did finally identify the potential for a First Amendment problem, it dismissed the question with misplaced reliance on Seattle Times v. Rhinehart, 467 U.S. 20, 81 L. Ed. 2d 17, 104 S. Ct. 2199 (1984). Seattle Times holds that parties to civil litigation do not have a right to disseminate information they have gained through participation in the discovery process. That case, however, does not govern the situation where an independent news agency, having gained access to sealed documents, decides to publish them.

In short, at no time—even to the point of entering a permanent injunction after two temporary restraining orders—did the District Court appear to realize that it was engaging in a practice that, under all but the most exceptional circumstances, violates the Constitution: preventing a news organization from publishing information in its possession on a matter of public concern.

We can only conclude that, had the District Court not been rushed to judgment by both parties and had it engaged in the proper constitutional inquiry, the injunction would never have been issued. Far from falling into that "single, extremely narrow class of cases" where publication would be so dangerous to fundamental government interests as to justify a prior restraint, New York Times Co. v. United States, 403 U.S. 713, 726, 29 L. Ed. 2d 822, 91 S. Ct. 2140 (1971) (Brennan, J. concurring), the documents in question are standard litigation filings that have now been widely publicized. The private litigants' interest in protecting their vanity or their commercial self-interest simply does not qualify as grounds for imposing a prior restraint. It is not even grounds for keeping the information under seal, as the District Court ultimately and correctly decided. Opinion and Order Granting Plaintiff's Motion for Leave to Amend its Complaint, J.A. at 33. The permanent injunction, therefore, was patently invalid and should never have been entered.

* * *

C. The Protective Order

Finally, the underlying protective order signed by Judge Rubin bears comment. While District Courts have the discretion to issue protective orders, that discretion is limited by the careful dictates of Fed. R. Civ. P. 26 and "is circumscribed by a long-established legal tradition" which values public access to court proceedings. Brown & Williamson Tobacco Corp. v. FTC, 710 F.2d 1165, 1177 (6th Cir.1983), cert. denied, 465 U.S. [*22] 1100, 80 L. Ed. 2d 127, 104 S. Ct. 1595 (1984). Rule 26(c) allows the sealing of court papers only "for good cause shown" to the court that the particular documents justify court-imposed secrecy. In this case, the parties were allowed to adjudicate their own case based upon their own self-interest. This is a violation not only of Rule 26(c) but of the principles so painstakingly discussed in Brown & Williamson.

The District Court cannot abdicate its responsibility to oversee the discovery process and to determine whether filings should be made available to the public. It certainly should not turn this function over to the parties, as it did here, allowing them to modify the terms of a court order without even seeking the consent of the court. The protective order in this case allows the parties to control public access to court papers, and it should be vacated or substantially changed.

III.   Conclusion

For the foregoing reasons, we REVERSE and VACATE the challenged orders.

■ [concurring opinion of Judge Martin and dissenting opinion of Judge Brown omitted]

QUESTIONS

A.   Is the First Amendment treated differently in *Proctor and Gamble* than in *Rhinehart*?

B.   If so, do factual differences in the two cases help account for the difference in treatment?

NOTE: POST–LITIGATION USE OF DISCOVERY MATERIAL

Cipollone v. The Liggett Group, 106 F.R.D. 573 (D.N.J.1985), *reversed and remanded* 785 F.2d 1108 (3d Cir.1986), *on remand* 113 F.R.D. 86, 87 (D.N.J.1986), *aff'd* 822 F.2d 335 (3d Cir.) *cert. denied* 479 U.S. 1043, 107 S.Ct. 907, 93 L.Ed.2d 857 (1987), was a products liability suit brought against a tobacco company. In discovery, attorneys for the plaintiff sought evidence which they believed would support their claim that the tobacco industry had conspired to suppress information concerning the harmful aspects of smoking. The defendant tobacco company sought a protective order preventing public disclosure of the material obtained in discovery and also preventing plaintiff's attorneys from disseminating the evidence obtained to other plaintiffs bringing similar tort suits.

The district court, citing *Seattle Times,* held that a protective order of the kind sought by defendants would be violative of the First Amendment. The Third Circuit Court of Appeals reversed and remanded, holding that the appropriate standard was not a *Seattle Times* balancing test, but whether defendants had shown "good cause" under Rule 26(c). On remand, the district court held that "good cause" did not exist for a blanket confidentiality order, but did approve a procedure whereby defendants could make an initial good faith determination of confidentiality subject to challenge by plaintiffs. In a subsequent order, the district court also ruled that confidential documents produced in the case could be used in related litigation, including future cigarette liability cases.

Given the rulings in *Cippolone* and the number of tobacco suits that followed in its wake, it is easy to see why many of the documents supporting the existence of a tobacco conspiracy have become public. It is not uncommon, prior to or in connection with the settlement of certain types of litigation, for the opposing parties to agree to a protective order which prohibits dissemination of confidential discovery materials, requires that all such material be destroyed or returned to defendants at the termination of the litigation, and agrees to sealing the court records relating to that litigation. If such a case is settled, might the price paid to plaintiff in the settlement reflect the value to defendants of keeping the information quiet as well as the value of plaintiff's claim? Concern that agreements to seal court records and/or keep discovery documents confidential might be contrary to the public interest has led some states to regulate or prohibit such agreements. Consider the following rule, applicable to all trial courts in the State of New York, which became effective on March 1, 1991:

> Section 216.1. Sealing of court records. (a) Except where otherwise provided by statute or rule, a court shall not enter an order in any action or

proceeding sealing the court records, whether in whole or in part, except upon a written finding of good cause, which shall specify the grounds thereof. In determining whether good cause has been shown, the court shall consider the interests of the public as well as of the parties. Where it appears necessary or desirable, the court may prescribe appropriate notice and an opportunity to be heard.

Shaver v. Yacht Outward Bound

United States District Court, Northern District of Illinois, 1976.
71 F.R.D. 561.

■ Leighton, District Judge.

I

Plaintiff Libby A. Shaver, Administratrix of the Estate of Robert D. Shaver, brought this suit against defendants Thomas F. Erickson, Goldman, Sachs & Co., and a yacht, the Outward Bound, pursuant to the Jones Act, 46 U.S.C. § 688, to recover for the conscious suffering and death of her husband, Robert D. Shaver. The issue before the court, arising from a controversy concerning production of documents, is whether the 1971, 1972 and 1973 federal income tax returns of the defendant Erickson are subject to discovery even though his income is not an issue in the case.

II

Count I of the four-count complaint alleged that Shaver was a seaman, a crewmember of the yacht, Debit V (renamed Outward Bound) which was owned by the defendant Erickson; that, at the time in question, Shaver was in the employ of Erickson and Goldman, Sachs; that on or about July 28, 1973, the yacht Outward Bound was afloat on the navigable waters of the United States on Lake Michigan and was being used by Erickson in the pursuit of his business as an employee of Goldman, Sachs; that while Shaver was in the performance of his duties as a crewmember aboard the yacht, assisting in the navigation of the vessel, he fell overboard and drowned; and that his death was not due to his negligence or fault, but was due in whole or in part to the negligence or fault of defendants Erickson, Goldman, Sachs, their employees, agents and servants.

On similar allegations, Counts II and III sought recovery under general maritime law for a crewmember and invitee against Erickson and Goldman, Sachs. Count IV sought recovery against the yacht Outward Bound, her engines, appliances and tackle.

Defendants filed separate answers to these allegations. In his, Erickson denied negligence on his part and further denied that Shaver was a seaman, crewmember or an employee either of Erickson or of Goldman, Sachs on the yacht Outward Bound. Although Erickson's answer admitted he was a Goldman, Sachs employee, and that the incident occurred on the date and at the place alleged, it denied that at the time he was engaged in the pursuit of Goldman, Sachs' business or that the yacht was being used by him for or on behalf of his employer.

Erickson was deposed concerning his knowledge of the events that led to this lawsuit. In the course of the deposition he stated that he had, at times, used his yacht, the Outward Bound, for business purposes. The notice for his deposition requested that he produce his federal income tax returns for the years 1971, 1972 and 1973, but he refused to do so. Thereafter, plaintiff moved for an order compelling production contending that the returns will reveal the extent to which the vessel had been used in a business capacity and, therefore, are relevant and material to the question whether the Outward Bound was being used for a business purpose on the occasion when Shaver was drowned. Erickson opposed the motion by arguing that production of the returns should not be ordered because his income is not in issue and that the occasional use of his yacht for business purposes is not relevant to the question whether it was being used in a business capacity on the day in question, he having sworn by affidavit that it was not being so used.

III

Rule 26 of the Federal Rules of Civil Procedure provides, in pertinent part, that "[p]arties may obtain discovery regarding any matter, not privileged, which is relevant to the subject matter involved in the pending action, whether it relates to the claim or defense of the party seeking discovery or to the claim or defense of any other party * * *. It is not ground for objection that the information sought will be inadmissible at the trial if the information sought appears reasonably calculated to lead to the discovery of admissible evidence." Rule 26(b)(1), Fed.R.Civ.P. The scope of discovery contemplated by the rule is broad, but not unlimited. See Corbett v. Free Press Ass'n, 50 F.R.D. 179 (D.C.Vt.1970); De Long Corp. v. Lucas, 138 F.Supp. 805 (S.D.N.Y. 1956). The matter sought to be discovered cannot be privileged and must be relevant to the subject involved in the action, whether it relates to a claim or defense of either party. * * *

As a general rule, federal income tax returns are subject to discovery in civil suits where a litigant tenders an issue as to the amount of his income. This rule is consistent with the public policy against unnecessary disclosures in order to encourage the filing by taxpayers of complete and accurate returns. Premium Service Corp. v. Sperry & Hutchinson Co., 511 F.2d 225 (9th Cir.1975). Nevertheless, federal returns are not absolutely privileged from discovery.[1]

---

1. For example, it is clear that the federal statutory provisions concerning inspection of income tax returns by state bodies, commissions or officials only restrict dissemination of tax returns by the government and does not otherwise make copies of tax returns privileged. See 26 U.S.C. § 6103; Heathman v. U.S. District Court for Central District of California, 503 F.2d 1032 (9th Cir.1974); Karlsson v. Wolfson, 18 F.R.D. 474 (D.C.Minn.1956). At least two federal courts have held, based on a convincing analysis of the authorities, that income tax returns are not privileged at all. See Connecticut Importing Co. v. Continental Distilling Corp., 1 F.R.D. 190 (D.C.Conn.1940); Konczakowski v. Paramount Pictures, 19 F.R.D. 361 (S.D.N.Y.1956).

But it is recognized that because they always have some character of confidentiality, their production should not be routinely required. Troglione v. McIntyre Aviation, Inc., 60 F.R.D. 511 (W.D.Pa.1973); Wiesenberger v. W.E. Hutton & Co., 35 F.R.D. 556 (S.D.N.Y.1964). And despite this restricting principle, a showing of good cause for the production of a federal tax return is no longer required. * * *

Accordingly, federal courts have been cautious in ordering the disclosure of tax returns insisting, at the very least, that it reasonably appear they are relevant and material to the matters in issue. June v. George C. Peterson Co., 155 F.2d 963, 967 (7th Cir.1946). In most instances, it has been held that production of a tax return should not be ordered unless there appears to be a compelling need for the information it contains, such as is not otherwise readily obtainable. See Copper v. Hallgarten & Co., 34 F.R.D. 482, 484 (S.D.N.Y.1964.)

IV

In this case, Count I of the complaint is grounded on the Jones Act. That statute creates a cause of action which can be brought by the personal representative of a seaman injured or killed in the course of his maritime employment. 42 U.S.C. § 688. The count alleges, but Erickson's answer denies, that at the time in question he, as owner of the yacht Outward Bound, was using it in the pursuit of his business as an employee of Goldman, Sachs & Co. and that Shaver was employed as a seaman and crewmember aboard the vessel. Therefore, a critical question raised by Erickson's denials is whether at the time Shaver was drowned Erickson's yacht was being used for a business purpose on Goldman, Sachs' behalf, or for a pleasure voyage.

In this court's view, the extent to which the vessel had been used for business purposes, as may be revealed by the business deductions shown on the federal tax returns requested of Erickson, is relevant to the factual issue raised by his denials. Indeed, it may be the only source of this information available to the plaintiff. As a party to this lawsuit, Erickson ought not be permitted to raise an issue upon which his tax returns may cast significant light and then claim that his returns are not subject to disclosure. See Rubenstein v. Kleven, 21 F.R.D. 183 (D.C.Mass.1957.)

For these reasons, his federal income tax returns for the years 1971, 1972 and 1973 are subject to discovery under the circumstances presented by this case, even though his income is not directly in issue. See Hawes v. C.E. Cooke & Co., 64 F.R.D. 222 (W.D.Mich.1974); Lavin v. A.G. Becker & Co., Inc., 60 F.R.D. 684 (N.D.Ill.1973). It is not enough that he examine the contents of the returns and swear by affidavit to what they contain. See Merriman v. Cities Service Gas Co., 11 F.R.D. 584 (W.D.Mo.1951); Reeves v. Pennsylvania R. Co., 80 F.Supp. 107 (D.C.Del.1948). Therefore, an order will be entered ordering that Erickson produce the requested tax returns for plaintiff's inspection at the continued deposition.

QUESTION

Did the Court apply the standard for disclosure of tax returns it sets out in Section III of the opinion? Did it order disclosure on different grounds?

Al–Site Corp. v. VSI International, Inc.

United States District Court, Southern District of Florida, 1993.
842 F. Supp. 507.

■ ATKINS, DISTRICT JUDGE

On November 17, 1992, Al–Site filed a Motion Seeking an Order Compelling Defendants to Respond to Certain Document Requests. Al–Site now appeals the portion of the Magistrate's order denying production of defendants' financial and tax records.

Al–Site contends that these materials are essential to prove punitive damages for its second cause of action arising under the Florida common law of unfair competition. While this contention may be accurate, Fla. Stat. Ch. 768.72 (1992) sets out certain conditions which must be met before a claimant may plead a claim for punitive damages. The statute provides:

> In any civil action, no claim for punitive damages shall be permitted unless there is a reasonable showing by evidence in the record or proffered by the claimant which would provide a reasonable basis for recovery of such damages. The claimant may move to amend his complaint to assert a claim for punitive damages as allowed by the rules of civil procedure. The rules of civil procedure shall be liberally construed so as to allow the claimant discovery of evidence which appears reasonably calculated to lead to admissible evidence on the issue of punitive damages. No discovery of financial worth shall proceed until after the pleading concerning punitive damages is permitted.

Fla. Stat. Ch. 768.72 (1992).

Therefore, if federal district courts must apply the Florida statute, the claimant must first show that evidence exists to support recovery of punitive damages before the trial court will allow a request for such damages. Similarly, no discovery of financial worth can be made without a comparable showing. *Wisconsin Invest. Bd. v. Plantation Square Assoc., Ltd.*, 761 F. Supp. 1569, 157681 (S.D.Fla.1991).

After an extensive analysis, this Court concludes that all of Fla. Stat. Ch. 768.72 must be applied here. This Court agrees with the court in Plantation Square, concluding that there are two elements to § 768.72: a pleading element and a discovery element. However, the two elements cannot be separated from each other as *Plantation Square* urges.

Plantation Square provides an extensive analysis of the Erie doctrine and its progeny, including *Guaranty Trust Co. v. York*, 326 U.S. 99, 89 L. Ed. 2079, 65 S. Ct. 1464 (1945), *Byrd v. Blue Ridge Rural Electric Co-op*, 356 U.S. 525, 2 L. Ed. 2d 953, 78 S. Ct. 893

(1958), and *Hanna v. Plumer*, 380 U.S. 460, 14 L. Ed. 2d 8, 85 S. Ct. 1136 (1965), to arrive at the conclusion "that § 768.72 is both a pleading rule and a discovery rule." 761 F. Supp. at 1572. The Court agrees with *Plantation Square's* conclusion and defers to that reasoning.

1. Discovery Aspect

This Court also agrees with *Plantation Square's* conclusion that federal courts must give effect to the discovery provision of Fla. Stat. Ch. 768.72. In brief, the court concluded that there is no conflict between § 768.72 and Federal Rule of Civil Procedure 26. The analysis continued under the twin aims of Erie: forum shopping and preventing a change of the character or result of the litigation. *Hanna*, 380 U.S. at 468. Under this analysis, if one of the aims was violated, then the court must apply the statute as substantive law. The *Plantation Square* court applied the discovery aspects of § 768.72 as substantive law because to do otherwise would lead to forum shopping.

a. Federal/State Conflict

Looking to the first test under *Hanna*, we must determine whether direct conflict exists between the Federal Rules of Civil Procedure and Florida's state law. The only potential conflicts exist between § 768.72 and Fed. R. Civ. P. 8 and 9. The Court will address each in inverse order.

First, Fed. R. Civ. P. 9(g) requires that "when items of special damage are claimed, they shall be specifically stated." There is no conflict between this rule and § 768.72 simply because the rule is silent with respect to the time in which items may be pled in the complaint. *Plantation Square*, 761 F. Supp. at 1574.

Neither does § 768.72 directly conflict with Fed. R. Civ. P. 8. Specifically, Rule 8(a)(2) requires that the pleading contain "a short and plain statement of the claim showing that the pleader is entitled to relief." On its face, section 768.72 does not affect the contents of the pleading. The Florida law merely requires the pleader to make a showing of specific facts before the court. If the court determines that a claimant has made a reasonable showing of evidence which would provide a reasonable basis for recovery of punitive damages, then the claimant would be granted leave to amend the complaint. See § 768.72. The amended pleading need only contain a "short and plain statement" showing that pleader is entitled to punitive damages.

b. Dual Aims of *Erie*

Since the first *Hanna* conflict requirement is not met, the court must proceed to the dual goals of *Erie*. *Hanna*, 380 U.S. at 468. *Erie* requires the Court to look at whether ignoring the state statute could lead to a significant change in the "character or result of the litigation" so as to "unfairly discriminate against citizens of the forum state" or to cause the plaintiff to prefer one forum over the other. *Hanna*, 380 U.S. at 468 n.9.

Recently, the Supreme Court of the United States adopted amendments to the Federal Rules of Civil Procedure pursuant to 28 U.S.C. § 2072. These amendments took effect on December 1, 1993, and govern all proceedings in civil cases, both newly commenced and pending.

These changes affect the forum shopping analysis presented in past cases and require a different result. Specifically, the Court amended the General Provisions Governing Discovery, Fed. R. Civ. P. 26.

* * *

As the committee notes describe, this subdivision imposes on parties a duty to disclose, without awaiting formal discovery requests, certain basic information that is needed in most cases to prepare for trial or make an informed decision about settlement. The rule requires all parties . . . early in the case to exchange information regarding potential witnesses, documentary evidence, damages, and insurance. . . .

Many litigants may interpret newly amended Rule 26 in a way to prematurely force production of financial information. In a Florida state court, punitive damages discovery would not be allowed prior to the evidentiary hearing described in § 768.72 under any circumstances. Under the new Rule 26, the opposite occurs—parties must immediately produce such information "without awaiting a discovery request." Fed. R. Civ. P. 26.

If the Court did not impose all of § 768.72's provisions, Florida plaintiffs may prefer federal courts over state courts; federal pleadings would be able to contain claims for punitive damages prior to hearings and judicial acceptance while state pleadings would not. Under this scenario, a claimant alleging a small punitive damages claim could obtain immediate access to "otherwise protected financial records" or use the threat of this discovery as an "unearned bargaining chip." *Plantation Square*, 761 F. Supp. at 157980. This forum shopping problem is the precise practice *Hanna* intended to restrain.

By its terms, Section 768.72 creates a substantive right not to be subjected to discovery without a "reasonable basis for recovery of [punitive] damages." The right is likewise demonstrated by the mandate that "no discovery of financial worth shall proceed until after the pleading concerning punitive damages is permitted." Fla. Stat. Ch. 768.72. Thus, discovery cannot occur without a successful hearing on amending the pleading. Under the confines of *Erie*, § 768.72 must be applied as substantive law.

South Florida Blood Serv. Inc. v. Rasmussen

District Court of Appeal of Florida, Third District, 1985.
467 So.2d 798.

■ NESBITT, JUDGE.

South Florida Blood Service, Inc. (SFBS) seeks review, by way of a petition for certiorari, of an order requiring it to produce the names and addresses of fifty-one volunteer blood donors. We grant the petition and quash the order under review.[1]

Donald Rasmussen has sued William DeLoatche and Leonel Levia Monterroso for personal injuries sustained when struck by a motor vehicle allegedly owned and operated by the defendants. It is that litigation which has led to the issue we must resolve.[2]

Rasmussen, while hospitalized because of the injuries he sustained in the accident, received fifty-one units of blood. He was subsequently diagnosed as having acquired immune deficiency syndrome (AIDS). Based on that diagnosis, and the opinion of a physician that the AIDS resulted from the transfusions received while hospitalized, Rasmussen served a subpoena duces tecum on SFBS. The subpoena sought "any and all records, documents and other material indicating the names and addresses of the blood donors identified on the attached records of St. Francis Hospital regarding the plaintiff herein, Donald Rasmussen."

SFBS, not a party to the lawsuit, moved to quash the subpoena or for a protective order on the grounds that Rasmussen had failed to show good cause or justifiable reason for the invasion of the private and confidential records of the blood service and its volunteer donors. The motion was denied and SFBS was ordered to produce the requested material.

AIDS

The 1980's have seen the emergence of a new and deadly disease, acquired immune deficiency syndrome or, as it is more commonly referred to, AIDS. The disease is characterized by an improperly functioning immune system which results in a lack of the normal body defense mechanisms and leaves the victim vulnerable to a wide variety of opportunistic diseases. Johnson, *AIDS*, 52 Medico–Legal Journal 3 (1984). At present, there is no known cause or cure and the mortality rate is high.[3]

Medical researchers have identified a number of groups which have a high incidence of the disease and are labeled "high risk" groups. The overwhelming percentage of AIDS victims are homosexual or bisexual males with multiple sexual partners (72%) and intravenous drug users (17%).[4]

1. A petition for certiorari is an appropriate vehicle for challenging the correctness of an order denying protection from discovery. East Colonial Refuse Services, Inc. v. Velocci, 416 So.2d 1276 (Fla. 5th DCA 1982).

2. Rasmussen died on June 11, 1984 and a suggestion of death was filed on June 12, 1984. To our knowledge, a personal representative has not yet been appointed. Consequently, Rasmussen's name is used throughout the opinion to describe the party seeking discovery.

3. The mortality rate may be as high as forty per cent (40%). Blodgert, *Despite the public's hands-off attitude towards AIDS, those who discriminate against the disease's victims are finding no immunity from the law*, 12 Student Law. 8 (Jan.1984).

4. Other high risk groups are hemophiliacs (1%), heterosexual partners of AIDS vic-

The public has reacted to the disease with hysteria. Reported accounts indicate that victims of AIDS have been faced with social censure, embarrassment and discrimination in nearly every phase of their lives, including jobs, education and housing.[5] It is with the above facts in mind that we analyze the respective interests in this case.

DISCOVERY

Florida Rule of Civil Procedure 1.280 allows for discovery of any matter, not privileged, that is relevant to the subject matter of the action. The scope of this rule, while recognized as being broad, Argonaut Insurance Co. v. Peralta, 358 So.2d 232 (Fla. 3d DCA), *cert. denied,* 364 So.2d 889 (Fla.1978), is not without limitation. First, as the rule indicates, irrelevant and privileged matter is not subject to discovery. Fla.R.Civ.P. 1.280(b)(1). *See also* East Colonial Refuse Service, Inc. v. Velocci, 416 So.2d 1276 (Fla. 5th DCA 1982); Malt v. Simmons, 405 So.2d 1018 (Fla. 4th DCA 1981). Second, the discovery of relevant, nonprivileged information may be limited or prohibited in order to prevent annoyance, embarrassment, oppression or undue burden of expense. Fla.R.Civ.P. 1.280(c); 1.410(b), (d)(1); Dade County Medical Association v. Hlis, 372 So.2d 117, 121 (Fla. 3d DCA 1979). We are dealing in this case only with this second limitation on discovery.

The discovery rules, enunciated pursuant to the supreme court's rule making authority under article V, section 2(a) of the Florida Constitution, grant courts authority to control discovery in all aspects in order to prevent harassment and undue invasion of privacy. Springer v. Greer, 341 So.2d 212, 214 (Fla. 4th DCA 1976), *appeal dismissed,* 351 So.2d 406 (Fla.1977). If a person seeking to prevent discovery establishes good cause, then a court may make any order necessary to protect the interests set out in the rules. In deciding whether good cause has been shown it is necessary to balance the competing interests that would be served by the granting or denying of discovery. * * *

Rasmussen's Interest

Rasmussen claims a need for the disputed information in order to adequately prove aggravation of his injuries and allow for full recovery. In other words, damages can be recovered for Rasmussen's death if it can be shown that the AIDS which resulted in his death was caused by the blood transfusions which were necessitated by the injuries he suffered in the accident. While this is a legitimate interest, its weight is mitigated because there is no indication that the discovery of the donors' names and addresses will add significantly to the proof

tims (1%), and blood transfusion recipients (1%). Centers for Disease Control, United States Public Health Service, *Morbidity and Mortality Weekly Report* (June 22, 1984) at 1–2.

5. *See, e.g.,* Flaherty, *A Legal Emergency Brewing Over AIDS,* Nat'l. L.J. July 9, 1984, at 1, col. 3; Pagano, *Quarantine Considered for AIDS Victims,* 4 Cal.Law. 17 (March 1984); Blodgert, *supra,* n. 3; Reaves, *AIDS and the Law,* 69 ABAJ 1014 (Aug. 1983).

of causation.[6] First, none of the fift-yone donors has been identified as an AIDS victim.[7] Second, even if discovery revealed that some of the donors are in high risk groups, that would not establish that any one of them has AIDS, much less that they transmitted it through a transfusion. Since the probative value of the evidence which might be discovered is questionable, Rasmussen's interest in the information is slight when compared with the opposing interests which we now discuss.

The Privacy Interests of the Donors

SFBS and the Council of Community Blood Centers (CCBC), as amicus curiae, argue that the donors' privacy rights are constitutionally based. *See e.g.,* City of Alcron v. Alcron Center for Reproductive Health, Inc., 462 U.S. 416, 105 S.Ct. 2481, 76 L.Ed.2d 687 (1983), Roe v. Wade, 410 U.S. 113, 93 S.Ct. 705, 35 L.Ed.2d 147 (1973); Griswold v. Connecticut, 381 U.S. 479, 85 S.Ct. 1678, 14 L.Ed.2d 510 (1965). See also, art I, § 23, Fla. Const.[8] We must decide whether a constitutionally protected privacy interest is at stake and, if so, whether that interest impacts on the discovery rules or court orders made pursuant to those rules.

There are two recognized zones of privacy. The first, the decision-making or autonomy zone of privacy interests, requires application of a compelling state interest test. That zone of privacy, however, is limited to decisionmaking interests in highly personal matters such as marriage, procreation, contraception, family relationships and education. Paul v. Davis, 424 U.S. 693, 96 S.Ct. 1155, 47 L.Ed.2d 405 (1976); Roe v. Wade; Shevin v. Byron, Harless, Schaffer, Reid & Associates, 379 So.2d 633 (Fla.1980). Such a privacy interest is not at issue in this case.

The second zone of privacy encompasses the interest in avoiding disclosure of personal matters. This is essentially an interest in confidentiality. It is evident Rasmussen needs more than just the names and addresses of the donors. His interest is in establishing that one or more of the donors has AIDS or is in a high risk group. Because the groups at highest risk are homosexuals, bisexuals, intravenous drug users and hemophiliacs, it is obvious that Rasmussen would have to probe into the most intimate details of the donors' lives, including their sexual practices, drug use and medical histories. Both the courts and the legislature have recognized these areas as sanctuaries of privacy entitled to protection. See Priest v. Rotary, 98 F.R.D. 755

---

6. It should be noted that Rasmussen already has the testimony of Dr. Kenneth Ratzen, Chief of The Division of Infectious Diseases at Mt. Sinai Medical Center, to the effect that "in all medical probability the cause of Mr. Rasmussen's AIDS was due to the multiple blood transfusions he received at St. Francis."

7. SFBS made this determination by checking the donors' names against the Dade County Health Services' list of AIDS victims.

8. SECTION 23. Right of privacy.—Every natural person has the right to be let alone and free from governmental intrusion into his private life except as otherwise provided herein. This section shall not be construed to limit the public's right of access to public records and meetings as provided by law.

(N.D.Cal.1983) (discovery of plaintiff's sexual history prohibited); Lampshire v. Procter & Gamble Co., 94 F.R.D. 58 (N.D.Ga.1982) (identity of subjects of a Centers for Disease Control study entitled to protection where the study contained information about medical history, personal hygiene, menstrual flow, sexual activity, contraceptive methods, pregnancies, douching and tampon use); *Argonaut Insurance Co.* (medical records of strangers to the suit entitled to protection); *Springer* (identity of nonparty patients entitled to protection in discovery of pharmacist's records). *See also* §§ 397.053, .096, 455.241(2), Fla.Stat. (1983) (legislative recognition of the confidentiality of drug abuse treatment and medical patient records). Certainly these fifty-one donors did not anticipate, when they altruistically donated blood, that some future litigant would intrude into these most personal aspects of their lives. Such probing by strangers into these areas of one's life is itself an invasion of privacy entitled to consideration. *Plante,* 575 F.2d at 1135.

It is also necessary to take into account the ramifications of possible disclosure to persons outside the litigation. The articles cited in note 5 demonstrate that AIDS is the modern day equivalent of leprosy. AIDS, or a suspicion of AIDS, can lead to discrimination in employment, education, housing and even medical treatment. If the donors' names were disclosed outside the litigation, they would be subject to this discrimination and embarrassment, even though most, if not all of the donors, would not be AIDS victims in fact, but only innocent suspected victims. It cannot be doubted that the donors have a strong interest in remaining free from both the intrusion of litigants into their private lives and the oppressive effects of possible disclosure outside the litigation. This interest is protected by the state and federal constitutions and falls within the disclosural privacy zone we previously identified.[9]

Having determined that the interests at stake are constitutionally based, we must analyze how these privacy rights relate to the discovery rules and orders issued pursuant to those rules. Court orders which compel, restrict or prohibit discovery constitute state action which is subject to constitutional limitations. Seattle Times Co. v. Rhinehart, 467 U.S. 20, 104 S.Ct. 2199, 81 L.Ed.2d 17 (1984) (subjecting a protective order to first amendment scrutiny and affirming Rhinehart v. Seattle Times Co., 98 Wash.2d 226, 654 P.2d 673 (1982), which affirmed a protective order granted on the ground that the discovery sought would infringe on constitutionally protected rights of privacy, religion and association); Calderbank v. Cazares, 435 So.2d 377, 379 (Fla. 5th DCA 1983). Therefore, an order allowing or compelling

9. Rasmussen argues that allowing the discovery would discourage those with AIDS or those in high risk groups from donating blood. That is unquestionably true. There are two problems, however, with the contention. First, the effect of disclosure will extend beyond the desired end because persons without AIDS and not in high risk groups will also be discouraged from donating. Second, the discovery rules were not designed to achieve such goals, but to fairly and reasonably aid the litigation process. It is for other agencies of government to act in detecting and preventing the spread of infectious diseases. *See, e.g.,* § 20.19(1)(g), Fla.Stat. (1983).

discovery could impinge on the constitutionally protected right to disclosural privacy.

In analyzing this particular privacy interest courts have applied a balancing test, comparing the interests served by the state action with the interests encroached upon by that action. Nixon v. Administrator of General Services, 433 U.S. 425, 97 S.Ct. 2777, 53 L.Ed.2d 867 (1977); Whalen v. Roe; Florida Board of Bar Examiners. In determining whether such an order is appropriate, the trial courts should balance the interests served by the rules of discovery against the interests of the party seeking protection. The discovery rules are designed to advance the state's interest in the fair and efficient resolution of disputes.[10] The more relevant and necessary the desired information is to a resolution of the case, the greater the state's interest in allowing discovery of the information. When possible, however, orders should be fashioned to minimize the impact on the competing interests. *See, e.g., Rhinehart,* 654 P.2d at 675, 690–91 (the discovery was allowed, thereby promoting the dispute resolution interest, but disclosure outside the litigation was prohibited in order to protect privacy interests).

This balancing test parallels the balancing test the courts have traditionally performed in good cause determinations under Rule 1.280(c). We find no infirmity in the fact that the rule places the burden of establishing good cause on the party seeking protection of a constitutional privacy right. The state's interest in fair and efficient resolution of disputes is great enough to justify a liberal discovery policy. The rule adequately accommodates privacy interests by providing for protection on a showing of good cause by the person whose privacy interest is at stake. Our decision today merely establishes that the state and federal constitutions are sources of privacy interests which must be scrutinized when raised in challenge of a discovery order.

Because we find that a balancing test, which is already utilized under Rule 1.280(c), is the appropriate standard to employ in deciding disclosural privacy claims, such a result will not unnecessarily or unreasonably impede the discovery process. Additionally, with regard to the state constitutional privacy provision, our interpretation is consistent with the language of section 23, which prohibits governmental intrusion into private lives and which was approved by the electors of this state.

The Institutional and Societal Interests

The institutional and public interests at stake are so interconnected that they are discussed together. SFBS, along with twenty-six other regional blood centers, is a member of the Council of Community Blood Centers (CCBC). CCBC is a national association which, together with the American Red Cross and the American Association of Blood

---

10. The value we place on our dispute resolution system is evidenced by article I, section 21 of the Florida Constitution which guarantees that "[t]he courts shall be open to every person for redress of any injury, * * *."

Banks, bears the responsibility for the nation's blood service system. One of the preeminent goals of these associations is to ensure the safety and adequacy of the nation's blood supply. An important means of attaining that goal is the promotion of an all-voluntary blood donation system. Such a voluntary system is encouraged by both the federal and state governments, *see* National Blood Policy, 39 Fed.Reg. 32701 (Sept. 10, 1974); § 381.601(3)(c), (4), Fla.Stat. (1983), because the blood of volunteer donors is less likely to be contaminated with infectious diseases than that of paid donors. National Blood Policy, 39 Fed.Reg. at 32702. SFBS and CCBC claim that confidentiality of blood service records is essential if they are to maintain a voluntary blood donation system which can meet the demands of society for blood and blood products, which task they are already experiencing difficulty in accomplishing.[11]

It cannot be questioned that the interests of these organizations are the interests of society as well. An all-volunteer blood donation system should be encouraged in order to maintain the life and health of individual members of society and, thus, society as a whole. As a corollary, it is in the public interest to discourage any serious disincentive to voluntary blood donation such as an intrusive probe into the most intimate details of one's life.[12] The public interest can be a sufficient reason for prohibiting the discovery of particular information. Numerous courts have found the interest in the free flow of information, ideas and advice sufficient to overcome the interest in the discovery of the reports of investigating committees and researchers. *See, e.g.,* Andrews v. Eli Lilly & Co., 97 F.R.D. 494 (N.D.Ill.1983) (quashing in part a subpoena seeking the records of a research repository); *Lampshire* (protecting the identity of research subjects); *Richards of Rockford, Inc.* (motion to compel disclosure of research information denied); *Hlis* (prohibiting discovery of a medical review committee report), and cases cited therein, 372 So.2d at 120; Head v. Colloton, 331 N.W.2d 870, 876 (Iowa 1983) (prohibiting disclosure of the identity of a potential bone marrow donor on statutory grounds, but noting the "possible chilling effect of disclosure upon medical research"). We likewise find the free flow of donated blood of sufficient public importance, when combined with the privacy interests of the donors in this AIDS-related litigation, to outweigh Rasmussen's interest in discovering the names and addresses.

11. SFBS argues that Florida Administrative Code Rules 10D–41.22, .34(5)(c) make the donors' names and addresses confidential. While we decline to hold that the rules make blood donors' names and addresses confidential for all purposes, we at least find support for the result we reach in the Department of Health and Rehabilitative Services' decision to make the reports of examinations of donors blood specimens confidential. It is indicative of society's and the government's desire to prevent the unwarranted intrusion of privacy interests.

12. The concern of the writer as to footnote 4 in Judge Schwartz' dissent is that it rests upon an assumption that a test has been devised which completely eliminates the possibility of a blood bank accepting a donation from anyone contaminated with AIDS. Until such an event occurs, the possibility of discouraging volunteer blood donors remains real and substantial. When such a test is developed, the time for revisiting this issue, if it is presented to the court, will have arrived.

We conclude by emphasizing that we are not deciding that a blood bank's records are immune from discovery in all cases. We are merely holding that on the facts of this case, after balancing all of the interests involved, the requested material should not be discovered. The complete denial of discovery is necessary to ensure the protection of both the donors' privacy interests and society's interest in a strong and healthy volunteer blood donation program.

Since the order denying SFBS' motion for protection from discovery was a departure from the essential requirements of law from which there is no adequate remedy by appeal, certiorari is granted and the order is quashed.[13]

■ SCHWARTZ, CHIEF JUDGE (dissenting).

Judge Nesbitt's opinion is carefully considered and well-crafted, but I profoundly disagree with both its general approach and its conclusion. While it is of course accurate to say that the present discovery controversy, like almost every other, is properly resolved by balancing the "competing interests to be served by granting discovery or by denying it," Dade County Medical Association v. Hlis, 372 So.2d 117, 121 (Fla. 3d DCA 1979); North Miami General Hospital v. Royal Palm Beach Colony, Inc., 397 So.2d 1033 (Fla. 3d DCA 1981), I think the court's opinion has put its thumb on the scale.

I

Treating first the *plaintiff's* interest in securing the information in question, it must be emphasized—although the court does not mention the fact—that the defendant below, apparently on the ground that Rasmussen may himself have been a member of a "high risk" group, severely contests the fact that he acquired AIDS in the blood transfusion process. Thus, far from a matter of purely tangential concern as in the cases cited supra, it is of absolute necessity to his and his survivors' right and ability to recover that they secure information that one or more of the donors is suffering from or is a potential carrier of the lethal affliction.[1]

II

On the other side of the balancing process, the court first places the so-called privacy interests of the individual blood donors. In doing so, it overlooks that the order before us requires only the revelation,

13. Because we find the issue presented to be of great public importance, we certify the following question to the Supreme Court of Florida, as provided for in article V, section 3(b)(4) of the Constitution of the State of Florida:

Do the privacy interests of volunteer blood donors and a blood service's and society's interest in maintaining a strong volunteer blood donation-system outweigh a plaintiff's interest in discovering the names and addresses of the blood donors in the hope that further discovery will provide some evidence that he contracted AIDS from transfusions necessitated by injuries which are the subject of his suit?

1. The fact that the petitioner has stated that none of the fifty-one is now suffering from AIDS is plainly insufficient. (In fact, without more, that representation unfairly weighs against Rasmussen's interests in proving his claim.) This is true both because the statement is a unilateral one which the plaintiff has no means of testing and because, we are told, one need not himself have developed the disease in order to transmit it.

within the litigation[2] of nothing more than the names and addresses of the donors—a subject as to which there is no statutory privilege, see Marshall v. Anderson, 459 So.2d 384 (Fla. 3d DCA 1984), no constitutional one of which I am aware, and no actual or practical one. Indeed, the donors have in fact already obviously revealed their identities to the blood bank—which, if it were concerned with the total anonymity of its donors, would not have even taken this information from them. Beyond this, I can think of no reason why the fifty-one persons would have any objection whatsoever to Rasmussen's relatives merely having their names—if they are not within one of the risk groups, a fact which would likely immediately become obvious to the plaintiff's lawyer without further inquiry or intrusion of any kind. If they *are* within such a group, or if they are otherwise presently or potentially AIDS carriers or victims, I should think both that they themselves would want to know about that and, more important, that their "right to privacy" must take second place to revealing and paying the price for the immense harm they may have done. None of the monstrous effects of the order below contemplated by the majority has actually occurred, and none may ever occur. If one should come to pass—that is, an unjustified or publicly revealed probe into the intimate details of the personal or sexual life of any donor, it will be time enough for the court to intervene. It is overkill of the worst kind, it seems to me, to cut the plaintiff off from any meaningful discovery to prevent a presently non-existent abuse of a dubious and non-asserted personal right.

The court's other ground for the decision to deny discovery—its perception that it promotes "institutional and societal interests" of which it approves—is, in my judgment, based on a combination of a sense of judicial self-importance and self-aggrandizement at the expense of the legislature on the one hand, and the presentation of a parade, indeed, a carnival of horribles on the other. It is that discovery of the fifty-one names will interfere with, perhaps destroy, the free flow of donated blood in our society. I can accept none of the premises upon which this prong of the court's opinion is based.

First, I believe it highly unlikely that our holding that the relatives of a deceased AIDS victim who have made a strong showing that he acquired the disease from a transfusion may learn the identities of those who gave him blood would even become known to potential donors, let alone adversely affect their decision to do so. Moreover, even if we take upon ourselves the task of answering the threshold question of whether encouraging voluntary blood donations is a good idea as a matter of public policy, but see 10 Fla.Jur.2d Constitutional Law § 147 (1979),[3] I do not understand upon what information the court relies in concluding that the denial of discovery here will promote that end in any way. If I had to speculate about it—and the

---

2. No public release even of the names is involved.

3. Ironically, one of the things which might be said against this policy is today's decision; the maintenance of the secrecy of donors' identity, which the majority says is required to preserve the system, but which operates to the serious disadvantage of those who are damaged by the system, may be too great a price to pay.

court's having done so makes it necessary to respond in kind—I would say that no one not in a risk group would be likely to have any hesitancy in giving blood no matter what we do in this case.[4] And, as I have already indicated, if those who *are* at risk are discouraged by the potential of the revelation of their names—when their blood causes AIDS—that is, I would have thought, a consummation devoutly to be wished.[5] With respect, I believe that the majority has no basis for disputing my analysis or to support its contrary prediction. As a matter of the inherent limitations of the institution, a court ought not, as has the majority, base a decision concerning the rights of those who come before it upon the supposed pragmatic consequences of that ruling when there is neither evidence in the record—nor means of acquiring it—as to what those results may be. All in all, Dean, later Judge, Goodrich might have been describing the majority opinion when he pointed out more than fifty years ago that

> Judges have laid down rules on the basis of public policy without the slightest support for the policy except preconceived opinion, and without either knowing or having means of knowing whether the policy declared was or was not aided by the particular decision rendered.

Goodrich, The Improvement of the Law, 4 Temp.L.Q. 311, 324–25 (1930).

III

However the "interests" advanced by the court may be character-ized—and I believe they are chimerical and hypothetical at best—they fade into total insignificance in the face of the rights of a blood donee to be free of AIDS and those of his survivors to recovery under the law when that horrendous result has in fact occurred. Because of the notion, founded solely upon its own unsupported suppositions about human conduct, that to do so will promote a policy which it alone has

4. Indeed, if the reported development of a blood test which reveals the presence of the AIDS virus is accurate and the use of such blood is thereby precluded, no future donor will ever acquire AIDS and no future donor will therefore ever have reason to be discouraged from giving by the court-created fear of what might happen in discovery if, as perhaps occurred here, that does take place. Thus, the court's denial of established rights to Rasmussen may well be for absolutely nothing. In any case, the essential point is that the determination of whether it is is not for this or any other court to make.

5. In answer, the court says at note 9:

Rasmussen argues that allowing the discovery would discourage those with AIDS or those in high risk groups from donating blood. That is unquestionably true. There are two problems, however, with the contention. First, the effect of disclosure will extend beyond the desired end because persons without AIDS and not in high risk groups will

also be discouraged from donating. Second, the discovery rules were not designed to achieve such goals, but to fairly and reasonably aid the litigation process. It is for other agencies of government to act in detecting and preventing the spread of infectious diseases. *See, e.g.,* § 20.19(1)(g), Fla.Stat. (1983).

Concerning the first response, the court does not know—and common sense indicates otherwise—that a non-high risk person will be discouraged from giving blood. The second response leaves me completely non-plussed. The majority seems not to recognize that the entire basis of its decision is not the forwarding of the litigation between Rasmussen and the tortfeasor, but, to the complete contrary, the vindication, by means the effect of which is dubious at best, of the voluntary system of blood donation. I entirely agree that this is not our business.

devised, the majority has seen fit to deny the ordinary discovery processes clearly provided in the rules to one who has done nothing but acquire AIDS and die. While we surely have the power to take that course, I do not think we have the right. I think the petition should be denied.[6a]

NOTES

A. Who do you think has the better of the argument, the majority or dissent?

B. Is the dissent right (at fn 4) that a blood test for donated blood will solve this problem?

C. In Belle Bonfils Memorial Blood Center v. District Court, 763 P.2d 1003 (Colo.1988), the court was faced with determining the permissible scope of discovery in a negligence action brought against a blood supplier by a hospital patient who tested positive for the HIV virus after being given blood supplied by the defendant. The blood in question had been obtained from an infected donor, allegedly as a result of the supplier's failure to follow its own screening procedures.

A sharply divided Colorado Supreme Court found (1) that there was a substantial need to interrogate the donor with respect to the details of the actions of defendant's technicians, particularly in view of ambiguities with respect to the donor's response to a screening questionnaire, and (2) that this information could be obtained by deposition on written questions (cf. FRCP 31) conducted through the clerk of the court without revealing the identity of the donor to the litigants.

Not all balancing is done judicially. Shortly before the decision in this case, the Colorado legislature created a privilege that would have precluded the discovery sought by plaintiff. That statute, relied upon by the dissent in *Belle Bonfils,* was held inapplicable by the majority because of its effective date.

Some opinions in this area are written broadly, with the sweep which large issues of public policy command; some are written narrowly focusing on factual detail. Thus *Belle Bonfils* is distinguished in *Doe v. American Red Cross Blood Services,* 125 F.R.D. 637 (D.S.C.1989) on the basis of the number of disqualifying responses on the questionnaire filled out by the donor.

D. The Florida legislature seems to have codified the result in *South Florida Blood Service.* A court order may be issued to disclose the identity of the person who has undergone a test for the HIV virus or the results of such a test only if the person seeking the results demonstrates a compelling need that cannot be accommodated by other means. Fla. Stat. Ch. 381.004(f) (1993). In assessing the compelling need, the statute requires the court to weigh the need for disclosure against the privacy interest of the test subject and the public interest that may be disserved by disclosure. The statute also provides that any pleadings which pertain to the disclosure of the results of such a test shall use a pseudonym in place of the true name of the test subject.

---

6. While I agree that the issue in this case is of great public importance and should be certified as such to the supreme court, I would prefer that the question be less argumentatively phrased than the one framed at note 12 of the majority opinion. I would propose the following, nonleading question:

Whether a plaintiff who presents a colorable claim that he acquired AIDS through blood transfusions required by treatment of injuries sustained in an accident may discover the names and addresses of the blood donors in an action against the party allegedly liable for the accident?

a. Affirmed by unanimous court, 500 S.2d 533 (Fla.1987).

The Florida legislature made findings that "the public health will be served by facilitating ... confidential use of tests designed to detect human immunodeficiency virus infection" and that "many members of the public are deterred from seeking [tests for the AIDS virus] because they ... fear that the test results will be disclosed without their consent." Fla. Stat. Ch. 381.004 (1993).

E. In *Sampson v. American National Red Cross*, 139 F.R.D. 95 (N.D.Tex. 1991), the court, considering a situation similar to that in *Belle Bonfils*, held that the infected donor's name should be revealed only to plaintiffs' counsel and experts on the issue of negligence, and that any documents containing the donor's name should be filed under seal. The opinion criticized the holdings in *South Florida Blood Service* and *Doe v. American Red Cross* that the public's interest in maintaining the blood supply outweighed plaintiffs' interest in identifying potential witnesses. These opinions were deficient, the *Sampson* court wrote, because they failed to cite data proving that identifying blood donors would deter blood donation.

(b) LIMITATIONS BASED ON CONSIDERATIONS OF COST

Clem v. Allied Van Lines

United States District Court, Southern District of New York, 1984.
102 F.R.D. 938.

■ KRAM, DISTRICT JUDGE.

The above-captioned action is before the Court upon plaintiff's motion, pursuant to Fed.R.Civ.P. 30(b)(7), for an order directing that his deposition be taken telephonically. For the reasons stated below, the motion is denied.

BACKGROUND

Clem is an American citizen stationed abroad in the course of his employment with Merrill Lynch International Incorporated. In August, 1978, Clem contracted with Allied Van Lines International Corporation ("Allied") for the transportation of certain of his household goods and personal effects from his home in Scottsdale, Arizona, to his foreign location of employment, then Tehran, Iran.

Allied received the items and commenced its transportation of them to Tehran. The state of affairs in Iran in late 1978 and early 1979, was, to say the least, turbulent. Clem was transferred from Tehran to Dubai, United Arab Emirates. In or about January, 1979, while Clem's goods were at the Port of Khorramshahr, Iran, Clem requested that the delivery be made to Dubai instead of Tehran. Sometime thereafter, the goods were apparently lost.

Clem commenced this action to recover compensation for his lost goods, valued by him at, at least, $119,600, and to recover the payment made for shipment, $12,383.30.

During the course of discovery, Allied served a Notice of Deposition upon Clem, scheduling his deposition for May 24, 1984, at the offices of Allied's attorneys in New York. Two days before his scheduled appearance, Clem filed the within motion requesting that his deposition be taken telephonically.

DISCUSSION

Plaintiff's motion is made pursuant to Rule 30(b)(7)[1] of the Federal Rules of Civil Procedure, which provides, in relevant part, that "the court may upon motion order that a deposition be taken by telephone." Plaintiff, however, relies on the general discovery provisions contained in Rule 26.

Rule 26 provides, in relevant part, as follows:

[(b)(1)] [t]he frequency or extent of use of the discovery methods * * * shall be limited by the court if it determines that * * * the discovery is unduly burdensome or expensive, taking into account the needs of the case, the amount in controversy, limitations on the parties' resources, and the importance of the issues at stake in the litigation.

* * *

[(c)] the court * * * may make any order which justice requires to protect a party or person from annoyance, embarrassment, oppression, or undue burden or expense, including one or more of the following: * * * (2) that the discovery may be had only on specified terms and conditions, including a designation of the time or place; (3) that the discovery may be had only by a method of discovery other than that selected by the party seeking discovery.

In addressing motions for protective orders pursuant to Rule 26(c), this Court has long enunciated the policy of requiring a nonresident plaintiff who chooses this district as his forum to appear for deposition in this forum absent compelling circumstances.

Plaintiff fails to cite a single case under Rule 30(b)(7) wherein the plaintiff was permitted to have his deposition taken telephonically.[2] This Court has not found any cases delineating the standards to be applied to a motion, pursuant to Rule 30(b)(7), seeking such relief. This Court expressly holds, however, that the policy discussed above is equally applicable to motions brought pursuant to Rule 30(b)(7): absent extreme hardship, the plaintiff should appear for deposition in his chosen forum. A telephonic deposition of Clem while he is abroad would be deemed to have been taken at the foreign situs, not within this forum. *See* Fed.R.Civ.P. 30(b)(7). Thus, Clem must demonstrate that taking his deposition here would impose an extreme hardship on him in order to be entitled to the relief sought.

Plaintiff claims that the cost of transportation to New York to attend a deposition here would be prohibitive. Affidavit of Andrew P. Saulitis, Esq., dated May 18, 1984, ¶ 4 ("Saulitis Aff.").[3] Plaintiff further

---

1. The Court is not at all certain that this motion is properly brought pursuant to Rule 30(b)(7) rather than Rule 26(c). The deposition was properly noticed prior to the filing of the motion; therefore, plaintiff is essentially seeking a protective order.

2. Indeed, plaintiff has failed to cite a single case.

3. During the period that this motion was *sub judice,* Clem was relocated from Dubai to Hong Kong. Plaintiff claims, without presenting the figures, that the cost of com-

argues that he "is not a wealthy man" and that "this is not a 'big case'." Saulitis Aff. ¶ 5.

The Court is not persuaded that deposing Clem in New York will impose an extreme hardship upon him. Clem has not sufficiently detailed his financial position so that this Court might assess the prohibitiveness of the deposition. The cost of transportation (approximately $3,000) would not, however, appear to be extreme, especially in light of the substantial claims involved here (in excess of $130,000, plus interest, plus attorneys' fees). Moreover, several issues in this case involve facts that are not in writing and will depend for their resolution upon the testimony of Clem, *e.g.,* Clem's reliance on oral statements made by employees of Allied. In such a situation, the defendant is entitled to depose the plaintiff face-to-face in order to adequately prepare for trial. *See, Slade,* 21 F.R.D. at 147. Finally, Clem does anticipate being in the United States in December of this year. His deposition should be taken in New York at that time to minimize the hardship on him and still adequately accord defendant its right to a face-to-face deposition in the forum of Clem's choosing.[4]

Accordingly, Plaintiff's motion is DENIED, and he will be required to submit to examination in this forum at a time and place to be agreed by counsel consistent with this decision, *i.e.,* during his stay in the United States.

NOTES

   A.   Who won the motion before the court?

   B.   Do you agree that a face to face deposition is strongly to be preferred over a telephonic deposition?

   C.   Do you think the standard for permitting telephonic depositions utilized in the *Clem* case is the appropriate one?

   D.   Contrast the approach of Enslen, J. in Rehau, Inc. v. Colortech, Inc., 145 F.R.D. 444, 446–447 (W.D.Mich.1993):

   I disagree with the approach of the district court for the Southern District of New York, which concluded that absent extreme hardship, the plaintiff should be required to appear for deposition in his or her chosen forum. Clem v. Allied Van Lines Int'l Corp., 102 F.R.D. 938 (S.D.N.Y.1984). Instead, I think that the rationale of Jahr v. IU Int'l Corp., 109 F.R.D. 429 (M.D.N.C.1986) is correct:

   > Nothing in the language of Rule 30(b)(7) requires that a telephonic deposition may only be taken upon a showing of necessity, financial inability, or other hardship ... by looking to a concomitant 1980 amendment to Rule 30, one discerns a purpose to encourage the courts to be more amenable to employing nontraditional methods for conducting depositions ... in order to reduce the cost of federal litigation.
   >
   > Because of the history and similar purpose of subsections (b)(4) and (b)(7), the Court concludes that leave to take telephonic depositions should be liberally

---

ing to New York would be even greater from Hong Kong.

   4. The Court is hopeful that the trial in this action, if indeed one remains necessary,

can also go forward during Clem's stay in the United States this December.

granted in appropriate cases.... Thus, upon giving a legitimate reason for taking a deposition telephonically, the movant need not further show an extraordinary need for the deposition. Rather, the burden is on the opposing party to establish why the deposition should not be conducted telephonically.

109 F.R.D. 429, 43031. The Jahr court's interpretation of Rule 30(b)(7) is consistent with Rule 1, which states that the Rules of Civil Procedure shall be "construed to secure the just, speedy, and inexpensive determination of every action." Civ. P. 1.

Defendants make no claim that the use of telephonic depositions in this case will be inaccurate or untrustworthy, and they do not argue that they will be prejudiced in any way. Defendants only state that they anticipate that each deposition will last one full day at the least.

There is no reason why a full day's deposition cannot be conducted by a conference call, and there is no indication that the integrity of the discovery process will be compromised in any way by doing so. The litigants in this action have managed to file 367 documents with this Court to date. Surely, the expenses to each side must be astronomical. I see positively no reason to add the cost of two trans-Atlantic flights and hotel accommodations to the tab when the same task can be accomplished with two simple phone calls. Therefore, plaintiff's motion on this point will be granted.

Cressler v. Neuenschwander

United States District Court for the District of Kansas, 1996.
170 F.R.D. 20.

■ SAFFELS, UNITED STATES DISTRICT JUDGE

This is a medical malpractice action in which the plaintiff claims that the defendants were negligent and departed from standard medical care. Now before the court is the plaintiff's Amended Motion for Order to Allow Telephonic Depositions of Dr. Golitz, Dr. Dreiling and Dr. Gonzales (Doc. 109).

The plaintiff seeks an order allowing the taking of the depositions of Loren Golitz, M.D., Lyndah Dreiling, M.D., and Rene Gonzales, M.D. by telephonic means in order to reduce costs. Fed. R. Civ. P. 30(b)(7) provides that "the parties may stipulate in writing or the court may upon motion order that a deposition be taken by telephone." The plaintiff also asks the court to order that neither the plaintiff's counsel nor defense counsel be present in person with the witnesses when the depositions are taken. The plaintiff maintains that if either attorney attends the depositions in person, the other attorney will feel obliged to also appear in person.

The defendants do not object to the plaintiff's appearing and deposing the witnesses via telephonic means. The defendants ask, however, that they not be precluded from being present in person at the depositions.

The party seeking to depose a witness telephonically must present a legitimate reason for its request. *Jahr v. IU Int'l Corp.*, 109 F.R.D. 429, 431 (M.D.N.C.1986). The burden then shifts to the opponent to show why the deposition should proceed by a more traditional method. *Id. at 431.* The court must consider whether the use of telephonic means would reasonably ensure accuracy and trustworthiness, and whether the opposing party would be prejudiced. *Rehau, Inc. v. Colortech, Inc.*, 145 F.R.D. 444, 447 (W.D.Mich.1993).

The plaintiff submits that Drs. Golitz, Dreiling, and Gonzales are located in Denver, Colorado, and that allowing him to depose the witnesses telephonically would reduce the costs of taking the depositions. The court finds that the plaintiff's desire to save money constitutes a legitimate reason to conduct the depositions telephonically. The defendants, however, claim that they would be prejudiced in several ways if precluded from personally attending the evidentiary depositions. The defendants assert that (1) they would be prevented from effectively evaluating the witnesses' demeanor; (2) it would be difficult for the court reporter to accurately record everything said by the witnesses and attorneys; and (3) the defendants would be unable to examine files maintained by the witnesses.

A party's ability to see a key witness and judge his demeanor are important considerations in the decision to permit a telephonic deposition. *Anguile v. Gerhart*, Civ. A. No. 93–934 (HLS), 1993 WL 414665, at *3 (D.N.J. Oct. 7, 1993) (granting plaintiff's motion for initial telephonic deposition, provided that second deposition would be in person). On the other hand, telephonic depositions inherently lack face-to-face questioning, and to deny a request to conduct a telephonic deposition solely because of the opponent's inability to observe the witness would be tantamount to repealing Fed. R. Civ. P. 30(b)(7). *Jahr*, 109 F.R.D. at 432. Similarly, the defendants' second proffered reason for conducting the depositions in person, i.e., that it would be difficult for the court reporter to accurately record everything that is said, would seem to be no more persuasive in this case than in any other in which telephonic depositions are sought.

The defendants' third reason for being present at the depositions, however, is more compelling. The defendants submit that it would be extremely difficult to identify, mark, and utilize the witnesses' extensive medical records during a telephonic deposition, or to use medical articles and journals to cross-examine the witnesses. The existence of voluminous documents which are central to a case may preclude a telephonic deposition. *Fireman's Fund Ins. Co. v. Zoufaly*, 1994 WL 583173, at *1 (S.D.N.Y. 1994); see also *Mercado v. Transoceanic Cable Ship Co.*, 1989 WL 83596 (E.D. Pa. 1989).

The court finds that the best solution in this case is to grant the plaintiff's motion for an order allowing the taking of the depositions of Drs. Golitz, Dreiling, and Gonzales by telephonic means, but to deny the plaintiff's request that the court order that neither plaintiff's counsel nor defense counsel attend the depositions in person. The plaintiff has provided the court with no authority, and the court has located none, which would restrain the defendant from being present during these depositions. See 4A James W. Moore, Moore's Federal Practice P 30.09[5], at 30–114 n.20 (2d ed. 1996) (Rule 30(b)(7) does not specify that a party may not be present during a telephonic deposition; so long as the voices of all the participants are transmitted, the deposition may fairly be characterized as taken by telephone under the rule). "If the party seeking the deposition is prepared to conduct its portion without a face-to-face encounter with the witness, there is no reason not to permit it to do so, with any other party free to question the witness in person, thus avoiding any prejudice while reducing expenses." *Fireman's Fund,* 1994 WL 583173, at *1; see also *Jahr,* 109 F.R.D. at 432 n.4 (where plaintiff lacked financial resources and defendant was concerned about lack of face-to-face questioning, procedure by which plaintiff took deposition over the telephone and defendant appeared in person "would eliminate all of defendants [sic] concerns and still accommodate plaintiff's desires as well").

IT IS THEREFORE BY THE COURT ORDERED that the plaintiff's Amended Motion for Order to Allow Telephonic Depositions of Dr. Golitz, Dr. Dreiling and Dr. Gonzales (Doc. 109) is granted in part and denied in part. The plaintiff's motion for an order allowing telephonic depositions of Drs. Golitz, Dreiling, and Gonzales is granted. The plaintiff's motion for an order that neither party's counsel be present in person when the depositions are taken is denied.

IT IS FURTHER ORDERED that the plaintiff's Motion for Order to Allow Telephonic Depositions of Dr. Golitz, Dr. Dreiling and Dr. Gonzales (Doc. 108) is denied as moot.

Stillman v. Nickel Odeon, S.A.

United States District Court, Southern District of New York, 1984.
102 F.R.D. 286.

■ SHARON E. GRUBIN, UNITED STATES MAGISTRATE:

Defendants Nickel Odeon, S.A., Jose Esteban Alenda, Jose Luis Garci, Simon/Reeyes/Landsburg Productions, Inc. and Twentieth Century–Fox Entertainment, Inc. move for an order pursuant to Rule 15(a) of the Civil Rules of this court requiring plaintiff's payment of said defendants' counsel's fees, travel and accommodation expenses for the depositions noticed by plaintiff of Shapira Films, Ltd. ("Shapira") by its President, Dahlia Shapira, and of Lennart Bjork to be taken in Israel and California, respectively. Local Rule 15(a) provides as follows:

> When a proposed deposition upon oral examination, including a deposition before action or pending appeal, is sought to be taken at a place more than one hundred (100) miles from the courthouse, the court may provide in the order or in any order entered under Rule 30(b), Federal Rules of Civil Procedure, that prior to the examination, the applicant pay the expense of the attendance including a reasonable counsel fee of one attorney for each adversary party at the place where the deposition is to be taken. The amounts so paid, unless otherwise directed by the court, shall be a taxable cost in the event that the applicant recovers costs of the action or proceeding.

Shapira is a codefendant in this action, although she has never appeared, and Bjork is allegedly Shapira's agent. Dahlia Shapira resides in Israel and Bjork in California. It is alleged by plaintiff that the Shapira deposition was originally noticed to take place in New York, but Dahlia Shapira became ill and has been instructed by her physicians to make no transatlantic trips.

Initially, it should be noted that Rule 15(a) is discretionary in nature, providing that the court "may" allow the relief sought by defendants. Moreover, although defendants have cited three cases to support their request, each of those cases involved the deposition of a nonparty witness rather than of a defendant and its agent.

In addition, although defendants rely upon the language in Henderson v. Adame, No. 81 Civ. 4591 (S.D.N.Y. September 24, 1982), to argue that "the courts in this district have consistently awarded expenses and counsel fees where depositions are noticed to be taken more than 100 miles from the courthouse," the four cases cited in *Henderson* to support this statement, as *Henderson* itself, involved circumstances quite different from those in this case. In Robbins v. Abrams, 79 F.R.D. 600 (S.D.N.Y.1978), plaintiffs sought the depositions of persons who the court found to be in defendants' control. Judge Werker ordered that defendants produce the witnesses in this district or, in the alternative, pay *plaintiffs'* costs of taking the depositions where the witnesses were located. In Worth v. Trans World Films, Inc., 11 F.R.D. 197 (S.D.N.Y.1951), plaintiff, who lived in Chicago but brought suit here, sought to have his *own* deposition, which had been noticed by defendant for this district, taken in Chicago and to have defendant pay the expenses of attendance of plaintiff's New York attorney. Judge Weinfeld understandably held that if the deposition were to be taken in Chicago, it was plaintiff who should pay defendant's expenses. The other cases cited in *Henderson* involved depositions of third-party witnesses. Moreover, in Ignacio Ituarte v. United Car Transport Corp., No. 81 Civ. 4901 (S.D.N.Y. February 23, 1982), Judge Haight found the payment of expenses warranted under the circumstances of that case under the court's inherent equitable powers in supervising discovery.

In addition to the foregoing, a controlling reason in the court's mind for not requiring plaintiff to pay defendants' expenses at this time arises from the 1983 amendments to the Federal Rules of Civil Procedure which encourage the district courts to take a strong supervisory role in discovery and to consider innovative cost-shifting concepts. For example, the Advisory Committee note to Rule 26(b)(1)(iii) explains that among the considerations for the court are the limitations on a financially weak litigant to withstand extensive opposition to a discovery program. Although the instant situation may not be one that the drafters had in mind, the philosophy underlying the new rules can appropriately be applied. The court is not unmindful of the fact that the financial burden on individual plaintiff Stillman, were he to be required to pay defendants' expenses, could seriously thwart his ability to pursue his case actively. On the other hand, all five defendants who are seeking these expenses are represented by the same attorney, and each would presumably have to pay only one-fifth of the cost.

I do not hold that a plaintiff who may be of more limited financial resources than a defendant should be entitled to shift the cost of the plaintiff's discovery onto the defendants. The parties should be aware that such is not this court's intention from previous decisions I have made in this case where such a theory has been argued by plaintiff. In the instant situation, given the fact that the depositions, which appear to be important to the issues in this case, are of a codefendant and its agent and given the other facts discussed above, it is only reasonable that each party continue to bear its own costs at this time. This holding is consistent with all prior holdings I have made in this case, and no justification has been offered for departing from the general rule that each party bear its own costs of discovery pending the outcome of the litigation.

However, the provision of the last sentence of local Rule 15(a) is hereby ordered in its converse: in the event that defendants are successful in the outcome of this case, their counsel fees, travel and accommodation expenses for the Shapira and Bjork depositions shall be taxed against plaintiff.

So Ordered.

NOTES

A. Do you agree that Magistrate Grubin is not determining whether to shift the cost of discovery based on the disparity in the parties' ability to pay?

B. Is there anything wrong with using disparity in the parties' financial resources as a criteria for allocating the costs of discovery?

Bicknell v. CBT Factors Corporation

Court of Appeals of Georgia, 1984.
171 Ga.App. 897, 321 S.E.2d 383.

■ BIRDSONG, JUDGE.

We granted interlocutory appeal of the trial court's protective order in this case, to determine whether the trial court abused its discretion in requiring the Georgia resident defendants either to depose the New York corporate plaintiff's agent in New York or to pay the New York plaintiff's expenses and costs of coming to Georgia. Appellants Bicknell contend the trial court's order abridges their constitutional and procedural rights to defend themselves in their resident forum, and their right to require CBT Factors Corp. ("CBT") to appoint an agent to be deposed in Georgia.

The plaintiff CBT sued the Bicknells on an account factored to CBT by its assignor "Kay Winds." The suit is for $2,916.76 plus interest. CBT filed a request for admissions as to the verity of an itemized statement of account for goods delivered to the Bicknells which statement was attached to the request and filed in the record; CBT also filed similar interrogatories. The Bicknells denied the request for admissions, said the statement of account was incorrect, and denied the indebtedness.

Three months passed without the defendants seeking any discovery. On March 25, 1983, the plaintiff CBT filed a motion for summary judgment with supporting affidavit and set the hearing date for April 28. On March 28, the Bicknells filed a "notice to take deposition of designated agent," requesting CBT to appoint a corporate agent (OCGA § 9–11–30(b)(6)). The deposition notice requested CBT's agent to testify to all transactions and business records concerning time, dates, names and places, and the ordering, shipment and inspection of goods, truth in lending disclosures and all matters concerning the assignment of account from Kay Winds to CBT. The deposition was set to take place April 5 in Columbus, Georgia. On April 4, CBT filed a motion for protective order, contending its witness would be from out of state, the time of notice was too short, the notice was filed for delay only, and that the Bicknells had already had much opportunity to schedule depositions but had done so only after CBT's motion for summary judgment was filed.

The trial court held: "This Court pursuant to the decisions of Karp v. Friedman, Alpren and Green, 148 Ga.App. 204 [250 S.E.2d 819]; and Global Van Lines, Inc. v. Daniel Moving and Storage, Inc., 159 Ga.App. 124 [283 S.E.2d 56] finds that discovery may be had by the Defendants only in the following manner:

"(a) By the use of Interrogatories, Request for Admissions directed to Plaintiff, Depositions on written questions and any other possible discovery and efforts allowable under the Civil Practice Act, but with the Court requiring that a deposition of an employee or designated agent of Plaintiff, a nonresident, can only be taken by the Defendants in Georgia if said Defendants shall pay the entire expense of said Plaintiff's employee, employees or designated agent to come to Georgia for the purpose of taking this deposition which would include travel, transportation, lodging and copying to be borne by said Defendants of any documents sought per Defendant's Notice to Produce; or in the alternative, if the Defendants seek a deposition of an employee, employees or designated agent of Plaintiff, then said deposition is to be taken in the offices of the Plaintiff outside the State of Georgia with the entire expense of the deposition including travel of Plaintiff's attorney and copying expense to be borne by Defendants.

"(b) The Defendants shall have ninety (90) days from the date of this Order to pursue any of the above enumerated methods of discovery according to the terms set out above." *Held:*

The trial court did not abuse its discretion in directing this order. See generally OCGA § 9–11–26(c). In Millholland v. Oglesby, 114 Ga.App. 745, 748, 152 S.E.2d 761, reversed on other grounds, 223 Ga. 230, we held: "Plaintiff objects to traveling from his home in Ohio to Atlanta for giving the deposition * * * [I]n similar situations in federal courts * * * it has been held many times that ordinarily one who chooses a forum should be required to make himself available for examination in that forum." We also held in *Millholland,* 114 Ga.App., at pp. 747–748, 152 S.E.2d 761, that the Georgia Civil Procedure Act was taken from the Federal Rules of Civil Procedure and "with slight immaterial variations its sections are substantially identical to corre-sponding rules. Because of this similarity it is proper that we give consideration and great weight to constructions placed on the Federal Rules by the federal courts. [Cits.]" The plaintiff in *Millholland* was dismissed because he did not seek a protective order and show good cause for being relieved of the deposition; he simply failed to show up.

In this case, CBT did seek relief by protective order and the trial court in its discretion found that CBT showed good cause for relief. We do not disagree with that finding. In 4 Moore's Federal Practice & Procedure, § 26.70, it is noted that the federal civil procedure rules (like the Georgia rules) do not fix the exact place for the taking of a deposition. "Since the plaintiff has selected the place for trial, it is held that he may be called upon to present himself at that place for the taking of his deposition. *This is not a fixed and inflexible rule, however, and it is within the discretion of the court to order that it be taken at some other place, often the place of his residence or business."* (Emphasis supplied.) Moore's, supra, 12, pp. 26–509, 26–512.

The trial court has the power under OCGA §§ 9–11–26(c) and 9–11–30(d) to control the details of time, place, scope and financing for the protection of the deponents and parties. See also 4 Moore's, § 26.69, p. 26–194. Where good cause is shown, such as insufficient time of notice, overburdensomeness of the record or amount and kind of testimony sought, or excessive expense or inconvenience, the trial court may order that other methods of discovery be pursued, and in appropriate (although rare) cases, refuse a deposition altogether. Moore's supra, § 26.71, p. 26–525.

It was within the trial court's discretion, and entirely appropriate to this case particularly in view of the size of the monetary claim (Moore's, § 26.71, p. 26–530), to suggest that the appellants pursue other discovery methods than to insist upon oral testimony. See generally Moore's, § 26.77, at pp. 26–529 and 26–530. The appellants are not prohibited from any discovery; but only from burdensome discovery. The appellants are given 90 days to complete discovery. The trial court's order is more than fair and we find no abuse of discretion. Neither Reams v. Composite State Bd. of Medical Examiners, 233 Ga. 742, 213 S.E.2d 640 nor any other case cited by appellants requires a contrary result. However, nothing stated herein should be construed to abrogate the general rule that a party who chooses a forum should be required to make himself available for examination in that forum.

Judgment affirmed.

■ CARLEY, JUDGE, concurring specially.

Based solely upon the facts and circumstances of this case, I concur in the judgment of the majority affirming the trial court's grant of the protective order at issue. However, I would like to point out that the issue is not one on which all courts agree. There is authority for applying almost without exception the rule that one who chooses a forum must make himself available for examination in that forum. The Supreme Court of Mexico was faced with a case in which the amount involved was even less than that at issue in the case at bar. Salitan v. Carrillo, 69 N.M. 476, 368 P.2d 149 (1961). In *Salitan,* the court was called upon to construe its Rules of Civil Procedure which, as is true with our CPA, are patterned upon the Federal Rules of Civil Procedure. In Salitan, the court reversed the trial court's grant of a protective order similar to the one involved in the case at bar and held that the fact that the amount in controversy was relatively small, in proportion to expense of travel from New York to New Mexico, was not sufficient to deprive the defendant of the right to depose the plaintiff in the forum which the plaintiff chose.

However, after thoroughly considering the balance that must be achieved in deciding an issue of this type, I am constrained to concur with the majority because to do otherwise would leave the door open to undue appellate restriction of the trial court's discretion in matters of discovery. Accordingly, I agree with Dr. Agnor that "[i]t would appear to be a better rule to consider each case on its specific facts rather than to follow the choice of the forum rule." Agnor, Use of Discovery Under the Ga. Civil Practice Act (3rd ed.), § 3–15, p. 86. Therefore, while I concur in the majority opinion, I especially wish to emphasize the last sentence of that opinion wherein it is held that "nothing stated herein should be construed to abrogate the general rule that a party who chooses a forum should be required to make himself available for examination in that forum."

NOTE

Does the Georgia Court of Appeals set forth a rule for determining when plaintiffs will or will not be required to appear for oral depositions in Georgia?

NOTE ON COST SHIFTING AND PROPOSED AMENDMENTS TO THE FEDERAL RULES

Rule 26(b)(2) presently authorizes the district court judge to limit the "frequency or extent of the use of the discovery methods permitted under these rules," if it determines that (1) the discovery sought is unreasonably cumulative or duplicative, (2) the party has already had an ample opportunity to obtain the information by discovery, or (3) the burden or expense of the proposed discovery outweighs its likely benefit.

The proposed 2000 amendments state that the judge may grant such marginal discovery on the condition that the party seeking it "pay part or all of the reasonable expenses incurred by the responding party." The Advisory Committee note states that, "In determining whether to order cost-bearing, the court should insure that only reasonable costs are included, and (as suggested by limitation (iii)) it may take account of the parties' relative resources in determining whether it is appropriate for the party seeking discovery to shoulder all or part of the cost of responding to the discovery."

NOTE ON DEPOSITION TACTICS

Sherman L. Cohn, New Developments in Federal Litigation: Discovery Defenses, AMERICAN INNS OF COURT FEDERAL PRACTICE DIGEST, 209–10 (Jan. 1994):

Hall v. Clifton Precision, 150 F.R.D. 525 (E.D.Pa.1993), laid down clear boundaries on defense tactics at depositions. Once the deposition opens, counsel may not confer with his client, even at the client's request, concerning any question asked or any other aspect of the deposition, except possible claims of privilege. That prohibition exists even during breaks and recesses.

Second, an attorney representing a deponent is prohibited from objecting that "since I cannot understand the question, my client can't understand the question." Moreover, attorneys are told they cannot instruct clients not to answer unless the question involves a matter of privilege, a matter that a court has ruled cannot be examined on in this deposition or a matter on which the attorney places on the record her intent to seek a protective order.

Finally, the attorney representing a client has no right to know, in advance of the deposition, what documents the deposing attorney will use to question the deponent

* * *

What does all this mean? It is a ruling of a judge who obviously has had enough of counsel's obstruction tactics at a deposition. The underlying purpose of a deposition is "getting to the truth," and obstructionist tactics that stand in the way—short of legitimate claims of privilege—are not to be tolerated. Many attorneys focus heavily on their duty of zealous advocacy, a term used in the Code of Professional Responsibility, but forgetting that the Code adds "within the law".

In issuing this order, this federal judge has joined the entire Eastern District of New York plus at least six other federal district judges who have issued similar orders. These orders spell out what one would have assumed that attorneys already knew: we are all officers of the court, protecting our clients' legitimate rights while engaged in a positive search for the truth. Some lawyers feel this is an idealistic view that doesn't reflect reality. As is clear from the *Hall* case, ... many judges are out to make clear that they will tolerate no less, and that the defense of "everyone's doing it" will no longer be heard.

TACTICS CONTINUED: HOW STRINGENT THE CONTROLS?

Once the courts begin to police attorney-client contacts during the taking of a deposition, counsel may be expected to attempt to push the boundaries of the doctrine to the outer limits. In *Odone v. Croda International PLC*, 170 F.R.D. 66 (D.C.D.C. 1997) plaintiff consulted with his attorney during a five minute recess, called by defendant, during the taking of a deposition. Defendant sought sanctions and the opportunity to depose plaintiff again. Motion denied.

C.   ADDITIONAL METHODS OF OBTAINING DISCOVERY

1.   Requests for Production

Cooper Industries Inc. v. British Aerospace

United States District Court, Southern District of New York, 1984.
102 F.R.D. 918 (S.D.N.Y.1984).

■ EDELSTEIN, DISTRICT JUDGE:

Plaintiff seeks to recover based upon strict liability and negligence in design for fire damage to an aircraft that plaintiff's predecessor purchased from defendant, British Aerospace, Inc. Plaintiff sought the production of certain documents that defendant asserted were not in its possession. Plaintiff believes, and defendant has not denied, that the documents are in the possession of defendant's British affiliate, British Aerospace Public Limited Co. ("British affiliate").

Defendant has now moved for a protective order based upon the Hague Convention on Taking Evidence Abroad in Civil or Commercial Matters, and plaintiff has cross-moved to compel production and for sanctions.

Defendant has waived any right to claim protection under the Hague Convention. Defendant made no effort to seek protective relief when the discovery request was served upon it. It simply failed to respond with respect to the British affiliate. Plaintiff was forced to request a conference on this matter. On April 12, 1984 at a pretrial conference defendant did not raise the Hague Convention, and the court ordered defendant either (1) to produce the documents if they were in its possession or in the possession of its British affiliate, or (2) if they were not found, to submit a detailed affidavit to the court explaining what steps were taken to find the documents, why they could not be found, what steps were taken to determine what had happened to them, and what the investigation revealed had happened to them.

Defendant, in defiance of this order, neither produced the documents, nor submitted the affidavit, nor sought any relief from the court. At plaintiff's request another pretrial conference was held on June 21, 1984. The court expressed to defendant its extreme dissatisfaction with defendant's failure to comply with the order. Defendant, for the first time, raised the argument that the discovery of these documents must be conducted under the procedures of the Hague Convention because the British affiliate is a foreign corporation and not a party to this action. The court found that defendant had waived its right to raise that basis for protection. The court found further that the Hague Convention did not bar the discovery as ordered. The court again ordered defendant to comply.

Defendant again failed to produce the documents or submit the required affidavit to the court, but instead moved for a protective order based upon the Hague Convention. At this stage, near the end of discovery, it is not the time, as a matter of efficient judicial administration, to engender further delays by proceeding under the Hague Convention; defendant should have raised these concerns earlier. Furthermore, the court finds that defendant, by its conduct, has waived any right to assert the Hague Convention. Murphy v. Reifenhauser KG Maschinefabrik, 101 F.R.D. 360, 363 (D.Vt.1984) (waiver based on delay even where no misconduct or bad faith).[1]

___

1. The court recognizes that not only defendant, but the British government also, has an interest in the application of the Hague Convention. That interest must be

Furthermore, defendant is wrong on the law. The cases cited by defendant on the Hague Convention are inapposite. The discovery demanded is proper under Fed.R.Civ.P. 34. The demand was made on defendant, a party to this action, for documents that are in its "possession or control."

Documents need not be in the possession of a party to be discoverable, they need only be in its custody or control. Fleming v. Gardner, 84 F.R.D. 217, 217–18 (E.D.Tenn.1978); Hubbard v. Rubbermaid, Inc., 78 F.R.D. 631, 635–37 (D.Md.1978); Advance Labor Service, Inc. v. Hartford Accident and Indemnity Co., 60 F.R.D. 632, 633–34 (N.D.Ill.1973).

The documents involved here are within the defendant's custody. The defendant sells and services planes to which the documents, mostly service manuals and blueprints, relate. The British affiliate is the manufacturer of these planes. When this law suit was filed, defendant was wholly owned by the British affiliate. Essentially defendant is the distributor and servicer in the United States of the British affiliate's planes.

Early in this law suit, when plaintiff attempted to obtain these documents from the British affiliate, counsel for defendant instructed plaintiff to make all such requests through him because he represented the British affiliate. *See* letter dated Nov. 2, 1983, Exhibit 5 to Affidavit of Robert S. Murphy in support cross motion, sworn to July 24, 1984 ("Murphy Affidavit"). In the contract of sale for the plane in question, defendant describes itself as an "affiliated company" of the British affiliate. *See* Exhibit 14 to Murphy Affidavit.

The documents plaintiff seeks all relate to the planes that defendant works with every day; it is inconceivable that defendant would not have access to these documents and the ability to obtain them for its usual business.[2] Defendant has submitted nothing more than conclusory statements to show that these documents are not in its custody or control.

The fact that the documents are situated in a foreign country does not bar their discovery. Marc Rich & Co. v. United States, 707 F.2d 663, 667 (2d Cir.1983) (grand jury investigation), *cert. denied,* 463 U.S. 1215, 103 S.Ct. 3555, 77 L.Ed.2d 1400; United States v. First National City Bank, 396 F.2d 897, 900–01 (2d Cir.1968) (grand jury investigation). These cases involving grand jury investigations are nonetheless applicable to the case at bar. The weighty needs of a criminal matter are merely one factor to consider by a court in determining, within the principles of comity, whether to allow this sort of discovery pursuant to Fed.R.Civ.P. 34. *Murphy, supra,* 101 F.R.D. at 363.

considered under the principles of comity, which this court considers *infra.*

2. The documents and records that a corporation requires in the normal course of its business are presumed to be in its control unless the corporation proves otherwise. Any other rule would allow corporations to improperly evade discovery. *Cf. In re Ironclad Mfg. Co.,* 201 F. 66, 68 (2d Cir.1912).

On balance Fed.R.Civ.P. 34 is the appropriate mechanism. The production demanded here does not infringe on British Sovereignty as it calls merely for documents, not a personal appearance. *Id.* Defendant cannot be allowed to shield crucial documents from discovery by parties with whom it has dealt in the United States merely by storing them with its affiliate abroad. Nor can it shield documents by destroying its own copies and relying on customary access to copies maintained by its affiliate abroad. If defendant could so easily evade discovery, every United States company would have a foreign affiliate for storing sensitive documents. Defendant has improperly resisted the orders of this court.

Furthermore, in defendant's moving papers and reply papers it has preoccupied itself with purported discovery malfeasances by plaintiff during the conduct of this litigation. These allegations, even if true, are entirely unrelated to the issue at hand. Interjecting them here constitutes a blatant, improper attempt to obfuscate the issues before the court.

Defendant must produce the documents demanded if the documents are found either in defendant's possession or in the possession of the British affiliate. Specifically defendant must produce documents as follows:

With respect to discovery demands dated December 12, 1983, defendants must produce: on demand 9(a), documents of title; on demand 10, documents in compliance—defendant's statement already produced is not responsive; on demand 11, the British affiliate's version of the manual unless it is exactly identical to what defendant has already produced, in which case defendant must so state; on demand 12, defendant's statement is satisfactory and defendant will be bound by it; on demand 15, the name of the designer(s) and the blueprints.

With respect to discovery demands dated April 10, 1983, defendant must comply with the outstanding demands, 4 and 5.

With respect to discovery demands dated June 26, 1983, defendant must comply fully.

If these documents are not found, defendant must submit a *detailed* affidavit to the court explaining what steps were taken to find the documents, why they could not be found, what steps were taken to determine what had happened to them, and what the investigation revealed happened to them.

This court might have narrowed these demands, on grounds other than the Hague Convention, had defendant raised them. At this stage, however, and after defendant's course of conduct, this court is not inclined to order anything but full compliance. Defendant shall have three weeks from the entry of this order to comply herewith, and thereafter shall be assessed $500 per day payable as a fine into the registry of the court, until compliance is complete. Discovery is extended for the purpose of defendant's production of these documents.

Plaintiff is awarded the costs of opposing defendant's motion and the costs of its cross motion. Plaintiff's motion to strike the answer is denied.

NOTES

A. How could the documents at issue in this case be in British Aerospace Inc.'s "custody" if they were not in its "possession"?

B. What will happen if the British affiliate still refuses to comply with the Judge Edelstein's order as set forth in this case?

C. Is the court's argument that British sovereignty is not infringed because only documents are involved persuasive?

NOTE ON DISCOVERY OF FOREIGN AND MULTINATIONAL CORPORATIONS

As *Cooper v. British Aerospace* indicates, a foreign or multinational corporation subject to the personal jurisdiction of an American court is potentially subject to the same discovery as a domestic defendant. It may be compelled to produce documents, even if they are stored abroad, and it may be compelled to produce its officers, directors or managing agents for oral depositions in the United States. *See* Fed. R.Civ.P. 30(b)(6); Financial General Bankshares v. Lance, 80 F.R.D. 22 (D.D.C. 1978). Of course, the court always retains the power to grant a protective order under Rule 26(c) to avoid undue burden and expense.

When evidence is sought from someone not subject to the personal jurisdiction of American courts, or where the U.S. court cannot or will not compel production in the United States, discovery must be sought in a foreign country where the party or witness may be found. Although Rule 28(b) provides that depositions may be taken in foreign countries by notice or before a person commissioned to take testimony by the United States court, these procedures will generally not be effective if the foreign witness does not agree to such discovery. The primary means of compelling production of evidence from a foreign party or witness are "letters of request", referred to in the *Hague Convention on the Taking of Evidence Abroad in Civil or Commercial Matters*, June 1, 1970, 23 U.S.T. 2555.

The Hague Convention is a multilateral treaty signed by 18 nations, including the United States. It sets forth procedures for obtaining discovery in civil litigation involving foreign parties. Under the letters of request procedure, a party seeking discovery must draft a letter of request describing the evidence being sought. (This may be a description of certain documents, a written set of questions to be asked of the witness, or both.) That letter is then submitted to the central authority designated by the foreign country for receiving such requests, which then forwards it to a domestic court in the foreign jurisdiction which then issues an order compelling production of the evidence. Obviously, this is a rather expensive and time consuming process. Moreover, since most countries provide far more limited discovery than the United States, and the national laws of some states (*e.g.* Switzerland) actually prohibit disclosure of certain types of information, there are likely to be substantial limitations on the evidence actually obtained under this procedure.

It has been argued that the Hague Convention provides the exclusive procedure for obtaining evidence from foreign defendants, since it represents a balance between the needs of domestic litigants for evidence and the comity interests of the United States in not intruding too greatly on the judicial sovereignty of other nations. Accordingly, it has been argued that the ordinary discovery provisions of the Federal Rules may not be available against foreign parties. (Note that this was an issue the court held waived in *British Aerospace.*)

In *Societe Nationale Industrielle Aerospatiale v. United States District Court for the District of Iowa*, 482 U.S. 522, 107 S.Ct. 2542, 96 L.Ed.2d 461 (1987), the Supreme Court held that while the Hague Convention was not the exclusive device for obtaining discovery from foreign defendants, it was an available method of doing so, and one which should be utilized by federal courts on a case by case basis, with due regard both to the need for expeditious litigation and for principles of comity and respect for comity. Four members of the Court would have gone further and created a presumption in favor of utilizing the Hague Convention procedures in taking discovery in foreign countries.

The 1993 amendments to Rule 28, which authorized depositions to be taken in foreign countries pursuant to "letters of request" were, according to the Advisory Committee "intended to make effective use of the Hague Convention".

Yablon, Stupid Lawyer Tricks: An Essay on Discovery Abuse

96 Columbia Law Review 1618, 1996.

On May 3, 1995, the normally unflappable readers of The Wall Street Journal were shocked to read of a new litigation tactic that further stretched the already elastic bounds of acceptable advocacy. In a pending defamation action brought by Philip Morris Company against the American Broadcasting Company, lawyers for ABC alleged that their adversaries, after some delay, had produced 25 boxes containing approximately one million documents. These were the "critically sensitive flavoring documents" which related to ABC's charge that Philip Morris spiked its cigarettes with nicotine.

The documents had been transferred onto a special dark red paper with squiggly lines, which made them harder to read and impossible to photocopy. The paper was also alleged to give off noxious fumes that made it "difficult to work with the altered copies for extended periods of time." The smelly paper was reported to have made one partner nauseous and given someone else a headache. The extent to which these documents were truly nauseating (that is, more nauseating than any other million documents that have to be reviewed) remains in dispute. Nonetheless, counsel for Philip Morris, New York's Wachtell, Lipton, Rosen and Katz and Richmond's Hunton and Williams, agreed to produce some of the documents on non-odiferous paper.

This pungent story has helped to air various perspectives on the vexing problem of discovery abuse. Responses to the stinky paper ploy revealed a serious difference of opinion about such tactics among the practicing bar. Some litigators, while not excusing counsels' action, sought to explain such excesses as an inevitable result of the current litigation climate, where aggression is equated with zealous advocacy and clients expect their lawyers to win at all costs. Other lawyers had a completely different reaction. They just wanted to know where they could buy some of that smelly paper.

Brand Name Prescription Drugs Antitrust Litigation

United States District Court for the Northern District of Illinois, Eastern Division.
878 F.Supp. 1078.

■ Kocoras, United States District Judge

This matter is before the Court on Class Plaintiffs' motion to compel CIBA–Geigy Corporation ("CIBA") to produce responsive, computer-stored electronic mail ("e-mail") at its own expense. For the reasons that follow, Class Plaintiffs' motion is granted, subject to the limitations set forth below.

DISCUSSION

At issue is the production of CIBA's e-mail, which is intra-corporate correspondence generated and stored within CIBA's computer system. CIBA does not dispute that it has responsive e-mail that is discoverable. Rather, CIBA contends that Class Plaintiffs' request is untimely, overly-broad and overly-burdensome such that the plaintiffs' request should be denied. In the alternative, CIBA asks that if Class Plaintiffs' request is granted, then we should require the plaintiffs to narrow the scope of their request, and further require the plaintiffs to bear the costs of production.

First of all, we agree with Class Plaintiffs that CIBA's e-mail is discoverable. Rules 26(b) and 34 of the Federal Rules of Civil Procedure instruct that computer-stored information is discoverable under the same rules that pertain to tangible, written materials.

CIBA argues that the plaintiffs have "waived" their right to seek e-mail by failing to diligently pursue their request. In support, CIBA tracks the parties' ongoing correspondence on the e-mail issue and argues that Class Plaintiffs' motion should be denied because they have been dilatory in pursuing their e-mail request. While we agree that Class Plaintiffs' performance in pursuing the e-mail issue has been less than exemplary, their conduct is not as egregious as CIBA suggests, and does not constitute an abuse of the discovery process. Accordingly, we reject CIBA's "waiver" argument.

We likewise reject CIBA's argument that the Class Plaintiffs should bear the costs for retrieving responsive e-mail. CIBA estimates that it has at least 30 million pages of e-mail data stored on its technical back-up tapes. CIBA states that in order to search the e-mail data for names of particular individuals and to eliminate duplicate messages CIBA will incur an estimated cost of $50,000 to $70,000 in compiling, formatting, searching and retrieving responsive e-mail. It is CIBA's position that the Class Plaintiffs should be required to reimburse CIBA for its costs because (a) the plaintiffs agreed to do so; and (b) the Manual for Complex Litigation contemplates reimbursement in circumstances such as these.

We find no support for CIBA's position that the plaintiffs somehow agreed to compensate CIBA for the $50,000 to 70,000 estimated retrieval costs. CIBA has failed to come forward with any express agreement where the Class Plaintiffs agreed to incur the estimated retrieval and production costs. At best, CIBA has shown that the parties discussed the issue of compensation, and that it was CIBA's "understanding" that the Class Plaintiffs would pay for the estimated retrieval costs. However, the correspondence leading up to this motion belies the notion that the parties agreed to anything regarding the e-mail issue.

The Manual for Complex Litigation lends some support to CIBA's position that Class Plaintiffs should be forced to incur the e-mail retrieval and production costs.[1] Nevertheless, relevant case law instructs that the mere fact that the production of computerized data will result in a substantial expense is not a sufficient justification for imposing the costs of production on the requesting party. Rather, in addition to considering whether the amount of money involved in producing the discovery is inordinate and excessive, the court may consider factors such as whether the relative expense and burden in obtaining the data would be greater to the requesting party as compared to the responding party, and whether the responding party will benefit to some degree in producing the data in question. See Bills v. Kennecott Corp., 108 F.R.D. 459, 464 (D.Utah 1985).

Indeed, parties obtaining information from another's computerized data typically are required to bear any special expense incident to this form of production.

Central to any determination of whether a cost should be shifted to a producing party is the issue of whether the expense or burden is "undue." In the context of the retrieval and production of computer-stored information issues of "undue burden" become complicated. On the one hand, it seems unfair to force a party to bear the lofty expense attendant to creating a special computer program for extracting data responsive to a discovery request. On the other hand, if a party chooses an electronic storage method, the necessity for a retrieval program or method is an ordinary and foreseeable risk. Faced with considerations similar to the ones presently confronting us, the United States Court of International Trade remarked:

> It would be a dangerous development in the law if new techniques for easing the use of information became a hindrance to discovery or disclosure in litigation. The use of excessive technical distinctions is inconsistent with the guiding principle that information which is stored, used, or transmitted in new forms should be available through discovery with the same openness as traditional forms.

* * *

The normal and reasonable translation of electronic data into a form usable by the discovering party should be the ordinary and

---

1. The Manual for Complex Litigation Second, § 21.446 (1993) provides as follows:
   Parties sometimes request production in a form that can be created only at substantial expense for additional programming; if so, payment of such costs by the requesting party should be made a condition to production.

foreseeable burden of a respondent in the absence of a showing of extraordinary hardship.

Daewoo Electronics Co. v. United States, 10 C.I.T. 754, 650 F. Supp. 1003, 1006 (Ct.Int'l Trade 1986).

Here, CIBA argues that devising and paying for a retrieval program is an extraordinary hardship which it should not be forced to bear. While we agree that an estimated retrieval cost of $50,000 to $70,000 is expensive, we do not believe that it is a burden that the Class Plaintiffs should bear, particularly where, as here, "the costliness of the discovery procedure involved is . . . a product of the defendant's record-keeping scheme over which the [plaintiffs have] no control." Delozier, 109 F.R.D. 161, 164 (citing *Kozlowski v. Sears Roebuck & Co.*, 73 F.R.D. 73 (D.Mass.1976)). CIBA essentially admits that part of the burden attendant to searching its storage files results from "the limitations of the software CIBA is using." Affidavit of Paul G. Keegan, Exhibit H to [CIBA's] Memorandum of Law in Opposition to Class Plaintiffs' Motion to Compel . . ., at P 7. Class Plaintiffs should not be forced to bear a burden caused by CIBA's choice of electronic storage. Moreover, we find it interesting that at least four other manufacturer defendants have produced e-mail without insisting that the Class Plaintiffs first agree to pay retrieval costs; at least two of these manufacturers had to conduct computer searches to retrieve the e-mail.

Based on the foregoing, we will not require the Class Plaintiffs to assume the costs associated with retrieving, formatting and electronically manipulating CIBA's e-mail data tapes and copying responsive e-mail documents. We will, however, require Class Plaintiffs to pay CIBA a $0.21 per page fee for e-mail that the Class Plaintiffs select for copying; this is consistent with the agreement already existing among counsel under which plaintiffs pay $0.21 per page for copies of documents selected from defendants' productions.

We will further require the Class Plaintiffs to narrow their request. Throughout its memorandum filed in opposition to Class Plaintiffs' motion CIBA asserts that its programming costs will be particularly time-consuming and burdensome because of the size of the data set requested by Class Plaintiffs. Therefore, for the purpose of containing costs we will require the parties to consult with each other and agree upon meaningful limitations on the scope of any e-mail search.

CONCLUSION

For the foregoing reasons, Class Plaintiffs' Motion to Compel is, for the most part, granted. CIBA will be required to produce its responsive, computer-stored e-mail at its own expense, with the exception that the Class Plaintiffs will pay CIBA the $0.21 per page fee for e-mail that the Class Plaintiffs select for copying. Class Plaintiffs are instructed to narrow the scope of their request. To that end, the parties are instructed to consult and agree upon meaningful limitations on the scope of any e-mail search.

2. Requests For Admissions

American Technology Corp. v. Mah

United States District Court for the District of Nevada, 1997.
174 F.R.D. 687.

■ JOHNSTON, UNITED STATES MAGISTRATE JUDGE.

On January 5, 1996, the Plaintiff, American Technology Corp. (ATC), filed a complaint against the Defendants alleging patent infringement; trade dress infringement and unfair competition in violation of Title *15, United States Code, Section 1125*(a); common law tort of palming off/passing off; false marketing; inducing infringement; common law unfair competition; and unjust enrichment. On August 13, 1996, ATC served Plaintiff's First Requests for Admission by mailing it to Defendant's attorney in accordance with Rule 36(a) and Rule 5 of the Federal Rules of Civil Procedure. See Plaintiff's First Requests for Admission to Defendants, attached to Renewed Motion (#43) as Exhibit 5. The Defendants did not respond to Plaintiff's requests. Thus, on October 10, 1996, after several telephonic attempts to confer, ATC's attorney sent a letter to the Defendants' counsel pointing out that the Defendants were delinquent in responding to Plaintiff's requests for admission and that Plaintiff would seek Court relief unless contacted. See Letter from Thorpe, North & Western, L.L.P., to John C. Lambertsen dated October 10, 1996, attached to Renewed Motion (#43) as Exhibit 2. The Defendants did not respond to the letter or the outstanding requests for admission.

On December 5, 1996, ATC filed its Motion for Order that Matters set Forth in Plaintiff's Request for Admissions be Deemed Admitted (#27). However, Plaintiff failed to serve the motion on Defendants. Therefore, the Court denied Plaintiff's Motion. ATC then filed a Corrected Motion for Order that Matters Set Forth in Plaintiff's Request for Admissions be Deemed Admitted (#37) on February 11, 1997. The Defendants responded by requesting an additional two weeks to complete the discovery requests. On April 4, 1997, Plaintiff filed a Renewed Motion for Order that Matters set Forth in Plaintiff's Request for Admissions be Deemed Admitted (#43), because Defendants still had not replied to Plaintiff's Requests for Admission.

DISCUSSION

Rule 36(a) of the Federal Rules of Civil Procedure provides that a request for admission is admitted if no written answer or objection is timely served on the requesting party. This basic tenet of Rule 36 is often recited by courts on the way to analyzing the sufficiency of answers or objections under the last paragraph of Rule 36(a). *Asea, Inc., v. Southern Pac. Transp. Co.*, 669 F.2d 1242, 1245 (9th Cir.1981). ("It is undisputed that failure to answer or object to a proper request for admission is itself an admission: the Rule itself so states.") However, the Defendants in this case did not serve any answers or objections to ATC's requests for admissions. Therefore, ATC seeks an order of the

Court confirming that the unanswered requests for admission are in fact admitted. Whether a requesting party must file a motion for a court order to conclusively establish the matters in the unanswered requests has not previously been addressed by the Court.

"The purpose of Rule 36(a) is to expedite trial by establishing certain material facts as true and thus narrowing the range of issues for trial." *Asea, Inc. v. Southern Pac. Transp. Co.*, 669 F.2d at 1245 (citations omitted). Once admitted under this rule, the matter is conclusively established and a party cannot deny the admission at trial, unless the court on motion permits withdrawal or amendment of the admission. If a court held otherwise, it would "overlook the purpose of Rule 36 and also . . . ignore the distinction between evidential admissions and judicial admissions. The salutary function of Rule 36 in limiting the proof would be defeated if the party were free to deny at the trial what he or she has admitted before trial." 8A C. Wright & A. Miller, Federal Practice and Procedure § 2264, at 573 (2d ed. 1994). An admission under Rule 36 falls into the category of judicial admissions similar to an admission in a pleading or a stipulation drafted by counsel for use at trial for the express purpose of limiting and defining the facts in issue.

A party who has been served with requests for admission has the option of not responding. However, a party's "failure to respond, either to an entire request or to a particular request, is deemed to be a [judicial] admission of the matter set forth in that request or requests." 8A C. Wright & A. Miller, Federal Practice and Procedure § 2259, at 549–550 (2d. ed. 1994). Since unanswered requests for admission are automatically deemed judicially admitted under Rule 36(a), no court intervention is required. The rule is explicit that a matter is admitted if a party fails to respond within thirty days or within a time period set by the court.

A motion to compel discovery pursuant to Rule 37 does not apply to a failure to respond to requests for admission. Generally, when a party fails to respond during pretrial discovery, the requesting party is authorized to seek an order compelling disclosure or discovery. Therefore, if a party fails to make a disclosure required by Rule 26(a); or a deponent fails to answer a question propounded or submitted under Rules 30 or 31; or a corporation or other entity fails to make a designation under Rules 30(b)(6) or 31(a); or a party fails to answer an interrogatory submitted under Rule 33; or if a party, in response to a request for inspection submitted under Rule 34, fails to respond that inspection will be permitted as requested or fails to permit inspection as requested, the discovering party may move for an order compelling an answer, or a designation, or an order compelling inspection in accordance with the request. Fed. R. Civ. P. 37(a)(2).

Recognizing the unavailability of a motion to compel answers to the requests for admission, the Plaintiff seeks an order from the Court confirming that the matters contained in the requests for admission are deemed admitted. Rule 36 does not require a motion for the Court's imprimatur on the unanswered requests for admission. The rule is self-executing. Schwarzer, Tashima & Wagstaffe, Federal Civil Procedure Before Trial P 11:812 (The Rutter Group 1997). A motion to establish or affirm the admissions upon a party's failure to admit or object is unnecessary under Rule 36(a). The resources of the parties and the Court should be devoted to other pursuits in the case.

Although the Court agrees with ATC that the Defendants have flagrantly disregarded their obligation to answer the requests for admission, Rule 36(a) does not mandate judicial intervention. Rule 36(a) provides its own enforcement mechanism, by automatically deeming the matters contained in the requests for admission as conclusively admitted. The Defendants' failure to respond to ATC's requests for admission automatically deemed the matters as admitted. Since court intervention is not required to invoke Rule 36(a), an order restating Rule 36 would be surplusage.

ORDER

Based on the foregoing and good cause appearing,

IT IS HEREBY ORDERED that Plaintiff's Plaintiff American Technology Corp.'s Renewed Motion for Order That Matters Set Forth in Plaintiff's Request for Admissions be Deemed Admitted (#43) is DENIED.

QUESTIONS

A. What was the effect of the court's denial of plaintiff's motion? Are the requested admissions deemed admitted for the purposes of the case?

B. If so, why would the court deny the plaintiff's motion?

Brook Village North Associates v. General Electric

United States Court of Appeals, First Circuit, 1982.
686 F.2d 66.

■ Rosenn, Circuit Judge.

The primary question on appeal in this diversity suit is the effect to be given admissions that are deemed to be made under Rule 36 of the Federal Rules of Civil Procedure because of a party's failure timely to respond to a request therefor, and the limits, if any, on the discretion of a trial judge to permit withdrawal of an admission once trial has commenced. We must also decide whether plaintiffs are entitled to prejudgment interest.

The plaintiffs, Brook Village North Associates ("Brook Village") and First Equity Associates, Inc. ("First Equity"), instituted suit in the United States District Court for the District of New Hampshire, to recover damages for breach of contract in the purchase of modular housing. After a bench trial, the trial judge declined to give conclusive effect to pretrial admissions of the defendant, General Electric Co., Re–Entry and Environmental Systems Division ("GE") under Rule 36, although the admissions had not been amended or withdrawn as proof of damages. Instead, the court awarded plaintiffs a lower sum based on evidence produced by the defendant at trial. The court also refused to award prejudgment interest. The plaintiffs appeal from the judgment awarding them $149,328.69. We reverse in part and remand.

I.

In partial fulfillment of its mandate to see that adequate housing is available to all Americans, the Department of Housing and Urban Development established a program entitled "Operation Breakthrough" to encourage mass-produced low and moderate income housing. On or about October 1, 1971, as part of this program First Equity entered into an agreement as contractor with GE under which GE agreed to supply 160 units of factory-produced modular housing, for erection into apartments in Nashua, New Hampshire, under the sponsorship of Brook Village.[1]

The modules, consisting of flat roofs and fabricated rooms complete with interior fixtures, were manufactured by GE in King of Prussia, Pennsylvania, and delivered to New Hampshire in early 1972. First Equity, employing its own crew, installed cement foundations and erected the modules according to GE's specifications.

Shortly after erection began, serious leaks developed in the flat roofs. By May of 1972 it became apparent that the roofs manufactured by GE were unsatisfactory and would not be able to withstand the elements. GE therefore arranged, at its sole cost, with a New Hampshire roofing company to install a "built-up" roof covering the entire complex. This was completed in the latter half of 1972. In 1973 further roof leaks developed, which were initially repaired at GE's expense. In July of 1973, however, GE refused to fund any further roof repairs. Plaintiffs were required to hire contractors to perform additional roof repairs and eventually, to forestall further leaks, to install pumps on the roof to remove water which "ponded."

Problems also developed when the front facia sheets on the doors and drawers of the kitchen cabinets furnished by GE began delaminating. In an effort to solve this problem, GE furnished plaintiffs with handles to be placed on all of the cabinets to correct the problem and prevent further delamination. Plaintiffs maintain that because the delamination was widespread and not confined to the doors, the handles were not used. Eventually, they were lost.

Plaintiffs brought suit in December 1975 under warranty and tort theories to recover damages for the defective roofing and cabinets. With respect to both problems, plaintiffs claimed that replacement of the offending structures was the only adequate solution. On October 31, 1977, they filed their first requests for admissions, seeking to establish the genuineness of certain documents and letters and the truth of statements contained therein pertaining to liability and dam-

---

1. The principals of Brook Village and First Equity appear to be the same individu-   als.

ages. After a period of more than nine months, on August 3, 1978, GE filed its reply to the requests for admissions. Brook Village immediately moved to strike GE's reply for untimeliness and the district court granted the motion. GE moved twice before trial as well as on the first day of trial for reconsideration of its request to allow late filing of answers to plaintiffs' requests for admissions or to strike the admissions; the court denied the motions and recognized the denial in its pretrial order.

On conclusion of the trial, the district court held that under the applicable law of Pennsylvania, the Uniform Commercial Code (UCC), GE had violated implied warranties of merchantability and fitness for a particular purpose in supplying the defective roof. The court assessed damages at $120,000 (the figure which the court determined to be the cost of replacement) plus $29,328.69, representing monies spent by plaintiffs to maintain the roof in a state of repair for the years 1974–1978. The court denied any recovery for the allegedly defective cabinets, concluding that "plaintiffs have failed to sustain their burden and are not entitled to recover on their claim of damages to the kitchen cabinets."

Plaintiffs then filed a motion under Fed.R.Civ.P. 59(e) to have the court amend its judgment. Plaintiffs sought reconsideration of both the amount assessed for the roof and the failure of the court to find liability for the kitchen cabinets. They also sought the addition of prejudgment interest to the award.

In its order denying plaintiffs' motion, the court rejected plaintiffs' argument that the court was bound by the prior admissions.

> Had plaintiffs desired, they could have refrained from attempting to introduce at trial the testimony of [their experts], thus depriving the Court of the opportunity to observe these witnesses live and under examination and to determine their credibility in comparison with the proof adduced by the defendant. But, having chosen to proceed with these witnesses, the Court in its function as factfinder and pursuant to the provisions of Rule 36(b), Fed.R.Civ.P., is not bound to accept the admission as proof of damages. This is particularly true where, as here, "presentation of the merits of the action will be subserved thereby and the party who obtained the admission fails to satisfy the court that withdrawal or amendment will prejudice him in maintaining his action or defense on the merits." [Citations omitted.]

> In short, the Court finds and rules that it would be blatantly unfair to permit plaintiffs at this late date, after they had full opportunity to present the veracity of witnesses and weight of their testimony to the trial court, to fall back on documents marked in evidence on the basis that they were admitted and cannot be contested.

Brook Village North Associates v. General Electric Co., No. 75–362, typescript op. at 2–3 (D.N.H. Apr. 30, 1981). The court also held that under Pennsylvania law the plaintiffs were not entitled to prejudgment interest. This appeal followed.

II.

Plaintiffs argue that they are entitled, at a minimum, to recover damages established as of 1975 in letters deemed admitted as true when GE failed timely to respond to the request for admissions and the district court repeatedly denied defendant's pretrial motions to allow its reply to be filed out of time. One of those letters, written by a roofing contractor, establishes that in 1975 the cost of replacing the defective roof was $194,720. Another letter, written by the manager of the kitchen division of Evans Products Company, reports that the lamination on the kitchen cabinet doors and drawer fronts in the complex is "totally unstable" and that the only solution is replacement throughout. It fixes the cost at $17,136 plus tax. Despite these admissions, plaintiffs had the writers of the letters testify, primarily for the purpose of establishing the increased cost of replacement at the time of trial. Plaintiffs' experts testified that the cost of replacing the roof had increased to $363,980, and the cabinets to $55,817.60. The district court allowed defendant to call an expert witness who testified that the cost of reroofing was $120,000, and the building manager who testified that he had only seen delaminated cabinets in some of the units. The court found the defendant's evidence more credible and awarded judgment in the lower amount for the roof and none for the kitchen cabinets.

A.

Rule 36 provides in relevant part:

(a) Request for Admission. A party may serve upon any other party a written request for the admission * * * of the truth of any matters * * * that relate to statements or opinions of fact or of the application of law to fact * * *.

* * * The matter is admitted unless, within 30 days after service of the request * * * the party to whom the request is directed serves upon the party requesting the admission a written answer or objection * * *.

* * *

(b) Effect of Admission. Any matter admitted under this rule is conclusively established unless the court on motion permits withdrawal or amendment of the admission. Subject to the provisions of Rule 16 governing amendment of a pretrial order, the court may permit withdrawal or amendment when the presentation of the merits of the action will be subserved thereby and the party who obtained the admission fails to satisfy the court that withdrawal or amendment will prejudice him in maintaining his action or defense on the merits.

Under Rule 36 in its present form (the rule was amended in 1970), if a party fails timely to answer a request for admissions, the requested items are deemed admitted. Any matter thus admitted under the Rule is conclusively established unless the court on motion permits withdrawal or amendment of the admission. And courts have not hesitated in appropriate cases to apply the sanction of Rule 36 to material facts that conclusively establish or preclude a party's claim.

The instant case poses the question of the discretion of a district court to permit withdrawal or amendment of an admission by default once trial has commenced. In general, the standard for being relieved of a failure to respond in a timely fashion to a request for admissions is permissive: a court may allow withdrawal or amendment of an admission "when the presentation of the merits of the action will be subserved thereby and the party who obtained the admission fails to satisfy the court that withdrawal or amendment will prejudice him in maintaining his action or defense on the merits." Fed.R.Civ.P. 36(b). The prejudice contemplated by the Rule is not simply that the party who initially obtained the admission will now have to convince the fact finder of its truth. Rather, it relates to the difficulty a party may face in proving its case, *e.g.,* caused by the unavailability of key witnesses, because of the sudden need to obtain evidence with respect to the questions previously answered by the admissions. *See* Westmoreland v. Triumph Motorcycle Corp., 71 F.R.D. 192 (D.Conn.1976).

The Rule understandably imposes a more restrictive standard, however, on the granting of a request to avoid the effect of an admission once trial had begun. Rule 36(b) specifies that the court can permit withdrawal or amendment of admissions "[s]ubject to the provisions of Rule 16 governing amendment of pretrial order." Rule 16 authorizes the conduct and defines the contours of a conference before trial. "The chief purposes of the pretrial conference are to define and simplify the issues, to lessen surprise at trial and the risk of judicial error, to conclude stipulations on matters of evidence, and to promote settlements." 3 J. Moore, *Moore's Federal Practice* ¶ 16.03 at 16–6 to 16–7 (2d ed.1982) (footnote omitted). To give effect to matters resolved at conference, Rule 16 provides for the court to make an order "which recites the action taken at the conference, the amendments allowed to the pleadings, and the agreements made by the parties as to any of the matters considered, and which limits the issues for trial to those not disposed of by admissions or agreement of counsel." The pretrial order, once entered, controls the subsequent course of action. "No proof need be offered as to matters stipulated to in the order, since the facts admitted at the pretrial conference and contained in the pretrial order stand as fully determined as if adjudicated at the trial." 3 J. Moore, *supra,* ¶ 16.19 at 16–40 to 16–41 (footnote omitted). The order can be modified at trial, but only "to prevent manifest injustice." Thus, Rule 16 by its terms sets a higher threshold for a trial judge to exercise his discretion to avoid the force of admissions under Rule 36 once trial has begun.

The district court in the instant case appears to have disregarded the existence of this higher threshold for opening up admissions after commencement of trial. In its order denying reconsideration of plaintiff's motion to amend the finding as to damages, the court held, first, that because plaintiff chose to proceed with the presentation of supplemental evidence touching on the matters governed by the admissions, plaintiffs waived their right to rely on them; and second, that because withdrawal of the admissions aided presentation of the merits and did not prejudice plaintiffs, the court as fact finder was no longer bound to accept them as proof of damages. This analysis stands at odds with the intendment of Rule 36.

The first rationale on which the district court relied, namely that if a plaintiff presents evidence which overlaps questions controlled by admissions by default he thereby waives the right to rely on the matters controlled by the admissions, works an unfair disadvantage on parties who properly seek to take advantage of Rule 36. Generally, the proof of a plaintiff's case may involve establishing a number of facts, some of which will be controlled by admissions and some of which will not. The party who obtains the admissions by default may be unsure what other facts must be established for him to prevail. Or he may, as in the present case, wish to present supplemental evidence in order to recover damages beyond those established by admission. In such cases, the waiver rule applied by the district court would either discourage parties from introducing additional evidence or would completely vitiate the conclusive effect of admissions by default obtained under the Rule.[4]

Requiring a party thus to elect between relying on admissions by default and introducing no evidence, and introducing evidence but foregoing the binding force of the admissions, unfairly forces a party who chooses to make use of admissions by default to limit his proof at trial to the scope of his request for admissions. We therefore hold that a party who obtains an admission by default does not waive his right to rely thereon by presenting evidence at trial that overlaps the matters controlled by the admission.

The district court, in adopting its second rationale for its conclusion that the admissions need not be viewed as binding, expressed a concern for "accord[ing] substantial justice over mere technical contentions." The court concluded, in effect, that having determined as fact finder that defendant's witnesses were more credible than plaintiffs', justice would be served if the court were free to consider anew the matters governed by the admissions.

To the extent that the court's analysis equates the standard for permitting withdrawal or amendment of admissions pretrial with the

---

4. The advisory committee note to the revised Rule 36 supports the conclusion that the district court's waiver analysis impermissibly undercuts the conclusive effect that the framers of the Rule intended admissions to have.

The new provisions give an admission a conclusively binding effect, for purposes only of the pending action, unless the admission is withdrawn or amended. In form and in substance a Rule 36 admission is comparable to an admission in pleadings or a stipulation drafted by counsel for use at trial, rather than to an evidentiary admission of a party. (Citations omitted.) Unless the party securing an admission can depend on its binding effect, he cannot safely avoid the expense of preparing to prove the very matters on which he has secured the admission, and the purpose of the rule is defeated. (Citations omitted.)

standard for opening up admissions once trial has begun, we reject it. Rule 36 plainly contemplates a more restrictive standard for foregoing the conclusive effect of admissions once trial has begun. *See supra,* at 70–71.

The court's ultimate conclusion is not, however, thereby disposed of. For framing the district court's argument in a way that renders it consonant with Rule 36's incorporation of Rule 16's standard for opening up admissions once trial has begun, the district court concluded that "to prevent manifest injustice," it was free to "allow withdrawal" of an admission after trial had commenced if the court as fact finder found evidence presented by the party bound by the admission to be more credible than the evidence presented by the party having the benefit of admission.

The district court cited a number of cases to support its decision. Most of the cases cited in which courts have allowed withdrawal of admissions involved questions raised at the pretrial stage, however, and are therefore not directly relevant. *See, e.g.,* Marshall v. Sunshine & Leisure, Inc., 496 F.Supp. 354, 355–56 (M.D.Fla.1980); St. Regis Paper Co. v. Upgrade Corp., 86 F.R.D. 355, 357 (W.D.Mich.1980); Pleasant Hill Bank v. United States, 60 F.R.D. 1 (W.D.Mo.1973). *Cf.* Westmoreland v. Triumph Motorcycle Corp., 71 F.R.D. 192, 192–93 (D.Conn.1976) (motion to strike untimely responses after entry of pretrial order but before trial allowed).

Two decisions cited by the parties squarely present the issue at bar. Warren v. International Brotherhood of Teamsters, 544 F.2d 334 (8th Cir.1976); Dependahl v. Falstaff Brewing Corp., 491 F.Supp. 1188 (E.D.Mo.1980), *rev'd in part on other grounds,* 653 F.2d 1208 (8th Cir.), *cert. denied,* 454 U.S. 968, 102 S.Ct. 512, 70 L.Ed.2d 384 (1981). In each, the court at trial allowed the introduction of evidence on questions covered by admissions that were obtained because requests therefor were not timely answered and subsequently ruled that the admissions would not be binding. Each case, however, involved other factors not present in the case at bar that supported the district court's action. In *Warren,* the sole reason for the failure to timely respond was a misreading by counsel of the time for filing provisions of the rule. 544 F.2d at 338–39. And in *Dependahl* the parties had unsuccessfully attempted to reach a settlement before trial. "Defendants' failure to timely deny is undoubtedly attributable in large part to plaintiffs' effort to enforce the settlement, and subsequent abandonment of that effort." 491 F.Supp. at 1194.

No similar extenuating circumstances are present in the case at bar. Plaintiffs immediately moved to strike the defendant's responses when more than nine months after the request of admissions was served, defendant finally responded. Defendant's motions for reconsideration to be allowed to file out of time were thrice denied prior to trial. This case therefore does not involve a simple, technical default, or a default in which the plaintiff shares responsibility.

A recent court of appeals decision reaches a result contrary to *Warren* and *Dependahl* on facts in many respects identical to those at bar. In Rainbolt v. Johnson, 669 F.2d 767 (D.C.Cir.1981), the appellate court reversed a decision of the district court confirming a Master's report because the Master had not given full effect to admissions by default. Although the district court had denied a motion to withdraw unanswered admissions,

> the Auditor–Master did not treat the admissions as "conclusively established." Instead, the Auditor–Master accepted some of the admitted facts and rejected others in the light of all of the evidence.

Id. at 769. Instead of awarding the plaintiffs damages in excess of $900,000, as established by the admissions, the Master substituted a figure of $175,391.68 based on his independent calculation of the amount to which plaintiffs were entitled. The court of appeals reversed with directions to enter partial summary judgment in the amount of $900,000.

We believe that the tack taken by the court in *Rainbolt* represents the sounder approach. Rule 36 plainly contemplates that a party seeking to avoid at trial the force of admissions obtained by default faces a higher burden than does a party seeking identical relief prior to the entry of the pre-trial order. We do not believe that the situation presented by this case, where the district court sitting as fact finder simply finds more credible the witnesses of the party against whom the admissions operate, rises to the level of "manifest injustice" required for relief from the effect of admissions, although permitting such relief may well subserve the presentation of the merits. To so hold would eradicate the distinction created under the Rules between pretrial and post-commencement of trial requests for relief from admissions. That the party found to be less credible may prevail because of the other side's failure to comply with the timeliness requirements of Rule 36 does not result in the type of manifest injustice contemplated under the Rules.

This does not mean that a district court is never free to permit withdrawal or amendment of admissions after considering the evidence presented at trial. For example, if a district court reviewing the evidence concludes that no rational fact finder could believe the facts established by the admissions to be true, the court might permit withdrawal or amendment so long as the party who obtained the admissions is not otherwise prejudiced. It is not enough, however, that the court as fact finder disbelieves one party's expert testimony.

We therefore hold that a district court is not free to permit amendment or withdrawal of admissions by default after trial merely because the parties presented evidence touching on matters governed by the admissions and the court finds more credible the evidence of the party against whom the admissions operate.

B.

By virtue of one of the untimely answered requests for admission defendant is deemed to have admitted the truth of plaintiffs' expert's letter of December 9, 1975. The letter describes the manner in which the roof is faulty, suggests how it can be corrected, and estimates the cost of reroofing at $194,770. Although the testimony at trial produced greatly disparate estimates by plaintiffs' and defendant's experts of the current cost to replace the roof—the plaintiffs' expert set the figure at $363,980, the defendant's at $120,000—we conclude that the district court could not have determined from all of the testimony that no rational fact finder could have found the amount established by the admissions to be correct. Defendant is therefore bound by the admission.

Moreover, plaintiffs may in fact have been prejudiced by the failure of the court to give conclusive effect to the admissions. The thrust of plaintiffs' proof was aimed at establishing the *current* cost of the roof repair. Plaintiffs did not, therefore, present evidence to establish that the roof repairs described in the admission were consistent with the quality of roof called for in the contract. The district court, however, concluded that plaintiffs were only entitled to a "Class C" roof, and therefore discounted plaintiffs' expert's testimony, which the court apparently believed described a roof of better than "Class C" quality. *See supra* note 7. Had plaintiffs known that the admissions would not be given conclusive effect they might well have presented evidence to bolster their claim, raised on appeal, that "Class C rating" as used in the contract refers to UL fire retardance only and not to the general quality of the roof.

Although the district court was not free to reject the admission of $194,720 as the cost of replacing the roof, the same constraints do not apply to its evaluation of the testimony of plaintiffs' expert at trial as to the increased cost of replacing the roof in 1978. As the fact finder, the court was free to discount this testimony in the face of other evidence. On the record before us, the district court's rejection of the $363,900.10 figure was not clearly erroneous. Accordingly, the district court having found the defendant liable to plaintiffs to replace the roof under implied warranty theories, GE is liable to plaintiffs in the sum of $194,720 for the replacement of the roof.

C.

By virtue of another untimely answered request for admission, defendant is deemed to have admitted the truth of plaintiffs' letter of October 15, 1974, relating to the kitchen cabinet doors and drawer fronts at the complex. The letter provides in relevant part:

> I have inspected the kitchen cabinet doors and drawer fronts of the above mentioned project and find that the plastic lamination is totally unstable. *The only solution would be to remove all the present doors and drawer fronts and replace them with new ones.* (Emphasis added.)

The letter sets the cost of replacement as of the date of the letter at $17,136.00 plus tax. In another request, defendant admits plaintiffs are "no[ ] more than 0% responsible for any kitchen cabinet delaminations."

At trial plaintiffs' expert testified that the current replacement cost was $55,817.60. The district court concluded, however, that plaintiff had failed to prove damages for the kitchen cabinets. The opinion notes that the project's maintenance manager testified that he saw delamination in only some of the apartments, and plaintiffs' expert only visited three apartments immediately before trial. The opinion also notes that GE, upon being advised of the delamination claims, sent handles intended to cure the damage, but the handles were never used and were eventually lost. Finally, the court observed that under the law of Pennsylvania "where one party to a contract is the cause of another's failure to perform, it cannot assert that failure against the other party."

We conclude that the district court erred in denying plaintiffs recovery for the kitchen cabinets. The admission respecting liability and damages for the cabinets is by itself sufficient to satisfy plaintiffs' burden of proof. The letter establishes that the defects exist throughout and sets the cost for correcting the problem.

Although the testimony was in conflict, it is not so blatantly onesided as to allow the district court to disregard the admissions. Not only does plaintiffs' expert's admitted letter note that the delamination extended throughout, but the letter dated October 29, 1974, of plaintiffs' counsel to John Smoltz, defendant's representative, specifically refers to "defective cabinet laminations in 160 units" of the complex. A later letter of April 29, 1975, to GE from plaintiffs' counsel asserts that "[t]he cabinet delamination has affected every apartment." Plaintiffs' witness Shaw also testified that he familiarized himself with the kitchen cabinets as the modules arrived at the project; described the nature of the delamination on the doors and drawers, and in response to a question as to how widespread was the delamination, replied "throughout."

The defendant is therefore bound by its admission that "the only solution" is total replacement of the cabinets at a cost of $17,136. Although the district court as fact finder is free to disbelieve plaintiffs' expert's testimony as to the increased cost of replacement, the admission should be viewed as setting the minimum amount of damages. The district court did not, however, consider whether plaintiffs' testimony as to the increased cost of replacement was in fact credible. We remand for that limited purpose.

IV.

In summary, the judgment of the district court will be vacated and the case remanded with instructions to the district court to enter judgment for the plaintiffs in the sum of $194,720 as damages for the roof and $29,329.69 for interim repairs, to make findings with respect to the damages for the kitchen cabinets in a sum not less than $17,135, and to enter judgment therefor. The claim for prejudgment interest is denied.

NOTES

    A. What is the difference between a request to admit and an interrogatory?

    B. Do you think the court's standard is too harsh?

3. Mental and Physical Examinations (and Further Consideration of the Discovery of Experts)

Schlagenhauf v. Holder

Supreme Court of the United States, 1964.
379 U.S. 104, 85 S.Ct. 234, 13 L.Ed.2d 152.

■ MR. JUSTICE GOLDBERG delivered the opinion of the Court.

This case involves the validity and construction of Rule 35(a) of the Federal Rules of Civil Procedure as applied to the examination of a defendant in a negligence action. * * *

I.

An action based on diversity of citizenship was brought in the District Court seeking damages arising from personal injuries suffered by passengers of a bus which collided with the rear of a tractor-trailer. The named defendants were The Greyhound Corporation, owner of the bus; petitioner, Robert L. Schlagenhauf, the bus driver; Contract Carriers, Inc., owner of the tractor; Joseph L. McCorkhill, driver of the tractor; and National Lead Company, owner of the trailer. Answers were filed by each of the defendants denying negligence.

Greyhound then cross-claimed against Contract Carriers and National Lead for damage to Greyhound's bus, alleging that the collision was due solely to their negligence in that the tractor-trailer was driven at an unreasonably low speed, had not remained in its lane, and was not equipped with proper rear lights. Contract Carriers filed an answer to this cross-claim denying its negligence and asserting "[t]hat the negligence of the driver of the * * * bus [petitioner Schlagenhauf] proximately caused and contributed to * * * Greyhound's damages."

Pursuant to a pretrial order, Contract Carriers filed a letter—which the trial court treated as, and we consider to be, part of the answer—alleging that Schlagenhauf was "not mentally or physically capable" of driving a bus at the time of the accident.

Contract Carriers and National Lead then petitioned the District Court for an order directing petitioner Schlagenhauf to submit to both mental and physical examinations by one specialist in each of the following fields:

    (1) Internal medicine;

    (2) Ophthalmology;

    (3) Neurology; and

    (4) Psychiatry.

For the purpose of offering a choice to the District Court of one specialist in each field, the petition recommended two specialists in internal medicine, ophthalmology, and psychiatry, respectively, and three specialists in neurology—a total of nine physicians. The petition alleged that the mental and physical condition of Schlagenhauf was "in controversy" as it had been raised by Contract Carriers' answer to Greyhound's cross-claim. This was supported by a brief of legal authorities and an affidavit of Contract Carriers' attorney stating that Schlagenhauf had seen red lights 10 to 15 seconds before the accident, that another witness had seen the rear lights of the trailer from a distance of three-quarters to one-half mile, and that Schlagenhauf had been involved in a prior accident.

* * *

While disposition of this petition was pending, National Lead filed its answer to Greyhound's crossclaim and itself "cross-claimed" against Greyhound and Schlagenhauf for damage to its trailer. The answer asserted generally that Schlagenhauf's negligence proximately caused the accident. The crossclaim additionally alleged that Greyhound and Schlagenhauf were negligent

> "[b]y permitting said bus to be operated over and upon said public highway by the said defendant, Robert L. Schlagenhauf, when both the said Greyhound Corporation and said Robert L. Schlagenhauf knew that the eyes and vision of the said Robert L. Schlagenhauf was [sic] impaired and deficient."

The District Court, on the basis of the petition filed by Contract Carriers, and without any hearing, ordered Schlagenhauf to submit to nine examinations—one by each of the recommended specialists—despite the fact that the petition clearly requested a total of only four examinations.

* * *

Rule 35 on its face applies to all "parties," which under any normal reading would include a defendant. Petitioner contends, however, that the application of the Rule to a defendant would be an unconstitutional invasion of his privacy, or, at the least, be a modification of substantive rights existing prior to the adoption of the Federal Rules of Civil Procedure and thus beyond the congressional mandate of the Rules Enabling Act.

* * *

Petitioner contends that even if Rule 35 is to be applied to defendants, which we have determined it must, nevertheless it should not be applied to him as he was not a party in relation to Contract Carriers and National Lead—the movants for the mental and physical examinations—at the time the examinations were sought. The Court of Appeals agreed with petitioner's general legal proposition, holding that the person sought to be examined must be an opposing party *vis-à-vis* the movant (or at least one of them). 321 F.2d, at 49. While it is clear that the person to be examined must be a party to the case,[12] we are of the view that the Court of Appeals gave an unduly restrictive interpretation to that term. Rule 35 only requires that the person to be examined be a party to the "action," not that he be an opposing party *vis-à-vis* the movant. There is no doubt that Schlagenhauf was a "party" to this "action" by virtue of the original complaint. Therefore, Rule 35 permitted examination of him (a party defendant) upon petition of Contract Carriers and National Lead (codefendants), provided, of course, that the other requirements of the Rule were met. Insistence that the movant have filed a pleading against the person to be examined would have the undesirable result of an unnecessary proliferation of crossclaims and counterclaims and would not be in keeping with the aims of a liberal, nontechnical application of the Federal Rules. See Hickman v. Taylor, supra, 329 U.S., at 500–501, 67 S.Ct., at 388–389.

While the Court of Appeals held that petitioner was not a party *vis-a-vis* National Lead or Contract Carriers at the time the examinations were first sought, it went on to hold that he had become a party *vis-a-vis* National Lead by the time of a second order entered by the District Court and thus was a party within its rule. This second order, identical in all material respects with the first, was entered on the basis of supplementary petitions filed by National Lead and Contract Carriers. These petitions gave no new basis for the examinations, except for the allegation that petitioner's mental and physical condition had been additionally put in controversy by the National Lead answer and crossclaim, which had been filed subsequent to the first petition for examinations. Although the filing of the petition for mandamus intervened between these two orders, we accept, for purposes of this opinion, the determination of the Court of Appeals that this second order was the one before it and agree that petitioner was clearly a party at this juncture under any test.

Petitioner next contends that his mental or physical condition was not "in controversy" and "good cause" was not shown for the examinations, both as required by the express terms of Rule 35.

* * *

It is notable, however, that in none of the other discovery provisions is there a restriction that the matter be "in controversy," and only in Rule 34[a] is there Rule 35's requirement that the movant affirmatively demonstrate "good cause."

* * *

12. Although petitioner was an agent of Greyhound, he was himself a party to the action. He is to be distinguished from one who is not a party but is, for example, merely the agent of a party. This is not only clear in the wording of the Rule, but is reinforced by the fact that this Court has never approved the Advisory Committee's proposed amendment to Rule 35 which would include within the scope of the Rule "an agent or a person in the custody or under the legal control of a party." Advisory Committee on Rules for Civil Procedure, Report of Proposed Amendments, 41–43 (1955). It is not now necessary to determine to what extent, if any, the term "party" includes one who is a "real party in interest" although not a named party to the action. Cf. Beach v. Beach, 72 App.D.C. 318, 114 F.2d 479, 131 A.L.R. 804.

a. Compare the language of Rule 34 as amended in 1970.

Rule 35, therefore, requires discriminating application by the trial judge, who must decide, as an initial matter in every case, whether the party requesting a mental or physical examination or examinations has adequately demonstrated the existence of the Rule's requirements of "in controversy" and "good cause," which requirements, as the Court of Appeals in this case itself recognized, are necessarily related. 321 F.2d, at 51. This does not, of course, mean that the movant must prove his case on the merits in order to meet the requirements for a mental or physical examination. Nor does it mean that an evidentiary hearing is required in all cases. This may be necessary in some cases, but in other cases the showing could be made by affidavits or other usual methods short of a hearing. It does mean, though, that the movant must produce sufficient information, by whatever means, so that the district judge can fulfill his function mandated by the Rule.

Of course, there are situations where the pleadings alone are sufficient to meet these requirements. A plaintiff in a negligence action who asserts mental or physical injury, cf. Sibbach v. Wilson & Co., supra, places that mental or physical injury clearly in controversy and provides the defendant with good cause for an examination to determine the existence and extent of such asserted injury. This is not only true as to a plaintiff, but applies equally to a defendant who asserts his mental or physical condition as a defense to a claim, such as, for example, where insanity is asserted as a defense to a divorce action.

Here, however, Schlagenhauf did not assert his mental or physical condition either in support of or in defense of a claim. His condition was sought to be placed in issue by other parties. Thus, under the principles discussed above, Rule 35 required that these parties make an affirmative showing that petitioner's mental or physical condition was in controversy and that there was good cause for the examinations requested. This, the record plainly shows, they failed to do.

The only allegations in the pleadings relating to this subject were the general conclusory statement in Contract Carriers' answer to the cross-claim that "Schlagenhauf was not mentally or physically capable of operating" the bus at the time of the accident and the limited allegation in National Lead's cross-claim that, at the time of the accident, "the eyes and vision of * * * Schlagenhauf was [sic] impaired and deficient."

The attorney's affidavit attached to the petition for the examinations provided:

"That * * * Schlagenhauf, in his deposition * * * admitted that he saw red lights for 10 to 15 seconds prior to a collision with a semi-tractor trailer unit and yet drove his vehicle on without reducing speed and without altering the course thereof.

"The only eye-witness to this accident known to this affiant * * * testified that immediately prior to the impact between the bus and truck that he had also been approaching the truck from the rear and that he had clearly seen the lights of the truck for a distance of three-quarters to one-half mile to the rear thereof.

"* * * Schlagenhauf has admitted in his deposition * * * that he was involved in a [prior] similar type rear end collision. * * *"

This record cannot support even the corrected order which required one examination in each of the four specialties of internal medicine, ophthalmology, neurology, and psychiatry. Nothing in the pleadings or affidavit would afford a basis for a belief that Schlagenhauf was suffering from a mental or neurological illness warranting wide-ranging psychiatric or neurological examinations. Nor is there anything stated justifying the broad internal medicine examination.[16]

The only specific allegation made in support of the four examinations ordered was that the "eyes and vision" of Schlagenhauf were impaired. Considering this in conjunction with the affidavit, we would be hesitant to set aside a visual examination if it had been the only one ordered. However, as the case must be remanded to the District Court because of the other examinations ordered, it would be appropriate for the District Judge to reconsider also this order in light of the guidelines set forth in this opinion.

The Federal Rules of Civil Procedure should be liberally construed, but they should not be expanded by disregarding plainly expressed limitations. The "good cause" and "in controversy" requirements of Rule 35 make it very apparent that sweeping examinations of a party who has not affirmatively put into issue his own mental or physical condition are not to be automatically ordered merely because the person has been involved in an accident—or, as in this case, two accidents—and a general charge of negligence is lodged. Mental and physical examinations are only to be ordered upon a discriminating application by the district judge of the limitations prescribed by the Rule. To hold otherwise would mean that such examinations could be ordered routinely in automobile accident cases.[18] The plain language of Rule 35 precludes such an untoward result.

Accordingly, the judgment of the Court of Appeals is vacated and the case remanded to the District Court to reconsider the examination order in light of the guidelines herein formulated and for further proceedings in conformity with this opinion.

Vacated and remanded.

---

16. Moreover, it seems clear that there was no compliance with Rule 35's requirement that the trial judge delineate the "conditions, and scope" of the examinations. Here the examinations were ordered in very broad, general areas. The internal medicine examination might for example, at the instance of the movant or its recommended physician extend to such things as blood tests, electrocardiograms, gastro-intestinal and other X-ray examinations. It is hard to conceive how some of these could be relevant under any possible theory of the case.

18. From July 1, 1963, through June 30, 1964, almost 10,000 motor vehicle personal injury cases were filed in the federal district courts. Administrative Office of the United States Courts, Annual Report of the Director, C2 (1964). In the Nation at large during 1963, there were approximately 11,-500,000 automobile accidents, involving approximately 20,000,000 drivers. National Safety Council, Accident Facts, 40 (1964 ed.).

■ MR. JUSTICE DOUGLAS, dissenting in part.[b]

While I join the Court in reversing this judgment, I would, on the remand, deny all relief asked under Rule 35. I do not suppose there is any licensed driver of a car or a truck who does not suffer from some ailment, whether it be ulcers, bad eyesight, abnormal blood pressure, deafness, liver malfunction, bursitis, rheumatism, or what not. If he or she is turned over to the plaintiff's doctors and psychoanalysts to discover the cause of the mishap, the door will be opened for grave miscarriages of justice. When the defendant's doctors examine plaintiff, they are normally interested only in answering a single question: did plaintiff in fact sustain the specific injuries claimed? But plaintiff's doctors will naturally be inclined to go on a fishing expedition in search of *anything* which will tend to prove that the defendant was unfit to perform the acts which resulted in the plaintiff's injury. And a doctor for a fee can easily discover something wrong with any patient—a condition that in prejudiced medical eyes might have caused the accident. Once defendants are turned over to medical or psychiatric clinics for an analysis of their physical wellbeing and the condition of their psyche, the effective trial will be held there and not before the jury. There are no lawyers in those clinics to stop the doctor from probing this organ or that one, to halt a further inquiry, to object to a line of questioning. And there is no judge to sit as arbiter. The doctor or the psychiatrist has a holiday in the privacy of his office. The defendant is at the doctor's (or psychiatrist's) mercy; and his report may either overawe or confuse the jury and prevent a fair trial.

The Court in Sibbach v. Wilson & Co., 312 U.S. 1, 61 S.Ct. 422, 85 L.Ed. 479, was divided when it came to submission of a plaintiff to a compulsory medical examination. The division was not over the constitutional power to require it but only as to whether Congress had authorized a rule to that effect. I accept that point as one governed by *stare decisis.* But no decision that when a *plaintiff* claims damages his "mental or physical condition" is "in controversy," within the meaning of Rule 35, governs the present case. The *plaintiff* by suing puts those issues "in controversy." A plaintiff, by coming into court and asserting that he has suffered an injury at the hands of the defendant, has thereby put his physical or mental condition "in controversy." Thus it may be only fair to provide that he may not be permitted to recover his judgment unless he permits an inquiry into the true nature of his condition.

A defendant's physical and mental condition is not, however, immediately and directly "in controversy" in a negligence suit. The issue is whether he was negligent. His physical or mental condition may of course be relevant to that issue; and he may be questioned concerning it and various methods of discovery can be used. But I balk at saying those issues are "in controversy" within the meaning of Rule 35 in every negligence suit or that they may be put "in controversy" by

b. The opinion of Justice Black, with whom Justice Clark joins, concurring in part   and dissenting in part, has been omitted.

the addition of a few words in the complaint. As I have said, Sibbach proceeded on the basis that a plaintiff who seeks a decree of a federal court for his damages may not conceal or make difficult the proof of the claim he makes. The defendant, however, is dragged there; and to find "waiver" of the "inviolability of the person" (Union Pacific R. Co. v. Botsford, 141 U.S. 250, 252, 11 S.Ct. 1000, 1001, 35 L.Ed. 734) is beyond reality.

Neither the Court nor Congress up to today has determined that any person whose physical or mental condition is brought into question during some lawsuit must surrender his right to keep his person inviolate. Congress did, according to *Sibbach,* require a plaintiff to choose between his privacy and his purse; but before today it has not been thought that any other "party" had lost this historic immunity. Congress and this Court can authorize such a rule. But a rule suited to purposes of discovery against defendants must be carefully drawn in light of the great potential of blackmail.

The Advisory Committee on Rules for Civil Procedure in its October 1955 Report of Proposed Amendments to the Rules of Civil Procedure for the United States District Courts proposed that Rule 35 be broadened to include situations where the mental or physical condition or "the blood relationship" of a party, or "of an agent or a person in the custody or under the legal control of a party," is "in controversy." We did not adopt that Rule in its broadened form. But concededly the issue with which we are now concerned was not exposed. It needs, in my opinion, full exposure so that if the Rule is to be applied to defendants as well as to plaintiffs, safeguards can be provided in the Rule itself against the awful risks of blackmail that exist in a Rule of that breadth.

This is a problem that we should refer to the Civil Rules Committee of the Judicial Conference so that if medical and psychiatric clinics are to be used in discovery against defendants—whether in negligence, libel, or contract cases—the standards and conditions will be discriminating and precise. If the bus driver in the instant case were not a defendant, could he be examined by doctors and psychiatrists? See Kropp v. General Dynamics Corp., D.C., 202 F.Supp. 207; 13 Buffalo L.Rev. 623 (1964). Lines must in time be drawn; and I think the new Civil Rules Committee is better equipped than we are to draw them initially.

* * *

NOTES

A. Was Schlagenhauf a party within the meaning of Rule 35?

B. Is the requirement of "good cause" under Rule 35 the same for plaintiffs and defendants? How does one obtain the evidence needed to make a showing of good cause?

C.   Why is there a higher standard for obtaining physical or mental examinations than other forms of discovery? Is it possible to obtain medical examinations of nonparties under the Federal Rules?

D.   An amendment to Rule 35 transmitted by the Supreme Court to Congress on April 30, 1991 (effective December 1, 1991), would no longer limit the examinations authorized by the Rule to physicians or clinical psychologists, but would permit the court to order a mental or physical examination by "any suitably licensed or certified examiner."

E.   In *Schuppin v. Unification Church, Sun Myung Moon, Founder and Owner*, 435 F.Supp. 603 (D.Vt.1977), *aff'd* 573 F.2d 1295 (2d Cir.1977), plaintiffs brought suit on their own behalf and as next friend of their daughter, Tamara, to remove her from the Unification Church. Tamara first "joined or otherwise became associated with" defendant church when she was approximately 18 years and 6 months old. The court notes that "The Unification Church has drawn much attention nationally due to highly publicized allegations that its members are recruited from among naive and vulnerable young people who are subjected to psychological programming or "brainwashing" which renders them powerless to resist or question the authority of Reverend Moon."

Tamara disassociates herself from the lawsuit. Further, she files an affidavit that she has never been adjudicated incompetent. Her parents seek a mental examination of Tamara, noting that they have made her present mental state an issue in the litigation.

What preliminary showing, if any, should be required of plaintiffs before the court orders the requested examination?

F.   You represent a defendant whose physical and mental condition has been placed in issue. As a result he has been examined by various specialists hired by plaintiff, examinations to which you agreed without requiring plaintiff to obtain a court order. You would like very much to see their reports. Are you entitled to them? What factors might you be wise to consider before requesting copies?

Hardy v. Essroc Materials, Inc.

United States District Court for the Eastern District of Pennsylvania, 1998.
1998 WL 103306.

■ KAUFFMAN, J.

AND NOW, this 18th day of February, 1998, upon consideration of the Motion of Defendant ESSROC Materials Inc. ("ESSROC") to Compel the Mental Examination of Plaintiff Candace M. Hardy ("Hardy"), and having heard Oral Argument on the matter, the Court holds as follows:

1.   In this sex discrimination suit, Hardy alleges discrimination in hiring, hostile work environment, and retaliation under both Title VII of the Civil Rights Act of 1964, *42 U.S.C. § 2000e* et seq. (1994), and the Pennsylvania Human Relations Act, 43 Pa.Stat.Ann. § 951 et seq. (West 1991 & Supp. 1997). Hardy seeks declaratory and injunctive relief, equitable back pay relief, compensatory damages for emotional distress, and punitive damages.

2.   ESSROC has moved to compel Hardy to submit to an examination by Dr. Peter Badgio, a psychologist, on the ground that Hardy

has placed her mental condition in controversy by seeking damages for, inter alia, emotional distress.

3.   Rule 35(a) of the Federal Rules of Civil Procedure empowers the court to order a mental examination of a party when the party's mental condition is "in controversy," and the party seeking the examination has demonstrated "good cause." These requirements

> are not met by mere conclusory allegations of the pleadings—nor by mere relevance to the case—but require an affirmative showing by the movant that each condition as to which the examination is sought is really and genuinely in controversy and that good cause exists for ordering each particular examination.

Schlagenhauf v. Holder, 379 U.S. 104, 118, 13 L. Ed. 2d 152, 85 S. Ct. 234 (1964).

4.   The "in controversy" requirement has spawned disagreement among the courts. *Bridges v. Eastman Kodak Co., 850 F. Supp. 216, 222 (S.D.N.Y.1994).* Most courts, however, have held that a defendant seeking to compel an examination under Rule 35(a) must show that the plaintiff's emotional distress claim is more than simply a component of her statutory cause of action. See, e.g., *E.E.O.C. v. Old W. Furniture Corp.,* 173 F.R.D. 444, 446 (W.D.Tex.1996); *Neal v. Siegel–Robert, Inc.,* 171 F.R.D. 264, 266 (E.D.Mo.1996); *O'Quinn v. New York Univ. Med. Ctr.,* 163 F.R.D. 226, 228 (S.D.N.Y.1995); *Turner v. Imperial Stores,* 161 F.R.D. 89, 97–98 (S.D.Cal.1995); *Curtis v. Express, Inc.,* 868 F. Supp. 467, 468–69 (N.D.N.Y.1994); *Bridges,* 850 F. Supp. at 222; *Robinson v. Jacksonville Shipyards, Inc.,* 118 F.R.D. 525, 531 (M.D.Fla.1988); *Cody v. Marriott Corp.,* 103 F.R.D. 421, 423 (D.Mass. 1984).[1]

5.   Courts tend to compel an employment discrimination plaintiff to undergo a mental examination only when the case involves, in addition to a claim of emotional distress, one or more of the following: (i) a separate tort cause of action for negligent or intentional infliction of emotional distress; see, e.g., *Lahr v. Fulbright & Jaworski, L.L.P.,* 164 F.R.D. 196, 199 (N.D.Tex.1995); (ii) an allegation of severe ongoing mental injury or a psychiatric disorder, see, e.g., *Lowe v. Philadelphia Newspapers, Inc.,* 101 F.R.D. 296, 298–99 (E.D.Pa.1983); (iii) the plaintiff's intent to offer expert testimony to support her emotional distress claim, see, e.g., *Shepherd v. American Broadcasting Cos.,* 151 F.R.D. 194, 213 (D.D.C.1993), *rev'd in part on other grounds,* 314 U.S. App. D.C. 137, 62 F.3d 1469 (D.C.Cir.1995); or (iv) the plaintiff's concession that her mental condition is in controversy, see, e.g., *Shirsat v. Mutual Pharmaceutical Co.,* 169 F.R.D. 68, 70 (E.D.Pa.1996).

6.   Hardy does not allege intentional or negligent infliction of emotional distress, does not allege a specific psychological or psychiat-

---

1. A few courts have held that a mental anguish claim alone puts a plaintiff's mental condition in controversy. See *Jansen v. Packaging Corp. of Am.,* 158 F.R.D. 409 (N.D.Ill. 1994); *Smedley v. Capps, Staples, Ward, Hastings & Dodson,* 820 F. Supp. 1227 (N.D.Cal. 1993); *Zabkowicz v. West Bend Co.,* 585 F. Supp. 635 (E.D.Wis.1984).

ric disorder, and has confirmed that she has no intention of offering expert testimony to prove her emotional distress. ESSROC contends that a mental examination is warranted because Hardy claims that the discrimination caused her to feel anxious and to have trouble sleeping. Under the case law interpreting Rule 35(a), such afflictions are not so severe as to warrant an order compelling a mental examination. The Court concludes that Hardy has not put her mental condition "in controversy" for purposes of Rule 35(a).

Accordingly, it is hereby ORDERED that Defendant's Motion to Compel Plaintiff's Mental Examination is DENIED.

NOTES

A. Should any claim of mental anguish or emotional distress put the mental state of the person making the claim "in controversy" and thus make them subject to mental examination?

B. The opinion notes that "[c]ourts tend to compel an *employment discrimination* plaintiff to undergo a mental examination only when the case involves" one of a number of things in addition to a claim of emotional distress. Should whether or not a plaintiff claiming emotional distress is subject to a mental examination depend on the legal basis of their claim? If so, what kind of claim should require that plaintiff's claiming emotional distress be subject to mental examinations?

C. In *Neal v. Siegel–Robert, Inc.,* 171 F.R.D. 264 (E.D.Mo.1996), the court held that an age discrimination plaintiff was not subject to a psychological examination simply because of his claim of emotional distress. The court drew a distinction between general emotional distress and complaints of "definable psychological symptoms." Only a claim of the latter would put the mental condition of the plaintiff "in controversy" and thus justify a mental examination. Is the distinction drawn by the court in *Neal* convincing?

Jakubowski v. Lengen

Supreme Court of New York, Appellate Division, Fourth Department, 1982.
86 A.D.2d 398, 450 N.Y.S.2d 612.

■ DOERR, JUSTICE.

In the course of a previously agreed upon physical examination of plaintiff by a physician designated by defendant in this personal injury action, it is claimed that a law clerk from the office of plaintiff's attorney unduly interfered with the conduct of the examination causing it to be terminated by the doctor. Briefly noted, the so-called interference occurred when plaintiff's representative refused to permit her to sign various releases and authorizations requested by the doctor, since all required authorizations had already been provided to defendant's attorney. A further dispute arose when, according to the doctor, the law clerk directed plaintiff not to remove her slacks for the examination as requested by the doctor. According to the law clerk, the doctor told plaintiff to remove her panties to which the law clerk objected. The clerk also objected to the scope of questions asked of plaintiff by the doctor's secretary. Defendant moved pursuant to CPLR 3124 for an order compelling plaintiff to submit to a physical examination. Neither the Notice of Motion nor the supporting affidavit of defendant's attorney sought to impose any conditions on the examination nor specifically to have plaintiff's attorney excluded from the physical examination. Special Term granted the motion and, inexplicably, ordered that the physical examination of plaintiff be conducted "in the absence of the plaintiff's attorneys or anyone representing the plaintiff's attorneys".

There is little law in New York on the subject of excluding plaintiff's attorney from a physical examination by defendant. This is probably explained by the longstanding and seldom challenged practice of attorneys accompanying and being with their clients at physical examinations. Neither CPLR 3121 (Physical or Mental Examination) nor the Uniform Calendar and Practice Rules of the Fourth Department (22 NYCRR 1024.25, Exchange of Medical Reports) provide for an attorney's presence at physical examinations and, more importantly, they do not provide for his exclusion. One of the commentators who addresses the parameters of CPLR 3121 states that there is "good ground" for a party's insisting that his doctor or attorney be present at the physical examination because "the practice reduces the possibility of misleading medical reports" and information obtained about the way the examination was conducted may be helpful on cross-examination (3A Weinstein–Korn–Miller, N.Y. Civ.Prac., § 3121.07).

Two lower court cases recognized these benefits and ordered a stenographer to record the psychiatric examinations conducted by defendant of plaintiff, the reporter to be stationed outside of the examining room, or in such a position so as not to interfere with the proper conduct of the examination (Murray v. Specialty Chems. Co., 100 Misc.2d 658, 660, 418 N.Y.S.2d 748; Milam v. Mitchell, 51 Misc.2d 948, 950, 274 N.Y.S.2d 326). In *Milam,* plaintiff's attorney did not ask that he be permitted to be present but instead requested the presence of a reporter so that a stenographic transcript could be made. Defendant's doctor, not defendant, objected to the presence of anyone in the room during the psychiatric examination on the grounds that it would interfere with his ability to examine and to prepare his report. In *Murray* the parties could not agree on the limits of the examination, the plaintiff refusing to be examined without the presence of her attorney.

Most litigation, of course, involves adversarial confrontation, not all necessarily confined to courtrooms or law offices. Perhaps in recognition of this fact of legal life, broad and generally liberally applied disclosure devices are provided for in CPLR Art. 31 which serve to accelerate disclosure when acceleration is needed, and to protect against disclosure when protection is appropriate. Pretrial disclosure has as its purpose the requirement that parties and witnesses shed their light before trial so as to avoid surprise and prevent litigation from becoming a game (Siegel, NY Practice, § 343, p. 419). Physical examinations serve these ends by narrowing, if possible, areas of medical dispute through the assistance of the medical profession, and eliminating most of the medical controversy in a personal injury case (Del Ra v. Vaughan, 2 A.D.2d 156, 154 N.Y.S.2d 336). In order to perform his function the examining physician should be allowed to ask such questions as, in his opinion, are necessary to enable him as a physician to determine and report freely on the nature and extent of the injuries complained of. This may include inquiry into the peculiar manner in which the injuries were received (see Wood v. Hoffman Co., 121 App.Div. 636, 106 N.Y.S. 308). The presence of plaintiff's attorney at such examination may well be as important as his presence at an oral deposition. A physician selected by defendant to examine plaintiff is not necessarily a disinterested, impartial medical expert, indifferent to the conflicting interests of the parties. The possible adversary status of the examining doctor for the defense is, under ordinary circumstances, a compelling reason to permit plaintiff's counsel to be present to guarantee, for example, that the doctor does not interrogate the plaintiff on liability questions in order to seek damaging admissions. This is not to suggest that counsel may interfere with the conduct of the physical examination or that the examining room should be turned into a hearing room with lawyers and stenographers from both sides participating. The lawyer's role at the physical examination should be limited to the protection of the legal interests of his client apart from the actual physical examination in which he has no role. If the attorney's participation intrudes upon the examination, appropriate steps may be taken by the court to provide the doctor with a reasonable opportunity to complete his examination. Whether to invoke conditions must be considered in the light of the facts and circumstances of each case.

The value of the attorney's presence at the physical examination of his client has been well stated in Sharff v. Superior Court, 44 Cal.2d 508, 510, 282 P.2d 896:

> Whenever a doctor selected by the defendant conducts a physical examination of the plaintiff, there is a possibility that improper questions may be asked, and a lay person should not be expected to evaluate the propriety of every question at his peril. The plaintiff, therefore, should be permitted to have the assistance and protection of an attorney during the examination.

On this record, we cannot say that plaintiff's representative interfered, unduly or otherwise, with the physical examination. The court below made no such finding and it was an abuse of discretion to direct a physical examination of plaintiff in secret without a compelling showing of the need for the examination to be conducted in this fashion. It is noted that the only sworn statement which the court had before it of a participant in the aborted examination was that of the law clerk (now an attorney) from the office of plaintiff's attorneys.

The order should be modified by deleting therefrom the third ordering paragraph in its entirety.

Order unanimously modified and as modified affirmed with costs to appellant, in accordance with Opinion.

NOTE

Neither Federal Rule 35 nor its New York counterpart says anything either way as to the presence of lawyers at physical or mental exams. Federal cases have tended to take a different view than *Jakubowski*, either prohibiting the presence of lawyers if the other party objects (Warrick v. Brode, 46 F.R.D. 427 (D.Del.1969)) or leaving the matter to the discretion of the trial court.

In *Tomlin v. Holecek*, 150 F.R.D. 628 (D.Minn.1993) plaintiff objected to examination of plaintiff by a psychologist unless plaintiff's lawyer was permitted to be present, the questions to be asked were submitted in advance, or a verbatim record was made of the session, for example by tape recording. The court, while recognizing contra authority, particularly in state cases, rejected each of the proposed restrictions and granted the motion to compel the examination.

Levin & Woolley, Dispatch and Delay: A Field Study of Judicial Administration in Pennsylvania

73–75 (1961).

Impartial Medical Experts

For our purposes it will be helpful to consider the systematic use of impartial medical experts as an adjunct of the pretrial conference. It is, of course, so much more than an adjunct of a preliminary procedure that obtaining impartial medical witnesses has, in its own right, been heralded as a major reform in judicial administration. Understandably, it is a reform associated with the process of trial itself, one addressed in large measure to eliminating the unseemly, and at times disgraceful, battle of the experts in court, the kind which so often gives the impression of having its roots less in professional disagreement than in compensated partisanship. We would not minimize the significance of improving the quality of evidence, of increasing the probability of a just result or of pointing the way to better diagnosis in the field of traumatic medicine, the last an unexpected byproduct of the New York Medical Expert Testimony Project. But the focus of our concern is the elimination of delay and in this the contribution of the impartial expert is by way of inducing settlements, much as is the case with pretrial. Moreover, where the major interest is in court congestion, the impartial expert is used in conjunction with pretrial: as a result of one conference and preliminary to a second.

The basic elements of an organized program of impartial opinion on disputed technical questions are simple enough. First, panels of experts in the various medical specialties are necessary. To insure a high level of professional competence, neutrality as regards the litigation and the litigants and unimpeachable ethical standards, it has been thought wise to have the membership of such panels determined by the medical societies themselves. Safeguards in connection with appointment from the panel to a particular case are necessary further to assure absence of bias. Finally, compensation should be either from an independent source or arranged in a manner that the expert finds it unconnected with either party.

Not every case in which there is some medical question needs the attention of a neutral expert. The parties may not be that far apart or the issue in dispute may not be central to the case. It is for the pretrial judge to screen the suits before him and, it must be readily apparent, those in which he finds particular need for an impartial view are precisely the cases which are resistant to settlement: the litigants, each viewing the case through the eyes of his own expert, are bargaining with respect to essentially different situations. An able professional, who if the case goes to trial will testify as such, creates a common ground. On occasion he may prove even more favorable to the plaintiff than the plaintiff's own expert; on occasion the jury may choose to disbelieve him if he does testify,[44] but it does seem unlikely that men of the professional calibre of those persuaded to man the panels in New York will continue the kind of record which previously had developed in that jurisdiction: one fourth of the cases with gross errors in the reading of x-rays; over a fourth with "essential tests to warrant a diagnosis" not made.

Critical analysis of the statistical evidence indicates that in the New York project settlements before trial were increased substantially. It also appears that this was at the expense of settlements during trial, but from the point of view of effective utilization of courts and judges, this is a most significant gain. It lends force to the argument that providing the parties with an advance view of what a neutral observer will tell the jury provides a new base from which to negotiate, and in a significant number of cases, to do so successfully.

The systematic use of impartial panels is gaining ground, having recently been instituted in the United States District Court for the Eastern District of Pennsylvania. Wherever in Pennsylvania the conditions for successful utilization of this device are present, and an adequate reservoir of professional talent appears to be one of these, the evidence presently available would warrant taking advantage of the impartial medical expert as an adjunct of the pretrial conference.

NOTE ON IMPARTIAL EXPERTS

Merryman, How Others Do It: The French and German Judiciaries, 61 S.Cal.L.Rev. 1865 (1988), provides the following comparative view:

"One example of the passive habits of our judges is their nonuse of the power that federal and many state judges have to appoint impartial experts as witnesses, referees, or special masters. Instead, our judges leave such matters to counsel, who introduce the testimony of partisan experts. Thus we are treated to the unseemly, expensive, often unhelpful, and frequently corrupt 'battle of the experts.' In France and Germany little use is made of party experts. Courts appoint their own experts and rely on their expertise, with the result that such matters are handled more efficiently and, in most cases, more expertly. My experience as a party expert witness in American judicial proceedings has made me an advocate of the French and German preference for court-appointed, impartial experts. I should add, however, that a distinguished colleague with imposing German credentials disagrees.

---

44. Professor Karlen describes a case in which Plaintiff's lawyer would have accepted $4500 to $5000 before trial. The verdict was for $65,000.

[citing Baade, Proving Foreign and International Law in Domestic Tribunals, 18 Va.J.Int.L. 619 (1978)]"

NOTE

Phoenix General Hospital v. Superior Court, 138 Ariz. 504, 675 P.2d 1323 (1984), involved an Arizona statute which provided that any action against a "health provider" must first go before a "medical liability review panel". The panel was to consist of a judge, a lawyer, and a medical expert in the field involved in that particular case. A proceeding would then be held before the panel with opening and closing statements, presentation of evidence, and most of the other procedures of a trial. The panel would then either find for the plaintiff or defendant. (Some states permit the panel to find for neither and simply remit the case for trial). The panel's finding has no adjudicatory effect but constitutes evidence which may be submitted to the finder of fact at trial.

In *Phoenix General* the plaintiff's attorney, apparently afraid of an adverse finding by the panel, appeared before the panel but refused to present any evidence to it. His plan was apparently to weaken the impact of the adverse finding he expected to get anyway, by arguing to the jury that the panel's finding was made without having heard the evidence in plaintiff's case. A previous Arizona case had established that review panel findings, like any other expert evidence, could be impeached at trial. The defendant hospital, characterizing the ploy as an "end run" around the review panels, sought summary judgment from the trial court dismissing plaintiff's action for failure to litigate in good faith before the malpractice panel. The trial court refused to issue such an order and it came to the Supreme Court of Arizona on mandamus.

The Arizona Supreme Court affirmed. It read the statute narrowly as requiring only that plaintiff appear before the malpractice panel. While noting that the tactics of plaintiff in this case might affect the "efficacy" of the statute, the Court was unwilling to impose any "good faith litigation" requirement on plaintiff. Noting that malpractice panels are not judicial tribunals under Arizona law, the Court was reluctant to make litigants' conduct before a nonjudicial body a matter requiring dismissal of the action. It also did not want to enmesh the courts in the problem of determining what constitutes "good faith litigation".

Were the tactics of plaintiff's attorney ethical? Why not simply give the malpractice panel power to decide the case?

D. JUDICIAL INTERVENTION IN THE DISCOVERY PROCESS

1. Sanctions

Rickels v. City of South Bend, Indiana Fara P. Evans, Appellee

United States Court of Appeals for the Seventh Circuit, 1994.
33 F.3d 785.

■ Easterbrook, Circuit Judge.

In the course of litigation against the police of South Bend, Indiana, Romane Rickels served discovery requests on Fara Evans, an attorney who had represented him in litigation against his former wife. The district court denied Rickels' requests to subpoena Evans and to add her as a party, ruling that any dispute Rickels had with Evans is unrelated to his grievance against the police and lacks an independent basis of federal jurisdiction. Rickels persisted, serving additional discovery requests that drove Evans to seek a protective order, which the district judge granted. See Fed. R. Civ. P. 26(c). Next the judge awarded Evans $1,386.78 under Fed. R. Civ. P. 37(a)(4) for the expenses of obtaining the protective order. From this decision Rickels appeals.

The appeal is foredoomed. Rule 37(a)(4) presumptively requires every loser to make good the victor's costs:

> If the motion is denied, the court may enter any protective order authorized under Rule 26(c) and shall, after affording an opportunity to be heard, require the moving party or the attorney filing the motion or both of them to pay to the party or deponent who opposed the motion the reasonable expenses incurred in opposing the motion, including attorney's fees, unless the court finds that the making of the motion was substantially justified or that other circumstances make an award of expenses unjust.

"The great operative principle of Rule 37(a)(4) is that the loser pays." Charles Alan Wright & Arthur R. Miller, 8 Federal Practice and Procedure § 2288 at 787 (1970). Fee shifting when the judge must rule on discovery disputes encourages their voluntary resolution and curtails the ability of litigants to use legal processes to heap detriments on adversaries (or third parties) without regard to the merits of the claims. Rickels lost and must pay.

A loser may avoid payment by establishing that his position was substantially justified. Appellate review of a decision that the position was not so justified is deferential, *Pierce v. Underwood*, 487 U.S. 552, 101 L. Ed. 2d 490, 108 S. Ct. 2541 (1988), and Rickels does not contend that the district court's conclusion was clearly erroneous. Apparently he believes that "other circumstances make an award of expenses unjust." But the only circumstance to which he points is correspondence received from Evans after the judge's order, correspondence in which Evans informed Rickels (correctly) that he must pay forthwith. Insistence on prompt reimbursement, even if conveyed in an impatient or condescending tone with many words underlined and capitalized, does not remove the justification for the award.

Evans (now represented by retained counsel) concludes her brief with a request for a remand so that the district court may award sanctions under Fed. R. Civ. P. 11 for what she characterizes as a frivolous appeal. Rule 11 applies, however, only to litigation in the district court. Sanctions for frivolous appeals are within the domain of Fed. R. App. P. 38.

Whether this appeal is frivolous matters only if the sum under Rule 37(a)(4)—"the reasonable expenses incurred in opposing the motion, including attorney's fees"—omits expenses incurred in obtaining and defending an award. If the district court had awarded sanctions under Rule 11, then the answer would be "yes." *Cooter & Gell v. Hartmarx Corp.*, 496 U.S. 384, 40509, 110 L. Ed. 2d 359, 110 S. Ct. 2447 (1990), holds that a person sanctioned for filing frivolous papers in the district court need not pay extra for taking an appeal, unless the appeal is independently frivolous and sanctionable under Rule 38. When the district court awards fees to the prevailing party as of course, by contrast, the costs of defending the award on appeal are added to that award as of course. E.g., *Commissioner of INS v. Jean*, 496 U.S. 154, 110 L. Ed. 2d 134, 110 S. Ct. 2316 (1990). The rationale of fee*shifting* rules is that the victor should be made whole—should be as well off as if the opponent had respected his legal rights in the first place. This cannot be accomplished if the victor must pay for the appeal out of his own pocket. Id. at 16365.

Rule 37(a)(4) is a fee-shifting rule. The winner is entitled to fees unless the opponent establishes that his position was "substantially justified." This is the same formulation employed in the Equal Access to Justice Act, the fee-shifting statute in *Jean*. When construing the EAJA, the Court concluded that the victor is entitled to recoup his full outlay, including the fees incurred in seeking fees and defending an award on appeal. The only potential obstacle to treating Rule 37(a)(4) the same way the Supreme Court treated the EAJA in *Jean* is that Rule 37, like the other civil rules, applies only in the district courts. *Cooter & Gell* emphasized this when discussing the relation between Civil Rule 11 and Appellate Rule 38. See 496 U.S. at 40607. Yet the Court also emphasized that Rule 11 is not a fee-shifting rule, id. at 408, implying that fee-shifting rules should be treated differently from rules designed to sanction frivolous positions. That Rule 37(a)(4) "applies" only in the district courts does not establish that its reference to "reasonable expenses incurred in opposing the motion, including attorney's fees," includes only the expenses incurred *prior* to the ruling on the motion. A sore loser who files repeated motions under Rules 59 and 60 in an effort to obtain relief from the award should expect to pay the tab, even though the opponent's expenses of opposing these requests may be distinguished from the expenses of opposing the discovery motion and obtaining the protective order.

If instead of pestering the victor with motions in the district court, the loser files equivalent documents in the court of appeals, the upshot should be the same. Under Rule 37 the district court makes the final award, so we remand for that purpose. Evans is entitled to the reasonable expenses, including attorneys' fees, incurred in obtaining the protective order and defending her entitlement to this reimbursement. Nothing less will make her whole; anything less would defeat the function of Rule 37(a)(4).

AFFIRMED AND REMANDED

NOTE: PUTTING SANCTIONS IN PERSPECTIVE

The text of Rule 37(a)(4) supports the conclusion of Judge Easterbrook in the principal case that the party forcing a discovery dispute into court has to pay the other side what this maneuver cost them, unless, of course, the court finds that the motion was "substantially justified," or that there is some other circumstance making the award of expenses "unjust." The same approach is evident in other provisions of Rule 37 and this, indeed, may be said to reflect the basic design of the federal rules.

Sound policy considerations support the principle: the added burdens in time and expense imposed by unjustified tactics do not come cost-free.

How most judges and litigants have actually treated Rule 37, over the years, is quite another matter. The authors of an important 1981 study of sanctions in federal cases state their conclusion in the following terms:

> The typical pattern of sanctioning that emerges from the reported cases is one in which the delay, obfuscation, contumacy, and lame excuses on the part of litigants and their attorneys are tolerated without any measured remedial action until the court is provoked beyond endurance. At that point the court punishes one side or the other with a swift and final termination of the lawsuit by dismissal or default. This "all or nothing" approach to sanctions results in considerable laxity in the day-to-day application of the rules. Attorneys are well aware that sanctions will be imposed only in the most flagrant situations.[1]

An earlier study had also found very few motions requesting sanctions, only about half of which were actually ruled on by the courts, and a grand total of 26 motions for sanctions granted out of 7,117 discovery requests—and three of these were conditional.[2]

Moreover, the basic pattern remains in most courts. Typically, lawyers involved in "ordinary" discovery disputes do not seek sanctions. Egregious conduct, such as that described under the headline "Sleazy in Seattle,"[3] is another matter. That conduct, once it came to light, led to an agreement "to pay $325,000 in sanctions for discovery abuse."[4] Moreover, it is far from clear that the sanctions agreed upon were adequate, either to compensate or to deter.[5]

National Hockey League et al. v. Metropolitan Hockey Club, Inc.

Supreme Court of the United States, 1976.
427 U.S. 639, 96 S.Ct. 2778, 49 L.Ed.2d 747.

■ Per Curiam.

This case arises out of the dismissal, under Fed.Rule Civ.Proc. 37, of respondents' antitrust action against petitioners for failure to timely

---

1. Robert E. Rodes, Jr., Kenneth F. Ripple, and Carol Mooney, Sanctions Imposable for Violations of the Federal Rules of Civil Procedure: A Report to the Federal Judicial Center from the Thomas J. and Alberta White Center for Law, Government and Human Rights, Notre Dame Law School, July, 1981, at 85.

2. Paul R. Connolly, Edith A. Holleman, and Michael J. Kuhlman, Judicial Controls and the Civil Litigative Process: Discovery, June, 1978, at 24.

3. Stuart Taylor, Jr., "Sleazy in Seattle," The American Lawyer, April, 1994, at 5, discussing Washington State P.I.E. & A. v. Fisons Corp., 858 P.2d 1054 (Wash.1993)

4. Id.

5. See Barbara J. Gorham, Note and Comment: "Fisons: Will it Tame the Beast of Discovery Abuse?" 69 Washington Law Review 765 (1994).

Altogether rare, but not unknown, is the imposition of $2.9 million of attorneys' fees as a sanction, affirmed in Religious Technology Center v. Church of the New Civilization, 1996 WL 171443 (9th Cir. 1996). The litigation involved a dispute between the Church of Scientology and a splinter group. The trial judge characterized the case in the following terms:

> The past 8 years have consisted mainly of a prolonged and ultimately unsuccessful, attempt to persuade or compel the plaintiff to comply with lawful discovery. These efforts have been fiercely resisted by plaintiffs. They have utilized every device that we on the District Court have ever heard of to avoid such compliance, and some that are new to us.

answer written interrogatories as ordered by the District Court, 63 F.R.D. 641. The Court of Appeals for the Third Circuit reversed the judgment of dismissal, finding that the District Court had abused its discretion, 531 F.2d 1188. The question presented is whether the Court of Appeals was correct in so concluding. Rule 37 provides in pertinent part as follows:

> "If a party * * * fails to obey an order to provide or permit discovery * * * the court in which the action is pending may make such orders in regard to the failure as are just, and among others the following:

> * * *

> (C) An order striking out pleadings or parts thereof, or staying further proceedings until the order is obeyed, or dismissing the action or proceeding or any part thereof, or rendering a judgment by default against the disobedient party."

This Court held in Societe Internationale v. Rogers, 357 U.S. 197, 212, 78 S.Ct. 1087, 1096, 2 L.Ed.2d 1255 (1958), that Rule 37

> "should not be construed to authorize dismissal of [a] complaint because of petitioner's noncompliance with a pretrial production order when it has been established that failure to comply has been due to inability, and not to willfulness, bad faith, or any fault of petitioner."

While there have been amendments to the Rule since the decision in *Rogers*, neither the parties, the District Court, nor the Court of Appeals suggested that the changes would affect the teachings of the quoted language from that decision.

The District Court, in its memorandum opinion directing that respondents' complaint be dismissed, summarized the factual history of the discovery proceeding in these words:

> "After seventeen months where crucial interrogatories remained substantially unanswered despite numerous extensions granted at the eleventh hour and, in many instances, beyond the eleventh hour, and notwithstanding several admonitions by the Court and promises and commitments by the plaintiffs, the Court must and does conclude that the conduct of the plaintiffs demonstrates the callous disregard of responsibilities counsel owe to the Court and to their opponents. The practices of the plaintiffs exemplify flagrant bad faith when after being expressly directed to perform an act by a date certain, viz., June 14, 1974, they failed to perform and compounded that noncompliance by waiting until five days afterwards before they filed any motions. Moreover, this action was taken in the face of warnings that their failure to provide certain information could result in the imposition of sanctions under Fed.R.Civ.P. 37. If the sanction of dismissal is not warranted by the circumstances of this case, then the Court can envisage no

set of facts whereby that sanction should ever be applied." 63 F.R.D. 641, 656 (1974).

The Court of Appeals, in reversing the order of the District Court by a divided vote, stated:

> "After carefully reviewing the record, we conclude that there is insufficient evidence to support a finding that M–GB's failure to file supplemental answers by June 14, 1974 was in flagrant bad faith, willful or intentional." 531 F.2d 1188, 1195 (1976).

The Court of Appeals did not question any of the findings of historical fact which had been made by the District Court, but simply concluded that there was in the record evidence of "extenuating factors." The Court of Appeals emphasized that none of the parties had really pressed discovery until after a consent decree was entered between petitioners and all of the other original plaintiffs except the respondents approximately one year after the commencement of the litigation. It also noted that respondents' counsel took over the litigation, which previously had been managed by another attorney, after the entry of the consent decree, and that respondents' counsel encountered difficulties in obtaining some of the requested information. The Court of Appeals also referred to a colloquy during the oral argument on petitioners' motion to dismiss in which respondents' lead counsel assured the District Court that he would not knowingly and willfully disregard the final deadline.

While the Court of Appeals stated that the District Court was required to consider the full record in determining whether to dismiss for failure to comply with discovery orders, see Link v. Wabash R. Co., 370 U.S. 626, 633–634, 82 S.Ct. 1386, 1390, 8 L.Ed.2d 734 (1962), we think that the comprehensive memorandum of the District Court supporting its order of dismissal indicates that the court did just that. That record shows that the District Court was extremely patient in its efforts to allow the respondents ample time to comply with its discovery orders. Not only did respondents fail to file their responses on time, but the responses which they ultimately did file were found by the District Court to be grossly inadequate.

The question, of course, is not whether this Court, or whether the Court of Appeals, would as an original matter have dismissed the action; it is whether the District Court abused its discretion in so doing. E.g., C. Wright & A. Miller, Federal Practice and Procedure: Civil § 2284, p. 765 (1970); General Dynamics Corp. v. Selb Mfg. Co., 481 F.2d 1204, 1211 (C.A.8 1973); Baker v. F & F Investment, 470 F.2d 778, 781 (C.A.2 1972). Certainly the findings contained in the memorandum opinion of the District Court quoted earlier in this opinion are fully supported by the record. We think that the lenity evidenced in the opinion of the Court of Appeals, while certainly a significant factor in considering the imposition of sanctions under Rule 37, cannot be allowed to wholly supplant other and equally necessary considerations embodied in that Rule.

There is a natural tendency on the part of reviewing courts, properly employing the benefit of hindsight, to be heavily influenced by the severity of outright dismissal as a sanction for failure to comply with a discovery order. It is quite reasonable to conclude that a party who has been subjected to such an order will feel duly chastened, so that even though he succeeds in having the order reversed on appeal he will nonetheless comply promptly with future discovery orders of the district court.

But here, as in other areas of the law, the most severe in the spectrum of sanctions provided by statute or rule must be available to the district court in appropriate cases, not merely to penalize those whose conduct may be deemed to warrant such a sanction, but to deter those who might be tempted to such conduct in the absence of such a deterrent. If the decision of the Court of Appeals remained undisturbed in this case, it might well be that *these* respondents would faithfully comply with all future discovery orders entered by the District Court in this case. But other parties to other lawsuits would feel freer than we think Rule 37 contemplates they should feel to flout other discovery orders of other district courts. Under the circumstances of this case, we hold that the District Judge did not abuse his discretion in finding bad faith on the part of these respondents, and concluding that the extreme sanction of dismissal was appropriate in this case by reason of respondents' "flagrant bad faith" and their counsel's "callous disregard" of their responsibilities. Therefore, the petition for a writ of certiorari is granted and the judgment of the Court of Appeals is reversed.[a]

QUESTIONS

A. Is the question of whether the failure to comply with discovery orders was "willful" an issue of fact or law?

B. Which individuals and what kind of conduct is the Court seeking to deter by its ruling in this case?

NOTE ON SANCTIONS FOR DISCOVERY ABUSE

Despite the availability of dismissal as a sanction for discovery violations under Rule 37(b)(2)(C) and the strong language of *National Hockey League,* dismissal of actions for discovery abuse remains an uncommon event. The Fifth Circuit's decision in Marshall v. Segona, 621 F.2d 763 (5th Cir.1980) illustrates some of the reasons for judicial reluctance to dismiss. The case was brought by the Secretary of Labor against the owner of two Louisiana truckstops, alleging that the owner had failed to pay his employees the minimum wage and required overtime premiums. The owner served interrogatories seeking precise information as to the names of the allegedly underpaid employees and the dates and locations worked. After repeated motions, the Labor Department answered the interrogatories, but over six months after the district court's initial order compelling production and four days after the final deadline set by the court had passed. Although the district court ordered

a. Dissent of Justice Brennan and Justice White omitted.

dismissal of the action, the Fifth Circuit reversed. In his opinion, Judge Brown stated:

"The bandwidth of the District Court's power to impose Rule 37 sanctions is broad indeed. We will not interfere unless important historical findings are clearly erroneous or—by the imposition of sanctions which are not 'just'—there has been an abuse of discretion. We are mindful that the use of even severe sanctions has a salutary deterrent effect on parties to other law suits and their counsel and that great army of yet unknowns who will for one reason or another have cases and counsel. National Hockey League v. Metropolitan Hockey Club, Inc., 427 U.S. 639, 643, 96 S.Ct. 2778, 2781, 49 L.Ed.2d 747, 751 (1976) (per curiam).[8]

"We have upheld the use of 'the draconian remedy of dismissal' in suitably 'extreme circumstances.' Bonaventure v. Butler, 593 F.2d 625, 626 (5th Cir.1979) (dismissal affirmed where plaintiff three times refused to appear for deposition). See Emerick v. Fenick Industries, Inc., 539 F.2d 1379 (5th Cir.1976) (default entered where defendant ignored three orders to produce documents); Jones v. Louisiana State Bar Association, 602 F.2d 94 (5th Cir.1979) (dismissal where plaintiff deliberately refused two orders to produce tape recording and notes which plaintiff admitted possession of); Venzara v. Continental Training Services, Inc., 615 F.2d 919 (5th Cir.1980) (Fifth Circuit Rule 21 affirmance of default judgments). Two other of our decisions which are similar yet distinguishable are Factory Air Conditioning Corp. v. Westside Toyota, Inc., 579 F.2d 334 (5th Cir.1978), and In re Liquid Carbonic Truck Drivers Chemical Poison Litigation, 580 F.2d 819 (5th Cir.1978). In the first, the defendant was ordered on May 16 to supplement its interrogatory answers by May 31. Nothing was filed, as the defendant was apparently disregarding the request of his own attorney for information. On July 20, the District Court entered yet a second order, allowing defendant until July 27 to answer. The plaintiff, on August 10, motioned again for default since as of that date answers had not been filed.[9] The motion was granted by the District Court and we affirmed.

"In *Liquid Carbonic,* the suits of five out of nine truck drivers were dismissed for repeated failures to adequately answer interrogatories. Because the five refused to cooperate with their own attorney (and after passage of the F.R.Civ.P. 33 period for answering interrogatories) an order was entered on June 15 which required answers by July 1. Subsequently, plaintiffs were six days late in filing answers. On August 10, the District Court found that the answers, which had been once amended at the Court's prodding, were still vague and incomplete. Accordingly, a second order was entered which allowed until August 15 to submit satisfactory answers. The answers were not filed, however, until August 16 or 17. The District Court dismissed the suits of the five *noncooperating* truck drivers, recounting a

---

8. In *National Hockey League* the Court considered the use of the most drastic sanction—dismissal—stating that it could be used when the failure to comply was due to "willfulness, bad faith, or * * * fault. * * * "427 U.S. at 640, 96 S.Ct. at 2779, 49 L.Ed.2d at 749 (quoting Societe Internationale v. Rogers, 357 U.S. 197, 212, 78 S.Ct. 1087, 1095, 2 L.Ed.2d 1255, 1267 (1958)). There the plaintiffs disregarded more than three Court orders to supplement interrogatory answers, and a year after the first order had not filed adequate answers. The answers were crucial to the defense and delay effectively prevented adequate discovery by the defendants since the inadequate answers were filed *after* the defendants' discovery cutoff date. See In re Professional Hockey Antitrust Litigation, 63 F.R.D. 641, 643–55 (E.D.Pa.1974). Accordingly, the District Court found the plaintiffs guilty of "callous disregard" of their responsibilities and of "flagrant bad faith" in their overall conduct. *Id.* at 656. The District Court reluctantly invoked the sanction of dismissal. The Court of Appeals overturned the dismissal sanction. Because the facts demonstrated no abuse of discretion, the Supreme Court reversed and upheld the dismissal.

9. The propriety of a default judgment is evaluated by the same standards as the sanction of dismissal. United Artists Corp. v. Freeman, 605 F.2d 854, 856–57 (5th Cir. 1979) (per curiam).

number of other discovery violations which had occurred. But the suits of the four truck drivers who had at least cooperated with the attorney were not dismissed. We upheld the dismissals, pointing out that the answers were not filed until 10 days before trial and that numerous other discovery violations occurred.

"But we have also recognized that dismissal is too harsh a sanction where a number of factors, singly or in combination, are present, or where the District Court's relevant findings of historical fact are clearly erroneous. First, dismissal is to be sparingly used and only in situations where its deterrent value cannot be substantially achieved by use of less drastic sanctions. Whether the other party's preparation for trial was substantially prejudiced is a consideration. 'Dismissal is generally inappropriate and lesser sanctions are favored where neglect is plainly attributable to an attorney rather than to his blameless client.' Nor does a party's simple negligence, grounded in confusion or sincere misunderstanding of the Court's orders, warrant dismissal. Finally, the Rule 'should not be construed to authorize dismissal * * * when it has been established that failure to comply has been due to inability * * *,' *National Hockey League, supra,* 427 U.S. at 640, 96 S.Ct. at 2779, 49 L.Ed.2d at 749, such as where requested information is not yet available, though it will later become so.[14]

"Present in this appeal in varying proportions are all of the factors which make dismissal inappropriate. We are furthermore of the 'definite and firm conviction'[15] that there was clear error in the District Court's perception of the facts relating to the amount of time during which the Secretary was obligated to supply the wage and hour information. *See* notes 2 and 3 and accompanying text *supra.* The record clearly shows that the Secretary was not under any F.R.Civ.P. 37(a) order until December 14, 1978. Even as of that date, good faith though partial compliance with Segona's discovery request had occurred since some 27 names and respective employment dates had been delivered.[16] The Secretary did not receive this order, with its thirty-day requirement, until December 19, 1978. As reflected by the third count of the Secretary's complaint, the inadequate state of Segona's wage and hour records made it most difficult for the Secretary to answer the interrogatories within the thirty days.[17] And Segona was also partly responsible for the Secretary's missing the final deadline—by four days—set for the filing of supplemental answers.

"There is also uncontroverted evidence that the Secretary's four-day noncompliance was caused by the good faith, sincere, but mistaken interpretation of the correct deadline of the District Court's order. This was at most simple negligence— a failure to completely understand the Court's order—and even then was negligence of the Secretary's lawyer, not the Secretary. It is also significant, though not controlling, that Segona was not prejudiced by the Secretary's inability to compile the wage and hour information."

14. Dorsey v. Academy Moving & Storage, Inc., 423 F.2d 858 (5th Cir.1970); Dunn v. Trans World Airlines, Inc., 589 F.2d 408 (9th Cir.1978). *Cf.* Read v. Ulmer, 308 F.2d 915 (5th Cir.1962) (default judgment).

15. *Cf.* Dorey v. Dorey, 609 F.2d 1128, 1136 (5th Cir.) (quoting from other cases), *rehearing en banc denied,* 613 F.2d 314 (5th Cir.1980).

16. We furthermore observe that the Secretary's August 29 responses to interrogatories numbered one through four may be viewed as objections, properly made under

F.R.Civ.P. 33(a). Segona's subsequent motion set in motion the overruling of those objections, but that was not done until the District Court's December 14 order. Viewed in this context, and contrary to the District Court's characterization, the Secretary's *only* actual discovery violation was its mistaken and inadvertent four-day noncompliance with the December 14 order.

17. We do not of course say that mere allegation of inadequate records excuses the plaintiff from compliance with discovery rules.

NOTE

As an examination of the authorities cited in *National Hockey* will demonstrate, defining when resort to dismissal as a sanction is appropriate is not limited to discovery abuse. Similarly, appellate reluctance to affirm resort to dismissal is reflected in connection with other rules. In *Adams v. Brewery Employees' Pension Trust Fund*, 29 F.3d 863 (3d Cir.1994) the court was obliged to consider dismissal as a sanction for failure to prosecute. "After a four and one-half year hiatus, the Pension Benefit Guaranty Corporation attempted to reopen its case against Pabst Brewing and Anheuser–Busch for unfunded benefits in a terminated pension fund."

The appellate court agreed that "PBGC's behavior was negligent and inexcusable," but (after many pages of discussion) reversed and remanded for imposition of a lesser sanction because dismissal with prejudice was too harsh.

2.   The Quest for Solutions

It is not possible to consider the problems of discovery in isolation. A major focus of the concern relates to the cost of litigation, a subject which is explored in some detail in the next chapter. In the search for solutions a great deal of attention has been focused on the role of the judge; more specifically, on what many consider the obligation of the judge to seize the initiative in managing civil litigation, a subject which is explored more fully infra in the chapter on the pretrial conference.

The Civil Justice Reform Act of 1990, introduced on January 25 by Senator Joseph R. Biden, Jr., chair of the Senate Judiciary Committee, recognizes this much, and yet it isolates certain steps that should be taken with respect to the control of discovery specifically.

In introducing the legislation Senator Biden noted that it was being co-sponsored by the ranking minority member, and that a companion bill was being introduced on the same day in the House with similar sponsorship. The following extract, focusing on discovery, is taken from Senator Biden's remarks on that occasion.[a]

Biden, Statement on the Introduction of the Civil Justice Reform Act of 1990

(January 25, 1990).

A central objective of the mandatory discovery-case management conference is to minimize discovery costs. Delineating the issues at an early stage of the litigation will minimize such costs, since the parties can then be steered away from aimless or redundant discovery. More than a decade ago, Judge William W. Schwarzer, of the U.S. District

---

a. As noted above, this bill was enacted into law in December 1990 and, in the process, was modified considerably. The compromises which preceded adoption of what is now known as the Civil Justice Reform Act of 1990, codified at 28 U.S.C. §§ 471–478, provided for greater flexibility on the part of the individual district courts. As enacted, the bill also provides for study of the impact of the legislation on cost and delay and for steps to be taken by the Judicial Conference of the United States following analysis of the results of that study. The following remains useful in setting forth the views of the author of the bill and in the continuing analysis of the problems of discovery.

Court for the Northern District of California, commented on the importance of a compulsory status conference, which, by setting discovery guidelines tailored to the case, can "reduce subsequent discovery disputes and piecemeal motions to compel or for protective orders, and tend to nip in the bud any notion by a party to wage an attrition campaign using discovery as a weapon."

The mandatory discovery-case management conference can also help the parties focus on possible grounds for dismissal or summary judgment. If it seems that motions are probable, the court should set dates and briefing schedules.

* * *

Some might argue that these conferences will themselves be costly, particularly in terms of judicial time they will require. This concern, in my view, is unfounded. Indeed, the best answer to it is provided by Judge Peckham, chief judge of one of our nation's busiest courts. Judge Peckham estimated that a judge could "easily conduct all status conferences for a full caseload in one day per month and certainly in no more than two." As he put it, "[t]his is very little time to expend in facilitating the prompt and fair disposition of cases."

* * *

The legislation attacks the discovery problem from several directions.

First, as I've mentioned, the tracking systems to be implemented in each district will include time periods for the completion of discovery. Specifically, Section 471(b)(6) requires "that each processing track in the district's tracking system establish presumptive time limits for the completion of discovery so that parties are apprised upon track assignment of the time within which discovery must be completed."

It's important to recognize that the discovery time limits are *presumptive*. This ensures that sufficient flexibility is retained for those cases warranting extensions of time. One example of a showing of "good cause" warranting an extension would be if additional discovery would not delay the trial. Absent such special circumstances, however, discovery should be limited according to the time frame set forth in the guidelines for the particular track to which the case has been assigned.

Second, Section 471(b)(7) requires that each district court include in its plan procedures for making the discovery process "track specific." Specifically, each district is to consider identifying and limiting the volume of discovery available, and phasing the use of discovery into two or more stages.

With respect to phasing discovery, I have been taken with the approach first suggested by Judge Peckham. The first stage is limited to developing information needed for a realistic assessment of the case. If the case does not terminate then, a second stage of discovery would commence, this one for the purpose of preparing for trial. Limiting discovery initially to those crucial issues that highlight the essential strengths and weaknesses of a case will often lead to considerable savings of time and money for clients and the court system. The information derived from the first stage should suffice for the disposal of many cases, without having to incur the expense of discovery that merely amplifies and cumulates already available evidence or that is directed to peripheral issues.

Another means of phasing discovery is to divide the use of interrogatories according to the stage of the case. The U.S. District Court for the Southern District of New York currently utilizes such a rule, which limits the type of interrogatories that may be served at particular stages of the litigation.

I should note that imposing discovery limitations is entirely consistent with the 1983 amendments to the Federal Rules of Civil Procedure. Rule 26(b)(1)(iii) was amended to permit the court to limit discovery where it would be "unduly burdensome or expensive, taking into account the needs of the case, the amount in controversy, limitations on the parties' resources and the importance of the issues at stake in the litigation." This was an extremely valuable addition to the rules, but for whatever reason, it has not been utilized to any great extent.

Third, Section 471(b)(8) requires that each district adopt as an element of its plan a rule that the parties attempt to resolve all discovery disputes informally before filing motion papers with the court.

I believe that these and other measures that the district courts may adopt will assist in reducing the costs of discovery.

NOTE: ATTORNEY OPINION OF THE FUTURE OF DISCLOSURE

The following information is taken from the Federal Judicial Center's 1997 Report entitled Discovery and Disclosure: Practice, Problems, and Proposals for Change. The Report presents findings from a national survey of attorneys who responded to a questionnaire regarding the levels, costs, and problems with discovery.

Do the discovery rules need to be changed? In what way should they be changed?

Although attorneys view judicial case management as the most promising approach to reducing discovery problems, 83% nonetheless want changes in the discovery rules. The desire for change centers on initial disclosure.

Regarding initial disclosure, a plurality of all respondents in the sample—41%—favor a uniform national rule requiring initial disclosure in every district. Another 27% favor a national rule with no requirement of initial disclosure and a prohibition on local requirements for disclosure. Close to a third—30%—favor the status quo. Attorneys who participated in initial disclosure in the sample case were considerably more likely to favor requiring disclosure than attorneys who did not (Table 39).

Table 39

Percentage of attorneys preferring certain types of uniform national roles, by participation in initial disclosure

Attorney opinion	Participation in initial disclosure	No participation in initial disclosure
National rule requiring initial disclosure in every district	52%	28%
National rule with no requirement for initial disclosure and a prohibition on local requirements for initial disclosure	22%	31%
Allowing local districts to decide whether or not to require initial disclosure (status quo)	23%	38%
Other	3%	2%

When should changes be made?

Among those who think the discovery rules should be revised, a majority (54%) favor making changes now ... Most of that group consists of attorney who want immediate consideration of change to Rule 26(a)(1).

CHAPTER V

THE COST OF LITIGATION

INTRODUCTORY NOTE

This chapter is divided into five sections. The first section deals with the cost of litigation as a problem in the delivery of justice, viewed from various perspectives: what percentage of the amount a defendant actually pays out mass tort cases, for example, reaches a successful plaintiff and how much is absorbed by transaction costs, including what the lawyers get? In terms of society as a whole, what trends are discernable in the percentage of the gross national product devoted to legal services?

The subsequent sections deal with a number of significant mechanisms for allocating the expense of litigation among parties: statutory shifting of attorneys' fees, payment of contingent fees from the recovery or settlement of a class action, taxation of costs, and court-imposed monetary sanctions.

A. THE COST OF LITIGATION—AN OVERVIEW

Containing the Cost of Litigation
A. Leo Levin and Denise D. Colliers.
37 Rutgers Law Review 219 (1985).

I. INTRODUCTION

The cost of litigation has become a matter of serious public concern. Front-page features in the daily press, extensive articles in popular magazines, and even the annual report of the president of Harvard University, have all discussed escalating legal costs. In light of these concerns, the Federal Rules of Civil Procedure have been amended twice in the last five years, and still further amendments are in prospect. The 1980 amendments were in large measure an effort to cope with escalating costs, and the intense debate and commentary surrounding their enactment reflected this concern. Considered inadequate by three Justices of the United States Supreme Court, the 1980 changes were followed by new amendments in 1983. The latter provided for mandatory sanctions intended to curb discovery abuse. Amendments currently under consideration focus upon economic incentives and disincentives associated with settlement offers.

Perhaps the most striking evidence of the existence of a serious problem comes from the lawyers themselves. Professor Wayne Brazil, reporting the results of an empirical study, recently wrote: "Even litigators who frankly admitted that they were becoming wealthy primarily because of fees attributable to discovery expressed amazement and concern about the rapid escalation of the expense of conducting and complying with discovery." Similarly, Francis Kirkham, a senior partner in a San Francisco law firm, declared during a colloquy on complex litigation: "If more is not done to reduce the expense of litigation, the legal profession will be destroyed. If the courts of this country cannot handle litigation at a reasonable expense, then some substitute mechanism for dispute settling will be needed." There may be an element of pardonable hyperbole in this last statement, but dissatisfaction with the present system is widespread. Indeed, leaders of the bar actively have sought the imposition of mandatory and potentially severe sanctions not only against litigants, but against other lawyers as well.

This is not to suggest that every civil case, even every federal case, involves inordinate expenditures and waste. The evidence is to the contrary. Yet costs even in litigation that must be described as in the middle-range—involving neither "mega-cases" nor petty claims—have become a source of serious concern; the five-year work of the American Bar Association's Action Commission to Reduce Court Costs and Delay clearly illustrates that concern. Whatever the extent of the problem, whatever the primary focus, it cannot be dismissed as de minimis.

This paper attempts to describe, at least in part, the nature and dimension of the problem and to suggest steps that can be taken to contain the costs of litigation. The time is propitious; as already noted, there exists today a fortunate mixture of altruism and self-interest on the part of many who are deeply concerned about the ultimate implications for the profession if present trends continue unchecked.

II. Increase in Cost and Volume of Litigation

A. *Legal Services and the Gross National Product*

Over the past decade, more and more of the country's wealth has been spent on legal services. In 1983, the portion of the gross national product (GNP) attributable to legal services was over $33 billion, representing a 58.6% increase in real terms, i.e., in constant dollars, over 1973. (See Figure 1.) In current dollars, this increase is in excess of $24 billion, or 244%, in a single decade. Moreover, these figures understate the dimensions of the change because they do not include the cost of in-house counsel or of government attorneys.

* * *

Justice Powell made the point succinctly and directly: "Delay and excessive expense now characterize a large percentage of all civil litigation. The problems arise in significant part, as every judge and litigator knows, from abuse of the discovery procedures available under the Rules." The litigation section of the American Bar Association concurred in a report that underscores the need "to reverse the trend toward increasingly expensive, time-consuming and vexatious use of the discovery rules."

Some examples are useful in understanding how discovery and other pretrial expenses can mount to the high levels they reach and in appreciating the magnitude of the sums involved. These examples are not offered as typical of the common tort or contract case; we will consider separately studies that shed light on the cost of litigation in the "ordinary" case.

In General William Westmoreland's libel suit against CBS, discovery produced 400,000 pages of documents. Of course, documents represent only a fraction of typical discovery costs. The case came to trial in October of 1984. During 1983, CBS spent an estimated $100,000 per month preparing for trial; plaintiff spent about $900,000 for the same year. Once the trial began, legal expenses escalated. Total legal expenses for the case, including the cost of an eighteen-week trial, were estimated at $8.3 million.

Patent litigation is frequently complex and typically expensive. A story in the press concerning one inventor's experience in vindicating his legal rights illustrates the point; the context was a patent infringement suit involving plastic-sheathed cable. For eleven years Frederic A. Lang battled large manufacturers of concrete cable. From 1972 to 1980, Mr. Lang spent more than $500,000 on pretrial legal expenses. In 1980, however, two years prior to the actual trial in the United States District Court for the District of Delaware, Mr. Lang could no longer afford to litigate with personal funds. He was able to continue his case only because he found attorneys willing to work on a contingency basis—for 40% of any final award or settlement. By the end of 1982, Lang had won victories in both the District of Delaware and the Eastern District of Virginia. Mr. Lang offered this advice to those considering bringing a patent infringement suit: "You shouldn't enter into enforcing a patent unless you have $1 million or resources equal to the opponent." With costs at this level, pretrial expenses alone can easily result in a denial of access to the courts.

Minimum resources of $1 million may be rather high for what is needed to commence litigation, but knowledgeable patent attorneys willing to discuss the subject do talk of six-figure minima. One patent lawyer recently suggested that the initial phases of a patent suit required an expenditure of approximately $250,000 by plaintiffs and that if the case were to go to trial, attorneys' fees and expenses easily could cost the plaintiff $500,000. Another patent attorney stated that he thought the above figures were high. He suggested that plaintiff would have to commit only $125,000 to start suit, but after a moment's reflection he added a caveat: "[I]f opposing counsel wants to make it an expensive case, he can."

A detailed depiction of lawyers' activities in the pretrial stage of litigation is provided in the fee petition submitted by counsel for the prevailing party in cases where the award of attorneys' fees is fixed by the court.

A case in point is the *Agent Orange Product Liability Litigation,* in which the fee of the principal attorneys was reduced from the requested $26 million to $5.9 million. Although much of the reduction was based on disallowance of any contingency multiplier, Judge Jack Weinstein also specifically criticized some of the activities for which fees and expenses were requested. One attorney had requested reimbursement for 4,956.25 hours in paralegal and law clerk time. Finding that the attorney's office was extensively over-staffed, the court reduced the number of compensable hours to 94.87. The same attorney "regularly ate and stayed at first-class restaurants and hotels and used courier services almost to the exclusion of first-class mail." Another attorney claimed "sometimes as many as nine hours per day for 'Federal Rules of Evidence Review'" even though he was "an accomplished student of the law of evidence, having distinguished himself in this subject at law school and in practice." These hours were also disallowed.

In the *Fine Paper Antitrust Litigation,* a case that was settled on the very first day of trial, plaintiffs' attorneys asked the court to approve a fee of $21 million and provided detailed documentation of what was done, by whom, and for how long. The underlying controversy was settled for slightly more than $50 million. The fee requested, then, was more than 40% of a very large recovery—in a case that did not even require a complete trial. Judge Joseph L. McGlynn, Jr., awarded only $5 million. Understandably, a number of plaintiffs' lawyers appealed. To some extent, they were successful. However, in the view of one of the appellants' attorneys, expressed in a press interview, the total award including increase on remand would not be in excess of $7.3 million—less than 35% of the original fee request.

This litigation offers many examples of inefficiency leading to excessive charges, of which two bear mention. The first is systemic. As the appellate court observed:

> [T]here is * * * considerable evidence in the fee petitions themselves that, whether because of friction between Harold Kohn and other lead counsel, or because of the complexity of the organizational structure, there was great duplication of effort. The committee structure resulted in assignment of discovery of individual defendants to subcommittee members. The work of the subcommittee members had to be forwarded and reviewed by an overall discovery committee and by lead counsel.

A second example involves a request for "approximately one-half million dollars for 1,446 hours of preparation, travel and attendance at pretrial conference," a rate of over $300 per hour. Judge McGlynn refused to approve this item, observing, "The class was ably represented at these conferences by lead counsel and * * * the attendance of the other lawyers who merely sat and watched was superfluous."

The excessive fee request in *Fine Paper* also resulted in substantial expenditure of judge time. Judge McGlynn was faced with the task of reviewing a "massive set of fee applications, which, if stacked in one pile, would amount to a pillar of paper 27 feet high." His original memorandum of decision in the case was almost 200 pages long. The opinion on appeal was also detailed and meticulous and invited still further detail on remand.

We are not suggesting that the size of the fee, in and of itself, implies abuse; in a sense, no matter how many millions are awarded, we cannot conclude automatically that the cost of litigation is "high." In *In re Corrugated Container Antitrust Litigation,* plaintiffs' attorneys requested fees in excess of $48 million, but the figure must be put in perspective. The case involved thirty-seven defendants, more than 200,000 class members, and a settlement, after trial, in excess of $500 million. More to the point, Chief Judge John V. Singleton, Jr., who presided at the trial, praised class counsel's handling of the litigation: "It is impossible to fault the management of this litigation and, instead, plaintiff counsel must be congratulated on the results achieved."

The *Fine Paper* case is, admittedly, a horror story, and horror stories are, by definition, atypical. Yet horror stories have a legitimate role to play—at the least they invite inquiry into the frequency with which they occur and into their significance. Serious medical pathology also occurs infrequently, but that is no reason for a concerned doctor to ignore such pathology when it does occur, particularly when there is high risk of contagion and a substantial probability of serious damage.

At this juncture it is important to attempt a sense of perspective. We do not suggest—and the available data do not support—any charge that discovery is an area of major difficulty in every federal case or in ordinary state litigation. Indeed, a Federal Judicial Center empirical study of more than 3,100 terminated cases involving more than 7,000 discovery requests (interrogatories, requests for documents, requests for admissions, and notices of deposition) revealed that discovery abuse did not permeate the vast majority of federal filings. In half the filings, there were no formal discovery, abusive or otherwise. In the remaining half, abuse—to the extent it existed—was more likely to be found in the *quality* of the discovery requests than in the *quantity* since fewer than 5% of the filings involved more than ten requests. Although it would be unwise to infer that there were no discovery problems, or that discovery in those cases was invariably conducted in the most economical fashion possible, the data militate against the conclusion that discovery is always a source of uneconomical, expensive litigation.

The Wisconsin Civil Litigation Research Project, a more recent work that examined the methods and the cost of resolving civil disputes in five distinct geographical areas, supports these conclusions. Court records of the cases studied in that project revealed no evidence of discovery in more than half of the cases. The percentage was almost identical in each of the studies. In those cases where there was evidence of discovery, rarely did the record reveal more than five discovery events. The Wisconsin Project, however, intentionally put to one side what were termed "extraordinary" cases—complex litigation involving substantial sums of money. Fifty-six percent of the cases studied involved $10,000 or less. Only 12% of the cases involved stakes of $50,000 or more, and the median value of the federal cases—

defined as the lawyer's estimate of what would be accepted in settlement—was more than three times that of the state cases: $15,000
versus $4,500. This project is not to be faulted for the decision to
study ordinary litigation, but if there are problems in the extraordinary
case, they should not be ignored. When a case is settled for $50
million, or damages in excess of $400 million are awarded, lawyers'
fees are in the millions, and, ultimately, these costs are paid by the
consumer. To return to an earlier analogy, we need not find that a
majority of the population has been afflicted with a disease to conclude that an outbreak has reached epidemic proportions, nor should
we dismiss any disease as insignificant where its effect is substantial
even though its incidence is relatively low.

There remains a final inquiry. Are legal expenses, particularly in
the ordinary case, "excessive"? Is too little of the total pie going to the
disputants and too much to the lawyers? Putting to one side methodo-
logical difficulties, against what standard are the data to be measured?
We make no effort to answer these questions.

* * *

III. Reflections on Cost-Benefit

Costs must be balanced against benefits. This much should be
realized by anyone who considers bringing an action or defending
against one. The evaluation, however, is frequently in terms of the
litigant's own interests. It is important to apply the same process to
the system, and to do so from the perspective of society. We have
examined the cost of litigation as a percentage of the gross national
product, focusing on its impact on society as a whole. It is therefore
appropriate that we consider the benefits of a civil justice system to
society. Though these benefits may be impossible to quantify, they are
nevertheless subject to description, analysis, and subjective evaluation.

Perhaps the point is best made by way of anecdote. A Texas law
firm, which at one time had been quite successful at representing
plaintiffs in employment discrimination cases, virtually stopped litigating such claims. The underlying reason, as one of the lawyers involved
explained, was economic. When Congress passed the controlling
statutes, blatant discrimination in employment was rampant, a condition which persisted for some time. Settling cases often posed no
difficulty, and victories after trial could be expected. The practice was
lucrative. After a period of years, however, hiring and promotion
practices changed. The more blatant forms of discrimination simply
ceased; the discrimination that remained was subtle. In short, legislation, appropriately enforced through civil litigation, had in fact resulted in changing the primary conduct of citizens. It is impossible to
ascribe a dollar figure to such a public good. But where a democrati-
cally elected Congress adopts a policy intended to govern the conduct
of citizens, and where the courts act to enforce that policy and to
make it a reality in the marketplace, the very embodiment of the
American ideal of democracy is reflected. If that costs money—taxpay-

er money for the courts and private funds for the costs of litigation—it is money well spent.

* * *

V. CONCLUSION

In this brief discourse there has been heavy emphasis on the prosaic details of litigation; the dollar sign has figured prominently throughout. It may seem that a preoccupation with efficiency and economy has displaced the weightier concern of the quality of justice. It is important to recognize, however, that expense and delay can serve to render the loftier goals unattainable. Some minimal level of efficiency and economy are preconditions to the delivery of justice to all. The point was well made by an ABA task force, chaired by Judge Griffin Bell, in a report published shortly after the Pound Revisited Conference:

> It is important to keep firmly in mind that neither efficiency for the sake of efficiency, nor speed of adjudication for its own sake are the ends which underlie our concern with the administration of justice in this country. The ultimate goal is to make it possible for our system to provide justice for all. Constitutional guarantees of human rights ring hollow if there is no forum available in fact for their vindication. Statutory rights become empty promises if adjudication is too long delayed to make them meaningful or the value of a claim is consumed by the expense of asserting it. Only if our courts are functioning smoothly can equal justice become a reality for all.[118]

Reinventing Civil Litigation: Evaluating Proposals for Change: Understanding Mass Personal Injury Litigation: a Socio–Legal Analysis

Deborah R. Hensler and Mark A. Peterson.
59 Brooklyn L. Rev. 961 (1993).

The 1980s marked the era of mass personal injury litigation. Hundreds of thousands of people sued scores of corporations for losses due to injuries or diseases that they attributed to catastrophic events, pharmaceutical products, medical devices or toxic substances. In some parts of the country, mass tort claims threatened to overwhelm the civil justice system, accounting for more than one-quarter of the entire civil caseload in certain courts. As a result of this wave of litigation, some businesses found that products once regarded as significant marketing successes now had the potential to drive them into bankruptcy. The specter of mass liability frightened insurers from some markets, and manufacturers from research and development in some product lines.

---

118. The Pound Conference: Perspectives on Justice in the Future 300 (A.L. Levin & R. Wheeler eds. 1979).

The mass litigation of the 1980s involved enormous stakes. Hundreds of thousands of plaintiffs received compensation for their injuries. Businesses and their insurers paid billions of dollars in indemnification. Plaintiffs', defense, and insurance lawyers received billions of dollars more.[4] As a result of mass personal injury litigation, trusts that were established to pay asbestos claimants now effectively own the Manville Corporation and several other major asbestos manufacturers.[5] Similarly, as a consequence of their mass litigation, the Dalkon Shield Claimants Trust received over seventy-five percent of the proceeds of the sale, in bankruptcy, of A.H. Robins, Co., the manufacturer of the Shield.[6] Asbestos and other mass tort claimants soon may own a dozen other businesses that are in or face possible bankruptcy.

Although there is disagreement about the causes and legitimacy of this litigation,[8] almost all of those involved would agree that the civil justice system has not performed well in response to the challenge of mass torts. The litany of criticisms is long and familiar: cases take an inordinately long time to reach disposition, sometimes concluding long after a plaintiff's death; outcomes are highly variable, often seeming to have little relationship to plaintiffs' injuries or defendants' culpability; transaction costs are excessive, far outstripping the amounts paid out in compensation.

Why the civil justice system has had such problems responding to mass personal injury litigation is itself a matter of some controversy. Some attribute these problems to a lack of fit between traditional civil procedure, with its reliance on individualized case treatment, and the demands imposed on courts by massive numbers of claims which, in practice, cannot be treated individually. This view has led to myriad proposals to facilitate aggregative treatment of mass tort claims, by amending Rule 23; extending multidistricting to include trial as well as

4. By 1982, a total of one billion dollars had been paid in compensation and transaction costs for asbestos worker injury litigation. See James S. Kakalik et al., *Variation in Asbestos Litigation Compensation and Expenses* (1984). In 1991, the total value of all pending asbestos worker injury claims was estimated at between $8 billion and $14 billion, not including legal fees. *In re Joint E. & S. Dist. Asbestos Litig., 129 B.R. 710, 931* (E. & S.D.N.Y. 1991). According to most estimates, for each dollar spent on indemnification of asbestos injury claims, more than two dollars are spent on legal fees and other transaction costs. [See Deborah Hensler, Fashioning A National Resolution of Asbestos Personal Injury Litigation: A Reply to Professor Brickman, 13 Cardozo L. Rev. 1967, 1977 (1992)]

5. Trusts established to pay asbestos claimants were given the majority of stock in Manville, UNR Industries, and a major subsidiary of National Gypsum. Eagle–Picher, Inc. and the asbestos claimants have agreed to support a bankruptcy reorganization plan

in which a claimants' trust would own all stock of that company. See Marianna S. Smith, Resolving Asbestos Claims: The Manville Personal Injury Settlement Trust, 53 Law & Contemp. Probs. 27, 30 (1990). On the development of claims facilities operated by trusts as a mechanism for compensating mass tort claimants, see Mark A. Peterson, Giving Away Money: Comparative Comments on Claims Resolution Facilities, 53 Law & Contemp. Probs. 113 (1990).

6. Over $2.3 billion dollars was placed in a trust to pay Dalkon Shield claimants by American Home Products, which bought A.H. Robins. See Kenneth R. Feinberg, The Dalkon Shield Claimants Trust, 53 Law & Contemp. Probs. 79, 103–04 (1990).

8. For an example of the diverse perspectives on the causes of mass tort litigation, see Colloquy: An Administrative Alternative to Tort Litigation to Resolve Asbestos Claims, 13 Cardozo L. Rev. 1817 (1992) (presenting views of judges, plaintiffs' and defense attorneys, a labor union leader and scholars on asbestos litigation).

pretrial preparation and state as well as federal cases; encouraging informal coordination between state and federal courts; creating a new "national disaster court," or removing some or all mass torts from the court system entirely.

At present, mass torts seem to have become a fixture on the litigation landscape. The specialized mass tort plaintiffs' bar that emerged during the 1980s has accumulated capital as a result of its success in litigating earlier mass claims, and is skillful and aggressive in identifying new investment opportunities. A mass tort defense bar has developed to counter these plaintiffs' attorney efforts. An elite of trial judges has come forward, ready to set aside traditional case-at-a-time disposition procedures in favor of aggregative procedures for disposing of hundreds or even thousands of cases. A cottage industry of experts and special masters supports their efforts by designing complex procedures and crafting complex settlements. Appellate courts wrestle with collective disposition of mass claims. Lawyers, judges, and business executives no longer wonder whether or not there will be another mass tort, but rather what the next mass tort will be.

NOTES

A.   A study of aviation accident cases found that plaintiffs received 71% of the total amount that defendants expended; the remaining 29% represented what it cost to prosecute the litigation, or what is frequently termed transaction costs. Kakalik, King, Traynor, Ebener & Picus, *Costs and Compensation Paid in Aviation Accident Litigation (Rand Institute for Civil Justice*, 1988) By way of contrast, in the "average tort case" plaintiffs receive only 50%, and in asbestos cases close to two-thirds (61%) of the monies paid out by defendants are consumed by transaction costs. Is it fair to say that the figures themselves make clear that a problem exists? Is this too simplistic a view? If a problem does exist, who has the responsibility of dealing with it?

B.   Brickman, *Contingent Fees Without Contingencies:* Hamlet *Without the Prince of Denmark?* 37 U.C.L.A. L.Rev. 29, 109 (1989), explains the aviation cases as follows: "Market forces have come to operate in aviation accident cases, and contingent fees in such cases have declined steadily in the past twenty-five years from the one-third level to an average of fifteen to twenty percent in 1984, with rates as low as ten percent noted. A principal reason for the reduction in the percentage charged is competition among attorneys for these very lucrative cases which usually have a zero risk of nonrecovery. This competition is accentuated by the public availability of the identities of the victims shortly after major aviation accidents. Attorneys quickly learn who the potential clients are and compete by bidding against each other for the cases." Contingent fees are discussed further *infra* at 465–467, 479, 481.

FRESH PERSPECTIVES AND THE QUEST FOR SOLUTIONS

Congress, too, has expressed its concern over expense and delay in civil litigation. The Senate Report accompanying The Judicial Improvements Act of 1990, which became law on December 1 of that year,[1] speaks in rather forceful terms:

---

1. P.L. 101–650. The Report accompanied S. 2648. The Act is codified at 28 U.S.C. §§ 471–482.

The Federal courts are suffering today under the scourge of two related and worsening plagues. First, the costs of civil litigation, and delays that contribute to those costs, are high and are increasing; they limit access to the courts to only those who can afford to pay the rising expenses; and they undermine the ability of American corporations to compete both domestically and abroad. Second, the Federal courts have a scarcity of resources, particularly Article III judges. This is especially true in jurisdictions that have high drug-related caseloads. * * *

A substantial majority of more than 1,000 experienced litigators and Federal trial judges said that the high cost of litigation unreasonably impedes access to the courts by the ordinary citizen. The burden of high litigation costs impacts American businesses as well. American corporations spend more than $20 billion annually on outside counsel defending lawsuits. The outside counsel expenses for some Fortune 100 companies exceed $30 million annually, and in one case exceed $100 million annually.[2]

Basically, the Act mandates that each District Court, aided by an Advisory Committee, formulate a plan to deal with expense and delay based on local conditions and local needs. The Act also recognizes that the difficulties encountered in achieving "the just, speedy, and inexpensive determination of every action," are due to a variety of causes, including, for example, the failure of Congress to provide an adequate number of federal judges.

In § 473(a), the Act lists six "principles of litigation management and cost and delay reduction" and in § 473(b) a number of "cost and delay reduction techniques," each of which the District Courts "shall consider and may include" in their respective plans. Among them are early involvement of a judicial officer in planning the progress of a case, limiting discovery, and utilizing various forms of alternative dispute resolution. We have already considered some of these in the chapter on discovery; others will be considered in the chapters on the pretrial conference and alternative dispute resolution.

B. ATTORNEYS' FEES

1. Cost Shifting Authorized by Statute

42 U.S.C.A. § 1988[a]

(b) Attorney's fees

In any action or proceeding to enforce a provision of sections 1981, 1981a, 1982, 1983, 1985, and 1986 of this title, title IX of Public Law 92–318, the Religious Freedom Restoration Act of 1993, title VI of the Civil Rights Act of 1964, or section 40302 of the Violence Against Women Act of 1994, the court, in its discretion, may allow the prevailing party, other than the United States, a reasonable attorney's fee as part of the costs, except that in any action brought against a judicial officer for an act or omission taken in such officer's judicial capacity such officer shall not be held liable for any costs, including attorney's fees, unless such action was clearly in excess of such officer's jurisdiction.

2. Report, pp. 1–2, 7.

a. Portions of this statute have been deleted.

(c) Expert fees

In awarding an attorney's fee under subsection (b) of this section in any action or proceeding to enforce a provision of section 1981 or 1981a of this title, the court, in its discretion, may include expert fees as part of the attorney's fee.

Spell v. McDaniel

United States Court of Appeals, Fourth Circuit, 1987.
824 F.2d 1380.

■ Before Phillips, Chapman and Wilkinson, Circuit Judges.

■ James Dickson Phillips, Circuit Judge:

This is a 42 U.S.C. § 1983 action in which after two trials Henry Spell was awarded substantial damages against the City of Fayetteville, North Carolina (the City), and Charles McDaniel, a City police officer, as a result of physical injury inflicted on Spell by McDaniel while Spell was in McDaniel's custody following Spell's arrest. McDaniel and the City have appealed, assigning various trial rulings as error and challenging as unreasonable the amount of attorney fees awarded to Spell as prevailing party.

We find no reversible error in the trials and therefore affirm the judgment on the merits against McDaniel and the City. Except for its inclusion of a "contingency multiplier," we also affirm the district court's award of attorney fees.

I

Spell, admittedly inebriated on alcohol and quaaludes, was stopped by Officer McDaniel while driving an automobile in the City of Fayetteville. After talking with Spell and finding a quantity of quaaludes in his automobile, McDaniel arrested him along with a passenger in Spell's automobile, handcuffed the two of them and took them in a patrol car to the police station. There Spell was subjected to various sobriety tests, including a breathalyzer test, and was formally charged with driving while impaired and with the possession of quaaludes.[1] Just after Spell completed the breathalyzer test and was returned, still handcuffed and inebriated, to McDaniel's direct custody, McDaniel, possibly angered by Spell's failure to respond to his questioning, and in any event without any physical provocation, brutally assaulted Spell. When Spell warded off a blow toward his head by raising his arms, McDaniel seized his handcuffed arms, pulled them down and violently kneed Spell in the groin. The blow to Spell's groin ruptured one of his testicles, necessitating its surgical removal. This resulted in irreversible sterility and of course in considerable associated pain and suffering.

---

1. Spell later pled guilty to the possession charge which was contained in a multicount indictment that also charged two counts of narcotics trafficking for which he was convicted after trial. At the time of trial of this § 1983 action, he was serving a seven year sentence growing out of those convictions, a fact brought out to the jury in Spell's own testimony on direct examination.

Spell then brought this § 1983 action naming as defendants McDaniel, the City of Fayetteville, the City Manager, the City Chief of Police, the Director of the police department's Internal Affairs Division and two police department command sergeants. He structured the action as one against McDaniel in his individual and official capacities; against the City Manager, Smith, the Police Chief, Dixon, the Internal Affairs Division Director, Johnson, and the two command sergeants, Dalton and Holman, in their several official capacities; and against the City as a suitable municipal corporation.

His pleaded theory of recovery against McDaniel individually was that McDaniel, acting under color of state law, had deprived him of rights secured by the fourth, fifth and fourteenth amendments by using excessive physical force against him in a custodial situation, thereby inflicting serious personal injuries. For this conduct he sought recovery of money damages against McDaniel in his individual capacity.

His pleaded theory of recovery against the City of Fayetteville was that the City was liable for damages under the doctrine of Monell v. Department of Social Services of the City of New York, 436 U.S. 658, 98 S.Ct. 2018, 56 L.Ed.2d 611 (1978), for the constitutional deprivation with consequent physical injuries directly inflicted by its employee McDaniel, because McDaniel's conduct was pursuant to a municipal "policy or custom." *Id.* at 694, 98 S.Ct. at 2037.

McDaniel denied inflicting any injury on Spell as a defense to the individual-capacity claim against him. The City also denied (for lack of sufficient knowledge or information) that McDaniel had inflicted injury on Spell, and alternatively denied that there was any basis for imposing municipal liability upon it under *Monell.*

The case then went to trial before a jury on the issues whether, as a matter of fact, McDaniel had assaulted Spell and was therefore liable individually, and if so, whether there existed a basis in law and fact for also imposing joint liability upon the City for the resulting constitutional deprivation.

After an 18–day trial, the jury returned verdicts finding McDaniel, in his individual capacity, and the City in its municipal capacity, jointly and severally liable. It awarded $1,000 in compensatory damages, and declined to award the punitive damages sought against McDaniel.

Spell then moved to set aside the $1,000 compensatory award as inadequate and for a new trial on the compensatory damages issue alone. The district court granted this motion, denying, *inter alia,* the defendants' counter-motion for new trial on all the issues if the verdict was to be set aside for inadequacy of the damage award.

On the re-trial of the damages issue, the jury returned a verdict for $900,000 compensatory damages. After denying defendants' renewed post-verdict motions for judgment n.o.v. or, alternatively, a new trial, the district court awarded Spell attorney fees and costs totalling $335,942.57. 616 F.Supp. 1069. Joint and several judgments against McDaniel and the City were then entered on the damage and fee awards.

This appeal followed.

Before us, the defendants join in contending that the district court erred in ordering a new trial on damages alone after setting aside as inadequate the first jury verdict; in making various evidentiary rulings; and in awarding unreasonably excessive attorney fees to Spell as prevailing party under 42 U.S.C. § 1988.

The City alone contends that the evidence did not warrant submission of the municipal liability issue to the jury and, in the alternative, that the court's jury instructions on that issue were prejudicially erroneous.

* * *

Assuming the credibility of the most critical oral testimony adduced by plaintiff and assessing the total evidence in its most favorable light, there emerged a picture of a police department whose members were either positively encouraged by training and deliberate cover-up to engage in uses of excessive force of the very type charged to McDaniel; or were tacitly encouraged to continue self-developed practices of this type by the deliberate failure of responsible municipal officials to exercise discipline or corrective supervision to halt the widespread, known practices; or were encouraged or authorized by both in combination.

To establish the existence of such a municipal policy or custom as the effective cause of Spell's injury, plaintiff relied principally upon the testimony of seven lay citizens of the City, eight present or former officers of the City police department, an assistant state district attorney, the former legal advisor to the police department and upon internal records of the City police department. This evidence was essentially concentrated upon a time period of three years preceding McDaniel's assault on Spell.

* * *

IV

The City's final assignment of error is to the district court's award of attorney fees to plaintiff as a prevailing party under 42 U.S.C. § 1988.

The court awarded Spell a total of $325,303.75 in attorney fees representing 1,964.5 hours billable at rates ranging from $100–125 per hour. A lodestar of $224,758.50 was enhanced by a "contingency" adjustment or "multiplier" of 1.5 to compensate Spell's counsel for the initial risk of not prevailing and thus not collecting a fee. *See* Spell v. McDaniel, 616 F.Supp. 1069, 1107–10 (E.D.N.C.1985). The defendants contend that the district court erred by including within the lodestar amount hours spent by Spell's attorneys on "non-legal" tasks such as serving subpoenas, photocopying documents, and filing pleadings; by allowing the $100–125 hourly rates requested by Spell's counsel despite their failure to offer evidence of their customary rates; by setting hourly rates of $100 for attorneys Holt and Richardson although each had less than five year's trial experience when this litigation commenced; by applying uniform rates to all services rendered regardless of the nature of the work performed; and by *presuming* the propriety of a contingency adjustment in § 1988 cases.

A

An allowance of attorney's fees by a district court, which has "close and intimate knowledge of the efforts expended and the value of the services rendered, must not be overturned unless it is 'clearly wrong.' " McManama v. Lukhard, 616 F.2d 727, 729 (4th Cir.1980) (*quoting* Barber v. Kimbrell's, Inc., 577 F.2d 216, 226 (4th Cir.1978)) (*citing* Lea v. Cone Mills Corp., 467 F.2d 277, 279 (4th Cir.1972) (*quoting* United States v. Anglin & Stevenson, 145 F.2d 622, 630 (10th Cir.1944))). Applying this standard to the careful analysis of the district court, we conclude that the defendants' contentions are without merit except as to the court's inclusion of a "contingency multiplier."

B

With respect to its inclusion within the lodestar amount of hours spent by Spell's counsel on "non-legal" tasks, the district court observed that the defendants' argument was "predicated on the erroneous assumption that a single, correct staffing pattern exists within every law firm for every lawsuit." 616 F.Supp. at 1096. Rather, as the court found, in some circumstances, it may be more efficient and reasonable for counsel to perform such tasks. Thus, for example, Spell's attorneys provided affidavits indicating that in many cases their service of subpoenas was accompanied by a final interview with witnesses; that personal service was often of particular importance because many of Spell's witnesses required constant reassurance; and that while photocopying documents, they screened, reviewed and arranged more than 14,000 pages of police department internal reports, "perhaps the most important time spent on this case by plaintiff's counsel." Id. at 1096–97. As a precautionary measure, the court nevertheless deducted ten hours from those requested "[t]o the extent secretaries could have been competently employed to perform some of this work." Id. at 1097.[17]

The § 1988 fee applicant bears the burden of establishing the reasonableness of the hourly rates requested. Specifically, the applicant must produce specific evidence of the "prevailing market rates in the relevant community" for the type of work for which he seeks an

---

17. In response to the defendants' related objection that the hours recorded by Spell's counsel reflected some duplication of effort, the court found that no evidence had been proffered which showed that duplicated time was unreasonable or unnecessary but nevertheless "employ[ed] a 5% across-the-board reduction in counsel's requested * * * hours in order to eliminate any unreasonable duplication that might have been overlooked, errors committed by this Court in denying defendants' excessive hours objections * * * and as a 'practical means of trimming any fat from [plaintiff's] fee petition.' " 616 F.Supp. at 1094–95, partially quoting New York State Association for Retarded Children v. Carey, 711 F.2d 1136, 1146 (2d Cir.1983).

award. Blum v. Stenson, 465 U.S. 886, 895–96 & n. 11, 104 S.Ct. 1541, 1547 & n. 11, 79 L.Ed.2d 891 (1984); National Association of Concerned Veterans v. Secretary of Defense, 675 F.2d 1319, 1325 (D.C.Cir. 1982). The prevailing market rate may be established through affidavits reciting the precise fees that counsel with similar qualifications have received in comparable cases; information concerning recent fee awards by courts in comparable cases; and specific evidence of counsel's actual billing practice or other evidence of the actual rates which counsel can command in the market. National Association of Concerned Veterans, 675 F.2d at 1325–26; Ramos v. Lamm, 713 F.2d 546, 555 (10th Cir.1983).

The district court acknowledged that Spell's counsel had "barely" made the required showing. Because they omitted information regarding their own billing practices and provided only a few generalized affidavits from local counsel, the district court was required to "substitute its personal knowledge and experiences in lieu of substantive evidence to a greater degree than it would have hoped." 616 F.Supp. at 1102. The court noted, however, that the defendants did not object to the rates requested, and that the factors articulated in Johnson v. Georgia Highway Express, Inc., 488 F.2d 714, 717–19 (5th Cir.1974), which were embraced by this court in Barber, 577 F.2d at 226[18] militate strongly in favor of compensating Spell's counsel at the rates sought. Among other things, the court found that the litigation presented challenging issues of both fact and law of considerable complexity and magnitude; that Spell's counsel incurred substantial opportunity costs in pursuing the litigation, given the drain of resources on their four-person firm and the unpopularity of their case within the community; and that the rates requested were in line with other awards in recent years in similar cases.[19] 616 F.Supp. at 1103–05. Although, as the district court observed, the rates allowed were at the "apogee of the range of rates that prevail in this district for lawyers of comparable qualifications and experience who handle cases of this sort," id. at 1105, we cannot say that they were "clearly wrong."

Nor can we say that the district court abused its discretion in allowing attorneys Holt and Richardson to charge their time at $100 per hour although each had less than five year's trial experience when this litigation commenced. Counsel's experience is only one of many

---

18. This court has summarized the Johnson factors to include: (1) the time and labor expended; (2) the novelty and difficulty of the questions raised; (3) the skill required to properly perform the legal services rendered; (4) the attorney's opportunity costs in pressing the instant litigation; (5) the customary fee for like work; (6) the attorney's expectations at the outset of the litigation; (7) the time limitations imposed by the client or circumstances; (8) the amount in controversy and the results obtained; (9) the experience, reputation and ability of the attorney; (10) the undesirability of the case within the legal community in which the suit arose; (11) the nature and length of the professional relationship between attorney and client; and (12) attorneys' fees awards in similar cases. Barber, 577 F.2d at 226 n. 28.

19. Although the court was unaware of any award of fees in a complex civil rights case within the district court in the last two years, Spell's counsel provided four affidavits from members of the Raleigh and Fayetteville Bars indicating that in similar cases they, or their colleagues, would charge the same rates as those requested. 616 F.Supp. at 1105.

factors to be considered in determining a reasonable fee. See Johnson, 488 F.2d 714.

As to the district court's application of uniform rates to all services rendered by Spell's counsel without regard to the nature of the work performed, we likewise cannot say that the result was "clearly wrong." As the district court noted, the lower courts have adopted varying approaches to the problem of valuing legal services, with some utilizing different rates for different types of work, particularly in-court and out-of-court or primary and secondary services, see e.g., Whitley v. Seibel, 676 F.2d 245, 253–54 (7th Cir.1982); Miles v. Sampson, 675 F.2d 5, 9 (1st Cir.1982); United Nuclear Corp. v. Cannon, 564 F.Supp. 581, 589 (D.R.I.1983); Langdon v. Drew Municipal Separate School District, 512 F.Supp. 1131, 1139 (N.D.Miss.1981), and others applying uniform rates for all services rendered, White v. City of Richmond, 713 F.2d 458, 461 (9th Cir.1983); Maceira v. Pagan, 698 F.2d 38, 40–41 (1st Cir.1983); Bonner v. Coughlin, 657 F.2d 931, 937 (7th Cir.1981). The district court applied flat rates in this case consistent with its own previous awards and with those of other judges within the district. 616 F.Supp. at 1103. The court found, moreover, that Spell's "counsel's knowledge, skills and abilities were as fully engaged in their out-of-court work as they were in-court." Id.

We therefore find no error in the district court's determination of the "lodestar fee."

C

As indicated, the district court, having computed the "lodestar" fee figure, then enhanced it by a 50% "multiplier," expressly to compensate counsel for the risk of not prevailing and therefore being paid nothing under their contingency fee contract.[20] Defendants challenge this primarily on the basis that the district court acted on a "presumption" of entitlement to a contingency multiplier rather than by a careful exercise of its discretion.

We disagree with this specific basis of challenge. The district court properly recognized that the "presumption" ran the other way: that the lodestar figure presumptively represented a reasonable fee, with the burden on the fee claimant to establish the propriety of an upward contingency adjustment. See 616 F.Supp. at 1107 n. 59. Based upon this understanding, the district court indeed undertook an extended, meticulous analysis of those factors it considered relevant to the use of a contingency multiplier under then controlling legal precedent. Noting that the general propriety of contingency multipliers had been expressly reserved by the Supreme Court, see 616 F.Supp. at 1107 (citing Blum v. Stenson, 465 U.S. at 901 n. 17, 104 S.Ct. at 1550 n. 17), the court relied for its allowance of a multiplier on a number of lower federal court decisions which had assumed their general propriety. See 616 F.Supp. at 1108–10.[21]

20. The court expressly declined to make a further upward "quality adjustment," 616 F.Supp. at 1110–11. This ruling is not challenged on appeal.

21. Among the decisions relied upon was that of another district court of this circuit which was later affirmed by this court,

It would be difficult to fault the district court's factual and legal analysis under the principles it understandably thought at the time controlled its discretionary allowance of the contingency multiplier. But the Supreme Court has in the interval now spoken to the question reserved in *Blum,* and in a way that we conclude makes a contingency multiplier inappropriate here as a matter of law.

In Pennsylvania v. Delaware Valley Citizens' Council for Clean Air, 483 U.S. 711, 107 S.Ct. 3078, 97 L.Ed.2d 585 (1987), a 5–4 majority of the Court held that a contingency multiplier may be permissible in appropriate cases,[22] though another 5–4 majority thought the multiplier used in the case before it not warranted.

Within the divided *Delaware Valley* Court, Justice O'Connor's position in concurrence controls on the circumstances in which a contingency multiplier may ever be allowable.[23] Critical to that concurring position as it affects the instant case are the propositions that (1) "no enhancement for risk is appropriate unless the applicant can establish that without an adjustment for risk the prevailing party 'would have faced substantial difficulties in finding counsel in the local or other relevant market,' " this being the basic purpose of § 1988, *id.* at 731–734, 107 S.Ct. at 3089–92; and (2) no enhancement for risk should be allowed on the basis of " 'legal' risks or risks peculiar to the case" since these risks are adequately taken into account in fixing the "lodestar" figure, *id.* at 734, 107 S.Ct. at 3091.

Specifically applying those constraints, Justice O'Connor provided the majority necessary to reverse allowance of the multiplier in that case on the alternative ground that it was inappropriate on the facts of the case even if not generally inappropriate. This majority emphasized

see Vaughns v. Board of Education, 770 F.2d 1244, 1246 (4th Cir.1985). The district court's allowance of a multiplier was therefore well within contemplation of emerging circuit law at the time.

22. The fee award at issue in *Delaware Valley* was made under § 304(d) of the Clean Air Act, 42 U.S.C. § 7604(d), but the Court's decision plainly applies as well to awards under 42 U.S.C. § 1988. *See Delaware Valley,* 483 U.S. at 722–725, 107 S.Ct. at 3085–86 (plurality opinion).

23. Justice White, writing for four Justices, being "unconvinced that Congress intended the risk of losing a lawsuit to be an independent basis for increasing the amount of any otherwise reasonable fee," *Delaware Valley,* 483 U.S. at 725, 107 S.Ct. at 3086 (plurality opinion), concluded in a plurality opinion that "multipliers or other enhancement of a reasonable lodestar fee to compensate for assuming the risk of loss is impermissible under the usual fee-shifting statutes," *id.* at 727, 107 S.Ct. at 3088. Lacking a majority for this *per se* position, Justice White then concluded that even if contingency multipliers were permissible

under the "typical fee-shifting statutes," they should only be allowed in "exceptional cases," and that on the facts of the particular case no enhancement was warranted. *Id.* at 728, 107 S.Ct. at 3087–90. Four Justices, for whom Justice Blackmun wrote in dissent, disagreed believing that fee enhancement for the risks of nonpayment was permissible in appropriate cases, and that remand for further fact findings would establish whether the case at issue was an appropriate one. *Id.* at 735–755, 107 S.Ct. at 3091–3102 (BLACKMUN, J., dissenting). Justice O'Connor, writing separately, agreed with the dissenting Justices that Congress did not intend flatly to foreclose all consideration of contingency in setting reasonable fees under such fee-shifting statutes as 42 U.S.C. § 1988. But she agreed with the other four justices that a "risk multiplier" was not warranted in the circumstances of the case before the Court, *id.* at 731–734, 107 S.Ct. 3089–92 thereby providing a majority for reversal. Justice O'Connor's position on the circumstances under which a "contingency multiplier" may be appropriate is therefore the pivotal one.

that there was no finding of record that an enhancement for risk was necessary in the relevant market to insure that "poor clients with good claims [could] secure competent help," *id.* at 730–731, 107 S.Ct. at 3089; and that the lower courts had instead found enhancement appropriate on the impermissible basis of the legal and practical risks peculiar to the particular case, rather than on the basis of any general difference in relevant market treatment of all comparable contingent fee cases, *id.* at 731–734, 107 S.Ct. at 3089–92.

We conclude that these same critical constraints make the allowance of a contingency multiplier inappropriate in the instant case.

Though the district court noted, and we can assume, that the case was an "unpopular" one in the community, there is no finding of record that a contingency enhancement was necessary to insure that competent counsel would nevertheless be willing to undertake contingency representation in such cases. More critically, we think that the record strongly suggests, if it does not compel, a directly opposite conclusion. In its lodestar analysis, the district court alluded to the fact that "there are a number of pending lawsuits in federal court against the [police department] and the City," and that plaintiff's counsels' time spent in conference with other counsel in those cases was for that reason practically justifiable. 616 F.Supp. 1099. From this we think it obvious that plaintiff here could not possibly show that "without risk-enhancement, plaintiff would have faced substantial difficulties in finding counsel in the local or other relevant market," *id.* 483 U.S. at 731, 107 S.Ct. at 3089 (plurality opinion). The picture that emerges from the entire record is instead that these counsel and others in related cases had no general reluctance to undertake contingency representation in this type case notwithstanding any general "unpopularity" they might have among the local lay populace. Indeed, it would appear that there was no dearth of competent counsel willing to take this and comparable cases on a contingency basis as being "good plaintiffs' cases" without any guarantee of special enhancement of reasonable "lodestar" fees.

Furthermore, here as did the lower courts in *Delaware Valley,* the district court essentially justified its allowance of a multiplier on the peculiar risks, complexities, and difficulties of the instant case rather than on any perception that enhancement was required to insure adequate representation in the run of like contingency fee cases. *See* 616 F.Supp. 1107–10. Specifically, the court, relying essentially on the mode of analysis followed by the Third Circuit in its pre-*Blum* decision in Lindy Brothers Builders v. American Radiator & Standard Sanitary Corp., 540 F.2d 102 (3d Cir.1976), looked primarily at the case-specific "burden" on the plaintiff in terms of the case's complexity, dubiety of success on the merits, and difficulty of proving damages; the case-specific practical risks of uncompensated time and expense assumed by counsel in undertaking representation; and the delay in receiving payment, *see* 616 F.Supp. at 1107–10. As we read *Delaware Valley,* a majority of the Supreme Court considered that these case-specific risk factors may not properly be drawn upon to enhance a "lodestar" fee with a "contingency multiplier." *See Delaware Valley,* 483 U.S. at 723–731, 107 S.Ct. at 3079–87 (plurality opinion); *id.* at 731, 107 S.Ct. at 3089 (concurring opinion).

Accordingly, we conclude that the "contingency multiplier" allowed in this case is not legally justified, and must be excised from the total fee award.

V

We therefore affirm the judgment against McDaniel and the City on the merits, and we vacate the district court's order awarding costs and attorney fees for modification in conformity with this opinion.

AFFIRMED IN PART; VACATED AND REMANDED IN PART.

Spell v. McDaniel

United States Court of Appeals, Fourth Circuit, 1988.
852 F.2d 762.

■ Before PHILLIPS, CHAPMAN and WILKINSON, CIRCUIT JUDGES.

■ PER CURIAM:

Henry Z. Spell, a successful civil rights plaintiff in a suit brought against Patrolman Charles McDaniel and the City of Fayetteville, North Carolina, see Spell v. McDaniel, 824 F.2d 1380 (4th Cir.1987), is again before this court on a motion for attorney's fees under 42 U.S.C. § 1988 for services performed in connection with the appeal and subsequent response to the appellant's petition for writ of certiorari. Plaintiff also seeks attorney's fees for time spent by his attorneys in preparing the present fee petition. Plaintiff seeks reimbursement of the amount he has already substantially paid his seven appellate counsel, five of whom joined the case post-trial, under a contractual fee agreement whereby counsel charged Spell for 1,886.1 hours of attorney time at rates varying from $80 to $150 per hour with an additional "contingency multiplier" of 1.5 applied to 1,362.3 of these hours and a bonus for winning of $15,000 resulting in a total attorney's fee of $383,236.25. In addition, plaintiff seeks from defendants the $5,482 he was charged for 98.2 hours attributed by his counsel to paralegal services, over $8,000 in costs and expenses, compensation for delay, and interest on the fee award. These sums are in addition to the $224,758.50 in attorney's fees and costs already awarded plaintiff in connection with the trial. We find that the amounts charged to Spell by his multiple appellate counsel represent a vast duplication of endeavors already performed at the trial level, a substantial degree of duplication and overkill in connection with the post-trial proceedings, an unconscionable exercise of billing judgment as to the reasonable number of hours expended and ultimately charged to plaintiff Spell, and an affront to the very purposes of the Civil Rights Attorney's Fees Awards Act of 1976, 42 U.S.C. § 1988. For these reasons, and as discussed more fully below, we award plaintiff the sum of $80,295.69 which we find represents a "reasonable" attorney's fee, expenses and adjustment for delay as contemplated by § 1988.

I

Plaintiff Spell brought the underlying § 1983 action against the defendant police officers and the City of Fayetteville, North Carolina, in 1984. After two jury trials, compensatory damages of $900,000 were awarded to plaintiff. Subsequently the district court awarded attorney's fees and costs for plaintiff's trial counsel, Gerald Beaver and William Richardson of the Fayetteville law firm of Beaver, Thompson, Holt & Richardson, P.A., in the amount of $335,942.57. The district court arrived at this figure by enhancing the reasonable lodestar figure of $224,758.50 by a 1.5 contingency multiplier. See Spell v. McDaniel, 616 F.Supp. 1069, 1107–10 (E.D.N.C.1985). The defendants appealed contesting both the fee award and the imposition of liability against them under 42 U.S.C. § 1983.

Plaintiff's trial counsel, Gerald Beaver, by affidavit in support of the present petition, states that as of May 1985 his four-member law firm was no longer able to shoulder the financial burden of representing Spell on the contingency basis which Spell's financial condition necessitated. Beaver and Richardson therefore took on a substantial additional case load and sought alternative or associate counsel to represent Spell on appeal. Beaver states that informal discussions with attorneys between the ages of 35 and 45 at several similarly small North Carolina law firms led him to believe that all such firms shared the same predicament as did his firm. He states further that he believed it unnecessary to contact larger firms because in his "personal experience" such firms "seldom, if ever, * * * take contingent work."

In September 1985, Beaver came in contact with Alfred Bryant, then of the seven-member Richmond, Virginia, firm of Obenshain, Hinnant, Ellyson, Runkle & Bryant (Obenshain), who after some discussion with his partners and with Beaver, agreed to represent Spell on appeal, and ultimately in subsequent proceedings, in association with Beaver and Richardson on a contingency basis. Bryant and Beaver agreed that the only way their representation could go forward given the size of their firms, and the limited time until the appellant's brief was due, January 21, 1986, was if Spell agreed, by written contract, to compensate Bryant and all Obenshain attorneys who worked on Spell's case at a base hourly rate of $150 with an additional contingency multiplier of 1.5 resulting in a total hourly rate of $225. By the terms of this same contract Beaver and Richardson were to be compensated at base hourly rates of $125 again enhanced by 1.5 to reach a total hourly rate of $187.50. In addition, Spell must separately reimburse counsel for paralegal services and out-of-pocket costs. Spell, then currently an inmate in state prison, signed this contract, and its enforceability is not in issue.

On appeal, this court affirmed the verdict for Spell on the merits. See 824 F.2d 1380, 1405. The district court's fee award was affirmed as to expenses and the $224,758.50 lodestar but vacated and remanded as to the application of the contingency multiplier in light of the Supreme Court's intervening decision in Pennsylvania v. Delaware Valley Citizens' Council for Clean Air, ___ U.S. ___, 107 S.Ct. 3078, 97 L.Ed.2d 585 (1987), and our determination that an enhancement for contingency was not necessary to attract competent trial counsel to represent plaintiffs such as Spell in this type of litigation. 824 F.2d at 1404–05.

The defendants then petitioned the Supreme Court for certiorari, which petition was denied on January 19, 1988. On January 20, 1988, the judgment, then totalling roughly $1,235,000 including interest, which had been stayed by this court pending the Supreme Court's action on the certiorari petition, was released from bond. At this time Spell made full payment on the bills submitted to him by counsel for which he now seeks full reimbursement from defendants through the exercise of this court's discretion under § 1988.

II

The Civil Rights Attorney's Fees Awards Act of 1976, 42 U.S.C. § 1988, provides that in federal civil rights actions such as the underlying action brought pursuant to 42 U.S.C. § 1983, "the court, in its discretion, may allow the prevailing party, other than the United States, a reasonable attorney's fee as part of the costs." "The purpose of § 1988 is to ensure 'effective access to the judicial process' for persons with civil rights grievances. H.R.Rep. No. 94–1558, p. 1 (1976). Accordingly, a prevailing plaintiff 'should ordinarily recover an attorney's fee unless special circumstances would render such an award unjust.' " Hensley v. Eckerhart, 461 U.S. 424, 429, 103 S.Ct. 1933, 1937, 76 L.Ed.2d 40 (1983) (citing S.Rep. No. 94–1011, p. 4 (1976), U.S.Code Cong. & Admin.News 1976, p. 5908). However, the burden of establishing entitlement to a fee award is upon the fee applicant. *See id.* at 437, 103 S.Ct. at 1941; *see also* 824 F.2d at 1402 (fee applicant must prove that hours spent and hourly rates are reasonable).

"The initial estimate of a reasonable attorney's fee is properly calculated by multiplying the number of hours *reasonably* expended on the litigation times a reasonable hourly rate." Blum v. Stenson, 465 U.S. 886, 888, 104 S.Ct. 1541, 1544, 79 L.Ed.2d 891 (1984) (emphasis added); *see* Daly v. Hill, 790 F.2d 1071, 1076–78 (4th Cir.1986). This sum is referred to as the lodestar. The hourly rate that can reasonably be charged by counsel reflects such factors as counsel's "experience and special skill" in the litigated area, *Blum,* 465 U.S. at 898, 104 S.Ct. at 1549, and the quality of counsel's representation. *Daly,* 790 F.2d at 1078; *see also id.* at 1075 n. 2 (discussing additional factors). The number of hours reasonably charged reflects such factors as the "novelty and complexity of the issues," *Blum,* 465 U.S. at 898, 104 S.Ct. at 1549, as well as the experience and skill of counsel. Hensley, 461 U.S. at 434, 103 S.Ct. at 1940 (excessive hours by inexperienced counsel should be reduced).

Where counsel take a case on a contingency basis it is, under certain circumstances, appropriate to enhance the lodestar figure as a whole or alternatively to apply a "multiplier" to the usual hourly rate charged by counsel in order to arrive at a "reasonable" fee award that furthers the underlying purpose of § 1988 of insuring "effective access to the judicial process for persons with civil rights grievances." *Hensley,* 461 U.S. at 429, 103 S.Ct. at 1937 (quoting H.R.Rep. No. 94–1558, p. 1 (1976)). But the Supreme Court recently has held that "a court may not enhance a fee award any more than necessary to bring the fee within the range that would attract competent counsel." *Delaware Valley,* 107 S.Ct. at 3091. This means that "no enhancement for risk is appropriate unless the applicant can establish that without an adjustment for risk the prevailing party 'would have to face substantial difficulties in finding counsel in the local or other relevant market.'" *Id.* at 3091; *see also* Spell v. McDaniel, 824 F.2d 1380, 1404 (4th Cir.1987). Finally, the risks for which the enhancement is made in a particular case are not the "legal and practical risks peculiar to the particular case," 824 F.2d at 1404, but rather the risk of not obtaining competent counsel because of a "general difference in relevant market treatment of all comparable contingent fee cases." *Id.* at 1404 (citations omitted). "[A]t all times the fee applicant bears the burden of proving the degree to which the relevant market compensates for contingency." *Delaware Valley,* 107 S.Ct. at 3090 (citations omitted).

Bearing these principles in mind, we now consider plaintiff's fee petition.

III

The specifics of plaintiff's fee petition for services rendered in conjunction with the post-trial proceedings in this case are laid out below:*

APPELLATE FEES:

Attorney	Hours × Hourly Rate = Base Fee			Adjustment Factor Where Requested	Requested Award
Bryant	481.1 × 150 =	72,165.00		1.5	108,247.50
Tucker	488.8 × 150 =	73,320.00		1.5	109,980.00
Marshall	166.4 × 150 =	24,960.00		1.5	37,440.00
Ellyson	12.5 × 150 =	1,875.00		1.5	2,812.50
Beaver	199.1 × 125 =	24,887.50			24,887.50
Richardson	83.2 × 125 =	10,400.00			10,400.00
Paralegal					
Mears	81.8 × 60 =	4,908.00			4,908.00
Totals	1,512.9	$212,515.50			$298,675.50

* Counsel for plaintiff also request that the Obenshain firm be awarded interest on the amount of fees presented in its bill to Spell dated December 5, 1986 until the date the bill was paid, January 20, 1988. An enhancement for delay is requested in conjunction with the fees of Beaver and Richardson for appellate services rendered since June 1986 and for which payment may not already have been tendered.

Attorney	Hours × Hourly Rate = Base Fee			Adjustment Factor Where Requested	Requested Award
Bonus					15,000.00
Expenses					5,282.07
Total Award					$318,957.57
CERTIORARI FEES					
Attorney					
Bryant	155.5 ×	150	= 23,325.00	1.5	34,987.50
Marshall	58 ×	150	= 8,700.00	1.5	13,050.00
Allen	83.6 ×	80	= 6,688.00		6,688.00
Beaver	93.25 ×	125	= 11,656.25		11,656.25
Paralegal					
Black	12.1 ×	35	= 423.50		423.50
Totals	402.45		$50,792.75		$66,805.25
Expenses					2,845.55
Total Award					$69,650.80
FEES FOR PREPARING FEE PETITION					
Attorney					
Bryant	35.4 ×	150	= 5,310.00		5,310.00
Marshall	6.3 ×	150	= 945.00		945.00
Allen	22.9 ×	80	= 1,832.00		1,832.00
Paralegal					
Black	4.3 ×	35	= 150.50		150.50
Totals	68.9		$8,237.50		$8,237.50
Expenses					541.67
Total Award					$8,779.17
TOTAL AMOUNT REQUESTED:			$397,387.54		

As reasons advanced in support of their request for nearly $400,-000 in fees and costs plus additional compensation for delay as well as interest in conjunction with their post-trial efforts, plaintiff's counsel argue that the case is one of great precedential value, that counsel deserve enhanced compensation because the case involved the investment of a great deal of their time on relatively short notice with a risk of no compensation whatsoever being received given the uncertainty that § 1983 litigation entails.

The defendants, in response, raise several objections to plaintiff's request for attorney's fees. In particular the defendants argue that the number of hours expended by plaintiff's counsel on appeal was not reasonable because the appeal was overstaffed resulting in an "overkill" for which the defendants cannot properly be charged; because the hours spent by appellate counsel were duplicative of those already spent by trial counsel for which an award of $224,758.50 had already been made, *see* 824 F.2d at 1401; and because appellate counsels' unwarranted practice of engaging in long daily conferences about the various issues on appeal resulted in an unreasonable escalation in the number of hours spent.

The defendants also contend that the hourly rate of $150 applied across the board to all Obenshain attorneys, regardless of their individual skill and experience, is not supported by specific evidence of "the prevailing market rates in the relevant community" as contemplated by the Supreme Court. *See Blum*, 465 U.S. at 895–96, 104 S.Ct. at 1547. Related objections are made to the hourly rates charged in connection with the paralegal services.

Defendants further contend, as they did with respect to trial counsel fees on appeal, that a contingency multiplier is inappropriate in this case because plaintiff's attorneys have not shown such multiplier to be necessary to attract competent counsel. The defendants emphasize that Mr. Beaver's affidavit indicates only that he did not want to or could not take the time to continue to represent Spell on appeal, not that he was not competent to do so.

By affidavits from attorneys at several larger North Carolina law firms, defendants seek to establish that Mr. Beaver did not properly act on his personal belief that only small law firms would consider taking Spell's case on a contingent basis.

We find many of defendants' objections to plaintiff's attorney's fee petition to be substantially meritorious and accordingly will address them *seriatim.*

IV

A. Reasonable Number of Hours Expended

As a preliminary matter, we observe that it is patently inconceivable that attorneys defending this overwhelming fact-supported jury verdict on appeal justifiably could expend a total of over 1,400 hours (175 working days) in roughly a five-month period to prepare and present written and oral arguments responsive to the issues raised by the appellants here. This is said without minimizing the substantial difficulty posed by the most critical issues raised, but in light of the fact that the arguments presented on those issues were not of outstanding quality and contributed little to the court's resolution of the appeal. It is similarly inconceivable that counsel, purportedly versed in appellate procedure, justifiably could have spent nearly 20 hours (2½ working days) reviewing the relevant procedures on this procedurally unexceptional appeal. In several other particulars, as discussed below, plaintiff's attorneys have allegedly expended and consequently charged their client for an unreasonable number of hours on both the appeal and the subsequent proceedings.

Because their petition claims such an inflated expenditure of time in so many particulars and overall that it is impossible for this court to cull in detail the justified from the unjustified, we find that reasonable, competent counsel representing a successful plaintiff on appeal such as that in the present case could easily have accomplished their task in no more than 420 total hours and that this sum is the reasonable number of hours assignable to counsel's appeal-related endeavors. This figure represents our view that the full month provided counsel to draft their responsive brief to appellants' brief was adequate time for two attorneys billing 35 hours per week to accomplish the task, having had two weeks to familiarize themselves with the record and potential arguments on appeal, as well as to tend to other tasks appropriately billed to their client. We consider this figure to represent the number of hours that reasonable counsel, exercising responsible "billing judgment," could have charged their own client in this regard. *See Hensley,* 461 U.S. at 434, 103 S.Ct. at 1940.

This figure also necessarily assumes a pre-existing familiarity with the record because, under § 1988, it is inappropriate to charge defendants with the time necessary for replacement appellate counsel to reach the level of familiarity with the case for which trial counsel had already been compensated, *see* Hickman v. Valley Local School Dist., 513 F.Supp. 659, 662 (S.D.Ohio 1981), especially where several of the legal issues had already been fully argued in the district court. *See* Sotomura v. County of Hawaii, 679 F.2d 152, 153 (9th Cir.1982). Even considering the change of counsel post-trial, however, the number of hours charged Spell by counsel is far outside the realm of a reasonable exercise of billing judgment.

In order to illustrate the inflated nature of the hours plaintiff's attorneys have charged plaintiff Spell and on whose behalf they seek reimbursement we here note a few particulars of the itemized bills which Bryant has presented to Spell on behalf of the Obenshain and McCarthy & Durrette law firms and for which full payment has been received. References to the time records kept by Beaver and Richardson are also included. These bills and time records are the bases of the lodestar sought by counsel on Spell's behalf.

Attorneys Bryant, Marshall, Tucker, Ellyson, Beaver, and Richardson seek reimbursement for 1,431.1 hours they claim to have spent in representing Spell on appeal through briefing, oral argument, and response to appellants' motions to file supplemental authority. As indicated, we consider that only 420 hours are reasonably allocated to these tasks. Although it is difficult to discern the exact number of hours allocated to particular tasks undertaken in connection with the appeal due to the varying degrees of particularity with which these six attorneys have recorded their time, we have been able to approximate these figures. Because the burden is on the party seeking the fee award to establish the reasonableness of the hours spent, *Hensley,* 461 U.S. at 437, 103 S.Ct. at 1941, where it is necessary for the court to approximate because of counsel's inadequate record-keeping we consider it just so to do in favor of the party contesting the fee award. *Cf. id.*

Our review of the itemized bill presented to Spell by Bryant, Marshall and Tucker, indicates that they have charged Spell for almost 20 hours of time spent either reviewing or ascertaining simple aspects of Fourth Circuit procedure. This amount was not properly charged to their client where counsel's appellate experience was a basis for their hourly rate nor therefore can it be charged to defendants under 42 U.S.C. § 1988. *See Hensley,* 461 U.S. at 434; *Daly,* 790 F.2d at 1079.

The attorneys also represent that at least 700 hours were spent researching and drafting their brief in response to the 10 specific issues raised in the appellants' brief. Additional hours were spent discussing these issues amongst themselves. Two of these issues were clearly frivolous and did not warrant discussion in this court's opinion. *See Spell*, 824 F.2d at 1399. Two of the remaining seven issues, designated as issues six and seven, were very simple evidentiary issues that warranted only limited discussion. *See id.* at 1400–01. However, it is clear from their time sheets that counsel spent in excess of 200 hours researching, briefing, and holding extensive conferences regarding these particular issues. We consider this time to have been unreasonable where these issues had been fully researched and discussed at the trial level, making the appellate endeavor largely duplicative, *see Sotomura*, 679 F.2d at 153; Hart v. Bourque, 798 F.2d 519, 522–23 (1st Cir.1986), and where less than 10 pages of their 47 page brief were even devoted to these issues. This particular work could reasonably have been accomplished in 50 hours or less.

Similarly, it appears from their time sheets that appellate counsel spent at least 100 hours researching, briefing, and discussing appellate issues designated numbers three and nine relating to the district court's grant of a new trial on the damages issue alone. Again these issues were fully treated at the trial level, merited relatively limited discussion by this court, *see* 824 F.2d at 1400, and were treated only briefly in appellee's brief. We find that the hours spent were clearly excessive and duplicative, the issues warranting at most 30 hours work in restructuring for appeal.

Of the remaining five issues, issue number 10, on which counsel allegedly spent roughly 30 hours, concerned objections raised by appellants to the district court's award of attorney's fees, specifically as to the lodestar and the use of a contingency multiplier. Appellee's brief included two pages devoted to this issue, arguing that the district court had meticulously exercised its discretion and that appellants had waived their right to take issue with the fee award due to lack of contemporaneous objection. On appeal, plaintiff prevailed as to the district court's lodestar determination, but was not a prevailing party as to the application of the contingency multiplier due to intervening Supreme Court authority. *See* 824 F.2d at 1404. Accordingly only a portion of the time purportedly devoted to the fee issue, which appears no less characterized by overkill than the other issues, is properly charged to defendants. *See Hensley*, 461 U.S. at 435, 103 S.Ct. at 1940. On the basis of the plaintiff's brief which simply quotes the district court's opinion in support of its own lodestar determination, we find that 10 hours would suffice to afford such reasonable treatment of appellants' objections to the lodestar.

The remaining issues raised on appeal we can only consider to have been as poorly managed regarding time allocation as the seven already discussed. It is impossible to determine the exact number of hours devoted to these issues but it appears to have been in excess of a total of at least 400. We find that it is necessary to substantially reduce these hours to account for the duplication of effort from the trial level, and the overstaffing and overkill that is characteristic of the entire fee petition. See Tasby v. Estes, 651 F.2d 287, 289 n. 1 (5th Cir.1981). It is especially appropriate to reduce the number of hours that reasonably could be charged to work on these issues because the appellee's brief upon them was singularly unilluminating, *see* Robins v. Harum, 773 F.2d 1004, 1011 (9th Cir.1985), suggesting either that the recorded amount of time was inflated or that the time claimed was spent in such a duplicative fashion that no single attorney actually spent enough time to grasp these most critical issues, those to which this court devoted the bulk of its opinion. *See* 824 F.2d at 1385–99. No more than 150 hours could reasonably have been devoted to preparing the briefs on these issues.

Counsel's time sheets also specifically reflect that between attorneys Marshall and Tucker approximately 150 hours were spent reviewing the record on appeal. An additional 12½ hours were spent by attorney Ellyson in indexing and cross-referencing the record. Between the five attorneys at least 30 hours were claimed to have been spent drafting the appellee's statement of the facts. In addition, at least 20 hours were spent preparing items from the record for inclusion in the appendix. All told, therefore, at the very least, 200 hours were allegedly spent by Spell's appellate counsel merely in digesting the record. We have already observed that it is inappropriate to charge defendants for duplicative endeavors and overkill on the part of newly acquired counsel. Defendants have already paid over $200,000 to plaintiff's trial counsel who can only be assumed to have had a substantial grasp of the record and the facts in this case. While we recognize that good appellate counsel must of course familiarize themselves with the record, we are satisfied that Spell's trial counsel working alone could easily have accomplished the task, including all indexing, cross-referencing, fact drafting, amongst other things, in well under 100 hours.

We have already noted that the obviously inflated claim of hours reasonably spent, the varying precision with which counsel maintained their time records, and counsel's failure to "make a good faith effort to exclude * * * hours that are excessive, redundant, or otherwise unnecessary," *Hensley,* 461 U.S. at 434, 103 S.Ct. at 1939–40, makes it impossible specifically to pinpoint the exact hours which particular attorneys reasonably gave to particular tasks. We have therefore found it necessary to determine, based on our awareness "that it is highly unusual, if not unique, that the cost of presenting a case on appeal is more than it was for trial," Hickman v. Valley Local School Dist., 513 F.Supp. 659, 662 (S.D.Ohio 1981), and our awareness of the practical demands of this particular case, that no more than 420 total hours (roughly 50 full working days) could reasonably have been spent in post-trial appellate work on this case. One need look no further than the over 170 hours (21 working days) allegedly spent by counsel in preparation for 30 minutes of oral argument after over 1,000 hours had purportedly already been spent on the appeal to realize the vastly inflated claim of hours reasonably devoted to these tasks.

We further find that the hours of counsel's paralegal staff for which plaintiff requests compensation reflect the same duplication of effort and unreasonable billing judgment attributable to the attorneys' own recorded hours. Paralegal Dru Mears allegedly spent 81.8 hours copying cases, punching holes, running errands, filing cases, and creating tabs and indexes as well as a small amount of proofreading, cite checking, and working on the table of cases for the appellate brief. Mr. Spell was charged an hourly rate of $60 for these services for a total of $4,908.00. We find that the number of hours claimed for this type work should be reduced in the same proportion that we have reduced counsel's hours. Plaintiff may therefore recover for 24.54 hours (81.8 × .30) of paralegal time in connection with the appeal at the reasonable hourly rate discussed *infra.* This reduction accounts not only for duplication but also for the fact that the attorney's own hourly rate can properly be considered to subsume the secretarial-type services identified as having been performed by their paralegals.

Finally, we find that the number of hours spent by counsel in connection with the post-appeal proceedings, including the hours spent preparing the fee petition in this case, as reflected in the McCarthy & Durrette firm's time records for September 24, 1987 through March 30, 1988, and Beaver's records for August 6, 1987 through January 6, 1988, reflect the same unreasonable expenditures of hours as do the fee statements related to the direct appeal to this court. By affidavit, Bryant admits that "the procedure followed in the preparation of plaintiff-respondent's brief for the Supreme Court was similar to that followed * * * in the preparation of the brief that was filed in the Fourth Circuit." We have already observed that this procedure obviously involved very substantial duplication of effort amongst at least four attorneys, that it was redundant of effort expended in earlier proceedings, and that it involved excessive conferences. We therefore find that the 390.35 hours recorded as having been spent by attorneys Bryant, Marshall, Allen, and Beaver and the 12.1 hours recorded as having been spent by paralegal Black on post-appeal services are properly reduced to 117.11 hours and 3.63 hours, respectively. Again, this reflects the roughly 70% reduction in hourly expenditures we have found necessary to apply to all of counsel's hours statements in order to find a basis for a reasonable attorney's fee in this case. A like reduction is properly applied to the simply incredible 64.6 hours that counsel contend in their supplemental motion they spent preparing the present fee petition. Nineteen attorney hours were sufficient to accomplish the initial task as well as to reply to defendants' objections. Cf. Sun Publishing Co. v. Mecklenburg News, Inc., 823 F.2d 818, 819–20 (4th Cir.1987). The secretarial-type services performed by McCarthy & Durrette's paralegal in connection with the fee petition are properly considered as part of counsel's overhead and do not merit an additional award.

B. Reasonable Hourly Rate

In our opinion in Spell v. McDaniel, 824 F.2d 1380 (4th Cir.1987), this court affirmed the district court's finding, based on evidence of relevant prevailing market rates, that $125 was a reasonable hourly rate for trial counsel Beaver considering, among other things, his experience and the type of issues involved in this case. *See id.* at 1402. In the present fee petition it is argued that Mr. Richardson, formerly compensated at a $100 hourly rate, having since gained experience and become a partner in the Fayetteville, North Carolina firm, can also reasonably charge $125. A flat hourly rate of $150 is submitted as reasonable for attorneys Bryant, Marshall, Tucker, and Ellyson. An award for time spent by paralegal Mears is sought at a rate of $60 per hour while paralegal Black's rate is only a requested $35 per hour. By affidavit, the lesser rate for Black is explained as reasonable in that she had never worked on the case before. A like reason applies to the requested hourly rate of $80 for attorney Allen.

Affidavits submitted in conjunction with the present motion, including those submitted by defendants, as well as those before the district court, *see* 824 F.2d at 1403 n. 19, support our prior conclusion, affirming that of the district court, that $125 is a reasonable and prevailing market rate for attorneys involved in cases similar to the present one. We therefore find that this is a reasonable rate for all attorney's hours billed in connection with the post-trial proceedings. Because "[c]ounsel's experience is only one of many factors to be considered in determining a reasonable fee," 824 F.2d at 1403 (citing Johnson v. Georgia Highway Express, Inc., 488 F.2d 714 (5th Cir. 1974)), and further because we have determined the number of hours that reasonably were expended in this case on the premise that one or two attorneys of like skill and experience were adequate to accomplish the various tasks in the stated numbers of hours, we decline to adjust the hourly rate of $125 either upward or downward to account for the slight variations of skill level and experience possessed by the seven attorneys who have represented Spell in post-trial proceedings. *Cf. Hensley,* 461 U.S. at 434, 103 S.Ct. at 1939–40 (holding that properly exercised billing judgment includes reductions in hours billed for attorneys of lesser skill and experience). Likewise a uniform rate for all services rendered is appropriate where the hours expended reflect only those "properly billed to one's client," *Id.* (citation omitted); 824 F.2d at 1403 (upholding district court's application of uniform rates).

Plaintiff's counsel have admitted that $35 per hour is a reasonable hourly rate for a paralegal who is new to an ongoing case. Defendants appear mainly to object to the $60 hourly rate charged for paralegal Mears' services. However, the focus of defendants' objection is the number of hours credited to paralegal work of a predominantly secretarial nature which is thus properly included in the office overhead rather than as a separate charge. *See* Ramos v. Lamm, 713 F.2d 546, 558–59 (10th Cir.1983). We find, therefore, that $35 per hour is a reasonable hourly rate for the paralegal services of Mears and Black where both, like their employers, were late additions to the case.

C. Expenses

A prevailing plaintiff in a civil rights action is entitled, under § 1988, to recover "those reasonable out-of-pocket expenses incurred by the attorney which are normally charged to a fee-paying client, in the course of providing legal services." Northcross v. Board of Educ. of Memphis City Schools, 611 F.2d 624, 639 (6th Cir.1979); *see Daly,* 790 F.2d at 1084. Plaintiff's counsel have submitted itemized bills pertaining to out-of-pocket expenses incurred in all post-trial proceedings in this matter. The total comes to $8,669.29, to which the defendants have not objected. We have reviewed the statements and find the items contained therein to be reasonable. We therefore award plaintiff the entire $8,669.29 requested.

D.   Contingency Multiplier

We have already concluded that, in light of the Supreme Court's holding in Pennsylvania v. Delaware Valley Citizens' Council for Clean Air, 483 U.S. 711, 107 S.Ct. 3078, 97 L.Ed.2d 585 (1987), "the 'contingency multiplier' allowed in this case [by the district court] is not legally justified." 824 F.2d at 1405. In particular we found that the record revealed "no dearth of competent counsel willing to take this and comparable cases on a contingency basis * * * without any guarantee of special enhancement of reasonable 'lodestar' fees." *Id.* This situation obviously could not have changed between the trial and appeal in this case, especially where plaintiff already had competent counsel and was now armed with a jury award of $900,000 which enjoyed a presumption of regularity on the appeal. Mr. Beaver's unsupported affidavits and hunches as to the possibilities of obtaining alternative or associate appellate counsel without application of a 1.5 contingency multiplier are not sufficient to establish that "enhancement for risk was necessary in the relevant market to insure that 'poor clients with good claims [could] secure competent help.' " *Spell,* 824 F.2d at 1404 (quoting 107 S.Ct. at 3089). Accordingly, we reject as not justified plaintiff's request for enhancement of the fees of attorneys Bryant, Tucker, Marshall, and Ellyson as well as the requested $15,000 bonus to the Obenshain firm.

E.   Interest and Compensation for Delay

The request from the Obenshain firm for interest on its appellate fee award from the December 5, 1986 billing date to January 20, 1988, is denied as unjustified. An eight percent enhancement for delay, or $1,126.70 (112.67 hours × $125 × .08) is, however, justified as to that portion of the fee attributable to Spell's trial counsel as reduced in accordance with this court's earlier judgment. *Cf.* 790 F.2d at 1081.

V

On the basis of the reasoning above, we find that a reasonable attorney's fee award for the post-trial proceedings in the present case is $69,513.75, which sum is arrived at by multiplying the $125 reasonable hourly rate by the 556.11 attorney hours reasonably spent on all of these proceedings combined. An additional $958.95 (28.17 hours × $35) is awarded for paralegal services; $8,669.29, for out-of-pocket expenses; and $1,126.70 for delay. Accordingly, the defendant-respondents are hereby ordered to pay the sum of $80,295.69 to plaintiff Henry Z. Spell as a final award of attorney's fees in connection with his successful § 1983 action against them.

To put things in perspective, it may be proper to close by emphasizing several critical aspects of this matter. The fee award claimed here is for services rendered in defending on appeal—not establishing at trial—a civil rights plaintiff's entitlement to a substantial damage award. The appeal presented no difficult problems of appellate procedure; in that sense it was quite simple and straightforward. While it did present a substantial and difficult substantive issue concerning the viability of plaintiff's legal theory of recovery, the jury verdict was overwhelmingly supported by the evidence within that theory. This was in fact a case so substantially proven and properly tried below that it could only be lost on appeal by judicial rejection of the basic legal theory upon which it was tried and submitted to the jury. Aside from one rather sticky problem involving the trial court's instructions on one aspect of the case, there were no other serious assignments of trial court error. While the verdict and judgment and the underlying legal theory were ultimately upheld on appeal, this cannot in candor, since the issue is raised, be attributed in any significant degree to the work of appellate counsel. This case was essentially won by trial counsel's efforts and simply not lost by appellate counsel's. Appellate counsel's claim for a fee award substantially in excess of the quite generous fee already awarded trial counsel is therefore completely at odds with the realities of the case and with a fair assessment of what went into making plaintiff a "prevailing party" in the end.

It Is So Ordered.

Quaratino v. Tiffany & Co.

United States District Court for the Southern District of New York, 1996.
948 F. Supp. 332.

■ John S. Martin, Jr., District Judge:

Presently before the Court is plaintiff's application for attorney's fees and costs in the amount of $139,022.68.

The most significant question is what proportion of the lodestar of $124,645.18 should be awarded given that the total judgment recovered by plaintiff was only $158,145. The resolution of this question raises fundamental issues of public policy which have been debated in both the Supreme Court and the Second Circuit. It is far from clear, however, how either of those courts would answer these questions today.

The basic question centers on the extent to which there should be a proportional relation between the amount of the fee and the amount of the plaintiff's recovery. This issue was squarely presented to the Supreme Court in *City of Riverside v. Rivera*, 477 U.S. 561, 106 S. Ct. 2686, 91 L. Ed. 2d 466 (1986) in which the Court sustained a fee award of $245,456.25, even though the plaintiffs had received a total award of only $33,350 in compensatory and punitive damages. In that case the Court rejected the argument of the petitioners, and the United States as amicus curiae, that attorneys' fees in civil rights cases should be analogized to fees in tort cases and should be proportionate to the amount of recovery.

Unfortunately for those seeking guidance from the Supreme Court there was no majority opinion in Rivera. The plurality opinion, authored by Justice Brennan, who was joined by Justices Marshall, Blackmun and Stevens, rejected applying the concept of proportionality on the ground that civil rights litigation seeks to vindicate important civil and constitutional rights that cannot be valued solely in monetary terms. In a strong dissent, Justice Rehnquist, joined by Chief Justice Burger and Justices White and O'Connor, argued that, in determining whether the time for which the prevailing attorney seeks compensation was reasonably spent, the district court should ask whether a competent attorney would reasonably have spent that amount of billable time on a matter that was likely to result in such a small recovery. Although Justice Rehnquist's dissent suggested that the "billing judgment" approach should control in most cases, it did recognize that there could be exceptions where the defendant's bad-faith conduct significantly increased the cost of litigation, or where the litigation produced substantial benefits for persons other than the plaintiff.

Any continuing authority of the plurality opinion in *Rivera* was cast in serious doubt by the Supreme Court's subsequent opinion in *Farrar v. Hobby*, 506 U.S. 103, 113 S. Ct. 566, 121 L. Ed. 2d 494 (1992). In that case the plaintiff had recovered only nominal damages but the district court awarded $280,000 in attorneys' fees. The Circuit Court reversed on the ground that a party who received only nominal damages should not be considered the prevailing party. The Supreme Court five person majority, in an opinion written by Justice Thomas, disagreed with the Circuit and held that the plaintiff was the prevailing party, but found that the award of nominal damages was such a limited success that it was reasonable to deny the plaintiff attorneys' fees altogether. Justice Thomas stated:

Once civil rights litigation materially alters the legal relationship between the parties, "the degree of the plaintiff's overall success goes to the reasonableness" of a fee award under Hensley v. Eckerhart. Indeed, "the most critical factor" in determining the reasonableness of a fee award "is the degree of success obtained." *Farrar*, 113 S. Ct. at 574 (citing *Hensley*, 461 U.S. at 436, 103 S. Ct. at 1941).

If I were deciding the present fee application with only the benefit of the relevant Supreme Court cases, I would conclude that in a case such as this, where the plaintiff sued solely to receive compensation for the damage that she personally suffered, the fee awarded must bear some relation to the amount she recovered. If a party who recovers nominal damages is entitled to a fee of zero because no significant monetary relief was obtained, then a party who receives only a limited recovery should only receive a fee that is reasonable in light of the amount of damages awarded. Indeed, in light of the opinion in Farrar, one would assume that a party who brought a civil rights action seeking monetary damages would rarely be entitled to an award that exceeded, or even approached, the amount of the damage award.

Yet, at least twice since the Supreme Court decided Farrar, the Second Circuit has sustained fee awards in individual employment discrimination cases that were out of proportion to the amount of the damages recovered. In *Reed v. A.W. Lawrence & Co.*, 95 F.3d 1170 (2d Cir.1996), the Second Circuit affirmed the award of attorneys' fees of approximately $54,417.28 to a plaintiff in an employment discrimination suit whose total recovery was $69,038.46. In *Saulpaugh v. Monroe Community Hospital*, 4 F.3d 134 (2d Cir.1993), the Circuit Court approved the award of $85,304.88 in attorneys' fees to a plaintiff who had been awarded only $38,282.90 in actual damages. In neither of the above cases did the Court mention the Supreme Court's decision in Farrar nor discuss the question of the relationship between the amount of the damage award and the amount of the fee.

The Second Circuit did take note of Farrar in *Lunday v. City of Albany*, 42 F.3d 131 (2d Cir.1994), a case where a plaintiff who obtained a total award of $35,000 against a police officer on an excessive force claim was awarded a total of $118,912.08 for attorney's fees and expenses. Although noting that Farrar provided that the degree of plaintiff's success is the most critical factor in determining reasonableness of a fee award, the Court stated "we consistently have resisted a strict proportionality requirement in civil rights cases. *Cowan v. Prudential Ins. Co. of America*, 935 F.2d 522, 525–28 (2d Cir.1991)." *Lunday*, 42 F.3d at 134–35.

Particular note has been taken of the identity of the judges involved in Cowan because in the most recent Second Circuit case on this issue, *Pino v. Locascio*, 101 F.3d 235 (2d Cir. 1996), a panel of Judges Winter, McLaughlin and Van Graafeiland, overturned an award of $50,590.80 in attorney's fees and costs of $4,842.49 to a plaintiff in an employment discrimination case who had recovered only nominal damages. Judge McLaughlin's opinion for the Court reiterates "the most important factor in determining the reasonableness of a fee award is the degree of success obtained. *Farrar*, 506 U.S. at 114." Pino, slip op. at 458.

Judge Kearse, the only other member of the Cowan panel still on the Circuit Court—Judge Pratt having retired—also was on a panel that, subsequent to Farrar, held that a plaintiff in a civil rights case who recovered only nominal damages was not entitled to an award of counsel fees. *Caruso v. Forslund*, 47 F.3d 27, 32 (2d Cir.1995). Thus, there is reason to doubt that the Circuit Judges involved in Cowan would consider that case as good law today.

The above analysis suggests that it is far from clear how the Circuit Court would resolve the fee question presented here. In part, the current lack of clarity on the issues stems from the fact that on the issue of the reasonableness of a fee award the appellate courts give substantial deference to the discretion of the district judge. *Clarke v.*

Frank, 960 F.2d 1146, 1153 (2d Cir.1992). While I would not change that rule, this appears to be an area where the district courts need guidance with respect to the factors that should be considered in exercising that discretion.

Given the uncertain state of the current law, I will follow the procedure adopted by Judge Winter in Cowan and calculate alternative fee awards, with the hope that a remand can be avoided should the Circuit Court disagree with the approach I adopt.

If *Cowan* and *Lunday* still represent the law of this Circuit, then it is appropriate to award the plaintiff the full amount of the lodestar, $124,645.18. The plaintiff prevailed on a substantial claim and, as already noted, the total amount of time expended would not have been reduced substantially had plaintiff pursued only the retaliation charge.

I will not award this amount, however, because the rationale of *Cowan* and *Lunday* appears inconsistent with *Farrar*, and with the views of at least five of the Justices who decided *Rivera*, as well as the recent decisions of the Second Circuit in *Pino v. Locascio*, and *Caruso v. Forslund*.

It seems most likely that, when squarely faced with this issue, the appellate courts will adopt the "billing judgment" approach suggested in Rivera by Chief Justice Rehnquist. This approach focuses on the judgment an attorney would exercise in determining the amount of time that should be devoted to a case in light of the anticipated recovery. While that approach would place heavy emphasis on the amount of the potential recovery in cases where the action was brought solely to recover damages sustained by an individual, it is flexible enough to provide reasonable guidance in the "infinitely variable" facts and circumstances alluded to by Justice Powell in *Rivera*. 477 U.S. at 585, 106 S. Ct. at 2700.

For example, in a case where a new legal principle of importance in the field of civil rights is involved, the appropriate billing judgment might be that of a public interest institution, such as the American Civil Liberties Union, and the question would be how much of the time of its lawyers would such an institution reasonably commit to a case brought to establish that principle. Public service institutions are always faced with the question of how much of their limited resources they can commit to a particular issue. In addition, the willingness of a private attorney to commit her time to a case where little monetary recovery may be expected may itself reflect a reasonable billing judgment that the issues presented are of overarching societal importance. The question whether the establishment of a particular rule of law is important enough to justify a substantial commitment of lawyers' time is one which the district courts are well-qualified to decide. See *Cabrera v. Jakabovitz*, 24 F.3d 372, 393 (2d Cir.1994).

In cases such as the present, the issue will be much more straight forward—what is a reasonable amount of time for a lawyer to spend at a given hourly rate in order to obtain the monetary award that one could reasonably anticipate.

A rational billing judgment would attempt to weigh the likely amount of any recovery against the risk of litigation. As Justice Rehnquist noted in *Rivera*, no rational lawyer would devote $25,000 of billable time to a matter where the potential recovery was only $10,000. See 477 U.S. at 592–93, 106 S. Ct. at 2703. Indeed, except in exceptional circumstances, no rational lawyer or client would commit to any case an amount for lawyer's fees that approaches the amount of the total recovery.

The use of a "billing judgment" approach in awarding attorney's fees should have the salutary effect of encouraging lawyers in cases such as this to limit pretrial discovery to that which is reasonable in light of the expected recovery. This Court has seen too many cases in which attorneys engage in excessive discovery in the apparent hope that if liability is established they will be compensated for the total time expended even though the resulting fee award is out of all proportion to the amount of the damages recovered.

In awarding fees on the "billing judgment" basis, it must be recognized that in some cases it is difficult for attorneys and clients to predict, at the outset, how much billable time it will take to obtain a particular result. In such circumstances, clients are often unwilling to make an open-ended commitment to fund the total costs of the litigation. The result may be a totally contingent fee arrangement or a retainer that provides a cap on the time charges and some contingent share by the lawyer in the recovery by plaintiff. Each of these varied situations involves a billing judgment with which the courts are familiar and which the courts can apply in determining a reasonable fee for a prevailing party in litigation such as this.

Turning to the facts of this case, it appears that a reasonable billing judgment would have placed a limit on the willingness of plaintiff to make an open-ended funding commitment to this case. First, a large compensatory damage award for lost wages could not have been anticipated. Plaintiff remained in defendant's employ throughout the period of the lawsuit and thus her damages were limited to the difference between the amount she was being paid and the higher rate of pay for the job she claimed she should have had. Plaintiff's damage expert—with the usual generosity one might anticipate from the plaintiff's expert—estimated the total damages for lost wages from 1992 to 1998 as $73,108. Although plaintiff had a claim for emotional distress and punitive damages, neither was so strong as to provide a reasonable expectation of a substantial award. A very generous evaluation of the case would have placed the maximum possible recovery at no more than $200,000. But then counsel and client would have had to factor in the risk that there might be no recovery at all—a substantial risk in this case. In these circumstances it appears that one of a number of reasonable billing judgments that an attorney and client would make is the one that, in fact, plaintiff and her attorney did make, i.e., an agreement that plaintiff's time charges would be capped at 50% of the recovery.

Quaratino v. Tiffany & Co.

United States Court of Appeals For The Second Circuit, 1999.
166 F.3d 422.*

■ JOSE A. CABRANES, CIRCUIT JUDGE:

Plaintiff-appellant Mary C. Quaratino appeals an order of the United States District Court for the Southern District of New York (John S. Martin, Jr., Judge) awarding attorney's fees in the amount of $79,072.50, exactly one-half of her recovery at trial on her pregnancy discrimination and retaliation claims against her employer, Tiffany & Co. ("Tiffany"), under Title VII of the Civil Rights Act of 1964, 42 U.S.C. § 2000e et seq. The district court decided not to award its calculated lodestar amount, and instead adopted a "billing judgment" approach. *Quaratino v. Tiffany & Co.*, 948 F. Supp. 332, 333, 336–38 (S.D.N.Y.1996) ("Quaratino II"). We decline to adopt this new fee award approach, and accordingly we vacate the district court's fee award, and remand with directions to award the lodestar attorney's fee, subject to limited recalculation.

In April 1993, Mary C. Quaratino filed suit in the United States District Court for the Southern District of New York, charging that Tiffany, her employer, had engaged in discrimination in violation of the Pregnancy Discrimination Act, 42 U.S.C. § 2000e(k), n2 of Title VII of the Civil Rights Act of 1964, 42 U.S.C. § 2000e et seq. She alleged that her discharge from employment in 1992 at the end of her maternity leave constituted unlawful pregnancy discrimination. Less than a month after the March 31, 1994 close of discovery, Quaratino initiated proceedings seeking to amend her complaint to add a claim of retaliation, alleging that in 1993 she was passed over for a promotion at Tiffany's (where she had since been rehired in a lower-level position) in retaliation for her pregnancy discrimination complaint. The district court denied Quaratino's motion to amend her complaint and granted summary judgment on the discrimination claim for Tiffany, but this Court reversed on both counts. See *Quaratino I*, 71 F.3d at 65–66.

In late July and early August of 1996, Quaratino's discrimination and retaliation claims were both tried to a jury, which returned a verdict for Tiffany on the pregnancy discrimination claim, but found for Quaratino on the retaliation claim. The jury awarded her $60,000 in compensatory damages and $98,145 in punitive damages—a total recovery of $158,145—on the retaliation claim.

---

* Pursuant to a sua sponte recall of the mandate, the matter was reheard by the Court of Appeals sitting in banc. After due consideration, and in light of this amended panel opinion, the in banc court has voted to dissolve itself. See Quaratino v. Tiffany, F.3d (2d Cir. 1998) (per curiam). We vacate our original opinion, see Quaratino v. Tiffany, 129 F.3d 702 (2d Cir.1997), which is superseded by This Opinion Substituted on Grant of Rehearing for Vacated Opinion of November 14, 1997.

Pursuant to Title VII's fee-shifting provision, 42 U.S.C. § 2000e–5(k), Quaratino filed a post-trial motion seeking attorney's fees. However, the court declined to award its calculated lodestar amount of $124,645.18, and instead awarded fees in the amount of one-half of the plaintiff's recovery at trial ($79,072.50). See *Quaratino II*, 948 F. Supp. at 336, 338.

A. "Billing Judgment"

Following an extended inquiry into the state of the law and the attributes of a preferred approach to fee awards, Judge Martin instead decided to award attorney's fees of exactly one-half of the plaintiff's $158,145 recovery at trial. He asserted that "it is far from clear how the Circuit Court would resolve the fee question presented here." *Id. at 333.*

In the face of this perceived uncertainty, the district court elected to craft what it termed a "billing judgment" approach. Under that approach, which the district court derived in part from the dissenting opinion of Justice Rehnquist in *City of Riverside v. Rivera*, 477 U.S. 561, 591–94, 91 L. Ed. 2d 466, 106 S. Ct. 2686 (1986), an attorney's requested fee would be judged "reasonable" if it were rationally related to the monetary recovery that the attorney could have anticipated ex ante. The district court would have had Quaratino's attorney estimate ex ante the total possible financial recovery in the case (the court forecast a "very generous" maximum of $200,000), discount that amount for the "substantial" risk of no recovery, and proceed to expend time on the case only up to the time value of an appropriate fraction of that expected recovery. See *Quaratino II*, 948 F. Supp. at 338. The validity of the attorney's ex ante predictions and ensuing expenditure of time would then be evaluated ex post by the district court to set a reasonable attorney's fee award.

Even setting aside considerable misgivings as to the feasibility of such precise ex ante calculations, we find that this approach conflicts with the legislative intent and rationales of the fee-shifting statute. Congress enacted fee-shifting in civil rights litigation precisely because the expected monetary recovery in many cases was too small to attract effective legal representation. See *Rivera*, 477 U.S. at 575 (plurality opinion) ("Congress did not intend for fees in civil rights cases . . . to depend on obtaining substantial monetary relief."). Were we to adopt the "billing judgment" approach that the district court advocates, we would contravene that clear legislative intent by relinking the effectiveness of a civil rights plaintiff's legal representation solely to the dollar value of her claim. As a near-unanimous Supreme Court reiterated in *Blanchard v. Bergeron*, 489 U.S. 87, 103 L. Ed. 2d 67, 109 S. Ct. 939 (1989), "a civil rights plaintiff seeks to vindicate important civil and constitutional rights that cannot be valued solely in monetary terms," *id. at 96* (quoting *Rivera*, 477 U.S. at 574), and we are unwilling to hold that the plaintiff's attorney should calculate the value of her client's rights in just those "monetary terms."

Nor is the district court's approach saved by its proposed exception, which would allow fees out of line with monetary recovery in "a case where a new legal principle of importance in the field of civil rights" or an "issue[] ... of overarching societal importance" is involved. *Quaratino II*, 948 F. Supp. at 337. Congress enacted fee-shifting statutes to compensate "private attorneys general" and thereby to encourage private enforcement of civil rights statutes, to the benefit of the public as a whole. See H.R. Rep. No. 94–1558, at 2 (1976) (citing *Newman v. Piggie Park Enters., Inc.*, 390 U.S. 400, 402, 19 L. Ed. 2d 1263, 88 S. Ct. 964 (1968) (per curiam)); see generally S. Rep. No. 94–1011 (1976). The public interest in private civil rights enforcement is not limited to those cases that push the legal envelope; it is perhaps most meaningfully served by the day-to-day private enforcement of these rights, which secures compliance and deters future violations. Congress meant reasonable attorney's fees to be available to the private attorneys general who enforce the law, see generally S. Rep. No. 94–1011, not only to those whose cases make new law.

The most direct response to the district court's fee calculation innovation, however, is that this Court does not follow, and has not suggested that it would be inclined to follow, the billing judgment rule that the district court developed. We believe that lodestar analysis, as developed and refined in the decade and a half of jurisprudence beginning with Hensley, is a flexible mechanism within whose parameters district courts should calculate the prevailing plaintiff's "reasonable" fee. We decline the district court's invitation to abandon that framework in favor of a billing judgment rule.

Instead, we restrict our analysis to the reasoning in fact employed by the district court in reaching its fee award—"billing judgment"—and, having found it flawed, remand for the award of a fee based on the actual lodestar.[9]

In sum, we find an error of law in the district court's abandonment of the lodestar method in favor of a "billing judgment" approach that requires vacatur of the district court's attorney's fee award. In light of this holding, as the district court anticipated, "it is appropriate to award the plaintiff the full amount of the lodestar." *Quaratino II*, 948 F. Supp. at 336.

ATTORNEY FEES AND ACCESS TO JUSTICE

What does *Spell* tell us about access to justice in this country? The two *Spell* opinions taken together tell us a great deal about Mr. Spell and his difficulties in financing the lawsuit he brought, which ultimately was successful. *Quaratino* illustrates the continuing difficulties courts face in determining what fees are reasonable. If we are to

---

9. Because the district court offered no basis other than "billing judgment" for its fee reduction, we intimate no view on the other circumstances that might—in other cases—warrant reduction of a fee award below the lodestar. The panel's initial (now superseded) opinion could be read to suggest that a district court may not reduce the fee award below the lodestar (a) because of the low degree of success, unless the plaintiff won no more than a nominal or technical victory, or (b) because of the triviality of the interest on which the plaintiff prevailed. We wish to clarify that neither question is presented on this appeal, and that we intimate no view on either one.

generalize beyond these cases, however, we must examine a broader canvas.

The American Rule and Fee Shifting Statutes: We begin with the general rule, typically referred to as the "American Rule," that each party pays for its own litigation costs, including attorney fees. In Alyeska Pipeline Service Co. v. Wilderness Society, 421 U.S. 240, 247, 95 S.Ct. 1612, 1616, 44 L.Ed.2d 141 (1975), the United States Supreme Court reaffirmed that rule and held that "it would be inappropriate for the Judiciary, without legislative guidance, to reallocate the burdens of litigation" in any fundamental manner. The "English" rule is that the losing party must pay all the costs and legal fees of the prevailing party. Since July 1995, U.K. litigants have been able to obtain insurance against potential liability for legal fees. For a premium of 85 pounds ($136) per case, the insurance will cover up to 100,000 pounds ($160,000) of costs and counsel fees. [See Law Society Gazette For The Record, 28 June 1995, page 1]

In this country, however, although the "American Rule" is the norm, there are close to 2,000 state statutes providing for fee shifting.[1] Similarly, there are over 150 similar federal statutes, some covering a wide range of civil litigation.[2] Among the most important are the Civil Rights Attorneys' Fees Award Act[3] and the Equal Access to Justice Act.[4] The following report describes some of the effects of those statutes with respect to claims against federal agencies.

United States General Accounting Office, Private Attorneys (Oct. 1995)

[We] are reporting data on the number of cases and amount of plaintiff attorneys' fees awarded over $10,000 against nine federal agencies, for cases closed during fiscal years 1993 and 1994. These data include the highest individual fees and hourly rates awarded under federal statutes against the nine federal agencies. The nine agencies are the Departments of Defense, Health and Human Services (HHS),[3] Housing and Urban Development (HUD), the Interior, Justice, Transportation, and the Treasury, the General Services Administration (GSA), and the U.S. Postal Service. In addition, we are providing attorneys' fee awards data reported in the fiscal year 1993 Equal Access to Justice Act annual reports and attorneys fee awards paid from the Judgment Fund during fiscal years 1993 and 1994.

---

1. See State Attorney Fee Shifting Statutes: Are We Quietly Repealing the American Rule? 47 L. & Contemp. Prob. 321, 323 (1984).

2. Percival and Miller, The Role of Attorney Fee Shifting in Public Interest Litigation, 47 L. & Contemp. Prob. 233 (1974).

3. 42 U.S.C. § 1988.

4. 5 U.S.C. § 504.

3. HHS did not provide data on attorneys' fee awards over $10,000 for Social Security Administration cases. It said that attorneys' fee awards were paid in thousands of cases, and it would be too burdensome to search these cases to find those that met our criteria. Many attorneys' fee awards against the Social Security Administration were awarded under the Equal Access to Justice Act. Also, because of the large volume of cases, HHS said it reviewed about one-half of the cases under the *Vaccine Injury Compensation Program*. It provided information on 64 cases that met our criteria.

Generally, the federal government may not be assessed attorneys' fee awards unless such awards are expressly authorized by law. The Congressional Research Service (CRS) identified approximately 180 federal statutes that authorize awards of attorneys' fees against the government in certain cases where an opposing party prevails against the government. Many of the statutes that authorize the award of attorneys' fees against the government specify that payment of those awards shall come from agency appropriations. Some of these statutes authorize a set hourly rate or a percentage of the plaintiff's award amount for determining attorneys' fee awards. Most of these statutes authorize reasonable attorneys' fees but do not specify how they are to be calculated.

One key statute, the Equal Access to Justice Act, allows a party who prevails against the United States to recover attorneys' fees and other expenses under certain circumstances. Portions of the act, codified at 5 U.S.C. § 504, allow specific categories of prevailing parties[8] to recover reasonable attorney fees, expert witness expenses, and related costs in adversary adjudications in administrative proceedings unless the hearing officer finds that the agency's position was substantially justified or that special circumstances make an award unjust. Under section 504, attorney fee rates are limited to $75 per hour unless the agency determines by regulation that an increase in the cost of living or a special factor, such as the limited availability of qualified attorneys or agents for the proceedings involved, justifies a higher fee. Fees and expenses awarded under section 504 are paid by the agency over which the party prevails from any funds made available to the agency by appropriation or otherwise.[b]

Portions of the act, codified at 28 U.S.C. 2412(b), authorize a court to award reasonable attorneys' fees and expenses to a prevailing party in civil actions brought by or against the United States. Under this subsection, the United States is to be liable for such fees to the same extent that any other party would be liable under the common law or under the terms of any federal statute that specifically provides for the award of such fees.

Subsection 2412(d) provides that a court shall award fees and other expenses to a party prevailing against the United States in any nontort civil action unless the court finds that the position of the United States was substantially justified or that special circumstances make an award unjust. Under this subsection, the hourly rate for attorney fees is not to exceed $75 per hour unless the court deter-

---

8. In order for the prevailing party to be paid attorneys' fees under 5 U.S.C. § 504 and 28 U.S.C. § 2412(d), it must be a "party" as defined in the act. In general, both provisions define "party" as an individual with net worth of not more than $2 million at the time the action was filed; any owner of an unincorporated business, or any corporation, partnership, association, local governmental unit or organization, with a net worth of not more than $7 million and not more than 500 employees at the time the action was filed; or a tax-exempt organization under 26 U.S.C. § 501(c)(3) or an agricultural cooperative under 12 U.S.C. § 1141j(a) regardless of net worth.

b. At least 21 states have enacted their own versions of the federal EAJA. These largely track the federal statute and the federal case law interpretations. Eds.

mines that an increase in the cost of living or a special factor, such as the limited availability of qualified attorneys for the proceedings involved, justifies a higher fee. Fees and expenses awarded under this subsection are to be paid by the agency over which the party prevails from any funds made available to the agency by appropriation or otherwise.

The 9 federal agencies reported 441 plaintiff attorneys' fee awards over $10,000 during fiscal years 1993 and 1994. These awards totaled about $20 million and were authorized under 19 federal statutes, including under the Equal Access to Justice Act. The highest single attorney's fee awarded during this 2–year period was $800,000 against HUD. The highest single hourly attorney rate, $320 per hour, was awarded in separate cases against three agencies: HHS, the Treasury, and GSA.

* * *

As for general civil litigation, only Alaska has a "loser pays" rule. There were complaints by two judges of the Alaska Supreme Court "that the weight of the burden imposed on a losing litigant by the award of attorneys fees must be considered in light of the litigant's constitutional right of access." A 1993 revision limits fees recoverable by prevailing defendants to 30% of its legal fees after trial and 20% of the lawsuit ends without a trial. See Vargo, The American Rule on Attorney Fee Allocation: The Injured Person's Access to Justice, 42 Amer. U. L. Rev. 1567, 1623–26 (1993).

What May the Lawyer Recover? The typical federal statute which provides for fee shifting requires the court to determine what constitutes a reasonable lawyer's fee, which sum is then assessed against the losing party. Does that judicial determination limit the amount the lawyer may recover from the client?

That precise question was raised in Venegas v. Mitchell, 495 U.S 82, 110 S.Ct. 1679, 109 L.Ed.2d 74 (1990). Plaintiff brought an action under 42 U.S.C. § 1983 alleging that police officers had falsely arrested him "and conspired to deny him a fair trial through the knowing presentation of perjured testimony." The trial court fixed the value of Mitchell's legal services at $75,000. Mitchell sought $406,000 based on a 40% contingent fee contract with the plaintiff.

Held: Nothing in the applicable statutes precludes a litigant contracting with his attorney and being required to perform according to its terms. White, J., speaking for a unanimous Court, noted that plaintiff had also argued that the fee in the instant case was "unreasonable under federal and state law." Since this contention had been rejected below and the Supreme Court found nothing in the record or briefs to disturb that conclusion, the Court had "no occasion to address the extent of the federal courts' authority to supervise contingency fees."

Contingent Fees: Fees contingent on a successful resolution of the lawsuit increase access to justice. They make it possible for impecunious and risk-averse plaintiffs to prosecute claims that they might otherwise be unable, or unwilling to bring.[3] Suppose a lawyer achieves a settlement in a tort case of $2,925,000. Is the recovery so large as to render a $975,000 fee unconscionable?[4] Suppose there was no risk, no real contingency, at least with respect to liability?[5]

There have been a series of bills introduced in the Congress which, among other things, limit the contingent fees lawyers may receive in various kinds of tort cases. None had been enacted by the end of May, 1996. The American Trial Lawyers Association (ATLA) earlier reported that 17 states limit contingent fees in various types of actions, mainly in medical malpractice suits. B. Franklin, *Learning Curve*, 81 A.B.A. J. 62, 63 (Aug., 1995).

The most recent and widely publicized effort at limitation of contingent fees is California's Initiative, Proposition 202 which applied to all tort cases not otherwise covered by state law. The workings of Proposition 202 require that early settlement offers be made. If the case is then settled within 60 days, the plaintiff s lawyer is limited to a contingent fee of 15% of the settlement amount. If the early settlement offer is rejected, the lawyer can get a higher percentage contingency fee, but calculated only on the amount recovered by later settlement or verdict in excess of the original offer. Proposition 202 was voted down on March 26, 1966.

Legislative Intervention: From time to time Congress enacts legislation designed to reduce legal fees in special situations. Thus, with respect to monetary claims made under laws administered by the Veterans' Administration the maximum fee that the client may pay his attorney is "$10 with respect to any one claim." Moreover, the statute imposes criminal sanctions for any violation, even by agreement. This provision was upheld against a due process challenge, Walters v. National Assn. of Radiation Survivors, 473 U.S. 305, 105 S.Ct. 3180 (1985), on the ground that "attorneys were not essential to vindicate the claims;" a system of service representatives provided without charge by organizations such as the American Legion, Disabled American Veterans and Veterans of Foreign Wars was not shown to be less effective than lawyers.

In U.S. Department of Labor v. Triplett, 494 U.S. 715, 110 S.Ct. 1428, 108 L.Ed.2d 701 (1990), the Court rejected a similar challenge to a provision in the Black Lung Benefits Act of 1972 that forbade a lawyer to take any fee unless approved in advance by the Department of Labor. More accurately, the challenge was to the administration of the provision by the Department. The Court held that to succeed in his challenge the objecting attorney had the obligation of showing "(1) that claimants could not obtain representation, and (2) that this unavailability of attorneys was attributable to the Government's fee regime," a burden which had not been met in the instant case.

---

3. Brickman, Contingent Fees Without Contingencies: *Hamlet* without the Prince of Denmark, 37 U.C.L.A.L.Rev. 29, 43 (1989).

4. See Gagnon v. Shoblom, 409 Mass. 63, 64, 565 N.E.2d 775 (1991) (allowing the fee in the absence of objection by the client).

5. See Brickman, supra note 3.

Professor Brickman reports that "many state legislatures have recently restructured contingent fee arrangements by establishing a sliding scale to govern contingent fee contracts in medical malpractice cases. The purpose of such statutory schemes is to combat the so-called 'insurance-crisis.' Under these schemes, the percentage fee declines as the dollar amount of recovery increases. For example, a New York statute allows a lawyer to receive as compensation thirty percent of the first $250,000 of recovery, twenty-five percent of the next $250,000, twenty percent of the next $500,000, fifteen percent of the next $250,000 and ten percent of any amount over $1.25 million."[6]

2. Attorneys' Fees in Class Actions and Class Action Settlements

Professors Macey and Miller point out that unlike the traditional model of litigation, where the attorney functions as an agent and under the control of the client, in class actions and derivative suits, particularly "large-scale small claim" litigation, plaintiffs' attorneys "function essentially as entrepreneurs who bear a substantial amount of the litigation risk and exercise nearly plenary control over all important decisions in the lawsuit." Jonathan R. Macey & Geoffrey P. Miller, The Plaintiffs' Attorney's Role in Class Action and Derivative Litigation: Economic Analysis and Recommendations For Reform, 58 U. Chicago L. Rev. 1, 3–7 (1991). Such arrangements lead to substantial "agency cost" problems, one of which is inadequate settlements. Plaintiffs' attorneys having a strong economic incentive to agree to smaller class settlements if they can obtain quick and substantial payments of their attorneys fees by defendants. As a solution to this problem, Professors Macey and Miller propose that some sort of auction of class and derivative claims be permitted, with law firms bidding for the right to bring such suits.

The prosecution of sizable and often complicated class and derivative actions is an expensive undertaking, even if settled short of trial, as nearly all are. To implement Macey and Miller's suggestion of an auction of bids for a single cash payment, a law firm would need considerable capital resources. This creates a formidable barrier to the participation of younger and maybe needier law firms which would enhance the competitive bidding. That is thought to be one reason that an auction technique—even short of a one-time cash payment—does not seem to bring in new law firms ready to bid and otherwise compete.

Professor John C. Coffee, Jr. points to the considerable and possibly overwhelming market power of the present active class action law firms (in security class actions.) Citing V. O'Brien and R. Hodges, A Study of Class Action Securities Fraud Cases, 1988–1993, he calculated that the top seven firms in market share, so to speak, were counsel or one of a few counsel in more than three-quarters of the 404 case

---

6. Brickman, supra note 3 at 125.

sample (86%). Coffee, *Regulating Plaintiffs' Attorneys*, N.Y.L.J. Sept. 22, 1994, p.1,5, and note 16.

Young lawyers cannot afford to invest the "one million or more dollars in annual costs and expenses that it may take to litigate a large, complex class action effectively." (id) One means of avoiding this relatively public problem is to allow some kinds of investment in the law firm's prosecution of a class action. The expenses may start early on, if the class certification is difficult or contested. Given the investment option, the law firm is then in a far better negotiating posture. The defendants know that dragging out the litigation and increasing the costs are tactics not likely to work. The law firm can invest in the necessary research and other preparation and cover the administrative costs as well. Note that Fed.R.Civ. Pro. 23 (a) (4) has been read to have the court consider the financial ability of the lawyers for the class as one factor in determining the adequacy of representation. Once the class has been certified the likelihood of a successful settlement is far greater than in most other kinds of law suits.

So long as the law firm and the investors can avoid the severest laws against champerty and maintenance, there is little problem with most forms of financing. Investments in law suits in one form or another seem to be widespread and growing. See Note, Litigation for Sale, 144 U. Pa. L. Rev. 1529 (1996).

In re Amino Acid Lysine Antitrust Litigation

United States District Court, Northern District of Illinois, 1996.
1996 WL 197671.

■ Shadur, Senior District Judge.

Before this opinion turns to the principal business at hand—the consideration of plaintiff's present motion stemming from a set of three proposed settlements—this Court is constrained to address what is clearly a basic misunderstanding in some quarters: the concept that there is some necessary correlation between, on the one hand, the inclusion of a maximum fee provision in the bid that was presented by the law firm that now represents the plaintiff class and, on the other hand, a less-than-adequate level of representation of the class by that law firm. It should be emphasized that this Court has made no judgment as to whether the now-proposed settlements are within the range of fairness, reasonableness and adequacy, let alone whether they meet those objective standards in ultimate terms—after these preliminary remarks are completed, this opinion will turn to the first of those questions. Instead what is being addressed at the outset is the suggestion, which has appeared in some of the media coverage, that the class counsel may have sold out too cheaply because of their unwillingness to invest all of the time that is required for the full representation of their clients' interests. * * *

But what is extraordinarily troublesome, both from what has appeared in the newspapers and from what this Court's law clerk has reported that he heard on National Public Radio, is that this view-point—this implicit accusation of a sellout—is also fed by one of the losing bidders who had hoped to represent the plaintiff class. Essentially Melvyn Weiss, Esq. of the Milberg Weiss firm charges that the existence of a cap on fees, which was self-imposed by the Kohn Swift & Graf firm as part of its bid, means that the latter firm is unwilling to exercise its best efforts on behalf of its clients, the class members, because the firm has nothing to gain in pushing for a larger recovery from the defendants. [T]he argument [is] that a lawyer will cease to exercise his or her fiduciary obligations to a client unless there's something extra in it for the lawyer * * * [It may] give us some unintended insight into how some lawyers may actually practice law. But in candor such a position is plainly unethical. * * *

Having mentioned the concept of hourly rates, this opinion pauses only another moment before going on to the current motion. Hourly rates and time spent are of course relevant if fees are based on the familiar lodestar concept. But anyone who has studied the subject is aware that particularly in recent years there has been a growing recognition that in a common fund situation, and especially in a class action where there is no one-to-one direct lawyer-client relationship, a fee based on a percentage of recovery, rather than on hourly rates multiplied by time spent, tends to strike the best balance in favor of the clients' interests while at the same time preserving the lawyers' self-interest. And not surprisingly, all eight law firms that chose to participate in seeking to represent the plaintiff class here—and it should be remembered that this Court neither prescribed nor suggested any formula or approach for the presentation of their bids—framed their bids in terms of a percentage of recovery.

As has already been said, only the Kohn firm opted to place a ceiling on its own fees. It was in that context, and in making the comparison between that bid and the only other one that was at all potentially close to it, that this Court's January 18 opinion spoke of what appeared, based on past experience, to be the unlikelihood that the case would be fully litigated within 12 months. And even that comparison, which was made on a purely hypothetical basis (as necessarily had to be the case at the outset), showed that the Kohn bid would be superior to the closest competing bid if even slightly more than $35 million were to be recovered from the defendants for the class.

Incidentally, since receiving the present motion this Court has plugged the figures that are represented by the currently proposed settlements into the various bids that had been received from the eight participants in the bidding process. Even if the now-proposed settlements were to be approved (something that, as will be seen, this Court has not yet decided to do), and even if no added recovery were to be made from the non-settling defendants—in other words, even on the worst-case scenario—the Kohn bid has indeed proved to provide the greatest benefit for the clients in comparison with all of the other bids. As the January 18 opinion reflected, only one of the seven other proposals came even close to the Kohn firm's bid. On the present figures, without reference to any possible improvement in the amount forthcoming from the settling defendants and without any account being taken of a possible further recovery from the nonsettling defendants, the existing settlement offers would still have to be $1 million higher than their present numbers for the plaintiff class to fare as well under that other close bid than it would under the Kohn firm's fee arrangement. Every other bid among the six other bidders, even on those most favorable assumptions, would have required at least $5 million more from Archer Daniels Midland before the plaintiff class would have come out as well as the clients would realize under the Kohn bid, taking into account its $3.5 million cap on fees. Among those six bids, the one from Milberg, Weiss would actually have required about $10.5 million more from ADM (over $35 million in settlement), failing which the plaintiff class—the clients—would have been worse off than with the Kohn firm at the helm.

But this discussion, which is really a side excursion, will end just as it began: by emphasizing that it is a total red herring to suggest that either the bidding process to obtain the best quality representation at the lowest cost to the plaintiff class members, or the cap on fees that the Kohn firm chose to include in its ultimately successful bid, has in any respect disadvantaged the plaintiff class. Instead precisely the opposite is true. Most importantly, nothing in either of those aspects of the case should deflect attention from the critical question whether the plaintiff class is well served by what has been put on the table. And this opinion now turns to that question.

In the class action context, Manual For Complex Litigation (1995 Third Edition) § 30.4 sets out the same procedure that was first marked out in this Circuit in Armstrong v. Board of School Directors, 616 F.2d 305, 314 (7th Cir.1980) and that our Court of Appeals has confirmed a number of times since then: the two-step process under Fed. R. Civ. P. 23(e) under which the court is to make the original determination whether the proposed settlement is within the range of fairness, reasonableness and adequacy so as to justify notifying the class members of the proposed settlement, followed by a fairness hearing to decide whether the proposal is indeed fair, reasonable and adequate in the ultimate sense. * * *

Armstrong has become the seminal case in this Circuit. Plaintiff's Mem. 7 has accurately encapsuled the factors identified in Armstrong and its progeny as relevant to the final approval of a proposed settlement: The most important factor is "the strength of plaintiffs' case on the merits balanced against the settlement offer...." Other factors to be considered are: a) the complexity, length and expense of continued litigation; b) the absence or presence of collusion in reaching a settlement; c) the opinion of competent counsel as to the reasonableness of the proposed settlement; d) the defendants' ability to pay; e) the stage of the proceedings and the amount of discovery completed; f) the reaction of the class members to the proposed settlement; and g) the opposition, if any, thereto.

By definition some of those factors cannot be known during the first step in the two-step process, when it is being decided whether the proposed settlement is sufficiently within the range of fairness, reasonableness and adequacy to justify notifying the class members and going to the second step. Those unknown factors are, of course, the reaction of the class members and the existence of any opposition to the proposed settlement. * * *

There is however one important exception, as to which this time this Court owes a debt of gratitude to the media coverage. What has been reported there is that the $25 million proposed to be contributed by Archer Daniels Midland toward settlement is smaller than the reserves that the company had set up for this litigation. In this Court's experience in representing public companies, or in separately representing the outside directors of public companies, it has found such reserves to be a material indicium of the fair value of a liability, estimated by those who are presumably in the best position to make such an evaluation. There is no reference to that factor in the current Plaintiff's Memorandum, nor is there any indication whether the negotiations or informal discovery that preceded entry into the agreement for the now-proposed settlement had taken that evaluation into account.

At a minimum this Court will require more extensive disclosure in that respect. It is of course recognized that a litigation reserve also includes the anticipated cost of litigation—an anticipated cost that is saved by an early settlement—but except for that cushion the reserve should normally reflect the defendant's informed judgment as to the discounted value of the risk involved. All parties should also understand that absent some persuasive argument as to why such should not be the case, such as factors that cause the reserve to be less than a reliable indicator, this Court would anticipate some potential difficulty in finding that a lesser figure comes within the range that is required for the first-step determination.

There is one final point that should be made now, given the added time that will be required to provide the just-described supplemental information. It is of course no secret that Archer Daniels Midland is under investigation for possible criminal prosecutions, stemming from the allegations of antitrust violations that also serve as the gravamen for the existing class action. And equally obviously this Court has no desire or intention to invade grand jury secrecy. But it would seem appropriate for the United States to receive notice of the present motion because of the possibility that it may, if it chooses, seek to express its view on the proposed settlement as one of the ingredients for consideration on my part.

General Motors Corporation v. Bloyed

Supreme Court of Texas, 1996.
916 S.W. 2d 949

■ JUSTICE CORNYN delivered the opinion of the Court, in which all Justices join.

The question in this appeal is whether the trial court abused its discretion under Texas Rule of Civil Procedure 42(e) when it approved the settlement of a class action involving about 645,000 owners of certain pickup trucks manufactured by General Motors Corporation (GMC). The plaintiffs claim that the trucks' side-saddle gas tanks, located outside the vehicle frame, make the trucks particularly vulnerable to combustion and fire after side impact. The plaintiffs sought only economic damages of diminished market value or cost of repair; the plaintiffs specifically excluded claims for personal injury or death.

The court of appeals determined that the trial court abused its discretion by approving a settlement agreed to by the class representatives, class counsel, and GMC. 881 S.W.2d 422. We granted the applications for writ of error filed by GMC and the class representatives challenging the court of appeals's conclusions that the settlement was not fair, adequate, and reasonable and that the notice to the class was deficient because it did not disclose the amount of attorney's fees that class counsel requested. We affirm the judgment of the court of appeals and remand this case to the trial court for further proceedings in accordance with this opinion.

I. Facts

On November 17, 1992, Tommy Dollar and six other people filed this action against GMC and others in Harrison County on behalf of all Texas residents who purchased, on or before October 16, 1992, full-size Chevrolet and GMC C/K or R/V series pickup trucks manufactured between 1973 and 1991. Four plaintiffs moved for certification of their case as a class action. Before the trial court ruled on the motion, however, the parties announced that they had reached a tentative settlement. The parties signed the settlement agreement on July 19, 1993. On that same day, GMC settled a national class action, which included GMC truck owners in every state but Texas, on terms that were nearly identical to those in this case. Compare 881 S.W.2d at 427 n. 2, with In re General Motors Corp. Pick–Up Truck Fuel Tank Prods. Liab. Litig., 55 F.3d 768, 780–81 & n. 4 (3d Cir.), cert. denied sub nom. General Motors Corp. v. French, 516 U.S. 824, 116 S.Ct. 88, 133 L.Ed.2d 45 (1995). In a well-reasoned and comprehensive opinion, the Third Circuit Court of Appeals set aside the national settlement and remanded the case due to the federal district court's failure to make the factual findings required to certify the class.

On July 20, 1993, the trial court certified the Texas case as a class action for settlement purposes only and ordered that notice of the terms of the proposed settlement be mailed to 645,312 registered Texas truck owners. Notices were also published in USA TODAY and the MARSHALL NEWS MESSENGER. The notice instructed class members who wished to opt out of the settlement class to send a written request to the district clerk by October 5, 1993. Class members wishing to object to the settlement were instructed to write to the district clerk, class counsel, and GMC by October 5, 1993. Class members Clyde Bloyed, Ron Godbey, Regina Godbey, and others filed objections to the proposed settlement. After considering affidavits and arguments of counsel, the trial court overruled all objections and rendered judgment approving the settlement on November 2, 1993.

Under the terms of the settlement approved by the trial court, each class member, upon written request, is entitled to receive a $1,000.00 certificate to use toward the purchase of a new Chevrolet or GMC truck or van. Each class member must redeem the certificate within fifteen months after class member receives notice that the certificates are available. The class member can use the certificate toward the down payment on a new vehicle, and the class member need not disclose an intent to use the certificate until striking his best deal with the dealer. The class member can also use the $1,000.00 certificate in conjunction with any marketing incentives or promotional offers available through GMC or General Motors Acceptance Corporation (GMAC).

Alternatively, the class member can transfer the certificate to an immediate family member who resides with the class member. Or, the class member can transfer the $1,000.00 certificate with the title to the settlement class vehicle, that is, to a third party who purchases the settlement class member's vehicle.

In lieu of a $1,000.00 certificate, and without transferring title to the settlement class vehicle, a class member may instead request that GMC issue a nontransferable $500.00 certificate to any third party except a GMC dealer or its affiliates. This $500.00 certificate is redeemable with the purchase of a new C/K series GMC or Chevrolet full-size pickup truck or its replacement model. The class member cannot use the $500.00 certificate in conjunction with any GMC or GMAC marketing incentive and is subject to the same fifteen-month redemption period.

In return, the settlement releases GMC from all claims related to the fuel system design of the trucks, excluding all claims arising out of any vehicular crash resulting in personal injury or death.

II. The Class Action's Uneasy Role in the Adversary System

Class action suits furnish an efficient means for numerous claimants with a common complaint to obtain a remedy "[w]here it is not economically feasible to obtain relief within the traditional framework of a multiplicity of small individual suits for damages." Deposit Guar. Nat'l Bank v. Roper, 445 U.S. 326, 339, 100 S.Ct. 1166, 1174, 63 L.Ed.2d 427 (1980); see also 1 Herbert B. Newberg & Alba Conte, Newberg on Class Actions § 1.06, at 1–20 (3d ed. 1992) (listing the objectives of class actions as: promoting efficiency, protecting defendants from inconsistent verdicts, protecting the rights of absent class members, allowing recovery by small claimants, and enforcing laws through private attorney general suits) [hereinafter Newberg & Conte]. Class actions also facilitate "the spreading of litigation costs among numerous litigants with similar claims." United States Parole Comm'n v. Geraghty, 445 U.S. 388, 403, 100 S.Ct. 1202, 1212, 63 L.Ed.2d 479 (1980). We do not doubt the salutary nature of this procedural device under appropriate circumstances. But, class actions are extraordinary proceedings with extraordinary potential for abuse. Therefore, among other prerequisites, before certifying a case as a class action, the trial court must first determine "that a class action is superior to other available methods for the fair and efficient adjudication of the controversy." TEX.R.CIV.P. 42(b)(4).

One of the foremost objectives of Rule 42 is to protect the interests of absent class members. The law generally requires notice of a lawsuit and an opportunity for a hearing before any person may be bound by a court's judgment. E.g., Cunningham v. Parkdale Bank, 660 S.W.2d 810, 813 (Tex.1983). By contrast, "[t]he judgment in an action maintained as a class action . . . whether or not favorable to the class, shall . . . be binding upon all those whom the court finds to be members of the class and who received notice as provided in subdivision (c)(2)." TEX.R.CIV.P. 42(c)(3). The United States Supreme Court has made it clear that due process requires adequate representation of the interests of absentee class members that the judgment will bind. Hansberry v. Lee, 311 U.S. 32, 42–43, 61 S.Ct. 115, 118–19, 85 L.Ed. 22 (1940).

In a class action, the absentee members of the class may not even learn of the proposed judgment until a tentative settlement has been struck on their behalf by the defendant, the class representative, and class counsel. When notice of a proposed settlement and notice of the class action are sent simultaneously, the absent class members may perceive it as a fait accompli. Mars Steel Corp. v. Continental Ill. Nat'l Bank & Trust Co., 834 F.2d 677, 680–81 (7th Cir.1987). The potential for conflicts of interest under these circumstances is substantial and to some extent unavoidable.

During the last decade scholars have expressed growing concern about the conflicts that may arise between the class and its counsel: "[T]hese attorneys are not subject to monitoring by their putative clients, they operate largely according to their own self-interest, subject only to whatever constraints might be imposed by bar discipline, judicial oversight, and their own sense of ethics and fiduciary responsibilities." Jonathan R. Macey & Geoffrey P. Miller, The Plaintiffs' Attorney's Role in Class Action and Derivative Litigation, 58 U.CHI.L.REV. 1, 7–8 n. 4 (1991); see also John C. Coffee, Jr., Rethinking the Class Action, 62 IND.L.J. 625, 628–29 (1987) (listing several factors that have contributed to entrepreneurial class action litigation, including the relatively low cost of filing dubious class action suits, the large amounts defendants are willing to pay in settling these suits, and the incentive for class counsel to invest little time and effort in protecting the absent class members); John C. Coffee, Jr., The Regulation of Entrepreneurial Litigation: Balancing Fairness and Efficiency in the Large Class Action, 54 U.CHI.L.REV. 877, 878, 878–79 (1987) (outlining proposed rule changes that would "manipulate the incentives that the law holds out so as to motivate" class counsel to defend the absent class members as they would any other client); Kenneth W. Dam, Class Actions: Efficiency, Compensation, Deterrence, and Conflict of Interest, 4 J.LEGAL STUD. 47, 61 (1975) (coining the phrase "lawyer-entrepreneur" in reference to class counsel). Judge Posner has noted that

> the absence of a real client impairs the incentive of the lawyer for the class to press the suit to a successful conclusion. His earnings from the suit are determined by the legal fee he receives rather than the size of the judgment. No one has an economic stake in the size of the judgment except the defendant, who has an interest in minimizing it. The lawyer for the class will be tempted to offer to settle with the defendant for a small judgment and a large legal fee, and such an offer will be attractive to the defendant, provided the sum of the two figures is less than the defendant's net expected loss from going to trial. Although the judge must approve the settlement, the lawyers largely control his access to the information—about the merits of the claim, the amount of work done by the lawyer for the class, the likely damages if the case goes to trial, etc.—that is vital to determining the reasonableness of the settlement.

Richard A. Posner, an Economic Analysis of Law 570 (4th ed. 1992) [hereinafter Posner, Economic Analysis].

The potential for abuse of the class action procedure points out the importance of the trial court's obligation to determine that the protective requirements of Texas Rule 42 are met when it approves a class action settlement. While the trial court generally plays a relatively detached role in most civil proceedings, in a class action the court is the guardian of the class interest. The trial court bears the burden under Rule 42 to police the proceeding to minimize conflicts of interest and, primarily, to protect absent class members:

> The drafters designed the procedural requirements of Rule 23, especially the requisites of subsection (a), so that the court can assure, to the greatest extent possible, that the actions are prosecuted on behalf of the actual class members in a way that makes it fair to bind their interests. The rule thus represents a measured response to the issues of how the due process rights of absentee interests can be protected and how absentees' represented status can be reconciled with a litigation system premised on traditional bipolar litigation.

In re General Motors Corp., 55 F.3d at 785.[1]

The trial court must assume its role as guardian of the class not only in approving class settlements, but also in deciding whether to certify a class in the first place. This means that Rule 42's certification requirements of numerosity, commonality, typicality, and adequacy of representation must always be met, even when cases are settled before certification of the class: "Without determining that the class claims are common and typical of the entire putative class and that the class

---

1. In our analysis of Texas Rule of Civil Procedure 42 we are guided by analysis of Federal Rule of Civil Procedure 23, from which Rule 42 was derived. See 1 McDonald, TEXAS CIVIL PRACTICE § 5:54, at 567 n. 445 (1992).

representatives and their counsel are adequate representatives, we have no assurance that the district court fully appreciated the scope and nature of the interests at stake." In re General Motors Corp., 55 F.3d at 797; see also 2 Newberg & Conte § 11.27, at 11–50 ("The actual class ruling is deferred in [settlement class actions] until after hearing on the settlement approval, following notice to the class. At that time, the court in fact applies the class action requirements to determine whether the action should be maintained as a class action. . . .").

Settlement classes, as we have indicated, raise special concerns. In setting aside the national class action settlement, the Third Circuit pointed out that:

> Settlement classes ... make it more difficult for a court to evaluate the settlement by depriving the judge of the customary structural devices of Rule 23 and the presumptions of propriety that they generate. Ordinarily, a court relies on class status, particularly the adequacy of representation required to maintain it, to infer that the settlement was the product of arm's length negotiations. . . . Where the court has not yet certified a class or named its representative or counsel, this assumption is questionable. . . . In particular, settlement classes create especially lucrative opportunities for putative class attorneys to generate fees for themselves without any effective monitoring by class members who have not yet been apprised of the pendency of the action.

In re General Motors Corp., 55 F.3d at 787–88; see also 2 NEWBERG & CONTE, § 11.09, at 11–14 (discussing the need for trial court oversight to minimize conflicts of interest between the class and class counsel). Some commentators have even warned that the class action device may be used in an offensive and collusive manner in order to foreclose future individual claims. See, e.g., John C. Coffee, Jr., Class Wars: The Dilemma of the Mass Tort Class Action, 95 COLUM.L.REV. 1343, 1350 (1995) ("Rather than serving as a vehicle by which small claimants can aggregate their claims in order to make litigation economically feasible . . ., the mass tort class action now often provides a means by which unsuspecting future claimants suffer the extinction of their claims even before they learn of their injury."). The gravity of these concerns mandates that a trial court independently determine that the requirements of Rule 42 have been scrupulously met, in their entirety, before approving any class action settlement. See In re General Motors Corp., 55 F.3d at 795–96.

III. The Court of Appeals's Error

Under Rule 42(e), the trial court is charged with the responsibility of determining that the settlement is fair, adequate, and reasonable. Approval of a class action settlement is within the sound discretion of the trial court and should not be reversed absent an abuse of that discretion. In other words, in reviewing the trial court's judgment, the appellate court must not merely substitute its judgment for that of the trial court.

Factors the court should consider in determining whether to approve a proposed settlement are: (1) whether the settlement was negotiated at arms' length or was a product of fraud or collusion; (2) the complexity, expense, and likely duration of the litigation; (3) the stage of the proceedings, including the status of discovery; (4) the factual and legal obstacles that could prevent the plaintiffs from prevailing on the merits; (5) the possible range of recovery and the certainty of damages; (6) the respective opinions of the participants, including class counsel, class representatives, and the absent class members. Ball, 747 S.W.2d at 423–24 (citing Parker v. Anderson, 667 F.2d 1204, 1209 (5th Cir.), cert. denied, 459 U.S. 828, 103 S.Ct. 63, 74 L.Ed.2d 65 (1982)). Put another way, the trial court must examine both the substantive and procedural aspects of the settlement: (1) whether the terms of the settlement are fair, adequate, and reasonable; and (2) whether the settlement was the product of honest negotiations or of collusion. Those defending the settlement must show that the evidence related to these factors supports approval of the settlement.

The trial court correctly analyzed the fairness of this settlement according to the six Ball factors. First, the trial court found that the agreement had been reached as a result of honest, arms' length negotiations and that there was no evidence of collusion or fraud. Second, the trial court found that the case involved extremely complex issues of liability and damages and that a jury trial would consume considerable time and resources. Third, the trial court also found that sufficient discovery had been conducted to allow the parties to make an informed decision about the relative merits of the case and the settlement. Fourth, the trial court found that only a fraction of one percent of the class had filed any objection to the terms of the settlement.

While the court of appeals acknowledged that these factors favored approval of the settlement, it nevertheless concluded that "[t]he trial court abused its discretion in approving the proposed settlement because this settlement is not fair, adequate, or reasonable to the class members as a whole, on whose behalf the action was initiated." 881 S.W.2d at 433. In essence, the court of appeals overturned the settlement because it decided that the potential windfall to GMC outweighed all the reasons supporting approval.

The primary basis for this conclusion was the apparent disparity between the value of the settlement to members of the class and the potential economic benefit to GMC. The court of appeals's opinion illustrates several areas of concern with the settlement in this case. First, the alleged defect in the gas tank design would not be corrected, leaving more than 600,000 class members driving what are allegedly unreasonably dangerous vehicles. Second, more than half of the class would be unable or unwilling to redeem the coupons in connection with the purchase of a new GMC truck within fifteen months of receiving the certificate.[2] Thus, more than half of the class would

---

2. The class's expert testified that 46% of the Texas class members would use the coupons, while the objectors' expert contended that only 10% would do so.

receive no benefit at all from the coupons, although all class members would be bound by the settlement. Third, the court objected to a settlement requiring claimants to pay up to $30,000.00 for a new truck, in order to receive a $1,000.00 benefit. In essence, the court of appeals questioned whether having to pay such a price for a relatively small rebate was fair. Fourth, as we have mentioned, the court worried that the coupons would translate into a sales bonanza for GMC. Evidence revealed that even with the $1,000.00 rebate provided by the certificates, GMC could expect a profit of $2,000.00–$3,000.00 on each new truck sale. Assuming 46% of the 645,000 claimants purchased new trucks, GMC stood to recover tremendous profits from this settlement.

We nevertheless agree with GMC and the class representatives that the court of appeals erred in holding that the trial court's approval of the settlement was an abuse of discretion. Although the settlement may well have translated into higher truck sales for GMC, the agreement was by no means one-sided in light of significant problems the class members faced on the merits of their claims.

In this vein, the trial court made the following findings of fact:

14.   The Court finds that there are substantial legal issues, including the statute of limitations and other issues, that make the likelihood of maintaining class certification through trial and recovery for plaintiffs uncertain. 15. The Court finds that there is uncertainty about the Plaintiffs' ability to prove liability. 16. The Court finds that there is uncertainty about Plaintiffs' ability to prove damages.

While we appreciate the uncertain value of this noncash settlement, the court of appeals erred in its preoccupation with the benefits of the settlement to GMC and its apparent disregard of the difficulties the trial court found with the plaintiffs' case on the merits. See In re General Motors Corp. Engine Interchange Litig., 594 F.2d 1106, 1132 n. 44 (7th Cir.), cert. denied, 444 U.S. 870, 100 S.Ct. 146, 62 L.Ed.2d 95 (1979) (stating that "the strength of the plaintiff's case on the merits balanced against the amount offered" is the crucial factor in evaluating the fairness of the settlement). As the trial court found, none of the class members reported any problems with the operation of their trucks, the market value of the trucks as measured by the Kelley Blue Book had not declined relative to comparable trucks manufactured by other companies, and no expert offered a reliable means of curing the alleged defect. See 881 S.W.2d at 429. In short, the individual class members faced considerable problems with proving any damages at all.

Furthermore, there was a strong likelihood that a large proportion of the class members' claims against GMC would have been barred by the statute of limitations. The side-saddle gas tank design had been advertised as early as 1973 and had been the subject of litigation since the early 1980s. Even if the discovery rule applied here, which we do not decide, the statute of limitations presented a serious impediment to recovery for almost all of the class members because this suit was not filed until November 1992.

It is also noteworthy that the trial court's assessment of the Texas plaintiffs' claims was echoed by the federal district court in the national class action, In re General Motors Corp. Pickup Truck Fuel Tank Prods. Liab. Litig., 846 F.Supp. 330, 336 (E.D.Pa.1993) ("Perhaps the greatest weakness in the plaintiffs' case is the lack of proof of economic damages."), rev'd, 55 F.3d 768 (3d Cir.), cert. denied, 516 U.S. 824, 116 S.Ct. 88, 133 L.Ed.2d 45 (1995), and by the Third Circuit. In re General Motors Corp., 55 F.3d at 814–17.

The class representatives apparently decided that accepting the certificates was preferable to proceeding with a lengthy lawsuit based on dubious evidence of damages, while GMC apparently opted for providing the certificates rather than exposing itself to continuing defense costs and potentially greater liability. In other words, both sides compromised. * * * In deciding that the potential windfall to GMC outweighed the reasons supporting the class compromise, we hold that the court of appeals substituted its judgment for that of the trial court as to what constituted a fair, adequate, and reasonable settlement.

IV. Notice of Attorney's Fees

Notwithstanding our conclusion that the court of appeals improperly substituted its judgment for that of the trial court in determining the fairness of the other provisions of the settlement, we nevertheless agree with the court of appeals that the settlement must be set aside because the class members did not receive adequate notice of all of the material terms of the proposed settlement, specifically the projected amount of attorney's fees and expenses.

After certifying the Texas claimants as a class for settlement purposes, the trial court set a fairness hearing for October 27, 1993. The court then ordered class counsel to notify all class members of the terms of the settlement and of their rights to opt out of the settlement or object to its terms. The notice contained only the following mention of attorney's fees:

> If the Court approves the settlement of the case, the Court will determine an award of attorneys' fees and reimbursement of costs and expenses, which would be paid solely by General Motors and would not reduce, directly or indirectly, any of the Settlement's benefits to Class members. GM reserves the right to oppose and appeal any application it deems unreasonable.

Class counsel mailed this notice to the class members in August 1993 and then filed its request for fees with the trial court on October 7, 1993. This notice was insufficient.

As we explained in Section II of this opinion, the potential conflict between absent class members and class counsel is one of the serious problems with class action settlements. We, therefore, hold that class action settlement notices must contain the maximum amount of attorney's fees sought by class counsel and specify the proposed method of calculating the award. The source of the fees—whether the fees are subtracted directly from the funds to be distributed among the class members or, as here, are paid by the defendant in an otherwise noncash settlement—is irrelevant. The class action settlement, including both the benefits conferred on the class and the fees awarded to class counsel, represents a total dollar figure that the defendant is willing to pay to avoid litigation. POSNER, ECONOMIC ANALYSIS at 570 (positing that defendants would approve a settlement with a small benefit to the class and a large fee for class counsel "provided the sum of the two figures is less than the defendant's net expected loss from going to trial"). Notwithstanding the trial court's finding that the attorney's fees awarded would not affect the benefits provided to the class members, we agree with the court of appeals that "[a]ttorneys' fees, even though they may not be technically deducted from the amount paid to the litigants, represent an integral part of the overall amount that the settling party is willing to pay, and as such, they have a direct effect on the net amount that will ultimately be paid to the litigants." 881 S.W.2d at 435–36.

Other courts have invalidated class action settlements based on a failure to notify the class members of the potential size of the class counsel's fee award. Moreover, any contention that providing fee information in a class action notice would be impracticable is belied by the routine inclusion of such information in class action notices. Notice of the attorney's fees sought by class counsel is essential because, without such notice, class members cannot "determine the possible influence of attorneys' fees on the settlement in considering whether to object to it." In re General Motors Corp. Engine Interchange Litig., 594 F.2d at 1130. Without this vital information, class members cannot make informed decisions about their right to challenge the fee award at the hearing, including the allocation of the settlement proceeds between the class and its attorneys.

V. On Remand

The trial court determined that the settlement in this class action was fair, adequate, and reasonable based solely on affidavits. In Jack B. Anglin Co. v. Tipps, 842 S.W.2d 266, 269 (Tex.1992), we wrote that as a general rule, "contested issues are decided after a plenary hearing, that is, a hearing at which witnesses present sworn testimony in person or by deposition rather than by affidavit." Even when deciding controverted material facts in a matter for which the Legislature has prescribed summary disposition, we require trial courts to conduct an evidentiary hearing to resolve those disputed facts. Id. Given the heightened responsibility of the trial court in approving class action settlements mandated by Rule 42(e), we think that a plenary hearing, with the opportunity for questioning by the court and vigorous cross-examination by counsel representing objecting class members, should be the general rule.

In conducting a plenary hearing on a proposed class action settlement, the trial court must resolve two primary issues: (1) whether to certify the class under the Rule 42 prerequisites of numerosity, commonality, typicality, and adequacy of representation; and, if so, (2) whether the settlement is fair, adequate, and reasonable, considering the six Ball factors and the amount of attorney's fees to be awarded class counsel.[3] It is important to understand that these two issues are separate and that findings approving the settlement as fair cannot substitute for the certification findings required by Texas Rule 42. See In re General Motors Corp., 55 F.3d at 795–96 (holding that findings regarding the fairness of the settlement cannot serve as "a surrogate for" certification findings because "the settlement approval inquiry is far different from the certification inquiry"); 2 NEWBERG & CONTE, § 11.27, at 11–50 (noting that the trial court must still make certification findings in the settlement class action context).

The trial court in this case made no determination regarding numerosity, commonality, typicality, and adequacy of representation, and the answers to the questions raised by these requirements are not obvious. For example, one striking feature of the settlement is that no fleet owner was designated as a class representative. There appears to be a serious intraclass conflict between individual truck owners and fleet owners, such as governmental entities, who will likely be constrained by competitive bidding and other purchasing requirements before they can take advantage of the settlement. See In re General Motors Corp., 55 F.3d at 781, 800–01. Concerns such as this led the Third Circuit to overturn the settlement in the national class action. Id.; see also Piambino v. Bailey, 610 F.2d 1306, 1329–30 (5th Cir.), cert. denied, 449 U.S. 1011, 101 S.Ct. 568, 66 L.Ed.2d 469 (1980) (vacating class certification for reconsideration of sharp conflicts of interest between two categories of plaintiffs).

While it did not conduct a plenary hearing on the Rule 42 requirements, the trial court did find that "there is uncertainty as to whether a class action could be properly certified and maintained through trial because there are potentially substantial individual questions of fact and law and obstacles to the manageability of the action on a class basis." If the trial court believed this to be the case, it should not have certified the class or approved the settlement as it did.

Both class action jurisprudence generally, see 2 NEWBERG & CONTE, § 11.65, at 11–183, and Texas law specifically impose fiduciary duties on attorneys in their relationship with their clients. This fiduciary relationship requires a full and fair disclosure of the terms of a proposed settlement. Tex.Disciplinary R.Prof.Conduct 1.02, 1.03, reprinted in Tex. Gov't Code, tit. 2, subtitl. G app. (State Bar Rules art. X, § 9). As we have already indicated, the divergent economic incentives of the class and its counsel create conflicting interests that

3. A fairness hearing should not be a full trial on the merits, In re General Motors Corp. Engine Interchange Litig., 594 F.2d at 1132 n. 44, but rather a preliminary assessment of the strength of the class's case.

warrant special scrutiny. See Andrew Rosenfield, An Empirical Test of Class–Action Settlement, 5 J.legal Stud. 113, 115 (1976) ("The crucial point is that costly transactions drive a wedge between the objectives of the class and the objectives of the attorney representing the class, thereby creating the possibility of advantageous trades among the class attorney and the defendant."). In other words, the clear divergence of financial incentives to settlement as between the class and class counsel creates the "danger ... that the lawyers might urge a class settlement at a low figure or on a less-than-optimal basis in exchange for a red-carpet treatment on fees." Weinberger v. Great N. Nekoosa Corp., 925 F.2d 518, 524 (1st Cir.1991); see also In re "Agent Orange" Prod. Liab. Litig., 818 F.2d 216, 224 (2d Cir.1987) ("The test to be applied is whether, at the time a fee sharing agreement is reached, class counsel are placed in a position that might endanger the fair representation of their clients and whether they will be compensated on some basis other than for legal services performed.").

In the event the parties on remand strike a new settlement that is approved by the trial court, then after appropriate notice to class members, the court must determine the amount of fees to award. Generally, there are two methods for calculating fees in the class action context: the percentage method, when the value of the settlement is subject to reasonably clear estimation, and the lodestar method, which calculates fees by multiplying the number of hours expended by an appropriate hourly rate determined by a variety of factors, such as the benefits obtained for the class, the complexity of the issues involved, the expertise of counsel, the preclusion of other legal work due to acceptance of the class action suit, and the hourly rate customarily charged in the region for similar legal work.

In this case, the trial court chose the percentage method and made the following finding regarding the amount of the attorney's fees award:

> 29. The Court concludes that the substantial value of the benefit secured for the class as a result of the efforts of counsel of record for the Plaintiffs and the class, the substantial hours devoted by counsel to the litigation, the nature and complexity of the issues involved in this case, the extent of the responsibilities assumed by counsel for Plaintiffs, and the level of skill and experience of class counsel support the award of nine million dollars as reasonable attorneys' fees for necessary services, that five hundred three thousand two hundred ninety-six dollars in expenses was reasonably incurred by counsel and necessary in prosecuting this case, and that the award of attorneys' fees and expenses is properly assessed against General Motors Corporation under the terms of the Agreement of Settlement. The Court finds that the attorneys' fees awarded represent less that ten percent of the value of the settlement based on consideration of the Affidavits submitted by Plaintiffs' experts and by certain objectors.

A comparison of the attorney's fees awarded both in the national class action and in this case raises serious questions about the methodology used by the trial court to set the amount of attorney's fees. In the national class action, the federal district court found the value of the settlement, which involved 5.7 million vehicles,[4] to be approximately between $1.98 billion and $2.18 billion, based upon projections that thirty-four to thirty-eight percent of the class would use the $1,000.00 certificates and eleven percent would sell them for $500.00. In re General Motors Corp., 55 F.3d at 807. Twenty-five law firms[5] in the national class action received a fee award in the amount of $9.5 million. In the Texas case, however, just two law firms received $9 million in attorney's fees plus costs, even though the Texas case involved roughly ten percent of the number of vehicles involved in the settlement of the national class action.

The lodestar method of calculating attorney's fees in class actions originated with Lindy Brothers Builders, Inc. v. American Radiator & Standard Sanitary Corp., 487 F.2d 161 (3d Cir.1973), appeal following remand, 540 F.2d 102 (3d Cir.1976) (listing four factors to be used in awarding attorney's fees). The lodestar method, though, has been criticized for, among other things, providing a financial incentive for counsel to expend excessive time in unjustified work and creating a disincentive to early settlement. Court Awarded Attorney Fees, 108 F.R.D. 237, 246–49 (3d Cir. Task Force 1985).

Both the percentage method and the lodestar method have their strengths and weaknesses, depending on the facts of the case. We do not here dictate any single method for the award of attorney's fees in a class action settlement, but leave that to the sound discretion of the trial court. As we have noted, when considering whether to approve the settlement of a class action, including the award of attorney's fees, the trial court should be particularly aware of the conflicting interests of the class and its counsel. The defendant's economic concerns consist only of the total value of the settlement, including attorney's fees and expenses. Unlike class counsel, the defendant has no economic interest in the allocation of settlement funds between the class members and counsel for the class. Thus, it is incumbent on the trial court to determine that the settlement's award of attorney's fees does not unfairly diminish the value of the settlement fund generated for the class's benefit.

In that connection, the trial court should require evidence that the attorney's fees sought by class counsel in this case were necessary to obtain benefits identical to those available in the parallel national class action. While valid reasons may exist in certain circumstances for proceeding with a separate state court class action instead of joining a national class action in federal court, nothing in the record here reveals the need for this separate class action beyond the single unexplained reference in Petitioner Dollar's Post–Submission Brief to

---

4. 6,450 owners objected to the national class action settlement and 5,203 opted out. In re General Motors Corp., 55 F.3d at 813 n. 32.

5. This is the undisputed contention of amici Public Citizen Inc. and the Consumer Federation of America, citing Docket Entry #107 In Re General Motors Corp. Pick-up Truck Fuel Tank Prods. Liab. Litig., MDL 961 (E.D.Pa.).

counsel's "serious concerns about subject matter jurisdiction in the federal court."

Regardless of the method by which attorney's fees are calculated, the terms of the nonmonetary settlement in this case raise additional concerns about the conflicting interests of class counsel and class members, because the value of the settlement can only be roughly estimated. Although the trial court found that the attorney's fees awarded here represent less than ten percent of the approximate value of the settlement, under a lodestar approach the fees awarded amount to a rate of approximately $1,500.00 per hour.[6] At a minimum, we think that on remand any fee awarded on a percentage basis should be tested against the lodestar approach to prevent grossly excessive attorney's fee awards and to minimize the inherent conflict between class counsel and the class members.

For the foregoing reasons, we affirm the judgment of the court of appeals. The cause is remanded to the trial court for further proceeding consistent with this opinion.

NOTES

A. Several commentators and case opinions discuss the arguments for and against what is termed a settlement class action, sometimes called a conditional class action. Before the action has been certified as a class action the lawyers will ask the court to approve the class action but only for purposes of settlement. The defendant is protected because if the case is not concluded there is no binding aspect to the court's order.

Despite the safeguards of FRCP 23, detailed in *General Motors Corp. v. Bloyed* [and more completely and elaborately stated in *General Motors Corp. Pick-up Truck Fuel Tank Products Liability Litigation*, 55 F.3d 768, 785 (3d Cit.1995) cert. denied sub nom. *General Motors Corp. v. French*, 516 U.S. 824, 116 S.Ct.88, 133 L.Ed.2d 45 (1995) ("nine factor test")] there are still scandals of varying gravity. These seem due to the workloads of the trial judges, their failure to follow exactly the requirements of Rule 23 or its state equivalent, and simply mistakes.

B. Egregious Examples of The Costs of Settlement Class Actions

The settlement of an airline price-fixing suit which gave the class plaintiffs coupons good for a $10 reduction in the cost of tickets for $240 or more. The total settlement was estimated at $438 million. The major beneficiaries would be the business firms who use air travel. Presumably their records would support the payment of many of the $10 coupons. Individual class members would have received little benefit. The class counsel were paid $16 million which is less than 4% of the gross settlement value. Probably a much smaller fee would have been allowed on a lodestar based calculation.

The Ford Bronco case was still pending in June, 1996 because the District Judge denied the motion by class counsel and Ford for approval of the proposed settlement. *In re Ford Motor Co. Bronco II Products Liability Litigation*, 1995 WL 373061 (E.D.La.) The class action did not include past or future personal injury

---

6. Class counsel asserted that they had spent 6,000 hours on this case. 881 S.W.2d at 436. Thus, an hourly rate of $1,500.00 for 6,000 hours would result in a $9 million fee award.

claims. The plaintiff class sought repayment of the purchase price, compensation for diminution in value of the Bronco II and perhaps an injunction requiring Ford to recall or retrofit all Bronco II's.

The proposed settlement provided for each member of the settlement class [this was a class temporarily certified for settlement purposes only] to receive, upon request a "utility vehicle video, a sun-visor warning sticker and an 'Owners' Guide Supplement.' " The case had involved about six months of pretrial litigation and some seven months of settlement negotiations. There was disagreement regarding the difficulty in plaintiffs' proving the essential facts of the case. The class member objectors (not their counsel in the class action) got discovery from Ford by court order after the fairness hearing. The material showed that Ford had settled 334 claims for personal injuries allegedly sustained in a Bronco II roll over accident for a total of about $113 million. Experts disagreed on whether Ford could retrofit the vehicle to reduce the propensity to roll over.

Class counsel sought fees and expenses of about $4 million. Affidavits were provided that class counsel had spent more than 3000 hours in prosecution of this action; and that an additional 300 to 500 hours would be needed to administer the settlements. Miscellaneous out-of-pocket expenses of $800,000 were anticipated by class counsel. From the information provided by class counsel, the court recalculated and found that the attorney fee request should have been $1,546,477.

That the interests of the defendants and the plaintiff class lawyers are apt to be coincident to the prejudice of the class members is not merely a theoretical construct. In addition to the cases noted, several recent contested and reported cases show this conflict between the class action lawyer and the class members. There is much anecdotal evidence. For example, it was reported that at a conference of mass tort defense lawyers, the participants were asked "how many of them had 'bought off' plaintiffs' counsel by offering to boost their fees in return for settling a class action. Roughly half the audience members raised their hands." M. Boot, *Stop Appeasing the Class Action Monster*, Wall St.J., May 8, 1996 at A15.

C.   COURT COSTS

In re Fialuridine ("FIAU") Products Liability Litigation
United States District Court for the District of Columbia, 1995.
163 F.R.D. 386.

■ LAMBERTH, DISTRICT JUDGE.

This case comes before the court on defendant Eli Lilly and Company's ("Lilly's") motion for a protective order under Federal Rule of Civil Procedure 26(c). Previously, plaintiffs requested, and the court ordered, under Federal Rule of Civil Procedure 34, the production of various documents pertaining to FIAU that were in the hands of Lilly's foreign affiliates. These documents, estimated by the parties to number close to one thousand, exist only in Italian, German, Japanese, and French.

Lilly filed this motion seeking a protective order that would require plaintiffs to reimburse Lilly for the costs of "formally"[1] translat-

---

1. Counsel for Lilly submitted samples of the documents to Berlitz Translation Services in Philadelphia for a cost estimate. According to counsel's representation, translation would cost over $200 per page.

ing these documents. Lilly claims that although plaintiffs do not specifically request translations of the documents, in order for it to first review the documents for privileged and proprietary information, it must translate them. In other words, Lilly claims that the practical effect of plaintiffs' request is to force Lilly to pay to translate the documents before producing them. Plaintiffs disagree and claim that they have not and will not request that Lilly translate the documents before producing them. Upon consideration of the submissions of counsel and the relevant law, the court will deny Lilly's motion.

A. Plaintiffs do not request translation.

Lilly attempts to bring plaintiffs' request under the holding in In re Puerto Rico Electric Power Authority, 687 F.2d 501 (1st Cir.1982) [hereinafter In re PREPA], the seminal case on the assessment of translation costs for Rule 34 productions, by alleging that plaintiffs' request for production is the functional equivalent of a request for translated documents. Under In re PREPA, a party cannot impose the cost of translating documents that exist in a foreign language on the producing party. 687 F.2d at 509. In that case, the Puerto Rico Electric Power Authority ("PREPA") had produced Spanish documents to the plaintiff, Mitsui & Co. ("Mitsui"). The plaintiff then specifically moved to compel PREPA to produce an English translation of the documents produced, or, in the alternative, to reimburse the plaintiff for the cost of such translation. As noted, the First Circuit held that a requesting party cannot impose translation costs on the producing party. Accord In re Korean Air Lines Disaster of Sept. 1, 1983, 103 F.R.D. 357 (D.D.C.1984).[2] It found that there is no general rule that requires a party to translate documents into the requesting party's native tongue, and it is the requesting party who bears the cost of translating the documents. Id. at 508–09.

In order to bring this motion under the First Circuit's holding in In re PREPA, Lilly contends (and indeed must show) that plaintiffs' request for the documents is the functional equivalent of a motion to compel Lilly to pay the cost of translation. If Lilly cannot establish this contention, its entire argument fails. To this end, Lilly first argues that in order for its counsel to adequately review the documents before producing them, the documents must be translated into English. Furthermore, absent plaintiffs' request, Lilly maintains that it would have no need to perform such translations. In this manner, Lilly argues, plaintiffs' request for the documents is a veiled attempt to shift the cost of translation onto Lilly, the producing party. Thus, if the court grants Lilly's motion, it does not shift the cost of translation onto

---

2. Cases following In re PREPA have arrived at the same conclusion. See, e.g., East Boston Ecumenical Community Council, Inc. v. Mastrorillo, 124 F.R.D. 14 (D.Mass.1989) (holding that the party seeking depositions bear the cost of interpreters for the deponents); Cook v. Volkswagen of Am., Inc., 101 F.R.D. 92 (S.D.W.Va.1984) (denying plaintiffs' motion to compel defendants to produce English translations of its documents); Rosado v. Mercedes–Benz of N. Am., Inc., 103 A.D.2d 395, 480 N.Y.S.2d 124 (1984) (relying on In re PREPA to deny plaintiff's motion to compel defendant to produce a translated brochure).

the plaintiffs; rather, it prevents the plaintiffs from shifting the cost onto Lilly. Finally, Lilly points out that the documents are useless to the plaintiffs unless they are first translated into English.

Plaintiffs, on the other hand, simply argue that they have not requested translated documents, therefore In re PREPA does not control. They counter that the translation of the documents by Lilly is not necessitated by their request. Because plaintiffs seek the documents as they currently exist, i.e., in various languages, how Lilly decides to "sanitize" them is its own decision; Lilly cannot shift the cost of translation onto the plaintiffs by claiming that the only way to review the documents is to formally translate them. Finally, plaintiffs remind the court of the general rule that a party bears the burden of producing its own documents. See In re PREPA, 687 F.2d at 507.

This court finds that the plaintiffs' request for the production of the foreign documents is not the functional equivalent of a motion to compel Lilly to translate the documents. Plaintiffs do not now move to require Lilly to produce translated documents, nor can Lilly convincingly argue that the only way to sanitize the documents is to first formally translate them at an excessive cost. Granting Lilly's motion would allow any party producing foreign documents to shift a potentially enormous economic burden onto the requesting party when it is unclear that any party actually needs to incur that cost. To be sure, before plaintiffs could use any of the documents in this litigation, they must be formally translated. However, not all the documents may be used. Plaintiffs may have access to any number of people who, for far less cost, could go through the documents and determine which ones contain useful information.[3] Because plaintiffs do not request translated documents and Lilly cannot demonstrate that formal translation is a necessary preliminary step before it can produce the documents, In re PREPA and its progeny do not apply.

B.   Lilly cannot show that plaintiffs' request is unduly burdensome.

As a general rule, a party bears the burden of producing its own documents unless "the discovery requests threaten to impose 'undue burden or expense' upon a respondent. . . ." In re PREPA, 687 F.2d at 507. In that event, "the district courts are specifically empowered to enter protective orders conditioning the request or requiring the requesting party to pay the expenses of production." Id. (citing Celanese Corp. v. E.I. duPont de Nemours & Co., 58 F.R.D. 606 (D.Del.1973); Currie v. Moore–McCormack Lines, Inc., 23 F.R.D. 660 (D.Mass.1959)); see also 8 Wright & Miller, Federal Practice & Procedure § 2038 at 505. In In re PREPA, the court pointed out that a production request that demanded translation would be unduly bur-

---

3. For that matter, Lilly need not formally translate the documents to sanitize them. It would seem that Lilly, the one who created the documents in the foreign language, would have better access to people who could review the documents for privileged and proprietary information.

densome, especially if the request comes at a time when the significance of the documents is not known. Id. at 509 n. 3.[4]

As discussed above, Lilly has failed to show that it must formally translate the documents in order to protect privileges and proprietary information. This court has already ruled that plaintiffs are entitled to discovery of the documents. Because translation is not required, this court cannot construe plaintiffs' request to be unduly burdensome. Moreover, if Lilly could require plaintiffs to front the cost of translation before the true significance of the documents are known, it could impose an unfair economic burden on plaintiffs. Ironically, Lilly's argument that the documents have no significance cuts both ways. It is precisely because the significance of the documents is not known that it would be unfair to allow Lilly to elect to translate them all at the expense of the plaintiffs. As a result, the court rejects Lilly's claim that plaintiffs' request imposes an undue burden.

C.   The court can award translation expenses at the conclusion of the litigation.

In the event that Lilly formally translates the documents before producing them, court can, in its discretion, award those costs to Lilly at the conclusion of the litigation. The D.C. Circuit has held that translation expenses can eventually be awarded to the prevailing party. See Quy v. Air America, Inc., 667 F.2d 1059, 1065–66 (D.C.Cir.1981) (awarding translation expenses under 28 U.S.C. § 1920(6)). If Lilly succeeds at trial, they can petition the court to award the translation fees in addition to any other recovery.

III.   Conclusion.

Accordingly, defendant Eli Lilly & Company's motion for a protective order is hereby DENIED.

Smith v. Southeastern Pennsylvania Transportation Authority

United States District Court Eastern District of Pennsylvania, 1994.
1994 WL 193907.

■ NORMA L. SHAPIRO, J.

Plaintiff brought this employment discrimination action under Title VII of the Civil Rights Act, as amended, 42 U.S.C. §§ 2000e— 2000e–17, and 42 U.S.C. § 1983. A jury trial was held on November 11 13, 1993; the jury found for defendant. Plaintiff appealed, and the Court of Appeals for the Third Circuit affirmed. The Clerk of Court taxed costs of $8,715.12 against plaintiff. Presently before the court is

4. It must be borne in mind that discovery of the sort involved here ranges far beyond basic and highly probative documents into large quantities of documents of the most marginal significance. To empower the discovering party to force his opponent to pay for translation of such materials long before their true significance can be known is to empower one party to impose a possibly crushing economic burden on the other. In re PREPA, 687 F.2d at 509 n. 3.

plaintiff's Motion to Review Clerk's Taxation of Costs. Plaintiff requests the court to reduce the award of costs to $4,357.56.

The Clerk's Bill of Costs consisted of $5,020.40 for transcripts of depositions and $3694.72 for photocopying costs. After the hearing on plaintiff's motion, the parties stipulated that defendant requested $4,488.98 in deposition costs and $2,439.20 in photocopy costs; defendant's total revised requested costs is $6,928.17.

Prevailing parties are entitled to costs as a matter of course unless otherwise directed by the court. Fed.R.Civ.P. 54(d). Title VII does not create an exception to this rule. Croker v. Boeing Co., 662 F.2d 975, 998 (3d Cir.1981). Nevertheless, the court has some discretion in awarding costs against a plaintiff. See Freidman v. Ganassi, 853 F.2d (3rd Cir.1988) ("Such taxable costs as the court finds to be established by the record will be awarded 'as of course' unless the district court concludes that such an award would be inequitable."); Croker, 662 F.2d at 998 ("The particular circumstances of each case may permit a district court to refuse to award costs altogether or to apportion them between the parties.").

In this district, two courts reduced taxed costs against the plaintiff in two recent cases. In Braxton v. UPS, 148 F.R.D. 527 (E.D.Pa.1993), plaintiff was a teacher at the Community College of Pennsylvania who "pursued a legitimate claim in good faith," id. at 528; defendants were United Parcel Service, which had earnings of $16.5 million in 1992, and Teamsters Union Local 623, "an unincorporated part of one of the nation's major labor unions." Id. at 529. Defendants were awarded summary judgment, and the Clerk taxed costs against plaintiff for $16,805.17. Given the "huge disparity of economic resources" between the parties, the court found that it would be inequitable for plaintiff to bear all of the defendants' costs and reduced the award of costs to $5,000.00. Id. In Ezold v. Wolf, Block, Schorr and Solis–Cohen, No. 90–0002, 1994 WL 156785 (E.D.Pa. April 28, 1994), plaintiff was awarded judgment at trial in an employment discrimination action; the Court of Appeals for the Third Circuit reversed, and judgment was entered for the defendant. The court reduced taxable trial costs from $24,822.84 to $12,411.42 because of the disparity of the parties' financial resources, the importance of the issues of public concern raised by the action, and the complexity and closeness of the case.

This action warrants a reduction of taxable costs for reasons similar to *Ezold* and *Braxton*. Plaintiff was employed as a cashier before termination by defendant and has limited financial resources; defendant is a large transportation authority with significant financial resources. Plaintiff pursued a legitimate claim in good faith and raised a serious legal issue regarding the preclusive effect of a prior administrative proceeding.[1] However, the amount at issue is not as large as in

---

1. There was reason to believe that plaintiff had been subjected to discrimination based on race and sex; however, her collective bargaining agreement required her to submit her claim to her union. Plaintiff claimed in a subsequent action that the union had failed

Ezold or *Braxton*. Under these circumstances, the court finds that a one-third reduction in defendant's revised requested costs will result in an equitable distribution of costs. Judgment will be awarded in favor of defendant and against plaintiff in the amount of $4,618.78.[2]

ORDER

AND NOW, this __ day of May, 1994, in consideration of plaintiff's Motion to Review Clerk's Taxation of Costs, defendant's response thereto, and after a hearing on May 11, 1994, it is ORDERED that plaintiff's Motion to Review Clerk's Taxation of Costs is GRANTED IN PART AND DENIED IN PART:

1. The motion is granted in that the February 10, 1994 Judgment of the Clerk of Court Costs is modified as follows: judgment is entered in favor of defendant Southeastern Pennsylvania Transportation Authority and against plaintiff Elizabeth Smith in the amount of $4,618.78.

2. The remainder of the motion is denied.

Smith v. Southeastern Pennsylvania Transportation Authority

United States Court of Appeals for the Third Circuit, 1995.
47 F.3d 97.

■ Before: BECKER, MANSMANN, and ALITO, CIRCUIT JUDGES.

■ PER CURIAM:

In this appeal, the Southeastern Pennsylvania Transportation Authority (SEPTA) has asked us to overturn a district court decision reducing an award of costs under Fed.R.Civ.P. 54(d). The district court made this reduction in large measure because of the great disparity between the parties' financial resources. We agree with SEPTA that the district court's reduction was not proper, and we therefore reverse in part.

Elizabeth Smith sued SEPTA under Title VII of the Civil Rights Act of 1964, 42 U.S.C. § 2000e et seq., and 42 U.S.C. § 1983, claiming that SEPTA had fired her because of race and gender. The case was tried before a jury. SEPTA defended on the ground that it had fired Smith because she failed a breathalyzer test that was administered based on reasonable suspicion that she was under the influence of alcohol. The jury returned a verdict for SEPTA, and our court affirmed the district court's judgment.

to adequately represent her and had discriminated against her on the basis of race and sex; that action was settled by the parties to that action.

2. Counsel for both parties contributed to the unusually high costs associated with this action. Plaintiff's counsel brought an extremely broad claim which may have increased the number and length of depositions. Plaintiff moved to disqualify defendant's counsel because of his conduct towards one of plaintiff's witnesses; the court ordered defense counsel to refrain from further contact with that witness. These factors were not considered by the court in determining the equitable level of costs to be borne by plaintiff.

SEPTA then filed a bill of costs in the district court. SEPTA sought $8,715.12—$5,020.40 for court reporter fees and $3,694.72 for photocopying costs. Smith objected, but the clerk of court taxed the full amount that SEPTA had sought. Smith then moved for review by the district court. Smith argued that certain costs were not taxable, and she also "beseech[ed] the Court, at the very least to reduce the award of costs to the amount of $4,357.56 (which represents 50% of the amount sought by defendant) in order to not punish plaintiff for filing suit and in order to not discourage the filing of civil rights suits." App. 206. After a hearing, the parties stipulated that the correct amount of taxable costs was $6,928.17, and the district court further reduced this amount to $4,618.78. The district court noted that two recent decisions in the district had reduced the costs taxed against the losing party based upon the "disparities" between the parties' "financial resources." Dist.Ct.Op. 2. The court then explained: This action warrants a reduction of taxable costs for reasons similar to [those in the two previous cases]. Plaintiff was employed as a cashier before termination by defendant and has limited financial resources; defendant is a large transportation authority with significant financial resources. Plaintiff pursued a legitimate claim in good faith and raised a serious legal issue. . . . Under these circumstances, the court finds that a one-third reduction in defendant's revised requested costs will result in an equitable distribution of costs. Judgment will be awarded in favor of defendant and against plaintiff in the amount of $4,618.78. SEPTA responded by taking the present appeal.

Before the adoption of the Federal Rules of Civil Procedure, "in the absence of a statutory provision otherwise providing, the prevailing party in an action at law was entitled to costs as of right; while in equity the allowance of costs to either party was subject to the court's discretion." 6 Moore's Federal Practice P 54.70[3] at 54–321 (2d ed. 1994) (citations omitted). Melding these two rules, Rule 54(d) provided a new standard for use in taxing costs in all cases. It states in pertinent part:

Except when express provision therefor is made either in a statute of the United States or in these rules, costs other than attorneys' fees shall be allowed as of course to the prevailing party unless the court otherwise directs; but costs against the United States, its officers, and agencies shall be imposed only to the extent permitted by law. Fed.R.Civ.P 54(d) (emphasis added). Under this rule, a prevailing party generally is entitled to an award of costs unless the award would be "inequitable." In describing the limits on a district court's discretion to deny costs to a prevailing party, we have also held that " 'the denial of costs to the prevailing party . . . is in the nature of a penalty for some defection on his part in the course of the litigation.' " ADM Corp. v. Speedmaster Packing Corp., 525 F.2d 662, 665 (3d Cir.1975) (quoting Chicago Sugar Co. v. American Sugar Refining Co., 176 F.2d 1, 11 (7th Cir.1949), cert. denied, 338 U.S. 948, 70 S.Ct. 486, 94 L.Ed. 584 (1950)). The Chicago Sugar case provides the following examples of a "defection" that would warrant denying costs to a prevailing party: "calling unnecessary witnesses, bringing in unnecessary issues or otherwise encumbering the record, or ... delaying in raising objection fatal to the plaintiff's case...." Institutionalized Juveniles v. Secretary of Public Welfare, 758 F.2d 897, 926 (3d Cir.1985).

Here, the district court reduced the costs taxed in favor of SEPTA based in large part on the disparity in the parties' financial resources, but we hold that this decision exceeded the district court's equitable discretion under Rule 54(d). We reject the general proposition that it is "inequitable" to tax costs in favor of a prevailing party with substantially greater wealth than the losing party. Acceptance of this general proposition would mean that large institutions such as SEPTA could be denied costs in most cases even when their unsuccessful adversaries could well afford to pay for them. In this instance this would be unfair to those who must ultimately bear the burden of SEPTA's costs—its customers and the taxpayers of the jurisdictions that subsidize it, though the public nature of SEPTA is not the basis for our discussion. If the losing party can afford to pay, the disparity in the parties' financial resources seems to us to be irrelevant for purposes of Rule 54(d).

If the losing party cannot afford to pay, that party is not automatically exempted from the taxation of costs. On the contrary, 28 U.S.C. § 1915(e) and cases decided thereunder make clear that costs may be taxed against a party who is permitted to proceed in forma pauperis. While these cases recognize that a district court may consider a losing party's indigency in applying Rule 54(d), the losing party in this case does not claim to be indigent, and the record does not establish that she is unable to pay the full measure of costs.

We therefore hold that neither the disparity between the parties' financial resources nor Smith's financial status provided a basis for reducing the costs sought by SEPTA. Moreover, after considering all of the factors cited by the district court and by Smith, we are convinced that the district court did not properly exercise its discretion in reducing the costs taxed in SEPTA's favor, for none of SEPTA's conduct in this litigation rendered the original fee award inequitable. We will therefore reverse the order of the district court in part and remand for the entry of a judgment taxing costs in SEPTA's favor in the amount of $6,928.17. Costs on appeal will also be taxed in favor of SEPTA.

Westwind Africa Line Ltd. v. Corpus Christi Marine Services Co.

United States Court of Appeals, Fifth Circuit, 1988.
834 F.2d 1232.

■ ALVIN B. RUBIN, CIRCUIT JUDGE:

The M/V TRADEWIND, a vessel owned by the Westwind Africa Line, ordered fuel from Corpus Christi Marine Services and Saber Petroleum Corporation for its return voyage from Corpus Christi, Texas, to Lagos, Nigeria. Twenty hours after leaving Corpus Christi, at a time when more than 50% of the fuel source was being drawn from the Corpus Christi bunkers, the ship's pump started to malfunction. Twice the engine room crew cleaned, repaired, or replaced affected parts, but, because of the damage, the ship's operations manager, after consulting with the chief engineer, decided to divert the vessel to Tampa, Florida, to take on substitute bunkers and replenish the supply of spare parts.

In Tampa, the ship discharged some of the Corpus Christi bunkers and sold them to a wholesaler. Westwind sent the money received for these bunkers to Marine Services and Saber. After taking on new bunkers and extra spare parts, the M/V TRADEWIND continued its voyage to Lagos. It chemically treated the portion of Corpus Christi bunkers that had been retained and used them as fuel, but it suffered some further difficulty en route.

Westwind brought an action against Marine Services and Saber, alleging that the fuel loaded in Corpus Christi had caused the M/V TRADEWIND's engine problems. Marine Services and Saber filed a counterclaim seeking to recover the full contract price of the bunkers they had furnished. The district court found that the fuel provided by Marine Services and Saber was neither merchantable nor fit for its intended use. It therefore held them liable for damages to the M/V TRADEWIND based on negligence and breach of contract. The court further held that Westwind was liable to Marine Services and Saber for the price realized for the fuel it resold in Tampa, but was not liable for the fuel retained on board and consumed. The court taxed costs against Marine Services and Saber, including costs of originals and copies of several deposition transcripts; travel expenses of a court reporter who went to Sweden to transcribe a deposition; and fees, travel expenses, and subsistence for two witnesses who came to Houston to have depositions taken rather than remaining in their hometowns and having the deposing attorneys come to them.

On appeal, Marine Services and Saber contend that:

* * *

6) The trial court abused its discretion in allowing certain items as taxable costs.

* * *

V.

We turn to the amounts allowed as taxable costs. In Crawford Fitting Co. v. J.T. Gibbons, Inc.[7] the Supreme Court held that, in cases in which there is no basis for an award of attorney's fees: 1) absent explicit statutory or contractual authorization to the contrary, courts may not tax items other than those listed in 28 U.S.C. § 1920 as costs against the losing party; 2) Federal Rule of Civil Procedure 54(d) allows trial courts to refuse to tax costs otherwise allowable, but it does not give them the power to tax items not elsewhere enumerated; and 3) insofar as there are statutory limits to the amounts that may be

---

7. 482 U.S. 437, 107 S.Ct. 2494, 96 L.Ed.2d 385 (1987).

taxed as costs, Rule 54(d) does not empower courts to exceed those limits. Because neither of the prevailing parties contends that there was contractual authorization for any of the disputed costs, the relevant question is whether there was any statutory authorization.

Title 28 U.S.C. § 1821(a)(1),[8] expressly authorizes the payment of a witness fee and a travel and subsistence allowance for attendance by a witness "before any person authorized to take his deposition." Under this authority, the district court taxed as costs the fees and allowances paid two expert witnesses for attendance at a deposition.

In order to attend the deposition, the witnesses travelled more than 100 miles. Although § 1821(c)(4) authorizes the taxation of "[a]ll normal travel expenses within and outside the judicial district," many courts have not allowed travel expenses for witnesses who travel more than 100 miles on the basis that, because a district court cannot use its subpoena power to compel a witness to travel more than 100 miles, a party who persuades witnesses to do so by paying their transportation expenses should not be able to tax those expenses to his adversary.

The statute contains no such limitation. Section 1821(c)(4) expressly states that "travel expenses within *and outside* the judicial district shall be taxable as costs * * *." (emphasis added). When the deposition of a witness who resides more than 100 miles outside the district must be taken, the lawyers must choose either to travel to the witness or to induce the witness to travel to the district. The witness's willingness to make the trip reduces litigation expenses, even if it increases taxable costs.

In *Farmer v. Arabian American Oil Co.,* the Court, in considering the taxation of the cost of transporting witnesses from Saudi Arabia to the United States, refused to "accept either the extreme position * * * that the old 100–mile rule has no validity for any purpose or [the] argument that a federal district court can never under any circumstances tax as costs expenses for transporting witnesses more than 100 miles." While it affirmed the district court's exercise of discretion in refusing to allow that expense, it stated that Rule 54(d) "quite plainly" vests some power in the court to allow such costs. As we have previously held, the allowance of expenses for travelling a distance in excess of one hundred miles is to be determined by trial courts using their usual sound discretion. In doing so, the trial court should consider the length of the journey, the necessity of the testimony, and the possibility of averting that expense. In this case, considering the necessity of the testimony of these witnesses and the expense saved by having them come to the lawyers rather than requiring the lawyers to go to them, we cannot say that the district judge abused his discretion.

Westwind also seeks to tax the cost of transporting a local court reporter to Sweden to transcribe the deposition of one of Westwind's witnesses. Section 1920 permits recovery only of the court reporter's fee for a transcript, not of the reporter's travel expenses. No other

---

8. (a)(1) Except as otherwise provided by law, a witness in attendance at any court of the United States * * * or before any person authorized to take his deposition pursuant to any rule or order of a court of the United States, shall be paid the fees and allowances provided by this section.

statutory provision defines court reporter's fees as including travel expenses in the way that § 1821 defines the amount allowed for the fees and expenses of witnesses. Accordingly, this item should have been disallowed.

Although § 1920 does not specifically mention depositions,[13] a number of courts have interpreted § 1920(2), which refers to "fees of the court reporter" and § 1920(4), which refers to "fees for exemplification and copies of papers necessarily obtained for use in [a] case," to authorize taxing the costs of deposition originals and deposition copies. In *United States v. Kolesar,* this court held that the cost of a deposition copy was taxable as a matter of statutory construction under § 1920(4), if the copy was necessarily obtained for use in the case. The trial judge is particularly qualified to decide whether a copy is necessary, and we reverse such a determination only for abuse of discretion. *Gibbons* limits judicial discretion with regard to the kind of expenses that may be recovered as costs; it does not, however, prevent courts from interpreting the meaning of the phrases used in § 1920.

The trial court awarded Westwind the costs of making copies of three depositions. The originals of two of those depositions were made part of the trial record and the copies were therefore necessary for use by Westwind during trial. Westwind expected that the third deposition would be made a part of the trial record and the copy would be used at trial. Under these circumstances, we cannot say that it was an abuse of discretion to award costs for the deposition copies. Accordingly, the cost of the deposition copies was properly taxed.

To summarize, Marine Services and Saber are entitled to:

     reduction of $2,371.40 for crew overtime in the damages the district court mistakenly awarded Westwind;

     reduction in damages for the value of the fuel used by the M/V TRADEWIND on its voyage from Tampa to Lagos;

reduction of the costs by $1,814.00, the cost of the court reporter's travel to Sweden.

The case is remanded for further proceedings consistent with this opinion.

D.   JUDICIAL POWER TO SANCTION BY AWARDING COSTS

In Chapter III we saw how Rule 11 of the Federal Rules of Civil Procedure authorizes the imposition of sanctions against lawyers and

---

13. § 1920 reads as follows:

A judge or clerk of any court of the United States may tax as costs the following:

    (1) Fees of the clerk and marshal;

    (2) Fees of the court reporter for all or any part of the stenographic transcript necessarily obtained for use in the case;

    (3) Fees and disbursements for printing and witnesses;

    (4) Fees for exemplification and copies of papers necessarily obtained for use in the case;

    (5) Docket fees under section 1923 of this title;

    (6) Compensation of court appointed experts, compensation of interpreters, and salaries, fees, expenses, and costs of special interpretation services under section 1828 of this title.

clients who assert claims or defenses in violation of that Rule. One of
the sanctions expressly permitted is "an order directing payment to
the movant of some or all of the reasonable attorneys' fees and other
expenses incurred as a direct result of the violation." The Private
Securities Litigation Reform Act, 15 U.S.C.A. § 78u–4(c)(1995), provides for mandatory sanctions if a violation of Rule 11(b) is found in a
private securities litigation, with a "presumption" that the appropriate
sanction will be an award of attorneys' fees and costs. The fee shifting
statutes we have studied in this Chapter can also be viewed as
authorizing the additional sanction of attorneys fees against defendants who have been found to have violated important statutory or
constitutional rights of plaintiffs. In the absence of such express
authorization, do the courts have any inherent power to assess costs
or attorneys fees against a party for conduct the court deems improper? That is the issue in the following case.

Eash v. Riggins Trucking

United States Court of Appeals, Third Circuit, 1985.
757 F.2d 557.

■ Adams, Circuit Judge.

This appeal presents an issue important to judicial administration,
namely, whether a district court may order an attorney to pay to the
government the cost of impanelling a jury for one day as a sanction for
the attorney's abuse of the judicial process.

I

The underlying action in this case was a personal injury suit
brought in a Pennsylvania state court in 1982 by plaintiffs Irvin and
Yvonne Eash. Upon motion by the defendants, the case was removed
to the District Court for the Western District of Pennsylvania, pursuant
to 28 U.S.C. § 1441 (1982). Settlement negotiations took place between the parties in the spring of 1983, leading to a stipulation to
dismiss the case. Consequently, on August 1, 1983, the district court
dismissed the action.

On August 12, 1983, without giving notice to the parties or
conducting a hearing, the district court entered an order requiring
defendants' counsel to pay $390 to the Clerk of Court. A copy of the
order appears in the appendix. The case was scheduled for trial before
a jury on May 23, 1983, and according to the district court judge,
plaintiffs' attorney made repeated attempts to communicate with
defendants' counsel regarding settlement possibilities during the week
of May 16, 1983. Receiving no response, plaintiffs' attorney prepared
for trial and came to court on May 23. At that point, defendants'
counsel proposed a settlement figure that plaintiffs accepted. The
district court believed, although this is disputed, that because defendants' attorney was scheduled for trial in state court that same day, the
settlement avoided a scheduling conflict.

The district court concluded that under the circumstances "settlement on the eve of trial was not justified. Defendants' attorney was given adequate notice by plaintiffs' counsel and by court personnel to attempt to reach an agreement." App. at 8A. The court therefore imposed a sanction of $390 on defendants' attorney, calculated as follows: $30, the per diem fee for each juror, multiplied by 13, the minimum number of persons necessary to select a jury. Subsequently the court denied a petition for reconsideration submitted by defendants' counsel, in which counsel disputed the factual basis of the order.

After a timely appeal was filed, the case was listed for resolution by a panel of this Court.[1] Because of the importance of the questions presented, however, the Court *in banc* has reviewed the case.

* * *

IV

A.

The amicus suggests that the district court's order is most properly viewed as an exercise of the court's inherent power. That courts have inherent powers—powers vested in the courts upon their creation, *see* Michaelson v. United States, 266 U.S. 42, 66, 45 S.Ct. 18, 20, 69 L.Ed. 162 (1924); * * * and not derived from any statute, *see* Link v. Wabash Railroad Co., 370 U.S. 626, 630, 82 S.Ct. 1386, 1388, 8 L.Ed.2d 734 (1962); * * *—is not disputed. Inherent power has been frequently invoked by the courts to regulate the conduct of the members of the bar as well as to provide tools for docket management. Courts have thus relied on the concept of inherent power to impose several species of sanctions on those who abuse the judicial process. For example, federal courts may dismiss a case for failure to prosecute, Link v. Wabash Railroad Co., 370 U.S. at 629–30, 82 S.Ct. at 1388–89; *see also* National Hockey League v. Metropolitan Hockey Club, Inc., 427 U.S. 639, 96 S.Ct. 2778, 49 L.Ed.2d 747 (1976) (per curiam); * * *. Similarly, the contempt power is rooted in the inherent power of the judiciary. *E.g.,* Levine v. United States, 362 U.S. 610, 615, 80 S.Ct. 1038, 1042, 4 L.Ed.2d 989 (1960). Commentators have also noted occasions in which, under its inherent power, a court has disbarred, suspended from practice, or reprimanded attorneys for abuse of the judicial process. *See* Comment, Financial Penalties Imposed Directly Against Attorneys in Litigation Without Resort to the Contempt Power, 26 UCLA L.Rev. 855, 856 (1979); Comment, Involuntary Dismissal for Disobedience or Delay: The Plaintiff's Plight, 34 U.Chi.L.Rev. 922, 937 n. 96 (1967); . . . . This Court has stated that in the absence of a statute, the taxation of costs in the appellate court "is a matter, inherently and necessarily within its general powers." *See* Island Development Co. v. McGeorge, 37 F.2d 345, 345 (3d Cir.1930);

---

1. The court appointed Robert J. Bartow, Professor, Temple University School of Law, to serve as amicus curiae and to assert a position, in the interest of informed decision-making, adverse to that of appellants.

see also Levin & Amsterdam, Legislative Control Over Judicial Rule–Making: A Problem of Constitutional Revision, 107 U.Pa.L.Rev. 1, 16 (1958). Courts, pursuant to inherent powers, have declared attorneys who choose to be absent from docket call "ready for trial," even though this may lead ineluctably to the entry of a default judgment. Williams v. New Orleans Public Service, Inc., 728 F.2d 730, 732 (5th Cir.1984); *see also* Schlesinger v. Teitelbaum, 475 F.2d 137, 142 (3d Cir.), *cert. denied,* 414 U.S. 1111, 94 S.Ct. 840, 38 L.Ed.2d 738 (1973) (an inherent power to set counsel fees in cases involving persons of presumed incapacity).

Despite historical reliance on inherent powers, including Supreme Court jurisprudence dating back to 1812, the notion of inherent power has been described as nebulous,[5] and its bounds as "shadowy." *See* Rosenberg, Sanctions to Effectuate Pretrial Discovery, 58 Colum.L.Rev. 480, 485 (1958). The conceptual and definitional problems regarding inherent power that have bedeviled commentators for years, *see* Burbank, Sanctions in the Proposed Amendments to the Federal Rules of Civil Procedure: Some Questions About Power, 11 Hofstra L.Rev. 997, 1004 (1983); *see also Sanctions Imposable, supra* n. 5, stem from several factors. First, perhaps because federal courts infrequently resort to their inherent powers or because such reliance most often is not challenged, very few federal cases discuss in detail the topic of inherent powers. *Cf.* Note, Power of Federal Courts to Discipline Attorneys for Delay in Pretrial Procedure, 38 Notre Dame Law. 158, 161 (1963).[6] More importantly, those cases that have employed inherent power appear to use that generic term to describe several distinguishable court powers. *Cf.* Williams, The Source of Authority for Rules of Court Affecting Procedure, 22 Wash.U.L.Q. 459, 473–74 (1937); Frankfurter & Landis, Power of Congress over Procedure in Criminal Contempts in "Inferior" Federal Courts—A Study in Separation of Powers, 37 Harv.L.Rev. 1010, 1023 (1924). To compound this lack of specificity, courts have relied occasionally on precedents involving one form of power to support the court's use of another. *See* Burbank, *supra,* 11 Hofstra L.Rev. at 1005.

These observations suggest that it is not always possible to categorize inherent power decisions. Nevertheless, it appears that the term inherent power has been employed in three general fashions. The first stems from the fact that once Congress has created lower federal courts and demarcated their jurisdiction, the courts are vested with judicial powers pursuant to Article III. This use of inherent power, which might be termed irreducible inherent authority, encompasses an extremely narrow range of authority involving activity so fundamental to the essence of a court as a constitutional tribunal that to divest the court of absolute command within this sphere is really to render practically meaningless the terms "court" and "judicial pow-

---

5. *See* R. Rodes, K. Ripple & C. Mooney, *Sanctions Imposable for Violations of the Federal Rules of Civil Procedure* 179 n. 466 (Federal Judicial Center 1981) [hereinafter *Sanctions Imposable*].

6. There is a plethora of state court cases regarding the powers of the state judiciary.

er." *See* Levin & Amsterdam, *supra,* 107 U.Pa.L.Rev. at 30–32. In this limited domain of judicial autonomy, courts may act notwithstanding contrary legislative direction. These inherent powers are grounded in the separation of powers concept, because to deny this power "and yet to conceive of courts is a self-contradiction." Frankfurter & Landis, *supra,* 37 Harv.L.Rev. at 1023; *see* Levin & Amsterdam, *supra,* 107 U.Pa.L.Rev. at 33; *see also* United States v. Klein, 80 U.S. (13 Wall.) 128, 147, 20 L.Ed. 519 (1900).

Boundaries for this sphere of minimal judicial integrity are not possible to locate with exactitude.[7] Certainly the power must be exercised with great restraint and caution. Whatever the proper limit of this form of inherent power may be, it is not the power to which the amicus has pointed as authority for the sanction imposed by the district court here.

The second, and most common, use of the term "inherent power" encompasses those powers sometimes said to arise from the nature of the court, *see Ex parte* Terry, 128 U.S. 289, 303, 9 S.Ct. 77, 79, 32 L.Ed. 405 (1888); * * *, but more often thought to be the powers "necessary to the exercise of all others." *E.g., Roadway,* 447 U.S. at 764, 100 S.Ct. at 2463 (quoting *Hudson*). Here courts are referring to powers implied from strict functional necessity. In *Roadway* the Supreme Court termed the contempt sanction "the most prominent" of these powers.[8] Historically, it has viewed this particular power as "essential to the administration of justice," *Michaelson,* 266 U.S. at 65, 45 S.Ct. at 20, and "absolutely essential" for the functioning of the judiciary. * * *

Because this second form of inherent power arises from necessity, on several occasions the Supreme Court has stated that while the authority "may be regulated within limits not precisely defined," it can "neither be abrogated nor rendered practically inoperative." *Michaelson,* 266 U.S. at 66, 45 S.Ct. at 20. Indeed, in one of its earliest decisions regarding the contempt power, the Supreme Court observed that congressional enactment of a contempt statute should "be considered, only as an instance of abundant caution, or a legislative declaration, that the power of punishing for contempt shall not extend

7. Levin & Amsterdam, *supra,* 107 U.Pa.L.Rev. at 33, note that courts have relied on this concept to void legislation requiring a written opinion in every case. Vaughan v. Harp, 49 Ark. 160, 4 S.W. 751 (1887); declaring within what time every case must be heard, Atchison, Topeka & Santa Fe Railway Co. v. Long, 122 Okla. 86, 251 P. 486 (1926); denying a court the power to issue its mandate until a prescribed period of time after the judgment has elapsed even if this renders the judgment meaningless, Burton v. Mayer, 274 Ky. 263, 118 S.W.2d 547 (1938); or providing for the automatic disqualification of judges simply upon the application of a party, State ex rel. Bushman v. Vandenberg, 203 Ore. 326, 329, 280 P.2d 344 (1955).

We do not pass on the validity of these holdings but only note that courts have sought to carve out a sphere of minimal autonomy based upon separation of powers notions.

8. Although now codified at 18 U.S.C. § 401 (1982) and in Fed.R.Crim.P. 42, the contempt power is rooted principally in the inherent power of the judiciary. *See* Levine v. United States, 362 U.S. 610, 615, 80 S.Ct. 1038, 1042, 4 L.Ed.2d 989 (1960); *Ex parte* Robinson, 86 U.S. (19 Wall.) at 510, 22 L.Ed. 205; *Sanctions Imposable, supra* note 5, at 74; Comment, Financial Penalties Imposed Directly Against Attorneys in Litigation Without Resort to the Contempt Power, 26 UCLA L.Rev. 855, 878 (1979).

beyond its known and acknowledged limits * * *." *Anderson,* 19 U.S. (6 Wheat.) at 226, 5 L.Ed. 242; *see also* * * * United States v. Hall, 198 F.2d 726, 728 (2d Cir.1952), *cert. denied,* 345 U.S. 905, 73 S.Ct. 641, 97 L.Ed. 1341 (1953) (statute merely "defines the acts toward which it may be directed").

The third form of authority subsumed under the general term inherent power implicates powers necessary only in the practical sense of being useful. An early example is *Ex parte* Peterson, 253 U.S. 300, 40 S.Ct. 543, 64 L.Ed. 919 (1920), in which the Supreme Court determined that "the court possesses the inherent power to supply itself" with an "auditor" to aid in its decisionmaking. *Id.* at 312, 40 S.Ct. at 547. "Courts have (at least in the absence of legislation to the contrary) inherent power to provide themselves with appropriate instruments required for the performance of their duties," and to appoint "persons unconnected with the court to aid judges in the performance of specific judicial duties." *Id.* * * *

This third category of inherent power has sometimes been said to be "rooted in the notion that a federal court, sitting in equity, possesses all of the common law equity tools of a Chancery Court (subject, of course, to congressional limitation) to process litigation to a just and equitable conclusion." ITT Community Development Corp. v. Barton, 569 F.2d 1351, 1359 (5th Cir.1978); *cf.* Hall v. Cole, 412 U.S. 1, 5, 93 S.Ct. 1943, 1946, 36 L.Ed.2d 702 (1973) (courts possess "inherent equitable power"); Johnston v. Marsh, 227 F.2d 528, 531 (3d Cir.1955) ("Our Federal judiciary has consistently recognized that at common law this inherent power existed."). In other cases this power is said to derive from necessity; for example, the court termed "essential" the appointment of an auditor in *Peterson,* 253 U.S. at 312, 40 S.Ct. at 547. Yet it is clear that such power is necessary only in the sense of being highly useful in the pursuit of a just result. *See* Note, Compulsory Reference in Actions at Law, 34 Harv.L.Rev. 321, 324 (1921).

As suggested by the above quotation from *Peterson,* courts may exercise this kind of inherent power only in the absence of contrary legislative direction. *See Williams, supra,* 22 Wash.U.L.Q. at 473; *see also* Alyeska Pipeline Service v. Wilderness Society, 421 U.S. 240, 259, 95 S.Ct. 1612, 1622, 44 L.Ed.2d 141 (1975) ("These exceptions are unquestionably assertions of inherent power in the courts to allow attorneys' fees in particular situations, unless forbidden by Congress * * *.").

The third form of power has also been invoked as "the underlying federal basis that permits the court to elect to use" a state mechanism for certification of a question of doubtful state law, Weaver v. Marine Bank, 683 F.2d 744 (3d Cir.1982); in order to grant bail in a situation not dealt with by statute, Johnston v. Marsh, 227 F.2d at 531; * * * and to dismiss a suit pursuant to the doctrine of *forum non conveniens,* Gulf Oil Corp. v. Gilbert, 330 U.S. 501, 502, 507 (1947).

Courts rarely have explained exactly what kind of authority they mean to invoke when using an inherent power to sanction an attorney. *See* Dowling, The Inherent Power of the Judiciary, 21 A.B.A.J. 635 (1935). Nevertheless, it seems quite clear that at least in the absence of contrary legislation, courts under their inherent powers have developed a wide range of tools to promote efficiency in their courtrooms and to achieve justice in their results. *E.g., Link,* 370 U.S. at 630–31, 82 S.Ct. at 1388–89 (where the Supreme Court stated that the authority to dismiss a case is an inherent "control necessarily vested in courts to manage their own affairs so as to achieve the orderly and expeditious disposition of cases").

B.

Nearly a quarter century ago, and more than fifteen years prior to the Supreme Court's decision in *Roadway,* this Court sitting in banc held that a district court lacked inherent authority to impose a "fine" on an attorney who had failed to file a pretrial memorandum in a timely fashion. Gamble v. Pope & Talbot, Inc., 307 F.2d 729 (3d Cir.), *cert. denied,* 371 U.S. 888, 83 S.Ct. 187, 9 L.Ed.2d 123 (1962). The plurality of the Court believed that the effect of the fine, whatever "it be called ... was to punish defendant's attorney for contempt in failing to file the defense pretrial memorandum within time." *Id.* at 731. The district court in *Gamble* did not, however, designate the lawyer's act as contempt nor did it invoke the formal contempt proceeding. On review, this Court noted that there was nothing in the Federal Rules of Civil Procedure which explicitly authorized the sanction that had been imposed. *Id.* While the plurality conceded that district courts have substantial local rulemaking power, it determined that such a "basic disciplinary innovation" as the sanction in question required a national "uniform approach." *Id.* at 732. The plurality believed that only a statute or Federal Rule could accomplish this. Significantly, while stating that no inherent authority for the fine existed, neither the plurality opinion nor the concurring statement of Judge Hastie discussed the doctrine of inherent powers, and neither opinion cited any case involving inherent power.

Judge Goodrich, dissenting, asserted that a judge "undoubtedly has inherent power to impose sanctions for the disciplining of lawyers who, in matters not amounting to contempt, do not obey rules." *Id.* at 737 (Goodrich, J., dissenting). In a separate dissent Chief Judge Biggs disputed the majority's perception that the fine carried any criminal connotation. He emphasized that unlike many of the penalties that courts impose for an attorney's failure to perform his or her duty, the monetary sanction did not punish clients for the shortcomings of their counsel. *Id.* at 734.[10]

The decision in *Gamble* was promptly and roundly criticized. *E.g.,* Note, Power of Federal Courts, 38 Notre Dame Law. 158; Comment,

---

10. Traditionally courts have treated the attorney as the client's agent so that the attorney's acts and omissions legally bind the client. *Sanctions Imposable, supra* note 5, at 70; *see generally Link,* 370 U.S. at 633–34, 82 S.Ct. at 1390–91. Because this approach ignores the realities of the lawyer-client relationship, *see* Comment, *Involuntary Dismissal for Disobedience or Delay: The Plaintiff's Plight,* 34 U.Chi.L.Rev. 922, 929 (1967), there has been a trend to seek to impose penalties upon only the offending lawyer.

Dismissal for Failure to Attend a Pretrial Conference and the Use of Sanctions at Preparatory Stages of Litigation, 72 Yale L.J. 819 (1963). And the case has continued to come under attack. *See, e.g.,* Renfrew, Discovery Sanctions, A Judicial Perspective, 67 Calif.L.Rev. 264, 270 (1979); Comment, Sanctions Imposed by Courts on Attorneys Who Abuse the Judicial Process, 44 U.Chi.L.Rev. 619, 635 (1977). Commentators have highlighted the curious and contradictory result created by the juxtaposition of *Link,* decided in 1962, and *Gamble,* decided one year later. Under *Link,* courts may invoke their inherent power to dismiss a plaintiff's entire case when a lawyer has failed without adequate excuse to appear at a scheduled pretrial conference, *Link,* 370 U.S. at 628–29, 82 S.Ct. at 1387–88, but under *Gamble* courts may not sanction financially a blameworthy attorney who filed a pretrial memorandum ten months late, *Gamble,* 307 F.2d at 730. *See, e.g.,* Comment, *Financial Penalties,* 26 UCLA L.Rev. at 877.

Recently a number of courts have rejected the result and reasoning of *Gamble* as unduly narrow. *See, e.g.,* Miranda v. Southern Pacific Transp. Co., 710 F.2d 516, 520 (9th Cir.1983) ("For the reasons stated by Judge Biggs, we decline to follow *Gamble.*"); Martinez v. Thrifty Drug & Discount Co., 593 F.2d 992, 993 (10th Cir.1979) (explicitly rejecting *Gamble*); *In re* Sutter, 543 F.2d 1030, 1037 (2d Cir.1976) ("We * * * decline to follow the Third Circuit."); *see also* Richman v. General Motors Corp., 437 F.2d 196, 200 (1st Cir.1971). A major factor in the decisions that have refused to follow *Gamble* has been the startling increase in the number and complexity of cases filed in the federal courts. The dramatic rise in litigation in the last decade has led trial judges to conclude that indulgent toleration of lawyers' misconduct is simply a luxury the federal court system no longer can afford. *See Renfrew, supra,* 67 Calif.L.Rev. at 275–76. Chief Justice Burger has recently observed that "a small handful [of lawyers] must not be permitted to abuse the system and preempt its time and machinery for purposes not intended, thus delaying and denying" access to courts to others in need of the courts' limited resources. Burger, Abuses of Discovery, Trial (Sept.1984). For example, the Second Circuit in *Sutter* upheld the imposition of juror costs based in part upon "intensified concerns" over "the increasing backlog of calendars." 543 F.2d at 1037. The *Martinez* court concluded that a sanction based on the cost of impanelling a jury had the "object and purpose of administering the court in an efficient manner." 593 F.2d at 994.

C.

With the foregoing discussion of inherent powers and the evolution of practice regarding attorney sanctions as background, we turn to the challenged order at issue here. Appellants, relying on the continuing vitality of the reasoning in *Gamble,* urge that a sanction in the form of juror costs improperly and "informally inflict[ed] a criminal" punishment, like contempt, without resort to the contempt statute. *Gamble,* 307 F.2d at 733. To a considerable extent, Judge Sloviter's dissent also rests on this view.

In *Gamble* this Court essentially was concerned with the imposition of a fine unrelated to any actual consequence of counsel's conduct and that knew no bounds other than each individual judge's notion of an appropriate penalty warranted by a counsel's misdeeds. The present case is significantly different in that the district court tied its sanction to specific costs that bore a direct relationship to the alleged misconduct and thus offered a nexus and a limit.

Moreover, and perhaps most significantly, the *Gamble* court's reasoning runs counter to the Supreme Court's observations that a court's broad power to discipline attorneys as officers of the court for misconduct not properly categorized as contempt is substantially different from the contempt power. The Supreme Court has noted, for example, that the " 'power to disbar an attorney proceeds upon very different grounds' from those which support a court's power to punish for contempt." Cammer v. United States, 350 U.S. at 408 n. 7, 76 S.Ct. at 460 n. 7 (quoting *Ex parte* Robinson, 86 U.S. (19 Wall.) 505, 512, 22 L.Ed. 205 (1873)). Similarly, we agree with the Ninth Circuit that a reasonable "monetary sanction for failure to carry out [an attorney's] special responsibility [to the court] * * * differs from the more severe infraction of contempt for which attorneys and members of the general public can become liable." *Miranda,* 710 F.2d at 521. The former is based simply on an unjustified failure to discharge an administrative responsibility as an officer of the court.

Relying in part on the Supreme Court's holding in Youngstown Sheet & Tube Co. v. Sawyer, 343 U.S. 579, 72 S.Ct. 863, 96 L.Ed. 1153 (1952), that the President was without inherent power to order the Secretary of Commerce to take possession of and actually operate most of the nation's steel mills, one dissenting opinion argues that the district court's assertion of authority to impose a sanction of $390 upon an attorney who has abused the judicial process somehow violates the doctrine of separation of powers. The Supreme Court has consistently recognized the federal court's powers—notwithstanding the absence of Congressional action—to sanction errant attorneys financially both for contempt and for conduct not rising to the level of contempt. *See, e.g., Roadway,* 447 U.S. at 765, 100 S.Ct. at 2463. Thus the dissent is relegated to arguing that the specific type of monetary sanction imposed here, one "unrelated to the other parties' costs," is akin to a criminal "fine" and "a fine can be imposed only to punish conduct that has been prohibited by the legislature." No authority has been offered for the proposition that financial sanctions by a federal court for abuse of the judicial process by an attorney before that court must be directly related to the other litigants' costs. Instead the dissent employs as an analog cases forbidding federal courts from creating federal common law crimes or from expanding the reach of criminal statutes. We agree with the Ninth Circuit that the imposition of juror costs when an attorney abuses the judicial process in a manner that forces the unnecessary calling of a jury does not carry any criminal connotation. *Miranda,* 710 F.2d at 521; *see* Comment, *Financial Penalties,* 26 UCLA L.Rev. at 890; *see also* Dowling, *supra,* 21 A.B.A.J. at 637.

The impact of the contrary position, moreover, would apparently be to invalidate many of the financial sanctions imposed by this Court and other courts of appeals, *cf., e.g., Miranda,* 710 F.2d at 521, for myriad violations of court rules, deadlines, or orders, such as the late-filing of a brief, or for conduct unbecoming a member of the bar. Although these financial penalties, payable to the government, are often based to some extent on Fed.R.App.P. 46(c), neither that Rule nor any Congressional enactment explicitly provides for such financial sanctions, nor expressly prohibits the conduct sanctioned by the court—a step Judge Sloviter's dissent argues is constitutionally mandated.

More fundamentally, we agree with those courts that have found the result in *Gamble* to be excessively restrictive in practice. While the judicious use of sanctions is a practical necessity in the management of caseloads, Comment, *Financial Penalties,* 26 UCLA L.Rev. at 875, the more traditional penalties based on a court's inherent powers, and the specialized sanctions of the Federal Rules of Civil Procedure, are at times inadequate to regulate the wide range of attorney misconduct. *Cf.* Miller, *The Adversary System: Dinosaur or Phoenix,* 69 Minn.L.Rev. 1, 25 (1984). For example, the court's power to dismiss a plaintiff's action because of the misdeeds of counsel, while unquestioned in principle after *Link,* must be exercised with great restraint because it subverts the sound public policy of deciding cases on their merits and punishes the client for the counsel's conduct. *E.g.,* Hritz v. Woma Corp., 732 F.2d 1178, 1181 (3d Cir.1984) ("we have repeatedly stated our preference that cases be disposed of on the merits whenever practicable"). The imposition of a modest monetary sanction on counsel is obviously considerably less severe than outright dismissal of an action, and is perhaps more appropriate in that the penalty is directed at the lawyer responsible for the infraction, rather than the litigant who may be completely innocent. *Id.; see also Miranda,* 710 F.2d at 521; *Gamble,* 307 F.2d at 734 (Biggs, C.J., dissenting); *Miller, supra,* 69 Minn.L.Rev. at 25, 27. The dissent, by denying the district courts this flexibility, would seem only to magnify the risk of a harsh and potentially inequitable response to attorney misconduct. The contempt sanction is similarly viewed as a drastic step. Contempt, concerned theoretically with the order, dignity, and decorum of a court, or with willful obstruction of justice, *see* Comment, Financial Penalties, 26 UCLA L.Rev. at 879, may be inappropriate in many situations of attorney misdeeds. *Miranda,* 710 F.2d at 521; Comment, Dismissal for Disobedience, 34 U.Chi.L.Rev. at 937; *see also Sanctions Imposable, supra* note 5, at 180–81 n. 470.

Judge Sloviter questions any reliance on "usefulness" as a factor relevant to the analysis, but we cannot overlook the language of the Supreme Court in *Link,* 370 U.S. at 630–31, 82 S.Ct. at 1388–89 stating that the "inherent power" to sanction an attorney was "governed not by rule or statute but by the control necessarily vested in courts to manage their own affairs so as to achieve the orderly and expeditious disposition of cases." If a court's inherent powers include the ability to do whatever is reasonably necessary to deter abuse of the judicial process, *cf. National Hockey League,* 427 U.S. at 643, 96 S.Ct. at 2781, courts must be able to impose reasonable sanctions for conduct by lawyers that falls short of contempt of court. *Sutter,* 543 F.2d at 1037; Renfrew, *supra,* 67 Calif.L.Rev. at 270; Comment, *Dismissal for Disobedience,* 34 U.Chi.L.Rev. at 937. A court's inherent power to manage its caseload, control its docket, and regulate the conduct of attorneys before it, provides authority to fashion tools that aid the court in getting on with the business of deciding cases. A recent study of sanctions in federal courts concluded that "the imposition of financial penalties is the only sanction both mild enough and flexible enough to use in day-to-day enforcement of orderly and expeditious litigation." *Sanctions Imposable, supra* note 5, at 86.

Referring to language in *Link* that the inherent power to dismiss a case was of "ancient origin," Judge Sloviter suggests that a lack of similar history fatally undermines the sanction used in the present case. It is true that historically most monetary sanctions imposed directly on attorneys, outside of the contempt context, have been related in some way to the expenses unnecessarily incurred by the opposing party. *Cf.* United States v. Blodgett, 709 F.2d at 611. Nevertheless we do not believe that a long-standing tradition need undergird every particular sanction imposed pursuant to the district court's inherent powers. *See* Note, Power of Federal Courts, 38 Notre Dame Law. at 165 ("courts have exercised vastly similar powers * * * for centuries," and the failure of many "courts to use this particular penalty does not prove the absence of the power to levy it"). The historical discussion in *Link* constituted a description; it did not establish a prerequisite to the employment of a sanction. Perhaps more telling is *Roadway,* in which the Supreme Court held that, despite the absence of Congressional authorization, in a proper case attorneys' fees may be assessed directly against a lawyer for abuse of the judicial process. The decision also reaffirmed a court's power to dismiss a case when a plaintiff fails to pursue the litigation diligently, and observed that the power of a court over the members of its bar must be at least as great as its authority over litigants. *Roadway,* 447 U.S. at 766, 100 S.Ct. at 2464. In upholding the taxing of counsel fees directly against an attorney, the Court was not dissuaded by the fact that this particular sanction did not have a long legal ancestry; in fact it ran counter to the "American rule" that each side pay its own fees. Rather, the Supreme Court emphasized the well acknowledged inherent power of a court to levy a reasonable sanction in response to abusive litigation practices. *Id.* at 765, 100 S.Ct. at 2463. Significantly, the Supreme Court cited Chief Judge Biggs' dissent in *Gamble* with approval in its discussion of the inherent power of a court to impose reasonable sanctions upon those admitted to its bar. *Id.* at 766 n. 12, 100 S.Ct. at 2464 n. 12 (citing *Gamble,* 307 F.2d at 735–36 (Biggs, C.J., dissenting)).

Roadway also would appear to refute the argument that the mere existence of the cost statutes, §§ 1920 & 1927, prevents reliance by courts on their inherent powers to support the imposition of a reasonable monetary sanction closely tied to the attorney's misconduct. Although there may be some inherent powers that a court may not exercise in the face of contrary legislation, *e.g., Alyeska,* 421 U.S. at 259, 95 S.Ct. at 1622, it would be an unwarranted extension of these precedents to argue that through §§ 1920 and 1927 Congress has pre-empted entirely the field of monetary sanctions against errant attorneys. In *Roadway,* the Court found that nothing in the statutes or their history suggests that Congress intended to preclude the use of a monetary sanction not expressly provided for in § 1920 and § 1927. Indeed, the Court acknowledged that although assessment of attorney's fees directly on an errant attorney was not a cost enumerated by Congress, the sanction was fully within the court's inherent powers. *Cf. Link,* 370 U.S. 626, 82 S.Ct. at 1386 (existence of Federal Rule permitting district court to dismiss case upon motion of party did not supersede court's inherent power to dismiss *sua sponte*); Note, Power of Federal Courts, 38 Notre Dame Law. at 169.

The present appeal does not raise one of the precise issues proffered in *Gamble, i.e.,* the propriety of a monetary sanction wholly unrelated to any costs incurred by a litigant, the court, or the government as a result of attorney misconduct. We do not resolve here the narrow question of what degree of nexus between sanction and misconduct is necessary. However, our fresh evaluation of the importance and necessity of some kind of sanction as one of the reasonable and flexible instruments for curbing abuse of the judicial process suggests that *Gamble* should no longer control this conceptual area. In light of the above described development of the law of sanctions, the persuasive reasoning of commentators, the combined wisdom of several other courts of appeals, and the fact that the Supreme Court significantly undercut *Gamble* in *Roadway,* we now most respectfully overrule *Gamble.*

We do not imply, in upholding the power of the district court to impose a sanction on an attorney in a proper case, that the imposition of a sanction was proper in the present case, *see infra* Part VI, nor do we express any view on what forms of attorney misconduct would justify the imposition of the sanction. Certainly, however, the district court must exercise discretion and sound judgment in dealing with the myriad methods with which lawyers may abuse the judicial process. Nor is anything in this opinion meant to suggest that settlement on the eve of trial is in and of itself improper. Frequently a settlement may be in the best interest of not only clients and their attorneys, but of the judicial system and society as a whole. The suggestion in the present proceeding, however, is that because of misconduct by an attorney a settlement took place at an unjustifiably late date thereby occasioning the waste of scarce judicial resources and the unnecessary expense of calling a jury.

V

The district court in the case at hand did not appear to base its sanction upon any local rule. The Supreme Court has stated, however, that a court's inherent authority over members of its bar is not limited to those specific facets of conduct covered by a local rule. In upholding a court's inherent power to dismiss a lawsuit, the Supreme Court in *Link* held:

> Petitioner's contention that the District Court could not act in the conceded absence of any local rule covering the situation here is obviously unsound. Federal Rule of Civil Procedure 83 expressly provides that "in all cases not provided for by rule, the district courts may regulate their practice in any manner not inconsistent with these rules."

Link, 370 U.S. at 633 n. 8, 82 S.Ct. at 1390 n. 8, *see also Sutter,* 543 F.2d at 1037. While we believe that the district court in imposing the sanction at issue here need not have relied on a local rule, we nevertheless suggest that if the district courts believe that there are occasions in which the imposition of such a sanction would be just, wise, and efficacious, a local rule on the imposition of such a sanction might well be salutary.

The rulemaking power of the district courts is now codified at 28 U.S.C. § 2071 (1982), which provides that the district courts may make rules prescribing the conduct of court business. The only statutory requirement is that the local rules promulgated be consistent with acts of Congress and the rules prescribed by the Supreme Court. The Federal Rules of Civil Procedure permit the district courts to make and amend rules governing their practice not at variance with the other Federal Rules. We agree with the Second, Ninth, and Tenth Circuits that the district courts have the power, absent a statute or rule promulgated by the Supreme Court to the contrary, to make local rules that impose reasonable sanctions where an attorney conducts himself in a manner unbecoming a member of the bar, fails to comply with any rule of court, including local rules, or takes actions in bad faith. *See Miranda,* 710 F.2d at 521–22; *Martinez,* 593 F.2d at 994; *Sutter,* 543 F.2d at 1037–38; *see also Sanctions Imposable, supra* note 5, at 265; Renfrew, *supra,* 67 Calif.L.Rev. at 270; Comment, Sanctions Imposed by Courts, 44 U.Chi.L.Rev. at 635; *accord* Fed.R.App.P. 46(b) (conduct unbecoming a member of the bar).

The *Gamble* plurality, in addition to finding the sanction imposed there to be unauthorized by inherent power, thought the "fine" assessed to be a "basic disciplinary innovation" and thus beyond the scope of the "local rulemaking power." 307 F.2d at 732. It is not clear, however, that the use of a reasonable, albeit nontraditional, sanction closely tied to the misconduct of the attorney fairly can be characterized as a "basic innovation." This is true especially given the universally recognized need to deter abuse of the judicial process. The *Gamble* court apparently was relying on language in Miner v. Atlass, 363 U.S. 641, 80 S.Ct. 1300, 4 L.Ed.2d 1462 (1960), which held that district courts could not introduce discovery into admiralty proceedings pursuant to local rule. Discovery was termed "one of the most significant innovations" of the Federal Rules of Civil Procedure, *id.* at 649, 80 S.Ct. at 1305, and thus a local rule governing discovery in the admiralty context was regarded at that time as improper. The Supreme

Court suggested, however, that a local rule might be more appropriate in situations involving "the necessary choice of a rule to deal with a problem which must have an answer, but need not have any particular one." *Id.*

More recently the Supreme Court has clarified the role of local rules in achieving procedural change. In Colgrove v. Battin, 413 U.S. 149, 93 S.Ct. 2448, 37 L.Ed.2d 522 (1973), it upheld the validity of a local rule providing for a jury of six in a civil trial. The Court declared that the "requirement of a six-member jury is not a 'basic procedural innovation.'" The Court went on to define the " 'basic procedural innovations' to which *Miner* referred" as "those aspects of the litigatory process which bear upon the ultimate outcome of the litigation." *Id.* at 164 n. 23, 93 S.Ct. at 2456 n. 23. A reasonable monetary sanction on an errant attorney is not a procedural innovation beyond the reach of a local rule since it is not outcome-determinative in the sense suggested by the Supreme Court.

Regarding the wisdom of a local rule on monetary sanctions, *Gamble* suggested that a national "uniform approach" was required. However, given that the district courts vary tremendously in size, volume of cases, calendar congestion, and types of cases, and that litigation tactics of attorneys may differ across the country, it is not readily apparent that a national rule is either required or desirable. *Cf.* Comment, *Financial Penalties,* 26 UCLA L.Rev. at 875. In the context of judicial disciplinary rules a recent commentator has noted that in "some instances the potential benefits of continuing experimentation are so obvious, and the costs arising from disuniformity so speculative, that requiring a uniform rule would be premature." Burbank, Procedural Rulemaking Under the Judicial Councils Reform and Judicial Conduct and Disability Act of 1980, 131 U.Pa.L.Rev. 283, 326 (1982). Others have observed that desirable differences in local rules stem in part from varying "local expectations and practice." Flanders, Local Rules in Federal District Courts: Usurpation, Legislation, or Information, 14 Loyola L.A.L.Rev. 213, 264 (1981).

Several courts have promulgated rules that provide for an assessment of juror and related costs, when a settlement occurs improperly shortly before trial.[11] "Such local rules occupy a vital role in the district courts' efforts to manage themselves and their dockets," *Flanders, supra,* 14 Loyola L.A.L.Rev. at 263, and are essential tools in implementing court policy. *Id.* at 218. The local rule device fulfills important informational purposes, placing the bar on notice of a court's policies. *Id.* at 263. Similarly, a local rule may well be the most effective means of ensuring that all members of the bar are aware that a particular practice is deemed improper, and thus subject to a sanction. Local rules may also alert rulemakers to the need for changes in national rules and supply an empirical basis for making such changes. Furthermore, a local rule may be a powerful implement for rationalizing

---

11. *See, e.g.,* D.Col.R. 11; D.Del.R. D.N.J.Gen.R. 20(G); D.N.M.R. 13(e); 5.5(D); N.D.Ill.Civ.R. 11; W.D.La.R. 5(g); W.D.Tenn.R. 6(b); E.D.Va.R. 20(e).

diverse court practices and imposing uniformity within a given district. *Id.* at 268, 269.

VI

Finally, appellants assert that the imposition of a monetary sanction by the district court without affording the attorney prior notice and an opportunity to be heard violates due process. We agree.

In the absence of extraordinary circumstances, procedural due process requires notice and an opportunity to be heard before any governmental deprivation of a property interest. Boddie v. Connecticut, 401 U.S. 371, 379, 91 S.Ct. 780, 786, 28 L.Ed.2d 113 (1971). The form which those procedural protections must take is determined by an evaluation of all the circumstances and an accommodation of competing interests. *See* Goss v. Lopez, 419 U.S. 565, 579, 95 S.Ct. 729, 738, 42 L.Ed.2d 725 (1975); *Renfrew, supra,* 67 Calif.L.Rev. at 281. The individual's right to fairness and accuracy must be respected, as must the court's need to act quickly and decisively.

In considering the imposition of a penalty upon attorneys, we note that the Court has cautioned that like "other sanctions, attorney's fees certainly should not be assessed lightly or without fair notice and an opportunity for a hearing on the record." *Roadway,* 447 U.S. at 767, 100 S.Ct. at 2464. Similarly, a court may not disbar an attorney without notice and a hearing. *Ex parte Bradley,* 74 U.S. (7 Wall.) 364, 372–74, 19 L.Ed. 214 (1868). Courts of appeals may not impose disciplinary sanctions on attorneys until "after reasonable notice and an opportunity to show cause to the contrary, and after hearing, if requested." Fed.R.App.Pro. 46(c). Although in *Link* the Supreme Court suggested that not every order entered without a preliminary adversary hearing offends due process. *Link,* 370 U.S. at 632, 82 S.Ct. at 1389, we believe that as a general practice a monetary detriment should not be imposed by a court without prior notice and some occasion to respond.

These procedural safeguards will ensure that the attorney has an adequate opportunity to explain the conduct deemed deficient. For example, in the present case, the attorney by affidavits disputes the factual predicate upon which the order was based. Furthermore, such procedures will afford the judge adequate time to evaluate the propriety of the particular sanction in light of the offending attorney's explanation as well as to consider alternatives. * * * Moreover, by providing a record, a hearing will facilitate appellate review. Miranda, 710 F.2d at 522–23; Renfrew, supra, 67 Calif.L.Rev. at 281. In some cases, it may be that the record developed at the time of the alleged misconduct will, itself, satisfy this need as long as the attorney has been afforded an opportunity to adduce the relevant facts. Upon imposing such a sanction it would seem appropriate for the district court to make adequate written findings.

A final point worth noting, although not raised in the briefs, is that the due process calculus may also be affected by the "knowledge which the circumstances show [the offending] party may be taken to have of the consequences of his own conduct." Link, 370 U.S. at 632, 82 S.Ct. at 1390. Thus, fundamental fairness may require some measure of prior notice to an attorney that the conduct that he or she contemplates undertaking is subject to discipline or sanction by a court. Consequently the absence, for example, of a statute, Federal Rule, ethical canon, local rule or custom, court order, or, perhaps most pertinent to the case at hand, court admonition, proscribing the act for which a sanction is imposed in a given case may raise questions as to the sanction's validity in a particular case.

As noted in Part V of this opinion there does not appear to be a local rule covering the conduct of the attorney in question. Nor is it apparent that any analogous form of actual or constructive notice was given to the attorney whose settlement conduct was deemed sanctionable by the district court, although there is no way of ascertaining that fact from the record before us. Therefore, a remand of the matter for consideration of this as well as the previously discussed due process issues is required.

VII

The order of the district court will be vacated and the case remanded for action consistent with this opinion.

■ SEITZ, CIRCUIT JUDGE, dissenting.

I read the majority opinion to hold that based on their inherent power and perhaps also on rights bestowed by the last sentence of Fed.R.Civ.P. 83,[1] district courts have the power, subject to certain equities, to assess jury costs against counsel when counsel settle a case on the eve of a jury trial. Although some of my colleagues attack this holding, my disagreement with the majority does not rest on a dispute as to the existence of the power of the district courts to act with respect to such subject matter. Rather, I am convinced that given the subject matter involved, the inherent power or the last sentence of Rule 83 cannot be employed by the district courts on an ad hoc basis.

In approaching the resolution of the present issue, it should be emphasized, as Justice Powell noted in Roadway Express, Inc. v. Piper, 447 U.S. 752, 764, 100 S.Ct. 2455, 2463, 65 L.Ed.2d 488 (1980): "[b]ecause inherent powers are shielded from direct democratic controls, they must be exercised with restraint and discretion." That caveat is particularly applicable here because the practice of last minute settlements which triggers these proceedings has not been thought by members of the bar to be reprehensible or otherwise impermissible. On the contrary, I take judicial notice that settling on the eve of trial has frequently been a "way of life" in the practice of law in this country for innumerable years. Indeed, such settlements were often thought to be in a client's best interests.

1. "In all cases not provided for by rule, the district courts may regulate their practice in any manner not inconsistent with these rules." See Link v. Wabash Railroad Co., 370 U.S. 626, 633, n. 8, 82 S.Ct. 1386, 1390 n. 8, 8 L.Ed.2d 734 (1962).

Given the long held understanding of the bar in this area, I believe fundamental fairness dictates that before an attorney may be subjected to the sanctions here implicated, he or she must be on notice, either actual or constructive, that such conduct may result in sanctions. This notice may take many forms. Certainly a local rule or some equivalent would be sufficient to put the practicing bar on notice that the particular practice may result in an assessment of jury fees. The record is barren of any such prior notice here.

This court has long recognized its inherent supervisory power to regulate significant procedural matters in the district courts. See Johnson v. Trueblood, 629 F.2d 302 (3d Cir.1980), *cert. denied,* 450 U.S. 999, 101 S.Ct. 1704, 68 L.Ed.2d 200 (1981) (invoking supervisory power to require notice and a hearing before district court may revoke attorney's pro hac vice status). Thus, due process implications apart, I believe that we should decide under our supervisory power that fairness dictates that if district courts desire under their inherent or other power to impose sanctions in connection with "late" settlement of scheduled jury trials, they must provide some form of advance notice to the bar by rule, or otherwise, that sanctions may attach for an eve of trial settlement in jury trials.[2] *See* In re United Corp., 283 F.2d 593 (3d Cir.1960) (appellate tribunal may reverse action of district court made pursuant to last sentence of Rule 83 if action is arbitrary or fundamentally unfair).

I do not wish my position here to be construed as any disagreement with the worthy objectives of saving the time of judicial personnel and preventing expense to the government arising from the payment of juror fees unnecessarily incurred. My position is based on principles of basic fairness. Notice of changes in the rules of the game should be conveyed to the players before the game is played.

I regard as a fundamental flaw the absence of prior notice that a sanction could flow from the particular conduct here involved. I would therefore not remand this case for a hearing and decision based on an after-the-fact notice. Rather, I would reverse the order of the district court.

■ Sloviter, Circuit Judge, with whom Judges Gibbons and Higginbotham join, dissenting.

* * *

NOTES: LIMITATIONS ON THE POWER TO SANCTION

A.   Roadway Express, Inc. v. Piper, 447 U.S. 752, 100 S.Ct. 2455, 65 L.Ed.2d 488 (1980), was a civil rights action alleging racial discrimination. The district court found plaintiffs' lawyers guilty of "deliberate inaction" in prosecuting the case and imposed, as a sanction, the attorneys' fees incurred by defendant. In the course of a careful review of various asserted sources of power, the Supreme Court upheld

---

2. I note that within our circuit, the district courts of Delaware and New Jersey have chosen to promulgate local rules to establish the type of sanction at issue here. *See* D.Del.R. 5.5(D); D.N.J.Gen.R. 20(G).

reliance on inherent power on the following analysis and with the following limitation: "If a court may tax counsel fees against a party who has litigated in bad faith, it certainly may assess those expenses against counsel who willfully abuse the judicial process * * *. Like other sanctions, attorney's fees certainly should not be assessed lightly or without fair notice and an opportunity for a hearing on the record. But in a proper case, such sanctions are within a court's powers."

B. Accepting the suggestion of the court in *Eash,* the Western District of Pennsylvania amended its local rules to include the following subsection of Rule 5:

IV. ASSESSING JURY COSTS FOR LATE SETTLEMENTS IN CIVIL CASES. Whenever the court finds, after 10 days notice and a reasonable opportunity to be heard, that any party or lawyer in any civil case before the court has acted in bad faith, abused the judicial process, or has failed to exercise reasonable diligence in effecting the settlement of such case at the earliest practicable time, the court may impose upon such party or lawyer the jury costs, including mileage and per diem, resulting therefrom.

The Court shall issue a rule to show cause and conduct a hearing of record to inquire into the facts prior to imposing any sanction.

Does the failure to exercise reasonable diligence support a finding of bad faith? If a local rule is specific in describing proscribed conduct and explicit in making clear that the conduct may be sanctionable, is a finding of bad faith necessary under *Eash?* See discussion in Levin & Golash, 37 U. of Fla.L.Rev. 29, 51 et seq. (1985).

C. In 1985 F.R.C.P. 83 was amended to eliminate any ambiguity. The last sentence of that rule now reads: "In all cases not provided for by rule, the district judges and magistrates may regulate their practice in any manner not inconsistent with these rules or with those of the district in which they act."

D. Most judges are reluctant to impose sanctions on the attorneys who practice before them. They are particularly reluctant to impose sanctions which reflect the added expense incurred by the taxpayers as a result of wasted judicial resources, whether court time or juror fees.

Two reasons account for this reluctance, the one technical and the other a matter of policy. On the technical level, money paid to the government, even when measured in terms of the resources that have been wasted, "smacks of a fine." Fines are criminal sanctions and may involve procedural safeguards of constitutional dimension. The point was made early on in an influential article by Judge Schwarzer, *Sanctions Under the New Federal Rule 11—A Closer Look,* 104 F.R.D. 181 (1985):

> [In c]riminal contempt proceedings * * * a right to a jury trial exists if the punishment exceeds a fine of $500 or imprisonment of six months. To impose a fine under Rule 11 without extending the procedural protections of criminal contempt proceedings risks reversal on appeal and is inadvisable.

Rule 11 proceedings, however, are civil and not criminal. So are hearings to consider sanctions for discovery abuse. Moreover, we are talking of orders imposing monetary sanctions which, although payable to the clerk of court, are set in an amount intended to compensate the public fisc for loss occasioned by the misconduct of the sanctioned party. It thus becomes particularly important to explore the underlying policy considerations. In Zambrano v. City of Tustin, 885 F.2d 1473 (9th Cir.1989), the court said:

> [W]e think it inappropriate for the court system to claim "compensation" for being "ill-used." The court system is not a private party that needs to be reimbursed for its inconvenience. Consequently, absent grossly negligent, reckless, or willful conduct, monetary penalties such as jury costs or judicial sanctions cannot be fairly levied against counsel for a violation of the local rules.

CHAPTER VI

THE PRETRIAL CONFERENCE

A. THE ROLE OF THE JUDGE IN CASE MANAGEMENT

Peckham, The Federal Judge as a Case Manager: The New Role in Guiding a Case From Filing to Disposition
60 Cal.L.Rev. 70 (1981).

Traditionally, judges have been depicted solely as dispensers of justice, weighing opposing evidence and legal arguments on their finely-calibrated scales to mete out rewards and punishments. Until quite recently the trial judge played virtually no role in a case until counsel for at least one side certified that it was ready for trial. But today's massive volume of litigation and the skyrocketing costs of attorney's fees and other litigation expenses have, by necessity, cast the trial judge in a new role, that of pretrial manager.

Federal district court filings have more than doubled during the last twelve years, and an increasing number of these cases are complex and protracted. In the last decade, the number of trials lasting over thirty days has increased by 344 percent. But in spite of burgeoning caseloads—perhaps because of them—federal courts have become more efficient. In the last twelve years, the median time from filing to disposition has dropped by twenty percent, and in the last year alone the case output per district judge has increased by six percent.

I suggest that it is the judge's new role as case manager that has made this impressive productivity record possible.

I am satisfied that the rise in judicial efficiency is primarily due to more effective use by judges of pretrial management procedures. Most important has been the increasingly widespread use of the early status conference, a device which enables a judge to intervene soon after the filing of a case to schedule all the activity that will occur before trial. Since only about six percent of all cases ever reach trial and more than twice as many cases terminate during pretrial than during or after trial, such pretrial management devices are among the case manager's most important tools.

Many judges will find the new emphasis on pretrial management techniques unfamiliar and uncomfortable. They may feel that their new role as case managers is somewhat less important than their traditional one as dispensers of ultimate justice. But the task is not directed toward efficiency for its own sake. Justice itself requires speedy, smooth, and inexpensive disposition of cases, because "justice delayed may be justice denied or justice mitigated in quality." Misman-agement or nonmanagement of cases can cause considerable delay, leading to uncertainty in business and personal affairs and, often, crushing expense to one or more of the parties.

Most members of the bench and bar agree that at least some pretrial procedures are vital for minimizing delay and expense in litigation and achieving the "just, speedy, and inexpensive determina-tion of every action." By defining the contested issues, mapping out a plan for discovery, forcing the attorneys to prepare themselves, and promoting settlement, pretrial procedures streamline litigation and thereby cut costs and help equalize the financial positions of the parties.

Resnik, Managerial Judges
96 Harv.L.Rev. 374 (1982).

The By-products of Judicial Management: The Erosion of Traditional Due Process Safeguards

In the rush to conquer case loads, few proponents of managerial judging have examined its side effects. Judicial management has its own techniques, goals, and values, which appear to elevate speed over deliberation, impartiality, and fairness. Ironically, the growth of federal judges' interest in management has coincided with their articulation of due process values, their emphasis on the relationship between proce-dure and just decisionmaking.

1. Vast New Powers.—Judges are very powerful: they decide contested issues, and they alone can compel obedience by the threat of contempt. As a result, those subject to judges' authority may challenge it only at great risk. Under the individual calendar system, a single judge retains control over all phases of a case. Thus, litigants who incur a judge's displeasure may suffer judicial hostility or even vengeance with little hope of relief.

Transforming the judge from adjudicator to manager substantially expands the opportunities for judges to use—or abuse—their power. In designing the pretrial schedule in *Paulson,* for example, Judge Kinser did not adjudicate a "case or controversy." Instead, he issued a series of directives before the parties had raised problems or asked for his help. Dissatisfied, the parties tried to convince him to change his procedural blueprint, but they knew that the decisions were ultimately Judge Kinser's alone. In an effort to induce settlement, the judge held separate meetings with the parties, challenged their arguments, and proposed specific settlement figures. Although he could not dictate a compromise, Judge Kinser made full use of his position to convince the parties to capitulate.

In addition to enhancing the power of judges, management tends to undermine traditional constraints on the use of that power. Judge Kinser created rules for the lawsuit, such as discovery timetables, but was not forced to submit his ideas to the discipline of a written justification or to outside scrutiny. His decisions were made privately, informally, off the record, and beyond the reach of appellate review.

Further, no explicit norms or standards guide judges in their decisions about what to demand of litigants. What does "good," "skilled," or "judicious" management entail? Judge Kinser hoped to speed pretrial preparation, because he thought quick preparation was better than slow preparation. Yet he had no guidelines, other than his own intuition, to inform him what was too slow or too fast. Judge Kinser wanted the parties to settle, because he believed that whatever outcomes settlement produced would be better—and less expensive—than those litigation could achieve. But how was he to determine, for the litigants and for the system as a whole, what was "better" or less "expensive"?

* * *

2. The Threat to Impartiality.—Privacy and informality have some genuine advantages; attorneys and judges can discuss discovery schedules and explore settlement proposals without the constraints of the formal courtroom environment. But substantial dangers also inhere in such activities. The extensive information that judges receive during pretrial conferences has not been filtered by the rules of evidence. Some of this information is received ex parte, a process that deprives the opposing party of the opportunity to contest the validity of information received. Moreover, judges are in close contact with attorneys during the course of management. Such interactions may become occasions for the development of intense feelings—admiration, friendship, or antipathy. Therefore, management becomes a fertile field for the growth of personal bias.

Further, judges with supervisory obligations may gain stakes in the cases they manage. Their prestige may ride on "efficient" management, as calculated by the speed and number of dispositions. Competition and peer pressure may tempt judges to rush litigants because of reasons unrelated to the merits of disputes. For example, Judge Kinser had interests of his own when he was advising settlement: he wanted *Paulson* off his calendar.

Unreviewable power, casual contact, and interest in outcome (or in aggregate outcomes) have not traditionally been associated with the "due process" decisionmaking model. These features do not evoke images of reasoned adjudication, images that form the very basis of both our faith in the judicial process and our enormous grant of power to federal judges. The literature of managerial judging refers only occasionally to the values of due process: the accuracy of decisionmaking, the adequacy of reasoning, and the quality of adjudication. Instead, commentators and the training sessions for district judges emphasize speed, control, and quantity. District court chief judges boast of vast statistics on the number of cases terminated, the number and type of discrete events (such as trial days and oral arguments) supervised, and the number of motions decided. The accumulation of such data may cause—or reflect—a subtle shift in the values that shape the judiciary's comprehension of its own mission. Case processing is no longer viewed as a means to an end; instead, it appears to have become the desired goal. Quantity has become all important; quality is occasionally mentioned and then ignored. Indeed, some commentators regard deliberation as an obstacle to efficiency.

Proponents of management may be forgetting the quintessential judicial obligations of conducting a reasoned inquiry, articulating the reasons for decision, and subjecting those reasons to appellate review—characteristics that have long defined judging and distinguished it from other tasks. Although the sword remains in place, the blindfold and scales have all but disappeared.

NOTE: FEDERAL RULE OF CIVIL PROCEDURE 16

A. The 1983 Amendments

In 1983 Rule 16 was re-titled and completely redrafted so that it dealt not only with the pretrial conference but also with scheduling of litigation and with case management.

The Civil Justice Improvements Act of 1990, 28 U.S.C. § 473(a)(2) further emphasized the importance of judicial management by suggesting "early and ongoing control of the pretrial process through involvement of a judicial officer in (A) assessing and planning the progress of a case * * * "

On December 1, 1993, FRCP Rule 16 was again amended. Rule 16(b) now provides that the court's initial scheduling order shall issue within 90 days after the defendant appears in the action (defendants appear either by answering the complaint or making a motion under Rule 12) or, if earlier, within 120 days after service of the complaint on a defendant.

Rule 16(c) was amended to set fourth certain additional subjects that may be considered at a pretrial conference, including presentation of evidence and various ways of structuring the trial. Rule 16(c)(9) makes specific reference to settlements and also invites attention to the possible use of "special procedures to assist in resolving the dispute when authorized by statute or local rule." Rule 16(f) contains a by now familiar provision relating to sanctions

For further discussion of the 1993 Amendments to Rule 16 see the Civil Advisory Committee Notes.

Executive Order 12988, Civil Justice Reform, February 5, 1996

By the authority vested in me as President by the Constitution and the laws of the United States of America, including section 301 of title 3, United States Code, and in order to improve access to justice for all persons who wish to avail themselves of court and administrative adjudicatory tribunals to resolve disputes, to facilitate the just and efficient resolution of civil claims involving the United States Government, to encourage the filing of only meritorious civil claims, to improve legislative and regulatory drafting to reduce needless litigation, to promote fair and prompt adjudication before administrative tribunals, and to provide a model for similar reforms of litigation practices in the private sector and in various states, it is hereby ordered as follows:

Section 1. Guidelines to Promote Just and Efficient Government Civil Litigation. To promote the just and efficient resolution of civil claims, those Federal agencies and litigation counsel that conduct or otherwise participate in civil litigation on behalf of the United States Government in Federal court shall respect and adhere to the following guidelines during the conduct of such litigation:* * *

(b) Settlement Conferences. As soon as practicable after ascertaining the nature of a dispute in litigation, and throughout the litigation, litigation counsel shall evaluate settlement possibilities and make reasonable efforts to settle the litigation. Such efforts shall include offering to participate in a settlement conference or moving the court for a conference pursuant to Rule 16 of the Federal Rules of Civil Procedure in an attempt to resolve the dispute without additional civil litigation.

* * *

Magistrate Judges handle most of the pretrial motions, discovery proceedings, and prisoners' civil rights petitions. A good analysis of FRCP 72 on the empowerment of the magistrate judges is in the 1996 pocket part to Volume 12 § 3076.1 (History and Purpose) of Wright, Miller, and Elliot, Federal Practice and Procedure. Note also that a full scale trial may be conducted by a magistrate judge with the consent of the parties under FRCP 73(b).

One may appropriately ask whether Rule 16 is designed to improve the quality or efficiency of a forthcoming trial or to induce the parties to accept a substitute. Is it appropriate to put the question in this either-or fashion, or might the rule have been designed to accomplish both, perhaps in the alternative?

Much of the material that follows is relevant to a consideration of the relationship between the twin problems of cost and delay in litigation and the role of the court in settlements and in facilitating resort to alternative mechanisms of dispute resolution, commonly known as A.D.R.

In a valuable and comprehensive article by Judge Charles R. Richey, the author suggests the following additional use of the pre-trial conference:

> * * * in my view, the Rule offers a means of addressing—albeit certainly not solving—one of the chronic problems facing litigators: the judge who simply will not decide a case. One of the virtues of Rule 16 is that it provides a legitimate means of getting the court's attention—of asking for the court's time—in order to address the progress of a lawsuit. Obviously, one insurmountable obstacle to any lawsuit is a judge's refusal (or inability) to decide an issue in the action, whether the issue is dispositive or otherwise. Of course, the problem need not arise from a judge's intransigence—in an era of 200 to 300—case dockets, it is a simple fact of life that some cases and motions fall through the cracks.

Richey, Rule 16: A Survey and Some Considerations for the Bench and Bar, 126 F.R.D. 599, 615–616 (1989).

B. THE ROLE OF THE JUDGE IN SETTLEMENTS

Provine, Settlement Strategies for Federal District Judges
(Federal Judicial Center 1986).

FOREWORD

A. Leo Levin

Trial judges are making greater efforts to promote settlements than ever before. These efforts, one aspect of increased involvement in the pretrial process, reflect judicial concern over the growing number of lawsuits, escalating costs, and increasingly complex claims and defenses.

Scheduling a firm date for trial has long been viewed as one of the most effective techniques for promoting settlements. Scheduling to establish a deadline for completion of discovery is important in making a trial date credible. Together, these procedures go far toward assuring a measure of both dispatch and economy, and to some extent they have been cast as requirements by recent amendments to the federal rules. These same amendments explicitly invite more direct judicial involvement in the settlement process. Neither the rules nor the notes of the Advisory Committee provide detailed guidance concerning what steps judges should take to encourage settlement, nor could they; what is appropriate in one situation may be totally inappropriate in another. More basically, there is less information and more controversy about the steps judges should take to facilitate settlement. That is the subject of this report, prepared by Marie Provine during her tenure as a judicial fellow in the Research Division of the Federal Judicial Center.

Judicial intervention to promote settlement casts the trial judge in a delicate role. Many lawyers desire more assistance from judges in removing psychological and informational barriers that stand in the way of settlement, but they do not want to lose control over their lawsuits or forgo their rights to proceed to trial. To serve the interests of the parties effectively, the judge must alter the relationship between the disputants so as to encourage—but not coerce—an early settlement. To serve the interests of the court, and indirectly the interests of the public, the judge must not spend more of the court's time than is warranted by the savings in trial time and litigation costs.

Trial judges across the United States are exploring and developing a variety of approaches to settlement. Judges are selecting cases for summary jury trial, for mediation, and in some situations for court-annexed arbitration, and they are hosting settlement conferences where they try out other ideas designed to encourage settlement. Most judges do not embrace a single approach to be applied in all circumstances—rather, there is a variation in methods selected depending on the judge's assessment of the critical elements of the case, the prior and continuing relationships of the parties, and the roles of the lawyers.

Professor Provine's report is based on insights provided by the burgeoning literature in this field, interviews with many of the leading judicial exponents of giving settlement effort a more central role in case processing, and, ultimately, a conference at which twenty of these leaders discussed the subject in terms ranging from abstract values to concrete hypothetical cases. Drawing on all these sources, she sorts through the settlement-oriented options available to judges, describing their premises, methods, and applications. Consideration is given to the timing of intervention and its intensity, to the degree of client participation, and to formality.

The author's objective has been to provide judges with a framework in which to consider alternative techniques for settlement and to identify those they find both congenial and appropriate so that, if they so choose, they may organize and plan comprehensive, cost-effective, and satisfying settlement strategies.

Heileman Brewing Co., Inc. v. Joseph Oat Corp.

United States Court of Appeals, Seventh Circuit, 1989.
871 F.2d 648.

■ Before BAUER, CHIEF JUDGE, CUMMINGS, WOOD, JR., CUDAHY, POSNER, COFFEY, FLAUM, EASTERBROOK, RIPPLE, MANION and KANNE, CIRCUIT JUDGES.

■ KANNE, CIRCUIT JUDGE.

May a federal district court order litigants—even those represented by counsel—to appear before it in person at a pretrial conference for the purpose of discussing the posture and settlement of the litigants' case? After reviewing the Federal Rules of Civil Procedure and federal district courts' inherent authority to manage and control the litigation before them, we answer this question in the affirmative and conclude that a district court may sanction a litigant for failing to comply with such an order.

I. BACKGROUND

A federal magistrate ordered Joseph Oat Corporation to send a "corporate representative with authority to settle" to a pretrial conference to discuss disputed factual and legal issues and the possibility of settlement. Although counsel for Oat Corporation appeared, accompanied by another attorney who was authorized to speak on behalf of the principals of the corporation, no principal or corporate representative personally attended the conference. The court determined that the failure of Oat Corporation to send a principal of the corporation to the pretrial conference violated its order. Consequently, the district court imposed a sanction of $5,860.01 upon Oat Corporation pursuant to Federal Rule of Civil Procedure 16(f). This amount represented the costs and attorneys' fees of the opposing parties attending the conference.

II. THE APPEAL

Oat Corporation appeals, claiming that the district court did not have the authority to order litigants represented by counsel to appear at the pretrial settlement conference. Specifically, Oat Corporation contends that, by negative implication, the language of Rule 16(a)(5) prohibits a district court from directing represented litigants to attend pretrial conferences. That is, because Rule 16 expressly refers to "attorneys for the parties and any unrepresented parties" in introductory paragraph (a), a district court may not go beyond that language to devise procedures which direct the pretrial appearance of parties represented by counsel. Consequently, Oat Corporation concludes that the court lacked the authority to order the pretrial attendance of its corporate representatives and, even if the court possessed such authority, the court abused its discretion to exercise that power in this case. Finally, Oat Corporation argues that the court abused its discretion to enter sanctions.

A. *Authority to Order Attendance*

First, we must address Oat Corporation's contention that a federal district court lacks the authority to order litigants who are represented by counsel to appear at a pretrial conference. Our analysis requires us to review the Federal Rules of Civil Procedure and district courts' inherent authority to manage the progress of litigation.

Rule 16 addresses the use of pretrial conferences to formulate and narrow issues for trial as well as to discuss means for dispensing with the need for costly and unnecessary litigation.

* * *

The pretrial settlement of litigation has been advocated and used as a means to alleviate overcrowded dockets, and courts have practiced numerous and varied types of pretrial settlement techniques for many years. *See, e.g.,* Manual for Complex Litigation 2d, §§ 21.1–21.4 (1985); Federal Judicial Center, Settlement Strategies for Federal District Judges (1988); Federal Judicial Center, The Judge's Role in the Settlement of Civil Suits (1977) (presented at a seminar for newly-appointed judges); Federal Judicial Center, The Role of the Judge in the Settlement Process (1977). Since 1983, Rule 16 has expressly provided that settlement of a case is one of several subjects which should be pursued and discussed vigorously during pretrial conferences.

The language of Rule 16 does not give any direction to the district court upon the issue of a court's authority to order litigants who are represented by counsel to appear for pretrial proceedings. Instead, Rule 16 merely refers to the participation of trial advocates—attorneys of record and *pro se* litigants. However, the Federal Rules of Civil Procedure do not completely describe and limit the power of the federal courts. * * * This authority likewise forms the basis for continued development of procedural techniques designed to make the operation of the court more efficient, to preserve the integrity of the judicial process, and to control courts' dockets.[4] Because the rules form and shape certain aspects of a court's inherent powers, yet allow the continued exercise of that power where discretion should be available, the mere absence of language in the federal rules specifically authorizing or describing a particular judicial procedure should not, and does not, give rise to a negative implication of prohibition. * * *

---

4. * * *

The practice of some district judges requiring represented parties to appear in person (or by corporate representative) has been part and parcel of such settlement conferences for many years. *See In re LaMarre,* 494 F.2d 753, 756 (6th Cir.1974) (court stating that it is well within the scope of a district court's authority to compel the appearance of a party's insurer at a pretrial conference and to enforce the order).

Obviously, the district court, in devising means to control cases before it, may not exercise its inherent authority in a manner inconsistent with rule or statute. * * * This means that "where the rules directly mandate a specific procedure *to the exclusion of others,* inherent authority is proscribed." Landau & Cleary, Ltd. v. Hribar Trucking, Inc., 867 F.2d 996, 1002 (7th Cir.1989) (emphasis added).

In this case, we are required to determine whether a court's power to order the pretrial appearance of litigants who are represented by counsel is inconsistent with, or in derogation of, Rule 16.

* * *

The wording of the rule and the accompanying commentary make plain that the entire thrust of the amendment to Rule 16 was to urge judges to make wider use of their powers and to manage actively their dockets from an early stage. We therefore conclude that our interpretation of Rule 16 to allow district courts to order represented parties to appear at pretrial settlement conferences merely represents another application of a district judge's inherent authority to preserve the efficiency, and more importantly the integrity, of the judicial process.

To summarize, we simply hold that the action taken by the district court in this case constituted the proper use of inherent authority to aid in accomplishing the purpose and intent of Rule 16. We reaffirm the notion that the inherent power of a district judge—derived from the very nature and existence of his judicial office—is the broad field over which the Federal Rules of Civil Procedure are applied. Inherent authority remains the means by which district judges deal with circumstances not proscribed or specifically addressed by rule or statute, but which must be addressed to promote the just, speedy, and inexpensive determination of every action.

B.   *Exercise of Authority to Order Attendance*

Having determined that the district court possessed the power and authority to order the represented litigants to appear at the pretrial settlement conference, we now must examine whether the court abused its discretion to issue such an order.

At the outset, it is important to note that a district court cannot coerce settlement. Kothe v. Smith, 771 F.2d 667, 669 (2d Cir.1985).[8] In this case, considerable concern has been generated because the court ordered "corporate representatives with authority to settle" to attend the conference. In our view, "authority to settle," when used in the context of this case, means that the "corporate representative" attending the pretrial conference was required to hold a position within the corporate entity allowing him to speak definitively and to commit the corporation to a particular position in the litigation. We do

---

8. Likewise, a court cannot compel parties to stipulate to facts. J.F. Edwards Constr. Co. v. Anderson Safeway Guard Rail Corp., 542 F.2d 1318 (7th Cir.1976) (per curiam). Nor can a court compel litigants to participate in a non-binding summary jury trial. *Strandell,* 838 F.2d at 887. In the same vein, a court cannot force a party to engage in discovery. Identiseal Corp. v. Positive Identification Sys., Inc., 560 F.2d 298 (7th Cir.1977).

not view "authority to settle" as a requirement that corporate representatives must come to court willing to settle on someone else's terms, but only that they come to court in order to consider the possibility of settlement.

* * *

If this case represented a situation where Oat Corporation had sent a corporate representative and was sanctioned because that person refused to make an offer to pay money—that is, refused to submit to settlement coercion—we would be faced with a decidedly different issue—a situation we would not countenance.

The Advisory Committee Notes to Rule 16 state that "[a]lthough it is not the purpose of Rule 16(b)(7) to impose settlement negotiations on unwilling litigants, it is believed that providing a neutral forum for discussing [settlement] might foster it." Fed.R.Civ.P. 16 advisory committee's note, subdivision (c) (1983). These Notes clearly draw a distinction between being required to attend a settlement conference and being required to participate in settlement negotiations. Thus, under the scheme of pretrial settlement conferences, the corporate representative remains free, on behalf of the corporate entity, to propose terms of settlement independently—but he may be required to state those terms in a pretrial conference before a judge or magistrate.

As an alternative position, Oat Corporation argues that the court abused its discretion to order corporate representatives of the litigants to attend the pretrial settlement conference * * * because its business was a "going concern" * * *.

This litigation involved a claim for $4 million—a claim which turned upon the resolution of complex factual and legal issues.[9] The litigants expected the trial to last from one to three months and all parties stood to incur substantial legal fees and trial expenses. This trial also would have preempted a large segment of judicial time—not an insignificant factor. Thus, because the stakes were high, we do not believe that the burden of requiring a corporate representative to attend a pretrial settlement conference was out of proportion to the benefits to be gained, not only by the litigants but also by the court.

---

9. G. Heileman Brewing Company hired RME Associates, Inc., a consulting firm, to build a waste water treatment plant at Heileman's brewery in LaCrosse, Wisconsin. Subsequently, RME entered into a contract with Joseph Oat Corporation whereby Oat Corporation agreed to design, engineer, construct and test the system. Oat Corporation was the exclusive licensee in the United States for the system's developer, N.V. Centrale Suicker Maatschappij (CSM), a Dutch corporation.

A contract dispute arose between Oat Corporation, Heileman, and RME involving the malfunctioning of the waste water treatment system. In December, 1982, Oat Corporation initiated federal diversity litigation against Heileman and RME in New Jersey. RME counterclaimed. The case was transferred to the court below. RME then joined CSM as a third-party defendant. On the same day, Heileman filed an action in Wisconsin state court against Oat Corporation and RME. RME cross-claimed against Oat Corporation and counter-claimed against Heileman.

In the early phase of trial preparation, Heileman and Oat Corporation agreed to withdraw all claims between them. In addition, Oat Corporation dismissed its complaint against RME. After these events, the lawsuit consisted of RME's claims against Oat Corporation and CSM.

Additionally, the corporation did send an attorney, Mr. Fitzpatrick, from Philadelphia, Pennsylvania to Madison, Wisconsin to "speak for" the principals of the corporation. It is difficult to see how the expenses involved in sending Mr. Fitzpatrick from Philadelphia to Madison would have greatly exceeded the expenses involved in sending a corporate representative from Camden to Madison. Consequently, we do not think the expenses and distance to be traveled are unreasonable in this case.

Furthermore, no objection to the magistrate's order was made prior to the date the pretrial conference resumed. Oat Corporation contacted the magistrate's office concerning the order's requirements and was advised of the requirements now at issue. However, Oat Corporation never objected to its terms, either when it was issued or when Oat Corporation sought clarification. Consequently, Oat Corporation was left with only one course of action: it had to comply fully with the letter *and* intent of the order and argue about its reasonableness later.

We thus conclude that the court did not abuse its authority and discretion to order a representative of the Oat Corporation to appear for the pretrial settlement conference on December 19.

C.   *Sanctions*

Finally, we must determine whether the court abused its discretion by sanctioning Oat Corporation for failing to comply with the order to appear at the pretrial settlement conference. Oat Corporation argues that the instructions directing the appearance of corporate representatives were unclear and ambiguous. Consequently, it concludes that the sanctions were improper.

Absent an abuse of discretion, we may not disturb a district court's imposition of sanctions for failure of a party to comply with a pretrial order. The issue on review is not whether we would have imposed these costs upon Oat Corporation, but whether the district court abused its discretion in doing so. National Hockey League v. Metropolitan Hockey Club, Inc., 427 U.S. 639, 642, 96 S.Ct. 2778, 2780, 49 L.Ed.2d 747 (1976) (citations omitted).

Oat Corporation contends that the presence of Mr. Fitzpatrick, as an attorney authorized to speak on behalf of the principals of Oat Corporation, satisfied the requirement that its "corporate representative" attend the December 19 settlement conference. Oat Corporation argues that nothing in either the November 19, 1984 order or the December 14, 1984 order would lead a reasonable person to conclude that a representative or principal from the Joseph Oat Corporation was required to attend the conference personally—in effect arguing that sanctions cannot be imposed because the order failed to require a particular person to attend the conference.

We believe that Oat Corporation was well aware of what the court expected. While the November order may have been somewhat ambiguous, any ambiguity was eliminated by the magistrate's remarks from the bench on December 14, the written order of December 18, and the direction obtained by counsel from the magistrate's clerk.

On December 14, in the presence of Oat Corporation's attorney of record and all those in the courtroom, the magistrate announced that the pretrial conference had been impaired because Oat Corporation[12] had not complied with Paragraph 5(c) of the November order requiring it to send to the conference a corporate representative.[13] The magistrate clearly stated that the order's purpose was to insure the presence of the parties personally at the conference. From that moment on, Oat Corporation had notice that it was ordered to send a corporate representative to the resumed conference. Moreover, prior to the December 19 conference, Oat Corporation's counsel contacted the magistrate's office to determine if the magistrate really intended for corporate representatives to be in Madison, Wisconsin, for the settlement conference. Counsel was assured that such was the case.

When the conference resumed on December 19, Mr. Possi was present acting in his capacity as Oat Corporation's attorney of record. Mr. Fitzpatrick, who was not an attorney of record in the case, asserted that he was directed to attend the conference and speak on behalf of Oat Corporation's principals.[14] Mr. Fitzpatrick also stated that he interpreted the November order not as requiring the presence of a principal of Oat Corporation at the conference scheduled for December 14, but as requiring the presence of the insurance carriers with authority to discuss settlement.

12. Except for the Oat Corporation, all the parties complied, sending their counsel and corporate representatives to the pretrial conference (a principal of CSM was standing by a telephone in the Netherlands). The Oat Corporation was represented by his [sic] attorney of record, John Possi. In addition, the Oat Corporation's liability insurance carrier, National Union Fire Insurance Company, was represented by an adjuster.

13. In pertinent part, the order stated:

5. A settlement conference, which shall include the Heileman Brewing Company, shall be held herein on December 14, 1984 at 2:00 p.m. * * *

In addition to counsel, each party shall be represented at the conference by a representative having full authority to settle the case * * *.

(Order of Nov. 19, 1984).

14. On December 19, the following dialogue took place between the magistrate and Mr. Fitzpatrick:

THE COURT: I made it clear on December 14th, that for purposes of this conference * * * that each party in addition to be [sic] represented by counsel would have present the party itself for purposes of authorizing or discussing settlement in this case, speaking specifically about the order which is dated December 18th but was entered I think clearly enough on the 14th. That in addition to counsel, each party * * * shall be represented at the conference in person by a representative having full authority to settle the case or make decisions relevant to all matters reasonably anticipated to come before the conference * * *.

As a matter of fact, Mr. Possi called yesterday to find out from my secretary if that is what I really meant * * * he was informed that it is what I really meant; and I would like to have your explanation as to why no one from Joseph Oat is here from [sic] that authority.

MR. FITZPATRICK: I am here as a representative of Joseph Oat which I understood your order to be. I have discussed this thing thoroughly with the principals of Joseph Oat. They directed me to come to the conference. They directed me that I could speak for them, with authority to speak for them. Their direction was I should make no offer to settle the case. That is their position. That is the position they choose to take and they designated me as the representative to communicate that to the Court.

(Transcript of Dec. 19, 1984).

The distinction is clearly drawn between an attorney representing a corporation and a corporate representative. As we define in this opinion—consistent with the meaning given by the magistrate—a corporate representative is a person holding "a position with the corporate entity." Although Mr. Fitzpatrick was representing the corporate principals and Mr. Possi the corporation, no corporate representative attended as required by the magistrate's order. We therefore conclude that the court properly sanctioned Oat Corporation pursuant to Rule 16(f) for failing to send a corporate representative to the settlement conference.

III. CONCLUSION

We hold that Rule 16 does not limit, but rather is enhanced by, the inherent authority of federal courts to order litigants represented by counsel to attend pretrial conferences for the purpose of discussing settlement. Oat Corporation violated the district court's order requiring it to have a corporate representative attend the pretrial settlement conference on December 19, 1984. Under these circumstances, the district court did not abuse its discretion by imposing sanctions for Oat Corporation's failure to comply with the pretrial order. The judgment of the district court is hereby AFFIRMED.

EASTERBROOK, CIRCUIT JUDGE, with whom POSNER, COFFEY and MANION, CIRCUIT JUDGES, join, dissenting.

Our case has three logically separate issues. First, whether a district court may demand the attendance of someone other than the party's counsel of record. Second, whether the court may insist that this additional person be an employee rather than an agent selected for the occasion. Third, whether the court may insist that the representative have "full settlement authority"—meaning the authority to agree to pay cash in settlement (maybe authority without cap, although that was not clear). Even if one resolves the first issue as the majority does, it does not follow that district courts have the second or third powers, or that their exercise here was prudent.

The proposition that a magistrate may require a firm to send an employee rather than a representative is puzzling. Corporate "employees" are simply agents of the firm. Corporations choose their agents and decide what powers to give them. Which agents have which powers is a matter of internal corporate affairs. Joseph Oat Corp. sent to the conference not only its counsel of record but also John Fitzpatrick, who had authority to speak for Oat. Now Mr. Fitzpatrick is an attorney, which raised the magistrate's hackles, but why should this count against him? Because Fitzpatrick is a part-time rather than a full-time agent of the corporation? Why can't the corporation make its own decision about how much of the agent's time to hire? Is Oat being held in contempt because it is too small to have a cadre of legal employees—because its general counsel practices with a law firm rather than being "in house"?

At all events, the use of outside attorneys as negotiators is common. Many a firm sends its labor lawyer to the bargaining table when a collective bargaining agreement is about to expire, there to dicker with the union (or with labor's lawyer). Each side has a statutory right to choose its representatives. 29 U.S.C. § 158(b)(1)(B). Many a firm sends its corporate counsel to the bargaining table when a merger is under discussion. See Ronald J. Gilson, Value Creation by Business Lawyers: Legal Skills and Asset Pricing, 94 Yale L.J. 239 (1984). Oat did the same thing to explore settlement of litigation. A lawyer is no less suited to this task than to negotiating the terms of collective bargaining or merger agreements. Firms prefer to send skilled negotiators to negotiating sessions (lawyers are especially useful when the value of a claim depends on the resolution of legal questions) while reserving the time of executives for business. Oat understandably wanted its management team to conduct its construction business.

As for the third subject, whether the representative must have "settlement authority": the magistrate's only reason for ordering a corporate representative to come was to facilitate settlement then and there. As I understand Magistrate Groh's opinion, and Judge Crabb's, the directive was to send a person with "full settlement authority". Fitzpatrick was deemed inadequate only because he was under instructions not to pay money. E.g.: "While Mr. Fitzpatrick claimed authority to speak for Oat, he stated that he had no authority to make a [monetary] offer. *Thus,* no representative of Oat or National having authority to settle the case was present at the conference as the order directed" (magistrate's opinion, emphasis added). On learning that Fitzpatrick did not command Oat's treasury, the magistrate ejected him from the conference and never listened to what he had to say on Oat's behalf, never learned whether Fitzpatrick might be receptive to others' proposals. (We know that Oat ultimately did settle the case for money, after it took part in and "prevailed" at a summary jury trial—participation and payment each demonstrating Oat's willingness to consider settlement.) The magistrate's approach implies that if the Chairman and CEO of Oat had arrived with instructions from the Board to settle the case without paying cash, and to negotiate and bring back for the Board's consideration any financial proposals, Oat still would have been in contempt.

Both magistrate and judge demanded the presence not of a "corporate representative" in the sense of a full-time employee but of a representative with "full authority to settle". Most corporations reserve power to *agree* (as opposed to power to discuss) to senior managers or to their boards of directors—the difference depending on the amounts involved. Heileman wanted $4 million, a sum within the province of the board rather than a single executive even for firms much larger than Oat. Fitzpatrick came with power to *discuss* and *recommend;* he could settle the case on terms other than cash; he lacked only power to sign a check. The magistrate's order therefore must have required either (a) changing the allocation of responsibility within the corporation, or (b) sending a quorum of Oat's Board.

Magistrate Groh exercised a power unknown even in labor law, where there is a duty to bargain in good faith. 29 U.S.C. § 158(d). Labor and management commonly negotiate through persons with the authority to discuss but not agree. The negotiators report back to management and the union, each of which reserves power to reject or approve the position of its agent. We know from Fed.R.Civ.P. 16—and especially from the Advisory Committee's comment to Rule 16(c) that the Rule's "reference to 'authority' is not intended to insist upon the ability to settle the litigation"—that the parties cannot be compelled to negotiate "in good faith". A defendant convinced it did no wrong may insist on total vindication. See Hess v. New Jersey Transit Rail Operations, Inc., 846 F.2d 114 (2d Cir.1988), and Kothe v. Smith, 771 F.2d 667 (2d Cir.1985), holding that a judge may not compel a party to make a settlement offer, let alone to accept one. Rule 68, which requires a party who turns down a settlement proposal to bear costs only if that party does worse at trial, implies the same thing. Yet if parties are not obliged to negotiate in good faith, on what ground can they be obliged to come with authority to settle on the spot—an authority agents need not carry even when the law requires negotiation? The order we affirm today compels persons who have committed no wrong, who pass every requirement of Rules 11 and 68, who want only the opportunity to receive a decision on the merits, to come to court with open checkbooks on pain of being held in contempt.

* * *

The majority does not discuss these problems. Its approach implies, however, that trial courts may insist that representatives have greater authority than labor negotiators bring to the table. And to create this greater authority, Oat Corp. might have to rearrange its internal structure—perhaps delegating to an agent a power state law reserves to the board of directors. Problems concerning the reallocation of authority are ubiquitous. For example, only the Assistant Attorney General for the Civil Division has authority to approve settlements of civil cases, and his authority reaches only to $750,000; above that the Deputy Attorney General must approve. 28 C.F.R. §§ 0.160(a)(2), 0.161. An attorney for the government, like Fitzpatrick, lacks the authority to commit his client but may negotiate and recommend. Does it follow that, in every federal civil case, a magistrate may require the presence of the Assistant or Deputy Attorney General or insist that they redelegate their authority? If such a demand would be improper for the Department of Justice, is it more proper when made of Joseph Oat Corporation?

These issues will not go away. The magistrate's order was to send a representative *with the authority to bind Oat to pay money.* What is the point of insisting on such authority if not to require the making of offers and the acceptance of "reasonable" counteroffers—that is, to require good faith negotiations and agreements on the spot? Fitzpatrick had the authority to report back to Oat on any suggestions; he had the authority to participate in negotiations. The only thing he lacked—the *only* reason Oat was held in contempt of court—was the ability to sign Oat Corp.'s check in the magistrate's presence. What the magistrate found unacceptable was that Fitzpatrick might say something like "I'll relay that suggestion to the Board of Directors", which might say no. Oat's CEO could have done no more. We close our eyes to reality in pretending that Oat was required only to be present while others "voluntarily" discussed settlement.[a]

Schwartzman v. ACF Industries and the United States of America

United States District Court for the District of New Mexico, 1996.
167 F.R.D. 694.

■ E. L. MECHEM, SENIOR UNITED STATES DISTRICT JUDGE

This matter came on for review of Magistrate Judge DeGiacomo's Memorandum Opinion and Recommendation entered May 22, 1996 recommending that the United States Department of Justice be sanctioned for failing to participate in good faith in the mandatory settlement conference set in this case.

This is an action for damages under the Federal Tort Claims Act alleging negligent disposal of industrial wastes causing soil and water contamination.

On August 17, 1995, Magistrate Judge DeGiacomo mailed to counsel for all parties, including the United States of America, a notice to appear at a mandatory settlement conference on September 26, 1995. The notice indicated that "counsel of record, Plaintiff(s) and Defendant(s), or where appropriate a designated representative, with final and complete settlement authority, must be present, in accordance with Rule 16(f)." (emphasis in original). The notice went on to say: "Any request to excuse a party or trial counsel from attendance at this settlement conference must be presented to the Court in writing." Lastly, the notice mandated that "prior to the conference, counsel are required to confer with one another in a good faith effort to resolve this litigation."

On August 24, 1995, trial counsel for the United States (hereinafter "Trial Counsel") mailed Magistrate Judge DeGiacomo a letter informing him that final settlement authority for the United States lay with Department of Justice officials in Washington, who were unable to attend the conference in person but who would be available by telephone. On September 21, 1995, Trial Counsel sent Magistrate Judge DeGiacomo another letter informing him that certain governmental representatives were also unavailable to attend the conference in person and would be available by telephone. Neither letter was framed as a request, however, Magistrate Judge apparently allowed the exception.

---

a. The dissenting opinions of Judges Posner, Coffey, Ripple, and Martin have been   omitted.

The Magistrate Judge issued another order on January 2, 1996 resetting the conference for Monday, February 26, 1996 at 9:00 a.m. This order reminded all counsel that "parties or personal representatives must have final and complete settlement authority so that no further decision or consultation upon the merits of any aspect of the litigation is required."

More than six weeks later, on the Friday afternoon before the settlement conference, at 4:41 p.m., Trial Counsel faxed Magistrate Judge DeGiacomo a letter indicating that he would be attending the settlement conference with "complete and final settlement authority within my preapproved limits." Trial Counsel now contends that "my purpose in sending this letter was to make clear to the Court that I did not have unlimited settlement authority." Exhibit B to United States' Objections, filed June 6, 1996.

The letter did not promise access to, much less personal participation of, anyone with final and complete settlement authority. Again, the letter was framed as notice, rather than request, and no further provision was made with the Court to ensure participation by the United States consonant with the Court's orders.

Trial Counsel's "pre-approved limits" turned out to be what Trial Counsel himself deemed "nuisance value" for the case. Trial Counsel finally revealed to the Magistrate Judge at the February 26, 1996 settlement conference that he had no authority to negotiate, much less to approve settlement, above what he characterized as "nuisance value".

Magistrate Judge DeGiacomo attempted to secure telephonic participation of Trial Counsel's superior in Washington, to no avail. In frustration, the Magistrate Judge continued the conference until the next day, ordering orally and in writing the personal attendance of a qualified decision-maker for the United States.

Virtually no time or effort was expended at the February 26, 1996 settlement conference in discussion of the prospects for settlement with the United States, even though a sizeable group of lawyers and party representatives had gathered for expressly that purpose. The entirety of the proceedings with the United States was directed to the problem of gaining access to a qualified representative for the purposes of conducting a good-faith settlement conference.

It also became apparent at the conference that no prior consultation had taken place to explore settlement with opposing counsel. The record reflects, and Defendant's own affidavits confirm, that Department of Justice officials conferred among themselves to arrive at their valuation of the case and then sent Trial Counsel as a messenger to the settlement conference to convey that message.

Ultimately the Magistrate Judge set the matter for an evidentiary hearing, at which he concluded that the United States had acted in bad faith, "causing continuous delays and needless expense to all parties to this litigation." The Magistrate Judge found, in effect, that the United States never came to the bargaining table, as it was ordered to do.("The result has been that for all these months the plaintiffs have been standing in line with the Court to buy a ticket on a train that had ceased to run."). Furthermore, the Magistrate Judge found that "the Department of Justice has established [a] policy of sending its attorneys to settlement conferences with limited authority, regardless of the Court's order." "The decisions were made not by [Trial Counsel] but by his superiors who were not before the Court. The settlement process was a mockery."

I agree that the Magistrate Judge was misled and his orders were disregarded. The United States disobeyed the Magistrate Judge's order to send a representative with final and complete authority to the settlement conference or to make advance provision in writing for adequate participation by other means. Counsel for the United States disobeyed the Magistrate Judge's order to confer with opposing counsel in a good-faith effort to resolve the litigation.

Substantial evidence supports a finding that counsel for the United States acted in bad faith, causing continuous delays and needless expense to all parties in the litigation. I further agree that sanctions should be applied against the United States Department of Justice, rather than against Trial Counsel, who was indisputably deprived by his superiors of full authority to pursue settlement. See e.g., In re Novak, 932 F.2d 1397, 1406 (11th Cir.1991) ("such an attorney serves simply as a courier").

II. DISCUSSION

In this appeal, the United States argues, essentially, that the sheer volume of cases involving the federal government precludes them from taking settlement conferences seriously. This is an ironic stance, given (1) that settlement conferences present the best opportunity we have conceived of so far to resolve disputes with dispatch, and (2) that the government's failure to participate properly in this instance has necessitated a much greater investment of Justice Department resources in the case than would otherwise have been required, including the entry of appearance of three additional Justice Department attorneys to represent the United States and Trial Counsel on the matter of sanctions alone, and (3) that there is probably no higher function assigned to the Department of Justice than to represent our country in connection with a claim of injury by one of its citizens.

The United States also argues, equally unconvincingly, that requiring them to send a fully authorized representative to settlement conferences amounts to unfair coercion to settle cases they have no intention of settling. See e.g., Kothe v. Smith, 771 F.2d 667, 669 (2d Cir. 1985) (Rule 16 "was not designed as a means for clubbing the parties—or one of them—into an involuntary compromise."). The United States is mistaken. It is not being reprimanded today for its refusal to settle this case, but for its refusal to come "to the bargaining table." United States' Objections at 23.

The United States' third and most distasteful argument is that this Court lacks the authority to compel participation in a settlement effort, or that the exercise of such authority against the Executive Branch violates the separation of powers doctrine. Again, the United States is mistaken.

This Court possesses at least three sources of power to compel participation in mandatory settlement conferences. First, Rule 16, which was expressly cited by the Magistrate Judge in his first notice to these litigants, was amended in 1993 to clarify and strengthen the authority of federal district courts to compel participation in settlement proceedings. The rule now states bluntly that "if appropriate, the court may require that a party or its representative be present or reasonably available by telephone in order to consider possible settlement of the dispute." Fed.R.Civ.P. 16(c).

The Civil Justice Reform Act of 1990 also authorized district courts to hold mandatory settlement conferences as part of civil justice and delay reduction plans. See 28 U.S.C.§ 473(b)(5). This effort arose out of the conclusion that "settlement conferences are valuable tools for district courts." In re Novak, supra 932 F.2d at 1404.

Third and most important, the district courts have inherent power "to manage their own affairs so as to achieve the orderly and expeditious disposition of cases." Id. at 1406 (quoting Link v. Wabash R.R., 370 U.S. 626, 630–31, 8 L. Ed. 2d 734, 82 S. Ct. 1386 (1962)). Even the cases predating the 1993 amendments to Rule 16 acknowledge that "subject to the abuse-of-discretion standard, district courts have the general inherent power to require a party to have a representative will full settlement authority present—or at least reasonably and promptly accessible—at pretrial conferences. This applies to the government as well as private litigants." In re Stone, 986 F.2d 898, 903 (5th Cir.1993).

Stripping away the Justice Department's bombast, what remains is a simple conflict, or perhaps no conflict at all, between the Court's insistence on a meaningful settlement effort and the Justice Department's intricate regulatory scheme for closure of federal government cases. The United States Congress has designated quite simply that "the Attorney General or his designee may arbitrate, compromise, or settle any claim" within the original jurisdiction of the federal courts. 28 U.S.C.§ 2677. However, the Department of Justice thereafter promulgated an exquisitely complicated network of regulations delegating the Attorney General's settlement authority among a small pool of high-ranking officials, subject to numerous approval and consultation requirements, leaving Justice Department attorneys not surprisingly to aver that they simply cannot make a meaningful appearance at the vast majority of settlement conferences across this country. See United States' Objections at 17 ("It would be virtually impossible for high-ranking Department of Justice officials to attend thousands of mediation and settlement conferences in which plaintiffs allege damages in excess of $500,000.").

Ultimately, if these regulations conflict with Rule 16, or interfere substantially with the inherent power of this Court, they must and do fail. Chilcutt v. U.S., 4 F.3d 1313, 1325, n. 31 (5th Cir.1993), cert.

denied, 513 U.S. 979, 130 L. Ed. 2d 367, 115 S. Ct. 460 (1994) ("if an inconsistency existed, however, the Federal Regulations, which do not have the force of a federal statute, would have to bow to the Federal Rules of Civil Procedure, which do.") (citing Sibbach v. Wilson and Co., 312 U.S. 1, 85 L. Ed. 479, 61 S. Ct. 422 (1941)). Ultimately, it is well within the "province" of this Court to "arrogate" itself into a review of Department of Justice settlement regulations.

Having briefly reviewed these regulations, however, I see no immediate, insurmountable conflict with Rule 16 as it is applied in this district. This Court is quite accustomed to presiding over settlement proceedings involving governmental entities, large and small. The Magistrate Judges regularly craft mechanisms to establish fruitful communications with officials who cannot be present and/or to secure settlement approval from various risk management agencies or boards consonant with their regulations and policies. See e.g. September 26, 1995 Settlement Conference (Tape 1), Magistrate Judge DeGiacomo speaking: "I can do all kinds of things, provided there is a willingness to talk." Indeed, such an invitation was explicitly made by Magistrate Judge DeGiacomo in this case.

Central to this effort, however, is the good faith participation of a qualified representative. See e.g., Advisory Committee Notes to Rule 16(c), 1993 Amendments ("Particularly in litigation in which governmental agencies or large amounts of money are involved, there may be no one with on-the-spot settlement authority, and the most that should be expected is access to a person who would have a major role in submitting a recommendation to the body or board with ultimate decision-making responsibility."). It is not the rank of this representative which concerns the Court, but rather his or her authority to confront the dispute, in dialog with the parties, opposing counsel, and the Magistrate Judge, and to participate fully in the attempt to resolve it.

Were the purpose of a settlement conference merely to exchange offer and demand, there would be no need for any mediator, much less a federal Magistrate Judge. To reiterate in the simplest terms: this Court construes Rule 16 to require, and to permit this Court to require, the participation of fully authorized representatives in mandatory settlement proceedings, by means approved by the Court, subject to an abuse of discretion standard.

The failure to participate in good faith in any Rule 16 conference is a serious matter which can have serious consequences. See e.g., Phillips USA, Inc. v. Allflex USA, Inc., 77 F.3d 493, 1996 WL 80448 (10th Cir.1996) (unpublished disposition) (dismissal); Held v. Shelter Systems Group Corp., 16 F.3d 416, 1994 WL 47157 (10th Cir.1994) (unpublished disposition) (default). The United States is no less subject to these penalties than any private party. See e.g., Bradley v. U.S., 866 F.2d 120, 126 (5th Cir.1989) ("All parties are expected to conform their conduct to these rules, or face sanctions of their failure to do so; this is even more true for the federal government, a party that regularly appears before the federal courts, knows the rules by which they operate, and is even at times a special beneficiary of those rules."). Moreover, the law is clear that Rule 16 sanctions may be imposed even if the court is later found to lack subject matter jurisdiction over the merits of the dispute, to wit, even if the United States ultimately prevails in its sovereign immunity motion in this case. Olcott v. Delaware Flood Co., 76 F.3d 1538, 1552–54 (10th Cir.1996).

Magistrate Judge DeGiacomo was persuaded that a monetary sanction would have little effect, given Defendant's contumacious posture, and recommends evidentiary sanctions. I find, however, that this case presents an opportunity which we should not eschew to craft a settlement procedure which accommodates, if possible, the regulatory settlement restrictions on Department of Justice attorneys while ensuring that the representatives participating in our settlement conferences have sufficient authority to pursue and procure settlement on behalf of the United States. See Olcott, supra at 1555 (when faced with a Rule 16 violation, district courts have substantial discretion to craft a remedial order which serves the interests of justice, relates specifically to the problem at hand, and seeks to deter similar sanctionable conduct in the future).

Accordingly, the following remedial order is hereby entered:

I.   Defendant United States of America, through its counsel, shall engage in good faith with Magistrate Judge DeGiacomo in an effort to craft a settlement procedure which accommodates, if possible, the regulatory settlement restrictions on Department of Justice attorneys while ensuring that the representatives participating in settlement conferences have sufficient authority to pursue and procure settlement on behalf of the United States.

2.   Defendant United States of America shall participate fully and in good faith in another settlement conference before Magistrate Judge DeGiacomo in this case.

3.   Prior to that settlement conference, counsel for the United States of America shall confer with opposing counsel in a good-faith effort to resolve this litigation.

4.   The United States Department of Justice shall pay all reasonable expenses, including attorney fees, incurred by all participants to the proceedings before Magistrate Judge DeGiacomo in this case on February 26, 1996, February 27, 1996 and March 20, 1996.

5.   This matter is recommitted to Magistrate Judge DeGiacomo:

a.   to admit evidence on the amount of expenses and attorney fees reasonably incurred by all participants to the February and March proceedings before him in this case, and to award those expenses and attorney fees against the United States Department of Justice;

b.   to craft, in consultation with the parties, a settlement procedure which accommodates the regulatory settlement restrictions on Department of Justice attorneys while ensuring that the representatives participating in settlement conferences have sufficient authority to pursue and procure settlement on behalf of the United States, OR to bring to my attention any insurmountable conflict with the regulations which appears to substantially interfere with this Court's exercise of Rule 16 or its inherent powers; and

    c.   to preside over another settlement effort in this case.

    IT IS SO ORDERED.

■ E.L. Mechem, Senior United States District Judge.

NOTES

A.   As the *Schwartzman* opinion notes, current Rule 16(c) expressly states that a district court may "require that a party or its representative may be present or reasonably available by telephone in order to consider possible settlement of the dispute." In effect, the 1993 amendments give courts the power to compel attendance through an explicit grant of authority rather than the inherent power relied on in *Joseph Oat*. Note, however, that the court in *Schwartzman* continues to rely on both Rule 16 and inherent powers in asserting its right to compel attendance by government representatives. The precise nature and extent of a court's inherent powers absent any grant of authority by rule or statute remains an important and somewhat mysterious question. As the court notes in *Joseph Oat,* a similar problem can arise in connection with participating in court-ordered programs of alternative dispute resolution. That subject will be explored in the next chapter.

McMunigal, The Costs of Settlements: The Impact of Scarcity of Adjudication on Litigating Lawyers
37 U.C.L.A. L.Rev. 833, 837, 881 (1990).

This Article, by comparison, focuses on the implications of lack of trial experience for litigating lawyers. Does lack of trial experience affect the way lawyers function in litigation? Does it influence their performance as advocates? As negotiators settling cases? Does it affect adherence to existing ethical standards such as those regarding competence and conflict of interest? Can one expect lawyers to understand, respect, and adhere to the values of an ethical and legal system premised, as ours is, upon a process of adjudication lawyers seldom, if ever, experience? Do the answers to these questions yield any insight for guiding reform of our adjudicatory process and the creation and use of alternatives to that process?

This Article concludes that lack of trial experience in a legal and ethical system premised on adjudication threatens the effective functioning and ethical conformity of litigating lawyers. Lack of such experience may already impair that functioning and contribute to some of the current practical and ethical problems in litigation, such as frivolous filings and discovery abuse. Contrary to many critiques of our present legal system, this Article suggests that we should worry about having too little rather than too much adjudication. Lawyers frequently speak of clients deserving their "day in court." This Article suggests that litigating lawyers need their "day in court" as well.

* * *

Conclusion

The debate over settlement and adjudication raises many issues: efficiency, justice, fairness, coercion, psychological and emotional cost, and the proper role of the judiciary. This Article has sought to broaden that debate to include the impact of lack of trial experience on the skills, roles, and values associated with the lawyers on whom we rely to operate our system of justice. Undoubtedly the image of the trial lawyer should be less dominant in our ethical and legal system. We need to supplement that image with others, such as counselor and mediator, and develop ethical rules modeled on these roles. But unless we do away with adjudication entirely, we have much to gain by making the trial lawyer not just an image, but a part of the experience of all litigators.

NOTES

A. Do you share McMunigal's concern? Does it provide sufficient reason for curtailing judicial efforts to achieve settlements?

B. Suppose a settlement has been reached, must it be entered on the docket? Is it important that the docket reflect that the dispute has been terminated? If so, how is that achieved? See F.R.C.P. 41(a) providing for voluntary dismissal.

C. Rule 41(a) has other uses and other problems. Suppose plaintiff is dissatisfied with a court-imposed discovery schedule and moves for a voluntary dismissal without prejudice. May the court dismiss with prejudice? May the court do so without affording plaintiff an opportunity to withdraw the motion? See Gravatt v. Columbia University, 845 F.2d 54 (2d Cir.1988).

THE CONFIDENTIALITY OF SETTLEMENT AGREEMENTS

Plaintiff, seriously injured in a fire which resulted from a gas tank rupturing in the course of an automobile accident, sues the manufacturer alleging faulty design with respect to the location of the gas tank. Settlement seems likely, but the defendant insists on keeping the terms of the settlement confidential. Defendant is concerned with the possibility of a substantial number of new lawsuits being brought as a result of the publicity. Should the court allow the terms of the settlement to remain confidential? Does the court have any authority to order disclosure?

The problem is a common one. It can arise in products liability cases like tobacco, asbestos or in other kinds of mass torts. It may even arise in connection with a defamation action involving a public figure.

We have already considered an analogous problem in connection with the sealing of depositions in Chapter 4. The problems, however, are not identical. It is clear that if injured plaintiff and defendant manufacturer come to an agreement before suit has been filed, no public records exist with a claim to disclosure. The settlement in our hypothetical, however, has come after the aid of the judicial system has been invoked; is there not a public interest in information that may avoid future injuries or, at the least, that may facilitate compensation of those already injured? Are there rules presently in place that would assure disclosure? If not, should there be? If so, what type of rule would you favor? For an extensive discussion of these issues see Laurie Kratky Dore Secrecy by Consent: The Use And Limits of Confidentiality in The Pursuit of Settlement, 74 Notre Dame L. Rev. 283 (1999)

REFUSAL TO ACCEPT A SETTLEMENT OFFER

Suppose plaintiff sues defendant for $500,000 for injuries sustained in an automobile accident. Defendant concedes liability, asserts that damages could not possibly exceed $75,000 and offers to pay plaintiff $75,000 without a trial. Plaintiff refuses and there is a verdict for plaintiff in the amount of $70,000. Should defendant, who incurred very substantial expenses in connection with what now appears to be a needless trial, be entitled to recoup some of those expenses, including attorney fees for the trial itself?

It is not easy to answer that question. Will the risk of substantial liability for the other party's expenses deter impecunious plaintiffs with claims that really ought to be litigated? Is it possible to fashion a rule that would be simple enough to be both predictable and equitable? Would the introduction of a judge's discretion solve the problem or simply add to unpredictability? Suppose there would be no fee shifting unless plaintiff fell short by a substantial percentage, e.g. 25%?

Federal Rule 68, which at first reading seems to point to allowing defendant some recovery for costs, is little used and attempts to amend it were vigorously opposed by public interest groups. Florida amended Rule of Civil Procedure 1.442 (offer of judgment) effective January 1, 1990, to provide for litigation expenses as sanctions, in the discretion of the judge, applicable to offers to pay and offers to accept payment, conditioned on a miscalculation of at least 25% and providing that, in determining "entitlement to and the amount of a sanction" the court may consider ten enumerated factors.

Kothe v. Smith

United States Court of Appeals, Second Circuit, 1985.
771 F.2d 667.

■ VAN GRAAFEILAND, CIRCUIT JUDGE:

Dr. James Smith appeals from a judgment of the United States District Court for the Southern District of New York (Sweet, J.), which directed him to pay $1,000 to plaintiff-appellee's attorney, $1,000 to plaintiff-appellee's medical witness, and $480 to the Clerk of the Court. For the reasons hereinafter discussed, we direct that the judgment be vacated.

Patricia Kothe brought this suit for medical malpractice against four defendants, Dr. Smith, Dr. Andrew Kerr, Dr. Kerr's professional corporation, and Doctors Hospital, seeking $2 million in damages. She discontinued her action against the hospital four months prior to trial.

She discontinued against Dr. Kerr and his corporation on the opening day of trial.

Three weeks prior thereto, Judge Sweet held a pretrial conference, during which he directed counsel for the parties to conduct settlement negotiations. Although it is not clear from the record, it appears that Judge Sweet recommended that the case be settled for between $20,000 and $30,000. He also warned the parties that, if they settled for a comparable figure after trial had begun, he would impose sanctions against the dilatory party. Smith, whose defense has been conducted throughout this litigation by his malpractice insurer, offered $5,000 on the day before trial, but it was rejected.

Although Kothe's attorney had indicated to Judge Sweet that his client would settle for $20,000, he had requested that the figure not be disclosed to Smith. Kothe's counsel conceded at oral argument that the lowest pretrial settlement demand communicated to Smith was $50,000. Nevertheless, when the case was settled for $20,000 after one day of trial, the district court proceeded to penalize Smith alone. In imposing the penalty, the court stated that it was "determined to get the attention of the carrier" and that "the carriers are going to have to wake up when a judge tells them that they want [sic] to settle a case and they don't want to settle it." Under the circumstances of this case, we believe that the district court's imposition of a penalty against Smith was an abuse of the sanction power given it by Fed.R.Civ.P. 16(f).

Although the law favors the voluntary settlement of civil suits, ABKCO Music, Inc. v. Harrisongs Music, Ltd., 722 F.2d 988, 997 (2d Cir.1983), it does not sanction efforts by trial judges to effect settlements through coercion. Del Rio v. Northern Blower Co., 574 F.2d 23, 26 (1st Cir.1978) (citing Wolff v. Laverne, Inc., 17 A.D.2d 213, 233 N.Y.S.2d 555 (1962)); see MacLeod v. D.C. Transit System, Inc., 283 F.2d 194, 195 n. 1 (D.C.Cir.1960); 89 C.J.S., Trial, § 577 at 355. In the Wolff case, cited with approval in Del Rio, supra, the Court said:

> We view with disfavor all pressure tactics whether directly or obliquely, to coerce settlement by litigants and their counsel. Failure to concur in what the Justice presiding may consider an adequate settlement should not result in an imposition upon a litigant or his counsel, who reject it, of any retributive sanctions not specifically authorized by law.

17 A.D.2d at 215, 233 N.Y.S.2d 555. In short, pressure tactics to coerce settlement simply are not permissible. Schunk v. Schunk, 84 A.D.2d 904, 905, 446 N.Y.S.2d 672 (1981); Chomski v. Alston Cab Co., 32 A.D.2d 627, 299 N.Y.S.2d 896 (1969). "The judge must not compel agreement by arbitrary use of his power and the attorney must not meekly submit to a judge's suggestion, though it be strongly urged." Brooks v. Great Atlantic & Pacific Tea Co., 92 F.2d 794, 796 (9th Cir.1937).

Rule 16 of the Fed.R.Civ.P. was not designed as a means for clubbing the parties—or one of them—into an involuntary compromise. See Padovani v. Bruchhausen, 293 F.2d 546, 548 (2d Cir.1961); Clark, To An Understanding Use of Pre–Trial, 1961, 29 F.R.D. 454, 456; Smith, Pretrial Conference—A Study of Methods, 1961, 29 F.R.D. 348, 353; Moskowitz, Glimpses of Federal Trials and Procedure, 1946, 4 F.R.D. 216, 218. Although subsection (c)(7) of Rule 16, added in the 1983 amendments of the Rule, was designed to encourage pretrial settlement discussions, it was not its purpose to "impose settlement negotiations on unwilling litigants." See Advisory Committee Note, 1983, 97 F.R.D. 205, 210.

We find the coercion in the instant case especially troublesome because the district court imposed sanctions on Smith alone. Offers to settle a claim are not made in a vacuum. They are part of a more complex process which includes "conferences, informal discussions, offers, counterdemands, more discussions, more haggling, and finally, in the great majority of cases, a compromise." J. & D. Sindell, Let's Talk Settlement 300 (1963). In other words, the process of settlement is a two-way street, and a defendant should not be expected to bid against himself. In the instant case, Smith never received a demand of less than $50,000. Having received no indication from Kothe that an offer somewhere in the vicinity of $20,000 would at least be given careful consideration, Smith should not have been required to make an offer in this amount simply because the court wanted him to.

Smith's attorney should not be condemned for changing his evaluation of the case after listening to Kothe's testimony during the first day of trial. As every experienced trial lawyer knows, the personalities of the parties and their witnesses play an important role in litigation. It is one thing to have a valid claim; it is quite another to convince a jury of this fact. It is not at all unusual, therefore, for a defendant to change his perception of a case based on the plaintiff's performance on the witness stand. We see nothing about that occurrence in the instant case that warranted the imposition of sanctions against the defendant alone.

Although we commend Judge Sweet for his efforts to encourage settlement negotiations, his excessive zeal leaves us no recourse but to remand the matter with instructions to vacate the judgment.

Schuck, The Role of Judges in Settling Complex Cases: The Agent Orange Example

53 U. of Chi.L.Rev. 337 (1986).

Although my study of the Agent Orange case includes a very detailed account of the settlement negotiations, a highly condensed (and thus somewhat distorted) synopsis must suffice for present purposes. From the moment that Judge Weinstein replaced Judge Pratt on October 21, 1983, the goal of settlement was uppermost in his mind. He believed that toxic tort cases like Agent Orange, involving mass exposures and causal relationships that are extremely difficult and costly to prove, could not be litigated properly or at an acceptable social cost under traditional rules. Absent settlement, he predicted a one-year trial with results that would remain inconclusive for years to come. Although he harbored genuine doubts about the veterans' evidence on causation, he deeply sympathized with their plight. In open court and in his written opinions, he denounced the "injustices" they suffered, believed that "[t]hey and their families should receive recognition, medical treatment and financial support," and shared the now-conventional view that the American people had failed to discharge "the nation's obligations to Vietnam veterans and their families." The prospect of having either to direct a verdict for the chemical companies or to reverse a jury verdict in favor of the veterans could not have been an appealing one. Unquestionably, he was prepared to do his duty if necessary, but a negotiated settlement offered the far more attractive possibility: everyone would gain something, soon, and at an acceptable social cost.

Earlier settlement discussions between the parties had failed.

The court, however, had not been involved in those negotiations. And since then, circumstances had changed—most particularly, the identity and judicial style of the presiding judge. Weinstein immediately established a May 7, 1984 trial date—a little more than six months away—and left no doubt of his implacable determination to hold to it. He did this despite—or perhaps because of—the fact that the parties had to that point conducted little discovery except on a single issue, the government contract defense. He dragged the United States back into the case, believing that the government's presence would greatly facilitate settlement. He also indicated that he would submit the issue of government liability to the jury on an "advisory" basis (the Federal Tort Claims Act precluded a binding jury decision). Finally, he revealed to the parties, albeit only as a "tentative," "preliminary," and, as it turned out, non-appealable matter, how he intended to rule on a number of important and complex legal issues, such as choice-of-law and governmental immunity.

In February 1984, Weinstein requested and obtained permission to retain, at the defendants' expense, an unnamed consultant to develop a settlement strategy and plan. That consultant was later revealed to be Ken Feinberg, a lawyer whom Weinstein knew and trusted. Feinberg was not only knowledgeable about toxic tort litigation, but also had a reputation as an effective mover, shaker, and conciliator. By mid-March, he had prepared a settlement plan. It stated no dollar amount but contained three sections: an analysis of the elements for determining the aggregate settlement amount, especially the various sources of uncertainty and the likely number and nature of claims; a discussion of alternative criteria for allocating any liability among the chemical companies; and a discussion of alternative criteria for distributing any settlement fund to claimants. This document, which the judge made available to the lawyers, occasioned considerable disagreement but succeeded in setting the terms for the negotiations that followed.

On April 10, less than three weeks before trial, Weinstein appointed three special masters for settlement.[29] Feinberg and David I. Shapiro, a prominent class action expert and skillful negotiator, would work with the lawyers. Leonard Garment, a Washington political insider, would explore what resources the government might contribute to a settlement. Feinberg and Shapiro immediately identified three major obstacles to settlement: the parties were more than *a quarter of a billion dollars* apart; each side was deeply divided internally over whether and on what terms to settle (and in defendants' case, how to allocate liability); and the government was manifestly unwilling to contribute toward a settlement fund or even to participate in settlement negotiations.

The judge and special masters decided to convene an around-the-clock negotiating marathon at the courthouse during the weekend before the trial. The lawyers were ordered to appear on Saturday morning, May 5, with their "toothbrushes and full negotiating authority." On that morning, while preliminary jury selection work was proceeding in another room, Weinstein met with the lawyers and gave them a "pep talk" about settlement. Then the special masters undertook a grueling two-day course of shuttle diplomacy, holding separate meetings with each side interspersed with private conferences with Judge Weinstein. On several occasions, the judge met privately with each side.

Several features of the discussion were particularly salient in generating the settlement agreement. First, the court did not permit the two sides to meet face-to-face until the very end, after the terms of the deal had been defined. This strategy preserved the court's control over the negotiations and prevented them from fragmenting. In particular, it stymied the plaintiffs' lawyers in their last-ditch effort to improve on the deal by settling with five of the defendants and isolating Monsanto and Diamond Shamrock, the two companies they thought most vulnerable to liability and punitive damages.

Second, the masters attempted to break log-jams in the negotiations by helping the lawyers to predict the consequences of the various approaches under consideration, and by proposing alternative solutions. For example, when the chemical companies' lawyers expressed the fear that a settlement would be rendered worthless if a large number of veterans decided to opt out of the class and sue on their own, Shapiro devised a "walk-away" provision that would minimize those concerns. The tax implications of a settlement were also questions that the masters helped to clarify.

Third, when especially difficult issues arose that threatened to derail the settlement, the parties agreed to be bound by the judge's decision. The most important example of the judge acting as arbitrator

---

29. Weinstein's appointment of special masters for *settlement*, rather than for discovery or remedy purposes, was itself a highly innovative action. For a subsequent example of settlement mastering, see Arthurs, *Master* *Lands Settlement That Almost Got Away*, Legal Times, Apr. 22, 1985, at 1. Litigants, acting on their own initiative, sometimes retain a third party for the same purposes.

involved perhaps the most difficult question facing the defendants—how to allocate liability among themselves. Another example involved the question of one of the defendants' "ability to pay" its share.

Fourth, the judge and his special masters, while being careful not to be duplicitous, did emphasize different things to each side. In their discussions with plaintiffs' lawyers, they stressed the weakness of the evidence on causation, the novelty of many questions of law in the case, the consequent risk of reversal on appeal of a favorable verdict, the prospect that they might lose everything if they rejected settlement, and the enormous costs of continued litigation. To the defendants' lawyers, they stressed the presumed pro-plaintiff sympathies of Brooklyn juries, the reputational damage that protracted litigation and unfavorable publicity would cause their clients, and the high costs of the trial and of the inevitable appeals.

Fifth, a common theme in all discussions was the pervasive *uncertainty* that surrounded the law, the facts, the duration and ultimate outcome of the litigation, and the damages likely to be awarded. By almost all accounts, it was this uncertainty that proved to be the decisive inducement to settlement.[30] On one count, however, Judge Weinstein left little doubt in the lawyers' minds: the court, having crafted and taken responsibility for the settlement, was in a position to make it stick.

Sixth, the imminence and ineluctability of trial "concentrated the minds" of the lawyers as nothing else could have done.[31] This deadline imparted to their deliberations an urgency and a seriousness that swept aside objections that might have undermined negotiations in less compelling circumstances. The lawyers' growing physical and mental exhaustion during that weekend of feverish intensity abetted the conciliatory effect. As one plaintiff's lawyer later complained in his challenge to the validity of the settlement, "the Judge wore us all down with that tactic."[32]

Seventh, the judge and special masters displayed a degree of skill, sophistication, imagination, and artistry in fashioning the settlement that almost all the participants viewed as highly unusual. But even this would not have availed had Judge Weinstein not inspired an extraordi-

---

30. This finding of a strong positive relationship between uncertainty of outcome and settlement, so apparent to all of the participants, suggests that the concept of uncertainty used in the model of the decision to litigate or to settle (especially as elaborated by Priest and Klein), which posits that uncertainty will actually *impede* settlement, is too broad. The concept needs to be unpacked and further specified if it is to have predictive power in complex cases, in which uncertainty of one kind or another is likely to be an important factor. *See* Priest & Klein, *supra* note 8, at 15–17; Priest, Selective Characteristics of Litigation, 9 J. Legal Stud. 399, 403 (1980). It is important to distinguish, for example, between those changes in the level of uncertainty that lead both parties to be more pessimistic, which will tend to encourage settlement, and those changes that lead them both to be more optimistic, which will tend to discourage it. *See infra* notes 52–53 and accompanying text.

31. For a less favorable view of the judicial tactic of setting immovable trial dates, see Hazard & Rice, Judicial Management of the Pretrial Process in Massive Litigation: Special Masters as Case Managers, 1982 Am.B.Found.Research J. 375, 386.

32. The "exhaustion factor" apparently has figured heavily in other settlements as well. *See, e.g.,* Arthurs, *supra* note 29, at 10.

nary measure of respect, even awe, in the lawyers, and had the special masters not been viewed as enjoying the authority to speak and make commitments for him.

Eighth, the settlement was negotiated without any agreement (or even any serious discussion) of how the settlement fund would be distributed among the claimants, and without reliable information as to the number of claims that would be filed.[33] The first, of course, was of great interest to the plaintiffs and a matter of indifference to the defendants. The second, however, was significant to both sides. It is not at all certain that settlement could have been reached had the parties been required to resolve these issues in advance. The problem was not simply that preparation of a distribution plan required an immense amount of analysis.[34] A protracted process of political compromise and education was also needed to gain support for the plan, a process whose results even now remain doubtful and perhaps legally vulnerable.

Ninth, the lawyers on the PMC[a] at the time of the settlement possessed very different personalities, ideologies, and incentives than those of the group of lawyers that had launched the case and carried it through its first five years. These differences likely affected the lawyers' disposition to settle. The veterans' passionate desire for vindication at trial, quite apart from their wish for compensation, had strongly driven their chosen lawyer, Victor Yannacone, during the earlier stages of the litigation. Yet the PMC's deliberations concerning the settlement were strongly influenced by lawyers who had only the most attenuated relationship to the veterans. And under the terms of an internal fee-sharing agreement, these lawyers would be secured financially by even a "low" settlement.

Finally, the court was prepared to allocate substantial resources to the quest for a settlement. Judge Weinstein devoted a great deal of his own time to thinking through and implementing a settlement strategy. His three special masters for settlement commanded high compensation and worked long hours. Their billings to the court totaled hundreds of thousands of dollars, even excluding the massive amount of work they later invested in connection with the distribution plan.

According to virtually all of the lawyers who participated in the negotiation of the Agent Orange settlement, Judge Weinstein's distinctive intervention was essential to the settlement. It is possible, of course, that the lawyers are wrong, and that a pretrial settlement would have been reached even without Weinstein's intervention—or, at the very least, that a settlement would have been reached after some witnesses had testified and "blood" had been drawn. But the court's settlement activity was regarded as crucial by those in the best position to know.

---

33. Indeed, the legality of the settlement has been challenged on the ground, inter alia, that any settlement lacking this information could not properly be approved.

34. It was not published until May 1985, a year after the settlement, and was hundreds of pages long.

a. Plaintiffs' Management Committee.

CHAPTER VII

ALTERNATIVE DISPUTE RESOLUTION

Alternative Dispute Resolution in Federal District Courts

A. Leo Levin and Deirdre Golash.
37 U. of Fla.L.Rev. 29 (1985).

As recently amended, Federal Rule of Civil Procedure 16(c)(7) invites the parties to a lawsuit to consider "use of extrajudicial procedures to resolve the dispute." This invitation can be expected to be a powerful stimulant to increased use of alternative dispute resolution (ADR) in the federal courts. The amendment also reflects the acceptance alternatives already have gained and is evidence of the change in judicial attitudes toward ADR. The judiciary, which once viewed private adjudication as an infringement on the jurisdiction of the courts, now sees alternatives as offering welcome relief to the courts while providing significant advantages to litigants. Proliferation of alternative dispute resolution programs has resulted in widespread interest in how they work and what they can be expected to accomplish.

Understandably, there has been no chorus of unanimous acclaim. Litigants required to participate in ADR programs have challenged the legality of the new procedures, and commentators have questioned the wisdom of altering what they view as the traditional roles of courts and judges. The purpose of this paper is to describe the programs currently in use in the federal courts, to assess, albeit in very preliminary fashion, what they appear to achieve, and to explore the legal bases for the promulgation of these programs. Because provisions for sanctions are so often an integral part of the programs themselves, we explore as well the legal foundation for fees and fines imposed by judges in the effort to make these programs work.

Alternative dispute resolution is an umbrella term; it encompasses a wide variety of techniques that range from informal, voluntary mediation to court-mandated arbitration that incorporates many of the formalities of trial. Under the same umbrella are small-claims procedures designed to accommodate pro se litigants, and the mini-trial, developed to serve the ends of corporate disputants anxious to reduce litigation costs and preserve business relationships.

At first blush, there appears to be no common principle underlying these diverse programs. There is not only a diversity of mechanisms, but a diversity of articulated goals as well. For example, a primary purpose of neighborhood justice centers is to further a sense of community in the constituencies they serve, while programs originating within the court system tend to be concerned primarily with relieving court congestion and delay. All ADR programs, however, seek to resolve disputes through some method other than a formal, adversary trial. Some programs succeed in avoiding litigation altogether; they are alternatives to bringing suit. In others, the ADR mechanism may be invoked only after pretrial proceedings have been completed. All ADR programs, however, have at least this much in common: they reflect the premise that alternative resolution of the dispute is preferable to trial. In short, there may be as many goals for alternative methods of dispute resolution as there are reasons for wanting to avoid trial.

Resorting to an alternative instead of proceeding to trial is not an end in itself, and certainly is not preferable in all cases. For some types of problems, and for some purposes, a formal trial is best. Sometimes the needs of litigants can be satisfied only by jury verdicts or by formal findings of fact and conclusions of law. Additionally, in some situations, only a judicial decision with precedential value can provide guidance for other litigants resolving similar disputes. The challenge for those who develop and administer ADR programs is to make optimal use of the programs without supplanting judicial decision-making where it, in fact, is the most appropriate mechanism to resolve the particular dispute.

I. The Programs

A. *Court–Annexed Arbitration*

In 1978, three federal district courts established experimental programs of court-annexed arbitration at the request of the Department of Justice, with funds provided by Congress. These programs continue today in two of the three courts—the Eastern District of Pennsylvania and the Northern District of California—and Congress recently approved funding for similar programs in eight additional districts.

In the Eastern District of Pennsylvania, all civil cases seeking only money damages not in excess of $75,000, except social security cases and prisoners' civil rights cases, are automatically assigned for arbitration. Cases are heard by a panel of three arbitrators, members of the bar of the court, who hear evidence as well as argument. If neither party objects to the arbitrators' award the court enters judgment on the award. Any party dissatisfied with the award may request a trial *de novo,* which will be conducted as though no arbitration had occurred. The party requesting the trial *de novo* must post a deposit in the amount of the arbitrators' fees; the deposit will be forfeited to the government unless that party improves on the arbitrators' award at trial. Because these fees amount only to $225, however, the sanction is minimal in comparison to the amount at stake, certainly in cases at the upper end of the scale.

The aims of court-annexed arbitration are to reduce the cost of litigation, to facilitate speedy disposition of claims, and to reduce the overall number of cases going to trial. Measured by these standards, and by the level of satisfaction of both bench and bar, court-annexed arbitration has done well. A Federal Judicial Center study by Lind and Shapard originally published in 1981, and updated in 1983, indicates that, after adoption of the Eastern District of Pennsylvania program, eighteen percent more cases were terminated within one year after filing.

An analysis of the number of terminations month by month after filing shows increased early dispositions for each month from the first through the twentieth, and the authors suggest that the eighteen percent figure "under-estimates the true effect of arbitration." The time savings result primarily from an increase in early settlement. It is the operation of the program, with its promise of a timely hearing, rather than the hearing itself that appears responsible for the early terminations. It should also be observed, however, that the number of cases in the arbitration program requiring a trial is strikingly low. By December 1984, just two percent of the 7100 terminated cases in the arbitration program had gone to trial.

Determining whether court-annexed arbitration results in lower litigation costs to the parties is a complex undertaking. In their 1981 report, Lind and Shapard stated: "We would be confident that expenses [to litigants] are generally reduced if the rule both reduces the incidence of trials and causes a large number of settlements in advance of the arbitration hearing itself." The 1983 update of the report indicates that these criteria may well be satisfied. Even if arbitration allows lawyers to spend less time on each dispute, however, the savings are not necessarily passed on to the parties. Recent research by the American Bar Association's Action Commission, in a study of state court innovations designed to save attorney time, showed that attorneys who were paid on an hourly basis—most typically representing defendants—did reduce their fees when time was saved. Nevertheless, the Commission also found that plaintiffs' attorneys working on a contingent fee basis did not reduce their fees in response to these time-saving devices. Additionally, the use of fixed-fee arrangements inhibited passing on the savings. Whether contingent fee rates have been adjusted to reflect the savings affected by arbitration, or whether they will be, is not a subject on which we can speak with any confidence. We do know that many contingent fee attorneys charge a lesser percentage when a case is settled before trial. Any conclusion about the precise effect of arbitration on costs to litigants must await the outcome of future developments and further study.

The benefits of court-annexed arbitration would count for little if the program did not deliver substantial justice to the participants. Agreement on objective standards of justice, however, is hard to come by. Perhaps more useful would be a comparison of arbitration awards with jury verdicts, but this would be a formidable, if not an impossible task. The best we can offer is some measure of the perceived fairness of awards in the eyes of litigants. On this standard, the Eastern District of Pennsylvania program has fared well. Most attorneys and litigants view the results of arbitration as fair and reasonable.

These findings are consistent with the findings of the Rand Institute of Civil Justice with respect to the state court-annexed arbitration program in Pittsburgh. The reasoning of those interviewed bears some emphasis: given a fair hearing and an impartial decision-maker, they preferred a timely, informal process to more formal proceedings that entailed both high cost and delay.[44]

A word of caution in interpreting what may be viewed as contrary data is necessary. Nejelsk and Zeldin report a thirty-four percent "reversal" rate at trial. Because so very few cases actually go to trial, these findings reflect an exceedingly small and unrepresentative sample of cases. Specifically, as of December 31, 1983, only thirty-six such "reversals" were recorded out of 6,081 cases in the program and 1,185 arbitration awards. Clearly, these cases are not representative; they go to trial precisely because one of the parties believes that the award did not reflect the probable outcome of trial. Of course, when a case does not go to trial, it is impossible to know whether the actual result is the same as one a judge or jury would have reached.

B. *Michigan Mediation/Valuation*

With their caseload rapidly increasing—by 300 percent over ten years—the Eastern District of Michigan in 1981 began looking for ways to reduce an overcrowded docket. The Third Judicial Circuit of Michigan had long been using a mediation program run by the Mediation Tribunal Association, an independent, non-profit organization created by the court itself. As much of the increase in federal filings was in diversity cases, the federal court took advantage of this state mechanism and arranged to refer a substantial number of its diversity cases to the mediation program.

Under Eastern District of Michigan Local Rule 32, cases may be referred to mediation upon motion of either party or by the court on its own initiative. Court referrals, rare in the early stages of the program, are becoming increasingly common. No dollar limit has been set and the only criterion is that the suit seek only money damages. Litigants each pay a $75 fee, making the program self-sustaining. Each case is heard by a panel of three mediators, one selected from a list compiled by the plaintiff's bar, one from a list prepared by the defense

---

44. The majority of individual litigants interviewed were quite satisfied with the program. Although winners were more satisfied than losers, a majority of the latter were at least somewhat satisfied with the program.

The survey also found that most litigants had a simple definition of what constituted a fair dispute resolution procedure: They wanted an opportunity to have their case heard and decided by an impartial third party. Most did not care whether a judge in black robes or an attorney in business attire heard and decided their case. Some Pittsburgh litigants

expressed a preference for the three-person panel rather than a judge because "three heads are better than one." Nor did most care whether their cases were heard in a formal courtroom, complete with bar and dais, or around a plain wood table in a small hearing room. As one Pittsburgh litigant said, "I wouldn't care if they held it in a closet!" For individual litigants what was important was that they had enough time to tell their story, that the arbitrators paid equal attention to the disputants—and that they could afford the process.

bar, and one from a list compiled jointly. Hearings take place approximately sixty days after referral.

Although commonly referred to as mediation, the Michigan program does not today involve mediation in the usual sense of the word. The parties do not negotiate, nor does the mediation panel attempt to conciliate the dispute. Rather, the panel of three mediators, after a thirty-minute hearing—fifteen minutes for each party—meets with each side separately in an attempt to reach a mutually acceptable solution. The mediators then confer among themselves and arrive at a valuation of the case, usually within a few minutes. A unanimous valuation by the panel becomes the judgment in the case unless one of the parties objects in writing within forty days. A party who rejects the mediators' valuation but fails to improve upon it at trial by more than ten percent may be required to pay court costs and the opponent's attorney's fees for trial. Complex provisions for fee shifting also are provided in situations where the valuation has been rejected by both parties. In practice, however, imposition of any penalty is not common. The program enjoys the support of both judges and attorneys.

The Western District of Michigan has a similar program in place as one of a number of alternatives available to the court and to the parties. In that part of the state, the federal court itself has provided for the creation of mediation panels.

C. *Summary Jury Trials*

Litigants often are unable to agree on settlement terms because they have widely differing views about how juries will perceive their cases. In cases where the applicable legal standard is a flexible one such as "reasonableness," attorneys have difficulty advising their clients with confidence concerning a likely jury verdict. Clients also have difficulty accepting such advice with confidence. To facilitate settlement in this kind of case, Judge Thomas A. Lambros of the Northern District of Ohio developed what has become known as the summary jury trial. Under this procedure, each party may present the substance of its case before a six-member jury selected from the regular jury pool. Each side is given one hour to summarize the evidence it would be prepared to present at trial. The judge then instructs the jurors on the law, and they retire to deliberate. While a consensus verdict is encouraged, if the jurors fail to agree they may instead report their individual views. The verdict is not binding; its purpose is to provide a basis for settlement discussions. Frequently, the result is that one or both parties realize that the outcome of trial might well be less favorable than anticipated. Such cases are commonly settled. Although Judge Lambros selects cases for summary jury trials because of his perception that the parties are highly unlikely to reach settlement, only four of eighty-eight cases he selected for the program failed to settle before trial.

Other federal judges have employed the summary jury trial and some have adopted variations of Judge Lambros' technique. In the District of Massachusetts, Judge McNaught uses five jurors to assure a majority decision. He permits live witnesses and some cross-examination. The judge's law clerk presides over the hearing while the judge sits as a silent juror. After the presentation, jurors retire and then return either a unanimous verdict or a "quotient" verdict, an averaging of the individual jurors' valuations of the case. The lawyers then are permitted to speak briefly with the jurors. Judge McNaught notes that, while the procedure is generally successful, an attempt to use it in an antitrust case was a mistake. The abbreviated proceeding did not give the jurors enough information to understand the issues. After they returned a verdict of $10 million for the plaintiff, the case was tried—and the defendant won. Judge Lambros however, reports the successful settlement of a $2.5 million antitrust case after a summary jury trial. Judge Lambros sometimes allocates as much as two days to summary jury trial in complex cases, which may account for his success here.

In the Western District of Michigan, a local rule authorizes summary jury trials at the option of the judge. The program, initiated by Judge Richard A. Enslen, is an adaption of Judge Lambros' program. Several weeks in advance of a summary jury trial, the magistrate meets with the attorneys to explain the procedure and to resolve questions about what evidence will be admitted. Either Judge Enslen or Magistrate Brenneman presides at the summary jury trial, which the principals are required to attend. The jurors are not informed until after they render their verdict that it will not be binding. After the hearing, the lawyers are permitted to talk to the jurors, and a settlement conference follows immediately.

Magistrate Brenneman points out that the need of some parties to be vindicated by a jury is met by summary jury trial. For example, when an insurance company refused to pay a claim because of suspected arson, the plaintiff sought both payment of his claim and removal of the stigma associated with the insurance company's position.

The summary jury trial, initiated in January 1983, is still relatively new in the Western District of Michigan. Preliminary reports indicate, however, that its success parallels that in the Northern District of Ohio.

D. *Mediation*

Mediation—the conciliation of a dispute through the non-coercive intervention of a third party—is one of the oldest and most familiar of all forms of alternative dispute resolution. Mediation procedure is flexible; a significant variable affecting its success is the choice of mediator. Some mediators are professionals, and judges may, in appropriate cases, call upon such professionals to assist in the settlement of pending litigation. Obviously, judges and magistrates who have extensive experience with settlement conferences in fact frequently serve as mediators in conducting such conferences. Accordingly, in this section we treat mediation broadly, including programs limited to non-judicial mediators, formal programs involving settlement efforts by judges and magistrates, and programs, such as that in the district of Kansas, that provide for both.

1.   Non-judicial Mediators

In the Western District of Washington, cases may be designated for compulsory mediation in the discretion of the assigned judge pursuant to Local Civil Rule 39.1. If a case is so designated, attorneys for all parties must meet once for a settlement conference without a mediator. If this effort fails, the parties select a mediator from a court-maintained list of qualified attorneys who have volunteered to serve. Mediation is generally scheduled following completion of discovery. If mediation fails, the parties may agree to binding or non-binding arbitration or go to trial. While use of the program declined after an initial spurt of activity, it generally is seen today as valuable, particularly by the lawyers. Indeed, the Federal Bar Association has recommended use of mediation in all civil cases. The Eastern District of Washington recently adopted a procedure similar to that of the Western District.

2.   Settlement Judges

The judge who will preside over the trial of a case stands in a very special relationship to the litigants. The control he or she has over the lawsuit may cause any suggestion that the case should be settled to be perceived as a threat. This certainly is true in the non-jury case, and the problem is intensified when the judge's involvement extends to suggesting settlement figures or to commenting on offers of settlement made by one of the parties. Litigants might also be unwilling to divulge their true positions to the judge who will preside at trial, particularly in non-jury cases. Many judges, sensitive to the risk that their efforts could be seen as coercive, have in the past refrained from active encouragement of settlement. Some even avoided broaching the subject, although a gentle query as to whether counsel have discussed settlement hardly seems objectionable. At the same time, the proportion of settlements to trials signifies that a calendar can be kept under control only through settlements. Moreover, judges have expressed concern about the waste of resources resulting from settlements that did not come until the first or second day of trial simply because the parties had never made serious pretrial settlement efforts. Some judicial involvement was recognized as highly desirable, especially when counsel asked the judge to participate. There were several steps a judge could take to avoid impropriety or the appearance of it. The judge could limit his involvement in the settlement negotiations, although that might serve to limit the judge's effectiveness as well. Alternatively, the judge could become as involved as necessary in the negotiations, but make it clear to the parties that he would not try the case. As one authority advised, you may

> have to indicate the possibility that you'll transfer the case to another judge for trial if it becomes apparent that, as a result of the negotiations, you are now prejudiced, or believe one side

thinks you're now prejudiced, to the point where you couldn't fairly try the case.

Another approach is also available. Concerned about these pitfalls and yet mindful of disadvantages in changing trial assignments, some judges developed the informal practice of asking another judge to hold the settlement conference. More recently, several federal courts have institutionalized this procedure. In the Western District of Oklahoma, a settlement judge may be assigned at the request of the parties or by the court on its own motion. The judge, usually a senior judge, conducts a confidential settlement conference and gives his or her view of the value of the case. Attendance of a person with settlement authority is required. The rule states that "[t]he parties, their representatives and attorneys are required to be completely candid with the settlement conference judge * * *." However, the entire proceeding is off the record and inadmissible at trial.

In 1984, the District of Kansas initiated a similar procedure. In that district, the judge may require the parties to attend a settlement conference conducted by a judge or magistrate. Alternatively, the parties may consent to a settlement conference before an attorney or panel of attorneys, in which event the mediators are paid by the parties. The court maintains a list of 30 attorneys qualified and willing to serve as mediators. Attorneys prefer judicial involvement in promoting settlement to a policy of "abstinence." A recent survey of 1900 lawyers who had recently litigated in federal court by Professor Wayne Brazil showed that "[a] staggering 85 percent of our respondents agree that 'involvement by federal judges in settlement discussions [is] likely to improve significantly the prospects for achieving settlement.' " A substantial majority of those surveyed agreed that judges should try to facilitate settlement even when they had not been asked to do so. These lawyers also indicated their preference for settlement discussions conducted by a judge other than the one who will preside at trial, particularly where the judges takes an active role in those discussions.

THE JUDICIAL IMPROVEMENTS AND ACCESS TO JUSTICE ACT OF 1988

Court-annexed arbitration was first introduced in three federal district courts by local rule, and promptly challenged on a number of legal grounds.

One, that the mandatory referral for an informal proceeding was an unconstitutional burden on the right to jury trial even though the award was not binding, deserves particular mention. In Mattos v. Thompson, 491 Pa. 385, 421 A.2d 190 (1980), the Supreme Court of Pennsylvania struck down a program of nonbinding arbitration for medical malpractice claims on the ground that, as administered, it did in fact create an impermissible burden on the right to jury trial. The court in that case recognized that similar statutes had been held constitutional in other jurisdictions, but after extensive analysis of a wealth of data, concluded that the program should not be allowed to continue. The court found, for example, that "six of the original 48 cases filed in 1976 remain unresolved, despite the passage of four years. No extraordinary circumstances have been offered to explain this intolerable delay. Furthermore, as of May 31, 1980, 38 per cent of the claims filed in 1977, 65 per cent of the claims filed in 1978, and 85 per cent of the claims filed in 1979 remain unresolved."

No such difficulties were encountered by the court-annexed arbitration program and it survived the challenge to its legality handily, Kimbrough v. Holiday Inn, 478 F.Supp. 566 (E.D.Pa.1979), and soon was adopted in a number of other districts. When it became necessary to obtain government funds for the administration of the program the courts went directly to the Appropriations Committees of the Congress, rather than to the Judiciary Committees, which had "substantive" jurisdiction over legislation affecting the courts. The program, it was explained, was viewed as experimental.

Which committee deals with such legislation involves a lot more than a technical turf battle. Different committees have different perspectives and different interests; staffs have different areas of expertise. When "substantive" legislation was finally enacted, as described below, it provided limitations on court annexed arbitration and included a sunset provision.

The Judicial Improvements and Access to Justice Act of 1988 included a chapter on court-annexed arbitration, which became effective in the spring of 1989. It lists ten districts by name as authorized to have such programs and then provides that the Judicial Conference of the United States may authorize ten additional districts to utilize court-annexed arbitration. There is a five-year sunset provision, limitations on jurisdictional amount and on permissible sanctions.

Perhaps one of the more interesting sections, particularly in light of the history of alternative dispute resolution in the federal courts, is section 904, which provides in its entirety: "Nothing in this title, or in chapter 44, as added by section 901 of this Act, is intended to abridge, modify, or enlarge the rule making powers of the Federal judiciary."

What does this provision say about the power of a court to promulgate a local rule which would institute an experimental program not authorized by Congress, perhaps one involving summary jury trial or some other form of alternative dispute resolution? See discussion in Levin, Local Rules as Experiments: A Study in the Division of Power, 139 U.Pa.L.Rev. 1567, 1587 (1991).

NOTES

A. One way in which some programs of alternative dispute resolution foster settlements is by exposing the strengths and weaknesses of a case to the litigants themselves, rather than merely to their lawyers. If a judge believes that a summary jury trial, described earlier in this chapter, might serve this purpose if the litigant herself were present at the proceedings, does the judge have the power to order a represented litigant to appear personally for such proceedings?

B.   Suppose a situation in which court annexed arbitration is mandatory and non-binding. May the lawyer for one of the parties simply appear, not participate and then request trial de novo? Suppose the lawyer participates, but only half-heartedly?

CIVIL JUSTICE REFORM ACT OF 1990

This legislation, designed to reduce expense and delay in civil litigation, puts heavy emphasis on the use of alternative dispute resolution. In introducing the bill, Senator Biden, its principal sponsor, quoted the Federal Courts Study Committee to the effect that ADR is currently "beyond the stage at which it should be limited to local experiments but not so advanced as to permit of uniform national rules," for which reason the Act encourages, indeed for certain courts it mandates, use of alternative dispute resolution.

A relatively new form of ADR, early neutral evaluation (ENE), is specifically mentioned in the statute. The program has been described as follows:

> The heart of ENE was to be an early, frank and thoughtful assessment of the parties' relative positions and the overall value of the case. Each evaluation was to be given by a neutral, very experienced and highly respected private attorney, called the evaluator. The confidential evaluation, based on the evaluator's reaction to the parties' written evaluation statements and oral presentations, was to be presented orally to the parties and their attorneys. The developers of ENE hoped to accomplish a variety of specific goals: (1) to force the parties to confront the merits of their own case and their opponents'; (2) to identify which matters of law and fact actually were in dispute as early as possible; (3) to develop an efficient approach to discovery; and (4) to provide a frank assessment of the case. Later, fostering early settlements was added as an explicit goal.

Levine, Northern District of California Adopts Early Neutral Evaluation to Expedite Dispute Resolution, 72 Judicature 235 (1989).

THE FEDERAL ARBITRATION ACT

Sharply to be distinguished from court-annexed arbitration is arbitration under the Federal Arbitration Act, 9 U.S.C. § 1 et seq. The former is mandatory, but not binding; the latter is consensual and binding.

In Shearson/American Express, Inc. v. McMahon, 482 U.S. 220, 107 S.Ct. 2332, 96 L.Ed.2d 185 (1987), plaintiffs charged defendant brokerage house and the registered representative of the house with violations of the Securities Exchange Act of 1934 and with civil RICO violations. Defendant relied on the following provision signed by plaintiff in a pre-dispute contract; "Unless unenforceable due to federal or state law, any controversy arising out of or relating to my accounts, to transactions with you for me or to this agreement or the breach thereof, shall be settled by arbitration in accordance with the rules, then in effect, of the National Association of Securities Dealers,

Inc. or the Boards of Directors of the New York Stock Exchange, Inc. and/or the American Stock Exchange, Inc. as I may elect."

Defendants moved to compel arbitration in accordance with the Federal Arbitration Act, and the Supreme Court held that they were entitled to do so. The Court noted that "The Act was intended to 'revers[e] centuries of judicial hostility to arbitration agreements.' "

Whether the particular contractual provision in question is part of a contract of adhesion, whether the particular arbitration program involved is both fair and efficient, and if not what instrument of government has the authority and the initiative to intervene, are separate questions.

The following case, which coincidentally also involves the Shearson brokerage house (perhaps not so coincidentally since NASD arbitration clauses have become a standard feature of securities brokerage agreements) illustrates the difficulties federal courts face in enforcing the FAA policy in favor of arbitration agreements while also giving effect to the intentions of the parties to the agreement.

Mastrobuono v. Shearson Lehman Hutton

Supreme Court of the United States, 1995.
514 U.S. 52; 115 S. Ct. 1212; 131 L.Ed. 2d 76.

■ JUSTICE STEVENS delivered the opinion of the Court.

New York law allows courts, but not arbitrators, to award punitive damages. In a dispute arising out of a standard-form contract that expressly provides that it "shall be governed by the laws of the State of New York," a panel of arbitrators awarded punitive damages. The District Court and Court of Appeals disallowed that award. The question presented is whether the arbitrators' award is consistent with the central purpose of the Federal Arbitration Act to ensure "that private agreements to arbitrate are enforced according to their terms." Volt Information Sciences, Inc. v. Board of Trustees of Leland Stanford Junior Univ., 489 U.S. 468, 479, 103 L. Ed. 2d 488, 109 S. Ct. 1248 (1989).

In 1985, petitioners, Antonio Mastrobuono, then an assistant professor of medieval literature, and his wife Diana Mastrobuono, an artist, opened a securities trading account with respondent Shearson Lehman Hutton, Inc. (Shearson), by executing Shearson's standard-form Client's Agreement. Respondent Nick DiMinico, a vice president of Shearson, managed the Mastrobuonos' account until they closed it in 1987. In 1989, petitioners filed this action in the United States District Court for the Northern District of Illinois, alleging that respondents had mishandled their account and claiming damages on a variety of state and federal law theories.

Paragraph 13 of the parties' agreement contains an arbitration provision and a choice-of-law provision. Relying on the arbitration provision and on §§ 3 and 4 of the Federal Arbitration Act (FAA), 9 U.S.C. §§ 3, 4, respondents filed a motion to stay the court proceedings and to compel arbitration pursuant to the rules of the National Association of Securities Dealers. The District Court granted that motion, and a panel of three arbitrators was convened. After conducting hearings in Illinois, the panel ruled in favor of petitioners.

In the arbitration proceedings, respondents argued that the arbitrators had no authority to award punitive damages. Nevertheless, the panel's award included punitive damages of $400,000, in addition to compensatory damages of $159,327. Respondents paid the compensatory portion of the award but filed a motion in the District Court to vacate the award of punitive damages. The District Court granted the motion, and the Court of Appeals for the Seventh Circuit affirmed. Both courts relied on the choice-of-law provision in paragraph 13 of the parties' agreement, which specifies that the contract shall be governed by New York law. Because the New York Court of Appeals has decided that in New York the power to award punitive damages is limited to judicial tribunals and may not be exercised by arbitrators, Garrity v. Lyle Stuart, Inc., 40 N.Y.2d 354, 353 N.E.2d 793, 386 N.Y.S.2d 831 (1976), the District Court and the Seventh Circuit held that the panel of arbitrators had no power to award punitive damages in this case. We granted certiorari, because the Courts of Appeals have expressed differing views on whether a contractual choice-of-law provision may preclude an arbitral award of punitive damages that otherwise would be proper. We now reverse.[1]

Earlier this Term, we upheld the enforceability of a predispute arbitration agreement governed by Alabama law, even though an Alabama statute provides that arbitration agreements are unenforceable. Allied–Bruce Terminix Cos. v. Dobson, 513 U.S. 265, 130 L. Ed. 2d 753, 115 S. Ct. 834 (1995). Writing for the Court, Justice Breyer observed that Congress passed the FAA "to overcome courts' refusals to enforce agreements to arbitrate." Id., at 270. See also Volt Information Sciences, Inc. v. Board of Trustees of Leland Stanford Junior Univ., 489 U.S. at 474; Dean Witter Reynolds Inc. v. Byrd, 470 U.S. 213, 220, 84 L. Ed. 2d 158, 105 S. Ct. 1238 (1985). After determining that the FAA applied to the parties' arbitration agreement, we readily concluded that the federal statute pre-empted Alabama's statutory prohibition.

Petitioners seek a similar disposition of the case before us today. Here, the Seventh Circuit interpreted the contract to incorporate New York law, including the Garrity rule that arbitrators may not award punitive damages. Petitioners ask us to hold that the FAA pre-empts New York's prohibition against arbitral awards of punitive damages because this state law is a vestige of the " ' "ancient" ' " judicial hostility to arbitration. Petitioners rely on Southland Corp. v. Keating, 465 U.S. 1, 79 L. Ed. 2d 1, 104 S. Ct. 852 (1984), and Perry v. Thomas,

---

1. Because our disposition would be the same under either a de novo or a deferential standard, we need not decide in this case the proper standard of a court's review of an arbitrator's decision as to the arbitrability of a dispute or as to the scope of an arbitration. We recently granted certiorari in a case that involves some of these issues. First Options of Chicago, Inc. v. Kaplan, 514 U.S. 938, 131 L. Ed. 2d 985, 115 S. Ct. 1920, now pending before the Court.

482 U.S. 483, 96 L. Ed. 2d 426, 107 S. Ct. 2520 (1987), in which we held that the FAA pre-empted two California statutes that purported to require judicial resolution of certain disputes. In *Southland*, we explained that the FAA not only "declared a national policy favoring arbitration," but actually "withdrew the power of the states to require a judicial forum for the resolution of claims which the contracting parties agreed to resolve by arbitration." 465 U.S. at 10.

Respondents answer that the choice-of-law provision in their contract evidences the parties' express agreement that punitive damages should not be awarded in the arbitration of any dispute arising under their contract. Thus, they claim, this case is distinguishable from *Southland* and *Perry*, in which the parties presumably desired unlimited arbitration but state law stood in their way. Regardless of whether the FAA pre-empts the *Garrity* decision in contracts not expressly incorporating New York law, respondents argue that the parties may themselves agree to be bound by *Garrity*, just as they may agree to forgo arbitration altogether. In other words, if the contract says "no punitive damages," that is the end of the matter, for courts are bound to interpret contracts in accordance with the expressed intentions of the parties—even if the effect of those intentions is to limit arbitration.

We have previously held that the FAA's proarbitration policy does not operate without regard to the wishes of the contracting parties. In Volt Information Sciences, Inc. v. Board of Trustees of Leland Stanford Junior Univ., 489 U.S. 468, 103 L. Ed. 2d 488, 109 S. Ct. 1248 (1989), the California Court of Appeal had construed a contractual provision to mean that the parties intended the California rules of arbitration, rather than the FAA's rules, to govern the resolution of their dispute. Noting that the California rules were "manifestly designed to encourage resort to the arbitral process," and that they "generally fostered the federal policy favoring arbitration," we concluded that such an interpretation was entirely consistent with the federal policy "to ensure the enforceability, according to their terms, of private agreements to arbitrate." After referring to the holdings in *Southland* and *Perry*, which struck down state laws limiting agreed-upon arbitrability, we added:

> "But it does not follow that the FAA prevents the enforcement of agreements to arbitrate under different rules than those set forth in the Act itself. Indeed, such a result would be quite inimical to the FAA's primary purpose of ensuring that private agreements to arbitrate are enforced according to their terms. Arbitration under the Act is a matter of consent, not coercion, and parties are generally free to structure their arbitration agreements as they see fit. Just as they may limit by contract the issues which they will arbitrate, see Mitsubishi [Motors Corp. v. Soler Chrysler–Plymouth, Inc., 473 U.S. 614, 628, 87 L. Ed. 2d 444, 105 S. Ct. 3346 (1985)], so too may they specify by contract the rules under which that arbitration will be conducted." Volt, 489 U.S. at 479.

Relying on our reasoning in *Volt*, respondents thus argue that the parties to a contract may lawfully agree to limit the issues to be arbitrated by waiving any claim for punitive damages. On the other hand, we think our decisions in *Allied–Bruce, Southland*, and *Perry* make clear that if contracting parties agree to include claims for punitive damages within the issues to be arbitrated, the FAA ensures that their agreement will be enforced according to its terms even if a rule of state law would otherwise exclude such claims from arbitration. Thus, the case before us comes down to what the contract has to say about the arbitrability of petitioners' claim for punitive damages.

Shearson's standard-form "Client Agreement," which petitioners executed, contains 18 paragraphs. The two relevant provisions of the agreement are found in paragraph 13. The first sentence of that paragraph provides, in part, that the entire agreement "shall be governed by the laws of the State of New York." The second sentence provides that "any controversy" arising out of the transactions between the parties "shall be settled by arbitration" in accordance with the rules of the National Association of Securities Dealers (NASD), or the Boards of Directors of the New York Stock Exchange and/or the American Stock Exchange. The agreement contains no express reference to claims for punitive damages. To ascertain whether paragraph 13 expresses an intent to include or exclude such claims, we first address the impact of each of the two relevant provisions, considered separately. We then move on to the more important inquiry: the meaning of the two provisions taken together.

The choice-of-law provision, when viewed in isolation, may reasonably be read as merely a substitute for the conflict-of-laws analysis that otherwise would determine what law to apply to disputes arising out of the contractual relationship. Thus, if a similar contract, without a choice-of-law provision, had been signed in New York and was to be performed in New York, presumably "the laws of the State of New York" would apply, even though the contract did not expressly so state. In such event, there would be nothing in the contract that could possibly constitute evidence of an intent to exclude punitive damages claims. Accordingly, punitive damages would be allowed because, in the absence of contractual intent to the contrary, the FAA would preempt the Garrity rule. Even if the reference to "the laws of the State of New York" is more than a substitute for ordinary conflict-of-laws analysis and, as respondents urge, includes the caveat, "detached from otherwise-applicable federal law," the provision might not preclude the award of punitive damages because New York allows its courts, though not its arbitrators, to enter such awards. See *Garrity*, 40 N.Y.2d at 358, 353 N.E.2d, at 796. In other words, the provision might include only New York's substantive rights and obligations, and not the State's allocation of power between alternative tribunals. Respondents' argument is persuasive only if "New York law" means "New York decisional law, including that State's allocation of power between courts and arbitrators, notwithstanding otherwise-applicable federal law." But, as we have demonstrated, the provision need not be read so broadly. It is not, in itself, an unequivocal exclusion of punitive damages claims.

The arbitration provision (the second sentence of paragraph 13) does not improve respondents' argument. On the contrary, when read separately this clause strongly implies that an arbitral award of punitive damages is appropriate. It explicitly authorizes arbitration in accordance with NASD rules; the panel of arbitrators in fact proceeded under that set of rules. The NASD's Code of Arbitration Procedure indicates that arbitrators may award "damages and other relief." NASD Code of Arbitration Procedure ¶ 3741(e) (1993). While not a clear authorization of punitive damages, this provision appears broad enough at least to contemplate such a remedy. Moreover, as the Seventh Circuit noted, a manual provided to NASD arbitrators contains this provision:

> "B. Punitive Damages

> "The issue of punitive damages may arise with great frequency in arbitrations. Parties to arbitration are informed that arbitrators can consider punitive damages as a remedy."

Thus, the text of the arbitration clause itself surely does not support—indeed, it contradicts—the conclusion that the parties agreed to foreclose claims for punitive damages.

Although neither the choice-of-law clause nor the arbitration clause, separately considered, expresses an intent to preclude an award of punitive damages, respondents argue that a fair reading of the entire paragraph 13 leads to that conclusion. On this theory, even if "New York law" is ambiguous, and even if "arbitration in accordance with NASD rules" indicates that punitive damages are permissible, the juxtaposition of the two clauses suggests that the contract incorporates "New York law relating to arbitration." We disagree. At most, the choice-of-law clause introduces an ambiguity into an arbitration agreement that would otherwise allow punitive damages awards. As we pointed out in Volt, when a court interprets such provisions in an agreement covered by the FAA, "due regard must be given to the federal policy favoring arbitration, and ambiguities as to the scope of the arbitration clause itself resolved in favor of arbitration." 489 U.S. at 476. See also Moses H. Cone Memorial Hospital v. Mercury Constr. Corp., 460 U.S. 1, 24–25, 74 L. Ed. 2d 765, 103 S. Ct. 927 (1983).

We hold that the Court of Appeals misinterpreted the parties' agreement. The arbitral award should have been enforced as within the scope of the contract. The judgment of the Court of Appeals is, therefore, reversed.

■ JUSTICE THOMAS, dissenting.

In Volt Information Sciences, Inc. v. Board of Trustees of Leland Stanford Junior Univ., 489 U.S. 468, 478, 103 L. Ed. 2d 488, 109 S. Ct. 1248 (1989), we held that the Federal Arbitration Act (FAA) simply requires courts to enforce private contracts to arbitrate as they would normal contracts—according to their terms. This holding led us to enforce a choice-of-law provision that incorporated a state procedural rule concerning arbitration proceedings. Because the choice-of-law provision here cannot reasonably be distinguished from the one in *Volt*, I dissent.

In *Volt*, Stanford University had entered into a construction contract under which Volt Information Sciences, Inc. was to install certain electrical systems on the Stanford campus. The contract contained an agreement to arbitrate all disputes arising out of the contract. A choice-of-law clause in the contract provided that "the Contract shall be governed by the law of the place where the Project is located," 489 U.S. at 470, which happened to be California. When a dispute arose regarding compensation, Volt invoked arbitration. Stanford filed an action in state court, however, and moved to stay arbitration pursuant to California Rules of Civil Procedure. Cal. Civ. Proc. Code Ann. § 1281.2(c) (West 1982). Opposing the stay, Volt argued that the relevant state statute authorizing the stay was preempted by the FAA.

We concluded that even if the FAA pre-empted the state statute as applied to other parties, the choice-of-law clause in the contract at issue demonstrated that the parties had agreed to be governed by the statute. Rejecting Volt's position that the FAA imposes a proarbitration policy that precluded enforcement of the statute permitting the California courts to stay the arbitration proceedings, we concluded that the Act "simply requires courts to enforce privately negotiated agreements to arbitrate, like other contracts, in accordance with their terms." 489 U.S. at 478. As a result, we interpreted the choice-of-law clause "to make applicable state rules governing the conduct of arbitration," *id.*, at 476, even if a specific rule itself hampers or delays arbitration. We rejected the argument that the choice-of-law clause was to be construed as incorporating only substantive law, and dismissed the claim that the FAA pre-empted those contract provisions that might hinder arbitration.

We so held in *Volt* because we concluded that the FAA does not force arbitration on parties who enter into contracts involving interstate commerce. Instead, the FAA requires only that "arbitration proceed in the manner provided for in [the parties'] agreement." 9 U.S.C. § 4. Although we will construe ambiguities concerning the scope of arbitrability in favor of arbitration, see Moses H. Cone Memorial Hospital v. Mercury Constr. Corp., 460 U.S. 1, 24–25, 74 L. Ed. 2d 765, 103 S. Ct. 927 (1983), we remain mindful that "as with any other contract, the parties' intentions control," Mitsubishi Motors Corp. v. Soler Chrysler–Plymouth, Inc., 473 U.S. 614, 626, 87 L. Ed. 2d 444, 105 S. Ct. 3346 (1985). Thus, if the parties intend that state procedure shall govern, federal courts must enforce that understanding. "There is no federal policy favoring arbitration under a certain set of procedural rules; the federal policy is simply to ensure the enforceability, according to their terms, of private agreements to arbitrate." *Volt*, 489 U.S. at 476.

In this case, as in *Volt*, the parties agreed to mandatory arbitration of all disputes. As in *Volt*, the contract at issue here includes a choice-of-law clause. Indeed, the language of the two clauses is functionally equivalent: Whereas the choice-of-law clause in *Volt* provided that "the Contract shall be governed by the law of [the State of California]," the one before us today states, in paragraph 13 of the Client's Agreement, that "this agreement . . . shall be governed by the laws of the State of New York." New York law prohibits arbitrators from awarding punitive damages, Garrity v. Lyle Stuart, Inc., 40 N.Y.2d 354, 353 N.E.2d 793, 386 N.Y.S.2d 831 (1976), and permits only courts to award such damages. As in *Volt*, petitioners here argue that the New York rule is "antiarbitration," and hence is pre-empted by the FAA. In concluding that the choice-of-law clause is ambiguous, the majority essentially accepts petitioners' argument. Volt itself found precisely the same argument irrelevant, however, and the majority identifies no reason to think that the state law governing the interpretation of the parties' choice-of-law clause supports a different result.

The majority relies upon two assertions to defend its departure from *Volt*. First, it contends that "at most, the choice-of-law clause introduces an ambiguity into an arbitration agreement." We are told that the agreement "would otherwise allow punitive damages awards," because of paragraph 13's statement that arbitration would be con- ducted "in accordance with the rules then in effect, of the National Association of Securities Dealers, Inc. [NASD]." It is unclear which NASD "rules" the parties mean, although I am willing to agree with the majority that the phrase refers to the NASD Code of Arbitration Procedure. But the provision of the NASD Code offered by the majority simply does not speak to the availability of punitive damages. It only states:

"The award shall contain the names of the parties, the name of counsel, if any, a summary of the issues, including the type(s) of any security or product, in controversy, the damages and other relief requested, the damages and other relief awarded, a statement of any other issues resolved, the names of the arbitrators, the dates the claim was filed and the award rendered, the number and dates of hearing sessions, the location of the hearings, and the signatures of the arbitrators concurring in the award." NASD Code of Arbitration Proce- dure § 41(e) (1985).

It is clear that § 41(e) does not define or limit the powers of the arbitrators; it merely describes the form in which the arbitrators must announce their decision. The majority cannot find a provision of the NASD Code that specifically addresses punitive damages, or that speaks more generally to the types of damages arbitrators may or may not allow. Such a rule simply does not exist. The code certainly does not require that arbitrators be empowered to award punitive damages; it leaves to the parties to define the arbitrators' remedial powers.

The majority also purports to find a clear expression of the parties' agreement on the availability of punitive damages in "a manual provided to NASD arbitrators." But paragraph 13 of the Client Agreement nowhere mentions this manual; it mentions only "the rules then in effect, of the [NASD]." The manual does not fit either part of this description: it is neither "of the [NASD]," nor a set of "rules."

Even if the parties had intended to adopt the manual, it cannot be read to resolve the issue of punitive damages. When read in context, the portion of the SICA manual upon which the majority relies seems only to explain what punitive damages are, not to establish whether arbitrators have the authority to award them[.]

Thankfully, the import of the majority's decision is limited and narrow. This case amounts to nothing more than a federal court applying Illinois and New York contract law to an agreement between parties in Illinois. Much like a federal court applying a state rule of decision to a case when sitting in diversity, the majority's interpretation of the contract represents only the understanding of a single federal court regarding the requirements imposed by state law. As such, the majority's opinion has applicability only to this specific contract and to no other. But because the majority reaches an erroneous result on even this narrow question, I respectfully dissent.

QUESTIONS

Do you agree with Justice Thomas that the issue in this case is "limited and narrow"? What result if New York law prohibited its courts from awarding punitive damages? What result if New York permitted courts to award punitive damages only if plaintiffs met an extremely high evidentiary standard?

CHAPTER VIII

ADJUDICATION WITHOUT TRIAL REVISITED; SUMMARY JUDGMENT

A. THE FUNCTIONAL UTILITY OF SUMMARY JUDGMENT

Cecil & Douglas, Summary Judgment Practice in Three District Courts
(Federal Judicial Center 1987).

FOREWORD

A. Leo Levin

With the cost of litigation of increasing concern to bench and bar alike, there has been renewed interest in the use of summary judgment as a potentially effective tool to avoid unnecessary trials. A finding that "there is no genuine issue as to any material fact" terminates the proceedings, subject always to appeal. Perhaps of greater significance, summary judgment can bring the costly process of discovery with in appropriate bounds by eliminating issues that are either frivolous or immaterial.

It bears emphasis that the rules provide for partial summary judgment, making it possible to eliminate particular issues that are not the subject of genuine controversy, even though there remain other issues requiring trial. Removing even one such issue from a complicated case can translate into significant savings, for the court and more particularly for the litigants.

Despite the potential utility of summary judgment, it has in recent years been used even less frequently than heretofore. As indicated in the present study, there was a sharp decline from 1975 to 1986 in the percentage of cases disposed of by this mechanism. The reasons for the decline remain unclear; perhaps some courts of appeals were perceived as being unreceptive to such motions, or perhaps there was a lack of clarity in the standards for imposition of summary judgment. For whatever the reason, summary judgment became a neglected tool at a time when the perceived need for precisely such a device was commanding increasing attention.

At professional meetings and circuit conferences lawyers have been heard to claim that the judges were unreceptive to motions for summary judgment. The trial judges, in turn, argued that the appeals courts were inhospitable to summary judgment and that the rates of reversal of dispositions following the grant of summary judgment had a chilling effect. However, as Chief Judge Wilfred Feinberg took occasion to point out recently in an important opinion,[a] misperception by both the bar and the trial bench of what the appellate courts were doing in fact may have been the root of the problem.

In any event, the Supreme Court has recently clarified that standards for summary judgment, and a number of courts of appeals have indicated a greater receptivity toward its use. Some early indicative data presented in this report suggest that summary judgment may today be expanding to occupy a more prominent role in the resolution of cases. This places the federal courts at a crucial point in the development of summary judgment. Without question, it is important to prevent abuse of a device that denies a litigant the right to trial, but a vigilant bench can prevent abuse. It will require careful balancing to achieve the potential for controlling frivolous filings and rights of parties to have genuine factual disputes resolved at trial. This report, focusing on what has been, is designed to be helpful in achieving that balance.

NOTE

This study was early, too soon after the "Trilogy" to take into account the impact of the changed summary judgment law. The case sample included selections until June 30, 1986. The researchers conclude (p.2) that their study "coincides with what may be the eve of a revitalization of the role of summary judgment" referring to the "Trilogy."

* * *

Knight v. U.S. Fire Ins. Co.

United States Court of Appeals, Second Circuit, 1986.
804 F.2d 9.

■ FEINBERG, CHIEF JUDGE:

Frederick W.A. Knight appeals from an order of the United States District Court for the Southern District of New York, Constance Baker Motley, Ch. J., granting summary judgment to defendant insurance companies. Knight argues that summary judgment was inappropriate because several genuine issues of material fact remain unresolved. Upon review, we conclude that no such issues are present. Therefore, we affirm the holding of the district court.

I.   Facts

The relevant facts are as follows: Between 1976 and 1979, Knight purchased in Thailand 222 antique stone and bronze statues for approximately $65,000. In 1980, an appraiser hired by Knight valued the collection at $20,205,000. The same appraiser revised his estimate to $27,000,000 in April 1981 and then to $30,307,500 in September

---

a.   Knight v. U.S. Fire Ins. Co., which follows in the text.

1981, the month in which he died. The appraiser was to receive for his services 5% of the proceeds from the eventual sale of the statues.

Meanwhile, Knight had transported the statuary from Thailand to Singapore. In February 1981, Knight obtained through the insurance brokerage firm of Hogg Robinson & Gardner Mountain (Marine) Ltd. (Hogg Robinson) coverage of $20,205,000 from London underwriters for shipment of the collection from Singapore to Holland. In May 1981, after receiving the first revised estimate from his appraiser, Knight requested and obtained through Hogg Robinson an additional $10,000,000 coverage for the voyage.

In June 1981, however, after the approximately $30 million risk had been placed, Robert Jensen, Knight's broker at Hogg Robinson, received two anonymous phone calls reporting that Knight was planning to perpetrate a fraud. Jensen conveyed this information to the lead London underwriters who, in response, ordered their own appraisal of the statuary. A few days later, Jensen sent a telex to Knight informing him that the underwriters had voided his policy because of his material nondisclosures and misrepresentations regarding his collection. Jensen stated in the telex that, based on their appraiser's inspection of some of the statues, the underwriters believed that the collection was "grossly over-valued and, in some, if not all cases, replicas.... The evidence currently available to underwriters suggests that the proper value of the consignment is nominal only (possibly approximately 1 pct of the value declared)."

In the spring of 1982, Knight again attempted to obtain insurance for the same statues, this time through a New York brokerage firm, H.E. Yerkes & Associates, Inc. Knight obtained $30 million of coverage with several American underwriters for a voyage from Singapore to France. However, the collection ultimately was not shipped and the policy lapsed.

In October 1982, Knight approached Yerkes & Associates to reinstate his $30 million of coverage, claiming that he was preparing to ship the statues to a purchaser in Greece. The brokers succeeded in placing $30,630,750 of risk for the voyage from Singapore to Greece with several American insurance companies. Many of these insurers had agreed to insure the earlier projected voyage from Singapore to France. These are the policies contested in this lawsuit. For convenience, we will refer to them hereafter as one policy (the New York policy).

In January 1983, the statues were loaded on board a vessel for the voyage from Singapore to Greece. On February 7, 1983, the ship sank in the Indian Ocean and the statues were lost.

After the loss of his statues, Knight attempted to collect on the insurance provided by defendant underwriters. Defendants refused and, instead, voided the New York policy ab initio because of Knight's alleged material nondisclosures and misrepresentations. Thereafter, Knight brought this lawsuit. Defendants moved for summary judgment before Judge Motley, and she granted the motion in a 16–page memorandum opinion. This appeal followed.

II. Summary Judgment

Rule 56(c) of the Federal Rules of Civil Procedure provides that a court shall grant a motion for summary judgment if it determines that "there is no genuine issue as to any material fact and that the moving party is entitled to a judgment as a matter of law." In considering the motion, the court's responsibility is not to resolve disputed issues of fact but to assess whether there are any factual issues to be tried, while resolving ambiguities and drawing reasonable inferences against the moving party. Anderson v. Liberty Lobby, Inc., 477 U.S. 242, 106 S.Ct. 2505, 2509–11, 91 L.Ed.2d 202 (1986); Eastway Constr. Corp. v. City of New York, 762 F.2d 243, 249 (2d Cir.1985).

Before rendering summary judgment, a court must also determine that any unresolved issues are not material to the outcome of the litigation. "[T]he mere existence of factual issues—where those issues are not material to the claims before the court—will not suffice to defeat a motion for summary judgment." Quarles v. General Motors Corp., 758 F.2d 839, 840 (2d Cir.1985) (per curiam). Nor may a party rely on mere speculation or conjecture as to the true nature of the facts to overcome a motion for summary judgment. Id. Similarly, a "bare assertion that evidence to support a fanciful allegation lies within the exclusive control of the defendants, and can be obtained only through discovery, is not sufficient to defeat a motion for summary judgment." Eastway, 762 F.2d at 251.

Properly used, summary judgment permits a court to streamline the process for terminating frivolous claims and to concentrate its resources on meritorious litigation. * * *

It appears that in this circuit some litigants are reluctant to make full use of the summary judgment process because of their perception that this court is unsympathetic to such motions and frequently reverses grants of summary judgment. Whatever may have been the accuracy of this view in years gone by, it is decidedly inaccurate at the present time, as borne out by a recent study by the Second Circuit Committee on the Pretrial Phase of Civil Litigation, chaired by Professor Maurice Rosenberg. The Committee analyzed the published and unpublished decisions of the Second Circuit for the period from July 1, 1983 to June 30, 1985 and found that the affirmance rate on appeals from orders granting summary judgment was 79%.[1] Final Report of the Second Circuit Committee on the Pretrial Phase of Civil Litigation 16–17 (June 1986). Thus it is evident that grants of summary judgment are upheld on appeal in most cases. That figure is comparable to this circuit's 84% affirmance rate for appeals in civil cases generally. Id. The widespread misperception regarding the disposition of appeals of summary judgment may be due to the fact that reversals are much more likely to be reported in published opinions than

---

1. Of course, there are few, if any, appeals from orders denying summary judgment, since such orders ordinarily are not appealable.

affirmances, which frequently are disposed of by unpublished orders under our Local Rule § 0.23. Id. We hope that the Committee's study dispels the misperception so that litigants will not be deterred from making justifiable motions for summary judgment.

III. Discussion

Judge Motley granted summary judgment for defendants in this case because Knight had failed to inform them of a material fact. After rejecting several alternative grounds for the voidance of the New York policy, Judge Motley ruled that Knight's nondisclosure of the prior London cancellation together with the cancelling underwriters' opinion that the statues were overvalued and inauthentic justified defendant underwriters' voidance of the policy ab initio. With respect to this nondisclosure, Judge Motley found that there was no genuine issue as to any material fact. Although Knight presents several challenges to Judge Motley's decision, his arguments center around two main issues: whether the omitted fact was material and whether the underwriters had knowledge of that fact.

A.

In evaluating whether particular facts are material, we must turn to the substantive law governing marine insurance. It is well-established under the doctrine of uberrimae fidei that the parties to a marine insurance policy must accord each other the highest degree of good faith. Puritan Ins. Co. v. Eagle S.S. Co. S.A., 779 F.2d 866, 870 (2d Cir.1985). This stringent doctrine requires the assured to disclose to the insurer all known circumstances that materially affect the risk being insured. Since the assured is in the best position to know of any circumstances material to the risk, he must reveal those facts to the underwriter, rather than wait for the underwriter to inquire. Id. The standard for disclosure is an objective one, that is, whether a reasonable person in the assured's position would know that the particular fact is material. Btesh v. Royal Ins. Co., 49 F.2d 720, 721 (2d Cir.1931). To be material, the fact must be "something which would have controlled the underwriter's decision" to accept the risk. Id. The assured's failure to meet this standard entitles the underwriter to void the policy ab initio. Puritan Ins. Co., 779 F.2d at 870–71.

Knight contends, however, that an assured's duty to disclose a prior cancellation is not triggered where the cancellation was based on fictitious or false information. He relies on the testimony of Leslie J. Buglass, an expert in marine insurance, that false information cannot materially affect risk. Arguing that his prior cancellation was caused by anonymous phone calls that were entirely groundless and an inspection that was performed by an unqualified appraiser, Knight maintains that it was error for Judge Motley to dismiss his allegations as irrelevant and to grant summary judgment.

The fact of the prior cancellation and the stated reasons for the cancellation are not disputed. In light of these circumstances, Judge Motley stated:

[A]s a matter of indisputable fact a prior underwriter's voidance of a thirty million dollar insurance policy on antiquities of dubious origin on the grounds that the goods were "grossly over-valued" and inauthentic would have been material to any subsequent underwriter's decision to accept the risk.... No reasonable juror could conclude, under the facts of this case, that defendants would not have declined to embrace plaintiff's requested thirty million dollar policy had they known of the prior London cancellation and of the incriminating contents of the telex from the London broker—at least not without subsequent opportunity for defendants to make their own investigation and perhaps adjust ... the amount insured.

We see no reason to disturb Judge Motley's conclusion that the fact of the prior cancellation and the stated reasons therefor would have materially affected defendants' decision to provide the thirty million dollar coverage. Although Knight devotes a substantial portion of his briefs to arguing that the prior cancellation was unfounded, that issue does not affect the materiality of the admitted nondisclosure. Regardless of the justifiability of the prior cancellation, the fact remains that the cancellation occurred because the London underwriters believed that the statues were overvalued and inauthentic. A reasonable assured in Knight's position would know that other insurers providing virtually the same coverage for the same statues would not take on the risk or maintain the same premium without at least investigating the prior cancellation, if informed of it and the stated reasons therefor. Cf. Solez v. Zurich General Accident & Liability Ins. Co., 54 F.2d 523, 526 (2d Cir.1931), cert. dismissed, 296 U.S. 668, 57 S.Ct. 756 (1932). We hold under these circumstances that the nondisclosure is material. Thus, the materiality of the nondisclosure does not depend on what an investigation would have revealed. The facts of this case illustrate the difficulty courts would face in determining retrospectively what an investigation would have uncovered, when the goods have already been lost. Instead, the insurer should be afforded the opportunity to investigate prior to its acceptance of the risk. Accordingly, the assured is required to communicate the information to the insurer before the policy is issued, so that the insurer can decide for itself at that time whether to accept the risk. This obligation is not burdensome to the assured and it comports with the open disclosure required by the doctrine of uberrimae fidei.

Knight's claim that the prior cancellation was unwarranted does not alter this conclusion. We are told that the materiality of information that an assured reasonably believes to be untrue is an issue of first impression, and we will assume for present discussion that Knight's belief in this case is reasonable. Under Knight's view, an assured would be permitted to withhold an otherwise material fact such as cancellation whenever he reasonably believed the basis for the cancellation to be unjustified. Such an approach would unnecessarily complicate litigation over nondisclosure. Deciding whether the basis for the undisclosed prior cancellation was well-founded would become a mini-trial in itself. The sounder approach is to require an assured to communicate the information to the insurer before a policy is issued, so that the insurer can decide whether to accept the risk despite the prior cancellation. Arnould's Law of Marine Insurance and Average ¶ 653 (M. Mustill & J. Gilman 16th ed. 1981) (hereinafter Arnould's Marine Insurance). Thus courts would not have to divine what would have occurred had there been full disclosure.[2]

We have also considered Knight's argument that a cancellation of prior insurance may be concealed, based on British cases holding that it is not necessary to disclose a prior refusal by another marine insurer to write a policy. See, e.g., Container Transport Int'l, Inc. & Reliance Group, Inc. v. Oceanus Mutual Underwriting Ass'n (Bermuda), 1982 2 Lloyd's L.R. 178, 190. This marine insurance rule is apparently "not followed" in other types of insurance. Arnould's Marine Insurance at ¶ 642 n. 75. The rule may be explainable by the unusual nature of marine risks, but seems anomalous in view of the doctrine that the parties to marine insurance must observe the highest degree of good faith. In any event, we are unpersuaded by the analogy. A refusal to write a policy is not the same as a cancellation, particularly when the latter resulted from the insurer's belief that the goods insured were overvalued and inauthentic.

Knight also argues that the materiality of a nondisclosure is a factual issue that can be decided only by a jury, because, he urges, live testimony is essential to such a determination. Judge Motley recognized that the materiality of a nondisclosure is a finding of fact that ordinarily is a jury question. In this case, though, since the only possible outcome as a matter of law, even if a trial had been conducted, is in favor of defendants, Judge Motley was correct in granting summary judgment. See R.G. Group, Inc. v. Horn & Hardart Co., 751 F.2d 69, 77 (2d Cir.1984); King v. Aetna Ins. Co., 54 F.2d 253, 255 (2d Cir.1931). Indeed, it is precisely under these kinds of circumstances that summary judgment serves salutary purposes.

B.

Knight claims that another genuine issue is whether defendants had knowledge, either actual or constructive, of the prior cancellation and the reasons for the cancellation. Such knowledge would defeat defendants' claim that the prior cancellation was not disclosed. Judge Motley's decision does not address this issue. After reviewing the record, we conclude that, even though Knight could have made these legal arguments more clearly in the district court, he did mention these basic contentions in his opposition to summary judgment. Accordingly, we will discuss the merits. Keeping in mind that we are reviewing a summary judgment, we consider the facts in a light most favorable to Knight.

---

2. Knight has made a motion to expand the record with an affidavit, not submitted to the district court, concerning the source of the anonymous telephone calls. Since we have determined that the justifiability of the prior cancellation is not relevant to the outcome of this appeal, we deny the motion.

Knight argues that he was not required to disclose the prior cancellation to defendants because some of the underwriters who reinsured a portion of the New York policy were primary insurers of part of the cancelled London policy. But defendants are the primary insurers of the New York policy, not the reinsurers, and there is no indication of actual knowledge of the prior cancellation on their part except for Knight's speculations. Knight's obligation was to communicate material facts to the primary insurers since they issued his policy.

Knight also maintains that two defendants—Insurance Company of North America (INA) and Centennial Insurance Company (Centennial)—had actual knowledge because of their relationship with two underwriters of the London policy—Insurance Company of North America, UK (INA(UK)) and Atlantic Mutual. He alleges that such knowledge existed because INA and INA(UK) are both subsidiaries of the same parent corporation and Centennial is a subsidiary of Atlantic Mutual. Again Knight offers only speculation that the two New York underwriters communicated with the two respective London underwriters about his policy prior to the loss of the statues. Speculation by itself is not enough to defeat a motion for summary judgment. Quarles, 758 F.2d at 840. The other circumstances described by Knight to show actual knowledge are even more speculative and do not require discussion.

Knight's claim of constructive knowledge is based on his alleged disclosure to INA of some of the circumstances surrounding his acquisition of the statues and his prior attempts to obtain insurance. See Luria Brothers & Co. v. Alliance Assurance Co., 780 F.2d 1082, 1091 (2d Cir.1986). He argues that the other defendants regarded INA as the lead underwriter and that they learned of any information known to the leader. Knight disclosed information such as the "very moderate" purchase price, the illegal export of the statues out of Thailand, his desire to avoid the London insurance market, and an earlier attempt to obtain "$15,000,000 upwards" coverage for the collection. None of this information, however, relates to the cancelled London policy. In view of the high burden of disclosure on the assured in the field of marine insurance, we conclude that this information falls short of providing sufficient notice so as to shift the obligation to defendants to inquire about a prior cancellation. Closely related to the claim of constructive knowledge is Knight's argument that defendants have not fulfilled their own obligations under uberrimae fidei. See Puritan Ins. Co., 779 F.2d at 870. He contends that they would have made inquiries and learned of the prior cancellation if they had been acting in the utmost good faith. Since the speculative assertions on which Knight relies do not establish a genuine issue with respect to any of these issues, these claims must fail.

IV.   Conclusion

We conclude that Judge Motley's grant of summary judgment was appropriate since Knight has not shown any genuine issue as to a material fact. The justifiability of the prior cancellation is not a material fact and defendants' knowledge of the prior cancellation is not a genuine issue. Therefore, we affirm Judge Motley's decision to grant summary judgment and to dismiss the case.

NOTES

1. Local Rule § 0.23 of the United States Court of Appeals for the Second Circuit provides:

§ 0.23   Dispositions in open court or by summary order

The demands of an expanding caseload require the court to be ever conscious of the need to utilize judicial time effectively. Accordingly, in those cases in which decision is unanimous and each judge of the panel believes that no jurisprudential purpose would be served by a written opinion, disposition will be made in open court or by summary order.

Where a decision is rendered from the bench, the court may deliver a brief oral statement, the record of which is available to counsel upon request and payment of transcription charges. Where disposition is by summary order, the court may append a brief written statement to that order. Since these statements do not constitute formal opinions of the court and are unreported and not uniformly available to all parties, they shall not be cited or otherwise used in unrelated cases before this or any other court.

2. Since then, federal courts have needed no encouragement to entertain summary judgment motions. Judge Wald's information from the District of Columbia is that about 22% of all terminations in 1996 were by summary judgment. Patricia M. Wald, Summary Judgment at Sixty, 76 Texas L. Rev. 1897, 1915 (1998).

B.   THE APPLICABLE STANDARD

Celotex Corporation v. Catrett

Supreme Court of the United States, 1986.
477 U.S. 317, 106 S.Ct. 2548, 91 L.Ed.2d 265.

■ JUSTICE REHNQUIST delivered the opinion of the Court.

The United States District Court for the District of Columbia granted the motion of petitioner Celotex Corporation for summary judgment against respondent Catrett because the latter was unable to produce evidence in support of her allegation in her wrongful-death complaint that the decedent had been exposed to petitioner's asbestos products. A divided panel of the Court of Appeals for the District of Columbia Circuit reversed, however, holding that petitioner's failure to support its motion with evidence tending to negate such exposure precluded the entry of summary judgment in its favor. Catrett v. Johns–Manville Sales Corp., 244 U.S.App.D.C. 160, 756 F.2d 181 (1985). This view conflicted with that of the Third Circuit in In re Japanese Electronic Products, 723 F.2d 238 (1983), rev'd on other grounds sub nom. Matsushita Electric Industrial Co. v. Zenith Radio Corp., 475 U.S. 574,

106 S.Ct. 1348, 89 L.Ed.2d 538 (1986.)[1] We granted certiorari to resolve the conflict, 474 U.S. 944, 106 S.Ct. 342, 88 L.Ed.2d 285 (1985), and now reverse the decision of the District of Columbia Circuit.

Respondent commenced this lawsuit in September 1980, alleging that the death in 1979 of her husband, Louis H. Catrett, resulted from his exposure to products containing asbestos manufactured or distributed by 15 named corporations. Respondent's complaint sounded in negligence, breach of warranty, and strict liability. Two of the defendants filed motions challenging the District Court's in personam jurisdiction, and the remaining 13, including petitioner, filed motions for summary judgment. Petitioner's motion, which was first filed in September 1981, argued that summary judgment was proper because respondent had "failed to produce evidence that any [Celotex] product ... was the proximate cause of the injuries alleged within the jurisdictional limits of [the District] Court." In particular, petitioner noted that respondent had failed to identify, in answering interrogatories specifically requesting such information, any witnesses who could testify about the decedent's exposure to petitioner's asbestos products. In response to petitioner's summary judgment motion, respondent then produced three documents which she claimed "demonstrate that there is a genuine material factual dispute" as to whether the decedent had ever been exposed to petitioner's asbestos products. The three documents included a transcript of a deposition of the decedent, a letter from an official of one of the decedent's former employers whom petitioner planned to call as a trial witness, and a letter from an insurance company to respondent's attorney, all tending to establish that the decedent had been exposed to petitioner's asbestos products in Chicago during 1970–1971. Petitioner, in turn, argued that the three documents were inadmissible hearsay and thus could not be considered in opposition to the summary judgment motion.

In July 1982, almost two years after the commencement of the lawsuit, the District Court granted all of the motions filed by the various defendants. The court explained that it was granting petitioner's summary judgment motion because "there [was] no showing that the plaintiff was exposed to the defendant Celotex's product in the District of Columbia or elsewhere within the statutory period." App. 217.[2] Respondent appealed only the grant of summary judgment in

---

1. Since our grant of certiorari in this case, the Fifth Circuit has rendered a decision squarely rejecting the position adopted here by the District of Columbia Circuit. See Fontenot v. Upjohn Co., 780 F.2d 1190 (1986)

2. Justice STEVENS, in dissent, argues that the District Court granted summary judgment only because respondent presented no evidence that the decedent was exposed to Celotex asbestos products in the District of Columbia. See post, at 2560–2561. According to Justice STEVENS, we should affirm the

decision of the Court of Appeals, reversing the District Court, on the "narrower ground" that respondent "made an adequate showing" that the decedent was exposed to Celotex asbestos products in Chicago during 1970–1971. See Ibid.

Justice STEVENS' position is factually incorrect. The District Court expressly stated that respondent had made no showing of exposure to Celotex asbestos products "in the District of Columbia or elsewhere." App. 217 (emphasis added). Unlike Justice STEVENS,

favor of petitioner, and a divided panel of the District of Columbia Circuit reversed. The majority of the Court of Appeals held that petitioner's summary judgment motion was rendered "fatally defective" by the fact that petitioner "made no effort to adduce any evidence, in the form of affidavits or otherwise, to support its motion." 244 U.S.App.D.C., at 163, 756 F.2d, at 184 (emphasis in original). According to the majority, Rule 56(e) of the Federal Rules of Civil Procedure, and this Court's decision in Adickes v. S.H. Kress & Co., 398 U.S. 144, 159, 90 S.Ct. 1598, 1609, 26 L.Ed.2d 142 (1970), establish that "the party opposing the motion for summary judgment bears the burden of responding only after the moving party has met its burden of coming forward with proof of the absence of any genuine issues of material fact." 244 U.S.App.D.C., at 163, 756 F.2d, at 184 (emphasis in original; footnote omitted). The majority therefore declined to consider petitioner's argument that none of the evidence produced by respondent in opposition to the motion for summary judgment would have been admissible at trial. Ibid. The dissenting judge argued that "[t]he majority errs in supposing that a party seeking summary judgment must always make an affirmative evidentiary showing, even in cases where there is not a triable, factual dispute." Id., at 167, 756 F.2d, at 188 (Bork, J., dissenting). According to the dissenting judge, the majority's decision "undermines the traditional authority of trial judges to grant summary judgment in meritless cases." Id., at 166, 756 F.2d, at 187.

We think that the position taken by the majority of the Court of Appeals is inconsistent with the standard for summary judgment set forth in Rule 56(c) of the Federal Rules of Civil Procedure. Under Rule 56(c), summary judgment is proper "if the pleadings, depositions, answers to interrogatories, and admissions on file, together with the affidavits, if any, show that there is no genuine issue as to any material fact and that the moving party is entitled to a judgment as a matter of law." In our view, the plain language of Rule 56(c) mandates the entry of summary judgment, after adequate time for discovery and upon motion, against a party who fails to make a showing sufficient to establish the existence of an element essential to that party's case, and on which that party will bear the burden of proof at trial. In such a situation, there can be "no genuine issue as to any material fact," since a complete failure of proof concerning an essential element of the nonmoving party's case necessarily renders all other facts immaterial. The moving party is "entitled to a judgment as a matter of law" because the nonmoving party has failed to make a sufficient showing on an essential element of her case with respect to which she has the burden of proof. "[T]h[e] standard [for granting summary judgment]

we assume that the District Court meant what it said. The majority of the Court of Appeals addressed the very issue raised by Justice STEVENS, and decided that "[t]he District Court's grant of summary judgment must therefore have been based on its conclusion that there was 'no showing that the plaintiff was exposed to defendant Celotex's product in the District of Columbia or elsewhere within the statutory period.'" Catrett v. Johns–Manville Sales Corp., 244 U.S.App. D.C. 160, 162, n. 3, 756 F.2d 181, 183, n. 3 (1985) (emphasis in original). In other words, no judge involved in this case to date shares Justice STEVENS' view of the District Court's decision.

mirrors the standard for a directed verdict under Federal Rule of Civil Procedure 50(a)...." Anderson v. Liberty Lobby, Inc., 477 U.S. 242, 250, 106 S.Ct. 2505, 2511, 91 L.Ed.2d 202 (1986).

Of course, a party seeking summary judgment always bears the initial responsibility of informing the district court of the basis for its motion, and identifying those portions of "the pleadings, depositions, answers to interrogatories, and admissions on file, together with the affidavits, if any," which it believes demonstrate the absence of a genuine issue of material fact. But unlike the Court of Appeals, we find no express or implied requirement in Rule 56 that the moving party support its motion with affidavits or other similar materials negating the opponent's claim. On the contrary, Rule 56(c), which refers to "the affidavits, if any" (emphasis added), suggests the absence of such a requirement. And if there were any doubt about the meaning of Rule 56(c) in this regard, such doubt is clearly removed by Rules 56(a) and (b), which provide that claimants and defendants, respectively, may move for summary judgment "with or without supporting affidavits" (emphasis added). The import of these subsections is that, regardless of whether the moving party accompanies its summary judgment motion with affidavits, the motion may, and should, be granted so long as whatever is before the district court demonstrates that the standard for the entry of summary judgment, as set forth in Rule 56(c), is satisfied. One of the principal purposes of the summary judgment rule is to isolate and dispose of factually unsupported claims or defenses, and we think it should be interpreted in a way that allows it to accomplish this purpose.

Respondent argues, however, that Rule 56(e), by its terms, places on the nonmoving party the burden of coming forward with rebuttal affidavits, or other specified kinds of materials, only in response to a motion for summary judgment "made and supported as provided in this rule." According to respondent's argument, since petitioner did not "support" its motion with affidavits, summary judgment was improper in this case. But as we have already explained, a motion for summary judgment may be made pursuant to Rule 56 "with or without supporting affidavits." In cases like the instant one, where the nonmoving party will bear the burden of proof at trial on a dispositive issue, a summary judgment motion may properly be made in reliance solely on the "pleadings, depositions, answers to interrogatories, and admissions on file." Such a motion, whether or not accompanied by affidavits, will be "made and supported as provided in this rule," and Rule 56(e) therefore requires the nonmoving party to go beyond the pleadings and by her own affidavits, or by the "depositions, answers to interrogatories, and admissions on file," designate "specific facts showing that there is a genuine issue for trial."

We do not mean that the nonmoving party must produce evidence in a form that would be admissible at trial in order to avoid summary judgment. Obviously, Rule 56 does not require the nonmoving party to depose her own witnesses. Rule 56(e) permits a proper summary judgment motion to be opposed by any of the kinds of evidentiary materials listed in Rule 56(c), except the mere pleadings themselves, and it is from this list that one would normally expect the nonmoving party to make the showing to which we have referred.

The Court of Appeals in this case felt itself constrained, however, by language in our decision in Adickes v. S.H. Kress & Co., 398 U.S. 144, 90 S.Ct. 1598, 26 L.Ed.2d 142 (1970). There we held that summary judgment had been improperly entered in favor of the defendant restaurant in an action brought under 42 U.S.C. § 1983. In the course of its opinion, the Adickes Court said that "both the commentary on and the background of the 1963 amendment conclusively show that it was not intended to modify the burden of the moving party ... to show initially the absence of a genuine issue concerning any material fact." Id., at 159, 90 S.Ct., at 1609. We think that this statement is accurate in a literal sense, since we fully agree with the Adickes Court that the 1963 amendment to Rule 56(e) was not designed to modify the burden of making the showing generally required by Rule 56(c). It also appears to us that, on the basis of the showing before the Court in Adickes, the motion for summary judgment in that case should have been denied. But we do not think the Adickes language quoted above should be construed to mean that the burden is on the party moving for summary judgment to produce evidence showing the absence of a genuine issue of material fact, even with respect to an issue on which the nonmoving party bears the burden of proof. Instead, as we have explained, the burden on the moving party may be discharged by "showing"—that is, pointing out to the district court—that there is an absence of evidence to support the nonmoving party's case.

The last two sentences of Rule 56(e) were added, as this Court indicated in Adickes, to disapprove a line of cases allowing a party opposing summary judgment to resist a properly made motion by reference only to its pleadings. While the Adickes Court was undoubtedly correct in concluding that these two sentences were not intended to reduce the burden of the moving party, it is also obvious that they were not adopted to add to that burden. Yet that is exactly the result which the reasoning of the Court of Appeals would produce; in effect, an amendment to Rule 56(e) designed to facilitate the granting of motions for summary judgment would be interpreted to make it more difficult to grant such motions. Nothing in the two sentences themselves requires this result, for the reasons we have previously indicated, and we now put to rest any inference that they do so.

Our conclusion is bolstered by the fact that district courts are widely acknowledged to possess the power to enter summary judgments sua sponte, so long as the losing party was on notice that she had to come forward with all of her evidence. See 244 U.S.App.D.C., at 167–168, 756 F.2d, at 189 (Bork, J., dissenting); 10A C. Wright, A. Miller, & M. Kane, Federal Practice and Procedure § 2720, pp. 28–29 (1983). It would surely defy common sense to hold that the District Court could have entered summary judgment sua sponte in favor of petitioner in the instant case, but that petitioner's filing of a motion requesting such a disposition precluded the District Court from ordering it.

Respondent commenced this action in September 1980, and petitioner's motion was filed in September 1981. The parties had conducted discovery, and no serious claim can be made that respondent was in any sense "railroaded" by a premature motion for summary judgment. Any potential problem with such premature motions can be adequately dealt with under Rule 56(f), which allows a summary judgment motion to be denied, or the hearing on the motion to be continued, if the nonmoving party has not had an opportunity to make full discovery.

In this Court, respondent's brief and oral argument have been devoted as much to the proposition that an adequate showing of exposure to petitioner's asbestos products was made as to the proposition that no such showing should have been required. But the Court of Appeals declined to address either the adequacy of the showing made by respondent in opposition to petitioner's motion for summary judgment, or the question whether such a showing, if reduced to admissible evidence, would be sufficient to carry respondent's burden of proof at trial. We think the Court of Appeals with its superior knowledge of local law is better suited than we are to make these determinations in the first instance.

The Federal Rules of Civil Procedure have for almost 50 years authorized motions for summary judgment upon proper showings of the lack of a genuine, triable issue of material fact. Summary judgment procedure is properly regarded not as a disfavored procedural short-cut, but rather as an integral part of the Federal Rules as a whole, which are designed "to secure the just, speedy and inexpensive determination of every action." Fed.Rule Civ.Proc. 1; see Schwarzer, Summary Judgment Under the Federal Rules: Defining Genuine Issues of Material Fact, 99 F.R.D. 465, 467 (1984). Before the shift to "notice pleading" accomplished by the Federal Rules, motions to dismiss a complaint or to strike a defense were the principal tools by which factually insufficient claims or defenses could be isolated and prevented from going to trial with the attendant unwarranted consumption of public and private resources. But with the advent of "notice pleading," the motion to dismiss seldom fulfills this function any more, and its place has been taken by the motion for summary judgment. Rule 56 must be construed with due regard not only for the rights of persons asserting claims and defenses that are adequately based in fact to have those claims and defenses tried to a jury, but also for the rights of persons opposing such claims and defenses to demonstrate in the manner provided by the Rule, prior to trial, that the claims and defenses have no factual basis.

The judgment of the Court of Appeals is accordingly reversed, and the case is remanded for further proceedings consistent with this opinion.

It is so ordered.

■ JUSTICE WHITE, concurring.

I agree that the Court of Appeals was wrong in holding that the moving defendant must always support his motion with evidence or affidavits showing the absence of a genuine dispute about a material fact. I also agree that the movant may rely on depositions, answers to interrogatories, and the like, to demonstrate that the plaintiff has no evidence to prove his case and hence that there can be no factual dispute. But the movant must discharge the burden the Rules place upon him: It is not enough to move for summary judgment without supporting the motion in any way or with a conclusory assertion that the plaintiff has no evidence to prove his case.

A plaintiff need not initiate any discovery or reveal his witnesses or evidence unless required to do so under the discovery Rules or by court order. Of course, he must respond if required to do so; but he need not also depose his witnesses or obtain their affidavits to defeat a summary judgment motion asserting only that he has failed to produce any support for his case. It is the defendant's task to negate, if he can, the claimed basis for the suit.

Petitioner Celotex does not dispute that if respondent has named a witness to support her claim, summary judgment should not be granted without Celotex somehow showing that the named witness' possible testimony raises no genuine issue of material fact. Tr. of Oral Arg. 43, 45. It asserts, however, that respondent has failed on request to produce any basis for her case. Respondent, on the other hand, does not contend that she was not obligated to reveal her witnesses and evidence but insists that she has revealed enough to defeat the motion for summary judgment. Because the Court of Appeals found it unnecessary to address this aspect of the case, I agree that the case should be remanded for further proceedings.

■ JUSTICE BRENNAN, with whom the CHIEF JUSTICE and JUSTICE BLACKMUN join, dissenting.

This case requires the Court to determine whether Celotex satisfied its initial burden of production in moving for summary judgment on the ground that the plaintiff lacked evidence to establish an essential element of her case at trial. I do not disagree with the Court's legal analysis. The Court clearly rejects the ruling of the Court of Appeals that the defendant must provide affirmative evidence disproving the plaintiff's case. Beyond this, however, the Court has not clearly explained what is required of a moving party seeking summary judgment on the ground that the nonmoving party cannot prove its case.[1]

---

1. It is also unclear what the Court of Appeals is supposed to do in this case on remand. Justice WHITE—who has provided the Court's fifth vote—plainly believes that the Court of Appeals should reevaluate whether the defendant met its initial burden of production. However, the decision to reverse rather than to vacate the judgment below implies that the Court of Appeals should assume that Celotex has met its initial burden of production and ask only whether the plaintiff responded adequately, and, if so, whether the defendant has met its ultimate burden of persuasion that no genuine issue exists for trial. Absent some clearer expression from the Court to the contrary, Justice WHITE's understanding would seem to be controlling. Cf. Marks v. United States, 430 U.S. 188, 193, 97 S.Ct. 990, 993, 51 L.Ed.2d 260 (1977).

This lack of clarity is unfortunate: district courts must routinely decide summary judgment motions, and the Court's opinion will very likely create confusion. For this reason, even if I agreed with the Court's result, I would have written separately to explain more clearly the law in this area. However, because I believe that Celotex did not meet its burden of production under Federal Rule of Civil Procedure 56, I respectfully dissent from the Court's judgment.

I

Summary judgment is appropriate where the Court is satisfied "that there is no genuine issue as to any material fact and that the moving party is entitled to a judgment as a matter of law." Fed.Rule Civ.Proc. 56(c). The burden of establishing the nonexistence of a "genuine issue" is on the party moving for summary judgment. 10A C. Wright, A. Miller, & M. Kane, Federal Practice and Procedure § 2727, p. 121 (2d ed. 1983) (hereinafter Wright) (citing cases); 6 J. Moore, W. Taggart & J. Wicker, Moore's Federal Practice ¶ 56.15[3] (2d ed. 1985) (hereinafter Moore) (citing cases). See also, ante, at 2551; ante, at 2553 (WHITE, J., concurring). This burden has two distinct components: an initial burden of production, which shifts to the nonmoving party if satisfied by the moving party; and an ultimate burden of persuasion, which always remains on the moving party. See 10A Wright, Miller & Kane § 2727. The court need not decide whether the moving party has satisfied its ultimate burden of persuasion[2] unless and until the Court finds that the moving party has discharged its initial burden of production. Adickes v. S.H. Kress & Co., 398 U.S. 144, 157–161, 90 S.Ct. 1598, 1608–10, 26 L.Ed.2d 142 (1970); 1963 Advisory Committee's Notes on Fed.Rule Civ.Proc. 56(e), 28 U.S.C.App., p. 626.

The burden of production imposed by Rule 56 requires the moving party to make a prima facie showing that it is entitled to summary judgment. 10A Wright, Miller & Kane § 2727. The manner in which this showing can be made depends upon which party will bear the burden of persuasion on the challenged claim at trial. If the moving party will bear the burden of persuasion at trial, that party

---

2. The burden of persuasion imposed on a moving party by Rule 56 is a stringent one. 6 Moore ¶ 56.15[3], pp. 56–466; 10A Wright, Miller & Kane § 2727, p. 124. Summary judgment should not be granted unless it is clear that a trial is unnecessary, Anderson v. Liberty Lobby, Inc., 477 U.S. 242, 255, 106 S.Ct. 2505, ___, 91 L.Ed.2d 202 (1986), and any doubt as to the existence of a genuine issue for trial should be resolved against the moving party, Adickes v. S.H. Kress & Co., 398 U.S. 144, 158–159, 90 S.Ct. 1598, 1608–09, 26 L.Ed.2d 142 (1970). In determining whether a moving party has met its burden of persuasion, the court is obliged to take account of the entire setting of the case and must consider all papers of record as well as any materials prepared for the motion. 10A Wright, Miller & Kane § 2721, p. 44; see, e.g., Stepanischen v. Merchants Despatch Transportation Corp., 722 F.2d 922, 930 (C.A.1 1983); Higgenbotham v. Ochsner Foundation Hospital, 607 F.2d 653, 656 (C.A.5 1979). As explained by the Court of Appeals for the Third Circuit in In re Japanese Electronic Products Antitrust Litigation, 723 F.2d 238 (1983), rev'd on other grounds sub nom. Matsushita Electric Industrial Co. v. Zenith Radio Corp., 475 U.S. 574, 106 S.Ct. 1348, 89 L.Ed.2d 538 (1986), "[i]f ... there is any evidence in the record from any source from which a reasonable inference in the [nonmoving party's] favor may be drawn, the moving party simply cannot obtain a summary judgment...." 723 F.2d, at 258.

must support its motion with credible evidence—using any of the materials specified in Rule 56(c)—that would entitle it to a directed verdict if not controverted at trial. Ibid. Such an affirmative showing shifts the burden of production to the party opposing the motion and requires that party either to produce evidentiary materials that demonstrate the existence of a "genuine issue" for trial or to submit an affidavit requesting additional time for discovery. Ibid.; Fed.Rules Civ.Proc. 56(e), (f).

If the burden of persuasion at trial would be on the non-moving party, the party moving for summary judgment may satisfy Rule 56's burden of production in either of two ways. First, the moving party may submit affirmative evidence that negates an essential element of the nonmoving party's claim. Second, the moving party may demonstrate to the Court that the nonmoving party's evidence is insufficient to establish an essential element of the nonmoving party's claim. See 10A Wright, Miller & Kane § 2727, pp. 130–131; Louis, Federal Summary Judgment Doctrine: A Critical Analysis, 83 Yale L.J. 745, 750 (1974) (hereinafter Louis). If the nonmoving party cannot muster sufficient evidence to make out its claim, a trial would be useless and the moving party is entitled to summary judgment as a matter of law. Anderson v. Liberty Lobby, Inc., 477 U.S. 242, 249, 106 S.Ct. 2505, 91 L.Ed.2d 202 (1986).

Where the moving party adopts this second option and seeks summary judgment on the ground that the nonmoving party—who will bear the burden of persuasion at trial—has no evidence, the mechanics of discharging Rule 56's burden of production are somewhat trickier. Plainly, a conclusory assertion that the nonmoving party has no evidence is insufficient. Such a "burden" of production is no burden at all and would simply permit summary judgment procedure to be converted into a tool for harassment. See Louis 750–751. Rather, as the Court confirms, a party who moves for summary judgment on the ground that the nonmoving party has no evidence must affirmatively show the absence of evidence in the record. Ante, at 2553. This may require the moving party to depose the nonmoving party's witnesses or to establish the inadequacy of documentary evidence. If there is literally no evidence in the record, the moving party may demonstrate this by reviewing for the court the admissions, interrogatories, and other exchanges between the parties that are in the record. Either way, however, the moving party must affirmatively demonstrate that there is no evidence in the record to support a judgment for the nonmoving party.

If the moving party has not fully discharged this initial burden of production, its motion for summary judgment must be denied, and the Court need not consider whether the moving party has met its ultimate burden of persuasion. Accordingly, the nonmoving party may defeat a motion for summary judgment that asserts that the nonmoving party has no evidence by calling the Court's attention to supporting evidence already in the record that was overlooked or ignored by the moving party. In that event, the moving party must respond by making an attempt to demonstrate the inadequacy of this evidence, for it is only by attacking all the record evidence allegedly supporting the nonmoving party that a party seeking summary judgment satisfies Rule 56's burden of production.[3] Thus, if the record disclosed that the moving party had overlooked a witness who would provide relevant testimony for the nonmoving party at trial, the Court could not find that the moving party had discharged its initial burden of production unless the moving party sought to demonstrate the inadequacy of this witness' testimony. Absent such a demonstration, summary judgment would have to be denied on the ground that the moving party had failed to meet its burden of production under Rule 56.

The result in Adickes v. S.H. Kress & Co., supra, is fully consistent with these principles. In that case, petitioner was refused service in respondent's lunchroom and then was arrested for vagrancy by a local policeman as she left. Petitioner brought an action under 42 U.S.C. § 1983 claiming that the refusal of service and subsequent arrest were the product of a conspiracy between respondent and the police; as proof of this conspiracy, petitioner's complaint alleged that the arresting officer was in respondent's store at the time service was refused. Respondent subsequently moved for summary judgment on the ground that there was no actual evidence in the record from which a jury could draw an inference of conspiracy. In response, petitioner pointed to a statement from her own deposition and an unsworn statement by a Kress employee, both already in the record and both ignored by respondent, that the policeman who arrested petitioner was in the store at the time she was refused service. We agreed that "[i]f a policeman were present, . . . it would be open to a jury, in light of the sequence that followed, to infer from the circumstances that the policeman and Kress employee had a 'meeting of the minds' and thus reached an understanding that petitioner should be refused service." 398 U.S., at 158, 90 S.Ct., at 1609. Consequently, we held that it was error to grant summary judgment "on the basis of this record" because respondent had "failed to fulfill its initial burden" of demonstrating that there was no evidence that there was a policeman in the store. Id., at 157–158, 98 S.Ct., at 1608–1609.

The opinion in Adickes has sometimes been read to hold that summary judgment was inappropriate because the respondent had not submitted affirmative evidence to negate the possibility that there was a policeman in the store. See Brief for Respondent 20, n. 30 (citing cases). The Court of Appeals apparently read Adickes this way and

---

3. Once the moving party has attacked whatever record evidence—if any—the nonmoving party purports to rely upon, the burden of production shifts to the nonmoving party, who must either (1) rehabilitate the evidence attacked in the moving party's papers, (2) produce additional evidence showing the existence of a genuine issue for trial as provided in Rule 56(e), or (3) submit an affidavit explaining why further discovery is necessary as provided in Rule 56(f). See 10A Wright, Miller & Kane § 2727, pp. 138–143. Summary judgment should be granted if the nonmoving party fails to respond in one or more of these ways, or if, after the nonmoving party responds, the court determines that the moving party has met its ultimate burden of persuading the court that there is no genuine issue of material fact for trial. See, e.g., First National Bank of Arizona v. Cities Service Co., 391 U.S. 253, 289, 88 S.Ct. 1575, 1592, 20 L.Ed.2d 569 (1968).

therefore required Celotex to submit evidence establishing that plaintiff's decedent had not been exposed to Celotex asbestos. I agree with the Court that this reading of Adickes was erroneous and that Celotex could seek summary judgment on the ground that plaintiff could not prove exposure to Celotex asbestos at trial. However, Celotex was still required to satisfy its initial burden of production.

II

I do not read the Court's opinion to say anything inconsistent with or different than the preceding discussion. My disagreement with the Court concerns the application of these principles to the facts of this case.

Defendant Celotex sought summary judgment on the ground that plaintiff had "failed to produce" any evidence that her decedent had ever been exposed to Celotex asbestos.[4] App. 170. Celotex supported this motion with a two-page "Statement of Material Facts as to Which There is No Genuine Issue" and a three-page "Memorandum of Points and Authorities" which asserted that the plaintiff had failed to identify any evidence in responding to two sets of interrogatories propounded by Celotex and that therefore the record was "totally devoid" of evidence to support plaintiff's claim. See id., at 171–176.

Approximately three months earlier, Celotex had filed an essentially identical motion. Plaintiff responded to this earlier motion by producing three pieces of evidence which she claimed "[a]t the very least . . . demonstrate that there is a genuine factual dispute for trial," id., at 143: (1) a letter from an insurance representative of another defendant describing asbestos products to which plaintiff's decedent had been exposed, id., at 160; (2) a letter from T.R. Hoff, a former supervisor of decedent, describing asbestos products to which decedent had been exposed, id., at 162; and (3) a copy of decedent's deposition from earlier workmen's compensation proceedings, id., at 164. Plaintiff also apparently indicated at that time that she intended to call Mr. Hoff as a witness at trial. Tr. of Oral Arg. 6–7, 27–29.

---

4. Justice STEVENS asserts that the District Court granted summary judgment on the ground that the plaintiff had failed to show exposure in the District of Columbia. He contends that the judgment of the Court of Appeals reversing the District Court's judgment should be affirmed on the "narrow ground" that it was "palpably erroneous" to grant summary judgment on this basis. Post, at 2561 (dissenting). The Court replies that what the District Court said was that plaintiff had failed to show exposure in the District of Columbia "or elsewhere." Ante, at 2560, n. 2. In my view, it does not really matter which reading is correct in this case. For, contrary to Justice STEVENS' claim, deciding this case on the ground that Celotex failed to meet its burden of production under Rule 56 does not involve an "abstract exercise in Rule construction." Post, at 2560 (STEVENS, J., dissenting). To the contrary, the principles governing a movant's burden of proof are straightforward and well established, and deciding the case on this basis does not require a new construction of Rule 56 at all; it simply entails applying established law to the particular facts of this case. The choice to reverse because of "palpable erro[r]" with respect to the burden of a moving party under Rule 56 is thus no more "abstract" than the choice to reverse because of such error with respect to the elements of a tort claim. Indeed, given that the issue of the moving party's burden under Rule 56 was the basis of the Court of Appeals' decision, the question upon which certiorari was granted, and the issue briefed by the parties and argued to the Court, it would seem to be the preferable ground for deciding the case.

Celotex subsequently withdrew its first motion for summary judgment. See App. 167.[5] However, as a result of this motion, when Celotex filed its second summary judgment motion, the record did contain evidence—including at least one witness—supporting plaintiff's claim. Indeed, counsel for Celotex admitted to this Court at oral argument that Celotex was aware of this evidence and of plaintiff's intention to call Mr. Hoff as a witness at trial when the second summary judgment motion was filed. Tr. of Oral Arg. 5–7. Moreover, plaintiff's response to Celotex' second motion pointed to this evidence—noting that it had already been provided to counsel for Celotex in connection with the first motion—and argued that Celotex had failed to "meet its burden of proving that there is no genuine factual dispute for trial." App. 188.

On these facts, there is simply no question that Celotex failed to discharge its initial burden of production. Having chosen to base its motion on the argument that there was no evidence in the record to support plaintiff's claim, Celotex was not free to ignore supporting evidence that the record clearly contained. Rather, Celotex was required, as an initial matter, to attack the adequacy of this evidence. Celotex' failure to fulfill this simple requirement constituted a failure to discharge its initial burden of production under Rule 56, and thereby rendered summary judgment improper.[6]

This case is indistinguishable from Adickes. Here, as there, the defendant moved for summary judgment on the ground that the record contained no evidence to support an essential element of the plaintiff's claim. Here, as there, the plaintiff responded by drawing the court's attention to evidence that was already in the record and that had been ignored by the moving party. Consequently, here, as there, summary judgment should be denied on the ground that the moving party failed to satisfy its initial burden of production.[7]

■ JUSTICE STEVENS, dissenting.

As the Court points out, petitioner's motion for summary judgment was based on the proposition that respondent could not prevail unless she proved that her deceased husband had been exposed to

---

5. Celotex apparently withdrew this motion because, contrary to the assertion made in the first summary judgment motion, its second set of interrogatories had not been served on the plaintiff.

6. If the plaintiff had answered Celotex' second set of interrogatories with the evidence in her response to the first summary judgment motion, and Celotex had ignored those interrogatories and based its second summary judgment motion on the first set of interrogatories only, Celotex obviously could not claim to have discharged its Rule 56 burden of production. This result should not be different simply because the evidence plaintiff relied upon to support her claim was acquired by Celotex other than in plaintiff's answers to interrogatories.

7. Although Justice WHITE agrees that "if [plaintiff] has named a witness to support her claim, summary judgment should not be granted without Celotex somehow showing that the named witness' possible testimony raises no genuine issue of material fact," he would remand "[b]ecause the Court of Appeals found it unnecessary to address this aspect of the case." Ante, at 2555–2556 (concurring). However, Celotex has admitted that plaintiff had disclosed her intent to call Mr. Hoff as a witness at trial before Celotex filed its second motion for summary judgment. Tr. of Oral Arg. 6–7. Under the circumstances, then, remanding is a waste of time.

petitioner's products "within the jurisdictional limits" of the District of Columbia.[1] Respondent made an adequate showing—albeit possibly not in admissible form[2]—that her husband had been exposed to petitioner's product in Illinois.[3] Although the basis of the motion and the argument had been the lack of exposure in the District of Columbia, the District Court stated at the end of the argument: "The Court will grant the defendant Celotex's motion for summary judgment there being no showing that the plaintiff was exposed to the defendant Celotex's product in the District of Columbia or elsewhere within the statutory period." App. 217 (emphasis added). The District Court offered no additional explanation and no written opinion. The Court of Appeals reversed on the basis that Celotex had not met its burden; the court noted the incongruity of the District Court's opinion in the context of the motion and argument, but did not rest on that basis because of the "or elsewhere" language.[4]

Taken in the context of the motion for summary judgment on the basis of no exposure in the District of Columbia, the District Court's decision to grant summary judgment was palpably erroneous. The court's bench reference to "or elsewhere" neither validated that decision nor raised the complex question addressed by this Court today. In light of the District Court's plain error, therefore, it is perfectly clear that, even after this Court's abstract exercise in Rule construction, we should nonetheless affirm the reversal of summary judgment on that narrow ground.[5]

1. See Motion of Defendant Celotex Corporation for Summary Judgment, App. 170 ("Defendant Celotex Corporation, pursuant to Rule 56(b) of the Federal Rules of Civil Procedure moves this Court for an Order granting Summary Judgment on the ground that plaintiff has failed to produce evidence that any product designed, manufactured or distributed by Celotex Corporation was the proximate cause of the injuries alleged within the jurisdictional limits of this Court") (emphasis added); Memorandum of Points and Authorities in Support of Motion of Defendant Celotex Corporation for Summary Judgment, id., at 175 (Plaintiff "must demonstrate some link between a Celotex Corporation product claimed to be the cause of the decedent's illness and the decedent himself. The record is totally devoid of any such evidence within the jurisdictional confines of this Court") (emphasis added); Transcript of Argument in Support of Motion of Defendant Celotex Corporation for Summary Judgment, id., at 211 ("Our position is . . . there has been no product identification of any Celotex products . . . that have been used in the District of Columbia to which the decedent was exposed") (emphasis added).

2. But cf. ante, at 2553 ("We do not mean that the nonmoving party must produce evidence in a form that would be admissible at trial in order to avoid summary judgment").

3. See App. 160 (letter from Aetna Life Insurance Co.) (referring to the "asbestos that Mr. Catrett came into contact with while working for Anning–Johnson Company" and noting that the "manufacturer of this product" was purchased by Celotex); id., at 162 (letter from Anning–Johnson Co.) (confirming that Catrett worked for the company and supervised the installation of asbestos produced by the company that Celotex ultimately purchased); id., at 164, 164c (deposition of Catrett) (description of his work with asbestos "in Chicago").

4. See Catrett v. Johns–Manville Sales Corp., 756 F.2d 181, 185, n. 14 (1985) ("[T]he discussion at the time the motion was granted actually spoke to venue. It was only the phrase 'or elsewhere,' appearing with no prior discussion, in the judge's oral ruling at the close of argument that made the grant of summary judgment even conceivably proper").

5. Cf. n. 2, supra. The Court's statement that the case should be remanded because the Court of Appeals has a "superior knowledge of local law," ante, at 2555, is bewildering because there is no question of local law to be decided. Cf. Bishop v. Wood, 426 U.S. 341, 345–347, 96 S.Ct. 2074, 2077–2079, 48 L.Ed.2d 684 (1976). The Court's decision to remand when a sufficient ground for affirmance is available does reveal, how-

I respectfully dissent.

NOTES

Before the trilogy, the federal courts generally did not use the summary judgement process for "controversies with heavy public policy implications." Judge Wald points out that since Celotex summary judgement practice in the federal courts is used in areas previously thought inappropriate for summary judgement. She lists 14 such areas, Freedom of Information; Privacy Act; Bank Insolvency; Insurance carrier liability cases; Defamation and libel cases; Federal Election Law; Title VII cases alleging discrimination in employment; Arbitration Reviews in labor disputes; Class actions based on allegedly miscalculated interest rates on home mortgages; Labor Management Reporting and Disclosure Act; Constitutional tort claims brought by prisoners; Airlines claims for reimbursement from the I.N.S.; Federal Advisory Committee Act cases; Age Discrimination in Employment Act. See Wald, Summary Judgement at Sixty, 76 Texas L. Rev. 1897, 1916–17 (1997).

A recent article by Tang and McMillian, Eighth Circuit Employment Discrimination Law: Hicks and its Impact on Summary Judgment, 41 St. L. L.J. 519, 520 (1997) states that in employment discrimination cases (which are nearly 9% of all new filings) there are rarely any witnesses who can testify as to the employer's mental processes. Motions for summary judgment are routinely filed by defendant employers; often granted by the district courts and usually affirmed on appeal. The authors conclude that the pretrial stage in employment discrimination cases is now the final procedural battleground.

Several studies agree that it is defendants who file the majority of summary judgment motions. Plaintiffs are handicapped because they usually have less money for investigation and often rely on discovery and even trial for full presentation of their case.

NOTES ON CELOTEX

1. The court did not decide whether the plaintiff's materials would defeat the motion for summary judgment. That issue was left to the Court of Appeals on remand. It decided the plaintiff's proffered documents were enough to withstand the motion. See Catrett v. Johns–Manville Sales Corp., 826 F.2d 33 (D.C.Cir.1987), cert. denied, 484 U.S. 1066 (1988).

2. Without more support, the two letters would be inadmissible as hearsay. Does Rule 56(c) require that the evidence be in an admissible form at the summary judgment stage?

3. Note that as influential as Celotex has been that it was a 5 to 4 decision and that no opinion gained a plurality.

ever, the Court's increasing tendency to adopt a presumption of reversal. See, e.g., New York v. P.J. Video, Inc., 475 U.S. 868, 884, 106 S.Ct. 1610, 1619, 89 L.Ed.2d 871 (1986) (MARSHALL, J., dissenting); Icicle Seafoods, Inc., v. Worthington, 475 U.S. 709, 715, 106 S.Ct. 1527, 1530, 89 L.Ed.2d 739 (1986) (STEVENS, J., dissenting); City of Los Angeles v. Heller, 475 U.S. 796, 800, 106 S.Ct. 1571, 1573, 89 L.Ed.2d 806 (1986) (STEVENS, J., dissenting); Pennsylvania v. Goldhammer, 474 U.S. 28, 31, 106 S.Ct. 353, 88 L.Ed.2d 183 (1985) (STEVENS, J., dissenting). As a matter of efficient judicial administration and of respect for the state and federal courts, I believe the presumption should be precisely the opposite.

NOTE: THE EFFECTS OF THE CHANGED SUMMARY JUDGMENT DOCTRINE

An empirical examination of the impact of the Supreme Court trilogy was conducted in the federal district courts in Ohio covering the six years before and after the trilogy. See Gregory A. Gordillo, Summary Judgment and Problems in Applying the Celotex Trilogy Standards, 42 Cleveland State Law Review 263, 278–79 (1994). There is a significant increase in defendants' summary judgment motions granted and in deciding summary judgment in favor of defendants generally. The author cautions that his review is limited to those decisions reported on WESTLAW and is therefore not exhaustive although the findings are consistent with earlier such studies.

* * *

As illustrated in the table below, research revealed 309 summary judgment opinions for the six years preceding the Celotex trilogy. During that period, plaintiffs moved for summary judgment in 11% of the opinions that did not involve motions by both parties, and defendants accounted for 89% of the motions. In comparison, research for the six years following Celotex revealed 319 summary judgment opinions. During this period, plaintiffs moved for summary judgment in 13% of the opinions that did not involve motions by both parties, and defendants accounted for 87% of the motions. Thus, the Celotex trilogy does not appear to have inspired defendants' counselors to move for summary judgment more often than before. Furthermore, even if the trilogy did increase the number of motions made, the influence appears to have affected plaintiff and defendant movants in a similar fashion rather than providing defendants with any greater incentive to move for summary judgment.

The Celotex trilogy has, however, altered the effectiveness of summary judgment as a defendants' tool. Prior to Celotex, when an opinion involved only one party moving for summary judgment, 8% of the motions resulted in the plaintiff prevailing. Of all those summary judgments entered during this time, 53% favored the defendant. After Celotex, 10% of these opinions favored plaintiffs and 69% favored the defendant. The difference in the effect on defendants becomes more apparent when comparing the relative rates of their motions being granted pre-Celotex. Before Celotex, courts granted 59% of defendant motions for summary judgment. After Celotex, courts granted 79% of defendant motions for summary judgment.

The 20% difference in defendant success rates is substantial; however, claims that Celotex shifted power from plaintiffs to defendants are less forceful in light of the relative plaintiff success for these pre-and post-Celotex years. Between 1979 and 1986, the courts granted 74% of plaintiff motions for summary judgment. Between 1986 and 1993, the courts granted 77% of plaintiff motions. Thus, while defendants prevail on their motions more often than before Celotex, the decision merely made the playing field more even rather than tipping it in favor of defendants. On the other hand, when considering the effect of the trilogy on the power of summary judgment as a tool for defendants, the fact that defendants are more likely to prevail now than prior to Celotex is probably more significant than the relative likelihood of plaintiffs' and defendants' success.

	1/1/79– 12/31/85	1/1/87– 12/31/92
Total Number of Cases	309	319
Cases with only 1 Movant	214	235
Percentage of Plaintiff Motions	11%	13%
Percentage of Defendant Motions	89%	87%
Percentage of all Motions Granted in Favor of Plaintiff	8%	10%
Percentage of all Motions Granted in Favor of Defendant	53%	69%
Percentage of Plaintiff Motions Granted	74%	77%
Percentage of Defendant Motions Granted	59%	79%

* * *

Liberty Lobby, Inc. v. Anderson

United States Court of Appeals, D. C. Circuit, 1984.
746 F.2d 1563.

■ SCALIA, CIRCUIT JUDGE:

To prevail in a libel trial, not only must the public-figure plaintiff prove the existence of actual malice; he must prove it with "convincing clarity," New York Times v. Sullivan, 376 U.S. at 254, 285–86 (1964), or to use the Court's more recent language, with "clear and convincing proof," Gertz v. Robert Welch, Inc., 418 U.S. 323, 342, 94 S.Ct. 2997, 3008, 41 L.Ed.2d 789 (1974). Moreover, judges are not merely to determine whether the finder of fact could reasonably find such "convincing clarity" to exist, but are "independently [to] decide" that point, "as expositors of the Constitution." Bose Corp. v. Consumers Union, 466 U.S. 485, 104 S.Ct. 1949, 1965, 80 L.Ed.2d 502 (1984). The issue we address in this portion of our opinion is whether these requirements of "convincing clarity" and "independent judicial determination" apply at the summary judgment stage. Even though this is a diversity case, that issue is governed by federal law—either because the Constitution imposes the more demanding requirements at the summary judgment stage, or because, if it does not, the matter is determined by the rules of the forum court under Erie R.R. v. Tompkins, 304 U.S. 64, 58 S.Ct. 817, 82 L.Ed. 1188 (1938).

* * *

With regard to the "clear and convincing evidence" requirement, the issue can be framed as follows: whether, in order to deny the defendant's motion for summary judgment, the court must conclude that a reasonable jury not only could (on the basis of the facts taken in the light most favorable to the plaintiff) find the existence of actual malice, but could find that it had been established with "convincing clarity." We conclude that the answer is no. Imposing the increased proof requirement at this stage would change the threshold summary judgment inquiry from a search for a minimum of facts supporting the plaintiff's case to an evaluation of the weight of those facts and (it would seem) of the weight of at least the defendant's uncontroverted facts as well. It would effectively force the plaintiff to try his entire case in pretrial affidavits and depositions—marshalling for the court all the facts supporting his case, and seeking to contest as many of the defendant's facts as possible. Moreover, a "clear and convincing evidence" rule at the summary judgment stage would compel the court to be more liberal in its application of that provision of FED.R.CIV.P. 56(e) which states that the court "may permit affidavits to be supplemented or opposed by depositions, answers to interrogatories, or further affidavits." In other words, disposing of a summary judgment motion would rarely be the relatively quick process it is supposed to be. Finally, if summary judgment were supposed to be based on a "clear and convincing" standard, it is hard to explain the Supreme Court's statement questioning the asserted principle that in public figure libel cases "summary judgment might well be the rule rather than the exception," and affirming to the contrary that "[t]he proof of 'actual malice' ... does not readily lend itself to summary disposition." Hutchinson v. Proxmire, 443 U.S. 111, 120 & n. 9, 99 S.Ct. 2675, 2680 & n. 9, 61 L.Ed.2d 411 (1979). There is slim basis for such a statement if, in order to survive a motion for summary judgment, the plaintiff must establish an arguably "clear and convincing" case.

* * *

We realize that some other courts have expressed a different rule. See, e.g., Yiamouyiannis v. Consumers Union, 619 F.2d 932, 940 (2d Cir.1980) ("a judge in denying a defendant's summary judgment motion must conclude that, based on the evidence asserted in the plaintiff's affidavits, 'a reasonable jury could find malice with convincing clarity,' " quoting Nader v. de Toledano, 408 A.2d 31, 50 (D.C. 1979), cert. denied, 444 U.S. 1078, 100 S.Ct. 1028, 62 L.Ed.2d 761 (1980)). Those formulations were set forth, however, with no analysis of the point here discussed. In fact, the courts' attention was directed to the question of whether the normal procedural standard governing summary judgment applied (i.e., the test "could a reasonable jury find," as opposed to some test more favorable to the defendant) rather than to the question of what burden of proof that standard should be applied to. Moreover, those courts' analyses of the facts demonstrate that they rested their decisions upon lack of evidence of malice, not upon lack of "convincing clarity" in that evidence. See Yiamouyiannis v. Consumers Union, supra, 619 F.2d at 942 ("no showing has been made that they were published with actual malice, let alone a showing that achieves 'convincing clarity' "); Nader v. de Toledano, supra, 408 A.2d at 56 ("[i]n sum, ... we agree with the trial court that appellant has demonstrated no genuine issue of fact as to whether Copley had reason to doubt de Toledano's veracity").

With regard to the Bose requirement of independent judicial determination we reach the same conclusion, for the same compelling practical reason: it is simply incompatible with the preliminary nature of the summary judgment inquiry. If it were to be applied at that early stage, summary judgment would be converted from a search for the minimum amount of evidence that could persuade a reasonable person into the final assessment of "actual malice" by the court itself—final, at least, if the court concludes actual malice has not been established. That would compel the plaintiff to present his full case prematurely, with the undesirable consequences described above. In addition, courts of appeal would be burdened with the unusual task of making the largely factual determination of actual malice in many cases where a judge or jury verdict against the plaintiff would render that unnecessary.

For the foregoing reasons, we believe that the constitutional requirements of "clear and convincing" proof and independent judicial determination of the ultimate issue of actual malice are to be applied only after the plaintiff has had an opportunity to present his evidence. We thus agree with the two-stage approach set forth by Judge Wright, joined by Judge Robinson, in his concurrence in Wasserman v. Time, Inc., 424 F.2d 920, 922 (D.C.Cir.), cert. denied, 398 U.S. 940, 90 S.Ct. 1844, 26 L.Ed.2d 273 (1970):

Unless the court finds, on the basis of pretrial affidavits, depositions or other documentary evidence, that the plaintiff can prove actual malice in the Times sense, it should grant summary judgment for the defendant. . . .

If the case survives the defendant's summary judgment motion, the trial court at the close of the plaintiff's case must decide whether actual malice has been shown with "convincing clarity."

* * *

V

The district court was correct in entering summary judgment in favor of the appellees on the foregoing twenty-one allegations, and we affirm its findings. As to each of them, one element of the cause of action—either defamatory content, factual nature or malice—is absent. Our examination of the record, however, reveals that a jury could reasonably conclude that the nine remaining allegations were defamatory, false, and made with actual malice. As to these claims, then, we must reverse and remand to the district court.

* * *

Allegation 11 asserts that Liberty Lobby occupies a building in Washington, D.C., owned by the Government Educational Foundation, "[t]he chairman and owner of [which] is Willis Carto, who bought the building with money contributed by many of Liberty Lobby's members in response to an urgent appeal"; and that Liberty Lobby pays the Government Educational Foundation $6,000 per month rent. The implication is that Carto is deriving personal profit from an excessive rental to Liberty Lobby. The plaintiffs deny all elements of the allegation, asserting that the building is not owned by the Government Educational Foundation, that Carto is neither chairman nor owner of that organization, and that Liberty Lobby pays no rent for the building. The sources allegedly relied upon by Bermant (other than Eringer, whose reliability for purposes of the good-faith defense is inadequate, as we shall discuss below) do not assert ownership of the Foundation by Carto or the payment of any rent, much less a specific figure of

$6,000. It is for a jury to determine the truth or falsity of these matters and whether, if false, they are defamatory. On the basis of evidence adduced at this stage, it is impossible to say that no actual malice could be found.

Allegation 15, in addition to once more characterizing Carto's movement among various right-wing groups as "drifting" * * * asserted that Carto "organized and promoted the Joint Council for Repatriation. What he meant by 'repatriation' was the forced deportation of all blacks to Africa." The published sources relied upon by defendants support the assertion that Carto created this organization, and that its purpose was to "send American blacks back to Africa." They do not establish, however, that the proposal envisioned "forced deportation"—in fact, to the contrary, one of them asserted that Carto (overtly at least) only sought "voluntary" repatriation. While the latter detail reduces not at all the repugnant racism of the scheme, it is possible to be a racist without being guilty of the quite separate fault of advocating the forced deportation of United States citizens. * * * Since the published sources referred to by the defendants not only do not establish this point but to the contrary assert that Carto's scheme was formally for "voluntary" repatriation, we think it is a jury question whether this allegation, if false, was made with actual malice.

We find that a jury could reasonably conclude that defamatory statements based wholly on the True article were made with actual malice. That article was the subject of a prior defamation action which was settled to Carto's satisfaction, a fact likely known to Bermant's editors, if not Bermant. Whether the particular statements relied on were false and whether the appellees were actually aware of that falsity are matters for a jury to determine. Allegation 19, the illustration suggesting that Carto emulated Hitler, and allegation 29, that Carto joined the singing of "Hitler's 'Horst Wessel Lied' " and delivered a speech in an attempt to emulate Hitler's style and charisma, were based solely on the True article. There is no other evidence that Carto emulates Hitler in appearance or in action, allegations the jury could find to be defamatory.

We turn next to the five allegations based solely upon the conversation with Robert Eringer:

> 13. Statement that Carto "conducts his business by way of conference calls from a public telephone," which arguably suggests criminality;

> 14. Claim that in 1968 a Carto front organization "used a direct mail blitz to support G. Gordon Liddy's Congressional campaign in New York" (since Liddy was later convicted of felony in connection with political activities, the allegation could be considered defamatory);

> 17. Illustration showing Carto secretly observing prospective employees through a one-way mirror;

> 23. One-way mirror allegation, in text;

27. Claim that a lead story in an issue of The Spotlight was a total hoax.

We find that a jury could reasonably conclude that Bermant made these allegations with a disregard for their truth or falsity that constituted actual malice. For one thing, there is only Bermant's word for the fact that Eringer ever said anything that supports the statements. The same was true for the statements, discussed earlier, attributed to Bartell and Suall—but as we noted, see pages 1576–1577, supra, those individuals were present at known locations in this country and could have been deposed by the plaintiffs, whereas the mysterious Mr. Eringer was thought to be somewhere in England. Moreover, Bermant's dealings with Eringer display a much lesser degree of care, despite the scurrilous allegations for which he is the sole source. Bermant not only did not inquire how Eringer came to know these details of Carto's operations; he never even looked the unknown Eringer in the eye until after the story was published, but spoke to him only once over the telephone. Anderson admits that he did not care whether Eringer was reliable. These actions came close to the hypothetical case of actual malice the Supreme Court described in St. Amant: a story "based wholly on an unverified anonymous telephone call." 390 U.S. at 732, 88 S.Ct. at 1326. Eringer was identified by name, but he was in all other respects unknown to the appellees. These allegations, which defendants claim were based solely on Eringer's assertions, should have gone to the jury.

* * *

We affirm the District Court's grant of summary judgment as to all claims of defamation except those addressed in Part V of this opinion. As to the latter, we reverse and remand for further proceedings consistent with this opinion.

So ordered.

Anderson v. Liberty Lobby, Inc.

Supreme Court of the United States, 1986.
477 U.S. 242, 106 S.Ct. 2505, 91 L.Ed. 2d 202.

■ JUSTICE WHITE delivered the opinion of the Court.

In New York Times Co. v. Sullivan, 376 U.S. 254, 279–280, 84 S.Ct. 710, 725–726, 11 L.Ed.2d 686 (1964), we held that, in a libel suit brought by a public official, the First Amendment requires the plaintiff to show that in publishing the defamatory statement the defendant acted with actual malice—"with knowledge that it was false or with reckless disregard of whether it was false or not." We held further that such actual malice must be shown with "convincing clarity." These New York Times requirements we have since extended to libel suits brought by public figures as well.

This case presents the question whether the clear-and-convincing-evidence requirement must be considered by a court ruling on a motion for summary judgment under Rule 56 of the Federal Rules of

Civil Procedure in a case to which New York Times applies. The United States Court of Appeals for the District of Columbia Circuit held that that requirement need not be considered at the summary judgment stage. We granted certiorari, because that holding was in conflict with decisions of several other Courts of Appeals, which had held that the New York Times requirement of clear and convincing evidence must be considered on a motion for summary judgment. We now reverse.

I

Respondent Liberty Lobby, Inc., is a not-for-profit corporation and self-described "citizens' lobby." Respondent Willis Carto is its founder and treasurer. In October 1981, The Investigator magazine published two articles: "The Private World of Willis Carto" and "Yockey: Profile of an American Hitler." These articles were introduced by a third, shorter article entitled "America's Neo–Nazi Underground: Did Mein Kampf Spawn Yockey's Imperium, a Book Revived by Carto's Liberty Lobby?" These articles portrayed respondents as neo-Nazi, anti-Semitic, racist, and Fascist.

Respondents filed this diversity libel action in the United States District Court for the District of Columbia, alleging that some 28 statements and 2 illustrations in the 3 articles were false and derogatory. Named as defendants in the action were petitioner Jack Anderson, the publisher of The Investigator, petitioner Bill Adkins, president and chief executive officer of the Investigator Publishing Co., and petitioner Investigator Publishing Co. itself.

Following discovery, petitioners moved for summary judgment pursuant to Rule 56. In their motion, petitioners asserted that because respondents are public figures they were required to prove their case under the standards set forth in New York Times. Petitioners also asserted that summary judgment was proper because actual malice was absent as a matter of law. In support of this latter assertion, petitioners submitted the affidavit of Charles Bermant, an employee of petitioners and the author of the two longer articles.[2] In this affidavit, Bermant stated that he had spent a substantial amount of time researching and writing the articles and that his facts were obtained from a wide variety of sources. He also stated that he had at all times believed and still believed that the facts contained in the articles were truthful and accurate. Attached to this affidavit was an appendix in which Bermant detailed the sources for each of the statements alleged by respondents to be libelous.

Respondents opposed the motion for summary judgment, asserting that there were numerous inaccuracies in the articles and claiming that an issue of actual malice was presented by virtue of the fact that in preparing the articles Bermant had relied on several sources that respondents asserted were patently unreliable. Generally, respondents charged that petitioners had failed adequately to verify their informa-

---

2. The short, introductory article was written by petitioner Anderson and relied exclusively on the information obtained by Bermant.

tion before publishing. Respondents also presented evidence that William McGaw, an editor of The Investigator, had told petitioner Adkins before publication that the articles were "terrible" and "ridiculous."

In ruling on the motion for summary judgment, the District Court first held that respondents were limited-purpose public figures and that New York Times therefore applied.[3] The District Court then held that Bermant's thorough investigation and research and his reliance on numerous sources precluded a finding of actual malice. Thus, the District Court granted the motion and entered judgment in favor of petitioners.

On appeal, the Court of Appeals affirmed as to 21 and reversed as to 9 of the allegedly defamatory statements. Although it noted that respondents did not challenge the District Court's ruling that they were limited-purpose public figures and that they were thus required to prove their case under New York Times, the Court of Appeals nevertheless held that for the purposes of summary judgment the requirement that actual malice be proved by clear and convincing evidence, rather than by a preponderance of the evidence, was irrelevant: To defeat summary judgment respondents did not have to show that a jury could find actual malice with "convincing clarity." The court based this conclusion on a perception that to impose the greater evidentiary burden at summary judgment "would change the threshold summary judgment inquiry from a search for a minimum of facts supporting the plaintiff's case to an evaluation of the weight of those facts and (it would seem) of the weight of at least the defendant's uncontroverted facts as well." The court then held, with respect to nine of the statements, that summary judgment had been improperly granted because "a jury could reasonably conclude that the ... allegations were defamatory, false, and made with actual malice."

II

A

Our inquiry is whether the Court of Appeals erred in holding that the heightened evidentiary requirements that apply to proof of actual malice in this New York Times case need not be considered for the purposes of a motion for summary judgment. Rule 56(c) of the Federal Rules of Civil Procedure provides that summary judgment "shall be rendered forthwith if the pleadings, depositions, answers to

3. In Gertz v. Robert Welch, Inc., 418 U.S. 323, 351, 94 S.Ct. 2997, 3012, 41 L.Ed.2d 789 (1974), this Court summarized who will be considered to be a public figure to whom the New York Times standards will apply:

"[The public figure] designation may rest on either of two alternative bases. In some instances an individual may achieve such pervasive fame or notoriety that he becomes a public figure for all purposes and in all contexts. More com-

monly, an individual voluntarily injects himself or is drawn into a particular public controversy and thereby becomes a public figure for a limited range of issues. In either case such persons assume special prominence in the resolution of public questions."

The District Court found that respondents, as political lobbyists, are the second type of political figure described by the Gertz court—a limited-purpose public figure.

interrogatories, and admissions on file, together with the affidavits, if any, show that there is no genuine issue as to any material fact and that the moving party is entitled to a judgment as a matter of law." By its very terms, this standard provides that the mere existence of some alleged factual dispute between the parties will not defeat an otherwise properly supported motion for summary judgment; the requirement is that there be no genuine issue of material fact.

As to materiality, the substantive law will identify which facts are material. Only disputes over facts that might affect the outcome of the suit under the governing law will properly preclude the entry of summary judgment. Factual disputes that are irrelevant or unnecessary will not be counted. This materiality inquiry is independent of and separate from the question of the incorporation of the evidentiary standard into the summary judgment determination. That is, while the materiality determination rests on the substantive law, it is the substantive law's identification of which facts are critical and which facts are irrelevant that governs. Any proof or evidentiary requirements imposed by the substantive law are not germane to this inquiry, since materiality is only a criterion for categorizing factual disputes in their relation to the legal elements of the claim and not a criterion for evaluating the evidentiary underpinnings of those disputes.

More important for present purposes, summary judgment will not lie if the dispute about a material fact is "genuine," that is, if the evidence is such that a reasonable jury could return a verdict for the nonmoving party. In First National Bank of Arizona v. Cities Service Co., 391 U.S. 253, 88 S.Ct. 1575, 20 L.Ed.2d 569 (1968), we affirmed a grant of summary judgment for an antitrust defendant where the issue was whether there was a genuine factual dispute as to the existence of a conspiracy. We noted Rule 56(e)'s provision that a party opposing a properly supported motion for summary judgment " 'may not rest upon the mere allegations or denials of his pleading, but ... must set forth specific facts showing that there is a genuine issue for trial.' " We observed further that

> "[i]t is true that the issue of material fact required by Rule 56(c) to be present to entitle a party to proceed to trial is not required to be resolved conclusively in favor of the party asserting its existence; rather, all that is required is that sufficient evidence supporting the claimed factual dispute be shown to require a jury or judge to resolve the parties' differing versions of the truth at trial." 391 U.S., at 288–289, 88 S.Ct., at 1592.

We went on to hold that, in the face of the defendant's properly supported motion for summary judgment, the plaintiff could not rest on his allegations of a conspiracy to get to a jury without "any significant probative evidence tending to support the complaint." Id., at 290, 88 S.Ct., at 1593.

Again, in Adickes v. S.H. Kress & Co., 398 U.S. 144, 90 S.Ct. 1598, 26 L.Ed.2d 142 (1970), the Court emphasized that the availability of summary judgment turned on whether a proper jury question was presented. There, one of the issues was whether there was a conspiracy between private persons and law enforcement officers. The District Court granted summary judgment for the defendants, stating that there was no evidence from which reasonably minded jurors might draw an inference of conspiracy. We reversed, pointing out that the moving parties' submissions had not foreclosed the possibility of the existence of certain facts from which "it would be open to a jury . . . to infer from the circumstances" that there had been a meeting of the minds. Id., at 158–159, 90 S.Ct., at 1608, 1609.

Our prior decisions may not have uniformly recited the same language in describing genuine factual issues under Rule 56, but it is clear enough from our recent cases that at the summary judgment stage the judge's function is not himself to weigh the evidence and determine the truth of the matter but to determine whether there is a genuine issue for trial. * * * there is no issue for trial unless there is sufficient evidence favoring the nonmoving party for a jury to return a verdict for that party. If the evidence is merely colorable, or is not significantly probative, summary judgment may be granted.

That this is the proper focus of the inquiry is strongly suggested by the Rule itself. Rule 56(e) provides that, when a properly supported motion for summary judgment is made,[4] the adverse party "must set forth specific facts showing that there is a genuine issue for trial."[5] And, as we noted above, Rule 56(c) provides that the trial judge shall then grant summary judgment if there is no genuine issue as to any material fact and if the moving party is entitled to judgment as a matter of law. There is no requirement that the trial judge make findings of fact.[6] The inquiry performed is the threshold inquiry of determining whether there is the need for a trial—whether, in other words, there are any genuine factual issues that properly can be resolved only by a finder of fact because they may reasonably be resolved in favor of either party.

Petitioners suggest, and we agree, that this standard mirrors the standard for a directed verdict under Federal Rule of Civil Procedure 50(a), which is that the trial judge must direct a verdict if, under the governing law, there can be but one reasonable conclusion as to the verdict. If reasonable minds could differ as to the import of the evidence, however, a verdict should not be directed. * * * The Court has said that summary judgment should be granted where the evidence is such that it "would require a directed verdict for the moving party." Sartor v. Arkansas Gas Corp., 321 U.S. 620, 624, 64 S.Ct. 724, 727, 88 L.Ed. 967 (1944). And we have noted that the "genuine issue" summary judgment standard is "very close" to the "reasonable jury"

---

4. Our analysis here does not address the question of the initial burden of production of evidence placed by Rule 56 on the party moving for summary judgment. See Celotex Corp. v. Catrett, 477 U.S. 317, 106 S.Ct. 2548, 91 L.Ed. 265 (1986). Respondents have not raised this issue here, and for the purposes of our discussion we assume that the moving party has met initially the requisite evidentiary burden.

5. This requirement in turn is qualified by Rule 56(f)'s provision that summary judgment be refused where the nonmoving party has not had the opportunity to discover information that is essential to his opposition. In our analysis here, we assume that both parties have had ample opportunity for discovery.

6. In many cases, however, findings are extremely helpful to a reviewing court.

directed verdict standard: "The primary difference between the two motions is procedural; summary judgment motions are usually made before trial and decided on documentary evidence, while directed verdict motions are made at trial and decided on the evidence that has been admitted." Bill Johnson's Restaurants, Inc. v. NLRB, 461 U.S. 731, 745, n. 11, 103 S.Ct. 2161, 2171, n. 11, 76 L.Ed.2d 277 (1983). In essence, though, the inquiry under each is the same: whether the evidence presents a sufficient disagreement to require submission to a jury or whether it is so one-sided that one party must prevail as a matter of law.

B

Progressing to the specific issue in this case, we are convinced that the inquiry involved in a ruling on a motion for summary judgment or for a directed verdict necessarily implicates the substantive evidentiary standard of proof that would apply at the trial on the merits. If the defendant in a run-of-the-mill civil case moves for summary judgment or for a directed verdict based on the lack of proof of a material fact, the judge must ask himself not whether he thinks the evidence unmistakably favors one side or the other but whether a fair-minded jury could return a verdict for the plaintiff on the evidence presented. The mere existence of a scintilla of evidence in support of the plaintiff's position will be insufficient; there must be evidence on which the jury could reasonably find for the plaintiff. The judge's inquiry, therefore, unavoidably asks whether reasonable jurors could find by a preponderance of the evidence that the plaintiff is entitled to a verdict—"whether there is [evidence] upon which a jury can properly proceed to find a verdict for the party producing it, upon whom the onus of proof is imposed." * * * Just as the "convincing clarity" requirement is relevant in ruling on a motion for directed verdict, it is relevant in ruling on a motion for summary judgment. When determining if a genuine factual issue as to actual malice exists in a libel suit brought by a public figure, a trial judge must bear in mind the actual quantum and quality of proof necessary to support liability under New York Times. For example, there is no genuine issue if the evidence presented in the opposing affidavits is of insufficient caliber or quantity to allow a rational finder of fact to find actual malice by clear and convincing evidence.

Thus, in ruling on a motion for summary judgment, the judge must view the evidence presented through the prism of the substantive evidentiary burden. This conclusion is mandated by the nature of this determination. The question here is whether a jury could reasonably find either that the plaintiff proved his case by the quality and quantity of evidence required by the governing law or that he did not. Whether a jury could reasonably find for either party, however, cannot be defined except by the criteria governing what evidence would enable the jury to find for either the plaintiff or the defendant: It makes no sense to say that a jury could reasonably find for either party without some benchmark as to what standards govern its deliberations and within what boundaries its ultimate decision must fall, and these standards and boundaries are in fact provided by the applicable evidentiary standards.

Our holding that the clear-and-convincing standard of proof should be taken into account in ruling on summary judgment motions does not denigrate the role of the jury. It by no means authorizes trial on affidavits. Credibility determinations, the weighing of the evidence, and the drawing of legitimate inferences from the facts are jury functions, not those of a judge, whether he is ruling on a motion for summary judgment or for a directed verdict. The evidence of the non-movant is to be believed, and all justifiable inferences are to be drawn in his favor. Adickes, 398 U.S., at 158–159, 90 S.Ct., at 1608–1609. Neither do we suggest that the trial courts should act other than with caution in granting summary judgment or that the trial court may not deny summary judgment in a case where there is reason to believe that the better course would be to proceed to a full trial.

In sum, we conclude that the determination of whether a given factual dispute requires submission to a jury must be guided by the substantive evidentiary standards that apply to the case. This is true at both the directed verdict and summary judgment stages. Consequently, where the New York Times "clear and convincing" evidence requirement applies, the trial judge's summary judgment inquiry as to whether a genuine issue exists will be whether the evidence presented is such that a jury applying that evidentiary standard could reasonably find for either the plaintiff or the defendant. Thus, where the factual dispute concerns actual malice, clearly a material issue in a New York Times case, the appropriate summary judgment question will be whether the evidence in the record could support a reasonable jury finding either that the plaintiff has shown actual malice by clear and convincing evidence or that the plaintiff has not.[7]

III

Respondents argue, however, that whatever may be true of the applicability of the "clear and convincing" standard at the summary judgment or directed verdict stage, the defendant should seldom if ever be granted summary judgment where his state of mind is at issue and the jury might disbelieve him or his witnesses as to this issue. They rely on Poller v. Columbia Broadcasting System, Inc., 368 U.S. 464, 82 S.Ct. 486, 7 L.Ed.2d 458 (1962), for this proposition. We do not understand Poller, however, to hold that a plaintiff may defeat a defendant's properly supported motion for summary judgment in a conspiracy or libel case, for example, without offering any concrete evidence from which a reasonable juror could return a verdict in his favor and by merely asserting that the jury might, and legally could, disbelieve the defendant's denial of a conspiracy or of legal malice.

---

7. Our statement in Hutchinson v. Proxmire, 443 U.S. 111, 120, n. 9, 99 S.Ct. 2675, 2680, n. 9 (1979), that proof of actual malice "does not readily lend itself to summary disposition" was simply an acknowledgment of our general reluctance "to grant special procedural protections to defendants in libel and defamation actions in addition to the constitutional protections embodied in the substantive laws." Calder v. Jones, 465 U.S. 783, 790–791, 104 S.Ct. 1482, 1487–1488, 79 L.Ed.2d 804 (1984).

The movant has the burden of showing that there is no genuine issue of fact, but the plaintiff is not thereby relieved of his own burden of producing in turn evidence that would support a jury verdict. Rule 56(e) itself provides that a party opposing a properly supported motion for summary judgment may not rest upon mere allegation or denials of his pleading, but must set forth specific facts showing that there is a genuine issue for trial. Based on that Rule, Cities Service, 391 U.S., at 290, 88 S.Ct., at 1593, held that the plaintiff could not defeat the properly supported summary judgment motion of a defendant charged with a conspiracy without offering "any significant probative evidence tending to support the complaint." As we have recently said, "discredited testimony is not [normally] considered a sufficient basis for drawing a contrary conclusion." Bose Corp. v. Consumers Union of United States, Inc., 466 U.S. 485, 512, 104 S.Ct. 1949, 1966, 80 L.Ed.2d 502 (1984). Instead, the plaintiff must present affirmative evidence in order to defeat a properly supported motion for summary judgment. This is true even where the evidence is likely to be within the possession of the defendant, as long as the plaintiff has had a full opportunity to conduct discovery. We repeat, however, that the plaintiff, to survive the defendant's motion, need only present evidence from which a jury might return a verdict in his favor. If he does so, there is a genuine issue of fact that requires a trial.

IV

In sum, a court ruling on a motion for summary judgment must be guided by the New York Times "clear and convincing" evidentiary standard in determining whether a genuine issue of actual malice exists—that is, whether the evidence presented is such that a reasonable jury might find that actual malice had been shown with convincing clarity. Because the Court of Appeals did not apply the correct standard in reviewing the District Court's grant of summary judgment, we vacate its decision and remand the case for further proceedings consistent with this opinion.

It is so ordered.

■ [The dissenting opinions of Justice Brennan and of Justice Rehnquist, joined by the Chief Justice are omitted. Eds.]

NOTE

1. Did plaintiff in Liberty Lobby have "a full opportunity to conduct discovery" given that Eringer, who was claimed to be the source of much of the published material, could not be deposed?

2. Most of the reported libel cases since Anderson have resulted in summary judgment for defendants. See Howley, John J.P., 34 N.Y. L. Sch. L. Rev. 201, note 99 (1989).

3. The Libel Defense Resource Center Report of September 30, 1997 states that the success rate of media defendants using summary judgment motions has risen significantly since 1986.

Brill v. Guardian Life Insurance Co.

Supreme Court of New Jersey, 1995.
142 N.J. 520, 666 A.2d 146.

The opinion of the Court was delivered by

■ COLEMAN, J.

This appeal involves a claim of negligence against a life-insurance broker and his agency for failing to advise a prospective insured of the possibility of securing immediate, temporary coverage upon completion of the application process. The trial court granted summary judgment holding the broker and his agency liable for the face value of the policy. The important question raised is whether the trial court incorrectly granted a summary judgment motion in favor of the insured. A subset of that question is whether the trial court engaged in an impermissible weighing of evidence to determine whether a genuine issue of material fact existed.

We hold that when deciding a motion for summary judgment under Rule 4:46–2, the determination whether there exists a genuine issue with respect to a material fact challenged requires the motion judge to consider whether the competent evidential materials presented, when viewed in the light most favorable to the non-moving party in consideration of the applicable evidentiary standard, are sufficient to permit a rational factfinder to resolve the alleged disputed issue in favor of the non-moving party. This assessment of the evidence is to be conducted in the same manner as that required under Rule 4:37–2(b).

I

Because the case was disposed of in a summary judgment proceeding, our statement of the facts is based on our consideration of the evidence in the light most favorable to the parties opposing summary judgment. Dairy Stores, Inc. v. Sentinel Publishing Co., Inc., 104 N.J. 125, 135, 516 A.2d 220 (1986); Judson v. Peoples Bank & Trust Co. of Westfield, 17 N.J. 67, 75, 110 A.2d 24 (1954).

In June 1989, Robert Brill, thirty-seven years old at the time with a wife and two minor children, decided his $10,000 in life insurance with Prudential was inadequate. He contacted his broker, Charles Gould, of the KRA Insurance Agency, Inc. (KRA), to purchase an additional $750,000 in term-life insurance.

Gould met with Brill on June 15, 1989, at Brill's office. Brill told Gould that he wanted a $750,000 term policy as soon as possible. Gould explained that a three-step process had to be completed before securing a policy: 1) completing and signing an application, 2) undergoing a medical examination and 3) giving a "binder check." Gould explained that the process would require about four to six weeks to complete an underwriting review before a policy would be issued by Guardian Life Insurance Co. (Guardian).

Gould read the application questions to Brill and recorded Brill's responses. Brill informed Gould that he had been treated for chronic stomach problems that were believed to have been caused by an ulcer. Brill expressed some concern that Guardian would issue him a rated policy (one surcharged with an additional premium). Gould's response was that Guardian would conduct its own medical investigation into Brill's health, and if a rated policy was issued "we'll deal with it then." Brill signed the application after Gould recorded the information.

At or about the time of completion of the application, Gould asked for a deposit. Brill, however, was unwilling to give money to the insurance company before he knew a standard policy would be issued.

The application stated that Brill's policy would become effective upon delivery of the policy to the named insured. The application also contained a provision for coverage prior to delivery of the policy. Paragraph Eleven of the application provided:

> I . . . further agree that no insurance shall take effect (except as provided in the Conditional Receipt if an advance payment has been made and acknowledged above and such Receipt issued) unless and until the Policy has been delivered to and accepted by me . . . and the first premium paid during the lifetime and prior to any change in health of the Proposed Insured as described in this Application.

However, Gould never advised Brill that he could obtain coverage virtually immediately in the form of a conditional receipt. Under the conditional-receipt concept, Brill would have been required to pass a medical examination conducted on behalf of Guardian. Passing the medical examination would have satisfied the requirement of being "acceptable as a standard risk." In addition, Brill would have been required to pay one-sixth of his annual premium for a standard policy, amounting to $141.87, upon signing the application.

Coverage under the conditional receipt would have existed for sixty days from the date of Guardian's medical examination. Conditional-receipt coverage would have (1) provided $500,000 in life insurance, (2) protected against any change in health requirement and (3) guaranteed that a standard policy, rather than a rated policy, would be issued in the amount of $750,000.

Gould also recorded the incorrect answer to a crucial question in the application that made Brill ineligible for a conditional receipt. Question 6(b) asked: "Have you, within the last 12 months . . . had an electrocardiogram because of chest pain or any other physical problem or taken medication for elevated blood pressure?" Gould answered "yes" to that question because Brill said that he had undergone an electrocardiogram in preparation for knee surgery that was performed in June 1988. Gould, however, failed to question Brill concerning the date and purpose of those procedures. Had he done so, he would have learned that the electrocardiogram was performed on May 31, 1988, and the surgery on June 6, 1988. Because both procedures were more than twelve months before the date of the application, and because the electrocardiogram was not related to chest pain, the answer to Question 6(b) should have been "no."

On June 19, 1989, four days after Brill completed his application, Dr. Mary Mazzarella performed a medical examination of Brill on behalf of Guardian. Dr. Mazzarella did not discover any health problems.

On June 28, 1989, Gould mailed Brill's completed application to Guardian's general agent. The agent then forwarded the application to Guardian for processing. As a supplement to Dr. Mazzarella's report, Guardian obtained a statement from Brill's personal physician, Dr. Jonathon Shapiro. Guardian's records reflect that Dr. Shapiro saw Brill in May 1989 for abdominal pain and bowel spasms, and that Dr. Shapiro made "no findings" at that time.

On July 21, 1989, Guardian issued a $750,000 standard life-insurance policy with Brill as the named insured. Brill's wife, plaintiff Robin Brill, was the primary beneficiary. After Guardian issued the policy, it was forwarded to Gould who was to deliver it to Brill. However, when Gould called Brill's office to set up a time for delivery, he was told that Brill was out of the office and would not return until August 20.

The parties agree that if Brill had obtained a conditional receipt, any change in Brill's health after June 19, 1989, the date Dr. Mazzarella examined him, would have been immaterial to the question of coverage under the standard policy.

On July 24, 1989, prior to delivery of Guardian's policy, Brill underwent a transverse colon resection and a liver biopsy. Brill was diagnosed post-operatively with colon cancer and "metastatic poorly differentiated carcinoma" of the liver.

On August 25, 1989, Gould delivered the Guardian policy to Brill and collected the first premium. Brill did not advise Gould that he had been diagnosed with and treated for cancer. Nor did Gould ask Brill whether he had undergone any change in health since the time of his June 15, 1989, application.

On June 29, 1990, Brill died of metastatic cancer of the liver and carcinoma of the colon. Shortly thereafter, Gould notified Guardian's general agent of Brill's death and submitted a claim on behalf of plaintiff. Guardian denied the claim on the grounds that Brill's policy was "null and void as of its effective date" because of the "change in health" experienced by Brill between the date of his application and receipt of the policy on August 25, 1989.

Following the denial of the claim for payment under the policy, plaintiff instituted the present litigation to compel payment of the face value of the policy. She alleged breach of contract, bad faith and breach of fiduciary duty against Guardian. She also alleged negligence and breach of fiduciary duty against KRA, Guardian's authorized agent, and Gould individually as agent for KRA. The theory of negligence against Gould was based on his failure to record the correct answer to

Question 6(b) and the failure to discuss a conditional receipt with Brill.

On May 28, 1993, the trial court granted summary judgment in favor of Guardian. The court reasoned that as a matter of law, the policy was null and void because Brill had failed to advise Guardian of an "egregious and monumental" change in his health that occurred between the date of his application and the date of delivery of the policy.

On the same date, the trial court also granted plaintiff's motion for summary judgment against Gould and KRA in the amount of $750,000. The court reasoned that it was "beyond dispute" that Gould incorrectly recorded the answer to Question 6(b) on Brill's application, thereby causing Brill to become ineligible for the conditional-receipt coverage that would have rendered moot the change-in-health feature of the policy. The court further stated: "It is beyond dispute, and no jury can find otherwise that Mr. Gould did not even tell Mr. Brill that the option was available to him." The court concluded:

> Through Gould's negligence, which is inescapable, Mr. Brill was denied the option to be bound in such a manner that the change in health feature of the policy would be moot. Had Mr. Gould not so behaved, Mr. Brill would have been bound over for five hundred thousand dollars until August 25 [1989]. It would have become seven hundred and fifty thousand dollars.

KRA and Gould appealed and the Appellate Division affirmed in an unreported opinion substantially for the reasons articulated by the trial court. We granted KRA's and Gould's petition for certification. 139 N.J. 288, 654 A.2d 469 (1994). We now affirm.

II

Defendants KRA and Gould argue that the grant of summary judgment against them was improper because the trial judge engaged in an improper "weighing of the facts" and "refused to consider the reasonable inferences to be drawn in favor of the defendant broker." They contend that the evidence presents two genuine issues of material fact: (1) whether Gould deviated from the standard of care required of insurance brokers; and (2) whether his alleged deviation from that standard of care was a proximate cause of damage to plaintiff.

They contend Gould was not negligent based on the opinion of their expert, insurance broker Armando Castellini, who concluded that "Gould and KRA did not breach any duty owed to Brill, and that the agent and agency did not fail to conform to generally accepted standards and practices in the industry." They argue that with respect to the issue of proximate cause, the facts justify an inference that even if Gould had discussed the conditional-receipt option with Brill, he would not have elected that option because "he was never going to give any deposit premium unless and until he had a non-rated policy in his hands."

They also contend that Brill learned of the conditional-receipt option when he reviewed the application before signing it and that this fact supports an inference of no negligence on the part of Gould, or, at the very least, creates an issue of comparative negligence requiring submission of the case to a jury. See Dancy v. Popp, 114 N.J. 570, 573, 556 A.2d 312 (1989).

III

A

Rule 4:46–2 provides that a court should grant summary judgment when "the pleadings, depositions, answers to interrogatories and admissions on file, together with the affidavits, if any, show that there is no genuine issue as to any material fact challenged and that the moving party is entitled to a judgment or order as a matter of law." [The federal summary judgment rule [is] the counterpart to Rule 4:46]
* * *

By its plain language, Rule 4:46–2 dictates that a court should deny a summary judgment motion only where the party opposing the motion has come forward with evidence that creates a "genuine issue as to any material fact challenged." That means a non-moving party cannot defeat a motion for summary judgment merely by pointing to any fact in dispute.

* * *

Recently, we emphasized:

> [Summary judgment] is designed to provide a prompt, business-like and inexpensive method of disposing of any cause which a discriminating search of the merits in the pleadings, depositions and admissions on file, together with the affidavits submitted on the motion clearly shows not to present any genuine issue of material fact requiring disposition at trial.

* * *

B

Today, we focus on how to determine when an alleged disputed issue of fact should be considered "genuine" for purposes of Rule 4:46–2 and when such an issue should be considered "of an insubstantial nature." While "genuine" issues of material fact preclude the granting of summary judgment, R. 4:46–2, those that are "of an insubstantial nature" do not. Judson, supra, 17 N.J. at 75, 110 A.2d 24.

After early debate about the breadth of the summary judgment power, the jurisprudence of summary judgment was rather uniform until 1986. In that year the United States Supreme Court upheld summary judgments in three cases: Matsushita Elec. Indus. Co., Ltd. v. Zenith Radio Corp., 475 U.S. 574, 106 S.Ct. 1348, 89 L.Ed.2d 538 (1986), Anderson v. Liberty Lobby, Inc., 477 U.S. 242, 106 S.Ct. 2505, 91 L.Ed.2d 202 (1986), and Celotex Corp. v. Catrett, 477 U.S. 317, 106 S.Ct. 2548, 91 L.Ed.2d 265 (1986). Matsushita was decided in March whereas Liberty Lobby and Celotex were decided the same day in June. The fact that the Court addressed the summary judgment standard three times within four months suggests how significant the issue had become.

* * *

Liberty Lobby involved a libel suit filed by a lobbying corporation and its founder against Jack Anderson, the publisher of a magazine, as well as against the magazine's president-chief executive officer, and the magazine itself, alleging they had libelled plaintiffs. * * * After completing discovery, defendants moved for summary judgment pursuant to Federal Rule of Civil Procedure 56(c).

In a libel action brought by a public official or public figure, a plaintiff is required by the First Amendment to prove that the defendant acted with actual malice and that actual malice must be shown with "convincing clarity." * * * In Liberty Lobby, the Court of Appeals for the District of Columbia found that although actual malice had to be proved by clear and convincing evidence, rather than by a preponderance, for purposes of summary judgment that "was irrelevant: To defeat summary judgment the [plaintiffs] did not have to show that a jury could find actual malice with 'convincing clarity.' "

The Supreme Court reversed and established a new standard for evaluating summary judgment motions under Federal Rule of Civil Procedure 56(c). * * *

Celotex involved a wrongful-death action against fifteen asbestos manufacturers. A factual issue was raised with respect to whether the decedent was exposed to Celotex asbestos products in Chicago in 1970–1971. The Court held that after passage of adequate time to complete the discovery, summary judgment should be granted "against a party who fails to make a showing sufficient to establish the existence of an element essential to that party's case, and on which that party will bear the burden of proof at trial." Celotex also held that the standard for granting summary judgment " 'mirrors the standard for a directed verdict under Federal Rule of Civil Procedure 50(a). . . .' " * * * Thus, Celotex established a weighing process in non-defamation summary judgment cases.

Read together, Matsushita, Liberty Lobby and Celotex adopted a standard that requires the motion judge to engage in an analytical process essentially the same as that necessary to rule on a motion for a directed verdict: "whether the evidence presents a sufficient disagreement to require submission to a jury or whether it is so one-sided that one party must prevail as a matter of law." Liberty Lobby, supra, 477 U.S. at 251–52, 106 S.Ct. at 2512, 91 L.Ed.2d at 214. That weighing process requires the court to be guided by the same evidentiary standard of proof—by a preponderance of the evidence or clear and convincing evidence—that would apply at the trial on the merits when deciding whether there exists a "genuine" issue of material fact.

* * *

The only distinction between 1) a directed verdict at the end of plaintiff's case pursuant to Rule 4:37–2(b), 2) a directed verdict pursuant to Rule 4:40–1 after all the evidence has been presented, 3) a judgment notwithstanding the verdict pursuant to Rule 4:40–2, and a summary judgment that allows a Rule 4:37–2(b) weighing of evidence to determine if a genuine issue of material fact exists, is that summary judgment motions are generally decided on documentary-evidential materials, while the directed verdicts are based on evidence presented during a trial. Under our holding today, the essence of the inquiry in each is the same: "whether the evidence presents a sufficient disagreement to require submission to a jury or whether it is so one-sided that one party must prevail as a matter of law." Liberty Lobby, supra, 477 U.S. at 251–52, 106 S.Ct. at 2512, 91 L.Ed.2d at 214.

Of course, there is in this process a kind of weighing that involves a type of evaluation, analysis and sifting of evidential materials. This process, however, is not the same kind of weighing that a factfinder (judge or jury) engages in when assessing the preponderance or credibility of evidence. On a motion for summary judgment the court must grant all the favorable inferences to the non-movant. But the ultimate factfinder may pick and choose inferences from the evidence to the extent that "a miscarriage of justice under the law" is not created. R. 4:49–1(a).

B

Measured by that standard, a dismissal under Rule 4:37–2(b), Rule 4:40–1, Rule 4:40–2 or for failure to allege or prove a prima facie case, does not unduly intrude into the province of the jury. In those instances, there simply is no issue to be decided by a jury based on the evidence. A jury resolves factual, not legal, disputes. If a case involves no material factual disputes, the court disposes of it as a matter of law by rendering judgment in favor of the moving or non-moving party on the issue of liability or damages or both. Thus, the right of trial by jury remains inviolate.

* * *

The majority of courts in other jurisdictions that have considered the Liberty Lobby–Celotex rule in non-First Amendment cases have adopted it. See, e.g., Orme School v. Reeves, 166 Ariz. 301, 802 P.2d 1000, 1003–09 (1990); [and citing to 28 other states' laws]

* * *

The Arizona Supreme Court has aptly described why so many jurisdictions have adopted the standard articulated in Celotex and Liberty Lobby. It stated:

We live in what is widely perceived as a time of great increase in litigation and one in which many meritless cases are filed, vastly increasing the dockets before our trial judges. As a result, the courts of this country have been urged to liberalize the standards

so as to permit summary judgment in a larger number of cases.
* * *

[Orme School, supra, 802 P.2d at 1003–04 (footnotes omitted).]

Consistent with this national trend, we hold that under Rule 4:46–2, when deciding summary judgment motions trial courts are required to engage in the same type of evaluation, analysis or sifting of evidential materials as required by Rule 4:37–2(b) in light of the burden of persuasion that applies if the matter goes to trial. Accordingly, we request the Civil Practice Committee to recommend appropriate rule changes on an expedited basis that are necessary to implement the standard we establish today.

Under this new standard, a determination whether there exists a "genuine issue" of material fact that precludes summary judgment requires the motion judge to consider whether the competent evidential materials presented, when viewed in the light most favorable to the non-moving party, are sufficient to permit a rational factfinder to resolve the alleged disputed issue in favor of the non-moving party. The "judge's function is not himself [or herself] to weigh the evidence and determine the truth of the matter but to determine whether there is a genuine issue for trial." Liberty Lobby, supra, 477 U.S. at 249, 106 S.Ct. at 2511, 91 L.Ed.2d at 212. Credibility determinations will continue to be made by a jury and not the judge. If there exists a single, unavoidable resolution of the alleged disputed issue of fact, that issue should be considered insufficient to constitute a "genuine" issue of material fact for purposes of Rule 4:46–2. Liberty Lobby, supra, 477 U.S. at 250, 106 S.Ct. at 2511, 91 L.Ed.2d at 213. The import of our holding is that when the evidence "is so one-sided that one party must prevail as a matter of law," Liberty Lobby, supra, 477 U.S. at 252, 106 S.Ct. at 2512, 91 L.Ed.2d at 214, the trial court should not hesitate to grant summary judgment.

* * *

The thrust of today's decision is to encourage trial courts not to refrain from granting summary judgment when the proper circumstances present themselves. Some have suggested that trial courts out of fear of reversal, or out of an overly restrictive reading of Judson, supra, 17 N.J. at 67, 110 A.2d 24, or a combination thereof, allow cases to survive summary judgment so long as there is any disputed issue of fact. As to fear of reversal, we believe our judges are made of sterner stuff and have sought conscientiously over the years to follow the law. We may have permitted an encrustation of the Judson standard that obscured its essential import. A summary judgment motion has in the past required and will in the future continue to require a searching review.

* * *

V

The trial court in the present case properly concluded that the evidence presented by KRA and Gould does not create a "genuine" issue of material fact under Rule 4:46–2. As the motion judge found, the competent evidential material presented leaves no doubt of any kind about whether Gould advised Brill of the availability of a conditional-receipt. By Gould's own unequivocal admission, he did not. The trial court thus correctly held that "[t]here is no evidence from which a jury could conclude that Mr. [Gould] offered the temporary option."

The fact that Brill reviewed and signed his insurance application does not alter the inescapable conclusion that Gould failed to make Brill aware of the conditional-receipt option. By signing that application, Brill did not acknowledge that he had been informed of the availability of a conditional receipt. Although the application contains a section devoted to the conditional-receipt option, there was no evidence to suggest that even if Brill read the option, he would understand its meaning.

The common law has long recognized that an insurance broker owes a duty to the insured to act with reasonable skill and diligence in performing the services of a broker. Carter Lincoln–Mercury, Inc. v. EMAR Group, Inc., 135 N.J. 182, 189, 638 A.2d 1288 (1994) (citations omitted). We have concluded previously that as a matter of law, the duty owed by a broker to an applicant for insurance includes the duty to inform the potential insured of the availability of immediate insurance coverage through a temporary binder. Id. at 190, 638 A.2d 1288 (citing Bates v. Gambino, 72 N.J. 219, 222–25, 370 A.2d 10 (1977)). Thus, if a broker does not inform the prospective insured of the availability of a temporary binder option, the broker has committed professional negligence. See Bates, supra, 72 N.J. at 225, 370 A.2d 10 (noting that this Court's case law sets forth the legal requirements of an insurance broker). We agree with the trial court that Gould was negligent as a matter of law. Carter, supra, 135 N.J. at 189–90, 638 A.2d 1288.

We are thoroughly convinced that Brill's refusal to provide a check for the entire amount of the policy premium is irrelevant to the issue of whether Gould was negligent for failing to advise Brill of the temporary binder option. That refusal can be considered only in the context of the facts known to Brill at the time. When Brill told Gould that he would not pay the policy premium in advance, Brill's knowledge of the relevant facts was incomplete. Indeed, when Brill made that statement, Gould had not made Brill aware of the conditional-receipt option that would have allowed Brill to obtain virtually immediately $500,000 in coverage for the very small sum of $141.87. Brill was also unaware that once he obtained a conditional receipt, any subsequent change in his health would be immaterial to coverage under the primary policy. Because Brill's statement refusing to provide a check for the full policy premium was based on insufficient knowledge of the available option to obtain a conditional receipt, it has no bearing on the issue of whether Gould acted negligently in failing to advise Brill of the availability of a conditional receipt or on the issue of proximate cause.

We likewise find that the opinion of defendants' expert broker does not create a genuine issue of material fact regarding Gould's negligence. Castellini stated specifically:

> The agent was prevented from issuing a Conditional Receipt, though it was Gould's practice to do so when possible, by Brill's refusal to make a premium payment with the application. There are a number of good and cogent reasons why producers—like Gould—want to take a premium deposit with the application. The agent, however, cannot force an applicant to do that which the applicant has refused to do.

Castellini's conclusion that Gould did not breach any duty owed to Brill is based on the false assumption that Gould performed all of his duties in the manner required by the applicable standard of care and that a conditional receipt was not issued because Brill refused to pay the entire premium. An expert's opinion of no negligence based on erroneous or nonexistent facts is worthless.

* * *

Finally, the competent evidential materials create no genuine issue of material fact with respect to whether Gould's failure to advise Brill of the conditional-receipt option was a proximate cause of damages to plaintiff. We are satisfied that no reasonable jury could conclude, based on the facts in the record, that Gould's negligence was not a proximate cause of Brill's lack of an effective Guardian life-insurance policy at the time of his death. It is clear from the record that Brill wanted to secure life-insurance coverage as quickly as possible. There can be no doubt, then, that had he been given the chance, Brill would have secured immediate, temporary coverage by paying the small sum of $141.87. Coverage under the conditional-receipt option would have become effective on June 19, 1989, the date of his successful medical examination. As of that date, Brill's change in health would have become immaterial to the existence of coverage under the primary policy. When the primary policy was issued on July 21, 1989, it would have replaced the coverage provided by the conditional receipt. Therefore, when Brill died, he would have been covered in the amount of $750,000. The evidence thus compels the unavoidable conclusion that because of Gould's negligence, plaintiff has been deprived of $750,000 that she otherwise would have received. That entitles plaintiff to judgment for the face value of the policy.

VI

In sum, we hold that the evidence in the record creates no "genuine" issue of material fact precluding the grant of summary judgment under Rule 4:46–2. It is undisputed, and no reasonable jury could conclude otherwise, that Gould failed to advise Brill of the availability of a conditional receipt. As a matter of law, that failure constituted a breach of the duty Gould owed to Brill. Finally, the record compels the unavoidable conclusion that Gould's negligence was a proximate cause of damages to plaintiff in the amount of $750,000.

The rule we adopt today shall apply to this case and all cases pending in the trial and appellate courts involving unresolved issues concerning summary judgment, including those cases in which summary judgment was denied previously.

NOTES

1. Summary judgement is usually considered on the papers alone, including affidavits, exhibits and the like. Hence in the federal courts the "prevailing rule is that appellate courts automatically exercise a de novo review of orders granting summary judgement." Schwarzer, Hirsh & Barrans, *The Analysis and Decision of Summary Judgement Motions,* 139 F.R.D. 441 (1992).

In Brill the standard for directed verdict, both after plaintiffs' case and after all the evidence has been presented, and judgement n.o.v. are said to be equivalent to those for a summary judgement. In motions for directed verdict, the trial judge has usually heard at least the plaintiff's presentation of his case and sometimes the full case; and in motions for judgement n.o.v. the trial judge presumably has heard the entire case and jury's verdict. Should the trial judge's rulings be subject to the same scope and standards of review in all four situations?

2. The judges and some commentators speak almost entirely of a more efficient legal system. The use of summary judgements would be better able "to deal with increasingly crowded dockets and rising litigation costs." See Schwarzer, Hirsch & Barrans, *The Analysis and Decision of Summary Judgement Motions*, 139 F.R.D. 441 (1992). It is "designed to expedite the resolution of cases and reduce costs and delay ..." Id. Consider the similar and strong commentary in Brill: we emphasized that summary judgement "is designed to provide a prompt, businesslike and inexpensive method of disposing of some cases."

3. Part of the rationale for the new standard announced in Brill is that it should help the courts control their dockets by curtailing the advancement of frivolous or very weak cases. Under the old standard, to defeat a summary judgement motion the non-movant only had to show that there was some doubt as to an issue of material fact. Under the new standard the non-movant must prove, bearing the burden which would apply at trial, that a reasonable finder of fact could find in his favor. This new standard requires a great deal more in terms of disclosing what the non-moving party is likely to present at trial. Thus under the new system an incentive, other than success(early and maybe enhanced discovery), exists for moving for summary judgement. Is it likely that weak motions will now be made to gain some tactical advantage?

4. Would it be desirable to include some domestic relations matters, such as divorce, property settlement, support payments, and child custody in the cases subject to summary judgement? Some states now exclude these from summary practice judgement.

5. In federal courts, although the trial judge is not required to write an opinion when granting summary judgment, most district judges do provide findings of fact and law. With specific reference Brill, the New Jersey rules of court impose an obligation on the judge. Rule of Court 4:46–2(c) requires that in summary judgment rulings the court must state the reasons for its actions. Denials are rarely explained, in the state courts or in the federal courts.

C. THE NEED FOR DISCOVERY

Dowling v. City of Philadelphia

United States Court of Appeals, Third Circuit , 1988.
855 F.2d 136. Rehearing and Rehearing In Banc Denied Sept. 19, 1988.

OPINION OF THE COURT

■ SLOVITER, CIRCUIT JUDGE.

Patricia Dowling was arrested by Philadelphia police officers and charged with defiant trespass and criminal conspiracy while she was protesting outside of an abortion clinic in Northeast Philadelphia. After the Philadelphia Municipal Court sustained a demurrer to the criminal charges. Dowling brought a civil rights action against the abortion clinic, its parent company, and the City of Philadelphia, alleging that her arrest and detention violated her constitutional rights and constituted the basis of state law torts as well. The district court gave summary judgment for the defendants. This appeal followed.

I.

Background

Dowling filed her civil rights complaint on November 5, 1986 in the Court of Common Pleas against the City of Philadelphia; the Northeast Women's Center, Inc. (NEWC), outside of which Dowling was arrested; and Humedco Corporation, NEWC's parent corporation. The action was removed to federal court.

NEWC and Humedco answered Dowling's amended complaint and asserted both a counterclaim against Dowling and a third-party claim against the Pro–Life Coalition of Southeastern Pennsylvania for trespass and intentional interference with business relations.[8] On April 1, 1987, the City filed a motion for a protective order from certain discovery Dowling sought, together with affidavits of its employees. On the same day, the City filed a motion for summary judgment, relying on Dowling's deposition and a partial transcript of the criminal proceeding containing the testimony of one of the arresting officers. Dowling responded without filing any affidavits. The district court entered an order on November 25, 1987 granting summary judgment to the City, NEWC and Humedco.

On December 11, 1987, the Pro–Life Coalition filed a motion for summary judgment on NEWC's and Humedco's third-party claim. On December 17, 1987, Dowling filed her notice of appeal from the

---

8. NEWC and Humedco labeled their claim against the Pro–Life Coalition a "counterclaim", see App. at 150, and the district court refers to it as a "cross claim", see App. at 159. Because defendants NEWC and Hu-

medco instituted the claim against the Pro–Life Coalition, it is more properly characterized as a third-party claim, see Fed.R.Civ.P. 14(a), and we will refer to it as such.

district court's November 25, 1987 order. Five days thereafter, on December 22, 1987, the district court entered an order granting the Pro–Life Coalition's motion for summary judgment on the third-party claim. Finally, on December 23, 1987 the district court dismissed the remaining claim, NEWC's and Humedco's counterclaim against Dowling.

* * *

III.

Discovery

We turn next to Dowling's argument that the district court abused its discretion by granting summary judgment to defendants before she had an adequate opportunity to obtain discovery and while the motion for a protective order was outstanding. To properly assess this contention we must consider the procedural history in some detail.

Dowling's complaint alleges that defendants "knew that they were without probable cause to arrest her," App. at 130, thereby depriving Dowling of her Fifth and Fourteenth Amendment due process and equal protection rights in violation of 42 U.S.C. § 1983 (1982). The complaint further alleges that Dowling's arrest and detention were part of a conspiracy motivated by anti-Catholic animus between the Philadelphia police, the District Attorney's office, NEWC and Humedco to deprive her of her constitutional rights, and that defendants' actions constituted the state law torts of malicious prosecution, false arrest, and false imprisonment.

The district court held a pretrial conference on February 24, 1987 and entered an order on March 2, 1987 which, inter alia, set May 1, 1987 as the date for completion of discovery. Defendants took Dowling's deposition on March 11, 1987, and on March 20, 1987 Dowling served defendants with a notice of depositions of eleven City employees and one employee of the corporate defendants. The City employees notice for deposition included the arresting officers, the Police Commissioner, two former Police Commissioners, the Deputy City Solicitor, and a former Deputy City Solicitor.

The City did not produce its employees for deposition. Instead, on April 1, 1987 it filed both a motion for a protective order and a motion for summary judgment. The motion for a protective order, filed on the grounds that the depositions scheduled were overbroad, oppressive and burdensome, sought a stay of Dowling's discovery "save for facts relevant to her response to Defendant's Motion for Summary Judgment." App. at 101.

Dowling stated in her answer to the City's motion for a protective order that she "must use some evidence obtained from defendants in the cours[e] of discovery to meet her burden" as part of her case in chief. App. at 124. Specifically, she stated that she needed to depose the present and former police commissioners "because Police Commissioner Tucker advised various members of the Pro–Life movement that he was merely continuing the policy of his predecessors in authorizing arrests that were similar to the plaintiff's arrest," and the present and former city solicitors because "there have been numerous references to directives from the City Solicitor to the police regarding the arrest policy of pro-life people." App. at 124. Dowling also explained that "[t]he very short period of time for discovery in this case necessitated the use of depositions rather than written interrogatories." App. at 125.

The district court entered summary judgment for defendants on November 25, 1987, without ever having ruled on the City's motion for a protective order. Dowling now complains that she was deprived of an opportunity for discovery and contends that the district court abused its discretion by entering summary judgment for defendants without first ruling on the protective order motion.

The court is obliged to give a party opposing summary judgment an adequate opportunity to obtain discovery. See Celotex Corp. v. Catrett, 477 U.S. 317, 322, 106 S.Ct. 2548, 2552, 91 L.Ed.2d 265 (1986); see also Costlow v. United States, 552 F.2d 560, 563–64 (3d Cir.1977). If, however, a party opposing a summary judgment motion believes that s/he needs additional time for discovery, Rule 56(f) of the Federal Rules of Civil Procedure specifies the procedure to be followed. Rule 56(f) provides:

> Should it appear from the affidavits of a party opposing the motion that the party cannot for reasons stated present by affidavit facts essential to justify the party's opposition, the court may refuse the application for judgment or may order a continuance to permit affidavits to be obtained or depositions to be taken or discovery to be had or may make such other order as is just.

This court has interpreted Rule 56(f) as imposing a requirement that a party seeking further discovery in response to a summary judgment motion submit an affidavit specifying, for example, what particular information is sought; how, if uncovered, it would preclude summary judgment; and why it has not previously been obtained. See Hancock Industries v. Schaeffer, 811 F.2d 225, 229–30 (3d Cir.1987) (Rule 56(f) motion, even if treated as an affidavit, insufficient because it failed to explain need for discovery and did not identify particular facts hoped to be uncovered); Koplove v. Ford Motor Co., 795 F.2d 15, 18 (3d Cir.1986) (Rule 56(f) affidavit insufficient because it did not specify what discovery was needed or why it had not previously been secured).

Moreover, "[M]ost courts which have considered the issue agree that filing an affidavit is necessary for the preservation of a Rule 56(f) contention that summary judgment should be delayed pending further discovery." Mid–South Grizzlies v. National Football League, 720 F.2d 772, 780 n. 4 (3d Cir.1983) (citing cases), cert. denied, 467 U.S. 1215, 104 S.Ct. 2657, 81 L.Ed.2d 364 (1984); see Falcone v. Columbia Pictures Industries, 805 F.2d 115, 117 n. 2 (3d Cir.1986); Gray v. Udevitz, 656 F.2d 588, 592 (10th Cir.1981); cf. Robin Construction Co. v. United States, 345 F.2d 610, 614 (3d Cir.1965) (to take advantage of

Rule 56(f) party "must state by affidavit the reasons for his inability" to obtain discovery).

Dowling did not file a Rule 56(f) affidavit with her response to the City's motion for summary judgment, and therefore, as a procedural matter alone, she has failed to comply with the rule. Even if we were to treat Dowling's answer to the City's motion for a protective order as a Rule 56(f) affidavit, it would be insufficient because the fact Dowling stated she hoped to uncover would not have precluded summary judgment. See Hancock, 811 F.2d at 230.

It obviously would have been preferable for the district court to have acted on the outstanding motion for a protective order before ruling on the summary judgment motion. However, the outstanding motion for a protective order did not alter Dowling's obligation under the federal rules to file a Rule 56(f) affidavit if she believed the outstanding discovery was necessary to her response.

Moreover, there is no basis for Dowling's claim that the mere existence of the City's motion for a protective order deprived her of "the opportunity to obtain any discovery from any original defendant in this case." Dowling's Brief at 15. By its very terms, the City's motion sought only to prevent Dowling from deposing eleven City employees on facts not "relevant to her response to [the City's] Motion for Summary Judgment," App. at 101, and thus explicitly left her free to seek any discovery necessary for her response to the summary judgment motion.

Moreover, the protective order motion did not prohibit Dowling from deposing the employees of either of the corporate defendants, nor from pursuing alternative avenues of discovery from any of the defendants, including the City. It did not prevent her from filing interrogatories or from seeking an extension of the court's May 1, 1987 discovery deadline. Had Dowling believed that the depositions she sought were essential to her case, she could have somehow brought that fact to the attention of the district court by, for example, filing a motion to compel.

Most important, there was absolutely nothing to prevent Dowling from filing her own affidavit and that of other protestors if she had any information that would have created a material issue of fact on a relevant issue. For some inexplicable reason, Dowling chose not to pursue any of these paths and instead did absolutely nothing to obtain discovery from any of the defendants in the approximately seven months that elapsed between the time Dowling filed her answer to the City's motions and the court granted the City's summary judgment motion.[3]

---

3. At oral argument before us, Dowling's attorney explained that she had not put any material on the record in response to the City's motion for summary judgment because she believed that "with what [the City] put on the record in front of the district court I couldn't believe that they could get summary judgment," and that she "didn't feel that [she] needed any [discovery] in response to the motion for summary judgment." This approach illustrates why the author of a leading federal practice manual admonishes that "it is clearly perilous for the opposing party neither to proffer any countering evidentiary

In view of the limits of the terms of the protective order motion, of Dowling's failure to pursue available discovery avenues, and of her failure to comply with Rule 56(f), we conclude that the district court acted within the permissible bounds of its discretion when it ruled on the City's summary judgment motion on the record before it.

* * *

V.

Conclusion

Nothing in this opinion derogates from the right of Dowling and others to exercise their First Amendment rights. However, the police have an obligation to take reasonable steps to attempt to insure that protestors do not cross the line between peaceful protest and violation of the law. Because Dowling has not made any showing that the defendants acted beyond this permissible objective and for the reasons set forth above, we will affirm the order of the district court.

■ SEITZ, CIRCUIT JUDGE, dissenting.

* * *

I turn now to the basis for my dissent, which I write, in part, for whatever energizing benefit it may have in the future. Given the then posture of the case, I believe the district court's action in granting summary judgment to the defendants was, at best, premature. More specifically, at the time of its decision, the district court had pending before it for a considerable period of time, defendants' opposed motion for a protective order with respect to Dowling's timely notice of the taking of the depositions of several individuals connected with the City of Philadelphia.

It is evident to me that the depositions were potentially relevant, at least in part, to issues asserted in the amended complaint. Had there been a disposition of the motion, any permitted depositions would have been before the district court when it ruled on the summary judgment motion. See Fed.R.Civ.P. 56(c). Indeed, in her memorandum in opposition to the motion for summary judgment, Dowling stated: "As of this writing, Defendant, City of Philadelphia has not provided one iota of discovery that was requested by the plaintiff. There are material issues of fact that only a fact finder can decide." It seems strange indeed to visit on Dowling the possibly negative consequences of the district court's inaction by holding that she was required to invoke the protection of Federal Rule of Civil Procedure 56(f) to avoid what is characterized as a failure to resist the summary judgment motion. I cannot believe under the circumstances that Dowling was required to file an affidavit under rule 56(f) pointing out that noticed discovery was awaiting a ruling on defendant's protective order and that the summary judgment determination should await such ruling.

---

materials nor file a Rule 56(f) affidavit." 6 J. Moore & J. Wicker, Moore's Federal Practice ¶ 56–22[2], at 56–773 (2d ed. 1988) (footnote omitted).

The majority suggest that Dowling was, in any event, free to pursue other avenues of discovery and that she is, in effect, the victim of her own inaction. There are two fundamental weaknesses in this suggestion. First, it assumes that the discovery sought would not be relevant. That determination was for the district court to make in the first instance. Dowling could then have evaluated where she stood and what course of action to pursue.

Second, and related to the first point, to say that other discovery was available should not foreclose Dowling from relying on the discovery evidence she sought, the protective order aside. Subject to judicial oversight of discovery, a litigant should be permitted to pursue discovery by the means that she believes most useful. If it be suggested that the district court's failure to rule on the motion for a protective order was harmless error, I ask, how can one tell?

Because I would reverse the district court order for failure to timely act on the motion for a protective order, I do not reach the merits of the summary judgment determination.

NOTES

1. An extra burden is imposed on the nonmoving party, the plaintiff in Dowling, by this interpretation of Rule 56(f). The requirement of "an affidavit specifying . . . what particular information is sought; how, if uncovered, it would preclude summary judgment; and why it has not been previously obtained." What is the court's justification for this interpretation of Rule 56(f)? What if the mandatory disclosure of Rule 26(a) had been in place?

2. In Eastman Kodak Co. v. Image Technical Services, Inc., 504 U.S. 451, 112 S. Ct. 2072, 119 L.Ed. 2d 265 (1992), Eastman Kodak filed its summary judgment motion before the plaintiffs had even started discovery. Rule 56(f) did not help the plaintiffs because apparently they could not specify how discovery would help them to resist the summary judgment motion. Although the issue arises only in a single paragraph and one footnote in the Supreme Court opinion, the Ninth Circuit Court of Appeals had pointed out that the record was not fully developed because only very limited discovery had been permitted by the trial judge. 540 U.S. at 458–59.

NOTE: POSTPONING DISCOVERY

In Palmer v. Tracor, Inc., 856 F.2d 1131 (8th Cir. 1988), plaintiff sued defendant parent company for wrongful death growing out of an accident in a munitions factory. Defendant moved to dismiss under Rule 12(b)(6) and, in the alternative, for summary judgment. The trial court granted both motions ruling on them in the same order. Plaintiff had requested the trial court to delay ruling on the motion for summary judgment until he had an adequate opportunity to conduct discovery. The trial court denied the request, noting that several months had passed without further pleading or discovery. On appeal plaintiff argued that it was unwilling to conduct full-scale discovery while the motion to dismiss was pending because it wished to avoid the expense of unnecessary discovery. HELD: reversed. The 12(b)(6) ruling was incorrect as a matter of law and the delay in conducting discovery pending that ruling was justified, thus rendering improper the grant of summary judgment.

CHAPTER IX

BOUNDARIES OF AN ACTION

INTRODUCTORY NOTE

Fixing the boundaries of an action has been a complex enterprise virtually over the entire history of civil procedure. The United States Supreme Court has told us, relatively recently, that under the Federal Rules "the impulse is toward entertaining the broadest possible scope of action consistent with fairness to the parties; joinder of claims, parties and remedies is strongly encouraged."[1] Moreover, Professors Friedenthal, Kane and Miller tell us that this "philosophy now has been adopted by a majority of states."[2]

Neither a philosophy nor an impulse, however, can serve as an adequate predictor of what courts will in fact allow or require in a field traditionally marked with technical distinctions and requirements. Moreover, the penalty for an erroneous prediction can be nothing less than loss of the claim itself. Identifying the problems and classifying them is the best way to begin.

Central to any analysis is the distinction between permissive joinder and what is sometimes termed compulsory joinder. Most, albeit not all of the cases discussed in this chapter will deal with what is permitted; what is mandated, under penalty of the most severe sanctions, is dealt with primarily in the chapter on Judgments.

We begin with a two-party action, one plaintiff and one defendant. Federal Rule of Civil Procedure 18(a) is explicit in allowing a party to join "as many claims, legal, equitable, or maritime, as the party has against an opposing party." There are many benefits that typically follow from allowing one suit to dispose of whatever disputes the parties have between them. However, as the Advisory Committee's Notes make clear, the fact that free joinder is allowed at the pleading stage does not mean that a single trial will necessarily best serve the interest of justice. If not, then at least three separate rules (20(b), 21 and 42(b)) allow the judge to sever claims for trial.

Expanding the lawsuit to bring in additional parties raises new problems. Under what circumstances is it desirable to allow a plaintiff to sue two or more defendants in the same action, or to allow a defendant to bring in a third party? These are questions that will be addressed in the materials, both in terms of the technical requirements of the rules and the practical considerations which motivated those who formulated those rules and continue to influence the judges who apply them.

---

1. United Mine Workers of America v. Gibbs, 383 U.S. 715, 86 S.Ct. 1130, 16 L.Ed.2d 218 (1966), quoted in Friedenthal, Kane & Miller, Civil Procedure 346–347 (1985).

2. Ibid.

The class action, or representative suit, provided for in F.R.C.P. 23 and in the typical state rules, is a device for expanding the boundaries of an action exponentially. Who stands to gain when an action is brought to force a defendant to disgorge millions allegedly made by overcharging thousands of class members less than $100 each?

Two additional types of problems will also command our attention. As F.R.C.P. 19 recognizes, sometimes there are "persons needed for just adjudication" who are not yet in the law suit. Shall the action proceed without them? What factors should control the response? Finally, suppose someone not in the lawsuit desires to become a party and to litigate. When is it appropriate to expand the boundaries of the action beyond what any of the original parties has requested?

The cases themselves and the notes that accompany them consider many of the relevant practical considerations.

It is important to recognize, however, that not all of the relevant factors are easily perceived. For example, in large metropolitan areas the concentration of the trial bar presents difficult problems of calendaring. An attorney who specializes in defending personal injury claims, usually for an insurance company, will have many suits coming to trial at the same time and he will, typically, be allowed to file "busy slips" to excuse his non-appearance while he is engaged in another trial. Where there are two defendants, each with his own busy lawyer, getting to trial becomes even more difficult. Is this a reason for restricting joinder? Is a "special listing", i.e. a fixed time set for trial some time in advance, often at the very beginning of a trial period, a satisfactory solution? What are the disadvantages of being too lenient in granting "special listings"?[3]

A. Permissive Joinder of Claims and Parties

Tanbro Fabrics Corp. v. Beaunit Mills and Amity Dyeing & Finishing Co.
Beaunit Mills v. Tanbro Fabrics Corp.
Tanbro Fabrics Corp. v. Amity Dyeing & Finishing Co.

Supreme Court of New York, Appellate Division, First Department, 1957.
4 A.D.2d 519, 167 N.Y.S.2d 387.

■ Breitel, Justice.

3. The problem of concentration of the trial bar is treated extensively in Zeisel, Kalven & Buchholz, Delay in the Court 190 (1959). They report that the busiest 10% of the defense lawyers in personal injury trials in the New York court which they studied handled 39% of the work, but suggest that "the concentration for the whole of New York City is greater than indicated by our tables." Id. at 195, 197. This valuable study focuses on loss of judicial time which occurs when the trial list breaks down and no case is ready for trial, despite a huge backlog of cases on the list. For treatment of the problem of concentration focused primarily on the delay caused the litigant, see Levin & Woolley, Dispatch and Delay: A Field Study of Judicial Administration in Pennsylvania 27–29 (1961) and authorities there cited.

Stripped of procedural details, the question here is whether a buyer of textile goods may obtain a single trial against the seller and the processor of the goods, either by joinder in a single action, or by consolidation of actions, to determine whether the goods are defective, and if so, whether the defect is the consequence of breach by the seller, or the processor, or both of them. Special Term held that such joinder or consolidation is not available. A contrary view is reached here. It is held that the buyer is entitled to have such a common trial, either by joinder in a single action or by a consolidation of actions.

The underlying business dispute spawned three lawsuits. In the first action (the second in the captioned title), the seller, Beaunit, sought to recover the purchase price of goods sold and delivered to Tanbro. The Buyer, Tanbro, counterclaimed for breach of warranty for improper manufacture, as a result of which the goods were subject to "yarn slippage". The seller replied to the counterclaim by denying that the slippage was due to improper manufacture. A portion of the goods still being in the hands of the processor, Tanbro initiated another action (the third in the captioned title), in replevin, to recover these goods. The processor, Amity, counterclaimed for its charges and asserted its claim to the goods under an artisan's lien. In the exchanges that preceded and attended the bringing of these lawsuits, the buyer Tanbro received Beaunit's assertion that the yarn slippage was caused by the processor's improper handling, while with equal force the processor charged the same defect to Beaunit as a consequence of its improper manufacture.

At this juncture, Tanbro, the buyer, brought the third lawsuit (the first in the captioned title) against Beaunit and Amity, charging the goods were defective because of yarn slippage and that such slippage was caused by either the seller, Beaunit, or alternatively the processor, Amity, or both. This is the main action before the court.

At Special Term, the buyer Tanbro moved to consolidate the three actions. Beaunit and Amity separately cross-moved to dismiss the complaint in the buyer's main action on the ground that there were prior actions pending between the parties with respect to the same cause of action. The motion to consolidate was denied and Beaunit's cross-motion to dismiss the complaint as against it was granted.

The order should be modified by granting the consolidation, denying the cross-motion of the seller Beaunit to dismiss the complaint as to it in the buyer's main action and otherwise affirming the order.

Both the seller and the processor resist consolidation. They do so on the ground that each had a separate and different relationship to the buyer, and that each was involved in a separate and independent contract. Therefore, they say, there is not involved the "same transaction or occurrence", nor any common question of law or fact to sustain either a joinder of parties or a consolidation of the actions.[1]

---

1. Both at Special Term and by the argument of the parties in this court it has been assumed that if a joinder of parties were permissible, then a consolidation of the ac-

They stress that the buyer Tanbro wishes to pit against each other the seller and the processor on the issue of responsibility for the alleged defect, while the buyer sits back free from the obligation to prove a full case, as it would otherwise have to do in separate actions against the seller and the processor. The buyer, on the other hand, argues that what is identical to the cases are the goods and the defect, with the common question of who is responsible for the defect. The buyer concedes that it would have to prove the defect, and also prove that the defect must have been caused by either the seller or the processor or both of them; that, therefore, this involves a single transaction or occurrence and involves a common question of fact.

The controlling statute is Section 212 of the Civil Practice Act. That section is a product of a codification revision in 1949 (L.1949, Ch. 147, Fifteenth Annual Report of N.Y. Judicial Council, 1949, p. 211 et seq.). The portion pertinent to the joinder of defendants reads as follows:

> "2. All persons may be joined in one action as defendants if there is asserted against them jointly, severally, or in the alternative, any right to relief in respect of or arising out of the same transaction, occurrence, or series of transactions or occurrences and if any question of law or fact common to all of them would arise in the action. Judgment may be given according to their respective liabilities, against one or more defendants as may be found to be liable upon all of the evidence, without regard to the party by whom it has been introduced."

A reading of the section by itself would suggest little or no difficulty in permitting a joinder of parties in the buyer's main action or a consolidation of the three actions. However, the section has a history, which has created some confusion as to the meaning and application of the section.

* * *

The emphasis in the legislative and decisional history is that the joinder statute is to be accorded broad liberality and interpretation in order to avoid multiplicity of suits and inconsistencies in determination. Moreover, the philosophy of broad joinder of parties has been followed in many jurisdictions. (See, 3 Moore's Federal Practice, 2d Ed., para. 20.04, at p. 2718.)

This then is the background for the present section 212 of the Civil Practice Act. It should be beyond argument, by now, that it is no longer a bar to joinder, and, by parallel reasoning, *a fortiori*, to consolidation, that there is not an identity of duty or contract upon which to assert alternative liability. It is still necessary, of course, that

tions was likewise authorized. As a matter of fact the statute authorizing consolidation is a much broader one than that permitting joinder of parties (see, Civil Practice Act, § 96). It is true, however, that on occasion tests justifying joinder have been used in determining whether consolidation was proper. (See, 2 Carmody–Wait, Cyc. of N.Y.Prac., p. 466 et seq., pp. 474–475). Such an assumed identity of test is not justified by the statutes. Nevertheless, for the purposes of this case, if the parties may be joined, a fortiori, the actions may be consolidated.

there be a finding that the alternative liability arises out of a common transaction or occurrence involving common questions of fact and law. But this is not a rigid test. It is to be applied with judgment and discretion, in the balancing of convenience and justice between the parties involved (2 Carmody–Wait, Cyc. of N.Y. prac., § 34, at p. 558 et seq.; 1 Bender's N.Y.Prac., § 6.02, para. 3, at p. 322.). Indeed, the buyer's situation prompted Special Term to comment that the buyer, Tanbro, "is in the unenviable position of not knowing possibly which of its contracting parties is responsible and in separate actions may find itself confronted with defeat in each event though the product as finally delivered may be defective."

On the other hand, the view taken here does not mean that the buyer is not obliged to make out a prima facie case. Of course, it must. Its situation would be, as the Judicial Council foresaw in its Fifteenth Annual Report (supra, at p. 220):

> "Similarly, when a party is in doubt as to the person from whom he is entitled to relief, the pleading of necessity will assert a right in the alternative; for only by asserting facts which in the alternative fasten liability either upon one or the other defendant can the plaintiff make out a cause of action and, by proving such facts, establish a prima facie case."

This is precisely the holding by the Court of Appeals in Chase Nat. Bank of City of N.Y. v. Battat, 297 N.Y. 185, 78 N.E.2d 465, a decision made at the same Term as the decision in the Great Northern case, supra. See, also, S. & C. Clothing Co. v. United States Trucking Corp., 216 App.Div. 482, 215 N.Y.S. 349; Klugman's Sons v. Oceanic Steam Navigation Co., D.C.S.D.N.Y., 42 F.2d 461.

In the light of this reasoning, the cross-motion dismissing the complaint in the buyer's main action against the seller, Beaunit, on the ground of prior action pending, should have been determined otherwise. It is in that action and under that complaint that both defendants are charged with alternative liability. While consolidation would bring all of the parties and their respective claims and cross-claims together, there would actually be no pleading which asserts alternative liability under Section 212. There is no reason why the issue should not be presented by a forthright pleading, although, concededly, so long as consolidation is granted the matter is not of the greatest moment.

The right of joinder and the privilege to obtain consolidation is always counterbalanced, of course, by the power of the court to grant a severance, or to deny a consolidation, if prejudice or injustice appear. In this case, the danger of separate trials, leading, perhaps, to an unjust and illogical result, is a possibility well worth avoiding. The buyer is entitled to a less hazardous adjudication of his dispute, so long as he is able to make out a prima facie case of alternative liability.

Accordingly, the order of Special Term insofar as it granted the cross motion to dismiss the complaint in the first described action as against the defendant Beaunit and denied the buyer Tanbro's motion to consolidate the three actions should be modified to deny the cross motion and to grant the motion to consolidate, and otherwise should be affirmed, on the law and in the exercise of discretion of the court, with costs to the appellant-respondent against the respondents-appellants.

Order unanimously modified to deny the cross motion to dismiss the complaint and to grant motion to consolidate, and as so modified, affirmed. Settle order on notice.

All concur.

Mohr v. State Bank of Stanley

Supreme Court of Kansas, 1987.
241 Kan. 42, 734 P.2d 1071.

■ MILLER, JUSTICE:

This is an appeal by the State Bank of Stanley from a judgment in a conversion action entered against it and in favor of the plaintiffs, Gene R. Mohr and Tri–County Farm Equipment Company, in the total amount of $422,650.26, following a jury trial in the District Court of Johnson County. The numerous issues raised on appeal will be stated and discussed separately in this opinion.

Tri–County Farm Equipment Company is a Missouri corporation qualified to do business in Kansas. Its principal activity was the sale of farm machinery at Olathe. Gene Mohr and James Loyd each owned 50% of the stock in Tri–County. The First National Bank of Olathe, Kansas, was designated as its depository bank. Tri–County's corporate resolution provided that all checks, drafts, or other orders for payment of money could be endorsed for deposit by stamp or personal endorsement of any officer or employee and deposited in the First National Bank. Tri–County had no banking relationship with the State Bank of Stanley.

Mohr and Loyd also started a leasing company, known as Mohr–Loyd Leasing, a partnership, for the purpose of leasing farm equipment. (For further background on these organizations see Executive Financial Services, Inc. v. Loyd, 238 Kan. 663, 715 P.2d 376 [1986].)

Additionally, Loyd had his own oil business known as Earthborn Energy. Mohr had no ownership interest in Earthborn Energy. So far as we are aware, Loyd was the sole owner and operator of Earthborn Energy, and its bank accounts were maintained in the State Bank of Stanley and in the First National Bank of Olathe.

Between January 25, 1982, and December 2, 1982, Loyd endorsed eight checks which were payable to Tri–County. He deposited those checks, not in the Tri–County account at the First National Bank of Olathe, but in Loyd's Earthborn Energy account in the State Bank of Stanley. Similarly, on August 25, and October 25, 1982, Loyd endorsed two checks which were the property of Mohr–Loyd Leasing, and deposited those checks in his Earthborn Energy account.

This action for conversion was commenced by Mohr and Tri–County. Mohr, as the successor in interest to Mohr–Loyd Leasing, sought the proceeds of the two checks payable to the leasing company which it never received. Tri–County brought suit on the eight checks made payable to it, the proceeds of which it never received, contending the State Bank of Stanley converted those checks. The jury returned a verdict in favor of Tri–County in the amount of the eight checks payable to it, $186,615.06, plus punitive damages of $76,000. It also returned a verdict in favor of Mohr for the two checks payable to Mohr–Loyd Leasing, in the amount of $57,455.92, plus punitive damages of $24,000. The trial court added 10% prejudgment interest to the actual damages (the face amount of all of the checks) in the total sum of $78,579.28. The Bank appeals.

* * *

The third issue is whether the trial judge erred in submitting the claims of Mohr, based on the two Mohr–Loyd Leasing checks, to the jury. Mohr successfully negotiated with the Bank of Stanley two loans for the partnership, Mohr–Loyd Leasing. Checks were issued by the Bank, one for $34,455.92 and the other for $23,000.00. The partnership never received the proceeds; Loyd deposited both checks in his Earthborn Energy account. Later, suit was filed by the Johnson County Airport Commission against the State Bank of Stanley, Johnson County Case No. 123284. Codefendants included the Bank, Mohr, Loyd, and Mohr–Loyd Leasing. The Bank filed a cross-claim against Mohr, seeking recovery on the loans to Mohr–Loyd Leasing. Mohr filed no claim against the Bank arising out of the loans and the embezzlement by Loyd of the check proceeds in that lawsuit.

The Bank contends here that Mohr's claim was a compulsory counterclaim in Johnson County Case No. 123284, and is barred pursuant to K.S.A.1986 Supp. 60–213(a). That section provides in pertinent part:

> "A pleading shall state as a compulsory counterclaim any claim which at the time of serving the pleading the pleader has against any opposing party, if it arises out of the transaction or occurrence that is the subject matter of the opposing party's claim * * *."

The Bank claims that it was error to submit these claims to the jury because they should have been asserted in the Johnson County Airport case, and were barred because not asserted. Mohr argues that because the Johnson County Airport case was subsequently dismissed, the claim on those two checks should not be barred. No authority is cited for the proposition, and we find none. The Bank raised this early in this proceeding. The matter was argued, and Judge McWilliams, who was then presiding, ruled that the claim was barred. This was some 30 days before the Johnson County Airport case was dismissed. Mohr, thus, had ample notice and opportunity to raise the claim in the Airport case.

Mohr also argues that the claim, if asserted in the Airport case, would have been a cross-claim, not a counterclaim, and that cross-claims are permissive, not compulsory. This argument is not persuasive. While the claim would have been against a codefendant, Mohr and the Bank were adverse parties in the Airport case, and Mohr's claim arose out of the transaction which formed the basis of the Bank's cross-claim against him. In 3 Moore's Federal Practice ¶ 13.12[1] (2nd ed. 1985), we find this explanation:

> "[I]f defendant X pleads a cross-claim against his co-party, defendant Y, the latter must plead as a counterclaim any claim which he (Y) has against X that arises out of the transaction or occurrence which is made the basis of X's cross-claim."

The Bank, as a codefendant with Mohr in the Airport case, was not obligated to assert a cross-claim against Mohr. Such action was permissive, not mandatory. Once a cross-claim was asserted, however, it became incumbent upon Mohr to file an answer to the cross-claim. See K.S.A. 60–207,–208. He then became subject to the compulsory counterclaim rule, K.S.A.1986 Supp. 60–213(a), which states:

> "A pleading shall state as a counterclaim any claim which at the time of serving the pleading the pleader has against any opposing party, if it arises out of the transaction or occurrence that is the subject matter of the opposing party's claim * * *."

K.S.A.1986 Supp. 60–213 speaks of presenting a counterclaim in a pleading. It does not limit the inclusion of counterclaims to answers. It also speaks of including any claim against any opposing party—not just a claim against the plaintiff. Here, Mohr had a compulsory counterclaim to the Bank's cross-claim in the Airport case. He was advised of that by the trial judge in this case almost a month before the Airport case was dismissed. No reason for his failure to assert his claim in the Airport case has been presented here. We hold that Mohr's claim against the Bank on the two Mohr–Loyd Leasing checks was a compulsory counterclaim which had to be raised in the Airport case. They were not raised there, with the result that they may not now be raised in a separate action, but are barred. The judgment on those two checks and related relief must be reversed.

NOTE: COUNTERCLAIMS AND CROSS–CLAIMS

A.   If P sues D on a contract, may D seek damages from P on an unrelated tort claim? Why?

B.   If P sues D alleging injury in an auto accident, caused by D's negligence, can D be forced to sue P in that action to recover for his injuries in that same accident? If not, will D suffer any penalty for failing to do so?

C.   If P's intestate was pancaked between a Chevy (C) and a Rolls Royce (R) (with most unfortunate consequences), and P sues C and R alleging negligence on the part of each, may C sue R in that action alleging that it was R's negligence that caused the accident and the resultant damage to C? Why?

D.   If in the immediately preceding case P sues C alone in Federal District Court in Philadelphia, Pennsylvania may C bring R into that action? May C do so if R is a resident of nearby Camden, New Jersey? See FRCP 4(f), 13, 14.

E.   In Hansen v. Shearson/American Express, 116 F.R.D. 246 (E.D.Pa.1987), one Guptill, a third-party defendant, filed a claim against one of the original defendants in the action under F.R.C.P. 13(h). That rule, however, appears to cover only persons "other than those made parties to the original action." What is the appropriate label for that pleading?. Said the trial judge: "At different times, this court has characterized Guptill's claim against Manfredo as either a permissive counterclaim (Memorandum/Order of October 13, 1983) or as a cross-claim (Memorandum of October 29, 1986). Upon further reflection neither characterization of Guptill's claim is correct."

More significantly, is the claim permitted under the rules? The court allowed the claim, relying on F.R.C.P. 1 in curing what "appears to be an oversight in the Rules."

B.   CLASS ACTIONS

Hazard, The Effect of the Class Action Device Upon the Substantive Law

58 F.R.D. 307 (1973).

Maitland put it that the substantive law is laid down in the interstices of procedure, and he was of course correct. Substantive law is shaped and articulated by procedural possibilities. Moreover, the function of procedure would be unintelligible if it were not to have substantive consequences. So the question here, as elsewhere, in the relation of substance and procedure is one of pace and of role: How quickly and how far should the courts go in using procedural devices that are in their disposal? The necessary technique is one of circumspect consideration of the appropriate role of the judicial institution in shaping the substantive consequences of procedures such as those established in Rule 23.

* * *

[T]he occasions generating the class suits were themselves mass production events. Consider the situation in cases such as Swarb v. Lennox, 405 U.S. 191,, 31 L.Ed.2d 138 92 S.Ct. 767, (1972). The legal question was that of overreaching on the terms of a promissory note. But the note was a printed form, used in substantially identical form by dozens or hundreds of retailers in behalf of dozens, and maybe more, money brokers—lenders to retailers who supplied the forms on which the retailers were to execute credit transactions. And the notes in this form were signed by thousands and perhaps millions of purchasers. Yet the law that is to govern those mass-production transactions finds its origin in the simple hand-tailored promissory note that was the subject of an over-reaching 300 years ago, perhaps between a London merchant and some down-county purchaser in rural England. The fraud, or the overreaching, if that's what it was in the original English case, was done one to one. In our modern case it was done by the technology of uniform documents, uniformly produced.

So with the securities cases. They also involve mass production wrongs, rather than single instances like their original prototype. The disclosure requirements of the Securities Act are prescribed in contemplation of a mass money market. But at the same time the legal principle involved is derived from basic principles of fraud and nondisclosure which in their origin were conceived and applied in single transactions.

This is true of the common law generally. The rules of the common law are legal responses to single transactions, each hand-tailored. Recall the origins of our own commercial law, regulating a commerce so heavily centered in the Fourth and Fifth Circuits, mainly in cotton and rice and the other commodities exchanged between the colonies and young states and Europe. The legal concepts in those cases were based on the assumption of hand-tailored transactions, each more or less unique unto itself. Today that commerce moves in a mass production of ships, airways, containers, and standardized documents.

Take another illustration, this time in the area of public nuisance. Public nuisance today is a great steel company with a computerized operation for specifying the precise tonnage of coal, the amount of iron ore, and the amount of limestone and other chemicals that it needs, arriving in carefully scheduled boxcars, piled in carefully scheduled piles, delivered into carefully scheduled furnaces, with carefully scheduled effluents that may pollute the air or the streams or the underground waters. It is a scheduled mass-production event. Where is the origin of the law that covers that case? It is of course the neighborhood kiln, the brick-oven case, found in the 18th Century Reports. You see the case there, a local incident between A and B, the immemorial parties to the cases in which our ideas of the law are conceived.

The thought I am trying to suggest is that, whereas our traditional ideas of substantive and procedural law derive from contemplating and reacting to "A v. B" as a single transaction, the world in which we must today make our legal concepts work is a world of many A's and many B's and many transactions.

We have recognized this problem in smaller scale in other procedural contexts besides the class suit. Joinder of multiple claims and multiple parties is an illustration. So is the extension of collateral estoppel in the multi-party tort situation and the modification of stare decisis through the "non-retroactive" doctrines. In a still broader sense, the mass-production characteristic of many modern legal wrongs, or claims of wrong, is reflected in the array of administrative regulations and agencies that are found in today's legal world. These devices are responses to the mass-production of legal problems. So is the class action such a response. Indeed the class action and regulation by administrative agency are in many respects alternatives and competitors as legal remedies.

Perhaps this helps put the class action in context. Its unique characteristic is the assertion that a large number of individuals are, in one aspect of their legal status, indistinguishable from each other and that they should therefore be considered essentially as one. The members of the class can say this of themselves precisely because in this aspect of their legal status, they were treated as one by their antagonist, or so they claim. Their contention, in others words, is that they were the result of mass production activities: The very identity of consequence is the product of an activity which itself was programmed for uniform results in the commercial areas, the programming typically went to the point that the people who were supposed to execute the transaction—the local loan officers, the brokers who actually sold the securities—were precluded by internal controls within the issuer from having any authority or discretion to vary the transaction to any significant degree.

I recite all this not as an advocate of the class action, for I share all the concerns about its fairness and utility. My purpose is only to show that we should not view the class action from a 19th Century perspective of substantive law. We have to view it in relation to the substantive legal problems of the 20th Century.

* * *

The legislative viewpoint involves thinking in large numbers, in terms of large classes and of sub-classes; thinking of the boundary lines between classes or sequences of events; and thinking in levels and alternative concepts of legal fault and responsibility. It requires formulating legal ideas in general or universal terms, rather than *ad hoc*. It is, of course, a different mode of thought than the case method.

The mode of thought of the legislator, more specifically the legislative consultant and draftsman, is the one that perhaps should be used in thinking of class suits. If we try to think of class suits as A v. B, plus A v. B, plus A v. B—single cases that have occurred simultaneously—we proceed on a wrong line of thought. Rather, we should bring in mind the method used in mathematics for designating an indefinitely large series: A_1, A_2, A_3 * * * A? where A_1 and A_2 and A? are specifically identified (representatives of the class), but where it is known also that there is a large and perhaps uncertainly enumerated group (the class) just like them in all material respects.

If we think this way, then we see that the important problem centers around the "A" characteristics of the individuals and the extent to which there are significant differences among the group in terms of this characteristic. Thus, to go back to concrete situations, we have to think about the members of the alleged class in terms of their position as purchasers of an issue of stock, their position as downstream riparian owners along a polluted river, their position as owners of property in the vicinity of smelter, or their position—to refer to a recent California case—of the objects of an aggressive sales campaign for frozen food and frozen food lockers.

If we adopt this frame of reference, it may prove to be a more comfortable, more manageable, more appropriate, more responsive way of thinking what the class suit problem is all about. That is not to say that in adopting a legislative viewpoint the courts can or should abandon the restrictions on role and competence that are properly imposed on the judiciary. It is not to say that the courts should convert themselves into legislatures. It is to say only that in thinking about class suits, one can usefully think about them as a problem of indefinite numbers and a problem of classification, as though one were in the legislature.

I now come to my second point. When one begins to think of legal problems from a legislative viewpoint, a central problem is presented that is usually obscure or latent when we think of legal problems case-by-case. This is the tension between the law's moral integrity and its practical effectiveness. Our law is characteristically infused with a high degree of moral enthusiasm, and we try to maximize it when we can. Hence, we like to think of making regulations that will purify the air, the waters, the marketplaces and relations between men generally. Very often statutes have preambles and judicial opinions have dicta to this effect. But when you get down to the enacting clauses of a statute or the holding of an opinion, the question becomes more complicated. Aside from what *ought* to be from a moral viewpoint the question becomes, what *can* be from a practical viewpoint? Do we really mean to hold people to the standard of conduct expressed or implied in the sweep of our moral major premises? It is nice to say that punitive damages should be awarded in the case of reckless behavior, and perhaps even satisfying to do it in a single case. But is this the right thing to do for every contract that fails to comply with a usury law or every automobile that fails to comply with a safety or emission-control standard?

Courts don't always face this kind of question when they decide cases one-to-one. At the same time, the legislature doesn't always face this question when it propounds the rules which the courts ultimately have to enforce. The legislature often pitches legislation at a higher level of expectation than it really intends to require. It anticipates a kind of discount for non-enforceability, and thereby enjoys a pleasant moral luxury in proclaiming high expectations. But one can't indulge that luxury, or its judicial equivalent in the form of expansive dicta, when one has to face up to enforcing the proposed rule. And that, of course, is what is involved in the class suit. That is why the strict liability rules of the securities legislation, the consumer protection laws, and the nuisance and warranty doctrines present so much difficulty in the class suit: substantive legal aspiration becomes reality through the procedural transformation of Rule 23. The class action is thus unique, perhaps, in forcing us simultaneously to think precisely about the terms of the substantive law's boundary lines, and to think seriously about what is involved in actually enforcing the law.

Eisen v. Carlisle & Jacquelin

Supreme Court of the United States, 1974.
417 U.S. 156, 94 S.Ct. 2140, 40 L.Ed.2d 732.

■ Mr. Justice Powell delivered the opinion of the Court.

On May 2, 1966, petitioner filed a class action on behalf of himself and all other odd-lot[1] traders on the New York Stock Exchange (the Exchange). The complaint charged respondents with violations of the antitrust and securities laws and demanded damages for petitioner and his class. Eight years have elapsed, but there has been no trial on the merits of these claims. Both the parties and the courts are still wrestling with the complex questions surrounding petitioner's attempt to maintain his suit as a class action under Fed.Rule Civ.Proc. 23. We granted certiorari to resolve some of these difficulties. 414 U.S. 908, 94 S.Ct. 235, 38 L.Ed.2d 146 (1973).

I

Petitioner brought this class action in the United States District Court for the Southern District of New York. Originally, he sued on behalf of all buyers and sellers of odd lots on the Exchange, but subsequently the class was limited to those who traded in odd lots during the period from May 1, 1962, through June 30, 1966. 52 F.R.D. 253, 261 (1971). Throughout this period odd-lot trading was not part of the Exchange's regular auction market but was handled exclusively by special odd-lot dealers, who bought and sold for their own accounts as principals. Respondent brokerage firms Carlisle & Jacquelin and DeCoppet & Doremus together handled 99% of the Exchange's odd-lot business. S.E.C., Report of Special Study of Securities Markets, H.R.Doc. No. 95, pt. 2, 88th Cong., 1st Sess., 172 (1963). They were compensated by the odd-lot differential, a surcharge imposed on the odd-lot investor in addition to the standard brokerage commission applicable to round-lot transactions. For the period in question the differential was ⅛ of a point (12½ per share on stocks trading below $40 per share and ¼ of a point (25 per share on stocks trading at or above $40 per share.[2]

Petitioner charged that respondent brokerage firms had monopolized odd-lot trading and set the differential at an excessive level in violation of §§ 1 and 2 of the Sherman Act, 15 U.S.C. §§ 1 and 2, and he demanded treble damages for the amount of the overcharge. Petitioner also demanded unspecified money damages from the Exchange for its alleged failure to regulate the differential for the protection of investors in violation of §§ 6 and 19 of the Securities Exchange Act of 1934, 15 U.S.C. §§ 78f and 78s. Finally, he requested attorneys' fees and injunctive prohibition of future excessive charges.

---

1. Odd lots are shares traded in lots of fewer than a hundred. Shares traded in units of a hundred or multiples thereof are round-lots.

2. On July 1, 1966, the $40 "break-point" was raised to $55.

A critical fact in this litigation is that petitioner's individual stake in the damages award he seeks is only $70. No competent attorney would undertake this complex antitrust action to recover so inconsequential an amount. Economic reality dictates that petitioner's suit proceed as a class action or not at all. Opposing counsel have therefore engaged in prolonged combat over the various requirements of Rule 23. The result has been an exceedingly complicated series of decisions by both the District Court and the Court of Appeals for the Second Circuit. To understand the labyrinthian history of this litigation, a preliminary overview of the decisions may prove useful.

In the beginning, the District Court determined that petitioner's suit was not maintainable as a class action. On appeal, the Court of Appeals issued two decisions known popularly as *Eisen I* and *Eisen II*. The first held that the District Court's decision was a final order and thus appealable. In the second the Court of Appeals intimated that petitioner's suit could satisfy the requirements of Rule 23, but it remanded the case to permit the District Court to consider the matter further. After conducting several evidentiary hearings on remand, the District Court decided that the suit could be maintained as a class action and entered orders intended to fulfill the notice requirements of Rule 23. Once again, the case was appealed. The Court of Appeals then issued its decision in *Eisen III* and ended the trilogy by denying class action status to petitioner's suit. We now review these developments in more detail.

Eisen I

As we have seen, petitioner began this action in May 1966. In September of that year the District Court dismissed the suit as a class action. 41 F.R.D. 147. Following denial of his motion for interlocutory review under 28 U.S.C. § 1292(b), petitioner took an appeal as of right under § 1291. Respondents then moved to dismiss on the ground that the order appealed from was not final. In *Eisen I,* the Court of Appeals held that the denial of class action status in this case was appealable as a final order under § 1291. 370 F.2d 119 (1966), cert. denied, 386 U.S. 1035, 87 S.Ct. 1487, 18 L.Ed.2d 598 (1967). This was so because, as a practical matter, the dismissal of the class action aspect of petitioner's suit was a "death knell" for the entire action. The court thought this consequence rendered the order dismissing the class action appealable under Cohen v. Beneficial Indus. Loan Corp., 337 U.S. 541, 546, 69 S.Ct. 1221, 1225, 93 L.Ed. 1528 (1949).

Eisen II

Nearly 18 months later the Court of Appeals reversed the dismissal of the class action in a decision known as *Eisen II.* 391 F.2d 555 (1968). In reaching this result the court undertook an exhaustive but ultimately inconclusive analysis of Rule 23. Subdivision (a) of the Rule sets forth four prerequisites to the maintenance of any suit as a class action: "(1) the class is so numerous that joinder of all members is impracticable, (2) there are questions of law or fact common to the class, (3) the claims or defenses of the representative parties are typical of the claims or defenses of the class, and (4) the representative parties will fairly and adequately protect the interests of the class." The District Court had experienced little difficulty in finding that petitioner satisfied the first three prerequisites but had concluded that petitioner might not "fairly and adequately protect the interests of the class" as required by Rule 23(a)(4). The Court of Appeals indicated its disagreement with the reasoning behind the latter conclusion and directed the District Court to reconsider the point.

In addition to meeting the four conjunctive requirements of 23(a), a class action must also qualify under one of the three subdivisions of 23(b). Petitioner argued that the suit was maintainable as a class action under all three subdivisions. The Court of Appeals held the first two subdivisions inapplicable to this suit[4] and therefore turned its attention to the third subdivision, (b)(3). That subdivision requires a court to determine whether "questions of law or fact common to the members of the class predominate over any questions affecting only individual members" and whether "a class action is superior to other available methods for the fair and efficient adjudication of the controversy." More specifically, it identifies four factors relevant to these inquiries. After a detailed review of these provisions, the Court of Appeals concluded that the only potential barrier to maintenance of this suit as a class action was the Rule 23(b)(3)(D) directive that a court evaluate "the difficulties likely to be encountered in the management of a class action." Commonly referred to as "manageability," this consideration encompasses the whole range of practical problems that may render the class action format inappropriate for a particular suit. With reference to this litigation, the Court of Appeals noted that the difficulties of distributing any ultimate recovery to the class members would be formidable, though not necessarily insuperable, and commented that it was "reluctant to permit actions to proceed where they are not likely to benefit anyone but the lawyers who bring them." 391 F.2d, at 567. The Court therefore directed the District Court to conduct "a further inquiry * * * in order to consider the mechanics involved in the administration of the present action." *Ibid.*

Finally, the Court of Appeals turned to the most imposing obstacle to this class action—the notice requirement of Rule 23(c)(2). The District Court had held that both the Rule and the Due Process Clause of the Fifth Amendment required individual notice to all class members who could be identified. 41 F.R.D., at 151. Petitioner objected that mailed notice to the entire class would be prohibitively expensive and argued that some form of publication notice would suffice. The

---

4. Before the Court of Appeals, petitioner dropped the contention that the suit qualified under subdivision (b)(1)(B). The court held subdivision (b)(1)(A) inapplicable on the ground that the prospective class consisted entirely of small claimants, none of whom could afford to litigate this action in order to recover his individual claim and that consequently there was little chance of "inconsistent or varying adjudications with respect to individual members of the class which would establish incompatible standards of conduct for the party opposing the class * * *." Subdivision (b)(2) was held to apply only to actions exclusively or predominantly for injunctive or declaratory relief. Advisory Committee's Note, Proposed Rules of Civil Procedure, 28 U.S.C. App., p. 7766.

Court of Appeals declined to settle this issue, noting that "[o]n the record before us we cannot arrive at any rational and satisfactory conclusion on the propriety of resorting to some form of publication as a means of giving the necessary notice to all members of the class on behalf of whom the action is stated to be commenced and maintained." 391 F.2d, at 569.

The outcome of *Eisen II* was a remand for an evidentiary hearing on the questions of notice, manageability, adequacy of representation, and "any other matters which the District Court may consider pertinent and proper." *Id.*, at 570. And in a ruling that aroused later controversy, the Court of Appeals expressly purported to retain appellate jurisdiction while the case was heard on remand.

Eisen III

After it held the evidentiary hearing on remand, which together with affidavits and stipulations provided the basis for extensive findings of fact, the District Court issued an opinion and order holding the suit maintainable as a class action. 52 F.R.D. 253 (1971). The court first noted that petitioner satisfied the criteria identified by the Court of Appeals for determining adequacy of representation under Rule 23(a)(4). Then it turned to the more difficult question of manageability. Under this general rubric the court dealt with problems of the computation of damages, the mechanics of administering this suit as a class action, and the distribution of any eventual recovery. The last-named problem had most troubled the Court of Appeals, prompting its remark that if "class members are not likely ever to share in an eventual judgment, we would probably not permit the class action to continue." 391 F.2d, at 567. The District Court attempted to resolve this difficulty by embracing the idea of a "fluid class" recovery whereby damages would be distributed to future odd-lot traders rather than to the specific class members who were actually injured. The court suggested that "a fund equivalent to the amount of unclaimed damages might be established and the odd-lot differential reduced in an amount determined reasonable by the court until such time as the fund is depleted." 52 F.R.D., at 265. The need to resort to this expedient of recovery by the "next best class" arose from the prohibitively high cost of computing and awarding multitudinous small damages claims on an individual basis.

Finally, the District Court took up the problem of notice. The court found that the prospective class included some six million individuals, institutions, and intermediaries of various sorts; that with reasonable effort some two million of these odd-lot investors could be identified by name and address;[5] and that the names and addresses of an additional 250,000 persons who had participated in special invest-

---

5. These two million traders dealt with brokerage firms who transmitted their odd-lot transactions to respondents Carlisle & Jacquelin and DeCoppet & Doremus via teletype. By comparing the odd-lot firms' computerized records of these teletype transactions and the general-services brokerage firms' computerized records of all customer names and addresses, the names and addresses of these two million odd-lot traders can be obtained.

ment programs involving odd-lot trading[6] could also be identified with reasonable effort. Using the then current first-class postage rate of six cents, the court determined that stuffing and mailing each individual notice form would cost 10 cents. Thus individual notice to all identifiable class members would cost $225,000,[7] and additional expense would be incurred for suitable publication notice designed to reach the other four million class members.

The District Court concluded, however, that neither Rule 23(c)(2) nor the Due Process Clause required so substantial an expenditure at the outset of this litigation. Instead, it proposed a notification scheme consisting of four elements: (1) individual notice to all member firms of the Exchange and to commercial banks with large trust departments; (2) individual notice to the approximately 2,000 identifiable class members with 10 or more odd-lot transactions during the relevant period; (3) individual notice to an additional 5,000 class members selected at random; and (4) prominent publication notice in the Wall Street Journal and in other newspapers in New York and California. The court calculated that this package would cost approximately $21,720.

The only issue not resolved by the District Court in its first opinion on remand from *Eisen II* was who should bear the cost of notice. Because petitioner understandably declined to pay $21,720 in order to litigate an action involving an individual stake of only $70, this question presented something of a dilemma:

"If the expense of notice is placed upon [petitioner], it would be the end of a possibly meritorious suit, frustrating both the policy behind private antitrust actions and the admonition that the new Rule 23 is to be given a liberal rather than a restrictive interpretation, Eisen II at 563. On the other hand, if costs were arbitrarily placed upon [respondents] at this point, the result might be the imposition of an unfair burden founded upon a groundless claim. In addition to the probability of encouraging frivolous class actions, such a step might also result in [respondents'] passing on to their customers, including many of the class members in this case, the expenses of defending these actions." 52 F.R.D., at 269.

Analogizing to the laws of preliminary injunctions, the court decided to impose the notice cost on respondents if petitioner could show a strong likelihood of success on the merits, and it scheduled a preliminary hearing on the merits to facilitate this determination. After this hearing the District Court issued an opinion and order ruling that petitioner was "more than likely" to prevail at trial and that respondents should bear 90% of the cost of notice, or $19,548. 54 F.R.D. 565, 567 (1972).

6. In the period from May 1962 through June 1968, 100,000 individuals had odd lot transactions through participation in the Monthly Investment Plan operated by the Exchange and 150,000 persons traded in odd-lots through participation in a number of payroll deduction plans operated by Merrill Lynch, Pierce, Fenner & Smith.

7. Adjusting this figure to reflect the subsequent 4increase in first-class postage would yield a figure of $315,000.

Relying on the purported retention of jurisdiction by the Court of Appeals after *Eisen II,* respondents on May 1, 1972, obtained an order directing the clerk of the District Court to certify and transmit the record for appellate review. Subsequently, respondents also filed a notice of appeal under 28 U.S.C. § 1291. Petitioner's motion to dismiss on the ground that the appeal had not been taken from a final order was denied by the Court of Appeals on June 29, 1972.

On May 1, 1973, the Court of Appeals issued *Eisen III,* 479 F.2d 1005. The majority disapproved the District Court's partial reliance on publication notice, holding that Rule 23(c)(2) required individual notice to all identifiable class members. The majority further ruled that the District Court had no authority to conduct a preliminary hearing on the merits for the purpose of allocating costs and that the entire expense of notice necessarily fell on petitioner as representative plaintiff. Finally, the Court of Appeals rejected the expedient of a fluid-class recovery and concluded that the proposed class action was unmanageable under Rule 23(b)(3)(D). For all of these reasons the Court of Appeals ordered the suit dismissed as a class action. One judge concurred in the result solely on the ground that the District Court had erred in imposing 90% of the notice costs on respondents. Petitioner's requests for rehearing and rehearing en banc were denied. 479 F.2d, at 1020.

Thus, after six and one-half years and three published decisions, the Court of Appeals endorsed the conclusion reached by the District Court in its original order in 1966—that petitioner's suit could not proceed as a class action. In its procedural history, at least, this litigation has lived up to Judge Lumbard's characterization of it as a "Frankenstein monster posing as a class action." *Eisen II,* 391 F.2d, at 572.

II

At the outset we must decide whether the Court of Appeals in *Eisen III* had jurisdiction to review the District Court's orders permitting the suit to proceed as a class action and allocating the cost of notice. Petitioner contends that it did not. Respondents counter by asserting two independent bases for appellate jurisdiction: first, that the orders in question constituted a "final" decision within the meaning of 28 U.S.C. § 1291[8] and were therefore appealable as of right under that section; and, second, that the Court of Appeals in *Eisen II* expressly retained jurisdiction pending further development of a factual record on remand and that consequently no new jurisdictional basis was required for the decision in *Eisen III.* Because we agree with the first ground asserted by respondents, we have no occasion to consider the second.

---

8. Section 1291 provides:

"The courts of appeals shall have jurisdiction of appeals from all final decisions of the district courts of the United States, the United States District Court States, the United States District Court for the District of the Canal Zone, the District Court of Guam, and the District Court of the Virgin Islands, except where a direct review may be had in the Supreme Court."

Restricting appellate review to "final decisions" prevents the debilitating effect on judicial administration caused by piecemeal appellate disposition of what is, in practical consequence, but a single controversy. While the application of § 1291 in most cases is plain enough, determining the finality of a particular judicial order may pose a close question. No verbal formula yet devised can explain prior finality decisions with unerring accuracy or provide an utterly reliable guide for the future.[9] We know, of course, that § 1291 does not limit appellate review to "those final judgments which terminate an action * * *," Cohen v. Beneficial Indus. Loan Corp., 337 U.S., at 545, 69 S.Ct., at 1225, but rather that the requirement of finality is to be given a "practical rather than a technical construction." *Id.,* at 546, 69 S.Ct., at 1226. The inquiry requires some evaluation of the competing considerations underlying all questions of finality—"the inconvenience and costs of piecemeal review on the one hand and the danger of denying justice by delay on the other." Dickinson v. Petroleum Conversion Corp., 338 U.S. 507, 511, 70 S.Ct. 322, 324, 94 L.Ed. 299 (1950) (footnote omitted).

We find the instant case controlled by our decision in Cohen v. Beneficial Indus. Loan Corp., *supra.* There the Court considered the applicability in a federal diversity action of a forum state statute making the plaintiff in a stockholder's derivative action liable for litigation expenses, if ultimately unsuccessful, and entitling the corporation to demand security in advance for their payment. The trial court ruled the statute inapplicable, and the corporation sought immediate appellate review over the stockholder's objection that the order appealed from was not final. This Court held the order appealable on two grounds. First, the District Court's finding was not "tentative, informal or incomplete." 337 U.S., at 546, 69 S.Ct., at 1225, but settled conclusively the corporation's claim that it was entitled by state law to require the shareholder to post security for costs. Second, the decision did not constitute merely a "step toward final disposition of the merits of the case * * *." *Ibid.* Rather, it concerned a collateral matter that could not be reviewed effectively on appeal from the final judgment. The Court summarized its conclusion in this way:

> "This decision appears to fall in that small class which finally determine claims of right separable from, and collateral to, rights asserted in the action, too important to be denied review and too independent of the cause itself to require that appellate consideration be deferred until the whole case is adjudicated." *Ibid.*

---

9. As long ago as 1892 the Court complained: "Probably no question of equity practice has been the subject of more frequent discussion in this court than the finality of decrees. * * * The cases, it must be conceded, are not altogether harmonious." McGourkey v. Toledo & Ohio C.R. Co., 146 U.S. 536, 544–545, 13 S.Ct. 170, 172, 36 L.Ed. 1079. In the intervening years the difficulty of resolving such questions has not abated. As Mr. Justice Black commented in Gillespie v. U.S. Steel Corp., 379 U.S. 148, 152, 85 S.Ct. 308, 311, 13 L.Ed.2d 199 (1964), "whether a ruling is 'final' within the meaning of § 1291 is frequently so close a question that decision of that issue either way can be supported with equally forceful arguments, and * * * it is impossible to devise a formula to resolve all marginal cases coming within what might well be called the 'twilight zone' of finality."

Analysis of the instant case reveals that the District Court's order imposing 90% of the notice costs on respondents likewise falls within "that small class." It conclusively rejected respondents' contention that they could not lawfully be required to bear the expense of notice to the members of petitioner's proposed class. Moreover, it involved a collateral matter unrelated to the merits of petitioner's claims. Like the order in *Cohen,* the District Court's judgment on the allocation of notice costs was "a final disposition of a claimed right which is not an ingredient of the cause of action and does not require consideration with it," *id.,* at 546–547, 69 S.Ct., at 1226, and it was similarly appealable as a "final decision" under § 1291. In our view the Court of Appeals therefore had jurisdiction to review fully the District Court's resolution of the class action notice problems in this case, for that court's allocation of 90% of the notice costs to respondents was but one aspect of its effort to construe the requirements of Rule 23(c)(2) in a way that would permit petitioner's suit to proceed as a class action.[10]

III

Turning to the merits of the case, we find that the District Court's resolution of the notice problems was erroneous in two respects. First, it failed to comply with the notice requirements of Rule 23(c)(2), and second, it imposed part of the cost of notice on respondents.

A

Rule 23(c)(2) provides that, in any class action maintained under subdivision (b)(3), each class member shall be advised that he has the right to exclude himself from the action on request or to enter an appearance through counsel, and further that the judgment, whether favorable or not, will bind all class members not requesting exclusion. To this end, the court is required to direct to class members "the best notice practicable under the circumstances *including individual notice to all members who can be identified through reasonable effort.*"[11] We think the import of this language is unmistakable. Individual notice must be sent to all class members whose names and addresses may be ascertained through reasonable effort.

The Advisory Committee's Note to Rule 23 reinforces this conclusion. See 28 U.S.C.App., p. 7765. The Advisory Committee described subdivision (c)(2) as "not merely discretionary" and added that the "mandatory notice pursuant to subdivision (c)(2) * * * is designed to fulfill requirements of due process to which the class action procedure is of course subject." *Id.,* at 7768. The Committee explicated its incorporation of due process standards by citation to Mullane v.

---

10. As explained in Part III of this opinion, we find the notice requirements of Rule 23 to be dispositive of petitioner's attempt to maintain the class action as presently defined. We therefore have no occasion to consider whether the Court of Appeals correctly resolved the issues of manageability and fluid-class recovery, or indeed, whether those issues were properly before the Court of Appeals under the theory of retained jurisdiction.

11. Emphasis added. * * *

Central Hanover Bank & Trust Co., 339 U.S. 306, 70 S.Ct. 652, 94 L.Ed. 865 (1950), and like cases.

In *Mullane* the Court addressed the constitutional sufficiency of publication notice rather than mailed individual notice to known beneficiaries of a common trust fund as part of a judicial settlement of accounts. The Court observed that notice and an opportunity to be heard were fundamental requisites of the constitutional guarantee of procedural due process. It further stated that notice must be "reasonably calculated, under all the circumstances, to apprise interested parties of the pendency of the action and afford them an opportunity to present their objections." *Id.,* at 314, 70 S.Ct., at 657. The Court continued:

> "But when notice is a person's due, process which is a mere gesture is not due process. The means employed must be such as one desirous of actually informing the absentee might reasonably adopt to accomplish it. The reasonableness and hence the constitutional validity of any chosen method may be defended on the ground that it is in itself reasonably certain to inform those affected." *Id.,* at 315, 70 S.Ct., at 657.

The Court then held that publication notice could not satisfy due process where the names and addresses of the beneficiaries were known.[12] In such cases, "the reasons disappear for resort to means less likely than the mails to apprise them of [an action's] pendency." *Id.,* at 318, 70 S.Ct., at 659.

In Schroeder v. City of New York, 371 U.S. 208, 83 S.Ct. 279, 9 L.Ed.2d 255 (1962), decided prior to the promulgation of amended Rule 23, the Court explained that *Mullane* required rejection of notice by publication where the name and address of the affected person were available. The Court stated that the "general rule" is that "notice by publication is not enough with respect to a person whose name and address are known or very easily ascertainable * * * " *Id.,* at 212–213, 83 S.Ct., at 282. The Court also noted that notice by publication had long been recognized as a poor substitute for actual notice and that its justification was " 'difficult at best.' " *Id.,* at 213, 83 S.Ct., at 283.

Viewed in this context, the express language and intent of Rule 23(c)(2) leave no doubt that individual notice must be provided to those class members who are identifiable through reasonable effort. In the present case, the names and addresses of 2,250,000 class members

---

12. The Court's discussion of the inadequacies of published notice bears attention:

"It would be idle to pretend that publication alone, as prescribed here, is a reliable means of acquainting interested parties of the fact that their rights are before the courts. * * * Chance alone brings to the attention of even a local resident an advertisement in small type inserted in the back pages of a newspaper, and if he makes his home outside the area of the newspaper's normal circulation the odds that the information will never reach him are large indeed. The chance of actual notice is further reduced when, as here, the notice required does not even name those whose attention it is supposed to attract, and does not inform acquaintances who might call it to attention." 339 U.S., at 315, 70 S.Ct., at 658.

are easily ascertainable, and there is nothing to show that individual notice cannot be mailed to each. For these class members, individual notice is clearly the "best notice practicable" within the meaning of Rule 23(c)(2) and our prior decisions.

Petitioner contends, however, that we should dispense with the requirement of individual notice in this case, and he advances two reasons for our doing so. First, the prohibitively high cost of providing individual notice to 2,250,000 class members would end this suit as a class action and effectively frustrate petitioner's attempt to vindicate the policies underlying the antitrust and securities laws. Second petitioner contends that individual notice is unnecessary in this case, because no prospective class member has a large enough stake in the matter to justify separate litigation of his individual claim. Hence, class members lack any incentive to opt out of the class action even if notified.

The short answer to these arguments is that individual notice to identifiable class members is not a discretionary consideration to be waived in a particular case. It is, rather, an unambiguous requirement of Rule 23. As the Advisory Committee's Note explained, the Rule was intended to insure that the judgment, whether favorable or not, would bind all class members who did not request exclusion from the suit. 28 U.S.C.App., pp. 7765, 7768. Accordingly, each class member who can be identified through reasonable effort must be notified that he may request exclusion from the action and thereby preserve his opportunity to press his claim separately or that he may remain in the class and perhaps participate in the management of the action. There is nothing in Rule 23 to suggest that the notice requirements can be tailored to fit the pocketbooks of particular plaintiffs.[13]

Petitioner further contends that adequate representation, rather than notice, is the touchstone of due process in a class action and therefore satisfies Rule 23. We think this view has little to commend it. To begin with, Rule 23 speaks to notice as well as to adequacy of representation and requires that both be provided. Moreover, petitioner's argument proves too much, for it quickly leads to the conclusion that no notice at all, published or otherwise, would be required in the present case. This cannot be so, for quite apart from what due process may require, the command of Rule 23 is clearly to the contrary. We therefore conclude that Rule 23(c)(2) requires that individual notice be sent to all class members who can be identified with reasonable effort.[14]

---

13. Petitioner also argues that class members will not opt out because the statute of limitations has long since run out on the claims of all class members other than petitioner. This contention is disposed of by our recent decision in American Pipe & Construction Co. v. Utah, 414 U.S. 538, 94 S.Ct. 756, 38 L.Ed.2d 713 (1974), which established that commencement of a class action tolls the applicable statute of limitations as to all members of the class.

14. We are concerned here only with the notice requirements of subdivision (c)(2), which are applicable to class actions maintained under subdivision (b)(3). By its terms subdivision (c)(2) is inapplicable to class actions for injunctive or declaratory relief maintained under subdivision (b)(2). Petitioner's effort to qualify his suit as a class action under subdivisions (b)(1) and (b)(2) was rejected by the Court of Appeals. See n. 4, *supra*.

B

We also agree with the Court of Appeals that petitioner must bear the cost of notice to the members of his class. The District Court reached the contrary conclusion and imposed 90% of the notice cost on respondents. This decision was predicated on the court's finding, made after a preliminary hearing on the merits of the case, that petitioner was "more than likely" to prevail on his claims. Apparently, that court interpreted Rule 23 to authorize such a hearing as part of the determination whether a suit may be maintained as a class action. We disagree.

We find nothing in either the language or history of Rule 23 that gives a court any authority to conduct a preliminary inquiry into the merits of a suit in order to determine whether it may be maintained as a class action. Indeed, such a procedure contravenes the Rule by allowing a representative plaintiff to secure the benefits of a class action without first satisfying the requirements for it. He is thereby allowed to obtain a determination on the merits of the claims advanced on behalf of the class without any assurance that a class action may be maintained. This procedure is directly contrary to the command of subdivision (c)(1) that the court determine whether a suit denominated a class action may be maintained as such "[a]s soon as practicable after the commencement of [the] action * * *." In short, we agree with Judge Wisdom's conclusion in Miller v. Mackey International, 452 F.2d 424 (C.A.5 1971), where the court rejected a preliminary inquiry into the merits of a proposed class action:

> "In determining the propriety of a class action, the question is not whether the plaintiff or plaintiffs have stated a cause of action or will prevail on the merits, but rather whether the requirements of Rule 23 are met." *Id.*, at 427.

Additionally, we might note that a preliminary determination of the merits may result in substantial prejudice to a defendant, since of necessity it is not accompanied by the traditional rules and procedures applicable to civil trials. The court's tentative findings, made in the absence of established safeguards, may color the subsequent proceedings and place an unfair burden on the defendant.

In the absence of any support under Rule 23, petitioner's effort to impose the cost of notice on respondents must fail. The usual rule is that a plaintiff must initially bear the cost of notice to the class. The exceptions cited by the District Court related to situations where a fiduciary duty pre-existed between the plaintiff and defendant, as in a shareholder derivative suit.[15] Where, as here, the relationship between the parties is truly adversary, the plaintiff must pay for the cost of notice as part of the ordinary burden of financing his own suit.

Petitioner has consistently maintained, however, that he will not bear the cost of notice under subdivision (c)(2) to members of the class as defined in his original complaint. See 479 F.2d, at 1008; 52

---

15. See, *e.g.*, Dolgow v. Anderson, 43 F.R.D. 472, 498–500 (E.D.N.Y.1968). We, of course, express no opinion on the proper allocation of the cost of notice in such cases.

F.R.D., at 269. We therefore remand the cause with instructions to dismiss the class action as so defined.[16]

The judgment of the Court of Appeals is vacated and the cause remanded for proceedings consistent with this opinion.

It is so ordered.

■ MR. JUSTICE DOUGLAS, with whom MR. JUSTICE BRENNAN and MR. JUSTICE MARSHALL, concur, dissenting in part.

While I am in general agreement with the phases of this case touched on by the Court, I add a few words because its opinion does not fully explore the issues which will be dispositive of this case on remand to the District Court.

Federal Rule Civ.Proc. 23(c)(4) provides: "When appropriate (A) an action may be brought or maintained as a class action with respect to particular issues, or (B) a class may be divided into subclasses and each subclass treated as a class, and the provisions of this rule shall then be construed and applied accordingly."

As Judge Oakes, speaking for himself and Judge Timbers, said below:

> "The plaintiff class might, for example, be divided into much smaller subclasses * * * of odd lot buyers for particular periods, and one subclass treated as a test case, with the other subclasses held in abeyance. Individual notice at what would probably be a reasonable cost could then be given to all members of the particular small subclass who can be easily identified." 479 F.2d 1005, 1023 (dissenting from denial of rehearing en banc).

Or a subclass might include those on monthly investment plans, or payroll deduction plans run by brokerage houses.[1] The possibilities, though not infinite, are numerous.

---

16. The record does not reveal whether a smaller class of odd-lot traders could be defined, and if so, whether petitioner would be willing to pay the cost of notice to members of such a class. We intimate no view on whether any such subclass would satisfy the requirements of Rule 23. We do note, however, that our dismissal of the class action as originally defined is without prejudice to any efforts petitioner may make to redefine his class either under Rule 23(c)(4) or Fed.Rule Civ.Proc. 15.

1. The parties and courts below concentrated on whether a class action could be sustained on behalf of all six million odd-lot investors, so that the record is limited in information bearing on what manageable subclasses could be created.

There is, nonetheless, indication that certain subclasses might be economically manageable. Counsel for respondent Carlisle & Jacquelin stated in oral argument before the Court of Appeals that 100,000 shareholders participate in his client's Monthly Invest-

ment Plan, and that Carlisle & Jacquelin corresponds with those investors, Merrill Lynch corresponds with 150,000 people participating in a payroll deduction investment plan. Whether Eisen or any other plaintiff who may come forward to intervene fits in such a subclass, we do not know. But if brokerage houses correspond regularly in the course of business with such odd-lot investors, the marginal cost of providing the individual notice required by Rule 23(c)(2) might be nothing more than printing and stuffing an additional sheet of paper in correspondence already being sent to the investor, or perhaps only programing a computer to type an additional paragraph at the bottom of monthly or quarterly statements regularly mailed by the brokers.

A subclass of those who had engaged in numerous transactions might also be defined, so that the recovery per class member might be large enough to justify the cost of notice and management of the action. A survey of only four of 14 wire firms revealed 2,000

The power to create a subclass is clear and unambiguous. Who should be included and how large it should be are questions that only the District Court should resolve. Notice to each member of the subclass would be essential under Rule 23(c)(2); and under Rule 23(c)(2)(A) any notified member may opt out. There would remain the question whether the subclass suit is manageable. But since the subclass could be chosen in light of the nonmanageability of the size of the class whose claims are presently before us, there is no apparent difficulty in that sense.

The statute of limitations, it is argued, has run or is about to run on many of these classes. We held in American Pipe & Construction Co. v. Utah, 414 U.S. 538, 94 S.Ct. 756, 38 L.Ed.2d 713, that the start of a class action prior to the running of the statute protects all members of the class. Whether that rule should obtain for the benefit of other members who could have been included in the subclass bringing suit, but for the manageability issue, is a question we have not decided.[2] Moreover, if the subclass sues and wins or sues and loses, questions covering the rights of members of the larger class who are not parties would be raised. These are questions we have not answered.[3] But the fact that unresolved questions of law would remain is not an insurmountable obstacle, and Rule 23(c)(4)(B) expressly authorizes subclasses to sue in lieu of a full class. Rule 23(c)(4)(B) may have had, as a forerunner, the proposal stated by Judge Weinstein in 1960:

> "When there is a question of law or fact common to persons of a numerous class whose joinder is impracticable, one or more of them whose claims or defenses are representative of the claims or

customers with 10 or more transactions between 1962 and 1966. 52 F.R.D. 253, 259, 267, and n. 10.

By defining more definite subclasses such as those discussed, moreover, the problems inherent in distributing an eventual judgment would be reduced. Class members would be more readily identifiable, with more readily accessible transaction records and individually provable damages.

2. In this case, the entire class was defined in the original complaint, and the defendants were put on notice within the period of limitation of their potential liability, serving the purpose of the statute of limitations even if the substantive merits were eventually to be prosecuted in the form of a subclass action with the class action held in abeyance. "Within the period set by the statute of limitations, the defendants have the essential information necessary to determine both the subject matter and size of the prospective litigation, whether the actual trial is conducted in the form of a class action, as a joint suit, or as a principal suit with additional intervenors." American Pipe & Construc-

tion Co. v. Utah, 414 U.S. 538, 555, 94 S.Ct. 756, 767, 38 L.Ed.2d 713. And see Wheaton, Representative Suits Involving Numerous Litigants, 19 Cornell L.Q. 399, 423 (1934).

3. If the subclass lost, it is argued that other investors not members of that subclass could not be precluded from prosecuting successful suits of their own, since they had never had their day in court or necessarily even been apprised of the subclass' action. See Hansberry v. Lee, 311 U.S. 32, 61 S.Ct. 115, 85 L.Ed. 22; F. James, Civil Procedure § 11.26 (1965); 1B J. Moore, Federal Practice ¶ 0.411[1] (1974). If the subclass won, strict application of the doctrine of mutuality of estoppel would limit the usefulness of that subclass victory in suits brought by investors not members of that subclass. See generally F. James, *supra*, § 11.31; 1B J. Moore, *supra*, ¶ 0.412[1] (and Supp.1973); and cases cited therein. And see Vestal, Preclusion/Res Judicata Variables: Parties, 50 Iowa L.Rev. 27, 55–59 (1964); Note, 35 Geo.Wash.L.Rev. 1010 (1967); Currie, Mutuality of Collateral Estoppel: Limits of the Bernhard Doctrine, 9 Stan. L.Rev. 281 (1957).

defenses of all and who will fairly and adequately protect the interests of all may sue or be sued on behalf of all."[4]

In explanation he added:

"Such a rule would provide six requirements for a class action: (1) a class, (2) numerous members, (3) common question of law or fact, (4) impracticability of joinder, (5) representative claim or defense, (6) fair and adequate protection of absentees.

"Almost any 'bond of association' in an event or status out of which a legal dispute arose is sufficient to constitute a class. The class must be numerous but need not be so large that, in itself, this factor makes it impracticable to bring them all before the court. A number of members sufficient to satisfy present Section 195 [of the New York Civil Practice Act] would satisfy the proposed rule. Size, modesty of monetary interest, inability to locate members and difficulty of obtaining jurisdiction should all be considered in determining impracticability of joinder."[5]

The Court permits Eisen to redefine his class either by amending his complaint pursuant to Fed.Rule Civ.Proc. 15, or by proceeding under Rule 23(c)(4). While Eisen may of course proceed by amending his complaint to define a subclass, it is clear that he need not do so.[6] Definition of the subclass would properly be accomplished by order of the District Court, as permitted by Rules 23(c)(4) and 23(c)(1), without amendment of the complaint as filed. While the complaint alleges that Eisen sues on his behalf and on behalf of all purchasers and sellers of odd lots, it adds, "Plaintiff will fairly insure the adequate representation of all such persons." Problems of manageability covered by Rule 23(b)(3)(D) arise only after issues are joined and the District Court is engaged in shaping up the litigation for a trial on the merits. If it finds that a subclass would be more appropriate, no new action need be started nor any amended complaint filed.

Rule 23(c)(1) provides: "As soon as practicable after the commencement of an action brought as a class action, the court shall determine by order whether it is to be so maintained. An order under this subdivision may be conditional, and may be altered or amended before the decision on the merits."

It is as plain as words can make it that the court which decides that a full class action can be maintained can alter or amend its order "before the decision on the merits." One permissible way in which the court's order may be changed is to have it "altered" as provided in

---

4. Weinstein, Revision of Procedure: Some Problems in Class Actions, 9 Buffalo L.Rev. 433, 458.

5. *Id.*, at 458–459 (footnotes omitted).

6. Were Eisen to be remitted to an individual action, as he would be if he refused to pay the cost of notice even to a subclass, amendment of the complaint might be called for by the District Court. Under Rule 23(d)(4), the District Court may in some in-stances require that pleadings be amended to eliminate class allegations. The Advisory Committee Notes indicate that this provision is to be applied only when a suit must proceed as a nonclass, individual action, not when, as here, an appropriate class exists and the action must be prosecuted in the first instance by a subclass only because of problems of manageability. See 28 U.S.C.App., p. 7767.

Rule 23(c)(1) by reducing the larger class to a subclass as provided in the same subsection—Rule 23(c)(4)(B). The prerequisites of a class cause of action are described in Rule 23(a). In the instant case that hurdle has been passed and we are at the stage of notice requirements and manageability. Not an iota of change is made in the cause of action by restricting it to a subclass.

The purpose of Rule 23 is to provide flexibility in the management of class actions, with the trial court taking an active role in the conduct of the litigation. See Dolgow v. Anderson, 43 F.R.D. 472, 481–482 (E.D.N.Y.); Green v. Wolf Corp., 406 F.2d 291, 298 (CA2), cert. denied, 395 U.S. 977, 89 S.Ct. 2131, 23 L.Ed.2d 766. Lower federal courts have recognized their discretion to define those subclasses proper to prosecute an action without being bound by the plaintiff's complaint. See, *e.g.,* Dolgow v. Anderson, *supra,* 43 F.R.D. at 491–493; Philadelphia Elec. Co. v. Anaconda American Brass Co., 43 F.R.D. 452, 462–463 (E.D.Pa.). See generally 7A C. Wright & A. Miller, Federal Practice and Procedure § 1790, p. 187; 3B J. Moore, Federal Practice ¶ 23.65. And, as Rule 23(c)(1) clearly indicates, the courts retain both the power and the duty to realign classes during the conduct of an action when appropriate. See, *e.g.,* Carr v. Conoco Plastics, Inc., 423 F.2d 57, 58 (CA5), cert. denied, 400 U.S. 951, 91 S.Ct. 241, 27 L.Ed.2d 257; Johnson v. ITT–Thompson Industries, Inc., 323 F.Supp. 1258, 1262 (N.D.Miss.); Ostapowicz v. Johnson Bronze Co., 54 F.R.D. 465, 466 (W.D.Pa.); Baxter v. Savannah Sugar Refining Corp., 46 F.R.D. 56, 60 (S.D.Ga.). That discretion can be fully retained only if the full-class complaint is preserved when a subclass is defined to prosecute the action. The bounds of the subclass can then be narrowed or widened by order of the District Court as provided in Rule 23(c)(1), without need to amend the complaint and without the constraints which might exist if the complaint had earlier been amended pursuant to Rule 15 to include only the subclass.

I agree with Professor Chafee that a class action serves not only the convenience of the parties but also prompt, efficient judicial administration.[7] I think in our society that is growing in complexity there are bound to be innumerable people in common disasters, calamities, or ventures who would go begging for justice without the class action but who could with all regard to due process be protected by it. Some of these are consumers whose claims may seem *de minimis* but who alone have no practical recourse for either remuneration or injunctive relief. Some may be environmentalists who have no photographic development plant about to be ruined because of air pollution by radiation but who suffer perceptibly by smoke, noxious gases, or radiation. Or the unnamed individual may be only a ratepayer being excessively charged by a utility or a homeowner whose assessment is slowly rising beyond his ability to pay.

The class action is one of the few legal remedies the small claimant has against those who command the status quo.[8] I would

---

7. Z. Chafee, Some Problems of Equity 149 (1950).

8. Judge Weinstein writing in the N.Y.Law Journal, May 2, 1972, p. 4, col. 3,

strengthen his hand with the view of creating a system of law that dispenses justice to the lowly as well as to those liberally endowed with power and wealth.

Castano v. American Tobacco Company

United States Court of Appeals for the Fifth Circuit, 1996.
84 F.3d. 734.

■ JERRY E. SMITH, CIRCUIT JUDGE

In what may be the largest class action ever attempted in federal court, the district court in this case embarked "on a road certainly less traveled, if ever taken at all," *Castano v. American Tobacco Co.*, 160 F.R.D. 544, 560 (E.D.La.1995) (citing Edward C. Lathan, The Poetry of Robert Frost, "The Road Not Taken" 105 (1969)), and entered a class certification order. The court defined the class as:

(a) All nicotine-dependent persons in the United States . . . who have purchased and smoked cigarettes manufactured by the defendants;

(b) the estates, representatives, and administrators of these nicotine-dependent cigarette smokers; and

(c) the spouses, children, relatives and "significant others" of these nicotine-dependent cigarette smokers as their heirs or survivors.

This matter comes before us on interlocutory appeal, under 28 U.S.C. § 1292(b), of the class certification order. Concluding that the district court abused its discretion in certifying the class, we reverse.

The plaintiffs filed this class complaint against the defendant tobacco companies and the Tobacco Institute, Inc., seeking compensation solely for the injury of nicotine addiction. The gravamen of their complaint is the novel and wholly untested theory that the defendants fraudulently failed to inform consumers that nicotine is addictive and manipulated the level of nicotine in cigarettes to sustain their addictive nature. The class complaint alleges nine causes of action: fraud and deceit, negligent misrepresentation, intentional infliction of emotional

said: "Where, however, public authorities are remiss in performance of this responsibility for reason of inadequate legal authority, excessive workloads or simple indifference, class actions may provide a necessary temporary measure until desirable corrections have occurred. The existence of class action litigation may also play a substantial role in bringing about more efficient administrative enforcement and in inducing legislative action.

"The matter touches on the issue of the credibility of our judicial system. Either we are committed to make reasonable efforts to provide a forum for adjudication of disputes involving all our citizens—including those deprived of human rights, consumers who overpay for products because of antitrust violations and investors who are victimized by insider trading or misleading information—or we are not. There are those who will not ignore the irony of courts ready to imprison a man who steals some goods in interstate commerce while unwilling to grant a civil remedy against the corporation which has benefited, to the extent of many millions of dollars, from collusive, illegal pricing of its goods to the public.

"When the organization of a modern society, such as ours, affords the possibility of illegal behavior accompanied by widespread, diffuse consequences, some procedural means must exist to remedy—or at least to deter—that conduct."

distress, negligence and negligent infliction of emotional distress, violation of state consumer protection statutes, breach of express warranty, breach of implied warranty, strict product liability, and redhibition pursuant to the Louisiana Civil Code.

Following extensive briefing, the district court granted, in part, plaintiffs' motion for class certification, concluding that the prerequisites of Fed. R. Civ. P. 23(a) had been met. The court rejected certification, under Fed. R. Civ. P. 23(b)(2), of the plaintiffs' claim for equitable relief. The court did grant the plaintiffs' motion to certify the class under Fed. R. Civ. P. 23(b)(3), organizing the class action issues into four categories: (1) core liability; (2) injury-in-fact, proximate cause, reliance and affirmative defenses; (3) compensatory damages; and (4) punitive damages. It then analyzed each category to determine whether it met the predominance and superiority requirements of rule 23(b)(3). Using its power to sever issues for certification under Fed. R. Civ. P. 23(c)(4), the court certified the class on core liability and punitive damages, and certified the class conditionally pursuant to Fed. R. Civ. P. 23(c)(1).

The court defined core liability issues as "common factual issues [of] whether defendants knew cigarette smoking was addictive, failed to inform cigarette smokers of such, and took actions to addict cigarette smokers. Common legal issues include fraud, negligence, breach of warranty (express or implied), strict liability, and violation of consumer protection statutes."

The court found that the predominance requirement of rule 23(b)(3) was satisfied for the core liability issues. Without any specific analysis regarding the multitude of issues that make up "core liability," the court found that under *Jenkins v. Raymark Indus.*, 782 F.2d 468 (5th Cir.1986), common issues predominate because resolution of core liability issues would significantly advance the individual cases. The court did not discuss why "core liability" issues would be a significant, rather than just common, part of each individual trial, nor why the individual issues in the remaining categories did not predominate over the common "core liability" issues.

The only specific analysis on predominance was on the plaintiffs' fraud claim. The court determined that it would be premature to hold that individual reliance issues predominate over common issues. Relying on *Eisen v. Carlisle & Jacquelin*, 417 U.S. 156, 40 L. Ed. 2d 732, 94 S. Ct. 2140 (1974), the court stated that it could not inquire into the merits of the plaintiffs' claim to determine whether reliance would be an issue in individual trials. Moreover, the court recognized the possibility that under state law, reliance can be inferred when a fraud claim is based on an omission. Accordingly, the court was convinced that it could certify the class and defer the consideration of how reliance would affect predominance.

The court also deferred substantial consideration of how variations in state law would affect predominance. Relying on two district court opinions, the court concluded that issues of fraud, breach of warranty, negligence, intentional tort, and strict liability do not vary so much from state to state as to cause individual issues to predominate. As for the consumer protection claims, the court also deferred analysis of state law variations, because "there has been no showing that the consumer protection statutes differ so much as to make individual issues predominate."

The court also concluded that a class action is superior to other methods for adjudication of the core liability issues. Relying heavily on *Jenkins*, the court noted that having this common issue litigated in a class action was superior to repeated trials of the same evidence. Recognizing serious problems with manageability, it determined that such problems were outweighed by "the specter of thousands, if not millions, of similar trials of liability proceeding in thousands of courtrooms around the nation."

Using the same methodology as it did for the core liability issues, the district court refused to certify the issues of injury-in-fact, proximate cause, reliance, affirmative defenses, and compensatory damages, concluding that the "issues are so overwhelmingly replete with individual circumstances that they quickly outweigh predominance and superiority."

In certifying punitive damages for class treatment, the court adopted the plaintiffs' trial plan for punitive damages: The class jury would develop a ratio of punitive damages to actual damages, and the court would apply that ratio in individual cases. As it did with the core liability issues, the court determined that variations in state law, including differing burdens of proof, did not preclude certification.

II

A district court must conduct a rigorous analysis of the rule 23 prerequisites before certifying a class. *General Tel. Co. v. Falcon*, 457 U.S. 147, 161, 72 L. Ed. 2d 740, 102 S. Ct. 2364 (1982); *Applewhite v. Reichhold Chemicals*, 67 F.3d 571, 573 (5th Cir.1995). The decision to certify is within the broad discretion of the court, but that discretion must be exercised within the framework of rule 23. *Gulf Oil Co. v. Bernard*, 452 U.S. 89, 100, 68 L. Ed. 2d 693, 101 S. Ct. 2193 (1981). The party seeking certification bears the burden of proof.

The district court erred in its analysis in two distinct ways. First, it failed to consider how variations in state law affect predominance and superiority. Second, its predominance inquiry did not include consideration of how a trial on the merits would be conducted.

Each of these defects mandates reversal. Moreover, at this time, while the tort is immature, the class complaint must be dismissed, as class certification cannot be found to be a superior method of adjudication .

A. Variations in State Law

In a multi-state class action, variations in state law may swamp any common issues and defeat predominance. See *Georgine v. Amchem Prods.*, 83 F.3d 610 (3d Cir.1996) (decertifying class because legal and factual differences in the plaintiffs' claims "when exponentially magnified by choice of law considerations, eclipse any common issues in this case.").

A district court's duty to determine whether the plaintiff has borne its burden on class certification requires that a court consider variations in state law when a class action involves multiple jurisdictions. "In order to make the findings required to certify a class action under Rule 23(b)(3) ... one must initially identify the substantive law issues which will control the outcome of the litigation." *Alabama v. Blue Bird Body Co.*, 573 F.2d 309, 316 (5th Cir.1978).

A requirement that a court know which law will apply before making a predominance determination is especially important when there may be differences in state law. See *In re Rhone–Poulenc Rorer, Inc.* ("Rhone–Poulenc"), 51 F.3d 1293, 1299–1302 (7th Cir.) (mandamus) (comparing differing state pattern instructions on negligence and differing formulations of the meaning of negligence), cert. denied, 133 L. Ed. 2d 122, 116 S. Ct. 184 (1995); *In re "Agent Orange" Prod. Liability Litig.*, 818 F.2d 145, 165 (2d Cir.1987) (noting possibility of differences in state products liability law), cert. denied, 484 U.S. 1004 (1988).

The district court's review of state law variances can hardly be considered extensive; it conducted a cursory review of state law variations and gave short shrift to the defendants' arguments concerning variations. In response to the defendants' extensive analysis of how state law varied on fraud, products liability, affirmative defenses, negligent infliction of emotional distress, consumer protection statutes, and punitive damages[15], the court examined a sample phase 1 jury interrogatory and verdict form, a survey of medical monitoring decisions, a survey of consumer fraud class actions, and a survey of punitive damages law in the defendants' home states. The court also relied on two district court opinions granting certification in multi-state class actions.

---

15. The *Castano* class suffers from many of the difficulties that the *Georgine* court found dispositive. The class members were exposed to nicotine through different products, for different amounts of time, and over different time periods. Each class member's knowledge about the effects of smoking differs, and each plaintiff began smoking for different reasons. Each of these factual differences impacts the application of legal rules such as causation, reliance, comparative fault, and other affirmative defenses.

Variations in state law magnify the differences. In a fraud claim, some states require justifiable reliance on a misrepresentation. States impose varying standards to determine when there is a duty to disclose facts.

Products liability law also differs among states. Some states do not recognize strict liability. Some have adopted RESTATEMENT (SECOND) OF TORTS § 402A. Among the states that have adopted the Restatement, there are variations.

Differences in affirmative defenses also exist. Assumption of risk is a complete defense to a products claim in some states. In others, it is a part of comparative fault analysis. Some states utilize "pure" comparative fault, others follow a "greater fault bar," and still others use an "equal fault bar,".

Despite these overwhelming individual issues, common issues might predominate. We are, however, left to speculate. The point of detailing the alleged differences is to demonstrate the inquiry the district court failed to make.

The court also failed to perform its duty to determine whether the class action would be manageable in light of state law variations. The court's only discussion of manageability is a citation to *Jenkins* and the claim that "while manageability of the liability issues in this case may well prove to be difficult, the Court finds that any such difficulties pale in comparison to the specter of thousands, if not millions, of similar trials of liability proceeding in thousands of courtrooms around the nation." Id. at 555–56.

The problem with this approach is that it substitutes case-specific analysis with a generalized reference to *Jenkins*. The *Jenkins* court, however, was not faced with managing a novel claim involving eight causes of action, multiple jurisdictions, millions of plaintiffs, eight defendants, and over fifty years of alleged wrongful conduct. Instead, Jenkins involved only 893 personal injury asbestos cases, the law of only one state, and the prospect of trial occurring in only one district.

B.   Predominance

The district court's second error was that it failed to consider how the plaintiffs' addiction claims would be tried, individually or on a class basis. The district court, based on *Eisen v. Carlisle & Jacquelin*, 417 U.S. 156, 177–78, 40 L. Ed. 2d 732, 94 S. Ct. 2140 (1974), and *Miller v. Mackey Int'l*, 452 F.2d 424 (5th Cir.1971), believed that it could not go past the pleadings for the certification decision. The result was an incomplete and inadequate predominance inquiry.

The crux of the court's error was that it misinterpreted *Eisen* and *Miller*. Neither case suggests that a court is limited to the pleadings when deciding on certification. Both, instead, stand for the unremarkable proposition that the strength of a plaintiff's claim should not affect the certification decision. In *Eisen*, the Court held that it was improper to make a preliminary inquiry into the merits of a case, determine that the plaintiff was likely to succeed, and consequently shift the cost of providing notice to the defendant. In *Miller*, this court held that a district court could not deny certification based on its belief that the plaintiff could not prevail on the merits.

The district court's predominance inquiry demonstrates why such an understanding is necessary. The premise of the court's opinion is a citation to *Jenkins* and a conclusion that class treatment of common issues would significantly advance the individual trials. Absent knowledge of how addiction-as-injury cases would actually be tried, however, it was impossible for the court to know whether the common issues would be a "significant" portion of the individual trials. The court just assumed that because the common issues would play a part in every trial, they must be significant. The court's synthesis of *Jenkins* and *Eisen* would write the predominance requirement out of the rule, and any common issue would predominate if it were common to all the individual trials.

III

In addition to the reasons given above, regarding the district court's procedural errors, this class must be decertified because it independently fails the superiority requirement of rule 23(b)(3). In the context of mass tort class actions, certification dramatically affects the stakes for defendants. Class certification magnifies and strengthens the number of unmeritorious claims. *Agent Orange*, 818 F.2d at 165–66. Aggregation of claims also makes it more likely that a defendant will be found liable and results in significantly higher damage awards.

In addition to skewing trial outcomes, class certification creates insurmountable pressure on defendants to settle, whereas individual trials would not. The risk of facing an all-or-nothing verdict presents too high a risk, even when the probability of an adverse judgment is low. *Rhone-Poulenc*, 51 F.3d at 1298. These settlements have been referred to as judicial blackmail.

It is no surprise then, that historically, certification of mass tort litigation classes has been disfavored. The traditional concern over the rights of defendants in mass tort class actions is magnified in the instant case. Our specific concern is that a mass tort cannot be properly certified without a prior track record of trials from which the district court can draw the information necessary to make the predominance and superiority requirements required by rule 23. This is because certification of an immature tort results in a higher than normal risk that the class action may not be superior to individual adjudication.

We first address the district court's superiority analysis. The court acknowledged the extensive manageability problems with this class. Such problems include difficult choice of law determinations, subclassing of eight claims with variations in state law, *Erie* guesses, notice to millions of class members, further subclassing to take account of transient plaintiffs, and the difficult procedure for determining who is nicotine-dependent. Cases with far fewer manageability problems have given courts pause. See, e.g., *Georgine*, 83 F.3d 610, 1996 WL 242442, at *19.

The district court's rationale for certification in spite of such problems i.e., that a class trial would preserve judicial resources in the millions of inevitable individual trials, is based on pure speculation. Not every mass tort is asbestos, and not every mass tort will result in the same judicial crises.

What the district court failed to consider, and what no court can determine at this time, is the very real possibility that the judicial crisis may fail to materialize.[26] The plaintiffs' claims are based on a new

---

[26] The plaintiffs, in seemingly inconsistent positions, argue that the lack of a judicial crisis justifies certification; they assert that the reason why individual plaintiffs have not filed claims is that the tobacco industry makes individual trials far too expensive and plaintiffs are rarely successful. The fact that a party continuously loses at trial does not justify class certification, however. The plaintiffs' argument, if accepted, would justify class treatment whenever a defendant has better attorneys and resources at its disposal.

The plaintiffs' claim also overstates the defendants' ability to outspend plaintiffs. Assuming arguendo that the defendants pool resources and outspend plaintiffs in individual trials, there is no reason why plaintiffs still cannot prevail. The class is represented by a consortium of well-financed plaintiffs' lawyers who, over time, can develop the expertise and specialized knowledge sufficient to

theory of liability and the existence of new evidence. Until plaintiffs decide to file individual claims, a court cannot, from the existence of injury, presume that all or even any plaintiffs will pursue legal remedies.

As he stated in the record, plaintiffs' counsel in this case has promised to inundate the courts with individual claims if class certification is denied. Independently of the reliability of this self-serving promise, there is reason to believe that individual suits are feasible. First, individual damage claims are high, and punitive damages are available in most states.

In a case such as this one, where each plaintiff may receive a large award, and fee shifting often is available, we find Chief Judge Posner's analysis of superiority to be persuasive:

> For this consensus or maturing of judgment the district judge proposes to substitute a single trial before a single jury. . . . One jury . . . will hold the fate of an industry in the palm of its hand. . . . That kind of thing can happen in our system of civil justice. . . . But it need not be tolerated when the alternative exists of submitting an issue to multiple juries constituting in the aggregate a much larger and more diverse sample of decision-makers. That would not be a feasible option if the stakes to each class member were too slight to repay the cost of suit. . . . But this is not the case. . . . Each plaintiff if successful is apt to receive a judgment in the millions. With the aggregate stakes in the tens or hundreds of millions of dollars, or even in the billions, it is not a waste of judicial resources to conduct more than one trial, before more than six jurors, to determine whether a major segment of the international pharmaceutical industry is to follow the asbestos manufacturers into Chapter 11.

Rhone–Poulenc, 51 F.3d at 1300.

So too here, we cannot say that it would be a waste to allow individual trials to proceed, before a district court engages in the complicated predominance and superiority analysis necessary to certify a class.

Fairness may demand that mass torts with few prior verdicts or judgments be litigated first in smaller units or even single-plaintiff, single-defendant trials until general causation, typical injuries, and levels of damages become established. Thus, "mature" mass torts like asbestos or Dalkon Shield may call for procedures that are not appropriate for incipient mass tort cases, such as those involving injuries arising from new products, chemical substances, or pharmaceuticals.

The remaining rationale for superiority, judicial efficiency, is also lacking. In the context of an immature tort, any savings in judicial resources is speculative, and any imagined savings would be over-

beat the tobacco companies at their own game.

whelmed by the procedural problems that certification of a sui generis cause of action brings with it.

The court's analysis of reliance also demonstrates the potential judicial inefficiencies in immature tort class actions. Individual trials will determine whether individual reliance will be an issue. Rather than guess that reliance may be inferred, a district court should base its determination that individual reliance does not predominate on the wisdom of such individual trials. The risk that a district court will make the wrong guess, that the parties will engage in years of litigation, and that the class ultimately will be decertified (because reliance predominates over common issues) prevents this class action from being a superior method of adjudication.

The complexity of the choice of law inquiry also makes individual adjudication superior to class treatment. The plaintiffs have asserted eight theories of liability from every state. Prior to certification, the district court must determine whether variations in state law defeat predominance. While the task may not be impossible, its complexity certainly makes individual trials a more attractive alternative and, ipso facto, renders class treatment not superior.

Another factor weighing heavily in favor of individual trials is the risk that in order to make this class action manageable, the court will be forced to bifurcate issues in violation of the Seventh Amendment. This class action is permeated with individual issues, such as proximate causation, comparative negligence, reliance, and compensatory damages. In order to manage so many individual issues, the district court proposed to empanel a class jury to adjudicate common issues. A second jury, or a number of "second" juries, will pass on the individual issues, either on a case-by-case basis or through group trials of individual plaintiffs.

The Seventh Amendment entitles parties to have fact issues decided by one jury, and prohibits a second jury from reexamining those facts and issues. Thus, the Constitution allows bifurcation of issues that are so separable that the second jury will not be called upon to reconsider findings of fact by the first:

> This Court has cautioned that separation of issues is not the usual course that should be followed, and that the issue to be tried must be so distinct and separable from the others that a trial of it alone may be had without injustice. This limitation on the use of bifurcation is a recognition of the fact that inherent in the Seventh Amendment guarantee of a trial by jury is the general right of a litigant to have only one jury pass on a common issue of fact. The Supreme Court explained ... that a partial new trial may not be "properly resorted to unless it clearly appears that the issue to be retried is so distinct and separable from the others that a trial of it alone may be had without injustice."

Alabama v. Blue Bird Body Co., 573 F.2d 309, 318 (5th Cir.1978)

(citations and footnotes omitted).

The plaintiffs' final retort is that individual trials are inadequate because time is running out for many of the plaintiffs. They point out that prior litigation against the tobacco companies has taken up to ten years to wind through the legal system. While a compelling rhetorical argument, it is ultimately inconsistent with the plaintiffs' own arguments and ignores the realities of the legal system. First, the plaintiffs' reliance on prior personal injury cases is unpersuasive, as they admit that they have new evidence and are pursuing a claim entirely different from that of past plaintiffs.

Second, the plaintiffs' claim that time is running out ignores the reality of the class action device. In a complicated case involving multiple jurisdictions, the conflict of law question itself could take decades to work its way through the courts. Once that issue has been resolved, discovery, subclassing, and ultimately the class trial would take place. Next would come the appellate process. After the class trial, the individual trials and appeals on comparative negligence and damages would have to take place. The net result could be that the class action device would lengthen, not shorten, the time it takes for the plaintiffs to reach final judgment.

We have once before stated that "traditional ways of proceeding reflect far more than habit. They reflect the very culture of the jury trial...." *In re Fibreboard Corp.*, 893 F.2d 706, 711 (5th Cir.1990). The collective wisdom of individual juries is necessary before this court commits the fate of an entire industry or, indeed, the fate of a class of millions, to a single jury. For the forgoing reasons, we REVERSE and REMAND with instructions that the district court dismiss the class complaint.

QUESTION

Does the decision in *Castano* indicate that the class action device is generally inappropriate for the adjudication of mass tort and product liability claims? If you were representing the plaintiffs in such a case, how could you structure the litigation to meet some or all of the Fifth Circuit's concerns?

NOTE: THE CLASS ACTION IN FEDERAL COURTS

The Supreme Court extended *Eisen* to preclude imposing on a defendant the cost of identifying the members of the class.[1] Clearly, the class action became a less attractive mechanism of righting civil wrongs. The notice requirement in *Eisen* was based on the Court's interpretation of Rule 23 and many states did not feel themselves constrained to follow the Supreme Court in interpreting their own class action rules.[2]

Another case, handed down the same term as *Eisen,* drastically reduced the availability of federal courts as a forum for 26(b)(3) class actions in which jurisdiction was based on diversity. It had long been held that diversity of citizenship, if it existed between the named parties, would not be defeated by that of the members of

---

1. Oppenheimer Fund, Inc. v. Sanders, 437 U.S. 340, 98 S.Ct. 2380, 57 L.Ed.2d 253 (1978).

2. See discussion in Friedenthal, Kane & Miller, Civil Procedure (1985) 751.

the class; the latter was irrelevant. In Zahn v. International Paper Co.,[3] however, the Court held that every member of the class must meet the jurisdictional amount requirement. The aggregate amount in controversy was irrelevant and the amount claimed by the named plaintiffs was similarly irrelevant. As the following note indicates, however, recent legislative changes have cast doubt on the continuing validity of Zahn.

NOTE ON FREE v. ABBOTT LABORATORIES

In *Free v. Abbott Laboratories*, 51 F.3d 524 (5th Cir.1995), the Fifth Circuit held that 28 U.S.C. § 1367, enacted as part of the Judicial Improvements Act of 1990, overruled the requirement of *Zahn v. International Paper Co.*, 414 U.S. 291, 38 L. Ed. 2d 511, 94 S. Ct. 505 (1973) that in a federal class action based solely on diversity, every class member must satisfy the jurisdictional amount requirement of 28 U.S.C. § 1332(a).

Free alleged a conspiracy by defendants to fix prices for infant formula in violation of Louisiana antitrust law. It was brought on behalf of Louisiana consumers. After affirming the district court's determination that the claims of the named plaintiffs exceeded $50,000, Judge Higginbotham then went on to consider whether the federal court also had jurisdiction over the claims of the other class members, which did not exceed the amount-in-controversy requirement. He stated:

> Section 1367(a) grants district courts supplemental jurisdiction over related claims generally, and § 1367(b) carves exceptions. Significantly, class actions are not among the exceptions. Some commentators have interpreted this silence to mean that Congress overruled *Zahn* and granted supplemental jurisdiction over the claims of class members who individually do not demand the necessary amount in controversy. Some of § 1367's drafters disagree. No appellate court has ruled on the question yet.

> Perhaps, by some measure transcending its language, Congress did not intend the Judicial Improvements Act to overrule *Zahn*. The House Committee on the Judiciary considered the bill that became § 1367 to be a "noncontroversial" collection of "relatively modest proposals," not the sort of legislative action that would upset any long-established precedent like *Zahn*. A disclaimer in the legislative history strives to make this point clear by stating: "The section is not intended to affect the jurisdictional requirements of 28 U.S.C. § 1332 in diversity-only class actions, as those requirements were interpreted prior to Finley."

>> We cannot search legislative history for congressional intent unless we find the statute unclear or ambiguous. Here, it is neither. The statute's first section vests federal courts with the power to hear supplemental claims generally, subject to limited exceptions set forth in the statute's second section. Class actions are not among the enumerated exceptions.

>> Omitting the class action from the exception may have been a clerical error. But the statute is the sole repository of congressional intent where the statute is clear and does not demand an absurd result. See *West Virginia Univ. Hosps., Inc. v. Casey*, 499 U.S. 83, 111 S. Ct. 1138, 1147, 113 L. Ed. 2d 68 (1991) (refusing to permit the Court's "perception of the 'policy' of the statute to overcome its 'plain language' "). Abolishing the strictures of *Zahn* is not an absurd result. Some respected commentators would welcome *Zahn's* demise. But the wisdom of the statute is not our affair beyond determining that overturning *Zahn* is not absurd. We are

---

3.   414 U.S. 291, 94 S.Ct. 505, 38 L.Ed.2d 511 (1973).

persuaded that under § 1367 a district court can exercise supplemental jurisdiction over members of a class, although they did not meet the amount-in-controversy requirement, as did the class representatives.

Amchem Products, Inc. v. George Windsor

Supreme Court of the United States, 1997.
521 U.S. 591, 117 S. Ct. 2231, 138 L.Ed. 2d 689.

■ Justice Ginsburg delivered the opinion of the Court.

This case concerns the legitimacy under Rule 23 of the Federal Rules of Civil Procedure of a class-action certification sought to achieve global settlement of current and future asbestos-related claims. The class proposed for certification potentially encompasses hundreds of thousands, perhaps millions, of individuals tied together by this commonality: each was, or some day may be, adversely affected by past exposure to asbestos products manufactured by one or more of 20 companies. Those companies, defendants in the lower courts, are petitioners here.

The United States District Court for the Eastern District of Pennsylvania certified the class for settlement only, finding that the proposed settlement was fair and that representation and notice had been adequate. That court enjoined class members from separately pursuing asbestos-related personal-injury suits in any court, federal or state, pending the issuance of a final order. The Court of Appeals for the Third Circuit vacated the District Court's orders, holding that the class certification failed to satisfy Rule 23's requirements in several critical respects. We affirm the Court of Appeals' judgment.

I

A

The settlement-class certification we confront evolved in response to an asbestos-litigation crisis. A United States Judicial Conference Ad Hoc Committee on Asbestos Litigation, appointed by The Chief Justice in September 1990, described facets of the problem in a 1991 report:

"[This] is a tale of danger known in the 1930s, exposure inflicted upon millions of Americans in the 1940s and 1950s, injuries that began to take their toll in the 1960s, and a flood of lawsuits beginning in the 1970s. On the basis of past and current filing data, and because of a latency period that may last as long as 40 years for some asbestos related diseases, a continuing stream of claims can be expected. The final toll of asbestos related injuries is unknown. Predictions have been made of 200,000 asbestos disease deaths before the year 2000 and as many as 265,000 by the year 2015.

"The most objectionable aspects of asbestos litigation can be briefly summarized: dockets in both federal and state courts continue to grow; long delays are routine; trials are too long; the same issues are litigated over and over; transaction costs exceed the victims' recovery by nearly two to one; exhaustion of assets threatens and distorts the process; and future claimants may lose altogether."

Real reform, the report concluded, required federal legislation creating a national asbestos dispute-resolution scheme. As recommended by the Ad Hoc Committee, the Judicial Conference of the United States urged Congress to act. See Report of the Proceedings of the Judicial Conference of the United States 33 (Mar. 12, 1991). To this date, no congressional response has emerged.

In the face of legislative inaction, the federal courts—lacking authority to replace state tort systems with a national toxic tort compensation regime—endeavored to work with the procedural tools available to improve management of federal asbestos litigation. Eight federal judges, experienced in the superintendence of asbestos cases, urged the Judicial Panel on Multidistrict Litigation (MDL Panel), to consolidate in a single district all asbestos complaints then pending in federal courts. Accepting the recommendation, the MDL Panel transferred all asbestos cases then filed, but not yet on trial in federal courts to a single district, the United States District Court for the Eastern District of Pennsylvania; pursuant to the transfer order, the collected cases were consolidated for pretrial proceedings before Judge Weiner. The order aggregated pending cases only; no authority resides in the MDL Panel to license for consolidated proceedings claims not yet filed.

B

After the consolidation, attorneys for plaintiffs and defendants formed separate steering committees and began settlement negotiations. Ronald L. Motley and Gene Locks—later appointed, along with Motley's law partner Joseph F. Rice, to represent the plaintiff class in this action—co-chaired the Plaintiffs' Steering Committee. Counsel for the Center for Claims Resolution (CCR), the consortium of 20 former asbestos manufacturers now before us as petitioners, participated in the Defendants' Steering Committee. Although the MDL order collected, transferred, and consolidated only cases already commenced in federal courts, settlement negotiations included efforts to find a "means of resolving . . . future cases."

In November 1991, the Defendants' Steering Committee made an offer designed to settle all pending and future asbestos cases by providing a fund for distribution by plaintiffs' counsel among asbestos-exposed individuals. The Plaintiffs' Steering Committee rejected this offer, and negotiations fell apart. CCR, however, continued to pursue "a workable administrative system for the handling of future claims."

To that end, CCR counsel approached the lawyers who had headed the Plaintiffs' Steering Committee in the unsuccessful negotiations, and a new round of negotiations began; that round yielded the mass settlement agreement now in controversy. At the time, the former heads of the Plaintiffs' Steering Committee represented thousands of plaintiffs with then-pending asbestos-related claims—claimants the parties to this suit call "inventory" plaintiffs. CCR indicated in these discussions that it would resist settlement of inventory cases absent "some kind of protection for the future." (CCR communicated to the inventory plaintiffs' attorneys that once the CCR defendants saw a rational way to deal with claims expected to be filed in the future, those defendants would be prepared to address the settlement of pending cases).

Settlement talks thus concentrated on devising an administrative scheme for disposition of asbestos claims not yet in litigation. In these negotiations, counsel for masses of inventory plaintiffs endeavored to represent the interests of the anticipated future claimants, although those lawyers then had no attorney-client relationship with such claimants.

Once negotiations seemed likely to produce an agreement purporting to bind potential plaintiffs, CCR agreed to settle, through separate agreements, the claims of plaintiffs who had already filed asbestos-related lawsuits. In one such agreement, CCR defendants promised to pay more than $200 million to gain release of the claims of numerous inventory plaintiffs. After settling the inventory claims, CCR, together with the plaintiffs' lawyers CCR had approached, launched this case, exclusively involving persons outside the MDL Panel's province—plaintiffs without already pending lawsuits.

C

The class action thus instituted was not intended to be litigated. Rather, within the space of a single day, January 15, 1993, the settling parties—CCR defendants and the representatives of the plaintiff class described below—presented to the District Court a complaint, an answer, a proposed settlement agreement, and a joint motion for conditional class certification.

The complaint identified nine lead plaintiffs, designating them and members of their families as representatives of a class comprising all persons who had not filed an asbestos-related lawsuit against a CCR defendant as of the date the class action commenced, but who (1) had been exposed—occupationally or through the occupational exposure of a spouse or household member—to asbestos or products containing asbestos attributable to a CCR defendant, or (2) whose spouse or family member had been so exposed. Untold numbers of individuals may fall within this description.

The complaint invoked the District Court's diversity jurisdiction and asserted various state-law claims for relief, including (1) negligent failure to warn, (2) strict liability, (3) breach of express and implied warranty, (4) negligent infliction of emotional distress, (5) enhanced risk of disease, (6) medical monitoring, and (7) civil conspiracy. Each plaintiff requested unspecified damages in excess of $100,000. CCR defendants' answer denied the principal allegations of the complaint and asserted 11 affirmative defenses.

A stipulation of settlement accompanied the pleadings; it proposed to settle, and to preclude nearly all class members from litigating against CCR companies, all claims not filed before January 15, 1993, involving compensation for present and future asbestos-related personal injury or death. An exhaustive document exceeding 100 pages, the stipulation presents in detail an administrative mechanism and a schedule of payments to compensate class members who meet defined asbestos-exposure and medical requirements. The stipulation describes four categories of compensable disease: mesothelioma; lung cancer; certain "other cancers" (colon-rectal, laryngeal, esophageal, and stomach cancer); and "non-malignant conditions" (asbestosis and bilateral pleural thickening). Persons with "exceptional" medical claims—claims that do not fall within the four described diagnostic categories—may in some instances qualify for compensation, but the settlement caps the number of "exceptional" claims CCR must cover.

For each qualifying disease category, the stipulation specifies the range of damages CCR will pay to qualifying claimants. Payments under the settlement are not adjustable for inflation. Mesothelioma claimants—the most highly compensated category—are scheduled to receive between $20,000 and $200,000. The stipulation provides that CCR is to propose the level of compensation within the prescribed ranges; it also establishes procedures to resolve disputes over medical diagnoses and levels of compensation.

Compensation above the fixed ranges may be obtained for "extraordinary" claims. But the settlement places both numerical caps and dollar limits on such claims. The settlement also imposes "case flow maximums," which cap the number of claims payable for each disease in a given year.

Class members, in the main, are bound by the settlement in perpetuity, while CCR defendants may choose to withdraw from the settlement after ten years. A small number of class members—only a few per year—may reject the settlement and pursue their claims in court. Those permitted to exercise this option, however, may not assert any punitive damages claim or any claim for increased risk of cancer. Aspects of the administration of the settlement are to be monitored by the AFL–CIO and class counsel. Class counsel are to receive attorneys' fees in an amount to be approved by the District Court.

D

On January 29, 1993, as requested by the settling parties, the District Court conditionally certified, under Federal Rule of Civil Procedure 23(b)(3), an encompassing opt-out class. The certified class included persons occupationally exposed to defendants' asbestos products, and members of their families, who had not filed suit as of January 15. Judge Weiner assigned to Judge Reed, also of the Eastern District of Pennsylvania, "the task of conducting fairness proceedings and of determining whether the proposed settlement is fair to the class." Various class members raised objections to the settlement stipulation, and Judge Weiner granted the objectors full rights to participate in the subsequent proceedings.[7]

Objectors raised numerous challenges to the settlement. They urged that the settlement unfairly disadvantaged those without currently compensable conditions in that it failed to adjust for inflation or to account for changes, over time, in medical understanding. They maintained that compensation levels were intolerably low in comparison to awards available in tort litigation or payments received by the inventory plaintiffs. And they objected to the absence of any compensation for certain claims, for example, medical monitoring, compensable under the tort law of several States. Rejecting these and all other objections, Judge Reed concluded that the settlement terms were fair and had been negotiated without collusion. He also found that adequate notice had been given to class members, and that final class certification under Rule 23(b)(3) was appropriate.

Subclasses were unnecessary, the District Court held, bearing in mind the added cost and confusion they would entail and the ability of class members to exclude themselves from the class during the three-month opt-out period. Reasoning that the representative plaintiffs "have a strong interest that recovery for all of the medical categories be maximized because they may have claims in any, or several categories," the District Court found "no antagonism of interest between class members with various medical conditions, or between persons with and without currently manifest asbestos impairment." Declaring class certification appropriate and the settlement fair, the District Court preliminarily enjoined all class members from commencing any asbestos-related suit against the CCR defendants in any state or federal court.

The objectors appealed. The United States Court of Appeals for the Third Circuit vacated the certification, holding that the requirements of Rule 23 had not been satisfied.

E

The Court of Appeals, in a long, heavily detailed opinion by Judge Becker, first noted several challenges by objectors to justiciability, subject-matter jurisdiction, and adequacy of notice. These challenges, the court said, raised "serious concerns." However, the court observed, "the jurisdictional issues in this case would not exist but for the [class action] certification." Turning to the class-certification issues and finding them dispositive, the Third Circuit declined to decide other questions.

On class-action prerequisites, the Court of Appeals referred to an earlier Third Circuit decision, In re General Motors Corp. Pick–Up Truck Fuel Tank Products Liability Litigation, 55 F.3d 768 (3d Cir.), cert. denied, 516 U.S. 824 (1995) (hereinafter GM Trucks), which held

---

7. These objectors, now respondents before this Court, include three groups of individuals with overlapping interests, designated as the "Windsor Group," the New Jersey "White Lung Group," and the "Cargile Group."

that although a class action may be certified for settlement purposes only, Rule 23(a)'s requirements must be satisfied as if the case were going to be litigated. The same rule should apply, the Third Circuit said, to class certification under Rule 23(b)(3). While stating that the requirements of Rule 23(a) and (b)(3) must be met "without taking into account the settlement," the Court of Appeals in fact closely considered the terms of the settlement as it examined aspects of the case under Rule 23 criteria..

The Third Circuit recognized that Rule 23(a)(2)'s "commonality" requirement is subsumed under, or superseded by, the more stringent Rule 23(b)(3) requirement that questions common to the class "predominate over" other questions. The court therefore trained its attention on the "predominance" inquiry. The harmfulness of asbestos exposure was indeed a prime factor common to the class, the Third Circuit observed. But uncommon questions abounded.

In contrast to mass torts involving a single accident, class members in this case were exposed to different asbestos-containing products, in different ways, over different periods, and for different amounts of time; some suffered no physical injury, others suffered disabling or deadly diseases. See "These factual differences," the Third Circuit explained, "translated into significant legal differences." State law governed and varied widely on such critical issues as "viability of [exposure-only] claims [and] availability of causes of action for medical monitoring, increased risk of cancer, and fear of future injury." "The number of uncommon issues in this humongous class action," the Third Circuit concluded, barred a determination, under existing tort law, that common questions predominated.

The Court of Appeals next found that "serious intra-class conflicts precluded the class from meeting the adequacy of representation requirement" of Rule 23(a)(4). Adverting to, but not resolving charges of attorney conflict of interests, the Third Circuit addressed the question whether the named plaintiffs could adequately advance the interests of all class members. The Court of Appeals acknowledged that the District Court was certainly correct to this extent: " 'The members of the class are united in seeking the maximum possible recovery for their asbestos-related claims.' " "But the settlement does more than simply provide a general recovery fund," the Court of Appeals immediately added; "rather, it makes important judgments on how recovery is to be allocated among different kinds of plaintiffs, decisions that necessarily favor some claimants over others."

In the Third Circuit's view, the "most salient" divergence of interests separated plaintiffs already afflicted with an asbestos-related disease from plaintiffs without manifest injury (exposure-only plaintiffs). The latter would rationally want protection against inflation for distant recoveries. See ibid. They would also seek sturdy back-end opt-out rights and "causation provisions that can keep pace with changing science and medicine, rather than freezing in place the science of 1993." Already injured parties, in contrast, would care little about such provisions and would rationally trade them for higher current payouts. These and other adverse interests, the Court of Appeals carefully explained, strongly suggested that an undivided set of representatives could not adequately protect the discrete interests of both currently afflicted and exposure-only claimants.

The Third Circuit next rejected the District Court's determination that the named plaintiffs were "typical" of the class, noting that this Rule 23(a)(3) inquiry overlaps the adequacy of representation question: "both look to the potential for conflicts in the class." Evident conflict problems, the court said, led it to hold that "no set of representatives can be 'typical' of this class."

The Court of Appeals similarly rejected the District Court's assessment of the superiority of the class action. The Third Circuit initially noted that a class action so large and complex "could not be tried." The court elaborated most particularly, however, on the unfairness of binding exposure-only plaintiffs who might be unaware of the class action or lack sufficient information about their exposure to make a reasoned decision whether to stay in or opt out. "A series of statewide or more narrowly defined adjudications, either through consolidation under Rule 42(a) or as class actions under Rule 23, would seem preferable," the Court of Appeals said.

The Third Circuit, after intensive review, ultimately ordered decertification of the class and vacation of the District Court's anti-suit injunction. Judge Wellford concurred, "fully subscribing to the decision of Judge Becker that the plaintiffs in this case had not met the requirements of Rule 23." He added that in his view, named exposure-only plaintiffs had no standing to pursue the suit in federal court, for their depositions showed that "they claimed no damages and no present injury."

We granted certiorari, and now affirm.

III

To place this controversy in context, we briefly describe the characteristics of class actions for which the Federal Rules provide. Rule 23, governing federal-court class actions, stems from equity practice and gained its current shape in an innovative 1966 revision. See generally Kaplan, Continuing Work of the Civil Committee: 1966 Amendments of the Federal Rules of Civil Procedure (I), 81 Harv. L. Rev. 356, 375–400 (1967) Rule 23(a) states four threshold requirements applicable to all class actions: (1) numerosity (a "class [so large] that joinder of all members is impracticable"); (2) commonality ("questions of law or fact common to the class"); (3) typicality (named parties' claims or defenses "are typical . . . of the class"); and (4) adequacy of representation (representatives "will fairly and adequately protect the interests of the class").

In addition to satisfying Rule 23(a)'s prerequisites, parties seeking class certification must show that the action is maintainable under Rule 23(b)(1), (2), or (3). Rule 23(b)(1) covers cases in which separate actions by or against individual class members would risk establishing

"incompatible standards of conduct for the party opposing the class,"
Fed. Rule Civ. Proc. 23(b)(1)(A), or would "as a practical matter be
dispositive of the interests" of nonparty class members "or substantially impair or impede their ability to protect their interests," Fed. Rule
Civ. Proc. 23(b)(1)(B). Rule 23(b)(1)(A) "takes in cases where the
party is obliged by law to treat the members of the class alike (a utility
acting toward customers; a government imposing a tax), or where the
party must treat all alike as a matter of practical necessity (a riparian
owner using water as against downriver owners)." Kaplan, Continuing
Work 388 . Rule 23(b)(1)(B) includes, for example, "limited fund"
cases, instances in which numerous persons make claims against a
fund insufficient to satisfy all claims.

Rule 23(b)(2) permits class actions for declaratory or injunctive
relief where "the party opposing the class has acted or refused to act
on grounds generally applicable to the class." Civil rights cases against
parties charged with unlawful, class-based discrimination are prime
examples.

In the 1966 class-action amendments, Rule 23(b)(3), the category
at issue here, was "the most adventuresome" innovation. Rule
23(b)(3) added to the complex-litigation arsenal class actions for
damages designed to secure judgments binding all class members save
those who affirmatively elected to be excluded. Rule 23(b)(3) "opt
out" class actions superseded the former "spurious" class action, so
characterized because it generally functioned as a permissive joinder
("opt in") device.

Framed for situations in which "class-action treatment is not as
clearly called for" as it is in Rule 23(b)(1) and (b)(2) situations, Rule
23(b)(3) permits certification where class suit "may nevertheless be
convenient and desirable." To qualify for certification under Rule
23(b)(3), a class must meet two requirements beyond the Rule 23(a)
prerequisites: Common questions must "predominate over any questions affecting only individual members"; and class resolution must be
"superior to other available methods for the fair and efficient adjudication of the controversy." In adding "predominance" and "superiority"
to the qualification-for-certification list, the Advisory Committee sought
to cover cases "in which a class action would achieve economies of
time, effort, and expense, and promote . . . uniformity of decision as
to persons similarly situated, without sacrificing procedural fairness or
bringing about other undesirable results." Sensitive to the competing
tugs of individual autonomy for those who might prefer to go it alone
or in a smaller unit, on the one hand, and systemic efficiency on the
other, the Reporter for the 1966 amendments cautioned: "The new
provision invites a close look at the case before it is accepted as a class
action. . . ."

Rule 23(b)(3) includes a nonexhaustive list of factors pertinent to
a court's "close look" at the predominance and superiority criteria:

> "(A) the interest of members of the class in individually control-
> ling the prosecution or defense of separate actions; (B) the extent
> and nature of any litigation concerning the controversy already

commenced by or against members of the class; (C) the desirability or undesirability of concentrating the litigation of the claims in the particular forum; (D) the difficulties likely to be encountered in the management of a class action."

In setting out these factors, the Advisory Committee for the 1966 reform anticipated that in each case, courts would "consider the interests of individual members of the class in controlling their own litigations and carrying them on as they see fit." They elaborated:

"The interests of individuals in conducting separate lawsuits may be so strong as to call for denial of a class action. On the other hand, these interests may be theoretic rather than practical; the class may have a high degree of cohesion and prosecution of the action through representatives would be quite unobjectionable, or the amounts at stake for individuals may be so small that separate suits would be impracticable."

While the text of Rule 23(b)(3) does not exclude from certification cases in which individual damages run high, the Advisory Committee had dominantly in mind vindication of "the rights of groups of people who individually would be without effective strength to bring their opponents into court at all." As concisely recalled in a recent Seventh Circuit opinion:

"The policy at the very core of the class action mechanism is to overcome the problem that small recoveries do not provide the incentive for any individual to bring a solo action prosecuting his or her rights. A class action solves this problem by aggregating the relatively paltry potential recoveries into something worth someone's (usually an attorney's) labor." Mace v. Van Ru Credit Corp., 109 F.3d 338, 344 (1997).

To alert class members to their right to "opt out" of a (b)(3) class, Rule 23 instructs the court to "direct to the members of the class the best notice practicable under the circumstances, including individual notice to all members who can be identified through reasonable effort." Fed. Rule Civ. Proc. 23(c)(2); see Eisen v. Carlisle & Jacquelin, 417 U.S. 156, 173–177,(1974) (individual notice to class members identifiable through reasonable effort is mandatory in (b)(3) actions; requirement may not be relaxed based on high cost).

In the decades since the 1966 revision of Rule 23, class action practice has become ever more "adventuresome" as a means of coping with claims too numerous to secure their "just, speedy, and inexpensive determination" one by one. See Fed. Rule Civ. Proc. 1. The development reflects concerns about the efficient use of court resources and the conservation of funds to compensate claimants who do not line up early in a litigation queue.

Among current applications of Rule 23(b)(3), the "settlement only" class has become a stock device. See, e.g., T. Willging, L. Hooper, & R. Niemic, Empirical Study of Class Actions in Four Federal District Courts: Final Report to the Advisory Committee on Civil Rules 61–62 (1996) (noting large number of such cases in districts studied).

Although all Federal Circuits recognize the utility of Rule 23(b)(3) settlement classes, courts have divided on the extent to which a proffered settlement affects court surveillance under Rule 23's certification criteria.

In GM Trucks, 55 F.3d at 799–800, and in the instant case, the Third Circuit held that a class cannot be certified for settlement when certification for trial would be unwarranted. Other courts have held that settlement obviates or reduces the need to measure a proposed class against the enumerated Rule 23 requirements. See, e.g., In re Asbestos Litigation, 90 F.3d at 975 (CA5) ("in settlement class context, common issues arise from the settlement itself"); White v. National Football League, 41 F.3d 402, 408 (C.A.8 1994) ("adequacy of class representation . . . is ultimately determined by the settlement itself"), cert. denied, 132 L. Ed. 2d 821, 115 S. Ct. 2569 (1995); In re A. H. Robins Co., 880 F.2d 709, 740 (CA4) ("if not a ground for certification per se, certainly settlement should be a factor, and an important factor, to be considered when determining certification"), cert. denied sub nom. Anderson v. Aetna Casualty & Surety Co., 493 U.S. 959, 107 L. Ed. 2d 362, 110 S. Ct. 377 (1989); Malchman v. Davis, 761 F.2d 893, 900 (C.A.2 1985) (certification appropriate, in part, because "the interests of the members of the broadened class in the settlement agreement were commonly held"), cert. denied, 475 U.S. 1143, 90 L. Ed. 2d 343, 106 S.Ct. 1798 (1986).

A proposed amendment to Rule 23 would expressly authorize settlement class certification, in conjunction with a motion by the settling parties for Rule 23(b)(3) certification, "even though the requirements of subdivision (b)(3) might not be met for purposes of trial." Proposed Amendment to Fed. Rule Civ. Proc. 23(b), 117 S. Ct. No. 1 CXIX, CLIV to CLV (Aug. 1996) (Request for Comment). In response to the publication of this proposal, voluminous public comments—many of them opposed to, or skeptical of, the amendment—were received by the Judicial Conference Standing Committee on Rules of Practice and Procedure. See, e.g., Letter from Steering Committee to Oppose Proposed Rule 23, signed by 129 law professors (May 28, 1996); Letter from Paul D. Carrington (May 21, 1996). The Committee has not yet acted on the matter. We consider the certification at issue under the rule as it is currently framed.

IV

We granted review to decide the role settlement may play, under existing Rule 23, in determining the propriety of class certification. The Third Circuit's opinion stated that each of the requirements of Rule 23(a) and (b)(3) "must be satisfied without taking into account the settlement." 83 F.3d at 626 (quoting *GM Trucks*, 55 F.3d at 799). That statement, petitioners urge, is incorrect.

We agree with petitioners to this limited extent: settlement is relevant to a class certification. The Third Circuit's opinion bears modification in that respect. But, as we earlier observed, the Court of Appeals in fact did not ignore the settlement; instead, that court homed in on settlement terms in explaining why it found the absentees' interests inadequately represented. The Third Circuit's close inspection of the settlement in that regard was altogether proper. Confronted with a request for settlement-only class certification, a district court need not inquire whether the case, if tried, would present intractable management problems, see Fed. Rule Civ. Proc. 23(b)(3)(D), for the proposal is that there be no trial. But other specifications of the rule—those designed to protect absentees by blocking unwarranted or overbroad class definitions—demand undiluted, even heightened, attention in the settlement context. Such attention is of vital importance, for a court asked to certify a settlement class will lack the opportunity, present when a case is litigated, to adjust the class, informed by the proceedings as they unfold.

And, of overriding importance, courts must be mindful that the rule as now composed sets the requirements they are bound to enforce. Federal Rules take effect after an extensive deliberative process involving many reviewers: a Rules Advisory Committee, public commenters, the Judicial Conference, this Court, the Congress. The text of a rule thus proposed and reviewed limits judicial inventiveness. Courts are not free to amend a rule outside the process Congress ordered, a process properly tuned to the instruction that rules of procedure "shall not abridge . . . any substantive right." § 2072(b). Rule 23(e), on settlement of class actions, reads in its entirety: "A class action shall not be dismissed or compromised without the approval of the court, and notice of the proposed dismissal or compromise shall be given to all members of the class in such manner as the court directs." This prescription was designed to function as an additional requirement, not a superseding direction, for the "class action" to which Rule 23(e) refers is one qualified for certification under Rule 23(a) and (b). Subdivisions (a) and (b) focus court attention on whether a proposed class has sufficient unity so that absent members can fairly be bound by decisions of class representatives. That dominant concern persists when settlement, rather than trial, is proposed.

Federal courts, in any case, lack authority to substitute for Rule 23's certification criteria a standard never adopted—that if a settlement is "fair," then certification is proper. Applying to this case criteria the rulemakers set, we conclude that the Third Circuit's appraisal is essentially correct. Although that court should have acknowledged that settlement is a factor in the calculus, a remand is not warranted on that account. The Court of Appeals' opinion amply demonstrates why—with or without a settlement on the table—the sprawling class the District Court certified does not satisfy Rule 23's requirements.

A

We address first the requirement of Rule 23(b)(3) that "[common] questions of law or fact . . . predominate over any questions affecting only individual members." The District Court concluded that predominance was satisfied based on two factors: class members' shared experience of asbestos exposure and their common "interest in receiving prompt and fair compensation for their claims, while minimizing the risks and transaction costs inherent in the asbestos litigation process as it occurs presently in the tort system." The settling parties also contend that the settlement's fairness is a common question, predominating over disparate legal issues that might be pivotal in litigation but become irrelevant under the settlement. The predominance requirement stated in Rule 23(b)(3), we hold, is not met by the factors on which the District Court relied. The benefits asbestos-exposed persons might gain from the establishment of a grand-scale compensation scheme is a matter fit for legislative consideration, but it is not pertinent to the predominance inquiry. That inquiry trains on the legal or factual questions that qualify each class member's case as a genuine controversy, questions that preexist any settlement.

The Rule 23(b)(3) predominance inquiry tests whether proposed classes are sufficiently cohesive to warrant adjudication by representation. The inquiry appropriate under Rule 23(e), on the other hand, protects unnamed class members "from unjust or unfair settlements affecting their rights when the representatives become fainthearted before the action is adjudicated or are able to secure satisfaction of their individual claims by a compromise." See 7B Wright, Miller, & Kane § 1797, at 340–341. But it is not the mission of Rule 23(e) to assure the class cohesion that legitimizes representative action in the first place. If a common interest in a fair compromise could satisfy the predominance requirement of Rule 23(b)(3), that vital prescription would be stripped of any meaning in the settlement context.

The District Court also relied upon this commonality: "The members of the class have all been exposed to asbestos products supplied by the defendants...." 157 F.R.D.at 316. Even if Rule 23(a)'s commonality requirement may be satisfied by that shared experience, the predominance criterion is far more demanding. Given the greater number of questions peculiar to the several categories of class members, and to individuals within each category, and the significance of those uncommon questions, any overarching dispute about the health consequences of asbestos exposure cannot satisfy the Rule 23(b)(3) predominance standard.

The Third Circuit highlighted the disparate questions undermining class cohesion in this case:

> "Class members were exposed to different asbestos-containing products, for different amounts of time, in different ways, and over different periods. Some class members suffer no physical injury or have only asymptomatic pleural changes, while others suffer from lung cancer, disabling asbestosis, or from mesothelioma.... Each has a different history of cigarette smoking, a factor that complicates the causation inquiry.

> "The [exposure-only] plaintiffs especially share little in common, either with each other or with the presently injured class members. It is unclear whether they will contract asbestos-related disease and, if so, what disease each will suffer. They will also

incur different medical expenses because their monitoring and treatment will depend on singular circumstances and individual medical histories."

Differences in state law, the Court of Appeals observed, compound these disparities.

No settlement class called to our attention is as sprawling as this one. Predominance is a test readily met in certain cases alleging consumer or securities fraud or violations of the antitrust laws. Even mass tort cases arising from a common cause or disaster may, depending upon the circumstances, satisfy the predominance requirement. The Advisory Committee for the 1966 revision of Rule 23, it is true, noted that "mass accident" cases are likely to present "significant questions, not only of damages but of liability and defenses of liability, . . . affecting the individuals in different ways." And the Committee advised that such cases are "ordinarily not appropriate" for class treatment. But the text of the rule does not categorically exclude mass tort cases from class certification, and district courts, since the late 1970s, have been certifying such cases in increasing number. The Committee's warning, however, continues to call for caution when individual stakes are high and disparities among class members great. As the Third Circuit's opinion makes plain, the certification in this case does not follow the counsel of caution. That certification cannot be upheld, for it rests on a conception of Rule 23(b)(3)'s predominance requirement irreconcilable with the rule's design.

B

Nor can the class approved by the District Court satisfy Rule 23(a)(4)'s requirement that the named parties "will fairly and adequately protect the interests of the class." The adequacy inquiry under Rule 23(a)(4) serves to uncover conflicts of interest between named parties and the class they seek to represent.

As the Third Circuit pointed out, named parties with diverse medical conditions sought to act on behalf of a single giant class rather than on behalf of discrete subclasses. In significant respects, the interests of those within the single class are not aligned. Most saliently, for the currently injured, the critical goal is generous immediate payments. That goal tugs against the interest of exposure-only plaintiffs in ensuring an ample, inflation-protected fund for the future.

The disparity between the currently injured and exposure-only categories of plaintiffs, and the diversity within each category are not made insignificant by the District Court's finding that petitioners' assets suffice to pay claims under the settlement. Although this is not a "limited fund" case certified under Rule 23(b)(1)(B), the terms of the settlement reflect essential allocation decisions designed to confine compensation and to limit defendants' liability. For example, as earlier described, the settlement includes no adjustment for inflation; only a few claimants per year can opt out at the back end; and loss-of-consortium claims are extinguished with no compensation.

The settling parties, in sum, achieved a global compromise with no structural assurance of fair and adequate representation for the diverse groups and individuals affected. Although the named parties alleged a range of complaints, each served generally as representative for the whole, not for a separate constituency. In another asbestos class action, the Second Circuit spoke precisely to this point:

> "Where differences among members of a class are such that subclasses must be established, we know of no authority that permits a court to approve a settlement without creating subclasses on the basis of consents by members of a unitary class, some of whom happen to be members of the distinct subgroups. The class representatives may well have thought that the Settlement serves the aggregate interests of the entire class. But the adversity among subgroups requires that the members of each subgroup cannot be bound to a settlement except by consents given by those who understand that their role is to represent solely the members of their respective subgroups." In re Joint Eastern and Southern Dist. Asbestos Litigation, 982 F.2d 721, 742–743 (2d Cir.1992), modified on reh'g sub nom. In re Findley, 993 F.2d 7 (2d Cir.1993).

The Third Circuit found no assurance here—either in the terms of the settlement or in the structure of the negotiations—that the named plaintiffs operated under a proper understanding of their representational responsibilities. That assessment, we conclude, is on the mark

C

Impediments to the provision of adequate notice, the Third Circuit emphasized, rendered highly problematic any endeavor to tie to a settlement class persons with no perceptible asbestos-related disease at the time of the settlement. Many persons in the exposure-only category, the Court of Appeals stressed, may not even know of their exposure, or realize the extent of the harm they may incur. Even if they fully appreciate the significance of class notice, those without current afflictions may not have the information or foresight needed to decide, intelligently, whether to stay in or opt out.

Family members of asbestos-exposed individuals may themselves fall prey to disease or may ultimately have ripe claims for loss of consortium. Yet large numbers of people in this category—future spouses and children of asbestos victims—could not be alerted to their class membership. And current spouses and children of the occupationally exposed may know nothing of that exposure. Because we have concluded that the class in this case cannot satisfy the requirements of common issue predominance and adequacy of representation, we need not rule, definitively, on the notice given here. In accord with the Third Circuit, however, we recognize the gravity of the question whether class action notice sufficient under the Constitution and Rule 23 could ever be given to legions so unselfconscious and amorphous.

V

The argument is sensibly made that a nationwide administrative claims processing regime would provide the most secure, fair, and efficient means of compensating victims of asbestos exposure. Congress, however, has not adopted such a solution. And Rule 23, which must be interpreted with fidelity to the Rules Enabling Act and applied with the interests of absent class members in close view, cannot carry the large load CCR, class counsel, and the District Court heaped upon it. As this case exemplifies, the rulemakers' prescriptions for class actions may be endangered by "those who embrace [Rule 23] too enthusiastically just as [they are by] those who approach [the rule] with distaste." C. Wright, Law of Federal Courts 508 (5th ed. 1994).

For the reasons stated, the judgment of the Court of Appeals for the Third Circuit is

Affirmed.

■ [Separate opinion of JUSTICE BREYER, with whom JUSTICE STEVENS joins, concurring in part an dissenting in part, omitted.]

C. CURRENT USES AND PROBLEMS OF THE STATE CLASS ACTION

Phillips Petroleum v. Shutts

Supreme Court of the United States, 1985.
472 U.S. 797, 105 S.Ct. 2965, 86 L.Ed.2d 628.

■ JUSTICE REHNQUIST delivered the opinion of the Court.

Petitioner is a Delaware corporation which has its principal place of business in Oklahoma. During the 1970's it produced or purchased natural gas from leased land located in 11 different States, and sold most of the gas in interstate commerce. Respondents are some 28,000 of the royalty owners possessing rights to the leases from which petitioner produced the gas: they reside in all 50 States, the District of Columbia, and several foreign countries. Respondents brought a class action against petitioner in the Kansas state court, seeking to recover interest on royalty payments which had been delayed by petitioner. They recovered judgment in the trial court, and the Supreme Court of Kansas affirmed the judgment over petitioner's contentions that the Due Process Clause of the Fourteenth Amendment prevented Kansas from adjudicating the claims of all the respondents, and that the Due Process Clause and the Full Faith and Credit Clause of Article IV of the Constitution prohibited the application of Kansas law to all of the transactions between petitioner and respondents. 235 Kan. 195, 679 P.2d 1139 (1984). We granted certiorari to consider these claims. 469 U.S. 879, 105 S.Ct. 242, 83 L.Ed.2d 181 (1984). We reject petitioner's jurisdictional claim, but sustain its claim regarding the choice of law.

Because petitioner sold the gas to its customers in interstate commerce, it was required to secure approval for price increases from what was then the Federal Power Commission, and is now the Federal Energy Regulatory Commission. Under its regulations the Federal Power Commission permitted petitioner to propose and collect tentative higher gas prices, subject to final approval by the Commission. If the Commission eventually denied petitioner's proposed price increase or reduced the proposed increase, petitioner would have to refund to its customers the difference between the approved price and the higher price charged, plus interest at a rate set by statute. See 18 CFR § 154.102 (1984).

Although petitioner received higher gas prices pending review by the Commission, petitioner suspended any increase in royalties paid to the royalty owners because the higher price could be subject to recoupment by petitioner's customers. * * * In three written opinions the Commission approved all of petitioner's tentative price increases, so petitioner paid to its royalty owners the suspended royalties of $3.7 million in 1976, $4.7 million in 1977, and $2.9 million in 1978. Petitioner paid no interest to the royalty owners although it had the use of the suspended royalty money for a number of years.

Respondents Iri Shutts, Robert Anderson, and Betty Anderson filed suit against petitioner in Kansas state court, seeking interest payments on their suspended royalties which petitioner had possessed pending the Commission's approval of the price increases. Shutts is a resident of Kansas and the Andersons live in Oklahoma. Shutts and the Andersons own gas leases in Oklahoma and Texas. Over petitioner's objection the Kansas trial court granted respondents motion to certify the suit as a class action under Kansas law. Kan.Stat.Ann. § 60–223 *et seq.* (1983). The class as certified was comprised of 33,000 royalty owners who had royalties suspended by petitioner. The average claim of each royalty owner for interest on the suspended royalties was $100.

After the class was certified respondents provided each class member with notice through first-class mail. The notice described the action and informed each class member that he could appear in person or by counsel; otherwise each member would be represented by Shutts and the Andersons, the named plaintiffs. The notices also stated that class members would be included in the class and bound by the judgment unless they "opted out" of the lawsuit by executing and returning a "request for exclusion" that was included with the notice. The final class as certified contained 23,100 members; 3,400 had "opted out" of the class by returning the request for exclusion, and notice could not be delivered to another 1,500 members, who were also excluded. Less than 1,000 of the class members resided in Kansas. Only a miniscule amount, approximately one quarter of one percent, of the gas leases involved in the lawsuit were on Kansas land.

After petitioner's mandamus petition to decertify the class was denied, Phillips Petroleum v. Duckworth, No. 82–54608 (Kan. June 25, 1982), cert. denied, 439 U.S. 1103, 103 S.Ct. 725, 74 L.Ed.2d 951

(1983), the case was tried to the court. The court found petitioner liable under Kansas law for interest on the suspended royalties to all class members. * * * The trial court did not determine whether any difference existed between the laws of Kansas and other States, or whether another State's laws should be applied to non-Kansas plaintiffs or to royalties from leases in states other than Kansas. 235 Kan., at 221, 679 P.2d at 1180.

Petitioner raised two principal claims in its appeal to the Supreme Court of Kansas. It first asserted that the Kansas trial court did not possess personal jurisdiction over absent plaintiff class members as required by International Shoe Co. v. Washington, 326 U.S. 310, 66 S.Ct. 154, 90 L.Ed. 95 (1945), and similar cases. Related to this first claim was petitioner's contention that the "opt-out" notice to absent class members, which forced them to return the request for exclusion in order to avoid the suit, was insufficient to bind class members who were not residents of Kansas or who did not possess "minimum contacts" with Kansas. Second, petitioner claimed that Kansas courts could not apply Kansas law to every claim in the dispute. The trial court should have looked to the laws of each State where the leases were located to determine, on the basis of conflict of laws principles, whether interest on the suspended royalties was recoverable, and at what rate.

The Supreme Court of Kansas held that the entire cause of action was maintainable under the Kansas class-action statute and the court rejected both of petitioner's claims. * * *

II

Reduced to its essentials, petitioner's argument is that unless out-of-state plaintiffs affirmatively consent, the Kansas courts may not exert jurisdiction over their claims. Petitioner claims that failure to execute and return the "request for exclusion" provided with the class notice cannot constitute consent of the out-of-state plaintiffs: thus Kansas courts may exercise jurisdiction over these plaintiffs only if the plaintiffs possess the sufficient "minimum contacts" with Kansas as that term is used in cases involving personal jurisdiction over out-of-state defendants. E.g., International Shoe Co. v. Washington, 326 U.S. 310, 66 S.Ct. 154, 90 L.Ed. 95 (1945); Shaffer v. Heitner, 433 U.S. 186, 97 S.Ct. 2569, 53 L.Ed.2d 683 (1977); World-wide Volkswagen Corp. v. Woodson, 444 U.S. 286, 100 S.Ct. 559, 62 L.Ed.2d 490 (1980). Since Kansas had no prelitigation contact with many of the plaintiffs and leases involved, petitioner claims that Kansas has exceeded its jurisdictional reach and thereby violated the due process rights of the absent plaintiffs.

In *International Shoe* we were faced with an out-of-state corporation which sought to avoid the exercise of personal jurisdiction over it as a defendant by Washington state court. We held that the extent of the defendant's due process protection would depend "upon the quality and nature of the activity in relation to the fair and orderly administration of the laws * * *." 326 U.S., at 319, 66 S.Ct. at 159. We noted that the Due Process Clause did not permit a State to make a binding judgment against a person with whom the State had no contacts, ties, or relations. *Ibid.* If the defendant possessed certain minimum contacts with the State, so that it was "reasonable and just, according to our traditional conception of fair play and substantial justice" for a State to exercise personal jurisdiction, the State could force the defendant to defend himself in the forum, upon pain of default, and could bind him to a judgment. *Id.,* at 320, 66 S.Ct., at 160.

* * *

Although the cases like *Shaffer* and *Woodson* which petitioner relies on for a minimum contacts requirement all dealt with out-of-state defendants or parties in the procedural posture of a defendant, cf. New York Life Ins. Co. v. Dunlevy, 241 U.S. 518, 36 S.Ct. 613, 60 L.Ed. 1140 (1916); Estin v. Estin, 334 U.S. 541, 68 S.Ct. 1213, 92 L.Ed. 1561 (1948), petitioner claims that the same analysis must apply to absent class-action plaintiffs. In this regard petitioner correctly points out that a chose in action is a constitutionally recognized property interest possessed by each of the plaintiffs. Mullane v. Central Hanover Bank & Trust Co., 339 U.S. 306, 70 S.Ct. 652, 94 L.Ed. 865 (1950). An adverse judgment by Kansas courts in this case may extinguish the chose in action forever through res judicata. Such an adverse judgment, petitioner claims, would be every bit as onerous to an absent plaintiff as an adverse judgment on the merits would be to a defendant. Thus, the same due process protections should apply to absent plaintiffs: Kansas should not be able to exert jurisdiction over the plaintiff's claims unless the plaintiffs have sufficient minimum contacts with Kansas.

We think petitioner's premise is in error. The burdens placed by a State upon an absent class-action plaintiff are not of the same order or magnitude as those it places upon an absent defendant. An out-of-state defendant summoned by a plaintiff is faced with the full powers of the forum State to render judgment *against* it. The defendant must generally hire counsel and travel to the forum to defend itself from the plaintiff's claim, or suffer a default judgment. The defendant may be forced to participate in extended and often costly discovery, and will be forced to respond in damages or to comply with some other form of remedy imposed by the court should it lose the suit. The defendant may also face liability for court costs and attorney's fees. These burdens are substantial, and the minimum contacts requirement of the Due Process Clause prevents the forum State from unfairly imposing them upon the defendant.

A class-action plaintiff, however, is in quite a different posture. The Court noted this difference in Hansberry v. Lee, 311 U.S. 32, 40–41, 61 S.Ct. 115, 117–118, 85 L.Ed. 22 (1940), which explained that a "class" or "representative" suit was an exception to the rule that one could not be bound by judgment *in personam* unless one was made fully a party in the traditional sense. *Ibid.*, citing Pennoyer v. Neff, 95 U.S. (5 Otto) 714, 24 L.Ed. 565 (1978). As the Court pointed out in

Hansberry, the class action was an invention of equity to enable it to proceed to a decree in suits where the number of those interested in the litigation was too great to permit joinder. The absent parties would be bound by the decree so long as the named parties adequately represented the absent class and the prosecution of the litigation was within the common interest. 311 U.S., at 41, 61 S.Ct. at 117.

Modern plaintiff class actions follow the same goals, permitting litigation of a suit involving common questions when there are too many plaintiffs for proper joinder. Class actions also may permit the plaintiffs to pool claims which would be uneconomical to litigate individually. For example, this lawsuit involves claims averaging about $100 per plaintiff; most of the plaintiffs would have no realistic day in court if a class action were not available.

In sharp contrast to the predicament of a defendant haled into an out-of-state forum, the plaintiffs in this suit were not haled anywhere to defend themselves upon pain of a default judgment. As commentators have noted, from the plaintiffs' point of view a class action resembles a "quasi-administrative proceeding, conducted by the judge." 3B J. Moore & J. Kennedy, Moore's Federal Practice ¶ 23.45[4.–5] (1984); Kaplan, Continuing Work of the Civil Committee: 1966 Amendments to the Federal Rules of Civil Procedure (I), 81 Harv.L.Rev. 356, 398 (1967).

A plaintiff class in Kansas and numerous other jurisdictions cannot first be certified unless the judge, with the aid of the named plaintiffs and defendant conducts an inquiry into the common nature of the named plaintiff's and the absent plaintiffs' claims, the adequacy of representation, the jurisdiction possessed over the class, and any other matters that will bear upon proper representation of the absent plaintiffs' interest. See, *e.g.,* Kan.Stat.Ann. § 60–223 (1983); Fed.Rule Civ.Proc. 23. Unlike a defendant in a civil suit, a class-action plaintiff is not required to fend for himself. See Kan.Stat.Ann. § 60–223(d) (1983). The court and named plaintiffs protect his interests. Indeed, the class-action defendant itself has a great interest in ensuring that the absent plaintiff's claims are properly before the forum. In this case, for example, the defendant sought to avoid class certification by alleging that the absent plaintiffs would not be adequately represented and were not amenable to jurisdiction. See Phillips Petroleum v. Duckworth, No. 82–54608 (Kan. June 29, 1982).

The concern of the typical class-action rules for the absent plaintiffs is manifested in other ways. Most jurisdictions, including Kansas, require that a class action, once certified, may not be dismissed or compromised without the approval of the court. In many jurisdictions such as Kansas the court may amend the pleadings to ensure that all sections of the class are represented adequately. Kan.Stat.Ann. § 60–223(d) (1983); see also e.g., Fed.Rule Civ.Proc. 23(d).

Besides this continuing solicitude for their rights, absent plaintiff class members are not subject to other burdens imposed upon defendants. They need not hire counsel or appear. They are almost never subject to counterclaims or cross-claims, or liability for fees or costs.[2] Absent plaintiff class members are not subject to coercive or punitive remedies. Nor will an adverse judgment typically bind an absent plaintiff for any damages, although a valid adverse judgment may extinguish any of the plaintiff's claim which was litigated.

Unlike a defendant in a normal civil suit, an absent class-action plaintiff is not required to do anything. He may sit back and allow the litigation to run its course, content in knowing that there are safe-guards provided for his protection. In most class actions an absent plaintiff is provided at least with an opportunity to "opt out" of the class, and if he takes advantage of that opportunity he is removed from the litigation entirely. This was true of the Kansas proceedings in this case. The Kansas procedure provided for the mailing of a notice to each class member by first-class mail. The notice, as we have previous-ly indicated, described the action and informed the class member that he could appear in person or by counsel, in default of which he would be represented by the named plaintiffs and their attorneys. The notice further stated that class members would be included in the class and bound by the judgment unless they "opted out" by executing and returning a "request for exclusion" that was included in the notice.

Petitioner contends, however, that the "opt out" procedure pro-vided by Kansas is not good enough, and that an "opt in" procedure is required to satisfy the Due Process Clause of the Fourteenth Amend-ment. Insofar as plaintiffs who have no minimum contacts with the forum State are concerned, an "opt in" provision would require that each class member affirmatively consent to his inclusion within the class.

Because States place fewer burdens upon absent class plaintiffs than they do upon absent defendants in nonclass suits, the Due Process Clause need not and does not afford the former as much protection from state-court jurisdiction as it does the latter. The Fourteenth Amendment does protect "persons," not "defendants," however, so absent plaintiffs as well as absent defendants are entitled to some protection from the jurisdiction of a forum State which seeks to adjudicate their claims. In this case we hold that a forum State may exercise jurisdiction over the claim of an absent class-action plaintiff, even though that plaintiff may not possess the minimum contacts with the forum which would support personal jurisdiction over a defen-dant. If the forum State wishes to bind an absent plaintiff concerning a claim for money damages or similar relief at law,[3] it must provide minimal procedural due process protection. The plaintiff must receive

---

2. Petitioner places emphasis on the fact that absent class members might be sub-ject to discovery, counterclaims, cross-claims or court costs. Petitioner cites no cases in-volving any such imposition upon plaintiffs, however. We are convinced that such burdens are rarely imposed upon plaintiff class mem-bers, and that the disposition of these issues is best left to a case which presents them in a more concrete way.

3. Our holding today is limited to those class actions which seek to bind known plain-tiffs concerning claims wholly or predomi-nately for money judgments. We intimate no view concerning other types of class action lawsuits, such as those seeking equitable re-lief. Nor, of course, does our discussion of personal jurisdiction address class actions where the jurisdiction is asserted against a *defendant* class.

notice plus an opportunity to be heard and participate in the litigation, whether in person or through counsel. The notice must be the best practicable, "reasonably calculated, under all the circumstances, to apprise interested parties of the pendency of the action and afford them an opportunity to present their objections." *Mullane,* 399 U.S., at 314–315, 70 S.Ct., at 657; cf. Eisen v. Carlisle & Jacquelin, 417 U.S. 156, 174–175, 94 S.Ct. 2140, 2151, 40 L.Ed.2d 732 (1974). The notice should describe the action and the plaintiffs' rights in it. Additionally, we hold that due process requires at a minimum that an absent plaintiff be provided with an opportunity to remove himself from the class by executing and returning an "opt out" or "request for exclusion" form to the court. Finally, the Due Process Clause of course requires that the named plaintiff at all times adequately represent the interests of the absent class members. *Hansberry,* 311 U.S., at 42–43, 45, 61 S.Ct., at 118–119, 120.

We reject petitioner's contention that the Due Process Clause of the Fourteenth Amendment requires that absent plaintiffs affirmatively "opt in" to the class, rather than be deemed members of the class if they do not "opt out." We think that such a contention is supported by little, if any precedent, and that it ignores the differences between class action plaintiffs, on the one hand, and defendants in non-class civil suits on the other. Any plaintiff may consent to jurisdiction. Keeton v. Hustler Magazine, Inc., 465 U.S. 770, 104 S.Ct. 1473, 79 L.Ed.2d 790 (1984). The essential question, then, is how stringent the requirement for a showing of consent will be.

We think that the procedure followed by Kansas, where a fully descriptive notice is sent first-class mail to each class member, with an explanation of the right to "opt out," satisfies due process. Requiring a plaintiff to affirmatively request inclusion would probably impede the prosecution of those class actions involving an aggregation of small individual claims, where a large number of claims are required to make it economical to bring suit. See, *e.g., Eisen, supra,* 417 U.S., at 161, 94 S.Ct. at 2144. The plaintiff's claim may be so small, or the plaintiff so unfamiliar with the law, that he would not file suit individually, nor would he affirmatively request inclusion in the class if such a request were required by the Constitution. If, on the other hand, the plaintiff's claim is sufficiently large or important that he wishes to litigate it on his own, he will likely have retained an attorney or have thought about filing suit, and should be fully capable of exercising his right to "opt out."

In this case over 3,400 members of the potential class did "opt out," which belies the contention that "opt out" procedures result in guaranteed jurisdiction by inertia. Another 1,500 were excluded because the notice and "opt out" form was undeliverable. We think that such results show that the "opt out" procedure provided by Kansas is by no means *pro forma,* and that the Constitution does not require more to protect what must be the somewhat rare species of class member who is unwilling to execute an "opt out" form, but whose claim is nonetheless so important that he cannot be presumed to consent to being a member of the class by his failure to do so. Petitioner's "opt in" requirement would require the invalidation of scores of state statutes and of the class-action provision of the Federal Rules of Civil Procedure, and for the reasons stated we do not think that the Constitution requires the State to sacrifice the obvious advantages in judicial efficiency resulting from the "opt out" approach for the protection of the *rara avis* portrayed by petitioner.

We therefore hold that the protection afforded the plaintiff class members by the Kansas statute satisfies the Due Process Clause. The interests of the absent plaintiffs are sufficiently protected by the forum State when those plaintiffs are provided with a request for exclusion that can be returned within a reasonable time to the court. See Insurance Corp. of Ireland, 456 U.S., at 702–703, and n. 10, 102 S.Ct. at 2104–2105, and n. 10. Both the Kansas trial court and the Supreme Court of Kansas held that the class received adequate representation, and no party disputes that conclusion here. We conclude that the Kansas court properly asserted personal jurisdiction over the absent plaintiffs and their claims against petitioner.

III

The Kansas courts applied Kansas contract and Kansas equity law to every claim in this case, notwithstanding that over 99% of the gas leases and some 97% of the plaintiffs in the case had no apparent connection to the State of Kansas except for this lawsuit. Petitioner protested that the Kansas courts should apply the laws of the States where the leases were located, or at least apply Texas and Oklahoma law because so many of the leases came from those States. The Kansas courts disregarded this contention and found petitioner liable for interest on the suspended royalties as a matter of Kansas law, and set the interest rates under Kansas equity principles.

Petitioner contends that total application of Kansas substantive law violated the constitutional limitations on choice of law mandated by the Due Process Clause of the Fourteenth Amendment and the Full Faith and Credit Clause of Article IV, § 1. We must first determine whether Kansas law conflicts in any material way with any other law which could apply. There can be no injury in applying Kansas law if it is not in conflict with that of any other jurisdiction connected to this suit.

[After determining that the law of Kansas was potentially in conflict with that of other states, the Court went on the state:]

* * * We think that the Supreme Court of Kansas erred in deciding on the basis that it did that the application of its laws to all claims would be constitutional.

Four Terms ago we addressed a similar situation in Allstate Ins. Co. v. Hague, 449 U.S. 302, 101 S.Ct. 633, 66 L.Ed.2d 521 (1981). In that case we were confronted with two conflicting rules of state insurance law. Minnesota permitted the "stacking" of separate uninsured motorist policies while Wisconsin did not. Although the decedent lived in Wisconsin, took out insurance policies and was killed there, he was employed in Minnesota and after his death his widow moved to Minnesota for reasons unrelated to the litigation, and was appointed personal representative of his estate. She filed suit in Minnesota courts, which applied the Minnesota stacking rule.

The plurality in *Allstate* noted that a particular set of facts giving rise to litigation could justify, constitutionally, the application of more than one jurisdiction's laws. The plurality recognized, however, that the Due Process Clause and the Full Faith and Credit Clause provided modest restrictions on the application of forum law. These restrictions required "that for a State's substantive law to be selected in a constitutionally permissible manner, that State must have a significant contact or significant aggregation of contacts, creating state interests, such that choice of its law is neither arbitrary nor fundamentally unfair." *Id.*, at 312–313, 101 S.Ct. at 639–640. The dissenting Justices were in substantial agreement with this principle. *Id.*, at 332, 101 S.Ct., at 650 (opinion of Powell, J., joined by Burger, C.J., and Rehnquist, J.). The dissent stressed that the Due Process Clause prohibited the application of law which was only casually or slightly related to the litigation, while the Full Faith and Credit Clause required the forum to respect the laws and judgments of other States, subject to the forum's own interests in furthering its public policy. *Id.*, at 333–336, 101 S.Ct. at 651–652.

The plurality in *Allstate* affirmed the application of Minnesota law because of the forum's significant contacts to the litigation which supported the State's interest in applying its law. *See id.* at 313–329, 101 S.Ct. at 640–648. Kansas contacts to this litigation, as explained by the Kansas Supreme Court, can be gleaned from the opinion below.

Petitioner owns property and conducts substantial business in the State, so Kansas certainly has an interest in regulating petitioner's conduct in Kansas. 223 Kan., at 210, 679 P.2d at 1174. Moreover, oil and gas extraction is an important business to Kansas, and although only a few leases in issue are located in Kansas, hundreds of Kansas plaintiffs were affected by petitioner's suspension of royalties; thus the court held that the State has a real interest in protecting "the rights of these royalty owners both as individual residents of [Kansas] and as members of this particular class of plaintiffs." *Id.*, at 211–212, 679 P.2d, at 1174. The Kansas Supreme Court pointed out that Kansas courts are quite familiar with this type of lawsuit, and "[t]he plaintiff class members have indicated their desire to have this action determined under the laws of Kansas." *Id.*, at 211, 222, 679 P.2d, at 1174, 1181. Finally, the Kansas court buttressed its use of Kansas law by stating that this lawsuit was analogous to a suit against a "common fund" located in Kansas. *Id.*, at 201, 211–212, 679 P.2d, at 1168, 1174.

We do not lightly discount this description of Kansas' contacts with this litigation and its interest in applying its law. There is, however, no "common fund" located in Kansas that would require or support the application of only Kansas law to all these claims. *See, e.g.,* Hartford Life Ins. Co. v. Ibs, 237 U.S. 662, 35 S.Ct. 692, 59 L.Ed. 1165

(1915). As the Kansas court noted, petitioner commingled the suspended royalties with its general corporate accounts. 235 Kan., at 201, 679 P.2d, at 1168. There is no specific identifiable res in Kansas, nor is there any limited amount which may be depleted before every plaintiff is compensated. Only by somehow aggregating all the separate claims in this case could a "common fund" in any sense be created, and the term becomes all but meaningless when used in such an expansive sense.

We also give little credence to the idea that Kansas law should apply to all claims because the plaintiffs, by failing to opt out, evinced their desire to be bound by Kansas law. Even if one could say that the plaintiffs "consented" to the application of Kansas law by not opting out, plaintiff's desire for forum law is rarely, if ever controlling. In most cases the plaintiff shows his obvious wish for forum law by filing there. "If a plaintiff could choose the substantive rules to be applied to an action * * * the invitation to forum shopping would be irresistible." *Allstate,* 449 U.S., at 337, 101 S.Ct., at 652 (opinion of POWELL, J.). Even if a plaintiff evidences his desire for forum law by moving to the forum, we have generally accorded such a move little or no significance. John Hancock Mut. Life Ins. Co. v. Yates, 299 U.S. 178, 182, 57 S.Ct. 129, 131, 81 L.Ed. 106 (1936); Home Ins. Co. v. Dick, 281 U.S. 397, 408, 50 S.Ct. 338, 341, 74 L.Ed. 926 (1930). In *Allstate* the plaintiff's move to the forum was only relevant because it was unrelated and prior to the litigation. 449 U.S., at 318–319, 101 S.Ct., at 643. Thus the plaintiffs' desire for Kansas law, manifested by their participation in this Kansas lawsuit, bears little relevance.

The Supreme Court of Kansas in its opinion in this case expressed the view that by reason of the fact that it was adjudicating a nationwide class action, it had much greater latitude in applying its own law to the transactions in question than might otherwise be the case:

> "The general rule is that the law of the forum applies unless it is expressly shown that a different law governs, and in case of doubt, the law of the forum is preferred * * *. Where a state court determines it has jurisdiction over a nationwide class action and procedural due process guarantees of notice and adequate representation are present, we believe the law of the forum should be applied unless compelling reasons exist for applying a different law * * *. Compelling reasons do not exist to require this court to look to other state laws to determine the rights of the parties involved in this lawsuit." 235 Kan., at 221–222, 679 P.2d, at 1181.

We think that this is something of a "bootstrap" argument. The Kansas class-action statute, like those of most other jurisdictions, requires that there be "common issues of law or fact." But while a state may, for the reasons we have previously stated, assume jurisdiction over the claims of plaintiffs whose principal contacts are with other States, it may not use this assumption of jurisdiction as an added weight in the scale when considering the permissible constitutional limits on choice of substantive law. It may not take a transaction with little or no relationship to the forum and apply the law of the forum in order to satisfy the procedural requirement that there be a "common question of law." The issue of personal jurisdiction over plaintiffs in a class action is entirely distinct from the question of the constitutional limitations on choice of law; the latter calculus is not altered by the fact that it may be more difficult or more burdensome to comply with the constitutional limitations because of the large number of transactions which the State proposes to adjudicate and which have little connection with the forum.

Kansas must have a "significant contact or aggregation of contacts" to the claims asserted by each member of the plaintiff class, contacts "creating state interests" in order to ensure that the choice of Kansas law is not arbitrary or unfair. *Allstate, supra,* 449 U.S., at 312–313, 101 S.Ct., at 639–640. Given Kansas' lack of "interest" in claims unrelated to that State, and the substantive conflict with jurisdictions such as Texas, we conclude that application of Kansas law to every claim in this case is sufficiently arbitrary and unfair as to exceed constitutional limits.

When considering fairness in this context, an important element is the expectation of the parties. See *Allstate, supra,* 449 U.S., at 333, 101 S.Ct., at 650 (opinion of Powell, J.). There is no indication that when the leases involving land and royalty owners outside of Kansas were executed, the parties had any idea that Kansas law would control. Neither the Due Process Clause nor the Full Faith and Credit Clause requires Kansas "to substitute for its own [laws], applicable to persons and events within it, the conflicting statute of another state," Pacific Employers Insurance Co. v. Industrial Accident Commission, 306 U.S. 493, 502, 59 S.Ct. 629, 633, 83 L.Ed. 940 (1939), but Kansas "may not abrogate the rights of parties beyond its borders having no relation to anything done or to be done within them." Home Insurance Co. v. Dick, *supra,* 281 U.S., at 410, 50 S.Ct. at 342.

Here the Supreme Court of Kansas took the view that in a nationwide class action where procedural due process guarantees of notice and adequate representation were met, "the laws of the forum should be applied unless compelling reasons exist for applying a different law." 235 Kan. at 221, 679 P.2d at 1181. Whatever practical reasons may have commended this rule to the Supreme Court of Kansas, for the reasons already stated we do not believe that it is consistent with the decisions of this Court. We make no effort to determine for ourselves which law must apply to the various transactions involved in this lawsuit, and we reaffirm our observation in *Allstate* that in many situations a state court may be free to apply one of several choices of law. But the constitutional limitations laid down in cases such as *Allstate* and Home Insurance Co. v. Dick, supra, must be respected even in a nationwide class action.

We therefore affirm the judgment of the Supreme Court of Kansas insofar as it upheld the jurisdiction of the Kansas courts over the plaintiff class members in this case, and reverse its judgment insofar as it held that Kansas law was applicable to all of the transactions which it sought to adjudicate. We remand the case to that Court for further proceedings not inconsistent with this opinion.[a]

D. COMPULSORY JOINDER—INDISPENSABLE PARTIES

Local 670 v. International Union, United Rubber

United States Court of Appeals, Sixth Circuit, 1987.
822 F.2d 613.

■ RALPH B. GUY, JR., Circuit Judge.

Local 670 of the United Rubber, Cork, Linoleum and Plastic Workers of America (URW) appeals the dismissal of its hybrid breach of contract/duty of fair representation claim pursuant to section 301 of the Labor Management Relations Act, 29 U.S.C. §§ 185 and 159(a). The district court, after a hearing on the matter, specifically found Local 670's grievance to be arbitrable but dismissed the suit in its entirety due to its inability to join a sister local out of California (Local 703), which the court found to be an indispensable party under Fed.R.Civ.P. 19 without which the court could not, in equity and good conscience, proceed. The employer, Armstrong Rubber Company (company) cross-appeals the finding of arbitrability. Although we agree that Local 670's claim is properly arbitrable, we find the district court's dismissal due to the absence of Local 703 improper under the circumstances of this case. Therefore, the decision below is affirmed in part and reversed in part, and the case is hereby remanded to the district court for further proceedings in accordance with this opinion.

I.

The facts relative to this appeal are simple and largely undisputed. Local 670, an unincorporated labor organization with principal offices in Madison, Tennessee, is one of five URW locals signatory to a master collective bargaining agreement with the company. Together the five locals comprise what is known as the "Armstrong chain," a nationwide group of local unions bargaining in concert with a common employer. The actual contract negotiating is conducted through the International Policy Committee (IPC), on which each local has at least one representative. In addition to the single master agreement, each local union also enters into local supplemental agreements addressing issues specific to that local and supplementing, but not contradicting or amending, the master agreement.

The underlying dispute centers on events during and just after negotiations for the parties' 1985 master agreement. A few weeks after all parties had signed both the master agreement and all five local supplemental agreements, the company approached Local 703 of

---

a. Opinion of Justice Stevens, concurring in part and dissenting in part, is omitted.

Hanford, California, in an attempt to enter into a wage reduction agreement with that local due to the unprofitability of the California plant. The company contended that, due to excess production capacity, the Hanford operation would be closed unless significant wage reductions were accepted. The company and Local 703 drafted two versions of the wage reduction agreement (the Hanford memoranda). The first Hanford memorandum provided that the agreement was "subject to approval by a majority of the local unions representing a majority of the membership and the International Executive Board." This memorandum was then submitted to a vote of the entire Armstrong chain and was soundly defeated. Immediately thereafter, the parties prepared the second Hanford memorandum with an even larger wage reduction objective than the first. In this memo, however, there was no longer a statement regarding the necessity of majority approval. The agreement was framed as one involving "labor grade changes," stating as follows:

> [I]n accordance with longstanding and clearly established practices by the parties and consistent with the Collective Bargaining Agreement, the Company and Union have negotiated the following labor grade changes for each specific job classification listed below * * *.

Despite deletion of the approval language, the International again submitted this memorandum to a majority vote. It was again defeated by a majority vote of all five locals, although it was approved by a majority of the members of Local 703. At this point, and with the approval of the vice-president of the International, the company implemented the agreement.

It was and is Local 670's contention that, by the express terms of the 1985 master agreement, the company had no right to alter the basic wage structure of one local in a local supplemental agreement, and, further, that the only way that any local supplemental agreement can be altered is upon approval by a majority of the local unions representing a majority of the union membership in the Armstrong chain. Because the International had been active in effecting the implementation of the Hanford agreement, Local 670 filed an internal union appeal against it for violations of Local 670's rights under the union constitution. The International Executive Board denied the appeal, stating in part that, since their "argument as to the proper interpretation of Paragraph 56 is obviously one of contract and not Constitutional interpretation ... the proper remedy is to pursue the matter through the grievance procedure."

On the day its internal union appeal was denied, the company laid off 64 members of Local 670. It is Local 670's contention that these layoffs were a direct result of the implementation of the drastic wage reductions accomplished by agreement with Local 703 in California. Local 670 then filed a grievance challenging the implementation of the Hanford memorandum and the attendant layoffs pursuant to Article VI of the master agreement. The company refused to process the grievance stating in part, "we do not think that Local 670 as a representative of the International, is in a position to claim that a breach has occurred." Local 670 then initiated the instant suit, after which the company furloughed an additional 141 employees from the Madison, Tennessee plant, bringing the number of displaced workers to over two hundred.

Defendants interposed motions to dismiss for failure to state a claim and failure to join an indispensable party, Local 703. Although the court found that the complaint stated a claim and that the company should be ordered to submit the grievance to arbitration, it further found that Local 703 was an indispensable party within the meaning of Fed.R.Civ.P. 19(a) since "it is the other contracting party with the defendant, Armstrong Rubber Company, in the contract which is the subject of the grievance which the court is directing to be arbitrated." It therefore ordered Local 670 to join Local 703 within ten days. Local 670 issued a summons and complaint to Local 703, along with a letter in which it offered to arbitrate the grievance in California at Local 703's customary site for arbitrations. Although Local 703 did not respond to the offer to arbitrate in California, they did file a motion to quash the service of summons due to lack of personal jurisdiction.

After a further hearing, the district court issued its second order, concluding that the court lacked personal jurisdiction over Local 703 and that its presence was so essential to the proceedings that the court was unable to satisfactorily resolve the issues or fashion an adequate remedy in its absence. Noting that "it appears that Local 670 has the ability to pursue its claims elsewhere," the court dismissed the suit.

II.

Arbitrability of the Grievance

* * *

We agree with the district court's finding that the grievance involves a dispute as to the "meaning, interpretation, scope, or application" of the 1985 master agreement and, as such, is clearly subject to arbitration. As the Supreme Court has recently reaffirmed, the presumption of arbitrability applies when, as here, the agreement contains a broad arbitration clause and there is no "express provision excluding a particular grievance from arbitration." *AT & T Technologies*, 106 S.Ct. at 1419. The Court reiterated that, in such cases, "only the most forceful evidence of a purpose to exclude the claim from arbitration can prevail * * * " *Id.* (quoting *Warrior & Gulf*, 363 U.S. at 584–85, 80 S.Ct. at 1353–54).

The company's claim that this dispute is a non-arbitrable internal union matter is without merit. Because the second Hanford memorandum was approved for implementation by the International's vice-president, the company now alleges that ratification of the agreement was strictly a union matter. However, the International's involvement does not relieve the company, as a party to the 1985 master agreement, of its duties thereunder. It is apparent that the company was well aware of the initial attempts to obtain approval of the Hanford agreement by vote of the membership of all five locals; therefore, it will not now be heard to say that it merely relied in good faith on assurances by the International concerning the required approval process. *See* Parker v. Local 413, International Brotherhood of Teamsters, 501 F.Supp. 440, 450 (S.D.Ohio 1980), *aff'd without opinion,* 657 F.2d 269 (6th Cir.1981) (acquiescence in challenged conduct with full knowledge of facts is not "good faith" reliance on union representations).

III.

Joinder of Local 703 and Rule 19 Dismissal

Assessment of the question of joinder under Rule 19 involves a three-step process. Initially, the court determines whether a person who is not a party should be joined in the action if possible. This first step is embodied in Rule 19(a): * * * If the court determines that the person or entity does not fall within one of these provisions, joinder, as well as further analysis, is unnecessary. However, if the court finds one of the criteria is satisfied, the person is one to be joined if feasible and the issue of the existence of personal jurisdiction arises. If personal jurisdiction is present, the party *shall* be joined; however, in the absence of personal jurisdiction (or if venue as to the joined party is improper), the party cannot properly be brought before the court. If such is the case, the court proceeds to the third step, which involves an analysis of the factors set forth in Rule 19(b) to determine whether the court may proceed without the absent party or, to the contrary, must dismiss the case due to the indispensability of that party. The four factors set forth in Rule 19(b) include:

> first, to what extent a judgment rendered in the person's absence might be prejudicial to him or those already parties; second, the extent to which, by protective provisions in the judgment, by the shaping of relief, or other measures, the prejudice can be lessened or avoided; third, whether a judgment rendered in the person's absence will be adequate; fourth, whether the plaintiff will have an adequate remedy if the action is dismissed for nonjoinder.

The rule is not to be applied in a rigid manner but should instead be governed by the practicalities of the individual case. Provident Tradesmens Bank & Trust Co. v. Patterson, 390 U.S. 102, 116 n. 12, 88 S.Ct. 733, 741, 19 L.Ed.2d 936 (1968). This court has noted that "[i]deally, all [the] parties would be before the court. Yet Rule 19 calls for a pragmatic approach; simply because some forms of relief might not be available due to the absence of certain parties, the entire suit should not be dismissed if meaningful relief can still be accorded." Smith v. United Brotherhood of Carpenters and Joiners of America, 685 F.2d 164, 166 (6th Cir.1982) (holding it error to have dismissed Title VII case due to absence of contractors hiring through union).

Before turning to our Rule 19 analysis, two issues require some clarification: our standard of review and the importance of the context of this hybrid section 301/unfair representation claim. With respect to the appropriate standard of review, we observe that this court has implicitly adopted the abuse of discretion standard for Rule 19 issues. See Jenkins v. Reneau, 697 F.2d 160, 163 (6th Cir.1983). However, this court and others have found "error" in a district court's dismissal under Rule 19 without resort to the abuse of discretion standard. Moreover, a determination that a party is "indispensable," thereby requiring dismissal of an action, represents a legal conclusion reached after balancing the prescribed factors under Rule 19. See e.g., Challenge Homes, Inc. v. Greater Naples Care Center, Inc., 669 F.2d 667, 669 n. 3 (11th Cir.1982). In that sense, it becomes a conclusion of law which this court reviews *de novo.* Taylor and Gaskin v. Chris–Craft Industries, 732 F.2d 1273, 1277 (6th Cir.1984). We note in this regard that the district court's conclusion that it was Local 703's contract with Armstrong that was "the subject of the grievance which the court is directing to be arbitrated" was also a conclusion of law reviewable by us *de novo.*

Insofar as context is concerned, it is important to keep in mind that this is a suit to determine whether the parties are required to submit their underlying dispute to arbitration, and not a ruling on the substantive dispute itself. Indeed, a court is *precluded* from ruling on the potential merits of the underlying claim. *AT & T Technologies,* 106 S.Ct. at 1419. Both this court and the district court have concluded that the dispute at issue is arbitrable. Under the parties' master collective bargaining agreement, to which all five locals are signatory, the parties have agreed to the voluntary dispute resolution process of binding arbitration. Arbitration takes place systemwide throughout the five-plant Armstrong chain, with an arbitrator chosen from a set panel of five persons agreed upon by all the parties.

This context is significant in at least two respects. First, unlike the vast majority of cases under Rule 19, in which the merits of a particular dispute are to be reached in the same forum which is applying Rule 19, here there is inevitably a two-tiered process. The role of the district court is solely to determine whether the parties have agreed to arbitrate a given dispute, whether there has been a breach of that agreement, and to compel arbitration if the answer to both of these questions is affirmative. The second tier occurs when, after the district court compels arbitration, the arbitrator adjudicates the parties' substantive claims pursuant to the voluntary dispute resolution process already agreed to by the parties. As a practical matter then, Local 703's substantive rights ultimately can be determined only by a procedure to which it already voluntarily has committed itself as one of five local unions in the Armstrong chain.

Second, the context is significant because of the compelling federal labor policy of requiring parties to honor their promises to arbitrate. The Supreme Court established long ago that an employer could be compelled to arbitrate a jurisdictional dispute, in which two separate unions laid claim to the same work under two different collective bargaining agreements, when only one of the unions was before the court. The Court reasoned:

> To be sure, only one of the two unions involved in the controversy has moved the state courts to compel arbitration. So unless the other union intervenes, the adjudication of the arbiter might not put an end to the dispute. *Yet the arbitration may as a practical matter end the controversy or put into movement forces that will resolve it.*

Carey v. Westinghouse Electric Corp., 375 U.S. 261, 265, 84 S.Ct. 401, 406, 11 L.Ed.2d 320 (1964) (emphasis added). Despite the possibility of a conflicting subsequent award, and implicitly, despite the absent union's interest, the Supreme Court in *Carey* held that the employer was compelled to arbitrate. The Court's focus on the practical realities of the arbitration process underscored the "pervasive, curative effect" of the voluntary dispute resolution process lying at the heart of federal labor relations. *Id.* at 272, 84 S.Ct. at 409.[7] The facts of the present case must be analyzed against the foregoing backdrop.

A. *Is Local 703 a "Party to be Joined if Feasible"?*

This is an extremely close issue. Local 703 clearly does not satisfy the criteria of Rule 19(a)(1) because complete relief (i.e., an order either compelling or denying arbitration) can be accorded to the parties before the court. However, under Rule 19(a)(2), Local 703's interest in upholding the validity of its wage reduction agreement and, thereby, the continuation of its workers' jobs, is sufficiently "related to" the subject of the action (the question of arbitrability) to make its joinder desirable. Further, we find that the company's risk of incurring inconsistent obligations as a result of arbitrating the question of the validity of its subsequent bilateral agreement without Local 703's presence also renders joinder the preferable course. Local 670 argues persuasively that the company's risk would *not* be substantial, due to the deference traditionally accorded previous arbitration findings as well as principles of collateral estoppel potentially applicable to local 703 in the face of its refusal to intervene in a proceeding which affects its interest in the contract and of which it clearly had notice. However, we do not consider it wise to subject the company to even this level of risk where, as here, it is easily avoided.[8]

---

7. Since this case arose in state court, no explicit Rule 19 analysis was applied. However, the Court's rationale and its recognition of the unique aspects of the labor arbitration context are highly relevant to Rule 19 analysis. The District of Columbia Circuit recently relied on *Carey* in holding that the lower court erred in enjoining a scheduled arbitration because of the possibility that a party would be subject to inconsistent arbitration awards. In re Meba Pacific Coast District, 114 L.R.R.M. 3431, 3436 (D.C.Cir.1983).

8. We stress that we consider it highly questionable whether Local 703 even qualifies as a person to be joined if feasible under Rule 19(a). However, Local 670 has voluntarily offered to participate in the arbitration proceeding in California, Local 703's home state. Therefore, due to the ease of fashioning relief under Rule 19(b) which will serve the interests of all the parties involved, we assume, without deciding, that Local 703 qualifies for joinder under Rule 19(a).

B. *Could the Court Obtain Personal Jurisdiction Over Local 703?*

We answer this question in the negative. In ruling on the jurisdictional issue, the district court interpreted section 301(c), 29 U.S.C. § 185(c), by its literal terms as defining the court's jurisdiction for the action to which Local 703 was joined.[9] The court then held that under the guidelines of section 301(c) it did not have jurisdiction over Local 703 and, therefore, it could not properly be joined in the action.

The parties now dispute whether section 301(c) is truly a jurisdictional statute or one which merely establishes proper venue for suits by and against labor organizations. Several courts have held, explicitly or implicitly, that the statute relates only to venue, and does not confine the jurisdictional inquiry. *See, e.g.,* Barefoot v. International Brotherhood of Teamsters, 424 F.2d 1001, 1002 (10th Cir.1970) (section constitutes venue provision); United Rubber, Cork, Linoleum and Plastic Workers of America v. Lee Rubber and Tire Corp., 394 F.2d 362, 364 (3d Cir.), *cert. denied,* 393 U.S. 835, 89 S.Ct. 106, 21 L.Ed.2d 105 (1968) (Congress referring to venue rather than jurisdiction); American Federation of Labor v. Western Union Telegraph Co., 179 F.2d 535, 536 (6th Cir.1950) (section sets forth where such actions may be *brought*). However, the analysis required under either section 301(c) or the traditional rules of "minimum contacts" is so similar as to render this issue a distinction without a difference.[10]

The trial court's analysis under section 301(c) included a consideration of Local 703's alleged "contacts" with Tennessee, including the facts that (1) it was a signatory of the 1985 master agreement; (2) it is a member of the IPC of the International Union; and (3) representatives of the International visited Tennessee "on Local 703's behalf" to advocate their position. The court found these contacts insufficient under section 301(c) and, in addition, declined to assert jurisdiction on the basis of Local 703's affiliation with the International alone, since such a ruling would obligate each local to defend lawsuits in every state in which the International has done business.[11] We agree.

---

9. Section 301(c) provides:

Jurisdiction

(c) For the purposes of actions and proceedings by or against labor organizations in the district courts of the United States, district courts shall be deemed to have jurisdiction of a labor organization (1) in the district in which such organization maintains its principal office, or (2) in any district in which its duly authorized officers or agents are engaged in representing or acting for employee members.

10. In support, we observe that Rule 19(a) specifically provides for the dismissal of a desirable party, upon objection, in all cases where "joinder would render the venue of the action improper."

11. We do not mean to imply that as International Union cannot exercise sufficient control and dominion over its member locals as to support a finding that they effectively act as an agent for each individual local in dealing with other locals. Such a theory might prevail upon a showing that the International so substantially participated in, condoned, ratified, or aided a particular local, at the request or instigation of the local, as to impute the International's actions for its benefit to that local. *See Bacino v. American Federation of Musicians,* 107 F.Supp. 548, 553–54 (N.D.Ill.1976). However, the International's actions here, which apparently consisted of polling the individual locals on their views as to whether Local 703's wage agreement was required to be put to a vote of all five units, does not rise to the requisite level to invoke agency status.

We acknowledge that the absence of physical contacts alone will not defeat jurisdiction if a commercial actor has purposefully directed activities toward out-of-state citizens and litigation results from injuries arising out of, or relating to, those activities. *See* Burger King Corp. v. Rudzswicz, 471 U.S. 462, 476, 105 S.Ct. 2174, 2184, 85 L.Ed.2d 528 (1985). However, Local 703 does not fit the traditional mold of a "commercial actor" in that its acts do not result in generating profit for its members by virtue of its out-of-state solicitations. Further, we cannot find that Local 703 in any sense "purposefully availed" itself of the privilege of conducting activities in Tennessee. *See* Asahi Metal Industry Co., Ltd. v. Superior Court of California, 480 U.S. 102, 107 S.Ct. 1026, 94 L.Ed.2d 92 (1987); World–Wide Volkswagen Corp. v. Woodson, 444 U.S. 286, 100 S.Ct. 559, 62 L.Ed.2d 490 (1980). In sum, we find Local 703's contacts with Tennessee to have been so attenuated as to insulate it from being forced to submit to suit there via the application of either section 301(c) or Tennessee's long-arm statute.[12] International Shoe Co. v. Washington, 326 U.S. 310, 316, 66 S.Ct. 154, 158, 90 L.Ed. 95 (1945).

C. *Was Local 703 an Indispensable Party?*

Analysis of the four factors of Rule 19(b) compels the conclusion that Local 703 was *not* an indispensable party to this action. In this regard, it is crucial to understand that Local 703's interest is its presence, not in the federal district court proceeding to compel arbitration, but in the actual arbitration that may affect any substantive rights it has regarding the Hanford agreement. This is the point which was misapprehended by the district court and which led it to conclude that Local 703 was an indispensable party to *this* action. The contract between Local 703 and Armstrong is *not* the contract which is the subject of Local 670's grievance here. Rather, the company's negotiation of that side agreement is merely the factual predicate for its claim that the company breached its master collective bargaining agreement *with Local 670.* So understood, it becomes clear that the contract between Local 703 and Armstrong is wholly collateral to the issue in this proceeding, which is the arbitrability of the alleged breach of the contract between the company and Local 670.

As counsel for Local 670 pointed out in oral argument, this is a two-tiered proceeding. In this first tier, no conclusion is reached as to the substantive rights of *any* of the parties. Our *sole* task is to determine whether Local 670 has succeeded in demonstrating that it and the company intended that this breach of contract claim be resolved through the process of arbitration. While Local 703's pres-

12. In pertinent part, Tenn.Code Ann. § 20–2–214 (1980) provides:

> 20–2–214 *Jurisdiction of persons unavailable to personal service in state— classes of actions to which actionable.—* (a) Persons who are nonresidents of Tennessee and residents of Tennessee who are outside the state and cannot be personally served with process within the state are subject to the jurisdiction of the courts of this state as to any action or claim for relief arising from:

> * * *

> (6) Any basis not inconsistent with the constitution of this state or of the United States.

ence at the arbitration proceeding may arguably be deemed "indispensable," that is not a question before the court at this time. Local 703's interest in *this* proceeding is adequately represented by the company, which has the identical interest in not only avoiding arbitration, with its attendant risk of voiding the Hanford agreement, but also in proceeding to arbitration, if necessary, in a location where Local 703 may participate so that the rights and duties of the company with respect to both locals can be effectively determined. Clearly, then, the district court erred in this portion of its analysis by looking solely to the consequences of the substantive outcome of an arbitration hearing conducted in Local 703's absence.[13]

The second provision of Rule 19(b) specifically confers upon the court the power to include "protective provisions in the judgment" to lessen or avoid any prejudice. Here, any prejudice to Local 703 of participating in an arbitration proceeding in Tennessee can be totally eliminated by ordering that the arbitration be held in California, a proposal already advanced by Local 670.[14] Such an order would be adequate to insure that the interests of all three parties are protected in the subsequent arbitration proceeding, thereby satisfying the third Rule 19(b) factor.

Finally, although it appears that Local 670 did have an alternate forum available at the time of the district court's dismissal, which occurred approximately four and one-half months after the likely accrual date of its cause of action, *see* DelCostello v. International Brotherhood of Teamsters, 462 U.S. 151, 103 S.Ct. 2281, 76 L.Ed.2d 476 (1983), that possibility was not clearly established. Upon filing in another court, Local 670 could have been subjected to claims of a statute of limitations bar depending on the date on which its claim was held to have begun accruing. *See* Shapiro v. Cook United, Inc., 762 F.2d 49 (6th Cir.1985) (claim accrues under section 10(b) when party discovers, or should have discovered, acts constituting alleged violation). Moreover, the potential existence of another forum does not, in and of itself, outweigh a plaintiff's right to the forum of his or her choice. Some additional interest of either the absent party, the other properly joined parties or entities, or the judicial system must also be present. *Pasco International,* 637 F.2d at 501.

13. Illustratively, the court stated that: "Although concerned with the loss of jobs by the workers represented by Local 670, the Court shares the same concern for the welfare of the workers at Armstrong's Hanford, California plant. Specifically, this Court is concerned that a ruling in Tennessee may result in job losses at the Hanford plant, despite the lack of any participation by Local 703 in the Tennessee decision-making process."

14. Local 670 additionally proffers the suggestion that the district court direct the company and Local 670 to agree that the company would petition the arbitrator unop-posed for an interpleader to compel Local 703's attendance as a party to the arbitration. Given that all the parties are signatories to the same master agreement, which gives a panel of designated arbitrators the commission to issue final and binding resolutions, it does not appear that an arbitral interpleader would face any jurisdictional bars. However, this is an issue for the district court to consider and, in view of the fact that we have indicated that the arbitration should be ordered conducted in California, any further attempt to insure Local 703's presence may be superfluous.

Based on the foregoing, this case is REMANDED to the district court for the entry of an appropriate order compelling arbitration under circumstances which will protect the interests of all involved parties. It will further be necessary for the district court to address Local 670's other contentions and claims for relief, e.g., its requests for the production of documents, injunctive relief, and damages, in conjunction with its order. We leave resolution of these ancillary matters to the district court's discretion.

Temple v. Synthes Corp., Ltd.

Supreme Court of the United States, 1990.
498 U.S. 5, 111 S.Ct. 315, 112 L.Ed.2d 263.

■ PER CURIAM.

Petitioner Temple, a Mississippi resident, underwent surgery in October 1986 in which a "plate and screw device" was implanted in his lower spine. The device was manufactured by respondent Synthes, Ltd. (U.S.A.) (Synthes), a Pennsylvania corporation. Dr. S. Henry LaRocca performed the surgery at St. Charles General Hospital in New Orleans, Louisiana. Following surgery, the device's screws broke off inside Temple's back.

Temple filed suit against Synthes in the United States District Court for the Eastern District of Louisiana. The suit, which rested on diversity jurisdiction, alleged defective design and manufacture of the device. At the same time, Temple filed a state administrative proceeding against Dr. LaRocca and the hospital for malpractice and negligence. At the conclusion of the administrative proceeding, Temple filed suit against the doctor and the hospital in Louisiana state court.

Synthes did not attempt to bring the doctor and the hospital into the federal action by means of a third-party complaint, as provided in Federal Rule of Civil Procedure 14(a). Instead, Synthes filed a motion to dismiss Temple's federal suit for failure to join necessary parties pursuant to Federal Rule of Civil Procedure 19. Following a hearing, the District Court ordered Temple to join the doctor and the hospital as defendants within twenty days or risk dismissal of the lawsuit. According to the court, the most significant reason for requiring joinder was the interest of judicial economy. App. C to Pet. for Cert. A–12. The court relied on this Court's decision in Provident Tradesmens Bank & Trust Co. v. Patterson, 390 U.S. 102, 88 S.Ct. 733, 19 L.Ed.2d 936 (1968), wherein we recognized that one focus of Rule 19 is "the interest of the courts and the public in complete, consistent, and efficient settlement of controversies." *Id.*, at 111, 88 S.Ct., at 739. When Temple failed to join the doctor and the hospital, the court dismissed the suit with prejudice.

Temple appealed, and the United States Court of Appeals for the Fifth Circuit affirmed. 898 F.2d 152 (1990) (judgment order). The court deemed it "obviously prejudicial to the defendants to have the separate litigations being carried on," because Synthes' defense might be that the plate was not defective but that the doctor and the hospital were negligent, while the doctor and hospital, on the other hand, might claim that they were not negligent but that the plate was defective. App. A to Pet. for Cert. A–3. The Court of Appeals found that the claims overlapped and that the District Court therefore had not abused its discretion in ordering joinder under Rule 19. A petition for rehearing was denied.

In his petition for certiorari to this Court, Temple contends that it was error to label joint tortfeasors as indispensable parties under Rule 19(b) and to dismiss the lawsuit with prejudice for failure to join those parties. We agree. Synthes does not deny that it, the doctor, and the hospital are potential joint tortfeasors. It has long been the rule that it is not necessary for all joint tortfeasors to be named as defendants in a single lawsuit. See Lawlor v. National Screen Service Corp., 349 U.S. 322, 329–330, 75 S.Ct. 865, 869, 99 L.Ed. 1122 (1955); Bigelow v. Old Dominion Copper Mining & Smelting Co., 225 U.S. 111, 132, 32 S.Ct. 641, 644, 56 L.Ed. 1009 (1912). See also Nottingham v. General American Communications Corp., 811 F.2d 873, 880 (C.A.5) (*per curiam*), cert. denied, 484 U.S. 854, 108 S.Ct. 158, 98 L.Ed.2d 113 (1987). Nothing in the 1966 revision of Rule 19 changed that principle. See *Provident Bank, supra,* 390 U.S., at 116–117, n. 12, 88 S.Ct., at 741–742, n. 12. The Advisory Committee Notes to Rule 19(a) explicitly state that "a tortfeasor with the usual 'joint-and-several' liability is merely a permissive party to an action against another with like liability." Advisory Committee's Notes on Fed.Rule Civ.Proc. 19, 28 U.S.C.App., p. 594, at 595. There is nothing in Louisiana tort law to the contrary. See Mullin v. Skains, 252 La. 1009, 1014, 215 So.2d 643, 645 (1968); La.Civ.Code Ann., Arts. 1794, 1795 (West 1987).

The opinion in *Provident Bank, supra,* does speak of the public interest in limiting multiple litigation, but that case is not controlling here. There, the estate of a tort victim brought a declaratory judgment action against an insurance company. We assumed that the policyholder was a person "who, under § (a), should be joined if 'feasible.'" 390 U.S., at 108, 88 S.Ct., at 737, and went on to discuss the appropriate analysis under Rule 19(b), because the policyholder could not be joined without destroying diversity. *Id.,* at 109–116, 88 S.Ct., at 737–741. After examining the factors set forth in Rule 19(b), we determined that the action could proceed without the policyholder; he therefore was not an indispensable party whose absence required dismissal of the suit. *Id.,* at 116, 119, 88 S.Ct., at 741, 743.

Here, no inquiry under Rule 19(b) is necessary, because the threshold requirements of Rule 19(a) have not been satisfied. As potential joint tortfeasors with Synthes, Dr. LaRocca and the hospital were merely permissive parties. The Court of Appeals erred by failing to hold that the District Court abused its discretion in ordering them joined as defendants and in dismissing the action when Temple failed to comply with the court's order. For these reasons, we grant the petition for certiorari, reverse the judgment of the Court of Appeals for the Fifth Circuit, and remand for further proceedings consistent with this opinion.

It is so ordered.

NOTE ON RHONE–POULENC v. INTERNATIONAL INSURANCE

Rhone–Poulenc v. International Insurance Co., 71 F.3d 1299 (7th Cir.1995), involved a company, Rhone Poulenc, that had incurred substantial clean-up costs as a result of environmental damage at several contaminated sites that had belonged to its predecessor. Rhone–Poulenc, however, was well insured. In addition to its ordinary Comprehensive General Liability Insurance, Rhone–Poulenc had purchased three "Environmental Impairment Liability" policies from International Insurance Co. which insured specifically for claims made for environmental damage.

When Rhone–Poulenc sought to assert claims under those policies, however, it was told by the insurer that they were "excess policies" and that no claims would be paid unless Rhone–Poulenc could show it had exhausted its other insurance. Rhone–Poulenc then sued in federal court, and the action was dismissed on the ground that Rhone–Poulenc's Comprehensive General Liability insurers (19 in number!) were indispensable parties that Rhone–Poulenc had failed to join as defendants and could not join, because to do so would destroy complete diversity of citizenship and with it federal jurisdiction over this suit.

On appeal, Judge Posner sought to determine, as a matter of Illinois law, whether the disputed policies were "primary" or "excess". He described the significance of this issue for the court's determination under Fed. R. Civ. Pro. 19(b):

> If the policies issued by International Insurance are pure primary policies, the district judge's ruling cannot stand. Other primary insurers may be indispensable parties in a suit by an insured against a primary insurer, but it depends on the circumstances of the case. Rule 19(b) sets forth a standard, not a rigid rule. so. A party is indispensable only if it would be unjust (against "equity and good conscience," in the words of the rule) to allow the litigation to proceed in his absence. It is not always unjust for an insured with several primary insurers not to proceed against all of them. A victim of wrongdoing is not generally required to sue all the wrongdoers. Certainly not in a tort case, where the rule of joint and several liability reigns; and not in a contract case either. In a case of multiple, overlapping coverage the insurers who are not sued will not be bound by determinations made in a suit to which they are not parties, and the insurers who are sued can if they lose seek contribution afterward from the others, though this may depend, as we shall see, on the precise wording of each insurance contract. If all the policies here are primary, the case would have to be remanded to allow the district judge to make a fresh determination whether any of the 19 primary insurers who were not sued are indispensable parties. There would be no presumption that they are.

> But if the policies that International Insurance issued to Rhone–Poulenc are excess, the ruling dismissing the suit for failing to join indispensable parties was well within the scope of the district judge's authority in applying the standard of Rule 19(b). If those policies are excess, it would mean that International Insurance's liability is contingent on the liability of the Comprehensive General Liability insurers to Rhone–Poulenc, a liability that cannot be determined in the absence of those insurers. On this ground it has been held in the only cases that we have found on the issue, none of them appellate cases, that a suit against an excess insurer cannot proceed in the absence of the

primary insurers until the latter have acknowledged their liability to the insured or have been determined by a court to be liable to him.

The court found the language of the insurance contracts ambiguous and remanded the case to the district court for further factual findings on that issue.

NOTE: FROM PERMISSIVE TO COMPULSORY JOINDER; AN UNCERTAIN JOURNEY

When a single plaintiff sues a single defendant, prevailing doctrine, as we have seen, allows free joinder of totally unrelated claims in the interest of efficiency. Such joinder is permissive rather than mandatory even though it is likely to be more efficient for the parties as well as the court to have one law suit rather than many.

Plaintiff does not enjoy unlimited options. It has long been accepted doctrine that plaintiff may not "split a cause of action," or, to use current terminology, "split a claim." The penalty for suing for only $50,000 of a $100,000 debt, or for injuries to one's arm and not to the leg injured in the same accident, is loss of the balance of the claim. The claim is said either to be merged in the judgment rendered in the first action or barred by it, and res judicata precludes a second suit.

Defining the boundaries of a single claim is not an exercise in the self-evident, nor has the law remained static. These are subjects explored in the chapter on judgments in connection with other aspects of the law of res judicata. But the theory remains as stated: we may redefine what constitutes a single claim, the effect may be to widen the scope of what plaintiff must include in the first suit, but there is no compulsory joinder of distinct claims.

Defendants, too, enjoy free joinder by way of permissive counterclaims they may enter against the plaintiff. The law, however, has introduced the concept of a compulsory counterclaim. Claims arising "out of the transaction or occurrence that is the subject matter of the opposing party's claim" must be pleaded in that law suit, minor exceptions aside, under pain of being lost. Here the interest of the parties and of the system in efficiency has prevailed, as illustrated by F.R.C.P. 13(a), although this provision is by no means law everywhere.

We turn to joinder of parties. Federal Rule of Civil Procedure 19, dealing with indispensable parties, is properly considered a rule of compulsory joinder, but the primary focus of its provisions is the protection of the utility and integrity of the law suit that has been brought. Fairness rather than efficiency is the dominant theme. The fact that joint tortfeasors are outside of its reach illustrates its limits.

Is there reason to move the line separating permissive from mandatory joinder of parties in the interest of the courts, the judicial process, and other litigants even where plaintiff has chosen not to join a putative defendant and the named defendant has chosen not to implead? If so, how can we best proceed to move the boundaries without harming litigants who relied on the locus of the old lines? These are the questions explored in the case that follows.

Cogdell v. Hospital Center at Orange

Supreme Court of New Jersey, 1989.
116 N.J. 7, 560 A.2d 1169.

■ HANDLER, J.

In this case, Ruth Cogdell, while under the care of Dr. Brown, an obstetrician, gave birth by an emergency cesarean section. The baby suffered permanent injuries at or shortly after her birth. She was diagnosed as having cerebral palsy of the severest spastic quadriparetic type with microcephaly and mental retardation. Mrs. Cogdell instituted a lawsuit on her own behalf, and as guardian ad litem, on behalf of her child, against Dr. Brown, and later against Dr. Snead, the emergency-room pediatrician. No other parties were named as defendants. Plaintiff's theory of the case was that the child's injuries were caused by Dr. Brown's negligent delay in deciding to perform the cesarean section and were further aggravated by improper resuscitation efforts by Dr. Snead.

The case was tried to conclusion, with the jury returning a verdict in favor of both defendants. Plaintiff then filed a notice of appeal. The appeal was dismissed in an unpublished opinion, the court concluding that it was barred under the terms of a settlement agreement that had been reached by the parties during the jury deliberations. Challenging only the issue of the preclusive effect of the settlement agreement, plaintiff filed a petition for certification to this Court, which was denied. 114 N.J. 517, 555 A.2d 631 (1989).

While the appeal was pending, plaintiff commenced a second action against the hospital, members of the operating team, and several hospital administrators. In this case, she alleged that the delay in performing the cesarean section, and the infant's resultant injuries, were caused by the negligence of these defendants in assembling the operating team necessary to assist in the delivery. The defendants moved to dismiss the action asserting that the entire controversy doctrine mandated their joinder as parties in the earlier action and therefore the current lawsuit against them was barred. Their motion was denied. Defendants then moved for leave to appeal, which was denied by the Appellate Division. Defendants filed a petition for certification, which this Court treated as a motion for leave to appeal and granted. 110 N.J. 519, 541 A.2d 1377 (1988).

I.

The first action, Cogdell v. Brown, 220 N.J.Super. 330, 531 A.2d 1379 (App.Div.1987), was brought by plaintiff against only the obstetrician and pediatrician on the theory that these doctors were guilty of professional negligence that caused the infant's serious injuries. Evidence of such negligence was suggested by the information disclosed in separate reports prepared by plaintiff's two expert medical witnesses.

The first was submitted by Dr. Mandelman in July 1984, who after noting that the patient was obviously and appropriately prepared for a cesarean section before Dr. Brown arrived, concluded that Dr. Brown's delay in starting the operation was "exceedingly prolonged and * * * blatantly deviant." In his opinion, the delay from the arrival of the patient on the labor floor to the time of delivery constituted a "deviation from good and accepted medical practice * * * [and] this delay * * * is the substantial cause of the Cogdell infant's present state." The second report, dated March 1985, prepared by Dr. Klaven, reached a similar conclusion.

Dr. Brown contended that he had not deviated from the accepted standard of medical care. Nevertheless, during his deposition in May 1985, Dr. Brown testified that there had been a delay in performing the cesarean section because of difficulty in assembling the operating team. Specifically he testified that he made the decision to perform an emergency cesarean section shortly after seeing Ruth Cogdell around 9:30 p.m. and began to assemble the required surgical team at that time. Dr. Brown could not "recall" how long it took the anesthesiologist or the pediatrician to arrive at the hospital but that "[t]here was a significant delay between the time of the decision that the cesarean was made and the time it was actually done, and we had to assemble the team, getting the nurses in and all that. That caused some problems." The evidence also revealed that the operation did not commence until approximately 11:00 p.m.

The plaintiffs then deposed all members of the operating team, along with Dr. Jones, the Chairman of the OB/GYN Department, between August and December 1985. The anesthesiologist and two operating nurses were relatively unspecific about their recollection of any delay in their own responses to the request to come to the hospital to perform the delivery. Similarly, in his deposition, Dr. Snead, the pediatrician, was unspecific about any delay but recalled no difficulty in arriving at the hospital that night. Dr. Jones did not indicate whether there was a delay in this case, although his testimony suggested there was probably none.

Nevertheless, there was additional evidence relating to the delay in undertaking the operation. A second obstetrician, Dr. Pinderhughes, in his deposition in October 1985, said that in reviewing the hospital records he observed that "it appears that there may have been a delay" in the delivery of the baby, although he did not explain the delay; moreover, he knew of no policy that set forth a time constraint for doing emergency cesarean sections in 1982. Further, in February 1986, Dr. Brown submitted a second report by another expert witness, Dr. Greenwald. After examining the hospital records, the reports of other expert witnesses, the plaintiff's and the defendants' answers to interrogatories, and Dr. Brown's and Ruth Cogdell's depositions, this expert reached the conclusion that there was delay attributable to the hospital and its staff.

The trial occurred in June 1987. The plaintiff proceeded only on the theory that the doctors were negligent. Dr. Brown was assertedly negligent because he did not decide to do a cesarean section immediately on arrival and he delayed in calling a surgical team together while he tried to induce natural labor. Plaintiff attempted to show that there was a period between Dr. Brown's initial examination and the time that the decision to operate was made. Plaintiff cross-examined Dr. Brown at length on whether he had initially tried to induce labor instead of making an immediate decision to operate to show that the delay was negligent. However, there was some indication that there were additional reasons for the delay. In plaintiff's cross-examination of Dr. Jones, he testified, contrary to his deposition and direct testimony, that there were problems assembling delivery teams at the hospital and that, on occasion, it took more than one hour to assemble an operating team.

As noted, following the jury's verdict in favor of defendants, plaintiff brought a second action against the hospital and its staff, the subject of this appeal. She charged these defendants with negligence in causing the delay that prevented the timely performance of the cesarean delivery with the resultant injuries to the newborn. Defendants contended that plaintiff knew at least two years before the first lawsuit was tried that Dr. Brown blamed the hospital for the delay in arranging for the cesarean section; moreover, plaintiffs had ample opportunity to amend their complaint to join the hospital and its responsible staff personnel as party-defendants when they added Dr. Snead in May 1986 as a defendant. As a result, plaintiffs should not be allowed "a second bite at the apple." Defendants argued without success that under these circumstances the entire controversy doctrine required such joinder and that the failure to join bars this second lawsuit based on essentially the same legal controversy.

II.

The issue on appeal is whether plaintiff was required to have joined as party-defendants the hospital and its staff in its original action against the obstetrician and pediatrician, and, if so, whether the failure to join these defendants operates as a bar to a second independent action against them. We are directed in the first instance to our Rule of practice, Rule 4:28–1(a), which governs the joinder of parties in New Jersey.

It provides in part:

> A person who is subject to service of process shall be joined as a party to the action if (1) in his absence complete relief cannot be accorded among those already parties, or (2) he claims an interest in the subject of the action and is so situated that the disposition of the action in his absence may either (i) as a practical matter impair or impede his ability to protect that interest or (ii) leave any of the persons already parties subject to a substantial risk of incurring double, multiple, or other inconsistent obligations by reason of his claimed interest.

This rule of mandatory joinder is not self-defining. Its provisions, however, do not suggest it would mandate joinder of these current defendants. Under the Rule's literal language, plaintiff and the defendants in the prior action could have secured complete relief between themselves without the current defendants. R. 4:28–1(a)(1). Nor is it apparent that the absence of the current defendants left them unable to protect their interest, their ability to disprove allegations of their own negligence, or adversely affected the obligations of any of the parties in the earlier action. R. 4:28–1(a)(2)(i), (ii).

In addition to the party-joinder Rule, Rule 4:5–1, is a pleading Rule that requires that if there is another pending action involving the same cause of action, the parties in that other action must be identified.[5] The Rule also requires the identification of "any other party who should be joined" without, however, otherwise defining this obligation. The Rule also contemplates that if during the litigation a person is discovered who might be required to be named, then the plaintiff should notify the court and parties, and the court itself might compel joinder. The Rule does not specify grounds for joinder nor does it indicate that a failure to notify under those circumstances will have any preclusionary effect.

Rule 4:5–1 was adopted following the decision of this Court in Crispin v. Volkswagenwerk, A.G., 96 N.J. 336, 476 A.2d 250 (1984). There, we determined that the entire controversy doctrine could bar an independent action against a party whose interest in that action was the same as that in a pending action but who had not been joined in the pending action. *Crispin,* however, did not directly address the issue of whether the failure to join such a party in an action, once that action has been concluded, can serve to bar a subsequent litigation against that party involving the same legal controversy. This case poses that situation, and we are impelled to consider again the underlying policies of the entire controversy doctrine.

The entire controversy doctrine embodies the principle that the adjudication of a legal controversy should occur in one litigation in only one court; accordingly, all parties involved in a litigation should at the very least present in that proceeding all of their claims and defenses that are related to the underlying controversy. *See* Comment, The Entire Controversy Doctrine: A Novel Approach to Judicial Efficiency, 12 Seton Hall L.Rev. 260 (1982). The doctrine has become such a fundamental aspect of judicial administration, it has achieved constitutional confirmation. Article 6, section 2, paragraph 4 of the 1947 Constitution states:

> Subject to rules of the Supreme Court, the Law Division and the Chancery Division shall each exercise the powers and functions of the other division when the ends of justice so require, and legal and equitable relief should be granted in any cause so that all matters in controversy between the parties may be completely determined.

5. Rule 4:5–1 provides in part:

Each party shall include with the first pleading a certification as to whether the matter in controversy is the subject of any other action pending in any court or of a pending arbitration proceeding, or whether any other action or arbitration proceeding is contemplated; and, if so, the certification shall identify such actions and all parties thereto. Further, each party shall disclose in the certification the names of any other party who should be joined in the action. Each party shall have a continuing obligation during the course of the litigation to file and serve on all other parties and with the court an amended certification if there is a change in the facts stated in the original certification. The court may compel the joinder of parties in appropriate circumstances, either upon its own motion or that of a party.

The purposes of the doctrine include the needs of economy and the avoidance of waste, efficiency and the reduction of delay, fairness to parties, and the need for complete and final disposition through the avoidance of "piecemeal decisions." 2 State of New Jersey Constitutional Convention of 1947, Committee on the Judiciary Report § II(J), at 1187 (1947). The entire controversy doctrine has evolved "to eliminate delay, prevent harassment of a party and unnecessary clogging of the judicial system, avoid wasting the time and effort of the parties, and promote fundamental fairness." *See* Barres v. Holt, Rinehart and Winston, Inc., 74 N.J. 461, 465, 378 A.2d 1148 (1977) (Schreiber, J., dissenting).

* * *

The purposes that have stimulated the growth of the claims-joinder rule, which has historically been equated with the entire controversy doctrine, are similar, if not identical, to those of the party-joinder rule. These goals are a recurrent refrain in the judicial explication of the doctrine, *see, e.g.,* Ajamian v. Schlanger, *supra,* 14 N.J. at 485, 103 A.2d 9; Massari v. Einsiedler, *supra,* 6 N.J. at 307, 313, 78 A.2d 572; Steiner v. Stein, *supra,* 2 N.J. at 377, 66 A.2d 719; Tumarkin v. Friedman, *supra,* 17 N.J.Super. at 25–26, 85 A.2d 304, as is the repeated concern for party fairness, *see* William Blanchard Co. v. Beach Concrete Co., Inc., 150 N.J.Super. 277, 297, 375 A.2d 675 (App.Div.) ("withholding [component of a controversy] is by definition unfair if its effect is to render the pending litigation merely one inning of the whole ball game."), certif. denied, 75 N.J. 528, 384 A.2d 507 (1977).

Nevertheless, traditionally the party-joinder rule differentiated "indispensable" parties from other persons whose participation in litigation was deemed only "necessary" or "proper." Thus, the mandatory joinder of "necessary" parties—those with only a material, albeit separable, interest in a controversy—in a single action has not generally been recognized as a constituent part of the entire controversy doctrine. *See, e.g.,* McFadden v. Turner, 159 N.J.Super. 360, 369, 388 A.2d 244 (App.Div.1978) (because "entire controversy doctrine [i]s a rule of mandatory joinder of claims, not of parties," plaintiff permitted to sue hospital nurses for injuries sustained under their care when he had already in a previous lawsuit, won a jury verdict for those same injuries against the hospital on the theory of respondeat superior); *see also* Aetna Ins. Co. v. Gilchrist Bros., 85 N.J. 550, 558, 428 A.2d 1254 (1981) ("the preclusive effect of nonjoinder of claims arising out of a single dispute or wrong between the parties may not automatically be applied to a failure to join a person as a party to the action.").

We perceive, nonetheless, that the commonality of purposes in both the party-joinder and claims-joinder rules indicates that they are conceptual subsets of the entire controversy doctrine. This explains their parallel, albeit uneven, development.

* * *

III.

It is contended by plaintiff that in *Crispin,* the extension of the entire controversy doctrine to include parties was limited. *Id.* at 343, 476 A.2d 250. We nevertheless there observed that "the complex web of causation that arises in cases of this nature suggests that joinder of known responsible parties in a single action be the norm." *Ibid.* Hence, if this appeal presents a case of "this nature," we must consider whether the "norm" for the "joinder of known responsible parties in a single action" applies. We are firmly of the belief that it does.

We can chart the application of the mandatory joinder of parties against the goals of the entire controversy doctrine. The comprehensive and conclusive determination of a legal controversy is an important objective of the entire controversy doctrine. While not always isolated or identified as a discrete goal of the doctrine, the values inherent in that objective have been consistently endorsed. A disposition that reflects only a partial glimpse of the merits, or that results from the participation of some but not all of the major or important parties to the legal contest, or that resolves only a segment of the controversy does not fully effectuate the judicial ideal of complete, not piecemeal, adjudications. *See, e.g.,* Newmark v. Gimbel's, Inc., *supra,* 54 N.J. 585, 258 A.2d 697; Vacca v. Stika, *supra,* 21 N.J. at 476, 122 A.2d 619.

In addition, party fairness is critical in the application of the entire controversy doctrine. In this modern era of litigation, particularly in the tort field with the advent of comparative negligence, it is highly desirable that all parties with a material interest, one that can affect or be affected by the judicial outcome of a legal controversy, should participate in its litigation. *See* Van Horn v. William Blanchard Co., *supra,* 88 N.J. at 108, 438 A.2d 552 (Handler, J., dissenting) ("the fairness of the resolution of tort claims follows a trial where all allegedly negligent parties are represented in a single action," (citing Prosser, "Comparative Negligence," 51 Mich.L.Rev. 465, 503–04 (1953)).

Judicial economy and efficiency—the avoidance of waste and delay—remain constants in the application of the entire controversy doctrine. Fragmented and multiple litigation takes its toll on not only the parties but the judicial institution and the public. This, if anything, is a more pressing concern today than it was in the past. The litigation explosion stretches judicial capabilities enormously and places extraordinary demands on the courts. These concerns have impelled the Court to pursue novel and creative measures to cope with the increase in caseloads. We are importuned to conserve judicial resources; judicial energy is not inexhaustible or endlessly renewable. Thus, a rule that can control litigational extravagance and reduce piecemeal litigation is a necessity.

Courts have not only the responsibility but authority commensurate to deal with such compelling policy concerns. This has been recognized from the early origins of the party-joinder rule. *See, e.g.,*

Broad St. National Bank v. Holden, *supra,* 109 N.J.Eq. at 256, 156 A. 827; McLaughlin v. Van Kueren and Schultz, 21 N.J.Eq. 379, 381 (E. & A.1869). Thus, a court could "correct the deficiency on its own motion by ordering process served upon the omitted necessary party whose presence or addition would give larger scope or effect to an adjudication of that claim as to the defendants already joined." Schnitzer and Wildstein, *N.J. Rules Service, supra* at A IV–980. In a given case a court can exercise broad judicial authority over joinder; it could raise the defense of failure to join an indispensable party on its own motion at any stage of the proceedings. *Id.* at A IV–974. It could also impose a "duty and obligation" on a plaintiff "to bring [an] action to resolve all the matters in one suit" and on defendants to include additional issues and parties to assure that end. *Id.* at AIV–940 (citing *Vacca v. Stika, supra,* 21 N.J. at 476, 122 A.2d 619).

The Court's joinder authority exemplifies the judicial rulemaking power that is derived from the Constitution, *N.J. Const.* of 1947, art. VI, § 2, ¶ 3, and is exclusive and plenary with respect to practice and procedure in the courts. George Siegler Co. v. Norton, 8 N.J. 374, 381, 86 A.2d 8 (1952); Winberry v. Salisbury, 5 N.J. 240, 74 A.2d 406 (1950). This authority is to be exercised to achieve efficient use of judicial resources, Winberry v. Salisbury, *supra,* 5 N.J. at 255, 74 A.2d 406, to expedite the business of the courts, to make practice just and simple, and to prevent unreasonable delay and expense, Milk Drivers & Dairy Employees Local 680 v. Shore Dairies, Inc., 8 N.J. 32, 38, 83 A.2d 609 (1951). It should be "devised and promulgated for the purpose of promoting reasonable uniformity in the expeditious and even administration of justice." Handelman v. Handelman, 17 N.J. 1, 10, 109 A.2d 797 (1954). "The Rules of Practice are not an end unto themselves, but a means of serving the ends of justice." Viviano v. CBS, Inc., 101 N.J. 538, 550–51, 503 A.2d 296 (1986).

All of the concerns that have energized our joinder rules under the entire controversy doctrine coalesce in the circumstances of this case. Thus, there can be little doubt that the participation of all potentially responsible persons as parties in the original action would have resulted in a fuller and fairer presentation of the relevant evidence and would have enabled the jury to make a more informed and complete determination of liability. It would have assured an ultimate determination that would be comprehensive, just and conclusive as to all persons implicated in the controversy.

Further, party fairness would have been served by joinder. The failure to have joined these defendants in the earlier action seems prejudicial and unfair. These defendants may well have concluded by the termination of the prior action that they were no longer targets. In addition, while technically their interests were not determined in the earlier action, they do not now have the same opportunity to persuade a jury that will be determining their liability that the former defendants are to be blamed. Moreover, such joinder would not be unfair to plaintiff. The plaintiff had sufficient information to have included these defendants in the earlier lawsuit. Plaintiff was aware that Dr. Brown believed that the hospital and its staff may have been responsible for the delay; the second pediatrician also commented on the delay and certainly did not ascribe the delay to Dr. Brown or exonerate the current defendants. Dr. Greenwald, as an expert, based on his review of available information—hospital records and pretrial discovery—concluded that these defendants were responsible for the delay. Indeed, when Dr. Jones testified at trial that these defendants were responsible for the delay, it was not a total surprise to plaintiff; his testimony was elicited on cross-examination in response to plaintiff's own leading questions that suggested an awareness that the delay was attributable to persons other than Dr. Brown.

In addition, the court is now confronted with a duplication of lawsuits, multiple actions each involving the identical controversy and the same witnesses. The second lawsuit, though technically separate and independent, is in truth not much more than a re-run of the earlier lawsuit. The waste and inefficiency are obvious.

In sum, the failure to have joined these defendants in the earlier lawsuit is more than an unfortunate inconvenience. It is inconsistent with all of the policies that surround the entire controversy doctrine.

We thus conclude that the entire controversy doctrine appropriately encompasses the mandatory joinder of parties. Accordingly, we now hold that to the extent possible courts must determine an entire controversy in a single judicial proceeding and that such a determination necessarily embraces not only joinder of related claims between the parties but also joinder of all persons who have a material interest in the controversy.

Therefore, the current Rule on party-joinder must be amended to require mandatory joinder of parties consistent with our explication of the entire controversy doctrine. In reaching this conclusion we are satisfied that it comports completely with the reasoning expressed in our opinions in *Crispin. See* Parks v. Colonial Penn Ins. Co., 98 N.J. 42, 50, 484 A.2d 4 (1984) (*dictum*); Burke v. Deiner, 97 N.J. 465, 482, 479 A.2d 393 (1984) (*dictum*); B.P. v. G.P., 222 N.J.Super. 101, 106–07, 536 A.2d 271 (App.Div.1987); Chiacchio v. Chiacchio, 198 N.J.Super. 1, 7–8, 486 A.2d 335 (App.Div.1984). To the extent decisions have eschewed application of a mandatory party-joinder rule with the understanding that the entire controversy doctrine does not encompass the joinder of parties, we disapprove their reasoning, without implying that in these cases good cause did not otherwise justify the non-joinder of parties in the particular circumstances. *See, e.g.,* Sentry Ins. Co. v. Cropski, 218 N.J.Super. 196, 527 A.2d 94 (App.Div.1987); Tall Timbers Property Owners Ass'n v. Tall Timbers, Inc., 217 N.J.Super. 119, 524 A.2d 1315 (App.Div.1987).

We recognized in *Crispin* that our decision to extend the doctrine in certain circumstances might pose problems, observing that the Court would "proceed on a step-by-step basis recognizing that the doctrine is one of judicial fairness and will be invoked in that spirit." 96 N.J. at 343, 476 A.2d 250. Justice O'Hern acknowledged that there are "many difficult problems that extension of the doctrine may pose," noting that the New Jersey Civil Practice Committee had recommended in 1982 that the entire controversy doctrine not be extended to parties because, in its view, the already time-consuming and expensive practice of modern litigation would be only further complicated. However, even the constitutional authors of the current entire controversy doctrine provision believed that a rule of mandatory joinder would not prevent courts from properly and effectively managing litigation. 2 State of New Jersey Constitutional Convention of 1947, *supra* at 1192. The mandatory joinder rule that we adopt is not unbounded. Its limits are reached when the joinder would result in significant unfairness or jeopardy to a clear presentation of the issues and just result. Implicit in the development of the entire controversy doctrine is the recognition that economies and the efficient administration of justice should not be achieved at the expense of these paramount concerns. The entire controversy doctrine does not demand monolithic adjudications. Any possible unfairness to litigants, confusion in the presentation of issues, administrative unmanageability, or distortion in the truth-determining process that may result from compulsory joinder of parties—or claims—can be eliminated or at least minimized by a trial court possessed of the discretion to excuse joinder or to order severance. [*Crispin, supra,* 96 N.J. at 354–55, 476 A.2d 250 (Handler, J., concurring).]

We add that the contours of this rule are not fixed precisely by this decision. Its contents and bounds can evolve with experience in the course of the exercise of this Court's regulatory authority over practice and procedure, either through formal rulemaking or case-by-case adjudications. *See, e.g.,* State v. Pillot, 115 N.J. 558, 560 A.2d 634 (1989); Crispin v. Volkswagenwerk, A.G., *supra,* 96 N.J. 336, 476 A.2d 250; State v. Gregory, 66 N.J. 510, 333 A.2d 257 (1975).

IV.

Although this Court is now establishing a mandatory party-joinder rule similar to the mandatory claim-joinder rule and consistent with the entire controversy doctrine, justice requires that it be applied only prospectively and to all cases not already on appeal. Understandably, plaintiff could have interpreted *Crispin* to have preserved the option of joining these defendants in the previous lawsuit or suing them in a separate action, an option that was not foreclosed by the specific or literal terms of the existing rules of practice. *See* R. 4:28–1(a); R. 4:5–1. Because our decision invokes our rulemaking, as well as our adjudicatory authority, fairness to plaintiff and others similarly situated impels us to follow the rule of prospectivity normally applied to legislative pronouncements.

Accordingly, the judgment below is affirmed.

■ CLIFFORD, J., dissenting in part.

I join in all but section IV of the Court's comprehensive opinion. Section IV applies the mandatory party-joinder rule prospectively only. I see nothing in the circumstances of the case or in considerations of fairness to justify depriving these defendants of the benefit of a rule that they advocated and have succeeded in establishing, one that we all agree advances the goals of judicial economy and efficiency, *ante* at 1176–1177. * * *

Allan R. Stein, Foreword to Symposium on Entire Controversy Doctrine

28 Rutgers L. J. 1 (1996).

On August 1, 1995, the Supreme Court of New Jersey decided four remarkable cases expanding the boundaries of its "Entire Controversy Doctrine." The doctrine took unique shape six years earlier when the Court ruled in Cogdell v. Hospital Center at Orange, that a plaintiff must join all potential defendants to an action, or forever be barred from asserting claims against those defendants in subsequent proceedings. The 1995 quartet collectively held that the rule applied even to claims partially litigated outside of New Jersey, even to settled claims dismissed with or without prejudice, and even to malpractice claims against the attorney who filed the earlier proceeding.

This is the stuff of law professors' dreams. While Entire Controversy is unique to New Jersey, the issues raised by these developments have broad implications. Courts and commentators across the country are grappling with the dilemma of complex litigation. The cost of litigation to both the parties and the courts seems to be eclipsing its remedial value. Courts nationwide are struggling with ways to trim the fat, to consolidate and to manage related litigation. Against this background, the New Jersey experience with Entire Controversy may have lessons for others.

E. INTERVENTION

Harris v. Pernsley

United States Court of Appeals, Third Circuit, 1987.
820 F.2d 592.

■ SEITZ, CIRCUIT JUDGE.

Ronald Castille, the District Attorney of Philadelphia County, appeals the orders of the district court denying his motion to intervene as of right, 113 F.R.D. 615, and approving the settlement agreement reached by the parties in this prison conditions litigation, 654 F.Supp. 1042. This court has appellate jurisdiction pursuant to 28 U.S.C. § 1291 (1982).

I.

In 1982 ten inmates at the Holmesburg Prison in Philadelphia filed a *pro se* complaint in federal district court seeking damages and injunctive relief for themselves and for a class consisting of all inmates of the Holmesburg prison since that date and all future Holmesburg inmates. Counsel appointed for the plaintiffs filed an amended complaint, pursuant to 42 U.S.C. § 1983 (1982), alleging that the conditions of the prison violated the eighth and fourteenth amendments. The amended complaint named as defendants the City of Philadelphia, the Philadelphia officials responsible for supervising the prisons, the Board of Trustees of the Philadelphia Prison System, the Warden of the Holmesburg Prison (collectively, the City Defendants or the City), and several state officials.

The district court dismissed the action on *res judicata* and abstention grounds in light of state court litigation, *Jackson v. Hendrick*, challenging the constitutionality of the Philadelphia prisons. This court reversed the district court's conclusion that the *Jackson v. Hendrick* litigation precluded hearing this action. Harris v. Pernsley, 755 F.2d 338 (3d Cir.1985). We denied the City's petition for rehearing on March 21, 1985. 758 F.2d 83 (3d Cir.1985). On November 4, 1985, the Supreme Court denied the defendants' petition for certiorari, 474 U.S.965, 106 S.Ct. 331, 88 L.Ed.2d 314 (1985).

After remand to the district court, the plaintiffs filed a second amended complaint expanding the plaintiff class to include the inmates of all the Philadelphia prisons and adding the wardens of the Detention Center and the House of Corrections as party defendants. The plaintiffs and City defendants then entered into settlement negotiations. On August 8, 1986, they informed the court that they had reached agreement. On this same date, the Mayor wrote the District Attorney a letter informing him that the parties had reached an agreement in this litigation and in the pending state court action.[1] A copy of a proposed consent decree was submitted to the district court on August 15.

On August 19 the District Attorney filed a motion to intervene as of right, pursuant to Fed.R.Civ.P. 24(a), as a full party defendant, or in the alternative, to intervene permissibly under Fed.R.Civ.P. 24(b). Both the City Defendants and the plaintiffs opposed this motion.

The parties then withdrew the proposed consent decree. After consulting with representatives of the District Attorney and the state courts, the City defendants renegotiated a settlement agreement with the plaintiffs. On October 3, the parties, except the state court defendants, submitted a second proposed consent decree to the court. It contained, among other things, a limit on the prison population.

After the second proposed consent decree was delivered to the district court, the District Attorney filed a proposed answer to the

---

1. *Jackson v. Hendrick* has been pending in the state courts since 1971. A three-judge state court panel held in 1972 that the prisoners' conditions of confinement amounted to cruel and unusual punishment, and ordered the appointment of a special master to assist the court in fashioning appropriate relief. The Pennsylvania Supreme Court affirmed this ruling. Jackson v. Hendrick, 457 Pa. 405, 321 A.2d 603 (1974). Between 1977 and 1983, the parties agreed to a series of consent decrees designed to alleviate overcrowding and other conditions in the prisons. In 1986, the supreme court remanded the case to the Philadelphia Common Pleas Court for consideration of whether the conditions in the Philadelphia prisons continued to violate the federal constitution. 509 Pa. 456, 503 A.2d 400 (1986).

plaintiffs' complaint denying that the conditions in the Philadelphia prisons were unconstitutional. In addition, he submitted a proposed cross-claim against the City Defendants, alleging that the proposed consent decree unlawfully interfered with his functions. The cross-claim sought a declaratory judgment that the City had no power to interfere with the District Attorney's duties, including entering an agreement that would result in the release of inmates who are serving sentences or who present either a threat to the community or a risk that they will fail to appear for trial. The District Attorney also sought a permanent injunction against the City to prevent it from entering any settlement that interfered with his duties.

The district court held two evidentiary hearings and heard oral argument on the District Attorney's motion to intervene. The District Attorney presented witnesses and introduced stipulated statements of a number of persons. Appellees did not present any evidence, but did cross-examine the District Attorney's witnesses.

Edward Rendell, the District Attorney from January 1978 to January 1986, testified that he had no knowledge of this litigation while he served as the District Attorney. He further testified that he believed that a cap on prison populations would affect the District Attorney's interest in prosecutions because those released without posting bail would not appear for their trials.

The present District Attorney testified that he did not learn of this litigation until August 1986. Deputy District Attorney Eric Henson testified that he became aware of this litigation in March 1985, when he read this court's opinion, and that he did not bring the case to the attention of the then District Attorney. He further stated that at that time he believed the City defendants were adequately representing the District Attorney's interest and that should the City decide not to litigate the case, it would inform the District Attorney before taking any action.

The District Attorney presented the testimony of Maria Terpolilli, the Senior Supervisor of the Bail Hearings Unit of the Pretrial Services Division of the Philadelphia Court of Common Pleas, to provide evidence of the failure to appear rates for persons under various release programs, including the one instituted by the *Jackson v. Hendrick* litigation, and of the rearrest rates for persons released under the *Jackson v. Hendrick* program.[2] The District Attorney attempted to show that the failure to appear and rearrest rates under the *Jackson v. Hendrick* program were extremely high. After cross-examination of Terpolilli, however, the district court refused to admit the ratios that Terpolilli derived from her statistics, finding the ratios "meaningless."

In addition, the District Attorney proffered statements from a number of state court officials as to their discussions with City officials

---

2. Under the *Jackson v. Hendrick* release mechanism, weekly lists of pretrial detainees are sent to a bail master who in turn holds hearings to determine who should be released. The District Attorney has the right to appear at these hearings, and may appeal the decisions of the bail master.

about the proposed agreements. Finally, the parties stipulated to statements from prison officials concerning the improvements in prison conditions since the *Jackson v. Hendrick* litigation was instituted. After hearing oral argument, the district court took the District Attorney's motion to intervene under advisement.

At the beginning of the hearing on the proposed consent decree, the district court informed the District Attorney that it was going to deny his motion to intervene. With the consent of the parties, however, the court permitted the District Attorney to present his objections to the proposed consent decree, both at the hearing and in written submissions. At the hearing, the District Attorney argued that the proposed settlement would endanger public safety, that there was no reason to enter such an agreement absent a finding that the conditions in the Philadelphia prisons were unconstitutional, that the consent decree went beyond what is required by the Constitution, and that the settlement would, in effect, undo the bail determinations and sentences of state court judges. The City and the plaintiffs reiterated their contention that the proposed settlement was fair and reasonable.

On December 31, the district court filed its opinion and order formally denying the District Attorney's motion to intervene, finding that he failed to meet any of the requirements of the rule for intervention of right. In addition, she denied his motion for permissive intervention. Because of these rulings it was not necessary for the district court to address the District Attorney's proposed answer to the complaint and proposed cross claim. On this same date, the district court entered its order approving the settlement agreement proposed by the plaintiffs and City defendants.[3] These appeals by the District Attorney followed.[4]

II.

The District Attorney asserts that, contrary to the district court's ruling, he has an absolute right to intervene in this action as a full-party defendant to litigate the constitutionality of the conditions of the Philadelphia prison system and the relief, if any, to which the plaintiffs may be entitled. Under Rule 24(a)(2),[5] a person is entitled to intervene if (1) the application for intervention is timely; (2) the applicant has a sufficient interest in the litigation; (3) the interest may be affected or impaired, as a practical matter, by the disposition of the action; and (4) the interest is not adequately represented by an existing party in

---

3. The state defendants are not a part of the consent decree, and none of the terms affect them. Two of the state defendants, Marks and Jeffes, were dismissed without prejudice at the same time as the district court entered its order approving the consent decree. The action is still pending against the other state defendant, Waldman.

4. On the motion of the District Attorney, we stayed the implementation of the consent decree's ceiling on the population pending the outcome of this appeal.

5. Rule 24(a) provides, in relevant part:

Upon timely application anyone shall be permitted to intervene in an action * * * (2) when the applicant claims an interest relating to the property or transaction which is the subject matter of the action and he is so situated that the disposition of the action may as a practical matter impair or impede his ability to protect that interest, unless the applicant's interest is adequately represented by existing parties.

the litigation. *See* Commonwealth of Pennsylvania v. Rizzo, 530 F.2d 501, 504 (3d Cir.), *cert denied sub nom.* Fire Fighters Union v. Pennsylvania, 426 U.S. 921, 96 S.Ct. 2628, 49 L.Ed.2d 375 (1976). Although these requirements are intertwined, each must be met to intervene as of right. *See, e.g.,* New Orleans Public Service, Inc. v. United Gas Pipe Line Co., 732 F.2d 452, 463 (5th Cir.) (in banc), *cert. denied sub nom.* Morial v. United Gas Pipe Line Co., 469 U.S. 1019, 105 S.Ct. 434, 83 L.Ed.2d 360 (1984); 3B J. Moore & J. Kennedy, Moore's Federal Practice ¶ 24.07[1] at 24–50 (2d ed. 1982); 7C C. Wright, A. Miller, & M. Kane, Federal Practice and Procedure: Civil 2d § 1908 at 262 (1986).[6]

A.

Because of its pervasive importance in the setting of the case, we at once focus on the second requirement: whether the District Attorney has shown a sufficient interest in this litigation. This circuit has not addressed what type of interests are necessary to entitle an applicant to intervene as of right. And as one court has noted, given the multitude of situations in which intervention controversies can arise, what constitutes such an interest "defies a simple definition." Restor–A–Dent Dental Laboratories, Inc. v. Certified Alloy Products, Inc., 725 F.2d 871, 874 (2d Cir.1984).

The Supreme Court has stated that under Rule 24(a)(2), an applicant's interest must be one that is "significantly protectable." Donaldson v. United States, 400 U.S. 517, 531, 91 S.Ct. 534, 542, 27 L.Ed.2d 580 (1971). Several circuits have concluded that an applicant must demonstrate a legal interest in the action to intervene as of right. Southern Christian Leadership Conference v. Kelley, 747 F.2d 777, 779 (D.C.Cir.1984) (the interest must be "legally protectable"); *New Orleans Public Service, Inc., supra,* 732 F.2d at 463 (intervention as of right requires a "direct, substantial, legally protectable interest in the proceedings"); Wade v. Goldschmidt, 673 F.2d 182, 185 (7th Cir.1982) (same). *But see* Smith v. Pangilinan, 651 F.2d 1320, 1324 (9th Cir. 1981) (an applicant "need not show that he has a legal or equitable interest in jeopardy * * * [but] must show that he has a 'protectable interest' in the outcome of the litigation of sufficient magnitude to warrant inclusion in the action.") (citations omitted). In addition, a number of courts have concluded that this interest must be "direct," as opposed to contingent or remote. *See Restor–A–Dent Dental Laboratories, supra,* 725 F.2d at 874; Air Lines Stewards and Stewardesses Association, Local 550 v. American Airlines, Inc., 455 F.2d 101, 105 (7th Cir.1972); 3B *Moore's Federal Practice, supra,* ¶ 24.07[2] at 24–59.

Courts have not been able to develop more than these general guidelines to answer what type of interest is necessary for interven-

---

6. As the Second Circuit has noted, however, a very strong showing that one of the requirements is met may result in requiring a lesser showing of another requirement. *See* United States v. Hooker Chemical & Plastics Corp., 749 F.2d 968, 983 (2d Cir. 1984).

tion. *See generally,* 3B *Moore's Federal Practice, supra,* ¶ 24.07[2] at 24–57 ("The exact nature of the interest required * * * has eluded a precise and authoritative judicial definition * * *."). Because Rule 24(a)(2) was designed to permit courts to solve intervention disputes in a pragmatic manner, it "requires consideration of all the competing and relevant interests raised by an application for intervention." United States v. Hooker Chemicals & Plastics Corp., 749 F.2d 968, 983 (2d Cir.1984); *see* Nuesse v. Camp, 385 F.2d 694, 700 (D.C.Cir.1967).

B.

With these rather conclusory guidelines in mind, we turn now to the District Attorney's argument that the district court erred in concluding that this litigation did not sufficiently implicate his interests to require intervention under Rule 24(a)(2). We must first determine the scope of review of the district court's determination denying the District Attorney's motion for intervention of right.

As we noted above, intervention controversies arise in many different contexts, and require the court to consider the pragmatic consequences of a decision to permit or deny intervention. The variety of situations in which an application may arise counsels against setting strict legal standards by which courts may measure applications under Rule 24(a)(2). *See* Shreve, Questioning Intervention of Right—Toward A New Methodology Of Decisionmaking, 74 Nw. U.L.Rev. 894, 916–24 (1980). This same reasoning supports an abuse of discretion standard of review, which we now adopt. *See* United States v. Hooker Chemicals & Plastics Corp., *supra,* 749 F.2d at 991. *But see* People of State of California v. Tahoe Regional Planning Agency, 792 F.2d 779, 781 (9th Cir.1986) (district court's denial of intervention as of right reviewed *de novo*).

We note, however, that our review of district court's decisions denying intervention of right is more stringent than the abuse of discretion review accorded to denials of motions for permissive intervention. Rule 24(a)(2) restricts the district court's discretion by providing that an applicant "shall be permitted to intervene" if he or she satisfies the requirements of the Rule. *See* Stringfellow v. Concerned Neighbors in Action, 480 U.S. 370, 382, 107 S.Ct. 1177, 1185 n. 1, 94 L.Ed.2d 389 (1987) (Brennan, J., concurring). We, therefore, will reverse a district court's determination on a motion to intervene of right if the court "has applied an improper legal standard or reached a decision that we are confident is incorrect." United States v. Hooker Chemicals & Plastics Corp., *supra,* 749 F.2d at 992; *see generally,* United States v. Criden, 648 F.2d 814, 817–19 (3d Cir.1981) (discussing the meaning of the "abuse of discretion" standard of review).

In this case, the District Attorney asserts a legal interest in support of his motion to intervene: his duties as a public official. The scope of his interest is defined by the scope of his legal duties under Pennsylvania law.[7] *See* Olden v. Hagerstown Cash Register, Inc., 619 F.2d 271,

---

7. Whether the legal duties as defined by Pennsylvania law are sufficient to give the District Attorney the right to intervene is, however, a question of federal law. *See New*

273 (3d Cir.1980). If his rights and duties, as defined by Pennsylvania law, may be affected directly by the disposition of this litigation, the District Attorney has a sufficient interest to intervene as of right in this action. *See* Blake v. Pallan, 554 F.2d 947, 953 (9th Cir.1977); Hines v. D'Artois, 531 F.2d 726, 738 (5th Cir.1976); *see also* Neusse v. Camp, *supra*, 385 F.2d at 700 (state banking commissioner has right to intervene in action brought by a state bank against the Comptroller where federal law incorporates the state's banking laws because he has an interest in the enforcement of the state laws' policies). We turn then to a recitation of the basic terms of the consent decree so that they may be juxtaposed with the authority accorded the District Attorney under Pennsylvania law.

At the time the consent decree was approved, there were 4300 inmates in the Philadelphia prison system; approximately two-thirds of the inmates were awaiting hearing or trial. The decree requires the inmate population in the present facilities to be reduced, in stages, to 3750 persons within six months. The ceiling on the prison population agreed to by the parties is higher than the ones that have been ordered by the Pennsylvania courts in the *Jackson v. Hendrick* litigation. *See, e.g.,* Jackson v. Hendrick, *supra,* 503 A.2d at 403; Jackson v. Hendrick, *supra,* 446 A.2d at 231.

If the inmate population of the prisons exceeds the maximum permissible under the consent decree, the agreement provides that the City "shall seek the release, through the mechanism of the Bail Master appointed by the *Jackson* court or otherwise, of persons being held either on the lowest bail or persons sentenced to the Philadelphia prisons with less than sixty days remaining to serve on their sentences."[8] The City will not seek the release of inmates charged with murder or forcible rape, or persons who, if released, posed an imminent threat to the public or themselves.

The settlement recognizes that the prison population fluctuates daily, and thus provides that the population may exceed the maximum temporarily, but not for more than seven days consecutively or twenty days out of any forty. If the population of a facility exceeds the limit for more than the allowable flux time, the decree provides that the City defendants cannot admit additional inmates to the facility. This provision does not apply to "persons charged with, or convicted of, murder, forcible rape, or a crime involving the use of a gun or knife in the commission of an aggravated assault or robbery."[9]

The statute establishing the office of district attorney provides, in relevant part: "The district attorney shall sign all bills of indictment and conduct in court all criminal and other prosecutions * * *." 16

Orleans Public Service, supra, 732 F.2d at 466 n. 29.

8. For a description of the release mechanism used by the *Jackson* court, *see, supra,* n. 2.

9. The consent decree also contains provision regulating certain living conditions for the inmates. The focus of the District Attorney's motion to intervene, however, is the fact the decree contains a cap on the prison conditions.

Pa.Stat.Ann. § 1402(a) (Purdon Supp.1986). The Pennsylvania Supreme Court has interpreted this statute as giving the District Attorney the power, and the duty, "to represent the Commonwealth's interests in the enforcement of its criminal laws." Commonwealth ex rel. Specter v. Bauer, 437 Pa. 37, 41, 261 A.2d 573, 575 (1970). The District Attorney is the "sole public official charged with the legal responsibility of conducting 'in court all criminal and other prosecutions.' " Id. at 43, 261 A.2d at 576 (citation omitted).

In particular, the District Attorney advocates specific bail levels and may appeal bail determinations with which he disagrees. See, e.g., Commonwealth of Pennsylvania v. Truesdale, 449 Pa. 325, 296 A.2d 829 (1972) (District Attorney appealing bail decision). The District Attorney also has the power to advocate sentences, to defend convictions in both state court actions and habeas actions in federal court, and to represent the Commonwealth in challenges to the constitutionality of the state's penal statutes. See Specter v. Bauer, supra, 437 Pa. at 42–43, 261 A.2d at 575–76. In short, the District Attorney is charged with the responsibility of enforcing the Commonwealth's criminal statutes.

The Philadelphia Home Rule Charter vests the Philadelphia Department of Public Welfare with the responsibility of supervising the Philadelphia prison, including the power to set the capacity of the institutions. 351 Pa.Admin.Code § 5.5–700(c) (1986). The Charter further provides that the Board of Trustees of the Philadelphia Prison System has the responsibility of managing the prisons. 351 Pa.Admin.Code § 5.5–701 (1986).

The Home Rule Charter, however, cannot provide the City with powers contrary to those granted by state statutes. 53 Pa.Stat.Ann. § 13133(b) (Purdon 1957). The Charter, thus, cannot provide support for the City to encroach on any duties vested in the District Attorney by state statute. Specter v. Bauer, supra, 437 Pa. at 43, 261 A.2d at 576.

Given the pertinent terms of the consent decree and the legal duties of the District Attorney, we must decide whether the duties enumerated above are implicated sufficiently in this prison overcrowding litigation that the District Attorney has the right to intervene. As we understand the District Attorney's position, he seeks to intervene in this action to litigate the prisoners' claims of unconstitutional conditions and to prevent a settlement to which he objects. According to the District Attorney, he has a right to intervene as a full-party defendant because limits on prison populations are a traditional response to a finding of unconstitutional conditions in prisons and this remedy would adversely affect his functions.

The District Attorney asserts that a limitation on the prison population will interfere with his prosecutorial powers in two ways. First, he argues that a prison cap will result in the release of inmates who have not posted the bond set by state court judges or inmates who have not served their full sentences. This, in turn, will result in his work going for naught and will hamper his ability to prosecute cases because those released without posting bond will not appear for their trials.

Second, he directs the court's attention to the fact the prison cap may make it impossible for the City prisons to admit additional persons. He contends that if the City refused to operate any jails, the refusal would interfere with his duties because his function as a prosecutor would be rendered meaningless. According to the District Attorney, it therefore follows that if some individuals are not admitted to prison because of the ceiling placed on the prison population, his role is rendered meaningless for those individuals.

In considering whether the District Attorney has a sufficient interest in this case, for intervention purposes, we will analyze the District Attorney's position in two stages: first, whether he has a right to intervene to oppose the plaintiff's claims of unconstitutional conditions on the merits and second, whether he has a right to participate in the formation of the remedy.

Given the nature of an applicant's interest, he or she may have a sufficient interest to intervene as to certain issues in an action without having an interest in the litigation as a whole.[11] *See* Howard v. McLucas, 782 F.2d 956, 962 (11th Cir.1986) (nonminority employees have the right to intervene to challenge the promotional remedy, but not to contest the existence of past discrimination); Bradley v. Milliken, 620 F.2d 1141, 1142 (6th Cir.1980) (representative of Hispanic community has right to intervene for the limited purpose of presenting evidence on question of *de jure* segregation of Hispanics); *see generally* Shapiro, *Some Thoughts on Intervention Before Courts, Agencies, and Arbitrators,* 81 Harv.L.Rev. 721, 752–56 (1968) (discussing limited intervention as of right). Examining an applicant's asserted interest in terms of discrete phases of an action seems particularly appropriate in institutional litigation. In institutional reform litigation, while only some individuals may be held liable for the unlawful conduct, and thus have an interest in the determination of liability, a larger number of persons' interests may be infringed on at the remedial stage of the litigation. *See, e.g.,* Equal Employment Opportunity Commission v. American Telephone and Telegraph Co., 506 F.2d 735 (3d Cir.1974).

C.

We thus turn to the District Attorney's contention that he has a right to intervene to litigate whether the conditions in the prison are unconstitutional. Under Pennsylvania law, the City defendants are vested with the responsibility of managing the prison system. It is the City, therefore, that would incur any liability, including attorney's fees

---

11. The Advisory Committee's Note to the 1966 Amendments acknowledge that intervention as of right "may be subject to appropriate conditions or restrictions responsive among other things to the requirements of efficient conduct of the proceedings." Although one authority has objected to placing limitations on those who intervene as of right, *see Wright, Miller & Kane, supra,* § 1922, we believe that, given the complexity of much public law litigation, permitting courts to limit intervention as of right to discrete phases of the litigation may be necessary in some cases.

under 42 U.S.C. § 1988 (1982), if the prison conditions were found to violate the Constitution.

The District Attorney, on the other hand, has no legal duties or powers with regard to the conditions in the Philadelphia prison system. He has no function in the administration of the prisons. His participation in the liability stage could not contribute to a greater understanding of the issues involved in this phase of the litigation.

Moreover, after five years in the federal courts, and fifteen years in the state courts, the City officials charged both with the duty of managing the prisons and presumably an awareness of the situation, have concluded that they should not litigate the issue of the constitutionality of the conditions in the prisons. This combination of circumstances leads us to conclude that the District Attorney, who has no role in the prison management and cannot be held liable for any unlawful conditions, does not have the right to prevent the City from effectuating its reasoned judgment that it is best not to litigate the action. Otherwise stated, the District Attorney has no interest entitling him to litigate the plaintiffs' contention that the conditions in the Philadelphia prison system are unconstitutional.

D.

We now address the more difficult question presented on appeal: whether the District Attorney has the right to intervene as a party in the formation of the terms of the settlement agreement in this case. The district court denied the District Attorney's motion because it found that the enforcement of the Commonwealth's penal statutes was not an issue in this case. It further stated that "[w]hile the final disposition of this action—either by settlement or by injunctive relief granted after a finding of unconstitutional conditions—could have some effect on the District Attorney's enforcement function, it is not the kind of direct, substantial interest that permits intervention as of right." The District Attorney asserts that the court committed a legal error in so concluding.

As discussed above, the District Attorney has the power and duty to advocate bail levels, to prosecute defendants, to recommend sentences once defendants are convicted, to defend convictions on appeal, and to defend challenges to the Commonwealth's penal statutes. He is the official who represents the Commonwealth's interests in criminal law enforcement.

The consent decree presented to, and approved by, the district court does not alter any of the duties enumerated above. The District Attorney is not prevented from performing his statutory duties. He is not obligated to take any action, or refrain from any action, by the decree; moreover, he could not be held in contempt under this decree. In short, none of his enumerated legal duties are taken away by the settlement approved in this case.

Because the consent decree does not alter the District Attorney's legal duties, Cobb v. Aytch, 539 F.2d 297 (3d Cir.1976), *cert. denied sub nom.* Engelfried v. Aytch, 429 U.S. 1103, 97 S.Ct. 1130, 51 L.Ed.2d 554 (1977), does not control this case. In *Cobb,* inmates of the Philadelphia prisons challenged the transfer of prisoners between the county and state prisons and named as defendants two state officials— the Attorney General and the Commissioner of Corrections—and three city officials—the District Attorney, the Commissioner of Police, and the Superintendent of the Philadelphia Prisons. The district court approved an agreement reached between the state officials and the plaintiffs, and the city officials appealed. We held that the court erred in approving the settlement over the objections of the Superintendent because, although the decree did not mention him, it took away his right, granted by state statute, to petition the state authorities to accept inmate transferees from the Philadelphia prisons. *Id.* at 300–01. In this case, by contrast, the decree does not limit the District Attorney's exercise of his statutory duties.

The District Attorney argues, however, that although the decree does not impinge expressly on his functions, his powers will be affected as a practical matter by the operation of the decree. In particular, he argues that the prison cap will hinder his ability to prosecute cases because some of the pre-trial detainees released will not appear for trial. He also asserts that if the City is forced to refuse admissions to the prisons, his role as a prosecutor will be rendered meaningless as to those not admitted. Finally, he asserts that his participation as a party is necessary to protect the public interest.

We agree with the District Attorney that Rule 24(a)(2) directs the courts to consider the practical consequences of the litigation in passing on an application to intervene as of right. As one court has noted, "the court is not limited to consequences of a strictly legal nature * * * [but] may consider any significant legal effect on the applicant's interest * * *." National Resources Defense Council, Inc. v. United States Nuclear Regulatory Commission, 578 F.2d 1341, 1345 (10th Cir.1978). Courts thus have found that an applicant has a sufficient interest to intervene when the action will have a significant *stare decisis* effect on the applicant's rights, *e.g.,* Smith v. Pangilinan, *supra,* 651 F.2d at 1325, or where the contractual rights of the applicant may be affected by a proposed remedy, *e.g.,* Little Rock School District v. Pulaski County Special School District, No. 1, 738 F.2d 82, 84 (8th Cir.1984); Equal Employment Opportunity Commission v. American Telephone and Telegraph Co., *supra,* 506 F.2d at 741–42.

At the same time, however, to have an interest sufficient to intervene as of right, "the interest must be 'a legal interest as distinguished from interests of a general and indefinite character.'" United States v. American Telephone and Telegraph Co., 642 F.2d 1285, 1292 (D.C.Cir.1980), quoting Radford Iron Co. v. Appalachian Elec. Power Co., 62 F.2d 940, 942 (4th Cir.1933). In many cases, especially class action litigation, the disposition of the action will have some impact on the interests of third parties. To intervene as of right as a party to the litigation, however, the applicant must do more than show that his or her interests may be affected in some incidental manner. Rather, the applicant must demonstrate that there is a tangible threat to a legally cognizable interest to have the right to intervene. *See, e.g.* United States v. Perry County Board of Education, 567 F.2d 277, 279 (5th Cir.1978).

Ceilings on prison population are a common remedy in prison overcrowding cases. *See, e.g.,* Inmates of Allegheny County Jail v. Wecht, 754 F.2d 120 (3d Cir.1985); Badgley v. Varelas, 729 F.2d 894 (2d Cir.1984); Duran v. Elrod, 713 F.2d 292 (7th Cir.1983), *cert. denied,* 465 U.S. 1108, 104 S.Ct. 1615, 80 L.Ed.2d 143 (1984). To the extent that the ceiling on the prison population, and any resultant release of inmates, may be required to maintain constitutional conditions in the prisons, the District Attorney has no legally protected interest in causing the constitutionally-imposed maximum to be exceeded. Simply stated, he can have no interest in assuring the incarceration of persons under unconstitutional conditions. *Cf.* Stotts v. Memphis Fire Dept., 679 F.2d 579, 582 (5th Cir.), *cert. denied,* 459 U.S. 969, 103 S.Ct. 297, 74 L.Ed.2d 280 (1982) ("There is no legally cognizable interest in promotional expectations which presumptively could only occur as the result of discriminatory practices."). The District Attorney argues, however, that the attempt by the City to agree to a prison ceiling interferes with his duties and thus, he has a right to intervene in this action.

We are persuaded that the District Attorney's argument that he has a right to be a party to this litigation overstates his role as the law enforcement officer of the Commonwealth. *But see* Jackson v. Hendrick, *supra* 446 A.2d at 232–34 (1982) (Nix, J., dissenting) (release of pretrial detainees affects the District Attorney's functions).[12] The District Attorney's argument assumes that he has the right to oversee the entire criminal justice system in Philadelphia. Under Pennsylvania law, however, a number of different actors have legal duties with respect to the system of criminal justice. For example, it is the duty of the state court judges to determine the bail status of those accused, 42 Pa.Cons. Stat.Ann. § 1123 (Purdon Supp.1986), and to set the sentences of those convicted. 42 Pa.Cons.Stat.Ann. § 9701 et seq. (Purdon 1982 and Supp.1986). The Mayor and City Council, moreover, have the authority to determine the size of the police force through their control of the City budget. 351 Pa.Admin.Code §§ 2.2–300, 4.4–101 (1986). Any action by one of actors in the system is likely to have some repercussions in terms of the other actors' duties.

We must respect the boundaries that the Commonwealth has chosen to draw as to the responsibilities of its public officials. But we decline to equate the District Attorney's function as the spokesperson for Pennsylvania's interest in criminal prosecutions with the responsibility for policing the entire criminal justice system. Although we agree

---

12. The majority in Jackson v. Hendrick, 498 Pa. 270, 446 A.2d 226 (1982), denied the District Attorney's motion to intervene on the ground that the motion was untimely. It did, however, note that the District Attorney "has failed to establish that the denial of intervention has harmed his interest," because he received the opportunity to submit his views on the appropriateness of the remedy. 446 A.2d at 230 n. 12.

with the District Attorney that the decree may result in some people not appearing for their scheduled trial dates and some individuals not having to post bond before being released, this by-product of the decree is not sufficient to give the District Attorney the right to become a party to any consent decree entered in this case. *Cf.* Graddick v. Alabama, 453 U.S. 928, 934–35, 102 S.Ct. 4, 8–9, 69 L.Ed.2d 1025 (1981) (Powell, J., in chambers) (expressing his doubt that the Attorney General of Alabama had standing to seek a stay of a court order releasing inmates from prison when the Governor, who was vested with the responsibility for the prison system, opposed the Attorney General's motion); *but cf. Id.* at 941–43, 102 S.Ct. at 11–12 (Rehnquist, J., in chambers) (explaining that he believes that the Attorney General has standing in light of his interest in law enforcement and the fact he was a party to the litigation).

Moreover, we reject the District Attorney's assertion that the City officials will be insensitive to concerns for public safety. Experience has demonstrated in similar cases that the officials in charge of the prisons are attuned to such concerns and will return to the court to seek a modification of the decree if the ceiling threatens the safety of the public. *See* Duran v. Elrod, 760 F.2d 756 (7th Cir.1985).

We therefore conclude that the District Attorney has not asserted a sufficient interest to intervene in this action as of right. This conclusion, moreover, is consistent with the approach that other circuits have taken when a public official has petitioned to intervene as of right. Where the public official has demonstrated only a general interest in the litigation, his motion to intervene has been denied. *See, e.g.,* Blake v. Pallan, *supra,* 554 F.2d at 953 (state securities commissioner does not have a sufficient interest in class action suit merely because the action contains some pendent state claims); People of State of California v. Tahoe Regional Planning Agency, *supra,* 792 F.2d at 782.

On the other hand, courts have found that the official had a sufficient interest to intervene in cases in which the subject of the suit came within the scope of his official duties. In Smith v. Pangilinan, *supra,* for example, the Ninth Circuit concluded that the Attorney General, as the official charged with the administration of the nation's immigration laws, had a sufficient interest to intervene in an action in which the plaintiffs sought to have the court determine whether they were persons who would, in the future, be able to become United States citizens. *See also* Hines v. D'Artois, *supra,* 531 F.2d at 738 (state examiner for the Civil Service has right to intervene where relief sought by plaintiff involved changes in the civil service examination); Neusse v. Camp, *supra,* 385 F.2d at 700 (state banking commissioner had an interest in action in which the federal law incorporated the substance of the state law because the litigation involved "the nature and protection of the state policy"). Because we believe that the District Attorney's interests fall within the first category of cases, we find that the district court did not abuse its discretion in denying the motion to intervene as of right.

Given our conclusion that the District Attorney does not have a sufficient interest to intervene of right as a party in this action, it is not necessary to review the correctness of the district court's determinations that the District Attorney did not meet the other requirements of the intervention rule. Moreover, we need not reach the issue of whether the district court abused its discretion in denying the District Attorney's motion for permissive intervention because he has not argued this issue on appeal and we deem it waived. *See* United States v. Hooker Chemical & Plastics Corp., *supra,* 749 F.2d at 969.

We would add that, although the District Attorney is not entitled to intervene as of right, we think it was entirely appropriate for the district court to permit the District Attorney to be heard on the terms of the consent decree, however his status may be otherwise legally characterized. Indeed, permitting persons to appear in court, either as friends of the court or as interveners for a limited purpose, may be advisable where third parties can contribute to the court's understanding of the consequences of the settlement proposed by the parties. *See, e.g.,* Kirkland v. New York State Dept. of Correctional Services, 711 F.2d 1117, 1125–27 (2d Cir.1983), *cert. denied sub nom.* Althiser v. New York State Dept. of Correctional Services, 465 U.S. 1005, 104 S.Ct. 997, 79 L.Ed.2d 230 (1984) (permitting nonminority employees to intervene to object to the affirmative action provisions in a proposed consent decree).

III.

The District Attorney also appeals the order of the district court approving the proposed consent decree. The source of the district court's authority to enter a consent decree is the parties' agreement. *See* Local No. 93, International Association of Firefighters v. City of Cleveland, 478 U.S.501, 106 S.Ct. 3063, 3076, 92 L.Ed.2d 405 (1986). As the Supreme Court has stated,

> Consent decrees are entered into by parties after careful negotiation has produced agreement on their precise terms. The parties waive their right to litigate the issues involved in the case and thus save themselves the time, expense and inevitable risk of litigation. Naturally, the agreement reached normally embodies a compromise; in exchange for the saving of cost and elimination of risk, the parties each give up something they might have won had they proceeded with the litigation.

United States v. Armour & Co., 402 U.S. 673, 681–82, 91 S.Ct. 1752, 1757, 29 L.Ed.2d 256 (1971).

Because a consent decree is an agreement between the parties to settle a case, one who is properly denied intervention cannot appeal the merits of the case. *See* Commonwealth of Pennsylvania v. Rizzo, *supra,* 530 F.2d at 508. The District Attorney's appeal of the merits, therefore, must be dismissed.[13]

---

13. Given our determination as well as the district court's ruling on intervention, we reject the District Attorney's contention that by hearing him on the terms of the consent

In dismissing the District Attorney's appeal of the consent decree, we do not intend to imply that a district court can avoid its independent obligation to determine that, as a matter of subject matter jurisdiction, such terms " 'come within the general scope of the case made by the pleadings.' " *Local No. 93, supra,* 478 U.S.501,526, 106 S.Ct. at 3063, 92 L.Ed.2d 405, *quoting* Pacific R. Co. v. Ketchum, 101 U.S. (11 Otto) 289, 297, 25 L.Ed. 932 (1879); Sansom Committee v. Lynn, 735 F.2d 1535, 1538 (3d Cir.); *cert. denied sub nom.* Trustees of University of Pennsylvania v. Sansom Committee, 469 U.S. 1017, 105 S.Ct. 431, 83 L.Ed.2d 358 (1984). That the relief comes within the scope of the pleadings, however, is not in question here. Moreover, because we conclude that the merits of the case are not properly before us, we are not called upon to decide in this case what legal and factual foundations are required for the district court to enter a consent decree.

IV.

In light of the foregoing, the order of the district court denying the District Attorney's motion to intervene as of right will be affirmed.

The appeal of the District Attorney from the order of the district court approving the consent decree will be dismissed.[a]

F. INTERPLEADER

NYLife Distributors v. The Adherence Group

United States Court of Appeals for the Third Circuit, 1995.
72 F.3d 371.

■ MANSMANN, CIRCUIT JUDGE.

[NYLife Distributors, administrator of the "Mainstay Mutual Fund", filed a complaint in interpleader in the district court against The Adherence Group ("TAG") and several TAG employees, including Gerasolo, the company's former President, and Bleach, its former Executive Vice President. There was sufficient diversity among the claimants to satisfy the requirements of 28 U.S.C.§ 1335.

In its complaint, NYLife asserted that it was subject to conflicting demands from the defendants for monies it was holding in Mainstay Mutual Fund accounts opened for TAG employees. One of the former TAG executives had demanded payment from the fund, but TAG's attorney had informed NYLife that monies from the Fund had been misappropriated from TAG. Claiming no interest in the money, NYLife deposited the total balance, $215,489.50, in the court's Registry. It requested that the defendants be required to interplead and settle among themselves their respective rights to the fund.

decree the district court, in effect, granted him limited intervention.

a. Dissenting opinion of Judge Garth omitted.

Gerasolo and Bleach filed an answer in which they asserted that TAG's claims were barred by certain settlement agreements. They brought a counterclaim against NYLife, alleging that NYLife's liquidation of their respective Fund accounts was a breach of contractual and fiduciary duties. They also brought cross-claims against TAG asserting their right to the disputed funds.

TAG also commenced an action in New Jersey state court against Gerasolo and Bleach, alleging that they had wrongfully appropriated TAG assets, including the monies deposited in the Mainstay Mutual Fund, through fraud, embezzlement and conversion.

On May 19, 1994, the district court issued an order granting NYLife's motion for a judgment in interpleader in the amount of $215,489.50, dismissing NYLife from the case and ordering that the defendants be enjoined from instituting any other action against NYLife or its affiliates based on NYLife's commencement of the interpleader action.

TAG then filed a motion asking the district court to dismiss the cross-claims Gerasolo and Bleach had asserted against it in the interpleader and to transfer the interpleaded fund to the Superior Court of New Jersey. In the alternative, TAG asked the court to retain the fund while the parties litigated their entitlement to the money in the action TAG had commenced in the New Jersey state court.

By order dated October 26, 1994, the district court granted TAG's motion. Of the view that its May 19, 1994 order, which granted NYLife's motion for judgment in interpleader, denied Gerasolo's and Bleach's cross-motion for dismissal of the interpleader action and dismissed the counterclaim against NYLife, had "eliminated" all federal claims in this case, the court invoked its discretion under 28 U.S.C. § 1367(c) (1993) and dismissed Gerasolo's and Bleach's state law cross-claims, and retained jurisdiction over the interpleaded fund pending the outcome of the state court litigation. Gerasolo and Bleach appealed.]

II

The federal interpleader statute, 28 U.S.C. § 1335 (1993), is a remedial device which enables a person holding property or money to compel two or more persons asserting mutually exclusive rights to the fund to join and litigate their respective claims in one action. The benefits of the device to both the stakeholder and the claimants are substantial. It relieves the stakeholder from determining at his peril the merits of competing claims and shields him from the prospect of multiple liability; it gives the claimant who ultimately prevails ready access to the disputed fund.

Section 1335 grants original jurisdiction to the district courts over interpleader actions and sets forth certain requirements that must be met before the action may be maintained. For example, although the citizenship of the stakeholder is irrelevant for jurisdictional purposes, the statute calls for diversity of citizenship between two or more of the adverse claimants, requires that the amount in controversy, which is measured by the value of the stake, be $500, and compels the stakeholder to deposit the money or property at issue in the court's Registry or, in the alternative, to give a bond payable to the clerk of courts in the appropriate amount. Additionally, 28 U.S.C. § 2361 (1994) provides for nationwide service on all claimants in statutory interpleader actions and allows a district court in a section 1335 interpleader case to enjoin any state or federal proceedings affecting the stake; 28 U.S.C. § 1397 (1993) provides that section 1335 interpleader cases may be brought where one or more of the claimants reside.

An action commenced under section 1335 typically involves two steps: during the first, the district court determines whether the requirements of the statute have been met and whether the stakeholder may be relieved from liability; during the second, it actually adjudicates the defendants' adverse claims to the interpleaded fund. The second stage, which proceeds like any other action, is ultimately resolved by the entry of a judgment in favor of the claimant who is lawfully entitled to the stake.

Here the district court completed the first step of interpleader on May 19, 1994, when it granted NYLife's motion for a judgment in interpleader and discharged NYLife from liability. The court did not, however, proceed to section 1335's second step—the unresolved dispute between the claimants for the interpleaded fund, which was, like the first, within the court's original jurisdiction. We thus hold that the district court's conclusion that all federal claims had been dismissed by virtue of its May 19, 1994 order was in error, and that its October 26, 1994 decision to terminate the case in favor of TAG's pending state court action on this basis was as well erroneous. It necessarily follows and we further conclude that the district court erred when it also dismissed Gerasolo's cross-claims under 28 U.S.C. § 1367(c)(3) (1993) on October 26, 1994, believing that all claims over which it had original jurisdiction had been eliminated from the case.

Our analysis, however, does not end here. We turn next to the legal principles that are implicated by that portion of TAG's motion which in effect requested that the interpleader action be dismissed so as to allow the parties to resolve their dispute over the Mainstay Mutual Fund monies in the New Jersey state court.

III

It is, of course, the general rule that the mere pendency of a similar action in a state court does not require, nor even permit, a federal court to refuse to hear or to stay an action that is properly within its jurisdiction, and that both state and federal actions should go forward until one of them results in a judgment that may be asserted as res judicata in the other.

Some fifty years ago, in *Brillhart v. Excess Ins. Co.*, 316 U.S. 491, 86 L. Ed. 1620, 62 S. Ct. 1173 (1942), the Supreme Court held that the district courts may decline to hear lawsuits brought under the Federal Declaratory Judgment Act, 28 U.S.C. § 2201(a), in favor of pending state actions for reasons of judicial economy, even where they have jurisdiction.

Later, in [*Colorado River Water Conservation Dist. v. United States*, 424 U.S. 800, 47 L. Ed. 2d 483, 96 S. Ct. 1236 (1976)], the Supreme Court revisited the propriety of a district court's decision to dismiss a federal suit in favor of a concurrent state court proceeding for reasons of judicial economy and efficiency. The Supreme Court confirmed that federal courts may, in appropriate circumstances, defer to state court proceedings for reasons of wise judicial administration, but, without discussing *Brillhart*, announced a very different standard. In *Colorado River* the Court referred to the "virtually unflagging obligation of the federal courts to exercise the jurisdiction given them", and set forth an "exceptional circumstances" test of several factors that the district courts should utilize.

Two years after its decision in *Colorado River*, the Court decided *Will v. Calvert Fire Ins. Co.*, 437 U.S. 655, 57 L. Ed. 2d 504, 98 S. Ct. 2552 (1978)., which concerned an action for an alleged violation of the federal securities laws commenced in federal court during the pendency of a related state court case. Relying on *Brillhart*, a plurality of the Court reversed the grant of a petition for a writ of mandamus ordering the district court to adjudicate the claim. Four Justices, however, joined Justice Brennan's dissent, which took issue with the plurality's reliance on *Brillhart* and its disregard for the *Colorado River* exceptional circumstances test.

Quite recently, the Supreme Court resolved the conflict in [Wilton v. Seven Falls Co., 515 U.S. 277, 132 L. Ed. 2d 214, 115 S. Ct. 2137 (1995)], holding that the *Brillhart* discretionary standard governs a district court's decision to stay a federal declaratory judgment action during the pendency of parallel state court proceedings. Its decision was premised on "distinct features of the Declaratory Judgment Act," which in the Court's view, "justify a standard vesting district courts with greater discretion in declaratory judgment actions than that permitted under the 'exceptional circumstances' test of *Colorado River*."

We turn now to the standard that governs a district court's decision to dismiss or stay an interpleader action commenced under 28 U.S.C. § 1335 (1993), due to the pendency of concurrent state court proceedings.

Our review has not produced nor have the parties suggested any cases which analyze the scope of a district court's discretion under 28 U.S.C. § 1335 (1993) to defer to state proceedings in light of the Supreme Court decisions we have discussed. We read the Supreme Court's decisions to instruct that the exceptional circumstances test is not universal and will yield in cases where the statute which grants a district court the authority to decide a matter "justifies [as does the Declaratory Judgment Act] a standard vesting district courts with greater discretion ... than that permitted under the 'exceptional circumstances' test."

Accordingly, we look to the interpleader statute to determine which standard—the discretionary approach taken in *Brillhart* or the exceptional circumstances test set forth in *Colorado River*—governs a district court's decision to dismiss a federal interpleader action in favor of pending state proceedings. We initially observe that historically and under the statute, interpleader is a suit in equity. A federal interpleader court, therefore, by the nature of its jurisdiction proceeds with broad discretion.

Against this backdrop, we turn to the text and structure, purpose and legislative history of section 1335 to determine the parameters of the district courts' discretion to decline jurisdiction and defer to state court proceedings for the sake of judicial administration and efficiency, looking specifically for any indication that Congress sought to limit a federal interpleader court's broad equitable discretion in such matters.

Starting with the statute's language and structure, we find that the text of section 1335, when considered with 28 U.S.C. § 2361 (1994), is inconclusive. Section 1335(b) of the interpleader statute provides that an action over which the district courts are granted original jurisdiction under section 1335(a) "may be entertained", even where the titles to or claims of the conflicting claimants are adverse and independent of one another. 28 U.S.C. § 1335(b). Although section 1335(b) is cast in discretionary terms, its permissive tone may relate solely to Congress' decision to abolish in the interpleader statute certain "historical limitations" that had been imposed on interpleader actions.

Section 2361, which authorizes the district courts to issue nationwide process and enjoin other actions affecting the stake, arguably suggests that a court may not decline to hear the case, stating that "[the] district court shall hear and determine the case, and may discharge the plaintiff from further liability, make the injunction permanent, and make all appropriate orders to enforce its judgment." 28 U.S.C. § 2361. We have not found any clues in other portions of section 1335 or section 2361 or in relevant legislative history to elucidate this language and its meaning. It does not seem likely, however, that at the same time Congress gave the district courts the considerable tool of nationwide process, retained their equitable power to order injunctive relief, and even granted them injunctive authority over state courts, it intended to narrow, if not eliminate, the district courts' discretion in deciding whether the issues raised in an interpleader action may be better resolved in a state court. We thus see section 2361 as a source of authority for the district courts, not as a command to the courts to exercise jurisdiction.

As to the purpose of section 1335, it has long been recognized that the interpleader statute is remedial, aimed at assisting a party who fears the vexation of defending multiple claims to a fund or property under his control by providing him the opportunity to satisfy his obligation in a single proceeding. See *State Farm Fire & Casualty Co.*

v. Tashire, 386 U.S. 523, 533, 18 L. Ed. 2d 270, 87 S. Ct. 1199 (1967). Indeed, the trend over the years has been directed toward increasing the availability of interpleader and relaxing historical, technical restraints on the device. This expansion of the remedy leads us to conclude that by the interpleader statute, Congress was more interested in providing an opportunity to litigants to resolve disputes, than in creating a duty in the district courts to exercise the jurisdiction given them therein.

We thus hold that the discretionary standard enunciated in *Brillhart* governs a district court's decision to dismiss an action commenced under the interpleader statute during the pendency of parallel state court proceedings.

■ [Dissent by JUDGE ROTH omitted]

State Farm Fire & Casualty Co. v. Tashire

Supreme Court of the United States, 1967.
386 U.S. 523, 87 S.Ct. 1199, 18 L.Ed.2d 270.

■ MR. JUSTICE FORTAS delivered the opinion of the Court.

Early one September morning in 1964, a Greyhound bus proceeding northward through Shasta County, California, collided with a southbound pickup truck. Two of the passengers aboard the bus were killed. Thirty-three others were injured, as were the bus driver, the driver of the truck and its lone passenger. One of the dead and 10 of the injured passengers were Canadians; the rest of the individuals involved were citizens of five American States. The ensuing litigation led to the present case, which raises important questions concerning administration of the interpleader remedy in the federal courts.

The litigation began when four of the injured passengers filed suit in California state courts, seeking damages in excess of $1,000,000. Named as defendants were Greyhound Lines, Inc., a California corporation; Theron Nauta, the bus driver; Ellis Clark, who drove the truck; and Kenneth Glasgow, the passenger in the truck who was apparently its owner as well. Each of the individual defendants was a citizen and resident of Oregon. Before these cases could come to trial and before other suits were filed in California or elsewhere, petitioner State Farm Fire & Casualty Company, an Illinois corporation, brought this action in the nature of interpleader in the United States District Court for the District of Oregon.

In its complaint State Farm asserted that at the time of the Shasta County collision it had in force an insurance policy with respect to Ellis Clark, driver of the truck, providing for bodily injury liability up to $10,000 per person and $20,000 per occurrence and for legal representation of Clark in actions covered by the policy. It asserted that actions already filed in California and others which it anticipated would be filed far exceeded in aggregate damages sought the amount of its maximum liability under the policy. Accordingly, it paid into court the sum of $20,000 and asked the court (1) to require all claimants to establish their claims against Clark and his insurer in this single proceeding and in no other, and (2) to discharge State Farm from all further obligations under its policy—including its duty to defend Clark in lawsuits arising from the accident. Alternatively, State Farm expressed its conviction that the policy issued to Clark excluded from coverage accidents resulting from his operation of a truck which belonged to another and was being used in the business of another. The complaint, therefore, requested that the court decree that the insurer owed no duty to Clark and was not liable on the policy, and it asked the court to refund the $20,000 deposit.

Joined as defendants were Clark, Glasgow, Nauta, Greyhound Lines, and each of the prospective claimants. Jurisdiction was predicated upon 28 U.S.C. § 1335, the federal interpleader statute,[1] and upon general diversity of citizenship, there being diversity between two or more of the claimants to the fund and between State Farm and all of the named defendants.

An order issued, requiring the defendants to show cause why they should not be restrained from filing or prosecuting "any proceeding in any state or United States Court affecting the property or obligation involved in this interpleader action, and specifically against the plaintiff and the defendant Ellis D. Clark." Personal service was effected on each of the American defendants, and registered mail was employed to reach the 11 Canadian claimants. Defendants Nauta, Greyhound, and several of the injured passengers responded, contending that the policy did cover this accident and advancing various arguments for the position that interpleader was either impermissible or inappropriate in the present circumstances. Greyhound, however, soon switched sides and moved that the court broaden any injunction to include Nauta and Greyhound among those who could not be sued except within the confines of the interpleader proceeding.

When a temporary injunction along the lines sought by State Farm was issued by the United States District Court for the District of Oregon, the present respondents moved to dismiss the action and, in the alternative, for a change of venue—to the Northern District of California, in which district the collision had occurred. After a hearing, the court declined to dissolve the temporary injunction, but continued the motion for a change of venue. The injunction was later broadened to include the protection sought by Greyhound, but modified to permit the filing—although not the prosecution—of suits. The injunc-

---

1. 28 U.S.C. § 1335(a) provides: "The district courts shall have original jurisdiction of any civil action of interpleader or in the nature of interpleader filed by any person, firm, or corporation, association, or society having in his or its custody or possession money or property of the value of $500 or more, or having issued a * * * policy of insurance * * * of value or amount of $500 or more * * * if

"(1) Two or more adverse claimants, of diverse citizenship as defined in section 1332 of this title, are claiming or may claim to be entitled to such money or property, or to any one or more of the benefits arising by virtue of any * * * policy * * *; and if (2) the plaintiff has * * * paid * * * the amount due under such obligation into the registry of the court, there to abide the judgment of the court * * *."

tion, therefore, provided that all suits against Clark, State Farm, Greyhound, and Nauta be prosecuted in the interpleader proceeding.

On interlocutory appeal, the Court of Appeals for the Ninth Circuit reversed. 363 F.2d 7. The court found it unnecessary to reach respondents' contentions relating to service of process and the scope of the injunction, for it concluded that interpleader was not available in the circumstances of this case. It held that in States like Oregon which do not permit "direct action" suits against insurance companies until judgments are obtained against the insured, the insurance companies may not invoke federal interpleader until the claims against the insured, the alleged tortfeasor, have been reduced to judgment. Until that is done, said the court, claimants with unliquidated tort claims are not "claimants" within the meaning of § 1335, nor are they "[p]ersons having claims against the plaintiff" within the meaning of Rule 22 of the Federal Rules of Civil Procedure.[3] *Id.*, at 10. In accord with that view, it directed dissolution of the temporary injunction and dismissal of the action. Because the Court of Appeals' decision on this point conflicts with those of other federal courts, and concerns a matter of significance to the administration of federal interpleader, we granted certiorari. 385 U.S. 811, 87 S.Ct. 90, 17 L.Ed.2d 52 (1966). Although we reverse the decision of the Court of Appeals upon the jurisdictional question, we direct a substantial modification of the District Court's injunction for reasons which will appear.

I.

Before considering the issues presented by the petition for certiorari, we find it necessary to dispose of a question neither raised by the parties nor passed upon by the courts below. Since the matter concerns our jurisdiction, we raise it on our own motion. Treinies v. Sunshine Mining Co., 308 U.S. 66, 70, 60 S.Ct. 44, 47, 84 L.Ed. 85 (1939). The interpleader statute, 28 U.S.C. § 1335, applies where there are "Two or more adverse claimants, of diverse citizenship * * *." This provision has been uniformly construed to require only "minimal diversity," that is, diversity of citizenship between two or more claimants, without regard to the circumstance that other rival claimants may be co-citizens. The language of the statute, the legislative purpose broadly to remedy the problems posed by multiple

---

3. We need not pass upon the Court of Appeals' conclusions with respect to the interpretation of interpleader under Rule 22, which provides that "(1) Persons having claims against the plaintiff may be joined as defendants and required to interplead when their claims are such that the plaintiff is or may be exposed to double or multiple liability * * *" First, as we indicate today, this action was properly brought under § 1335. Second, State Farm did not purport to invoke Rule 22. Third, State Farm could not have invoked it in light of venue and service of process limitations. Whereas statutory interpleader may be brought in the district where any claimant resides (28 U.S.C. § 1397), Rule interpleader based upon diversity of citizenship may be brought only in the district where all plaintiffs or all defendants reside (28 U.S.C. § 1391(a)). And whereas statutory interpleader enables a plaintiff to employ nationwide service of process (28 U.S.C. § 2361), service of process under Rule 22 is confined to that provided in Rule 4. See generally 3 Moore, Federal Practice ¶ 22.04. [Amendments to the general venue statute since the date of this case apply to Rule interpleader as well, and the Court's statement concerning application of 28 U.S.C. § 1391(a) should be modified accordingly.— Eds.]

claimants to a single fund, and the consistent judicial interpretation tacitly accepted by Congress, persuade us that the statute requires no more. There remains, however, the question whether such a statutory construction is consistent with Article III of our Constitution, which extends the federal judicial power to "Controversies * * * between citizens of different States * * * and between a State, or the Citizens thereof, and foreign States, Citizens or Subjects." In Strawbridge v. Curtiss, 3 Cranch 267, 2 L.Ed. 435 (1806), this Court held that the diversity of citizenship statute required "complete diversity": where co-citizens appeared on both sides of a dispute, jurisdiction was lost. But Chief Justice Marshall there purported to construe only "The words of the act of congress," not the Constitution itself. And in a variety of contexts this Court and the lower courts have concluded that Article III poses no obstacle to the legislative extension of federal jurisdiction, founded on diversity, so long as any two adverse parties are not co-citizens. Accordingly, we conclude that the present case is properly in the federal courts.

II.

We do not agree with the Court of Appeals that, in the absence of a state law or contractual provision for "direct action" suits against the insurance company, the company must wait until persons asserting claims against its insured have reduced those claims to judgment before seeking to invoke the benefits of federal interpleader. That may have been a tenable position under the 1926 and 1936 interpleader statutes. These statutes did not carry forward the language in the 1917 Act authorizing interpleader where adverse claimants "may claim" benefits as well as where they "are claiming" them. In 1948, however, in the revision of the Judicial Code, the "may claim" language was restored. Until the decision below, every court confronted by the question has concluded that the 1948 revision removed whatever requirement there might previously have been that the insurance company wait until at least two claimants reduced their claims to judgments. The commentators are in accord.

Considerations of judicial administration demonstrate the soundness of this view which, in any event, seems compelled by the language of the present statute, which is remedial and to be liberally construed. Were an insurance company required to await reduction of claims to judgment, the first claimant to obtain such a judgment or to negotiate a settlement might appropriate all or a disproportionate slice of the fund before his fellow claimants were able to establish their claims. The difficulties such a race to judgment pose for the insurer, and the unfairness which may result to some claimants, were among the principal evils the interpleader device was intended to remedy.

III.

The fact that State Farm had properly invoked the interpleader jurisdiction under § 1335 did not, however, entitle it to an order both enjoining prosecution of suits against it outside the confines of the interpleader proceeding and also extending such protection to its insured, the alleged tortfeasor. Still less was Greyhound Lines entitled to have that order expanded so as to protect itself and its driver, also alleged to be tortfeasors, from suits brought by its passengers in various state or federal courts. Here, the scope of the litigation, in terms of parties and claims, was vastly more extensive than the confines of the "fund," the deposited proceeds of the insurance policy. In these circumstances, the mere existence of such a fund cannot, by use of interpleader, be employed to accomplish purposes that exceed the needs of orderly contest with respect to the fund.

There are situations, of a type not present here, where the effect of interpleader is to confine the total litigation to a single forum and proceeding. One such case is where a stakeholder, faced with rival claims to the fund itself, acknowledges—or denies—his liability to one or the other of the claimants. In this situation, the fund itself is the target of the claimants. It marks the outer limits of the controversy. It is, therefore, reasonable and sensible that interpleader, in discharge of its office to protect the fund, should also protect the stakeholder from vexatious and multiple litigation. In this context, the suits sought to be enjoined are squarely within the language of 28 U.S.C. § 2361, which provides in part:

"In any civil action of interpleader or in the nature of interpleader under section 1335 of this title, a district court may issue its process for all claimants and enter its order restraining them from institution or prosecuting *any proceeding* in any State or United States court *affecting the property, instrument or obligation involved in the interpleader action * * *.*" (Emphasis added.)

But the present case is another matter. Here, an accident has happened. Thirty-five passengers or their representatives have claims which they wish to press against a variety of defendants: the bus company, its driver, the owner of the truck, and the truck driver. The circumstance that one of the prospective defendants happens to have an insurance policy is a fortuitous event which should not of itself shape the nature of the ensuing litigation. For example, a resident of California, injured in California aboard a bus owned by a California corporation should not be forced to sue that corporation anywhere but in California simply because another prospective defendant carried an insurance policy. And an insurance company whose maximum interest in the case cannot exceed $20,000 and who in fact asserts that it has no interest at all, should not be allowed to determine that dozens of tort plaintiffs must be compelled to press their claims—even those claims which are not against the insured and which in no event could be satisfied out of the meager insurance fund—in a single forum of the insurance company's choosing. There is nothing in the statutory scheme, and very little in the judicial and academic commentary upon that scheme, which requires that the tail be allowed to wag the dog in this fashion.

State Farm's interest in this case, which is the fulcrum of the interpleader procedure, is confined to its $20,000 fund. That interest receives full vindication when the court restrains claimants from seeking to enforce against the insurance company any judgment obtained against its insured, except in the interpleader proceeding itself. To the extent that the District Court sought to control claimants' lawsuits against the insured and other alleged tortfeasors, it exceeded the powers granted to it by the statutory scheme.

We recognize, of course, that our view of interpleader means that it cannot be used to solve all the vexing problems of multiparty litigation arising out of a mass tort. But interpleader was never intended to perform such a function, to be an all-purpose "bill of peace." Had it been so intended, careful provision would necessarily have been made to insure that a party with little or no interest in the outcome of a complex controversy should not strip truly interested parties of substantial rights—such as the right to choose the forum in which to establish their claims, subject to generally applicable rules of jurisdiction, venue, service of process, removal, and change of venue. None of the legislative and academic sponsors of a modern federal interpleader device viewed their accomplishment as a "bill of peace," capable of sweeping dozens of lawsuits out of the various state and federal courts in which they were brought and into a single interpleader proceeding. * * *

In light of the evidence that federal interpleader was not intended to serve the function of a "bill of peace" in the context of multiparty litigation arising out of a mass tort, of the anomalous power which such a construction of the statute would give the stakeholder, and of the thrust of the statute and the purpose it was intended to serve, we hold that the interpleader statute did not authorize the injunction entered in the present case. Upon remand, the injunction is to be modified consistently with this opinion.

IV.

The judgment of the Court of Appeals is reversed, and the case is remanded to the United States District Court for proceedings consistent with this opinion.

It is so ordered.[a]

NOTE

Is there need for both statutory interpleader and F.R.C.P. 22?

a. The dissenting opinion of Justice Douglas is omitted.

CHAPTER X

TRIAL

A. RIGHT TO JURY TRIAL

Armster v. United States District Court

United States Court of Appeals, Ninth Circuit, 1986.
792 F.2d 1423.

■ REINHARDT, CIRCUIT JUDGE:

Petitioners, plaintiffs in civil cases pending before the District Court for the Central District of California and the District Court for the District of Alaska, seek emergency writs of mandamus against those two district courts prohibiting them from suspending civil jury trials because of an alleged insufficiency of funds appropriated for the payment of juror fees. The threatened suspensions were based on advice from the Administrative Office of the United States Courts and the Executive Committee of the Judicial Conference that, as a result of a budgetary crisis, a nationwide suspension of the civil jury trial system was required from June 16, 1986 to October 1, the commencement of the next fiscal year.

* * *

Joseph Walters, one of the petitioners, is the plaintiff in a civil suit pending in the Central District of California. Walters made a timely jury trial demand and his case was scheduled to go to trial earlier this Spring. As of Friday, June 13, his case was trailing, pending completion of an ongoing trial before the district judge to whom the case was assigned. Late Friday afternoon, Walters' counsel was informed by the district judge's clerk that because insufficient funds had been appropriated to pay jurors during the current fiscal year, neither the district judge nor any other judge of the Central District would start any new jury trials until after October 1, 1986, the date on which the next fiscal year commences. The other petitioners, all represented by Walters' counsel, also are plaintiffs in cases with civil jury trials scheduled to commence prior to October 1, including one scheduled for Tuesday, June 17. All the cases are civil rights actions brought under 42 U.S.C. § 1983.

* * *

It is clear from the record before us that, at the direction of the Executive Committee of the Judicial Conference, the Administrative Office informed all district judges that the Anti–Deficiency Act requires the nationwide suspension of all new civil jury trials, and that on the basis of the Administrative Office memorandum the district judge, through his clerk, notified Walters that, because of the ordered suspension, his trial would not be held until the next fiscal year. The issue before us is whether district judges are legally obligated to empanel civil juries during the remainder of the current fiscal year, notwithstanding the Anti–Deficiency Act and the anticipated shortage in appropriated funds.

The proceeding before us raises both statutory and constitutional questions. For prudential reasons we avoid deciding constitutional questions unnecessarily. Hospital and Service Employees Union, Local 399 v. NLRB, 743 F.2d 1417, 1427 (9th Cir.1984). Ordinarily, if a case presents a potentially dispositive statutory question we decide that question before turning to the constitutional issue. In this case, however, the Justice Department has urged us to decide the constitutional question first, and we agree that it is necessary to do so. The petition was presented to us as an emergency motion. It raises a most serious issue regarding a continuing deprivation of a fundamental constitutional right, a deprivation that may well be occurring in every district throughout the circuit—and, in fact, the nation. The speediest possible decision is required. The constitutional question has been fully briefed and argued, and is relatively straightforward. The statutory questions are considerably more complicated; the legal issues involved have not been adequately briefed or argued by either party, and the record lacks certain facts that might be necessary to a proper resolution of those questions. Thus, this is not a case in which "the record presents some other ground upon which the case may be disposed of," Rescue Army v. Municipal Court of Los Angeles, 331 U.S. 549, 569, 67 S.Ct. 1409, 1419, 91 L.Ed. 1666 (1947). Because of the need to decide this case at the earliest possible time, it is unavoidable that we reach the constitutional question now.

Walters claims that the suspension of civil jury trials following receipt of the memorandum from the Administrative Office violates the seventh amendment and, specifically, his right to a civil jury trial. The Justice Department contends that the seventh amendment does not guarantee that a civil jury trial must take place at a particular time and that, therefore, a three and one-half month suspension of jury trials does not violate the seventh amendment in general, or Walters' right in particular. In support of its argument, the Justice Department notes that, while the sixth amendment guarantees a speedy *criminal* jury trial, the seventh amendment does not guarantee a speedy *civil* jury trial. It also notes that district courts frequently postpone scheduled civil jury trials for reasons other than the lack of funds to pay jurors. These reasons include calendar congestion, lack of a sufficient number of judges, and the priority accorded to trying criminal cases before civil actions.

The petition before us does not involve a judge's determination, after exercising his discretion in good faith, that the number of cases that are ready for trial exceeds the inherent limitations on his ability to try them immediately, and that he must therefore schedule future trial dates for some of those cases. Nor does it involve a judge's attempts to balance the competing demands of the sixth and seventh amendments. We recognize that calendar delays resulting from the current high volume of litigation are all too common, and we have frequently said that the district courts must have wide discretion to handle such matters. In such circumstances, the proper exercise of discretion by district judges implicates no seventh amendment right.

Here, as the Administrative Office memorandum makes clear, what is proposed is not any exercise of judicial discretion by individual district judges. Rather, we are confronted with the wholesale nondiscretionary suspension of the civil jury trial system and a blanket moratorium on all civil jury trials for a three and one-half month period. The Director of the Administrative Office, in his affidavit, acknowledges that the Constitution would prohibit a similar suspension of criminal jury trials not only "because [of] the constitutional and statutory mandates for speedy trials of criminal cases, [but also because of] the constitutional right to a criminal jury trial." However, the Director contends that there is no constitutional bar to the suspension of civil jury trials, at least where financial considerations require such action. The Justice Department agrees with this contention. We disagree, most emphatically.

The Supreme Court has emphasized, in no uncertain terms, the importance of the right to a civil jury trial and the need for the courts to be vigilant in guarding against the erosion of that right:

> The right of jury trial in civil cases at common law is a basic and fundamental feature of our system of federal jurisprudence which is protected by the Seventh Amendment. A right so fundamental and sacred to the citizen * * * should be jealously guarded by the courts.

Jacob v. New York City, 315 U.S. 752, 752–53, 62 S.Ct. 854, 854, 86 L.Ed. 1166 (1942).

The Supreme Court has adopted a most rigorous standard for reviewing any potential infringement of the right to a civil trial. The Court has said more than once that " '[m]aintenance of the jury as a fact-finding body is of such importance and occupies so firm a place in our history and jurisprudence that any seeming curtailment of the right to a jury trial should be scrutinized with the utmost care.' " Beacon Theatres v. Westover, 359 U.S. 500, 501, 79 S.Ct. 948, 951, 3 L.Ed.2d 988 (1959) (quoting Dimick v. Schiedt, 293 U.S. 474, 486, 55 S.Ct. 296, 301 (1935)).

Thus, our duty is clear. We must vigilantly protect the right to civil jury trials, and we must scrutinize in the most rigorous manner possible any action that appears to limit in any way the availability of that right.

We begin by repeating some past observations. We have previously noted that the cost of the civil jury system nationwide is "minimal at best," that in 1979 the cost was about equal to that of "two jet fighters," and that the cost factor is not a justification for restricting the use of civil juries. These observations, set forth in In re U.S. Financial Securities Litigation, 609 F.2d 411, 430 & n. 71 (9th Cir. 1979), *cert. denied, sub nom.* Gant v. Union Bank, 446 U.S. 929, 100 S.Ct. 1866, 64 L.Ed.2d 281 (1980), are equally relevant today. We would only add that in 1986 the total cost of providing both the civil and criminal jury system nationwide, (including the three and one-half month period at issue here) is but *one-sixtieth* the cost of building one new space shuttle.[12]

Next, we proceed directly to the heart of the issue, the relationship between constitutional rights and the public fisc. The answer to the fundamental question before us is, as the Justice Department has suggested, simple. It is not, however, the one the Department has proffered. We conclude that the availability of constitutional rights does not vary with the rise and fall of account balances in the Treasury. Our basic liberties cannot be offered and withdrawn as "budget crunches" come and go, nor may they be made contingent on transitory political judgments regarding the advisability of raising or lowering taxes, or on pragmatic or tactical decisions about how to deal with the perennial problem of the national debt. In short, constitutional rights do not turn on the political mood of the moment, the outcome of cost/benefit analyses or the results of economic or fiscal calculations. Rather, our constitutional rights are fixed and immutable, subject to change only in the manner our forefathers established for the making of constitutional amendments. The constitutional mandate that federal courts provide civil litigants with a system of civil jury trials is clear. There is no price tag on the continued existence of that system, or on any other constitutionally-provided right.

We conclude that the civil jury trial system may not be suspended for lack of funds. Specifically, we conclude that the seventh amendment right to a civil jury trial is violated when, because of such a suspension, an individual is not afforded, for any significant period of time, a jury trial he would otherwise receive. We do not suggest that a suspension of any duration whatsoever would be constitutional. We need only decide here that a suspension for a significant period is barred by the seventh amendment. The suspension of civil jury trials described in the Administrative Office memorandum clearly falls within the parameters of that term. In fact, we believe three and a half months constitutes far more than a significant period, given the mandate of the seventh amendment. We recognize that the suspension in this case may be shortened if supplemental appropriations become

12. *See* New York Times, May 25, 1986, at 1, J.N. Wilford, "Reagan Is Reported Near Decision To Approve a New Space Shuttle." (Cost of new space shuttle estimated to be $2.3 billion). Other estimates of the cost of a new space shuttle include improvements and range from $5 to $8 billion, *see* New York Times, May 16, 1986; *see also* n. 3 *supra* (total juror costs for fiscal year 1986 estimated to be $46.2 million; amount appropriated 43.4 million).

The total cost of operating the federal judicial system, including the salaries of judges and all other personnel, is only slightly more than a third the cost of a single space shuttle, *see* Departments of Commerce, Justice, and State, the Judiciary, and Related Agencies Appropriation Act Pub.L. No. 99–180, 99 Stat. 1136, 1153–55 (1985). If the higher estimate of the space shuttle cost is correct, our entire federal court system costs only one-eighth as much as a single shuttle.

available. However, the possibility of future changed circumstances cannot affect our decision. We take the suspension as we find it, and we apply the rigorous scrutiny that the law requires. *See* Beacon Theatres v. Westover, 359 U.S. at 501, 79 S.Ct. at 951. Nor would our view be any different if there were no specific time period set forth in connection with the suspension of civil jury trials and if, instead, a moratorium were imposed only "until further notice." Any suspension other than a most minimal one would, we believe, be for a significant period.

Despite our conclusion that the suspension of the civil jury trial system is unconstitutional, we do not believe a writ of mandamus is required in this instance. Mandamus is a drastic remedy that should be invoked only in extraordinary circumstances. Kerr v. United States District Court, 426 U.S. 394, 402, 96 S.Ct. 2119, 2123, 48 L.Ed.2d 725 (1976). Considering the rapid and confused sequence of events that gave rise to this proceeding, and the seemingly mandatory language of the Administrative Office memorandum, the district judge's action is readily understandable. We are confident, however, that the judges of the Central District who are presiding over the cases that are the subject of this petition will now act in light of the principles set forth in this opinion, that they will follow their normal procedures and exercise their customary and reasonable judicial discretion in scheduling and holding civil jury trials, and that they will do so without regard to the availability or unavailability of appropriated funds for the payment of juror fees.

Tull v. United States

Supreme Court of the United States, 1987.
481 U.S. 412, 107 S.Ct. 1831, 95 L.Ed.2d 365.

■ JUSTICE BRENNAN delivered the opinion of the Court.

The question for decision is whether the Seventh Amendment guaranteed petitioner a right to a jury trial on both liability and amount of penalty in an action instituted by the Federal Government seeking civil penalties and injunctive relief under the Clean Water Act, 62 Stat. 1155, as amended, 33 U.S.C. § 1251 *et seq.*

I

The Clean Water Act prohibits discharging, without a permit, dredged or fill material into "navigable waters," including the wetlands adjacent to the waters. 33 U.S.C. §§ 1311, 1344, and 1362(7); 33 CFR § 323.2(a)(1)–(7) (1986). "Wetlands" are "swamps, marshes, bogs and similar areas." 33 CFR § 323.2(c) (1986). The Government sued petitioner, a real estate developer, for dumping fill on wetlands on the island of Chincoteague, Virginia. The Government alleged in the original complaint that petitioner dumped fill on three sites: Ocean Breeze Mobile Homes Sites, Mire Pond Properties, and Eel Creek. The Government later amended the complaint to allege that petitioner also placed fill in a manmade waterway, named Fowling Gut Extended, on the Ocean Breeze property.[1]

Section 1319 enumerates the remedies available under the Clean Water Act. Subsection (b) authorizes relief in the form of temporary or permanent injunctions. Subsection (d) provides that violators of certain sections of the Act "shall be subject to a civil penalty not to exceed $10,000 per day" during the period of the violation. The Government sought in this case both injunctive relief and civil penalties. When the complaint was filed, however, almost all of the property at issue had been sold by petitioner to third parties. Injunctive relief was therefore impractical except with regard to a small portion of the land.[2] App. 110, 119. The Government's complaint demanded the imposition of the maximum civil penalty of $22,890,000 under subsection (d). App. 31–34.

Petitioner's timely demand for a trial by jury was denied by the District Court. During the 15–day bench trial, petitioner did not dispute that he had placed fill at the locations alleged and did not deny his failure to obtain a permit. Petitioner contended, however, that the property in question did not constitute "wetlands." 615 F.Supp. 610, 615–618 (E.D.Va.1983). The Government concedes that triable issues of fact were presented by disputes between experts involving the composition and nature of the fillings. Tr. of Oral Arg. 44.

The District Court concluded that petitioner had illegally filled in wetland areas on all properties in question, but drastically reduced the amount of civil penalties sought by the Government. With respect to the Ocean Breeze Mobile Homes Sites, the court imposed a civil fine of $35,000, noting that petitioner had sold seven lots at a profit of $5,000 per lot. The court fined petitioner another $35,000 for illegal fillings on the Mire Pond Properties, and $5,000 for filling that affected a single lot in Eel Creek, although petitioner had realized no profit from filling in these properties. In addition, the court imposed on petitioner a $250,000 fine to be suspended, however, "on the specific condition that he restore the extension of Fowling Gut to its former navigable condition ." Although petitioner argued that such restoration required purchasing the land from third parties at a cost of over $700,000, thus leaving him no choice but to pay the fine, the court refused to alter this order. The court also granted separate injunctive relief: it ordered the restoration of wetlands on the portions of Mire Pond and Eel Creek still owned by petitioner, and further ordered the removal of fillings on five lots of the Ocean Breeze Mobile Home Sites

---

1. Additionally, the Government alleged that petitioner's dumping of fill in Fowling Gut Extended violated another statute, the Rivers and Harbors Act, which prohibits the placement of fill in navigable waters without the authorization of the Secretary of the Army. 33 U.S.C. § 403. Petitioner does not base his Seventh Amendment claim on the Government's prosecution under this statute, which provides for injunctive relief but not for civil penalties.

2. The Government's complaint alleged violations involving over 1 million square feet of land. The Government obtained injunctive relief, however, relating to only 6,000 square feet.

unless petitioner were granted an "after-the-fact permit" validating the fillings.

The Court of Appeals affirmed over a dissent, rejecting petitioner's argument that, under the Seventh Amendment, he was entitled to a jury trial. 769 F.2d 182 (C.A.4 1985). The court expressly declined to follow the decision of the Court of Appeals for the Second Circuit in United States v. J.B. Williams Co., 498 F.2d 414 (1974), which held that there was a Seventh Amendment " 'right of jury trial when the United States sues * * * to collect a [statutory civil] penalty, even though the statute is silent on the right of jury trial.' " 498 F.2d, at 422–423 (quoting 5 J. Moore, Federal Practice ¶ 38.–31[1], pp. 232–233 (2d ed. 1971)). The Court of Appeals in this case also found unpersuasive the dictum in Hepner v. United States, 213 U.S. 103, 115, 29 S.Ct. 474, 479, 53 L.Ed. 720 (1909), and in United States v. Regan, 232 U.S. 37, 46–47, 34 S.Ct. 213, 216–217, 58 L.Ed. 494 (1914), that the Seventh Amendment's guarantee applies to civil actions to collect a civil penalty. The court concluded that, while in *Hepner* and *Regan* the civil penalties were statutorily prescribed fixed amounts, the District Court in the present case exercised "statutorily conferred equitable power in determining the amount of the fine." 769 F.2d, at 187. The Court of Appeals also noted that the District Court fashioned a " 'package' of remedies" containing both equitable and legal relief with "one part of the package affecting assessment of the others."

In Atlas Roofing Co. v. Occupational Safety and Health Review Comm'n, 430 U.S. 442, 449, n. 6, 97 S.Ct. 1261, 1266, n. 6, 51 L.Ed.2d 464 (1977), we explicitly declined to decide whether the dictum of *Hepner* and *Regan* "correctly divines the intent of the Seventh Amendment." To resolve this question and the conflict between Circuits, we granted certiorari. 476 U.S. 1139, 106 S.Ct. 2244, 90 L.Ed.2d 691 (1986). We reverse.

II

The Seventh Amendment provides that, "[i]n Suits at common law, where the value in controversy shall exceed twenty dollars, the right of trial by jury shall be preserved * * *."[3] The Court has construed this language to require a jury trial on the merits in those actions that are analogous to "Suits at common law." Prior to the Amendment's adoption, a jury trial was customary in suits brought in the English *law* courts. In contrast, those actions that are analogous to 18th-century cases tried in courts of equity or admiralty do not require a jury trial. *See* Parsons v. Bedford, 3 Pet. 433 (1830). This analysis applies not only to common-law forms of action, but also to causes of

---

3. Before initiating the inquiry into the applicability of the Seventh Amendment, "[w]e recognize, of course, the 'cardinal principle that this Court will first ascertain whether a construction of the statute is fairly possible by which the [constitutional] question may be avoided.' " Curtis v. Loether, 415 U.S. 189, 192, n. 6, 94 S.Ct. 1005, 1007, n. 6, 39 L.Ed.2d 260 (1974) (citation omitted); see also Pernell v. Southall Realty, 416 U.S. 363, 365, 94 S.Ct. 1723, 1724, 40 L.Ed.2d 198 (1974). Nothing in the language of the Clean Water Act or its legislative history implies any congressional intent to grant defendants the right to a jury trial during the liability or penalty phase of the civil suit proceedings. Given this statutory silence, we must answer the constitutional question presented.

action created by congressional enactment. *See* Curtis v. Loether, 415 U.S. 189, 193, 94 S.Ct. 1005, 1007, 39 L.Ed.2d 260 (1974).

To determine whether a statutory action is more similar to cases that were tried in courts of law than to suits tried in courts of equity or admiralty, the Court must examine both the nature of the action and of the remedy sought. First, we compare the statutory action to 18th-century actions brought in the courts of England prior to the merger of the courts of law and equity. *See, e.g.,* Pernell v. Southall Realty, 416 U.S. 363, 378, 94 S.Ct. 1723, 1731, 40 L.Ed.2d 198 (1974); Dairy Queen, Inc. v. Wood, 369 U.S. 469, 477, 82 S.Ct. 894, 899, 8 L.Ed.2d 44 (1962). Second, we examine the remedy sought and determine whether it is legal or equitable in nature. *See, e.g.,* Curtis v. Loether, *supra,* 415 U.S., at 196, 94 S.Ct., at 1009; Ross v. Bernhard, 396 U.S. 531, 542, 90 S.Ct. 733, 740, 24 L.Ed.2d 729 (1970).[4]

A

Petitioner analogizes this Government suit under § 1319(d) to an action in debt within the jurisdiction of English courts of law. Prior to the enactment of the Seventh Amendment, English courts had held that a civil penalty suit was a particular species of an action in debt that was within the jurisdiction of the courts of law. *See, e.g.,* Atcheson v. Everitt, 1 Cowper 382, 98 Eng.Rep. 1142 (K.B.1776) (characterizing civil penalty suit as a type of action in debt); Calcraft v. Gibbs, 5 T.R. 19, 101 Eng.Rep. 11 (K.B.1792) (granting new jury trial in an action in debt for a civil penalty).

After the adoption of the Seventh Amendment, federal courts followed this English common law in treating the civil penalty suit as a particular type of an action in debt, requiring a jury trial. *See, e.g.,* United States v. Mundell, 27 F.Cas. 23 (No. 15,834) (CC Va.1795) (bail not required in a civil penalty case tried by a jury because it was an action in debt); Jacob v. United States, 13 F.Cas. 267 (No. 7,157) (CC Va.1821) (action in debt by United States to recover civil penalty of $500 and costs of violation of an Act of Congress); Lees v. United States, 150 U.S. 476, 479, 14 S.Ct. 163, 164, 37 L.Ed. 1150 (1893) ("[A]lthough the recovery of a penalty is a proceeding criminal in nature, yet in this class of cases it may be enforced in a civil action, and in the same manner that debts are recovered in the ordinary civil courts"). Actions by the Government to recover civil penalties under statutory provisions therefore historically have been viewed as one type of action in debt requiring trial by jury.

It was against this historical background that the Court in Hepner v. United States, 213 U.S. 103, 29 S.Ct. 474, 53 L.Ed. 720 (1909), considered the propriety of a directed verdict by a District Court Judge

---

4. The Court has also considered the practical limitations of a jury trial and its functional compatibility with proceedings outside of traditional courts of law in holding that the Seventh Amendment is not applicable to administrative proceedings. *See, e.g.,* Atlas Roofing Co. v. Occupational Safety and Health Review Comm'n, 430 U.S. 442, 454, 97 S.Ct. 1261, 1268, 51 L.Ed.2d 464 (1977); Pernell v. Southall Realty, *supra,* 416 U.S. at 383, 94 S.Ct. at 1733. But the Court has not used these considerations as an independent basis for extending the right to a jury trial under the Seventh Amendment.

in favor of the Government where there was undisputed evidence that a defendant had committed an offense under § 8 of the Alien Immigration Act of 1903, which provided for a $1,000 civil penalty. The Court held that a directed verdict was permissible and did not violate the defendant's right to a jury trial under the Seventh Amendment. The Court said:

> "The objection made in behalf of the defendant, that an affirmative answer to the question certified could be used so as to destroy the constitutional right of trial by jury, is without merit and need not be discussed. *The defendant was, of course, entitled to have a jury summoned in this case,* but that right was subject to the condition, fundamental in the conduct of civil actions, that the court may withdraw a case from the jury and direct a verdict, according to the law if the evidence is uncontradicted and raises only a question of law." 213 U.S., at 115, 29 S.Ct., at 479 (emphasis added).

In United States v. Regan, 232 U.S. 37, 34 S.Ct. 213, 58 L.Ed. 494 (1914), the Court assumed that a jury trial was required in civil penalty actions. In that case, the Court upheld the validity of a jury instruction in an action brought by the Government under the Alien Immigration Act of 1907. The Court stated that the instruction requiring proof beyond a reasonable doubt was incorrect because:

> "While the defendant was entitled to have the issues tried before a jury, this right did not arise from Article III of the Constitution or from the Sixth Amendment, for both relate to prosecutions which are strictly criminal in their nature, but it derives out of the fact that in a civil action of debt involving more than twenty dollars a jury trial is demandable." 232 U.S., at 47, 34 S.Ct., at 216 (citation omitted).

In the instant case, the Government sought penalties of over $22 million for violation of the Clean Water Act and obtained a judgment in the sum of $325,000. This action is clearly analogous to the 18th-century action in debt, and federal courts have rightly assumed that the Seventh Amendment required a jury trial.

The Government argues, however, that—rather than an action in debt—the closer historical analog is an action to abate a public nuisance. In 18th-century English law, a public nuisance was "an act or omission 'which obstructs or causes inconvenience or damage to the public in the exercise of rights common to all Her Majesty's subjects.'" W. Prosser, Law of Torts 583 (4th ed. 1971) (hereinafter Prosser) (footnote omitted). The Government argues that the present suit is analogous to two species of public nuisances. One is the suit of the sovereign in the English courts of equity for a "purpresture" to enjoin or order the repair of an enclosure or obstruction of public waterways; the other is the suit of the sovereign to enjoin "offensive trades and manufactures" that polluted the environment. 4 W. Blackstone, Commentaries *167.

It is true that the subject matter of this Clean Water Act suit—the placement of fill into navigable waters—resembles these two species of public nuisance. Whether, as the Government argues, a public nuisance action is a better analogy than an action in debt is debatable. But we need not decide the question. As Pernell v. Southall Realty, 416 U.S., at 375, 94 S.Ct., at 1729, cautioned, the fact that the subject matter of a modern statutory action and an 18th-century English action are close equivalents "is irrelevant for Seventh Amendment purposes," because "that Amendment requires trial by jury in actions unheard of at common law." It suffices that we conclude that both the public nuisance action and the action in debt are appropriate analogies to the instant statutory action.

The essential function of an action to abate a public nuisance was to provide a civil means to redress "a miscellaneous and diversified group of minor criminal offenses, based on some interference with the interests of the community, or the comfort or convenience of the general public." Prosser 583.[5] Similarly, the essential function of an action in debt was to recover money owed under a variety of statutes or under the common law. Both of these 18th-century actions, then, could be asserted by the sovereign to seek relief for an injury to the public in numerous contexts.

We need not rest our conclusion on what has been called an "abstruse historical" search for the nearest 18th-century analog. *See* Ross v. Bernhard, 396 U.S., at 538, n. 10, 90 S.Ct., at 738, n. 10. We reiterate our previously expressed view that characterizing the relief sought is "[m]ore important" than finding a precisely analogous common-law cause of action in determining whether the Seventh Amendment guarantees a jury trial. Curtis v. Loether, 415 U.S., at 196, 94 S.Ct., at 1009.[6]

B

A civil penalty was a type of remedy at common law that could only be enforced in courts of law. Remedies intended to punish

---

5. Public nuisances included "interferences with the public health, as in the case of a hogpen, the keeping of diseased animals, or a malarial pond; with the public safety, as in the case of the storage of explosives, the shooting of fireworks in the streets, harboring a vicious dog, or the practice of medicine by one not qualified; with public morals, as in the case of houses of prostitution, illegal liquor establishments, gambling houses, indecent exhibitions, bullfights, unlicensed prize fights, or public profanity; with the publice [sic] peace, as by loud and and disturbing noises, or an opera performance which threatens to cause a riot; with the public comfort, as in the case of bad odors, smoke, dust and vibration; with public convenience, as by obstructing a highway or a navigable stream, or creating a condition which makes travel unsafe or highly disagreeable, or the collection of an inconvenient crowd; and in addition, such unclassified offenses as eaves-dropping on a jury, or being a common scold." Prosser 583–585 (footnotes omitted).

6. The Government contends that both the cause of action and the remedy must be legal in nature before the Seventh Amendment right to a jury trial attaches. It divides the Clean Water Act action for civil penalties into a cause of action and a remedy, and analyzes each component as if the other were irrelevant. Thus, the Government proposes that a public nuisance action is the better historical analog for the cause of action, and that an action for disgorgement is the proper analogy for the remedy. We reject this novel approach. Our search is for a single historical analog, taking into consideration the nature of the cause of action and the remedy as two important factors. *See* Pernell v. Southall Realty, 416 U.S., at 375, 94 S.Ct., at 1729; Curtis v. Loether, 415 U.S., at 195–196, 94 S.Ct., at 1008–1009.

culpable individuals, as opposed to those intended simply to extract compensation or restore the status quo, were issued by courts of law, not courts of equity. *See, e.g.,* Curtis v. Loether, *supra,* at 197, 94 S.Ct., at 1009 (punitive damages remedy is legal, not equitable, relief); Ross v. Bernhard, *supra,* 396 U.S. at 536, 90 S.Ct. at 737 (treble-damages remedy for securities violation is a penalty, which constitutes legal relief).[7] The action authorized by § 1319(d) is of this character. Subsection (d) does not direct that the "civil penalty" imposed be calculated solely on the basis of equitable determinations, such as the profits gained from violations of the statute, but simply imposes a maximum penalty of $10,000 per day of violation. The legislative history of the Act reveals that Congress wanted the district court to consider the need for retribution and deterrence, in addition to restitution, when it imposed civil penalties. 123 Cong.Rec. 39191 (1977) (remarks of Sen. Muskie citing Environmental Protection Agency (EPA) memorandum outlining enforcement policy).[8] A court can require retribution for wrongful conduct based on the seriousness of the violations, the number of prior violations, and the lack of good-faith efforts to comply with the relevant requirements. *Ibid.* It may also seek to deter future violations by basing the penalty on its economic impact. *Ibid.* Subsection 1319(d)'s authorization of punishment to further retribution and deterrence clearly evidences that this subsection reflects more than a concern to provide equitable relief. In the present case, for instance, the District Court acknowledged that petitioner received no profits from filling in properties in Mire Pond and Eel Creek, but still imposed a $35,000 fine. App. to Pet. for Cert. 60a. Thus, the District Court intended not simply to disgorge profits but also to impose punishment. Because the nature of the relief authorized by § 1319(d) was traditionally available only in a court of law, petitioner in this present action is entitled to a jury trial on demand.

The punitive nature of the relief sought in this present case is made apparent by a comparison with the relief sought in an action to abate a public nuisance. A public nuisance action was a classic example of the kind of suit that relied on the injunctive relief provided

---

7. The Government distinguishes this suit from other actions to collect a statutory penalty on the basis that the statutory penalty here is not fixed or readily calculable from a fixed formula. We do not find this distinction to be significant. The more important characteristic of the remedy of civil penalties is that it exacts punishment—a kind of remedy available only in courts of law. Thus, the remedy of civil penalties is similar to the remedy of punitive damages, another legal remedy that is not a fixed fine. *See, e.g.,* Curtis v. Loether, *supra,* at 189–190, 94 S.Ct., at 1005–1006 (defendant entitled to jury trial in an action based on a statute authorizing actual damages and punitive damages of not more than $1,000).

8. When Congress enacted the 1977 amendments to the Clean Water Act, it en-

dorsed the EPA's then-existing penalty calculation policy. 123 Cong.Rec. 39190–39191 (1977) (remarks of Sen. Muskie). This policy was developed to guide EPA negotiators in reaching settlements with violators of the Act. The policy instructed negotiators to consider a number of factors: the seriousness of the violations, the economic benefits accrued from the violations, prior violations, good-faith efforts to comply with the relevant requirements, and the economic impact of the penalty. After the Court heard argument in this case, § 1319(d) was amended to require the trial court to consider these factors in determining the amount of a civil penalty along with "such other matters as justice may require." § 313(d), Water Quality Act of 1987, Pub.L. 100–4, 101 Stat. 47.

by courts in equity. Prosser 603. "Injunctive relief [for enjoining a public nuisance at the request of the Government] is traditionally given by equity upon a showing of [peril to health and safety]." Steelworkers v. United States, 361 U.S. 39, 61, 80 S.Ct. 1, 186, 4 L.Ed.2d 12 (1959) (Frankfurter, J., concurring). The Government, in fact, concedes that public nuisance cases brought in equity sought injunctive relief, not monetary penalties. Brief for United States 24, n. 17. Indeed, courts in equity refused to enforce such penalties. See James, Right to a Jury Trial in Civil Actions, 72 Yale L.J. 655, 672 (1963).

The Government contends, however, that a suit enforcing civil penalties under the Clean Water Act is similar to an action for disgorgement of improper profits, traditionally considered an equitable remedy. It bases this characterization upon evidence that the District Court determined the amount of the penalties by multiplying the number of lots sold by petitioner by the profit earned per lot. Tr. of Oral Arg. 27. An action for disgorgement of improper profits is, however, a poor analogy. Such an action is a remedy only for restitution—a more limited form of penalty than a civil fine. Restitution is limited to "restoring the status quo and ordering the return of that which rightfully belongs to the purchaser or tenant." Porter v. Warner Holding Co., 328 U.S. 395, 402, 66 S.Ct. 1086, 1091, 90 L.Ed. 1332 (1946). As the above discussion indicates, however, § 1319(d)'s concerns are by no means limited to restoration of the status quo.

The Government next contends that, even if the civil penalties under § 1319(d) are deemed legal in character, a jury trial is not required. A court in equity was empowered to provide monetary awards that were incidental to or intertwined with injunctive relief. The Government therefore argues that its claim under § 1319(b), which authorizes injunctive relief, provides jurisdiction for monetary relief in equity. Brief for United States 38. This argument has at least three flaws. First, while a court in equity may award monetary restitution as an adjunct to injunctive relief, it may not enforce civil penalties. *See* Porter v. Warner Co., *supra,* at 399, 66 S.Ct., at 1089. Second, the Government was aware when it filed suit that relief would be limited primarily to civil penalties, since petitioner had already sold most of the properties at issue. A potential penalty of $22 million hardly can be considered incidental to the modest equitable relief sought in this case.

Finally, the Government was free to seek an equitable remedy in addition to, or independent of, legal relief. Section 1319 does not intertwine equitable relief with the imposition of civil penalties. Instead each kind of relief is separably authorized in a separate and distinct statutory provision. Subsection (b), providing injunctive relief, is independent of subsection (d), which provides only for civil penalties. In such a situation, if a "legal claim is joined with an equitable claim, the right to jury trial on the legal claim, including all issues common to both claims, remains intact. The right cannot be abridged by characterizing the legal claim as 'incidental' to the equitable relief sought." Curtis v. Loether, 415 U.S. at 196, n. 11, 94 S.Ct. at 1009, n. 11. Thus, petitioner has a constitutional right to a jury trial to determine his liability on the legal claims.

III

The remaining issue is whether petitioner additionally has a Seventh Amendment right to a jury assessment of the civil penalties. At the time this case was tried, § 1319(d) did not explicitly state whether juries or trial judges were to fix the civil penalties. The legislative history of the 1977 Amendments to the Clean Water Act shows, however, that Congress intended that trial judges perform the highly discretionary calculations necessary to award civil penalties after liability is found. 123 Cong.Rec. 39190–39191 (1977) (remarks of Sen. Muskie citing letter from EPA Assistant Administrators of Enforcement of Dec. 14, 1977) ("[P]enalties assessed by judges should be sufficiently higher than penalties to which the Agency would have agreed in settlement to encourage violators to settle"). We must decide therefore whether Congress can, consistent with the Seventh Amendment, authorize judges to assess civil penalties.

The Seventh Amendment is silent on the question whether a jury must determine the remedy in a trial in which it must determine liability.[9] The answer must depend on whether the jury must shoulder this responsibility as necessary to preserve the "substance of the common-law right of trial by jury." Colgrove v. Battin, 413 U.S. 149, 157, 93 S.Ct. 2448, 2452, 37 L.Ed.2d 522 (1973). Is a jury role necessary for that purpose? We do not think so. " 'Only those incidents which are regarded as fundamental, as inherent in and of the essence of the system of trial by jury, are placed beyond the reach of the legislature.' " *Id.*, at 156, n. 11, 93 S.Ct. at 2452, n. 11 (quoting Scott, Trial by Jury and the Reform of Civil Procedure, 31 Harv.L.Rev. 669, 671 (1918)). *See also* Galloway v. United States, 319 U.S. 372, 392, 63 S.Ct. 1077, 1088, 87 L.Ed. 1458 (1943) ("[T]he Amendment was designed to preserve the basic institution of jury trial in only its most fundamental elements"). The assessment of a civil penalty is not one of the "most fundamental elements." Congress' authority to fix the penalty by statute has not been questioned, and it was also the British practice, see, *e.g.,* Atcheson v. Everitt, 1 Cowper 382, 98 Eng.Rep. 1142 (K.B.1776). In the United States, the action to recover civil penalties usually seeks the amount fixed by Congress. *See, e.g.,* United States v. Regan, 232 U.S., at 40, 34 S.Ct., at 213; Hepner v. United States, 213 U.S., at 109, 29 S.Ct., at 477. The assessment of civil

9. Nothing in the Amendment's language suggests that the right to a jury trial extends to the remedy phase of a civil trial. Instead, the language "defines the kind of cases for which jury trial is preserved, namely 'suits at common law.' " Colgrove v. Battin, 413 U.S. 149, 152, 93 S.Ct. 2448, 2450, 37 L.Ed.2d 522 (1973). Although " '[w]e have almost no direct evidence concerning the intention of the framers of the seventh amendment itself,' the historical setting in which the Seventh Amendment was adopted highlighted a controversy that was generated * * * by fear that the civil jury itself would be abolished." *Ibid.* (footnote and citation omitted). We have been presented with no evidence that the Framers meant to extend the right to a jury to the remedy phase of a civil trial.

penalties thus cannot be said to involve the "substance of a common-law right to a trial by jury," nor a "fundamental element of a jury trial."

Congress' assignment of the determination of the amount of civil penalties to trial judges therefore does not infringe on the constitutional right to a jury trial. Since Congress itself may fix the civil penalties, it may delegate that determination to trial judges. In this case, highly discretionary calculations that take into account multiple factors are necessary in order to set civil penalties under the Clean Water Act. These are the kinds of calculations traditionally performed by judges. *See* Albemarle Paper Co. v. Moody, 422 U.S. 405, 442–443, 95 S.Ct. 2362, 2384–2385, 45 L.Ed.2d 280 (1975) (Rehnquist, J., concurring). We therefore hold that a determination of a civil penalty is not an essential function of a jury trial, and that the Seventh Amendment does not require a jury trial for that purpose in a civil action.

IV

We conclude that the Seventh Amendment required that petitioner's demand for a jury trial be granted to determine his liability, but that the trial court and not the jury should determine the amount of penalty, if any. The judgment of the Court of Appeals is therefore reversed, and the case is remanded for further proceedings consistent with this opinion.

■ JUSTICE SCALIA, with whom JUSTICE STEVENS joins, concurring in part and dissenting in part.

I join the Court's disposition, and Parts I and II of its opinion. I do not join Part III because in my view the right to trial by jury on whether a civil penalty of unspecified amount is assessable also involves a right to trial by jury on what the amount should be. The fact that the Legislature could elect to fix the amount of penalty has nothing to do with whether, if it chooses not to do so, that element comes within the jury-trial guarantee. Congress could, I suppose, create a private cause of action by one individual against another for a fixed amount of damages, but it surely does not follow that if it creates such a cause of action *without* prescribing the amount of damages, that issue could be taken from the jury.

While purporting to base its determination (quite correctly) upon historical practice, the Court creates a form of civil adjudication I have never encountered. I can recall no precedent for judgment of civil liability by jury but assessment of amount by the court. Even punitive damages are assessed by the jury when liability is determined in that fashion. One is of course tempted to make an exception in a case like this, where the Government is imposing a noncompensatory remedy to enforce direct exercise of its regulatory authority, because there comes immediately to mind the role of the sentencing judge in a criminal proceeding. If criminal trials are to be the model, however, determination of liability by the jury should be on a standard of proof requiring guilt beyond a reasonable doubt. Having chosen to proceed in civil fashion, with the advantages which that mode entails, it seems to me the Government must take the bitter with the sweet. Since, as the Court correctly reasons, the proper analogue to a civil-fine action is the common-law action for debt, the Government need only prove liability by a preponderance of the evidence; but must, as in any action for debt, accept the amount of award determined not by its own officials but by 12 private citizens. If that tends to discourage the Government from proceeding in this fashion, I doubt that the Founding Fathers would be upset.

I would reverse and remand for jury determination of both issues.

Markman v. Westview Instruments, Inc.

Supreme Court of the United States, 1996.
517 U.S. 370, 116 S. Ct. 1384, L. Ed. 2d.

■ JUSTICE SOUTER delivered the opinion for a unanimous Court.

The question here is whether the interpretation of a so-called patent claim, the portion of the patent document that defines the scope of the patentee's rights, is a matter of law reserved entirely for the court, or subject to a Seventh Amendment guarantee that a jury will determine the meaning of any disputed term of art about which expert testimony is offered. We hold that the construction of a patent, including terms of art within its claim, is exclusively within the province of the court.

I

The Constitution empowers Congress "[t]o promote the Progress of Science and useful Arts, by securing for limited Times to Authors and Inventors the exclusive Right to their respective Writings and Discoveries." U.S. Const., Art I, § 8, cl. 8. Congress first exercised this authority in 1790, when it provided for the issuance of "letters patent," Act of Apr. 10, 1790, ch. 7, § 1, 1 Stat. 109, which, like their modern counterparts, granted inventors "the right to exclude others from making, using, offering for sale, selling, or importing the patented invention," in exchange for full disclosure of an invention, H. Schwartz, Patent Law and Practice 1, 33 (2d ed.1995). It has long been understood that a patent must describe the exact scope of an invention and its manufacture to "secure to [the patentee] all to which he is entitled, [and] to apprise the public of what is still open to them." McClain v. Ortmayer, 141 U.S. 419, 424, 12 S.Ct. 76, 77, 35 L.Ed. 800 (1891). Under the modern American system, these objectives are served by two distinct elements of a patent document. First, it contains a specification describing the invention "in such full, clear, concise, and exact terms as to enable any person skilled in the art ... to make and use the same." 35 U.S.C. § 112; see also 3 E. Lipscomb, Walker on Patents § 10:1, pp. 183–184 (3d ed. 1985) (Lipscomb) (listing the requirements for a specification). Second, a patent includes one or more "claims," which "particularly poin[t] out and distinctly clai[m] the subject matter which the applicant regards as his invention." 35

U.S.C. § 112. "A claim covers and secures a process, a machine, a manufacture, a composition of matter, or a design, but never the function or result of either, nor the scientific explanation of their operation." 6 Lipscomb § 21:17, at 315–316. The claim "define[s] the scope of a patent grant," 3 id., § 11:1, at 280, and functions to forbid not only exact copies of an invention, but products that go to "the heart of the invention but avoid the literal language of the claim by making a noncritical change," Schwartz, supra, at 82.[1] In this opinion, the word "claim" is used only in this sense peculiar to patent law.

Characteristically, patent lawsuits charge what is known as infringement, and rest on allegations that the defendant "without authority ma[de], use[d] or [sold the] patented invention, within the United States during the term of the patent therefor...." 35 U.S.C. § 271(a). Victory in an infringement suit requires a finding that the patent claim "covers the alleged infringer's product or process," which in turn necessitates a determination of "what the words in the claim mean." Schwartz, supra, at 80.

Petitioner in this infringement suit, Markman, owns United States Reissue Patent No. 33,054 for his "Inventory Control and Reporting System for Drycleaning Stores." The patent describes a system that can monitor and report the status, location, and movement of clothing in a dry-cleaning establishment. The Markman system consists of a keyboard and data processor to generate written records for each transaction, including a bar code readable by optical detectors operated by employees, who log the progress of clothing through the dry-cleaning process. Respondent Westview's product also includes a keyboard and processor, and it lists charges for the dry-cleaning services on barcoded tickets that can be read by portable optical detectors.

Markman brought an infringement suit against Westview and Althon Enterprises, an operator of dry-cleaning establishments using Westview's products (collectively, Westview). Westview responded that Markman's patent is not infringed by its system because the latter functions merely to record an inventory of receivables by tracking invoices and transaction totals, rather than to record and track an inventory of articles of clothing. Part of the dispute hinged upon the meaning of the word "inventory," a term found in Markman's independent claim 1, which states that Markman's product can "maintain an inventory total" and "detect and localize spurious additions to inventory." The case was tried before a jury, which heard, among others, a witness produced by Markman who testified about the meaning of the claim language.

After the jury compared the patent to Westview's device, it found an infringement of Markman's independent claim 1 and dependent

---

1. Thus, for example, a claim for a ceiling fan with three blades attached to a solid rod connected to a motor would not only cover fans that take precisely this form, but would also cover a similar fan that includes some additional feature, e.g., such a fan with a cord or switch for turning it on and off, and may cover a product deviating from the core design in some noncritical way, e.g., a three-bladed ceiling fan with blades attached to a hollow rod connected to a motor. H. Schwartz, Patent Law and Practice 81–82 (2d ed.1995).

claim 10.[2] The District Court nevertheless granted Westview's deferred motion for judgment as a matter of law, one of its reasons being that the term "inventory" in Markman's patent encompasses "both cash inventory and the actual physical inventory of articles of clothing." 772 F.Supp. 1535, 1537–1538 (E.D.Pa.1991). Under the trial court's construction of the patent, the production, sale, or use of a tracking system for dry cleaners would not infringe Markman's patent unless the product was capable of tracking articles of clothing throughout the cleaning process and generating reports about their status and location. Since Westview's system cannot do these things, the District Court directed a verdict on the ground that Westview's device does not have the "means to maintain an inventory total" and thus cannot "detect and localize spurious additions to inventory as well as spurious deletions therefrom," as required by claim 1. Id., at 1537.

Markman appealed, arguing it was error for the District Court to substitute its construction of the disputed claim term "inventory" for the construction the jury had presumably given it. The United States Court of Appeals for the Federal Circuit affirmed, holding the interpretation of claim terms to be the exclusive province of the court and the Seventh Amendment to be consistent with that conclusion. 52 F.3d 967 (1995). Markman sought our review on each point, and we granted certiorari. 515 U.S.1192, 116 S.Ct. 40, 132 L.Ed.2d 921 (1995). We now affirm.

II

The Seventh Amendment provides that "[i]n Suits at common law, where the value in controversy shall exceed twenty dollars, the right of trial by jury shall be preserved...." [Since 1812] we have understood that "[t]he right of trial by jury thus preserved is the right which existed under the English common law when the Amendment was adopted." Baltimore & Carolina Line, Inc. v. Redman, 295 U.S. 654, 657, 55 S.Ct. 890, 891, 79 L.Ed. 1636 (1935). In keeping with our long-standing adherence to this "historical test," Wolfram, The Constitutional History of the Seventh Amendment, 57 Minn. L.Rev. 639, 640–643 (1973), we ask, first, whether we are dealing with a cause of action that either was tried at law at the time of the Founding or is at least analogous to one that was, see, e.g., Tull v. United States, 481 U.S. 412, 417, 107 S.Ct. 1831, 1835, 95 L.Ed.2d 365 (1987). If the action in question belongs in the law category, we then ask whether the particular trial decision must fall to the jury in order to preserve the substance of the common-law right as it existed in 1791.

A

As to the first issue, going to the character of the cause of action, "[t]he form of our analysis is familiar. 'First we compare the statutory action to 18th-century actions brought in the courts of England prior

2. Dependent claim 10 specifies that, in the invention of claim 1, the input device is an alpha-numeric keyboard in which single keys may be used to enter the attributes of the items in question

to the merger of the courts of law and equity.' " Granfinanciera, S.A. v. Nordberg, 492 U.S. 33, 42, 109 S.Ct. 2782, 2790, 106 L.Ed.2d 26 (1989) (citation omitted). Equally familiar is the descent of today's patent infringement action from the infringement actions tried at law in the 18th century, and there is no dispute that infringement cases today must be tried to a jury, as their predecessors were more than two centuries ago. See, e.g., Bramah v. Hardcastle, 1 Carp. P.C. 168 (K.B.1789).

B

This conclusion raises the second question, whether a particular issue occurring within a jury trial (here the construction of a patent claim) is itself necessarily a jury issue, the guarantee being essential to preserve the right to a jury's resolution of the ultimate dispute. In some instances the answer to this second question may be easy because of clear historical evidence that the very subsidiary question was so regarded under the English practice of leaving the issue for a jury. But when, as here, the old practice provides no clear answer, we are forced to make a judgment about the scope of the Seventh Amendment guarantee without the benefit of any foolproof test.

The Court has repeatedly said that the answer to the second question "must depend on whether the jury must shoulder this responsibility as necessary to preserve the 'substance of the common-law right of trial by jury.' " Tull v. United States, supra, at 426.

The "substance of the common-law right" is, however, a pretty blunt instrument for drawing distinctions. We have tried to sharpen it, to be sure, by reference to the distinction between substance and procedure. We have also spoken of the line as one between issues of fact and law.

But the sounder course, when available, is to classify a mongrel practice (like construing a term of art following receipt of evidence) by using the historical method, much as we do in characterizing the suits and actions within which they arise. Where there is no exact antecedent, the best hope lies in comparing the modern practice to earlier ones whose allocation to court or jury we do know, seeking the best analogy we can draw between an old and the new.

C

"Prior to 1790 nothing in the nature of a claim had appeared either in British patent practice or in that of the American states," Lutz, Evolution of the Claims of U.S. Patents, 20 J. Pat. Off. Soc. 134 (1938), and we have accordingly found no direct antecedent of modern claim construction in the historical sources. Claim practice did not achieve statutory recognition until the passage of the Act of 1836, and inclusion of a claim did not become a statutory requirement until 1870. * * *

The closest 18th-century analogue of modern claim construction seems, then, to have been the construction of specifications, and as to that function the mere smattering of patent cases that we have from this period shows no established jury practice sufficient to support an argument by analogy that today's construction of a claim should be a guaranteed jury issue. Few of the case reports even touch upon the proper interpretation of disputed terms in the specifications at issue. * * *

III

Since evidence of common law practice at the time of the Framing does not entail application of the Seventh Amendment's jury guarantee to the construction of the claim document, we must look elsewhere to characterize this determination of meaning in order to allocate it as between court or jury. We accordingly consult existing precedent and consider both the relative interpretive skills of judges and juries and the statutory policies that ought to be furthered by the allocation.

A

The two elements of a simple patent case, construing the patent and determining whether infringement occurred, were characterized by the former patent practitioner, Justice Curtis.[11] "The first is a question of law, to be determined by the court, construing the letters-patent, and the description of the invention and specification of claim annexed to them. The second is a question of fact, to be submitted to a jury." Winans v. Denmead, 15 How., at 338.

B

Where history and precedent provide no clear answers, functional considerations also play their part in the choice between judge and jury to define terms of art. We said in Miller v. Fenton, 474 U.S. 104, 114, 106 S.Ct. 445, 451, 88 L.Ed.2d 405 (1985), that when an issue "falls somewhere between a pristine legal standard and a simple historical fact, the fact/law distinction at times has turned on a determination that, as a matter of the sound administration of justice, one judicial actor is better positioned than another to decide the issue in question." So it turns out here, for judges, not juries, are the better suited to find the acquired meaning of patent terms.

The construction of written instruments is one of those things that judges often do and are likely to do better than jurors unburdened by training in exegesis. Patent construction in particular "is a special occupation, requiring, like all others, special training and practice. The judge, from his training and discipline, is more likely to give a proper interpretation to such instruments than a jury; and he is, therefore, more likely to be right, in performing such a duty, than a jury can be expected to be." Parker v. Hulme, 18 F. Cas., at 1140. Such was the understanding nearly a century and a half ago, and there is no reason to weigh the respective strengths of judge and jury differently in relation to the modern claim; quite the contrary, for "the claims of patents have become highly technical in many respects as the result of

11. See 1 A Memoir of Benjamin Robbins Curtis, L L. D., 84 (B. Curtis ed. 1879).

special doctrines relating to the proper form and scope of claims that have been developed by the courts and the Patent Office." Woodward, Definiteness and Particularity in Patent Claims, 46 Mich. L.Rev. 755, 765 (1948).

Markman would trump these considerations with his argument that a jury should decide a question of meaning peculiar to a trade or profession simply because the question is a subject of testimony requiring credibility determinations, which are the jury's forte. It is, of course, true that credibility judgments have to be made about the experts who testify in patent cases, and in theory there could be a case in which a simple credibility judgment would suffice to choose between experts whose testimony was equally consistent with a patent's internal logic. But our own experience with document construction leaves us doubtful that trial courts will run into many cases like that. In the main, we expect, any credibility determinations will be subsumed within the necessarily sophisticated analysis of the whole document, required by the standard construction rule that a term can be defined only in a way that comports with the instrument as a whole. Thus, in these cases a jury's capabilities to evaluate demeanor, to sense the "mainsprings of human conduct," or to reflect community standards, are much less significant than a trained ability to evaluate the testimony in relation to the overall structure of the patent. The decisionmaker vested with the task of construing the patent is in the better position to ascertain whether an expert's proposed definition fully comports with the specification and claims and so will preserve the patent's internal coherence. We accordingly think there is sufficient reason to treat construction of terms of art like many other responsibilities that we cede to a judge in the normal course of trial, notwithstanding its evidentiary underpinnings.

C

Finally, we see the importance of uniformity in the treatment of a given patent as an independent reason to allocate all issues of construction to the court. As we noted in General Elec. Co. v. Wabash Appliance Corp., 304 U.S. 364, 369, 58 S.Ct. 899, 902, 82 L.Ed. 1402 (1938), "[t]he limits of a patent must be known for the protection of the patentee, the encouragement of the inventive genius of others and the assurance that the subject of the patent will be dedicated ultimately to the public." Otherwise, a "zone of uncertainty which enterprise and experimentation may enter only at the risk of infringement claims would discourage invention." It was just for the sake of such desirable uniformity that Congress created the Court of Appeals for the Federal Circuit as an exclusive appellate courts for patent cases, H.R.Rep. No. 97–312, pp. 20–23 (1981), observing that increased uniformity would "strengthen the United States patent system in such a way as to foster technological growth and industrial innovation."

Uniformity would, however, be ill served by submitting issues of document construction to juries. Making them jury issues would not, to be sure, necessarily leave evidentiary questions of meaning wide open in every new court in which a patent might be litigated, for principles of issue preclusion would ordinarily foster uniformity. But whereas issue preclusion could not be asserted against new and independent infringement defendants even within a given jurisdiction, treating interpretive issues as purely legal will promote (though it will not guarantee) intrajurisdictional certainty through the application of stare decisis on those questions not yet subject to interjurisdictional uniformity under the authority of the single appeals court.

* * *

Accordingly, we hold that the interpretation of the word "inventory" in this case is an issue for the judge, not the jury, and affirm the decision of the Court of Appeals for the Federal Circuit.

It is so ordered.

QUESTIONS

1. What if the jury had decided against Markman? Would the trial judge do nothing?

2. Would the result be no change in the law because there would be no *Markman* case before the Supreme Court?

3. Are there any other terms for which "judges, not juries, are the better suited to find" their "acquired meaning?"

4. If the writing to be construed is by a lay person are juries likely to do better than judges in finding the correct meaning?

5. What evidence or what kind of evidence might there be to support the court's proposition that "[t]he construction of written instruments is one of those things that judges often do and are likely to do better than jurors unburdened by training in exegesis."?

NOTE ON ROSS v. BERNHARD

Ross v. Bernhard, 396 U.S. 531, 90 S.Ct. 733, 24 L.Ed.2d 729 (1970), was a stockholders' derivative action brought against the directors of an investment company and its broker. The suit alleged that by causing the company to pay excessive brokerage fees, the defendants had breached their fiduciary duty to the corporation, breached brokerage contracts and wasted corporate assets. The Court of Appeals for the Second Circuit had held that derivative actions were entirely equitable in nature and that there was no Seventh Amendment right to a jury trial with respect to any issue in the case.

The Supreme Court reversed. It analyzed the derivative action as consisting of two parts. The first part, which established the right of the stockholder to sue on behalf of the corporation, was equitable in nature. The second part, however, the suit by the corporation against directors or third parties, could involve legal as well as equitable claims. Justice White, writing for the majority, noted that since legal and equitable actions had been merged in the federal courts under the Federal Rules of Civil Procedure, the Seventh Amendment required the parties to be afforded a right to a jury trial on any legal issues that had been joined with equitable ones. The Court, in a footnote, stated a three-part test for determining whether an issue was "legal" in nature:

[F]irst, the pre-merger custom with reference to such questions; second, the remedy sought; and third, the practical abilities and limitations of juries.

396 U.S. at 538.

Justice White went on to note that even though legal as well as equitable issues in derivative suits had historically been tried in equity courts, that had been justified by the corporation's failure to pursue its own legal claims, which created the "lack of an adequate remedy at law". Justice White stated that this historical rule had become "obsolete" since the merger of law and equity, holding that: "We think the Seventh Amendment preserves to the parties in a stockholder's suit the same right to a jury trial that historically belonged to the corporation and to those against whom the corporation pressed its legal claims."

NOTES: RIGHT TO JURY TRIAL IN STATUTORILY CREATED ACTIONS

The federal courts have held that civil rights claims seeking damages under 42 U.S.C. §§ 1981 and 1983 for racial discrimination in employment confer a right to a trial by jury. *See,* Wade v. Orange County Sheriff's Office, 844 F.2d 951, 953 (2d Cir.1988); Bibbs v. Jim Lynch Cadillac, Inc., 653 F.2d 316, 318 (8th Cir.1981). However, employment discrimination claims under Title VII of the Civil Rights Act of 1964, 42 U.S.C. § 2000e *et seq.,* whose statutory remedies provide only for reinstatement and payment of back pay, have been held to be equitable in nature and not to confer a right to trial by jury. *See,* Great American Federal Savings & Loan Ass'n v. Novotny, 442 U.S. 366, 375 & n. 19, 99 S.Ct. 2345, 2350 & n. 19, 60 L.Ed.2d 957 (1979).

In 1978, Congress amended the Age Discrimination in Employment Act, 29 U.S.C. §§ 621–34, to provide expressly for a right to jury trial "of any issue of fact in any such action for recovery of amounts owing as a result of violation of this Act" 29 U.S.C. § 626(c)(2) (Supp. III 1979). Do you think Congress expected this change in the mode of trial to have a substantive impact on the number and size of awards in age discrimination cases?

In Deborah Leslie, Ltd. v. Rona, Inc., 630 F.Supp. 1250 (D.R.I.1986) plaintiff sued for damages under the National Stamping Act, alleging that certain castings marked sterling silver did not have sufficient pure silver to meet the Congressionally imposed standard. The statute provided for injunctive relief as well as money damages. The court held that defendant was entitled to a jury trial.

Frequency of Civil Jury Trials

There are relatively few civil jury trials in the federal and state court systems. They are, however, more influential than the numbers would suggest. Jury tried verdicts often become a kind of benchmark on which settlement negotiations are based.

The federal district courts conduct some 5000 civil jury trials each year. This is about 2% of all the civil cases terminated in federal courts. In the state courts civil jury trials are estimated to make up about 1% of the more than nine million civil claims disposed of annually.

More than half of all federal civil trials are before judges without juries. The proportion of bench tried cases in the state courts is even higher.

For federal cases in which the parties had a right to chose a jury trial, about 31% are selected to be bench tried. Much depends on the type of case: personal injury cases are tried primarily by juries; other lawsuits are mostly bench tried.

Sometimes, with the consent of the parties, the trial may be conducted by a federal magistrate. FRCP 73(c) and the statutory authority of 28 U.S.C. § 636 allow for that.

B. Limitations on Right to Jury Trial

Washington v. New York City Bd. of Estimate

United States Court of Appeals, Second Circuit, 1983.
709 F.2d 792.

■ Kearse, Circuit Judge:

Washington, an employee of the Board since 1972, commenced this action pro se on April 16, 1981. In 1978 he had held the position of clerk and office aide, and had taken a promotional examination for the position of Office Associate. Of the seven Board employees who took the test, Washington's "score," a combination of his test results and his seniority, was the highest. Washington was not promoted. His complaint alleged chiefly that the Board had denied him promotion on the basis of his race, color, gender, and age. The only defendant named in the complaint was the Board.

* * *

Section 4(c) of the ADEA, as amended, provides that a person suing for redress of age discrimination in violation of the ADEA is entitled to a trial by jury. 29 U.S.C. § 626(c)(2) (Supp. V 1981). *See also* Lorillard v. Pons, 434 U.S. 575, 585, 98 S.Ct. 866, 872, 55 L.Ed.2d 40 (1978). * * *

Washington made his first request for a jury trial on his ADEA claim many months past the deadline set by Rule 38(b). He contends that the district court erred in denying his belated request because there was no basis on which the court could find that he had waived his right to a jury trial knowingly and intelligently. This argument misperceives the test for waiver under Rule 38.

Rule 38 "proceed[s] on the basic premise that a jury trial is waived unless a timely demand is filed," Cascone v. Ortho Pharmaceutical Corp., 702 F.2d 389, 391 (2d Cir.1983). When Rule 38(b) has not been followed,

> it is clear that the test of waiver that is applied to other constitutional rights, that there must have been "an intentional relinquishment or abandonment of a known right or privilege," is not applicable to the right of trial by jury.

9 C. Wright & A. Miller, Federal Practice and Procedure § 2321, at 101 (1971) (footnotes omitted). Thus, a "[w]aiver by failure to make a timely demand is complete even though it was inadvertent and unintended and regardless of the explanation or excuse." *Id.* at 102.[4]

---

4. In determining whether a party has waived his right to a jury trial, we have distinguished between acts—or failures to act—prior to the time set by Rule 38(b) for

We are unpersuaded by Washington's argument that the application of Rule 38 to a pro se litigant is unfair "absent some notification of its operation."[5] (Appellant's brief on appeal at 7.) The operation of the Rule imposes no greater burden on pro se litigants than on represented litigants, as the unintentional or unknowing failures of all litigants to comply with Rule 38 are dealt with equally. Thus, we have concluded that there was waiver where the party's attorney wrongly believed that a timely demand had been made, Noonan v. Cunard Steamship Co., 375 F.2d 69 (2d Cir.1967), and where the attorney's failure to make a timely demand resulted from the removal of the case from state court, where a written request was not required, to federal court where the different procedure of Rule 38 applied, Galella v. Onassis, 487 F.2d 986, 996–97 (2d Cir.1973). The same rule of waiver has been applied to pro se litigants. *See* Scharnhorst v. Independent School District, 686 F.2d 637, 641 (8th Cir.1982); McCray v. Burrell, 516 F.2d 357, 371 (4th Cir.1975) (en banc), *cert. dismissed,* 426 U.S. 471, 96 S.Ct. 2640, 48 L.Ed.2d 788 (1976).

Finally, we note that Federal Rule 39(b) provides that even if a jury demand has not been made in compliance with Rule 38, if the action is one "in which such a demand might have been made of right, the court in its discretion upon motion may order a trial by a jury of any or all issues." We see no abuse of discretion here in the district court's refusal to relieve Washington of his waiver on the ADEA claim.

the making of a demand, and failures to make a timely demand in accordance with Rule 38. In effect we have applied a presumption against waiver in the former circumstances and a presumption in favor of waiver in the latter. *Compare* National Equipment Rental, Ltd. v. Hendrix, 565 F.2d 255, 258 (2d Cir.1977) (no waiver by signing of a contract having a jury waiver clause buried in the fine print), *and* Heyman v. Kline, 456 F.2d 123 (2d Cir.) (no waiver of right to have counterclaim tried to a jury by mere failure to assert right at a pretrial conference that preceded service of counterclaim), *cert. denied,* 409 U.S. 847, 93 S.Ct. 53, 34 L.Ed.2d 88 (1972), *with* Galella v. Onassis, 487 F.2d 986 (2d Cir.1973) (waiver by failure to follow Rule 38 after removal of action from state court), *and* Noonan v. Cunard Steamship Co., 375 F.2d 69 (2d Cir.1967) (waiver by inadvertent failure to follow Rule 38).

It should be noted as well that if a timely demand has been made pursuant to Rule 38, Rule 39(a) provides stringent formal safeguards against an inadvertent subsequent waiver. *See* Palmer v. United States, 652 F.2d 893, 896 (9th Cir.1981). Where the right has been appropriately demanded, "any seeming curtailment of the right to a jury trial should be scrutinized with the utmost care." Dimick v. Schiedt, 293 U.S. 474, 486, 55 S.Ct. 296, 301, 79 L.Ed. 603 (1935).

5. The present practice of the pro se office of the Southern District of New York, a practice not yet in effect when Washington commenced this action, is to provide pro se litigants with a document that reads as follows:

JURY TRIAL

In some kinds of cases you are entitled to a trial by jury. However, you lose your right to a jury trial if you do not ask for it early enough.

If you want a jury trial you should write "JURY TRIAL DEMANDED" on your complaint to the right of the caption. You can also demand a jury trial within 10 days of service of the answer.

If you have already lost your right to a jury trial, the judge might let you have a jury trial anyway if you make a motion for a jury trial, explaining why you did not ask earlier. The judge does not have to grant this motion. If you have any questions, contact the Pro-Se Clerk's Office.

We commend this practice. In so doing, however, we in no way intimate that any failure of the pro se office to supply such information would relieve the pro se litigant of his obligation to make timely demand for a jury trial. *Cf.* Fed. R.Civ.P. 77(d).

Indeed, it has not been suggested that Washington had any desire for a jury trial, until his attorney entered the case. Certainly in proceeding for more than a year pro se Washington evinced no timidity about demanding from the court whatever relief he did desire. His pro se motions included requests for stays or adjournments; a motion to amend the complaint, as discussed in Part A above; a request, shortly after the Board filed its answer, that the court proceed with the action; a request for a trial; a request for the appointment of an attorney to represent him; a request that answers to his interrogatories be submitted under oath; a motion to compel the Board to respond to his unanswered interrogatories, his document demand, and his request for a list of trial witnesses; and a request that the court call a conference of all parties. Washington's pro se request for a trial did not mention a jury; nor did his attorney suggest that Washington had believed he was thereby seeking a trial by jury. Indeed, any such suggestion would apparently be belied by Washington's reaction to the Board's suggestion that a trial might be unnecessary because summary judgment might be appropriate: Washington responded that "a summary judgment would not allow the court to get a total view of the situation * * *." (Document filed November 12, 1981).

■ OAKES, CIRCUIT JUDGE (dissenting):

I respectfully dissent as to the age discrimination claim on the jury trial point.

In respect to the age discrimination claim, I believe that Washington, as a pro se claimant, was entitled to a jury trial. A pro se claimant should not be deemed to waive a demand for jury trial absent a procedure by which he is made aware of his constitutional right to trial by jury. There is no showing in this case that Washington was informed of his right to a jury trial and of the necessity of making a written demand under Fed.R.Civ.P. 38.

The majority cites Cascone v. Ortho Pharmaceutical Corp., 702 F.2d 389 (2d Cir.1983), which held, following Higgins v. Boeing Co., 526 F.2d 1004 (2d Cir.1975) (per curiam), in a removed case, that the district court has discretion to permit the untimely filing of a jury demand. *See also* Cox v. C.H. Masland & Sons, Inc., 607 F.2d 138, 144 (5th Cir.1979). It is true that the Second Circuit as in Noonan v. Cunard Steamship Co., 375 F.2d 69, 70 (2d Cir.1967), has taken a view that the district court's discretion is exercisable only where there are special circumstances excusing the untimely demand. This is as opposed to the broader view held by some other courts that the court should grant a jury trial in the absence of strong and compelling reasons to the contrary, *see* 9 C. Wright and A. Miller, Federal Practice and Procedure § 2334, at 113 (1971). Nevertheless even under a narrow view it seems to me that the paradigm case for permitting untimely filing is that of a pro se plaintiff, at least one who is not himself a lawyer or should not otherwise be presumed to have familiarity with the Federal Rules of Civil Procedure. This is within the spirit not only of Haines v. Kerner, 404 U.S. 519, 92 S.Ct. 594, 30 L.Ed.2d 652 (1972), but of Johnson v. Zerbst, 304 U.S. 458, 58 S.Ct.

1019, 82 L.Ed. 1461 (1938). It also adheres more closely to our own Cascone v. Ortho Pharmaceutical Corp., supra, and it is a very simple matter as pointed out in the majority opinion, footnote 5, for the pro se claimant to be provided with the information necessary to claim or waive jury trial.

So far as I know this is the first case in this circuit passing upon waiver of a jury trial on the part of a pro se plaintiff. The Rules, I recollect, are to be construed "to secure the just, speedy, and inexpensive determination of every action." Fed.R.Civ.P. 1. In this day of six person juries, less-than-unanimous verdicts and facile waiver, I fear that I am one of those old-fashioned few who still believes that the emphasis of Rule 38(a) should be maintained on its last five words: "The right of trial by jury as declared by the Seventh Amendment to the Constitution or as given by a statute of the United States shall be preserved to the parties inviolate."

Leasing Service Corp. v. Crane

United States Court of Appeals, Fourth Circuit, 1986.
804 F.2d 828.

■ JAMES DICKSON PHILLIPS, CIRCUIT JUDGE:

This is an appeal and cross-appeal from a judgment rendered in a diversity action involving a disputed lease of drilling equipment. After defendants Fred and Donald Crane (the Cranes) leased a drill rig from a supplier, the lessor-supplier assigned the lease to plaintiff Leasing Service Corporation (Leasing Corp.). When the Cranes fell behind in their payments under the lease, Leasing Corp. sued in diversity, seeking damages for breach and repossession of the rig under provisions of the lease. The Cranes counterclaimed seeking damages for breach of contract, slander of title, and statutory unfair trade practices. In a bench trial, the district court dismissed all of the Cranes' counterclaims and awarded repossession of the rig and damages, limited by a side agreement, to Leasing Corp.

* * *

II

We consider first the Cranes' contention that the lower court's enforcement of a contractual waiver of the right to a jury trial deprived them of their seventh amendment right to jury trial. We disagree and affirm the denial of a jury trial.

The seventh amendment right is of course a fundamental one, but it is one that can be knowingly and intentionally waived by contract. See K.M.C. Co. v. Irving Trust Co., 757 F.2d 752, 755–56 (6th Cir. 1985); National Equipment Rental, Ltd. v. Hendrix, 565 F.2d 255, 258 (2d Cir.1977). Where waiver is claimed under a contract executed before litigation is contemplated, we agree with those courts that have held that the party seeking enforcement of the waiver must prove that consent was both voluntary and informed. See, e.g., Hendrix, 565 F.2d at 258; *but see K.M.C. Co.*, 757 F.2d at 758 (burden is on party seeking to avoid waiver to show not voluntary and knowing).

The Cranes contend that Leasing Corp. has failed to prove such a waiver in light of the circumstances. Specifically, they point out that the waiver provision at issue here is situated on the reverse side of a two-page, standardized, fine print contract provided by Leasing Corp. and Credit Alliance Corporation. The waiver, which stipulates that "Lessor and Lessee waive any and all right to a trial by jury in any action or proceeding based hereon or relating to the subject matter hereof," is not set off in a paragraph of its own. It is in the ninetieth line of print and is in the middle of a thirty-eight line paragraph.

We cannot declare the district court's finding of waiver clearly erroneous on the evidence. There are other factors than those emphasized by the Cranes that make the finding a completely plausible one.

The lease agreement was only two pages long. The parties were not manifestly unequal in bargaining positions. Despite their lack of formal education, the Crane brothers were manifestly shrewd businessmen who had been in a generally successful drilling business for sixteen years. Fred Crane had held both a dealer's and a salesman's license for the purchase and the sale of equipment. The circumstances surrounding the lease negotiations in fact reveal both the Cranes' general business acumen and their specific understanding of the Equipment Lease Agreement. The Cranes engaged in protracted negotiations with Nesbit at the Cranes' shop, while a Nesbit competitor waited outside in the event the Cranes did not obtain a favorable agreement. Fred Crane's wife reviewed the two page lease agreement closely enough to locate, object to, and have lined out the provision in the middle of the document which granted the lessor a security interest in all other assets belonging to the lessee. Finally, the Cranes' insistence on the execution of the handwritten agreement which limited the lessor's remedies in the event of a default indicates their understanding of the situation and of their interests.

These factors taken together persuade us that the district court did not err in finding that the Cranes knowingly and voluntarily waived their right to a jury trial.

C. Composition of the Jury

The major repeated objections to the use of civil juries are that jury decisions are irrational and unpredictable. Frequently cited examples of such huge and unforeseeable punitive damage awards are those against McDonalds for damage caused by hot coffee ($2.9 million punitive damage award reduced to $480,000) and the verdict in BMW v. Gore ($4 million punitive damage award reduced to $2 million by the state appellate court. Reversed and remanded by the U.S. Supreme Court.)

It seems questionable that, taken as a set of cases over time, jury awards are either huge, irrational or unpredictable. Three recent empirical studies put these assertions at issue. The Department of Justice and the National Center for State Courts [Civil Jury Cases and Verdicts in Large Counties 1995]; two American Bar foundation scholars, S. Daniels & J. Martin, [Civil Juries and the Politics of Reform 1995], and—the largest and most broadly based study—that by Professor Michael Rustad, In Defense of Punitive Damages, 78 Iowa L. Rev. 1 (1992) which, at 26–29, also briefly examines earlier empirical studies of punitive damage awards in product liability cases.

A second common and forcefully argued objection to jury decisions is that they "generate widespread uncertainty, anxiety, and aversion to risk in those who must respond to them." Peter H. Schuck, Mapping the Debate on Jury Reform, Chapter 9 in Verdict, Assessing The Civil Jury System, Ed R.E. Litan (1993). If true, these are undesirable effects on the behavior of others. Could these effects be measured?

It is contended that jurors do not understand the issues and the evidence presented to them; and even if the presentation process was greatly improved, in too much of contemporary litigation, a jury of lay persons simply cannot make an informed decision. The examples abound. The trial of Liggett & Myers v. Brown & Williamson narrated in Chapter 4 of S.J. Adler, The Jury (1994), describes a conscientious group of six citizens, as jurors, quite unable to comprehend oligopoly, LIFO decrement avoidance tax benefit, FIFO, double inference tests, average variable costs, and so on. The judge's charge to the jury took up 81 pages of the trial transcript. The shared experience of the jurors is a wonderful statement about community and the civic experiences of jurors.

Prospective jurors have been qualified in several different ways. Jury pool lists have been compiled from a variety of sources: voter registration lists, telephone directories, property tax rolls, driver's license registrations, and utility bills.

The Federal Jury Selection and Service Act [28 USC § 1861] governs the selection of jurors in federal district courts. Criteria for disqualifying individuals from the jury pool include

(2) is unable to read, write and understand the English language with a degree of proficiency sufficient to fill out satisfactorily the juror qualification form;

(3) is unable to speak the English language;

(5) has been charged with a crime or convicted of a crime punishable by imprisonment for more than one year "and his civil rights have not been restored." 28 USC § 1865 (b)(1988) [note that in New York there has to be a conviction; not merely a charge]. Apart from the constitutionally based inhibitions on the composition of the jury pool and the petit jury, the Federal Act proscribes the exclusion of certain cognizable classes from jury service. Citizens may not be excluded from jury service on account of race, color, religion, national origin, or economic status.

The usual juror qualifications call for the ability to read and write the English language. The New York statute is typical. It requires a person not to have been convicted of a felony and that the prospective juror have "a degree of proficiency sufficient to fill out satisfactorily the juror qualification questionaire and be able to speak the English language in an understandable manner." N.Y. Jud. Law § 510 (McKinney 1992) §§ 4 and 5.

A recent Note, A Challenge to the English Language Requirement of the Juror Qualification Provision of New York's Judiciary Law, 29 N.Y.L.S.L. Rev. 479 (1994), cites the latest census figures that some 25% of the New York City population is Hispanic and that almost half of them (48%) are excluded from jury service because of the language requirement. The felony exclusion provision may well lose for jury service a sizable fraction of the young black male population, although not as much as the Federal juror exclusions.

The jury pool, or venire, is assembled on the first day of the trial; then begins the process of selecting jurors to serve on the petit jury. This involves the questioning of the jurors in voir dire. In the federal courts most of the district judges permit no direct attorney participation in voir dire. The practices vary from state to state. The lawyers may then challenge for cause. Such challenges are ordinarily created by statute. They are unlimited in number but are restricted in scope. Typical bases for exclusion are persons who are blood relatives or friends, and persons who had business dealings with the lawyers or parties. Obviously persons who have fixed ideas about the case or feelings about the parties or lawyers are subject to challenge for cause. Then there are peremptory challenges. These are usually quite limited in number (three each in the federal district courts by statute, 28 U.S.C. § 1870, referred to in FRCP 47(b)). The peremptory challenge to a juror being seated is, historically, a claim made without cause being shown. It is not used to select jurors but to reject them. The peremptory challenge is not for the purpose of questioning the competence or qualifications of an individual juror.

The litigant in a civil case may not use peremptory challenges to exclude prospective jurors on account of their race or sex. This violates the equal protection rights of the excluded jurors. The opposing litigant has third party standing to raise the excluded juror's rights for the opposing litigant's own benefit.

FRCP 48 provides that juries will consist of six to twelve members and that verdicts must be unanimous. All but 17 states allow verdicts on something less than unanimity.

Purkett v. Elem

Supreme Court of the United States, 1995.
514 U.S. 765, 115 S. Ct. 1769, 131 L. Ed. 2d 834.

■ PER CURIAM.

Respondent was convicted of second-degree robbery in a Missouri court. During jury selection, he objected to the prosecutor's use of peremptory challenges to strike two black men from the jury panel, an objection arguably based on Batson v. Kentucky, 476 U.S. 79, 106 S.Ct. 1712, 90 L.Ed.2d 69 (1986). The prosecutor explained his strikes: "I struck [juror] number twenty-two because of his long hair. He had long curly hair. He had the longest hair of anybody on the panel by far. He appeared to not be a good juror for that fact, the fact that he had long hair hanging down shoulder length, curly, unkempt hair. Also, he had a mustache and a goatee type beard. And juror number twenty-four also has a mustache and goatee type beard. Those are the only two people on the jury . . . with facial hair. . . . And I don't like the way they looked, with the way the hair is cut, both of them. And the mustaches and the beards look suspicious to me." App. to pet. for Cert. A–41. The prosecutor further explained that he feared that juror number 24, who had had a sawed-off shotgun pointed at him during a supermarket robbery, would believe that "to have a robbery you have to have a gun, and there is no gun in this case."

The state trial court, without explanation, overruled respondent's objection and empaneled the jury. On direct appeal, respondent renewed his Batson claim. The Missouri Court of Appeals affirmed, finding that the "state's explanation constituted a legitimate 'hunch'" and that "[t]he circumstances fail[ed] to raise the necessary inference of racial discrimination." State v. Elem, 747 S.W.2d 772, 775 (Mo.App. 1988).

Respondent then filed a petition for habeas corpus under 28 U.S.C. § 2254, asserting this and other claims. Adopting the magistrate judge's report and recommendation, the District Court concluded that the Missouri courts' determination that there had been no purposeful discrimination was a factual finding entitled to a presumption of correctness under § 2254(d). Since the finding had support in the record, the District Court denied respondent's claim.

The Court of Appeals for the Eighth Circuit reversed and remanded with instructions to grant the writ of habeas corpus. It said: "[W]here the prosecution strikes a prospective juror who is a member of the defendant's racial group, solely on the basis of factors which are facially irrelevant to the question of whether that person is qualified to serve as a juror in the particular case, the prosecution must at least articulate some plausible race-neutral reason for believing that those factors will somehow affect the person's ability to perform his or her duties as a juror. In the present case, the prosecutor's comments, 'I don't like the way [he] look[s], with the way the hair is cut. . . . And the mustache and the beard look suspicious to me,' do not constitute such legitimate race-neutral reasons for striking juror 22." 25 F.3d 679, 683 (1994).

Under our Batson jurisprudence, once the opponent of a peremptory challenge has made out a prima facie case of racial discrimination (step 1), the burden of production shifts to the proponent of the strike to come forward with a race-neutral explanation (step 2). If a race-neutral explanation is tendered, the trial court must then decide (step 3) whether the opponent of the strike has proved purposeful racial discrimination. Hernandez v. New York, 500 U.S. 352, 358–359, 111 S.Ct. 1859, 1865–1866, 114 L.Ed.2d 395 (1991) (plurality opinion); id., at 375, 111 S.Ct., at 1874 (O'CONNOR, J., concurring in judgment); Batson, supra, at 96–98, 106 S.Ct., at 1722–1723. The second step of this process does not demand an explanation that is persuasive, or even plausible. "At this [second] step of the inquiry, the issue is the facial validity of the prosecutor's explanation. Unless a discriminatory intent is inherent in the prosecutor's explanation, the reason offered will be deemed race neutral." Hernandez, 500 U.S., at 360, 111 S.Ct., at 1866 (plurality opinion); id., at 374, 111 S.Ct., at 1874 (O'CONNOR, J., concurring in judgment).

The Court of Appeals erred by combining Batson's second and third steps into one, requiring that the justification tendered at the second step be not just neutral but also at least minimally persuasive, i.e., a "plausible" basis for believing that "the person's ability to perform his or her duties as a juror" will be affected. 25 F.3d, at 683. It is not until the third step that the persuasiveness of the justification becomes relevant—the step in which the trial court determines whether the opponent of the strike has carried his burden of proving purposeful discrimination. Batson, supra, at 98, 106 S.Ct., at 1723; Hernandez, supra, at 359, 111 S.Ct., at 1865 (plurality opinion). At that stage, implausible or fantastic justifications may (and probably will) be found to be pretexts for purposeful discrimination. But to say that a trial judge may choose to disbelieve a silly or superstitious reason at step 3 is quite different from saying that a trial judge must terminate the inquiry at step 2 when the race-neutral reason is silly or superstitious. The latter violates the principle that the ultimate burden of persuasion regarding racial motivation rests with, and never shifts from, the opponent of the strike. * * *

The prosecutor's proffered explanation in this case—that he struck juror number 22 because he had long, unkempt hair, a mustache, and a beard—is race-neutral and satisfies the prosecution's step 2 burden of articulating a nondiscriminatory reason for the strike. "The wearing of beards is not a characteristic that is peculiar to any race." EEOC v. Greyhound Lines, Inc. 635 F.2d 188, 190, n. 3 (C.A.3 1980). And neither is the growing of long, unkempt hair. Thus, the inquiry properly proceeded to step 3, where the state court found that the prosecutor was not motivated by discriminatory intent.

Accordingly, respondent's motion for leave to proceed in forma pauperis and the petition for a writ of certiorari are granted. The judgment of the Court of Appeals is reversed, and the case is remanded for further proceedings consistent with this opinion.

It is so ordered.

■ [The dissent of JUSTICE STEVENS, with whom JUSTICE BREYER joined, is omitted]

NOTE

In *Batson v. Kentucky*, 476 U.S. 79 (1986), the Supreme Court had stated a test for trial judges in deciding whether a prosecutor had violated the Equal Protection clause in the use of a peremptory challenge. The test applies as well to civil juries and all participants. The complaining party must be one of a cognizable group. Usually, the stricken juror must be a member of the same group. But a prosecutor's striking of blacks where the defendant was white was also nullified. *Powers v. Ohio*, 499 U.S. 400 (1991). Then as stated in *Purkett* the trial judge must accept that the relevant circumstances raise an inference of discrimination. If, in the trial court's opinion, the complaining party has made a prima facie case of purposeful discrimination, the party doing the peremptory striking must proffer a nondiscriminatory explanation. Although the reasons given must relate to the case, *Purkett* reaffirms that the reasons need not rise to the level justifying exercise of a challenge for cause. It may be difficult to prove a negative but the reasons given in *Purkett* seem less than persuasive.

What are the cognizable groups that begin the analysis? Under existing doctrine, those that are cognizable racial or ethnic groups and thus entitled to special protection, are American Indians, Hispanics, probably Asian–Americans, and, of course, black persons, white persons and females.

Criminal law practitioners and some commentators think *Purkett* portends the end of the safeguards against discriminatory use of peremptory challenges. Although the per curiam treatment of such an important issue seems amiss, all that may be corrected on the remand ordered. There is little doubt that whatever the interpretation of the rule in *Purkett*, it will promptly be applied to civil juries.

If recent history is a good guide, the various rules regarding jurors in criminal trials will be extended to all civil litigation. Edmonson v. Leesville Concrete Concrete Co., 500 U.S. 614, 114 L. Ed. 2d 660, 111 S. Ct. 2077 (1991) held that race-based peremptory challenges violate equal protection rights in a civil case. J.E.B. v. Alabama ex rel. T.B., 511 U.S. 127, 128 L. Ed. 2d 89, 114 S. Ct. 1419 (1994) held that the state in a civil action for child support cannot use peremptory strikes to exclude jurors because of sex.

Professor George P. Fletcher, Political Correctness in Jury Selection, 29 Suffolk L. Rev. 1 (1995), notes these two rules that flow from *Batson* and the cases that followed it: (1) The members of one's own cognizable group (and maybe of others') cannot be stricken from the jury by peremptory challenge without a strong showing of neutrality; and (2) a stricken juror has a constitutional right to serve on a jury which can serve as the basis for a complaint by a party. He asks some questions about this.

(1) Why is it unfair to try a case without "members of a defendant's own race having a fair opportunity to sit on the jury?"

(2) Are we to presume that "whites, Asians and Hispanics, properly chosen for a jury, cannot judge a [black] defendant impartially?" "If that is the case, shouldn't a [black] defendant have a right to" an all black jury?

(3) Does it, therefore, follow that "all defendants should be tried by a jury consisting of solely their race [(or their cognizable group)]?"

(4) In *J.E.B. v. Alabama*, the court assumed that the State violated the constitutional rights of men whom the prosecution excluded from serving on the jury. Professor Fletcher asks, "why should this defendant, having received a fair and impartial trial, secure a reversal of the judgment against him just because the prosecutor violated the rights of some other unnamed man?"

Minetos v. City University of New York

United States District Court, Southern District of New York, 1996.
925 F. Supp. 177.

■ CONSTANCE BAKER MOTLEY, DISTRICT JUDGE

This case was tried to a jury before this court from October 16, 1995 to October 26, 1995. Plaintiff, Fior D'Aliza Minetos, who had worked as an office assistant in the Music Department of Hunter College from 1981 until 1991, charged that: (1) defendants City University of New York and Hunter College had discriminated against her on the basis of her national origin and Hispanic accent in violation of Title VII of the Civil Rights Act of 1964 ("Title VII"), 42 U.S.C. sec. 2000(e) et seq.; (2) defendants City University of New York and Hunter College had discriminated against her on the basis of her age in violation of the Age Discrimination in Employment Act (the "ADEA"), 29 U.S.C. sec. 621 et seq.; and (3) defendants Peter Basquin, Ruth DeFord (Kotecha), L. Michael Griffel, Russel Oberlin and James S. Harrison had tortiously interfered with her contractual rights in violation of New York State law. The jury found in favor of defendants on plaintiff's Title VII and ADEA claims and this court entered judgment as a matter of law in favor of defendants on plaintiff's state law claim. Plaintiff now moves for a new trial based on this court's finding of Batson error by defendants at the time of jury selection or, in the alternative, for a new trial on her state law claim for tortious interference with contractual relations. For the reasons set forth below, plaintiff's motions are denied.

I. Background Facts

Jury selection in this case occurred on October 16, 1995. During this process, plaintiff objected that defendants' peremptory challenges were racially motivated in violation of Batson v. Kentucky, 476 U.S. 79, 90 L. Ed. 2d 69, 106 S. Ct. 1712 (1986). Plaintiff claimed (and this court agreed) that defendants had used three peremptories to exclude two African–Americans and one Hispanic from the prospective jury. After plaintiff's objection, defendants passed on their fourth and final peremptory (as to an alternate juror) and allowed a Hispanic female to sit. This juror was the only minority member of the jury. Plaintiff requested that, in remedy, all excused jurors be recalled and added to the jury. This court agreed that defendants had committed so-called Batson error, denied plaintiff's request and, at that stage of the proceedings, expressed the view that plaintiff would be entitled to a new trial if the jury found for defendants .. However, the court also noted on the record defendants' objection that plaintiff had used all of her peremptories to strike only white males.

The trial commenced and, at the end of plaintiff's case, defendants moved for judgment as a matter of law pursuant to Fed. R. Civ. P. 50. This court reserved decision on defendants' motion and the trial continued. At the conclusion of the trial, special interrogatories were given to the jury, and the jury answered in favor of defendants, in relevant part as follows:

Has the plaintiff sustained her burden of proving, by a fair preponderance of the credible evidence, that she was discharged or constructively discharged by defendants?

1. Hunter College   YES

2. Peter Basquin   YES

3. James Harrison   YES

4. Ruth DeFord   YES

5. L. Michael Griffel   YES

6. Russell Oberlin   YES

If the answer to [the above question] question is YES as to any defendant, has the plaintiff sustained her burden of proving, by a fair preponderance of the credible evidence, that her discharge was motivated, in whole or in part, by her national origin or her age or both?

National Origin   NO

Age   NO

Defendants have offered legitimate, non-discriminatory reasons for transferring plaintiff out of the Music Department of Hunter College to another department.

Do you find that this reason was a pretext for the transfer? NO.

See Special Interrogatory To The Jury, filed November 1, 1995.

Although the jury's findings disposed of plaintiff's ADEA and Title VII claims, its conclusion that plaintiff was "discharged or constructively discharged" caused a dispute between the parties over whether plaintiff's tortious interference with contractual relations claim under state law should be separately submitted to the jury. The court heard oral argument on this point, reviewed the parties' proposed jury charges, and then granted defendants' earlier motion for judgment as a matter of law on this claim. The court did not, at that time, grant defendants' motion for judgment as a matter of law on plaintiff's federal claims because it would have been superfluous to do so in light of the jury's verdict.

On November 1, 1995, in keeping with the jury's special interrogatories and this court's judgment as a matter of law, plaintiff's complaint was dismissed and costs awarded to defendants. Shortly thereafter, on November 7, 1995, plaintiff made the instant motion for a new trial on all her claims or, in the alternative, for a new trial on her state law claim for tortious interference with contractual relations. On April 29, 1996 plaintiff's motion was the subject of a hearing before this court and both sides submitted further briefing. The court now addresses plaintiff's motion for a new trial as well as defendant's motion for a directed verdict on plaintiff's federal claims.

II.   Use Of Peremptory Challenges

In Batson v. Kentucky, the Supreme Court held that the equal protection clause of the Fourteenth Amendment forbids a prosecutor to use peremptory challenges to exclude African Americans from jury service because of their race. 476 U.S. at 96–98. This was later extended to civil litigants, who are considered "state actors" when exercising peremptory challenges. Edmonson v. Leesville Concrete Co., 500 U.S. 614, 621, 114 L. Ed. 2d 660, 111 S. Ct. 2077 (1991).

The three-step test originally enunciated by the Supreme Court to prove Batson error was recently reiterated by the Court in Purkett v. Elem: "once the opponent of a peremptory challenge has made out a prima facie case of racial discrimination (step 1), the burden of production shifts to the proponent of the strike to come forward with a race-neutral explanation (step 2). If a race-neutral explanation is tendered, the trial court must then decide (step 3) whether the opponent of the strike has proved purposeful racial discrimination." 514 U.S. 765; 115 S. Ct. 1769, 131 L. Ed. 2d 834, 1995 WL 283453, at *2 (1995) (citing Hernandez v. New York, 500 U.S. 352, 359, 114 L. Ed. 2d 395, 111 S. Ct. 1859 (1991) (plurality opinion); and Batson, 476 U.S. at 96–98).

Purkett however, gave a new spin to step two of this test. While the Supreme Court in Batson had held that "the prosecutor ... must articulate a neutral explanation related to the particular ease to be tried" and give a "clear and reasonably specific" explanation of his "legitimate reasons for exercising the challenge," 476 U.S. at 98, the Supreme Court in Purkett has asserted that the second step "does not demand an explanation that is persuasive, or even plausible." Id.

Purkett's variation on Batson's test did not escape criticism from Justices Stevens and Breyer:

> Today, without argument, the Court replaces the Batson standard with the surprising announcement that any neutral explanation, no matter how "implausible or fantastic" ... even if it is "silly or superstitious," is sufficient to rebut a prima facie case of discrimination. . . . The Court's unnecessary tolerance of silly, fantastic and superstitious explanations ... demeans the importance of the values vindicated by our decision in Batson.

Purkett, 115 S. Ct. 1769, 131 L. Ed. 2d 834, 1995 WL 283453 at *6–7 (Stevens, J. dissenting). Indeed, Purkett leaves one wondering what explanation would not satisfy its second step, and brings to mind Justice Marshall's concurrence in Batson, in which he stated: "[Lawyers] are left free to discriminate ... in jury selection provided that they hold discrimination to an 'acceptable' level." 476 U.S. at 105 (Marshall, J., concurring).

During jury selection, this court determined in response to plaintiff's objection that defendants were using their peremptory challenges to strike African–American and Hispanic venire persons based on their race and ethnicity. Specifically, plaintiff made a prima facie showing that defendants were exercising their peremptory challenges in a race-based fashion, and defendants proffered the requisite "facially race-neutral" reasons for their strikes, as follows:

[The Court]: What do you say [in response to plaintiff's challenge of Batson error]?

[Defendants' Counsel: Well, we have non-discriminatory reasons for each of the three exercises of our peremptory challenges.

[The Court]: You can put them on the record.

[Defendants' Counsel]: The individual Eddie Rosa indicated that he didn't feel that people necessarily needed to speak English on the job. And the question of accent and foreign language is right at the heart of this case. That's one of the charges. [Plaintiff] was identified as Hispanic on account of her accent the plaintiff claims. With respect to the black woman, her name was Victoria Simmons, and she was a teacher in the New York City public school system which is exactly what the plaintiff is. The plaintiff has spent two of the last several years between these events and the present working as a full time substitute teacher in the New York City public schools so we felt the identification was a matter of concern to us. Mr. Judd is a blue collar worker with no office experience whatsoever, which is a factor for us. People who have never worked in an office we feel would have difficulty understanding the office dynamics which are very important to this case.

Since defendants struck exclusively Hispanic and African–American venirepersons and created an unmistakable "pattern" as warned about in Batson, this court determined that their race-neutral explanations hid discriminatory intent.

Defendants then raised the objection that plaintiff had likewise committed Batson error by striking only white male members from the prospective jury. In connection with this charge, the following exchange took place at side bar:

[Defendants' Lawyer]: The court could extend an additional challenge to plaintiff's counsel at this point in time so that they can remove another white professional male from the jury.

[Plaintiff's Lawyer]: I think as I've indicated before, Your Honor, I think if Your Honor finds, as you have so found, that they have acted in a discriminatory fashion, then there has to be some form of punishment. And I think the only appropriate punishment is to—

[The Court]: What about defendants' claim now made that you've used your challenges to remove white males?

[Plaintiff's Lawyer]: No. What I did was to exclude individuals who we viewed as pro-management. . . .

[The Court]: . . . . I think this case illustrates what some Supreme Court justices have noted before, particularly I think, maybe it was a concurring opinion in Batson, that peremptory challenges should be eliminated altogether, because like you just pointed out, you think the plaintiffs are using theirs to exclude white males in a case like this. If we have challenge for cause, that should be sufficient. How do you control really a situation like this in a case involving discrimination? It comes up in every case. So maybe this is a case that can be used as a reason why we shouldn't have any peremptory challenges. That applies to both sides. Let's proceed.

On further review of the full process of jury selection in this case as well as the record of the trial and of the hearing on the instant motion, this court agrees with defendants. This court does not find plaintiff's proffered reason for striking the white males credible. In New York City the business community is overwhelmingly and disproportionately white. Thus the "pro-management" excuse offers easy cover for those with discriminatory motives in jury selection. This court also notes that striking a venireperson based on his or her employment is explicitly presumed pretextual under guidelines set forth by the appellate courts in New York.

Moreover, plaintiff's argument that defendants' lack "standing" to make this objection because the jury was, in the end, white, exposes plaintiff's basic misunderstanding of the rights protected by Batson. The Supreme Court has reiterated time and again that "racial bias mars the integrity of the judicial system and prevents the idea of democratic government from becoming reality." Edmonson, 500 U.S. at 628. Race discrimination, in any form, frustrates the meaningful administration of justice. A recent decision by the New York Court of Appeals confirms this. See People v. Jones, 215 N.Y.L.J. 89 (May 8, 1996). The Court of Appeals reviewed three cases of so-called reverse-Batson claims, in which black defendants' had struck white jurors and given reasons found by the trial courts to be pretextual for discriminatory motives. There, the prosecutors had objected on behalf of the excluded jurors. The Court of Appeals noted that "the Batson rule circumscribes racially-rooted peremptory excusals by lawyers for both the defense and the prosecution equally," and then emphasized the need to "promulgate protocols designed to condemn, expose and root out such practices. . . ."

It has, thankfully, remained unquestioned since Batson that "racial discrimination in the qualification or selection of jurors offends the dignity of persons and the integrity of the courts" and "to permit racial exclusion in this official forum compounds the racial insult inherent in judging a person by the color of his or her skin." Id. (citing Powers v. Ohio, 499 U.S. 400, 402, 113 L. Ed. 2d 411, 111 S. Ct. 1364 (1991) (holding that a defendant, regardless of his or her race, may object to a prosecutor's race-based exclusion of persons from the jury)).

For these profound reasons, the Supreme Court squarely upheld, as a uniform matter, a litigant's third party standing to assert a prospective juror's equal protection rights in situations precisely like the one at hand, i.e., civil proceedings. Edmondson, 500 U.S. at 629. In fact "[the] sole purpose [of peremptory challenges] is to permit litigants to assist the government in the selection of an impartial trier of fact." Thus plaintiff's discriminatory use of her peremptory challenges defies the only reason for having them and violates each excluded juror's rights, irrespective of the final racial makeup of the jury. Plaintiff's "unclean hands" in this regard leave her poorly situated to complain about unfair treatment at trial and counsels strongly against the grant of a new one.

This case illustrates the bedeviling problems associated with peremptory challenges which, by their very nature, invite corruption of the judicial process. This is particularly true in Title VII cases, where parties are obviously tempted to exclude jurors on the basis of race or sex or national origin alone. As Mr. Justice Marshall stated in his concurrence to Batson:

> Much ink has been spilled regarding the historic importance of ... peremptory challenges.... But this Court has also repeatedly stated that the right of the peremptory challenge is not of constitutional magnitude, and may be withheld altogether without impairing the constitutional guarantee of impartial jury and fair trial.... I applaud the Court's holding that the racially discriminatory use of peremptory challenges violates the Equal Protection Clause, and I join in the Court's opinion. However, only by banning peremptories entirely can such discrimination be ended.

476 U.S. at 108 (Marshall, J., concurring)

Time has proven Mr. Justice Marshall correct. Ten frustrating years have now passed since the Supreme Court's decision in Batson. Purkett promises to add more years of vexatious litigation over a right lacking constitutional stature in our jurisprudence. All peremptory challenges should now be banned as an unnecessary waste of time and an obvious corruption of the judicial process. Such a change would have the added benefit of putting an end to the awkward analyses set forth in Batson and its progeny which have proved over ten years to be uncertain in their application and which have caused great consternation in the courts.

A brief review of the case law shows that judicial interpretations of Batson are all over the map.

In an effort to lend method to the madness, the New York Appellate Courts have drawn up some "Guidelines" to help trial courts apply Batson's second step. Under these guidelines, certain reasons for striking jurors, offered in response to a challenge of Batson error, will be presumed pretextual on their face and certain reasons will be presumed not pretextual. Reasons that will be presumed pretextual include: (1) the juror's employment; (2) the juror's being an employee in a hierarchical company; (3) the attorney's concern for a balanced jury; (3) the juror's living in the same or an adjacent community; (4) the juror's being too old or too young; (5) the attorney's lack of time to question the juror; (6) the attorney's belief that the juror would not be fair; (7) the juror's lack of strength; (8) the juror's clothing, where other juror's clothing was not an issue; (8) the attorney's general reassurance that the strike was in good faith; (9) the attorney's feeling that the juror "did not appeal" to him or her.

Reasons that will be presumed non-pretextual are more numerous, and include: (1) the juror's having a job that is police-related; (2) the juror gives inconsistent statements regarding his or her leanings;

(3) prior criminal jury service by the juror; (4) the juror's familiarity with the defendant; (5) the juror's familiarity with the crime scene; (6) the juror's statement that he or she cannot be fair; (6) the juror is employed in a creative field; (7) the juror's lack of mental capacity; (7) the juror's criminal record; (8) the juror's membership in a sympathetic religion; (8) the juror's knowledge of the language that is to be interpreted; (9) the juror's expressed disapproval of the defendant not testifying; (10) the juror's tardiness; (11) the juror's related expertise; (12) the juror's equivocal attitude about having been assaulted; (13) the juror's displeasure concerning past dealings with the police; (14) the juror's friendliness with a policeperson.

Subjective reasons offered by counsel to justify peremptory challenges (such as the juror's hairstyle, bad facial expression, body language, or over-responsiveness to opposing counsel) will be evaluated by the trial court and the peremptory challenge will be sustained if the trial court confirms there is a sound and credible basis for it. Of course, listing in this manner has the unfortunate effect of creating a how-to guide for defeating Batson challenges. Such guidelines do not ensure that juror strikes are not racially motivated—only that advocates are on notice of which reasons will best survive judicial review. Further, as observed by Mr. Justice Marshall ten years ago:

> "It is even possible that an attorney may lie to himself in an effort to convince himself that his motives are legal." A prosecutor's own conscious or unconscious racism may lead him easily to the conclusion that a prospective black juror is "sullen" or "distant," a characterization that would not have come to his mind if a white juror had acted identically. A judge's own conscious or unconscious racism may lead him to accept such an explanation as well supported."

Batson, 476 U.S. at 106–07 (Marshall, J., concurring) (citations omitted).

It is time to put an end to this charade. We have now had enough judicial experience with the Batson test to know that it does not truly unmask racial discrimination. In short, lawyers can easily generate facially neutral reasons for striking jurors and trial courts are hard pressed to second-guess them, rendering Batson and Purkett's protections illusory. After ten years, this court joins in Justice Marshall's call for an end to peremptory challenges and the racial discrimination they perpetuate.

Accordingly, this court vacates its prior oral decision at the time of jury selection to the effect that plaintiff's remedy for defendants' Batson violation, in the event of a verdict for defendants, would be a new trial. This court now holds that, given plaintiff's own Batson error, equity does not favor granting her a new trial on this basis. This court also holds that judicial experience with peremptory challenges proves that they are a cloak for discrimination and, therefore, should be banned.

For the reasons set forth above, plaintiff's claim to a new trial based on Batson error by defendants is denied, as is plaintiff's motion for a new trial under Fed. R. Civ. P. 59 on both her federal and state law claims. Moreover, since the only reasonable verdict in light of the evidence would have been one in favor of defendants on all claims, defendants' motion for judgment as a matter of law is now granted as to plaintiff's Title VII and ADEA claims.

NOTE

See Developments in the Law: The Civil Jury, 110 Harv. L. Rev. 1408 (1997).

D. JUDICIAL CONTROL OF THE JURY PROCESS: NEW TRIAL, REMITTITUR, JUDGMENT AS A MATTER OF LAW

Anderson v. City of Atlanta

United States Court of Appeals, Eleventh Circuit, 1985.
778 F.2d 678.

■ CLARK, CIRCUIT JUDGE:

I. FACTS

A. *Procedural History*

This civil rights action, filed pursuant to 42 U.S.C. § 1983, alleges constitutional violations which plaintiffs contend resulted in the death of Larry Gene Anderson while he was in custody at the Atlanta Pre-trial Detention Center. Named as defendants were the individual police officers involved in the arrest of Larry Gene Anderson, R.L. Kelly, W.R. Burks, A. Bieri and M.T. Pickering. Also named as defendants were George Napper, the Commissioner of the Department of Public Safety; Morris Redding, the Chief of Police of the Atlanta Bureau of Police Services; J.D. Hudson, the Director of Bureau of Corrections of the City of Atlanta; and the City of Atlanta.[1]

The trial of this case began on March 13, 1984. On March 19, 1984, after receiving special interrogatories from the court specifically setting out the degree of liability necessary for finding each defendant liable, the jury returned a verdict for plaintiffs. The jury awarded $1 nominal damages and $25,000 punitive damages against J.D. Hudson and $175,000 compensatory damages against the City of Atlanta. On May 15, 1984, the trial judge, on motion by defendants, granted judgment notwithstanding the verdict. He further granted a new trial if the Eleventh Circuit disagreed with his decision to grant the judgment notwithstanding the verdict. This appeal followed.

---

1. The entire City Council of the City of Atlanta and Mayor Andrew Young were originally named as defendants. Their motion to dismiss was granted by the court and that order is not appealed.

B. *The Facts Surrounding the Death of Larry Anderson*

In the early morning hours of January 4, 1983, while on routine patrol, Officer Kelly, of the Atlanta Police Department, observed an automobile, carrying six passengers and being driven by a white female, pull into the parking lot of a closed business. Officer Kelly observed the woman exit the car and walk around in a manner which indicated she was unsteady on her feet. He investigated and determined that the woman, Sherry Nelson, was intoxicated. He then arrested her for driving under the influence. Larry Gene Anderson, one of the passengers in the car, then approached Officer Kelly and stated that he was the person driving the vehicle. He subsequently changed his statement and maintained that he was not driving the vehicle. Based upon Anderson's statement and the fact that Officer Kelly had seen the woman driving the car, Mr. Anderson was arrested for making a false statement to a police officer. While Officer Kelly was verifying information given to him by Ms. Nelson, Elizabeth Jones, another passenger in the car, attempted to shift gears in the vehicle and gave Officer Kelly the impression she was attempting to leave. Officer Kelly then arrested Ms. Jones for driving under the influence. While Officer Kelly was filling out his paper work, Billy Moncus, another occupant of the vehicle, approached Officer Kelly in order to ask several questions regarding the arrest of his friends. As Mr. Moncus walked back to the vehicle, Officer Kelly observed the outline of what he believed to be a gun in Mr. Moncus' back pocket. Moncus was then arrested for carrying a concealed weapon. A paddy wagon was called to transport the prisoners and a female officer was summoned in order to search the female prisoners. Officer Pickering arrived with a paddy wagon and Officer Anna Bieri responded to the call for a female officer.[2]

The search of the female prisoners revealed that Elizabeth Jones possessed controlled substances. During the search, it also appeared that Ms. Jones had swallowed some of the pills which were found on her person.

Once Mr. Anderson and Mr. Moncus were transferred to the paddy wagon, Officer Pickering searched Mr. Moncus and found a small amount of what he believed to be marijuana in his shirt pocket. He then observed Mr. Anderson remove a bottle of pills from his right sock and pass the bottle to Mr. Moncus. Officer Pickering then went around to open the paddy wagon and discovered that the contents of the bottle, approximately 50 red and blue capsules, had been emptied onto the floor of the van. The pills were then confiscated. The female prisoners were placed in Officer Kelly's patrol car, which was searched. Numerous pills and capsules of various kinds were found under the seat. Shortly thereafter, Mr. Moncus passed out in the rear of the paddy wagon. Mr. Anderson informed the officers that Moncus had swallowed a number of tuonols, a barbiturate. He indicated to

---

2. When Officer Kelly initially observed the vehicle being driven by Ms. Nelson, he indicated by radio that he was taking action. Sergeant Burks who was Officer Kelly's immediate supervisor, was in the vicinity and overheard the call. As a result, he drove by the parking lot. Upon observing that Officer Kelly had the situation under control, defendant Burks left the scene but returned a short time later.

Officer Burks that Mr. Moncus and Ms. Jones, as well as himself, had taken pills.

Mr. Moncus was transported by ambulance to Grady Memorial Hospital for treatment. Ms. Nelson and Ms. Jones were transported to the detention center at Grady Memorial Hospital to receive sobriety tests in connection with their driving under the influence charges. On the way to Grady, Ms. Jones became unconscious in the back of Officer Kelly's patrol car. Mr. Anderson was the only detainee transported to the Atlanta Pre-trial Detention Center. Upon arrival at the pre-trial detention center, Officer Pickering gave custody of Mr. Anderson to the corrections intake officer, Michael Marshall. According to Officer Marshall, Officer Pickering told him that Mr. Anderson had taken a "large quantity of pills." Officer Pickering denied making the statement as well as having any knowledge that Anderson had used drugs.

Mr. Anderson was initially processed by Officer Marshall. During the intake process, Officer Marshall allegedly completed a medical screening form on Mr. Anderson and noted on the form that he was under the influence of drugs and had taken a large quantity of pills. Officer Marshall testified that Mr. Anderson told him that he was overdosing on drugs. The shift commander, Lieutenant Irvin, was present at the time Officer Marshall repeated to her that Mr. Anderson had stated that he was overdosing on drugs. She instructed Officer Marshall to make sure that he noted on Mr. Anderson's medical screening form that he was overdosing. Lieutenant Irvin further instructed Officer Marshall to put Mr. Anderson in a single cell and keep a close watch on him. Accordingly, Anderson was placed in a single cell. Another detainee was subsequently placed in the cell along with Mr. Anderson.

Mr. John Carl Weisgerber, a detainee at the pre-trial detention center that night, indicated that he saw Mr. Anderson and that he was obviously under the influence of drugs and that he heard Mr. Anderson tell the officers that he was sick and needed to go to the hospital.

Officer Marshall testified that he spoke to Mr. Anderson at 4:30 A.M. and again at 6:00 A.M. and that both Officer Marshall and his relieving officer, Tommy Smith, stated that they made Mr. Anderson get up and come to the door of his cell at 7:00 A.M. Doctor Stivers, the Fulton County Medical Examiner, testified, however, that Mr. Anderson in all likelihood died between 4:00 A.M. and 5:00 A.M. and that he was probably in a coma for some time prior to death. Mr. Anderson was found dead in his cell at approximately 9:25 A.M.

There are two issues on appeal: (1) Whether the trial court properly granted the City of Atlanta's and J.D. Hudson's motion for a judgment notwithstanding the verdict; and (2) Whether the trial court properly granted a new trial should this court not agree with its decision to grant a judgment notwithstanding the verdict.

II. THE LEGAL ISSUES IN CONTEXT

A. *Did the District Court Properly Grant Defendants' Motion for Judgment Notwithstanding the Verdict*

1. *The district court's decision and the Standard of Review*

The district court in granting defendants' motion for judgment notwithstanding the verdict stated:

> The court finds that there is no evidence of record to support 42 U.S.C. § 1983 liability against either defendant, J.D. Hudson, a supervisor with no personal participation, or the municipality itself, the City of Atlanta. All defendants having any actual participation in the incarceration of plaintiff's deceased had verdicts rendered in their favor. *See also* Parratt v. Taylor, 451 U.S. 527 [101 S.Ct.1908, 68 L.Ed.2d 420] (1981).

In reviewing the district court's decision to grant the motion for judgment N.O.V., we must consider all of the evidence in the light and with all reasonable inferences most favorable to the party opposed to the motion. If the inferences point so strongly and overwhelmingly in favor of the movant that reasonable persons could not have arrived at a contrary verdict, then the district court's decision to grant the motion was proper. Dresco Mechanical Contractors, Inc. v. Todd–Cea, Inc., 531 F.2d 1292, 1296 (5th Cir.1976). If there was substantial evidence opposed to the motion, i.e., evidence of such quality and weight that reasonable and fair-minded persons in the exercise of impartial judgment might reach different conclusions, then the district court's decision to grant the motion would be improper. Boeing Company v. Shipman, 411 F.2d 365, 374 (5th Cir.1969) (en banc).

2. *A review of the evidence*

In this case we believe that the district court's decision to grant defendant's motion for judgment notwithstanding the verdict was erroneous. The evidence indicates the following. Several police officers testified that the pre-trial detention center was inadequately staffed and that it was very difficult to do one's job properly. For example, Officer Marshall testified that he often worked a double shift at both the new and old detention centers because "there was a shortage of officers."[3] (TR V at 66–67). Most importantly for the purpose of this case he testified that they were short four or five officers on his shift, i.e., 11:00 P.M. to 7:00 A.M., on January 3 and 4, 1983, when Larry Gene Anderson died at the pre-trial detention center. (TR V at 69). Additionally, he testified that he was in receiving alone that night because another officer assigned to receiving, Officer Snipes, was off doing someone else's job. (TR V at 77).

He testified that Officer Pickering, who brought Anderson to the detention center, informed him that Mr. Anderson had taken a large quantity of pills. (TR V at 72).[4] However, Officer Pickering denied

---

3. He testified that he worked a double shift on the day of Mr. Anderson's death.

4. According to Officer Marshall's testimony, the screening form that Marshall filled out also indicated Mr. Anderson was under

having any knowledge that Mr. Anderson had taken any drugs and also denied making the statement to Officer Marshall. (TR IV at 57). However, Pickering did testify that Mr. Anderson appeared intoxicated. (TR IV at 69). Mr. Anderson also told Officer Marshall that he was overdosing on drugs and that he was sick and needed to go to the hospital. (TR V at 77 and 87). Marshall testified that he took no action because there was no medical staff present on that shift. (TR V at 80 and 89). Additionally, he testified that there was only one officer on duty on each floor in the pre-trial detention center on the night of January 3rd and 4th even though two officers were required. Finally, he indicated that it was very busy and hectic that evening and due to the shortage of staff it was impossible to check on the inmates as often as needed. (TR V at 90).

Lieutenant Sarah B. Irvin, the shift commander that evening, testified that no medical staff worked on her shift from 12:00 A.M. to 7:00 A.M.

* * *

Officer Tommy Smith testified that at times on his shift, i.e., 7:00 A.M. to 3:00 P.M., there were as few as sixteen officers working when approximately 25 were required.

* * *

Plaintiff also called two expert witnesses. Dr. Paul Siehl, a physician employed by Correctional Medical Systems, testified regarding minimum health care standards at jails. Essentially he testified that if a correctional officer knows or has reason to believe that a detainee has taken a large quantity of drugs, he should immediately notify the health care provider to examine the patient. (TR IV at 37–38). William Alexander was also called. He was employed by Correctional Medical Systems as a director of operations overseeing the health care in a number of correctional institutions in Georgia. (TR IV at 40–41). The Fulton County Jail was one of the facilities. (TR IV at 41). He testified that if an individual detainee states that he is overdosing on drugs, the person needs to be referred to someone who can properly evaluate the complaint, preferably medical personnel at the facility. If none is available, the detainee should be referred to a community hospital or an outside facility where health care can be provided. (TR IV at 45–57). Mr. Alexander testified for plaintiff under subpoena and not voluntarily. (TR IV at 47).

Thomas J. Pocock, the deputy director of the Bureau of Corrections with specific responsibility for the Detention Center, also testified. (TR VI at 346). He stated that if the screening officer, upon observing the physical appearance of the prisoner, detects no serious illness or injury, then the prisoner is admitted to the facility. (TR VI at 352). He testified that the jail had a minimum staffing level of twenty

---

the influence of drugs and had said he was overdosing. However, the form itself could not subsequently be located. Director Hudson disputed whether Marshall ever in fact filled it out. (TR VI at 373).

personnel per watch, irrespective of food service personnel, medical personnel, etc. (TR VI at 363). He further testified that there were twenty persons on duty the night Mr. Anderson died. (TR VI at 364). Additionally, he maintained that in obtaining federal funds for the new facility, the City had to accommodate various aspects of the new jail, including staffing to meet certain standards. (TR VI at 365). Thus, he stated strongly that the jail was adequately staffed on January 4, 1983. (TR VI at 370).

J.D. Hudson, Director of Bureau of Corrections for the City of Atlanta, testified that as Director of the Bureau of Corrections, he established the formal policies of the City of Atlanta to insure the health and safety of the inmates. (TR V at 244). According to his testimony, the minimum number of officers required on any given shift at the Atlanta Pre–trial Detention Center was 23. (TR V at 216). He also testified that it was his belief that the average number of officers on duty at the pre-trial detention center on any given shift was 13. (TR V at 217). Director Hudson, however, did not at any time admit that the jail was understaffed. He testified, "[t]he jail that we operate is a state of the art. We have adequate staff that has been trained and retained * * *. We have some of the best officers, the most professional officers in the country, and one of the best jails in the country. It is not understaffed." (TR V at 217).

He did indicate, reluctantly, that he had received complaints from officers that more personnel was needed. (TR V at 222). Furthermore, Standard Operating Procedure No. 81–10–SOP–BCS, issued and signed by him as director, set out the duties to be performed by the health care provider during all shifts, including the 11:00 P.M. to 7:00 A.M. shift; however, no health care provider was required to be at the center on the 11:00 P.M. to 7:00 A.M. shift. Medical personnel were on call, either by beeper or phone. (TR VI at 239). The standard operating procedures and special orders issued by Hudson further called for a full complement of staffing of health care personnel at the Pre–trial Detention Center on a 24 hour, seven day a week basis. (TR VI at 243). A nurse was required to be on duty to make a visual observation of each detainee brought into the Pre–trial Detention Center to assess normal appearance and conditions versus abnormal appearance and to inspect the detainee's physical anatomy. (TR VI at 249). However, no nurse was ever hired to perform these duties on the 11:00 P.M. to 7:00 A.M. shift. (TR VI at 250–251). Mr. Hudson further testified that part of the standard operating procedures required for the detention areas to be checked every 30 minutes for the health and well-being of the detainees. (TR VI at 243).

Carl J. Weisgerber, who was a detainee at the Pre-trial Detention Center at the time of Mr. Anderson's death, testified that he tried to explain to the duty officer on the 11:00 P.M. to 7:00 A.M. shift that he was on heart pills and needed to see a doctor or nurse but was continually told that he would have to wait. (TR V at 189). He also testified that he overheard an officer complain to another officer that he was the only one on the floor and could not do the entire job himself.

Most importantly, for the purposes of this case, he testified that he saw Mr. Anderson that night at the Detention Center and that he could not walk without the support of the officers and that Mr. Anderson told the officers that he was having trouble seeing and that he was sick and needed to go to a hospital. (TR V at 185). He further indicated that it was obvious from Mr. Anderson's looks that he was heavily under the influence of drugs and that he could not stand alone, his eyes were very red, and he was slobbering. (TR V at 185). Additionally, he testified that the officers were complaining about the lack of personnel and that they could not do their jobs properly. (TR V at 190).[9]

The Fulton County Medical Examiner, Doctor Stivers also testified at trial. He stated that Mr. Anderson could have lived from the amount of drugs that he ingested. His testimony was that Mr. Anderson died at approximately 4:00 A.M. from acute barbiturate intoxication. (TR V at 141). His death was in all probability preceded by at least some period in a coma. (TR V at 143). Despite the officers' testimony that they checked on Mr. Anderson at 4:30 A.M. and at 6:00 A.M., his testimony indicated that this was unlikely. He did not believe that Mr. Anderson could have spoken or stood up at these times. (TR V at 145). This testimony was based upon his examination and autopsy of Larry Gene Anderson. Mr. Anderson was not found dead in his cell until about 9:25 A.M. At this time, full rigor mortis and lividity had set in and Dr. Stivers stated that this process took at least several hours after death. He placed the time of death somewhere between 4:00 A.M. and 5:00 A.M. (TR V at 145).

3. *Municipal liability*

The Supreme Court recently reiterated in City of Oklahoma City v. Tuttle,471 U.S. 808, 105 S.Ct. 2427, 85 L.Ed.2d 791 (1985), that a municipality cannot be subjected to § 1983 liability "based upon theories akin to *respondeat superior.*" *Tuttle, supra,* 105 S.Ct. at 2433. Thus, only deprivations arising from municipal custom or policy can result in municipal liability.

* * *

Contrary to appellees' assertions, the verdict against the City in this case was not based upon single incident liability. A municipality can generally not be liable for a single act of negligence or misconduct. *See Tuttle, supra; Gilmere, supra* (no municipal liability where failure properly to train one police officer is not attributable to city policy or custom). If the City's evidence had shown that the jail was understaffed on the evening in question as an isolated event, this case would be within the parameters of *Tuttle, supra.* However, the jury instruction specifically required the jury to find a pattern or practice of

9. Mr. Pocock testified that he did not believe, based upon the physical layout of the Detention Center, that it would have been possible for Weisgerber to have seen Anderson. (TR VI at 357–59).

incidents of indifference. There was sufficient proof here to support such a finding. Several officers testified that understaffing was a persistent problem and that complaints had been lodged with their supervisors, including J.D. Hudson. Certainly this is sufficient to show a custom or policy of understaffing. Furthermore, the evidence was sufficient to show an affirmative link between the policy and the death of Mr. Anderson.

* * *

The special interrogatory pertaining to the City of Atlanta stated very clearly the degree of proof necessary to find liability on the part of the City. Nothing in the interrogatory mentioned liability under *respondeat superior* principles. The interrogatory states:

> Do you find from a preponderance of the evidence that the City of Atlanta through its supervisory officials, whose acts may fairly represent official policy, deprived Larry Gene Anderson of his legal right to necessary medical care by an established pattern or practice showing deliberate indifference or tacit authorization of the wrongful conduct?

To this the jury unanimously answered, "Yes."

Because the evidence was sufficient to support plaintiff's position and the jury was properly instructed and given special interrogatories containing the proper standards of liability, we conclude that the district court improperly granted the defendant City's motion for a judgment notwithstanding the verdict.

5. *The punitive damages award against J.D. Hudson*

However, we affirm the district court's decision to grant a judgment notwithstanding the verdict in one respect, the punitive damages award against J.D. Hudson. Generally, before an award of punitive damages is authorized in a civil rights action the jury must find, and the evidence must support its decision, that the defendant was motivated by an evil motive or intent, or there must be reckless or callous indifference to federally protected rights. Smith v. Wade, 461 U.S. 30, 103 S.Ct. 1625, 75 L.Ed.2d 632 (1983). Consistent with *Smith v. Wade,* the district court instructed the jury:

> The function of [punitive damages] is to punish the defendants for malicious or grossly wrong [conduct] and to deter similar [conduct] by others. Whether you decide to award punitive damages should be based upon whether or not you find that the defendants have been willful or malicious in their violation of plaintiff's constitutional rights, or that their acts were intentional in gross disregard of his constitutional rights.

(TR VII at 462).

The evidence offered by plaintiffs in this case does not support an award of punitive damages. There was no evidence that Director Hudson had an evil motive to infringe upon Mr. Anderson's constitutional right to life or that his actions were so egregious as to constitute reckless or callous indifference. Therefore, the award of punitive damages cannot stand.

B.   *The District Court's Decision to Grant a New Trial*

In the district court's order he stated that in the event that the Eleventh Circuit did not agree with his decision to grant a judgment notwithstanding the verdict he would grant defendant's motion for a new trial because he believed that "the verdict was based principally on adverse reaction by the jury to the defendant Hudson's impatient and defensive demeanor while on the stand rather than to the substance of his testimony or any other evidence of record—in other words, that he antagonized the jury."[15]

J.D. Hudson was not only a witness but a defendant. He was called as a witness by plaintiff for the purpose of cross-examination in order to make out plaintiff's case. In any case of this nature, many of the witnesses that a plaintiff will have to use will necessarily be correctional officers and supervisory personnel, as was Director Hudson. Thus the jury must pay close attention to the witnesses and judge them not only by their responses to the questions but by their demeanor, credibility, appearance, etc. Furthermore, in this case the judge specifically instructed the jury to that effect:

> You may be guided by the appearance and the conduct of the witness, the manner in which the witness testifies, the character of the testimony given or by evidence to the contrary. You should carefully scrutinize all the testimony given as I have said and consider each witness's intelligence, motive, state of mind, demeanor and manner while on the stand. Consider also any relation each witness may bear to either of the side[s] of the case, the manner which each witness may be affected by the verdict, and the extent to which, if at all, he is either supported or contradicted by other evidence in this case.

(TR VII at 468–469). This is a standard jury charge in a case of this nature, and properly so. A review of his testimony does indicate that Hudson was defensive and evasive on the stand. However, our review of the record does not indicate his conduct was so egregious that it both antagonized and influenced the jury to render a verdict adverse to the City. Rather as we have indicated in our discussion of the trial court's decision to grant defendant's motion for judgment notwithstanding the verdict, there was sufficient evidence upon which a properly instructed jury could return a verdict against the City, which

---

15. Generally, a district court's decision to grant a motion for a new trial is not appealable. However, if an appeal is properly taken from a judgment notwithstanding the verdict, the appellate court, on holding that the J.N.O.V. was erroneous, has the power to review a conditional order of the trial court granting a new trial. Fed.R.Civ.P. 50(c); *see also* Wright & Miller, *Federal Practice and Procedure,* § 2818, at 115. In this case the district court alternatively granted the motion for a new trial because it believed that Hudson antagonized the jury. When the district court grants a new trial for reasons unrelated to the weight of the evidence but rather having to do with what it believes to be some "distortion" in the trial process, then we review the district court's decision only for abuse of discretion. O'Neil v. W.R. Grace & Co., 410 F.2d 908 (5th Cir.1969).

it did. Therefore, the decision of the district court to grant defendant's motion for a new trial is reversed.

JUDGMENT AS A MATTER OF LAW

Under the amendments to the Federal Rules of Civil Procedure transmitted by the Supreme Court to Congress on April 30, 1991 (effective December 1, 1991), the terms "directed verdict" and "judgment notwithstanding the verdict" in Rule 50 have been replaced by the term "judgment as a matter of law."

Pursuant to the amended Rule, a motion for judgment as a matter of law may be made "at any time before submission of the case to the jury" and may be granted if "a party has been fully heard with respect to an issue and there is no legally sufficient evidentiary basis for a reasonable jury to have found for that party with respect to that issue." The motion for judgment as a matter of law, if made but not granted at the close of all the evidence, may be renewed not later than 10 days after entry of judgment.

The Committee Notes to these revisions make clear that they are not intended to change existing standards or procedures for pre-and post-verdict motions, but to revise a nomenclature which the drafters believed was "freighted with anachronisms" and "misleading as a description of the relationship between judge and jury."

Scogin v. Century Fitness, Inc.

United States Court of Appeals, Eighth Circuit, 1985.
780 F.2d 1316.

■ BRIGHT, CIRCUIT JUDGE:

David Scogin brought suit against Century Fitness, Inc. (Century), alleging that he was assaulted and battered or negligently struck and injured by Tony West, a Century employee, acting within the scope of his employment. The parties tried the case in federal district court before a six-person jury, which returned a special verdict in a bifurcated submission. The jury determined that Century's employee did not assault Scogin but that Scogin's injury and damage resulted from his assumption of the risk together with the negligence of Century's employee. In addition, the jury attributed 55% of the fault to Scogin and 45% of the fault to Century. Thereafter, the district court under Arkansas' comparative negligence statute[2] dismissed the action. It subsequently denied Scogin's motion to examine jurors or obtain affidavits in order to establish that the jury rendered a quotient verdict

2. The law in Arkansas is that:

If the fault chargeable to a party claiming damages is of less degree than the fault chargeable to the party or parties from whom the claiming party seeks to recover damages, then the claiming party is entitled to recover the amount of his damages after they have been diminished in proportion to the degree of his own fault. If the fault chargeable to a party claiming damages is equal to or greater in degree than any fault chargeable to the party or parties from whom the claiming party seeks to recover damages, then the claiming party is not entitled to recover such damages.

Ark.Stat.Ann. § 27–1765 (1979).

and his motion for a new trial. In this appeal from the adverse judgment, Scogin argues that the district court erred in rejecting his post-trial motion for a new trial. He contends that the jury rendered an impermissible quotient verdict, that the jury was confused by the instructions and interrogatories and therefore rendered a verdict that was not its true intent, and that the evidence was insufficient to support the jury's verdict. We reject Scogin's contentions and affirm.

* * *

In April 1983, David Scogin began taking tae-kwon-do lessons from a recreational center in Fayetteville, Arkansas operated by Century Fitness. While attending a group lesson on December 1, 1983, and while sparring with the instructor, Tony West, Scogin received a kick to his head which fractured his cheekbone.

Thereafter, he brought this suit in federal district court, jurisdiction resting on diversity of citizenship and requisite amount in controversy, against Century Fitness alleging alternatively that he was assaulted and battered or negligently struck and injured by West, a Century Fitness employee.

The principal issues presented on appeal surfaced after the jury had returned its verdict finding that Scogin was more at fault for his injuries than Century Fitness. After the trial judge stated to the jury that it had performed its duty and could be discharged, one of the jurors, who was apparently surprised by this advice, inquired whether another paper (probably a verdict form) needed to be signed by the jurors. The district court answered the inquiry in the negative. At that point in the proceedings, Scogin's counsel asked to voir dire the jury at a future time concerning possible confusion about the attribution of fault interrogatory. The district court denied the request.

Scogin subsequently moved to examine or obtain affidavits from jurors concerning the means by which the jury had apportioned fault between the parties. He also moved for a new trial on the grounds that the jury rendered an impermissible quotient verdict, that the jury was confused by the instructions and interrogatories and therefore rendered a verdict that was not its true intent, and that the evidence was insufficient to support the jury's verdict. Scogin supported the motions by affidavits from a court bystander and from one of his attorneys. Following the denial of his post-trial motions, Scogin brought this appeal from the adverse judgment.

II. DISCUSSION

A. Quotient Verdict

Scogin first argues that he should have been granted a new trial because the jury rendered an impermissible quotient verdict. Scogin relies on an affidavit from a court bystander, Charles A. McDaris, to support his argument. McDaris states in his affidavit that immediately following the trial Roger Burke, the jury foreperson, told him that the percentage figures attributing fault to each of the parties had been determined by a quotient method, that is by adding up percentage figures given by each juror and then striking an average for the fault attributable to Scogin and to Century's employee, West.

It is well established that a juror may not impeach his or her verdict, with the exception that a juror may testify about extraneous prejudicial information or improper influence in the jury room. McDonald v. Pless, 238 U.S. 264, 269, 35 S.Ct. 783, 785, 59 L.Ed. 1300 (1915); United States v. Eagle, 539 F.2d 1166, 1169–70 (8th Cir.1976), *cert. denied*, 429 U.S. 1110, 97 S.Ct. 1146, 51 L.Ed.2d 563 (1977); Fed.R.Evid. 606(b).[5] In *McDonald,* the Supreme Court upheld the trial court's refusal to allow a juror to testify regarding the jury's alleged use of a quotient verdict procedure. Justice Lamar, writing for the Court, explained:

> But let it once be established that verdicts solemnly made and publicly returned into court can be attacked and set aside on the testimony of those who took part in their publication and all verdicts could be, and many would be, followed by an inquiry in the hope of discovering something which might invalidate the finding. Jurors would be harassed and beset by the defeated party in an effort to secure from them evidence of facts which might establish misconduct sufficient to set aside a verdict. If evidence thus secured could be thus used, the result would be to make what was intended to be a private deliberation, the constant subject of public investigation—to the destruction of all frankness and freedom of discussion and conference.

McDonald v. Pless, 238 U.S. at 267–68, 35 S.Ct. at 784. The Eighth Circuit has applied the rule enunciated in *McDonald* to hold that the affidavits of jurors may not be used to show a quotient verdict. Barry v. Legler, 39 F.2d 297, 302 (8th Cir.1930); Manhattan Oil Co. v. Mosby, 72 F.2d 840, 847 (8th Cir.1934).

The rule against a juror impeaching his or her verdict is now stated in Fed.R.Evid. 606(b), which reads:

> *Upon an inquiry into the validity of a verdict or indictment, a juror may not testify as to any matter or statement occurring*

---

5. Federal decisions have focused upon insulating jury deliberations, including discussions, statements, mental and emotional reactions, votes, and any other feature of the process. Thus testimony or affidavits of jurors have been held incompetent to show a quotient verdict, McDonald v. Pless, 238 U.S. 264, 269, 35 S.Ct. 783, 785, 59 L.Ed. 1300 (1915); a compromise verdict, Hyde v. United States, 225 U.S. 347, 382–84, 32 S.Ct. 793, 807–09, 56 L.Ed. 1114 (1912); speculation as to insurance coverage, Holden v. Porter, 405 F.2d 878, 879 (10th Cir.1969), Farmers Co-op. Elevator Ass'n v. Strand, 382 F.2d 224, 230 (8th Cir.), *cert. denied*, 389 U.S. 1014, 88 S.Ct. 589, 19 L.Ed.2d 659 (1967); misinterpretations of instructions, *Farmers Co-op. Elev. Ass'n v. Strand, supra;* mistake in returning a verdict, United States v. Chereton, 309 F.2d 197, 200 (6th Cir.1962), *cert. denied,* 372 U.S. 936, 83 S.Ct. 883, 9 L.Ed.2d 767 (1963); interpretation of guilty plea by one defendant as implicating others, United States v. Crosby, 294 F.2d 928, 949 (2d Cir. 1961), *cert. denied,* 368 U.S. 984, 82 S.Ct. 599, 7 L.Ed.2d 523 (1962). The policy does not, however, foreclose testimony by jurors as to prejudicial extraneous information or influences injected into or brought to bear upon the deliberative process. Thus a juror is recognized as competent to testify to statements by the bailiff or the introduction of a prejudicial newspaper account into the jury room, Mattox v. United States, 146 U.S. 140, 148–49, 13 S.Ct. 50, 52–53, 36 L.Ed. 917 (1892). *See also* United States v. Delaney, 732 F.2d 639, 643, n. 6 (8th Cir.1984); Government of Virgin Islands v. Gereau, 523 F.2d 140, 148–50 (3d Cir.1975), *cert. denied,* 424 U.S. 917, 96 S.Ct. 1119, 47 L.Ed.2d 323 (1976).

during the course of the jury's deliberations or to the effect of anything upon his or any other juror's mind or emotions as influencing him to assent to or dissent from the verdict or indictment or concerning his mental processes in connection therewith, except that a juror may testify on the question whether extraneous prejudicial information was improperly brought to the jury's attention or whether any outside influence was improperly brought to bear upon any juror. *Nor may his affidavit or evidence of any statement by him concerning a matter about which he would be precluded from testifying be received for these purposes.*

Fed.R.Evid. 606(b) (emphasis added).[6]

The present case does not concern extraneous prejudicial information or outside influence being brought to bear upon any juror. Therefore, neither statements or affidavits from jurors themselves, nor McDaris' affidavit may be used to impeach the jury verdict. Because the record is devoid of competent proof that the jury reached its verdict by a quotient method, the district court did not err in denying Scogin's motion for a new trial on that ground.

B. Jury Confusion

Scogin also argues that the district court should have granted his motion for a new trial because the jurors were confused by the instructions and interrogatories and, consequently, the verdict did not reflect their true intent. Scogin relies on the affidavit of Erwin L. Davis, one of his attorneys, to support this argument. Davis' affidavit states that after the jury had been discharged some of the members expressed dismay at the verdict because they had thought that Scogin would recover a portion of his damages.

Scogin's argument regarding jury confusion fails for reasons similar to those discussed above regarding the reaching of a quotient verdict. We have consistently held that the testimony or affidavits of jurors are incompetent to show that jury instructions were misinterpreted. In Chicago, Rock Island & Pacific Railroad v. Speth, 404 F.2d 291, 295 (8th Cir.1968), this court stated that "[i]t is well settled that a jury's misunderstanding of testimony, misapprehension of law, errors in computation or improper methods of computation, unsound reasoning or other improper motives cannot be used to impeach a verdict. These matters all inhere in the verdict itself." *See also* Farmers Co-operative Elevator Association v. Strand, 382 F.2d 224, 230 (8th Cir.1967); Fed.R.Evid. 606(b). Accordingly, we hold that the district

---

6. The draft of Fed.R.Evid. 606(b) passed by the House of Representatives would have permitted juror testimony about objective matters occurring during the jury's deliberation, such as the reaching of a quotient verdict. H.R.Rep. No. 93–650, 93rd Cong., 2nd Sess. (1974), *reprinted in* 1974 U.S.Code Cong. & Ad.News 7051, 7075, 7083–84. The Senate version, however, which was approved by the Joint Conference Committee, expressly denounced such a practice. S.Rep. No. 93–1277, 93rd Cong., 2nd Sess. (1974), *reprinted in* 1974 U.S.Code Cong. & Ad.News 7051, 7060; Conf.Rep. No. 93–1597, 93rd Cong., 2nd Sess. (1974), *reprinted in* 1974 U.S.Code Cong. & Ad.News 7098, 7102.

court did not err in denying Scogin's motion for a new trial on the basis of jury confusion.[7]

C. Insufficient Evidence

Finally, Scogin contends that there was insufficient evidence of fault on his part to support the jury verdict. In ruling on a motion for a new trial, the district court, after reviewing all of the evidence, must exercise its independent judgment in determining whether the verdict was against the clear weight of the evidence. Firemen's Fund Insurance Co. v. Aalco Wrecking Co., 466 F.2d 179, 186 (8th Cir.1972) *cert. denied* 410 U.S. 930, 93 S.Ct. 1371, 35 L.Ed.2d 592 (1973). We review the district court's ruling on the motion for a new trial under an abuse of discretion standard, and do not upset its ruling absent a strong showing of abuse. Moran v. Vermeer Manufacturing Co., 742 F.2d 456, 457 (8th Cir.1984); Lincoln Carpet Mills, Inc. v. Singer Co., 549 F.2d 80, 81 (8th Cir.1977).

In this case, there is sufficient evidence to support the jury's verdict. Accordingly, no abuse of discretion is shown.

Smith v. City of Seven Points, Texas

United States District Court, Eastern District of Texas, 1985.
608 F.Supp. 458.

■ STEGER, DISTRICT JUDGE:

* * *

I. BACKGROUND

The events culminating in this civil action occurred in the early morning hours of November 3, 1983. Defendants Mark Jordan and Frank Barina, acting as law enforcement officers for the City of Seven Points, Texas, stopped the plaintiff because they believed he was

---

7. The district court submitted the issues to the jury in separate stages. First, the court asked the jury to decide two questions: whether Century through its agent Tony West, assaulted Scogin and/or whether Century negligently injured Scogin. The jury answered the assault issue negatively, and the negligence issue affirmatively. Second, and after the jury returned, the court submitted two more interrogatories to the jury, one on whether Scogin assumed the risk (the jury said: "Yes") and an additional interrogatory requesting the jury to attribute fault on a percentage basis to each party, to which, as we have noted, the jury answered 55% attributable to plaintiff and 45% attributable to the defendant. Had the jury attributed greater fault to the defendant the court evidently planned another round of deliberation for assessment of damages.

While neither party objected to the piecemeal submission and the matter is not before

us as a matter of appellate review, the writer of this opinion observes that such submission hardly seems advisable in a relatively straightforward one-day trial of this kind. One may suspect that there is at least a possibility of jury confusion where the judge instructs fully on a number of issues, and then sends the jury out to decide the interrogatories piecemeal with damages to be fixed, if necessary, only in a final separate submission.

Moreover, this procedure varies somewhat from the language of Fed.R.Civ.P. 49(a) which specifies that "[t]he court may require a jury to return only a special verdict in the form of a special written finding upon each issue of fact * * * [and] shall give to the jury such explanation and instruction concerning the matter thus submitted as may be necessary to enable the jury to make its findings upon each issue."

driving while intoxicated. At the time, plaintiff C.E. Smith, then age 73, was returning home from a local bar where he had won a shuffleboard tournament. He had with him a passenger named Wesley Bonner.

After he stopped and emerged from his pick-up truck, Smith was asked to perform a test to determine whether he was intoxicated. The test required Smith to walk along the broken shoulder of the road, a feat he refused to attempt because of an old foot injury.

At this point a fracas erupted. There was conflicting testimony concerning the cause of this altercation, but the jury's answers to the interrogatories clearly evince their conviction that Officers Jordan and Barina were most culpable.

There is little dispute over the results of the scuffle. Officer Barina struck Mr. Smith several times with a blackjack. Mr. Smith was knocked to the ground, handcuffed, arrested, and taken into custody. He suffered a cut on his head, a serious bruise on his left cheek, various other abrasions, and his clothes were dirtied. Much more significantly, Mr. Smith suffered an injury to his dignity.

For the sake of completeness, it should be noted that Officer Jordan was occupied in a struggle with Mr. Bonner during much of the time that Smith and Barina were tussling. No suit arose out of the Jordan and Bonner skirmish. It was also apparent that Officer Barina did not emerge unscathed after his encounter with Mr. Smith. He also suffered a cut on his head and some abrasions, though he did not suffer the indignity of an arrest.

A trial of this action commenced on March 4, 1985, and the jury returned its verdict on March 6, 1985. The jury decided that Officers Barina and Jordan unlawfully arrested Mr. Smith, and used excessive force in making the arrest. They also found Doug Curry, Chief of the Seven Points Police Department, liable for the injuries suffered by Smith because he failed to control his officers' known propensity for violence. Finally, the jury found that the unlawful arrest was undertaken as part of the official policy of the City of Seven Points, making the city liable along with its officers.

The jury awarded plaintiff $150,000.00 in actual damages, and assessed an additional sum of $50,000.00 each against Officer Jordan, Officer Barina, and Chief Curry as punitive damages. The total award thus amounted to exactly $300,000.00. It is the magnitude of this award that has excited the passions of counsel for the defendants and led to the three motions now to be discussed.

* * *

III. CITY OF SEVEN POINTS' MOTION FOR JUDGMENT NOTWITHSTANDING THE VERDICT

The city has requested judgment in its favor on the basis that there was no evidence that the actions of Officers Barina and Jordan were taken pursuant to official city policy. There was, however, evidence that members of the city council were aware that excessive force was used by the police force. The evidence was slim, but in the Court's opinion was sufficient to raise a fact question for the jury to decide. By their answers to the interrogatories, the jury indicated their belief that use of excessive force was a persistent, widespread practice of the city that was so common and well-settled that it constituted a custom representing city policy.

* * *

B. New Trial or Remittitur

As noted earlier, the defendants' central contention is that in light of the evidence presented, the enormity of the verdict establishes beyond doubt that the jury was motivated by bias or prejudice. Because of this, defendants have asked this Court to either grant a new trial or order a remittitur of a substantial portion of the damages awarded.

Decisions on motions for new trial are committed to the sound discretion of the trial court. Reeves v. General Foods Corp., 682 F.2d 515, 519 (5th Cir.1982); Valley View Cattle Co. v. Iowa Beef Processors, 548 F.2d 1219, 1220 n. 2 (5th Cir.1977). If the trial court feels that a remittitur is more appropriate, it must first offer plaintiff a choice between accepting a reduction in damages or proceeding with a new trial. Higgins v. Smith International, Inc., 716 F.2d 278, 281 (5th Cir.1983). In reducing the level of damages, the court may not simply substitute its opinion concerning the proper amount for that of the jury. Consequently, the court may not reduce the award below the maximum amount that is supported by the evidence. Bonura v. Sea Land Service, Inc., 505 F.2d 665, 669 (5th Cir.1974).

Trial courts should employ remittitur for those verdicts that are so large as to be contrary to right reason, while requiring a new trial on issues infected by passion or prejudice. Westbrook v. General Tire and Rubber Co., 754 F.2d 1233, 1241 (5th Cir.1985). If it is clear that the issue of damages is independent of those issues relating to liability, the new trial, if any, may be limited to the question of damages. Westbrook, 754 F.2d at 1242; citing Gasoline Products Co. v. Champlin Refining Co., 283 U.S. 494, 500, 51 S.Ct. 513, 515, 75 L.Ed. 1188 (1931).

Summarizing the preceding discussion, it appears that this Court must answer four questions before deciding the defendants' motion for new trial. First, was the verdict excessive? Second, was the excessiveness of the verdict, if any, caused by passion or prejudice on the part of the jury? Third, if the verdict was excessive, what was the maximum amount that the jury could have awarded given the evidence submitted? Finally, if it is found to be appropriate, how much should the damages be reduced in order to set a proposed remittitur?

1. Excessiveness of the Verdict

This Court has concluded that the verdict entered in this action was excessive in light of the evidence presented at trial. The only evidence of past medical expenses was a dental bill for just under $900.00. Mr. Smith had this work done in late September of 1984, almost eleven months after his unlawful arrest on November 4, 1983. By deposition, the dentist indicates that plaintiff was suffering from periodontal disease that would have necessitated dental work even if the arrest had never occurred. At best, a blow from Officer Barina to Mr. Smith's mouth may have cracked a denture, accounting for a portion of the $900.00 dental bill. Mr. Smith did not receive medical attention after his arrest beyond first aid treatment administered by employees of the City of Seven Points. There was no evidence of future medical expenses.

Plaintiff's response to defendants' motion for new trial describes the "obvious pain and suffering" caused by a brutal beating. It may have been brutal in the sense that it was ruthless or unfeeling, but not in the sense that it was severe. Plaintiff refused to go to the hospital for examination or treatment after the arrest. Evidence as to severity was limited to testimony from plaintiff's wife and children saying that he looked very bad—i.e., badly bruised—the next day and for several days after the arrest.

Plaintiff's primary injury was described in his response to defendants' motion as the "shame, embarrassment, humiliation, and other mental anguish and suffering" resulting from the manner of his arrest. All of these items really amount to one thing: A loss of self-respect, with the best descriptive word being "humiliation." It is difficult to determine how much humiliation Mr. Smith suffered, however.

Humiliation, and the pain and suffering described earlier, are abstract and speculative elements of damage that are not susceptible to precise calculation. Since there was no evidence of any actual monetary loss other than the dental bills, however, at least $149,-000.00 of the $150,000.00 award for actual damages must be assigned to these abstract and speculative elements of damage. Although they may not be precisely calculated, this Court is convinced that $149,-000.00 "is simply not in the universe of rational awards on the evidence" in this action. Howell v. Marmpegaso Compania Naviera, S.A., 536 F.2d 1032, 1034 (5th Cir.1976), *citing* Bonura v. Sea Land Service, Inc., 505 F.2d at 669–670.

To help place the extravagance of this award in perspective, the Court has examined several jury awards in other police abuse cases. While the excessiveness of a verdict cannot be determined solely by comparison to awards in other cases, and has not been determined that way in this case, it is still helpful to review other verdicts. Each of the cited cases differs from the present case in some or many respects. Each, however, is similar to the extent that it involved the use of excessive force by law enforcement officers making a custodial arrest.

In Bauer v. Norris, 713 F.2d 408 (8th Cir.1983), the plaintiffs, Mr. and Mrs. Bauer, were walking back to their home from a restaurant at 11:00 p.m. They were stopped by a deputy sheriff one block from their home. He demanded identification. The Bauers responded by pointing to their home, explaining that they were headed in that direction. The deputy met them at their house after they had continued walking, demanded identification, and then engaged in an exchange of epithets with Mr. Bauer. After being threatened with physical harm, both Bauers were arrested, tightly handcuffed, and taken into custody. They were acquitted at a subsequent trial for disorderly conduct. After filing a § 1983 action in federal court, a federal jury awarded the Bauers a total of $15,000.00 for the physical and emotional injuries they suffered. This award was upheld by the court of appeals after being challenged by the defendants.

In Raley v. Fraser, 747 F.2d 287 (5th Cir.1984), the plaintiff was arrested for public intoxication by Officer Fraser. The officer applied four choke holds on Raley, leaving Raley with bruised arms, a scraped face, welts on his wrists from the handcuffs, and a sore throat that required two visits to a doctor. The trial court awarded just $1,000.00 for pain and mental suffering on a pendent assault claim. The plaintiffs' § 1983 claims were dismissed on the basis that the officer used reasonable force to subdue Raley.

Circumstances more similar to those in the present case were presented in Keyes v. Lauga, 635 F.2d 330 (5th Cir.1981). A group of deputies appeared at the Keyes' residence at 5:00 a.m. to execute arrest warrants for both Mr. and Mrs. Keyes. Fearing for their children, Mr. Keyes left the house and was immediately arrested. Mrs. Keyes came out of the house, then returned to call other authorities with three of the deputies close behind. According to Mrs. Keyes' testimony, the deputies made a quick search of the house, then went after Mrs. Keyes, kicking her and beating her with nightsticks before taking her into custody. On the way to the jail and again after she was placed in her cell, Mrs. Keyes testified that she was beaten with fists and "a big black stick" by two deputies. She was charged with resisting arrest, assaulting a police officer, and disturbing the peace. These charges were ultimately dropped. 635 F.2d at 334 n. 3.

The jury awarded $75,000.00 in damages, $37,500.00 from each of the two deputies responsible for the beating. In reviewing the award, the Fifth Circuit noted that Mrs. Keyes had suffered a low-grade concussion, numbness in her left thumb, multiple bruises, and continuing headaches, nightmares, and nervousness. Her past medical expenses totalled $329.00.

The Court noted that over $74,000.00 of the verdict was directed to speculative items of recovery, including pain and suffering and humiliation. (With regard to Mrs. Keyes' humiliation, it should be noted that her 13–year–old son witnessed the beating she received in her home.) The court nevertheless concluded that based on the evidence in the record, $75,000.00 was "beyond the maximum possible recovery" that could be awarded, and remanded the action with instructions to the district court to determine an appropriate remittitur.

Given the evidence presented in this action, it is manifest that $150,000.00 for actual damages plus another $150,000.00 in punitive damages is excessive. Plaintiff deserves compensation for his humiliation, but not a princely treasure.

2.   Passion or Prejudice

Having determined that $300,000.00 is an excessive verdict based on the evidence presented, the Court must now determine if the jury arrived at this total through the machinations of passion and prejudice. If this was the case, the only proper remedy is to order a new trial. In the alternative, this Court could decide that the verdict was contrary to right reason, but was not the product of passion or prejudice, thus justifying the offer of a choice between remittitur or new trial.

The resolution of this issue requires a great reliance upon the discretion of the court. Based on his or her observation of the trial, the trial judge must determine whether the jury was impassioned or prejudiced against the defendants. In effect, the judge must speculate on the deliberations of the jury, guessing at their probable mental state. The process is ripe for abuse, whether consciously or subconsciously, depending on the trial judge's willingness to preside over a new trial.

Cognizant of these dangers, this Court has concluded that the jurors in this case were not infected by passion or prejudice. The size of the award, both in terms of the actual and punitive damages, clearly reflects the jury's desire to punish these defendants. The desire to punish, however, can be a product of reason rather than emotion, and can result from a rational deduction that such action is necessary. The Court believes that the jury acted on this kind of deduction in the present case, and did not act solely out of emotion or passion. In addition, there was nothing in the jury's behavior to indicate that they were predisposed—i.e. prejudiced—in the plaintiff's favor.

In light of this conclusion, the Court is of the opinion that a remittitur is appropriate.

3.   Maximum Award

Having determined that remittitur is appropriate, the Court must next identify the maximum verdict supported by the evidence. Compensatory and punitive damages will be considered separately.

As noted earlier, nearly all of the actual injury suffered by Mr. Smith falls into a nebulous, intangible category that cannot be accurately calculated. It is difficult to place a price on humiliation and the infringement of a right.

The evidence presented does cast some light on the degree of humiliation that plaintiff experienced. The City of Seven Points has fewer than 1,000 occupants, including the immediate outlying areas. As in most small communities, word of plaintiff's arrest probably travelled quickly. In light of the evidence presented concerning the violent tendencies of the city's police force, however, it is also probable that many of the area's residents sympathized with Mr. Smith.

Rather than being a cause for ridicule, his arrest was likely a cause for consolation and encouragement on the part of many people. The overall effect on plaintiff was possibly less a sense of humiliation and more a desire for revenge or vindication. While it occurred after the fact and is not a proper consideration for damages, the positive effect on Mr. Smith's self-respect caused by this favorable verdict should not be overlooked. The jury's decision alone vindicates Mr. Smith; the only question is the amount of money that will properly compensate him.

In light of these and other considerations, and after carefully reviewing the evidence presented, this Court is of the opinion that $50,000.00 is the maximum possible recovery for the injuries suffered by C.E. Smith.

The question of punitive damages is different in many respects. The jury was instructed to consider the following five factors in assessing punitive damages: (1) The nature of the wrong, (2) the character of the conduct involved, (3) the degree of culpability of the wrongdoer, (4) the situation and sensibility of the parties, and (5) the extent to which the defendants' conduct offends a public sense of justice and propriety. *See generally* Hansen v. Johns–Manville Products Corp., 734 F.2d 1036, 1047 (5th Cir.1984). In more general terms, an award of punitive damages is generally designed to punish the wrong-doer and deter future wrongs. Maxey v. Freightliner Corp., 665 F.2d 1367, 1378 (5th Cir.1982). The jury has wider discretion in assessing punitive damages while bearing in mind the five factors listed above.

In reviewing the jury's award for exemplary damages, the court must consider the Texas rule that they must be reasonably proportioned to the amount of actual damages. *See Hansen,* 734 F.2d at 1047. In addition, exemplary damages are subject to the same "maximum recovery" rule that applies to compensatory damages. *See Bonura,* 505 F.2d at 669.

At $150,000.00, the punitive damages awarded in this case are not unreasonably disproportionate to the actual damages of $50,000.00. That sum is, however, greater than the maximum recovery supported by the evidence. The $50,000.00 assessed against each of the three individual defendants is probably greater than twice their annual gross salary from the city. In the case of Officer Barina, an unpaid reserve officer, it is even more disproportionate. Such a sum goes too far in punishing these defendants and deterring future wrongful conduct, just as an award of twice a corporation's annual gross proceeds would be too large.

The five factors listed above also must not be ignored. In large part, Texas law proportions punitive damages to actual damages so that the punishment will fit the wrong.

In this case, the Court determined that actual damages could not have exceeded $50,000.00. This was a reduction of two-thirds of the original award. The Court believes an equivalent reduction in punitive damages is appropriate, thus bringing that total down to $50,000.00, or approximately $16,666.67 per individual defendant. This is the maximum possible recovery for punitive damages. It more than adequately punishes the individual defendants and should serve to deter future similar conduct.

4.   Remittitur or New Trial

It is the opinion of this Court that the maximum recovery shown by the evidence in this case is $100,000.00—$50,000.00 in actual damages and $50,000.00 in punitive damages.

It is, therefore, ORDERED that defendants' Motion for New Trial be GRANTED on the following conditions:

(1) If plaintiff agrees to a reduction in actual and punitive damages of $200,000.00, then defendants' motion will be DENIED and judgment will be entered in plaintiff's favor for $50,000.00 in actual damages and $50,000.00 in punitive damages.

(2) Plaintiff must indicate acceptance of the remittitur in writing on or before June 10, 1985. If this notice is not received by that date, a new trial will be scheduled.

(3) If plaintiff accepts the remittitur, plaintiff's counsel will then be given sufficient time to submit documents in support of a claim for attorneys' fees pursuant to 42 U.S.C. § 1988. Defendants will be given time to respond to this claim, and a hearing, if necessary, will be scheduled.

(4) If a new trial is necessary, it will include both the issue of liability and damages. Given the nature of this claim, plaintiff could not prove either actual or punitive damages without repeating the previous testimony regarding the occurrence in question. As such, the questions concerning liability are not "sufficiently distinct and independent" from questions concerning damages so that a new trial on the latter issue alone could be justified.

NOTE ON ADDITUR

Smith v. City of Seven Points involved a conditional exercise of remittitur, that is, the power of the court to reduce the amount of damages awarded by the jury. Does the court also have the power of additur, the power to increase the amount awarded by the jury? In federal courts, the answer is no. In Dimick v. Schiedt, 293 U.S. 474, 482, 55 S.Ct. 296, 299, 79 L.Ed. 603 (1935), the Supreme Court held that a federal court order increasing the size of a jury award would violate the Seventh Amendment. Justice Sutherland's opinion was based primarily on his holding that:

"[W]hile there was some practice to the contrary in respect of *decreasing* damages, the established practice and rule of the common law, as it existed in England at the time of the adoption of the Constitution, forbade the court to *increase* the amount of damages awarded by a jury in actions such as that here under consideration.

While this rule forbidding additur has been criticized, by, among others, Justice Stone in his dissent in *Dimick, supra,* 293 U.S. at 488, 55 S.Ct. at 301, it remains the law for the federal courts. The Seventh Amendment, however, does not apply to the states, and many state court systems, including California, permit the use of additur.

A recent article by D. Baldus, J. MacQueen & G. Woodworth, Improving Judicial Oversight of Jury Damages Assessments* * *, 80 Iowa L. Rev. 1109, 1128– 30 (1995), notes the "relative infrequency of additur/remittitur review". It describes a study of post trial settlements which estimated that in two large jurisdictions, "25% of cases resulting in plaintiff verdicts resulted in post-trial reductions of the plaintiff's award. Of those reductions, 62% were the product of a post-trial settlement between the parties, while only 23% were reduced by trial or appellate courts."

BMW of North America v. Gore

Supreme Court of the United States, 1996.
517 U.S. 559, 116 S. Ct. 1589, 134 L. Ed.2d 809.

■ STEVENS, J., delivered the opinion of the Court, in which O'CONNOR, KENNEDY, SOUTER, and BREYER, JJ., joined. BREYER, J., filed a concurring opinion, in which O'CONNOR and SOUTER, JJ., joined. SCALIA, J., filed a dissenting opinion, in which THOMAS, J., joined. GINSBURG, J., filed a dissenting opinion, in which REHNQUIST, C. J., joined.

■ JUSTICE STEVENS delivered the opinion of the Court.

The Due Process Clause of the Fourteenth Amendment prohibits a State from imposing a " 'grossly excessive' " punishment on a tortfeasor. TXO Production Corp. v. Alliance Resources Corp., 509 U.S. 443, 454, 125 L. Ed. 2d 366, 113 S. Ct. 2711 (1993) (and cases cited). The wrongdoing involved in this case was the decision by a national distributor of automobiles not to advise its dealers, and hence their customers, of predelivery damage to new cars when the cost of repair amounted to less than 3 percent of the car's suggested retail price. The question presented is whether a $2 million punitive damages award to the purchaser of one of these cars exceeds the constitutional limit.

In January 1990, Dr. Ira Gore, Jr. (respondent), purchased a black BMW sports sedan for $40,750.88 from an authorized BMW dealer in Birmingham, Alabama. After driving the car for approximately nine months, and without noticing any flaws in its appearance, Dr. Gore took the car to "Slick Finish," an independent detailer, to make it look " 'snazzier than it normally would appear.' " 646 So. 2d 619, 621 (Ala.1994). Mr. Slick, the proprietor, detected evidence that the car had been repainted. Convinced that he had been cheated, Dr. Gore brought suit against petitioner BMW of North America (BMW), the American distributor of BMW automobiles. Dr. Gore alleged, inter alia, that the failure to disclose that the car had been repainted constituted suppression of a material fact. The complaint prayed for $500,000 in compensatory and punitive damages, and costs.

At trial, BMW acknowledged that it had adopted a nationwide policy in 1983 concerning cars that were damaged in the course of manufacture or transportation. If the cost of repairing the damage exceeded 3 percent of the car's suggested retail price, the car was placed in company service for a period of time and then sold as used. If the repair cost did not exceed 3 percent of the suggested retail price, however, the car was sold as new without advising the dealer that any repairs had been made. Because the $601.37 cost of repainting Dr. Gore's car was only about 1.5 percent of its suggested retail price, BMW did not disclose the damage or repair to the Birmingham dealer.

Dr. Gore asserted that his repainted car was worth less than a car that had not been refinished. To prove his actual damages of $4,000, he relied on the testimony of a former BMW dealer, who estimated that the value of a repainted BMW was approximately 10 percent less than the value of a new car that had not been damaged and repaired. To support his claim for punitive damages, Dr. Gore introduced evidence that since 1983 BMW had sold 983 refinished cars as new, including 14 in Alabama, without disclosing that the cars had been repainted before sale at a cost of more than $300 per vehicle. Using the actual damage estimate of $4,000 per vehicle, Dr. Gore argued that a punitive award of $4 million would provide an appropriate penalty for selling approximately 1,000 cars for more than they were worth.

The jury returned a verdict finding BMW liable for compensatory damages of $4,000. In addition, the jury assessed $4 million in punitive damages, based on a determination that the nondisclosure policy constituted "gross, oppressive or malicious" fraud.

BMW filed a post-trial motion to set aside the punitive damages award. The company introduced evidence to establish that its nondisclosure policy was consistent with the laws of roughly 25 States defining the disclosure obligations of automobile manufacturers, distributors, and dealers. The most stringent of these statutes required disclosure of repairs costing more than 3 percent of the suggested retail price; none mandated disclosure of less costly repairs. Relying on these statutes, BMW contended that its conduct was lawful in these States and therefore could not provide the basis for an award of punitive damages.

BMW also drew the court's attention to the fact that its nondisclosure policy had never been adjudged unlawful before this action was filed. Just months before Dr. Gore's case went to trial, the jury in a similar lawsuit filed by another Alabama BMW purchaser found that BMW's failure to disclose paint repair constituted fraud. Yates v. BMW of North America, Inc., 642 So. 2d 937, 1993 WL 93670 (Ala. 1993). Before the judgment in this case, BMW changed its policy by taking steps to avoid the sale of any refinished vehicles in Alabama and two other States. When the $4 million verdict was returned in this case, BMW promptly instituted a nationwide policy of full disclosure of all repairs, no matter how minor.

The trial judge denied BMW's post-trial motion, holding, inter alia, that the award was not excessive. On appeal, the Alabama Supreme Court also rejected BMW's claim that the award exceeded the constitutionally permissible amount. 646 So. 2d 619 (1994).

The Alabama Supreme Court did, however, rule in BMW's favor on one critical point: The court found that the jury improperly computed the amount of punitive damages by multiplying Dr. Gore's compensatory damages by the number of similar sales in other jurisdictions. Having found the verdict tainted, the court held that "a constitutionally reasonable punitive damages award in this case is $2,000,000," and therefore ordered a remittitur in that amount. The court's discussion of the amount of its remitted award expressly disclaimed any reliance on "acts that occurred in other jurisdictions"; instead, the court explained that it had used a "comparative analysis" that considered Alabama cases, "along with cases from other jurisdictions, involving the sale of an automobile where the seller misrepresented the condition of the vehicle and the jury awarded punitive damages to the purchaser."

Because we believed that a review of this case would help to illuminate "the character of the standard that will identify constitutionally excessive awards" of punitive damages, see Honda Motor Co. v. Oberg, 512 U.S. 415, (1994) we granted certiorari, 513 U.S. 1125 (1995).

II

Punitive damages may properly be imposed to further a State's legitimate interests in punishing unlawful conduct and deterring its repetition. Gertz v. Robert Welch, Inc., 418 U.S. 323, 350, 41 L. Ed. 2d 789, 94 S. Ct. 2997 (1974); Newport v. Fact Concerts, Inc., 453 U.S. 247, 266–267, 69 L. Ed. 2d 616, 101 S. Ct. 2748 (1981); Haslip, 499 U.S. at 22. In our federal system, States necessarily have considerable flexibility in determining the level of punitive damages that they will allow in different classes of cases and in any particular case. Most States that authorize exemplary damages afford the jury similar latitude, requiring only that the damages awarded be reasonably necessary to vindicate the State's legitimate interests in punishment and deterrence. See TXO, 509 U.S. at 456; Haslip, 499 U.S. at 21, 22. Only when an award can fairly be categorized as "grossly excessive" in relation to these interests does it enter the zone of arbitrariness that violates the Due Process Clause of the Fourteenth Amendment. Cf. TXO, 509 U.S. at 456. For that reason, the federal excessiveness inquiry appropriately begins with an identification of the state interests that a punitive award is designed to serve.

No one doubts that a State may protect its citizens by prohibiting deceptive trade practices and by requiring automobile distributors to disclose presale repairs that affect the value of a new car. But the States need not, and in fact do not, provide such protection in a uniform manner. Some States rely on the judicial process to formulate and enforce an appropriate disclosure requirement by applying principles of contract and tort law. Other States have enacted various forms of legislation that define the disclosure obligations of automobile manufacturers, distributors, and dealers. The result is a patchwork of rules representing the diverse policy judgments of lawmakers in 50 States.

That diversity demonstrates that reasonable people may disagree about the value of a full disclosure requirement.

We may assume, arguendo, that it would be wise for every State to adopt Dr. Gore's preferred rule, requiring full disclosure of every presale repair to a car, no matter how trivial and regardless of its actual impact on the value of the car. But while we do not doubt that Congress has ample authority to enact such a policy for the entire Nation, it is clear that no single State could do so, or even impose its own policy choice on neighboring States. Similarly, one State's power to impose burdens on the interstate market for automobiles is not only subordinate to the federal power over interstate commerce, Gibbons v. Ogden, 22 U.S. 1, 9 Wheat. 1, 194–196, 6 L. Ed. 23 (1824), but is also constrained by the need to respect the interests of other States, see, e.g., Healy v. Beer Institute, 491 U.S. 324, 335–336, 105 L. Ed. 2d 275, 109 S. Ct. 2491 (1989) (the Constitution has a "special concern both with the maintenance of a national economic union unfettered by state-imposed limitations on interstate commerce and with the autonomy of the individual States within their respective spheres" (footnote omitted)); Edgar v. MITE Corp., 457 U.S. 624, 643, 73 L. Ed. 2d 269, 102 S. Ct. 2629 (1982).

We think it follows from these principles of state sovereignty and comity that a State may not impose economic sanctions on violators of its laws with the intent of changing the tortfeasors' lawful conduct in other States. Before this Court Dr. Gore argued that the large punitive damages award was necessary to induce BMW to change the nation-wide policy that it adopted in 1983. But by attempting to alter BMW's nationwide policy, Alabama would be infringing on the policy choices of other States. To avoid such encroachment, the economic penalties that a State such as Alabama inflicts on those who transgress its laws, whether the penalties take the form of legislatively authorized fines or judicially imposed punitive damages, must be supported by the State's interest in protecting its own consumers and its own economy.

In this case, we accept the Alabama Supreme Court's interpretation of the jury verdict as reflecting a computation of the amount of punitive damages "based in large part on conduct that happened in other jurisdictions." The Alabama Supreme Court therefore properly eschewed reliance on BMW's out-of-state conduct, id., at 628, and based its remitted award solely on conduct that occurred within Alabama. The award must be analyzed in the light of the same conduct, with consideration given only to the interests of Alabama consumers, rather than those of the entire Nation. When the scope of the interest in punishment and deterrence that an Alabama court may appropriately consider is properly limited, it is apparent—for reasons that we shall now address—that this award is grossly excessive.

III

Elementary notions of fairness enshrined in our constitutional jurisprudence dictate that a person receive fair notice not only of the conduct that will subject him to punishment but also of the severity of the penalty that a State may impose. Three guideposts, each of which indicates that BMW did not receive adequate notice of the magnitude of the sanction that Alabama might impose for adhering to the nondisclosure policy adopted in 1983, lead us to the conclusion that the $2 million award against BMW is grossly excessive: the degree of reprehensibility of the nondisclosure; the disparity between the harm or potential harm suffered by Dr. Gore and his punitive damages award; and the difference between this remedy and the civil penalties authorized or imposed in comparable cases. We discuss these considerations in turn.

Degree of Reprehensibility

Perhaps the most important indicium of the reasonableness of a punitive damages award is the degree of reprehensibility of the defendant's conduct. As the Court stated nearly 150 years ago, exemplary damages imposed on a defendant should reflect "the enormity of his offense." Day v. Woodworth, 54 U.S. 363, 13 How. 363, 371, 14 L. Ed. 181 (1851).

In this case, none of the aggravating factors associated with particularly reprehensible conduct is present. The harm BMW inflicted on Dr. Gore was purely economic in nature. The presale refinishing of the car had no effect on its performance or safety features, or even its appearance for at least nine months after his purchase. BMW's conduct evinced no indifference to or reckless disregard for the health and safety of others. To be sure, infliction of economic injury, especially when done intentionally through affirmative acts of misconduct, or when the target is financially vulnerable, can warrant a substantial penalty. But this observation does not convert all acts that cause economic harm into torts that are sufficiently reprehensible to justify a significant sanction in addition to compensatory damages.

Dr. Gore contends that BMW's conduct was particularly reprehensible because nondisclosure of the repairs to his car formed part of a nationwide pattern of tortious conduct.

In support of his thesis, Dr. Gore advances two arguments. First, he asserts that the state disclosure statutes supplement, rather than supplant, existing remedies for breach of contract and common-law fraud. Thus, according to Dr. Gore, the statutes may not properly be viewed as immunizing from liability the nondisclosure of repairs costing less than the applicable statutory threshold.

We recognize, of course, that only state courts may authoritatively construe state statutes. As far as we are aware, at the time this action was commenced no state court had explicitly addressed whether its State's disclosure statute provides a safe harbor for nondisclosure of presumptively minor repairs or should be construed instead as supplementing common-law duties. A review of the text of the statutes, however, persuades us that in the absence of a state-court determination to the contrary, a corporate executive could reasonably interpret the disclosure requirements as establishing safe harbors.

During the pendency of this litigation, Alabama enacted a disclosure statute which defines "material" damage to a new car as damage requiring repairs costing in excess of 3 percent of suggested retail price or $500, whichever is greater. Ala. Code § 8–19–5(22) (1993). After its decision in this case, the Alabama Supreme Court stated in dicta that the remedies available under this section of its Deceptive Trade Practices Act did not displace or alter pre-existing remedies available under either the common law or other statutes. Hines v. Riverside Chevrolet–Olds, Inc., 655 So. 2d 909, 917, n. 2 (Ala.1994). It refused, however, to "recognize, or impose on automobile manufacturers, a general duty to disclose every repair of damage, however slight, incurred during the manufacturing process." Instead, it held that whether a defendant has a duty to disclose is a question of fact "for the jury to determine." In reaching that conclusion it overruled two earlier decisions that seemed to indicate that as a matter of law there was no disclosure obligation in cases comparable to this one.

Dr. Gore's second argument for treating BMW as a recidivist is that the company should have anticipated that its actions would be considered fraudulent in some, if not all, jurisdictions. This contention overlooks the fact that actionable fraud requires a material misrepresentation or omission. This qualifier invites line drawing of just the sort engaged in by States with disclosure statutes and by BMW. We do not think it can be disputed that there may exist minor imperfections in the finish of a new car that can be repaired (or indeed, left unrepaired) without materially affecting the car's value. There is no evidence that BMW acted in bad faith when it sought to establish the appropriate line between presumptively minor damage and damage requiring disclosure to purchasers. For this purpose, BMW could reasonably rely on state disclosure statutes for guidance.

Finally, the record in this case discloses no deliberate false statements, acts of affirmative misconduct, or concealment of evidence of improper motive, such as were present in Haslip and TXO. Haslip, 499 U.S. at 5, TXO, 509 U.S. at 453. We accept, of course, the jury's finding that BMW suppressed a material fact which Alabama law obligated it to communicate to prospective purchasers of repainted cars in that State. But the omission of a material fact may be less reprehensible than a deliberate false statement, particularly when there is a good-faith basis for believing that no duty to disclose exists.

That conduct is sufficiently reprehensible to give rise to tort liability, and even a modest award of exemplary damages, does not establish the high degree of culpability that warrants a substantial punitive damages award. Because this case exhibits none of the circumstances ordinarily associated with egregiously improper conduct, we are persuaded that BMW's conduct was not sufficiently reprehensible to warrant imposition of a $2 million exemplary damages award.

Ratio

The second and perhaps most commonly cited indicium of an unreasonable or excessive punitive damages award is its ratio to the actual harm inflicted on the plaintiff. See TXO, 509 U.S. at 459; Haslip, 499 U.S. at 23. The principle that exemplary damages must bear a "reasonable relationship" to compensatory damages has a long pedigree. Scholars have identified a number of early English statutes authorizing the award of multiple damages for particular wrongs. Some 65 different enactments during the period between 1275 and 1753 provided for double, treble, or quadruple damages. Our decisions in both Haslip and TXO endorsed the proposition that a comparison between the compensatory award and the punitive award is significant.

In Haslip we concluded that even though a punitive damages award of "more than 4 times the amount of compensatory damages," might be "close to the line," it did not "cross the line into the area of constitutional impropriety." Haslip, 499 U.S. at 23–24. TXO, following dicta in Haslip, refined this analysis by confirming that the proper inquiry is " 'whether there is a reasonable relationship between the punitive damages award and the harm likely to result from the defendant's conduct as well as the harm that actually has occurred.' " TXO, 509 U.S. at 460 (emphasis in original), quoting Haslip, 499 U.S. at 21. Thus, in upholding the $10 million award in TXO, we relied on the difference between that figure and the harm to the victim that would have ensued if the tortious plan had succeeded. That difference suggested that the relevant ratio was not more than 10 to 1.

The $2 million in punitive damages awarded to Dr. Gore by the Alabama Supreme Court is 500 times the amount of his actual harm as determined by the jury. Moreover, there is no suggestion that Dr. Gore or any other BMW purchaser was threatened with any additional potential harm by BMW's nondisclosure policy. The disparity in this case is thus dramatically greater than those considered in Haslip and TXO.

Of course, we have consistently rejected the notion that the constitutional line is marked by a simple mathematical formula, even one that compares actual and potential damages to the punitive award. TXO, 509 U.S. at 458. n37 Indeed, low awards of compensatory damages may properly support a higher ratio than high compensatory awards, if, for example, a particularly egregious act has resulted in only a small amount of economic damages. A higher ratio may also be justified in cases in which the injury is hard to detect or the monetary value of noneconomic harm might have been difficult to determine. It is appropriate, therefore, to reiterate our rejection of a categorical approach. Once again, "we return to what we said . . . in Haslip: 'We need not, and indeed we cannot, draw a mathematical bright line between the constitutionally acceptable and the constitutionally unacceptable that would fit every case. We can say, however, that [a] general concern of reasonableness . . . properly enters into the constitutional calculus.' " TXO, 509 U.S. at 458 (quoting Haslip, 499 U.S., at 18). In most cases, the ratio will be within a constitutionally acceptable range, and remittitur will not be justified on this basis. When the ratio is a breathtaking 500 to 1, however, the award must surely "raise a suspicious judicial eyebrow." TXO, 509 U.S. at 482 (O'CONNOR, J., dissenting).

Sanctions for Comparable Misconduct

Comparing the punitive damages award and the civil or criminal penalties that could be imposed for comparable misconduct provides a third indicium of excessiveness. As JUSTICE O'CONNOR has correctly observed, a reviewing court engaged in determining whether an award of punitive damages is excessive should "accord 'substantial deference' to legislative judgments concerning appropriate sanctions for the conduct at issue." Browning–Ferris Industries of Vt., Inc. v. Kelco Disposal, Inc., 492 U.S. at 301 (O'CONNOR, J., concurring in part and dissenting in part). In Haslip, 499 U.S. at 23, the Court noted that although the exemplary award was "much in excess of the fine that could be imposed," imprisonment was also authorized in the criminal context. n38 In this case the $2 million economic sanction imposed on BMW is substantially greater than the statutory fines available in Alabama and elsewhere for similar malfeasance.

IV

The fact that BMW is a large corporation rather than an impecunious individual does not diminish its entitlement to fair notice of the demands that the several States impose on the conduct of its business. Indeed, its status as an active participant in the national economy implicates the federal interest in preventing individual States from imposing undue burdens on interstate commerce. While each State has ample power to protect its own consumers, none may use the punitive damages deterrent as a means of imposing its regulatory policies on the entire Nation.

As in Haslip, we are not prepared to draw a bright line marking the limits of a constitutionally acceptable punitive damages award. Unlike that case, however, we are fully convinced that the grossly excessive award imposed in this case transcends the constitutional limit. Whether the appropriate remedy requires a new trial or merely an independent determination by the Alabama Supreme Court of the award necessary to vindicate the economic interests of Alabama consumers is a matter that should be addressed by the state court in the first instance.

■ [concurring opinion of JUSTICE BREYER omitted]

■ JUSTICE SCALIA, with whom JUSTICE THOMAS joins, dissenting.

Today we see the latest manifestation of this Court's recent and increasingly insistent "concern about punitive damages that 'run wild.'" Pacific Mut. Life Ins. Co. v. Haslip, 499 U.S. 1, 18, 113 L. Ed. 2d 1, 111 S. Ct. 1032 (1991). Since the Constitution does not make that concern any of our business, the Court's activities in this area are an unjustified incursion into the province of state governments.

The most significant aspects of today's decision—the identification of a "substantive due process" right against a "grossly excessive" award, and the concomitant assumption of ultimate authority to decide anew a matter of "reasonableness" resolved in lower court proceedings—are of course not new. Haslip and TXO revived the notion, moribund since its appearance in the first years of this century, that the measure of civil punishment poses a question of constitutional dimension to be answered by this Court. Neither of those cases, however, nor any of the precedents upon which they relied, actually took the step of declaring a punitive award unconstitutional simply because it was "too big." At the time of adoption of the Fourteenth Amendment, it was well understood that punitive damages represent the assessment by the jury, as the voice of the community, of the measure of punishment the defendant deserved. See, e.g., Barry v. Edmunds, 116 U.S. 550, 565, 29 L. Ed. 729, 6 S. Ct. 501 (1886); Missouri Pacific R. Co. v. Humes, 115 U.S. 512, 521, 29 L. Ed. 463, 6 S. Ct. 110 (1885); Day v. Woodworth, 54 U.S. 363, 13 How. 363, 371, 14 L. Ed. 181 (1851). See generally Haslip, supra, at 25–27 (SCALIA, J., concurring in judgment). Today's decision, though dressed up as a legal opinion, is really no more than a disagreement with the community's sense of indignation or outrage expressed in the punitive award of the Alabama jury, as reduced by the State Supreme Court. It reflects not merely, as the concurrence candidly acknowledges, "a judgment about a matter of degree," but a judgment about the appropriate degree of indignation or outrage, which is hardly an analytical determination.

One might understand the Court's eagerness to enter this field, rather than leave it with the state legislatures, if it had something useful to say. In fact, however, its opinion provides virtually no guidance to legislatures, and to state and federal courts, as to what a "constitutionally proper" level of punitive damages might be.

In Part III of its opinion, the Court identifies "three guideposts" that lead it to the conclusion that the award in this case is excessive: degree of reprehensibility, ratio between punitive award and plaintiff's actual harm, and legislative sanctions provided for comparable misconduct. The legal significance of these "guideposts" is nowhere explored, but their necessary effect is to establish federal standards governing the hitherto exclusively state law of damages.

Of course it will not be easy for the States to comply with this new federal law of damages, no matter how willing they are to do so. In truth, the "guideposts" mark a road to nowhere; they provide no real guidance at all. As to "degree of reprehensibility" of the defendant's conduct, we learn that " 'nonviolent crimes are less serious than crimes marked by violence or the threat of violence,' " and that " 'trickery and deceit' " are "more reprehensible than negligence,". As to the ratio of punitive to compensatory damages, we are told that a " 'general concern of reasonableness . . . enters into the constitutional calculus,' "—though even "a breathtaking 500 to 1" will not necessarily do anything more than " 'raise a suspicious judicial eyebrow,' " ante, at 23 (quoting TXO, supra, at 481 (O'CONNOR, J., dissenting), an opinion which, when confronted with that "breathtaking" ratio, approved it). And as to legislative sanctions provided for comparable misconduct, they should be accorded " 'substantial deference,' " ibid. One expects the Court to conclude: "To thine own self be true."

■ Justice Ginsburg, with whom the Chief Justice joins, dissenting.

The Court, I am convinced, unnecessarily and unwisely ventures into territory traditionally within the States' domain, and does so in the face of reform measures recently adopted or currently under consideration in legislative arenas.

The respect due the Alabama Supreme Court requires that we strip from this case a false issue: no impermissible "extraterritoriality" infects the judgment before us; the excessiveness of the award is the sole issue genuinely presented.

Because the jury apparently (and erroneously) had used acts in other states as a multiplier to arrive at a $4 million sum for punitive damages, the Alabama Supreme Court itself determined " 'the maximum amount that a properly functioning jury could have awarded.' " 646 So. 2d at 630 (Houston, J., concurring specially) (quoting Big B, Inc. v. Cottingham, 634 So. 2d 999, 1006 (Ala.1993)). The per curiam opinion emphasized that in arriving at $2 million as "the amount of punitive damages to be awarded in this case, [the court did] not consider those acts that occurred in other jurisdictions." 646 So. 2d at 628 (emphasis in original). As this Court recognizes, the Alabama high court "properly eschewed reliance on BMW's out-of-state conduct and based its remitted award solely on conduct that occurred within Alabama." Ante, at 13 (citation omitted). In sum, the Alabama Supreme Court left standing the jury's decision that the facts warranted an award of punitive damages—a determination not contested in this Court—and the state court concluded that, considering only acts in Alabama, $2 million was "a constitutionally reasonable punitive damages award." 646 So. 2d at 629.

The Court finds Alabama's $2 million award not simply excessive, but grossly so, and therefore unconstitutional. The decision leads us further into territory traditionally within the States' domain, and commits the Court, now and again, to correct "misapplication of a properly stated rule of law." But cf. S. Ct. Rule 10 ("A petition for a writ of certiorari is rarely granted when the asserted error consists of erroneous factual findings or the misapplication of a properly stated rule of law."). n4 The Court is not well equipped for this mission. Tellingly, the Court repeats that it brings to the task no "mathematical formula," ante, at 22, no "categorical approach," ante, at 23, no "bright line," ante, at 26. It has only a vague concept of substantive due process, a "raised eyebrow" test, see ante, at 23, as its ultimate guide.

For the reasons stated, I dissent from this Court's disturbance of the judgment the Alabama Supreme Court has made.

APPENDIX TO DISSENTING OPINION OF GINSBURG, J.
STATE LEGISLATIVE ACTIVITY REGARDING PUNITIVE DAMAGES

State legislatures have in the hopper or have enacted a variety of measures to curtail awards of punitive damages. At least one state legislature has prohibited punitive damages altogether, unless explicitly provided by statute. See N. H. Rev. Stat. Ann. § 507:16 (1994). We set out in this appendix some of the several controls enacted or under consideration in the States. The measures surveyed are: (1) caps on awards; (2) provisions for payment of sums to state agencies rather than to plaintiffs; and (3) mandatory bifurcated trials with separate proceedings for punitive damages determinations.

[list of state statutes deleted]

NOTE: IMPOSING RATIONAL LIMITS ON PUNITIVE DAMAGES

On remand, BMW of North America v. Gore, 701 So. 2d 507 (Ala.1997), the Supreme Court of Alabama ordered a new trial unless the purchaser filed a remittitur limiting damages to $50,000. The opinions speak of the permissible limits in terms of multiples of actual damages. If actual damages are relatively small, does this argue for larger or smaller punitive awards?

Suppose a corporate defendant contemplates taking action that will save it money, but will cause a small amount of damage to many people. Management calculates that although savings in each individual occurrence will be small, the potential aggregate savings will be substantial, even if defendant will have to pay compensatory damages to any individual who brings a lawsuit. (Defendant expects such claims to be rare, however, because the potential damages in each case are small.) Does this situation call for small or large punitive damages to be added to the recovery of those plaintiffs who do choose to litigate? Is this an argument for no limits on what a plaintiff may recover as punitive damages? How does the availability of punitives change the plaintiff's incentive to litigate? How does it affect defendant's original decision to take the contemplated harmful action?

NOTE: THE APPROPRIATE STANDARD AS A FUNCTION OF THE NATURE OF THE CLAIM

In Thornton v. Gulf Fleet Marine Corp., 752 F.2d 1074 (5th Cir.1985) Judge Williams pointed out that in the case of a claim of unseaworthiness a directed verdict or judgment nov is justified only "if the facts and inferences point so strongly and overwhelmingly in favor of one party that the court believes that reasonable men could not arrive at a contrary verdict." However, he added, in a Jones Act case the standard is "much stricter," being identical to that applied in federal Employers' Liability Act cases, requiring that there be "a complete absence of probative facts to support the verdict," or no more than "a scintilla of evidence."

SPECIAL VERDICTS AND SPECIAL INTERROGATORIES

In most civil cases in most jurisdictions, juries are asked to set forth their decision in the form of a *general verdict.* That is, the jury need only state whether the plaintiff or the defendant has prevailed in the lawsuit, and are not asked to set forth the reasons for their decisions or state the findings they have made on any intermediate factual issues in the case. (If plaintiff has prevailed, the jury will also usually be asked to state the amount of damages to be recovered.)

In most jurisdictions, however, alternative verdict forms may be used which require juries to set forth the grounds for their decisions with greater particularity. The Federal Rules of Civil Procedure provide for two such devices. The *special verdict,* pursuant to Rule 49(a), requires a jury to make special written findings with respect to each issue of fact. The *general verdict accompanied by answer to interrogatories,* pursuant to Rule 49(b), provides an intermediate position between general and special verdicts. It permits the jury to render a general verdict, but requires them to supplement that verdict with findings on one or more factual issues whose determination is necessary to the verdict.

The pros and cons of general and special verdicts have been debated for a long time. *See, e.g.* Sunderland, *Verdicts, General and Special,* 29 Yale L.J. 259 (1920). Some see the special verdict as adding efficiency and precision to the deliberation process, enabling a judge to detect errors and inconsistencies in the jury's reasoning. Others feel that a special verdict improperly impinges on the jury's freedom to view the case from many perspectives and decide it as a totality.

In most states, as in the federal system, judges retain broad discretion to decide when to use special verdicts or interrogatories, although a few states have sought to encourage their use. Texas, for example, at one time had a rule of civil procedure which required issues to be submitted to the jury "distinctly and separately", but that rule was later amended to require that "In all jury cases the court shall, whenever feasible, submit the cause upon broad form questions." Tex.R.Civ.P. 227.

One problem (or perhaps advantage) of special verdicts and interrogatories is that they can reveal inconsistencies in the jury's reasoning that would be hidden in a general verdict. Such inconsistencies, if they cannot be resolved, require an order granting a new trial. Judges, however, have both a doctrinal obligation and a practical interest in harmonizing potential inconsistencies whenever possible.

For example, in Van Cleve v. Betts, 16 Wash.App. 748, 559 P.2d 1006 (1977), a case involving a pedestrian injured by an automobile in which the driver of the car claimed that plaintiff had "walked into" the side of his car, the jury answered interrogatories stating that plaintiff was negligent but that her negligence was not the proximate cause of her injuries. The appellate court, noting that it had a legal obligation to read the interrogatory answers "harmoniously", noted that it was "conceivable" that the jury felt that plaintiff was negligent, not for walking into the side of the car, but for not maintaining a "proper lookout". It reconciled the two findings by stating the jury might have concluded that "even if Mrs. Van Cleve had maintained a proper lookout, the speed and direction of the travel of the car would have made it impossible for her to avoid a collision."

E. APPELLATE REVIEW OF FINDINGS BY THE COURT

When a case is tried to the court and there is no jury, or there is only an advisory jury, review of the findings of fact is by appeal. The standard, however, is quite deferential to the trial court: a finding of fact may be reversed only if it is "clearly erroneous." See F.R.C.P. 52(a).

Precisely what does it mean to say that a finding is clearly erroneous? Justice White in Anderson v. City of Bessemer City, N.C., 470 U.S. 564, 574, 105 S.Ct. 1504, 1511, 84 L.Ed.2d 518 (1985), recognized that the meaning of the phrase "is not immediately apparent," and articulated the general principles, derived from previous cases decided by the Supreme Court, that govern the appellate court's power to reverse on this ground:

> The foremost of these principles, as the Fourth Circuit itself recognized, is that "[a] finding is 'clearly erroneous' when although there is evidence to support it, the reviewing court on the entire evidence is left with the definite and firm conviction that a mistake has been committed." United States v. United States Gypsum Co., 333 U.S. 364, 395, 68 S.Ct. 525, 542, 92 L.Ed. 746 (1948). This standard plainly does not entitle a reviewing court to reverse the finding of the trier of fact simply because it is convinced that it would have decided the case differently. The reviewing court oversteps the bounds of its duty under Rule 52(a) if it undertakes to duplicate the role of the lower court. "In applying the clearly erroneous standard to the findings of a district court sitting without a jury, appellate courts must constantly have in mind that their function is not to decide factual issues *de novo.*"

Where evaluation of the evidence depends in whole or in part on demeanor, as is almost always true of oral testimony, the advantage enjoyed by the trial court is readily apparent. A "dead transcript" is hardly the equal of live testimony when it comes to assessing credibility. Suppose, however, that the finding of fact is based entirely on documentary evidence, is there any reason for deference to the trial judge? Are not three heads better than one? Courts had divided on that issue.

Rule 52(a), as amended, makes it perfectly clear that the clearly erroneous standard applies in that situation as well. In *Anderson,* handed down shortly before the amendment to Rule 52(a) was promulgated by the Supreme Court, Justice White provided the rationale:

> The rationale for deference to the original finder of fact is not limited to the superiority of the trial judge's position to make determinations of credibility. The trial judge's major role is the determination of fact, and with experience in fulfilling that role comes expertise. Duplication of the trial judge's efforts in the court of appeals would very likely contribute only negligibly to the accuracy of fact determination at a huge cost in diversion of judicial resources. In addition, the parties to a case on appeal have already been forced to concentrate their energies and resources on persuading the trial judge that their account of the facts is the correct one; requiring them to persuade three more judges at the appellate level is requiring too much. As the Court has stated in a different context, the trial on the merits should be

"the 'main event' * * * rather than a 'tryout on the road.' "
Wainwright v. Sykes, 433 U.S. 72, 90, 97 S.Ct. 2497, 2508, 53
L.Ed.2d 594 (1977). For these reasons, review of factual findings
under the clearly-erroneous standard—with its deference to the
trier of fact—is the rule, not the exception.

JUDGMENT ON PARTIAL FINDINGS

Sometimes a single, relatively simple issue will be dispositive of
what would otherwise be a long and complicated case. For example, a
legally valid release or a waiver of a condition in a contract may make
irrelevant proof of damages. Where the case is being tried to the court
and the judge finds against one of the parties on such an issue, is
there any point to continuing? Under the amendments to the Federal
Rules of Civil Procedure transmitted by the Supreme Court to Congress on April 30, 1991 (effective December 1, 1991) section (c) has
been added to Rule 52 to make clear that judgment may be entered
"on partial findings."

The rule provides: "if during a trial without a jury a party has
been fully heard with respect to an issue and the court finds against
the party on that issue, the court may enter judgment as a matter of
law against that party" on any claim that, as a matter of substantive
law, requires a favorable finding on such an issue. Findings of fact and
conclusions of law are required, as they are under Rule 52(a).

CHAPTER XI

JUDGMENTS

A. RELIEF FROM JUDGMENTS

Great Coastal Express v. International Brotherhood of Teamsters

United States Court of Appeals, Fourth Circuit 1982.
675 F.2d 1349, *cert. denied* 459 U.S. 1128, 103 S.Ct. 764, 74 L.Ed.2d 978 (1983).

■ INGRAHAM, SENIOR CIRCUIT JUDGE.

These proceedings were initiated by the International Brotherhood of Teamsters, Chauffeurs, Warehousemen and Helpers of America ("IBT" or "the Union") in an effort to obtain relief from a judgment the Union argues was procured through fraud on the court.

This dispute arises out of a 1970 strike by IBT against Great Coastal. Great Coastal subsequently brought suit against IBT on two theories: (1) damages to property and equipment caused by union violence; and (2) lost business caused by illegal secondary boycotting. The union violence claim was eliminated from the case by directed verdict at the close of Great Coastal's case in chief. The jury then awarded over $1,000,000 in damages on the secondary boycott claim, which prompted a new trial on damages alone and a second, reduced verdict. The judgment was affirmed as to both liability and damages by this court. Great Coastal Express, supra. IBT subsequently uncovered evidence that the company itself had planned and executed several of the acts of violence described during the suit, and petitioned the district court and this court for relief from the judgment. The district court concluded that company witnesses had indeed perjured themselves in the original trial, but that such facts did not constitute a fraud on the court under Hazel–Atlas Glass Co. v. Hartford-Empire Co., 322 U.S. 238, 64 S.Ct. 997, 88 L.Ed. 1250 (1944), or support an independent action for relief. For reasons developed below, we affirm the denial of relief and deny the direct petition in this court.

I. *Background*

    A. History of this Litigation.

Great Coastal is an interstate truck carrier based in Richmond, Virginia. In 1970, the company's employees were represented by Local 592, an affiliate of the IBT. From 1964 to March 31, 1970, the parties were signatories to the National Master Freight Agreement. Negotiations for a new agreement were unsuccessful and Local 592 went on strike in August 1970. On December 10, 1970, Great Coastal filed an action in a Virginia state court which was removed by IBT to the Eastern District of Virginia pursuant to 28 U.S.C. § 1441(b), as an action purporting to state a claim under § 8(b)(4) of the Labor-Management Relations Act, 29 U.S.C. 158(b)(4), over which the United States District Courts have original jurisdiction.

The case was tried before a jury on the two theories described above, damages caused by union violence and illegal secondary boycotting. From the outset, union counsel objected to the introduction of evidence of violence that was not shown to be connected to the union. On the proffer of Great Coastal that all such evidence would ultimately be linked to the IBT, the district court permitted the company to go forward. Company witnesses testified to wide-spread and savage acts of violence directed towards its employees and property. At the close of the company's case, however, the district court granted the union's motion for directed verdict on the violence claims, holding that the company had failed to meet its burden under United Mine Workers v. Gibbs, 383 U.S. 715, 735–37, 86 S.Ct. 1130, 1143–44, 16 L.Ed.2d 218 (1966), of linking the acts of violence to IBT. The secondary boycott claim was allowed to go to the jury, and the jury found liability on this ground.

Although counsel for Great Coastal stated during closing argument that it had shown actual damages proximately resulting from the unlawful secondary boycott activities amounting to $942,065, the jury returned a verdict of $1,300,000. On the union's motion for judgment notwithstanding the verdict, the district court concluded that "the damage award ... was substantially out of touch with damages allegedly proven." 350 F.Supp. 1377, 1380 (E.D.Va.1972). The excessive verdict, in the court's opinion, suggested that:

> The jury, while well intentioned, was in spite of the Court's instructions to the contra influenced in its consideration of damages by the gross and vicious conduct attributed to the members of the local union and their sympathizers.

The court denied the motion for JNOV as to the remaining issues raised by the union, but directed a retrial on damages alone. The second jury reached a verdict of $806,093 and judgment was entered on the secondary boycott claim in that amount.

On appeal to this court, IBT argued that the district court erred in submitting to the jury the question whether the local union and its members were agents of the International; that the company had failed to demonstrate what part of its losses were caused by illegal activity as distinguished from legal activity; that the court erred in restricting the new trial to damages; and that the instructions to the second jury were inconsistent and improper. This court affirmed on all issues. Great Coastal Express, supra, 511 F.2d at 841. With respect to the partial new trial issue, the opinion of the court observed that "the union does not contest the fact that there was evidence from which a jury could find an illegal secondary boycott," id. at 842, and further, "it goes without saying that the jury had abundant evidence" to find that IBT had committed unlawful secondary boycotting. Id. at 844. We concluded there was no basis for believing that the evidence of violence had so inflamed the jury as to fatally infect the liability verdict with prejudice, particularly in light of the district court instructions, and that IBT had not overcome the presumption of validity of a verdict. Id. at 847. Certiorari was denied by the Supreme Court and the union paid Great Coastal a total of $961,653.67, representing the judgment plus interest and costs.

In February of 1977, counsel for IBT first received information that the company had deliberately sabotaged its own equipment on at least one occasion, and had committed other acts of violence in the evident expectation that responsibility for these acts could be laid on the union. Counsel investigated these matters between March and December 1977 and turned over the results of their investigation to the Justice Department. The Department's response in August 1978 was that the applicable statute of limitations precluded any criminal action with respect to the allegations. The Department made a similar response to an inquiry by the district court in November 1979.

IBT filed its motion to set aside the judgment in the district court on December 14, 1978. The court allowed post-judgment discovery and held a two-day evidentiary hearing. At the hearing, two of the company's witnesses from the 1972 trial admitted that part or all of their testimony had been false, and other evidence of fraudulent company practices was introduced. Stressing that the allegations of fraud on the court all were instances of either perjury or fabricated evidence, the district court considered it unnecessary to address the evidence in greater detail but denied relief as a matter of law. The court's decision may be briefly summarized as follows: relief under Federal Rule of Civil Procedure 60(b)(3) would be forthcoming except that the union had not filed its motion within the Rule's one-year time limitation, and this limitation could not be evaded through use of 60(b)(6); perjury and fabricated evidence do not rise to the level of fraud on the court under the savings provisions of Rule 60(b), and that IBT had not shown attorney involvement in the fraud; and similarly that perjury and fabricated evidence were "intrinsic" rather than "extrinsic" forms of fraud and would not support an independent action in equity for relief from a judgment. Great Coastal Express v. International Brotherhood of Teamsters, 86 F.R.D. 131, 136–40 (E.D.Va.1980). This is the principal decision appealed from.

The case was briefed and argued before this panel at the November 1980 sitting. We remanded, 639 F.2d 780, with directions that the district court supplement the record with specific findings of fact based upon the evidentiary hearing that had been held. The district court provided these findings by memorandum dated August 27, 1981, and we allowed supplemental briefing and further oral argument.

B. The District Court's Findings of Perjury and Fabricated Evidence.

The district court found that in October of 1970 during the strike Robert Seward, an employee of Great Coastal, was ordered by Terminal Manager William Funai to get a brick or rock, take a company truck out on the road and "tear it up some." Seward drove the company truck to Route 33 past New Kent, Virginia, broke the windshield of the truck with a brick, and fired three shots into the front of the trailer with a small caliber hand gun. Seward thereafter executed several false affidavits describing this incident, concealing the true events and claiming "unidentified persons" had sabotaged the truck. One of these affidavits was incorporated into Great Coastal's answers to interrogatories as "direct evidence of specific instances of violence, intimidation and secondary boycotting activity." Evidence was also adduced that Funai sent Seward and other company employees to the yards of competing companies that had hired some of the striking Great Coastal drivers, and sabotaged trucks in those yards.

After the strike, and after Local 592 had been decertified as representative of the company's employees as the result of an election, Seward received a $500 payment from C. E. Estes, president of the company. Estes told Seward to keep the payment to himself and to consider it a "Christmas bonus or pay for a job well done." The $500 is not reflected anywhere on the company's books and records. Funai also received a payment, a share of the IBT judgment, of approximately $12,000. This payment was ostensibly part of the company's profit-sharing plan; however, Funai was not employed by the company at the time of the recovery of the IBT judgment, and therefore payment of this share to Funai was contrary to company policy regarding profit-sharing.

The district court found that Seward had falsely testified in the 1972 trial, as to the New Kent incident and the company's role in fabricating acts of violence, and also that Funai failed to tell the complete truth in violation of his oath as a witness in that trial. The court concluded as follows:

> The Court is satisfied and finds as a fact that much of the testimony offered by the plaintiff in the first trial dealing with the alleged acts of violence by the defendant were perjured.

> Just as the perjurors are, regrettably, free from prosecution for perjury by virtue of the statute of limitations, the one year limitation precludes the instant defendant from relief under Rule 60(b)(3) for the reasons stated in the Court's memorandum of February 29, 1980.

II. *Discussion*

At the outset, Great Coastal urges that the fraud uncovered by the union, inasmuch as it relates to acts of violence, became immaterial once the violence claim was eliminated by directed verdict. The judgment under attack, the company continues, is a secondary boycott judgment that this court has already affirmed in no uncertain terms. We note that this argument is, in effect, that any fraud in the case was harmless error, and that strictly speaking discussion of such a question should be preceded by the threshold determination of whether error has occurred at all (or, in this case, whether the fraud is the type justifying relief from judgment). Nevertheless, we will briefly consider the company's argument here because the parties have given it some priority and it is the principal point stressed in all of the company's submissions to this court.

The position of IBT is that once fraud enters the case in any manner, the judgment must be vitiated without further inquiry as to the materiality or effect of the fraud on the judgment, citing Hazel–Atlas Glass Co. v. Hartford–Empire Co., 322 U.S. 238, 64 S.Ct. 997, 88 L.Ed. 1250 (1944). In Hazel–Atlas, the successful litigant had used an article in a trade publication in support of a patent application, and subsequently defended the patent in the federal courts. However, in its zeal to assure the success of the patent, company officials had fraudulently attributed the authorship of the article to a nationally known, supposedly impartial figure when in reality the article was authored by a company patent attorney. The Supreme Court noted that whatever influence the article may or may not have had on the patent office and the courts, the company clearly thought it was material and went to some trouble to procure it. The IBT particularly relies on the following language: "(T)hey urged the article upon the Circuit Court and prevailed. They are in no position now to dispute its effectiveness." 322 U.S. at 247, 64 S.Ct. at 1002.

No doubt in cases like Hazel–Atlas, where a single cause of action is involved, the IBT's position has merit. A case such as ours, where separate and independent causes of action were alleged, is in that respect somewhat different and we do not believe Hazel–Atlas provides a complete answer. We might be receptive to the company's position that the secondary boycott judgment was insulated from the fraud if in fact the violence claim was effectively and entirely eliminated from the jury's consideration. In such a case, materiality may well be a proper inquiry. Cf. Alberta Gas Chemicals, Ltd. v. Celanese Corp., 650 F.2d 9, 12 (2d Cir.1981); Wilkin v. Sunbeam Corp., 466 F.2d 714, 717 (10th Cir.1972), cert. denied, 409 U.S. 1126, 93 S.Ct. 940, 35 L.Ed.2d 258 (1973); Mas v. Coca Cola, 163 F.2d 505, 508 (4th Cir.1947).

We cannot say with complete confidence, however, that the fraud was harmlessly excised from the case. This is primarily because of the following factual considerations. First, at the close of the first trial in 1972 the district court did instruct the jury that they were not to consider the evidence of acts of violence in reference to any damages from secondary boycotting, and that the jury should only concern itself with the second boycott claim. However, near the close of his instructions the district court also stated:

> Don't get off on those despicable acts that were testified to. We are not involved with that anymore with reference to the issue right before you except as a totality of circumstances which may or may not have any bearing on it.

Thus, there is the possibility that the perjury and fabricated evidence at issue may have been considered by the jury as part of the "totality of circumstances." As we have noted above, in the course of ordering a partial new trial, the district court acknowledged that the jury may have been improperly influenced by the evidence of acts of violence.

Secondly, the company's brief to this court on its prior appeal contained repeated references to the evidence of violence, with specific reference to the New Kent incident and sabotage of equipment. The company argued:

> The Union's efforts to persuade non-striking employees to stop work were not restricted to peaceful means. Again and again, during the long period of the strike, resort was had to extreme violence. . . . It would have been permissible for the jury to find, upon these facts, that the Union drew upon the force of the violent acts for its benefit. In combination with the other illegal hot cargo and secondary boycott activity, which was inextricably tied in with the violence, the company's business was brought to a total standstill.

Such argumentation falls directly within the prescription of Hazel–Atlas quoted above, see also 322 U.S. at 241, 64 S.Ct. at 999, and we are precluded from inquiring as to its materiality or effect on this court's decision.

A.   Relief from Judgments Under Rule 60(b).

Respect for the finality of judgments is deeply engrained in our legal system. As Justice Story observed, "(i)t is for the public interest and policy to make an end to litigation. . . ." so that "suits may not be immortal, while men are mortal." Ocean Ins. Co. v. Fields, 18 F.Cas. 532, 539 (No. 10,406) (C.C.D.Mass. 1841) (Story, J. sitting as Circuit Judge). See also Southern Pacific RR Co. v. United States, 168 U.S. 1, 49, 18 S.Ct. 18, 27, 42 L.Ed. 355 (1897). Equally compelling circumstances may arise, however, in which parties are entitled to be relieved of an unjust judgment arrived at through mistake, ignorance, inadvertence or misconduct. See, e.g., Publicker v. Shallcross, 106 F.2d 949, 952 (3d Cir.1939), cert. denied, 308 U.S. 624, 60 S.Ct. 379, 84 L.Ed. 521 (1940) ("We believe truth is more important than the trouble it takes to get it.")

Federal Rule of Civil Procedure 60 provides the terms on which these two principles are balanced. Rule 60(b)(3) allows a court to relieve a party from final judgment on the grounds of "fraud (whether heretofore denominated intrinsic or extrinsic), misrepresentation, or other misconduct of an adverse party." A motion under 60(b)(3), however, must be made within one year after the judgment was entered. Thus, the Rule suggests that equitable considerations prevail in such cases for one year, and that the interest in finality of judgments prevails thereafter.

We are in complete accord with the conclusions of the district court that 60(b)(3) would have provided relief in this case had the union's motion been timely, and also that 60(b)(6) ("any other reason justifying relief") cannot be used to circumvent the one-year limitation for grounds specified previously in the rule. 86 F.R.D. at 136–37. See also Kerwit Medical Products, Inc. v. N & H Instruments, Inc., 616 F.2d

833, 836–37 n. 8 (5th Cir.1980). We therefore turn to the savings provisions in Rule 60(b).

B. "Fraud on the Court".

IBT has continuously asserted that it seeks relief from fraud on the court under Hazel–Atlas Glass Co. v. Hartford–Empire Co., 322 U.S. 238, 64 S.Ct. 997, 88 L.Ed. 1250 (1944). Rule 60(b) specifically provides that "this rule does not limit the power of a court to ... set aside a judgment for fraud upon the court," and the 1946 Notes of the Advisory Committee cites Hazel–Atlas "as an illustration of this situation."

The Supreme Court's opinion in Hazel–Atlas reveals the following facts. Hartford–Empire Company had sought a patent for a device that manufactured glass by a process known as "gob-feeding." Faced with "apparently insurmountable Patent Office opposition," Hartford officials devised a scheme for the deliberate purpose of deceiving the hostile Patent Office into awarding them a patent. The scheme was to have a Hartford patent attorney prepare an article praising the process and then procure the signature of an ostensibly disinterested and respected pseudo-author. This plan was carried out and, with the article included in the application, a patent was granted. Shortly thereafter Hartford brought suit in a federal district court charging Hazel-Atlas with infringing the patent. Although the article was part of the voluminous record, the district court dismissed the suit without reference to the article on the ground no infringement was proved. On appeal, however, Hartford directed the court's attention to the article and the court of appeals reversed, quoting the article at some length.

Hazel–Atlas had received preliminary information during the litigation that the authorship of the article was fraudulent. Following the court of appeals decision, investigation began in earnest. Although investigators for Hazel-Atlas reported little success from their discussions with the ostensible author, Hartford representatives who had been in clandestine contact with him reported "very successful results," specifically that the "author" was cooperative and would be of great assistance. In the weeks that followed, Hartford paid the author $8000, explaining the payments as a "moral obligation" of the company although there was no prior agreement between the parties that the individual would be compensated.

Hazel–Atlas eventually brought suit only after the facts were fully disclosed in a separate lawsuit. The court of appeals denied relief on the grounds that the fraud was not newly discovered, that the article was not a primary basis of its earlier decision, and that it lacked the power to set aside a decree after the expiration of the court term in which the decree was rendered. The Supreme Court reversed.

The pertinent parts of the Supreme Court's analysis are as follows: The Court first reasserted the historical equity power of courts to set aside judgments, the enforcement of which would be manifestly unconscionable. The Court characterized the fraud as a "deliberately planned and carefully executed scheme to defraud not only the Patent Office but the Circuit Court of Appeals." 322 U.S. at 245–46, 64 S.Ct. at 1000–01. Furthermore, the litigation involved did not merely concern the private parties but also "issues of great public moment" associated with the legal monopoly afforded by a patent. Id. at 246, 64 S.Ct. at 1001. The court concluded that the "term rule" was not a bar to equitable relief in such circumstances and directed that the original judgment be set aside. Id. at 248–51, 64 S.Ct. at 1002–04.

IBT urges that this case presents all the critical elements of fraud in the Hazel–Atlas case: specifically, that the fabricated testimony here was intended to "help along" the company's damage suit, just as Hartford used the article to help along its patent application; and that both Hartford and Great Coastal tried to buy the silence of the conspirators. The analogy is indeed close in some respects, however we must ultimately reject it.

The federal courts that have struggled with the definition of "fraud on the court" in the context of Rule 60(b) have found such a definition elusive, see, e.g., Toscano v. Commissioner, 441 F.2d 930, 933–34 (9th Cir.1971), but have generally agreed that the concept should be construed very narrowly, see, e.g., Kerwit Medical Products, Inc. v. N & H Instruments, 616 F.2d 833, 836–37 (5th Cir.1980); Senate Realty Corp. v. Commissioner, 511 F.2d 929, 931, 932–33 (2d Cir.1975). The principal concern motivating narrow construction is that the otherwise nebulous concept of "fraud on the court" could easily overwhelm the specific provision of 60(b)(3) and its time limitation and thereby subvert the balance of equities contained in the Rule. See Kupferman v. Consolidated Research & Manufacturing Corp., 459 F.2d 1072, 1078 (2d Cir.1972); 7 Moore's Federal Practice § 60.33 at 511 (1971). Not all fraud is "fraud on the court." 11 Wright & Miller, Federal Practice and Procedure § 2870 at 253 (1973). Thus "fraud on the court" is typically confined to the most egregious cases, such as bribery of a judge or juror, or improper influence exerted on the court by an attorney, in which the integrity of the court and its ability to function impartially is directly impinged. See Addington v. Farmers Elevator Mutual Ins. Co., 650 F.2d 663, 668 (5th Cir.), cert. denied, 454 U.S. 1098, 102 S.Ct. 672, 70 L.Ed.2d 640 (1981); Lockwood v. Bowles, 46 F.R.D. 625, 630 (D.D.C.1969). Professor Moore's suggested formulation is often cited, although the Toscano court observed that it still leaves many aspects of the issue unresolved:

> "Fraud upon the court" should, we believe, embrace only that species of fraud which does or attempts to, defile the court itself, or is a fraud perpetrated by officers of the court so that the judicial machinery can not perform in the usual manner its impartial task of adjudging cases that are presented for adjudication. Fraud inter partes, without more, should not be a fraud upon the court, but redress should be left to a motion under 60(b)(3) or to the independent action.

7 Moore's Federal Practice § 60.33 at 515 (1971); see also Martina Theater Corp. v. Schine Chain Theaters, 278 F.2d 798 (2d Cir.1960) (following Moore).

In this light we cannot say that the fraud in this case presents a deliberate scheme to directly subvert the judicial process, sufficient to constitute fraud on the court. It is also apparent that the fraud here primarily concerns the two parties involved and does not threaten the public injury that a fraudulently-obtained legal monopoly did in Hazel-Atlas. Cf. Comment, 60 Cal.L.Rev. 531, 557 (1972).

Despite the confusion inherent in this doctrine, we are not totally without guideposts. We concur in the appraisal of the district court that the fraud here consists of perjury and fabricated evidence. Early in the Court's analysis in Hazel–Atlas, the Court commented "This is not simply a case of a judgment obtained with the aid of a witness who, on the basis of after-discovered evidence, is believed possibly to have been guilty of perjury." 322 U.S. at 245, 64 S.Ct. at 1000. Motivated at least in part by this language, courts confronting the issue have consistently held that perjury or fabricated evidence are not grounds for relief as "fraud on the court." See, e.g., Pfizer, Inc. v. International Rectifier Corp., 538 F.2d 180, 193–95 (8th Cir.1976), cert. denied, 429 U.S. 1040, 97 S.Ct. 738, 50 L.Ed.2d 751 (1977); Serzysko v. Chase Manhattan Bank, 461 F.2d 699, 702 (2d Cir.), cert. denied, 409 U.S. 883, 93 S.Ct. 173, 34 L.Ed.2d 139 (1972); Porcelli v. Joseph Schlitz Brewing Co., 78 F.R.D. 499 (E.D.Wisc. 1978), aff'd without opinion, 588 F.2d 838 (7th Cir.1978); Konigsberg v. Security National Bank, 66 F.R.D. 439, 442 (S.D.N.Y.1975); Lockwood v. Bowles, 46 F.R.D. 625, 630 (D.D.C.1969). See also Restatement of Judgments § 126(2)(b). This conclusion is consistent with the general definitional principles just described. Perjury and fabricated evidence are evils that can and should be exposed at trial, and the legal system encourages and expects litigants to root them out as early as possible. In addition, the legal system contains other sanctions against perjury. See Lockwood v. Bowles, 46 F.R.D. 625 (D.D.C.1969); Shammas v. Shammas, 9 N.J. 321, 88 A.2d 204 (1952) (Brennan, J.). Fraud on the court is therefore limited to the more egregious forms of subversion of the legal process already suggested, those that we cannot necessarily expect to be exposed by the normal adversary process.

IBT also takes exception to the district court's conclusion that fraud on the court requires involvement by attorneys. Involvement of an attorney, as an officer of the court, in a scheme to suborn perjury would certainly be considered fraud on the court. IBT points out, however, that the record in Hazel–Atlas indicates that the company "attorney" who prepared the article with the intent that it be signed by another was in fact a "patent attorney," a title given at least at that time to any registered patent agent, and that he had not attended law school and was not the member of any bar. Other circuits have also recognized that fraud on the court can occur without the involvement of attorneys. See Toscano v. Commissioner, 441 F.2d 930, 933–34 (9th Cir.1971); Lim Kwock Soon v. Brownell, 369 F.2d 808 (5th Cir.1966).

However, in view of our holding that the type of fraud in this case does not rise to the level of fraud on the court, we need not consider the question of attorney involvement.

We therefore conclude that the company's actions, however reprehensible, are not tantamount to fraud on the court.

C.   Independent Action in Equity.

While the IBT initially proceeded under the theory of fraud on the court under Hazel–Atlas and not under the second savings provision of Rule 60(b), the independent action in equity, the district court nevertheless considered and rejected the applicability of this doctrine and IBT has addressed the issue in its briefs. The district court followed the intrinsic/extrinsic fraud distinction described in United States v. Throckmorton, 98 U.S. 61, 25 L.Ed. 93 (1878). Under this doctrine, fraud must be "extrinsic" to justify relief, that is, fraud that actually prevented an issue from being joined or a party from making a valid claim or defense. See Bizzell v. Hemingway, 548 F.2d 505 (4th Cir.1977) (collusion between plaintiff's attorney and opposing party). Notwithstanding the considerable criticism leveled against the intrinsic/extrinsic distinction, see, e.g., 11 Wright & Miller, Federal Practice and Procedure § 2868 at 240 (1973), and the debate regarding the effect of Marshall v. Holmes, 141 U.S. 589, 12 S.Ct. 62, 35 L.Ed. 870 (1891), on the question, it is clear that perjury and false testimony are not grounds for relief in an independent action in the Fourth Circuit for many of the same reasons that apply to fraud on the court. See Durham v. New Amsterdam Casualty Co., 208 F.2d 342, 345 (4th Cir.1953); Aetna Casualty & Surety Co. v. Abbott, 130 F.2d 40, 43–44 (4th Cir.1942); Chrysler Corp. v. Superior Dodge, Inc., 83 F.R.D. 179, 186 (D.Md.1979); Prickett v. Duke Power Co., 49 F.R.D. 116, 118 (D.S.C.1970).

Referring, apparently, to the extrinsic/intrinsic distinction, IBT argues that the independent action doctrine requires only that the fraud, if disclosed, "would have made a difference in the way ... counsel approached the case or prepared for trial," citing Rozier v. Ford Motor Co., 573 F.2d 1332, 1339–42 (5th Cir.1978). Under such a formula, the union claims if it had known the truth in this case it would have thoroughly impeached the company's witnesses. We believe the more complete inquiry is described in Addington v. Farmers Elevator Mutual Ins. Co., 650 F.2d 663, 667–68 (5th Cir.), cert. denied, 454 U.S. 1098, 102 S.Ct. 672, 70 L.Ed.2d 640 (1981):

> (1) a judgment which ought not, in equity and good conscience, to be enforced; (2) a good defense to the alleged cause of action on which the judgment is founded; (3) fraud, accident, or mistake which prevented the defendant in the judgment from obtaining the benefit of his defense; (4) the absence of fault or negligence on the part of defendant; and (5) the absence of any adequate remedy at law.

The particular element that is lacking in this case is a good defense to the action that the IBT was prevented from discovering or asserting because of the fraud. Both parties recognize that the judgment under attack here is the secondary boycott judgment: the union has not proffered any defense to liability for secondary boycotting that it was precluded from asserting because of the company's perjury and we frankly cannot perceive one in light of the comments on the evidence made on the prior appeal, quoted in part supra. Relief was properly denied on this ground as well.

III. *Conclusion*

We affirm the district court's denial of relief in No. 80–1217 and dismiss the petitions in Nos. 73–2393 and 73–2448. The company's appeal No. 81–2073 is dismissed.

SO ORDERED.

■ BUTZNER, CIRCUIT JUDGE, dissenting:

I agree with the district court and part II A of the majority opinion that the union would be entitled to prevail had it filed its motion to set aside the judgment, which the company fraudulently obtained, within the one-year period of limitations prescribed by Rule 60(b). But I do not agree that the one-year limitation bars relief to the union. Because the union did not institute proceedings to set aside Great Coastal's judgment within one year after its entry, it must show that Great Coastal practiced fraud upon the court. The rule provides that this type of fraud is not subject to the one-year limitation.

I dissent from the majority's conclusion that Great Coastal's fraud does not rise to the level of fraud on the court. The facts satisfy the requirements of fraud on the court that are set forth in Hazel–Atlas Glass Co. v. Hartford–Empire Co., 322 U.S. 238, 64 S.Ct. 997, 88 L.Ed. 1250 (1944). Rule 60(b) was amended in 1946 to reflect the principles expounded in Hazel–Atlas, and the Notes of the Advisory Committee clarify the concept of fraud on the court by citing Hazel–Atlas as "an illustration of this situation" which the amended rule addresses.

I

Pursuant to the directions of this court, the district court made supplementary findings of fact derived from the 1979 evidentiary hearing on the union's motion for relief from the judgment granted Great Coastal. The district court's findings on remand clearly establish that the officers and employees of Great Coastal engaged in an extensive, deliberate scheme to subvert justice by perpetrating a fraud on administrative and judicial tribunals. Because the district court's findings are essential for the resolution of this appeal, they are quoted as follows:

[Approximately four printed pages reviewing the evidence in great detail are deleted.]

* * *

III

Hazel–Atlas explains that a court's power to grant equitable relief against a fraudulent judgment is not a creature of statute; nor, I might add, is it a creature of Rule 60(b). The Court stated:

It is a judicially devised remedy fashioned to relieve hardships which, from time to time, arise from a hard and fast adherence to another court-made rule, the general rule that judgments should not be disturbed after the term of their entry has expired. Created to avert the evils of archaic rigidity, this equitable procedure has always been characterized by flexibility which enables it to meet new situations which demand equitable intervention, and to accord all the relief necessary to correct the particular injustices involved in these situations. 322 U.S. at 248, 64 S.Ct. at 1002.

Hazel–Atlas requires proof of two elements to establish fraud on the court for the purpose of setting aside a civil judgment when the court itself has not been compromised by bribery or corruption. These two elements distinguish fraud on the court from the type of fraud that Rule 60(b) requires to be asserted within one year. The first is that the judgment involves an issue "of great moment to the public...." 322 U.S. at 246, 64 S.Ct. at 1001. A dispute that concerns only private litigants is not enough. See S & E Contractors, Inc. v. United States, 406 U.S. 1, 15, 92 S.Ct. 1411, 1419, 31 L.Ed.2d 658 (1972) (dictum).

Hazel–Atlas dealt with an affront to the public's interest in the integrity of the nation's patent laws. This case involves an assault on the public's interest in the integrity of the laws governing our national labor policy. There can be no doubt that the dispute between the company and the union implicated interests beyond those of the litigants. Section 1 of the Labor Management Relations Act, 1947, 29 U.S.C. § 141, states in part:

> It is the purpose and policy of this chapter, in order to promote the full flow of commerce ... to define and proscribe practices on the part of labor and management which affect commerce and are inimical to the general welfare, and to protect the rights of the public in connection with labor disputes affecting commerce.

Just as a litigant in Hazel–Atlas deceived the patent office by fabricated evidence, Great Coastal deceived the National Labor Relations Board in administrative proceedings pertaining to the same strike that is the subject of this case by fabricating evidence of union violence. Just as a litigant in Hazel–Atlas invoked in judicial proceedings the patent laws that are designed both to grant a monopoly and advance the public interest, Great Coastal invoked the Labor Management Relations Act, particularly 29 U.S.C. §§ 158(b)(4), 185, and 187. As the congressional declaration of purpose and policy states, 29 U.S.C. § 141, these laws, too, are designed to protect the public as well as litigants.

I therefore conclude that the litigation culminating in the judgment for Great Coastal satisfied the first requirement of Hazel–Atlas. This litigation involved more than a controversy between private parties, and the fraud by which it was prosecuted debased the laws enacted to assure the free flow of commerce for the benefit of the public.

IV

The second requirement of Hazel–Atlas is best described in the words of the Court, 322 U.S. at 245–46, 64 S.Ct. at 1000–01:

> This is not simply a case of a judgment obtained with the aid of a witness who, on the basis of after-discovered evidence, is believed possibly to have been guilty of perjury. Here ... we find a deliberately planned and carefully executed scheme to defraud not only the Patent Office but the Circuit Court of Appeals.

The unrefuted evidence of the 1979 hearing conducted by the district court and the court's supplementary findings establish beyond doubt that Great Coastal, its officers, and employees engaged in "a deliberately planned and carefully executed scheme to defraud" the National Labor Relations Board, the district court, and the court of appeals. Their fraud was no isolated instance of perjury. To achieve their purposes, the officers and employees created spurious evidence, deceived the Virginia State Police, answered interrogatories under oath untruthfully, filed false affidavits and gave perjured testimony in administrative and judicial proceedings, introduced fabricated exhibits, and filed a corrupt brief and appendix on appeal.

By payments and promises of payments, Great Coastal frustrated discovery of its fraud through the judicial processes afforded by the Rules of Civil Procedure. Moreover, its scheme did not end with the entry of judgment. Like the litigant in Hazel–Atlas, it later attempted to forever seal its deception by the payment of large sums of money to the participants in its fraudulent scheme. And, as in Hazel–Atlas, it succeeded in cloaking its wrong for several years.

I therefore conclude that this case satisfies the second requirement of Hazel-Atlas.

V

Finally, I find no merit in Great Coastal's argument that the fraud did not taint its recovery of damages. While the evidence concerning the secondary boycott was sufficient to sustain a verdict, this issue presented questions for the jury both on liability and damages. As part II of the majority opinion points out, it cannot be said "with complete confidence * * * that the fraud was harmlessly excised from the case." Indeed, the majority opinion states: "We are in complete accord with the conclusions of the district court that 60(b)(3) would have provided relief in this case had the union's motion been timely."

Great Coastal's argument is similar to the argument rejected in Hazel–Atlas that the fabricated evidence was not "basic" to the judgment under attack. 322 U.S. at 246. There the Court did not attempt to appraise the effect of the fraud on the decision making process. Instead, it pointed out that the fraudulent litigant deemed the spurious document to be material. The litigant contrived the fraud to deceive the patent office and the court. The litigant, therefore, was "in no position now to dispute its effectiveness." 322 U.S. at 247, 64 S.Ct. at 1002.

Great Coastal is in the same posture as the fraudulent litigant in Hazel-Atlas. Great Coastal's fraud was conceived and used to deceive the National Labor Relations Board and both trial and appellate courts. The jury that found liability was exposed to the fraud. On appeal Great Coastal argued that violence-which the district court later found was self-inflicted-was inextricably tied in with the secondary boycott. Like the litigant in Hazel–Atlas, Great Coastal is in no position to dispute the effectiveness of its fraud.

I would reverse the order of the district court, afford the union equitable relief on its petition filed in this court, and set aside the judgment because, tested by Hazel–Atlas, Great Coastal committed a fraud upon the court.

Brandon v. Chicago Board of Education

United States Court of Appeal for the Seventh Circuit, 1998.
143 F.3d 293, *cert. denied*, 525 U.S. 948, 119 S.Ct. 374, 142 L. Ed. 2d 309 (1998).

■ Ilana Diamond Rovner, Circuit Judge.

Lorenzo Brandon sought Rule 60 relief from a judgment entered against him for failure to prosecute his case. The district court denied relief and Brandon now appeals. The facts are unusual. Indeed, Brandon claims they are unique. Brandon filed his Americans with Disabilities action against the Chicago Board of Education on August 2, 1995. His attorneys, Paul F. Peters and James C. Reho, entered appearances in the case, listing as their address the Law Offices of Paul F. Peters, One North LaSalle Street, Chicago. It is undisputed that in docketing the case, the Clerk of the United States District Court erroneously entered Paul A. Peters, another Chicago attorney, who is located at 10 South LaSalle Street, Chicago, as attorney for the plaintiff. As a result of this error, subsequent mailings from the court were directed to the wrong attorney at the wrong address. Admirably, Paul A. Peters actually took the time to write to the Clerk of the district court, informing the Clerk that he was not counsel of record in the case, had no connection to the case, and was returning any materials sent to him.

Unfortunately, the Clerk's office still did not understand the nature of its error, and continued to send all minute orders and other mailings to the wrong address. As a result, Brandon's counsel never received notice of two different status hearings, and failed to appear. After failing to appear for the second status hearing, the court dismissed the case for want of prosecution on December 13, 1995. The order dismissing the case was also sent to the wrong address. A little more than a year passed before plaintiff's counsel began to wonder what happened to the case. Upon visiting the Clerk's office in late 1996, he discovered his case had been quite active without him. Included in the court's file was the letter from Paul A. Peters, orders setting status hearings, and the order dismissing the case for want of prosecution.[1]

On December 16, 1996, one year and three days after the dismissal, Paul F. Peters filed a Rule 60 motion to vacate the judgment. Astonishingly, yet another clerical error, this one caused by plaintiff's counsel, caused the motion to be spindled under the wrong case number. When plaintiff's counsel noticed this error on the day the motion was to be heard, he pointed it out to the Clerk's office. The Clerk's office told him the motion would not be heard that day, and would have to be re-noticed. Plaintiff's counsel then refiled the motion under the correct case number. Before the new date for the hearing, however, plaintiff's counsel received a minute order from the court, granting the motion. As a courtesy, plaintiff's counsel sent a letter to defendant's counsel, stating that the motion had been granted and no appearance was necessary on the date set for hearing the motion. Nevertheless, defendant's counsel appeared in court on the day of the hearing and persuaded the court to vacate its order granting Rule 60 relief. After briefing on the motion, the court ultimately denied Rule 60 relief.

On appeal, Brandon argues that he cannot be faulted for a lack of diligence when he was never notified by the court that there was anything he was supposed to be doing. He never ignored a court order, he contends, because he never knew about any orders. Rather, the clerical error in the Clerk's office was the source of the problem, and the district court abused its discretion in refusing to grant Rule 60 relief. Although Brandon initially moved for relief under Rule 60(a), he subsequently argued (and argues on appeal) that he is entitled to relief under Rule 60(b)(6). He admitted at oral argument that he is abandoning any claim to relief under Rule 60(a), which by its own terms applies only to clerical mistakes in "judgments, orders or other parts of the record and errors therein arising from oversight or omission."[2] The Chicago Board of Education focuses its response on Brandon's lack of entitlement to relief under Rule 60(b)(1), stating that it is the only conceivably relevant subsection.

---

1. The Board of Education filed two motions early in the case, one to extend the time to answer, and the other to file the answer instanter. Brandon received a notice for each of these motions, and opposed neither. The court entered minute orders granting the motions and, as before, the Clerk mailed the minute orders to the wrong attorney. The Board rightly points out that Brandon should have known something was amiss when he failed to receive either order.

2. Brandon is correct to abandon his Rule 60(a) argument. See Wesco Products Co. v. Alloy Automotive Co., 880 F.2d 981, 984 (7th Cir.1989). We noted there that district courts often have difficulty determining whether motions are brought to correct a clerical error (as opposed to some other kind of error). "In this circuit, we have identified the relevant distinction as being between changes that implement the result intended by the court at the time the order was entered and changes that alter the original meaning to correct a legal or factual error. Thus, '[i]f the flaw lies in the translation of the original meaning to the judgment, then Rule 60(a) allows a correction; if the judgment captures the original meaning but is infected by error, the parties must seek another source of authority to correct the mistake.'" Id. (citing United States v. Griffin, 782 F.2d 1393, 1396–97 (7th Cir.1986)) (internal citations omitted). In the instant case, as in Wesco, the dismissal for want of prosecution accurately reflected the court's intention at the time it was entered. Thus, the error, to the extent there was one, was not in the transcription, but in the court's decision, a ground for relief not contained in Rule 60(a).

We begin by examining Rule 60(b),

* * *

Neither side argues that subsections (2) through (5) are applicable. Instead, Brandon argues that he is entitled to relief under subsection (b)(6), the catchall section. The Board contends that subsection (b)(1) is the only applicable section. The parties agree that we may not reverse a trial court's denial of a Rule 60(b) motion absent an abuse of discretion. See Dickerson v. Board of Education of Ford Heights, Illinois, 32 F.3d 1114, 1116 (7th Cir.1994) (trial court's denial of Rule 60(b) motion reviewed under a highly deferential standard, and reversed only for abuse of discretion). Moreover, because a court's dismissal for failure to prosecute is itself reviewed only for abuse of discretion, "a court's decision under Rule 60(b) not to reinstate a case dismissed for want of prosecution has been described as 'discretion piled on discretion.' " Id., 32 F.3d at 1117.

> "Inherent in the structure of Rule 60(b) is the principle that the first three clauses and the catchall clause are mutually exclusive. Thus, if the asserted grounds for relief fall within the terms of the first three clauses of Rule 60(b), relief under the catchall provision is not available." Wesco Products Co. v. Alloy Automotive Co., 880 F.2d 981, 983 (7th Cir.1989) (internal citations omitted). Therefore, we must first determine if the relief sought falls within Rule 60(b)(1). We noted in Wesco that Rule 60(b)(1) applies to errors by judicial officers as well as parties. 880 F.2d at 984–85. The district court here appeared to be analyzing the motion pursuant to Rule 60(b)(1), finding that "[t]here was a lack of diligence," and that this was "certainly not excusable neglect." See Transcript of Proceedings before the Honorable George W. Lindberg, Feb. 11, 1997, at p. 8. The district court also acknowledged that Rule 60(b)(1) applies to errors by the court, stating that "if the rules mean anything, and the Seventh Circuit jurisprudence means anything, it means that lawyers must follow their cases. They cannot rely on the Judge, the law clerks or the courtroom deputies or the Clerk's office. They must follow their case." Id.

We agree with the district court that Rule 60(b)(1) is the appropriate mechanism for analyzing Brandon's request for relief. Indeed, the facts here demonstrate an unusual combination of error by the Clerk's office and neglect by the attorney.[3] Rule 60(b)(1) covers both. Having found that Rule 60(b)(1) applies, we must necessarily find that Rule 60(b)(6) does not apply. Wesco, 880 F.2d at 983. By its own terms, a motion brought pursuant to Rule 60(b)(1) must be made within one year of the date the judgment was entered. "[T]he one year time limit is jurisdictional and may not be extended in any event...." Wesco,

---

3. The instant case is distinguishable from the cases cited in the Wesco dissent, where various court clerks affirmatively misled parties as to the status of their cases. See 880 F.2d at 986–87 (Ripple, Circuit Judge, dissenting). Here, the Clerk did not affirma-tively mislead plaintiff's counsel in any way. Indeed, when plaintiff's counsel finally went to the Clerk's office to determine the status of the case, the Clerk provided a complete and accurate record of the proceedings.

880 F.2d at 985. No one disputes that Brandon brought his motion one year and three days after judgment was entered against him. We therefore conclude that the district court did not abuse its discretion in denying relief.

AFFIRMED.

B. Claim Preclusion

F.R.C.P. 8(c) lists res judicata as an affirmative defense. Thus, that issue would, in the normal case, be raised in the answer. If the defendant omits the issue of res judicata, used here in its generic sense which includes both claim preclusion and issue preclusion, that defense may be lost. Commentators, however, think most federal courts allow the preclusive effect of a prior judgment to be raised for the first time in a motion for summary judgment. A Rule 56 motion is often "the most appropriate vehicle for determining the validity of a defense of preclusion." Wright, Miller & Kane, Fed. Practice & Procedure § 2735.

THE RATIONALE OF CLAIM PRECLUSION AND ITS LIMITATIONS

A. If plaintiff prevails in the first law suit, we say that her claim is merged into the judgment: plaintiff may not sue again on the same claim, even to recover items of damage not previously litigated. By the same token, if plaintiff sues on the judgment, in another state, for example, defendant may not avail herself of defenses that might have been, but were not litigated in the first action.

The Restatement of the Law of Judgments, Second, § 18 (1982) explains the doctrine as follows:

a. The doctrine of merger. When the plaintiff recovers a valid and final personal judgment, his original claim is extinguished and rights upon the judgment are substituted for it. The plaintiff's original claim is said to be "merged" into the judgment. It is immaterial whether the defendant had a defense to the original action if he did not rely on it, or if he did rely on it and judgment was nevertheless given against him. It is immaterial whether the judgment was rendered upon a verdict or upon a motion to dismiss or other objection to the pleadings or upon consent, confession, or default.

Illustrations:

1. A brings an action against B for negligently causing injury to A. At trial A is unable to prove any serious injury to his person. Verdict is given for A for $100 and judgment is entered thereon. Thereafter it appears that A's injuries are more serious than proved at the trial. A is precluded by the judgment from maintaining a second action against B for the collision.

2. The facts are the same as stated in Illustration 1, except that at the trial of the first action A offers evidence of nervous shock, and the court erroneously excludes such evidence. A is precluded by the judgment from maintaining a second action against B for the collision.

B. If defendant prevails at the first suit, that judgment is said to bar a second action. The Restatement, at § 19, explains the doctrine as follows:

a. *Rationale.* It is frequently said that a valid and final personal judgment for the defendant will bar another action on the same claim only if the judgment is rendered "on the merits." The prototype case continues to be one in which the merits of the claim are in fact adjudicated against the plaintiff after trial of the substantive issues. Increasingly, however, by statute, rule, or court decision, judgments not passing directly on the substance of the claim have come to operate as a bar. Although such judgments are often described as "on the merits," that terminology is not used here in the statement of the general rule because of its possibly misleading connotations.

The rule that a defendant's judgment acts as a bar to a second action on the same claim is based largely on the ground that fairness to the defendant, and sound judicial administration, require that at some point litigation over the particular controversy come to an end. These considerations may impose such a requirement even though the substantive issues have not been tried, especially if the plaintiff has failed to avail himself of the opportunities to pursue his remedies in the first proceeding, or has deliberately flouted orders of the court.

The general rule stated in this Section requires that errors underlying a judgment be corrected on appeal or other available proceedings to modify the judgment or to set it aside, and not made the basis for a second action on the same claim.

C. Claim Preclusion, whether by way of merger or bar, operates to extinguish a claim even if all possible theories of recovery had not been litigated in the first law suit. The Restatement, supra at § 24, states the general rule as follows:

The claim extinguished includes all rights of the plaintiff to remedies against the defendant with respect to all or any part of the transaction, or series of connected transactions, out of which the action arose.

(2) What factual grouping constitutes a "transaction," and what groupings constitute a "series," are to be determined pragmatically, giving weight to such considerations as whether the facts are related in time, space, origin, or motivation, whether they form a convenient trial unit, and whether their treatment as a unit conforms to the parties' expectations or business understanding or usage.

Illustrations:

3.   A lends goods to B on the understanding that B will return them in good condition. Upon B's failure to return A's goods to him, A might conceivably have rights against B upon alternative theories of negligent loss of the goods, breach of a contractual duty to return the goods, or wrongful conversion of goods, depending on the precise facts proved or varying emphasis put upon the facts, and A's relief might be for the return of the goods or for money damages (possibly calculated in various ways). The transaction is single and it follows that if A sues upon it and a judgment is rendered which extinguishes the claim under the rules of merger or bar, A is precluded from suing B a second time , even on a view of the facts or a theory not presented, or a form or measure of relief not sought, in the first action.

5.   A brings an action against B Co., a street railway company, alleging that the motorman was negligent in starting the car while A was alighting and that as a result A broke his arm. After a verdict and judgment for A, A brings a new action against B Co. alleging that after alighting from the car he fell into a trench negligently left by B. Co. beside the road and broke his leg. The action is precluded.

6.   On the false accusation that A was engaging in disorderly conduct at a racetrack, B Co., the owner of the track, caused A in successive acts to be assaulted, slandered, physically detained, and prosecuted criminally. A sues B Co. for the assault and slander. If a judgment is rendered that extinguishes the claim, A may not maintain a second action for the detention or for malicious prosecution.

7.   B owes A $500 on an obligation that matured on February 1. A visits B on June 1 and requests payment, whereupon B commits an unprovoked assault upon A. A sues B on the debt and recovers. A may maintain a second action against B based on the assault.

D.   It is usually prudent to treat claim preclusion as an inexorable rule; judges are likely to treat it precisely that way. This is understandable because res judicata is intended to protect the judicial system itself or, more accurately, the interests of litigants waiting for court time. Yet, there are exceptions, infrequently—indeed, rarely—applied, but available in a few highly unusual situations. Defendant's doctor has assured plaintiff that his headaches are temporary. Plaintiff sues and recovers for his other injuries, and then the headaches turn into permanent blindness. The mistake may have been innocent, but it was defendant's doctor's mistake and there is much to be said for not applying claim preclusion.

Normally, a change in the applicable law will not suffice to preclude claim preclusion. Suppose, however, there has been a change in constitutional doctrine of major proportions and a great public interest—in the area of racial discrimination, for example—relitigation may be preferable to leaving the parties where a prior judgment put them.

The restatement text seems straightforward. But several of the terms have different meanings in some state and federal courts. What is the same claim? When is a judgment final? How do you determine whether a judgment is on the merits and, especially in issue preclusion, whether a particular determination was essential to the judgment.

Federal law is that judgments are final for purposes of preclusion even though an appeal is still pending. Some states require that an appeal have been finally decided.

The most widely accepted standard for determining if a claim has been precluded by a prior judgment is whether the actions arise out of the same transaction or series of transactions. The Restatement test in section 24(2) states, "What factual grouping constitutes a 'series,' are to be determined pragmatically, giving weight to such considerations as whether the facts are related in time, space, origin, or motivation, ..." But there are narrower variations. One is mentioned in the Matsushita v. Epstein opinion quoting from the opinion of the Delaware Supreme Court in Nottingham Partners v. Dana, 564 A.2d 1089, 1106 (Del.1989): " ...a court may permit the release of a claim based on the identical factual predicate as that underlying the claims in the settled class action ..."

C.   ISSUE PRECLUSION

Parklane Hosiery Co. v. Shore

Supreme Court of the United States, 1979.
439 U.S. 322, 99 S.Ct. 645, 58 L.Ed.2d 552.

■ MR. JUSTICE STEWART delivered the opinion of the Court.

This case presents the question whether a party who has had issues of fact adjudicated adversely to it in an equitable action may be collaterally estopped from relitigating the same issues before a jury in a subsequent legal action brought against it by a new party.

The respondent brought this stockholder's class action against the petitioners in a Federal District Court. The complaint alleged that the petitioners, Parklane Hosiery Co., Inc. (Parklane), and 13 of its officers, directors, and stockholders, had issued a materially false and misleading proxy statement in connection with a merger.[4] * * * The complaint sought damages, rescission of the merger, and recovery of costs.

---

4. The amended complaint alleged that the proxy statement that had been issued to the stockholders was false and misleading because it failed to disclose: (1) that the president of Parklane would financially benefit as a result of the company's going private; (2) certain ongoing negotiations that could have resulted in financial benefit to Parklane; and (3) that the appraisal of the fair value of Parklane stock was based on insufficient information to be accurate.

Before this action came to trial, the SEC filed suit against the same defendants in the Federal District Court, alleging that the proxy statement that had been issued by Parklane was materially false and misleading in essentially the same respects as those that had been alleged in the respondent's complaint. Injunctive relief was requested. After a 4–day trial, the District Court found that the proxy statement was materially false and misleading in the respects alleged, and entered a declaratory judgment to that effect. SEC v. Parklane Hosiery Co., 422 F.Supp. 477. The Court of Appeals for the Second Circuit affirmed this judgment. 558 F.2d 1083.

The respondent in the present case then moved for partial summary judgment against the petitioners, asserting that the petitioners were collaterally estopped from relitigating the issues that had been resolved against them in the action brought by the SEC.[5] The District Court denied the motion on the ground that such an application of collateral estoppel would deny the petitioners their Seventh Amendment right to a jury trial. The Court of Appeals for the Second Circuit reversed, holding that a party who has had issues of fact determined against him after a full and fair opportunity to litigate in a nonjury trial is collaterally estopped from obtaining a subsequent jury trial of these same issues of fact. 565 F.2d 815. The appellate court concluded that "the Seventh Amendment preserves the right to jury trial only with respect to issues of fact, [and] once those issues have been fully and fairly adjudicated in a prior proceeding, nothing remains for trial, either with or without a jury." Id., at 819. Because of an inter-circuit conflict,[6] we granted certiorari. 435 U.S. 1006, 98 S.Ct. 1875, 56 L.Ed.2d 387.

I

The threshold question to be considered is whether, quite apart from the right to a jury trial under the Seventh Amendment, the petitioners can be precluded from relitigating facts resolved adversely to them in a prior equitable proceeding with another party under the general law of collateral estoppel. Specifically, we must determine whether a litigant who was not a party to a prior judgment may nevertheless use that judgment "offensively" to prevent a defendant from relitigating issues resolved in the earlier proceeding.[7]

5. A private plaintiff in an action under the proxy rules is not entitled to relief simply by demonstrating that the proxy solicitation was materially false and misleading. The plaintiff must also show that he was injured and prove damages. Mills v. Electric Auto–Lite Co., 396 U.S. 375, 386–390, 90 S.Ct. 616, 622–624, 24 L.Ed.2d 593. Since the SEC action was limited to a determination of whether the proxy statement contained materially false and misleading information, the respondent conceded that he would still have to prove these other elements of his prima facie case in the private action. The petitioners'

right to a jury trial on those remaining issues is not contested.

6. The position of the Court of Appeals for the Second Circuit is in conflict with that taken by the Court of Appeals for the Fifth Circuit in Rachal v. Hill, 435 F.2d 59.

7. In this context, offensive use of collateral estoppel occurs when the plaintiff seeks to foreclose the defendant from litigating an issue the defendant has previously litigated unsuccessfully in an action with another party. Defensive use occurs when a defendant seeks to prevent a plaintiff from asserting a claim the plaintiff has previously litigated and lost against another defendant.

A

Collateral estoppel, like the related doctrine of res judicata,[8] has the dual purpose of protecting litigants from the burden of relitigating an identical issue with the same party or his privy and of promoting judicial economy by preventing needless litigation. Blonder-Tongue Laboratories, Inc. v. University of Illinois Foundation, 402 U.S. 313, 328–329, 91 S.Ct. 1434, 1442–1443, 28 L.Ed.2d 788. Until relatively recently, however, the scope of collateral estoppel was limited by the doctrine of mutuality of parties. Under this mutuality doctrine, neither party could use a prior judgment as an estoppel against the other unless both parties were bound by the judgment.[9] Based on the premise that it is somehow unfair to allow a party to use a prior judgment when he himself would not be so bound,[10] the mutuality requirement provided a party who had litigated and lost in a previous action an opportunity to relitigate identical issues with new parties.

By failing to recognize the obvious difference in position between a party who has never litigated an issue and one who has fully litigated and lost, the mutuality requirement was criticized almost from its inception.[11] Recognizing the validity of this criticism, the Court in Blonder–Tongue Laboratories, Inc. v. University of Illinois Foundation, supra, abandoned the mutuality requirement, at least in cases where a patentee seeks to relitigate the validity of a patent after a federal court in a previous lawsuit has already declared it invalid. The "broader question" before the Court, however, was "whether it is any longer tenable to afford a litigant more than one full and fair opportunity for judicial resolution of the same issue." 402 U.S., at 328, 91 S.Ct., at 1442. The Court strongly suggested a negative answer to that question * * *

B

The Blonder–Tongue case involved defensive use of collateral estoppel—a plaintiff was estopped from asserting a claim that the

---

8. Under the doctrine of res judicata, a judgment on the merits in a prior suit bars a second suit involving the same parties or their privies based on the same cause of action. Under the doctrine of collateral estoppel, on the other hand, the second action is upon a different cause of action and the judgment in the prior suit precludes relitigation of issues actually litigated and necessary to the outcome of the first action.

9. *E. g.*, Bigelow v. Old Dominion Copper Co., 225 U.S. 111, 127, 32 S.Ct. 641, 642, 56 L.Ed. 1009 ("It is a principle of general elementary law that estoppel of a judgment must be mutual"); Buckeye Powder Co. v. E. I. DuPont De Nemours Powder Co., 248 U.S. 55, 63, 39 S.Ct. 38, 39, 63 L.Ed. 123; Restatement of Judgments § 93 (1942).

10. It is a violation of due process for a judgment to be binding on a litigant who was not a party or a privy and therefore has never had an opportunity to be heard. Blon-

der–Tongue Laboratories, Inc. v. University of Illinois Foundation, 402 U.S. 313, 329, 91 S.Ct. 1434, 1443, 28 L.Ed.2d 788; Hansberry v. Lee, 311 U. S. 32, 40, 61 S.Ct. 115, 117, 85 L.Ed. 22.

11. This criticism was summarized in the Court's opinion in Blonder-Tongue Laboratories, Inc. v. University of Illinois Foundation, supra, 402 U.S., at 322–327, 91 S.Ct., at 1439–1442. The opinion of Justice Traynor for a unanimous California Supreme Court in Bernhard v. Bank of America Nat. Trust & Savings Assn., 19 Cal.2d 807, 812, 122 P.2d 892, 895, made the point succinctly:

"No satisfactory rationalization has been advanced for the requirement of mutuality. Just why a party who was not bound by a previous action should be precluded from asserting it as res judicata against a party who was bound by it is difficult to comprehend."

plaintiff had previously litigated and lost against another defendant. The present case, by contrast, involves offensive use of collateral estoppel—a plaintiff is seeking to estop a defendant from relitigating the issues which the defendant previously litigated and lost against another plaintiff. In both the offensive and defensive use situations, the party against whom estoppel is asserted has litigated and lost in an earlier action. Nevertheless, several reasons have been advanced why the two situations should be treated differently.

First, offensive use of collateral estoppel does not promote judicial economy in the same manner as defensive use does. Defensive use of collateral estoppel precludes a plaintiff from relitigating identical issues by merely "switching adversaries." Bernhard v. Bank of America Nat. Trust & Savings Assn., 19 Cal.2d, at 813, 122 P.2d, at 895.[12] Thus defensive collateral estoppel gives a plaintiff a strong incentive to join all potential defendants in the first action if possible. Offensive use of collateral estoppel, on the other hand, creates precisely the opposite incentive. Since a plaintiff will be able to rely on a previous judgment against a defendant but will not be bound by that judgment if the defendant wins, the plaintiff has every incentive to adopt a "wait and see" attitude, in the hope that the first action by another plaintiff will result in a favorable judgment. E. g., Nevarov v. Caldwell, 161 Cal. App.2d 762, 767–768, 327 P.2d 111, 115; Reardon v. Allen, 88 N.J.Super. 560, 571–572, 213 A.2d 26, 32. Thus offensive use of collateral estoppel will likely increase rather than decrease the total amount of litigation, since potential plaintiffs will have everything to gain and nothing to lose by not intervening in the first action.[13]

A second argument against offensive use of collateral estoppel is that it may be unfair to a defendant. If a defendant in the first action is sued for small or nominal damages, he may have little incentive to defend vigorously, particularly if future suits are not foreseeable. The Evergreens v. Nunan, 141 F.2d 927, 929 (CA2); cf. Berner v. British Commonwealth Pac. Airlines, 346 F.2d 532 (CA2) (application of offensive collateral estoppel denied where defendant did not appeal an adverse judgment awarding damages of $35,000 and defendant was later sued for over $7 million). Allowing offensive collateral estoppel may also be unfair to a defendant if the judgment relied upon as a basis for the estoppel is itself inconsistent with one or more previous judgments in favor of the defendant[14]. Still another situation where it might be unfair to apply offensive estoppel is where the second action

12. Under the mutuality requirement, a plaintiff could accomplish this result since he would not have been bound by the judgment had the original defendant won.

13. The Restatement (Second) of Judgments § 88(3) (Tent. Draft No. 2, Apr. 15, 1975) provides that application of collateral estoppel may be denied if the party asserting it "could have effected joinder in the first action between himself and his present adversary."

14. In Professor Currie's familiar example, a railroad collision injures 50 passengers all of whom bring separate actions against the railroad. After the railroad wins the first 25 suits, a plaintiff wins in suit 26. Professor Currie argues that offensive use of collateral estoppel should not be applied so as to allow plaintiffs 27 through 50 automatically to recover. Currie, supra, 9 Stan.L.Rev., at 304. See Restatement (Second) of Judgments § 88(4), supra.

affords the defendant procedural opportunities unavailable in the first action that could readily cause a different result.[15]

C

We have concluded that the preferable approach for dealing with these problems in the federal courts is not to preclude the use of offensive collateral estoppel, but to grant trial courts broad discretion to determine when it should be applied.[16] The general rule should be that in cases where a plaintiff could easily have joined in the earlier action or where, either for the reasons discussed above or for other reasons, the application of offensive estoppel would be unfair to a defendant, a trial judge should not allow the use of offensive collateral estoppel.

In the present case, however, none of the circumstances that might justify reluctance to allow the offensive use of collateral estoppel is present. The application of offensive collateral estoppel will not here reward a private plaintiff who could have joined in the previous action, since the respondent probably could not have joined in the injunctive action brought by the SEC even had he so desired.[17] Similarly, there is no unfairness to the petitioners in applying offensive collateral estoppel in this case. First, in light of the serious allegations made in the SEC's complaint against the petitioners, as well as the foreseeability of subsequent private suits that typically follow a successful Government judgment, the petitioners had every incentive to litigate the SEC lawsuit fully and vigorously.[18] Second, the judgment in the SEC action was not inconsistent with any previous decision. Finally, there will in the respondent's action be no procedural opportunities available to the petitioners that were unavailable in the first action of a kind that might be likely to cause a different result.[19]

---

15. If, for example, the defendant in the first action was forced to defend in an inconvenient forum and therefore was unable to engage in full scale discovery or call witnesses, application of offensive collateral estoppel may be unwarranted. Indeed, differences in available procedures may sometimes justify not allowing a prior judgment to have estoppel effect in a subsequent action even between the same parties, or where defensive estoppel is asserted against a plaintiff who has litigated and lost. The problem of unfairness is particularly acute in cases of offensive estoppel, however, because the defendant against whom estoppel is asserted typically will not have chosen the forum in the first action. See id., § 88(2) and Comment d.

16. This is essentially the approach of id., § 88, which recognizes that "the distinct trend if not the clear weight of recent authority is to the effect that there is no intrinsic difference between 'offensive' as distinct from 'defensive' issue preclusion, although a stronger showing that the prior opportunity to litigate was adequate may be required in

the former situation than the latter." Id., Reporter's Note, at 99.

17. SEC v. Everest Management Corp., 475 F.2d 1236, 1240 (CA2) ("[T]he complicating effect of the additional issues and the additional parties outweighs any advantage of a single disposition of the common issues"). Moreover, consolidation of a private action with one brought by the SEC without its consent is prohibited by statute. 15 U.S.C. § 78u(g).

18. After a 4-day trial in which the petitioners had every opportunity to present evidence and call witnesses, the District Court held for the SEC. The petitioners then appealed to the Court of Appeals for the Second Circuit, which affirmed the judgment against them. Moreover, the petitioners were already aware of the action brought by the respondent, since it had commenced before the filing of the SEC action.

19. It is true, of course, that the petitioners in the present action would be entitled to a jury trial of the issues bearing on

We conclude, therefore, that none of the considerations that would justify a refusal to allow the use of offensive collateral estoppel is present in this case. Since the petitioners received a "full and fair" opportunity to litigate their claims in the SEC action, the contemporary law of collateral estoppel leads inescapably to the conclusion that the petitioners are collaterally estopped from relitigating the question of whether the proxy statement was materially false and misleading.

II

The question that remains is whether, notwithstanding the law of collateral estoppel, the use of offensive collateral estoppel in this case would violate the petitioners' Seventh Amendment right to a jury trial.[20]

A

"[T]he thrust of the [Seventh] Amendment was to preserve the right to jury trial as it existed in 1791." Curtis v. Loether, 415 U.S. 189, 193, 94 S.Ct. 1005, 1007, 39 L.Ed.2d 260. At common law, a litigant was not entitled to have a jury determine issues that had been previously adjudicated by a chancellor in equity. Hopkins v. Lee, 6 Wheat. 109; Smith v. Kernochen, 7 How. 198, 217–218, 12 L.Ed. 666; Brady v. Daly, 175 U.S. 148, 158–159, 20 S.Ct. 62, 66, 44 L.Ed. 109; Shapiro & Coquillette, The Fetish of Jury Trial in Civil Cases: A Comment on Rachal v. Hill, 85 Harv.L.Rev. 442, 448–458 (1971).[21]

Recognition that an equitable determination could have collateral-estoppel effect in a subsequent legal action was the major premise of this Court's decision in Beacon Theatres, Inc. v. Westover, 359 U.S. 500, 79 S.Ct. 948, 3 L.Ed.2d 988. In that case the plaintiff sought a declaratory judgment that certain arrangements between it and the defendant were not in violation of the antitrust laws, and asked for an injunction to prevent the defendant from instituting an antitrust action to challenge the arrangements. The defendant denied the allegations and counterclaimed for treble damages under the antitrust laws, requesting a trial by jury of the issues common to both the legal and equitable claims. The Court of Appeals upheld denial of the request, but this Court reversed, stating:

> "[T]he effect of the action of the District Court could be, as the Court of Appeals believed, 'to limit the petitioner's opportunity fully to try to a jury every issue which has a bearing upon its

whether the proxy statement was materially false and misleading had the SEC action never been brought—a matter to be discussed in Part II of this opinion. But the presence or absence of a jury as factfinder is basically neutral, quite unlike, for example, the necessity of defending the first lawsuit in an inconvenient forum.

20. The Seventh Amendment provides: "In Suits at common law, where the value in controversy shall exceed twenty dollars, the right to jury trial shall be preserved...."

21. The authors of this article conclude that the historical sources "indicates that in the late eighteenth and early nineteenth centuries, determinations in equity were thought to have as much force as determinations at law, and that the possible impact on jury trial rights was not viewed with concern.... If collateral estoppel is otherwise warranted, the jury trial question should not stand in the way." 85 Harv.L.Rev., at 455–456. This common-law rule is adopted in the Restatement of Judgments § 68, Comment j (1942).

treble damage suit,' for determination of the issue of clearances by the judge might 'operate either by way of res judicata or collateral estoppel so as to conclude both parties with respect thereto at the subsequent trial of the treble damage claim.' "Id., at 504, 79 S.Ct., at 953.

It is thus clear that the Court in the Beacon Theatres case thought that if an issue common to both legal and equitable claims was first determined by a judge, relitigation of the issue before a jury might be foreclosed by res judicata or collateral estoppel. To avoid this result, the Court held that when legal and equitable claims are joined in the same action, the trial judge has only limited discretion in determining the sequence of trial and "that discretion . . . must, wherever possible, be exercised to preserve jury trial." Id., at 510, 79 S.Ct., at 956.[22]

Both the premise of Beacon Theatres, and the fact that it enunciated no more than a general prudential rule were confirmed by this Court's decision in Katchen v. Landy, 382 U.S. 323, 86 S.Ct. 467, 15 L.Ed.2d 391. In that case the Court held that a bankruptcy court, sitting as a statutory court of equity, is empowered to adjudicate equitable claims prior to legal claims, even though the factual issues decided in the equity action would have been triable by a jury under the Seventh Amendment if the legal claims had been adjudicated first. The Court stated:

> "Both Beacon Theatres and Dairy Queen recognize that there might be situations in which the Court could proceed to resolve the equitable claim first even though the results might be dispositive of the issues involved in the legal claim." Id., at 339, 86 S.Ct., at 478.

Thus the Court in Katchen v. Landy recognized that an equitable determination can have collateral-estoppel effect in a subsequent legal action and that this estoppel does not violate the Seventh Amendment.

B

Despite the strong support to be found both in history and in the recent decisional law of this Court for the proposition that an equitable determination can have collateral-estoppel effect in a subsequent legal action, the petitioners argue that application of collateral estoppel in this case would nevertheless violate their Seventh Amendment right to a jury trial. The petitioners contend that since the scope of the Amendment must be determined by reference to the common law as it existed in 1791, and since the common law permitted collateral estoppel only where there was mutuality of parties, collateral estoppel cannot constitutionally be applied when such mutuality is absent.

The petitioners have advanced no persuasive reason, however, why the meaning of the Seventh Amendment should depend on

---

22. Similarly, in both Dairy Queen, Inc. v. Wood, 369 U.S. 469, 82 S.Ct. 894, 8 L.Ed.2d 44, and Meeker v. Ambassador Oil Corp., 375 U.S. 160, 84 S.Ct. 273, 11 L.Ed.2d 261, the Court held that legal claims should ordinarily be tried before equitable claims to preserve the right to a jury trial.

whether or not mutuality of parties is present. A litigant who has lost because of adverse factual findings in an equity action is equally deprived of a jury trial whether he is estopped from relitigating the factual issues against the same party or a new party. In either case, the party against whom estoppel is asserted has litigated questions of fact, and has had the facts determined against him in an earlier proceeding. In either case there is no further factfinding function for the jury to perform, since the common factual issues have been resolved in the previous action. Cf. Ex parte Peterson, 253 U.S. 300, 310, 40 S.Ct. 543, 547, 64 L.Ed. 919 ("No one is entitled in a civil case to trial by jury, unless and except so far as there are issues of fact to be determined").

The Seventh Amendment has never been interpreted in the rigid manner advocated by the petitioners. On the contrary, many procedural devices developed since 1791 that have diminished the civil jury's historic domain have been found not to be inconsistent with the Seventh Amendment. See Galloway v. United States, 319 U.S. 372, 388–393, 63 S.Ct. 1077, 1086–1088, 87 L.Ed. 1458 (directed verdict does not violate the Seventh Amendment); Gasoline Products Co. v. Champlin Refining Co., 283 U.S. 494, 497–498, 51 S.Ct. 513–514, 75 L.Ed. 1188 (retrial limited to question of damages does not violate the Seventh Amendment even though there was no practice at common law for setting aside a verdict in part); Fidelity & Deposit Co. v. United States, 187 U.S. 315, 319–321, 23 S.Ct. 120, 121–122, 47 L.Ed. 194 (summary judgment does not violate the Seventh Amendment).[23]

The Galloway case is particularly instructive. There the party against whom a directed verdict had been entered argued that the procedure was unconstitutional under the Seventh Amendment. In rejecting this claim, the Court said:

> "The Amendment did not bind the federal courts to the exact procedural incidents or details of jury trial according to the common law in 1791, any more than it tied them to the common-law system of pleading or the specific rules of evidence then prevailing. Nor were 'the rules of the common law' then prevalent, including those relating to the procedure by which the judge regulated the jury's role on questions of fact, crystalized in a fixed and immutable system.

> "The more logical conclusion, we think, and the one which both history and the previous decisions here support, is that the Amendment was designed to preserve the basic institution of jury trial in only its most fundamental elements, not the great mass of procedural forms and details, varying even then so widely among

---

23. The petitioners' reliance on Dimick v. Schiedt, 293 U.S. 474, 55 S.Ct. 296, 79 L.Ed. 603, is misplaced. In the Dimick case the Court held that an increase by the trial judge of the amount of money damages awarded by the jury violated the second clause of the Seventh Amendment, which provides that "no fact tried by a jury, shall be otherwise reexamined in any Court of the United States, than according to the rules of the common law." Collateral estoppel does not involve the "re-examination" of any fact decided by a jury. On the contrary, the whole premise of collateral estoppel is that once an issue has been resolved in a prior proceeding, there is no further factfinding function to be performed.

common-law jurisdictions." 319 U.S., at 390, 392, 63 S.Ct., at 1087 (footnote omitted).

The law of collateral estoppel, like the law in other procedural areas defining the scope of the jury's function, has evolved since 1791. Under the rationale of the Galloway case, these developments are not repugnant to the Seventh Amendment simply for the reason that they did not exist in 1791. Thus if, as we have held, the law of collateral estoppel forecloses the petitioners from relitigating the factual issues determined against them in the SEC action, nothing in the Seventh Amendment dictates a different result, even though because of lack of mutuality there would have been no collateral estoppel in 1791.

The judgment of the Court of Appeals is Affirmed.

■ Mr. Justice Rehnquist, dissenting.

It is admittedly difficult to be outraged about the treatment accorded by the federal judiciary to petitioners' demand for a jury trial in this lawsuit. Outrage is an emotion all but impossible to generate with respect to a corporate defendant in a securities fraud action, and this case is no exception. But the nagging sense of unfairness as to the way petitioners have been treated, engendered by the imprimatur placed by the Court of Appeals on respondent's "heads I win, tails you lose" theory of this litigation, is not dispelled by this Court's antiseptic analysis of the issues in the case. It may be that if this Nation were to adopt a new Constitution today, the Seventh Amendment guarantee-ing the right of jury trial in civil cases in federal courts would not be included among its provisions. But any present sentiment to that effect cannot obscure or dilute our obligation to enforce the Seventh Amendment, which was included in the Bill of Rights in 1791 and which has not since been repealed in the only manner provided by the Constitution for repeal of its provisions.

The right of trial by jury in civil cases at common law is funda-mental to our history and jurisprudence. Today, however, the Court reduces this valued right, which Blackstone praised as "the glory of the English law," to a mere "neutral" factor and in the name of procedural reform denies the right of jury trial to defendants in a vast number of cases in which defendants, heretofore, have enjoyed jury trials. Over 35 years ago, Mr. Justice Black lamented the "gradual process of judicial erosion which in one hundred fifty years has slowly worn away a major portion of the essential guarantee of the Seventh Amendment." Galloway v. United States, 319 U.S. 372, 397, 63 S.Ct. 1077, 1090, 87 L.Ed. 1458 (1943) (dissenting opinion). Regrettably, the erosive process continues apace with today's decision.

I

The history of the Seventh Amendment has been amply docu-mented by this Court and by legal scholars, and it would serve no useful purpose to attempt here to repeat all that has been written on the subject. Nonetheless, the decision of this case turns on the scope and effect of the Seventh Amendment, which, perhaps more than with any other provision of the Constitution, are determined by reference to the historical setting in which the Amendment was adopted. See Colgrove v. Battin, 413 U.S. 149, 152, 93 S.Ct. 2448, 2450, 37 L.Ed.2d 522 (1973). It therefore is appropriate to pause to review, albeit briefly, the circumstances preceding and attending the adoption of the Seventh Amendment as a guide in ascertaining its application to the case at hand.

The founders of our Nation considered the right of trial by jury in civil cases an important bulwark against tyranny and corruption, a safeguard too precious to be left to the whim of the sovereign, or, it might be added, to that of the judiciary. Those who passionately advocated the right to a civil jury trial did not do so because they considered the jury a familiar procedural device that should be continued; the concerns for the institution of jury trial that led to the passages of the Declaration of Independence and to the Seventh Amendment were not animated by a belief that use of juries would lead to more efficient judicial administration. Trial by a jury of laymen rather than by the sovereign's judges was important to the founders because juries represent the layman's common sense, the "passional elements in our nature," and thus keep the administration of law in accord with the wishes and feelings of the community. O. Holmes, Collected Legal Papers 237 (1920). Those who favored juries believed that a jury would reach a result that a judge either could not or would not reach. It is with these values that underlie the Seventh Amendment in mind that the Court should, but obviously does not, approach the decision of this case.

B

The Seventh Amendment requires that the right of trial by jury be "preserved." Because the Seventh Amendment demands preservation of the jury trial right, our cases have uniformly held that the content of the right must be judged by historical standards. If a jury would have been impaneled in a particular kind of case in 1791, then the Seventh Amendment requires a jury trial today, if either party so desires.

To be sure, it is the substance of the right of jury trial that is preserved, not the incidental or collateral effects of common-law practice in 1791.

I think it is clear that petitioners were denied their Seventh Amendment right to a jury trial in this case. Neither respondent nor the Court doubts that at common law as it existed in 1791, petitioners would have been entitled in the private action to have a jury determine whether the proxy statement was false and misleading in the respects alleged. The reason is that at common law in 1791, collateral estoppel was permitted only where the parties in the first action were identical to, or in privity with, the parties to the subsequent action. It was not until 1971 that the doctrine of mutuality was abrogated by this Court in certain limited circumstances. Blonder–Tongue Laboratories, Inc. v. University of Illinois Foundation, 402 U.S. 313, 91 S.Ct. 1434, 28 L.Ed.2d 788. But developments in the judge-made doctrine of collateral estoppel, however salutary, cannot, consistent with the Seventh Amendment, contract in any material fashion the right to a jury trial that a defendant would have enjoyed in 1791. In the instant case, resort to the doctrine of collateral estoppel does more than merely contract the right to a jury trial: It eliminates the right entirely and therefore contravenes the Seventh Amendment.

The Court responds, however, that at common law "a litigant was not entitled to have a jury [in a subsequent action at law between the same parties] determine issues that had been previously adjudicated by a chancellor in equity," and that "petitioners have advanced no persuasive reason ... why the meaning of the Seventh Amendment should depend on whether or not mutuality of parties is present." But that is tantamount to saying that since a party would not be entitled to a jury trial if he brought an equitable action, there is no persuasive reason why he should receive a jury trial on virtually the same issues if instead he chooses to bring his lawsuit in the nature of a legal action. The persuasive reason is that the Seventh Amendment requires that a party's right to jury trial which existed at common law be "preserved" from incursions by the government or the judiciary. Whether this Court believes that use of a jury trial in a particular instance is necessary, or fair or repetitive is simply irrelevant. If that view is "rigid," it is the Constitution which commands that rigidity. To hold otherwise is to rewrite the Seventh Amendment so that a party is guaranteed a jury trial in civil cases unless this Court thinks that a jury trial would be inappropriate.

* * * [T]he development of nonmutual estoppel is a substantial departure from the common law and its use in this case completely deprives petitioners of their right to have a jury determine contested issues of fact. I am simply unwilling to accept the Court's presumption that the complete extinguishment of petitioners' right to trial by jury can be justified as a mere change in "procedural incident or detail."

II

Even accepting, arguendo, the majority's position that there is no violation of the Seventh Amendment here, I nonetheless would not sanction the use of collateral estoppel in this case. The Court today holds:

> "The general rule should be that in cases where a plaintiff could easily have joined in the earlier action or where, either for the reasons discussed above or for other reasons, the application of offensive estoppel would be unfair to a defendant, a trial judge should not allow the use of[20] offensive collateral estoppel."

In my view, it is "unfair" to apply offensive collateral estoppel where the party who is sought to be estopped has not had an opportunity to have the facts of his case determined by a jury. Since in

---

20. The Court's decision today may well extend to other areas, such as antitrust, labor, employment discrimination, consumer protection, and the like, where a private plaintiff may sue for damages based on the same or similar violations that are the subject of government actions.

this case petitioners were not entitled to a jury trial in the Securities and Exchange Commission (SEC) lawsuit. I would not estop them from relitigating the issues determined in the SEC suit before a jury in the private action. I believe that several factors militate in favor of this result.

First, the use of offensive collateral estoppel in this case runs counter to the strong federal policy favoring jury trials, even if it does not, as the majority holds, violate the Seventh Amendment. Today's decision will mean that in a large number of private cases defendants will no longer enjoy the right to jury trial. Neither the Court nor respondent has adverted or cited to any unmanageable problems that have resulted from according defendants jury trials in such cases. I simply see no "imperative circumstances" requiring this wholesale abrogation of jury trials.

Second, I believe that the opportunity for a jury trial in the second action could easily lead to a different result from that obtained in the first action before the court and therefore that it is unfair to estop petitioners from relitigating the issues before a jury. This is the position adopted in the Restatement (Second) of Judgments, which disapproves of the application of offensive collateral estoppel where the defendant has an opportunity for a jury trial in the second lawsuit that was not available in the first action.[22] The Court accepts the proposition that it is unfair to apply offensive collateral estoppel "where the second action affords the defendant procedural opportunities unavailable in the first action that could readily cause a different result." Differences in discovery opportunities between the two actions are cited as examples of situations where it would be unfair to permit offensive collateral estoppel. But in the Court's view, the fact that petitioners would have been entitled to a jury trial in the present action is not such a "procedural opportunit[y]" because "the presence or absence of a jury as factfinder is basically neutral, quite unlike, for example, the necessity of defending the first lawsuit in an inconvenient forum."

As is evident from the prior brief discussion of the development of the civil jury trial guarantee in this country, those who drafted the Declaration of Independence and debated so passionately the proposed Constitution during the ratification period, would indeed be astounded to learn that the presence or absence of a jury is merely "neutral," whereas the availability of discovery, a device unmentioned in the Constitution, may be controlling. It is precisely because the Framers believed that they might receive a different result at the hands of a jury of their peers than at the mercy of the sovereign's judges, that the Seventh Amendment was adopted. And I suspect that anyone who litigates cases before juries in the 1970's would be equally amazed to

---

22. Restatement (Second) of Judgments § 88(2), Comment d (Tent. Draft No. 2, Apr. 15, 1975). Citing Rachal v. Hill, 435 F.2d 59 (C.A.5 1970), cert. denied, 403 U.S. 904, 91 S.Ct. 2203, 29 L.Ed.2d 680 (1971), the Reporter's Note states: "The differences between the procedures available in the first and second actions, while not sufficient to deny issue preclusion between the same parties, may warrant a refusal to carry over preclusion to an action involving another party." Restatement, supra, 100.

hear of the supposed lack of distinction between trial by court and trial by jury. The Court can cite no authority in support of this curious proposition. The merits of civil juries have been long debated, but I suspect that juries have never been accused of being merely "neutral" factors.

Contrary to the majority's supposition, juries can make a difference, and our cases have, before today at least, recognized this obvious fact. The ultimate irony of today's decision is that its potential for significantly conserving the resources of either the litigants or the judiciary is doubtful at best. That being the case, I see absolutely no reason to frustrate so cavalierly the important federal policy favoring jury decisions of disputed fact questions. The instant case is an apt example of the minimal savings that will be accomplished by the Court's decision. As the Court admits, even if petitioners are collaterally estopped from relitigating whether the proxy was materially false and misleading, they are still entitled to have a jury determine whether respondent was injured by the alleged misstatements and the amount of damages, if any, sustained by respondent. Thus, a jury must be impaneled in this case in any event. The time saved by not trying the issue of whether the proxy was materially false and misleading before the jury is likely to be insubstantial. It is just as probable that today's decision will have the result of coercing defendants to agree to consent orders or settlements in agency enforcement actions in order to preserve their right to jury trial in the private actions. In that event, the Court, for no compelling reason, will have simply added a powerful club to the administrative agencies' arsenals that even Congress was unwilling to provide them.

NOTES

If you represented a defendant in the *Parklane* situation, what better alternatives might be available? Would you, in settlement negotiations with the SEC, give more if that could get your client a consent decree without any admission of fact? When the SEC sued, might you prevail in moving the district court to delay the SEC trial or to accelerate the process to trial in the class action, so as not to deprive your client of its right to a trial by jury?

Note that the nonparty plaintiffs in *Parklane* did not sit back and await the outcome of the SEC action. Their class action had been started earlier and they could not join in the SEC action unless the SEC consented which it would not do.

Edward I. Koch, v. Consolidated Edison Company of New York, Inc.

New York Court of Appeals, 1984.
62 N.Y.2d 548, 479 N.Y.S.2d 163, 468 N.E.2d 1.
Cert. denied, 469 U.S. 1210, 105 S.Ct. 1177, 84 L.Ed.2d 326 (1985).

■ JONES, JUDGE.

The determination made in a prior action that Con Edison was grossly negligent in connection with the 1977 blackout in the City of

New York is binding and conclusive on Con Edison in this action. Although plaintiffs may recover damages for physical injury to persons and property directly resulting from the service interruption, including damages resulting from looting and vandalism by rioters, they may not recover damages for additional expenditures, occasioned by the blackout, made by plaintiffs in the performance of their governmental functions, nor may they recover for loss of revenues assertedly attributable to the blackout.

On July 13, 1977 at approximately 9:36 p.m. there was a complete failure of electrical service in the City of New York except for an area in the Borough of Queens which was supplied by the Long Island Lighting Company. The blackout lasted for approximately 25 hours with power not being completely restored until approximately 10:40 p.m. on July 14.

The present action was instituted on September 7, 1978 by the City of New York and 14 public benefit corporations to recover damages allegedly sustained as a result of Con Edison's gross negligence and reckless and willful conduct with respect to the blackout.

Plaintiffs moved for partial summary judgment with respect to Con Edison's liability for gross negligence "on the ground that, under the doctrine of collateral estoppel, a prior determination in another lawsuit (Food Pageant, Inc. v. Consolidated Edison Co., Inc., Supreme Court, Bronx County, Index No. 16971/77)[1] that the July 13–14, 1977 electric power failure * * * resulted from the gross negligence of the defendant Consolidated Edison, is conclusive and binding on the defendant Consolidated Edison in this action". Con Edison thereupon made a cross motion for partial summary judgment, so far as pertinent for the purposes of the present appeal

Special Term granted plaintiffs' motion and denied Con Edison's motion as described above. The Appellate Division, 95 A.D.2d 988, 465 N.E.2d 99, affirmed, without opinion, and granted both plaintiffs and Con Edison leave to appeal to our court. We modify the determination at the Appellate Division.

We agree with both courts below that on the issue of Con Edison's liability for gross negligence in connection with the blackout, Con Edison is precluded by the adverse determination of the issue in Food Pageant v. Consolidated Edison Co., 54 N.Y.2d 167, 445 N.Y.S.2d 60, 429 N.E.2d 738. The applicable principle in this case is that of third-party issue preclusion.[2]

---

1. When this case reached our court we upheld the jury verdict which found Con Edison to have been grossly negligent in causing the 1977 blackout and which awarded plaintiff grocery store chain damages in the sum of $40,500 for food spoilage and loss of business. (Food Pageant v. Consolidated Edison Co., 54 N.Y.2d 167, 445 N.Y.S.2d 60, 429 N.E.2d 738).

2. Issue preclusion between the same parties is to be distinguished from third-party issue preclusion. In the former case as stated in section 27 of the Restatement of Judgments, Second—"When an issue of fact or law is actually litigated and determined by a valid and final judgment, and the determination is essential to the judgment, the determination is conclusive in a subsequent action between the parties, whether on the same or a different claim", subject to a very narrow range of exceptions (id., § 28). By some contrast the principle of third-party issue preclu-

It is plaintiffs who seek to invoke the principle of third-party issue preclusion to bar Con Edison from relitigating its liability for gross negligence. It is not disputed that this issue was actually litigated and determined by a valid and final judgment in Food Pageant and that the determination of that issue was essential to the judgment in that case. Plaintiffs contend, therefore, that the determination in Food Pageant is binding and conclusive in this case. Con Edison, having the burden to demonstrate that the circumstances of the prior determination justify affording it an opportunity to relitigate the issue of liability, advances several arguments in support of its contention that the determination in Food Pageant is not to be given preclusive effect.[4] These arguments, taken singularly or in combination, do not warrant the result for which

sion is that, again in the phraseology of the Restatement (§ 29)—"A party precluded from relitigating an issue with an opposing party, in accordance with §§ 27 and 28, is also precluded from doing so with another person". The range of circumstances which may lead to avoidance of preclusion, however, is now much broader—"unless the fact that he lacked full and fair opportunity to litigate the issue in the first action or other circumstances justify affording him an opportunity to relitigate the issue." With respect to the distinction between issue preclusion between the same parties and third-party issue preclusion, see Matter of American Ins. Co. (Messinger–Aetna Cas. & Sur. Co.), 43 N.Y.2d 184, 190, 401 N.Y.S.2d 36, 371 N.E.2d 798.

4. The relevant factors to be considered are set out in section 29 of the Restatement of Judgments, Second, and in Schwartz. Section 29 provides in full as follows:

§ 29. Issue Preclusion in Subsequent Litigation with Others

"A party precluded from relitigating an issue with an opposing party, in accordance with §§ 27 and 28, is also precluded from doing so with another person unless the fact that he lacked full and fair opportunity to litigate the issue in the first action or other circumstances justify affording him an opportunity to relitigate the issue. The circumstances to which considerations should be given include those enumerated in § 28 and also whether:

"(1) Treating the issue as conclusively determined would be incompatible with an applicable scheme of administering the remedies in the actions involved;

"(2) The forum in the second action affords the party against whom preclusion is asserted procedural opportunities in the presentation and determination of the issue that were not available in the first action and could likely result in the issue being differently determined;

"(3) The person seeking to invoke favorable preclusion, or to avoid unfavor-

able preclusion, could have effected joinder in the first action between himself and his present adversary;

"(4) The determination relied on as preclusive was itself inconsistent with another determination of the same issue;

"(5) The prior determination may have been affected by relationships among the parties to the first action that are not present in the subsequent action, or apparently was based on a compromise verdict or finding;

"(6) Treating the issue as conclusively determined may complicate determination of issues in the subsequent action or prejudice the interests of another party thereto;

"(7) The issue is one of law and treating it as conclusively determined would inappropriately foreclose opportunity for obtaining reconsideration of the legal rule upon which it was based;

"(8) Other compelling circumstances make it appropriate that the party be permitted to relitigate the issue."

The articulation in Schwartz appears at page 72, 298 N.Y.S.2d 955, 246 N.E.2d 725, as follows: "A decision whether or not the plaintiff drivers had a full and fair opportunity to establish their non-negligence in the prior action requires an exploration of the various elements which make up the realities of litigation. A comprehensive list of the various factors which should enter into a determination whether a party has had his day in court would include such considerations as the size of the claim, the forum of the prior litigation, the use of initiative, the extent of the litigation, the competence and experience of counsel, the availability of new evidence, indications of a compromise verdict, differences in the applicable law and foreseeability of future litigation."

Con Edison contends, and Con Edison has not tendered sufficient proof in admissible form to require trial of any issue of fact or reversal of the exercise of judgment by the courts below.

It is first contended that third-party issue preclusion should not apply because there are other judicial determinations concluding that Con Edison was not guilty of gross negligence in connection with the blackout. Whatever might be said of the effect properly to be given to inconsistent determinations of like judicial stature, in this instance it suffices to dismiss Con Edison's contention to observe that the inconsistent determinations on which it would rely are those in cases tried in the Small Claims Part of the Civil Court of New York City as to which informal and simplified procedures are applicable and which by express statutory provision are not to be deemed an adjudication of any fact at issue (other than the amount involved) with respect to any other action.

Con Edison next argues that there is now available exculpatory evidence which in fairness requires that it be permitted to relitigate the issue of liability. Reference is made to investigative reports, in particular to the so-called Clapp Report. These reports were available and offered but rejected in the Food Pageant trial. Nothing suggests that the exclusion of this hearsay evidence was there error (and any contention that it was could have been subjected to appellate review on the appeal in that case), and no persuasive argument is now advanced to support admissibility in this case.

Con Edison next makes an oblique plea that we should reintroduce the former requirement of mutuality which we declared "a dead letter" in B.R. DeWitt, Inc. v. Hall, 19 N.Y.2d 141, 147, 278 N.Y.S.2d 596, 225 N.E.2d 195. To grant this plea would, of course, be entirely to eliminate third-party issue preclusion. It is understandable that Con Edison should express concern, in the light of the multiplicity of claims arising out of the blackout, that the issue of its gross negligence will have been established in each case. Nevertheless, no sufficient justification is advanced to turn the clock back with respect to so fundamental a legal development as the elimination of the requirement of mutuality. We have been committed since DeWitt, and indeed even before (Israel v. Wood Dolson Co., 1 N.Y.2d 116, 151 N.Y.S.2d 1, 134 N.E.2d 97), to the proposition that efficient utilization of the judicial system is served by preclusion of relitigation of issues as to which a litigant has had a full and fair opportunity for resolution, irrespective of the identity of his particular opponent. Nor does Con Edison advance any intermediate position warranting a different application of the principles of third-party issue preclusion with respect to a multiplicity of claims arising out of a community-wide disaster such as the blackout in this case.

It is then argued that the determination in Food Pageant should not be given preclusive effect because of indications that it was the result of compromise in the jury room. No tender has been made, however, of proof in admissible form sufficient to require trial of this factual issue. The arguments of Con Edison are grounded only in speculation, and it cannot be said as a matter of law that the Food Pageant verdict was the result of impermissible compromise.

The circumstance, to which Con Edison next points, that the claim in Food Pageant and the amount of the jury's verdict ($40,500) may be said to be "small in absolute terms and particularly so when compared to the aggregate of over $200 million in claims against Con Edison arising out of the 1977 blackout", provides no basis to deny application of third-party issue preclusion. In Food Pageant, Con Edison had a full and fair opportunity to litigate the issue of gross negligence, the forum and applicable procedures were the same, the burden of persuasion was the same, and Con Edison, explicitly then recognizing the potential preclusive effects of an adverse determination in that case, had every incentive to defend that action fully and vigorously.

Nor does the adoption of a rule of comparative negligence in New York (CPLR art. 14–A) foreclose application of third-party issue preclusion in the circumstances of this case. No contention whatsoever is put forth by Con Edison that any action or omission to act on the part of any of plaintiffs contributed to cause the blackout. There simply is no issue of comparative negligence involved in the question of Con Edison's responsibility for the blackout. It may be, however, that principles of mitigation will require consideration of certain action or inaction on the part of plaintiffs in the determination of damages.

Finally with respect to the preclusion issue, we reject as wholly without merit Con Edison's assertion that to apply third-party issue preclusion would be to deprive it of the due process to which it is constitutionally entitled. The characterization of this appeal as "presenting a question of fundamental fairness" neither concludes nor advances the argument. Con Edison cites no authority, and we know of none, which now regards the application of third-party issue preclusion as posing a question of constitutional dimension where in the prior action a full and fair opportunity to litigate has been afforded.

For the reasons stated we conclude that the prior determination in Food Pageant with respect to Con Edison's liability for gross negligence in connection with the 1977 blackout is binding and conclusive on Con Edison in this action.

* * *

For the reasons stated, the order of the Appellate Division should be modified, without costs, to grant Con Edison's motion for partial summary judgment dismissing plaintiffs' claims for damages on account of expenditures made for additional governmental services furnished in consequence of the blackout and for loss of revenue and similar economic damage asserted to be attributable to the blackout, and as so modified, affirmed.

NOTES

A. The Court in *Parklane Hosiery* concluded that it was preferable not to preclude application of res judicata, but to vest "broad discretion" in the trial judge as to whether the doctrine should be applied in the particular case. In whom is this discretion vested, the trial judge who first heard the case? No issue concerning relitigation arose in that case; it was not until the second case that any question about issue preclusion came before the court. It is the trial judge in the second case in whom the discretion is vested , for it is she who will have to examine the relevant factors and rule on the defense of res judicata. The decision being "discretionary," at the time of the first case it is impossible for either party to know with any certitude whether that litigation will or will not be held to have preclusive effect. Is this desirable? Does it make for an efficient system?

B.   In addition to the obvious concerns that there have been a full and fair opportunity to litigate the issues, the *Parklane* opinion states the most cogent fairness factors that go into the decision whether issue preclusion is appropriately applied. One might add the unfairness of there being different burdens of proof in the two cases and differences in the applicable law and cases where the claims are different although the specific issue might be the same. Related lawsuits with some common issues can be brought in the courts of more than one state and in state courts and federal courts. Such cases can create complexities in the choice(s) of applicable law, and, obviously, can bring about difficulties in the determination of fairness. It may be that a party to a prior adjudication cannot realistically foresee the various possibilities of issue preclusion.

C.   The stated benefits of issue preclusion are judicial economy, efficiency and reduced costs to the parties and the public. Presumably, the trial courts will have more time to devote to other cases. But the application of issue preclusion is always discretionary. The court must decide whether issue preclusion would be fair.

D.   Some jurisdictions do not allow offensive use of issue preclusion if the plaintiff could have but did not become part of the first lawsuit. See Rest. (2d) Judgments, § 29(3) and especially Comment (e). New York, along with the federal courts however, has not required compulsory intervention by nonparties. See Rest. (2d) Judgments § 29(1)-(7) Exceptions. As Koch v. Con Edison shows, this rule can be a tactical advantage for nonparties (and perhaps current plaintiffs).

E.   The N.Y. Court of Appeals opinion justifies issue preclusion as an "efficient utilization of the judicial system [which] is served by preclusion of relitigation of issues as to which a litigant has had a full and fair opportunity for resolution ..." The opinion also speaks of "Con Edison explicitly then recognizing the potential preclusive effects of an adverse determination in that case ..." Food Pageant v. Consolidated Edison Co., 54 N.Y.2d 167, 445 N.Y.S.2d 60, 429 N.E.2d 738.

F.   Sometimes offensive issue preclusion will not be permitted if there have been inconsistent prior judgments. The N.Y. Court of Appeals did not consider those cited in note 5 because all were tried in small claims court which are not considered courts of record.

G.   What tactical steps might have been available had Con Edison anticipated issue preclusion? A defensive class action might have helped. Even if the total damage awards were about the same, the costs of litigation would have been sharply reduced. Otherwise Con Edison might have been subjected to jury trials on the individual damage claims.

H.   What if Con Edison never appealed the Food Pageant decision? See *Berner v. British Comm.* 346 F2d 532 (2d Cir. 1965) (application of offensive collateral estoppel denied where defendant did not appeal an adverse judgment awarding damages of $35,000 and defendant was later sued for over $7 million.)

THE SCOPE OF ISSUE PRECLUSION: TO WHAT ISSUES DOES IT APPLY?

A.   Creditor sues debtor for the interest due on a note. Debtor defends on the ground that creditor had executed a valid instrument releasing debtor from the obligation to pay any interest on the note. The issue is contested and creditor wins. Six months later creditor sues for the next installment of interest. Debtor is precluded from relitigating the issue of the release, but she is not precluded from defending on the ground that the original note was procured by fraud.

We say that issue preclusion applies only where an issue is actually litigated and, in addition, is "necessary to the judgement." The issue of fraud in obtaining the note has not been litigated; it may be raised now. This is the most significant difference between claim preclusion and issue preclusion. The former operates to preclude litigation of what was actually litigated and, in addition, of what might have been litigated. The latter does not.; in this regard it is far more restricted in scope. Of course, as we have seen, it is far broader in scope with respect to the parties who may invoke it and the claims to which it may be applied.

B.   Suppose defendant introduces several defenses, any one of which would result in victory in that law suit. For example, defendant, sued for personal injuries resulting from a defective ladder, defends on the ground that (1) she did not manufacture the ladder, (2) the ladder was not defective, and (3) plaintiff's injuries did not result from the fall of the ladder. The trier of fact finds that defendant was the manufacturer of the ladder, that the ladder was defective, but that the injuries did not result from the fall of the ladder. (Perhaps they were incurred in a little private brawl that took place at the same location.) In subsequent litigation is defendant precluded from litigating whether the ladder was defective? No, relitigation of that issue is not precluded because that finding was not "necessary to the judgment."

Probably the easiest way to understand this result is to recognize that defendant won the first suit. As the victor, she had neither the right to appeal nor incentive to appeal. Why should an appellate court take the time to decide an appeal that would not change the result below? Moreover, once defendant prevails on one defense, the others become irrelevant and can be viewed as dictum, if you will.

C.   The classic example illustrating the same point involves litigation following an automobile accident. P sues D who defends on the ground that he, D, was not negligent while P was guilty of contributory negligence, where victory on rather issue was sufficient to defeat the action. The trier of fact finds them both negligent. Thus, D wins. D now sues P for damages incurred in the same accident, and no rule relating to compulsory counterclaims bars the suit. The finding in the first suit that D was negligent will not preclude relitigation of that issue in the second suit.; it was not necessary to the judgment. What of the finding that P has been contributorily negligent? Will that finding now relieve D of proving P's negligence in the second suit?

D.   D is prosecuted for arson and is acquitted. In a subsequent civil action against the insurance company to recover damages incurred in the same fire, the insurance company defends on the ground that the policy does not cover fires intentionally started by D. D claims res judicata based on his acquittal. What ruling?

NOTE ON VACATUR

How might losing defendants avoid the sometimes drastic consequences of issue preclusion? Defendants want to prevent a judgment from being a precedent for purposes of preclusion. To avoid the preclusive effects of an earlier adjudication, usually a trial court judgment, the plaintiff as winner can be offered a generous settlement. Defendant will pay the amount of the judgment and an additional amount for plaintiff's agreement to join in a motion to have the judgment erased. This is done by vacatur which means that the judgment has no legal effect as a precedent and cannot be the basis for later preclusion.

All opposing parties must request vacatur. In the usual situation, after the trial court judgment and even while the case is on appeal, the parties agree to a settlement with the condition that the trial court vacate its judgment. Only when that is done is the settlement effective. Like most settlements of civil cases the court need not approve the other terms of the settlement although the circumstances that vacatur be ordered by the court gives the court leverage regarding the settlement.

Vacatur in somewhat different form is permitted in several states and is routinely granted in some, notably California and Texas. In the federal courts, it is quite the other way. The Supreme Court in U.S. Bancorp Mortgage Co. v. Bonner Mall Partnership, 513 U.S. 18 (1994) required federal courts to exercise what amounts to a presumption against vacatur which may be granted only in exceptional circumstances. It is not enough that the parties agree on a settlement that includes vacatur.

D. SPECIAL SITUATIONS

Rivet v. Regions Bank of La.

Supreme Court of the United States, 1998.
522 U.S. 470, 118 S. Ct. 921, 139 L. Ed. 2d 912.

■ JUSTICE GINSBURG delivered the opinion of the Court.

Congress has provided for removal of cases from state court to federal court when the plaintiff's complaint alleges a claim arising under federal law. Congress has not authorized removal based on a defense or anticipated defense federal in character. This case presents the question whether removal may be predicated on a defendant's assertion that a prior federal judgment has disposed of the entire matter and thus bars plaintiffs from later pursuing a state-law-based case. We reaffirm that removal is improper in such a case. In so holding we clarify and confine to its specific context the Court's second footnote in Federated Department Stores, Inc. v. Moitie, 452 U.S. 394, 397, n. 2, 101 S.Ct. 2424, 2427, n. 2, 69 L.Ed.2d 103 (1981). The defense of claim preclusion, we emphasize, is properly made in the state proceeding, subject to this Court's ultimate review.

I

This case arose out of a series of mortgages and conveyances involving a parcel of real property in New Orleans. In 1983, a partnership that owned the Louisiana equivalent of a leasehold estate in the property mortgaged that interest to respondent Regions Bank of Louisiana (Bank). One year later, to secure further borrowing, the partnership granted a second mortgage to petitioners Mary Anna Rivet, Minna Ree Winer, Edmund G. Miranne, and Edmund G. Miranne, Jr. The partnership thereafter filed for bankruptcy, and the bankruptcy trustee sought court permission to sell the leasehold estate free and clear of all claims.

In June and August 1986 orders, the Bankruptcy Court first granted the sale application and later approved sale of the leasehold estate to the Bank, sole bidder at the public auction. The court also directed the Recorder of Mortgages for Orleans Parish to cancel all liens, mortgages, and encumbrances, including the mortgages held by the Bank and petitioners. Nonetheless, petitioners' mortgage remained inscribed on the mortgage rolls of Orleans Parish. Subsequently, in 1993, the Bank acquired the underlying land from respondents Walter L. Brown, Jr., and Perry S. Brown. The Bank then sold the entire property to the current owner, respondent Fountainbleau Storage Associates (FSA).

On December 29, 1994, petitioners filed this action in Louisiana state court. They alleged that the 1993 transactions violated Louisiana law because the property was transferred without satisfying petitioners' superior rights under the second mortgage. In their prayer for relief, petitioners sought recognition and enforcement of their mortgage or, alternatively, damages. Respondents removed the action to the District Court for the Eastern District of Louisiana. Federal-question jurisdiction existed, they contended, because the prior Bankruptcy Court orders extinguished petitioners' rights under the second mortgage.

In federal court, petitioners filed a motion to remand and respondents moved for summary judgment. The District Court denied the remand motion. Relying on the Fifth Circuit's decision in Carpenter v. Wichita Falls Independent School Dist., 44 F.3d 362 (1995), the District Court held that removal was properly predicated on the preclusive effect of the 1986 Bankruptcy Court orders. The Court then granted summary judgment to the Bank and FSA on the ground that the Bankruptcy Court's adjudication barred petitioners' suit. The District Court also granted summary judgment to the Browns, ruling that petitioners failed to state a claim against them.

The Fifth Circuit affirmed. 108 F.3d 576 (1997). It agreed with the District Court that under Carpenter a defendant could remove " 'where a plaintiff files a state cause of action completely precluded by a prior federal judgment on a question of federal law.' "108 F.3d, at 586 (quoting Carpenter, 44 F.3d, at 370). Carpenter's holding, the Court of Appeals thought, was dictated by the second footnote to our decision in Moitie, 452 U.S., at 397, n. 2, 101 S.Ct., at 2427 n. 2.

In dissent, Judge Jones maintained that removal is appropriate under Moitie only where a plaintiff loses in federal court on an "essentially federal" claim and, recharacterizing the claim as one based on state law, files again in state court. 108 F.3d, at 594. She concluded that removal here was improper because there was nothing federal about petitioners' claim.

The circuit courts have adopted differing views regarding the propriety of removing a state court action to federal court on the ground that the claim asserted is precluded by a prior federal judgment. We granted certiorari, 521 U.S. 1152, 118 S.Ct. 31, 138 L.Ed.2d 1060 (1997), to resolve the matter.

II

A

A state court action may be removed to federal court if it qualifies as a "civil action . . . of which the district courts of the United States have original jurisdiction," unless Congress expressly provides otherwise. 28 U.S.C. § 1441(a). In this case, respondents invoked, in support of removal, the district courts' original federal-question jurisdiction over "[a]ny civil action . . . founded on a claim or right arising under the Constitution, treaties or laws of the United States." 28 U.S.C. § 1441(b); see also 28 U.S.C. § 1331.

We have long held that "[t]he presence or absence of federal-question jurisdiction is governed by the 'well-pleaded complaint rule,' which provides that federal jurisdiction exists only when a federal question is presented on the face of the plaintiff's properly pleaded complaint." A defense is not part of a plaintiff's properly pleaded statement of his or her claim. ("To bring a case within the [federal-question removal] statute, a right or immunity created by the Constitution or laws of the United States must be an element, and an essential one, of the plaintiff's cause of action.") Thus, "a case may not be removed to federal court on the basis of a federal defense, . . . even if the defense is anticipated in the plaintiff's complaint, and even if both parties admit that the defense is the only question truly at issue in the case." Franchise Tax Bd. of Cal. v. Construction Laborers Vacation Trust for Southern Cal., 463 U.S. 1, 14, 103 S.Ct. 2841, 2848, 77 L.Ed.2d 420 (1983).

Allied as an "independent corollary" to the well-pleaded complaint rule is the further principle that "a plaintiff may not defeat removal by omitting to plead necessary federal questions." Id., at 22, 103 S.Ct., at 2853. If a court concludes that a plaintiff has "artfully pleaded" claims in this fashion, it may uphold removal even though no federal question appears on the face of the plaintiff's complaint. The artful pleading doctrine allows removal where federal law completely preempts a plaintiff's state-law claim.

B

Petitioners' complaint sought recognition and enforcement of a mortgage. The dispute involved Louisiana parties only, and petitioners relied exclusively on Louisiana law. Respondents defended their removal of the case from state court to federal court on the ground that petitioners' action was precluded, as a matter of federal law, by the earlier Bankruptcy Court orders. We now explain why the removal was improper.

Under the doctrine of claim preclusion, "[a] final judgment on the merits of an action precludes the parties or their privies from relitigating issues that were or could have been raised in that action." Moitie, 452 U.S., at 398, 101 S.Ct., at 2428; see also Baker v. General Motors Corp., 522 U.S. 222, 233, n. 5, 118 S.Ct. 657, 664, n. 5, 139 L.Ed.2d 580 (1998) ("a valid final adjudication of a claim precludes a second action on that claim or any part of it"). Claim preclusion (res judicata), as Rule 8(c) of the Federal Rules of Civil Procedure makes clear, is an affirmative defense. See also Blonder–Tongue Laboratories, Inc. v. University of Ill. Foundation, 402 U.S. 313, 350, 91 S.Ct. 1434, 1453, 28 L.Ed.2d 788 (1971) ("Res judicata and collateral estoppel [issue preclusion] are affirmative defenses that must be pleaded.") (italics omitted).

A case blocked by the claim preclusive effect of a prior federal judgment differs from the standard case governed by a completely preemptive federal statute in this critical respect: The prior federal judgment does not transform the plaintiff's state-law claims into federal claims but rather extinguishes them altogether. See Commissioner v. Sunnen, 333 U.S. 591, 597, 68 S.Ct. 715, 719, 92 L.Ed. 898 (1948) ("The judgment puts an end to the cause of action, which cannot again be brought into litigation between the parties upon any ground whatever, absent fraud or some other factor invalidating the judgment."). Under the well-pleaded complaint rule, preclusion thus remains a defensive plea involving no recasting of the plaintiff's complaint, and is therefore not a proper basis for removal.

In holding removal appropriate here, the Court of Appeals relied on a footnote—the second one—in our Moitie opinion. The Fifth Circuit is not alone in concluding from the Moitie footnote that removal properly may rest on the alleged preclusive effect of a prior federal judgment. The Moitie footnote, however, was a marginal comment and will not bear the heavy weight lower courts have placed on it.

We granted certiorari in Moitie principally to address the Ninth Circuit's "novel exception to the doctrine of res judicata." 452 U.S., at 398, 101 S.Ct., at 2427. In that case, several actions alleging price-fixing by department stores in California were consolidated in federal court and dismissed. Most of the plaintiffs appealed and obtained a reversal, but two chose instead to file separate claims in state court. The defendants removed the actions to federal District Court, where plaintiffs unsuccessfully moved to remand and defendants successfully moved to dismiss the actions on preclusion grounds. The Court of Appeals for the Ninth Circuit agreed that removal was proper, but held that preclusion did not apply in the unique circumstances of the case. 611 F.2d 1267 (1980).

In the course of reversing the Ninth Circuit's holding on preclusion, we noted, without elaboration, our agreement with the Court of Appeals that "at least some of the claims had a sufficient federal character to support removal." 452 U.S., at 397, n. 2, 101 S.Ct., at 2427, n. 2. In that case-specific context, we declined to "question . . . [the District Court's] factual finding" that the plaintiffs "had attempted to avoid removal jurisdiction by artfully casting their essentially federal[-]law claims as state-law claims." Ibid. (internal quotation marks omitted).

"Moitie's enigmatic footnote," Rivet, 108 F.3d, at 584, we recognize, has caused considerable confusion in the circuit courts. We therefore clarify today that Moitie did not create a preclusion exception to the rule, fundamental under currently governing legislation, that a defendant cannot remove on the basis of a federal defense.

In sum, claim preclusion by reason of a prior federal judgment is a defensive plea that provides no basis for removal under § 1441(b). Such a defense is properly made in the state proceedings, and the state courts' disposition of it is subject to this Court's ultimate review.

For the foregoing reasons, the judgment of the Court of Appeals for the Fifth Circuit is reversed, and the case is remanded for further proceedings consistent with this opinion.

It is so ordered.

NOTE

There is complete preemption of state law claims by some federal laws. Justice Ginsburg's opinion mentions ERISA and LMRA. In these limited areas, removal will result despite the federal law issues being raised in a complaint to support a preemption defense. Rivet is the more common situation. Federal question jurisdiction is not created by pleading an affirmative defense such as preclusion as part of the complaint.

NOTE ON FORESEEABILITY

It has been contended that preclusion should not apply and that parties should be permitted to relitigate issues the importance of which were not foreseeable at the time of the first lawsuit and those issues the existence of which could not have been forseen because of intervening changes in the law. Some cases and the Restatement(Second) of Judgments (1980) § 28(5) so hold. The anticipated public and private benefits of preclusion presuppose that persons will change their behavior given their knowledge of the doctrine of preclusion. But that premise is negated if the application (or non-application) of preclusion rules was not reasonably foreseeable at the time of the first lawsuit. There is also the feeling that fairness requires that the party be able to anticipate the consequences of a judgment before he undertakes a lawsuit.

Matsushita Electric Industrial Co. v. Epstein

Supreme Court of the United States, 1996.
516 U.S. 367, 116 S. Ct. 873, 134 L. Ed. 2d 6.

■ JUSTICE THOMAS delivered the opinion of the Court.

This case presents the question whether a federal court may withhold full faith and credit from a state-court judgment approving a class-action settlement simply because the settlement releases claims within the exclusive jurisdiction of the federal courts. The answer is no. Absent a partial repeal of the Full Faith and Credit Act, 28 U.S.C. § 1738, by another federal statute, a federal court must give the judgment the same effect that it would have in the courts of the State in which it was rendered.

I

In 1990, petitioner Matsushita Electric Industrial Co. made a tender offer for the common stock of MCA, Inc., a Delaware corporation. The tender offer not only resulted in Matsushita's acquisition of MCA, but also precipitated two lawsuits on behalf of the holders of MCA's common stock. First, a class action was filed in the Delaware Court of Chancery against MCA and its directors for breach of fiduciary duty in failing to maximize shareholder value. The complaint was later amended to state additional claims against MCA's directors for, inter alia, waste of corporate assets by exposing MCA to liability under the federal securities laws. In addition, Matsushita was added as a defendant and was accused of conspiring with MCA's directors to violate Delaware law. The Delaware suit was based purely on state-law claims.

While the state class action was pending, the instant suit was filed in Federal District Court in California. The complaint named Matsushita as a defendant and alleged that Matsushita's tender offer violated Securities Exchange Commission (SEC) Rules. Section 27 of the Exchange Act confers exclusive jurisdiction upon the federal courts for suits brought to enforce the Act or rules and regulations promulgated thereunder. See 15 U.S.C. § 78aa. The District Court declined to certify the class, entered summary judgment for Matsushita, and dismissed the case. The plaintiffs appealed to the Court of Appeals for the Ninth Circuit.

After the federal plaintiffs filed their notice of appeal but before the Ninth Circuit handed down a decision, the parties to the Delaware suit negotiated a settlement. In exchange for a global release of all claims arising out of the Matsushita–MCA acquisition, the defendants would deposit $2 million into a settlement fund to be distributed pro rata to the members of the class. As required by Delaware Chancery Rule 23, which is modeled on Federal Rule of Civil Procedure 23, the Chancery Court certified the class for purposes of settlement and approved a notice of the proposed settlement. The notice informed the class members of their right to request exclusion from the settlement class and to appear and present argument at a scheduled hearing to determine the fairness of the settlement. In particular, the notice stated that "[b]y filing a valid Request for Exclusion, a member of the Settlement Class will not be precluded by the Settlement from individually seeking to pursue the claims alleged in the . . . California Federal Actions, . . . or any other claim relating to the events at issue in the Delaware Actions." App. to Pet. for Cert. 96a. Two such notices were mailed to the class members and the notice was also published in the national edition of the Wall Street Journal. The Chancery Court then held a hearing. After argument from several objectors, the Court found the class representation adequate and the settlement fair.

The order and final judgment of the Chancery Court incorporated the terms of the settlement agreement, providing: "All claims, rights and causes of action (state or federal, including but not limited to claims arising under the federal securities law, any rules or regulations promulgated thereunder, or otherwise), whether known or unknown that are, could have been or might in the future be asserted by any of the plaintiffs or any member of the Settlement Class (other than those who have validly requested exclusion therefrom), . . . in connection with or that arise now or hereafter out of the Merger Agreement, the Tender Offer, the Distribution Agreement, the Capital Contribution Agreement, the employee compensation arrangements, the Tender Agreements, the Initial Proposed Settlement, this Settlement . . . and including without limitation the claims asserted in the California Federal Actions . . . are hereby compromised, settled, released and discharged with prejudice by virtue of the proceedings herein and this Order and Final Judgment." In re MCA, Inc. Shareholders Litigation, C.A. No. 11740 (Feb. 22, 1993). The judgment also stated that the notice met all the requirements of due process. The Delaware Supreme Court affirmed. In re MCA, Inc., Shareholders Litigation, 633 A.2d 370 (1993) (judgment order).

Respondents were members of both the state and federal plaintiff classes. Following issuance of the notice of proposed settlement of the Delaware litigation, respondents neither opted out of the settlement class nor appeared at the hearing to contest the settlement or the representation of the class. On appeal in the Ninth Circuit, petitioner Matsushita invoked the Delaware judgment as a bar to further prosecution of that action under the Full Faith and Credit Act, 28 U.S.C. § 1738.

The Ninth Circuit rejected petitioner's argument, ruling that § 1738 did not apply. Epstein v. MCA, Inc., 50 F.3d 644, 661–666 (1995). Instead, the Court of Appeals fashioned a test under which the preclusive force of a state court settlement judgment is limited to those claims that "could . . . have been extinguished by the issue preclusive effect of an adjudication of the state claims." Id., at 665. The lower courts have taken varying approaches to determining the preclusive effect of a state court judgment, entered in a class or derivative action, that provides for the release of exclusively federal claims. We granted certiorari to clarify this important area of federal law. 515 U.S. 1141, 115 S.Ct. 2576, 132 L.Ed.2d 826 (1995).

II

The Full Faith and Credit Act mandates that the "judicial proceedings" of any State "shall have the same full faith and credit in every court within the United States . . . as they have by law or usage in the courts of such State . . . from which they are taken." 28 U.S.C. § 1738.

The Act thus directs all courts to treat a state court judgment with the same respect that it would receive in the courts of the rendering state. Federal courts may not "employ their own rules ... in determining the effect of state judgments," but must "accept the rules chosen by the State from which the judgment is taken." Kremer v. Chemical Constr. Corp., 456 U.S. 461, 481–482, 102 S.Ct. 1883, 1898, 72 L.Ed.2d 262 (1982). Because the Court of Appeals failed to follow the dictates of the Act, we reverse.

A

The state court judgment in this case differs in two respects from the judgments that we have previously considered in our cases under the Full Faith and Credit Act. As respondents and the Court of Appeals stressed, the judgment was the product of a class action and incorporated a settlement agreement releasing claims within the exclusive jurisdiction of the federal courts. Though respondents urge "the irrelevance of section 1738 to this litigation," Brief for Respondents 25, we do not think that either of these features exempts the judgment from the operation of § 1738.

That the judgment at issue is the result of a class action, rather than a suit brought by an individual, does not undermine the initial applicability of § 1738. The judgment of a state court in a class action is plainly the product of a "judicial proceeding" within the meaning of § 1738. Cf. McDonald v. West Branch, 466 U.S. 284, 287–288, 104 S.Ct. 1799, 1801–1802, 80 L.Ed.2d 302 (1984) (holding that § 1738 does not apply to arbitration awards because arbitration is not a "judicial proceeding"). Therefore, a judgment entered in a class action, like any other judgment entered in a state judicial proceeding, is presumptively entitled to full faith and credit under the express terms of the Act.

Further, § 1738 is not irrelevant simply because the judgment in question might work to bar the litigation of exclusively federal claims. Our decision in Marrese v. American Academy of Orthopaedic Surgeons, 470 U.S. 373, 105 S.Ct. 1327, 84 L.Ed.2d 274 (1985), made clear that where § 1738 is raised as a defense in a subsequent suit, the fact that an allegedly precluded "claim is within the exclusive jurisdiction of the federal courts does not necessarily make § 1738 inapplicable." Id., at 380, 105 S.Ct., at 1332 (emphasis added). In so holding, we relied primarily on Kremer v. Chemical Constr. Corp., supra, which held, without deciding whether Title VII claims are exclusively federal, that state court proceedings may be issue preclusive in Title VII suits in federal court. Kremer, we said, "implies that absent an exception to § 1738, state law determines at least the ... preclusive effect of a prior state judgment in a subsequent action involving a claim within the exclusive jurisdiction of the federal courts." Marrese, 470 U.S., at 381, 105 S.Ct., at 1332. Accordingly, we decided that "a state court judgment may in some circumstances have preclusive effect in a subsequent action within the exclusive jurisdiction of the federal courts." Id., at 380, 105 S.Ct., at 1332.

In Marrese, we discussed Nash County Board of Education v. Biltmore Co., 640 F.2d 484 (C.A.4), cert. denied, 454 U.S. 878, 102 S.Ct. 359, 70 L.Ed.2d 188 (1981), a case that concerned a state court settlement judgment. In Nash, the question was whether the judgment, which approved the settlement of state antitrust claims, prevented the litigation of exclusively federal antitrust claims. See 470 U.S., at 382, n. 2, 105 S.Ct., at 1333, n. 2. We suggested that the approach outlined in Marrese would also apply in cases like Nash that involve judgments upon settlement: that is, § 1738 would control at the outset. In accord with these precedents, we conclude that § 1738 is generally applicable in cases in which the state court judgment at issue incorporates a class action settlement releasing claims solely within the jurisdiction of the federal courts.

B

Marrese provides the analytical framework for deciding whether the Delaware court's judgment precludes this exclusively federal action. When faced with a state court judgment relating to an exclusively federal claim, a federal court must first look to the law of the rendering State to ascertain the effect of the judgment. See id., at 381–382. If state law indicates that the particular claim or issue would be barred from litigation in a court of that state, then the federal court must next decide whether, "as an exception to § 1738," it "should refuse to give preclusive effect to [the] state court judgment." Id., at 383, 105 S.Ct., at 1333. See also Migra v. Warren City School Dist. Bd. of Ed., 465 U.S. 75, 80, 104 S.Ct. 892, 896, 79 L.Ed.2d 56 (1984) ("[I]n the absence of federal law modifying the operation of § 1738, the preclusive effect in federal court of [a] state-court judgment is determined by [state] law").

1

We observed in Marrese that the inquiry into state law would not always yield a direct answer. Usually, "a state court will not have occasion to address the specific question whether a state judgment has issue or claim preclusive effect in a later action that can be brought only in federal court." 470 U.S., at 381–382, 105 S.Ct., at 1332. Where a judicially approved settlement is under consideration, a federal court may consequently find guidance from general state law on the preclusive force of settlement judgments. See, e.g., id., at 382–383, n. 2, 105 S.Ct., at 1333, n. 2 (observing in connection with Nash that "[North Carolina] law gives preclusive effect to consent judgment[s]"). Here, in addition to providing rules regarding the preclusive force of class-action settlement judgments in subsequent suits in state court, the Delaware courts have also spoken to the particular effect of such judgments in federal court.

Delaware has traditionally treated the impact of settlement judgments on subsequent litigation in state court as a question of claim preclusion. Early cases suggested that Delaware courts would not afford claim preclusive effect to a settlement releasing claims that could not have been presented in the trial court. See Ezzes v.

Ackerman, 234 A.2d 444, 445–446 (Del.1967) ("[A] judgment entered either after trial on the merits or upon an approved settlement is res judicata and bars subsequent suit on the same claim. . . . [T]he defense of res judicata . . . is available if the pleadings framing the issues in the first action would have permitted the raising of the issue sought to be raised in the second action, and if the facts were known or could have been known to the plaintiff in the second action at the time of the first action"). As the Court of Chancery has perceived, however, "the Ezzes inquiry [was] modified in regard to class actions," In re Union Square Associates Securities Litigation, C.A. No. 11028, 1993 WL 220528, *3 (June 16, 1993), by the Delaware Supreme Court's decision in Nottingham Partners v. Dana, 564 A.2d 1089 (1989).

In Nottingham, a class action, the Delaware Supreme Court approved a settlement that released claims then pending in federal court. In approving that settlement, the Nottingham Court appears to have eliminated the Ezzes requirement that the claims could have been raised in the suit that produced the settlement, at least with respect to class actions: " '[I]n order to achieve a comprehensive settlement that would prevent relitigation of settled questions at the core of a class action, a court may permit the release of a claim based on the identical factual predicate as that underlying the claims in the settled class action even though the claim was not presented and might not have been presentable in the class action.' " 564 A.2d, at 1106 (quoting TBK Partners, Ltd. v. Western Union Corp., 675 F.2d 456, 460 (C.A.2 1982)). These cases indicate that even if, as here, a claim could not have been raised in the court that rendered the settlement judgment in a class action, a Delaware court would still find that the judgment bars subsequent pursuit of the claim.

The Delaware Supreme Court has further manifested its understanding that when the Court of Chancery approves a global release of claims, its settlement judgment should preclude on-going or future federal court litigation of any released claims. In Nottingham, the Court stated that "[t]he validity of executing a general release in conjunction with the termination of litigation has long been recognized by the Delaware courts. More specifically, the Court of Chancery has a history of approving settlements that have implicitly or explicitly included a general release, which would also release federal claims." 564 A.2d, at 1105 (citation omitted). Though the Delaware Supreme Court correctly recognized in Nottingham that it lacked actual authority to order the dismissal of any case pending in federal court, it asserted that state-court approval of the settlement would have the collateral effect of preventing class members from prosecuting their claims in federal court. Perhaps the clearest statement of the Delaware Chancery Court's view on this matter was articulated in the suit preceding this one: "When a state court settlement of a class action releases all claims which arise out of the challenged transaction and is determined to be fair and to have met all due process requirements, the class members are bound by the release or the doctrine of issue preclusion. Class members cannot subsequently relitigate the claims barred by the settlement in a federal court." In re MCA, Inc. Shareholders Litigation, 598 A.2d 687, 691 (1991).[4] We are aware of no Delaware case that suggests otherwise.

Given these statements of Delaware law, we think that a Delaware court would afford preclusive effect to the settlement judgment in this case, notwithstanding the fact that respondents could not have pressed their Exchange Act claims in the Court of Chancery. The claims are clearly within the scope of the release in the judgment, since the judgment specifically refers to this lawsuit. As required by Delaware Court of Chancery Rule 23, see Prezant v. De Angelis, 636 A.2d 915, 920 (1994), the Court of Chancery found, and the Delaware Supreme Court affirmed, that the settlement was "fair, reasonable and adequate and in the best interests of the . . . Settlement class" and that notice to the class was "in full compliance with . . . the requirements of due process."

2

Because it appears that the settlement judgment would be res judicata under Delaware law, we proceed to the second step of the Marrese analysis and ask whether § 27 of the Exchange Act, which confers exclusive jurisdiction upon the federal courts for suits arising under the Act, partially repealed § 1738. Section 27 contains no express language regarding its relationship with § 1738 or the preclusive effect of related state court proceedings. Thus, any modification of § 1738 by § 27 must be implied. In deciding whether § 27 impliedly created an exception to § 1738, the "general question is whether the concerns underlying a particular grant of exclusive jurisdiction justify a finding of an implied partial repeal of § 1738." Marrese, 470 U.S., at 386, 105 S.Ct., at 1334. "Resolution of this question will depend on the particular federal statute as well as the nature of the claim or issue involved in the subsequent federal action. . . . [T]he primary consideration must be the intent of Congress."

As an historical matter, we have seldom, if ever, held that a federal statute impliedly repealed § 1738.

Nor does § 27 evince any intent to prevent litigants in state court—whether suing as individuals or as part of a class—from voluntarily releasing Exchange Act claims in judicially approved settlements. While § 27 prohibits state courts from adjudicating claims arising under the Exchange Act, it does not prohibit state courts from approving the release of Exchange Act claims in the settlement of suits over which they have properly exercised jurisdiction, i.e., suits arising under state law or under federal law for which there is concurrent jurisdiction. In this case, for example, the Delaware action was not "brought to enforce" any rights or obligations under the Act. The Delaware court asserted judicial power over a complaint asserting

---

4. In fact, the Chancery Court rejected the first settlement, which contained no opt-out provision, as unfair to the class precisely because it believed that the settlement would preclude the class from pursuing their exclusively federal claims in federal court. See In re MCA Inc. Shareholders Litigation, 598 A.2d 687, 692 (1991) ("[I]f this Court provides for the release of all the claims arising out of the challenged transaction, the claims which the Objectors have asserted in the federal suit will likely be forever barred").

purely state law causes of action and, after the parties agreed to settle, certified the class and approved the settlement pursuant to the requirements of Delaware Rule of Chancery 23 and the Due Process Clause. Thus, the Delaware court never trespassed upon the exclusive territory of the federal courts, but merely approved the settlement of a common-law suit pursuant to state and nonexclusive federal law. See Abramson v. Pennwood Investment Corp., 392 F.2d 759, 762 (C.A.2 1968) ("Although the state court could not adjudicate the federal claim, it was within its powers over the corporation and the parties to approve the release of that claim as a condition of settlement of the state action"). While it is true that the state court assessed the general worth of the federal claims in determining the fairness of the settlement, such assessment does not amount to a judgment on the merits of the claims.

Taken together, these [cited]cases stand for the general proposition that even when exclusively federal claims are at stake, there is no "universal right to litigate a federal claim in a federal district court." Allen v. McCurry, 449 U.S., at 105, 101 S.Ct., at 420. If class action plaintiffs wish to preserve absolutely their right to litigate exclusively federal claims in federal court, they should either opt out of the settlement class or object to the release of any exclusively federal claims. In fact, some of the plaintiffs in the Delaware class action requested exclusion from the settlement class. They are now proceeding in federal court with their federal claims, unimpeded by the Delaware judgment.

In the end, §§ 27 and 1738 "do not pose an either-or proposition." Connecticut Nat. Bank v. Germain, 503 U.S. 249, 253, 112 S.Ct. 1146, 1149, 117 L.Ed.2d 391 (1992). They can be reconciled by reading § 1738 to mandate full faith and credit of state court judgments incorporating global settlements, provided the rendering court had jurisdiction over the underlying suit itself, and by reading § 27 to prohibit state courts from exercising jurisdiction over suits arising under the Exchange Act. Cf. C. Wright, A. Miller, & E. Cooper, Federal Practice and Procedure § 4470 pp. 688–689 (1981) ("[S]ettlement of state court litigation has been held to defeat a subsequent federal action if the settlement was intended to apply to claims in exclusive federal jurisdiction as well as other claims.... These rulings are surely correct"). Congress' intent to provide an exclusive federal forum for adjudication of suits to enforce the Exchange Act is clear enough. But we can find no suggestion in § 27 that Congress meant to override the "principles of comity and repose embodied in § 1738," Kremer v. Chemical Constr. Corp., 456 U.S., at 463, 102 S.Ct., at 1888, by allowing plaintiffs with Exchange Act claims to release those claims in state court and then litigate them in federal court. We conclude that the Delaware courts would give the settlement judgment preclusive effect in a subsequent proceeding and, further, that § 27 did not effect a partial repeal of § 1738.

C

The Court of Appeals did not engage in any analysis of Delaware law pursuant to § 1738. Rather, the Court of Appeals declined to apply § 1738 on the ground that where the rendering forum lacked jurisdiction over the subject matter or the parties, full faith and credit is not required. 50 F.3d, at 661, 666. See Underwriters Nat. Assurance Co. v. North Carolina Life & Accident & Health Ins. Guaranty Assn., 455 U.S. 691, 704–705, 102 S.Ct. 1357, 1366, 71 L.Ed.2d 558 (1982) (" '[A] judgment of a court in one State is conclusive upon the merits in a court in another State only if the court in the first State had power to pass on the merits—had jurisdiction, that is, to render the judgment' ") (quoting Durfee v. Duke, 375 U.S. 106, 110, 84 S.Ct. 242, 244, 11 L.Ed.2d 186 (1963)). The Court of Appeals decided that the subject-matter jurisdiction exception to full faith and credit applies to this case because the Delaware court acted outside the bounds of its own jurisdiction in approving the settlement, since the settlement released exclusively federal claims. See 50 F.3d, at 661–662, and n. 25.

As explained above, the state court in this case clearly possessed jurisdiction over the subject matter of the underlying suit and over the defendants. Only if this were not so—for instance, if the complaint alleged violations of the Exchange Act and the Delaware court rendered a judgment on the merits of those claims—would the exception to § 1738 for lack of subject-matter jurisdiction apply. Where, as here, the rendering court in fact had subject-matter jurisdiction, the subject-matter jurisdiction exception to full faith and credit is simply inapposite. In such a case, the relevance of a federal statute that provides for exclusive federal jurisdiction is not to the state court's possession of jurisdiction per se, but to the existence of a partial repeal of § 1738.

The judgment of the Court of Appeals is reversed and remanded for proceedings consistent with this opinion.

■ [The dissent of JUSTICE STEVENS is omitted.]

■ JUSTICE GINSBURG, concurring in part and dissenting in part.

I join the Court's judgment to the extent that it remands the case to the Ninth Circuit. I agree that a remand is in order because the Court of Appeals did not attend to this Court's reading of 28 U.S.C. § 1738 in a controlling decision, Kremer v. Chemical Constr. Corp., 456 U.S. 461, 102 S.Ct. 1883, 72 L.Ed.2d 262 (1982). But I would not endeavor, as the Court does, to speak the first word on the content of Delaware preclusion law. Instead, I would follow our standard practice of remitting that issue for decision, in the first instance, by the lower federal courts. See, e.g., Marrese v. American Academy of Orthopaedic Surgeons, 470 U.S. 373, 387, 105 S.Ct. 1327, 1335, 84 L.Ed.2d 274 (1985).

I write separately to emphasize a point key to the application of § 1738: A state-court judgment generally is not entitled to full faith and credit unless it satisfies the requirements of the Fourteenth Amendment's Due Process Clause. See Kremer, 456 U.S., at 482–483, 102 S.Ct., at 1898–1899. In the class action setting, adequate representation is among the due process ingredients that must be supplied if the judgment is to bind absent class members. See Phillips Petroleum Co. v. Shutts, 472 U.S. 797, 808, 812, 105 S.Ct. 2965, 2972, 2974, 86

L.Ed.2d 628 (1985); Prezant v. De Angelis, 636 A.2d 915, 923–924 (Del.1994).

Suitors in this action (called the "Epstein plaintiffs" in this opinion), respondents here, argued before the Ninth Circuit, and again before this Court, that they cannot be bound by the Delaware settlement because they were not adequately represented by the Delaware class representatives. They contend that the Delaware representatives' willingness to release federal securities claims within the exclusive jurisdiction of the federal courts for a meager return to the class members, but a solid fee to the Delaware class attorneys, disserved the interests of the class, particularly, the absentees. The inadequacy of representation was apparent, the Epstein plaintiffs maintained, for at the time of the settlement, the federal claims were sub judice in the proper forum for those claims—the federal judiciary. Although the Ninth Circuit decided the case without reaching the due process check on the full faith and credit obligation, that inquiry remains open for consideration on remand.

NOTES

A.   On remand, the Ninth Circuit denied recognition to the Delaware judgment and the universal release it had affirmed. Epstein v. MCA, Inc. 126 F.3d 1235 (9th Cir. 1997). The majority of the panel ruled that a member of the class who had not opted out of the class can collaterally attack the judgment on the ground that the class was not adequately represented in the original state court class action.

B.   In Part I of its opinion, the panel ruled that a class action is binding on absent class members only if they were adequately represented. The panel then found (Part II) that the representation leading to the Delaware state court settlement was inadequate. The panel found support in such factors as that the Delaware state court could not hear federal claims (because lacking subject matter jurisdiction) and that the federal and state claims were based on entirely different operative facts without any overlapping issues of fact.

C.   The panel carefully examined the respective bargaining positions of the clients and lawyers to determine whether there could be adequate representation. It found "that the Delaware settlement was the product of a one-sided bargaining process . . ." There could be no trial on the federal claim in the state court, nor could there be discovery regarding the federal claims to estimate their possible value.

D.   Finally, since the state and federal claims "shared no common issues of material fact, a judgment on the state claims could not be used as an "offensive" estoppel in future litigation," 126 F.3d at 1249.

Baker v. General Motors Corporation

Supreme Court of the United States, 1998.
522 U.S. 222, 118 S.Ct. 657, 139 L.Ed. 2d 580.

■ JUSTICE GINSBURG delivered the opinion of the Court.

This case concerns the authority of one State's court to order that a witness' testimony shall not be heard in any court of the United States. In settlement of claims and counterclaims precipitated by the discharge of Ronald Elwell, a former General Motors Corporation (GM) engineering analyst, GM paid Elwell an undisclosed sum of money, and the parties agreed to a permanent injunction. As stipulated by GM and Elwell and entered by a Michigan County Court, the injunction prohibited Elwell from "testifying, without the prior written consent of [GM], ... as ... a witness of any kind ... in any litigation already filed, or to be filed in the future, involving [GM] as an owner, seller, manufacturer and/or designer...." GM separately agreed, however, that if Elwell were ordered to testify by a court or other tribunal, such testimony would not be actionable as a violation of the Michigan court's injunction or the GM–Elwell agreement.

After entry of the stipulated injunction in Michigan, Elwell was subpoenaed to testify in a product liability action commenced in Missouri by plaintiffs who were not involved in the Michigan case. The question presented is whether the national full faith and credit command bars Elwell's testimony in the Missouri case. We hold that Elwell may testify in the Missouri action without offense to the full faith and credit requirement.

I

Two lawsuits, initiated by different parties in different states, gave rise to the full faith and credit issue before us. One suit involved a severed employment relationship, the other, a wrongful-death complaint. We describe each controversy in turn.

A

The Suit Between Elwell and General Motors

Ronald Elwell was a GM employee from 1959 until 1989. For fifteen of those years, beginning in 1971, Elwell was assigned to the Engineering Analysis Group, which studied the performance of GM vehicles, most particularly vehicles involved in product liability litigation. Elwell's studies and research concentrated on vehicular fires. He assisted in improving the performance of GM products by suggesting changes in fuel line designs. During the course of his employment, Elwell frequently aided GM lawyers engaged in defending GM against product liability actions. Beginning in 1987, the Elwell-GM employment relationship soured. GM and Elwell first negotiated an agreement under which Elwell would retire after serving as a GM consultant for two years. When the time came for Elwell to retire, however, disagreement again surfaced and continued into 1991.

In May 1991, plaintiffs in a product liability action pending in Georgia deposed Elwell. The Georgia case involved a GM pickup truck fuel tank that burst into flames just after a collision. During the deposition, and over the objection of counsel for GM, Elwell gave testimony that differed markedly from testimony he had given when serving as an in-house expert witness for GM. Specifically, Elwell had several times defended the safety and crash worthiness of the pickup's fuel system. On deposition in the Georgia action, however, Elwell testified that the GM pickup truck fuel system was inferior in comparison to competing products.

A month later, Elwell sued GM in a Michigan County Court, alleging wrongful discharge and other tort and contract claims. GM counterclaimed, contending that Elwell had breached his fiduciary duty to GM by disclosing privileged and confidential information and misappropriating documents. In response to GM's motion for a preliminary injunction, and after a hearing, the Michigan trial court, on November 22, 1991, enjoined Elwell from:

> "consulting or discussing with or disclosing to any person any of General Motors Corporation's trade secrets[,] confidential information or matters of attorney-client work product relating in any manner to the subject matter of any products liability litigation whether already filed or [to be] filed in the future which Ronald Elwell received, had knowledge of, or was entrusted with during his employments with General Motors Corporation."

Elwell v. General Motors Corp., No. 91–115946NZ (Wayne Cty.) (Order Granting in Part, Denying in Part Injunctive Relief, pp. 1–2), App. 9–10.

In August 1992, GM and Elwell entered into a settlement under which Elwell received an undisclosed sum of money. The parties also stipulated to the entry of a permanent injunction and jointly filed with the Michigan court both the stipulation and the agreed-upon injunction. The proposed permanent injunction contained two proscriptions. The first substantially repeated the terms of the preliminary injunction; the second comprehensively enjoined Elwell from

> "testifying, without the prior written consent of General Motors Corporation, either upon deposition or at trial, as an expert witness, or as a witness of any kind, and from consulting with attorneys or their agents in any litigation already filed, or to be filed in the future, involving General Motors Corporation as an owner, seller, manufacturer and/or designer of the product(s) in issue."

Order Dismissing Plaintiff's Complaint and Granting Permanent Injunction (Wayne Cty., p. 2, Aug. 26, 1992), App. 30.

To this encompassing bar, the consent injunction made an exception: "[This provision] shall not operate to interfere with the jurisdiction of the Court in ... Georgia [where the litigation involving the fuel tank was still pending]." No other noninterference provision appears in the stipulated decree. On August 26, 1992, with no further hearing, the Michigan court entered the injunction precisely as tendered by the parties.

Although the stipulated injunction contained an exception only for the Georgia action then pending, Elwell and GM included in their separate settlement agreement a more general limitation. If a court or other tribunal ordered Elwell to testify, his testimony would "in no way" support a GM action for violation of the injunction or the settlement agreement:

" 'It is agreed that [Elwell's] appearance and testimony, if any, at hearings on Motions to quash subpoena or at deposition or trial or other official proceeding, if the Court or other tribunal so orders, will in no way form a basis for an action in violation of the Permanent Injunction or this Agreement.' "

Settlement Agreement, at 10, as quoted in 86 F.3d 811, 820, n. 11 (8th Cir. 1996).

In the six years since the Elwell–GM settlement, Elwell has testified against GM both in Georgia (pursuant to the exception contained in the injunction) and in several other jurisdictions in which Elwell has been subpoenaed to testify.

B

The Suit Between the Bakers and General Motors

Having described the Elwell–GM employment termination litigation, we next summarize the wrongful-death complaint underlying this case. The decedent, Beverly Garner, was a front-seat passenger in a 1985 Chevrolet S–10 Blazer involved in a February 1990 Missouri highway accident. The Blazer's engine caught fire, and both driver and passenger died. In September 1991, Garner's sons, Kenneth and Steven Baker, commenced a wrongful death product liability action against GM in a Missouri state court. The Bakers alleged that a faulty fuel pump in the 1985 Blazer caused the engine fire that killed their mother. GM removed the case to federal court on the basis of the parties' diverse citizenship. On the merits, GM asserted that the fuel pump was neither faulty nor the cause of the fire, and that collision impact injuries alone caused Garner's death.

The Bakers sought both to depose Elwell and to call him as a witness at trial. GM objected to Elwell's appearance as a deponent or trial witness on the ground that the Michigan injunction barred his testimony. In response, the Bakers urged that the Michigan injunction did not override a Missouri subpoena for Elwell's testimony. The Bakers further noted that, under the Elwell–GM settlement agreement, Elwell could testify if a court so ordered, and such testimony would not be actionable as a violation of the Michigan injunction.

After in camera review of the Michigan injunction and the settlement agreement, the Federal District Court in Missouri allowed the Bakers to depose Elwell and to call him as a witness at trial. Responding to GM's objection, the District Court stated alternative grounds for its ruling: (1) Michigan's injunction need not be enforced because blocking Elwell's testimony would violate Missouri's "public policy," which shielded from disclosure only privileged or otherwise confidential information; (2) just as the injunction could be modified in Michigan, so a court elsewhere could modify the decree.

At trial, Elwell testified in support of the Bakers' claim that the alleged defect in the fuel pump system contributed to the postcollision fire. In addition, he identified and described a 1973 internal GM memorandum bearing on the risk of fuel-fed engine fires. Following trial, the jury awarded the Bakers $11.3 million in damages, and the District Court entered judgment on the jury's verdict.

The United States Court of Appeals for the Eighth Circuit reversed the District Court's judgment, ruling, inter alia, that Elwell's testimony should not have been admitted. 86 F.3d 811 (8th Cir. 1996). Assuming, arguendo, the existence of a public policy exception to the full faith and credit command, the Court of Appeals concluded that the District Court erroneously relied on Missouri's policy favoring disclosure of relevant, nonprivileged information, see id., at 818–819, for Missouri has an "equally strong public policy in favor of full faith and credit," id., at 819.

The Eighth Circuit also determined that the evidence was insufficient to show that the Michigan court would modify the injunction barring Elwell's testimony. See id., at 819–820. The Court of Appeals observed that the Michigan court "has been asked on several occasions to modify the injunction, [but] has yet to do so," and noted that, if the Michigan court did not intend to block Elwell's testimony in cases like the Bakers', "the injunction would . . . have been unnecessary." Id., at 820.

We granted certiorari to decide whether the full faith and credit requirement stops the Bakers, who were not parties to the Michigan proceeding, from obtaining Elwell's testimony in their Missouri wrongful death action.

II

A

The Constitution's Full Faith and Credit Clause provides:

"Full Faith and Credit shall be given in each State to the public Acts, Records, and judicial Proceedings of every other State. And the Congress may by general Laws prescribe the Manner in which such Acts, Records and Proceedings shall be proved, and the Effect thereof." U.S. Const., Art. IV, § 1.

Pursuant to that Clause, Congress has prescribed:

"Such Acts, records and judicial proceedings or copies thereof, so authenticated, shall have the same full faith and credit in every court within the United States and its Territories and Possessions as they have by law or usage in the courts of such State, Territory or Possession from which they are taken." 28 U.S.C. § 1738.[5]

The animating purpose of the full faith and credit command, as this Court explained in Milwaukee County v. M.E. White Co., 296 U.S. 268, 56 S.Ct. 229, 80 L.Ed. 220 (1935),

---

5. The first Congress enacted the original Full Faith and Credit statute in May 1790. See Act of May 26, 1790, ch. 11, 1 Stat. 122 (codified as amended at 28 U.S.C. § 1738) ("And the said records and judicial proceedings authenticated as aforesaid, shall have such faith and credit given to them in every court within the United States, as they have by law or usage in the courts of the state from whence the said records are or shall be taken."). Although the text of the statute has been revised since then, the command for full faith and credit to judgments has remained constant.

"was to alter the status of the several states as independent foreign sovereignties, each free to ignore obligations created under the laws or by the judicial proceedings of the others, and to make them integral parts of a single nation throughout which a remedy upon a just obligation might be demanded as of right, irrespective of the state of its origin." Id., at 277, 56 S.Ct., at 234. See also Estin v. Estin, 334 U.S. 541, 546, 68 S.Ct. 1213, 1217, 92 L.Ed. 1561 (1948) (the Full Faith and Credit Clause "substituted a command for the earlier principles of comity and thus basically altered the status of the States as independent sovereigns").

Our precedent differentiates the credit owed to laws (legislative measures and common law) and to judgments. "In numerous cases this Court has held that credit must be given to the judgment of another state although the forum would not be required to entertain the suit on which the judgment was founded." Milwaukee County, 296 U.S., at 277, 56 S.Ct., at 234. The Full Faith and Credit Clause does not compel "a state to substitute the statutes of other states for its own statutes dealing with a subject matter concerning which it is competent to legislate." Pacific Employers Ins. Co. v. Industrial Accident Comm'n, 306 U.S. 493, 501, 59 S.Ct. 629, 632, 83 L.Ed. 940 (1939); see Phillips Petroleum Co. v. Shutts, 472 U.S. 797, 818–819, 105 S.Ct. 2965, 2977–2978, 86 L.Ed.2d 628 (1985). Regarding judgments, however, the full faith and credit obligation is exacting. A final judgment in one State, if rendered by a court with adjudicatory authority over the subject matter and persons governed by the judgment, qualifies for recognition throughout the land. For claim and issue preclusion (res judicata) purposes, in other words, the judgment of the rendering State gains nationwide force. See, e.g., Matsushita Elec. Industrial Co. v. Epstein, 516 U.S. 367, 373, 116 S.Ct. 873, 878, 134 L.Ed.2d 6 (1996); Kremer v. Chemical Constr. Corp., 456 U.S. 461, 485, 102 S.Ct. 1883, 1899, 72 L.Ed.2d 262 (1982); see also Reese & Johnson, The Scope of Full Faith and Credit to Judgments, 49 Colum. L.Rev. 153 (1949).

A court may be guided by the forum State's "public policy" in determining the law applicable to a controversy. See Nevada v. Hall, 440 U.S. 410, 421–424, 99 S.Ct. 1182, 1188–1190, 59 L.Ed.2d 416 (1979).[6] But our decisions support no roving "public policy exception" to the full faith and credit due judgments. See Estin, 334 U.S., at 546, 68 S.Ct., at 1217 (Full Faith and Credit Clause "ordered submission . . . even to hostile policies reflected in the judgment of another State, because the practical operation of the federal system, which the Constitution designed, demanded it."); Fauntleroy v. Lum, 210 U.S. 230, 237, 28 S.Ct. 641, 643, 52 L.Ed. 1039 (1908) (judgment of Missouri court entitled to full faith and credit in Mississippi even if Missouri judgment rested on a misapprehension of Mississippi law). In

6. See also Paulsen & Sovern, "Public Policy" in the Conflict of Laws, 56 Colum. L.Rev. 969, 980–981 (1956) (noting traditional but dubious use of the term "public policy" to obscure "an assertion of the forum's right to have its [own] law applied to the [controversy] because of the forum's relationship to it").

assuming the existence of a ubiquitous "public policy exception" permitting one State to resist recognition of another State's judgment, the District Court in the Bakers' wrongful-death action, see supra, at 662, misread our precedent. "The full faith and credit clause is one of the provisions incorporated into the Constitution by its framers for the purpose of transforming an aggregation of independent, sovereign States into a nation." Sherrer v. Sherrer, 334 U.S. 343, 355, 68 S.Ct. 1087, 1092–1093, 92 L.Ed. 1429 (1948). We are "aware of [no] considerations of local policy or law which could rightly be deemed to impair the force and effect which the full faith and credit clause and the Act of Congress require to be given to [a money] judgment outside the state of its rendition." Magnolia Petroleum Co. v. Hunt, 320 U.S. 430, 438, 64 S.Ct. 208, 213, 88 L.Ed. 149 (1943).

The Court has never placed equity decrees outside the full faith and credit domain. Equity decrees for the payment of money have long been considered equivalent to judgments at law entitled to nationwide recognition. We see no reason why the preclusive effects of an adjudication on parties and those "in privity" with them, i.e., claim preclusion and issue preclusion (res judicata and collateral estoppel), should differ depending solely upon the type of relief sought in a civil action.

Full faith and credit, however, does not mean that States must adopt the practices of other States regarding the time, manner, and mechanisms for enforcing judgments. Enforcement measures do not travel with the sister state judgment as preclusive effects do; such measures remain subject to the even-handed control of forum law. See McElmoyle ex rel. Bailey v. Cohen, 13 Pet. 312, 325, 10 L.Ed. 177 (1839) (judgment may be enforced only as "laws [of enforcing forum] may permit"); see also Restatement (Second) of Conflict of Laws § 99 (1969) ("The local law of the forum determines the methods by which a judgment of another state is enforced.").[8]

Orders commanding action or inaction have been denied enforcement in a sister State when they purported to accomplish an official act within the exclusive province of that other State or interfered with litigation over which the ordering State had no authority. Thus, a sister State's decree concerning land ownership in another State has been held ineffective to transfer title, see Fall v. Eastin, 215 U.S. 1, 30 S.Ct. 3, 54 L.Ed. 65 (1909), although such a decree may indeed preclusively adjudicate the rights and obligations running between the parties to the foreign litigation, see, e.g., Robertson v. Howard, 229 U.S. 254, 261, 33 S.Ct. 854, 856, 57 L.Ed. 1174 (1913) ("[I]t may not be doubted that a court of equity in one State in a proper case could compel a defendant before it to convey property situated in another

---

8. Congress has provided for the inter-district registration of federal court judgments for the recovery of money or property. 28 U.S.C. § 1963 (upon registration, the judgment "shall have the same effect as a judgment of the district court of the district where registered and may be enforced in like manner"). A similar interstate registration procedure is effective in most States, as a result of widespread adoption of the Revised Uniform Enforcement of Foreign Judgments Act, 13 U.L.A. 149 (1964). See id., at 13 (Supp.1997) (Table) (listing adoptions in 44 States and the District of Columbia).

State.''). And antisuit injunctions regarding litigation elsewhere, even if compatible with due process as a direction constraining parties to the decree, see Cole v. Cunningham, 133 U.S. 107, 10 S.Ct. 269, 33 L.Ed. 538 (1890), in fact have not controlled the second court's actions regarding litigation in that court. See, e.g., James v. Grand Trunk Western R. Co., 14 Ill.2d 356, 372, 152 N.E.2d 858, 867 (1958); see also E. Scoles & P. Hay, Conflict of Laws § 24.21, p. 981 (2d ed.1992) (observing that antisuit injunction ''does not address, and thus has no preclusive effect on, the merits of the litigation [in the second forum]''). Sanctions for violations of an injunction, in any event, are generally administered by the court that issued the injunction. See, e.g., Stiller v. Hardman, 324 F.2d 626, 628 (C.A.2 1963) (nonrendition forum enforces monetary relief portion of a judgment but leaves enforcement of injunctive portion to rendition forum).

B

With these background principles in view, we turn to the dimensions of the order GM relies upon to stop Elwell's testimony. Specifically, we take up the question: What matters did the Michigan injunction legitimately conclude? As earlier recounted, the parties before the Michigan County Court, Elwell and GM, submitted an agreed-upon injunction, which the presiding judge signed.[10] While no issue was joined, expressly litigated, and determined in the Michigan proceeding,[11] that order is claim preclusive between Elwell and GM. Elwell's claim for wrongful discharge and his related contract and tort claims have ''merged in the judgment,'' and he cannot sue again to recover more. See Parklane Hosiery Co. v. Shore, 439 U.S. 322, 326, n. 5, 99 S.Ct. 645, 649, n. 5, 58 L.Ed.2d 552 (1979) (''Under the doctrine of res judicata, a judgment on the merits in a prior suit bars a second suit involving the same parties or their privies based on the same cause of action.''); see also Restatement (Second) of Judgments § 17 (1980). Similarly, GM cannot sue Elwell elsewhere on the counterclaim GM asserted in Michigan. See id., § 23, Comment a, p. 194 (''A defendant who interposes a counterclaim is, in substance, a plaintiff, as far as the counterclaim is concerned, and the plaintiff is, in substance, a defendant.'').

Michigan's judgment, however, cannot reach beyond the Elwell–GM controversy to control proceedings against GM brought in other States, by other parties, asserting claims the merits of which Michigan has not considered. Michigan has no power over those parties, and no basis for commanding them to become intervenors in the Elwell–GM

---

10. GM emphasizes that a key factor warranting the injunction was Elwell's inability to assure that any testimony he might give would steer clear of knowledge he gained from protected confidential communications. See Brief for Respondent 28–29; see also id., at 32 (contending that Elwell's testimony ''is pervasively and uncontrollably leavened with General Motors' privileged information''). Petitioners assert, and GM does not dispute, however, that at no point during Elwell's

testimony in the Bakers' wrongful-death action did GM object to any question or answer on the grounds of attorney-client, attorney-work product, or trade secrets privilege. See Brief for Petitioners 9.

11. In no event, we have observed, can issue preclusion be invoked against one who did not participate in the prior adjudication. * * *

dispute. See Martin v. Wilks, 490 U.S. 755, 761–763, 109 S.Ct. 2180, 2184–2185, 104 L.Ed.2d 835 (1989). Most essentially, Michigan lacks authority to control courts elsewhere by precluding them, in actions brought by strangers to the Michigan litigation, from determining for themselves what witnesses are competent to testify and what evidence is relevant and admissible in their search for the truth. See Restatement (Second) of Conflict of Laws, §§ 137–139 (1969 and rev.1988) (forum's own law governs witness competence and grounds for excluding evidence); cf. Societe Nationale Industrielle Aerospatiale v. United States Dist. Court for Southern Dist. of Iowa, 482 U.S. 522, 544, n. 29, 107 S.Ct. 2542, 2556, n. 29, 96 L.Ed.2d 461 (1987), (foreign "blocking statute" barring disclosure of certain information "do[es] not deprive an American court of the power to order a party subject to its jurisdiction to produce [the information]"); United States v. First Nat'l City Bank, 396 F.2d 897 (2d Cir. 1968) (New York bank may not refuse to produce records of its German branch, even though doing so might subject the bank to civil liability under German law).

As the District Court recognized, Michigan's decree could operate against Elwell to preclude him from volunteering his testimony. But a Michigan court cannot, by entering the injunction to which Elwell and GM stipulated, dictate to a court in another jurisdiction that evidence relevant in the Bakers' case—a controversy to which Michigan is foreign—shall be inadmissible. This conclusion creates no general exception to the full faith and credit command, and surely does not permit a State to refuse to honor a sister state judgment based on the forum's choice of law or policy preferences. Rather, we simply recognize that, just as the mechanisms for enforcing a judgment do not travel with the judgment itself for purposes of Full Faith and Credit, see McElmoyle ex rel. Bailey v. Cohen, 13 Pet. 312, 10 L.Ed. 177 (1839); see also Restatement (Second) of Conflict of Laws § 99, and just as one State's judgment cannot automatically transfer title to land in another State, see Fall v. Eastin, 215 U.S. 1, 30 S.Ct. 3, 54 L.Ed. 65 (1909), similarly the Michigan decree cannot determine evidentiary issues in a lawsuit brought by parties who were not subject to the jurisdiction of the Michigan court. Cf. United States v. Nixon, 418 U.S. 683, 710, 94 S.Ct. 3090, 3108–3109, 41 L.Ed.2d 1039 (1974) ("[E]xceptions to the demand for every man's evidence are not lightly created nor expansively construed, for they are in derogation of the search for truth.").[12]

12. Justice Kennedy inexplicably reads into our decision a sweeping exception to full faith and credit based solely on "the integrity of Missouri's judicial processes." The Michigan judgment is not entitled to full faith and credit, we have endeavored to make plain, because it impermissibly interferes with Missouri's control of litigation brought by parties who were not before the Michigan court. Thus, Justice Kennedy's hypothetical, see ibid., misses the mark. If the Bakers had been parties to the Michigan proceedings and had actually litigated the privileged character of Elwell's testimony, the Bakers would of course be precluded from relitigating that issue in Missouri. See Cromwell v. County of Sac, 94 U.S. 351, 354, 24 L.Ed. 195 (1876) ("[D]etermination of a question directly involved in one action is conclusive as to that question in a second suit between the same parties. . . .").

The language of the consent decree is informative in this regard. Excluding the then-pending Georgia action from the ban on testimony by Elwell without GM's permission, the decree provides that it "shall not operate to interfere with the jurisdiction of the Court in ... Georgia." Elwell v. General Motors Corp., No. 91–115946NZ (Wayne Cty.) (Order Dismissing Plaintiff's Complaint and Granting Permanent Injunction, p. 2), App. 30 (emphasis added). But if the Michigan order, extended to the Georgia case, would have "interfer[ed] with the jurisdiction" of the Georgia court, Michigan's ban would, in the same way, "interfere with the jurisdiction" of courts in other States in cases similar to the one pending in Georgia.

In line with its recognition of the interference potential of the consent decree, GM provided in the settlement agreement that, if another court ordered Elwell to testify, his testimony would "in no way" render him vulnerable to suit in Michigan for violation of the injunction or agreement. See 86 F.3d, at 815, 820, n. 11. The Eighth Circuit regarded this settlement agreement provision as merely a concession by GM that "some courts might fail to extend full faith and credit to the [Michigan] injunction." Ibid. As we have explained, however, Michigan's power does not reach into a Missouri courtroom to displace the forum's own determination whether to admit or exclude evidence relevant in the Bakers' wrongful-death case before it. In that light, we see no altruism in GM's agreement not to institute contempt or breach-of-contract proceedings against Elwell in Michigan for giving subpoenaed testimony elsewhere. Rather, we find it telling that GM ruled out resort to the court that entered the injunction, for injunctions are ordinarily enforced by the enjoining court, not by a surrogate tribunal.

In sum, Michigan has no authority to shield a witness from another jurisdiction's subpoena power in a case involving persons and causes outside Michigan's governance. Recognition, under full faith and credit, is owed to dispositions Michigan has authority to order. But a Michigan decree cannot command obedience elsewhere on a matter the Michigan court lacks authority to resolve. See Thomas v. Washington Gas Light Co., 448 U.S. 261, 282–283, 100 S.Ct. 2647, 2661, 65 L.Ed.2d 757 (1980) (plurality opinion) ("Full faith and credit must be given to [a] determination that [a State's tribunal] had the authority to make; but by a parity of reasoning, full faith and credit need not be given to determinations that it had no power to make.").

For the reasons stated, the judgment of the Court of Appeals for the Eighth Circuit is reversed, and the case is remanded for further proceedings consistent with this opinion.

It is so ordered.

■ JUSTICE SCALIA, concurring in the judgment.

I agree with the Court that enforcement measures do not travel with sister-state judgments as preclusive effects do. It has long been established that "the judgment of a state court cannot be enforced out of the state by an execution issued within it." McElmoyle ex rel. Bailey

v. Cohen, 13 Pet. 312, 325, 10 L.Ed. 177 (1839). To recite that principle is to decide this case.

General Motors asked a District Court in Missouri to enforce a Michigan injunction. The Missouri court was no more obliged to enforce the Michigan injunction by preventing Elwell from presenting his testimony than it was obliged to enforce it by holding Elwell in contempt. The Full Faith and Credit Clause " 'did not make the judgments of other States domestic judgments to all intents and purposes, but only gave a general validity, faith, and credit to them, as evidence. No execution can issue upon such judgments without a new suit in the tribunals of other States.' " Thompson v. Whitman, 18 Wall. 457, 462–463, 21 L.Ed. 897 (1873) (emphasis added) (quoting J. Story, Conflict of Laws § 609). A judgment or decree of one State, to be sure, may be grounds for an action (or a defense to one) in another. But the Clause and its implementing statute

> "establish a rule of evidence, rather than of jurisdiction. While they make the record of a judgment, rendered after due notice in one State, conclusive evidence in the courts of another State, or of the United States, of the matter adjudged, they do not affect the jurisdiction, either of the court in which the judgment is rendered, or of the court in which it is offered in evidence. Judgments recovered in one State of the Union, when proved in the courts of another government, whether state or national, within the United States, differ from judgments recovered in a foreign country in no other respect than in not being reexaminable on their merits, nor impeachable for fraud in obtaining them, if rendered by a court having jurisdiction of the cause and of the parties."

Wisconsin v. Pelican Ins. Co., 127 U.S. 265, 291–292, 8 S.Ct. 1370, 1375, 32 L.Ed. 239 (1888) (citation omitted).

The judgment that General Motors obtained in Michigan " 'does not carry with it, into another State, the efficacy of a judgment upon property or persons, to be enforced by execution. To give it the force of a judgment in another State, it must be made a judgment there; and can only be executed in the latter as its laws may permit.' " Lynde v. Lynde, 181 U.S. 183, 187, 21 S.Ct. 555, 556, 45 L.Ed. 810 (1901) (quoting McElmoyle, supra, 13 Pet. at 325). See, e.g., Watts v. Waddle, 6 Pet. 389, 392, 8 L.Ed. 437 (1832), a case involving a suit to obtain an equity decree ordering the conveyance of land, duplicating such a decree already issued in another State.

Because neither the Full Faith and Credit Clause nor its implementing statute requires Missouri to execute the injunction issued by the courts of Michigan, I concur in the judgment.

■ JUSTICE KENNEDY, with whom JUSTICES O'CONNOR and THOMAS join, concurring in the judgment.

I concur in the judgment. In my view the case is controlled by well-settled full faith and credit principles which render the majority's extended analysis unnecessary and, with all due respect, problematic in some degree.

Issue Preclusion Against the United States Government

70 Iowa L.Rev. 113 (1984).
A. Leo Levin and Susan M. Leeson.

I. *Mendoza and Stauffer*

A. *Background*

In recent years, the Supreme Court has followed the general trend of modern cases to expand the scope of issue preclusion, broadening it beyond traditional common-law limits. For example, the Court has held that a patent holder whose patent has been declared invalid can be precluded from relitigating the validity of the patent against another alleged infringer. It has held that a litigant who was not a party to a federal suit may make offensive use of preclusion against the party who lost on the relevant issue in the first suit. The Court consistently has given preclusive effect to issues decided by state courts when a party seeks to relitigate in federal court. And it has held that when a criminal defendant in a state court has had a full and fair opportunity to litigate a search and seizure issue, preclusion prevents relitigation of the search and seizure issue in federal court under 42 U.S.C. § 1983.

In each of these cases, the Court used traditional preclusion analysis. It asked whether the party sought to be precluded already had a full and fair opportunity to litigate, whether preclusion would be unfair to either party, and whether judicial economy would be served by preclusion. The 1983 Term cases required the Court to consider not only these traditional factors, but also other concerns that arise when the United States government is a litigant.

B. *Mendoza v. United States*

Dr. Sergio Elejar Mendoza was a 73–year-old Filipino physician who filed a petition for naturalization in 1978 under a statute that had expired thirty-two years earlier. Mendoza claimed that he had been denied due process of law by the government's administration of the statute, specifically because naturalizations in the Philippines were halted for a nine-month period between October 1945 and August 1946. The district court and the Ninth Circuit Court of Appeals held that the government could not relitigate the due process issue because the issue had been decided against the government several years earlier in a decision that the government had not appealed.

The opinion of the court of appeals is noteworthy on several grounds and deserves careful analysis. The court framed the central issue on appeal as follows: Whether the trial court abused its discretion in precluding the government from relitigating the due process issue it had lost in 1975 in *In re Naturalization of 68 Filipino War Veterans.* Relying heavily on the Supreme Court's grant of broad discretion to trial courts to apply collateral estoppel offensively, a unanimous panel held that there was no abuse of discretion and affirmed.

Central to the court's holding that it was not unfair to preclude government relitigation was the fact that the government had withdrawn its appeal in *68 Filipinos.* The government's justification for failure to prosecute the appeal was that it had miscalculated the impact of the district court's holding. Specifically, the government claimed that in 1975 the State Department was of the view that the holding made possible no more than 25,000 naturalization petitions, but subsequently, the government became persuaded that the correct number was between 60,000 and 80,000. As a result, the government sought to relitigate an issue in 1982 that it had been willing to drop in 1975. The Ninth Circuit's opinion may be read as holding that the government should bear the consequences of its failure to understand the implications of its 1975 loss and its consequent acquiescence in the judgment of the trial court.

Permeating the opinion, however, is a sense that preclusion doctrine was viewed by the court primarily as a mechanism for achieving a desired result in a particular case. The Ninth Circuit seemed particularly concerned with fairness to Mendoza. The opinion went to great pains to point out that the persons who qualified to take advantage of *68 Filipinos* were of necessity over sixty years of age. All had fought with United States troops in World War II, and many, like Mendoza, had suffered imprisonment by the Japanese, and had survived the Bataan Death March. In the court's view, Congress' commitment to naturalization should be honored as a matter of simple justice. Estopping the government from relitigating the issue it lost in *68 Filipinos* was the vehicle for accomplishing that goal, and the estoppel was considered to be well within the discretion of the trial judge. The panel was not impressed by the government's "numbers theory," in part because its assertions were not supported by the record. The appellate court believed that the government had had a full and fair opportunity to litigate *68 Filipinos* no matter what its subsequent understanding of the significance of the decision might be. Hence, it was not unfair to preclude the government from relitigating; on the other hand, the result might have serious consequences for Mendoza if the court were to hold to the contrary.

The United States Supreme Court reversed the Ninth Circuit in a unanimous opinion written by Justice Rehnquist. It held that *"Parklane Hosiery*'s approval of nonmutual offensive collateral estoppel is not to be extended to the United States." Justice Rehnquist noted that the Supreme Court benefits from allowing several courts of appeals to explore difficult questions before the Court grants certiorari. This "percolation" of issues among the circuit courts can be helpful to the development of the law, and the Court typically waits for such intercircuit conflicts before granting petitions for certiorari. A rule that provided for nonmutual collateral estoppel against the government in such cases would "substantially thwart the development of important questions of law by freezing the first final decision rendered on a particular legal issue." The Justices agreed unanimously that the better policy is to allow thorough development of legal doctrine through litigation in multiple forums.

The purpose of collateral estoppel, of course, is to "relieve parties of the cost and vexation of multiple lawsuits, conserve judicial resources, and, by preventing inconsistent decisions, encourage reliance on adjudication." Paradoxically, as Justice Rehnquist explained, application of nonmutual estoppel against the government might serve to waste rather than to conserve judicial resources. This paradox finds its matrix in the dramatic differences between the litigation conduct of the government and that of private parties.

Only a small fraction of the cases lost by the government are ever appealed. The Solicitor General determines when to appeal from a judgment adverse to the United States and such appeals are not authorized routinely. The Solicitor General is even more circumspect in seeking Supreme Court review. The state of the Supreme Court's docket is an important factor in that decision, as is the Court's practice of waiting for intercircuit conflicts before granting the government's petitions for certiorari. n46 Moreover, these policies affect thousands of cases each year.

Application of nonmutual estoppel against the United States would force the Solicitor General to seek review of virtually all adverse decisions. Phrased differently, such a rule might result in "requiring the government to abandon virtually any exercise of discretion in seeking to review judgments unfavorable to it." Allowing the government to relitigate thus contributes to the conservation of appellate court resources.

The focus of the Supreme Court, understandably, is on the appellate phase of litigation. Failure to apply preclusion against the government, however, appears to have rather different implications for trial court resources. Quite aside from the burdens borne by individual litigants, relitigation places heavy burdens on trial courts. The point was made effectively by Judge Meanor in *Pharmadyne Laboratories v. Kennedy,* a case involving the Food and Drug Administration:

[T]he institutional interests of the lower federal courts and those of the Supreme Court may differ. The lower courts, overburdened as they are, might like to be free from repetitive litigation over the same issue in different districts and circuits, unless, perhaps, there is at stake an issue of overriding public importance. The Supreme Court has a somewhat contrary interest to the end that it receive only well refined and precise issues. To achieve that often may take multiple decisions on a given point.

A further reason for refusing to preclude the government in *Mendoza,* however, had little to do with traditional preclusion rationale. Over the years executive branch policies change. Policy choices made by one Administration often are reevaluated by another Administration. In a sense, that is what democratic elections are all about. The Supreme Court recognized as much. For this reason, courts must "be careful" when they seek to apply expanding rules of preclusion in government litigation. Preclusion in the instant case, said Justice Rehnquist, would freeze into law the immigration policy of one Administration that had been properly rejected by another. It is not for the judicial branch to constrict such flexibility.

NOTE: NONMUTUAL PRECLUSION AGAINST STATES

Mendoza has evoked much discussion and some disagreement from the commentators. The federal case law is not entirely consistent. As the most conspicuous exception to the federal rule that mutuality (as in *Parklane Hosiery*) is not required, it gives the federal government a special status. Should the *Mendoza* rule allow nonmutual issue preclusion against state governments? Judging from the reported opinions of the state courts, there is no clear consensus on whether issue preclusion should apply against state governments.

CHAPTER XII

APPEALS

A. THE FINAL JUDGMENT RULE AND ITS EXCEPTIONS

The frequency of trials in civil cases in the federal courts has declined sharply, by about four-fifths, over the past 50 years. More law suits are settled and also more law suits are adjudicated through dispositive rulings (at law and in practice) by the trial courts. The settlements are not subject to any kind of appellate review. Many of the important pretrial and pre-judgment rulings are not reviewed by an appellate court largely because of the restrictions of the final judgment rule.

Professor Stephen C. Yeazell in The Misunderstood Consequences of Modern Civil Process, 1994 Wisconsin Law Review 631, 636–637 thinks these changes are due to the impact of Federal Rules of Civil Procedure which focus not on the trial but on a variety of pretrial motions and other activities prior to trial. He points out that 60 years ago, 63% of the adjudicated terminations of civil cases were trials and directed verdicts (whose results are dependent on the evidence submitted at trial). By1990, trials accounted for only 11% of all adjudications; the remainder were disposed of before trial, the majority by pretrial motion.

Professor Yeazell thinks these procedural changes involve a considerable reallocation of judicial powers. "Trial courts now enjoy effective insulation from appellate review for a greater proportion of their decisions than was the case 50 years ago." One of his observations is that "the final judgment rule results in late and little review."

Apart from historical reasons, the major justifications for the final judgment rule, which prohibits the immediate appeal of most federal district court orders other than final judgments, are (1) that appeals from interlocutory orders create delay; (2) that permitting extensive interlocutory appeals would indicate a lack of respect for the decisions of federal district judges; (3) that combining all the issues in a case into a single appeal saves time (for appellate courts) and (4) that reserving appeal until after the final judgment emphasizes the deference that Courts of Appeals in the federal system feel they owe to trial judges, who must often make very diverse rulings with relative promptness.

Interlocutory orders are those made at the prejudgment stage, mostly before the trial has even begun. Critics of the final judgment rule contend that more such rulings can be appealed without interfering with other aspects of the progress of litigation. Some pretrial rulings, even if not final and therefore not appealable as of right, may effectively end the lawsuit. Suppose defendant is sued in an out-of-state forum which he believes will not be sympathetic to him or his case and in which it will be expensive to litigate. If his motion to dismiss for lack of personal jurisdiction or for a change of venue is denied, the defendant will have no right to challenge the ruling immediately on appeal because it is not a final order. Even if he thinks the district court is wrong, the defendant may feel it prudent under those circumstances to settle the case, thereby foreclosing any possibility of appellate review. This was likely the situation in Helicopteros (Chapter II) and Piper Aircraft v. Reyno (Chapter II). Consider also Justice Scalia's comment concurring in Lauro Lines v. Chasser (Chapter II): "While it is true . . . that the right not to be sued elsewhere than in Naples is not fully vindicated—indeed to be utterly frank, it is positively destroyed—by permitting the trial to occur and reversing the outcome, . . ."

Firestone Tire & Rubber Co. v. Risjord

Supreme Court of the United States, 1981.
449 U.S. 368, 101 S.Ct. 669, 66 L.Ed.2d 571.

■ JUSTICE MARSHALL delivered the opinion of the Court.

This case presents the question whether a party may take an appeal, pursuant to 28 U.S.C. § 1291, from a district court order denying a motion to disqualify counsel for the opposing party in a civil case. The United States Court of Appeals for the Eighth Circuit held that such orders are not appealable, but made its decision prospective only and therefore reached the merits of the challenged order. We hold that orders denying motions to disqualify counsel are not appealable final decisions under § 1291, and we therefore vacate the judgment of the Court of Appeals and remand with instructions that the appeal be dismissed for lack of jurisdiction.

I

Respondent is lead counsel for the plaintiffs in four product-liability suits seeking damages from petitioner and other manufacturers of multipiece truck tire rims for injuries caused by alleged defects in their products. The complaints charge petitioner and the other defendants with various negligent, willful, or intentional failures to correct or to warn of the supposed defects in the rims. Plaintiffs seek both compensatory and exemplary damages.

Petitioner was at all relevant times insured by Home Insurance Co. (Home) under a contract providing that Home would be responsible only for some types of liability beyond a minimum "deductible" amount. Home was also an occasional client of respondent's law firm. Based on these facts, petitioner in May 1979 filed a motion to disqualify respondent from further representation of the plaintiffs.

* * *

Under § 1291, the courts of appeals are vested with "jurisdiction of appeals from all final decisions of the district courts . . . except where a direct review may be had in the Supreme Court." We have consistently interpreted this language as indicating that a party may not take an appeal under this section until there has been "a decision by the District Court that 'ends the litigation on the merits and leaves nothing for the court to do but execute the judgment.' " Coopers & Lybrand v. Livesay, 437 U.S. 463, 467, 98 S.Ct. 2454, 2457, 57 L.Ed.2d 351 (1978), quoting Catlin v. United States, 324 U.S. 229, 233, 65 S.Ct. 631, 633, 89 L.Ed. 911 (1945). This rule, that a party must ordinarily raise all claims of error in a single appeal following final judgment on the merits, serves a number of important purposes. It emphasizes the deference that appellate courts owe to the trial judge as the individual initially called upon to decide the many questions of law and fact that occur in the course of a trial. Permitting piecemeal appeals would undermine the independence of the district judge, as well as the special role that individual plays in our judicial system. In addition, the rule is in accordance with the sensible policy of "avoid[ing] the obstruction to just claims that would come from permitting the harassment and cost of a succession of separate appeals from the various rulings to which a litigation may give rise, from its initiation to entry of judgment." Cobbledick v. United States, 309 U.S. 323, 325, 60 S.Ct. 540, 541, 84 L.Ed. 783 (1940). See DiBella v. United States, 369 U.S. 121, 124, 82 S.Ct. 654, 656, 7 L.Ed.2d 614 (1962). The rule also serves the important purpose of promoting efficient judicial administration. Eisen v. Carlisle & Jacquelin, 417 U.S. 156, 170, 94 S.Ct. 2140, 2149, 40 L.Ed.2d 732 (1974).

Our decisions have recognized, however, a narrow exception to the requirement that all appeals under § 1291 await final judgment on the merits. In *Cohen v. Beneficial Industrial Loan Corp., supra,* we held that a "small class" of orders that did not end the main litigation were nevertheless final and appealable pursuant to § 1291. Cohen was a shareholder's derivative action in which the Federal District Court refused to apply a state statute requiring a plaintiff in such a suit to post security for costs. The defendant appealed the ruling without awaiting final judgment on the merits, and the Court of Appeals ordered the trial court to require that costs be posted. We held that the Court of Appeals properly assumed jurisdiction of the appeal pursuant to § 1291 because the District Court's order constituted a final determination of a claim "separable from, and collateral to," the merits of the main proceeding, because it was "too important to be denied review," and because it was "too independent of the cause itself to require that appellate consideration be deferred until the whole case is adjudicated." Id., at 546, 69 S.Ct. at 1225. Cohen did not establish new law; rather, it continued a tradition of giving § 1291 a "practical rather than a technical construction." Ibid. See, e. g., United States v. River Rouge Improvement Co., 269 U.S. 411, 413–414, 46 S.Ct. 144, 70 L.Ed. 339 (1926); Bronson v. LaCrosse & Milwaukee R. Co., 67 U.S. 524–531, 2 Black 524, 530–531, 17 L.Ed. 347 (1862); Forgay v. Conrad, 47 U.S. 201, 203, 6 How. 201, 203, 12 L.Ed. 404

(1848); Whiting v. Bank of the United States, 38 U.S. 6, 15, 13 Pet. 6, 15, 10 L.Ed. 33 (1839). We have recently defined this limited class of final "collateral orders" in these terms: "[T]he order must conclusively determine the disputed question, resolve an important issue completely separate from the merits of the action, and be effectively unreviewable on appeal from a final judgment." Coopers & Lybrand v. Livesay, supra, 437 U.S. at 468, 98 S.Ct. at 2457 (footnote omitted). See Abney v. United States, 431 U.S. 651, 658, 97 S.Ct. 2034, 2039, 52 L.Ed.2d 651 (1977).

* * *

To be appealable as a final collateral order, the challenged order must constitute "a complete, formal and, in the trial court, final rejection," Abney v. United States, supra, 431 U.S. at 659, 97 S.Ct. at 2040, of a claimed right "where denial of immediate review would render impossible any review whatsoever," United States v. Ryan, 402 U.S. 530, 533, 91 S.Ct. 1580, 1582, 29 L.Ed.2d 85 (1971). Thus we have permitted appeals prior to criminal trials when a defendant has claimed that he is about to be subjected to forbidden double jeopardy, Abney v. United States, supra, or a violation of his constitutional right to bail, Stack v. Boyle, 342 U.S. 1, 72 S.Ct. 1, 96 L.Ed. 3 (1951) because those situations, like the posting of security for costs involved in Cohen, "each involved an asserted right the legal and practical value of which would be destroyed if it were not vindicated before trial." United States v. MacDonald, 435 U.S. 850, 860, 98 S.Ct. 1547, 1552, 56 L.Ed.2d 18 (1978). By way of contrast, we have generally denied review of pretrial discovery orders, see, e. g., United States v. Ryan, supra; Cobbledick v. United States, supra. Our rationale has been that in the rare case when appeal after final judgment will not cure an erroneous discovery order, a party may defy the order, permit a contempt citation to be entered against him, and challenge the order on direct appeal of the contempt ruling. See Cobbledick v. United States, supra, at 327, 60 S.Ct. at 542. We have also rejected immediate appealability under § 1291 of claims that "may fairly be assessed" only after trial, United States v. MacDonald, supra, at 860, and those involving "considerations that are 'enmeshed in the factual and legal issues comprising the plaintiff's cause of action.'" Coopers & Lybrand v. Livesay, 437 U.S., at 469, 98 S.Ct., at 2458, quoting Mercantile National Bank v. Langdeau, 371 U.S. 555, 558, 83 S.Ct. 520, 522, 9 L.Ed.2d 523 (1963).

An order refusing to disqualify counsel plainly falls within the large class of orders that are indeed reviewable on appeal after final judgment, and not within the much smaller class of those that are not. The propriety of the district court's denial of a disqualification motion will often be difficult to assess until its impact on the underlying litigation may be evaluated, which is normally only after final judgment. The decision whether to disqualify an attorney ordinarily turns on the peculiar factual situation of the case then at hand, and the order embodying such a decision will rarely, if ever, represent a final rejection of a claim of fundamental right that cannot effectively be reviewed following judgment on the merits. In the case before us, petitioner has made no showing that its opportunity for meaningful review will perish unless immediate appeal is permitted. On the contrary, should the Court of Appeals conclude after the trial has ended that permitting continuing representation was prejudicial error, it would retain its usual authority to vacate the judgment appealed from and order a new trial. That remedy seems plainly adequate should petitioner's concerns of possible injury ultimately prove well founded. As the Second Circuit has recently observed, the potential harm that might be caused by requiring that a party await final judgment before it may appeal even when the denial of its disqualification motion was erroneous does not "diffe[r] in any significant way from the harm resulting from other interlocutory orders that may be erroneous, such as orders requiring discovery over a work-product objection or orders denying motions for recusal of the trial judge." Armstrong v. McAlpin, 625 F.2d 433, 438 (1980), cert. pending, No. 80–431. But interlocutory orders are not appealable "on the mere ground that they may be erroneous." Will v. United States, 389 U.S. 90, 98, n. 6, 88 S.Ct. 269, 275, n. 6, 19 L.Ed.2d 305 (1967). Permitting wholesale appeals on that ground not only would constitute an unjustified waste of scarce judicial resources, but also would transform the limited exception carved out in Cohen into a license for broad disregard of the finality rule imposed by Congress in § 1291. This we decline to do.[13]

III

We hold that a district court's order denying a motion to disqualify counsel is not appealable under § 1291 prior to final judgment in the underlying litigation. Insofar as the Eighth Circuit reached this conclusion, its decision is correct. But because its decision was contrary to precedent in the Circuit, the court went further and reached the merits of the order appealed from. This approach, however, overlooks the fact that the finality requirement embodied in § 1291 is

---

13. Although there may be situations in which a party will be irreparably damaged if forced to wait until final resolution of the underlying litigation before securing review of an order denying its motion to disqualify opposing counsel, it is not necessary, in order to resolve those situations, to create a general rule permitting the appeal of all such orders. In the proper circumstances, the moving party may seek sanctions short of disqualification, such as a protective order limiting counsel's ability to disclose or to act on purportedly confidential information. If additional facts in support of the motion develop in the course of the litigation, the moving party might ask the trial court to reconsider its decision. Ultimately, if dissatisfied with the result in the District Court and absolutely determined that it will be harmed irreparably, a party may seek to have the question certified for interlocutory appellate review pursuant to 28 U.S.C. § 1292(b), and, in the exceptional circumstances for which it was designed, a writ of mandamus from the court of appeals might be available. See In re Continental Investment Corp., supra, 637 F.2d, at 7; Community Broadcasting of Boston, Inc. v. FCC, 178 U.S.App.D.C., at 262, 546 F.2d, at 1028. See generally Comment, The Appealability of Orders Denying Motions for Disqualification of Counsel in Federal Courts, 45 U.Chi.L.Rev. 450, 468–480 (1978). We need not be concerned with the availability of such extraordinary procedures in the case before us, because petitioner has made no colorable claim that the harm it might suffer if forced to await the final outcome of the litigation before appealing the denial of its disqualification motion is any greater than the harm suffered by any litigant forced to wait until the termination of the trial before challenging interlocutory orders it considers erroneous.

jurisdictional in nature. If the appellate court finds that the order from which a party seeks to appeal does not fall within the statute, its inquiry is over. A court lacks discretion to consider the merits of a case over which it is without jurisdiction, and thus, by definition, a jurisdictional ruling may never be made prospective only. We therefore hold that because the Court of Appeals was without jurisdiction to hear the appeal, it was without authority to decide the merits. * * *

NOTES

A.   What relief will be ordered if this case proceeds to trial, plaintiff wins, and the appeals court then determines that defendant's disqualification motion should have been granted? Would it save judicial time and energy to have that issue fully adjudicated prior to trial? Whose judicial time and energy?

B.   Why does the Supreme Court say that a rule like the one enunciated in Firestone Tire can never be prospective only?

C.   The often considerable impact of interlocutory rulings extends to transfers of venue in the federal courts. In recent federal civil cases, researchers found that the plaintiff's rate of winning drops from 59% where there is no transfer to 29% in transferred cases. "This dramatic effect prevails over the range of substantively different types of cases." K. Clermont & T. Eisenberg, Exorcising the Evil of Forum Shopping, 80 Cornell L.Rev. 1507 (1995).

Lauro Lines S.R.L. v. Chasser

Supreme Court of the United States, 1989.
490 U.S. 495, 109 S.Ct. 1976, 104 L.Ed.2d 548.

See Chapter II

Behrens v. Pelletier

Supreme Court of the United States, 1996.
516 U.S. 299, 116 S.Ct. 834, 133 L.Ed. 2d 773.

■ Justice Scalia delivered the opinion of the Court.

In Mitchell v. Forsyth, 472 U.S. 511, 105 S.Ct. 2806, 86 L.Ed.2d 411 (1985), we held that a district court's rejection of a defendant's qualified-immunity defense is a "final decision" subject to immediate appeal under the general appellate jurisdiction statute, 28 U.S.C. § 1291 (1994 ed.). The question presented in this case is whether a defendant's immediate appeal of an unfavorable qualified-immunity ruling on his motion to dismiss deprives the court of appeals of jurisdiction over a second appeal, also based on qualified immunity, immediately following denial of summary judgment.

I

In 1983, South Coast Savings and Loan Association, a new institution, applied to the Federal Home Loan Bank Board (FHLBB or Board) for the approval necessary to obtain account insurance from the

Federal Savings and Loan Insurance Corporation (FSLIC).[12] Under FHLBB regulations, approval of new institutions was to be withheld if their "financial policies or management" were found to be "unsafe" for any of various reasons, including "character of the management." Accordingly, when FHLBB approved South Coast for FSLIC insurance in March 1984, it imposed a number of requirements, including the condition that South Coast "provide for employment of a qualified full-time executive managing officer, subject to approval by the Principal Supervisory Agent"—FHLBB's term for the president of the regional Home Loan Bank when operating in his oversight capacity on behalf of FHLBB. Resolution No. 84–164, ¶ 10(p) (Mar. 29, 1984). The Board's resolution also required that, for a period of three years, any change in South Coast's chief management position be approved by FHLBB.

Shortly after obtaining FHLBB's conditional approval, South Coast was succeeded in interest by Pioneer Savings and Loan Association, another new institution. Pioneer named respondent Pelletier as its managing officer, subject to FHLBB consent, which Pioneer sought in mid-May 1985. Only a few weeks earlier, however, on April 23, 1985, FHLBB had declared insolvent Beverly Hills Savings and Loan Association, where respondent had at one time held a senior executive position. An inquiry by FSLIC pointed to potential misconduct by high-level management of the failed institution, which ultimately became the subject of a FSLIC lawsuit against several Beverly Hills officers, including respondent.

The FSLIC suit had not yet been filed at the time Pioneer sought the Board's consent to hire respondent; but FSLIC's pending investigation into Beverly Hills' collapse caused petitioner Behrens, the FHLBB "Supervisory Agent" then responsible for monitoring Pioneer's operations, to write Pioneer on May 8, 1986, withholding approval and advising that respondent be replaced. On receipt of the letter Pioneer asked respondent to resign and, when he refused, fired him.

Three years later, in 1989, respondent brought suit in federal court, naming petitioner as defendant in a complaint that included Bivens damages claims for two alleged constitutional wrongs. See Bivens v. Six Unknown Fed. Narcotics Agents, 403 U.S. 388, 91 S.Ct. 1999, 29 L.Ed.2d 619 (1971). Respondent charged, first, that petitioner's action in writing a letter that had effectively discharged him from his post at Pioneer, in summary fashion and without notice or opportunity to be heard, violated his right to procedural due process. Second, he claimed that he had been deprived of substantive due process by petitioner's alleged interference with his "clearly established and Constitutionally protected property and liberty rights . . . to specific employment and to pursue his profession free from undue governmental interference." The complaint alleged that petitioner's letter, along with other, continuing efforts to harm his reputation, had

---

12. FHLBB, FSLIC and the regulatory scheme described in this opinion no longer exist, having been eliminated by the Financial Institutions Reform, Recovery, and Enforcement Act of 1989, 103 Stat. 183.

cost respondent not only his position at Pioneer, but also his livelihood within the savings and loan industry. * * *

Petitioner filed a motion to dismiss or, in the alternative, for summary judgment. With regard to the Bivens claims, he asserted a statute-of-limitations defense and claimed qualified immunity from suit on the ground that his actions, taken in a governmental capacity, "did not violate clearly established statutory or constitutional rights." Harlow v. Fitzgerald, 457 U.S. 800, 818, 102 S.Ct. 2727, 2738, 73 L.Ed.2d 396 (1982). The District Court [denied petitioner's motion]. The court also denied petitioner's summary judgment motion, without prejudice, on the ground that it was premature given the lack of discovery.

Petitioner immediately appealed the District Court's implicit denial of his qualified-immunity defense regarding the remaining Bivens claim. The Court of Appeals entertained the appeal, notwithstanding its interlocutory nature, holding that "a denial of qualified immunity is an appealable 'final' order under the test set forth in Cohen v. Beneficial Indust. Loan Corp., 337 U.S. 541, 69 S.Ct. 1221, 93 L.Ed. 1528 (1949) . . ., regardless of whether that denial takes the form of a refusal to grant a defendant's motion to dismiss or a denial of summary judgment." Pelletier v. Federal Home Loan Bank of San Francisco, 968 F.2d 865, 870 (C.A.9 1992). It said in dictum, however, that a defendant claiming qualified immunity could not "take advantage of the several opportunities for immediate appeal afforded him by bringing repeated pretrial appeals," and that "[o]ne such interlocutory appeal is all that a government official is entitled to and all that we will entertain." On the merits of the appeal, the court rejected the argument that petitioner enjoyed qualified immunity because he had not violated any "clearly established right." It said that the question whether respondent had a constitutionally protected property interest in his Pioneer employment (subject, as it was, to regulatory approval) was not properly before the court, since the claims relating specifically to his discharge had been dismissed as time-barred. (The Court of Appeals noted in dictum, however, that the District Court had applied an unduly short limitations period.) With respect to the claimed deprivation of post-Pioneer employment, the court held that the "nebulous theories of conspiracy" set out in respondent's complaint—although "insufficient to survive a motion for summary judgment"—made out a proper Bivens claim.

Upon remand, the District Court reversed its earlier statute-of-limitations ruling in light of the Court of Appeals' dictum, and reinstated the claims relating to employment at Pioneer. After discovery, petitioner moved for summary judgment on qualified-immunity grounds, contending that his actions had not violated any "clearly established" right of respondent regarding his employment at Pioneer or elsewhere. The District Court denied the motion with the unadorned statement that "[m]aterial issues of fact remain as to defendant Behrens on the Bivens claim." Petitioner filed a notice of appeal, which, on respondent's motion, the District Court certified as frivolous. In an unpublished order, the Ninth Circuit dismissed the appeal "for lack of jurisdiction."

II

Section 1291 of Title 28, U.S.C., gives courts of appeals jurisdiction over "all final decisions" of district courts, except those for which appeal is to be had to this Court. The requirement of finality precludes consideration of decisions that are subject to revision, and even of "fully consummated decisions [that] are but steps towards final judgment in which they will merge." Cohen, supra. It does not, however, bar review of all prejudgment orders. In Cohen, we described a "small class" of district court decisions that, though short of final judgment, are immediately appealable because they "finally determine claims of right separable from, and collateral to, rights asserted in the action, too important to be denied review and too independent of the cause itself to require that appellate consideration be deferred until the whole case is adjudicated." The issue in the present case is the extent to which orders denying governmental officers' assertions of qualified immunity come within the Cohen category of appealable decisions.

As set forth in Harlow v. Fitzgerald, 457 U.S. 800, 102 S.Ct. 2727, 73 L.Ed.2d 396 (1982), the qualified-immunity defense "shield[s] [government agents] from liability for civil damages insofar as their conduct does not violate clearly established statutory or constitutional rights of which a reasonable person would have known," Harlow adopted this criterion of "objective legal reasonableness," rather than good faith, precisely in order to "permit the defeat of insubstantial claims without resort to trial." Unsurprisingly, then, we later found the immunity to be "an entitlement not to stand trial or face the other burdens of litigation, conditioned on the resolution of the essentially legal [immunity] question." Mitchell v. Forsyth, 472 U.S., at 526, 105 S.Ct., at 2815. And, as with district-court rejection of claims to other such entitlements distinct from the merits, see, e.g., Puerto Rico Aqueduct, supra, at 145–146, 113 S.Ct., at 688–689, (Eleventh Amendment immunity); Abney v. United States, 431 U.S. 651, 662, 97 S.Ct. 2034, 2041–2042, 52 L.Ed.2d 651 (1977) (right not to be subjected to double jeopardy), we held that "a district court's denial of a claim of qualified immunity, to the extent that it turns on an issue of law, is an appealable 'final decision' within the meaning of 28 U.S.C. § 1291 notwithstanding the absence of a final judgment." Mitchell, supra, at 530.

While Mitchell did not say that a defendant could appeal from denial of a qualified immunity defense more than once, it clearly contemplated that he could raise the defense at successive stages:

> "Unless the plaintiff's allegations state a claim of violation of clearly established law, a defendant pleading qualified immunity is entitled to dismissal before the commencement of discovery. Even if the plaintiff's complaint adequately alleges the commission of acts that violated clearly established law, the defendant is entitled to summary judgment if discovery fails to uncover evidence

sufficient to create a genuine issue as to whether the defendant in fact committed those acts." 472 U.S., at 526 (citation omitted).

Thus, Mitchell clearly establishes that an order rejecting the defense of qualified immunity at *either* the dismissal stage or the summary-judgment stage is a "final" judgment subject to immediate appeal. Since an unsuccessful appeal from a denial of dismissal cannot possibly render the later denial of a motion for summary judgment any less "final," it follows that petitioner's appeal falls within § 1291 and dismissal was improper.

Indeed, it is easier to argue that the denial of summary judgment—the order sought to be appealed here—is the more "final" of the two orders. That is the reasoning the First Circuit adopted in holding that denial of a motion to dismiss on absolute-immunity grounds was not "final" where the defendant had stated that, if unsuccessful, he would later seek summary judgment on qualified-immunity grounds: "Since the district court has not yet determined whether [the defendant] has qualified immunity, and that he will have to stand trial, its decision is not an appealable collateral order." The problem with this approach, however, is that it would logically bar any appeal at the motion-to-dismiss stage where there is a possibility of presenting an immunity defense on summary judgment; that possibility would cause the motion-to-dismiss decision to be not "final" as to the defendant's right not to stand trial. The First Circuit sought to avoid this difficulty by saying that the defendant could render the motion-to-dismiss denial final by waiving his right to appeal the summary-judgment denial. But quite obviously, eliminating the ability to appeal the second order does not eliminate the possibility that the second order will vindicate the defendant's right not to stand trial, and therefore does not eliminate the supposed reason for declaring the first order nonfinal.

The source of the First Circuit's confusion was its mistaken conception of the scope of protection afforded by qualified immunity. Harlow and Mitchell make clear that the defense is meant to give government officials a right, not merely to avoid "standing trial," but also to avoid the burdens of "such pretrial matters as discovery . . . , as '[i]nquiries of this kind can be peculiarly disruptive of effective government.'" Mitchell, supra, at 526 (emphasis added) (quoting from Harlow, supra, at 817). Whether or not a later summary-judgment motion is granted, denial of a motion to dismiss is conclusive as to this right. We would have thought that these and other statements from Mitchell and Harlow had settled the point, questioned by Justice BREYER, that this right is important enough to support an immediate appeal. If it were not, however, the consequence would be, not that only one pretrial appeal could be had in a given case, as Justice BREYER proposes, but rather, that there could be no immediate appeal from denial of a motion to dismiss but only from denial of summary judgment. That conclusion is foreclosed by Mitchell, which unmistakably envisioned immediate appeal of "[t]he denial of a defendant's motion for dismissal or summary judgment on the ground of qualified immunity."

The Court of Appeals in the present case, in the first of its two decisions, rested its "one-appeal" pronouncement upon the proposition that resolving the question of entitlement to qualified immunity "should not require more than one judiciously timed appeal." Pelletier, 968 F.2d, at 871. It did not explain how this proposition pertains to the question of finality, but we suppose it could be argued that a category of appeals thought to be needless or superfluous does not raise a claim of right "too important to be denied review," as our Cohen finality jurisprudence requires, see 337 U.S., at 546, 69 S.Ct., at 1225–1226. In any event, the proposition is not sound. That one appeal on the immunity issue may not be enough is illustrated by the history of respondent's claims for loss of employment at Pioneer in the present case. Because these claims had initially been dismissed as time-barred, the Court of Appeals refused to decide (and thus evidently regarded as an open question) whether one who holds his job subject to regulatory approval can assert a constitutionally cognizable expectation of continued employment. Thus, the question whether petitioner was entitled to immunity on these claims was not presented to any court until petitioner's summary-judgment motion—and, by operation of the Ninth Circuit's one-appeal rule, has never been addressed by an appellate court.

That is assuredly an unusual set of circumstances, but even in a case proceeding in a more normal fashion resolution of the immunity question may "require more than one judiciously timed appeal," because the legally relevant factors bearing upon the Harlow question will be different on summary judgment than on an earlier motion to dismiss. At that earlier stage, it is the defendant's conduct as alleged in the complaint that is scrutinized for "objective legal reasonableness." On summary judgment, however, the plaintiff can no longer rest on the pleadings, see Fed. Rule Civ. Proc. 56, and the court looks to the evidence before it (in the light most favorable to the plaintiff) when conducting the Harlow inquiry. It is no more true that the defendant who has unsuccessfully appealed denial of a motion to dismiss has no need to appeal denial of a motion for summary judgment, than it is that the defendant who has unsuccessfully made a motion to dismiss has no need to make a motion for summary judgment.

The Court of Appeals expressed concern that a second appeal would tend to have the illegitimate purpose of delaying the proceedings. Undeniably, the availability of a second appeal affords an opportunity for abuse, but we have no reason to believe that abuse has often occurred. To the contrary, successive pretrial assertions of immunity seem to be a rare occurrence. Moreover, if and when abuse does occur, as we observed in the analogous context of interlocutory appeals on the issue of double jeopardy, "it is well within the supervisory powers of the courts of appeals to establish summary procedures and calendars to weed out frivolous claims." Abney, 431 U.S., at 662, n. 8, 97 S.Ct., at 2042, n. 8. In the present case, for example, the District Court appropriately certified petitioner's immunity appeal as "frivolous" in light of the Court of Appeals' (unfortunately erroneous) one-appeal precedent. This practice, which has been embraced by several Circuits, enables the district court to retain jurisdiction pending summary disposition of the appeal, and thereby minimizes disruption of the ongoing proceedings. In any event, the question before us here—whether there is jurisdiction over the appeal, as opposed to whether the appeal is frivolous—must be determined by focusing upon the category of order appealed from, rather than upon the strength of the grounds for reversing the order. "Appeal rights cannot depend on the facts of a particular case." Carroll v. United States, 354 U.S. 394, 405, 77 S.Ct. 1332, 1339, 1 L.Ed.2d 1442 (1957). As we have said, an order denying qualified immunity, to the extent it turns on an "issue of law," Mitchell, 472 U.S., at 530, is immediately appealable.

III

Our rejection of the one-interlocutory-appeal rule does not dispose of this case. Respondent proposes two other reasons why appeal of denial of the summary-judgment motion is not available. First, he argues that no appeal is available where, even if the District Court's qualified-immunity ruling is reversed, the defendant will be required to endure discovery and trial on matters separate from the claims against which immunity was asserted. Respondent reasons that a ruling which does not reach all the claims does not "conclusively determin[e] the defendant's claim of right not to stand trial," id., at 527, and thus the order denying immunity cannot be said to be "final" within the meaning of Cohen.

It is far from clear that, given the procedural posture of the present case, respondent would be entitled to the benefit of the proposition for which he argues; but we will address the proposition on its merits. The Courts of Appeals have almost unanimously rejected it, and so do we. The Harlow right to immunity is a right to immunity from certain claims, not from litigation in general; when immunity with respect to those claims has been finally denied, appeal must be available, and cannot be foreclosed by the mere addition of other claims to the suit. Making appealability depend upon such a factor, particular to the case at hand, would violate the principle discussed above, that appealability determinations are made for classes of decisions, not individual orders in specific cases. Apart from these objections in principle, the practical effect of respondent's proposal would be intolerable. If the district court rules erroneously, the qualified-immunity right not to be subjected to pretrial proceedings will be eliminated, so long as the plaintiff has alleged (with or without evidence to back it up) violation of one "clearly established" right; and both that and the further right not to be subjected to trial itself will be eliminated, so long as the complaint seeks injunctive relief (for which no "clearly established" right need be alleged).

Second, respondent asserts that appeal of denial of the summary-judgment motion is not available because the denial rested on the ground that "[m]aterial issues of fact remain." This, he contends, renders the denial unappealable under last Term's decision in Johnson v. Jones, 515 U.S., at 313–315, 115 S.Ct., at 2156–2157. That is a misreading of the case. Denial of summary judgment often includes a determination that there are controverted issues of material fact, see Fed. Rule Civ. Proc. 56, and Johnson surely does not mean that every such denial of summary judgment is nonappealable. Johnson held, simply, that determinations of evidentiary sufficiency at summary judgment are not immediately appealable merely because they happen to arise in a qualified-immunity case; if what is at issue in the sufficiency determination is nothing more than whether the evidence could support a finding that particular conduct occurred, the question decided is not truly "separable" from the plaintiff's claim, and hence there is no "final decision" under Cohen and Mitchell. See 515 U.S., at 313–316, 115 S.Ct., at 2156–2157. Johnson reaffirmed that summary-judgment determinations are appealable when they resolve a dispute concerning an "abstract issu[e] of law" relating to qualified immunity, id., at 317, 115 S.Ct., at 2158—typically, the issue whether the federal right allegedly infringed was "clearly established."

Here the District Court's denial of petitioner's summary-judgment motion necessarily determined that certain conduct attributed to petitioner (which was controverted) constituted a violation of clearly established law. Johnson permits petitioner to claim on appeal that all of the conduct which the District Court deemed sufficiently supported for purposes of summary judgment met the Harlow standard of "objective legal reasonableness." This argument was presented by petitioner in the trial court, and there is no apparent impediment to its being raised on appeal. And while the District Court, in denying petitioner's summary-judgment motion, did not identify the particular charged conduct that it deemed adequately supported, Johnson recognizes that under such circumstances "a court of appeals may have to undertake a cumbersome review of the record to determine what facts the district court, in the light most favorable to the nonmoving party, likely assumed." Johnson, supra, at 139, 115 S.Ct., at 2159. That is the task now facing the Court of Appeals in this case.

The judgment of the Court of Appeals is reversed, and the case is remanded for proceedings consistent with this opinion.

It is so ordered.

■ JUSTICE BREYER, with whom JUSTICE STEVENS joins, dissenting.

I do not agree with the Court's holding that those asserting a defense of qualified immunity are entitled, as a matter of course, to more than one interlocutory appeal. Rather, in my view, the law normally permits a single interlocutory appeal, and not more than one such appeal, from denials of a defendant's pretrial motions to dismiss a case on grounds of qualified immunity. The "collateral order" doctrine's basic rationale, this Court's precedents, and several practical considerations lead to this conclusion.

* * *

Judges have . . . created what is, in effect, a nonstatutory exception, authorizing a special set of interlocutory appeals, where a trial court's interlocutory order is a "collateral order" that satisfies the statutory term "final" for purposes of § 1291. See Cohen v. Beneficial Industrial Loan Corp., 337 U.S. 541, 545–547, 69 S.Ct. 1221, 1225–1226, 93 L.Ed. 1528 (1949). The trial court's interlocutory order is "collateral" (and "final"), however, only where it meets certain requirements. It must (1) "conclusively determine [a] disputed question," (2) "resolve an important issue completely separate from the merits of the action," and (3) "be effectively unreviewable on appeal from a final judgment." Coopers & Lybrand v. Livesay, 437 U.S. 463, 468, 98 S.Ct. 2454, 2458, 57 L.Ed.2d 351 (1978).

These requirements explain why the courts have created the "collateral order" exception. The "effective unreviewability" requirement means that failure to review the order on appeal now may cause a litigant permanent harm. The "conclusive determination" requirement means that appellate review now is likely needed to avoid that harm. The "separability" requirement means that review now will not likely force an appellate court to consider the same (or quite similar) questions more than once. Taken together, these requirements, as set forth in the Court's cases, help pick out a class of orders where the error-correcting benefits of immediate appeal likely outweigh the costs, delays, diminished litigation coherence, and waste of appellate court time potentially associated with multiple appeals.

In Mitchell v. Forsyth, 472 U.S. 511, 105 S.Ct. 2806, 86 L.Ed.2d 411 (1985), the Court applied this rationale to a district court order denying a claim of qualified immunity. The Court concluded that the district court order, by sending the case to trial, could cause the litigant what (in terms of the immunity-doctrine's basic trial-avoiding purpose) would amount to an important harm. And, the legal issue (where purely legal, see Johnson, supra, at 313–317, 115 S.Ct., at 2156–2158), would often prove "separate" enough from the more basic substantive issues in the case to avoid significant duplication of appellate court time and effort. Hence, the "collateral order" doctrine's basic rationale supported interlocutory appeal.

That same rationale, however, does not support two pretrial interlocutory appeals, the first from a denial of a motion to dismiss a complaint, the second from a later, post-appeal, denial of a motion for summary judgment. Consider the "separability" requirement. Both orders satisfy the literal terms of that requirement because the qualified immunity issues they resolve are both "separate," in equal measure, from the merits of the plaintiff's claim. But, the reasoned principles and purposes underlying the "separability" requirement are not served by a rule that permits both orders to be appealed because the issues they raise are not normally "separate" one from the other.

Rather, they will often involve quite similar issues, likely presented to different appellate court panels, thereby risking the very duplication and waste of appellate resources that the courts intended the "separability" requirement to avoid. See 15A C. Wright, A. Miller, & E. Cooper, Federal Practice and Procedure § 3911, pp. 333–334 (2d ed.1992)

Similarly, given the law's promise of one pretrial interlocutory appeal, a litigant's need for a second is much less pressing. The single interlocutory appeal can avoid much of, though not all of, the harm that Mitchell found. And, the remaining harm, as I shall next discuss, is not of a kind that the law considers important enough to justify an interlocutory appeal.

* * *

Because one pretrial appeal would normally prove sufficient to protect a government defendant's qualified immunity interest in not standing trial, the right to take multiple interlocutory appeals will normally protect only the defendant's additional interest in avoiding such pretrial burdens as discovery. Thus, the question, as Justice SCALIA has pointed out, is whether this anti-discovery interest is "sufficiently important to overcome the policies militating against interlocutory appeals." Lauro Lines, supra, at 503, (emphasis added). The relevant precedent indicates that, in the context of qualified immunity, it is not.

■ [The concurring opinion of Justice Rehnquist is omitted.]

NOTE

Congress amended the Rules Enabling Act in 1990 to provide that the power granted to the United States Supreme Court under that Act to promulgate and amend the Federal Rules of Appellate Procedure shall also include the power to "define when a ruling of a district court is final for purposes of appeal under section 1291."

No amendment of the rules to define finality has been proposed and none is in prospect, apparently because of a lack of interest on the part of the appellate judiciary. Such a lack of interest is ambiguous. It may be because the appellate judges whose suggestions were solicited did not perceive a serious problem or it may be that the judges did not believe that promulgation of a definition would make a significant contribution to solving it.

Contrast the following two statements:

The state of the law on when a district court ruling is appealable because it is "final," or is an appealable interlocutory action, strikes many observers as unsatisfactory in several respects. The area has produced much purely procedural litigation. Courts of appeals often dismiss appeals as premature. Litigants sometimes face the possibility of waiving their right to appeal when they fail to seek timely review because it is unclear when a decision is "final" and the time for appeal begins to run. Decisional doctrines–such as "practical finality" and especially the "collateral order" rule–blur the edges of the finality principle, require repeated attention from the Supreme Court, and may in some circumstances restrict too sharply the opportunity for interlocutory review.

Federal Courts Study Comm., Judicial Conference of the United States, Report of the Federal Courts Study Committee 95 (1990).

> By and large, the [final judgment] rule and the exceptions appear to have worked together reasonably well in establishing effective levels of certainty and flexibility.

15A Wright, Miller & Cooper, Federal Practice & Procedure: Jurisdiction 2d § 3901 (1992).

The authors of this authoritative treatise add that "both flexibility and certainty may be enhanced" by wise use of the rulemaking power granted by Congress. Does this lead you to believe that the rule and its exceptions may not be working quite as well as statement (2) suggests?

NOTES ON INTERLOCUTORY APPEALS

A. In both *Firestone Tire* (at fn. 13) and *Lauro Lines*, the court refers to the fact that an appeal as of right may not be available under § 1292(b). Note the requirements under that statute for certification of a "controlling question of law" whose immediate appeal "may materially advance the ultimate termination of the litigation". Even if the district court grants an order certifying an interlocutory appeal, it remains within the discretion of the court of appeals whether or not to hear that appeal.

B. If the district court refuses to certify an interlocutory appeal, is there any way for a party to obtain immediate appellate review of an interlocutory order? Consider the procedural posture (and the caption) of Asahi Metal Industries v. Superior Ct. of California (see Chapter II, *supra*). That case involved a "writ of mandate" (referred to in the federal system and many states as a writ of mandamus) to obtain immediate appellate review of the Superior Court of California's interlocutory order which refused to quash service against Asahi on the grounds of lack of personal jurisdiction.

The writ of mandamus derives from early English legal practice. *See* Jenks, The Prerogative Writs in English Law, 32 Yale L.J. 523 (1923). Technically, it is an original proceeding, instituted in the appellate court to prevent a court (or judicial officer) from exceeding its power or jurisdiction (hence the appearance of the Superior Court of California as the respondent in the *Asahi* case). In effect, it is a way of obtaining immediate appellate review of lower court orders which are alleged to violate clear legal obligations.

As footnote 13 of *Firestone Tire* indicates, mandamus is only granted under "exceptional circumstances". The standard for granting the writ cannot be precisely stated, and varies to some degree among different jurisdictions. California appellate courts, for example, are somewhat freer in granting mandamus than most federal courts of appeals. The power cannot be used, however, to review mere errors of law by the trial court, but is confined to circumstances where the lower court's action can be described as exceeding its power or violating its mandatory obligations in some significant way. Consider three cases we have read in which an "extraordinary writ" was used. *World Wide Volkswagen* (Chap. II) involved a writ of prohibition, issued to prevent a lower court from acting beyond its power by asserting personal jurisdiction over defendants. *Asahi* (Chap. II) involved a "writ of mandate" ordering a lower court to quash a summons where the issuance of such a summons was claimed to violate the Due Process Clause. In *Schlagenhauf v. Holder*, (Chap. IV), petitioner sought mandamus to quash an interlocutory order requiring mental and physical examinations that allegedly violated not just Rule 35 of the FRCP but the Congressional grant of power to the federal courts under the Rules Enabling Act.

C. A third basis of interlocutory appeal is authorized for the federal courts in 28 U.S.C. § 1292 (a) which provides an express right to appeal from certain interlocutory orders, including orders "granting, continuing, modifying, refusing or dissolving injunctions." Accordingly, judicial orders granting or denying preliminary injunctions are almost always subject to immediate appeal as of right. As the following case illustrates, however, it is not always easy to determine whether a particular order constitutes a preliminary injunction.

Fernandez–Roque v. Smith

United States Court of Appeals, Eleventh Circuit, 1982.
671 F.2d 426.

■ TUTTLE, CIRCUIT JUDGE:

The present action is a consolidation of three suits filed by various groups of Cuban nationals. These plaintiffs-appellees represent a class of approximately 1800 Cubans who were detained by the Immigration and Naturalization Service upon their arrival in the United States as part of the 1981 Freedom Flotilla.[1] The original complaints sought only relief from detention. Appellees later amended their complaints alleging that they were "refugees" as that term is defined in the 1951 Convention Relating to the Status of Refugees and the 1967 Protocol Relating to the Status of Refugees,[2] (hereinafter Convention & Protocol), 19 U.S.T. 6223, T.I.A.S. 6577. Seeking the protections allegedly afforded them by the Convention & Protocol, the appellees asserted that they had a well-founded fear of persecution, if deported, because of their membership in a social group-the Freedom Flotilla.[3]

During a hearing conducted on August 19, 1981, the Cuban detainees expressed their concern that the government might deport them during the pendency of this litigation. The district court first attempted to obtain assurances from the government counsel that they

---

1. Unlike the other approximately 122,-000 Cubans who were granted parole status upon entry in the United States, the appellees were detained because it was believed that they had committed various crimes either in Cuba or the United States. A substantial number of these Cuban detainees were, however, subsequently found to be excludable solely due to lack of entry papers. Fernandez–Roque v. Smith, No. C81–1084A (Aug. 20, 1982). Moreover, during the oral argument of this case, the government indicated that nearly 1000 of the Cuban detainees have now been determined to be releasable pending final determination of their status.

2. The 1967 Protocol is a treaty to which the United States is a signatory party. The Protocol was opened for signature on January 21, 1967, and entered into force on October 4, 1967, 19 U.S.T. 6223 T.I.A.S. No. 6577, 606 U.N.T.S. 267 (entered into force for U.S. Nov. 1, 1968). Although the United States is not a party to the 1951 Convention, opened for signature on July 28, 1951, entered into force on April 22, 1954, 184

U.N.T.S. 137, the Protocol incorporates by reference the substantive provisions of the Convention. Nicosia v. Wall, 442 F.2d 1005, 1006, n. 4 (5th Cir.1971).

3. In support of these allegations, appellees filed separate affidavits of thirteen Cuban nationals who had voluntarily returned to Cuba. In their affidavits these Cubans stated that upon arrival in Cuba, they were incarcerated, tortured and subsequently set adrift in the ocean by Castro without supplies or navigational equipment. Appellees also filed a copy of the Country Report on Human Rights Practices–Cuba, prepared by the State Department, which described the cruel treatment accorded some refugees before they left Cuba. The government filed an affidavit of a state department official. This affidavit reflected the State Department's opinion that the only returning Cubans believed to have suffered persecution are those who returned without the Cuban government's consent and those who sought to remove relatives.

would provide the Court with advance notice prior to deporting any of the Cuban detainees. When this endeavor proved unsuccessful, the district court entered a temporary restraining order enjoining the government from deporting any of the Cuban detainees pending further order of the court. This order, entered on August 19, 1981, remains in effect at this time.

On October 16, 1981, the government filed a notice of appeal on the theory that the TRO had ripened into a preliminary injunction and thus appellate jurisdiction exists pursuant to 28 U.S.C. § 1292(a)(1) (1976). The proper role of the judiciary with respect to the detention or release of excludable aliens is not implicated in this appeal. Rather, the only issue before us is the propriety of the district court's actions relating to the asylum claims. The government seeks to have the district court's order dissolved on the ground that the district court had no authority to interject itself into the statutory scheme provided for by the immigration laws. Specifically, the government contends that the district court was without habeas corpus jurisdiction because the appellees have failed to exhaust their administrative remedies and because the immigration statute requires individual rather than class-wide determinations of appellees' asylum claims.

* * *

It is incumbent upon this Court to first determine whether our power to declare the law has been properly invoked. It is well established that as a general rule a temporary restraining order is not appealable. A preliminary injunction is, however, an interlocutory decision reviewable by a court of appeals. 28 U.S.C. § 1292(a)(1) (1976). Thus, our jurisdiction in this appeal turns on the proper characterization of the district court's order. Since the "label attached to an order by the trial court is not decisive," we are required to consider several factors in reaching a decision concerning the true nature of the order.

One inherent characteristic of a temporary restraining order is that it has the effect of merely preserving the status quo rather than granting most or all of the substantive relief requested in the complaint. The circumstances of the instant case indicate that in issuing this order, the district court intended merely to preserve the status quo in the face of the stated intention of the government to deport the appellees without notice to the court.

* * *

Another, and perhaps more important, characteristic of a temporary restraining order is the limitation on its duration. Rule 65 of the Federal Rules of Civil Procedure provides in pertinent part:

> Every temporary restraining order granted without notice shall
> . . . expire by its terms within such time after entry, not to exceed
> 10 days, as the court fixes, unless within the time so fixed the
> order, for good cause shown, is extended for a like period or

unless the party against whom the order is directed consents that it may be extended for a longer period * * *

Fed.Rule Civ.Proc. 65(b) (emphasis added). This rule has been interpreted to mean that a temporary restraining order continued without the consent of the parties beyond the twenty day maximum may be treated as a preliminary injunction. Conversely, a temporary restraining order issued or extended with the consent of all parties remains a nonappealable order. Ross v. Evans, 325 F.2d 160 (5th Cir.1963); cf. Haitian Refugee Center v. Civiletti, 614 F.2d 92 (5th Cir.1980) (preliminary injunction entered upon the consent of all parties cannot be appealed).

On the facts of this case, we must conclude that the government consented to the extension of the temporary restraining order. * * * Indeed, at a September 10, 1981 conference, government counsel informed the court that it was "[n]ot at this point" seeking a hearing. Moreover, during the September 24, 1981 conference, the following colloquy occurred:

> THE COURT: The next question, what do you want to do with the TRO? Are the parties satisfied to let the matter-let the temporary restraining order continue until some further time? That was the posture at which we left it at the September 10th meeting.

> GOVERNMENT COUNSEL: At this point I don't now (sic) what the Government's position is. We do, in fact, have serious concerns about the jurisdictional question of the Court's authority to enter the injunction at all * * *

> THE COURT: I will be happy to vacate the restraining order as long as I get a representation by the Government that I get two days notice before you try and deport anybody.

> GOVERNMENT COUNSEL: What I would like to do is leave it up in the air right now . . .

Finally, we note that the district court stated in its order of November 4, 1981, that it "construed the representations of the government's attorneys, and the government's failure to move to dissolve the TRO, as consent to its extension."

We conclude that the order entered by the district court was clearly intended only to preserve the status quo in this case. We further conclude that since the government consented to the continuation of this order, the order remains nonappealable. Recognizing, however, that the essence of the government's complaint is the district court's failure to rule on the jurisdictional issue, we have decided to treat the government's appeal as a petition for a writ of mandamus. See Huckeby v. Frozen Food Express, 555 F.2d 542, 549 n. 14 (5th Cir.1977); Hartland v. Alaska Airlines, 544 F.2d 992, 1001 (9th Cir. 1976); United States v. Briggs, 514 F.2d 794, 808 (5th Cir.1975); International Products Corp. v. Koons, 325 F.2d 403, 407 (2d Cir. 1963).

A district court possesses inherent powers of equity sufficient to enable it to preserve the status quo until the question of its jurisdiction can be resolved.

* * *

Moreover, the district court's decision on the jurisdictional issues will initially control its otherwise discretionary power to conduct an evidentiary hearing on the merits of the appellees' group asylum claim. The government's contention that such a hearing would violate the separation of powers doctrine requires us to consider the policies underlying the statutory provision for certification. See Gillespie v. United States Steel Corp., 379 U.S. 148, 154, 85 S.Ct. 308, 312, 13 L.Ed.2d 199 (1964); 28 U.S.C. § 1292(b) (1976). In the absence of an initial decision clarifying the various jurisdictional claims made by the appellees, we are today unable effectively to render an enlightened decision on the propriety of the district court's holding such a hearing on the merits. Accordingly, we believe that this case presents the truly "rare" situation in which it is appropriate for this court to require certification of a controlling issue of national significance. See Ex Parte Tokio Marine & Fire Insurance Co., 322 F.2d 113, 115 (5th Cir.1963); see also Gillespie v. United States Steel Corp., supra; Nelson v. Heyne, 491 F.2d 352, 354 (7th Cir.), cert. denied, 417 U.S. 976, 94 S.Ct. 3183, 41 L.Ed.2d 1146 (1974); compare Ernst & Ernst v. United States District Court, Southern District of Texas, 439 F.2d 1288, 1293–94 (5th Cir.1971), Supp. Op., 457 F.2d 1399 (5th Cir.1972). Under these exceptional circumstances, we find it necessary to invoke our discretionary powers under the All Writs Act, 28 U.S.C. § 1651(a) (1976), in order to supervise the judicial administration of this case and to prevent the defeat of appellate review. Schlagenhauf v. Holder, 379 U.S. 104, 85 S.Ct. 234, 13 L.Ed.2d 152 (1964); LaBuy v. Howes Leather Co., 352 U.S. 249, 77 S.Ct. 309, 1 L.Ed.2d 290 (1957); United States v. Denson, 603 F.2d 1143 (5th Cir.1979).

Since we find it imperative for the district court to resolve the question of its jurisdiction, we remand this case with the direction that it conduct forthwith only such hearing as is necessary to a determination of whether subject matter jurisdiction exists. Such hearing should be conducted without any discovery as to issues other than that of jurisdiction. Upon the conclusion of such hearing, the district court shall enter an opinion setting forth the reasons for its decision. To the extent, if any, that the appellees have altered the nature of the relief sought in their amended complaint, the district court shall specify the exact nature of the claim or claims as to which jurisdiction is now alleged to reside in the district court. The question of subject matter jurisdiction shall then be certified to this Court, pursuant to 28 U.S.C. § 1292(b), upon request by any party.

Appeal Dismissed

Treating the appeal as a petition for mandamus, we remand the case to the District Court with directions.

The mandate shall issue forthwith.

NOTE

If the plaintiffs in *Fernandez-Roque* lose their motion for a preliminary injunction, will the court be able to grant them full relief after the trial on the merits? Should this factor be considered in determining whether a temporary restraining order or preliminary injunction should be granted? Should it be dispositive?

NOTE ON FINAL JUDGMENTS BEFORE A TRIAL COURT HAS CONCLUDED THE ENTIRE LITIGATION

Liberal rules that facilitate joinder of claims and joinder of parties can lead to very complex, time-consuming litigation. The trial court may dispose of one of the claims, or of all claims against a particular party, relatively early in the litigation, with the likelihood that final judgment in the case may still be years away. May an aggrieved party appeal that determination without awaiting final judgment that will dispose of the entire case?

Rule 54(b) permits entry of final judgment "as to one or more but fewer than all of the claims or parties," but "only upon an express determination that there is no just reason for delay and upon an express direction for the entry of judgment." If the trial court fails to make that express determination, there is no appealable judgment; if, however, it makes what is generally referred to as the 54(b) certification and judgment is entered, an aggrieved party must file a timely notice of appeal or lose the right to appellate review.

The determination is itself subject to appellate review. A recent case, Novacor Chemicals Inc. v. GAF Corp. v. BASF Corp., 164 F.R.D. 640 (E.D.Tenn.1996), is illustrative. The court was asked to enter a 54(b) certification of an interlocutory appeal certification under § 1292 (b). Almost three years had already elapsed since the case was filed and there was virtually no prospect of early disposition of the entire litigation. The court states the case as follows:

> The suit for contribution and indemnification under the Comprehensive Environmental Response, Compensation and Liability Act of 1980 (CERCLA), involves complex factual and legal issues. Issues involving chlorinated organic chemicals, ground water contamination, possible land contamination, successive corporate liability, and responsibility for clean up under CERCLA must be resolved. The Court must also address issues involving privity of contract, "facility," breach of contract, contract applicability and interpretation.

> In part because of the complicated nature of the lawsuit, extensive pleadings have been filed in this case. Counsel for each side have very ably argued their respective positions. There is no doubt the parties have expended considerable sums and efforts in the litigation thus far. As this case continues, additional expense and effort will not be necessary. The Court, therefore, understands and is sympathetic to the desire of defendant to obtain an advance ruling from the appellate court so as to "avoid protracted and expensive litigation with regard to difficult rulings."

In this circuit, trial courts are required to consider the following factors when making a Rule 54(b) determination:

> (1) the relationship between the adjudicated and unadjudicated claims; (2) the possibility that the need for review might or might not be mooted by future developments in the district court; (3) the possibility that the reviewing court might be obliged to consider the same issue a second time; (4) the presence or absence of a claim or counterclaim which would result in set-off against the judgment sought to be made final; (5) miscellaneous factors such as delay,

economic and solvency considerations, shortening the time of trial, frivolity of competing claims, expense, and the like. Depending upon the facts of the particular case, all or some of the above factors may bear upon the propriety of the trial court's discretion in certifying a judgment as final under Rule 54 (b).

After considering the above factors, the Court does not find this case a suitable one for immediate appeal. First, issues in any interlocutory appeal would be substantially similar to the issues in any appeal after judgment. Both appeals would involve a myriad of similar complex legal issues based on CERCLA, i.e., the obligations under federal law of landowners, past and present, regarding the cleanup of hazardous waste and the definition of a "facility." "A similarity of legal or factual issues will weigh heavily against entry of judgment under Rule 54(b)." Assuming that the decision to grant summary judgment to BASF is not reversed, the only adjudicated claims are those between GAF and BASF. GAF has asserted defenses to liability that might well prevail at trial. Should GAF prevail at trial, its claims against BASF would be moot. Second, future developments in the case may nullify the need for review and make any appellate decision on this interlocutory issue unnecessary. Third, if review is needed, it would be in one appeal before one panel, instead of in separate appeals before two of more panels. Last, considerations of delay and the administration of justice militate against certification.

NOTE ON DIFFERING STATE SYSTEMS

As noted above, even the federal courts permit some exceptions to the rule that only final orders are appealable as of right, and many state court systems provide far broader rights of interlocutory appeal.

(1) New York

Section 5701 of the Civil Practice Law and Rules, permits an appeal as of right to the intermediate appellate court from any order which, among other things, grants or refuses a provisional remedy, involves some part of the merits, or affects a substantial right. As one might expect, appeals from interlocutory orders occur far more frequently in New York than they do in the federal system.

The Appellate Division of the Supreme Court (the trial court of general jurisdiction) in New York usually sits in panels of five judges. A Report of the Appellate Division Task Force (November, 1990) in a unanimous conclusion recommended that "No further restrictions should be placed on the appealability of interlocutory orders ..." The Task Force said (at 36) "The review of intermediate orders is an important provision by which the Appellate Division exercises both its supervisory and error correcting roles. It provides the Appellate Division with means for elaborating the law and providing guidance to the trial courts on matters of pre-trial practice."

The basis for its judgment was "[A]n extensive two year study in interlocutory appeals by the Association of the Bar of the City of New York which concluded that approximately 35% of interlocutory appeals resulted in reversal or modification, a rate significant enough to persuade that Association and the members of the Task Force to conclude that the Appellate Divisions play an important error correcting role in their review of interlocutory orders."

The Task Force also was unanimous in recommending that the Appellate Divisions sit in panels of five judges.

(2) Massachusetts

Massachusetts also allows immediate appeal of all interlocutory orders by various trial courts. The appeal is decided by one judge from two appellate courts. Each judge decides such appeals for one month. See David Scheffel, Comment, Interlocutory Appeals in New York—Time Has Come for a More Efficient Approach, 16 Pace Law Review 607, 623–624 (on the Mass. Practice), 613–616 (on the NY practice).

B. THE SCOPE OF REVIEW

Cooter & Gell v. Hartmarx Corp.

Supreme Court of the United States, 1990.
496 U.S. 384, 110 S.Ct. 2447, 110 L.Ed.2d 359.

See Chapter III

National Hockey League v. Metropolitan Hockey Club

Supreme Court of the United States, 1976.
427 U.S. 639, 96 S.Ct. 2778, 49 L.Ed. 2d 747.

See Chapter IV

NOTES

A. You are a federal court of appeals judge hearing an appeal from a district court order imposing Rule 11 sanctions after a warning notice on plaintiff's attorney for instituting suit based on a novel theory of law. After carefully reviewing the record on appeal, you conclude that the novel claim, while appropriately dismissed by the district court, was warranted by a good faith argument for the extension of existing law. Under *Cooter & Gell*, does your conclusion justify reversal of the trial court's judgment? What further inquiry must be made?

B. Suppose, in question A above, you conclude that a Rule 11 sanction was warranted, but the particular sanction applied was too harsh. What standard will you use to decide whether your disagreement with the sanction justifies a reversal?

C. In *National Hockey League*, why is the Supreme Court willing to review the trial court's ruling under an abuse of discretion standard, but will not apply the same standard to the ruling of the court of appeals?

NOTE ON STANDARDS OF REVIEW

There are a number of technical terms utilized to describe the standard of review to be employed by an appellate court. Sometimes these are incorporated in specific rules. *See, e.g.* FRCP 52(a). Sometimes they are developed judicially. Thus, we speak of *de novo* review, typically applicable to a question of law, *clearly erroneous*, typically applicable to a factual finding in a non-jury case, and an *abuse of discretion* standard, applicable, for example, to the trial court's choice of sanction for abuse of discovery. Appellate courts have even utilized all three in determining an appeal from the same case. *See* the legal discussion in *Cooter & Gell*. With respect to "mixed questions of law and fact," the federal courts in different circuits apply a number of different standards of appellate review. *See generally*, Lee,

Principled Decisionmaking and the Proper Role of Federal Appellate Courts: Mixed Questions Conflict, 64 So.Cal.L.Rev. 235 (1991).

Determining the precise meaning and applicability of each of these terms is not without its difficulties. *See* Justice White's comment regarding the clearly erroneous standard in *Anderson v. City of Bessemer City, N.C.* 470 U.S. 564, 574, 105 S.Ct. 1504, 1511, 84 L.Ed.2d 518 (1985). (Chapter X) Note Justice O'Connor's use of the term "deferential" to describe the appropriate standard of review in *Cooter & Gell.*

Roger J. Traynor, The Riddle of Harmless Error

14–24 (1970).

The harmless-error statues require appellate courts to substitute judgment for automatic application of rules; to preserve review as a check upon arbitrary action and essential unfairness in trials, but at the same time to make to process perform that function without giving men fairly convicted the multiplicity of loopholes which any highly rigid and minutely detailed scheme of errors, especially in relation to procedure, will engender and reflect in a printed record.

We can readily agree on the common sense of a harmless-error rule in the foregoing context. There had to be an end to battles of bright or dull wits in the courtroom on witless technicalities.

There remains the large task of articulating what should be the limitations on an appellate court's discretion to determine whether or not an error is harmless.

* * *

There is obvious need of guidelines to control appellate discretion in the evaluation of error. They are not to be found in the broad directives of the harmless-error statutes. The federal statute, for example, simply directs appellate courts to disregard harmless errors that do not "affect the substantial rights of the parties." Such language, although adequate in the case of inconsequential errors, provides no standards for determining when nontechnical errors are harmless. A determination that an error has affected a substantial right does no more than set the stage for the basic inquiry: Was the error harmless? There are countless possible variations of error. There are also countless possible exponential factors that may determine what effect, if any, an error in the course of litigation may have upon a judgment.

* * *

In each case a court must determine whether a right at issue is substantial, whether it has been denied or impaired, and if so whether the error had an effect on the judgment. Litigation rights designed to insure a fair trial are ordinarily substantial and the difficult problems of harmlessness usually turn, not on whether a right is substantial or technical. But on whether error has affected the judgment.

Apart from the federal statute, there is a condition in the Federal Rules of Civil Procedure that no judgment or verdict shall be disturbed unless failure to do so "appears to the court inconsistent with substantial justice."

A large word like justice, incorporated into a rule governing harmless error, compels an appellate court to concern itself not alone with a particular result but also with the very integrity of the judicial process. In this context we can compare various tests.

The "Not Clearly Wrong Result" Test of Harmless Error

Of course a court must reverse if it concludes that the judgment is clearly wrong, as when there is no substantial evidence to support it, or when a verdict should have been directed for the appellant or a judgment entered for him notwithstanding the verdict. Should a court always affirm when the judgment is not clearly wrong? There are advocates of this arbitrary test. They contend that an appellate court should not reverse such a judgment even though it appears that it was or might have been affected by an error.

Under the *not clearly wrong result* test, few errors would be reversible. However egregious the errors, and however great the likelihood that absent the error a different judgment would have to discount the error as harmless. Such a test operates to diminish judicial responsibility. The emphasis should not be on whether the judgment is not clearly wrong; how could an appellate court rest easy in the fact of doubt? The emphasis should be on whether the judgment is not clearly right, so long as there is a substantial chance that error brought it about.

In sum, although a clearly wrong judgment can automatically be equated with a miscarriage of justice, it is perilous to assume that a judgment not clearly wrong, but still dubious, can be equated with justice.

The "Correct Result" Test of Harmless Error

This test assumes that there is never anything dubious about a judgment that has reached the correct result. Does it follow that when a result is correct, it cannot be a "miscarriage of justice" or "inconsistent with substantial justice"? Can a correct result automatically be equated with justice?

There are advocates of such an equation, though it is not less mechanical than the *not clearly wrong result* test. They readily concede that in equating a correct result with justice, an appellate court necessarily envisages what result it would have reached as a trier of fact, thereby substituting itself for the actual trial court or jury. In their view an appellate court is bound to do so. They find the mandate in the words "appears to the court" in the federal rule and "the court shall be of the opinion" in the federal rule and "the court shall be of the opinion" in the California rule. These words, they say, call for an independent decision by an appellate court on the justice of the result based upon its independent evaluation of the correctness of the result.

The correct result advocates add as makeweight that since an appellate judge necessarily exercises discretion in applying any test of harmless error, he cannot keep in limbo his subjective evaluation of the result below. In their view, despite the separation of appellate court and trial court functions, an ad hoc merging of functions in evaluating error is essential to the conservation of judicial resources.

The conservation of judicial resources, though itself a worthy objective is a strange terminal point for an argument purportedly concerned with precluding miscarriages of justice. The argument goes off course because of its assumption at the outset that a correct result is necessarily a just one.

What could be more misleading than such an equation? It is one thing to tolerate as harmless the errors that involve only the "mere etiquette of trials" or the "formalities or minutiae of procedure." It is quite another also to tolerate as harmless the errors that do such violence to the substantial rights of litigants as to debase the judicial process itself, whose very purpose is to assure justice. One such violence is tolerated, no one could enter a courtroom confident of a fair trial. Would that matter? Would justice suffer? Yes. Concededly, not one of us can draw a picture of justice or state its dimensions in words. Nonetheless, we know from this country's long experience in giving substance to the concept of a fair trial that for use, at least, it is an essential element of justice.

We know also from experience the danger of mechanical formulas that tend to replace discriminating judgment. We no longer tolerate the dissipation of judicial resources by the crafty use of essentially harmless error to propel a reversal. We cannot now tolerate the debasement of the judicial process itself by a shortsighted preoccupation with correct results regardless of what violence may have been done to the substantial rights of litigants.

A rational test of harmless error must operate to preserve such rights even as it serves to screen out innocuous errors. Since the right to a fair trial underlies all other rights, a litigant has a right to something more than a decision by a specified tribunal. He has a right to objective consideration of all proper evidence by triers of fact without violations of any substantial rights he may have as a litigant. He is entitled, not to a trial free of all possible error, but to a trial free of harmful error.

The concept of fairness extends to reconsideration of the merits when a judgment has been or might have been influenced by error. In that event they should be a retrial in the trial court, time-consuming or costly though it may be. The short-cut alternative of reconsidering the merits in the appellate court, because it is familiar with the evidence and aware of the error, has the appeal of saving time and money. Unfortunately it does not measure up to accepted standards of fairness.

The conventional arguments against such a quasi trial on appeal can be briefly summarized. It deprives the appellant of a trial in a trial court to which he is entitled. The appellate court is limited to the mute record made below. Many factors may affect the probative value of testimony, such as age, sex, intelligence, experience, occupation, demeanor, or temperament of the witness. A trial court or jury before whom witnesses appear is at least in a position to take note of such factors. An appellate court has no way of doing so. It cannot know whether a witness answered some questions forthrightly but evaded others. It may find an answer convincing and truthful in written form that may have sounded unreliable at the time it was given. A well-phrased sentence in the record may have seemed rehearsed at the trial. A clumsy sentence in the record may not convey the ring of truth that attended it when the witness groped his way to its articulation. What clues are there in the cold print to indicate where the truth lies? What clues are there to indicate where the half-truth lies?

* * *

The foregoing criticism of the *correct result* test still applies even if one revises the question "Was the result correct?" or "Would the same result be reached on a retrial?" There is a superficial appeal to the argument that if a new trial without error would clearly have the same result, justice would be delayed and judicial resources wasted by requiring it. Such an argument, however, assumes that the evidence would be the same, that counsel's tactics and the trial judge's rulings, aside from the error, would be the same, and that the reactions of the trial judge or jury would be the same as those of the previous judge or jury. Even in a context of these assumptions, the question does not qualify as a test of harmless error. The crucial question is not what might happen tomorrow on an edited rerun, but what did happen yesterday on the actual.

Even overwhelming evidence in support of a verdict does not necessarily dispel the risk that an error may have played a substantial part in the deliberation of the jury and thus contributed to the actual verdict reached, for the jury may have reached its verdict because of the error without considering other reasons untainted by error that would have supported the same result. Overwhelming evidence may provide support, even conclusive support, for holding the error harmless, but it is not invariably conclusive. If the error was so forceful as to leave its mark on the judgment, the trial itself was contaminated. An appellant whose right to a fair trial in a trial court has been vitiated should be accorded that right anew. Retrial is a small price to pay for insuring the right to a fair trial.

The "Effect on the Judgment" Test of Harmless Error

At this juncture it is important to keep in mind that in any test of harmless error, and in any case, an appellate court has only probabilities to go on, not certainties. Nonetheless, when it undertakes to evaluate the probabilities in terms of an error's effect on the judgment, instead of merely looking at the result as the test of harmlessness, the judicial process at the trial level as well as in appellate review stands to make a long-term gain in fairness without any long-term loss in efficiency. In the long run there would be a closer guard against error at the trial, if appellate courts were alert to reverse, in case of doubt, for error that could have contaminated the judgment.

Ordinarily an appellate court would have reason for doubt, for there are no scientific answers to the ultimate question whether the trier of fact was influenced by an error. How can anyone determine what went on in the mind of another or of twelve others who served as triers of fact? The only source of direct evidence would be their own testimony. If the facts had been tried by a jury, such testimony would be precluded by the rule forbidding affidavits or evidence of any sort that tends to contradict, impeach, or defeat the jury's verdict. Thus, there is no possibility of tapping the only source of direct evidence on the effect, if any, of an error upon the jury's verdict.

Answers to special interrogatories, however, might indicate that an error was or was not harmless. A special verdict, for example, might be in favor of the appellant on an issue to which the error related, thus demonstrating that it had not effect on the verdict. Special verdicts in jury trials could be considerable assistance to appellate courts as they grapple with the problem of harmless error. Are there any compelling reasons against their use, apart from criminal cases where they could operate to inhibit the jury's prerogative to temper the law with mercy? We should not lack judges and lawyers able and willing to draft special interrogatories skillful enough to disclose the actual basis of decision.

The fact is that they seldom do so. Thus, even though special interrogatories are permissible in California, they are seldom used.

C.   APPELLATE PROCEDURE

NOTES ON FEDERAL APPELLATE PROCEDURE

A. The basic procedure for taking an appeal to a United States court of appeals is set forth in the Federal Rules of Appellate Procedure ("FRAP"). (Appeals to the United States Supreme Court are governed by that Court's own set of rules.) All of the federal courts of appeals also have their own local rules which supplement FRAP.

B. An appeal as of right from an order or judgment of a United States district court is taken by filing a "notice of appeal" with the *district court* which issued the order (FRAP 3(a)). The content of the notice of appeal is prescribed by FRAP 3(c), and the time for filing the notice (generally 30 days from the entry of the order or judgment appealed from) is prescribed by FRAP 4. Filing of the notice of appeal is jurisdictional. Failure to file within the requisite time will deprive the court of appeals of subject matter jurisdiction to hear the appeal. But there is a provision for limited extension of time in FRAP 4(a)(5).

C. Once the notice of appeal is filed, the party taking the appeal, known in the federal system as the "appellant", must take various actions designed to permit the clerk of the district court to prepare and transmit the "record on appeal" in accordance with the provisions of FRAP 10 & 11. This will include making sure that transcripts of any relevant proceedings have been made (FRAP 10(b)) and filed with the district court. The record will also contain the original papers and exhibits filed in the district court and a certified copy of the docket entries in the case. Once prepared, the record on appeal is then transmitted from the district court clerk's office to the office of the clerk of the court of appeals.

D.   The appellant will also be required, pursuant to a schedule issued by the court of appeals, to submit a brief (FRAP 28) setting forth appellant's legal arguments on appeal and an appendix reproducing certain portions of the record on appeal as prescribed by FRAP 30. The opposing party, known in the federal system as the "appellee" (but in some states, and in certain federal and state proceedings, as "respondent") submits a brief in response to appellant's brief. Appellant then has a right to file a "reply brief" (FRAP 28(c)).

E.   Finally, FRAP 34 requires that oral argument be allowed in all cases, unless a local rule is promulgated that permits a panel of judges, by unanimous agreement, to dispense with oral argument under conditions set forth in FRAP 34. In fact, all the circuits have such local rules, and decision on the merits without oral argument is not at all unusual in the federal courts of appeals. In 1988, 50% of the cases decided on the merits in all federal courts of appeals were decided without oral argument. The percentage of cases in which oral argument was heard varied among the circuits, ranging from a low of 30.2% in the Fifth Circuit to a high of 82.5% in the Second. Report of the Director of the Administrative Office of the United States Courts (1988) Table S–3.

F.   Largely as a consequence of the 1990 Civil Justice Reform Act, there is now far less uniformity in the practices of the federal appellate courts. As one commentator notes, "Many of the local rules adopted by the individual circuits are in sharp conflict with the FRAP. These rules thereby deprive the federal regime of much of its force and deny counsel the right to rely . . . upon those rules adopted by the Supreme Court through the more visible and regular national judicial rulemaking process. Local circuit variations on and supplementation of the FRAP raise technical obstacles to the efficient prosecution and defense of federal appeals." Gregory C. Sisk, The Balkanization of Appellate Justice: The Proliferation of Local Rules in the Federal Circuits, 68 U. Colo. L. Rev. 1 (1997).

Miami International Realty Co. v. Paynter

United States Court of Appeals, Tenth Circuit, 1986.
807 F.2d 871.

■ BARRETT, CIRCUIT JUDGE.

After examining the briefs and the appellate record, this three-judge panel has determined unanimously that oral argument would not be of material assistance in the determination of this appeal. See Fed.R.App.P. 34(a); Tenth Cir.R. 10(c). The cause is therefore ordered submitted without oral argument.

Miami International Realty Company (Miami), appeals from an order of the district court staying execution of a judgment pending appeal. In this appeal, we are asked to review under what circumstances, if any, may a stay be granted pursuant to Fed.R.Civ.Proc. Rule 69, 28 U.S.C. without a supersedeas bond for the full amount of the judgment. The relevant facts are not in dispute.

Miami filed this action against Richard T. Paynter (Paynter) and the law firm of Paynter & Hensick, P.C., alleging malpractice. After trial to a jury, Miami was found to have been damaged in amount of $3,000,000, reduced to $2,100,000 upon the jury's finding that Miami was 30% negligent. Judgment was entered in favor of Miami for $2,100,000 on December 20, 1985. Paynter subsequently moved for judgment notwithstanding the verdict or, in the alternative, for a new trial. On February 6, 1986, the district court, in a detailed order, denied Paynter's motion.

Commencing on February 13, 1986, Miami served various writs of garnishment upon parties holding funds of Paynter, including American Home Assurance Company (American), Paynter's malpractice insurance carrier. American's malpractice coverage on Paynter had a $500,000 policy limit.

On February 21, 1986, Paynter moved for a stay of execution and waiver of supersedeas bond or, in the alternative, approval of a supersedeas bond for less than the $2,100,000 judgment entered in favor of Miami. * * *

During the discovery hearing,[4] Paynter acknowledged that: on December 23, 1985, three days after the jury had awarded the $2,100,-000 verdict in Miami's favor, he had closed his bank account by withdrawing $111,865.88; after paying his personal bills, he lost between $60,000 and $70,000 gambling in Las Vegas; he closed his law office on February 12, 1986 at which time many records were destroyed; and that he had no significant accounts receivable. Although our transcript of the March 19, 1986, hearing is incomplete, Paynter's responses during the hearing indicate that he did not have any significant assets.

On March 28, 1986, a hearing was held on Miami's motion for reconsideration of Paynter's requested stay. After a brief hearing, an order was entered by the court on April 30, 1986. The order provided in part:

The stay of execution herein ordered shall be and is expressly conditioned upon Defendants' compliance with the following events and conditions:

a.   Defendants, through American Home Assurance Company, shall within five (5) days of the date of this Order, post and file with the Clerk of this Court the sum of $500,000. . . .

b.   Richard T. Paynter, Jr. shall submit to all reasonable post-judgment discovery pursuant to Rule 69 of the Federal Rules of Civil Procedure.

c.   Pending the time required for an appeal of the judgment in this matter, Defendant Richard T. Paynter, Jr. shall not sell, transfer, convey, encumber, pledge or in any other manner, other than is reasonably necessary for purposes of providing for his cost

---

4. Fed. R. Civ. Pro. Rule 69(a), 28 U.S.C. provides in part:

"In aid of the judgment or execution, the judgment creditor * * * may obtain dis-

covery from any person, including the judgment debtor, in the manner provided in these rules * * *."

of living and practicing or engaging in a profession or occupation, dissipate any asset or assets . . . or any other things or right of any value whatsoever.

(R., Vol. I, Def's Exh. B, pp. 1–2).

On appeal, Miami contends that Rule 62(d) requires a supersedeas bond for the full amount of a judgment as a condition for a stay of execution absent extraordinary circumstances and that the district court abused its discretion in granting the stay of execution.

Rule 62(d) provides:

> When an appeal is taken the appellant by giving a supersedeas bond may obtain a stay. . . . The bond may be given at or after the time of filing the notice of appeal or of procuring the order allowing the appeal, as the case may be. The stay is effective when the supersedeas bond is approved by the court.

Miami argues that Rule 62(d) ordinarily requires a supersedeas bond for the full amount of the judgment as a condition for stay of execution. It also acknowledges, however, that "some courts have held that Rule 62(d) does not prohibit a court, in extraordinary circumstances, from permitting an alternate form of security for a stay pending appeal."

* * *

Miami is correct in arguing that the purpose of a supersedeas bond is to secure an appellee from loss resulting from the stay of execution and that a full supersedeas bond should be the requirement in normal circumstances.

District courts, however, have inherent discretionary authority in setting supersedeas bonds. In Texaco, Inc., v. Pennzoil Company, 784 F.2d 1133, 1154, 1155 (2d Cir.1986), the court stated:

> A judgment creditor's primary concern when a judgment in his favor is stayed pending appeal is that he be "secure . . . from loss resulting from the stay of execution. . . ." In making that determination we look to general equitable principles. Accordingly, when setting supersedeas bonds courts seek to protect judgment creditors as fully as possible without irreparably injuring judgment debtors. . . . A full supersedeas bond may be required "where there is some reasonable likelihood of the judgment debtor's inability or unwillingness to satisfy the judgment in full upon ultimate disposition of the case and where posting adequate security is practicable", whereas no bond or a reduced bond would suffice when the creditor's interest, due to unusual circumstances, would not be unduly endangered. . . .

* * *

We hold that the district court's stay was valid under Rule 62(d). The court did not err in granting a stay without a supersedeas bond for the full amount of Miami's judgment inasmuch as: Paynter's motion for a stay was supported by an affidavit in which Paynter stated that he did not have sufficient assets to post a supersedeas bond for $1,600,000 above his malpractice coverage insurance of $500,000 (and thereby fully cover Miami's $2,100,000 judgment) and that execution of the judgment would cause him irreparable harm and place him in insolvency; on March 10, 1986, the district court, following a hearing on Paynter's motion for a stay, concluded that Paynter "has no ability to post the full amount of the bond and I think ... we should proceed as the plaintiff [Miami] suggested ... which is to say that the insurance company should put the full amount of the insurance policy into some escrow account";

* * *

Although Miami argues that the court erred and abused its discretion by not requiring Paynter to post a full supersedeas bond, Miami has not contradicted Paynter's evidence that he was financially unable to post a full bond and that execution on the judgment would place him in insolvency. Under such circumstances, we decline to hold that the court erred in granting the stay without a full supersedeas bond. *Texaco, Inc. v. Pennzoil Company, supra*, ("when setting supersedeas bonds courts seek to protect judgment creditors as fully as possible without irreparably injuring judgment debtors".)

Affirmed

NOTES

A. Why would Paynter be "irreparably injured" if no stay of execution of the judgment against him were granted pending appeal?

B. Suppose the relief ordered by the district court did not involve a money judgment, but an order prohibiting defendant from practicing law. Could Paynter obtain a stay of such an order pending appeal? From which court should he seek such a stay? *See* FRAP 8(a).

NOTE ON UNPUBLISHED AND UNSIGNED OPINIONS

Law school materials and instruction tend to emphasize signed, published opinions of appellate judges to the point where students may get the mistaken impression that such opinions are the primary way in which appellate courts resolve the cases before them. They are not. Statistics from the Administrative Office of the United States Courts indicate that in 1990, an active judge on a federal court of appeals produced an average of 133 "written decisions". Of these, 51 were signed opinions of the sort familiar to readers of law school casebooks. Another 67 were "unsigned", defined in the report as "unsigned opinions of the court which state the legal and factual elements and judgment rationale." An average of 15 more cases were decided "without comment", defined as "unsigned opinions/orders which do not state the legal and factual elements and judgment rationale." 1990 Federal Court Management Statistics (Administrative Office of the United States Courts) pp. 31, d.

Moreover, many written opinions of the appellate courts are never published. Most of the federal courts of appeals do not publish even half of their decisions on the merits. Robel, The Myth of the Disposable Opinion: Unpublished Opinions and Government Litigants in the United States Courts of Appeals, 87 Mich.L.Rev. 940

n. 2 (1989). Most of the circuits have also adopted rules which attempt to curtail use of these unpublished opinions by limiting their distribution and forbidding their citation in all but certain limited situations. Seventh Circuit Rule 53, for example, provides that unpublished orders may only be distributed to counsel for the parties, circuit judges, the lower court judge or agency who decided the case below, and the news media. It also states that such orders shall not be cited or used as precedent, except to support a claim of res judicata, collateral estoppel or law of the case.

These rules were intended to save judicial time in preparation of opinions (the assumption being that opinions not intended for publication can be less elaborate and more quickly and easily written), and to avoid burdening courts, lawyers and law libraries with published opinions that involve no novel legal issues. Many have criticized the widespread use of unpublished opinions, however, as creating a body of secret law that is likely to be available only to litigants appearing frequently before the appellate courts, like government attorneys. *See* Robel, *supra*, (finding that many lawyers for federal agencies maintain files of unpublished appellate opinions and use them in litigation decisions and in preparing briefs). They also express the view that cases judged by the court to be of no precedential value may, in fact, be of use to other judges and lawyers.

As an aspiring lawyer looking forward to many years of legal research, which system would you favor: one which requires publication of all appellate opinions, which would assure you that all potentially useful precedents are available, but at the cost of forcing you to slog through yet more case reporters and longer computer searches, or a system which limits publication to cases the judges deem important?

INDEX

References are to page

1-56662-755-9

90000

9 781566 627559